1500

Children Moving

NINTH EDITION

Children Moving

A REFLECTIVE APPROACH TO TEACHING PHYSICAL EDUCATION

George Graham
PE Central (www.pecentral.org)

Shirley Ann Holt/Hale
Linden Elementary School, Oak Ridge, Tennessee

Melissa Parker
University of Northern Colorado

McGraw Hill

Connect
Learn
Succeed™

CHILDREN MOVING: A REFLECTIVE APPROACH TO TEACHING PHYSICAL EDUCATION

Published by McGraw-Hill, an imprint of The McGraw-Hill Companies, Inc., 1221 Avenue of the Americas, New York, NY 10020. Copyright © 2013 by The McGraw-Hill Companies, Inc. All rights reserved. Printed in the United States of America. Previous editions © 2010, 2008, and 2006. No part of this publication may be reproduced or distributed in any form or by any means, or stored in a database or retrieval system, without the prior written consent of The McGraw-Hill Companies, Inc., including, but not limited to, in any network or other electronic storage or transmission, or broadcast for distance learning.

Some ancillaries, including electronic and print components, may not be available to customers outside of the United States.

This book is printed on acid-free paper.

1 2 3 4 5 6 7 8 9 0 DOW/DOW 1 0 9 8 7 6 5 4 3 2

ISBN: 978-0-07-802259-3
MHID: 0-07-802259-2

Vice President & Editor-in-Chief: *Michael Ryan*
Vice President of Specialized Publishing: *Janice M. Roerig-Blong*
Publisher: *David Patterson*
Sponsoring Editor: *Christopher Johnson*
Marketing Coordinator: *Colleen P. Havens*
Development Editor: *Darlene M. Schueller*
Project Manager: *Melissa M. Leick*
Design Coordinator: *Margarite Reynolds*
Cover Design: *Studio Montage, St. Louis, Missouri*
Cover/Interior Images: © *George Graham, Shirley Ann Holt/Hale, and Melissa Parker*
Buyer: *Susan Culbertson*
Media Project Manager: *Sridevi Palani*
Typeface: *9.5/12 ITC Stone Serif*
Compositor: *Aptara®, Inc.*
Printer: *R.R. Donnelley*

Library of Congress Cataloging-in-Publication Data
Graham, George, 1943–
    Children moving : becoming a reflective teacher / George Graham,
Shirley Ann Holt, Melissa Park.—9th ed.
        p. cm.
    Includes index.
    ISBN 978-0-07-802259-3 (alk. paper)
    1. Physical education for children—Study and teaching—United States. 2. Physical education for children—Curricula—United States. 3. Movement education—United States.
I. Holt/Hale, Shirley Ann. II. Parker, Melissa. III. Title.
GV443.G73 2013
372.86′044—dc23
                                                                              2011044388

To Austin, Carter, Savanna, and Lois
  GG

To the staff at Linden Elementary School
  SHH

To my family and colleagues who have both inspired my thinking and endured my distractions
  MP

PART FOUR

Movement Concepts Development   207

CHAPTER 13

Space Awareness   209

CHAPTER 14

Effort   226

CHAPTER 17

Chasing, Fleeing, and Dodging   292

CHAPTER 18

Bending, Stretching, Curling, and Twisting   309

CHAPTER 22

Kicking and Punting 406

CHAPTER 26

Striking with Long-Handled Implements 523

Children! Impressionable, innocent, enthusiastic, eager to learn, and all different. In fact, if you believe that all children are identical—same interests, same abilities, same size—then *Children Moving* is not the book for you. The authors of *Children Moving* recognize that each child is unique and different. One size does not fit all! The purpose of *Children Moving* is to guide you in the process of learning to teach a curriculum that is differentiated for a range of skill abilities and fitness levels. If all children were the same, we would be able to "package" a curriculum—the same games, gymnastic stunts, and dances you would do with all of the children as if they were identical. *Children Moving* will introduce you to a process of teaching—the reflective approach—that will provide the background for you to adapt, adjust, and modify lessons so they are interesting and worthwhile for all of the children you teach—from the lowest to the highest skill and fitness levels. The ultimate goal, of course, is to guide youngsters in the process of becoming physically active for a lifetime.

The importance of physical activity for one's health is recognized today as never before. As we write this ninth edition, virtually no one questions the value of participating in 60 minutes, or more, of physical activity each day. *Children Moving* focuses on building the competence and confidence in children that leads to a lifetime of physical activity. It's easy to recommend that children, and adults, become and remain physically active. As you may know it's much harder to do it.

Children Moving is not simply a description of games and activities for kids. Instead it emphasizes the importance of children actually learning to move by focusing on skill themes that are used in virtually all sports and physical activities. This text contains a variety of rich, tested lesson ideas that have the potential to assist children in becoming good movers. Competent movers typically enjoy physical activity and are eager participants. In contrast, incompetent movers who are poorly skilled are far more likely to avoid physical activity. Each logical, developmentally appropriate skill theme progression is described with word-for-word examples of what teachers actually say to the children during the lessons. This is especially valuable for novice teachers and those with little experience teaching by skill themes.

In addition to providing detailed examples of lessons for each of the skill themes, *Children Moving* also devotes nine chapters to the process of teaching (Parts 2 and 3). These pedagogical skills are based in the research literature and also years and years of teaching experience. If you want to become a good teacher, you understand effective teachers do a lot more than just keep kids "busy, happy and good." They develop logical skill progressions that are the foundation of sports skills and physical activities and then they provide copious amounts of encouraging feedback that lets the children know how they are doing—and what they need to work on.

Children Moving is far more than a collection of fun, unrelated physical activities for children. If you wanted to be a popular parent, you might let your children eat nothing but desserts. Yet you know that doing so would be terrible for the health of your children. The authors of *Children Moving* feel the same about physical education. Simply playing a bunch of unrelated games with no progression or feedback is not in the children's best interest. For this reason the authors of *Children Moving* have built on the literature about teaching, and children, to develop a solid, experience-tested, evidence-based approach to teaching children physical education. We hope you enjoy reading and implementing the skill theme approach. We also believe the children you teach will benefit enormously.

When the first edition of *Children Moving* was published in 1980, the skill theme approach was new to many in our profession. Today, an increasing number of teachers follow the developmentally appropriate guidelines and practices outlined in this book. We have blended the literature on effective teaching with research on physical activity and teacher preparation into a practical format designed to help you understand, and successfully implement, the skill theme approach with children—an approach that provides a program of physical education appropriate for all children, not just the athletically gifted or physically fit youngsters.

In 1980 the research documenting the benefits of physical activity and the importance of physical education in the school curricula was nonexistent, as was the universal lack of understanding about the importance of physical activity for children. Today, with the increasing epidemic of obesity and the associated health problems, there is little need to convince parents, administrators, and the medical community of the importance of regular physical activity for children.

It has now been more than a decade since the Surgeon General's report on physical activity and the first edition of the *National Standards for Physical Education* were published. Today they are landmark documents. Increasingly quality programs of physical education are aligning their curricula with national and state standards with clear and obvious goals. In this era of increased accountability and testing, state legislatures and school districts are mandating that teachers document what students have and have not learned, often through high-stakes testing with highly publicized results. Physical education programs that do not have sound educational goals and practices guiding their instruction are now more vulnerable than ever before.

Developmentally Appropriate Physical Education Practices for Children (1992, 2000) and *Appropriate Practices for Elementary School Physical Education* (third edition, 2009), all published by the National Association for Sport and Physical Education (NASPE), offer counsel for the structure of quality physical education programs along with suggested content.

The authors of *Children Moving* have been involved with these and other national, regional, and state projects in various ways. Our involvement is one of the key reasons for the match between *Children Moving* and the recent national and state advances substantiating the importance of physical activity. This edition includes literally hundreds of practical learning experiences and assessments for reaching the goals and objectives outlined in the combined editions of the *National Standards* and various state standards.

In this edition we have continued to expand, clarify, and update the content and teaching process suggested in the documents of the mid-1990s. Our goal, however, is to keep the book both informal and practical. What we wrote in the preface to the first edition remains true today: "We are teachers of children first. And writers second. Individual insights gained during years of teaching experience and ideas to enhance teacher success are sprinkled throughout the text. We hope that by sharing these experiences with you we can help others to enrich the lives of children."

At the outset of the ninth edition, we want to thank those professors and instructors who have used *Children Moving* in the past. We think you will be pleased to see the major changes we have made to this edition. For students and teachers who are reading this text for the first time, you will be pleased to know that this edition is easier to understand, and use, than past editions. We have also continued to stay abreast of recent developments in our profession and, as you will see, these changes are reflected throughout this edition.

In this section of the Preface, we want to highlight some of the specific changes we have made to this edition of *Children Moving*. The Introduction to the skill theme approach (Part 1) now contains revised chapters. Chapter 1 highlights the benefits of physical activity for children as well as the components of a quality physical education program for children. Chapters 2 and 3 define the skill theme approach.

The four chapters in Part 2 of this edition focus specifically on the process of becoming a reflective teacher. Chapter 4 defines and gives examples of reflective teaching. One of the tenets of reflective teaching is that we base our lessons on the skills, abilities and interests of the children. Chapter 5 describes our system for determining the content the children are ready to learn based on their developmental needs and interests—an alternative to organizing the content by grade levels or age (generic levels of skill proficiency). Our new Chapter 6 is an extremely important one as it conveys a four-part process describing how reflective teachers plan their lessons and programs to maximize the benefit for children. As you will read in this chapter, planning in the skill theme approach involves a lot more than just finding games or activities that will keep the children "busy, happy, and good" for 30 minutes or so. The last chapter in Part 2 is designed to assist you in analyzing your teaching to better understand your effectiveness and progress as a reflective teacher. It provides a number of practical examples to provide you with feedback about your teaching.

Part 3 of *Children Moving* also focuses on the teaching skills (pedagogy) of effective teaching. The first two chapters describe the process of creating a positive learning environment with your classes (Chapter 8) and strategies for maintaining that environment after it has been created (Chapter 9). Chapter 8 describes the process of creating an atmosphere conducive to learning and includes sections on safety and legal liability. In this chapter we introduce the safety icon ⚠ as an alert for a strong emphasis on safety in a given situation. Chapter 9 introduces a multitude of strategies that can be used to help all students stay on task and ensure the environment that was created initially continues throughout the year. If you don't know it now, you will when you start teaching—these are two very important chapters to read, understand, and refer to as a teacher. Chapter 10 describes a variety of instructional approaches teachers use to heighten children's ability to gradually become independent learners. An analysis is provided that allows teachers to determine how any given approach may be more or less appropriate than others based on the students' needs and the teacher's pedagogical skills. This chapter provides links of various instructional approaches to specific learning tasks in the skill theme chapters. The process of observing the children with understanding is a critical pedagogical skill to determining the lesson and program content that will be most beneficial to the children. Once again in the ninth edition, we have devoted an entire chapter to the observation process because we believe it is so important to becoming an effective reflective teacher (Chapter 11). The final chapter in Part 3 provides a plethora of practical ideas you can use to answer questions such as, Are the children I am teaching improving? Are they grasping the important concepts? Assessment icons ✓ are used throughout the text to indicate performance assessments that are explained in detail in Chapter 12—and assist you in answering these two questions. In addition suggestions for checking for cognitive understanding are indicated with the icon ✿. All assessment items are aligned with the *National Standards*.

The next two parts of the book provide detailed and practical examples of the movement concepts (Part 4) and skill themes (Part 5). The movement concept chapters (Chapters 13–15) describe how the concepts of space awareness, effort, and relationships are taught in the skill theme approach and include references to both editions of the *National Standards* for content and assessment ideas. They are followed by the skill theme chapters (Chapters 16–26), which contain hundreds of learning experiences designed to help children develop the motor skills necessary for successful participation in and enjoyment of a variety of physical activities and sports.

Each skill theme chapter begins with an overview of the content followed by a description of a series of tasks, the critical elements or cues necessary to succeed at these tasks, and challenges designed to maintain children's interest in learning the tasks. The tasks are organized according to the generic levels of skill proficiency in a spiral progression from beginning to advanced. Assessment options for the skill theme chapters are keyed to the assessment chapter (Chapter 12). Many of the skill theme chapters also take advantage of a new photographic technique allowing us to provide movement sequences of many of the skill themes labeled with the cues (critical elements) that are so important for children to learn the fundamental motor and sport skills that are the building blocks for successful and enjoyable participation in sports and physical activities for a lifetime.

Part 6 begins with a chapter focusing on teaching children important concepts related to physical activity and wellness (Chapter 27). It also describes a process for using physical fitness tests in developmentally appropriate ways that are designed to motivate all of the children in a program—not only the youngsters who are already physically fit. The next three chapters describe how the skill themes and movement concepts are applied to dance, gymnastics, and games (Chapters 28, 29, and 30). These chapters describe predesigned and child-designed learning experiences, with a focus on teachers guiding children to develop their own games, gymnastic sequences, and dances. Chapter 31 focuses on teaching children with special needs and addressing the diversity within our gymnasiums and classrooms. The last chapter in Part 6 (Chapter 32) provides examples of how classroom and physical education teachers can work together to reinforce the literacy, mathematics, science, social studies, and other concepts that are taught in the classroom, in the gymnasium, and on the playground.

The final part of *Children Moving* (Part 7) contains two chapters. Chapter 33 describes some of the ways physical educators can garner support for their program for various constituents that are critical for the development of a thriving, contemporary program of physical education. Chapter 34 contains our dreams for the future. You may want to read this chapter any time. We think it says a great deal about the authors of *Children Moving* and our vision of the future.

New to This Edition

If you have read previous editions of *Children Moving*, you will see that we have reorganized some chapters, combined several, and written a new chapter. We will describe these changes in more detail in the next part of the Preface, but here is a brief list of the major changes.

- We divided the book into seven related parts. We did this to emphasize even more than in the past the process of becoming a reflective teacher (Part 2).
- To better explain the relationship between movement concepts, skill themes, and what we have termed *content areas*—physical fitness, games, gymnastics and dance—we have created a new section (Part 6) that explains this relationship after, not before, the movement concept and skill theme chapters.
- We have revised the content development and planning chapters into a single chapter that better explains the process of reflective teaching.
- The movement analysis framework (the wheel) has been revised to make it easier to understand and use. Now each part of the wheel corresponds to one of the movement concept or skill theme chapters.
- In the spirit of making the skill theme approach easier to understand, we have a new chapter entitled "Bending, Stretching, Curling, and Twisting" (Chapter 18).
- We have color-coded the skill theme and movement concept chapters to correspond with the colors on the wheel to make it easier to understand and use.
- Last, but certainly not least, we have taken advantage of a new photography process called stromotion that

allows us to include action photographs, labeled with cues, that will make it much easier to analyze the movement of the children when you are teaching.

Evidence-Based Support

This new edition highlights many examples of the latest research in the field, such as findings that suggest a connection between ongoing physical activity and obesity, and between movement and learning; the use of heart rate monitors and pedometers in learning more about movement; the creation of a learning environment and motivation in physical education; and safety and liability issues that need to be addressed.

Whenever possible we have cited research evidence to support the skill theme approach. These citations are noted throughout the chapters, and complete references are included at the end of many chapters. In some instances you will see research cited that may be a number of years old. In these instances the research cited is relevant today, even though it was done some time ago. In other instances there are no recent relevant studies of which the authors are aware.

Successful Features

The Skill Theme Approach

The skill theme focus of this book guides teachers in helping children develop their motor skills with developmentally appropriate activities that are directed toward their skill level rather than their grade level. Designed for both classroom teachers and physical education teachers, the skill theme approach highlights practical ways of teaching physical education to children.

Basic Teaching Skills

This book emphasizes the foundation for teaching skills with topics such as planning, organizing, assessing, and evaluating. It offers a strong background in educationally sound theory and explains how to apply that knowledge to become an effective teacher. The focus is on reflective teaching, which involves adjusting both the content and teaching process to match the needs of students.

Classroom Conversations

The scripted format of the skill theme chapters offers new teachers examples of real conversations that take place in the classroom or gymnasium. In this way teachers can learn how to participate in the different dialogues that are instrumental to child-centered education.

Advocacy of Physical Education

This text focuses on physical education and its relationship to physical fitness. Recognizing the value of physical education as a part of total fitness, this book incorporates the concepts of fitness and wellness throughout all chapters. Virtually every movement concept and skill theme activity avoids asking the children to wait in lines or wait for turns.

Promotion of Inclusion

The idea of inclusion is central to *Children Moving*. Examples of how all individuals can be included in high-quality physical education are found throughout this text. In essence this is the foundation of the reflective teaching process that is described throughout the book.

Small-Sided Games

Demonstrating the value of small-sided games in the skill theme approach, this book offers examples of how to design such games and make them a valuable part of your physical education program. It discusses ideas about developing versatile games players who understand strategies and skills for playing well.

Pedagogical Aids

Key Concepts   Each chapter begins with a list of Key Concepts to help students focus their attention on the main topics as they begin studying the chapter. This learning tool also offers an accessible and practical method of review.

Safety   Throughout the text discussions, the symbol ⚠ indicates a safety alert for a particular situation. This tool keeps the new teacher attuned to making safety a basic element in physical education activities and helps avoid accidents.

Tasks   The skill theme and movement concept chapters feature a suggested progression of tasks, or extensions, for children. Highlighted by the symbol Ⓣ, each task is worded in a conversational style that can be used to give instructions to the children about how to perform the task.

Cues   Cues, or refinements, can be used to help the children perform a skill more efficiently. A selection of cues—such as "Heads Up" or "Light on Your Feet"—is presented at the beginning of each series of tasks for skill themes and movement concepts. The teacher can select a cue that is appropriate to help children perform the skill correctly. Many of these cues are illustrated in sequences of photos of children actually performing the skills.

Challenges   Challenges, or applications, are indicated by the symbol Ⓒ in the skill theme and movement concept chapters. They are designed to maintain the children's interest in a particular task. Teachers can either use the challenges listed along with the tasks or create ones that seem appropriate for the children with whom they are working. Challenges allow the reflective teacher to avoid making tasks too difficult before the children are ready.

Assessment Ideas   Assessment tools are designed to see what students have learned in relation to the goals set by the teacher. The symbol ✓ identifies suggested assessments that can be used as part of a lesson (formative) rather than as a separate entity at the end of the unit (summative). These assessment ideas include an array of options, from exit (or entrance) slips that can be used to quickly assess cognitive and affective learning, to teacher observation checklists and digital analysis to verify psychomotor skills.

Summaries   The chapter summaries highlight the major topics and concepts discussed in the chapter. They can be used for clarification or for review for examinations.

Reading Comprehension Questions   A set of questions appears at the end of each chapter that will allow you to test your understanding of the content. These questions also offer a means of reviewing and analyzing the material.

References/Suggested Readings   This list at the end of each chapter includes references that support the text discussion and additional sources for study and exploration.

Appendix   The Appendix to this book offers two sample school-year overviews based on the material in *Children Moving*. It includes a two-day-a-week scope and sequence for an inexperienced class (grades K–2) and a five-day-a-week program (scope and sequence) for an experienced (grades 3–6) class. These overviews can be followed exactly as presented or used as a model for developing individualized programs.

Supplements

Computerized Test Bank

The test bank is designed for use with McGraw-Hill's EZ Test computerized testing software. EZ Test is a flexible and easy-to-use electronic testing program that allows instructors to create tests from book-specific items. It accommodates a wide range of question types, and instructors may add their own questions. Multiple versions of the test can be created, and any test can be exported for use with course management systems such as WebCT or BlackBoard. Additional help is available at www.mhhe.com/eztest.

On the Move: Lesson Plans to Accompany Children Moving, *Ninth Edition,* by Shirley Ann Holt/Hale

These lesson plans are designed to offer learning experiences for children that assist them in developing a broad base of movement skills coupled with an enjoyment of physical activity that will translate into a physically active, healthy lifestyle for a lifetime. Some of the highlights are (1) instructional objectives attainable within a single lesson; (2) content development with a focus on a skill rather than on broad exploration; (3) maximum practice of the focus skill; (4) concentration on one cue at a time; (5) challenges throughout the lessons; and (6) both cognitive and performance assessments.

Special features include a series of physical fitness concept lesson plans; sample lessons for integrated discipline activities; and a separate section devoted to *Children Moving* challenges written for the classroom teacher and designed for the recess or playground environment, with a focus on physical activities with minimum instruction and maximum participation for all students. Also included is a discussion of curriculum mapping with a skill theme approach and a sample curriculum plan to assist teachers in the process of planning by mapping. Tasks within the lesson plan book that are directly from *Children Moving* are highlighted in a different font to provide an easy reference to *Children Moving*. New to the ninth edition: Lesson plans are coded to show the direct reference to the chapters in Children Moving from which the lesson plan evolved.

Children Moving Web site

www.mhhe.com/graham9e
The Web site to accompany this text offers resources for both students and instructors. Visit this Web site to find useful materials such as:

For the Instructor

- Instructor's Manual
- Sample syllabi
- State curriculum guides
- The wheel and activities
- Downloadable PowerPoint presentations
- Lesson plan Web sites
- Lecture outlines
- Links to professional resources

For the Student

- State curriculum guides
- NASPE curriculum standards
- Sample lesson plan
- National organizations
- Student success strategies
- Lesson Plan Web sites
- eWheel
- Quizzes
- Self-scoring chapter quizzes
- Lesson plan template
- Fitness and nutrition journal
- Videos

McGraw-Hill Create™

Craft your teaching resources to match the way you teach! With McGraw-Hill Create™, you can easily rearrange chapters, combine material from other content sources, and quickly upload content you have written like your course syllabus or teaching notes. Find the content you need in Create by searching through thousands of leading McGraw-Hill textbooks. Arrange your book to fit your teaching style. Create even allows you to personalize your book's appearance by selecting the cover and adding your name, school, and course information. Order a Create book and you'll receive a complimentary print review copy in 3–5 business days or a complimentary electronic review copy (eComp) via email in minutes. Go to www.mcgrawhillcreate.com today and register to experience how McGraw-Hill Create empowers you to teach *your* students *your* way.

Electronic Textbook Option

This text is offered through CourseSmart for both instructors and students. CourseSmart is an online resource where students can purchase the complete text online at almost half the cost of a traditional text. Purchasing the eTextbook allows students to take advantage of CourseSmart's Web tools for learning, which include full text search, notes and highlighting, and email tools for sharing notes between classmates. To learn more about CourseSmart options, contact your sales representative or visit www.CourseSmart.com.

Acknowledgments

Children Moving continues to be a work in progress. Over the past 30 plus years, we have been fortunate to work with a number of dedicated professionals who have assisted and inspired us to continue to improve each edition. We would like to acknowledge many of the people who assisted us with this edition and previous ones. We are grateful for their efforts to work with us to continue to improve *Children Moving*.

- Eloise Elliott, Concord University, Athens, West Virginia, for writing Chapter 32, "Integrating the Skill Theme Approach Across the Curriculum," as well as for developing the instructor materials for the third through the sixth editions.
- Martin Block, University of Virginia, for his inspiration and shared philosophy concerning children with special needs.
- Kevin Patton, California State University, Chico, for developing the instructor materials for the last three editions of the book; your continual insight and reflection into preservice and inservice teacher development enhances what we do.
- Linda Sharp, J.D., of the University of Northern Colorado, for her ongoing expert advice related to the legal aspects of teaching physical education.
- Pat Petrie, research assistant, for her countless hours of assistance and attention to details.
- Rosa Edwards, Shawn Fortner, Liz Harkrader, Sharn Nicholson, John Pomeroy, Andy Lloyd, Larry Satchwell, Casey Jones, Lizzy Ginger, Karla Drury, Tia Ziegler, Nancy McNamee, and so many other children's physical education teachers—for your inspiration, dedication to children, and example in serving as role models for countless other teachers and thousands of children.
- The children at St. Mary's Elementary School, Grand Forks, North Dakota; Bluff Elementary School, Bluff, Utah; The Accelerated School, Los Angeles, California; and Madison Elementary School, Greeley, Colorado, who continually added to our understanding of linking skill themes with the development of personal and social responsibility.
- The children at Linden Elementary School in Oak Ridge, Tennessee, who create as well as follow our dreams of physical education for children.
- Marina Bonello for her insightful, analytic, copious questions and suggestions throughout this process.

Our Friday morning coffees were an invaluable contribution to the development of the ninth edition.

- Barbara Adamcik, for her ability to capture children's movement through photography.
- Josh Trout, Kevin Patton, Derek Sine, Van Tucker, and the Visual Anthropology Department of California State University, Chico, for making the seemingly impossible possible with photography that brought to life the critical elements of skill. We dreamed it; you did it. The children of Beth Giese's fifth/sixth class at Hooker Oak Elementary School and youngsters from the greater Chico, California, area who selflessly endured our "do it one more time" photography sessions.
- Tia Ziegler and the children of Chappelow K–8 Magnet School, Evans, CO; Karla Drury, Lizzy Ginger, and the children of Shawsheen and Monfort Elementary Schools, Greeley, CO; and Nathan and Dillon Patton for the children's drawings used throughout the book.
- Lans Hayes of Mayfield Publishing Company, who, in 1977, took a huge risk on four unknown authors with a radical idea.
- Jill Eccher, our freelance developmental editor for the eighth and ninth editions, as well as production editor for the seventh, eighth, and ninth editions, for her guidance, patience, gentle nagging, and unconditional support. She went way beyond the "call of duty," and we are most grateful for her efforts on our behalf.
- Deborah Kopka, our copyeditor for this edition, for her attention to detail, her patience with us as authors, and her love of children's physical education and movement.
- The entire McGraw-Hill book team who worked on this edition: Janice Roerig-Blong, Darlene Schueller, Melissa Leick, Colleen Havens, and Margarite Reynolds.
- We would like to offer special thanks to the countless teachers and students who have made so many positive and helpful comments since the first edition of *Children Moving* was published. Your support and encouragement continue to be much appreciated.
- Finally, we would like to thank the reviewers of this edition for their insights:

Sarah Bingham
Longwood University

Christine Brett
East Stroudsburg University

Nancy Estes
Florida Atlantic University-Davie

Julie Knutson
Saint Cloud State University

Patricia McDiarmid
Springfield College

Shaunna McGhie
Utah Valley University Orem

Laura Valley
University of Nevada-Reno

Kathryn Wiggins
Depaul University

Michael Wright
California State University-Sacramento

Students, are you looking for practical teaching techniques? Working hard to develop the skill theme approach with children? Trying to improve your grade? The features in *Children Moving* will help you do this and more! Take a look.

23
CHAPTER

Throwing and Catching

Key Concepts

Each chapter, or each part in the skills theme chapters, begins with a list of key concepts to help you focus your attention on the main topics as you begin studying each chapter. This learning tool also offers an accessible and practical method of review.

---

66   PART 2 Becoming a Reflective Teacher

www.mhhe.com/graham9e

Key Concepts

- Reflective teachers plan and revise their plans over the course of a career as they continue to strive to provide the most productive and enjoyable learning experiences for children.
- Planning is divided into four steps in this chapter.
- The first planning step is the development of a curriculum scope that outlines the content to be taught for several years.
- The second planning step is to decide how many lessons will be devoted to each of the skill themes and movement and fitness concepts during a year.
- The third planning step is the development of benchmarks or assessments that allow the reflective teacher to determine if the children are learning what is being taught.
- The final planning step is the development of daily lesson plans that are interesting and beneficial to youngsters.
- Ideally, lessons encourage students to be physically active during the majority of the lesson. Typically this occurs when children are able to be successful and consider the lesson fun.
- Just because a lesson is fun does not mean that it is a productive learning experience for children.

confusion; tasks that are interesting, enjoyable, and worthwhile; and, in some instances, less off-task behavior. In short, well-planned classes assist children to learn the concepts and skills being taught.

Reflective Planning

If all schools, all children, all facilities, all teachers, all communities, and all equipment were the same, we could simply provide you with a book of prepackaged lesson plans that would be successful with every class you teach, no matter the situation. As you know, however, that isn't the case. Reflective teachers plan lessons—and entire programs—that consider the various unique characteristics of their teaching situation (Graham et al. 1993; Housner and Griffey 1985).

The reflective planner considers many factors when trying to devise the best lessons possible under the circumstances. Planning can't be reduced to an exact formula, but certain factors will always influence lesson effectiveness. Each factor is important, and all interact to determine the teaching environment for which the reflective teacher must plan. As we described in Chapter 4, reflective teachers consider class size, frequency of class meetings, available equipment and facilities,

Reflective teachers are planners. Any good program begins with a good plan. Failure to plan appropriately can lead to disastrous lessons. Disorganization and spending an excessive amount of time on management characterize the lessons of the teacher who hasn't planned effectively.

Inappropriate planning can also have long-term implications. One important task of physical education is to provide a variety of learning experiences that give children a broad foundation of movement abilities (Stodden et al. 2008). Children who are skillful in only a few activities, typically games, may be the products of programs characterized by inefficient planning. Instructors who don't plan are likely to teach only what they know well and what the children enjoy, which often results in an unbalanced program over the years.

Because planning is typically done during the teacher's own time rather than during school time, there are strong temptations to avoid it. It can be much more pleasant to watch television, go to a ball game, or just go to bed early. But planning, even though you may consider it as onerous as homework, is necessary.

The benefits of effective planning include classes that run more smoothly with less interruption and

Effective teachers use many resources to plan successful lessons.

Online Learning Center Resources

Want a better grade? This address appears throughout to remind you about the study aids and other resources available at our Online Learning Center.

Box 22-2

Key Observation Points: Kicking a Stationary Ball in the Air

Arms extend forward

Foot placement alongside ball

Contact slightly below center

Contact with shoelaces

Slight backward lean of trunk

Follow through

successful physical activity within and beyond the school day. The skills of the tap/dribble and all its combinations are in the sport of soccer from beginning to advanced levels. The punt increases in accuracy, distance, and placement as the youngster advances from mastery of the skill to punting in football and soccer. The entire spectrum of kicking experiences, from precontrol through proficiency, is represented in our progression spiral on page 407. The tasks are stated in terms that imply a direct approach (see Chapter 10), but teachers are encouraged to vary the approach according to the purpose of the lesson and the characteristics of the class.

Precontrol Level (GLSP): Activities for Exploration of Kicking

At the precontrol level children are challenged to make contact with a stationary ball and with the gentle tap/tap of kicking a ball from foot to foot.

Kicking a Stationary Ball from a Stationary Position

Setting: A variety of plastic, foam, and rubber balls for kicking, placed around the gymnasium approximately 10 feet from the wall.

Tasks/Challenges:

Ⓣ Stand behind a kicking ball. Kick the ball really hard so it travels to the wall.

Ⓒ Practice until you can kick the ball three times in a row to the wall.

Ⓣ Practice kicking with one foot and then with the other foot.

Ⓣ Practice kicking the ball, making it go sometimes along the ground, sometimes in the air.

♟ What determines whether the ball travels along the ground or in the air?

Illustration Program

Instructional full-color illustrations and photographs throughout the book enhance learning with an exciting visual appeal.

Dribbling a ball past a defender into a goal is a dynamic game-like skill experience.

experiences don't occur in every lesson; they are only a part of the total physical education program.

We have divided games playing experiences into predesigned experiences and child-designed experiences. Each has its own inherent strengths and weaknesses.

Predesigned Games-Playing Experiences

There are three types of predesigned games-playing experiences: ready-made, modified ready-made, and teacher designed.

Ready-Made Games Ready-made games are those described in textbooks or learned in methods classes and taught to children without modification. The textbooks imply that such games will be appropriate, as well as interesting, for children. Brownies and Fairies; Duck, Duck, Goose; Red Rover; Four Square; and Steal the Bacon are well-known ready-made games.

Ready-made games are easy to teach because they require little preparation or teaching skill. The teacher selects a game and explains it to the children. When the children understand the game, they start to play, and the game continues until the lesson ends or the teacher changes the activity.

It has been our experience that few ready-made games are appropriate for all the children in a class. A few skilled children often dominate such games, whereas others are minimally involved, both physically and emotionally. Some (Belka 2004b) say these games should be discarded. However, you may occasionally encounter a situation in which a particular ready-made game is appropriate for a class or group of children. Usually, though, you'll find that although

many of the ideas in a ready-made game are worthwhile, you have to extensively modify the structure of the game to the abilities and interests of different children (Belka 2004b).

Nettie Wilson (1976) conducted a study to determine the number of throwing, catching, and kicking opportunities in the game of kickball as played by third- and fourth-grade children under the direction of a classroom teacher. Her findings include the following:

* *Less than half of the game was actually spent using the criterion skills.*
* *The average number of catches attempted in the kickball games was slightly more than two—35 percent of the children never caught the ball. Of the children who didn't catch the ball, 83 percent were girls.*
* *The average number of throws made in the kickball games, excluding those made by the pitcher and catcher, was slightly more than one—52 percent of the children never threw the ball at all during the entire game, and 67 percent of those who never threw the ball were girls.*

When I first started teaching, I was looking for games that were recommended for first-grade children and did not require a great deal of game skill. Brownies and Fairies, a simple running and chasing game, was prescribed in one text as appropriate for six-year-olds. The first time the game was played, two children fell down and bloodied their knees when they tried to run in a crowd of children. They could run by themselves without falling. But when they were placed in a dynamic situation that involved both running and dodging, they were unsuccessful. They probably forgot that experience many years ago—once their knees healed. I haven't.

Modified Ready-Made Games Modifying ready-made games requires greater planning and organizing ability. Yet by modifying a ready-made game, you can do much to make the game more appropriate for a particular class.

Both Rink (2010) and Stiehl, Morris, and Sinclair (2008) provide useful ideas for modifying ready-made games. The teacher can change the rules (e.g., allow two tries instead of only one); the equipment used (e.g., larger and lighter; the number of players involved (generally, it's best to decrease the number); the playing area (e.g., larger or smaller); or the skills involved (e.g., throwing instead of striking). Many teachers modify

Vignettes and Quotations

The authors and seasoned teachers provide real examples of experiences with students that relate to the topics discussed, for more insight into the dynamics of teaching.

Tasks/Challenges

The skill theme and movement concept chapters feature a suggested progression of tasks for children. Each task is worded in a conversational style that can be used to give instructions to the children about how to perform the task. Challenges are designed to maintain the children's interest in a particular task. Teachers can either use the challenges listed along with the tasks or create ones that seem appropriate for the children with whom they are working.

T As you're stretching to catch, don't forget to keep trying to catch in different places. So the task should be like this: Stretch and reach to catch in different places around your body.

The child's success with the previous tasks depends a great deal on the child's ability to throw so she or he has to stretch. It helps to practice stretching without the throw or simply throwing away from the body. If the students aren't catching on as you think they should, see if the reason is the throw.

Throwing Overhand at a High Stationary Target

Setting: Targets about 5 or 6 feet high on the wall, one for each student (paper plates with pictures on them make good targets); a spot for each child (to help maintain their spacing); a ball for each child.

When drawing targets for children to throw at, we do not draw faces on the targets. Putting faces on targets subtly reinforces the idea of throwing at people, a violent concept we do not support in physical education programs.

More Targets for Throwing

Two student teachers came up with a great target for Throwing Overhand at a Stationary Target. They partially filled self-tie plastic kitchen trash bags with old aluminum cans. On the outside of each bag they drew a target and then inserted a coat hanger in the top of each bag, closed it, taped it for reinforcement, and hung each one from various things in the gym. The children loved it—the targets were big and made noise when they were hit. The cleanup was much simpler than with plates, more than one child could work at a target, and the targets were reusable.

Throwing at a large target challenges youngsters at the control level.

Cues

| Eyes on Target | (Your eyes should be on the target all the time.) |
| Side, Arm, Step, Follow | (Don't forget the cues for throwing—always use them.) |

Tasks/Challenges:

T This time you're going to throw at targets. You'll have to keep your eyes on the target. Each of you has a target in your own space. See how often you can hit it.

T When you can hit your target three times in a row, take a giant step backward and try from that distance.

This same task can be changed for underhand throwing by lowering the targets to 2 to 3 feet from the floor. The second cue would change from Side to Face, Arm, Step, Follow.

Assessment Example

From the National Standards for Physical Education

Peer Observation

Using an appropriate size ball, students practice throwing at a target on the wall, alternating with a partner in five-throw turns. The students should be instructed to concentrate on the critical elements of throwing as taught by the instructor (i.e., ready position, arm preparation, opposite side to the target, step with leg opposite the throwing arm, follow-through, accuracy of throw). After each bout of five throws the partner gives feedback on one of the critical elements by drawing a smiley face on a score sheet each time the element was employed as instructed. Note changes in performance with subsequent five-throw bouts.

Skill Theme Development Progression
Throwing and Catching

Proficiency Level

Throwing and catching while using simple offense and defense in a small-sided invasion game
Throwing, catching, and dribbling in a small-sided invasion game
Throwing and catching with a football in a small-sided invasion game
Throwing and catching with a flying disc in a small-sided invasion game
Throwing and catching in a small-sided keep-away type invasion game
Throwing at a stationary object while being defended
Throwing and catching in a small-sided invasion game
Throwing to avoid a defender
Throwing and catching in a field, run, and score game-like situation
Throwing and catching a flying disc in different places around the body with a partner

Utilization Level

Throwing while in the air
Catching to throw quickly to a target
Catching to throw quickly to a partner
Throwing flying discs at targets
Throwing at a target from different distances
Throwing for distance and accuracy
Throwing to a moving target
Throwing to make a partner move to catch
Throwing on the move
Throwing and catching while traveling
Moving to catch

Control Level

Catching off a bounce
Throwing and catching over a net with a partner
Throwing and catching with a partner
Throwing for distance
Throwing a ball against a wall and catching the rebound
Catching off the fly
Catching with a scoop
Throwing a flying disc
Throwing backhand to a target
Throwing to high targets
Throwing underhand to targets: hoops
Throwing underhand to targets: jugs
Throwing overhand at a low stationary target
Throwing overhand at a high stationary target
Catching in different places around the body
Throwing an object to different levels and catching it
Bouncing a ball to self and catching it
All three throwing patterns: over, under, and side
Throwing sidearm
Throwing overhand
Throwing underhand

Precontrol Level

Tossing to self and catching
Drop–Catch
Catching from a skilled thrower
Catching a rolling ball
Throwing at a large target
Throwing a yarn ball against the wall

Skill Theme Development Sequences

The skill theme chapters contain hundreds of learning experiences designed to help children learn. Motor skills are organized according to the generic levels of skill proficiency in a spiral progression from beginning to advanced.

As you're stretching to catch, don't forget to keep trying to catch in different places. So the task should be like this: Stretch and reach to catch in different places around your body.

The child's success with the previous tasks depends a great deal on the child's ability to throw so she or he has to stretch. It helps to practice stretching without the throw or simply throwing away from the body. If the students aren't catching on as you think they should, see if the reason is the throw.

Throwing Overhand at a High Stationary Target

Setting: Targets about 5 or 6 feet high on the wall, one for each student (paper plates with pictures on them make good targets), a spot for each child (to help maintain their spacing); a ball for each child.

When drawing targets for children to throw at, we do not draw faces on the targets. Putting faces on targets subtly reinforces the idea of throwing at people, a violent concept we do not support in physical education programs.

More Targets for Throwing

Two student teachers came up with a great target for Throwing Overhand at a Stationary Target. They partially filled self-tie plastic kitchen trash bags with old aluminum cans. On the outside of each bag they drew a target and then inserted a coat hanger in the top of each bag, closed it, taped it for reinforcement, and hung each one from various things in the gym. The children loved it—the targets were big and made noise when they were hit. The cleanup was much simpler than with plates, more than one child could work at a target, and the targets were reusable.

Throwing at a large target challenges youngsters at the control level.

Cues	
Eyes on Target	(Your eyes should be on the target all the time.)
Side, Arm, Step, Follow	(Don't forget the cues for throwing—always use them.)

Tasks/Challenges:

This time you're going to throw at targets. You'll have to keep your eyes on the target. Each of you has a target in your own space. See how often you can hit it.

When you can hit your target three times in a row, take a giant step backward and try from that distance.

This same task can be changed for underhand throwing by lowering the targets to 2 to 3 feet from the floor. The second cue would change from Side to Face, Arm, Step, Follow.

Assessment Example

From the National Standards for Physical Education

Peer Observation
Using an appropriate size ball, students practice throwing at a target on the wall, alternating with a partner in five-throw turns. The students should be instructed to concentrate on the critical elements of throwing as taught by the instructor (i.e., ready position, arm preparation, opposite side to the target, step with leg opposite the throwing arm, follow-through, accuracy of throw). After each bout of five throws the partner gives feedback on one of the critical elements by drawing a smiley face on a score sheet each time the element was employed as instructed. Note changes in performance with subsequent five-throw bouts.

Cues

Cues can be used to help children perform a skill more efficiently. A selection of cues is presented at the beginning of each series of tasks. The teacher can choose a cue that is appropriate for a particular child to make the task easier for that child to perform. Many of the cues are illustrated in color photographic sequences to allow the child to perform the skill correctly.

Assessment Ideas

Assessment tools are designed to see what students have learned in relation to the goals set by the teacher. These assessment ideas include an array of options from exit (or entrance) slips that can be used to quickly assess cognitive and affective learning to teacher observation checklists and digital analysis to verify psychomotor skills.

---

they are continually self-analyzing their teaching in order to improve. They don't teach the same lessons over and over, year after year. They change their lessons from class to class, day to day, and year to year based on their reflections about how and what might be improved.

We wish that simply reading and understanding *Children Moving* would be enough to become a reflective teacher. It's not! If you have become a good athlete, an excellent musician or artist, or made the dean's list every semester, you know how much time and hard work it takes to attain your level of achievement. Reflective teachers are no different. As you know by now, becoming an excellent teacher takes many, many hours of hard work. Just because a teacher has 10 or 15 years of teaching experience and a master's degree does not mean he or she has become an excellent teacher. The process of reflective teaching is no different. *Children Moving* will guide you in the process of beginning to become a reflective teacher. We hope you find your journey both enjoyable and worthwhile.

Summary

Six major variables necessitate the need for reflective teaching, or differentiated instruction: the values of the teacher, class size, the number of class sessions per week, facilities and equipment, student behavior, and the context of the school. The reflective teacher considers the characteristics of each class and the abilities of the individual students. A reflective teacher doesn't expect all children to respond in the same way or to achieve the same level of skill. Reflective teachers continually observe and analyze, a process that enables them to revise their expectations and adapt all the components of the program, thereby constantly improving the program's effectiveness. The reflective approach requires that teachers constantly and accurately monitor their teaching as they attempt to design and implement a physical education program for a given school. Reflective teachers also have a wealth of content knowledge that allows them to adapt and modify tasks for individuals of varying abilities. The process of becoming a reflective teacher takes time and practice. *Children Moving* is designed to guide you in this process.

Reading Comprehension Questions

1. What is reflective teaching? What are its basic characteristics?
2. What does a linear approach to teaching mean? What is a prepackaged curriculum? How is it different from the skill theme approach?
3. Provide three examples of how class size influences the way a teacher teaches a lesson.
4. Provide an example of a teacher who rolls out the ball. Contrast that teacher with a reflective teacher. What do they do differently in their planning, teaching, and assessment of their teaching?
5. In the previous two chapters you have learned about skill themes and movement concepts. Explain the difference(s) between skill themes and games like Duck, Duck, Goose or elimination dodgeball.
6. In your own words, explain the major implication of reflective teaching, or differentiated instruction.

References/Suggested Readings

Allen, D. 1975. The future of education: Where do we go from here? *Journal of Teacher Education* 26: 41–45.

Foster, H. L. 1974. *Ribbin', jivin' and playin' the dozens: The unrecognized dilemma of inner-city schools.* Cambridge, MA: Ballinger.

Good, T. L., B. J. Biddle, and J. E. Brophy. 1975. *Teachers make a difference.* New York: Holt, Rinehart & Winston.

Graham, G. 2008. *Teaching children physical education: Becoming a master teacher.* 2nd ed. Champaign, IL: Human Kinetics.

Graham, G., C. Hopple, M. Manross, and T. Sitzman. 1993. Novice and experienced children's physical education teachers: Insights into their situational decision-making. *Journal of Teaching in Physical Education* 12: 197–217.

Summaries

The chapter summaries highlight the major topics and concepts discussed in the chapter. They can be used for clarification or for review for examinations.

Reading Comprehension Questions

A set of questions appears at the end of each chapter to allow you to test your understanding of the content. This tool offers a means of reviewing and analyzing the material.

References/Suggested Readings

At the end of each chapter are references that support the text discussion and additional sources for study and exploration.

---

they are continually self-analyzing their teaching in order to improve. They don't teach the same lessons over and over, year after year. They change their lessons from class to class, day to day, and year to year based on their reflections about how and what might be improved.

We wish that simply reading and understanding *Children Moving* would be enough to become a reflective teacher. It's not! If you have become a good athlete, an excellent musician or artist, or made the dean's list every semester, you know how much time and hard work it takes to attain your level of achievement. Reflective teachers are no different. As you know by now, becoming an excellent teacher takes many, many hours of hard work. Just because a teacher has 10 or 15 years of teaching experience and a master's degree does not mean he or she has become an excellent teacher. The process of reflective teaching is no different. *Children Moving* will guide you in the process of beginning to become a reflective teacher. We hope you find your journey both enjoyable and worthwhile.

Summary

Six major variables necessitate the need for reflective teaching, or differentiated instruction: the values of the teacher, class size, the number of class sessions per week, facilities and equipment, student behavior, and the context of the school. The reflective teacher considers the characteristics of each class and the abilities of the individual students. A reflective teacher doesn't expect all children to respond in the same way or to achieve the same level of skill. Reflective teachers continually observe and analyze, a process that enables them to revise their expectations and adapt all the components of the program, thereby constantly improving the program's effectiveness. The reflective approach requires that teachers constantly and accurately monitor their teaching as they attempt to design and implement a physical education program for a given school. Reflective teachers also have a wealth of content knowledge that allows them to adapt and modify tasks for individuals of varying abilities. The process of becoming a reflective teacher takes time and practice. *Children Moving* is designed to guide you in this process.

Reading Comprehension Questions

1. What is reflective teaching? What are its basic characteristics?
2. What does a linear approach to teaching mean? What is a prepackaged curriculum? How is it different from the skill theme approach?
3. Provide three examples of how class size influences the way a teacher teaches a lesson.
4. Provide an example of a teacher who rolls out the ball. Contrast that teacher with a reflective teacher.
5. In the previous two chapters you have learned about skill themes and movement concepts. Explain the difference(s) between skill themes and games like Duck, Duck, Goose or elimination dodgeball.
6. In your own words, explain the major implication of reflective teaching, or differentiated instruction.

References/Suggested Readings

Allen, D. 1975. The future of education: Where do we go from here? *Journal of Teacher Education* 26: 41–45.

Foster, H. L. 1974. *Ribbin', jivin' and playin' the dozens: The unrecognized dilemma of inner-city schools.* Cambridge, MA: Ballinger.

Good, T. L., B. J. Biddle, and J. E. Brophy. 1975. *Teachers make a difference.* New York: Holt, Rinehart & Winston.

Graham, G. 2008. *Teaching children physical education: Becoming a master teacher.* 2nd ed. Champaign, IL: Human Kinetics.

Graham, G., C. Hopple, M. Manross, and T. Sitzman. 1993. Novice and experienced children's physical education teachers: Insights into their situational decision-making. *Journal of Teaching in Physical Education* 12: 197–217.

Sample Two-Day-a-Week Lesson Topics for Primary Grade Classes (72 Days a Year)

Week	Chapter	Day	
1	8	1	Establishing an Environment for Learning (pgs. 99–125)
	8	2	Establishing an Environment for Learning (cont.) (pgs. 99–125)
2	13	1	Exploring Self-Space (p. 212)
	13	2	Exploring General Space (p. 214)
3	13	1	Traveling in Different Directions (p. 217)
	13	2	Traveling and Freezing at Different Levels (p. 218)
4	27	1	Teaching Physical Fitness, Physical Activity, and Wellness (p. 561)
	23	2	Throwing at a Large Target (p. 439)
5	23	1	Catching a Rolling Ball (p. 440); Catching from a Skilled Thrower (p. 440)
	16	2	Traveling with Different Locomotor Patterns (p. 271): Sliding; Galloping; Hopping; Skipping (p. 274)
6	16	1	Performing Locomotor Sequences (p. 276)
	17	2	Traveling to Flee (p. 295); Fleeing from a Partner (p. 296)
7	17	1	Traveling to Dodge (p. 295); Dodging the Obstacles (p. 296)
	22	2	Kicking a Stationary Ball from a Stationary Position (p. 408)
8	22	1	Approaching a Stationary Ball and Kicking (p. 409); Kicking in the Air (p. 410)
	22	2	Dropping, Bouncing, and Kicking Lightweight Balls (p. 425); Dropping and Punting (p. 425)
9	19	1	Jumping and Landing: Basic Patterns (p. 326)
	27	2	Teaching Physical Fitness, Physical Activity, and Wellness (p. 561)
10	24	1	Volleying Balloons in the Air (p. 466)
	24	2	Volleying a Ball Upward (Underhand Pattern) (p. 468)
11	24	1	Bouncing a Ball Down (Dribbling) Continuously (p. 483)
	24	2	Dribbling and Walking (p. 483)
12	14	1	Exploring Time (p. 229)
	14	2	Exploring Force (p. 234)
13	14	1	Traveling and Changing Force Qualities (p. 234)
	8	2	Establishing an Environment for Learning (p. 101)
14	13	1	Exploring Pathways (p. 219)
	13	2	Exploring Extensions (p. 223)
15	16	1	Moving to Rhythms (p. 278)
	27	2	Teaching Physical Fitness, Physical Activity, and Wellness (p. 561)
16	25	1	Striking Down; Striking Up (pp. 504, 505)
	25	2	Striking Up and Down (p. 505)
17	19	1	Jumping over Low Obstacles: Hoops (p. 329); Jumping over Low Obstacles: Hurdles (p. 329)
	19	2	Jumping a Turned Rope (p. 330); Jumping a Self-Turned Rope (p. 331)
18	15	1	Identifying Body Parts (p. 244); Balancing on Matching and Nonmatching Parts (p. 245)
	15	2	Traveling and Freezing in Different Body Shapes (p. 247)
19	27	1	Teaching Physical Fitness, Physical Activity, and Wellness (p. 561)
	16	2	Leaping (p. 268)
20	15	1	Over, Under, Around, In Front Of, and Behind Concepts (p. 252)
	16	2	Locomotors and Rhythm: The Follow-Me Dance (p. 280)
21	21	1	Rocking on Different Body Parts (p. 388); Rocking to Match a Partner (p. 387)
	21	2	Rolling Sideways (p. 387); Rolling Forward (p. 389)
22		1	Special Event
	15	2	Matching (p. 256); Mirroring (p. 257); Matching and Mirroring (p. 257)
23	20	1	Balancing on Different Bases of Support (pp. 345, 348)
	20	2	Balancing in Different Body Shapes (pp. 346, 349)
24	21	1	Rolling in a Long, Narrow Position (Log Roll) (p. 387)
	21	2	Rocking Backward (p. 388); Rocking Backward over the Shoulders (p. 391)
25	21	1	Transferring Weight to Hands Momentarily (p. 370)
	21	2	Transferring Weight to Hands Across Mats (p. 371)
26	23	1	Throwing Overhand (p. 441); Throwing Underhand (p. 441); Throwing Sidearm (p. 442)
	23	2	Throwing a Ball Against a Wall and Catching the Rebound (p. 448)

(continued)

Appendix

The Appendix to this book offers two sample school-year overviews (scopes and sequences) based on the material in *Children Moving*. These overviews can be followed exactly as presented or used as a model for developing your own quality physical education program.

Introduction and Content Overview

Trent

A quality program of physical education for children is much more than simply a bunch of activities that children enjoy for 30 minutes or so several times a week. A quality program of physical education has a definite purpose and long-term goals, and is developmentally and instructionally appropriate; in short, it makes a difference for children that lasts well beyond elementary school. Part 1 of *Children Moving* contains the first three chapters and documents the importance of a quality program of physical education for children and also introduces you to the skill theme approach.

Chapter 1, "The Value and Purpose of Physical Education for Children," answers three important questions as an introduction and overview to the book. The first two answers respond to the need for, and the importance of, physical education for children. The last answer provides insights into the characteristics of a physical education program for children that is positive and guides them in the process of becoming physically active for a lifetime. As you will see, these responses are based on recent publications written by some of the leading experts in physical activity for children. Together they define a clear and unified direction (outcomes) for programs of physical education while also suggesting a process (developmentally appropriate) that is consistent with contemporary approaches for teaching children.

Chapter 2, "The Skill Theme Approach," answers many of the questions that teachers often ask when they are first exposed to the skill theme approach. Because the skill theme curriculum is organized by skills and concepts rather than by games, gymnastics, and dance, for example, some teachers initially find the approach confusing. In Chapter 2, we use a question-and-answer format to respond to these questions.

Then, in Chapter 3, "Skill Themes, Movement Concepts, and the *National Standards*," we define the skill themes and movement concepts. Chapter 3 also includes the rationale for the skill theme approach in children's physical education and demonstrates how it is aligned with national physical education standards as well as state and district standards that have adopted or adapted the national standards.

The Value and Purpose of Physical Education for Children

As the old man walked the beach at dawn, he noticed a young man ahead of him picking up starfish and flinging them into the sea. Finally catching up with the youth, he asked him why he was doing this. The answer was that the stranded starfish would die if left until the morning sun.

"But the beach goes on for miles and there are millions of starfish," countered the old man. "How can your effort make any difference?"

The young man looked at the starfish in his hand and then threw it to the safety of the waves. "It makes a difference to this one," he said.

—DONALD QUIMBY (1988)

If you don't take care of your body, where are you going to live?

—AUTHOR UNKNOWN

What if you could give the children you teach a gift to help them live longer, happier, healthier lives? Of course you are thinking "sure I would like to do that." You also have numerous questions. What is involved? Would this program be for every child? Would it be expensive? How long would it take? Can I really do that?

As a teacher the gift you can give the children you teach is a love and enjoyment of sports and physical activity that leads to fun, frequent participation in physical activity as children, adolescents, and adults. *Children Moving* describes, in detail, how to develop a quality program of elementary school physical education. Many experts believe programs like this provide a foundation that leads to developing the competence that leads to confidence and the enjoyment of physical activity for a lifetime. This book provides a complete blueprint for teachers who are interested in starting children on the path to obtain the skills, knowledge, and attitudes that lead to a physically active lifestyle.

Children, especially young children, love to move. They enjoy squirming, wriggling, crawling, running, chasing, jumping, rolling, balancing, kicking, throwing, and many other activities. For parents and teachers the challenge is getting the children to stop moving—for just a few minutes. And then, at about 10 or 12 years of age, this torrent of physical activity becomes a trickle for far too many children. Why? What can be done to encourage children, all children, to continue this enjoyment of movement into their teen and adult years? In short, what can teachers and schools do to encourage children to continue moving throughout their lifetime?

Children Moving attempts to provide answers to many of these questions. The goal of this book is to describe both a curriculum and the companion teaching skills that are designed to guide youngsters in the process of becoming physically active for a lifetime. There is general agreement that skillfulness, the ability to perform fundamental and sports-related motor skills, is an important prerequisite for adopting a physically active lifestyle (Clark 2007). Our goal is also to teach children to value physical activity for all the benefits that are described later in this chapter—as well as the pure enjoyment and satisfaction that comes from successful and enjoyable participation in sports and physical activity.

Why are some adults physically active and others not? We don't have the research to answer this question. We have limited evidence suggesting that physically active children become physically active adolescents and adults (Barnett et al. 2008; Ennis 2011; Malina 2001; Stodden, Langendorfer, and Roberton 2009). And we have a solid evidence base that physically active children, as well as adults, derive substantial benefits from being physically active (USDHHS 1996).

Children Moving is based on the premise that to truly enjoy many of the physical activities and sports participated in by adults, one needs a certain level of skillfulness. The ideal time to learn these foundational motor and sports skills is when children are young and they so enjoy moving in any form. One of the important characteristics of motor skills is that once they are learned, they are retained for a lifetime. Swimming and riding a bike are two good examples. While we may not be as adept at these skills if we have not done them for 20 years or so, our bodies (kinesthetic memory) don't forget. Thus the goal of *Children Moving* is to describe effective techniques and strategies to assist children in acquiring many of the foundational motor skills that children and adults use in sports and physical activities. In short, we are assisting children to develop the physical literacy they will need to enjoy physical activity for a lifetime.

Positive physical education programs emphasize enjoyable participation in physical activity and "help students develop the knowledge, attitudes, motor skills, behavioral skills, and confidence needed to adopt and maintain physically active lifestyles" (NCCDPHP 1997, 205). Our goal is to keep the love of movement (exercise) alive in youngsters so that they associate exercise with enjoyment and fun!

It is important to emphasize that quality programs do far more than simply provide opportunities for children to be physically active for the few minutes they are in physical education class (NASPE 2006). As will be explained throughout the book, quality physical education programs actually teach children the fundamental motor and sports skills used in all types of physical activities and sports— while also keeping the children physically active throughout the lesson (NASPE 2011). It is analogous to teaching reading or mathematics—children learn the fundamental skills in elementary school and then apply them in middle school and high school—and throughout their lives. As you will learn in this book, physical education for children is far more than just playing a few games or learning a dance or two. It is a process of providing learning experiences that lead to competence and confidence in physical activity and sports.

Since 1996, when the Surgeon General of the United States released his report documenting the important contribution regular physical activity can make to good health (USDHHS 1996), the importance of physical activity has been recognized as never before. In 2005 Strong and his colleagues reviewed 850 research studies and concluded that "school age youth should participate daily in 60 minutes or more of moderate to vigorous physical activity that is developmentally appropriate, enjoyable and involves a variety of activities" (Strong et al. 2005, 732). In 2008, the U.S. Department of Health and Human Services (USDHHS) issued *Physical Activity Guidelines for Americans*, which provide science-based recommendations to help persons age 6 or older improve their health through physical activity. The guidelines recommend that children and adolescents should have 60 minutes or more of physical activity daily (USDHHS 2008). Quality programs of physical education contribute to the recommended 60 minutes or more of daily physical activity—but they do far more than provide opportunities for children to be physically active.

This chapter answers three questions about physical education and physical activity:

1. Why do children need quality physical education programs?
2. What health benefits are associated with a lifetime of physical activity?

3. What components of a physical education program encourage youngsters to maintain physically active lifestyles?

Why Children Need Physical Education

Why do children need physical education? A quality program of physical education can lead children to a lifetime of physical activity—and the enormous health, cognitive, and social benefits associated with participation in sports and physical activity.

Look at the list below from the Centers for Disease Control (CDC) in 2011 that outlines how regular physical activity can improve health. Physical activity, including sports, does the following:

- Reduces the risk of dying prematurely
- Reduces the risk of dying from heart disease
- Reduces the risk of developing diabetes
- Reduces the risk of developing high blood pressure
- Helps reduce blood pressure in people who already have high blood pressure
- Reduces the risk of developing colon cancer
- Reduces feelings of depression and anxiety
- Helps control weight
- Helps build and maintain healthy bones, muscles, and joints
- Helps older adults become stronger and better able to move about without falling
- Promotes psychological well-being (CDC, 2011).

Children *and* adults need physical activity for these and other reasons outlined later.

Physical activity and sports are more than fun— they are a great way to lessen the chance of the health risks cited above. Physical education is the subject in elementary school that teaches children the importance of physical activity and also provides them with the foundation of motor skills necessary for enjoyable participation in physical activity.

In addition to the health benefits associated with regular physical activity documented by the CDC above, numerous related benefits have been summarized by the National Association for Sport and Physical Education (NASPE 2002, 7) and are adapted here. They include:

Regular, healthful physical activity According to the American Heart Association (AMA 2011) regular physical activity, as well as an appropriate diet, are the best antidotes to turn around the current obesity epidemic and also provide a positive alternative to television and computer screen time.

Skill development In a quality physical education program, children learn the fundamental motor and sport skills that enable them to develop the competence that creates confidence and leads to safe and successful participation in a wide range of sports and physical activities as adults (Chapters 16–26).

Improved physical fitness Children are encouraged to improve their muscular and cardiovascular endurance, strength, and flexibility (Chapter 27).

Reinforcement of subjects taught in the classroom Movement can be used to reinforce the understanding of many subjects taught in the classroom (e.g., mathematics and reading). Movement is also associated with enhanced brain functioning (Chapter 32).

Self-discipline Youngsters can learn valuable lessons about accepting responsibility for their personal motor skill and fitness development (Chapter 9).

Goal setting Physical education classes are an excellent laboratory for helping youngsters understand the process of setting and achieving goals, especially physical fitness.

> *Girls who do not participate in sports before the age of 10 have less than a 10 percent chance of doing so at age 25.*
>
> —DONNA LOPIANO, Women's Sports Foundation

Leadership and cooperation Many physical education activities require youngsters to work in groups to solve problems or as a team. These opportunities become an excellent laboratory for developing both leadership and cooperation skills.

Enhanced self-efficacy The motor domain is especially important to young children who have yet to fully develop their verbal communication skills. Thus, confidence in physical abilities may lead to positive feelings of self-esteem.

Stress reduction A good workout helps ease stress, tension, and anxiety and may result in better attention in the classroom.

Strengthened peer relationships Sports and physical activity are excellent ways to meet and make new friends. Confidence in one's physical abilities encourages youngsters, and later adults, to socialize more easily and fit into a variety of situations.

This list briefly summarizes many of the benefits experts agree are outcomes that accrue to those who are physically active. There are also serious consequences related to not being physically active (Box 1-1).

Box 1-1

The Physically Uneducated Adult

Adults who are physically uneducated often find themselves in awkward and unpleasant situations. For example, they may:

- Be overweight partly as a result of physical inactivity
- Have chronic lower back pain
- Have painful memories of being picked last when teams were chosen
- Remember being laughed at because they couldn't catch a softball or were afraid of a volleyball
- Recall being last whenever they ran laps
- Dread the memory of never being able to do even one pull-up on the physical fitness test
- Be uncomfortable starting and maintaining an exercise program
- Feel like a klutz and make excuses to avoid physical activity
- Believe that athletes were born that way
- Not understand there are virtually hundreds of ways to exercise and they would enjoy some of them

It is estimated that 65 percent of adults today are overweight or obese.

Box 1-2

Significant Seminal Surgeon Report Linking Physical Activity and Health Benefits

In 1996 the Surgeon General of the United States published a significant report that documented, for the first time, the relationship between regular physical activity and health. Here are some of the research-based observations in the report (USDHHS 1996). These findings have also been supported in the recently released document *Physical Activity Guidelines for Americans* (USDHHS 2008).

- Significant health benefits can be obtained by including a moderate amount of physical activity (e.g., 30 minutes of brisk walking or raking leaves, 15 minutes of running, or 45 minutes of volleyball) on most, if not all, days of the week. Through a modest increase in daily activity, most Americans can improve their health and quality of life (4).

- Additional health benefits can be gained through greater amounts of physical activity. People who can maintain a regular regimen of activity that is of longer duration or of more vigorous intensity are likely to derive greater benefit (4).
- Consistent influences on physical activity patterns among adults and young people include confidence in one's ability to engage in regular physical activity (e.g., self-efficacy), enjoyment of physical activity, support from others, positive beliefs concerning the benefits of physical activity, and lack of perceived barriers to physical activity (249).
- Physical activity appears to improve health-related quality of life by enhancing psychological well-being and by improving physical functioning in persons compromised by poor health (8).

Children Moving introduces you to the skill theme approach that is designed for every child, from the least skilled child in a class to the most athletic youngster. The book explains the ways you can guide all children in positive directions, as referenced in the Surgeon General's Report (Box 1-2), enabling them to develop the competence that leads to confidence in their physical abilities. This competence and confidence eventually culminate in a desire to participate regularly in physical activity because it has become an enjoyable and important part of their lives as children, as teens, and later as adults.

Clearly, the accumulated evidence suggests that youngsters who develop physically active lifestyles stand to gain enormous health, social, and emotional benefits. However, this doesn't happen automatically. Programs must be carefully designed and implemented if they are to guide youngsters to become physically active for a lifetime.

As anyone who knows children will quickly acknowledge, however, fears of heart disease, stress, or back pain in later years are not major concerns for most 8- or 10-year-olds. To them, 40 seems old! Fortunately children enter school loving to move and be

Children enjoy seeing how they can take their weight on their hands on a beautiful sunny day outside.

active. One of the early tasks of primary-grade classroom teachers is to teach children to listen and stay in their seats. Most youngsters would prefer to be up and moving. Physical educators' challenge is not so much to instill a love of movement as it is to keep alive and channel this inborn urge to move so that as individuals enter their adult years they will continue to enjoy being physically active and will derive all the physical, emotional, and social benefits that come to those who have been physically active throughout their lifetimes.

Characteristics of a Quality Physical Education Program

At this point in the chapter you may be asking how the program described in *Children Moving* is different from the program you had in elementary school. We hope that most of the characteristics described apply to the program you experienced in elementary school. Once again we look to the National Association for Sport and Physical Education (NASPE) for its definition of a quality physical education program (NASPE 2002, 7) and guidelines developed by the United States Department of Health and Human Services in its *School Health Index* (USDHHS 2000, 3–8). Some of the characteristics of a positive, or quality, program of physical education are straightforward and require little or no explanation. Others are lengthier because they are not as obvious or easily understood. The characteristics are bulleted, rather than numbered, because they are all important parts of a positive physical education program that leads to the benefits described in the first two sections of this chapter.

The Physical Activity Hourglass

Opportunities to be physically active can be depicted as an hourglass. Young children have plenty of opportunities to be physically active. Playgrounds, parks, and an increasing number of fast-food chains have equipment for children to climb on, over, around, and through. Young children also are encouraged to run and chase their friends and siblings. Many communities also have soccer, basketball, and softball or baseball leagues for young children. There are also opportunities to be on a swim team and take lessons in dance or martial arts.

Unfortunately, once a youngster enters middle school, many of these opportunities are reduced, unless a youngster is athletic. Too often if a middle school sponsors athletic teams, only a relatively few "make the team." The same is true at the high school level for athletics and intramurals. If intramurals are offered, many are limited to team sports after school. Also, in many schools it is not "cool" to play intramurals or have your parents drive you to a dance lesson.

After high school, however, there are once again a plethora of physical activities for adults. They include weight and fitness clubs, recreation programs, and simply walking, jogging, or biking activities that were not "cool" in secondary school but are acceptable to an adult, especially as one ages and/or puts on additional pounds.

Physical Activity Hourglass

Preschool and elementary
Multitude of opportunities

Secondary school
Limited to school sports and intramurals

Adults
Multitude of opportunities

- *Time* Ideally children have physical education for at least 150 minutes each week (USDHHS 2000). This is especially important if they are to develop the fundamental motor skills that are so necessary for successful and enjoyable participation in sports and physical activities in later years. NASPE recommends 150 minutes per week in elementary school and 225 minutes for middle and high school.
- *Class size* The number of children in a physical education class should be the same number as in the classroom.
- *Sequential, developmental curriculum* Teachers follow a carefully planned curriculum scope and sequence that progressively builds on past experiences and incorporates new experiences when children are developmentally ready. (The Appendix provides examples of curricular scopes and sequences based on the content in this book.) Lessons are not simply selected randomly with no obvious connection to past and future lessons or just as a way to keep children busy, happy, or good for 30 minutes.
- *Minimum of 50 percent MVPA* Physical education is a moving experience. In quality physical education programs, teachers find ways to actively engage all children in moderate to vigorous physical activity (MVPA) for the majority of every lesson while they are also learning motor and sports skills (USDHHS 2000).

- *Plenty of practice opportunities* In addition to being actively engaged, children also need plenty of opportunities to practice the skill or concept being taught that day. In a game of kickball, children average fewer than two chances to throw, kick, and catch during an entire game. And girls have fewer chances than boys (Wilson 1976)! Quality programs provide many practice opportunities (opportunities to learn) for children to develop their motor skills, sometimes alone, sometimes with a partner, and sometimes in small-sided games or with groups.

- *High rates of success* In addition to copious practice opportunities, teachers also design lessons so that youngsters of all abilities have high rates of success (Chapter 10). When youngsters, especially the unskilled, experience success, they are more likely to continue practicing and working to improve than when they fail continually. This is especially important in physical education because success and failure are so readily observable. For this reason, many programs have switched from a curriculum consisting predominantly of low-organized games and team sports (e.g., kickball, basketball, dodgeball, and soccer) to the skill theme approach as described in *Children Moving.* Thus the athletic youngsters, all too often boys, are no longer allowed to dominate (Portman 1995), and physical education is for every youngster, especially the poorly coordinated, overweight, or awkward children who stand to benefit the most from a quality program of physical education.

- *Positive emotional environment* Quality physical education classes, in addition to promoting successful learning experiences, are also emotionally warm, nurturing environments in which children are encouraged to practice learning new motor skills and improve their physical fitness without feeling embarrassed or humiliated by the teacher or their peers (Chapter 8).

Children derive lifetime benefits from becoming physically active.

Developmentally and Instructionally Appropriate Experiences

In the early 1990s the National Association for the Education of Young Children (NAEYC) published a series of articles and documents describing developmentally appropriate educational experiences for young children (Bredekamp 1992). The ideas in these documents were extremely popular with educators and parents. Several years later the Council on Physical Education for Children (COPEC 1992) used the same format to describe developmentally and instructionally appropriate elementary school physical education experiences for children. This position statement was also highly popular. Since 1992, similar documents have been published by NASPE for preschool, middle school, high school, and college physical education programs (COPEC 2000; MASSPEC 2001, 2004; NASPE 2009). These documents can be purchased from NASPE or downloaded from the Internet by clicking on the publications section of the NASPE Web site: www.aahperd.org/naspe/.

Quality physical education is both developmentally and instructionally suitable for the specific children being served. Developmentally appropriate practices in physical education are those that recognize children's changing capacities to move and those that promote such change. A developmentally appropriate physical education program accommodates a variety of individual characteristics, such as developmental status, previous movement experiences, fitness and skill levels, body size, and age. Instructionally appropriate physical education incorporates the best known practices, derived from both research and experiences teaching children, into a program that maximizes opportunities for learning and success for all children (COPEC 1992, 3).

In addition to defining *developmentally and instructionally appropriate,* these documents describe in easy-to-follow, straightforward terms the tenets of the new physical education that has been evolving over the past three decades. They emphasize, for example, that:

- Children develop at different rates, and therefore educators should recognize these variances by designing experiences that allow for individual differences in abilities.
- For learning to occur, youngsters need lots of opportunities to practice a skill or movement at high rates of success.
- It is inappropriate to use exercise as punishment.
- The physical education curriculum should have a clear scope and sequence, with observable outcomes that can be assessed.
- Allowing captains to pick teams, overemphasizing competition, and giving fitness tests to one student at a time while the rest of the class watches are inappropriate educational practices.

These documents clearly make the point that physical education curriculums that consist solely of large-group games, often played with one ball, are both developmentally and instructionally inappropriate.

- *Teacher background* The teacher has an extensive background in both the content and pedagogy of physical education for children, typically obtained as a physical education major in college. There are also classroom teachers who provide excellent movement experiences for their youngsters despite their relatively limited background. For this reason *Children Moving* is written for both the physical education major, or specialist, as well as the classroom teacher.
- *Realistic expectations* Teachers with an extensive background in children's physical education are able to develop realistic programs when their time is less than the recommended 150 minutes per week. The emphasis is on "developing basic motor skills that allow participation in a variety of physical activities" (NCCDPHP 1997, 209).
- *Adequate equipment and facilities* Many excellent physical education programs have substandard facilities and equipment. Ideally, however, every program has both an indoor and outdoor facility and a wide variety of equipment so children do not have to wait for turns to use equipment.
- *Enjoyability* Quality physical education classes are also fun classes. Children should enjoy and look forward to coming to physical education class. The best teachers find ways to make learning fun.

The 60-Second One-Ball Test

Principals and parents typically do not have time to spend hours observing a physical education class to determine if it is a quality program. A rough estimate can be made in a short amount of time, however, by using the 60-second one-ball test. Here are the directions.

When you walk (or drive) by a physical education lesson, observe how many balls are in use (obviously this applies only to lessons in which balls are being used). If there is only one ball for an entire class of 20 youngsters or more, make a mental note. This typically takes less than 60 seconds, as the intent is not to observe an entire lesson. As you notice more lessons, keep track of the number of balls being used.

After observing five or more lessons, you will have an idea of the amount of practice opportunities children are getting in their physical education classes. If all the lessons use only one ball, then you know the amount of practice is severely limited, just as if a reading class was using only one book for an entire class. In contrast, if every child had a ball in the lessons you observed, then you know the teacher is attempting to maximize practice opportunities for children. Although this is hardly a scientific approach, it does provide one generalized indicator about the quality of a program.

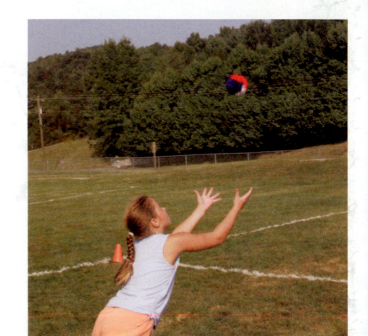

Catching is a skill used in many sports and physical activities.

- *Physical (psychomotor), cognitive, and affective domains* Although the major emphasis in physical education is on the physical or psychomotor domain, quality programs also take every opportunity to emphasize cognitive concepts and to develop an environment that encourages positive social experiences and attitude development.

Cognitive Domain

If you are or plan to be teaching in the classroom, you will find this section on the cognitive domain especially interesting. There is a rapidly accumulating body of research that has documented positive relationships between physical activity and brain function/learning Ahamed et al. (2007), Carlson et al. (2008), Chomitz et al. (2009), Grissom (2005), Coe et al. (2006), Jensen (2000), and Ratey (2008) all believe that encouraging children to be physically active throughout the day will help them learn more effectively than having them sit at desks all day. As explained in Chapter 32, there are many ways that children can learn math, science, reading, and social studies while they move.

Major studies in California (Grissom 2005) and the Texas Education Agency (2009) have also documented the relationship between physical fitness and reading and math scores. This research can be summarized as follows: The brain is stimulated by physical activity, so providing plenty of opportunities throughout the day for children to be physically active may actually help them do better in subjects typically taught while children are sitting still in a classroom. If you are interested in reviewing the research on physical activity and academic achievement, go to the research section on PE Central, the health and physical education Web site for educators, for an up-to-date bibliography (www.pecentral.org/research/index.asp).

Affective Domain

In addition to stimulating brain function/learning, physical education provides numerous opportunities for social and emotional learning experiences. The most obvious examples are assisting children understand the feelings related to winning and losing; that success is a result of hard work and practice; sports are a great way to make friends and learn to cooperate with others as a team, and to value and recognize the feelings of joy and elation that are a by-product of sports and physical activity. Chapter 10 focuses on some of the ways teachers encourage children to develop positive attitudes toward themselves and physical activity by creating safe and enjoyable learning environments.

We hope this chapter has helped you to understand why a quality physical education program can be so important in a youngster's life, especially for a child who is inclined not to be a physically active adolescent or adult. This chapter also provides an overview of the components of a quality, or positive, physical education (see Box 1-3). The next two chapters describe in detail the components of the skill theme approach designed to maintain the torrent of physical activity and love of movement, which is so characteristic of young children, into the middle and high school years.

Box 1-3

National Standards for Physical Education

Physical activity is critical to the development and maintenance of good health. The goal of physical education is to develop physically educated individuals who have the knowledge, skills, and confidence to enjoy a lifetime of physical activity.

A physically educated person:

Standard 1: Demonstrates competency in motor skills and movement patterns needed to perform a variety of physical activities.

Standard 2: Demonstrates understanding of movement concepts, principles, strategies, and tactics as they apply to the learning and performance of physical activities.

Standard 3: Participates regularly in physical activity.

Standard 4: Achieves and maintains a health-enhancing level of physical fitness.

Standard 5: Exhibits responsible personal and social behavior that respects self and others in physical activity settings.

Standard 6: Values physical activity for health, enjoyment, challenge, self-expression, and/or social interaction.

Source: National Association for Sport and Physical Education, *Moving into the future: National standards for physical education,* 2nd ed. (Reston, VA: National Association for Sport and Physical Education, 2004), 11. With permission from the National Association for Sport and Physical Education (NASPE), 1900 Association Drive, Reston VA 20191-1599.

PE Central www.pecentral.org

Throughout the ninth edition of *Children Moving,* we will be referring to a variety of documents that can be accessed directly via the Internet. PE Central is the most comprehensive Web site for K–12 physical educators in the world. Virtually all the documents referred to in this edition can be located through PE Central. In addition to links to the developmentally appropriate documents, the Surgeon General's report, and the *National Standards for Physical Education* (NASPE 2004), numerous developmentally appropriate lessons and assessment ideas are available free on the Web site. There are also descriptions of best practices, conference and job announcements, kids' quotes, and links to many other Web sites. The Web address, or URL, for PE Central is www .pecentral.org. You will also find easy-to-use forms for sharing your lesson and assessment ideas with other physical educators.

Mark Manross currently serves as the executive director, and Dave Hinman and Jan Bierschbach are senior editors. In addition, hundreds of physical educators have published their ideas on PE Central and/or work on it in an editorial capacity. George Graham, a coauthor of this book, is the chief executive officer for PE Central.

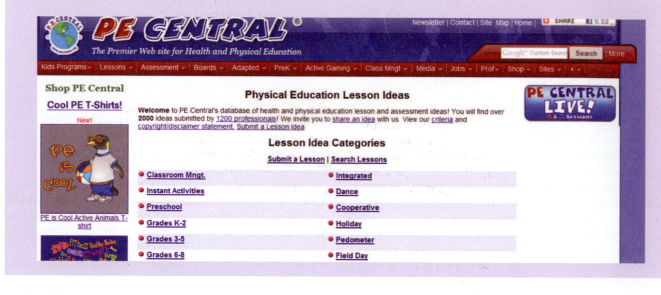

Summary

Quality physical education programs for children have never been more important than they are today. The three overarching questions in this chapter provide an introduction to the program and teaching process described in the text. The responses to the questions taken from the recent literature (1) provide reasons why children need quality physical education, (2) summarize the health benefits that may accrue to those who remain physically active for a lifetime, and (3) define a quality physical education program for children as one that is developmentally and instructionally appropriate.

Reading Comprehension Questions

1. The introduction to Chapter 1 described the purpose of a quality physical education program. Explain your reasons for agreeing or disagreeing with the purpose.
2. Chapter 1 provides a list of reasons children need quality physical education. Which of those reasons do you think are most important? Least important? Explain your reasons.
3. Categorize the reasons for a quality physical education program into two categories. The first category (column) will consist of those reasons that are predominantly the responsibility of the physical education program. In the second column, list the reasons for which other programs may also share responsibility (i.e., they are also goals for the teachers in the classroom and not specifically those of the physical education program).
4. The Physical Activity Hourglass suggests that opportunities for many youngsters are reduced once they

enter secondary school. Analyze the opportunities for middle school and high school youth to be physically active in your community. Contrast the opportunities with those provided for young children. Describe what your community might do to create more environmental invitations to become physically active, especially for the youngsters who are not on athletic teams.

5. Chapter 1 describes the characteristics of a quality physical education program. Make a three-column table listing these characteristics in the left-hand-column. In the second column, grade your elementary school program on each of these characteristics from A to F. In the third column, explain your reason for each grade. If you did not have an elementary

school physical education program, analyze your middle or high school physical education program.

6. Assume that someone asks you why youngsters need physical education. Prepare an argument using the information from this chapter to convince the person that physical education is as important as many other subjects in school.

7. It is recommended that children be physically active for 60 minutes or more most days of the week. Physical education classes are often 30 minutes in length. What would you recommend to a class of third graders about how they could acquire the recommended physical activity minutes on days they do not have physical education? Make five fun and interesting recommendations.

References/Suggested Readings

Ahamed, Y., H. MacDonald, K. Reed, P. J. Naylor, T. Liu-Amrose, and H. McKay. 2007. School-based physical activity does not compromise children's academic performance. *Medicine and Science in Sports and Exercise* 39: 371–76.

[AMA] American Heart Association. 2011. Physical activity and children. **http://www.heart.org/HEARTORG/GettingHealthy/Physical-Activity-and-Children_UCM_304053_Article.jsp#.TqbNk3FJB7o.**

Barnett, L. M., P. J. Morgan, E. van Beurden, and J. R. Beard. 2008. Perceived sports competence mediates the relationship between childhood and adolescent motor skill proficiency and fitness. *International Journal of Behavioral Nutrition and Physical Activity* 10: 5–40.

Bredekamp, S. 1992. What is developmentally appropriate and why is it important? *Journal of Physical Education, Recreation and Dance* 63(6): 31–32.

Carlson, S. A., J. E. Fulton, S. M. Lee, L. M. Maynard, D. R. Brown, H. W. Kohl, and W. H. Dietz. (Feb. 28, 2008). Physical education and academic achievement in elementary school: Data from the Early Childhood Longitudinal Study. *American Journal of Public Health.*

[CDC] Centers for Disease Control. 2011. *Physical activity and health.* **http://www.cdc.gov.**

Chomitz, V., M. Slining, R. McGowan, S. Mitchell, G. Dawson, and K. Hacker. 2009. Is there a relationship between physical fitness and academic achievement? Positive results from public school children in the northeastern United States. *Journal of School Health* 79(1): 30–37.

Clark, J. E. 2007. On the problems of motor skill development. *Journal of Physical Education, Recreation & Dance* 78(5): 39–44.

Coe, D. P., J. M. Pivarnik, C. J. Womack, M. J. Reeves, and R. M. Malina. 2006. Effect of physical education and activity levels on academic achievement in children. *Medicine and Science in Sports and Exercise* 38: 1515–19.

[COPEC] Council on Physical Education for Children. 1992. *Developmentally appropriate physical education practices for children: A position statement of the council on physical education for children.* Reston, VA: National Association for Sport and Physical Education.

[COPEC] Council on Physical Education for Children. 2000. *Appropriate practices for elementary school physical education: A position statement of the National Association for Sport and Physical Education developed by the Council on Physical Education for Children (COPEC).* Reston, VA: National Association for Sport and Physical Education. **http://www.aahperd.org/naspe.**

Ennis, C. E. (2011). Physical education curriculum priorities: Evidence for education and skillfulness. *Quest* 63: 5–18.

Furth, H. G. 1970. *Piaget for teachers.* Englewood Cliffs, NJ: Prentice Hall.

Grissom, J. B. (2005). The relationship between physical fitness and academic achievement. *Journal of Exercise Physiology-online* 8(1): 11–25.

Jensen, E. 2000. Brain-based learning: A reality check. *Educational Leadership* 57(7): 76–79.

Malina, R. M. 2001. Adherence to physical activity from childhood to adulthood. *Quest* 53(3): 346–55.

[MASSPEC] Middle and Secondary School Physical Education Council. 2001. *Appropriate practices for middle school physical education: A position statement of the National Association for Sport and Physical Education developed by the Middle and Secondary School Physical Education Council (MASSPEC).* Reston, VA: National Association for Sport and Physical Education. **http://www.aahperd.org/naspe.**

[MASSPEC] Middle and Secondary School Physical Education Council. 2004. *Appropriate practices for high school physical education: A position statement of the National Association for Sport and Physical Education Developed by the Middle and*

Secondary School Physical Education Council (MASSPEC). Reston, VA: National Association for Sport and Physical Education. **http://www.aahperd.org/naspe**.

[NASPE] National Association for Sport and Physical Education. 2002. *2001 shape of the nation report*. Reston, VA: National Association for Sport and Physical Education.

[NASPE] National Association for Sport and Physical Education. 2004. *Moving into the future: National standards for physical education*. 2nd ed. Reston, VA: National Association for Sport and Physical Education.

[NASPE] National Association for Sport and Physical Education. 2006. *Is it physical education or physical activity?* **http://www.aahperd.org/naspe/publications/ teachingTools/PAvsPE.cfm**.

[NASPE] National Association for Sport and Physical Education. 2009. *Appropriate practices for elementary school physical education*. 3rd ed. Reston, VA: National Association for Sport and Physical Education. **http://www.aahperd.org/ naspe/standards/nationalGuidelines/Apppracticedoc .cfm**.

[NASPE] National Association for Sport and Physical Education. 2011. *Key points of a quality physical education program.* **http://www.aahperd.org/naspe/publications/ teachingTools/key-points-of-QPE.cfm**.

[NCCDPHP] National Center for Chronic Disease Prevention and Health Promotion, Centers for Disease Control and Prevention. 1997. Guidelines for school and community programs to promote lifelong physical activity among your people. *Journal of School Health* 76(6): 202–19.

Portman, P.A. 1995. Who is having fun in physical education classes? Experiences of sixth grade students in elementary and middle schools. *Journal of Teaching in Physical Education* 14(4): 445–53.

Quimby, D. 1988. The starfish. *TEAM* 2(6).

Ratey, J. 2008. Spark: *The revolutionary new science of exercise and the brain*. New York: Little Brown.

Sanders, S., and G. Graham. 1995. Kindergarten children's initial experiences in physical education: The relentless persistence of play clashes with the zone of acceptable responses. *Journal of Teaching in Physical Education* 14(4): 372–83.

Shephard, R. 1996. Habitual physical activity and academic performance. *Nutrition Reviews* 54(4): 32–35.

Stodden, D., S. Langendorfer, and M. A. Roberton. 2009. The association between skill competence and physical fitness in adults. *Research Quarterly for Exercise and Sports* 80: 229–33.

Strong, W. B., R. M. Malina, J. R. Cameron, R. Bumke, S. R. Daniels, R. K. Dishman, B. Gutin, et al. 2005. Evidence based physical activity. *Journal of Pediatrics* 146: 732–7.

Texas Education Agency. Mar. 9, 2009. *Physically fit students more likely to do well in school, less likely to be disciplinary problems*. Austin, TX: Texas Education Agency.

[USDHHS] U.S. Department of Health and Human Services. 1996. *Physical activity and health: A report of the Surgeon General*. Atlanta: Centers for Disease Control and Prevention, National Center for Chronic Disease Prevention and Health Promotion.

[USDHHS] U.S. Department of Health and Human Services. 2000. *School health index for physical activity and healthy eating: A self-assessment and planning guide for elementary school*. Atlanta: Centers for Disease Control and Prevention. Available for free download from **http:// www.cdc.gov/HealthyYouth**.

[USDHHS] U.S. Department of Health and Human Services. 2008. *Physical activity guidelines for Americans*. **http://www.health.gov/paguidelines**.

Wilson, N. 1976. The frequency and patterns of selected motor skills by third and fourth grade girls and boys in the game of Kickball. Unpublished master's thesis, University of Georgia, Athens.

The Skill Theme Approach

Physical fitness, movement skills, concept and affective development should be emphasized throughout the curriculum. The greatest emphasis during the preschool and early elementary grades should be upon movement skill acquisition.

—COUNCIL ON PHYSICAL EDUCATION FOR CHILDREN (1992)

Motor skills do not develop miraculously from one day to the next or through maturation; they must be nurtured, promoted, and practiced. Physical education must promote both physical activity and motor skill development. If we want students to become physically active for life, we need to help them acquire the motor skills that will allow them to participate in a wide range of physical activities.

—JANE CLARK (2007)

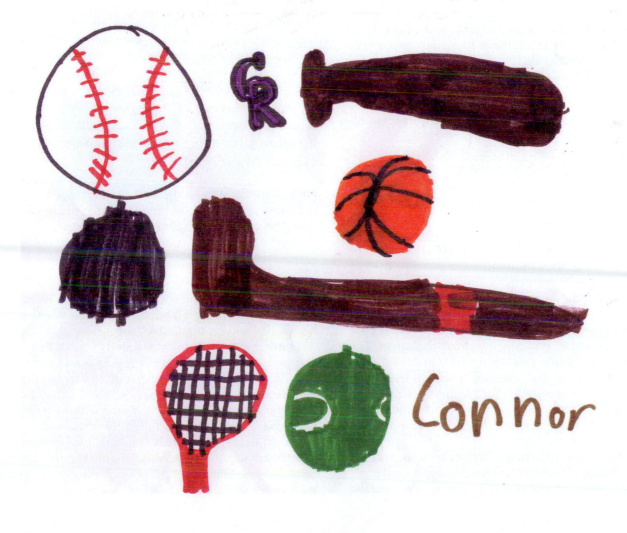

Key Concepts

- The skill theme approach describes both the content and pedagogy for physical education.

- The skill theme approach is based on developmentally appropriate principles that recognize children have different interests, abilities, and motor skills.

- The development of fundamental motor skills and their application to a variety of sports and physical activities create the basis for the skill theme approach.

- The Curriculum Diamond suggests the content to be taught in elementary, middle school, and high school physical education programs.

- Children's abilities and interests as opposed to age or grade level are used to guide the selection of content in the skill theme approach.

- Skill themes are initially practiced in isolation; as youngsters develop their motor skills, they practice them in sports, games, gymnastics, and dance contexts.

- Skill themes are revisited throughout the year rather than in units of several weeks.

- Cognitive, affective, and physical concepts are interwoven throughout the skill theme approach rather than taught as isolated units.

Chapter 1 answered questions that provided important insights into why physical education is so important in children's lives today, followed by an overview of the characteristics of a quality, or positive, physical education program. This chapter also answers a question: What is the skill theme approach to children's physical education?

Over the years we have observed many elementary school teachers whose curriculum consists solely of games. Each day the children play a game or two. In these programs the teacher's role is to explain the game, provide the equipment, keep score, and referee. The teacher pays no attention to the development of motor or sport skills. The athletes in the classes are happy because they typically dominate the games. The poorly skilled children survive from day to day—devoid of both enjoyment and learning. The skill theme approach offers an alternative for teachers who want to make a difference in children's lives by helping them become skillful movers who enjoy sports and physical activity.

The skill theme approach describes both the content (what to teach) of children's physical education (Parts 3 and 4 of *Children Moving* detail the curriculum) and the

teaching process, or pedagogy (how to teach, which is described in Part 2). A question-and-answer format will help you understand the characteristics of the skill theme approach. You will discover how it differs from traditional games programs, and how dance, games, gymnastics, and physical fitness are incorporated in it.

What Are Skill Themes?

Skill themes are initially the fundamental movements that form the foundation for success in sports and physical activities in later years. Reflective teachers, as will be explained throughout the text, adapt the skill themes to match the ability level of the students in a class. Initially we focus on one skill at a time; in later grades as children become more skillful, skills are combined and used in more complex settings, such as those in dance, games, and gymnastics. The intent is to help children develop the building blocks for a variety of locomotor, nonmanipulative, and manipulative skills that provide the foundation to enjoyably and confidently play a sport, for example, or perform a dance consisting of an intricate set of movements. If you watch college or professional athletes practicing their sport, you will observe the skill themes in their most advanced stage, for example, throwing to a batter in baseball, striking a tennis ball, dancing with a partner, diving and rolling in volleyball.

What Are the Characteristics of the Skill Theme Approach?

Four characteristics of the skill theme approach (content and pedagogy combined) clearly distinguish it from the games curriculum described above.

Characteristic 1

A major purpose of the skill theme approach is competence in performing a variety of locomotor, nonmanipulative, and manipulative motor skills.

Think of a sport or physical activity you know well. If you were asked to write a progression (a series of tasks) starting with novices (beginners) up to varsity athletes, you would be able to develop a series of tasks or drills that would, over a period of years and with a lot of practice, lead to the students (athletes) becoming highly skilled in that sport. This is the basic idea behind the skill theme approach. Each skill theme begins with the fundamental skills and concepts, is gradually combined with other skills (e.g., dribbling while running), and

Box 2-1

Critical Elements in the Skill Theme Approach

One of the sample benchmarks for second graders in the *National Standards* suggests that children be able to "identify four characteristics of a mature throw" (NASPE 1995, 20). In the skill theme approach, as you will see in later chapters, we focus on children learning the critical elements. Manross (2000) interviewed 25 children who had been taught using a skill theme approach (at Pendleton Elementary School) and 25 children whose curriculum consisted primarily of low-organized games (at Eckland). As part of his study he asked the children to identify the critical elements (cues) of the overhand throw. It was clear that the children in the skill theme approach at Pendleton could describe many of the critical elements of a mature overhand throw, whereas the children at Eckland had not learned the critical elements. The table contains their responses.

Answer Stated	No. of Times
Pendleton (Skill Theme Approach)	
Turn your side to the target	17
Step with the opposite foot	15
Arm way back	10
Aim at target	9
Follow through	3
Step through with other foot	2
Let elbow lead	1
Twist body at waist	1
Bring arm straight over, not sidearm	1

Eckland (Low-Organized Games)	
Get straight in front of target	4
Hold ball with tight grip	3
Bring hand back behind shoulder	3
Follow through	2
Try your best	2
Don't know	2
Practice	2
Don't be scared of the ball	2
Take a forward step	2
Throw hard	2
Aim at target	2
Don't strain arm	2
Try to throw sidearm	1
Hold your hand straight	1
Work on stance	1
Don't throw hard	1
Pretend it is hot object	1
Don't get nervous	1
Keep mind on throwing	1
Make sure they see good	1
Have a strong arm	1
Keep eye on ball	1

eventually leads to success and enjoyment in full-sided games (e.g., five-against-five basketball).

The skill theme approach reflects the growing concern that some, perhaps many, children who participate in programs that emphasize game playing rather than motor skill learning don't necessarily improve their motor ability (Graham 1987; Manross 2000). The logical implication, of course, is that adults with inefficient motor skills tend to avoid physical activities that require them to use these poorly learned skills and as a consequence develop tendencies toward "couch potatoism." See Box 2-1 for one example of the difference in outcomes of the two approaches.

A basic assumption is that a curriculum that is "scoped and sequenced" by skill themes (Appendix) introduces students to the requisite skills for enjoyably participating in adult versions of sports, dance, and the myriad other physical activities available today—and those that will be invented tomorrow. As physical educators we're able to help children learn these skills more quickly and with less frustration than they would if they attempted to learn the skills on their own.

The skill themes are generic in the sense that they are not tied to any single sport or activity. Rather, they transcend, or cut across, structured sports. As shown in Figure 2.1, which illustrates a dribbling progression that might be used in basketball, introductory or beginning tasks for each skill theme start at the most basic level. The children are asked to practice the motor skill—with no defenders, for example—and the fundamental critical components or cues are emphasized, such as throwing a ball hard against a wall while focusing on opposition (that is, stepping with the foot opposite the throwing hand). As children demonstrate the ability to perform the skill using the critical components, the tasks require children to combine the skill with other skills and concepts, such as throwing while running to a partner who is also running. When the children are ready, the skill theme tasks may involve developing dance and gymnastic routines with

Figure 2.1 The skill theme of dribbling is initially studied as an isolated skill. As the children become more skillful, it is combined with other skills and concepts. Eventually, dribbling is used in teacher- or children-designed routines, games, or small-sided basketball games.

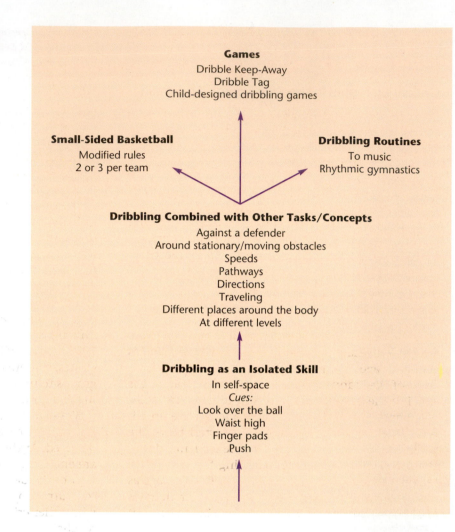

their classmates or playing small-sided games. Some skills (e.g., jumping and landing) are used in games, dance, gymnastics, track and field, for example. Other skills such as dribbling are more specific to games or sports.

Although some skill themes are typically associated with a specific sport, most are used in a variety of sports or physical activities. This is illustrated by using the skill theme of dribbling with the hands (Chapter 24). Dribbling is typically associated with basketball. The initial dribbling tasks focus on children dribbling a ball in a self-space without traveling or moving. As they gain dribbling skill, children are challenged to dribble and travel in different pathways, at different speeds, and around stationary and eventually moving obstacles. If there is sufficient time for practice, eventually the children will be ready to dribble in complex situations that might be small-sided basketball games; children may also be challenged to create dribbling routines to music or to dribble in keep-away or tag games. In some instances the teacher designs

the routine or game; in other instances the children design their routine or invent their game. Figure 2.1 illustrates how the skill theme of dribbling is developed with youngsters based on the tasks described in Chapter 24.

Some skill theme chapters (e.g., Chapters 22, 23, and 24) include rules for games, but these rules are suggested as part of the skill theme progression for children at more advanced levels (e.g., utilization and proficiency levels, as described in Chapter 5). To reach the more advanced levels, the children will need to spend considerable time on tasks devoted to learning these skills—initially in rather static environments—before using them successfully within the dynamic setting of an organized game, for example. In this book, games are carefully selected (or designed) to enhance skill acquisition as part of a long-term progression rather than simply as a way to keep children busy, happy, and good for 30 minutes or so.

We also encourage teachers to explain to their classes that skillfulness typically involves practicing outside of school the skills taught in class. Unfortunately, in many physical education programs there is just not enough time to devote to the skill themes and movement concepts to enable children to dramatically improve their skill levels. It is important that children understand this reality so they do not develop unrealistic expectations about how much practice it takes to become skillful.

In addition to including a progression (sequence) of tasks for developing each skill theme from the beginning through the advanced levels (Part 4), each chapter includes information (written descriptions, diagrams, and/or photos) to help the teacher observe children (this process is first described in Chapter 11) and to help the youngsters develop efficient and biomechanically correct motor patterns (see Chapter 12).

Characteristic 2

The skill theme approach is designed to provide experiences appropriate to a child's developmental level, as opposed to age or grade level.

One of the many challenges of reflective teaching is matching the content of the lesson to students' abilities (Chapter 10). Both grade level and age are unreliable indices of ability. A second characteristic of the skill theme approach is that it uses the students' developmental level as a guide for selecting the content to be taught. It may be easier to use grade level or age as an indicator, but children develop at different rates and reflective teachers attempt to take this into account (NASPE 1995).

The generic levels of skill proficiency (Chapter 5) serve as guides for assessing the children's abilities and then selecting tasks that are matched to their abilities. If the majority of children in a class, for example, were unable to hit a ball against a wall continually using a paddle so that it returned on a single bounce, we wouldn't require them to participate in a game requiring an even greater ability to strike the ball—for example, a game that required them to hit a ball to a partner (Chapter 25).

In the skill theme approach, the tasks are selected according to the children's abilities and not according to a predetermined calendar that implies all children of the same grade develop at the same rate. This is especially important, for example, when children's skill development may be limited because they have physical education classes only one or two days a week (Graham, Metzler, and Webster 1991). In practice, this means that if an experienced teacher taught three consecutive fourth-grade classes using a skill theme approach, one class might be challenged with a more difficult series of tasks than another (Graham et al. 1993). And within each of the three fourth-grade classes, students might be challenged individually or in groups to undertake different tasks as will be explained in Chapter 6.

We can use the skill of throwing (Chapter 23) to illustrate how a skill theme is developmentally sequenced. At the most basic level (precontrol), children are encouraged to throw a ball hard or far. These tasks lead to the development of greater trunk rotation and foot–arm opposition, for example, which combine with other critical components to form a mature (biomechanically efficient) throwing pattern. Throwing for distance, however, is only one type of throwing. As the children learn the components of an overhand

Fitness is built into the skill theme approach as children hop in general space.

throw for distance, they are challenged by tasks that involve throwing at targets, throwing to a partner, and throwing while moving. At more advanced levels (utilization and proficiency), they might be invited to participate in a game of Keep-Away involving throwing, such as two against two or three against one (three throwers, one defender). The reflective teacher bases these decisions, however, on the children's readiness rather than on age or grade level. Throwing efficiently and effectively then becomes a focus that is interwoven and revisited as variations of throwing throughout the program.

Characteristic 3

The scope and sequence of the skill themes are designed to reflect students' varying needs and interests over a period of years.

The third characteristic of the skill theme approach can be found within the scope and sequence recommendations (see Chapter 6 and the Appendix). Rather than focusing on the same skill theme for several weeks (in a three- or six-week unit, for example), we focus on a skill theme for brief periods and then revisit it at various times during the year. At the beginning levels (precontrol and control), we might spend only

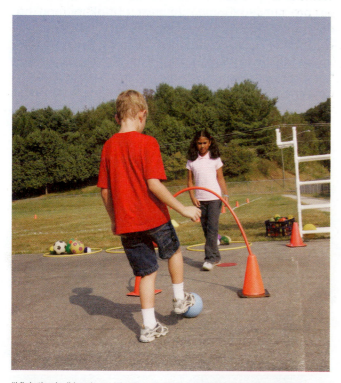

"Kick the ball back and forth with your partner; try to make it go through the arch" is a task skill theme teachers use to develop kicking skills.

two or three days in a row on a skill theme. In fact, we might not even spend an entire class period on a single skill theme. As children gain proficiency, expanding their motor repertoire, they become more interested in spending larger amounts of time (three or four days) on the same skill theme because the tasks are more complex and involved and their success rate is higher.

Revisiting the same skill theme several times during a year, as depicted in the progression spiral in Chapter 3, also allows the teacher to teach virtually the same lesson that was taught two or three months before. This is often necessary when the children's skill doesn't improve noticeably. A teacher who remains on the same skill theme for many days in a row, however, is tempted to make the tasks harder (in an effort to alleviate the children's and the teacher's boredom) than the children may be ready for. The skill theme curriculum begins with the development of foundational skills and abilities and gradually, over the years, introduces more complex and difficult skills (NASP, 1995).

Characteristic 4

The skill theme approach emphasizes instructional alignment. Teachers decide what students can learn in a lesson (objectives) (Chapter 6), develop a series of tasks designed to assist the children accomplish the lesson objective(s) (Chapters 13–26), and then assess the objective (Chapter 12) to determine if the lesson objective(s) have been accomplished. The assessment then serves as a guide for future lessons. According to Tannehill, a teacher "tells students what is important for them to know and be able to do (the objectives), designs appropriate tasks that allow them to practice what you taught them, and assesses them on what they have been practicing" (Tannehill 2001, 19). For example, if a teacher wants her class to learn the grapevine step, she would demonstrate and explain the step, devise tasks that allow them to practice it, and then assess their ability to do the grapevine to determine if they need more practice. This process, called instructional alignment, is emphasized throughout *Children Moving*. Each lesson has objectives that reflect what teachers want the children to learn that are aligned with district, state, and national standards.

What Is Developmentally Appropriate Physical Education?

Another characteristic of the skill theme approach is that it is developmentally appropriate. Motor development research studies the "process of change in an individual's movement behaviors" (Barnett and Merriman 1992, 5; NASPE 1995). The skill theme approach is developmentally appropriate because it reflects important motor development principles in curriculum design and in the teaching process. Some of the important motor development principles upon which *Children Moving* is based are briefly explained below.

Children Develop at Different Rates

One critical premise of motor skill development is that children develop at different rates. Some kindergarten children can skip; others are not ready to skip. Some are able to track a ball in motion; others are not visually ready yet. Developmentally appropriate physical education recognizes this premise and therefore does not expect all children to be able to perform the same task identically. As you will see in subsequent chapters detailing the skill theme approach, we recognize and value the developmental differences in children's abilities, although it's not easy with 25 or more in a class.

Age Does Not Predict Motor Ability

If age was a predictor of motor ability, then all adults would be skillful athletes. Although there are certain advantages to aging (e.g., quicker reflexes, visual tracking ability), the only way individuals become skillful in motor skills is to use, or practice, them. Thus most adults are reasonably efficient at walking. Many, however, are inefficient at catching a ball or striking an object with a racket. They are inefficient because they have not used the skills regularly over a period of years and not because they do not have the potential to be skillful.

Children Develop Motor Skills Naturally through Play

Children today have fewer and fewer opportunities to develop motor skills on their own. Television viewing, computer games, the Internet, and fear of playing outside in many communities combine to mean fewer chances to be physically active. Although there is some evidence that motor skills may develop through informal play (hours and hours of basketball or soccer, for example), this possibility is becoming less and less probable in society today. The simple fact is that physical education is becoming increasingly important for children because their playtime is severely limited. This is especially true for overweight youngsters who have little or no physical activity built into their lives.

The Myth of the Natural Athlete

One sports myth is that there are natural athletes. Although some youngsters are physically (genetically) disposed to do better at some sports than others, the fact is that highly skilled children have participated in one or many sports from very early ages. Some children begin kindergarten with mature throwing and catching patterns, for example. They were not born this way. They played a lot of catch with parents, siblings, or friends from a young age and thus enter school more highly skilled than their peers. In time, however, their less-skilled peers can catch up if they, too, practice and use the motor skill thousands of times as they play with friends, on teams, or with a parent.

Differences in Physical Abilities between Boys and Girls

On average, boys are more physically active than girls (USDHHS 1996). This may be one reason boys tend to be more highly skilled than girls in certain sports. Developmentally, however, girls have the potential to be equally as skillful as boys. As more and more girls play sports and become physically active, we can expect to see a decline in any gap that exists between physical abilities. As teachers we emphasize this continually in our programs so that the girls in our classes understand that skillfulness is a result of practice, not heredity or gender.

Boys tend to be taller than girls and have wider bones (AAOS 2005). As with motor skills, however, girls can dramatically improve their strength. Just as we are seeing an increasing number of girls playing sports, so, too, we are seeing more girls and women who have improved their strength through practice and exercise.

In summary, developmentally appropriate physical education recognizes that youngsters develop at different rates and have different abilities, and that the environment plays a critical role in the development of motor skills. The chapter continues with a question-and-answer format that answers many questions typically asked when folks are initially introduced to the skill theme approach.

Why Don't You Describe Such Activities as Duck, Duck, Goose and Kickball?

We don't include many of the so-called traditional activities for three major reasons. First, activities such as these, in which children are singled out to perform solo with everyone watching them, can be both embarrassing and discouraging when the less-skilled children are "on center stage." Children (or adults, for that matter) who are embarrassed or made to feel inadequate are hardly motivated to participate. One of our primary goals is to encourage children to develop positive attitudes about themselves and about physical activity so they choose to be physically active throughout their lives. Games such as those named above are developmentally inappropriate because they do not take into account the varying skill abilities of children within a class (NASPE 2009) and thereby force some children into situations that make them unhappy and may lead them to dislike physical activity.

Second, these games emphasize winning more than learning. Another of our primary goals is to help children develop the movement competence that enables them to enjoy and participate in physical activity successfully. While keeping score and attempting to win are enjoyable for some children, others prefer games and activities in which score is not kept. When children are encouraged to design their own games (Chapter 31), you will see that some keep score and others do not.

Finally, many of these traditional games encourage only a few youngsters to be physically active. The less-skilled, overweight, or less physically fit youngsters often find ways to avoid actively participating in games with one ball or tag games with one person who is "it." The skill theme approach was designed with the underlying premise that children have different skill levels and abilities.

What Is the Curriculum Diamond?

The Curriculum Diamond (Figure 2.2), created by physical educators Dawn McCrumb and Wendy Mustain in 1995, illustrates the concept of a motor skill foundation leading to successful participation in sports and physical activities. George Graham, Ken Bell, and Catherine Himberg expanded and elaborated on this model in 1996. It is intended to help physical educators think about and design curriculums that will guide youngsters in the process of becoming physically active for a lifetime. It is important to understand that it takes time, and practice—a lot of practice—to successfully perform complex, sport-related skills in game, gymnastics, and dance contexts. In fact, it is virtually impossible to become proficient without the foundational motor skills described in the skill theme approach (NASPE 1995). Clearly, decisions about when to introduce different content will need to be based on the progress students make in a given program (e.g., number of days per week, length of the classes, equipment, and facilities).

The Curriculum Diamond suggests a curricular focus corresponding to the grade-level structure of most school districts across the United States—elementary, middle, and high school. (Grade levels are suggested in the model for illustration purposes only). It follows the recommendations of the National Center for Chronic

Games like Duck, Duck, Goose are fun for a few, but most of the children are inactive.

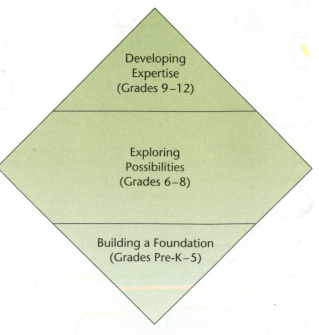

Developing Expertise (Grades 9–12)

Exploring Possibilities (Grades 6–8)

Building a Foundation (Grades Pre-K–5)

Figure 2.2 The Curriculum Diamond.

Disease Prevention and Health Promotion (NCCD-PHP/CDC 1997) and the National Standards for Physical Education (NASPE 2004) by developing a broad foundation of motor skills at the elementary and middle school levels and then focusing on proficiency in a few movement forms at the high school level. It provides a brief, albeit oversimplified, answer to the question, How can elementary, middle, and high school physical education programs work together to guide youngsters in the process of becoming physically active for a lifetime?

Building a Foundation (Preschool through Grade 5)

The bottom part of the diamond represents the earliest ages at which children are introduced to skill themes and movement concepts. The initial focus is on developing a functional (applied) understanding of the concepts of space awareness, effort, and relationships (Chapters 13–15). As children develop, they are introduced to skill themes designed to encourage and assist them in beginning to acquire the fundamental competencies that will become the foundation skills for many of the sports and physical activities they will pursue as adolescents and adults (Chapters 16–26). Notice that this section of the diamond widens as each layer is laid upon the foundational layer that precedes it. This is intended to represent how skill themes and concepts are combined in the upper elementary grades. (Some have suggested that a more appropriate geometric representation might be a trapezoid. This figure would suggest that the skill themes and movement concepts would be wider at the base, the broader foundation, and gradually narrow toward the top. What do you think?)

Exploring Possibilities (Grades 6–8)

In the middle school years, the focus shifts from building a foundation to using the skills and concepts in a variety of movement forms. Skills continue to be developed and learned, but the focus is on exposing students to wide variety of sports and physical activities designed to stimulate interest in health-enhancing lifetime activities. Ideally this is the age when adolescents begin to discover the various sports and physical activities that are or are not personally appealing. Some youngsters, for example, like team sports; others may prefer individual sports. Others will enjoy yoga, dance, martial arts, or mountain biking. The goal is to introduce youngsters to many different movement forms and then assist them to discover the types of activities that are personally enjoyable and meaningful to them.

Developing Expertise (Grades 9–12)

Ideally the exposure to many movement options in middle school stimulates student interest in a handful of health-enhancing lifetime activities. When students enter high school, the diamond begins to narrow, suggesting that students will begin to make decisions about the activities they enjoy and desire to become proficient in. At this point students choose electives based on the possibilities they explored in middle school. As students approach the peak, the focus narrows. This is the time when students develop the expertise that enables them to participate in several activities enjoyably and confidently, thereby allowing them to accrue the benefits that come to those who remain physically active for a lifetime. This is the time when students refine the skill themes and movement concepts they learned in the early years for use in specific sports and physical activities.

Is It Difficult to Maintain Youngsters' Interest in a Program That Emphasizes the Fundamentals?

We hope by now you understand why skill themes are important as the building blocks for enjoyable participation in physical activities and sports. Some, who haven't been taught using a skill theme approach, wonder about maintaining children's interest in fundamentals. Ideally, children begin this program in preschool when this is really the only program they know, so their interest remains high. When we introduce skill themes to children in the fourth and fifth grades for the first time, some children initially have a difficult time adjusting, particularly the highly skilled who enjoy playing games they dominate. In time, however, children learn to enjoy this program because they're improving. As reflective teachers we also attempt to adjust the activities to the youngsters' skill level, and this makes the lessons more interesting. It is important to understand, however, that students do play games, albeit small sided, in the skills theme approach, but only when they have the necessary skills to do so. As you may have experienced, games, even small-sided ones, are no fun when you haven't learned the necessary skills to play them.

What Does "Adjusting the Activities" Mean?

"Adjusting the activities" is the concept of reflective teaching (Chapter 4). It means that the teacher adapts the lesson for the children rather than allowing them to fail. If a boy can't catch a ball, for example, he isn't going to enjoy playing a game of softball in which the score is kept and winning is important. Thus, we provide noncompetitive activities for this child in which he can succeed. In the same class, however, a girl may have played softball on a team for several years and be very good. We try to provide her with game-like activities related to softball in which she and a group of classmates may choose to keep score. For more effective learning in reading and math classes, children are grouped by ability (differentiated instruction). Although it's harder to do this in physical education, we do provide different tasks based on the youngsters' ability. This system for determining students' skill level is explained in Chapter 4 as are techniques like teaching by invitation and intratask variation (Chapter 8). In addition, the tasks in each skill theme chapter are organized into a logical sequence.

Where Is Physical Fitness in the Skill Theme Approach?

Physical fitness is an important part of the skill theme approach. As we explain in Chapter 27, it is interwoven throughout the program rather than confined to one separate unit. Our emphasis is not on training children so they score well on a physical fitness test battery. Rather, we try to provide experiences that help them to understand and value the importance of physical fitness and physical activity. We also try to help children enjoy physical activity so they choose to make it a part of their daily lives for a minimum of 60 minutes a day (CDC 2011) The success of the physical fitness component within the skill theme approach is measured not by the children's scores on a physical fitness test battery, but by an assessment of their understanding of, attitudes toward, and enjoyment of physical activity.

Some of our lessons are devoted primarily to helping children understand and apply the important fitness concepts. In virtually every lesson we teach, however, we try to ensure that children are moderately to vigorously active a minimum of 50 percent of the lesson (USDHHS 2005) to enhance their cardiovascular benefits. We also find that running laps or doing jumping jacks, for example, seems to be a waste of time when children can obtain the same benefits

"Travel under the shape made by your partner" is an example of a task used to develop the ability to transfer weight from feet to hands to feet.

while learning and enjoying physical activity by, for example, playing tag games, learning new jump rope tricks, or perfecting a sequence of jumping and landing and rolling.

Where Does the Cognitive Domain Fit into the Skill Theme Approach?

As explained in Chapter 1, the cognitive domain is a critical aspect of the skill theme approach for two reasons. The first is the increasing recognition of the important link between physical activity and cognitive functioning (Ratey and Hagerman 2008). As suggested in their book *Spark,* there is an increasing body of evidence that physical activity has a number of positive influences on brain function in youth and adults.

The second related reason that the cognitive domain is an important part of the skill theme approach is the correlation between physical activity and academic achievement (Carlson et al. 2008; Coe et al. 2006). "High amounts of physical education may be associated with an academic benefit" (Carlson et al. 2008, 721).

The skill theme approach, as you will see, encourages children to think on their feet as they move. The movement concepts, for example, which we introduce in the early grades, teach them an important movement vocabulary they will use throughout their lives. The skill theme approach focuses not only on children's physical movements, but also on how and why they move certain ways as well as the most efficient and effective ways to do so. Chapter 10 provides specific examples of problem solving and guided discovery that encourage the children to find solutions to movement problems teacher present.

As with physical fitness, we weave cognitive concepts and principles into virtually every lesson we teach. We do not teach separate lessons, or units, on cognitive concepts, because we believe it is far more effective to emphasize these concepts and principles in every lesson we teach.

Many physical educators who use the skill theme approach also work closely with the classroom teachers at their schools. They incorporate concepts taught in the classroom into their physical education lessons. Chapter 32 describes in detail how teachers integrate the skill themes with many subjects taught in the classroom, such as math, reading, and science. This chapter also describes how classroom teachers use physical activity to teach many of the subjects in their curriculum.

Where Does the Affective Domain Fit into the Skill Theme Approach?

Just as with the cognitive domain, as explained in Chapter 1, we emphasize the affective domain in virtually every lesson we teach. Children's feelings, emotions, and self-concept can never be ignored. We attempt to design our lessons so they are developmentally appropriate and recognize that children have different abilities, attitudes, and feelings about being in our classes. We carefully follow the appropriate practice guidelines developed by the National Association for Physical Education and Sport (NASPE 2009; www.naspeinfo.org) to ensure that children are treated fairly, compassionately, and equitably.

From years of teaching and observing children's physical education classes, we are increasingly convinced that lifelong attitudes and feelings toward physical activity and exercise are developed during the

elementary school years. We want children to enjoy and feel good about their participation in physical education because our goal is to do our part to lead them to adopt and value a lifetime of physical activity. For this reason, we are continually aware of the affective domain in every lesson we teach. We want children to learn while they enjoy themselves in our classes. Thus we focus on helping them be successful learners and we also recognize that peer interactions are a critical part of every lesson we teach. Chapters 8 and 9 describe in detail how we create these positive learning environments for children.

What about Dance and Gymnastics?

Our initial focus in the skill theme approach is on helping children develop and learn the fundamental motor skills. As children acquire these building blocks, they are placed into the contexts of dance and gymnastics (and games) (Figure 2.3). It's important to understand that the purpose of dance, gymnastics, and games extends beyond simply skill improvement. Dance is a form of expression by moving to rhythm alone or with others. Gymnastics is a series of acrobatic skills combined into smooth, repeatable sequences performed on the floor and/or on an apparatus to demonstrate strength, balance, and body control. Games are organized activities that require manipulative skills and are played for the enjoyment and satisfaction of cooperating and competing with others.

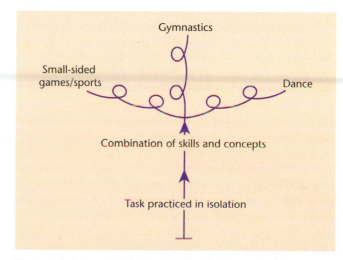

Figure 2.3 Skill themes are practiced initially in isolation, then in combination with other skills and concepts leading to their use in games, dance, and gymnastics.

The fundamental motor skill of balancing has many uses.

Dance, gymnastics, and games require skills that are best learned initially outside these complex contexts. It's ineffective to always practice the skills in isolation, however, so the contexts of dance, gymnastics, and games are interwoven throughout the movement concept and skill theme chapters (Parts 4 and 5). The chapters on dance, gymnastics, and games (Chapters 28, 29, and 30, respectively) illustrate this technique.

An analogy with reading also illustrates this point. Most children learn to read in elementary school; as adults, they choose what they'll read. In the skill theme approach, we teach the fundamental motor skills that are thought to provide the foundation for a lifetime of enjoyable, hopefully regular, physical activity. The children might tell us they aren't interested in some skills now. But 20 years from now, who knows?

How Do Classroom Teachers Feel about the Skill Theme Approach?

Classroom teachers are positive about the skill theme approach because they can relate it directly to their work in the classroom—in teaching children vocabulary, for example. They also appreciate the fact that the program accommodates the variation in abilities typical of any class of children. Many teachers also consider the program's deemphasis of competition a welcome alternative to those programs that constantly pit one team against another in games in which the score is kept. They feel not only that this is more consistent with the approaches they use in the classroom, but also that it makes their jobs easier; the children don't come angrily into their rooms after physical education class, arguing about the scores or who cheated, for example. As detailed in Chapter 32, classroom teachers also are able to use movement to teach reading, writing, and math, for example.

How Do Middle (Junior) and High School Physical Education Teachers Feel about the Skill Theme Approach?

Clearly there are many views. Some middle school teachers are enthusiastically supportive, realizing the importance of ensuring that children maintain positive attitudes about physical activity. Their job is much harder if their students have been turned off to physical education. Interestingly, a number of middle school teachers have actually started focusing on skill themes in their programs in response to their students' poor motor skill development. These teachers realize it's extremely difficult to excite students about sports and lifetime physical activity if they have yet to acquire the basic motor or sports skills. The skill theme approach has no age or grade limits. It can be valuable for people of any age.

Summary

The skill theme approach describes both the content (what is taught) and the pedagogy (how it is taught) that are used in a developmentally appropriate program of physical education. This approach recognizes that age or grade levels are inappropriate indicators of physical ability; therefore lessons are designed to consider different abilities and interests. The Curriculum Diamond provides an overview of how content can be sequentially developed so that elementary, middle school, and high school programs work together to provide a solid movement foundation for youngsters to attain the competence and confidence to remain physically active throughout a lifetime.

Initially the skill theme approach emphasizes the development of fundamental motor skills (e.g., throwing, balancing, striking). As the children progress in ability, the skill themes are taught in sports, games, dance, and gymnastics contexts. Because of the rapid changes in children's development, skill themes are revisited throughout the year rather than taught in units of several weeks. Concepts related to physical fitness and the cognitive and affective domains are interwoven throughout the lessons.

Reading Comprehension Questions

1. Why aren't games such as basketball and Duck, Duck, Goose included in this book?
2. In your own words describe the skill theme approach. Use the Curriculum Diamond (Figure 2.2) as part of your explanation.
3. Four characteristics of the skill theme approach are listed in this chapter. In your opinion, which provides the most compelling reason for using a skill theme approach? Why?
4. When are children ready for organized games? Why is it incorrect to respond to this question by suggesting an age or grade level?
5. This chapter suggests that children should be taught that becoming skillful will probably require practicing at home. Write a brief explanation to the children for a physical education Web page that you might use to explain why they need to practice outside of physical education class if they want to become good at a sport or physical activity.
6. Physical fitness is an important part of the skill theme approach, yet only one chapter addresses it. How can this be explained?
7. Do you think the skill theme approach should be used in middle schools? Why or why not?
8. As explained at the beginning of this chapter, some teachers' programs consist entirely of games. Use the content in this chapter to develop an argument as to why teaching only games is not in children's best interests.

References/Suggested Readings

[AAOS] American Academy of Orthopaedic Surgeons. 2005. Men and women not created equal in terms of predisposition to musculoskeletal problems. Press release, July 5. **http://www6.aaos.org/news/Pemr/press_release .cfm?PRNumber=384 (accessed July 14, 2008).**

Barnett, B. E., and W. J. Merriman. 1992. Misconceptions in motor development. *Strategies* 5(3): 5–7.

Bernhardt, D., T., J. Gomez, B. M. D. Johnson, T. B. Martin, T. W. Rowland, E. Small, C. LeBlanc, et al. 2001. Strength training by children and adolescents. *Pediatrics* 107(6): 1470–72.

Carlson, S. A., J. E. Fulton, S. M. Lee, L. M. Maynard, D. R. Brown, H. W. Kohl, and W. H. Dietz. 2008. Physical education and academic achievement in elementary school: Data from the Early Childhood Longitudinal Study. *American Journal of Public Health* 98(4): 721–27.

[CDC] Centers for Disease Control and Prevention. 2011. How much physical activity do children need? **http:// www.cdc.gov/physicalactivity/everyone/guidelines/ children.html.**

Clark, J. E. 2007. On the problem of motor skill development. *Journal of Physical Education, Recreation & Dance* 78(5): 39–44.

Coe, D. P., J. M. Pivarnik, C. J. Womack, M. J. Reeves, and R.M. Malina. 2006. Effect of physical education and activity levels on academic achievement. *Medicine and Science in Sports and Exercise* 38: 1515–19.

[COPEC] Council on Physical Education for Children. 1992. *Developmentally appropriate physical education practices for children: A position statement of the Council on Physical Education for Children.* Reston, VA: National Association for Sport and Physical Education.

Graham, G. 1987. Motor skill acquisition: An essential goal of physical education programs. *Journal of Physical Education, Recreation and Dance* 58(8): 44–48.

Graham, G., C. Hopple, M. Manross, and T. Sitzman. 1993. Novice and expert children's physical education teachers: Insights into their situational decision-making. *Journal of Teaching in Physical Education* 12(2): 197–214.

Graham, G., M. Metzler, and G. Webster. 1991. Specialist and classroom teacher effectiveness in children's physical education. *Journal of Teaching in Physical Education* 10(4): 321–426.

Manross, M. 2000. Learning to throw in physical education class: What I learned from 4th and 5th graders: Part 3. *Teaching Elementary Physical Education* 11(3): 26–29.

[NASPE] National Association for Sport and Physical Education. (1995). *Looking at physical education from a developmental perspective: A guide to teaching.* Position statement. Reston, VA: National Association for Sport and Physical Education.

[NASPE] National Association for Sport and Physical Education. 1995. *Moving into the future: National standards for physical education.* Reston, VA: National Association for Sport and Physical Education.

[NASPE] National Association for Sport and Physical Education. 2004. *Moving into the future: National standards for physical education.* 2nd ed. Reston, VA: National Association for Sport and Physical Education.

[NASPE] National Association for Sport and Physical Education. 2009. *Appropriate practices for elementary school physical education.* 3rd ed. Reston, VA: National Association for Sport and Physical Education.

[NCCDPHP/CDC] National Center for Chronic Disease Prevention and Health Promotion, Centers for Disease Control and Prevention. 1997. Guidelines for school and community programs to promote lifelong physical activity among young people. *Journal of School Health* 76(6): 202–19.

Ratey, J. J., and E. Hagerman.2008. *Spark: The revolutionary new science of exercise and the brain.* New York: Little, Brown.

Tannehill, D. 2001. Using the NASPE content standards. *Journal of Teaching Physical Education, Recreation and Dance* 72(8): 19.

[USDHHS] U.S. Department of Health and Human Services. 1996. *Physical activity and health: A report of the Surgeon General.* Atlanta: Centers for Disease Control and Prevention, National Center for Chronic Disease Prevention and Health Promotion.

[USDHHS] U.S. Department of Health and Human Services. 2005. *School health index for physical activity and healthy eating: A self-assessment and planning guide for elementary school.* Atlanta: Centers for Disease Control and Prevention. Available for free download from: **http://www.cdc.gov/nccdphp/dash.**

Skill Themes, Movement Concepts, and the *National Standards*

A physical education program for children which begins with an organized sport is analogous to a language arts program beginning with a Shakespearean sonnet.

—Iris Welsh, student

Children are not little adults. Their responses to activity are quite different from those of adults. Activity programs should be planned with these differences in mind.

—Oded Bar-Or (1995)

Key Concepts

- Children need to become sufficiently competent in basic motor skills if they are going to eventually enjoy playing sports or games as teens and adults.

- In elementary school, the emphasis is placed on practicing the fundamental motor and sport skills rather than learning rules or the structures of sports.

- Skill themes are analogous to verbs (i.e., they are action words). They are subdivided into three categories: locomotor, nonmanipulative, and manipulative skills.

- Movement concepts are analogous to adverbs (i.e., they describe how an action is performed). They are also subdivided into three categories: space awareness, effort, and relationships.

- In the primary grades, movement concepts are taught before the skill themes.

- The movement analysis framework "wheel" describes how the skill themes and movement concepts interact with one another.

- The "spirals" outline a developmentally appropriate progression for each of the skill themes.

- *Children Moving* aligns directly with the national and many state physical education standards.

Our primary goal in the skill theme approach is to provide children with a degree of competence leading to the confidence that encourages them to become, and remain, physically active for a lifetime. Our intent is to help children gain enough skills and confidence to participate enjoyably in many activities, not just a few traditional team sports, and to avoid the abysmal failure and embarrassment that often result from a total lack of skill. By focusing on learning and practicing skills rather than on the rules or structure of a game or sport, we can dramatically increase the amount of practice the children actually receive, thereby heightening their opportunities to learn the fundamental motor skills that form the foundation for becoming a lifetime mover. We are also able to do this in ways that children find enjoyable.

Essentially, the notion is that these elements (fundamental motor skills) are learned in early life through the various activities performed (such as jumping, throwing, striking, and the like), and then when a new act is to be learned in later life, the student can piece together these elements in a more efficient way to achieve the new motor goal. The assumption is that by jumping over objects of various sizes, shapes, heights, etc., the student will have more effective "elements" for the performance of the next jumping tasks (e.g., the running long jump in high school).

—RICHARD SCHMIDT, "Schema Theory: Implications for Movement Education," (1977)

Typically, children who are learning to read are taught first to recognize letters, then parts of words, then complete words, and finally sentences. Children who are studying mathematics learn to solve problems after they've grasped the basic functions of numbers and signs. Children learning to play a musical instrument typically study the scale before attempting a song. In physical education, however, all too often children are taught games, dances, or complex gymnastic stunts before they're able to adequately perform fundamental motor skills. Too often, children know the rules for a game or the formation of a dance, but they don't have the motor skills needed for successful and enjoyable participation. Our way of teaching children how to participate effectively in various activities is to focus on the development of the necessary motor skills. We call this approach teaching by skill themes.

One of the easiest ways to understand skill themes is to think of a popular sport. Let's pick softball. The major skills people use to play softball include throwing, catching, batting, and running. In another popular sport—basketball—throwing, catching, running, dribbling with hands, jumping and landing, and chasing and fleeing skills are used frequently (Table 3.1). Obviously we could list a number of other sports. The point is that some of the same skills—for example, throwing, catching, and running—are used in both sports, and in many more. Thus if children learn to throw and catch, for example, their odds of playing and enjoying a sport such as softball or basketball increase because they have a reasonable chance to succeed at that sport. We have termed these skill themes because they apply to many different sports, although the way they are used (the context) differs from one sport to another. Table 3.1 lists various skill themes and indicates which sports emphasize them.

Characteristics of Themes

In music, a theme recurs in different parts of a song, sometimes in exactly the same way, at other times in a slightly different form. *The Random House Dictionary of*

Table 3.1 Skill Themes Used in Sports*

Skill Themes	Aerobics	Basketball	Football	Dance	Golf	Hockey	Martial Arts	Rock Climbing	Soccer	Softball	Tennis	Track and Field	Tumbling	Ultimate Frisbee	Volleyball
Traveling	×	×	×	×	×	×	×	×	×	×	×	×	×	×	×
Chasing, fleeing, dodging		×	×			×	×		×	×				×	
Jumping, landing	×	×	×	×			×	×	×	×	×	×	×	×	×
Balancing	×	×	×	×	×	×	×	×	×	×	×	×	×	×	×
Transferring weight	×	×	×	×	×	×	×	×	×	×	×	×	×	×	×
Rolling			×	×			×						×		×
Kicking	×		×	×			×		×						
Punting			×						×						
Throwing		×	×						×	×		×		×	×
Catching		×	×						×	×				×	
Volleying									×						×
Dribbling		×				×			×						
Striking with rackets											×				
Striking with golf clubs					×										
Striking with bats										×					
Striking with hockey sticks						×									

*This table is intended only to suggest how various skill themes are applied in sports contexts.

the English Language defines theme as "a short melodic subject from which variations are developed." In physical education, various movements can be thought of as a theme. Skill themes are initially practiced as fundamental motor skills and then in increasingly more complex contexts, with other skill themes and concepts, as the children become more skillful. Skill themes are the foundation or building blocks for successful and enjoyable participation in sports, gymnastics, dance, and other physical activities. By revisiting a movement—sometimes in the previous context and sometimes in a radically different one—we provide children with variations of a skill theme. These variations lead to proficiency as well as diversity. Jumping, for example, can be presented as jumping from an object—a box or a table—and landing softly. This movement can be revisited with a slight variation: jumping from an object and landing facing a different direction from the takeoff position. Jumping for distance or leaping in synchronization with the leap of a partner would be radically different, yet the theme would still be jumping (Gallagher 1984). The high jump and the long jump for track and field athletes as well as jumping to catch a ball in football, softball, or basketball are also variations on the theme of jumping. Whenever possible, we point out to students the similarities in movements used in different contexts to enhance their cognitive understanding of the principles that underlie successful performance of a movement. We're not certain that this influences skill performance (transfer of learning), but it doesn't seem to have any adverse effects.

The instructor who teaches by themes can focus on helping children become skillful movers. Youngsters will have plenty of opportunities as they grow older to learn the rules, tactics, and cooperation associated with games, sports, dance, and gymnastics activities, but first they must learn the basic motor skills needed for successful participation.

> *Fundamental activities such as running, jumping, skipping, sliding, catching, kicking, and striking are the basic components of the games, sports, and dances of our society. Children who possess inadequate motor skills are often relegated to a life of exclusion from the organized and free play experiences of their peers, and subsequently, to a lifetime of inactivity because of their frustrations in early movement behavior.*
>
> —VERN SEEFELDT, JOHN HAUBENSTRICKER, AND SAM REUSCHLEIN

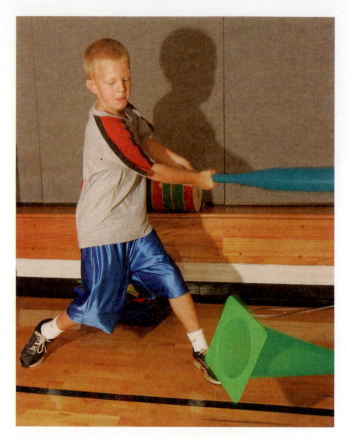

Try to bat the ball without hitting the cone is the challenge used by this child's physical educator.

Many adults choose not to play tennis or swim or dance. They don't enjoy these activities because they don't possess the skills needed to participate successfully. An unskilled adult attempting to learn a complex set of dance steps may be embarrassed and frustrated, as well as the adult who is trying to learn to play tennis but cannot even hit the ball into the opponent's court. Our goal in the skill theme approach is to help youngsters become skillful adults who enjoy a variety of physical activities and sports.

As children acquire the fundamental skills, the reflective teacher combines skill themes and movement concepts into the movement contexts we typically identify as games, sports, gymnastics, and dance. The key word, however, is ready. We lead children to these experiences gradually rather than forcing them into adult settings prematurely. Let's use the batting skill theme as an example. In Chapter 26 we explain a variety of enjoyable ways children can practice the skill of batting without placing them in an adult-rules nine-against-nine softball game. Constantly striking out in a softball game in front of your classmates is hardly conducive to wanting to play softball as an adult. Therefore we have developed a sequence of batting tasks and activities that gradually progress into fun batting games that also provide plenty of practice opportunities. We do the same for each of the other skill themes (Part 5).

Skill Themes and Movement Concepts

We hope by now you understand the rationale for the skill theme approach. In this section two tables and two figures are especially important to a thorough understanding of the skill theme approach. The movement concept categories and components are listed in Table 3.2 and the skill theme categories, themes, and

Table 3.2 Movement Concept Categories and Components

Movement Concept Categories	Movement Concepts	Components
Space Awareness (Chapter 13) (where the body moves)	Location	Self-space and general space
	Directions	Forward, backward; sideways (right and left); clockwise and counterclockwise
	Levels	Low, middle, and high
	Pathways	Straight, curved, and zigzag
	Extensions	Large, small; far, near
Effort (Chapter 14) (how the body moves)	Time	Fast, slow
	Force	Strong, light
	Flow	Bound and free; smooth and jerky
Relationships (Chapter 15) (of body parts, with objects, with people)	Of body parts	Round, narrow, wide, and twisted; symmetrical and nonsymmetrical
	With objects and/or people	Over/under; on/off; near/far; in front/behind, alongside; along, through; meeting/parting, surrounding, around
	With people	Leading/following; mirroring/matching; unison/contrast; alone in a mass, solo, partners, groups, between groups

*This table represents many of the movement concepts taught in elementary school physical education. It is not meant to be all-inclusive but to provide examples of movement concepts.

Table 3.3 Skill Theme Categories, Skill Themes, and Components*

Skill Theme Categories	Skill Themes	Sample Components
Locomotor	Traveling (Chapter 16)	Walking, running, hopping, leaping, sliding, galloping and skipping • in general space • in pathways • in different directions • at different speeds • in bound and free flow • in games, sports, and gymnastics
	Chasing, Fleeing, and Dodging (Chapter 17)	Traveling to chase, flee, and dodge; dodging to avoid obstacles and people; chasing, fleeing, and dodging in games with others
Nonmanupulative	Bending, Stretching, Twisting and Curling (Chapter 18)	Traveling and jumping while twisting, curling, and stretching; stretching to catch with a ball thrown by a partner while traveling.
	Jumping and Landing (Chapter 19)	Jumping for distance and height; five basic jumping-and-landing patterns; jumping over obstacles; jumping rope; buoyant and yielding landings; jumping to throw and catch; partner jumping
	Balancing (Chapter 20)	Balancing on different bases of support; in different shapes; on benches; inverted balances; balancing sequences with other skill themes.
	Transferring Weight and Rolling (Chapter 21)	Transferring weight from feet to hands, on and off equipment; traveling weight onto and off apparatus; transferring weight sequences. Rolling forward, backward, and sideways; rolling at different speeds; transferring weight and rolling; rolling onto and off equipment; rolling sequences.
Manipulative	Kicking and Punting (Chapter 22)	Kicking for distance; to targets; dribbling with feet; to a partner; one-on-one soccer; kicking in small-sided games. Punting for distance; for accuracy; running and punting; in small-sided games.
	Throwing and Catching (Chapter 23)	Throwing for distance; underhand, overhand, and sidearm; at targets; throwing with a partner; flying discs. Catching from a self-toss; from a partner; while running; while jumping. In small-sided games.
	Volleying and Dribbling (Chapter 24)	Dribbling in self-space and general space; at different levels; and traveling; and changing speeds, changing directions, in pathways, against a defender; in a small-sided game. Striking balloons (and other objects) in the air with different body parts; over a net; partner volleying; modified volleyball.
	Striking with Rackets and Paddles (Chapter 25)	Striking balloons and suspended balls; striking up, down, and at targets; striking at different levels; striking over a net; partner striking.
	Striking with Long-Handled Implements (Chapter 27)	Striking with golf clubs, bats, and hockey sticks for distance and accuracy.

*This table represents many of the skill themes taught in physical education. It is not meant to be all-inclusive but to provide examples of skill themes. The major source for this explanation of skill themes and movement concepts is from the work of Sheila Stanley, *Physical education: A movement orientation,* 2nd ed. (New York: McGraw-Hill, 1977). She analyzed and applied the work of Rudolf Laban for American physical educators.

components in Table 3.3. These tables organize the content (fundamental skills and concepts) to be taught in physical education, not by sports, but by an analysis of movements used in most sports and physical activities. The tables also serve as a guide to be certain that we teach all the important movements and do not leave any out. The skill themes and movement concepts are defined and thoroughly explained in Parts 4 and 5. There are 3 movement concept chapters (Part 4) and 11 skill theme chapters.

The movement analysis framework, which has been termed "the wheel" (Figure 3.1), is intended to show how the skill themes and movement concepts interact with each other. The sample spiral (Figure 3.2) is an example of one of the 16 developmentally appropriate progressions we have created for each of the 16 skill themes in Part 5. (There are 16 progression spirals because some of the related skill themes are combined within the same chapter. Transferring weight and rolling are combined in Chapter 21, for example. Batting, striking with hockey sticks and golf clubs are combined in Chapter 26).

Both the movement analysis framework and the progression development spirals are explained later in this chapter. Obviously the content of our program consists of more than just skill themes. In fact, it's difficult to focus on a skill theme for long without introducing one or more movement concepts. The two terms, *skill themes*

Children enjoy learning the vocabulary of the skill theme approach. This teacher has posted her skill themes on the gym wall.

and *movement concepts*, differentiate the movements (skill themes) from the adverbs (movement concepts) used to modify or enrich the range and effectiveness of skill employment. Chapters 13–15 are devoted specifically to ideas and examples for teaching the movement concepts, while Chapters 16–26 do the same for skill themes. At this point, however, it is important to understand the differences between them.

The distinction between movement concepts (Table 3.2) and skill themes (Table 3.3) can be clarified by a comparison to grammar. Skill themes are always verbs—they're movements that can be performed. Movement concepts are always modifiers (adverbs)—they describe how a skill is to be performed. This distinction also clarifies how movement concepts are employed to embellish, enhance, or expand the quality of a movement. A verb by itself—strike, travel, roll—is typically less interesting than one that is modified by an adverb—strike hard, travel jerkily, roll smoothly. Skills can stand by themselves. You can roll or gallop or jump, but you can't low or high or under without moving. Concepts modify skills.

Skill themes perform three related functions.

1. They link the skills to the concepts, for example, running fast or slow; balancing in a symmetrical on nonsymmetrical shape; striking a ball hard or easy.
2. Skill themes also link one skill with another skill, for example, jumping and catching; running and kicking; twisting and dodging.
3. Skill themes are also linked to dance, gymnastics, and games contexts.

Our initial focus with the primary-grade children is on learning and understanding the movement concept vocabulary (see Table 3.2 and Chapters 13–15); for this reason, the movement concepts are taught before the skill themes (see Table 3.3 and Chapters 16–26). We focus on movement concepts before skill themes because children in preschool and the primary grades spend a great deal of time studying vocabulary (learning new words), and many of the movement concepts can be part of this vocabulary. This is also the time when children truly enjoy the challenge of learning and moving as they demonstrate their understanding of such movement concepts as symmetrical, zigzag, and twisted.

When the children are learning the movement concepts, they are also practicing the skill themes. As soon as the children begin to move, they are practicing one or more skill themes, even though they may not be thinking about it at the time. For example, if we ask children to skip in a curved pathway, they may be thinking about the curve, but they are also practicing skipping. If we ask them to land in a low level from a jump (Chapter 13), they are also getting jumping and landing practice. In later grades, the teacher's focus will shift from the low level (movement concept) to providing cues for soft, safe landings—from the concept to the skill (Chapter 19). The skill themes and movement concepts are constantly interacting as the children move—it is the emphasis of the teacher that changes.

The Wheel (Movement Analysis Framework)

The movement concepts and skill themes work together. In fact, one cannot teach a movement concept without including a skill theme, unless, of course, the children are just sitting and listening and not moving. Our goal, however, is to have children moving because this is the

Figure 3.1 Movement analysis framework (wheel) depicting the interaction of movement concepts and skill themes. An interactive wheel is located inside the back cover of this book.*

only way to effectively teach the movement concepts and the skill themes. So right now you need to refer to Tables 3.2 and 3.3 (pages 32–33) and Figure 3.1, the wheel. (The wheel included with your text actually moves and will better help you understand our explanation.)

The movement concepts and the skill themes are listed in Tables 3.2 and 3.3. The left column of Table 3.2 lists the three categories of movement concepts (space awareness, effort, and relationships) and the left column of Table 3.3 lists the three categories of skill themes (locomotor, nonmanipulative, and manipulative). The

*Some movement analysis frameworks include the concept of space (direct and flexible) as a quality of movement. In our teaching, however, we use this concept so infrequently that we don't include it in our discussion of the qualities of movement.

middle columns in both tables list the actual movement concepts and skill themes. The right column in each table lists the components of the movement concepts and skill themes that become the actual focus of individual lessons.

Now look at the wheel, a term our students coined. You will see that the outermost circle consists of three movement concept *categories*—space awareness, effort, and relationships. Each *category* consists of several *movement concepts* listed in the second circle from the outside. The *movement concept category* of space awareness, for example, consists of five *movement concepts*. They are location, directions, levels, pathways, and extensions. The effort movement concept category has three *movement concepts* (time, force, and flow), and the relationship category also has three *movement concepts* (of body parts, with objects and/or people, and with people).

The third circle from the outside contains the *components* that become the focus of individual lessons. So, for example, if you were teaching the concept of time, you would be focusing on teaching the children to move at slow speeds, fast speeds, and speeds in between. If you were teaching the movement concept of flow, you would be guiding children to move using both the components of bound and free flow. (These ideas are explained fully in Chapter 17 along with a variety of tasks (activities) used to teach the effort movement concept and components.

The skill themes are organized the same way as the movement concepts (Table 3.3). There are three skill theme *categories*—locomotor, nonmanipulative and manipulative. These are in the innermost circle of the wheel. Moving outward, the actual skill themes are listed around the next circle. So you will see that there are two skill themes (traveling and chasing, fleeing and dodging) in the locomotor *category*. There are four skill themes in the nonmanipulative *category* (bending, stretching, twisting and curling; jumping and landing, transferring weight and rolling, and balancing). The third skill theme *category*, manipulative, has five skill themes. They are kicking and punting, throwing and catching, volleying and dribbling, striking with paddles and rackets and striking with long handled implements (bats, golf clubs, and hockey sticks). The skill theme *components*, what we focus on in specific lessons, are listed in Table 3.3 in right-hand last column.

We know the wheel is not easy to understand. So here's a test for you. How many skill themes are in the locomotor skill theme category? If you said two you would be correct: (1) traveling and (2) chasing, fleeing, and dodging. How many movement concepts make up the effort movement concept category? Remember that the skill themes and movement concepts are then

subdivided into *components*, what we actually teach the children in individual lessons.

The interaction between the movement concepts and the skill themes listed in Tables 3.2 and 3.3 is represented schematically by five concentric circles (Figure 3.1). The two inner circles of the wheel (movement analysis framework) represent the skill themes (Table 3.3); the three outer circles represent the movement concepts (Figure 3.1). The three outermost circles refer to the movement concepts (Figure 3.1.) The innermost circle contains the three categories of skill themes: manipulative, nonmanipulative, and locomotor skills. The next inner circle names the skill themes. For example, traveling (Chapter 19) and chasing, fleeing, and dodging (Chapter 20) are the two skill themes in the locomotor skills category. Some of the skill themes also list the components of a skill theme. Striking with long handled implements (Chapter 26), for example, is subdivided into three components—striking with golf clubs, bats, and hockey sticks.

We hope by now you are beginning to understand how skill themes and movement concepts are arranged on the wheel. Now we will look at how the wheel is designed to work. Again, look at the interactive wheel that was in your book. You will see that the two innermost circles representing the skill themes are stationary. The three outer circles are connected to each other but can rotate around the two inner circles. The purpose of designing the wheel to rotate is to show that the same movement concept can be used to enhance the development of different skill themes. The concept of levels in space, for example, is useful for refining such skills as catching, striking, volleying, and balancing (e.g., catching at high level). The concept of fast and slow can be applied to the study of such skills as traveling, rolling, dribbling, transferring weight, and dodging (e.g., rolling at a slow speed). At times, some concepts blend with other concepts. For example, fast or slow may modify pathways, and forward and backward may modify over and under (e.g., galloping slowly forward in a zigzag pathway).

Do you understand now how the wheel works? If so that's great! If not, reread the paragraphs above and, once again, refer to the interactive wheel that came with your book. Once you grasp the concept behind the design of the wheel, you will understand the movement concept and skill theme chapters and are on your way to doing movement analyses for your students.

Progression Spiral

The progressional development spiral is much easier to understand than the wheel. As you no doubt understand, just learning the terminology for the movement concepts (Table 3.2) and the skill themes (Table 3.3) is not enough to begin actually teaching them to children. Subsequent chapters present explanations for each of the movement concepts and skill themes, along with a plethora of practical, easy-to-use activities (Chapters 13–26). In each of these chapters we provide tasks and activities (lesson ideas) in a progression from the easiest to the hardest, and from less to more complex. The content in each of the skill theme chapters is outlined in a figure we call a progression spiral (Figure 3.2). The spiral is intended to be read from the bottom to the top—that is, the easiest tasks are at the bottom, the hardest at the top. It also suggests that tasks may need to be retaught when, for example, it has been several months since the children have practiced that skill or it is the beginning of a school year.

Each line on the spiral corresponds to a section in the skill theme chapters. The lesson ideas are arranged in a progression from easy to hard. So, for example, if you were teaching a class that was predominantly at the control level, as explained in Chapter 5, you might want to teach the children how to punt for distance and/or punt for accuracy (Figure 3.2.). Chapter 22, pages 427 to 428, contains lesson ideas for actually teaching children to punt accurately and for distance. To make it easier for you to use the skill theme approach, all of the skill theme lesson ideas correspond directly (Chapters 16–26) to the progressions outlined in the spirals.

As you begin to plan using the tasks and activities in the skill theme chapters, you will see how the movement concepts and skill themes work together. The movement concepts of fast and slow, for example, can be used to make a task more interesting or challenging. The skill theme of rolling or transferring weight can be made more difficult by challenging the children to move more slowly. But with a skill such as dribbling, which is easier to perform at a slower rate, the challenge "dribble faster" increases the complexity of the task. In short, there's no standard formula that can be used as a guide for varying the contexts in which all skill themes are studied. Each skill theme is different as are the children. The 16 spirals in the skill theme chapters suggest a progression that will help you both understand and teach the skill themes effectively.

Notice in Figure 3.2 that the spirals do not suggest the length of time, or the number of lessons, to be spent studying a particular theme. In reflective teaching, as Chapter 4 details, these decisions are based on the time allocated for physical education classes (e.g., two days a week versus daily), the children and their home backgrounds, and the opportunities available in the community. In other words, it would be impossible

PUNTING

Proficiency Level
Playing Punt-Over
Punting while traveling
Receiving and punting against
   opponents

Utilization Level
Playing rush the circle
Punting within a limited time
Receiving a pass, then punting
Punting to a partner
Punting at angles

Control Level
Punting for height
Punting for accuracy
Using punting zones
Punting for distance
Punting different types of balls
Punting with an approach
Punting over low ropes
Punting for consistency

Precontrol Level
Dropping and punting
Dropping, bouncing, and kicking
   lightweight balls

Figure 3.2 Progression spiral illustrating the contextual variations in which skill themes can be studied.

for us to use the same yearly and weekly sequence of lessons for every physical education program in the country unless they were all identical—which, as you know, they are certainly not!

Finally, the spirals provide a progression from the precontrol (beginner or novice) level up to the proficiency level (varsity athlete) (see Chapter 5). The movement concept and skill theme progressions in Parts 4 and 5 are based on our knowledge of the pertinent literature and on years of teaching experience. But you may find that a different ordering of the tasks (activities) is more appropriate for a particular teaching situation. Each child, each class, each teaching environment differs from all others, and the reflective teacher adapts to these differences. So we suggest you start with the tasks and activities outlined in the content chapters (13–26) and then change and adapt your lessons and sequence based on your particular teaching situation. See Box 3-1 for an example of one school's use of skill themes in its physical education curriculum.

Adapting the Skill Theme Approach

Since the first edition of *Children Moving* was published in 1980, a number of school districts throughout the United States have based their curriculums on skill themes. In Gwinnett County (near Atlanta, Georgia), an overview of each area of the curriculum is described on a poster that many elementary schools in the county display on their walls. The poster is prominently displayed alongside math, reading, and science posters, an arrangement conveying the message that the teachers of Gwinnett County are dedicated to educating the total child.

Physical Education
K–5 Curriculum

The fundamental objective of the physical education program is to provide opportunities for the development of motor skills and physical fitness.

Skill Themes and Fitness Concepts
Students in grades K–5 will experience a developmentally designed program of skill and fitness development, including educational games, educational dance, and educational gymnastics. The following motor skills and fitness concepts are included:

- body awareness
- balancing
- chasing, fleeing, dodging
- kicking and punting
- striking with implements (short and long handled)
- rolling
- throwing and catching
- traveling
- volleying and dribbling
- transferring weight
- jumping and landing
- cardiorespiratory endurance
- flexibility
- muscular strength and endurance
- fitness testing

Becoming physically educated is a developmental process that begins in early childhood and continues throughout life. The physical education program involves the total child and includes physical, mental, social, and emotional growth experiences. The physical education program provides instruction that will enable the pursuit of physical fitness and a lifetime of physical activity.

Gwinnett County Public Schools

The *National Standards* and the Skill Theme Approach

In this ninth edition of *Children Moving*, we attempt to show how our program fits with the content of the National Association for Sport and Physical Education's *Moving into the Future: National Standards for Physical Education* (NASPE 2004). We think this will be especially useful for those teachers who are interested in revising their programs to reflect the content suggested in the National Standards. Before describing how *Children Moving* can be used as a guide to developing a program designed on the National Standards, it is important to provide a brief background of the process that led to the development of those standards.

Background of *National Standards* Development

In the late 1980s, the National Association for Sport and Physical Education (NASPE) formed a blue-ribbon task force and asked its members to:

- Define a person who is "physically educated"
- Define "outcomes" and "benchmarks" that could serve as guidelines for constructing physical education program curriculums

The Outcomes Task Force worked on the project for more than five years; each year, at NASPE's national conference, physical educators from throughout the United States were invited to review and critique the work. The task force then revised its work based on these recommendations and presented it again the following year. Over several years, hundreds of physical educators reviewed the work of the task force that, as a result, reflects the collective wisdom of much of the profession. The result of this work, published in 1992, was a document entitled *The Physically Educated Person* (NASPE 1992, v), which defined a physically educated person as an individual who:

- HAS learned skills necessary to perform a variety of physical activities
- IS physically fit
- DOES participate regularly in physical activity
- KNOWS the implications of and the benefits from involvement in physical activity
- VALUES physical activity and its contributions to a healthful lifestyle

Outcome statements were also developed for each of the five parts of the definition, along with benchmarks for kindergarten, second, fourth, sixth, eighth, tenth, and twelfth grades.

Using the same process, NASPE built upon the foundation of the "Outcomes Project" to develop national content standards for physical education, including examples for assessment. The standards were initially published in 1995 (NASPE 1995) and were revised in 2004 (NASPE 2004). They were especially important because they paralleled work that was also being done in other disciplines, such as mathematics, science, and geography. The skill theme approach, as defined in *Children Moving*, is aligned with the National Standards for Physical Education.

Skill Themes and the Content Standards

Box 1-3 in Chapter 1 lists the six content standards for physical education from the National Standards. *Children Moving* addresses all the standards throughout the text. Once you understand the skill theme approach, the content chapters in Parts 4 and 5 will be especially helpful for designing, delivering, and assessing the first two content standards. When you read these two standards and the paragraphs that follow each standard, it will be easy to see how closely the content of *Children Moving* aligns with the national standards.

1. A physically educated person demonstrates competency in motor skills and movement patterns needed to perform a variety of physical activities.

   The intent of this standard is development of the physical skills needed to enjoy participation in physical activities. Mastering movement fundamentals establishes a foundation to facilitate continued motor skill acquisition and gives students the capacity for successful and advanced levels of performance to further the likelihood of participation on a daily basis. In the primary years, students develop maturity and versatility in the use of fundamental motor skills (e.g., running, skipping, throwing, striking) that are further refined, combined, and varied during the middle school years. These motor skills, now having evolved into specialized skills (e.g., a specific dance step, chest pass, catching with a glove, or the use of a specific tactic), are used in increasingly complex movements . . . through the middle school years (NASPE 2004, 12).

2. A physically educated person demonstrates understanding of movement concepts, principles, strategies, and tactics as they apply to the learning and performance of physical activities.

   The intent of this standard is facilitation of learners' ability to use cognitive information to understand and enhance motor skill acquisition and performance. . . . In the lower elementary grades, emphasis is placed on establishing a movement vocabulary and applying introductory concepts. Through the upper elementary and middle school years, an emphasis is placed on applying and generalizing these concepts to real-life physical activity situations (NASPE 2004, 12).

The content chapters (13–26) provide the tasks and activities (lesson ideas) that align with the skills and concepts suggested in the National Standards. It will also help to refer to Boxes 3-2 and 3-3, which contain sample performance outcomes from the National Standards, and Box 3-4, which contains guidelines for promoting lifelong physical activity from the National Center for Chronic Disease Prevention and Health Promotion (NCCDPHP). After each sample benchmark you will see one or more chapter references that indicate where you can learn more about that specific benchmark and the activities that teachers use to help children achieve the suggested goal. Again this will assist you to see how we have aligned the content of *Children Moving* with the national standards.

In many chapters we have also quoted sample performance outcomes from the National Standards to help you understand how the content of the *Children Moving* chapters can be developed to meet these benchmarks. When appropriate, we have also included assessment examples in those chapters to help you determine how well your students are progressing with regard to the benchmarks.

As we conclude this section on skill themes and movement concepts and how they are described in the National Standards, it is important to remember that the standards are not intended as a prescribed set of goals or outcomes to be achieved by all physical education programs. The National Standards document is not a national curriculum! As detailed in Chapter 4, "Reflective Teaching," you will need to determine the goals of your program based on the specific characteristics of the schedule, the children, and the community—as well as your district and state standards. The suggested grade levels, for example, are only that—suggestions. The

---

Box 3-2

Sample Performance Indicators for National Standard 1: Movement Forms

A more detailed description of each performance indicator, along with activities to teach it, is included in the *Children Moving* chapter(s) listed below at the end of each benchmark. The critical elements (cues) of a mature form are also described in these chapters.

Grades K–2

- Skips (or hops, gallops, slides, etc.) using mature form (Chapter 16)
- Performs a simple dance step in keeping with a specific tempo (Chapter 28)
- Demonstrates clear contrasts between slow and fast movements when skipping (hopping, galloping, sliding, etc.) (Chapters 14, 16)
- Travels forward and sideways, changing directions quickly in response to a signal or obstacle using a variety of motor skills (Chapters 13, 14, 15)
- Demonstrates a smooth transition between locomotor skills in time to music (Chapters 14, 16)
- Drops a ball and catches it at the peak of the bounce (Chapter 23)
- Throws a ball underhand using mature form (Chapter 23)
- Discovers how to balance on different body parts, at different levels, becoming "like" a statue while making symmetrical and nonsymmetrical shapes (Chapters 13, 20)

Grades 3–5

- Balances with control on a variety of objects (e.g., balance board, large apparatus, skates) (Chapter 20)
- Catches a fly ball using a mature form (Chapter 23)
- Jumps vertically and lands using mature form (Chapter 19)
- Throws a ball overhand and hits a target on the wall (Chapter 23)
- Develops and refines a gymnastics sequence (or creative dance sequence) demonstrating smooth transitions (Chapters 28, 29)
- Dribbles, then passes a ball to a moving receiver (Chapter 24)
- Throws a ball to a partner 15 yards away using mature form (Chapter 23)

Grades 6–8

- Serves a volleyball underhand using a mature form (Chapter 24)
- Dribbles a ball while preventing an opponent from stealing the ball (Chapter 24)
- Places the ball away from an opponent during a tennis rally (Chapter 25)
- Designs and performs gymnastics (or dance) sequences that combine traveling, rolling, balancing, and weight transfer into smooth, flowing sequences with intentional changes in direction, speed, and flow (Chapters 13–16, 21)

Box 3-3

Sample Performance Indicators for National Standard 2: Movement Concepts

A more detailed description of each performance indicator, along with activities to teach it, is included in the *Children Moving* chapter(s) listed below at the end of each performance indicator.

Grades K–2

- Identifies correctly various body parts (e.g., knee, foot, arm, palm) (Chapter 13)

Grades 3–5

- Identifies four characteristics of a mature throw (Chapter 23)
- Uses concepts of space awareness and movement control to run, hop, and skip in different ways in a large group without bumping or falling (Chapters 13, 16)

- Identifies and demonstrates the major characteristics of mature walking, running, hopping, and skipping (Chapter 16)

Grades 6–8

- Transfers weight from feet to hands at fast and slow speeds using large extensions (e.g., mule kick, handstand, cartwheel) (Chapter 21)
- Accurately recognizes the critical elements of a throw made by a fellow student and provides feedback to that student (Chapter 23)
- Consistently strikes a softly thrown ball with a bat or paddle, demonstrating an appropriate grip (Chapters 25, 26)

Box 3-4

Guidelines for Promoting Lifelong Physical Activity

Almost 30 years ago the NCCDPHP made the following recommendations for "developing students' mastery of and confidence in motor and behavioral skills for participating in physical activity." They still apply today:

- Students should become competent in many motor skills and proficient in a few to use in lifelong physical activities.
- Elementary school students should develop basic motor skills that allow participation in a variety of physical activities.
- Older students should become competent in a select number of physical activities they enjoy and succeed in.

- Students' mastery of and confidence in motor skills occur when these skills are broken down into components and the tasks are ordered from easy to hard.
- Students need opportunities to observe others performing the skills and receive encouragement, feedback, and repeated opportunities for practice during physical education class.
- Active student involvement . . . that focuses on building confidence may increase the likelihood that children and adolescents will enjoy and succeed in physical education and physical activity.

Source: NCCDPHP 1977, 209.

National Standards can be immensely helpful, however, because they represent the professional judgment of hundreds of physical education teachers and professors about the content of a quality physical education curriculum that provides the movement foundation for a lifetime of physical activity.

We must emphasize, however, that the National Standards are designed for programs that have daily physical education for grades K–12. Even then, however, the standards may represent optimistic goals. The challenge for many schools and districts that have

physical education only one or two days a week is to carefully select the standards they can truly accomplish in the amount of time they have allocated for their physical education programs. The standards can also provide the foundation for a strong argument for more time for physical education in the school day. It is always difficult to decide which of the standards a school or district will ignore because of the lack of time allocated for physical education.

Since the National Standards were first published in 1995, a number of states have revised or developed state standards, many of them based on the National Standards. Go to PE Central (www.pecentral.org/professional/statestandards.html) to see if your state has revised or developed state standards. It would also be interesting to see how your state standards compare to the ones developed at the national level.

Summary

Teaching by skill themes focuses on developing children's competence in a variety of motor skills and movement concepts that, if practiced frequently outside of the school setting, will eventually enable the children to acquire confidence and enjoy physical activity throughout their lifetimes. They are closely aligned with the national standards for physical education developed by the National Association for Physical Education and Sport. Games, sports, gymnastics, and dance typically require children to use combinations of motor skills and movement concepts that are developed only after a substantial amount of practice.

Teaching by themes also involves revisiting the same skills or concepts continually throughout the program at different times and in different contexts. In preschool and the primary grades, the focus is on learning the vocabulary associated with the movement concepts (Chapters 13–15). Once the vocabulary has been learned, the emphasis shifts to the skill themes (Chapters 16–26). The skill themes and movement concepts constantly interact, as depicted in the movement analysis framework (the wheel). The progression and activities for each of the skill themes are outlined in the progression spirals in the skill theme chapters (16–26). The spirals are visual reminders that the child revisits each task to enhance skill acquisition and retention and that skills are best learned when they are presented in a progression from basic to advanced.

Support for the skill theme approach can be found in three national statements, the *National Standards for Physical Education* (NASPE 1995, 2004); *Developmentally Appropriate Physical Education Practices for Children* (COPEC 1992); and *Appropriate Practices for Elementary School Physical Education* (COPEC 2000; NASPE 2009). Essentially, these sources recommend that physical education programs at the preschool and elementary school levels focus on helping children improve their fundamental motor skills. Cognitive and affective goals are interwoven throughout the program.

Reading Comprehension Questions

1. What do children need to learn in physical education before they're ready to play a game successfully and enjoyably? Why?
2. What is the difference between a movement concept and a skill theme?
3. In your own words explain how the wheel works. Then briefly explain why it is important.
4. Find the dribbling progression spiral in Chapter 24. One of the progressions on the spiral is entitled "dribbling and looking." This refers to teaching children to look away from the ball when they are dribbling. On what page in the chapter are the tasks for teaching children to look away from the ball? Briefly summarize the two tasks that are described.
5. What three skill themes relate most directly to teaching dance? To games? To gymnastics? You may not use the same skill theme twice.
6. Select a team sport (or physical activity) you are familiar with. List skills that are needed to play the sport enjoyably. List three movement concepts that are also important for success in that sport.
7. Attempt to locate your state physical education standards at PE Central (www.pecentral.org/professional/statestandards.html). (If your state has not posted them, you can refer to the national standards.) Find three examples of state (national) standards for the elementary school grades that directly address the teaching of movement concepts or skill themes. Copy the standard (include the grade level and standard number) and indicate which skill theme or movement concept the standard addresses.

References/Suggested Readings

Bar-Or, O. 1995. Health benefits of physical activity during childhood and adolescence. In *President's Council on Physical Fitness and Sports Research Digest*. Washington, DC: President's Council on Physical Fitness and Sports.

[COPEC] Council on Physical Education for Children. 1992. *Developmentally appropriate physical education practices for children: A position statement of the Council on Physical Education for Children*. Reston, VA: National Association for Sport and Physical Education.

[COPEC] Council on Physical Education for Children. 2000. *Appropriate practices for elementary school physical education: A position statement of the National Association for Sport and Physical Education*. Reston, VA: National Association for Sport and Physical Education.

Gallagher, J. 1984. Making sense of motor development: Interfacing research with lesson planning. In *Motor skill development during childhood and adolescence*, ed. J. Thomas, 123–38. Minneapolis: Burgess.

[NASPE] National Association for Sport and Physical Education. 1992. *The physically educated person*. Reston, VA: National Association for Sport and Physical Education.

[NASPE] National Association for Sport and Physical Education. 1995. *Moving into the future: National standards for physical education*. Reston, VA: National Association for Sport and Physical Education.

[NASPE] National Association for Sport and Physical Education. 2004. *Moving into the future: National standards for physical education*. 2nd ed. Reston, VA: National Association for Sport and Physical Education.

[NASPE] National Association for Sport and Physical Education. 2009. *Appropriate practices for elementary school physical education*. 3rd ed. Reston, VA: National Association for Sport and Physical Education.

[NCCDPHP] National Center for Chronic Disease Prevention and Health Promotion, Centers for Disease Control and Prevention. 1977. Guidelines for school and community programs to promote lifelong physical activity among young people. *Journal of School Health* 76(6): 202–19.

Schmidt, R. A. 1977. Schema theory: Implications for movement education. *Motor Skills: Theory into Practice* 2: 36–48.

Stanley, S. 1977. *Physical education: A movement orientation*. 2nd ed. New York: McGraw-Hill.

Becoming a Reflective Teacher

The four chapters in Part 2 introduce you to the concept of reflective teaching and the process of becoming a reflective teacher. Chapter 4, "Reflective Teaching," describes how teachers adapt their programs according to the particular characteristics of their school (for example, the number of days per week they teach physical education, the available facilities and equipment) and their children (for example, background, experience, type of community). The process of reflective teaching is contrasted with programs that assume all children have identical physical abilities and fail to adapt and change their programs to meet the needs of their students. Typically these programs consist primarily of games with little or no teacher instruction provided.

Chapter 5, "Determining Generic Levels of Skill Proficiency," introduces a system for analyzing the children's skills and abilities in a class in order to present content that is developmentally appropriate and beneficial in terms of learning. The Generic Levels of Skill Proficiency present a viable alternative to organizing the content by grade level or age.

Chapter 6, "Planning and Developing the Content," explains how reflective teachers plan their school years. The first three steps focus on long-term planning that answers the questions, What do I teach and when? The fourth step provides a practical, yet detailed, example of how to plan lessons. It demonstrates how to develop the content to match children's abilities by using the Reflective Planning Grid.

Chapter 7, "Analyzing Reflective Teaching," provides practical techniques for analyzing the process of reflective teaching. It gives a three-step cycle that teachers can use to reflect on their own teaching. In a nutshell Chapter 7 provides insights into the question, "How am I doing as a reflective teacher?"

Reflective Teaching

The good teacher must relate his teaching to the world of his students as it is, not as he or she would like it to be.

—HERBERT FOSTER (1974)

A search for rigid prescriptions of the right way to teach has largely been replaced with the search for propositional rules and principles to guide practice.

—JUDITH E. RINK (1966)

By Esmeralda Michelle Mejia

Ball

Key Concepts

- The reflective teacher believes that students, classes, and teaching situations are different and develops lessons and the curriculum accordingly.

- The number of students in a class, frequency and length of classes, facilities, equipment, behavior of the students, and characteristics of the school are all factors reflective teachers take into account as they develop their lessons and programs.

- The teacher's personal value system is the most important characteristic of a reflective or of an invariant teacher.

- Invariant teachers rarely reflect on their effectiveness, continuing to teach the same lessons and content year after year, ignoring the students' progress and interest.

- Reflective teachers are continually thinking about what they need to change, or do differently, to heighten their teaching and program effectiveness.

Chapters 1–3 provided an introduction to the purpose and characteristics of a quality physical education program, along with an overview of skill themes and concepts of movement. This short but important chapter also provides an overview—of reflective teaching and the reasons for reflective, as opposed to invariant, teaching (Table 4.1).

This chapter defines reflective teaching and why we believe it is so important for teachers today. One of the guiding concepts in education today is differentiation of instruction. This concept recognizes that all children are not identical and that teachers should attempt to vary their teaching, both what and how they teach, based on children's abilities. The authors of *Children Moving*, and many other respected educators, do not believe that a prepackaged curriculum can meet the needs and abilities of all children in a class. We want every child we teach to experience success, pleasure, and a sense of competence that leads to their becoming physically active for a lifetime. In order to do so, we differentiate our instruction—that is, we are reflective teachers who create quality programs of physical education that recognize one size does not fit all (NASPE 2009).

We know you agree that no two children are exactly alike. There are obvious physical differences and more subtle personality and individual differences. What is exciting to one child is boring to another. Some youngsters can accomplish a great deal on their own; other children require almost constant monitoring to make progress. For each child who delights in the challenge and camaraderie of a team game, another prefers the challenge and satisfaction of individual activities.

Schools are also different. Some school buildings have open designs, and others are divided into permanent

Table 4.1 Comparison of Reflective Teaching and Invariant Teaching

Variable	Reflective Teachers	Invariant Teachers
Planning	Adjust lesson plans to differences between classes and children	Use the same plan for each primary grade and the same plan for each intermediate grade
Progression within and between lessons	Base progression on such factors as youngsters' (1) rate and extent of improvement; (2) physical skill needs; (3) interest in a particular topic or activity	Base progression on such factors as (1) six-week units; (2) amount of material to be covered in a semester or year; (3) a predetermined formula for progression
Methodology	Vary the methodology according to such factors as (1) characteristics of children in the class; (2) purpose of the lesson; (3) ability of the children to accept responsibility	Employ the same methodology with all classes and hope that the children will eventually fulfill the teacher's expectations
Curriculum	Design curriculum for each unique class of children after examining the children to determine their abilities and needs	Use predetermined curricular content without considering such factors as children's ability, community influences, or children's interests
Equipment and facilities	Modify activities and lessons to available equipment and facilities	Teach activities and lessons that use available equipment and facilities
Discipline	Attempt to understand management problems and then seek the causes, modifying teaching procedure accordingly	Assume that the children are misbehaving and resort to punitive measures to modify individual and class behavior
Assessment	Regularly assess the children and seek constructive criticism about their teaching from children and colleagues	Assess sporadically and often base assessment on whether children liked the lesson, how long they remained interested, and how well they behaved

classrooms. Administrators can be strict, stultifying, or supportive. Fellow teachers can be cooperative or competitive, helpful, or obstructive. Gymnasiums, plentiful physical education equipment, adequate field space, and small class sizes are basic necessities in some elementary schools; other schools view such facilities as frills. Parents may be concerned, meddlesome, apathetic, helpful, or unavailable.

How is a teacher to succeed amid this diversity? We have no magical answers. But we are convinced that a prepackaged (linear) approach* to teaching is not effective, and so we coined the term *reflective teaching*. The reflective teacher achieves success and professional satisfaction by differentiating instruction in an attempt to challenge both the high- and low-skilled children in a class. She also changes lessons from one class to another, recognizing that all third-grade classes, for example, are not identical.

What Is Reflective Teaching?

Reflective teaching is recognizing that children are different—and doing something about it. It could also be called adapted teaching because the teacher adapts the content, and his teaching, to suit the needs of individual students and classes. Reflective teaching is directly related to the concept of developmentally appropriate teaching, which acknowledges that students develop at different rates and stages (NASPE 2009). Invariant teaching, the opposite of reflective teaching, assumes

*Dwight Allen defined linear thinking as searching for the answer to a problem by investigating a single solution without considering feasible alternatives (Allen 1975).

that all children have the same abilities, interests, and level of physical fitness (Table 4.1).

The concept of reflective teaching is not new. In fact, the teachers in one-room schoolhouses were no doubt models of reflective teaching because they had to teach children of many ages in the same classroom. The results of attempting to teach prepackaged lessons without considering the unique characteristics of a class have been disastrous for both the children and many teachers. As stated in a recent review of the importance of physical activity for school-age youth: "Coaching and teaching styles are particularly relevant to the self-concept in organized sport and physical education" (Strong et al. 2005).

In *Children Moving*, reflective teaching doesn't refer to any particular methodology or style of teaching; it refers to the many teaching skills employed by individuals who are respected as master teachers (Graham 2008). The reflective teacher designs and implements an educational program that is congruent with the idiosyncrasies of a particular school situation. Invariant teaching is characterized by the use of one approach, and often identical content, in all teaching situations. Invariant teachers often rely on prepackaged curriculums that provide the same lessons organized by grade level, thereby assuming that all children have the same abilities and that one school is virtually identical to another school.

The Need for Reflective Teaching

If all schools, classes, and youngsters were identical, there would be no need for reflective teaching. We would simply provide you with prepackaged lesson

Some teachers teach most of their lessons outdoors.

Figure 4.1 Interacting factors that contribute to the unique ecology of each school.

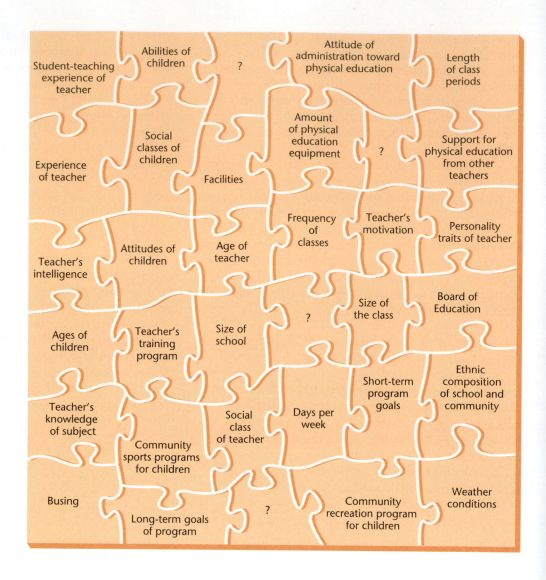

plans for each grade level, and you could follow them exactly. You know, however, that schools, programs, and youngsters are different. Figure 4.1 illustrates some of the obvious differences. Its puzzle shape indicates that teaching is a constant challenge as we attempt to fit the pieces together into a unified, consistent program that provides youngsters with the active learning experiences they need. Reflective teachers take these differences into account and continuously modify and change their teaching and curriculum based on the needs of the students at their school. We want to focus on six of these variables that are major factors in any program necessitating reflective teaching: values of the teacher, class size, the number of class sessions per week, facilities and equipment, student behavior, and the context of the school. Although they may seem obvious, it has been our experience that far too many invariant teachers fail to account for

these variables in their teaching. We'll now discuss them in detail.

Values of the Teacher

Clearly one of the most important variables is the personal disposition (attitudes and beliefs) we, as teachers, bring to our teaching situation. Some physical education teachers, for example, are more interested in coaching than teaching—and their programs reflect a lack of planning and interest in high-quality physical education. Other physical education teachers are totally dedicated to their programs and spend countless hours planning new and interesting activities, as well as volunteering time with children before and after school. Still other physical education teachers view physical education as merely a break for the children from the routine of the classroom, so their programs consist primarily of activities with virtually no purpose or emphasis on learning.

In many schools, physical education is also the classroom teacher's responsibility. Like physical education teachers, classroom teachers vary in their views of the purpose and importance of physical activity in children's lives. Some classroom teachers, for example, find time in their hectic schedules to develop programs for children that truly enhance the development of positive attitudes and learning, as suggested in Chapter 1. In contrast, other classroom teachers view physical education as a break for the children and themselves—and rely on such old standbys as kickball, dodgeball, and Duck, Duck, Goose to keep the children entertained during physical education class.

Ideally, every classroom teacher or physical education teacher would appreciate the importance of physical education and physical activity for children and develop programs that are developmentally appropriate—and effective—for children. Realistically, however, there will always be some teachers who fall back on the ways things were done in the past rather than working to develop innovative programs. In addition to the teacher's values, a number of other variables contribute to the ease or difficulty of developing quality physical education programs.

Class Size

A variable that has particular impact on what a teacher is able to accomplish in physical education is the size of the classes. Physical education classes are all too often the largest classes in a school. A person doesn't need much teaching experience to realize that the number of students within a given class, other variables excluded, significantly dictates what a teacher can accomplish. Lessons that are possible with 25 children are difficult, if not impossible, with 100 children. This is the primary reason it is recommended that physical education classes be the same size as in the classroom (NASPE 2011; USDHHS 2000).

For teachers to do more than provide directions to a mass of children, they must have opportunities to observe and analyze and give children feedback. The logistical problems of providing individual instruction for each child in a class of 50 children who meet for 30 minutes are overwhelming. The educational literature supports this viewpoint: "The more successful teachers did more tutorial teaching. They spoke to the class as a whole in order to provide structure and give general direction, but most of their actual instruction was given in small groups or to individuals" (Good, Biddle, and Brophy 1975, 70). Class size strongly influences the teaching approach that a given teacher can use to foster a successful educational experience.

Number of Class Sessions per Week

In addition to the teacher's values and the size of classes, another influential variable that must be considered is the number of class sessions per week. Children in some schools, for example, have "organized" physical education only one day a week. Children in other schools have daily physical education. Obviously, children who have instructional physical education 180 days a year can learn significantly more than those who have physical education only 36 days a year (NASPE 2002; USDHHS 2000). The challenge for the

Some teachers teach in gymnasiums that are used only for physical education.

teacher is to make the difficult decisions about what can be learned in one or two days a week so the children truly benefit from the program rather than simply being exposed to a variety of activities (Graham, Metzler, and Webster 1991; NASPE 2009). This also means that the teacher, or the district, will have to decide which state or national standards to exclude because of time constraints.

In schools where children don't have daily physical education, the classroom teacher can play a vital role in reinforcing what the specialist has taught—and vice versa. When the classroom teachers and the physical education specialist work together closely, the children reap the benefits.

Facilities and Equipment

A fourth variable is the adequacy of the facilities and equipment in a particular school. Established physical education programs often include adequate equipment and a reasonable solution to the use of indoor space during inclement weather. In contrast, fledgling physical education programs may lack equipment. In some schools, physical education classes are forced to use classrooms, cafeterias, or even hallways on rainy days.

Some teachers are masters of improvisation, but others can't function without adequate facilities and equipment. The teaching skills acquired during student teaching, when equipment and facilities were ideal, often must be adapted to less desirable conditions. You may find that there is only one ball per class instead of one ball per child. You may find yourself on a rainy afternoon teaching in a classroom instead of on a playground. Different environments call for different teaching skills.

At the heart of complexity in the gym is numbers. That the teacher is one and the learners are many is a fact of life which shapes every aspect of the teacher's experience. What many outsiders fail to appreciate is that an average class contains a lot of kids for one person to handle even if there were no intent to teach anything. This failure particularly is true of parents who often feel qualified as experts on child management because they deal more or less successfully with their own children in groups rarely exceeding three or four.

—Larry Locke, The Ecology of the Gymnasium: What the Tourist Never Sees (1975)

Student Behavior

Another variable that contributes to the need for reflective teaching is student behavior. The ability to manage children effectively is a major concern in education today among parents as well as teachers.

The ability to manage a class of children effectively is also one of the few teaching skills that educators agree is a prerequisite to successful teaching. A teacher must be able to create and maintain an appropriate environment if children are to learn. Some teachers are able to maintain desirable student behavior simply by glancing occasionally at certain children in a class. Other teachers spend most of their time trying to maintain order. We believe that specific teaching skills can be effectively employed to create and sustain an appropriate environment (see Chapters 8 and 9).

Unfortunately, many textbooks—and many teachers—underplay the role of discipline. These texts and teachers assume that a "good" teacher doesn't have discipline problems (Siedentop and Tannehill 2000). Our experience suggests otherwise. During a teaching career, a teacher encounters many kinds of classes. Some will test the teacher's ability to maintain appropriate behavior; others are cooperative. Successful teachers are able to work effectively with both types of classes.

Context of the School

A sixth and equally important variable that supports the need for reflective teaching is the context of the school. Some schools today are populated predominantly by children in transient situations, many of whom will move before the end of the school year. An increasing number of children are from homes in which both parents work outside the home and consequently are generally unavailable during the day or when the children return home after school. Rural schools continue to have children with needs different from those of children in suburban or inner-city schools. Moreover, it is typical today to have one or more children in a class who do not speak English, and it seems that more classes have mainstreamed children than ever before. Each of these situations, as well as the many variations that have not been described, presents interesting challenges to teachers— challenges that have no standard answers. The one constant in all of these situations is that children need caring, dedicated teachers, perhaps more than ever.

Some inner-city youngsters often test their teachers according to rules governing their street corner behavior rather than by their teachers' middle-class rules and expectations. This testing by street corner rules happens to teachers and administrators in inner-city schools every day. And most of the teachers and administrators neither realize nor understand what is happening. Indeed, until you actually experience this testing—when all your middle-class niceties do not count a damn and you wonder why this kid is doing that to you because you are not as prejudiced as the others and you really want to help—it will be hard, if not impossible, for you to understand what I am talking about.

—HERBERT FOSTER, *Ribbin', Jivin' and Playin' the Dozens* (1974)

Do I Want to Become a Reflective Teacher?

The first step to becoming a reflective teacher is believing that it is important to become a reflective, rather than invariant, one. This may be especially challenging for physical education majors who were athletes. Many physical educators were athletes; consequently we loved playing sports and frequently did very well in physical education classes. In fact, for many majors it was our best class. We really enjoyed physical education when it consisted of games, typically team sports because we dominated the games with our friends. Many physical educators, for example, enjoyed elimination games such as dodgeball. We could hardly wait to play these games. The intent of *Children Moving*, however, is to convince you there is an alternative to programs that are predominantly based on team sports—that are still enjoyable for athletes but also beneficial for all of the children in a class.

Can you recall many of your classmates in your physical education classes? Some were overweight, some were poorly skilled, some disliked competition, and some didn't enjoy physical activity in general. Now as a teacher you have responsibility for all of the children in your class—not only the athletes! What are you going to do for these youngsters who may not like sports and physical activity? Reflective teachers worry about these children: What can they do to provide interesting, fun, beneficial learning experiences for them? The answer is that they will not teach as they did in the past because there are newer and better ways. The goal of *Children Moving* is to guide you to become a reflective teacher and deliver a new and improved physical education for all of the children in a class.

How Do I Become a Reflective Teacher?

How do you become a reflective teacher? Chapters 5, 6, and 7 are designed to get you started on that journey.

Chapter 5 provides an alternative to grouping children by age or grade level. This will help you to plan lessons based on the children's abilities at your school and also differentiate your instruction. This is an important first step in becoming a reflective teacher.

Chapter 6 describes a planning process that will help you develop lessons (the content) that are not only enjoyable but also beneficial so children will be physically active and, most important, will be developing the motor and sports skills that lead them to develop competence and confidence in their physical abilities. Reflective teaching involves planning and designing lessons that are enjoyable learning experiences. This is the opposite of "rolling out the ball" whereby teachers simply present activities that keep the children busy, happy, and good—with no learning intended. No single prepackaged curriculum or program works for all teachers in every school. If you accept this premise, you are well on your way to becoming a reflective teacher.

The next step in the process of becoming a reflective teacher is learning some of the techniques (systems) for analyzing your teaching to determine how you are actually interacting with the children and whether your teaching is effective. One of the predominant characteristics of reflective teachers is that

Reflective teachers are constantly observing their classes to determine the children's needs, interests, and abilities.

they are continually self-analyzing their teaching in order to improve. They don't teach the same lessons over and over, year after year. They change their lessons from class to class, day to day, and year to year based on their reflections about how and what might be improved.

We wish that simply reading and understanding *Children Moving* would be enough to become a reflective teacher. It's not! If you have become a good athlete, an excellent musician or artist, or made the dean's list every semester, you know how much time and hard work it takes to attain your level of achievement. Reflective teachers are no different. As you know by now, becoming an excellent teacher takes many, many hours of hard work. Just because a teacher has 10 or 15 years of teaching experience and a master's degree does not mean he or she has become an excellent teacher. The process of reflective teaching is no different. *Children Moving* will guide you in the process of beginning to become a reflective teacher. We hope you find your journey both enjoyable and worthwhile.

Summary

Six major variables necessitate the need for reflective teaching, or differentiated instruction: the values of the teacher, class size, the number of class sessions per week, facilities and equipment, student behavior, and the context of the school. The reflective teacher considers the characteristics of each class and the abilities of the individual students. A reflective teacher doesn't expect all children to respond in the same way or to achieve the same level of skill. Reflective teachers continually observe and analyze, a process that enables them to revise their expectations and adapt all the components of the program, thereby constantly improving the program's effectiveness. The reflective approach requires that teachers constantly and accurately monitor their teaching as they attempt to design and implement a physical education program for a given school. Reflective teachers also have a wealth of content knowledge that allows them to adapt and modify tasks for individuals of varying abilities. The process of becoming a reflective teacher takes time and practice. *Children Moving* is designed to guide you in this process.

Reading Comprehension Questions

1. What is reflective teaching? What are its basic characteristics?
2. What does a linear approach to teaching mean? What is a prepackaged curriculum? How is it different from the skill theme approach?
3. Provide three examples of how class size influences the way a teacher teaches a lesson.
4. Provide an example of a teacher who rolls out the ball. Contrast that teacher with a reflective teacher. What do they do differently in their planning, teaching, and assessment of their teaching?
5. In the previous two chapters you have learned about skill themes and movement concepts. Explain the difference(s) between skill themes and games like Duck, Duck, Goose or elimination dodgeball.
6. In your own words, explain the major implication of reflective teaching, or differentiated instruction.

References/Suggested Readings

Allen, D. 1975. The future of education: Where do we go from here? *Journal of Teacher Education* 26: 41–45.

Foster, H. L. 1974. *Ribbin', jivin' and playin' the dozens: The unrecognized dilemma of inner-city schools.* Cambridge, MA: Ballinger.

Good, T. L., B. J. Biddle, and J. E. Brophy. 1975. *Teachers make a difference.* New York: Holt, Rinehart & Winston.

Graham, G. 2008. *Teaching children physical education: Becoming a master teacher.* 2nd ed. Champaign, IL: Human Kinetics.

Graham, G., C. Hopple, M. Manross, and T. Sitzman. 1993. Novice and experienced children's physical education teachers: Insights into their situational decision-making. *Journal of Teaching in Physical Education* 12: 197–217.

Graham, G., M. Metzler, and G. Webster. 1991. Specialist and classroom teacher effectiveness in children's physical education: A 3-year study [monograph]. *Journal of Teaching in Physical Education* 4: 321–426.

Housner, L. D., and D. C. Griffey. 1985. Teacher cognition: Differences in planning and interactive decision making between experienced and inexperienced teachers. *Research Quarterly for Exercise and Sport* 56: 56–63.

Locke, L. F. 1975, Spring. *The ecology of the gymnasium: What the tourist never sees.* Southern Association for Physical Education of College Women Proceedings: 38–50.

[NASPE] National Association for Sport and Physical Education. 2002. *2001 Shape of the nation report: Status of physical education in the USA.* Reston, VA: American Alliance for Health, Physical Education, Recreation and Dance.

[NASPE] National Association for Sport and Physical Education. 2009. Appropriate practices for elementary school physical education. Reston, VA: National Association for Sport and Physical Education. **http://www.naspeinfo.org.**

[NASPE] National Association for Sport and Physical Education. 2011. *Key points of a quality physical education program.* **http://www.aahperd.org/naspe/publications/teachingTools/key-points-of-QPE.cfm.**

Rink, J. 1996. Effective instruction in physical education. In *Student learning in physical education,* ed. S. J. Silverman and C. D. Ennis, 171–98. Champaign, IL: Human Kinetics.

Siedentop, D., and D. Tannehill. 2000. *Developing teaching skills in physical education.* 4th ed. Mountain View, CA: Mayfield.

Strong, W. B., R. M. Malina, C. J. Blimkie, S. R. Daniels, R. K. Dishman, B. Gutin, A. C. Hergenroeder, et al. 2005. Evidence-based physical activity for school-age youth. *Journal of Pediatrics* 146: 732–37.

[USDHHS] U.S. Department of Health and Human Services. 2000. *School health index for physical activity and healthy eating: A self-assessment and planning guide for elementary school.* Atlanta: Centers for Disease Control and Prevention. Available for free download from **http://www.cdc.gov/HealthyYouth.**

Determining Generic Levels of Skill Proficiency

Where parents have a voice in physical education programs, they usually insist that the curriculum includes the dances, games, and sports skills of their culture. At the elementary level these activities are often preceded by the fundamental skills that are combined into more complex tasks as age and skill levels increase. . . . Teachers are to concentrate on the process of learning by selecting the appropriate content for whatever level of development the child demonstrates.

—VERN SEEFELDT (1979)

by . Janette

Key Concepts

- The generic levels of skill proficiency (GLSP) provide a relatively quick and easy way to assess the abilities of entire classes of children.
- The GLSP apply to the skill themes, not the movement concepts.
- The GLSP serve as a guide to matching the difficulty of a task (activity) to the ability of the students so they can have success and yet still be challenged.
- At the precontrol level, the beginner or novice level, successful performances are typically accidents and are rarely repeated.
- At the control level, tasks require intense concentration if they are to be performed successfully. Learners at this level are easily distracted.
- At the utilization level, learners are ready to combine several skills together or practice in dynamic, unpredictable contexts.
- Proficiency level is the expert, or mastery, level.
- It is unreasonable to expect children to advance from the precontrol to the proficiency level in a skill theme if they practice that skill only during physical education classes.
- Adults can be at the precontrol level in skill themes they have had little or no opportunity to practice.

Think about a group of your friends or maybe a class you are teaching. If your friends or students were asked to dribble a ball with their feet through a general space, would they all be able to do it successfully? Would some, perhaps those on a soccer team, be much more proficient than others? Would some keep losing control of the ball?

You probably answered yes to the last two questions. Obviously age, or grade level, is not an accurate predictor of developmental level. If all fifth graders had identical motor skill abilities, this chapter would not be necessary. Typically, however, in a fifth-grade class, there is a wide range of motor abilities—and that range only increases with age. Therefore as a reflective teacher you want to design lessons that are both interesting and developmentally appropriate for the classes you teach.

One of the major challenges of reflective teaching (Chapter 4) is matching a task (activity) to the child's ability. If a task is appropriate—that is, not too hard and not too easy—the child will typically be successful and therefore remain interested, continue trying, and learn. If a task is too easy, however, the child will become bored and lose interest; too hard, and the child will want to do something else because of the frustration level. Matching tasks to abilities is complicated drastically by the fact that we don't teach one child at a time—we typically teach 25 or more in a class. And the range of abilities within any class is typically wide. Some of the children may never have tried an activity, whereas others may have been playing it at home after school or on a team for several years.

In writing this book, we knew from the outset that describing and organizing activities according to the children's grade level (or age) would be inadequate. We needed a classification system that would help us communicate with one another—and with you.

As we reviewed the literature, we came across a classification system developed by Sheila Stanley (1977), which we found to be descriptive and helpful in communicating the range of abilities related to a skill. She proposed four levels, which we have termed the generic levels of skill proficiency (GLSP): precontrol, control, utilization, and proficiency.

The term *generic* is synonymous with terms such as *universal*, *all-purpose*, *covering a broad spectrum*. We thought it would be too difficult and confusing if we created a different classification system for each skill theme. Thus, we use the term *generic* to mean that the same classification system can be used to analyze youngsters' ability levels for all of the different skill themes. *Levels of skill proficiency* is the phrase we use to identify children's developmental level for each of the skill themes. We are not suggesting that the GLSP are precise, exact measures of motor ability. They are, however, immensely helpful as a way to observe a class of youngsters to quickly determine their overall ability and make an informed decision about which task is appropriate for the overall skill level of the class. The GLSP system also enables the teacher to assess individual youngsters quickly when attempting to manage an entire class.

We have organized and sequenced the content in the skill theme chapters by the GLSP. As you become familiar with these terms, we think you, too, will find them more descriptive and helpful than the beginner-to-advanced classifications that might have been used. We also hope you understand the connection between the GLSP and reflective teaching. The teacher who teaches as if all of her students have the same motor abilities is not only doing the children a disservice, but also falling into the trap of boring some students and frustrating others. Before describing how we have used the GLSP throughout the text, we first need to define and describe each of the four skill levels.

Box 5-1

Observable Characteristics of the Generic Levels of Skill Proficiency

Precontrol Level

- Child is unable to repeat movements in succession; one attempt doesn't look like another attempt to perform the same movement.
- Child uses extraneous movements that are unnecessary for efficiently performing the skill.
- Child seems awkward and frequently doesn't even come close to performing the skill correctly.
- Correct performances are characterized more by surprise than by expectancy.
- When the child practices with a ball, the ball seems to control the child.

Control Level

- The child's movements appear less haphazard and seem to conform more to the child's intentions.
- Movements appear more consistent, and repetitions are somewhat alike.
- The child begins to perform the skill correctly more frequently.
- The child's attempt to combine one movement with another or perform the skill in relation to an unpredictable object or person is usually unsuccessful.
- Because the movement isn't automatic, the child needs to concentrate intensely on what he or she is doing.

Utilization Level

- The movement becomes more automatic and can be performed successfully with concentration.
- Even when the context of the task is varied (slightly at first), the child can still perform the movement successfully.
- The child has developed control of the skill in predictable situations and is beginning to move skillfully in unpredictable situations. The child can execute the skill the same way consistently.
- The child can use the skill in combination with other skills and still perform it appropriately.

Proficiency Level

- The skill has become almost automatic, and performances in a similar context appear almost identical.
- The child is able to focus on extraneous variables—an opponent, an unpredictable object, the flow of travel—and still perform the skill as intended.
- The movement often seems effortless as the child performs the skill with ease and seeming lack of attention.
- The movement can be performed successfully in a variety of planned and unplanned situations as the child appears to modify performance to meet the demands of the situation.

Identifying Generic Levels of Skill Proficiency

Observable characteristics of each generic level of skill proficiency are discussed below and listed in Box 5-1.

Precontrol Level

The precontrol (beginner) level is characterized by lack of ability to either consciously control or intentionally replicate a movement. For example, a child at the precontrol level who is bouncing a ball spends more time chasing after the ball than bouncing it—the ball seems to control the child. A child who tries to do a forward roll may complete a revolution on a mat or may get stuck, not rolling at all or rolling half forward and half to the side and finishing flat on the back. A child's efforts to strike a ball with a racket are characterized by frequent misses, mishits, and an inefficient and inconsistent striking pattern. Successful skill performances

are a surprise! Most preschool and kindergarten children are at the precontrol level. By the time children are in the first grade, however, you'll observe some of them entering the control level.

Control Level

The control (advanced beginner) level is characterized by less haphazard movements—the body appears to respond more accurately to the child's intentions. The child's movements often involve intense concentration because the movements are far from automatic. A movement that is repeated becomes increasingly uniform and efficient. At this level, a cartwheel the child performs is more or less identifiable as a cartwheel; the child is able to travel in a previously identified direction while briefly taking full weight on the hands. When the child tries to throw a ball at a target, the ball usually travels in the direction of the target.

Some primary-grade children are at the control level. You'll begin to observe that a few children involved in certain youth sports programs are at the next level, the utilization level. This is true only for their sport, however. For example, children involved in after-school gymnastics programs may be approaching the utilization level in the skill themes of rolling or transferring weight, but they may be at the precontrol level for throwing and catching or kicking a ball.

Utilization Level

The utilization (intermediate) level is characterized by increasingly automatic movements. A child at this level is able to use a movement in a variety of ways because he or she doesn't need to think as much about how to execute the movement. Dribbling a ball in a game situation is appropriate for a child at the utilization level. When children at the previous level (control) try to dribble a ball, they spend more time chasing the ball than dribbling because they're unable to focus on dribbling a ball while trying to travel away from an opponent. A cartwheel, as one in a sequence of three movements, is also an appropriate task for a child at the utilization level.

As children get older, the gap between the skill levels widens. Children in the fourth and fifth grades who are involved in youth sports programs are often at the utilization level in the skill themes used in their sport but not necessarily used in other skills. In the same class, however, it's not uncommon to have children who have remained at the precontrol level, primarily because of their lack of activity beyond formally organized physical education classes.

Proficiency Level

The fourth level, proficiency (advanced), is characterized by somewhat automatic movements that begin to seem effortless. At this level, the child gains control of a specific movement and is challenged by the opportunities to employ that skill in changing environments that may require sudden and unpredictable movements (open skill). The challenge of repeating movements exactly and with ever-increasing degrees of quality (closed skill) is also appropriate for children at this level. Rarely are elementary school children at the proficiency level in a skill. In almost every instance, their proficiency is a result of their extensive involvement in after-school youth sports programs.

One Child, More than One Level

Now that you understand the four levels of skill proficiency, we can expand our use of the term *generic*. Once again, our jobs as teachers would be much easier

if every child had the same ability—not only within a grade, but also for every skill. If this were so, we could, for example, merely observe a child kicking a ball at the utilization level and thereby determine that the child was also at the utilization level in throwing, balancing, and jumping and landing. As you know, however, this is not the case. A child may be at the utilization level in one skill and at the precontrol level in another. It's not uncommon for children in our classes to be skillful (utilization-level) throwers and catchers and be at the precontrol level in the nonmanipulative skills of rolling, balancing, and transferring weight. By generic, then, we mean that the terms *precontrol, control, utilization,* and *proficiency* are used to describe a child's ability in every skill we teach—we don't use a different set of terms to describe the skill level for balancing, for example, and still another set of terms to describe the skill level for volleying. The hypothetical example in Figure 5.1 illustrates two points: (1) the GLSP apply to all the skills we teach, and (2) children are typically at different skill levels for different skills. The reflective teacher accounts for these differences in the way he plans his lessons (Chapter 6), the way he establishes the learning environment (Chapter 8) and also the way he teaches the lessons (Chapter 10). The unreflective teacher assumes that all children have identical motor skills and abilities.

Figure 5.1 also suggests that age is not an accurate indicator of ability. If it were, all adults would be skillful

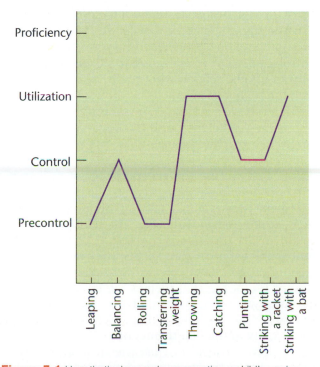

Figure 5.1 Hypothetical example representing a child's varying levels of proficiency in different skills.

at striking with a racket, for example, and we know this isn't true. Fourth and fifth graders are often at the precontrol level when a new skill is introduced that they have never practiced. Generally, however, because of their physical maturation and previous experiences, they move from the precontrol level more rapidly than the primary-grade children (although there are always exceptions).

Using the Generic Levels of Skill Proficiency in Teaching

The generic levels of skill proficiency provide a broad guideline for answering two important questions for the reflective teacher:

1. What is the motor ability level of this class?
2. Which tasks and activities work best for a class at this GLSP?

Although there will be a range of skill levels within any class, we as reflective teachers make a judgment about the overall ability of the class. Then we modify the tasks for individuals using teaching by invitation and intratask variation, as discussed in Chapter 8.

Tasks that succeed with one third-grade class may need to be changed (made easier or harder) to meet the needs of the next third-grade class. The GLSP provide us with broad guidelines for doing so. For example, it is generally safe to assume that most of the children in school through first grade will be at the precontrol level.

In the upper grades, however, we typically find a few children who are at precontrol level, a number at control level, some at utilization level, and a few, especially in middle school, who might be at proficiency level: the higher the grade level, the greater the range of skill levels within a class. The reflective teacher recognizes these differences and teaches accordingly. The unreflective teacher assumes that one third grade is identical to the next.

Note that we use the generic levels of skill proficiency to describe a youngster's proficiency for each skill theme—for example, kicking, jumping and landing, or striking a ball with a bat. The skill levels do not pertain to the movement concepts (Chapters 13–15) because the concepts aren't skills; they represent cognitive understanding expressed through versatile and efficient use of the skill themes. As you read further, this point will become clearer. For now, however, just remember that the four generic levels of skill proficiency apply to the skill themes only.

As reflective teachers we use the GLSP in two ways. First, we observe the students to determine their overall skill level. Second, we attempt to match the tasks to the skill level of the children in the class. For example, if we determine that the majority of the children in a class are at the precontrol level for the skill of kicking, we would not ask them to play a proficiency-level game such as Alley Soccer or Cone Soccer (Chapter 22). Instead, we would ask them to practice precontrol tasks, such as kicking a stationary ball from a standing position and then running to kick the ball.

Which Task?

As teachers gain experience in reflective teaching and learn to use the GLSP, they become able to assess the overall skill level of a class rather quickly and determine which tasks will be productive for that group (Graham et al. 1993; Housner and Griffey 1985). For those who are new to the skill theme approach, or perhaps new to a school, it will take time and experience to learn the tasks that work with different grade and ability levels. Veteran teachers who have been teaching by skill themes know which tasks will work—and which will not. Beginning teachers, in contrast, will learn with practice the tasks that are most effective and how to make them interesting and appealing to children of various generic levels. As you plan, especially when you start working with the skill theme approach, we recommend being prepared to deliver a series of 10 to 15 tasks in a lesson—not just 1 or 2! Extensive planning will also help you learn the progression of tasks for each skill theme and movement concept. The chapters on planning and observation techniques (Chapters 6 and 11) will also help you better understand how to plan for skill theme lessons—and when to use a task and when to change to a new one.

Finally, it is important to remember that there is no single, correct way to deliver the tasks in a lesson. Some teachers, for example, prefer to start at the precontrol level (for a class at the control level) and quickly progress up the spiral with a series of tasks that serve as a warm-up and review for the children. Others prefer to start with a task or activity that most closely matches that class's GLSP. If a task is too hard and children have high rates of failure and frustration, then a teacher who has planned well can move down the spiral to an easier task. That's why it is so important for the reflective teacher to plan a series of tasks rather than only one or two for a lesson.

How to Know if a Task Works

Chapter 11, "Observing Student Responses," explains in more detail how to know if a task works, but a quick overview of the process is helpful here. A task works when youngsters are provided numerous chances to be successful—and they want to keep doing the task. Tasks that are too hard or too easy lead to frustration or boredom. The GLSP will help you match tasks to the ability level of the majority of the class so that children are not frustrated or bored. This is why we did not organize the book by grade levels: There is such a wide range of variance among classes at the same grade level. As you increase your understanding of the skill theme approach, you will find it is relatively easy to change tasks and activities with classes.

When a class is required to play a sport or participate in a predesigned game—that is, a game designed with no knowledge of the class of children being taught—the teacher implicitly assumes that all the youngsters have the same abilities and interests. The response of a sixth-grade boy to an opinion poll about a "flag football" unit (Figure 5.2) provides one potent example of how some children feel when they are all required to play a sport that requires proficiency-level skills. Obviously this lesson (unit) was not taught by a reflective teacher. It also suggests why teaching the

prerequisite skills for successful game playing, as opposed to playing games, is so important at the elementary school level—especially for those youngsters who have yet to reach the utilization or proficiency level.

Insights about the Generic Levels of Skill Proficiency

Now that you're familiar with the four levels that constitute the GLSP, we want to suggest four insights that will enhance your understanding of the levels and help you apply them in your teaching situation.

Multiple Skill Levels in a Class

The first insight is that in the upper-elementary and middle school grades, you can expect to have children

Figure 5.2 Sixth-grader's evaluation of a flag football unit.

Personal Opinion

Age: 12½   Sex: m

Answer the following questions:

1) What is the most important thing you have learned in flag football?

   In flag football I learned, hold on I can sum it up with a couple of words! Absolutely nothing!

2) Did you enjoy the unit? Why? Why not?

   NO! I hated this unit! I'm sorry, but it stank! I pretty much hate any outdoor activity! Except Rollerblading, riding bicycles and basketball!

3) Is flag football appropriate to your age? Why?/Why not?

   I don't know, and don't care! I Hate Football.

in the same class at three different levels: precontrol, control, and utilization. Your challenge as a reflective teacher is to determine the predominant skill level and then make adjustments for individuals through teaching by invitation or intratask variation (Chapter 8) and task sheets (Chapter 10) for example. In the preschool and primary grades, in contrast, many children will be at the precontrol and control levels—although there will always be exceptions.

Control Level in Two Days a Week

The second insight we can offer is that in programs of elementary school physical education in which children have physical education classes only once or twice a week, the children will reach the utilization level of most of the skill themes only if they do something outside of class (Graham, Metzler, and Webster 1991), i.e. with a parent, siblings, or on athletic teams. Unfortunately, an increasing number of children today are not physically active after school and on weekends. It is our observation that, along with the decline in physical activity beginning in the middle school years (Chapter 1), children are also experiencing a decline in their skill levels from past years. The implication, of course, is that it is not uncommon for a teacher to use control-level tasks for children in the fourth and fifth grades—because the majority of students haven't developed their skills beyond that level. If we develop lessons using utilization- and proficiency-level tasks, we end up frustrating these children and convincing them that physical activity is not enjoyable because they are so inept.

Proficiency Level Is Rare

Our third insight is that children at the proficiency level in a skill are the exception. Remember that the GLSP apply to skills, not ages. Thus anyone, regardless of age, can be at the precontrol level. The standards or criteria for each of the skill levels apply across the board to all skills and all ages. Consequently, we do not see many children at the proficiency level. In fact, it seems unlikely that many children can reach proficiency level simply by participating in a physical education program— unless that program is a quality, daily program. Typically children reach the proficiency level in a skill because they've been involved in an after-school sports program in which they practice the skill frequently or because a parent or older sister or brother is involved in a sport and the child consequently spends a lot of time practicing and receiving instruction in the backyard.

Overall, however, we do not observe children at proficiency level very often. For this reason, you will probably use the proficiency-level tasks we have listed in each of the chapters more as part of teaching by invitation and intratask variation (differentiated instruction) (Chapter 8) than with entire classes of children. This does not mean, of course, that some of the children don't want to perform the proficiency-level tasks, especially the skill themes used in popular games. Children who are new to the skill theme approach, particularly those in the upper-elementary and middle school grades, constantly ask the question, "When do we get to play the real 'official' game?" Our standard answer is, "At recess. At home. On the weekends." In time, as the children become accustomed to the skill theme approach and we're able to individualize the program to a greater extent, they no longer ask the question—at least, not as often.

Unfortunately, some teachers succumb to the pressure from the children to "play the game." In the long run, the children end up shortchanged, just as they do when their diet consists primarily of unhealthy snacks and fast food. Although it may not be as much fun (for some) as playing games such as kickball and dodgeball, a focus on learning and improving has the potential to help children eventually derive the benefits of regular involvement in physical activity (Barnett et al. 2008; Malina 2001; Stodden et al. 2008). Failure to help children develop the prerequisite motor skills may mean that, as they age, children come to feel inadequate and incompetent in physical activity. Just as it's easier for parents to let their children sit in front of the television five or six hours a day, it's easier for teachers to let the children play kickball and dodgeball every day. But is this better for the children?

Assessment Using the GLSP?

As you will see in Chapter 12 on assessment, we do not suggest that the generic skill proficiency levels be used to assess children's progress in physical education. After reading this chapter, you can understand why. Change from one level to another (e.g., control to utilization) is primarily dependent on copious amounts of practice and experiences using the skill themes. Unfortunately, in too many programs of physical education, there is simply not enough time to reasonably expect children to progress from one skill level to another over a semester or even a year. For this reason, we assess what children can reasonably learn in the time allotted for physical education. Thus our final insight to conclude this chapter is that the GLSP are immensely helpful for determining the overall skill level of a class and the ability level of individual children. It seems unreasonable, however, to expect that we will see dramatic changes in skill level from year to year if children practice the skills only during physical education class. For this reason, we do not recommend that the GLSP be used to assess, or grade, individual students' progress.

Summary

Organizing curriculum by grade level or age is convenient. Yet because of the range of skills found at any grade level or age, these are inadequate indicators of children's skill levels. We have adopted the concept of generic levels of skill proficiency (GLSP). Assessing children's skills in terms of these levels is a basis for planning appropriate activities. The four generic levels of motor skill proficiency are (1) precontrol, (2) control, (3) utilization, and (4) proficiency.

Children at the precontrol level are unable to consciously control or replicate a particular movement. At the control level, the child's body appears to respond more accurately to the child's intentions, and movements become increasingly similar. Movements are even more automatic and reflexive at the utilization level; children can use a movement in a variety of contexts. At the proficiency level, the child has gained control of a movement and is challenged by the goal of repeating movements exactly or using movements effectively in dynamic, unpredictable situations.

The generic levels of skill proficiency are task related—that is, a child at the utilization level in one motor skill may be at the control level in another skill. Age and skill level are not necessarily related. The reflective teacher uses this information to plan enjoyable and effective lessons—rather than assuming that all children in a grade have identical physical abilities.

Reading Comprehension Questions

1. What is the purpose of the GLSP? How are they used?
2. In your own words, explain the differences between the four generic levels of skill proficiency.
3. What do we mean by generic?
4. Why isn't age, or grade level, an indicator of motor skill proficiency?
5. Pick a skill theme, and describe how a reflective teacher would use the GLSP to help her make decisions about which tasks to include in a lesson. Contrast your explanation with how an unreflective teacher would teach a lesson.
6. Figure 5.1 shows a hypothetical example of a child's proficiency level at several skills. Use the following

10 Skills

form to create your own graph. Select 10 of the skill themes that represent your range of abilities. Graph your skill levels. Which skill themes do you need to work on most? Why are you less advanced at these skills than at the others? Did you rate yourself at the proficiency level for any of these skills? If so, why do you think you attained the proficiency level for that skill? Answer the same questions if you're at the precontrol level for any of the 10 skills you selected.

7. In Figure 5.2, a sixth-grade boy responds to three questions about a flag football unit. Why do you think he responded as he did? What do think his GLSP were for throwing, catching, chasing, and fleeing? What would you do if he were in your class to help him enjoy the unit?

References/Suggested Readings

Barnett, L., P. Morgan, E. van Beurden, and J. Beard. 2008. Perceived sports competence mediates the relationship between childhood motor skill proficiency and adolescent physical activity and fitness. *International Journal of Behavioral Nutrition and Physical Activity* 5(40): 1–12.

Graham, G., C. Hopple, M. Manross, and T. Sitzman. 1993. Novice and experienced children's physical education teachers: Insights into their situational decision-making. *Journal of Teaching in Physical Education* 12(2): 197–214.

Graham, G., M. Metzler, and G. Webster. 1991. Specialist and classroom teacher effectiveness in children's physical education: A 3-year study [monograph]. *Journal of Teaching in Physical Education* 4: 321–426.

Housner, L. D., and D. C. Griffey. 1985. Teacher cognition: Differences in planning and interactive decision making between experienced and inexperienced teachers. *Research Quarterly for Exercise and Sport* 56: 56–63.

Malina, R. M. 2001. Adherence to physical activity from childhood to adulthood. *Quest* 53: 350.

Seefeldt, V. 1979. Developmental motor patterns: Implications for elementary school physical education. In *Psychology of motor behavior and sport,* ed. C. Nadeau, W. Halliwell, K. Newell, and C. Roberts. Champaign, IL: Human Kinetics.

Stanley, S. 1977. *Physical education: A movement orientation.* 2nd ed. New York: McGraw-Hill.

Stodden, D., J. Goodway, S. Langedorfer, M. Roberton, M. Rudisill, C. Garcia, and L. Garcia. 2008. A developmental perspective on the role of motor skill competence in physical activity. *Quest* 60: 290–306.

Planning

"Will you please tell me which way I ought to go from here?"
"That depends a good deal on where you want to get to," said the Cat.
"I don't care much where," said Alice.
"Then it doesn't matter which way you go," said the Cat.

—LEWIS CARROLL

If you don't know where you are going, you will be lost when you get there.

—YOGI BERRA

If you want kids to learn to skip, teach them the essential components of skipping, let them practice skipping, and then assess how well they can skip.

—NASPE (2004, 3)

Key Concepts

- Reflective teachers plan and revise their plans over the course of a career as they continue to strive to provide the most productive and enjoyable learning experiences for children.

- Planning is divided into four steps in this chapter.

- The first planning step is the development of a curriculum scope that outlines the content to be taught for several years.

- The second planning step is to decide how many lessons will be devoted to each of the skill themes and movement and fitness concepts during a year.

- The third planning step is the development of benchmarks or assessments that allow the reflective teacher to determine if the children are learning what is being taught.

- The final planning step is the development of daily lesson plans that are interesting and beneficial to youngsters.

- Ideally, lessons encourage students to be physically active during the majority of the lesson. Typically this occurs when children are able to be successful and consider the lesson fun.

- Just because a lesson is fun does not mean that it is a productive learning experience for children.

Reflective teachers are planners. Any good program begins with a good plan. Failure to plan appropriately can lead to disastrous lessons. Disorganization and spending an excessive amount of time on management characterize the lessons of the teacher who hasn't planned effectively.

Inappropriate planning can also have long-term implications. One important task of physical education is to provide a variety of learning experiences that give children a broad foundation of movement abilities (Stodden et al. 2008). Children who are skillful in only a few activities, typically games, may be the products of programs characterized by inefficient planning. Instructors who don't plan are likely to teach only what they know well and what the children enjoy, which often results in an unbalanced program over the years.

Because planning is typically done during the teacher's own time rather than during school time, there are strong temptations to avoid it. It can be much more pleasant to watch television, go to a ball game, or just go to bed early. But planning, even though you may consider it as onerous as homework, is necessary.

The benefits of effective planning include classes that run more smoothly with less interruption and confusion; tasks that are interesting, enjoyable, and worthwhile; and, in some instances, less off-task behavior. In short, well-planned classes assist children to learn the concepts and skills being taught.

Reflective Planning

If all schools, all children, all facilities, all teachers, all communities, and all equipment were the same, we could simply provide you with a book of prepackaged lesson plans that would be successful with every class you teach, no matter the situation. As you know, however, that isn't the case. Reflective teachers plan lessons—and entire programs—that consider the various unique characteristics of their teaching situation (Graham et al. 1993; Housner and Griffey 1985).

The reflective planner considers many factors when trying to devise the best lessons possible under the circumstances. Planning can't be reduced to an exact formula, but certain factors will always influence lesson effectiveness. Each factor is important, and all interact to determine the teaching environment for which the reflective teacher must plan. As we described in Chapter 4, reflective teachers consider class size, frequency of class meetings, available equipment and facilities,

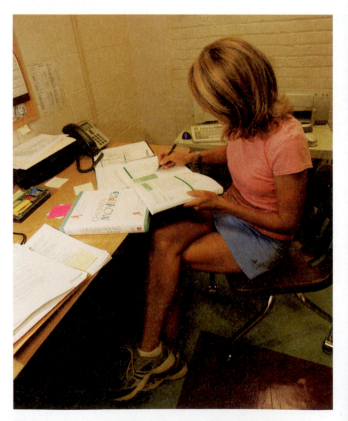

Effective teachers use many resources to plan successful lessons.

personal characteristics of the children, and children's skill levels and interests in their teaching and planning.

A Four-Step Planning Process

We suggest a four-step planning process that provides children with a progression of learning experiences over several years.

Step 1: Develop a curriculum scope for the entire five or six years of the program. This is designed to answer the question, What am I going to teach and when over the entire program?

Step 2: Develop a yearly plan from the program scope, deciding approximately how many days you will devote to the various movement and fitness concepts and skill themes for each grade taught that year.

Step 3: Decide which part of each of the skill themes and movement and fitness concepts you'll focus on, with special attention to the cues or refinements you will be emphasizing. These are referred to as benchmarks or checkpoints and are aligned with national, state, and district standards.

Step 4: Write daily lesson plans.

An analogy may help explain the process. Imagine you and a friend are going on a trip. You are planning to drive several thousand miles. You would probably ask and answer questions similar to the four steps:

1. Where do we plan to end up? What do we plan to visit along the way?
2. How many days do we plan to stay in each location?
3. What will we use as our performance indicators (or benchmarks) along the way to determine how well our plan is working?
4. How will we organize each day?

Effective teachers ask, and answer, essentially the same four questions as they plan their programs. The following sections describe (with examples) the planning process used by teachers employing a skill theme approach of asking and answering these four questions. We caution you that the process may appear complex, but, just as with a long journey, taking it step by step makes it much easier.

Step 1: Developing the Scope for a Skill Theme Curriculum

The scope is what you plan to teach over several years. Imagine the children you teach live in a community where soccer or basketball is extremely popular. Are you going to spend a lot of your classes teaching the

skills of basketball: hand dribbling, shooting (throwing), guarding an opponent (relationship with a partner)? Or, are you going to spend a lot of time teaching soccer skills: kicking, foot dribbling, moving in relation to others? Or are you going to devote relatively few lessons to these skills because you assume that many of the children you teach are already at the utilization or proficiency levels (Chapter 5) and therefore need to practice and learn skills for other sports and activities? Your curriculum scope will reflect the decisions you make.

Look at Tables 6.1 and 6.2. They provide a scope suggesting when to teach the movement concepts and skill themes. (These examples are organized by grade levels to be consistent with the National Association for Sport and Physical Fitness's National Standards (NASPE 1995, 2004). The grade levels merely serve as a general indicator, however; the decisions about what and when to teach are based on observing the actual classes of children we teach). Table 6.1, for example, suggests that by the end of first grade the children will have learned the concepts of self and general space, so these would not be the major focus of lessons in grades 2–5, although you would certainly review them. Table 6.2 suggests that throwing and catching would not be the major focus of lessons until grade 2. In what grade do the authors suggest that you begin teaching striking with bats, golf clubs, and hockey sticks?

Table 6.1 Sample of Movement Concept Scope and Sequence for Grades K–5 (Step 1 in Planning)

Movement Concept	K	1	2	3	4	5
Space Awareness						
Self-space	X	X				
General space	X	X	X			
Levels	X	X	X			
Directions	X	X	X			
Pathways	X	X	X			
Extensions			X	X		
Effort						
Time/speed	X	X	X	X	X	
Force			X	X	X	X
Flow			X	X	X	X
Relationships						
Body part identification	X					
Shapes	X	X	X			
Relationships with objects	X	X	X	X		
Relationships with people			X	X	X	X

Notes: This chart is intended only as an example. Reflective teachers will want to adapt this chart for their school.

X denotes that a movement concept is the major focus of lessons at a grade level. Concepts are studied at other grade levels but not as the primary focus of the lesson.

Table 6.2 Sample Skill Theme Scope and Sequence for Grades K–5 (Step 1 in Planning)

Skill Theme	K	1	2	3	4	5
Traveling						
Walking	X	X				
Running	X	X				
Hopping	X	X	X			
Skipping	X	X	X			
Galloping	X	X	X			
Leaping	X	X	X	X		
Sliding	X	X	X	X		
Chasing, Fleeing, Dodging			X	X	X	X
Bending, Stretching, Twisting and Curling			X	X	X	X
Jumping and Landing	X	X	X	X	X	X
Balancing	X	X	X	X	X	
Transferring Weight			X	X	X	X
Rolling	X	X	X	X	X	X
Kicking			X	X	X	X
Punting					X	X
Throwing			X	X	X	X
Catching			X	X	X	X
Volleying				X	X	X
Hand Dribbling			X	X	X	X
Foot Dribbling			X	X	X	X
Striking with Rackets			X	X	X	X
Striking with Long-Handled Implements						
Bats				X	X	X
Golf clubs				X	X	X
Hockey sticks				X	X	X

Notes: This chart is intended only as an example. Reflective teachers will want to adapt this chart for their school.

X denotes that a skill theme is the major focus of lessons at a grade level. Concepts are studied at other grade levels but not as the primary focus of the lesson.

As a reflective teacher, you will make changes as you learn more about the children you are teaching, your program, and you as a teacher. You may also want to include additional topics. The point of developing a scope that is translated into a school year overview, however, is to determine what you will teach, and in which grades, during the years you are teaching the children. Again we suggest that if you are new to the skill theme approach, you begin by using the overviews in the Appendix to get started and then change them as you gain experience and learn more about the children you are teaching and the program itself.

Step 2: Devising a Yearly Overview

So how long might you spend teaching these movement concepts and skill themes, i.e. how many lessons a year? Table 6.3 provides an example of a scope translated into a school year. In this example the children have two lessons a week, about 72 days per year. If you

Table 6.3 Sample Yearly Overview of Number of Lessons for a Two-Day-a-Week Program: Grades K, 2, and 4 (Step 2 in Planning)

Concept/Theme/Activity	K	2	4
Establishing a Learning Environment	6	4	3
Space Awareness	10	4	2
Effort	4	4	3
Relationships	6	3	2
Traveling	10	3	1
Chasing, Fleeing, Dodging	3	5	3
Bending, Stretching, Twisting and Curling	0	3	2
Jumping and Landing	4	4	3
Rolling	2	4	4
Balancing	4	4	4
Transferring Weight	2	3	4
Kicking and Punting	4	4	4
Throwing and Catching	4	6	6
Volleying	0	2	4
Dribbling	1	2	3
Striking with Rackets	2	3	4
Striking with Hockey Sticks	0	1	2
Striking with Golf Clubs	0	1	2
Striking with Bats	0	1	2
Fitness/Wellness Concepts	5	7	9
Field Day and Other Events	5	4	5
Total Days per Year	72	72	72

Note: Numbers represent days per year that a concept theme will be the major focus of a lesson. Numbers are intended for discussion only; the overview will differ from teacher to teacher.

look at the first line in the table you will see that the teacher plans to spend six lessons for her kindergarten classes focused on establishing a learning environment (Chapter 8), four days with the second-grade classes, and three with the fourth-grade classes. In this example the teacher plans to devote 10 lessons for the kindergarten classes on the movement concept of space awareness (Chapter 13) and only four lessons on effort concepts (Chapter 14). Do you agree with this?

If you have not taught by skill themes before, or if you are a beginning teacher, we have provided two sample scopes in the Appendix. We have termed them sample school year overviews because, as you will see, they break down the school year into lesson topics for each day the children have physical education. One of them is for a two-day-a-week program for the primary grades, and one is for daily physical education programs (five days a week) for intermediate grades. Each overview begins with a scope indicating how many days that year will be devoted to the different movement concepts and skill themes, followed by suggested topics for each lesson of the year. Thus there are 72 lesson topics for two-day-a-week programs and 180 lesson topics for the daily program. Obviously you will need to adapt these overviews if, for example, your classes only meet one day a week (about 36 days a year) or three or four days a week.

This may be a bit confusing, so more examples may be useful. If you look at the example in the Appendix for a two-days-a week program, you will see that for each of the 36 weeks in the school year there are two lesson topics suggested for each week. So find week nine in the Appendix (page A-6). You will see that the first lesson of the week focuses on the basic jumping and landing patterns (Chapter 19, page 323). The second lesson of the week focuses on teaching the physical fitness concepts related to recommended amounts of physical activity (60 minutes a day) (Chapter 27).

Let's look at another example from the same Appendix (page A-6). In the 32nd week of the school year, we suggest the first lesson focus on tasks related to teaching the children to throw and catch with a partner (Chapter 23, pages 434–449). The second lesson of the week is focused on teaching the children to strike a ball rebounding from a wall with a racket or paddle

(Chapter 25, page 506). These are examples to provide you with a place to start developing your own scopes, sequences, and lessons. If you have not taught elementary school physical education, however, they are an excellent place to start.

Once you have adopted, or adapted, one of the yearly overviews from the Appendix, you'll translate it into a yearly calendar. Essentially, this involves deciding which skill themes or concepts you'll emphasize during which days of the school year. Figure 6.1 shows one type of planning calendar.

Based on what we know about how children learn, it seems wise to distribute the throwing lessons over the year rather than to mass them together (Schmidt and Wrisberg 2008). If, for example, a teacher planned to focus on throwing (Chapter 23) for eight days of the year, three of the lessons might be scheduled in September, two in January, and three more in April. A teacher with a three-day-a-week program might have a total of five throwing lessons. In such a case, the teacher might decide to devote three lessons in a row

Figure 6.1 Yearly planning calendar.

to throwing, but it's still better to distribute the total number of lessons throughout the year rather than mass them all together (Schmidt and Wrisberg 2008). Continuing to revisit lessons helps the children better remember the key points. Spending several days on a skill or concept and then not reviewing it for another year is much less effective. Also when a skill theme is taught in the fall, some of the children who were not developmentally ready in October may be ready in April. Again, it's important to emphasize that the children will actually practice throwing in more classes than just the ones that focus primarily on throwing. For example, the sessions dedicated to catching will typically offer many opportunities to throw. In these sessions, however, the teacher will focus on the way the children catch, not on the way they throw. Obviously, children don't reach the utilization level in three lessons per year—it takes much more time and practice. It is possible for them to learn some of the fundamental cues to the overhand throw, however, in three lessons a year. It is reasonable to expect, for example, that they can learn to step with the foot opposite the throwing hand or turn their nondominant side toward the target.

Another advantage of distributing the lessons throughout the year, rather than teaching them as a single unit, is that you can essentially teach the same lesson again later in the school year. This is especially important for children at the precontrol level because the options to change tasks and activities without making them too difficult are limited when the children are first learning a skill.

If you are new to the skill theme approach, you may find it difficult to sequence the lessons, i.e., some take longer than others. With experience, however, you'll learn to predict, with increasing accuracy, the appropriate number of lessons for a skill theme or concept with a given class. And experience helps you adjust the lesson sequence to account for individual differences within a class and among classes. Once you have outlined a sequence, you can rearrange it without losing sight of the intended direction or progression of the skill theme or movement concept.

Here are helpful guidelines for developing your yearly overviews:

- The first time you introduce a concept or theme, the children will need several lessons in a row to grasp the major ideas. Later in the year, they'll need less time. Mass the practice in the beginning of the year; distribute it later (Schmidt and Wrisberg 2008). During weeks 4 and 6, for example, you may devote four lessons to jumping and landing. For the remainder of the year, jumping and landing are the major focus of the lesson only two days in a row.

This same principle applies to any skill theme or movement concept: massed practice during initial learning, distributed practice later.

- The older the children, the longer they're able to remain on the same skill theme. For example, children designing games or dances typically need several days in a row for this task. As the children become more skilled, you'll notice that it becomes easier to remain on a skill theme than it was initially.

- It isn't effective to focus on a skill once a year and then never revisit it. Three weeks of practice in February on the skill theme of rolling, for example, probably won't lead to the long-term learning that three weeks of practice—one week each in October, February, and April—will. That is why we organize the skill theme curriculum by skills and concepts, unlike traditional approaches that organize the physical education curriculum as a series of units.

- To get you started, a major task is generally appropriate for the focus of a day's lesson. If you think the children will find a single task too strenuous or uninteresting, you may combine a major task from two different chapters. For example, you may combine the ideas under the heading Jumping a Turned Rope (Chapter 19) with the major task Traveling in Different Pathways (Chapter 16). This will give the children variety. Although most of our lessons focus on one major movement concept or skill theme, there's no reason not to focus on two themes or concepts in a single lesson, especially with the younger children who are the precontrol and control levels (Chapter 5).

Once you've written your outline, use it only as a guide and change it as often and as much as the particular situation requires. Write your outlines in pencil, leaving plenty of space for changes.

Learning is not totally predictable. If the study of a particular topic is going especially well, we don't change simply because the daily outline tells us to change. If several lessons on a particular topic have proven ineffective, it's possible to change to a different focus even though the daily outline calls for teaching three more lessons on that topic.

The children's needs and interests are the guide for the lessons to be presented. No outline, however theoretically sound it may be, can unfailingly reflect the progress and interests of all the children being taught.

Step 3: Determining Benchmarks (Performance Indicators or Checkpoints)

The authors of *Children Moving* worked closely with the National Association for Sport and Physical Education in the development of benchmarks and the national physical education standards. As a result, the skill theme curriculum is closely aligned both with the national standards and also many state physical education standards that have been adapted from the national standards. Consequently, these standards and benchmarks can be used to determine the progress the children are making throughout their programs.

Reflective teachers develop checkpoints to be sure the children are learning what they want them to be learning—and then constantly assess their progress along the way—in all subjects, not only physical education. These teachers don't wait until the fifth grade, for example, to assess what the children have learned (or not learned). They continually check to be sure the children are getting it before moving on—and revisit areas that have not been clear to the children or areas in which they simply need additional time to practice.

The first edition of the National Standards for Physical Education (NASPE 1995) included a comprehensive list of sample benchmarks designed to serve as guides to what students are expected to be learning in our physical education programs. They are intended to serve as checkpoints along the way, assuring us that we are on the right course in guiding youngsters in the process of becoming physically active for a lifetime. They represent the learnable pieces that, when combined, result in skillful performance and the development of positive self-efficacy.

Often the benchmarks are the critical elements or cues for various skills. Thus once a teacher makes the decision to spend a certain number of days on the skill of catching, for example, she will need to decide what the students are going to learn about catching—that is, the critical elements of catching. Remember, students will not become proficiency-level catchers in one year, but they can learn one or more catching cues that year. The skill theme chapters (16–24) also provide cues (critical elements) to assist you in determining the objective(s) for your lessons.

Table 6.4 provides one example of how a teacher might define the various critical elements of catching that will be emphasized from year to year. Assume that a teacher decides to teach the four catching cues in Table 6.4 and also in Chapter 23, "Throwing and Catching." (This is one example of Content Standard 2 of the National Standards, which states, "Demonstrates understanding of movement concepts, principles, strategies and tactics as they apply to the learning and performance of physical activities" [NASPE 2004, 11].) The teacher could then decide which cues to emphasize each year to serve as benchmarks of student progress. These four critical elements would provide a checkpoint to be sure that the children were actually

Table 6.4 Sample Critical Elements (Cues) for Assessing Progress in Catching

Grade	Critical Element (Cues)
2	Eye contact (track the ball)
3	Ready position (quick feet)
4	Hand and arm position (hands up)
5	Absorption of force (give)

remembering and applying these cues, which would assist them in becoming competent and confident catchers. (The next section of this chapter explains how to teach to these cues so students can understand and apply them.)

For younger children, the teacher might teach the movement concepts of levels and the difference between symmetrical and nonsymmetrical movements, as described in the chapter on space awareness (Chapter 13). The assessment from the National Standards for grades K–2 that could be used to measure the children's progress is "discovers how to balance on different body parts, at different levels, becoming 'like' a statue while making symmetrical and nonsymmetrical shapes" (NASPE 2004, 16). Then the teacher could use other balancing performance objectives from the National Standards to develop the performance indicators or benchmarks shown in Table 6.5.

In summary, the question we suggest you ask and answer for Step 3 of the planning process is this: "What are the benchmarks or checkpoints I will use to assess my students' progress?" For example, if a teacher wants students to know how to position their hands correctly to catch a ball above the waist, or below the waist, most children should be able to demonstrate this cue correctly. If, however, most of them still cannot

Table 6.5 Sample Performance Outcomes for Balancing, Grades K–8

Grade Range	Performance Outcome
K–2	Discovers how to balance on different body parts, at different levels, becoming "like a statue" while making symmetrical and nonsymmetrical shapes
3–5	Balances with control on a variety of objects, such as balance board, large apparatus, skates
6–8	Designs and performs gymnastic (or dance) sequences that combine traveling, rolling, balancing, and weight transfer into smooth, flowing sequences with intentional changes in direction, speed, and flow

Source: NASPE 2004, pp. 16–18.

demonstrate the proper way to position their hands, then the teacher needs to reteach the skill so the students can eventually become successful softball or basketball players. Unfortunately we observe far too many students who have been in physical education programs who have not learned to throw, to catch, to jump, to move in relation to others, etc. We believe physical education should be an educational learning experience for all children—not just a few minutes to simply be physically active during the school day.

Less Is More

"Less is more" is a popular saying that refers to the fact that we often try to do more than we have time for. This is especially true in planning your curriculum. Many physical education programs expose children to a variety of motor skills and sports, but there is little, if any, learning that occurs as a result of this exposure. As you design your curriculum, keep this in mind. The classroom teacher easily describes what the children have learned in math or reading for that year. How will you respond if asked what the children have learned in your program? That response is quite different from simply explaining what you "did" in physical education that year.

Step 4: Developing Daily Lesson Plans

Now you know the content you want to teach during the year (the scope) (Step 1), how you plan to organize the content (the yearly overview, Step 2), and performance objectives (benchmarks) that will provide checkpoints to determine children's progress (Step 3). This may appear to be a lot of work—and it is. But again we want to remind you that the Appendix provides a solid starting point for you to begin so you don't have to start from scratch. We are certain you will want to make changes in what we have provided—but at least you have an initial place to begin.

The final step is to translate the first three steps into actual lesson plans. We are going to show you a lesson planning format (Box 6-1) that we use to develop lessons in the skill theme approach adapted from the work of Judy Rink (2010). We call it the Reflective Planning Grid. The purpose of this sample lesson is to work toward the outcome stated in the national standards for catching: "Catches a fly ball using mature form (e.g., has eyes on ball, moves to position, reaches with hands, caught with hands only rather than trapping the ball, bends elbows to pull ball into chest to absorb force)" (NASPE 2004, 17). These cues or critical elements will serve as the

benchmarks (outcomes) along the way to formatively assess the progress the children are making as explained in the previous section.

The first part of the lesson plan (Box 6-1) consists of information you want at the beginning of your lesson plan—e.g., name of the class you are teaching, grade level, skill level of the class, time the class begins and ends, topic for the lesson (typically a skill theme or movement concept), an outline of the objective(s) for the lesson, and the materials/equipment you will need for the lesson. The lesson begins with an instant activity (Graham 2008) or warm-up followed by the purpose of the lesson (set induction or anticipatory set) [Graham 2008] and what we want the children to do to start the lesson. Box 6-1 illustrates the initial part of the lesson plan (planning grid). This information is typically included in most lesson planning formats. The next part of the plan, however, contains the actual grid used to guide the reflective teacher in developing lessons that vary from class to class based on the children's abilities and interests.

The reflective planning grid consists of five parts organized into columns to make it easier to use in a dynamic teaching situation (Rink 2010). The first column in this example from Chapter 23 refers to the page number in *Children Moving* that contains the tasks, cues, and challenges that comprise the lesson content. For the reflective planning grid in Box 6-1, we have chosen the skill theme of catching for a class in which most children are at the control level (441–450). The second column contains the tasks (activities, drills) for the lesson. The tasks are marked with the following symbol (T) that will make it easier for you to locate them and see their progression. In Box 6-1, there are nine control-level tasks organized in a progression from easier to harder (441–450). With some classes the reflective teacher may use all of these tasks—and need even more. With other classes he may use only one or two of the tasks. Clearly this depends on the children in the classes and all of the other variables that make each class and child unique. We suggest that beginning teachers who are new to the skill theme approach plan 15 tasks for their lessons until they learn more about the abilities of different classes and understand more about content development. This process of content development is also used when differentiating instruction for children of differing abilities (teaching by invitation and intratask variation).

The third column in the reflective planning grid contains the cues (critical elements) that the teacher has decided to reinforce during the lesson. Notice that the cue is in the same row as the task. This is both intentional and important because the cue needs to align with the task to be useful and effective. We will expand on this later in the chapter. The cues link directly to

Box 6-1

Lesson Plan (Reflective Planning Grid) to Teach the Skill of Catching to a Control-Level Class

Class Name (Grade) _____ **Skill Level** Control/Utilization

Lesson Length 30 minutes   10:20–10:50 a.m.

Number of Meetings per Week 2

Number of Students 25

Lesson Focus Catching

Objective(s): At the end of this lesson the children will be able to:
1. Reach and pull the ball into their body by bending the elbows
2. Move into position by moving their feet
CUES: Reach and pull (watch, reach, give)
Move your feet

Materials/ Equipment 25 poly spots, 25 softball-size foam round balls that bounce, tape for wall and floor markings; nets or ropes suspended from poles or trees

Instant Activity Find a rope and a space far away from others and start practicing your jumping tricks. Try to keep jumping until the music ends *(3-4 minutes)*.

Set Induction What sports or games do you play, or want to play, that involves catching a ball? *(Children respond with sports like basketball, softball, football, playing catch with my friends, etc.).* Today we are going to practice catching so that you will be better when you play these sports on a team or in your backyard.

Content Development

Introduction (Informing)

We are going to focus on two catching cues. The first is reaching and pulling. *(Demonstrate and then ask the children to show you "reaching and pulling" as they pretend to catch a ball. Check for understanding to see that they are reaching and giving.)* We are also going to focus on moving our feet to get into position to catch. Show me how to move your feet to catch a ball that is in front of you, behind you, to your side. *(Watch to see that children are moving their feet to catch an imaginary ball.)* When I say go, find a ball and stand on one of the poly spots that are spread throughout the gym.

Page in CM	Task	Cue	Challenge	Organization/Safety
440	**T** Find a poly spot and practice throwing and catching a ball to yourself.		**C** Each time you catch the ball say a letter of your first name? your last name? the street you live on.	Observe to be certain the children remain on their poly spots
442	**T** Remain on your poly spot and bounce the ball and catch it.	Watch, reach, pull	**C** Can you catch 5 in a row without a miss?	Observe to be certain the children remain on their poly spots
443	**T** Throw the ball (or bean bag) and try to catch it at middle level. High level. Low level.	Watch, reach, pull	**C** How high can you make your catch? How close to the ground?	Observe to be certain the children remain on their poly spots
443	**T** Now try to catch the ball (bean bag) on the side of your body? The other side? Now try catching on the side at different levels.	Watch, reach, pull	**C** Can you catch the ball at all three levels on your right side? Your left side? Without a miss?	Observe to be certain the children remain on their poly spots
447	**T** Now get a scoop and practice catching a bean bag with it. Throw with one hand and catch with the scoop.	Watch, reach, give	**C** If this is easy you may want to try catching a ball with your scoop.	Observe to be certain the children remain on their poly spots

Box 6-1 (continued)

Page in CM	Task	Cue	Challenge	Organization/Safety
447	**T** In a group of 3 or 4 you will need one bean bag and one playground ball. We are going to play a game called flying bean bag. Bounce the ball with the bean bag on it. The person closest the bean bag when it flies off tries to catch it.	Move your feet	**C** How many flying bean bags can your group catch in a row?	You may want to have the children use cones or ropes to define their group spaces. Some groups will bounce the playground ball hard and the bean bag will fly high so it is a good idea to remind them to remain in their group space.
448	**T** Now you are going to stand on one of the poly spots with your side to the wall. You will need one tennis ball. Throw the ball, let it bounce once and then catch it. Then on a fly.	Move your feet	**C** I'll time you for one minute. How many catches can you make in the air? We'll do it several times so you can see if you are getting better.	Be certain children are spaced properly on the poly spots. Watch to be certain that they return to their poly spot before they make the next throw.
449	**T** Now find a partner and practice catching underhand throws.	Move your feet	**C** Can you make 3 catches in a row without miss? 5? 7?	Scattered in general space about 10 feet apart depending upon the skill level. Use poly spots to mark the places you distance between the partners.

Closure

"Today we practiced two cues for catching. Can you show me how you hands should be when you are trying to catch a ball? *(Check for understanding to see if the children are "reaching and giving" with their hands.)* Can you show me what your feet should be doing when you are trying to catch a ball? *(Check for understanding that they are moving their feet to get into position to catch the object.)* Great! Before our next lesson I would like you to practice at least 100 catches. You may do it alone with a ball or a bean bag or with a friend or maybe one of your parents. See you next class. We will practice catching with partners again."

Reflection/Insights/Comments

Use this space to write down your thoughts and insights about what worked, what didn't work, and thoughts about future catching lessons.

the lesson objectives. This is critical if the lesson is going to be an educational experience for the children. The cues also guide the teacher in providing specific, congruent feedback as explained in Chapter 10.

The fourth column in the Reflective Planning Grid contains challenges. Challenges do not change the tasks children are working on but rather encourage the children to continue practicing a task when their interest or attention begins to wane. The challenges are marked in the movement concept and skill theme chapters (Chapters 13–26) with the symbol **C**. Again, notice in Box 6-1 that the challenges are in the same row as the task and cue so the challenge aligns with the task the children are practicing. The challenge is not a new task but merely an incentive to keep the children practicing the task they continue to need work on. Challenges are expressed as sentences or phrases the teachers use as incentives to motivate children to continue practicing the task given. As you will see, there are a variety of ways challenges can be presented, e.g., successful repetitions, number done in a given period of time, repetition of a task.

Challenges are useful for two reasons. They provide opportunities for the children to apply the tasks in different contexts (e.g., successful repetitions, number done in a given period of time, repetition of a task). As stated above, challenges also encourage the children to remain practicing a task that they have yet to learn. All too often teachers make tasks harder before the children are ready, and this can be both discouraging and frustrating to some children in a class.

The last column is a place to note any organization or safety reminders that are important not only for the lesson but for each task. Once again, these reminders are aligned in the same row with the tasks, cues, and challenges to help you remember these important parts of the lesson. Box 6-1 illustrates several examples of these reminders.

Closure

The closure, or conclusion, typically lasts no more than two or three minutes. The teacher calls the children together and quickly reviews the key points (the learnable pieces) of the lesson that were stated in the lesson objectives and emphasized throughout the class. As the sample lesson in Box 6-1 indicates, the teacher can phrase the closure in the form of questions. This is an especially important time to remind children of what has been emphasized throughout the class. It can also provide the teacher with an informal assessment about whether the children have attained the lesson objectives or not (Graham 2008).

Effective closures typically have three characteristics: (a) they review the cue(s) of the day, (b) they link what was taught in the lesson with past and future lessons (scaffolding), and (c) they suggest ways students can obtain more practice outside of the school setting.

Lesson Reflection

In a perfect world, there would be time at the end of every lesson for a teacher to sit at her desk and reflect on the lesson just completed. Did I accomplish my objectives? Which tasks worked well? Which needed to be changed? What do I need to emphasize the next time I teach catching to this class? Unfortunately this is not always the case but when possible, it is really useful to record your thoughts about what worked, what didn't work, and what you might do next time you teach catching.

Planning Insights Gained from Years of Teaching Experience

In this section we offer additional insights about planning that relate directly to the four steps we have outlined in the planning process. They provide insights we think you will find extremely useful as your develop your reflective planning skills. You might also call them lesson planning tips. They are important, and we think you will find them especially helpful for understanding the planning process we have outlined in this chapter and for gaining insights into the planning process.

Insights About Task Development (Column Two)

Once the children have been provided with a starting task or activity, the reflective teacher observes the children to determine whether the task is too easy (the children are able to do it easily with no apparent challenge); too hard (the children are occasionally successful, but many are unable to do the task with success); or simply unproductive (the children just aren't benefiting [learning] from doing the task). In any of these cases, the teacher will want to change the task so more of the children can be successful.

Tasks that are "just right" allow children to succeed at the task about 80 percent of the time (Siedentop and Tannehill 2000). The 80 percent success rate is a rough estimate, but it provides a guideline for determining the appropriateness of a task. High rates of success typically motivate children to keep trying and working at the task. Tasks that are too easy or too hard prompt off-task behavior or questions like, "When can we do something else?" "When do we get to play the game?"

Task progression, however, is not always about making a task harder. In some instances you will want to make a task easier. The advantage of the Reflective Planning Grid (Box 6-1) is that you can move up or down the task column (column 2) based on the children you are teaching. This provides a more dynamic way to think about the content. Veteran teachers have years of experience and are able to think about task progression without writing detailed lesson plans as suggested here. Engaging in the process we have described here, however, will help you develop a plethora of tasks that eventually you will remember and use dynamically when teaching your classes.

An analogy about moving is useful here. When you move to a town, for example, you rely on a lot on maps and probably need to ask directions frequently. Once you lived in that town for a few years, you rarely consult maps or ask for directions to get around town. The same is true for veteran teachers who spend a lot of time planning in their first few years—eventually they have a mental repertoire of effective tasks for teaching the movement concepts and skill themes.

Insights About Cues (Refinements) (Column Three)

Once a task is judged to be appropriate (not too easy or too hard), the teacher can provide cues (or refinements) to help the children perform the skill more efficiently. Cues are also referred to as critical elements. Providing cues is one of the most valuable roles a teacher can perform (Graham 2008; Landin 1994; Masser 1987, 1993; Rink 2010). Cues help children understand how to perform a skill and shortcut the learning process as well as encourage the children to practice proper techniques. In the overhand throw for distance, for example, it is important that children learn to step with the foot opposite the throwing hand. When landing from a jump, it is important that the children learn to bend not only at the knees but also at the hips and ankles. These tips or cues help children learn skills more efficiently than they would by trial and error. The cues (critical elements) are listed at the beginning of each series of tasks in the skill theme chapters (Chapters 16–26). In addition to helping the children learn the correct ways of performing a skill, emphasizing cues can also provide the children with a checklist of the important critical elements they will need when they decide to play a sport on their own outside of school. Children who attend physical education class for an hour or less a week obviously don't have enough time to reach the utilization or proficiency level. We do know, however, that they can learn the critical elements, so at least they will recall how to perform a skill appropriately (Manross 1992).

When you begin to use the information in the skill theme chapters, you will notice that no cues are provided with the tasks at the precontrol level of the generic levels of skill proficiency (GLSP; Chapter 7). This is because youngsters at that level have had minimal experience with even attempting a given movement. We want them to first explore the skill until they have at least a general idea of how it feels and what is required to do it successfully (Schmidt and Wrisberg 2008). For example, if you have never attempted a movement, being told four or five cues will have little meaning and probably won't stick with you. Obviously

we must emphasize safety, but explanation and demonstration of the critical elements can begin once youngsters have a basic understanding of the movement and are at the control level. At this point in the learning curve, they are often more receptive to learning the cues because they have discovered they are not adept at the skill and would like to know how to do it more efficiently and effectively.

You will also notice there is a progression of cues from the control to the utilization and then the proficiency level. This is because the movements are different at each of the GLSP. For example, youngsters at the proficiency level in landing from a jump do not need to be told to "bend their knees"—they learned that when they were at the control level. Just as the tasks change for each of the GLSP, so do the cues.

Each of the skill theme development chapters provides numerous cues that the children will find helpful for enhancing the quality of their movements. The challenge for you as a teacher is to select the cue that will be most helpful for your class. Much of this analysis is completed as part of the lesson planning when you develop the progression of tasks and the appropriate cues. Beware of the temptation to tell the children too much at once. As suggested in the National Association for Sport and Physical Education's National Standards (NASPE 1995; 2004), we want the children not only to hear the cues, but also to recall and apply them.

Insights About Challenges (Applications) (Column Four)

In addition to informing (providing information to the children), presenting a logical progression of tasks and activities, and providing cues, a teacher may also present challenges (applications) to the children to maintain their interest in a task. Even when children are doing a task and succeeding at high rates, there comes a time when they become disinterested and are ready to move on to another task. The problem is that we are not always able to provide another task that is just a little bit harder; in some instances, a task is much harder, and if we ask the children to do this task before they are ready, many of the children will fail. Many challenges that will motivate the children to continue practicing are "invented" as part of the planning process. The important point to remember is that the task stays the same, but the challenge is designed to motivate the children to keep practicing that same task.

Let's take the example of batting. A logical progression from striking a ball from a batting tee is to strike a pitched ball (Chapter 26). Hitting a pitched ball is much more difficult for the children, especially at young ages when many children's throwing (pitching) skills are not yet refined. The right kind of challenge at the right time, however, will motivate the children to continue practicing batting from a tee. This will allow the teacher time to continue providing feedback about the way the children are (or aren't) stepping with the lead foot when they bat. The following list gives some examples of batting challenges. Note that all the tasks still require the children to keep batting from a tee, the task they had been working on before the teacher decided to provide a challenge.

- "If this is easy for you, you may want to try batting a smaller ball; if it is hard for you, you may want to try batting a larger ball. (object size challenge)
- "Every time you bat the ball without hitting the tee with the bat, say a letter of your last name. Try to spell your whole name." (repetition challenge)
- "See how many times in a row you can hit the ball without hitting the tee or missing the ball." (keeping score challenge)
- "Try to hit the fence (wall) with the ball on a fly three times in a row." (repetition challenge)

These challenges do not substantively change the task; rather, they are designed to maintain the children's interest in that task. In game-like settings, a challenge of keeping score, either cooperatively or competitively, would be a logical application for that task.

Some teachers find it easier than others to use challenges in their teaching. As we increase our understanding of how children at different ages think—and their sense of humor—it becomes easier to create challenges for them. Preschool children, for example, can be challenged simply by being asked to perform a task with a ball, hoop, or carpet square of a different color. Some middle school children enjoy the challenge of competing against a friend to see who can be more successful (keeping score). Others enjoy seeing if they can surpass their previous personal records (keeping score). We have provided a few examples of challenges in the subsequent chapters, but the best ones are those you create as you come to know the children you are teaching.

Insights About Additional Ideas (Content) for Lessons

The movement concepts and skill theme chapters (13–26) provide an excellent starting point for content development. Obviously, however, there are many other sources for lesson ideas, such as notes from classes, your own and others' observations, books, workshops, conferences, articles, and discussions with other teachers. The Internet is another great source. PE Central, for example, has a plethora of excellent lesson ideas that are aligned with movement concepts and skill themes. Go the main page of PE Central (www.pecentral.org) and click on the Lessons tab of the drop-down menu.

Planning for lessons involves sifting through sources and then designing lessons to match the needs and characteristics of your students to help them learn the benchmarks developed in the previous step of the planning process. We've found few, if any, prepackaged lessons that worked for us as they supposedly worked for their authors. So instead of including specific lesson plans in *Children Moving* (with the exception of Box 6-1), we provide tasks for development to encourage you to develop your own plans.

Insights About Developing Lesson Objectives

As explained at the beginning of this chapter, lesson objectives, or outcomes, are critical if the children are going to increase their understanding and skillfulness. Effective objectives state what we want the children to learn in the lesson rather than what they are to do. For example, stating that the children will throw and catch a ball in self-space is not an objective—it is a task. "The children will learn to catch a ball" is a goal. Unfortunately, this goal cannot be accomplished in a 30-minute lesson; it will take many lessons, perhaps thousands of practice catches, before a child can truly be able to catch a ball.

The objectives, then, are "learnable pieces" based on the benchmarks—something a child has a reasonable chance to learn in a single lesson. In the sample lesson in Box 6-1, the teacher will focus on two aspects (critical elements) of successful catching: teaching the children (1) to move their hands into a ready position before catching the ball and (2) to move their feet so they are in a good position to make the catch. The teacher decided on these two cues after reading the chapter on catching (Chapter 23) and reviewing the National Standards for Physical Education (NASPE 2004). The teacher will not simply provide chances to practice catching but will demonstrate and provide individual feedback related to using the hands and arms appropriately to catch a ball or an object. During the lesson, she will continually pause and remind the children of the cue they need to work on. Sometimes she will demonstrate the cue. Sometimes she will pinpoint other youngsters as they use the critical elements in their catching. As the children practice, the teacher will also move among them and provide specific congruent feedback (Chapter 11) about how well they are using the cues. You will hear her constantly remind individual children to "get their hands into the 'ready' position" or to "move your feet."

The Kids Love It

One of the comments often heard from teachers whose goal is to keep youngsters busy, happy, and good is that the kids love the game or activity. Although it is certainly desirable for youngsters to enjoy an activity, it is not our sole criterion. For example, some children would love to eat ice cream or doughnuts or potato chips for every meal. Obviously, however, it would not be in these children's best interest if that was all they ate. The same is true for the classroom. There are many fun reading, math, and science games. But the successful teacher always evaluates these games or activities to be certain that if the children play them, they actually lead to better reading, more effective computing, or understanding of science concepts. So when we hear that youngsters love a game or an activity, we can't help but wonder: Are the children really learning something? Is the activity truly a learning experience? Should the fact that kids love it be the sole, or major, criterion to determine the success of a lesson? Our goal is to keep youngsters busy, happy, and good—but also learning! If they aren't learning, then what are we teaching them?

Insights About Organization/Management/Safety (Column Five)

Column Five of the planning grid entitled Organization/Safety provides the teacher with a place to write down and/or draw the different organizations and formats that will be used during a lesson. Although this may not be necessary for experienced teachers, it's very helpful for beginning teachers; it leads them to think through the organizational formats they might use during the lesson, thereby avoiding some of the problems that might occur—for example, when a teacher hasn't thought about how the children will move from throwing against a wall to finding a partner to throw and catch with. If not planned for carefully, these transitions can lead to wasted time, confusion, and even misbehavior.

Keeping Track of Your Lessons

We have suggested a lesson planning format that works for many teachers (Box 6-1). Certainly, however, changes are made to make our lesson plans work for us. If you use the content development format of the planning grid (the five columns), it is relatively easy to add or delete content and continue to use the plans over a number of years.

A well-developed plan can be somewhat lengthy, especially for beginning teachers. For this reason, many teachers find it helpful to write a brief outline on a 5-by-8-inch card they carry with them during the lesson as a handy reminder.

Making Planning Enjoyable

Planning is hard work. It takes time and energy to plan effective lessons that are exciting and interesting to children. Teachers who fail to plan well are tempted to return to old standbys—kickball, dodgeball, and Four Square—that contribute minimally to children's learning in physical education.

You'll always be able to find something to do that is more interesting than planning lessons. So it's a good idea to devise ways to make planning easier and more fun. We've found the following ideas helpful:

- Set aside some time each day specifically for planning. Then you won't be constantly trying to find time to plan. Some people find that planning at school before they leave for home is effective; others prefer to arrive at school early to plan the day.
- Try to become excited about your plans. When you're excited about trying to present an idea in a new and interesting way, planning is fun, and you communicate your enthusiasm to your students. Reading books and journals, attending conferences, talking to colleagues, and searching the Internet are some ways you can find new and interesting ideas to incorporate into your plans. Remember, however, that less is more, so be sure to take something out for every new activity you add into your scope.
- Don't hesitate to experiment. The worst that can happen is that a lesson won't work as planned. When this happens, we tell the children we were trying a new idea and it didn't work. Children understand and sometimes make worthwhile suggestions about how the idea might be improved.

When you set aside appropriate amounts of time, discover new ideas, and attempt to make lessons exciting, planning becomes more enjoyable and your attitude toward teaching will be affected. Most of us experience uncertainty when beginning a lesson (or anything else) for which we're unprepared. When you've planned a lesson thoroughly, the assurance and enthusiasm you feel can be contagious.

Recording Progress

A reflective teacher records the progress that a particular class, group, or individual makes during a lesson. An elementary school physical education specialist may teach 8 to 12 classes a day. Each group and each student will progress to a different degree and in a different way. A reflective teacher, whose approach takes these differences into consideration, will need notes on which to base the next day's (or week's) lessons.

You can write brief comments in a standard planning book or on index cards. Some teachers use handheld computers or a tape recorder—or your cell phone may include a tape recording application. Notes summarizing what was accomplished during a lesson help you plan the next day's lessons. Ideally, the day's schedule will include 5 or 10 minutes between classes; you can use this time for recording observations and, if necessary, arranging equipment for the next class. Teachers who use handheld computers to keep track of their students' progress have the advantage of easily downloading the information into a computer for ease of use and future reference. Whether you use note cards, a tape recorder, a handheld computer, or some other technique, it will certainly help you plan more efficiently. What seems clear at 9 a.m. is often opaque by 4 p.m.

Lesson Design

If children are to develop into skillful movers, they must do more than play games. Children need opportunities to practice skills in contexts that are meaningful and enjoyable to them. A successful teacher creates practice situations that are enjoyable, appropriately designed, and allow for maximum participation. The teacher who can design interesting and exciting practice situations will rarely hear the question asked so often by highly skilled, unchallenged children, "When do we get to play a game?"

Interesting Lessons

Many children, particularly younger ones, don't understand the need to practice to become more skillful. Children typically are interested only in the present and have little concern about future years. Thus young children more easily accept and enjoy lessons with immediate meaning. For example, we wouldn't teach second graders how to turn on one foot (pivot) by having them perform a mass drill because such an exercise would have little meaning or interest to them. We might, however, have them jog around the gym and instruct them, "Spin around on one foot when you hear the drum and then continue jogging." On the next drumbeat we might say, "Pivot on the other foot" or "Spin in the opposite direction." Later, when the children are able to travel dribbling a ball, we might say, "Spin on the drumbeat while continuing to dribble a ball." We don't teach skills as if all children really

want to learn the skill because they intend to play on a varsity team in high school—they don't.

Variety in a lesson also makes the lesson more enjoyable. We try to give children a number of related practice opportunities in a single lesson rather than having them practice the same skill the same way the entire lesson. The only way to accomplish this goal of providing variety is through extensive and thorough planning.

Appropriate Lessons

Children want to be challenged and successful at the same time. The ideal task is difficult enough so the child can't do it as intended every time, yet easy enough so the child is successful much of the time. If small children try to shoot a basketball through a 10-foot-high basket, their success rate may be so low they'll quickly lose interest. If the same children are given options—for example, shooting at a basket 7 feet high or shooting through a hoop suspended from a pole—their interest will remain higher for longer periods, and their skills will therefore improve.

Maximum Participation

One of the clearest differences between more effective and less effective teachers is that the students of more effective teachers actually spend more time practicing than do the children of less effective teachers (Rink, 2010; Siedentop and Tannehill 2000). The value of practice may seem obvious, yet practice is frequently neglected, particularly in teaching games. When a class of 30 children practices a skill such as throwing or catching and they use only three or four balls, the children's skills will improve less than the skills of children whose teacher designs the same lesson with a ball for every two children in the class.

Remember, not all children have learned to practice on their own. Making more equipment available doesn't guarantee increased practice time. In fact, we've observed instances in which the children in a class actually practiced more when there were only three or four balls available because most of the students in the class hadn't yet learned to work on their own.

One study (Graham et al. 1993) that compared student teachers with experienced teachers found that veteran teachers provided children with far fewer tasks than the novice teachers. The novices believed that they had to "get through all of the tasks in their plan." In contrast, the veteran teachers were focused on the children. If a task was "right," they stayed with it for long periods of time.

Parting Thought

The planning process described above no doubt seems complex, time consuming, and maybe even unnecessary. It's not! Think again about planning your trip. Time spent planning can heighten the enjoyment dramatically. Being lost, confused, or in the wrong place at the wrong time is no fun; neither is a poorly planned lesson that is uninteresting, dominated by a few highly skilled children (unless, of course, you are one of the highly skilled), or simply unproductive. If you want to become a highly successful teacher, it is going to take a lot of work—and the journey starts with planning.

The Relationship Between Planning and Content Development

Planning is the process of developing a progression of learning experiences that are productive, beneficial, and interesting to the children. Reflective teachers use planning as a well-thought-out guide that provides a clear direction designed to accomplish the program's goals and objectives. Planning is typically done ahead of the lesson delivery before or after school, at home, or in the office at school.

Developing the content is the process of implementing the plan in the gym or on the playground. Essentially it is transferring the written plan to a series of learning experiences during the actual lesson. Rarely, however, do reflective teachers deliver the plans learning exactly as designed. Plans are meant to be dynamic and change according the GLSP in a particular class, students' interest on a given day, how quickly the children are grasping the content, etc. One lesson rarely is identical to another lesson. The process of developing the content, therefore, makes lesson planning come to life as it evolves to cater for the unique children in a class.

Invariant teachers, in contrast, appear to make the assumption that "one size fits all." They teach virtually identical lessons, typically games, and provide little or no feedback and/or encouragement to the children they are teaching. It appears they are attempting to keep the children busy, happy and good rather than providing worthwhile learning experiences for all children. Invariant teachers typically use an identical lesson plan for several grades, irrespective of the children's needs, interests, and skill levels. Reflective teachers, in contrast, develop the content by adapting the progression of tasks to the children in a given class. Rarely, if ever, do they teach identical lessons—even though the grade level may be same for three classes in a row.

Summary

Planning is a crucial part of the teaching process. Successful teachers plan effectively—not only their daily lessons, but also the entire program, as well as each year of the program. Plans are guides, not cast in stone. As you learn more about the school, the children, and the context of the teaching situation, plans change!

This chapter described four steps in the planning process. Step 1 is the development of a curriculum scope for all of the grades you will be teaching. Essentially, the first step answers the questions "What will I teach?" and "In what grades?" Step 2 involves making difficult

decisions about how many days you will be able to focus on various skills and concepts—and which ones should receive more or less emphasis. Benchmarks (learnable pieces) are formulated in Step 3 as you determine when and how you will check to see what your children are learning. Step 4 is the creation of daily lesson plans. This section describes a process for planning including the Reflective Planning Guide for content development. It concludes with insights and suggestions related to creating interesting, appropriate lessons that provide for the children's maximum participation and success.

Reading Comprehension Questions

1. What is meant by the term *reflective planning*? Think about your elementary school: Which contextual factors influenced the program and the way the teacher planned?
2. What might happen when a teacher does not bother to do Steps 1 and 2 in the planning process and only plans day to day?
3. Tables 6.1 and 6.2 present sample scopes for the movement concepts and skill themes. In your own words, explain why some concepts and skills are not taught at various grade levels. Use specific concepts and skills in your explanation.

4. Using Table 6.3 as a guide, select first, third, or fifth grade, and do a yearly overview for that grade. Then write a brief analysis explaining what you changed from the grade before and after. For example, if you choose third grade, explain how your guide is different from those for second and fourth grades.

5. Use the guide for planning daily lessons (Box 6-1) to plan one of your own lessons. Use one of the skill theme chapters as a guide, but do not use the skills of throwing and catching. Include at least 10 tasks.

Use the five-column Reflective Planning Grid format described in this chapter.

6. Veteran teachers typically spend less time planning than do beginning teachers. Why might this be the case?

7. Explain how the concept "less is more" applies to developing a curriculum. What happens when a teacher attempts to jam too many skill themes into a year for the time allotted?

References/Suggested Readings

Graham, G. 2008. *Teaching children physical education*. 2nd ed. Champaign, IL: Human Kinetics.

Graham, G., C. Hopple, M. Manross, and T. Sitzman. 1993. Novice and experienced children's physical education teachers: Insights into their situational decision-making. *Journal of Teaching in Physical Education* 12(2): 197–217.

Holt/Hale, S. 2010. *On the move: Lesson plans to accompany Children Moving*. New York: McGraw-Hill.

Housner, L., and D. Griffey. 1985. Teacher cognition: Differences in planning and interactive decision making between experienced and inexperienced teachers. *Research Quarterly for Exercise and Sport* 56: 56–63.

Kelly, L. E. 1989. Instructional time: The overlooked factor in PE curriculum development. *Journal of Physical Education, Recreation and Dance* 60: 29–32.

Landin, D. 1994. The role of verbal cues in skill learning. *Quest* 46(3): 299–313.

Manross, M. 1992. What children think, feel, and know about the overhand throw. Unpublished master's thesis, Virginia Polytechnic Institute and State University, Blacksburg, Virginia.

Masser, L. 1987. The effects of refinement on student achievement in a fundamental motor skill in grades K

through 6. *Journal of Teaching in Physical Education* 6(2): 174–82.

Masser, L. 1993. Critical cues help first grade students' achievement in handstands and forward rolls. *Journal of Teaching in Physical Education* 12(3): 301–12.

[NASPE] National Association for Sport and Physical Education. 1995. *Moving into the future: National standards for physical education*. St. Louis, MO: Mosby.

[NASPE] National Association for Sport and Physical Education. 2004. *Moving into the future: National standards for physical education*. 2nd ed. Reston, VA: National Association for Sport and Physical Education.

Rink, J. E. (2010). *Teaching physical education for learning*. 6th ed. New York: McGraw Hill.

Schmidt, R. A., and C. A. Wrisberg. 2008. *Motor learning and performance*. 4th ed. Champaign, IL: Human Kinetics.

Siedentop, D., and D. Tannehill. 2000. *Developing teaching skills in physical education*. 4th ed. New York: McGraw-Hill.

Stodden, D. F., J. D. Goodway, S. J. Langendorfer, M. A. Roberton, M. E. Rudisill, C. Garcia, and L.E. Garcia. 2008. A developmental perspective on the role of motor skill competence in physical activity. *Quest:* 290–306.

Analyzing Reflective Teaching

Of all the things teachers undertake, the most important, it seems to me, is doing the thinking of teaching or the reflecting about the complexities of their work. . . . Learning is continuous as reflective teachers engage in the work of thinking and doing. . . . In this way, learning is central to teaching.

—ANNA RICHERT (1995)

It's not the doing that matters; it's the thinking about the doing.

—JOHN DEWEY

Key Concepts

- Reflection on teaching is an essential aspect of continual growth as a teacher.

- Reflective teachers follow a cycle of describing teaching, critiquing teaching, and setting goals.

- Regular self-reflection on teaching allows teachers to describe their teaching and determine more specific information to gather.

- Systematic observation allows reflective teachers to critique their teaching by obtaining clear and detailed information about various effective teaching aspects.

- Systematic observation techniques include unassisted techniques, student-assisted techniques, and peer-assisted techniques.

- Collecting information on feedback and lesson content development are unassisted techniques.

- Student-assisted techniques that provide more observable information include such things as information on interaction patterns with students and the quantity of practice opportunities the students have.

- Peer-assisted techniques allow for a still-higher level of detail and include the quality and quantity of practice opportunities and feedback, the use of time in class, and the clarity of demonstrations.

- Goal setting provides reflective teachers with a mechanism to determine if there are changes to teaching.

- Professional learning communities allow teachers to analyze teaching learning environments with the support of others.

Quite simply, reflective teachers reflect. One implication of Chapter 4, "Reflective Teaching," is that teaching is an incredibly complex activity. While *Children Moving* can provide multiple ideas for teaching, at the end of the day a reflective teacher is thoughtful and intentional about implementing correct strategies and content at precise moments to meet the needs of all students that results in student learning. As we teach, we have to take into consideration a variety of influences, including our experience as a teacher, the facilities in which we work, the frequency of our class meetings, the number of students in our classes, children's attitudes toward physical education, our beliefs as a teacher, and the like. Beyond taking into account those influences, as teachers we perform multiple and distinct tasks. We have to choose the content to teach, determine how to deliver it meaningfully, deliver it to meet all learners' needs, and assess the results. In addition, we have to interact with children, administrators, parents, custodians, and other teachers. We have to comfort the fearful child and assure concerned parents. What is more, we inspire hope, coax curiosity, and celebrate success (Richert 1995). This list of "jobs" could go on and on, and as Locke (1975) indicates, it represents only a portion of what is necessary to do the work of good teaching. Yet our job doesn't end here. Reflective teachers share the ownership of the teaching and learning process.

Some have asked us why we even include this chapter on analyzing reflective teaching in *Children Moving*. It is precisely because this continuing to wonder, worry, and reflect on what is happening in their gymnasiums and classrooms and on their playgrounds is what separates effective from ineffective teachers. Effective teachers are reflective teachers who learn by inquiring into their practice. They not only think about their experiences in order to make sense of them, but analyze specific aspects of teaching and student learning (Lorson, Goodway, and Hovatter 2007). When faced with a situation for which there is no easy or certain answer, they engage in reflective inquiry. They gather as much information as possible about a situation that puzzles them and then scrutinize the information to determine how they will act in the future. Most often this process is informal—we all engage in it to some extent to answer the millions of questions we daily encounter in our work—but occasionally the process is more formal. Either way, the constant and ongoing process of reflection provides the basis for learning in teaching. It is this process of learning in teaching that makes good teaching responsive to the uncertainties of the rapidly changing world of which teaching is a part (Richert 1995) and allows teachers to differentiate instruction (see Chapter 5). Reflective teachers work to improve their students' learning by improving their teaching throughout their careers. Unfortunately, reflection and inquiry into teaching are left largely to the individual teacher. Historically, the culture of schools has been one of isolation and individualism, where teachers work under conditions long ago imposed by administration, school board policy, and state guidelines, and there is little instruction-related conversation (Glickman, Gordon, and Ross-Gordon 2010). This lack of instructional sharing is often coupled with a lack of shared technical language, difficult work assignments, and unclear expectations. Compounding the issue is the lack of meaningful (and sometimes inaccurate) feedback provided to teachers. For example, an assessment based on how much the students like a teacher doesn't provide much useful information about that teacher's performance, nor does a principal's evaluation based on a five-minute, once-a-year visit to the gymnasium. Some student teachers receive helpful and accurate feedback from their supervisors. Few teachers, however, continue to receive throughout their teaching careers the amount and type of feedback vital to improving teaching performance.

The notion that, upon certification, a teacher knows all there is to know about how and what to teach and requires little, if any, assistance is quickly being discredited (Stroot 2001). In its place is growing acceptance of the belief that teachers can benefit from reflection, guidance, and assistance if they are going to progress in their teaching. If you are fortunate, your school district provides an ongoing mentoring program coupled with continuing professional development. Some school districts provide, even require, that novice teachers are paired with veteran teachers. These mentors enhance the likelihood that new teachers will be provided assistance in reflecting on teaching. Increasingly, as it becomes apparent that teacher growth and change are part of a lifelong process requiring constant support, school districts are also arranging for ongoing reflection and development opportunities throughout the teaching years in the form of learning communities (Darling-Hammond and Richardson, 2009).

Regardless of the support, reflection begins with the teacher. Good reflection is cyclical. It involves a description of your teaching, a critique of your teaching performance, and setting goals to continue to develop your teaching skills throughout your career (NASPE 2009). This chapter provides strategies and techniques for reflecting on your teaching to make it congruent with your beliefs about school, children, physical education, and effective teaching and learning environments. This will allow you to "see" yourself through self-reflection, systematic observation, and support groups. Chapter 11 provides you with techniques to allow you to "see" your students.

Elementary school physical education teachers have been observed who clocked as little as three and a half minutes of significant face-to-face contact with other adults between the hours of 7:30 a.m. and 4:30 p.m. The teacher can be psychologically alone in a densely populated world. The physical (architectural) isolation of the gym located away from the political heartland of the school and the social isolation of the physical educator role, which may make the teacher peripheral to the real business of the school, both seem to sustain and intensify the feelings of isolation.

Teaching physical education in some schools is a lonely job, awash in an endless sea of children.

—LARRY LOCKE, "The Ecology of the Gymnasium: What the Tourist Never Sees" (1975)

Self-Reflection: Describing Your Teaching

Continuous reflection regarding one's knowledge, beliefs, instructional practices, and teaching effectiveness is essential to ongoing professional growth (Banville and Rikard 2001; Housner 1996). Self-reflection allows a teacher to thoughtfully describe and contemplate the struggles and successes encountered in teaching (Stroot and Whipple 2003). Self-reflection is best accomplished as an ongoing and purposeful process that creates a permanent product of your thoughts. Most often this is through a written journal or an audiotaped log. Regardless of how self-reflection is accomplished, there are two keys to its success. First, be consistent with it. Set a time frame for self-reflection. It might be daily, biweekly, or weekly. But regardless of the time period you choose, do it consistently. Second, whether your reflection is written or verbal, review it periodically. These reflections often lead teachers to identify concerns and begin to think about how to reduce problems and enhance the learning environment. When specific concerns are identified or interests arise, systematic observation can be employed to obtain more formal and reliable information.

Systematic Observation: Critiquing Your Teaching

Consistent self-reflection allows us to determine points of exploration about our teaching; systematic observation allows us to obtain more objective information about those points. Systematic observation is the orderly and focused collection of specific and defined information about teaching. Again, in view of the usual lack of assistance teachers receive, many techniques we include in this chapter can be carried out on your own or with the assistance of another teacher, digital recordings, or an untrained observer.

Getting Started

Regardless of who is collecting the information about your teaching, the most important aspect is deciding what teaching action to look at or target. Although it may seem as if we are stating the obvious, we have

Actions of Effective Teachers

Research has shown that effective teachers—whether class-room or physical education teachers—share similar behaviors. Effective teachers:

- Give students time to learn by devoting a high percentage of time to the academic subject.
- Communicate high, yet realistic, expectations for students.
- Establish routines and organizational structures that lead to a positive classroom management climate.
- Present meaningful and challenging tasks in which students are highly successful.
- Move the class forward with determined direction.
- Communicate the content clearly and hold students accountable for completing tasks.
- Assess students' skill progress closely and change practice to fit students' needs.
- Communicate warmth through clear, enthusiastic presentations.

Source: B. Cusimano, P. Darst, and H. van der Mars, Improving your teaching through self-evaluation, *Strategies*, 7, no. 8 (1993): 28.

Determining What to Observe

If you're having problems with inappropriate student behavior, select one or more of the following:

- Look at your plans for potential breakdowns.
- Transcribe all your instructions to the class, and check for clarity. Did you know what was supposed to happen? Did you mix the organizational and content portions of your instruction?
- Videotape a lesson to analyze your use of time. Was there an extreme amount of management time? Waiting time?
- Record your feedback. Did you handle inappropriate behavior promptly and consistently, or did you nag often?

To check the atmosphere of your class, do one or more of the following:

- Tally your feedback. Was there a large percentage of negative feedback?
- Check student interaction patterns. Did you favor one group over another?
- To assess the instructional environment, select from the following:
- Check your task development. Did you disperse challenges throughout the lesson or only at the end?
- Assess each student's practice opportunities. Did children have lots of practice chances?
- Check the general use of class time.
- Tally feedback with specific attention to skill feedback.
- Evaluate the quality of the demonstrations provided to your class.

seen more than one teacher collect information about his or her teaching without having a clear purpose. These targets may stem directly from your self-reflection or from the variables that have been shown to be related to effective teaching. Box 7-1 enumerates some of the actions, gleaned from research on teaching, of effective teachers. In Chapter 8 we stated that establishing a learning environment is a necessary but not sufficient condition for student learning and that the class environment indicates what you believe about children and physical education. Therefore, if nothing else seems to fit, determining whether you have set up a learning environment and what that environment is like may be a good place to start. The checklists in Box 7-2 can help you decide what to look for, based on your questions about teaching.

Unassisted Techniques

You can learn much about your teaching without relying on others for observation, interpretation, or analysis. Unassisted analysis techniques for analyzing your teaching performance involve either digital audio or video recording. Audio recording can easily be done by placing a recorder in a pocket. Video recording using a wireless microphone will lend itself to gathering even more information (without a wireless microphone, the noise in the gym makes almost impossible to hear the conversations between teacher and children). The children quickly become accustomed to seeing the audio or video recorder, and before long they forget about it.

You can gain a wealth of information from listening to your teaching. For example, you can learn the answers to such important questions as:

- What percentage of a lesson did I spend talking to the entire class? To groups? To individuals?
- Are my verbal comments clear? Do I repeat myself frequently?

- What percentage of my comments to the children is positive? Negative? Neutral? Do I nag the children?
- Do I interact with many children in a class? Or do I focus on just a few, constantly calling their names?
- How do I develop the lesson content?

You can answer these and many other questions by making digital recordings. Finding the answers involves defining what you want to assess, listening to the tape, tallying the number of times each behavior occurs or recording the length of time something occurs, and then determining percentages. We often use this kind of recording to analyze the feedback we give to students and how we develop content with individual classes.

Feedback Analysis Feedback, the information the teacher provides to individual or small groups of children about the quality of their movement or behavior, based on observation, is one teaching aspect on which you can reflect from an audio or video tape. The teacher feedback form (Figure 7.1) allows you to analyze your feedback by tallying each comment you make to children. Depending on the lesson and your interest, you may simply want to total the amount and type of feedback you give. You may also want to determine which children receive your feedback—and what type of feedback they receive. If you want to analyze total feedback, simply tally each statement, placing it in one of the feedback categories shown in Figure 7.1 and defined below. (If you want to analyze feedback to individual children, see the later discussion of Figure 7.5.) You may want to use all these categories, or just one or two.

Your first choice of feedback type is specific versus general feedback. Specific feedback has to do with either the child's skill or the child's behavior. However, if there is no way for the child to tell (based just on your statement) whether your comment is about skill or behavior, the feedback is general. "Good" is probably the most common general feedback statement heard in physical education lessons, followed closely by "OK." If the feedback is specific, the next step is to determine whether it is about skill (movement) or behavior. Then, ask yourself whether the child to whom the comments were provided would perceive them as positive, corrective, or negative. In addition, you may want to determine whether the feedback was congruent or incongruent with the lesson cues—specifically, with what you asked the children to think about when you last gave instruction. Congruent feedback relates directly to what you said immediately before the children began their activity. Incongruent feedback, in contrast, might be about something the children were never told or

hadn't been reminded of for several weeks. (Note that if you code congruent/incongruent feedback, it will be a "double tally" in a row. One for positive, corrective, or negative, and one for congruent/incongruent.) This sounds complicated, but as the process is broken down, it will become easier.

Assume, for instance, that the children are practicing striking with paddles (Chapter 25), and the teacher is focusing on teaching them to turn their sides to the target so they can swing more efficiently. Following are some examples of feedback and the way each statement would be coded on the teacher feedback form in Figure 7.1:

- "Marilyn, that swing was great! You really turned your side to the target." (specific, skill, positive, congruent)
- "Terrific." (general, positive)
- "Mark, remember to keep your eye on the ball." (specific, skill, corrective, incongruent)
- "Christine, stay in your own space." (specific, behavior, scold)
- "Kakki, way to keep your side to the target." (specific, skill, positive, congruent)
- "Good side, Rosie." (specific, skill, positive, congruent)
- "Kevin, that's wrong." (general, negative)
- "Side, Steve." (specific, skill, corrective, congruent)
- "Juan, you are facing the target; don't do that." (specific, skill, negative, congruent)

When you tally your various feedback statements, you will have a profile that lets you know what type of feedback you tend to give. In addition, you can determine a feedback rate per minute by dividing the total number of statements into the elapsed time to find out how much feedback you give. While the information on the types of feedback necessary is mixed (Rink 2003), a good pattern to strive for is skill-specific, corrective, and congruent feedback to enhance learning, and positive behavior feedback to promote an appropriate environment. Don't worry if your pattern doesn't initially appear as you would like it to be; after all, anything we do takes practice. The good news is that adjusting feedback is relatively easy (van der Mars 1987).

Lesson Content Another useful type of information you can collect for reflection is how content is developed in your lesson. As described in Chapter 6, there are three categories of information you may wish to collect regarding your lessons: the tasks you give the children, the cues you provide, and the challenges you offer. The tasks are the activities you actually ask the students to do, such as dribbling a ball in self-space or bouncing a ball while traveling in general space. Cues, or critical elements, are the hints you provide the children to

Teacher Feedback

Teacher: _____ Date: _____

Grade/Activity: _____ # of Pupils: _____

Start time: _____ End time: _____ Elapsed time: _____

FEEDBACK	BEHAVIOR FEEDBACK		SKILL FEEDBACK						
	Praise	Scold	Positive	Corrective	Negative	Congruent	Incongruent	Total	Rate/ Minute
Specific									
General									
Total									
Rate/Minute									

Rate/Minute _____ _____ _____ _____ _____ _____ _____ _____

COMMENTS:

Figure 7.1 Teacher feedback form.

help them perform the task more effectively or correctly. Examples would be "use finger pads" and "bend your knees." Cues always seek to improve the quality of the student performance and are listed at the beginning of each task segment in the skill theme chapters. Challenges shift the focus to using the skill in a more demanding or testing situation. These are most often self-testing or competitive situations.

Figure 7.2 shows a graph you can use to determine how content is developed in a lesson. Before filling in the graph, listen to your recording and write down, in order, every task, cue, and challenge presented during the class session. Then categorize each as a task, cue, or challenge. (For this project, record only tasks, cues, or challenges given to the entire class, not feedback or suggestions given to individual students.)

After you have labeled the tasks, cues, and challenges, plot them on the graph in the order in which they occurred. Once you have finished, you will have a picture of how your lesson progressed. Although

there is no perfect pattern of content development, a good rule of thumb is that the graph should reflect a zigzag pattern and not steps. The use of tasks, cues, and challenges should be mixed across the lesson rather than practice, practice, practice, game. This mix allows children to progressively develop their skills while staying motivated and focused.

Student-Assisted Techniques

Mature, responsible students can occasionally help you assess your teaching performance by using techniques they can learn in just a few minutes. These methods can provide information that cannot be obtained by the two unassisted techniques described above. The determination of teacher interaction patterns with students and the number of practice opportunities children receive are two techniques that provide a great deal of information about the class learning environment.

CONTENT DEVELOPMENT

TEACHER: _____ DATE: _____ GRADE: _____ NO. OF STUDENTS:_____

DIRECTIONS: Write down, in order, the statements made to the entire class about motor skills. At times you may need to leave out a few words, but try to get down the intent of the statement. After the lesson is over, classify each statement as a task, cue, or challenge, and then graph the statements in the order they occurred. Use the back of the sheet if necessary.

1.

2.

3.

4.

5.

6.

7.

8.

9.

10.

Challenge

Cue

Task

1   2   3   4   5   6   7   8   9   10

Activities

Definitions:

    Tasks: Activities that present the skill to be practiced
    Cues: Words that focus on the critical elements of the skill
    Challenges: Self-testing or competitive experiences

Analysis: Number of tasks, cues, or challenges/Total number of activities = %

_____ % tasks
_____ % cues
_____ % challenges

Figure 7.2 Content development graph.

Interaction Patterns It's important to interact, verbally or nonverbally, with each child during each lesson. You can use an interaction checklist (Figure 7.3) to obtain information about your interaction patterns with an entire class.

Select a student who knows the names of all the children in the class. Give that student a checklist on which you've listed the names of the entire class. The student can then make a tally, in the appropriate column, across from the name of each child you talk to, touch, or smile at during one class period. At the conclusion of the lesson, you can use the completed checklist to analyze your interaction patterns and determine if there is differential treatment of children.

On another level, you may be able to determine whether there's a disparity in your interactions with different groups of children. Are you interacting more with the most-skilled children than with the least-skilled ones? Are you interacting with boys more than girls? Are you interacting with one race more than the others? Or do the interaction patterns indicate some other distribution of attention? For example, identify a most-skilled and a least-skilled group—each group should include about 25 percent of the class. From an analysis of the interactions with each group and a comparison of these two interaction patterns, you determine the group to whom you are devoting more time.

Practice Opportunities Effective teachers give children plenty of practice opportunities. One way to indirectly assess the number of practice opportunities students are getting in a class is to teach a student helper to observe and record the number of practices

Figure 7.3 Interaction checklist.

INTERACTION CHECKLIST

Date: _____

Teacher: _____ Observer: _____
Start Time: _____ End Time: _____

Student's Name	Types of Interaction			
	Talked To	Made Eye Contact	Nodded Approval	Total
Nick	‖		ǀ	3
Tom	‖ǀ	ǀ		4
Carlos	‖			2
Naomi		ǀ		1
Abbey	‖‖‖		‖	7
Total Interactions	12	2	3	17

COMMENTS:

Figure 7.4 Practice opportunities checklist.

```
                                                          Date _____
       Teacher _____ Observer_____
       Theme of Lesson _____

                        OBSERVATIONAL DATA

                                         Practice Opportunities
```

Name of Child	ROLL	CATCH	KICK	THROW

for selected students (Figure 7.4). You may want to select the children to be observed, or the student helper can select two or more children to observe. This technique works best when the lesson focuses on discrete skills—such as rolls, catches, or kicks—that can be written on the form before the lesson.

Peer-Assisted Techniques

Some children could learn to use the data-gathering systems described below, but for these methods it's more realistic to seek the assistance of a colleague who is willing to help you assess your teaching performance. Such an arrangement can be mutually beneficial because the systems described in this section can be easily adapted for use in a classroom setting. Thus, if

there's only one physical education specialist in the school, a classroom teacher could work as peer assistant with the specialist. The techniques presented here allow you to gain more detailed information about practice opportunities and feedback, to determine how time was used during the class, and to assess the quality of the demonstrations given to the children.

Practice Opportunities and Feedback Checklist   This system goes a bit further than the practice opportunities checklist (Figure 7.4) and the teacher feedback form (Figure 7.1). Using the form shown in Figure 7.5, a colleague selects several children without your knowledge and records their practice opportunities, circling successful attempts. He or she also records feedback statements you make to the students being

Figure 7.5 Practice opportunities and teacher feedback checklist.

Date _FEBRUARY 12_

Teacher _WANDA_   Observer _JUDY_

Theme of Lesson _KICKING AND CATCHING_

OBSERVATIONAL DATA

Name of Child	Practice Opportunities — KICKING	CATCHING	Teacher Feedback — MOVEMENT — POSITIVE	NEGATIVE	BEHAVIOR — POSITIVE	NEGATIVE
MARK	①‖①①① ①‖①①① ①	①①‖‖‖①	‖			‖	
CARMELITA	‖①①① ‖	‖‖	‖‖‖		‖	
TODD	①①①①① ①①①①①① ①①①‖‖① ①	‖①①① ①①①①① ‖①①① ①①①	‖‖		①	①
ARIAM	①①①‖‖ ①‖①①①	①①‖‖‖ ①①①①		‖‖‖‖	①	‖‖
SUSIE	①①①①① ‖①①①① ①①①	①①‖①① ①‖①①①	‖‖		‖	①

observed. Each statement is marked as related to the child's movement or behavior, and, when possible, as positive or negative. Neutral statements are not recorded under the behavior heading. For example, the statement "Nice catch, Carmelita" would be marked on the teacher feedback part of the checklist under "movement, positive." The statement "Jeff, you never listen!" would be marked under "behavior, negative." This observation system is relatively simple to learn and can be used reliably after just a few minutes of practice.

Duration Recording System   Duration recording allows you to reflect on how you use time in your physical education class. It provides a look at what students are actually doing and for how long. This system, which is a bit more difficult to use than the teacher feedback

form, divides the use of class time into four categories: activity time, instruction time, management time, and waiting time. The total amount of time, in minutes and seconds, is determined for each of the four categories, allowing the teacher to see how the class spent its time. Minutes and seconds can be converted into percentages so you can compare one lesson with another.

The duration recording form (Figure 7.6) contains five time bars, each representing 7 minutes, marked off in 15-second increments. The form defines the codes the peer assistant should use to report what is happening: A for activity, I for instruction, M for management, and W for waiting. The peer assistant records the exact time the lesson begins—the time at which the children enter the gym or playground. (Alternatively, you can analyze a videotaped lesson.) From that moment until the end of the lesson, the peer assistant,

During instructional time, the opportunity to learn is present, but the students aren't active.

Figure 7.6 Duration recording form.

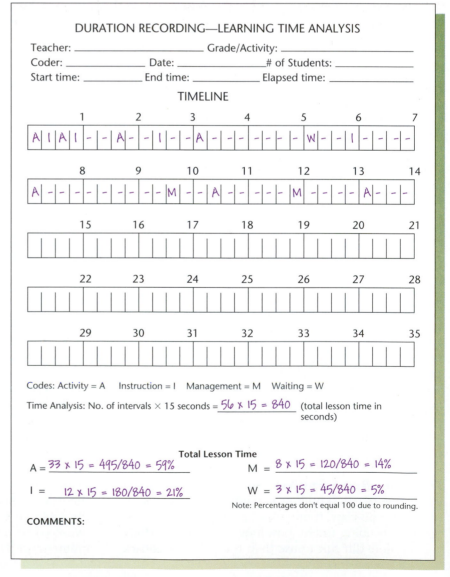

DURATION RECORDING—LEARNING TIME ANALYSIS

Teacher: _____ Grade/Activity: _____
Coder: _____ Date: _____ # of Students: _____
Start time: _____ End time: _____ Elapsed time: _____

TIMELINE

1		2		3		4		5		6		7
A	I	A	I	-	-	A	-	-	I	-	-	A	-	-	-	-	-	-	W	-	-	I	-	-	-	-

| 8 | | 9 | | 10 | | 11 | | 12 | | 13 | | 14 |

| A | - | - | - | - | - | - | - | - | M | - | - | A | - | - | - | - | - | M | - | - | - | - | A | - | - | - |

Codes: Activity = A   Instruction = I   Management = M   Waiting = W

Time Analysis: No. of intervals × 15 seconds = 56 × 15 = 840 (total lesson time in seconds)

Total Lesson Time

A = 33 × 15 = 495/840 = 59%   M = 8 × 15 = 120/840 = 14%

I = 12 × 15 = 180/840 = 21%   W = 3 × 15 = 45/840 = 5%

Note: Percentages don't equal 100 due to rounding.

COMMENTS:

Table 7.1 Coding Guide for the Duration Recording System

Category	Definition	Examples
Activity time	Time when most students (51 percent or more) are involved with physical movement consistent with the goals of the particular lesson.	Practicing a skill; designing a game, dance, or gymnastic sequence; participating in a group or individual game; providing assistance for a partner
Instruction	Time when students have an opportunity to learn. They may be receiving verbal and nonverbal information. Most students (51 percent or more) are engaged in cognitive activity about the lesson focus.	Listening to a lecture, watching the teacher or another student demonstrate a skill, participating in a class discussion, answering teacher's questions.
Management	Time when the opportunity to learn is *not* present. Most students (51 percent or more) are involved in activities only indirectly related to the class learning activity. There is no instruction, demonstration, or practice.	Changing activities, forming groups, listening for roll call, getting out or putting away equipment, getting into line.
Waiting	Time not defined by the other three categories.	Waiting for class to begin, or waiting for instruction to resume when it has been interrupted by another teacher, student messenger, parent, principal, or public address system; waiting in line for a turn.

using a watch that allows for the determination of seconds, marks the time bars to reflect what is happening in the class. When there is a change in student behavior, the assistant indicates the change by writing the appropriate letter in the next space on the bar. At the end of the lesson, the time is recorded. The peer assistant uses the definitions and examples in Table 7.1 as guides to accurate coding. It is important to remember to code what 51 percent (or more than half) of the students are doing and to code what is happening for the majority of the segment. So, if only 10 of 25 students are active or if 15 students are active but only for 5 seconds of the 15-second segment, a W would be recorded (if the students are waiting for a turn).

After the lesson, the teacher uses the information on the duration recording form to calculate what percentage of class time was spent in each category. The following procedure should be used: Calculate the total number of 15-second intervals recorded and multiply by 15 for the total number of seconds in the lesson. Then determine the number of 15-second intervals for each of the four time categories and multiply by 15. Next, divide each number by the total number of seconds for the lesson. The result is the percentage of time in each category.

In the beginning, the peer assistant may be uncertain about how to code a particular event. This is not uncommon when one is learning to use any type of analysis system. The assistant should make a decision and then code other such events the same way. That will enable you to compare a succession of lessons to determine what progress you're making.

Waiting time can include the minutes when students are waiting in line for their turn with an activity.

During activity time, the children are involved in movement that is consistent with the teacher's goals.

There are no hard-and-fast rules as to how time should be distributed within a lesson; however, a major consideration is the focus of the lesson. If the focus is learning a motor skill, the majority of the time in a lesson (more than 50 percent) should be spent practicing the skill. If students are waiting or listening, they are not able to practice. There is a bit of a catch here—there may be such a thing as too much practice time. If there is no instruction, it may be an indication that students are not receiving the information they need to practice correctly. Thus more than 70 percent practice time may be an indicator that the lesson is simply a physical activity session and not physical education.

Demonstration Checklist   Peers can also help reflect on your demonstrations. Most young students are visual learners; therefore, the demonstrations you give them often influence their skill responses as well as their ability to perform a task the way you designed it. Accurate demonstrations are vital to task clarity. By analyzing your demonstrations using the demonstration checklist in Figure 7.7, you can determine if your demonstrations are enhancing the clarity of your instruction and your students' skill. If after analyzing the information from the form you discover that the demonstration was not performed correctly, it could explain why some students were off task.

The time taken to retrieve equipment is considered management.

Demonstration Checklist

Teacher: _____ Observer: _____ Date: _____ Time: _____

Grade: _____ Class Size: _____ Content: _____

DIRECTIONS: Answer the following questions "yes" or "no" based on the instructor's demonstration of the skills.

Components	Task 1	Task 2	Task 3
1. Was the whole skill/action shown early in the demonstration?			
2. Was the skill/action performed at correct (full) speed?			
3. Was the skill performed at more than one angle?			
4. Was a student used to demonstrate the skill (if practical)?			
5. Did the demonstration use the same organizational format that is required for practicing/using the skill?			
6. Were the major common errors (nonexamples) shown?			
7. Were the essential, accurate cues to the performance verbalized?			
8. Were the cues emphasized more than once?			
9. Was noncritical information left out?			
10. Was a check for understanding done?			
11. Do you think students were able to form an accurate mental image of the skill/action as a result of the demonstration?			
12. Was information provided that showed why the skill should be performed as it was demonstrated?			
13. Was the demonstration done in a location similar to where students will perform the skill/action?			

COMMENTS (reference specific comments by number):

Figure 7.7 Demonstration checklist.

Making Sense of It All: Combining and Adapting Techniques and Setting Goals

Many observation systems have been developed to analyze the teaching performance of physical education teachers (Darst, Zakrajsek, and Mancini 1989; Rink 2010; Siedentop and Tannehill 2000). The preceding examples have all been about "standard" effective teaching constructs. As presented, they may or may not fit your needs. You need to make the technique yours. You can do this in a number of ways. First, you can combine instruments and begin to code teacher and student behavior simultaneously—for example, record how many students are off task at a particular moment or how many positive and negative feedback statements you make.

Second, you can develop your own coding instrument based on your environment and particular needs. For most of the questions you want to ask about your teaching, you can develop similar, uncomplicated systems that will give you the specific information you want to know. The secret to developing such systems is to define the behavior (what you want to observe or listen to) very precisely so you can tell when it does and doesn't happen. It doesn't help very much to say, "I want to find out if I was clear when I talked to students"; you need to define what "clear" means to you. It could mean that students didn't have to ask you questions about how to do a task after you gave it; it could mean you didn't mumble and slur your words when you gave a task; or it could mean you didn't have to turn the recorder up to 9 to be able to hear yourself. Whatever it is, define it, and then try to assess it by listening to your tape.

After obtaining data about his or her teaching performance, the reflective teacher reflects on the information, draws conclusions, and sets goals. The improvement can be measured over a period of weeks or months. For example, you may want to set a goal of interacting at least once with every child in the class or to have at least 80 percent of your comments positive. As you set goals be gentle with yourself; set reasonable and progressive goals. If your feedback was at a rate of .25 per minute the first week, increasing to a rate of 2.0 per minute the next week may be unreasonable. When you listen to the recording after a class, you'll learn whether you've achieved your goal. Remember, what is measured or how it is measured is less important than the continuing effort to systematically assess and improve your teaching performance. Relying on your subjective judgment ("I think I'm getting better") or that of a colleague ("That lesson looked good") is not nearly as effective as collecting and analyzing relatively objective data you can refer back to in a few days, months, or even years.

Being Observed

Because many of us are reluctant to be observed while we teach, it may be less threatening to begin your assessment process with the unassisted or student-assisted techniques. When you've progressed to the point where you want more complex data and can no longer use students to help obtain data, be thoughtful about whom you ask to observe you. We've found it easier and more comfortable to use a colleague who is a nonjudgmental friend, someone you're willing to expose both your good points and weaknesses to. For most of us, it takes a while to build up to this point—take it slowly.

Always remember you're obtaining this information to help improve your teaching. The information is yours to do with as you wish; no one else needs to see it unless you want them to. When viewed this way, assessing your teaching performance can be interesting and challenging, not threatening (Hellison and Templin 1991).

Linking and Finding Out More

Equally as important as collecting information about your teaching is knowing what you want to collect information about. The information about your teaching should link directly to what you want to know about teaching, and the ability to collect such information comes from reflection on your teaching situation and goals. It is useless to collect information just for the sake of doing so.

The observation and reflection techniques just discussed are based to a large degree on information from research on teaching—the things that have been found to affect student learning of skills. Many teachers may want to find out more—they may want to know if their teaching is successfully accomplishing the student learning they desire. To find this out, use the assessment for learning options discussed in Chapter 12 and found throughout the skill theme chapters. If you consistently find that students do not learn what you intend them to, use some of the techniques outlined in this chapter to discover if some of the basic constructs of effective teaching are not aligned in your teaching the way you want them to be.

In addition, many of the techniques discussed in this chapter relate largely to student learning of psychomotor and cognitive goals (e.g., activity time relates directly to the learning of psychomotor goals). If you have affective and cognitive goals in your lesson, you may want to revise these instruments or devise others that allow you to discover how much time you are spending on these goals. Again, a number of teachers have found that keeping a teacher journal, much like a diary, allows them to look back on their own teaching over time and provides revealing insights into the nature of their work. The important point to remember is to reflect on your own teaching in an effort to continually find ways to enhance student learning. Employing systematic observation without the purpose of improving teaching to improve learning is a fruitless, time-consuming undertaking that often produces only defensive behavior.

Professional Learning Communities

The techniques described for analyzing one's teaching are effective approaches to improving performance. But successful teaching is more than using specific teaching behaviors in predetermined ways. Teaching can never be totally reduced to specific formulas of behavior that guarantee success for all teachers with all classes (Glickman, Gordon, and Ross-Gordon 2010). However, systematic observation can help answer some questions and provide information that can influence a teacher's success. Other questions require careful thought and analysis, and they cannot be answered through self-reflection or solely by systematic observation. Sometimes we need to sit down with colleagues who'll listen carefully and help us understand (analyze) a particular situation. This is what professional learning communities (PLCs) do. Teachers form professional learning communities to build relationships that allow them to learn from and with each other. These communities are founded on a basis of trust, collegiality, and a desire to learn; within them individuals share their concerns, questions, dreams, and hopes about themselves as teachers.

If you're not careful, teaching can be a lonely and difficult profession. As a poster depicting an exhausted teacher at the end of an obviously difficult day reminds us: "No one ever said teaching was going to be easy." When your teaching isn't going well, or when you've had a spectacular day, a support group can provide comfort and encouragement or share your excitement. It's reassuring to have a stable group of colleagues who'll listen carefully, verbally applaud your successes, and help you analyze your concerns. For those of us in physical education, it is important to seek out those professional learning communities that are discipline or content specific. Often PLCs are established at the school level; the most beneficial PLCs for physical education teachers may be at the district level.

Most teachers occasionally complain about teaching conditions, parents, administrators, or fellow teachers. We all have our down days. Within a PLC, however, complaining is inappropriate because it's often toxic and tends to contaminate others' thinking. PLCs are designed to enhance teaching and learning by empowering teachers as learners.

Teaching will never be an exact, predictable science. There will always be an art to teaching effectively. Self-reflection, systematic observation techniques, and support groups are three approaches to improving both teaching performance and one's personal satisfaction and enthusiasm for teaching.

Summary

Reflective teaching is a developmental process and because effective teaching involves learning, it is a continuous, lifelong process. Teachers who want to become more effective invoke a reflective cycle that includes describing teaching, critiquing teaching, and setting goals to guide their thinking about teaching.

Describing teaching through self-reflection involves the thoughtful contemplation of the act of teaching. It usually results in a permanent product much like a diary or journal. Systematic observation can be used to gather an orderly and focused collection of specific and defined information to critique teaching. It can be classified into three categories: (1) unassisted, (2) student-assisted, and (3) peer-assisted techniques. Goal setting allows reflective teachers to determine if they are making changes to their practices that enhance student learning.

A valuable aid in the teacher reflective process is a PLC, or professional learning community. These groups, made up of fellow teachers, can not only provide comfort and encouragement, but also an environment in which teachers learn from and with each other. When a group of peers actively listen to each other's questions and help clarify each other's thoughts, the teaching skills and knowledge of all the members are improved.

Reading Comprehension Questions

1. Why is this chapter included in *Children Moving?* What is the value of self-reflection?
2. What is a reflection cycle? What three aspects are included in it?
3. What purpose does self-reflection serve in the reflective cycle?
4. How does systematic observation allow a reflective teacher to critique his or her teaching? Identify two systematic observation techniques you can use by yourself. What information can you obtain from each technique?
5. What type of content development pattern would you deem optimal in your teaching situation? How could you use the content development form to compare what actually happens to your desired pattern? What various types of feedback can be determined from recording teacher feedback? What goals would you set if student learning was the focus of your teaching?
6. What kind of analysis can you make from student–teacher interactions?
7. How does the combined practice opportunities and teacher feedback checklist (Figure 7.5) work?
8. What is duration recording? What categories does it contain? How is each category defined? How does a duration recording system work?
9. Why is the use of systematic observation without a clear purpose of improving teaching to improve student learning counterproductive?
10. What is the key to goal setting?
11. What are professional learning communities? What is their value?

References/Suggested Readings

Banville, D., and Rikard, L. 2001. Observational tools for teacher reflection. *Journal of Physical Education, Recreation, and Dance* 72(4): 46–49.

Boyce, B. A. 2003. *Improving your teaching skills: A guide for student teachers and practitioners.* Boston: McGraw-Hill.

Cusimano, B., P. Darst, and H. van der Mars. 1993, October. Improving your teaching through self-evaluation. *Strategies* 7(8): 26–29.

Darling-Hammond, L., and N. Richardson. 2009. Teacher learning: What matters? *Educational Leadership* 66(5), 46–53.

Darst, P. W., D. B. Zakrajsek, and V. H. Mancini, eds. 1989. *Analyzing physical education and sport instruction.* Champaign, IL: Human Kinetics.

Glickman, C., S. Gordon, and J. Ross-Gordon. 2010. *Supervision and instructional leadership: A developmental approach.* 8th ed. Upper Saddle River, NJ: Pearson.

Hellison, D., and T. Templin. 1991. *A reflective approach to teaching physical education.* Champaign, IL: Human Kinetics.

Housner, L. 1996. Innovation and change in physical education. *In Student learning in physical education: Applying research to enhance instruction,* eds. S. Silverman and C. Ennis, 367–89. Champaign, IL: Human Kinetics.

Locke, L. F. 1975, Spring. *The ecology of the gymnasium: What the tourist never sees.* Southern Association of Physical Education for College Women Proceedings: 38–50.

Lorson, K., J. Goodway, and R. Hovatter. 2007. Using goal-directed reflection to make reflection more meaningful. *Journal of Physical Education, Recreation, and Dance* 78(4), 42–47.

[NASPE] National Association for Sport and Physical Education. 2009. *National standards for beginning physical education teachers.* 3rd ed. Reston, VA: National Association for Sport and Physical Education.

Richert, A. 1995. Introduction. In *Teachers who teach teachers: Reflections on teacher educations,* eds. T. Russell and F. Korthagen, 1–7. London: Falmer Press.

Rink, J. 2003. Effective instruction in physical education. In *Student learning in physical education,* 2nd ed., eds. S. Silverman and C. Ennis, 165–86. Champaign, IL: Human Kinetics.

Rink, J. 2010. *Teaching physical education for learning.* 6th ed. New York: McGraw-Hill.

Siedentop, D., and D. Tannehill. 2000. *Developing teaching skills in physical education.* 4th ed. New York: McGraw-Hill.

Stroot, S. 2001. Once I graduate, am I an expert? *Teaching Elementary Physical Education* 12(2): 18–20.

Stroot, S., and C. Whipple. 2003. Organizational socialization: Factors impacting beginning teachers. *In Student learning in physical education: Applying research to enhance instruction,* 2nd ed., eds. S. Silverman and C. Ennis, 311–28. Champaign, IL: Human Kinetics.

van der Mars, H. 1987. Effects of audiocueing of teacher verbal praise on students' managerial and transitional task performance. *Journal of Teaching in Physical Education* 66(1): 48–59.

Active Teaching Skills

Part 3 contains five chapters describing many of the teaching skills reflective teachers use to help children learn and enjoy physical activity. Unlike Parts 4 and 5 that focus on the content (what to teach), the chapters in Part 3 focus on the teaching process, or pedagogy—how to teach.

Chapters 8 and 9 provide concrete examples related to creating a learning environment conducive to student learning. Chapter 8, "Establishing an Environment for Learning," describes many of the techniques teacher use to create positive attitudes toward physical education, ideas for fostering an atmosphere conducive to learning, and safety procedures for teaching inside and outside. This is a critical chapter. Teachers who don't follow these or similar procedures often spend a great deal of their time managing and dealing with off-task behavior

Invariably, however, there will be some children who are off-task, and Chapter 9, "Maintaining Appropriate Behavior," provides practical ideas for maintaining a productive environment, including approaches for working both with individual children and with entire classes. Specific examples from actual teaching situations illustrate how to increase appropriate behavior, decrease inappropriate behavior, and maintain proper behavior. Additional techniques described in Chapter 9 include how to interact positively with children; how to work with them one on one; how to apply "punishment," such as time-outs and desists; and how to follow worthwhile reward systems, such as class rewards and tokens.

Chapter 10, "Instructional Approaches," provides an overview of the pedagogy of skill themes by describing a variety of different instructional techniques used to create active learning experiences for children. This chapter explains a number of approaches that go beyond direct interactive instruction to indirect instruction—including task sheets, stations, peer teaching, cooperative learning, guided discovery, and child-designed instruction. Each of these alternatives provides a more engaging way for children to learn and more fully addresses the cognitive and affective goals of our physical education classes.

One of the critical teaching skills for a reflective teacher is the ability to observe with understanding. For this reason we dedicate an entire chapter to this process. Chapter 11, "Observing Student Responses," focuses on observing children's responses to movement tasks and includes a format for observing classes that includes safety, on-task behavior, and the movements of the entire class and individual children. Two observation techniques of back-to-the-wall and scanning are suggested as effective ways in which to observe.

Chapter 12, "Assessing Student Learning," helps answer the question, "Are my students learning what I want them to learn as a result of my teaching?" In recent years, educators have started to use alternative methods of assessing children. These tech-

niques are ongoing (formative) rather being than a culminating experience at the end of a series of lessons or at the end of several years. Many of them are designed by teachers to assess specifically what they have been teaching in their programs. Chapter 12 includes explanations and examples of some of these techniques, such as journals, exit slips, student drawings, and displays. In addition, scoring rubrics are explained as a way to determine how well children have learned what was taught.

Parts 4 and 5 (Chapters 13–26) focus on the content of the skill theme approach. These are important chapters, but teachers who fail to understand the teaching process described in Chapters 8–12 lessen their chances of providing worthwhile, enjoyable learning experiences for their students.

Establishing an Environment for Learning

A well run lesson that teaches nothing is just as useless as a chaotic lesson in which no academic work is possible.

—WALTER DOYLE (1979)

Key Concepts

- A learning environment is the condition the teacher creates in a classroom that supports (or hinders) learning by the students.

- A learning environment consists of two components, a managerial component and an instructional component, both of which are necessary if physical education is to reach its full learning potential.

- The managerial component establishes the structures that allow the classroom to function effortlessly.

- The instructional component refers to the subject matter activities that allow students to learn physical education content.

- The development of a managerial component is a necessary, but not sufficient, condition for student learning.

- As part of the managerial component, reflective teachers develop protocols, including rules and routines that ensure smooth existence in the gymnasium and on the playground.

- Rules are general expectations for behavior that cover a wide variety of situations; routines are procedures for accomplishing specific duties within a class.

- Rules and routines are most effective when they reflect a positive environment while teaching children to be responsible for their own behavior.

- The development of protocols is an integral and critical part of maintaining a safe environment.

- As part of the instructional component, reflective teachers develop content purposely and progressively, communicate effectively, provide focused feedback, and accommodate individual differences.

- Content development includes the use of tasks, cues, and challenges.

- The KISS principle, using one cue at a time, clear demonstrations, and pinpointing are all aspects of communication.

- Congruent feedback provides focused information to children about the skill they are practicing.

- Individual differences can be accommodated through the use of teaching by invitation and intratask variation.

- A major responsibility of every reflective teacher is to provide students with a physically and psychologically safe learning environment.

Teaching is complex. As teachers it is our responsibility to design and maintain an environment in which learning is supported and allowed to take place—the creation, development, and utilization of processes resulting in a gymnasium or playground conducive to learning. We have to set the stage for student learning by making physical education a place that is warm, supportive, and encourages student performance and achievement. Such an environment is a necessary, though not sufficient, condition for learning (Rink 2010). This means that without such an environment, there is little chance learning will occur; with it, learning is still not possible unless the instructional activities are carried out and appropriate curriculum is in place.

Establishing a learning environment involves two separate components, managerial and instructional, to place students in contact with—and to keep them in contact with—the subject matter at a high success rate for as long as possible. Others have analogized these components to systems, and, similar to a smoothly operating piece of machinery, both must be present for the classroom to operate (Tousignant and Siedentop 1983). Regardless of the term used, both instructional and managerial structures must be present to establish an environment that has the potential for learning. One without the other is not adequate. You can manage without teaching, but you cannot teach without managing.

A component can be defined as a regular pattern of practices used to accomplish the class functions. The word cloud in Figure 8.1 indicates the multitude of learning environment aspects that need to be developed and maintained; it is obvious that this is an intricate task, but it is not magic. The managerial component refers to the non–subject-matter activities necessary for a class to run smoothly and efficiently over a period of time. The instructional component refers to the subject-matter activities designed to see that children learn what is desired by participating in physical education. Both components need to be developed when establishing a learning environment. All too often, physical education teachers establish a managerial aspect (Mowling et al. 2004) but neglect to focus on an instructional aspect or component. This chapter and Chapter 9 are about the managerial components of the learning environment. This chapter plus Chapters 6, 10, 11, and 12 are about the instructional components of the learning environment.

For each of these components, certain teacher practices ensure that the component achieves what the teacher desires. A well-operating component, either managerial or instructional, establishes and maintains student responsibility for appropriate conduct, task involvement, and learning outcomes (see Chapter 6 and "The Instructional Component" section in this chapter). The practices that accomplish this are known as

Figure 8.1 Learning environment word cloud.

accountability measures (Doyle 1980; Hastie and Siedentop 2007). Whether personal or imposed, these accountability measures are so important that without them both the instructional and managerial components become lax and may not even operate (Doyle 1980). Traditional accountability measures in physical education include tests, grades, attendance, teacher reprimands, and punishment. These types of accountability measures are now thought to be largely inappropriate if student learning is the intended outcome of physical education. In fact, they undermine learning and communicate to the public that physical education has little to teach other than to dress and show up for class. This chapter introduces you to a variety of other teacher practices that serve as accountability measures in establishing the managerial and instructional components necessary for a smoothly running class in which learning occurs.

Although the development of a component sounds rigid and sterile, the type of component developed and how it is implemented reflect what we believe not only about physical education, but also about education, children, and society. It mirrors what we feel is important about our school, our gymnasium, our students, and ourselves. All components must accomplish certain things—smooth and consistent gymnasium operation—yet it is how the component is put into action that says who we are. For example, a managerial component that is solely teacher developed and directed indicates a belief that

student input or helping students learn to make decisions isn't important. On the other hand, the complete lack of a managerial component could indicate a teacher's abdication of all responsibility and a belief that it doesn't make any difference what we do (Ennis 1995). However, components that seek student voice and help students learn to make decisions about managerial (noninstructional) situations and instructional (learning) situations indicate that we value students and have taken the responsibility not only to teach psychomotor content, but also to teach the larger goals of personal and social responsibility (Dyson, 2006; Helion 1996; Parker, Kallusky, and Hellison 1999; Parker and Stiehl 2010). The National Standards indicate that one of the goals of physical education is to develop students who demonstrate responsible personal and social behavior in physical activity settings (NASPE 2004). Although the accountability and managerial literature have largely developed from behavior management and business, where efficiency is paramount, there are models in which the development of responsibility and self-direction are important (Hellison 2011). In these models, although initial efficiency may be slightly compromised and the teacher must be willing to relinquish some control, students gradually move toward more independent learning and responsibility.

It is our belief that physical education is child centered and that students should develop increasing responsibility for their own behavior, attitudes, and learning. Therefore the prevailing philosophy of this chapter is the development of components designed to accomplish the goals of self-directed learning and behavior. In other words, just like fitness and motor skill development, responsibility is part of the content with which students must stay in contact. See Box 8-1 for sample recommendations for establishing a learning environment from the Appropriate Practice Guidelines.

Classroom management helps run an effective classroom, but doesn't solve the social problems.

—DON HELLISON

Gymnasium Atmosphere

When the weather forecaster announces an impending low-pressure system, we know what it will feel like—heavy, humid, and often accompanied by rain or snow. Similarly, with high-pressure systems, we know to expect fair weather and dry air. The atmosphere of

Box 8-1

Selected Appropriate and Inappropriate Physical Education Practices

Components: The Learning Environment and Instructional Strategies

Appropriate Practice

- Physical educators systematically plan for, develop, and maintain a positive learning environment focused on maximizing learning and participation, in an atmosphere of respect and support from the teacher and the peers of the child.
- The environment is supportive of all children, and promotes the development of a positive self-concept. Children are given chances to try, to fail, and to try again, free of criticism or harassment from the teacher or other students.
- Programs are designed to guide children to take responsibility for their own behavior and learning. Emphasis is on intrinsic, rather than extrinsic, incentives.
- Fair and consistent classroom management practices encourage student responsibility for positive behavior. Students are often included in the process of developing class rules/agreements.
- Bullying and inappropriate student remarks and behaviors are dealt with immediately and firmly.
- Physical educators make every effort possible to create a safe learning environment for students (e.g., safety considerations and plans are a part of every daily lesson plan). Routines and rules are developed with safety in mind.
- Activities are carefully selected to ensure they match the ability level of the students and are also safe for all of the students regardless of their ability level.
- Facilities and equipment are maintained and closely inspected daily for safety hazards (e.g., free of glass, proper ground cover under equipment).
- The physical educator creates an environment that is inclusive and supportive of all students regardless of their race, ethnic origin, gender, sexual orientation, religion, or physical ability. These differences are acknowledged, appreciated, and respected.
- All children (boys and girls, all skill levels) have equal opportunities for participation and interaction with the teacher (e.g., leadership, playing "skilled" positions, teacher feedback).
- All children, regardless of developmental level and ability, are challenged at an appropriate level.
- Both boys and girls are encouraged, supported, and socialized toward successful achievement in all of the content that is taught in physical education (e.g., dance is for everyone).

- Physical educators use gender-neutral language (e.g., students).
- Clear goals and objectives for student learning and performance are communicated to students, parents, and administrators.
- Physical educators form pairs, groups, and teams in ways that preserve the dignity and self-respect of every child (e.g., randomly, by fitness or skill level when necessary, or by a class system such as birthdays, squads, colors, numbers).

Inappropriate Practice

- The environment is not supportive or safe. As a result, some children feel embarrassed, humiliated, and generally uncomfortable in physical education class (e.g., teacher makes degrading or sarcastic remarks).
- Only highly skilled or physically fit children are viewed as successful learners. The teacher and peers overlook and/or ignore students if they are not highly skilled or physically fit.
- Children behave appropriately because they are fearful of receiving a poor grade or other punishment if they do not follow the teacher's rules.
- The rules are unclear and may vary from day to day.
- Verbal or nonverbal behavior that is hurtful to other children is overlooked and ignored.
- Teachers allow or ignore unsafe practices in their classes. Children are permitted to ignore the safety of others in the class (e.g., pushing, shoving, or tackling children in ball games) or use equipment unsafely (e.g., swinging bats in close proximity to others).
- Human target games (dodgeball) and/or drills that allow aggressive behaviors toward other students are permitted.
- No regular facility safety inspection occurs. Dangerous, broken, or outdated equipment is used.
- The physical education environment supports highly skilled children more fully than children who have less skill development (e.g., posters on display are predominantly of male professional athletes from the major sports).
- Teachers inadvertently promote exclusion by allowing student captains to pick teams or by arbitrarily separating teams by gender or skill level (e.g., popular or highly skilled students are chosen first and cliques are evident).

Source: National Association for Sport and Physical Education, *Appropriate instructional practice guidelines for elementary school physical education.* 3rd ed. (Reston, VA: National Association for Sport and Physical Education, 2009). Reprinted with permission.

the gym is much the same except it is created by the teacher, not by weather systems. Regardless of the component—managerial or instructional—the atmosphere in the gym needs to be emotionally safe and positive. If this atmosphere is not created, then the remainder of this book is probably useless.

As discussed in Chapter 4, of all the teacher practices involved in establishing a positive learning environment, one of the most important pieces is also one of the least tangible and most easily compromised: teacher attitude or approach to teaching and children. This is essentially the translation of a teacher's beliefs into practice. The teacher's self-image and feelings about teaching, about physical education, and about children all influence atmosphere. The enthusiastic teacher conveys this attitude to the children and as a result heightens their enthusiasm for physical education. The teacher who views physical education as a time for learning and work communicates this feeling to the children in the way he or she demands that all the children adhere to certain criteria for behavior. Likewise, the teacher who believes that children are vessels to be molded and should be compliant with teacher expectations, whether they seem reasonable or not, communicates to children that they are not capable of making significant decisions.

Even though children's motivation for participation in physical education changes with age (Xiang, McBride, and Guan 2004), children at any age need to belong and feel competent, useful, potent, and optimistic in order to be motivated to learn. When those needs are met, people commit wholeheartedly to an endeavor (Sagor 2002). The study of physical activity settings has yielded similar findings (Deutsch 1999; Herbel and Parker 1995; Galvan and Parker, 2011). The teacher–student relationship is at the heart of this notion of class management/atmosphere that supports student learning.

In looking at thousands of teachers, Marzano and Marzano (2003) found three aspects contributed to the teacher–student relationship. First, teachers who had a positive relationship with youngsters displayed teacher dominance. While sounding negative, this is actually a positive trait that means teachers provide a clear purpose and strong guidance in content and behavior by establishing clear expectations and consequences as well as clear learning goals and the assertive behaviors to accomplish those goals. Second, appropriate levels of cooperation (characterized by strong feelings of membership, engagement, and commitment) were present in classrooms where real learning occurs. To create these levels of cooperation, the teacher provided students with flexible learning goals, took a personal interest in students, and used positive and equitable

(not equal) classroom behaviors. Finally, the teacher–student relationship was enhanced by the teacher's awareness of high-need students (including those who were passive-aggressive, had attention problems, were perfectionists, or were socially inept). It is this atmosphere that we must create in the gym if we want all children to be attracted to being physically active for a lifetime.

It is our belief that few teachers would argue with the notion of creating an environment that empowers children; however, the act of doing it is difficult. Several strategies may help make your gym a place that attracts children to physical activity for a lifetime while helping them become self-directed, responsible learners.

1. *Change, challenge, choice.* The practices of change, challenge, and choice (Stiehl, Morris, and Sinclair 2008) can be employed as a way to differentiate instruction and to ensure the gymnasium is a place where all learners feel competent, useful, potent, optimistic, and empowered. Though slightly modified here, the premise of Stiehl, Morris, and Sinclair's work is that any aspect of an activity can (and should) be changed so the learner is allowed to be successful at the appropriate level. For example, equipment, space, or the task itself can be modified (see intratask variation examples later in this chapter). The challenges listed in Chapters 16–26 allow tasks to be adapted to more appropriately challenge all children. Choice empowers and intrinsically motivates children by allowing them input that meets their needs (Mowling et al. 2004). Choice can be offered in anything from the type of equipment used to how far apart partners stand. The technique of teaching by invitation provides a mechanism for allowing choice in activities. See Chapter 31 for additional examples of change, challenge, and choice in physical education.

2. *Use positive interactions.* Positive reinforcement and praise need to dominate interactions with children. Unfortunately, the reverse is usually true. Subtle nagging statements such as, "I am waiting for you to be quiet" and "Anytime now" are more often heard than "I like the way you came in and began your warm-up" or "Thanks for listening; it makes my job easier."

3. *People are not for hurting.* Children should be psychologically as well as physically safe in physical education. Hurting refers to everything from physical safety to inappropriate practices, such as games that pinpoint and demean (e.g., dodgeball and the like) to name-calling and making fun.

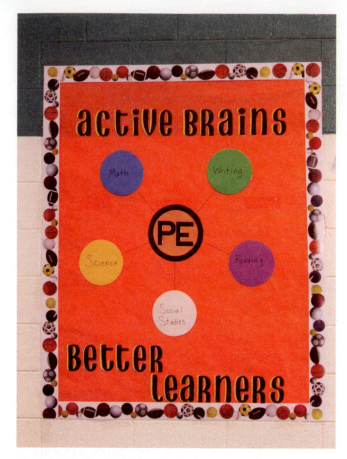

Physical education bulletin board.

It is wise to check yourself regarding these practices on a weekly basis to make sure you haven't slipped into an unproductive pattern.

When establishing the learning environment, the focus is on fostering acceptable behavior and creating an atmosphere appropriate for a physical education class. As in any class, some discipline may be required in a physical education class. An established, consistent, positive environment in the gymnasium and appropriate tasks, however, allow students to know exactly what is expected of them and stimulate enthusiasm for learning. The remainder of this chapter deals with ways teachers have successfully developed both managerial and instructional components to establish a productive learning environment. Remember, you can't maintain a learning environment if it has not been established.

The Managerial Component

Some educators use the terms *management* and *discipline* synonymously; we don't. Developing the managerial component is proactive; discipline is reactive. Discipline is required when a child's behavior is disruptive and the teacher needs to prevent the disruption from occurring again. The managerial component could be considered a "first base" skill because it establishes structures or protocols through which the physical education class becomes predictable and operates smoothly (Rink 2010; Siedentop and Tannehill 2000). This component essentially consists of two aspects: creating the learning environment (this chapter) and maintaining it (Chapter 9). The creation involves the development of protocols, the rules and routines that allow the gymnasium to function.

When they begin school, most children have few preconceptions about how a physical education learning environment will be structured. Within a short time they learn to function according to the teacher's expectations. The managerial component establishes the limits for behavior and the teacher's expectations for the students. Because of our belief in children developing responsibility for themselves and our dislike for constantly feeling as if it is our job to control students, the managerial components we develop focus on establishing an appropriate learning environment and also on having students take more and more responsibility for it. If youngsters are allowed to develop unacceptable behavior in physical education class, the teacher will find it increasingly difficult to alter their behavior. Thus it's crucial for teachers establish an appropriate learning environment during

4. **Never use sarcasm.** As adults we have become used to sarcasm. Children take it literally. It has no place in the gym.

5. **There are no stupid questions.** As a friend of ours puts it, "It is OK not to know, but it is not OK to continue not knowing" (Stiehl 2011). The implication is that we need to make our gymnasiums places where children are free to ask questions.

6. **Physical education is for everyone.** Sports are for those who choose to participate in them. They are usually dominated by the highly skilled and sometimes aggressive children. Physical education is an educational activity designed for every child of every skill level. This means multiple forms of equipment, multiple types of games at the same time, and intratask variation are all needed.

7. **Walk your talk.** We chose to be teachers. We are role models.

8. **Decorate.** For many, the gym is a scary place. Make your gym an attractive place to be—decorate the walls, paint with bright colors, keep the gym sparkling clean, and make sure the lights are bright.

their very first lessons with the students. How well they do this sets the tone for the remainder of the year. We've found the following techniques helpful in developing and holding students accountable for managerial components.

Developing Protocols

Research indicates that effective teachers develop gymnasium protocols that help their gyms run smoothly and minimize disruptions, thus maximizing students' learning time (Jones and Jones 2010). These protocols consist of both rules and routines. Rules identify general expectations for behavior that cover a variety of situations. Though rules are intended to address both acceptable and unacceptable behavior, they quite often focus on inappropriate behavior. A concept that some teachers have found useful in changing to a positive focus is explaining rules as guidelines to help children examine their behavior and attitudes as they affect themselves and others (Jones and Jones 2010). Routines are procedures for accomplishing specific duties in a class. They are different from rules in that they usually refer to specific activities and are usually aimed at accomplishing tasks rather than forbidding behavior. Evidence has shown that effective teachers spend the first few days of the year teaching their classes protocols (Brophy and Good 1986; Fink and Siedentop 1989).

Protocols generally stay in effect for the school year (unless you find one that isn't working or discover that something has been neglected). It is frustrating and time consuming to repeat the protocols for new students or for students who were absent when they were taught. Thus we have found it valuable to videotape the lessons at the beginning of the year when protocols are presented and taught. When a new student joins the class, the videotape can be used at school or at home to orient that student to your gymnasium protocols. The tape is also a useful resource to share classroom procedures with parents at parent–teacher meetings or, if needed, to document the teaching of safety procedures, rules, and routines to a class. This is also a good way to remind students of safety procedures.

Establishing Rules and Expectations That Reflect a Positive Environment

Establishing rules is more than provide the gymnasium "laws"; it also sets the general atmosphere of the gym and conveys the teacher's beliefs about control and responsibility. For example, if all the rules are developed by the teacher, are written as a series of don'ts, and are narrow and punitive, this sends the message that the teacher is the ultimate control figure and children are merely people to be controlled. However, if children provide input and the rules are guiding and broader, allowing children some part in the decision making, then the message is that children are people learning to be responsible; they are capable of making decisions and have self-worth. These messages may appear subtle, but they are powerful to students. Therefore our choice in the development of rules and routines is to be broad and guiding rather than narrow and restricting. They are essentially guidelines by which our classes have agreed to operate.

Children who understand the expectations within which they are to function are less likely to test the teacher's flexibility and more likely to cooperate. A few rules that the teacher states clearly and adheres to consistently can be helpful to everyone. One set of guidelines we have found effective—that help children examine their behaviors and attitudes—is an adaptation of Hellison's five levels of responsibility (Hellison 2011; see Box 8-2). These guidelines are broad enough to encompass the aspects necessary for safe group survival in the gym while guiding students well beyond simple compliance into responsibility.

Figure 8.2 shows how these guidelines can be translated into class rules. A discussion of the guidelines can cover many things normally included in narrower rules. For example, respect for the rights and feelings of others can include all aspects of pushing, stopping, and looking when the teacher talks, sportspersonship, interrupting, use of equipment, and the like. Participation and effort is broad enough to include the whole idea of trying hard (even when you might not want to), giving 100 percent, and similar ideas. Interestingly enough, these two guidelines alone encompass most of the rules we are accustomed to seeing in the gymnasium. The third and fourth guidelines in Figure 8.2 provide an extension we consider important in our teaching. The third indicates that students should be able to work on their own, without the teacher's constant attention—a concept most of us relish. The fourth is one of our ultimate goals—that students care for and help each other. This can include actions as small as handing stray balls back to their owners or as broad as helping another student learn a skill. We have found that when we establish these types of guidelines and constantly adhere to them, students learn to manage themselves and develop the concepts of personal and social responsibility we desire as outcomes of our programs. With such a managerial component developed and in place, we find that we are "managing" less, have more time for teaching, and have more fun teaching because we do not need to behave like police officers.

Box 8-2

Responsibility Levels

Level I: Respecting the Rights and Feelings of Others

Self-control
The right to be included
The right to peaceful conflict resolution

Level II: Participation and Effort

Exploring effort
Trying new things
A personal definition of success

Level III: Self-Direction

On-task independence
Personal plan
Balancing current and future needs
"Striving against external forces"

Level IV: Caring about and Helping Others

Prerequisite interpersonal skills
Compassion
Contributing member of the community and beyond
Without rewards

Level V: Going Beyond

Being responsible at home and school, with friends
Positive role model

Source: D. Hellison, *Teaching responsibility through physical activity,* 3rd ed. (Champaign, IL: Human Kinetics, 2011).

Gymnasium Rules

Be nice to classmates, the teacher,
and the equipment.

Try everything—and try hard.

Do what you are supposed to do,
even when the teacher isn't looking.

Help others.

Figure 8.2 Translation of Hellison's (2011) responsibility levels into rules.

Rules are necessary for group well-being and development. The picture on page 109 shows another set of gymnasium rules teachers have found successful in eliciting the learning environment they desire. You may wish to establish different rules; if so, the following general guidelines may help you:

- Explain why the rules are necessary. Children are far more cooperative with rules that make sense to them than with seemingly arbitrary regulations. In some cases, children can help make the necessary rules.
- State rules positively. Whenever possible, avoid using the words *don't*, *not*, and *no*. In essence, it is more productive to tell children what to do than what not to do.
- Keep the number of rules to a minimum. A good guide is to state no more than five rules.
- Post rules in an attractive fashion so they can be seen and read easily.
- Make sure the children understand the rules. To teach rules most efficiently, first describe and demonstrate the desired behavior, then have the children rehearse the correct behavior (this usually takes more than one rehearsal). Finally, provide feedback, especially the first time you ask the children to use a routine (the first days of school).
- Design, teach, post, and practice the consequences of breaking the rules.
- Especially in the beginning, prompt students toward appropriate behavior, and reinforce appropriate behavior. Let students know when they've done something correctly.

One of the obvious questions, although students don't always ask it, is, What happens when one of the rules is broken? No matter how well we teach, some of the children will break some of the rules, so we find it helps at the outset of the year to describe the consequences for breaking a rule. These consequences are for relatively minor offenses; major offenses are discussed in Chapter 9.

The teacher needs to develop consequences appropriate to the particular teaching situation. Many teachers use a series of consequences similar to the following, which allow children to first take responsibility for their actions before the teacher does.

1. The first time a child violates a rule—for example, the child fails to stop and listen—give the child a verbal prompt.
2. The second time a child violates a rule in the same class period, ask if the child "needs to sit out for a while." The child's response to this question is usually amazingly honest, and the question places the responsibility on the child for his or her actions. To increase student refection and responsibility, the child can reenter class when ready without consulting the teacher.
3. The third time a child violates a rule, tell the child to take a time-out. As in the previous step, the child may reenter class when he or she feels ready.
4. The fourth time a child violates the same rule, have the child sit out until a personal plan can be developed regarding his or her actions (see Chapter 9). This usually means the remainder of the class. Although sitting out the remainder of the class may seem a bit harsh, as teachers we need to be able to teach. A continually disruptive child takes our attention away from other children who deserve it just as much. Be aware that some lapse in following rules may be minor or a nonproblem, whereas other actions are major problems that can escalate. Be sure not to overreact to minor problems so children do not respect the actions taken. See Chapter 9 for further discussion of maintaining the learning environment.

As much as possible, the consequences for violating a rule should be noninterruptive. We try to deliver a consequence with a word or two and avoid interfering with the learning experiences of the rest of the class. One final comment about time-outs: They are effective when the children find the lesson interesting. If the lesson is uninteresting, dull, or inappropriate for a child, then the time-out becomes a reward rather than a consequence for off-task behavior.

Establishing Gymnasium Routines

Routines are protocols designed to help the gymnasium run smoothly and efficiently. Remember, routines are specific ways to accomplish certain tasks in a lesson; they should remain consistent as much as

Attractively posting classroom rules is an effective way to guide children's actions.

possible. Routines also reflect what we feel is important. Here are key areas in which physical education teachers find routines to be effective: entry to and exit from the gymnasium/playground; ways to obtain, handle, and return equipment; signals for attention and starting and stopping activity; the use of space; boundaries for work spaces; and housekeeping activities such as going to the restroom, getting drinks, and leaving the room.

Routines do much to reflect what we think of students and what we believe about them and thus send clear messages to students. How routines are implemented can tell students they are competent and capable or dependent and not to be trusted. Martinek (1988) found that teachers developed learned helplessness in students by creating low expectations for them. Conversely, when given and taught seemingly high expectations for things such as responsibility and their own learning, students lived up to the expectations (Ward and Parker, 2009). Although some of the actions may be subtle, the difference in the two scenarios appears to center around how much perceived control the students have over some basic decisions. Routines that rob students of basic decisions or allow no alternative seem to cause resentment and let the students transfer responsibility for their actions to the teacher. Alternatively, routines that allow students some flexibility and decision making seem to empower them. Consider using some of the following suggestions as you develop routines for your classes.

Entering and Leaving the Gym   We have found it beneficial to have a standardized way of entering and leaving the gym. It is helpful to have the classroom teacher bring students to the gym, and to have a set routine when the students get to the gym. Some teachers have children sit on the center circle or line; others post an initial activity often called DIN (Do It Now); still others have children in predetermined groups go to a predetermined part of the gym to warm up on their own. Children need to have something to do when they arrive or they will make something up themselves. Exiting should be the same as entering. Most schools require students to walk quietly in lines to and from places in the school. It is helpful if classroom teachers meet their classes in the gym for return to the classroom.

Stopping and Listening Skills   In a successful learning environment, noise rarely exceeds a reasonable level that can be thought of as productive noise. Hollering, shrieking, and yelling, although appropriate at recess, are not appropriate in physical education. The children shouldn't be expected to be silent, but they should be able to hear a teacher speaking in a reasonable tone considerably below a shout.

One of the seemingly hardest routines to teach children in physical education is to stop activity quickly and listen to the teacher. When a teacher must spend time quieting the children so the entire class can hear an explanation or comment, the amount of time left for activities is decreased. Thus it's imperative that children learn to respond quickly and appropriately to the teacher's signal for quiet. We have seen teachers use a variety of signals, including dimming of the lights, verbal cues such as "freeze," turning music off and on, a hand drum or tambourine, or simply the raising of a hand. Regardless of the signal, it should be clear what the students are to do when the signal is given—hands on knees, eyes on teacher, equipment on floor, and the like. Listening games (Box 8-3) can be used to teach children to listen as they move and to respond quickly to the teacher's signals.

Equipment   Getting and putting away equipment seem to be two of the biggest issues in class. We have found several things to be helpful. Have equipment ready before class starts and available in various locations. For example, hula hoops create great storage areas for balls, but be sure to have multiple locations so all children are not going to one place to get equipment. It is also important for youngsters to walk rather than run and push to get equipment. The same is true for returning equipment at the end of activity; children need to walk and place it in its spot—not shoot

---

Box 8-3

Listening Games

While using movement concepts and skills as the physical activity, these listening games are management activities designed to help the children learn to stop and listen quickly. As you use them, do not single out children who are slow to respond, and don't use penalties as a form of discipline. Embarrassment and punishment are both counterproductive; you want children to enjoy exercise, not to think of it as unpleasant. Remember, learning management protocols takes the same practice as learning motor skills.

Stop and Go

Children travel in general space in a scattered formation. Once the children are able to (1) walk without touching others and (2) stay far away from others as they walk, you can begin to play Stop and Go. When you say "Stop," the children should stop and freeze instantly. When you say "Go," they should begin to travel again. Don't shout the signals—*speak* them so the children become accustomed to listening for your voice at a reasonable level. Vary the time of each movement segment, usually keeping the movement time to no more than about 10 seconds. This should be a very lively activity.

Hocus Pocus

One of the cleverest variations of Stop and Go we have seen recently was the use of the phrase *hocus pocus* by two student teachers, Jessica Segura and Cristian Sarmento. Whenever students were practicing and heard "hocus pocus," they

Box 8-3 (continued)

responded with "time to focus," put their equipment on the floor, and put their hands on their knees and their eyes on the teacher. Youngsters seemed to love saying "time to focus," and the protocol worked like a charm.

Body Parts

This game focuses on the different body parts. Once the children have adjusted to Stop and Go, they enjoy the challenge of touching the floor with different body parts—elbow, seat, knee, wrist, waist, left hand, or right foot—as quickly as they can when you say "Stop."

Traveling

Once the children have learned to travel using different locomotor patterns, variations in these patterns are appropriate. Call out different ways of traveling—skipping, hopping, crab-walking, galloping—and challenge the children to change from one to another as rapidly as possible. You can increase the challenge of this game by combining traveling and the concept of direction—for example, gallop backward or hop to the right.

Shapes

This game can be played on a painted playground surface or in a gymnasium. Before class, draw circles, triangles, squares, etc., on the ground. The object is for the children to move as quickly as possible to the shape you name; for example, if you call out "circle," the children stand on a circle as quickly as possible. You can use colors instead of or in combination with shapes if the surface you're using is painted various colors. The terms you use will be determined by your pupils' knowledge of colors and shapes.

Numbers

In one version of this game, the children stop with the appropriate number of body parts touching the ground. For example, if you call out "three," the children should stop with three body parts touching the ground.

In a second version, the children stop in groups. The number the teacher calls determines the size of the group. This game is helpful when you want the children to form into groups of three, four, or five in a hurry.

Combinations

As children learn each variation, they find it challenging and fun to play several games at once. For example, you might call out a body part, a color, a locomotor pattern, or a number. Children thrive on increasingly difficult games.

Switch and Rotate

The purpose of this game is primarily to teach listening, but it's more appropriate for older children. The object of the game is to stay so close to a partner that when the teacher says "stop" and the players freeze, the follower can still touch the leader. When the teacher says "switch," the partners change roles, and the follower becomes the leader.

You can make this game more difficult by increasing the size of the group to three, then four, then five. The object of the game remains the same: Each child should be able to touch the person in front as soon as you say "Stop." When you add the challenge "Rotate," the leader goes to the end of the line and becomes a follower. Children find the challenge of listening and responding instantly while trying to remain close to the children in front of them fascinating. You can make this game more challenging by varying the locomotor patterns—for example, from walking to skipping to hopping to galloping to running.

You might initially assign a criterion of five seconds as a reasonable amount of time for the children to stop and listen after they hear the stop signal. If the entire class stops and listens in five seconds or less, praise them. If they don't, explain that taking more than five seconds is too slow and have them practice again. Gradually raise the standard as the children become more proficient. The children often view these races against the clock as fun games and delight in the teacher's praise when they perform well. They also enjoy trying to beat their own records. This approach provides far more time for activity and instruction. As the children learn the value of spending less time on management tasks, you can eliminate these races against the clock. Teachers must be clear, concise, and to the point. As a general rule, once a class has begun, we try to keep our verbal explanations to less than one minute. Although this isn't always possible (or even appropriate), it does help to increase the children's willingness to stop and listen to us.

from the center of the gym. In the beginning it may be useful to have selected groups of students—all those wearing red, for example—get equipment, and then have other groups go. The two least effective ways to get equipment are to hand it out individually and to have it all in one place.

Once children get equipment, they need to know what to do with it. Tell them, for example, "Walk, get a paddle and ball, carry it to your space, and wait for directions," or "Walk, get a ball, carry it to your space, and begin throwing and catching by yourself." As with entering the gym, if you don't tell them what to do, children

Spreading equipment out and providing equipment options are two routines that promote student responsibility.

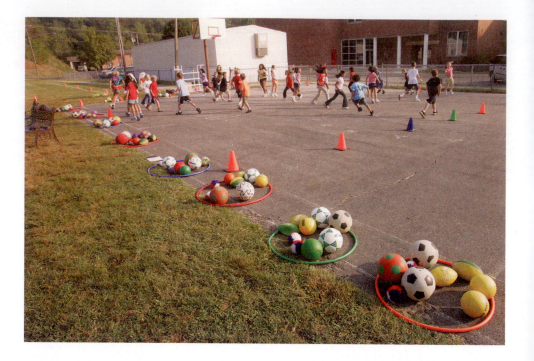

will devise something to do with the equipment themselves, and it usually is not what you had in mind.

The final aspect of using equipment is what to do with it when the teacher is talking. Children, like adults, have a hard time holding on to equipment without playing with it. Many teachers will ask students to place the ball on the floor, to hold it like a pro under one elbow, or even to hold it on their heads. Regardless of the technique, children need to have something to do with the equipment when the teacher is talking.

Partners and Groups   When choosing partners or teams, the more teachers choose partners for children, the more we disenfranchise them. It is important to have children learn how to appropriately choose their own partners. Box 8-4 has routines for choosing partners that have worked for us.

Other Routines   Other helpful routines involve getting water, responding to accidents, using the bathroom, and dressing appropriately. Table 8.1 compares gymnasium routines that enable and don't enable students to show responsibility. Any decisions we can help students learn to make on their own build independence, competence, self-worth, and confidence, thus reducing behavior problems. Taking away decisions students are capable of making fosters dependence and usually creates behavior problems. The key factor is first teaching students to make deci-

sions competently. The net result of this instruction is that we as teachers are freed from trivial decisions that detract from our ability to teach—and we have a classroom that manages itself.

Getting Off to a Good Start

Typically, the first day a class meets, the teacher goes over the logistical and organizational rules and procedures she or he feels are essential for effective class functioning. Many times we've seen this done only in the first lesson via a lecture; the rules and procedures are never taught and never reviewed again unless something goes wrong.

> *Students don't need to be fearful of teachers to listen to them.*
>
> —**MARK MURDOCK,** practicum student, after his first time teaching sixth grade

It has become increasingly obvious how important the first few days of school are (Brooks 1985; Brophy and Good 1986; Krouscas 1996): The first days establish the environment for the entire year. The students learn what behavior and attitude are appropriate in the gymnasium and what will be expected of them in physical education. It is then that they learn the stated and unstated class rules. When a situation arises and is consistently

Box 8-4

Forming Partners or Groups

Though the days of having a class divide into two teams and play against each other are largely over in physical education, on many occasions children need to form partners or small groups. In some classes, the act of finding a partner creates many behavior problems. Children argue over who is going to be whose partner, other children are left out, the time used in deciding partners takes longer than the task itself, and then children want to change partners. The same problems occur, even more so, when dividing children into groups. We've found the following techniques helpful in avoiding such problems as much as possible.

Getting Partners

- Put a time limit on how long children can take to choose partners, such as "by the time I count from five to one, you should have your partner and be standing in your own space."
- Put restrictions on who may be partners—for example, "someone you've never worked with before," "the person sitting next to you," "the person who sits next to you in class," or "someone you know you can work with in a productive manner." A note here: children can understand the word *productive* if we teach it to them.
- Decide ahead of class who will be partners.
- Hand out color codes (pieces of paper, stickers, or marking-pen marks on the hand) at the beginning of class; the children who match up are partners.

Dividing into Groups

- Have children choose partners; then put one partner in one group and one in another. This works well for making groups equal.
- Assign each student a color or number (the number of colors or numbers equals the number of groups you desire) at the beginning of the year or month. When groups are to be formed, simply say, "Reds here," "Blues here," "Purples here," and "Greens here." (This is also an efficient way to take roll in your class.) Be sure to change colors or numbers by grading period so the groups are varied.
- Divide teams by certain generic characteristics, such as eye color, month of birth, number of siblings, or number of letters in first name.
- Divide groups ahead of time.
- Create a deck of cards (or shapes, letters, or numbers) that has the number of groups you desire. For example, if you want groups of four, configure the deck so you use four triangles, four circles, four squares, four stars, and four rectangles. Pass out the cards randomly and have the four that match become a group.

Whatever you do, don't take more than 60 seconds and, most important, don't alienate anyone. Under no circumstances should selecting partners or dividing children into groups be a popularity contest.

Table 8.1 Routines That Promote (and Don't Promote) Decision Making

Task	Promotes	Doesn't Promote
Getting equipment	Spread equipment and have students walk to pick it up.	Hand out equipment.
Entering the gymnasium	Post initial activity; students begin to practice as soon as they enter.	Students line up, waiting for the teacher.
Choosing partners	Students choose partners with whom they can practice productively.	Teacher assigns partners.
Dress	Students choose appropriate clothing that allows them to participate freely.	Student wears uniforms.
Getting water/bathroom	Students get a drink or use the restroom when they need it if no one else is at the drinking fountain or in the restroom.	Drinking and/or restroom use is permitted only before or after class.

treated the same way, the students know the teacher means what has been said. This establishes the behavior and attitude that will typify a class for the remainder of the year. We've found the following suggestions helpful for getting off to a good start, and Figure 8.3 provides a checklist to ensure you're ready for the beginning of the school year. For those of you who are reading *Children Moving* and are about to begin a field experience, your beginning of the year is the first day you see your students. While you will not want to vary much from what your cooperating teacher does, you can use the same suggestions for letting students know that you know what goes on in the gym.

- *Ready the gym* Be certain that your gymnasium and materials are ready before the beginning of the year.
- *Plan protocols* Even if you plan is to have students provide input into the rules and routines of the gymnasium, decide before you meet your students what general rules (consequences) and routines are important and necessary for you. What is the general atmosphere you wish to create? In what ways can you guide students? Teachers who have the students decide on protocols often come prepared with generic guidelines (such as participation; treatment of others—students and teachers; safety; equipment)

Figure 8.3 Checklist for the beginning of school.
Source: Adapted from C. Evertson, E. Emmer, and M. Worsham, *Classroom management for elementary teachers,* 7th ed. (Boston: Allyn & Bacon, 2009).

CHECKLIST FOR THE BEGINNING OF SCHOOL		
Item	Check When Done	Notes
Are your teaching areas and equipment ready?		
Have you decided on your class protocols?		
Are you familiar with the parts of the school that you may use (halls, cafeteria, multipurpose room, etc.) and any procedures associated with their use?		
Do you have complete class rosters for each class you teach?		
Do you have file information on your students, including any comments from previous teachers and information on health problems?		
Do you know if you have any students with disabilities who should be accommodated for in your instruction?		
Do you have an adequate amount of equipment for your students?		
Have you established the procedure for the arrival and departure of the students from the physical education area?		
Are the children's name tags ready? Do you have some blank ones for unexpected students?		
Do you have your first day's plan of activities?		
Do you have rainy-day activities planned?		
Have you inspected all facilities for safety issues?		
Do you have a letter ready to send home to the parents with information about the school year and expectations?		
Do you know how to obtain assistance from school staff members (e.g., school nurse, office personnel, and the custodians)?		

for operation of the gym. Students can then form specific rules within those guidelines. If you decide to develop the rules and consequences of the gym yourself, have them ready and posted before children arrive.

- *Plan beginning-of-school activities* Develop activities for the first few days of physical education that will involve students at a high success rate and have a whole-group focus (see Chapter 10). This gives you an opportunity to see who follows directions and to reinforce appropriate behavior and attitudes. Don't begin independent work until you are certain individuals know what is expected of them. Teach the rules of behavior and expected attitudes as well as classroom routines (e.g., what to do when arriving in class; how to take out, set up, and take down equipment; what to do in a fire drill). You can most easily do this by planning what the routines will be, designing situations that allow students to practice the routines, and teaching those routines in the gym. Spending time teaching behavior and attitudes at the beginning of the school year allows you to spend more time during the rest of the year teaching skills and much less time repeating what should already have become habit.
- *Communicating with parents* Many teachers find it valuable to communicate via a written newsletter or flyer the expectations of physical education class as well what to expect in terms of learning in the gym. The newsletter can include what themes will be taught and when, a bit about special events, the safety rules of the gym and playground, and how to contact you. Some teachers leave a place for comments on the flyer and request that a signed copy be returned.
- *Developing strategies for potential problems* Anticipate problems both in terms of content (e.g., what will be too hard for some students) or gymnasium routines (e.g., how students might potentially misunderstand a certain routine), and develop ways to prevent or reduce those problems.
- *Monitoring* In the early days, routinely check with students individually to determine how they're settling in and to gain other information relevant to the physical education and school setting.
- *Creating accountability* Develop procedures that help students learn to be responsible for their actions (Chapter 9) and work (Chapter 12).

School-Wide Programs

Many schools have adopted school-wide behavior management programs for all children in all disciplines. These programs, the most common of which is Positive Behavioral Interventions & Supports (PBIS), have as a focus positive behavior, rewarding children for positive behavior, and acceptance of responsibility for that behavior. Behavioral expectations are positively stated, easy for the children to remember, and pertinent to the specific school setting. For additional information on PBIS, contact www.PBIS.org. If your school has such a program, it is important to adopt that program for physical education if it is going to be successful. Many schools and physical education programs have adapted the school logo as a way to make the expectations clear; the physical education teacher(s) and the students working together then develop specific guidelines that mesh with the school expectations. Figure 8.4 shows how one physical education program adapted school-level guidelines for physical education.

Chappelow Magnet School (the Cheetahs) developed PRIDE as the aconymn for what was expected for all students in the school. At their school, Cheetah PRIDE stands for Personal Responsibility, Respect, Integrity, Determination, and Empathy.

To help the children better translate the abstract ideas into actions, specific behaviors were identified by letter.

  P: I own my choices, words, and actions.

  R: I honor myself, others, and my environment.

  I: I am honest and make the right choices.

  D: I try my best and don't give up.

  E: I am kind and considerate.

In physical education, PRIDE was translated into the class rules of:

- Being responsible for yourself and your learning
- Respecting others and equipment
- Telling the truth and being honest during game play or any other movement activity
- Working hard by practicing tasks and not giving up
- Caring for others and being helpful

Figure 8.4 Cheetah PRIDE.
Source: Tia Ziegler, physical education teacher, Chappelow Magnet School, Evans, CO.

Teaching Skills for Establishing the Managerial Aspects of the Learning Environment

The preceding sections emphasized the importance of a managerial component as well as the tasks necessary to create it. Effective teachers also use a number of generic teaching skills to help create and maintain a component. Such skills include teaching the protocols, setting performance standards, and maintaining consistency.

Teaching Protocols

When children are learning psychomotor skills, we commonly give them much practice; when they make mistakes, we provide feedback. We would never think about punishing a child who did not learn to throw correctly, especially after one try. The same is true with teaching rules and routines. For children to learn rules and routines, teach them just as you would teach content—using the same effective teaching skills. The following four aspects are some of the most important when teaching protocols.

1. ***Describe, demonstrate, and expect the desired behavior.*** Some people call this setting performance standards. Effective teachers set high but reasonable expectations for students and communicate them to the children. We've found that an easy way to do this is to teach with a critical demandingness (Brophy and Evertson 1976), which means that we set standards and consistently adhere to them so the children know exactly what is expected. For example, we've established performance standards for many daily management tasks, such as putting away equipment or lining up to go back to the classroom. Performance standards are really a way for teachers to communicate exactly what they expect. When these expectations are clear, the children understand what the teacher wants.

    Use both words and actions to convey what specific behaviors are acceptable. For example, do not simply tell children you want them to display good sportspersonship, but tell them what good means—for example, say thank you to others, walk to get equipment, put equipment down and listen when the teacher or others are talking, walk around others to retrieve lost equipment. Second, demonstrate what each behavior looks like. Many children will have a different idea than you do about what walking means. Setting performance standards helps define the atmosphere of the classroom and maintain safety.

2. ***Practice the behaviors.*** Practice helps children learn the appropriate behavior and at the same time allows you to see if the youngsters understand and can follow a procedure. Box 8-5 gives an example of a practice activity for rules and procedures. Note that the primary purpose of this activity is to help students learn the protocols of the gymnasium by performing a variety of activities. All the activities involve working together productively as a group, which focuses on the atmosphere of the gym itself.

3. ***Provide feedback.*** Protocols, just like motor skills, are learned, and children don't often get them right the first time. After students have successfully practiced the protocol for the first time, be sure to tell them they did it correctly and then praise them. If improvement is needed, tell them exactly what is needed and practice again. Even after youngsters seem to know a protocol, be prepared to prompt and give feedback if they forget.

4. ***Maintain consistency.*** When establishing a classroom atmosphere, to avoid slippage (letting the children become lax as the year progresses), it's important that teachers be consistent in what they expect from one day to the next.

    Students learn best when the gymnasium is a predictable place to be. Rules and routines must be followed habitually. For example, if children are allowed to take out equipment mats by dragging them across the floor on one day, but on the next day four people are required to carry each mat, what Doyle (1979) calls ambiguity exists: The students don't know what is expected of them and are confused. Therefore, after behaviors have been described and taught (performance standards set), the protocols practiced, and feedback given, you must be consistent with your actions if youngsters are to really understand your expectations.

The Instructional Component

It is not enough to create a reasonable place in which students are able to learn; we must also teach so students can learn. Learning motor skills and fitness concepts is the unique goal of physical education. It guides our actions as teachers and directs student attention as well as participation and attitudes. The instructional component of the learning environment consists of subject-matter functions designed to see that children learn the intended content. Students are more likely to learn when expectations about learning are communicated. More learning occurs when students understand and value learning goals; when the task is appropriate and has a definite aim or focus; and when content is made personal, concrete, and familiar.

Box 8-5

Teaching Protocols with Group Practice: Ring the Bell

Equipment

For an average-size class:

- Four sets of large cards, each with a protocol practice activity written on one side (see below). Each set of cards should be a different color.
- Four medium bells.
- Any equipment necessary to practice the card-activities.

Organization

After protocols have been explained and demonstrated, divide the class into four groups. Give each group a color to match the cards. All cards are spread out face down in the middle of the gym and mixed. When instructed, one member of each group retrieves a card for his or her group, takes it to the group, and they complete the activity. One member then returns to the middle, rings the cowbell, hands the card to the teacher, and retrieves another card. The activity continues until all cards have been completed.

Sample Card Activities

- At the regroup area, finger-spell your first name.
- Go get a drink of water. One at a time, please.
- Go to the blue neighborhood and do 10 push-ups of any kind.
- Go to the planning-time area (see Chapter 10) and review the rules with each other.
- Measure the length of the gym using your bodies. Lie down on the floor head-to-toe.
- Go to the bathroom pass area and show your group your favorite safe balance.
- Go to the red neighborhood, get a ball, and dribble it 15 times with your right hand and 15 times with your left hand.

Assessment

This would be an opportune time to check for understanding by using a student drawing or an exit slip (see Chapter 12) asking about one or two protocols.

Source: Adapted from material by Chet Bunting, Riverside Elementary School, Thornton, CO. Used with permission.

If students are to be held accountable for learning the expectations we have set, it is essential that they accomplish the task as intended. Accountability in a managerial component is clear: If a student is asked to walk but runs instead, he or she is asked to start over again and walk. Accountability also exists with motor performance, but the strategies differ. Typically we have used testing as the major accountability component for learning in physical education. Unfortunately, testing occurs infrequently and only at the end of a unit. Alternative assessment practices have helped alleviate that problem (see Chapter 12). Yet, to truly learn and understand, students need ongoing accountability components. Effective teachers utilize a variety of practices to create effective instructional components that keep students on task, focused, and motivated to improve their performance. Four concepts are foundational to creating an instructional environment primed for learning: content development (discussed in Chapter 6 and reinforced here), communication, feedback, and accommodating differences.

Content Development

Content development is the use of four functions that the teacher performs: informing, extending, refining, and applying (Rink 2010) to help children learn movement concepts and skill themes. (See Chapter 6 for a complete explanation of content development.) Varying the type of task builds student accountability for learning. In *Children Moving*, extensions are the tasks that allow students to progress a skill to more complex situations, while refinements are the cues that provide focus on the critical aspects of a skill to make it successful. Using challenges (applications) on a regular basis gives students the opportunity to focus their work and informally assess their learning between tests. Chapter 7, "Analyzing Reflective Teaching," provides you with a way to determine how you are developing the content (see Figure 7.2). Ideally, you will find that your lessons include a number of cues that relate to the tasks the children are doing in that lesson. Lessons that consist entirely of tasks followed by challenges are considered undesirable sequences. Though there is no magic number or mix, desirable task sequences consist of a more varied pattern that includes a mix of tasks, relevant cues, and challenges as needed (Belka and Short 1991). In other words, there is no formula that can be used for content development (task, cues, challenges). It always depends on the abilities and interests of the class being taught—as well as the amount of time and effort the teacher has spent on planning interesting, enjoyable, and worthwhile lessons. In addition, it has been our finding that appropriate, challenging content eliminates about 90 percent of the potential behavior problems in class.

Communication

Effective teachers are good communicators (Graham et al. 1993; Rink 2010). They provide clear and interesting explanations and descriptions so the children can easily understand the information. As you will see in the movement concept and skill theme chapters (Chapters 13–26), each section (activity) begins by providing the children with some information about how a particular task is to be done—for example, the equipment needed, the space in which the activity will occur, the rules, and whether the children will be working alone or with others. This information is considered instructional and thus not designated as tasks, cues, or challenges. Ideally, the instructional part of the lesson is both brief and clear so the children can quickly begin practicing the starting task with few questions. When we provide this information, we also follow the KISS principle.

The KISS Principle
The KISS principle (Keep It Short and Simple) is a good guideline to follow when talking to children. The problem we face as teachers is that we have much to tell the children about a concept or skill, but the children aren't really interested in listening for long because they want to move. We try to limit our instruction to just what the children need to know, although there are exceptions to this.

One trap teachers easily fall into is spending five or more minutes telling (and demonstrating) all they know about a skill or activity. There is a lot to tell the children—the problem is that the children can't possibly remember all that information when it is provided in a single minilecture. Think of a skill or exercise you know well. It would be easy for you to talk for five minutes, for example, on how to hit a ball with a bat or the correct way to do a crunch. The children won't remember all of this, however. If you don't believe it, try an experiment with one of your classes. Give them a minilecture. During the following class, use the Helping Murgatroid technique (see Chapter 12, page 181) to see what they actually are able to recall from your lecture. We believe you'll find that information provided in small bits throughout a lesson is more effective than long-winded explanations children don't remember.

Demonstrations
In addition to keeping our explanations brief and to the point, we also demonstrate whenever possible (Graham 2008; Rink 2010). This is helpful to the children who are visual as opposed to auditory learners, and it's necessary for the increasing number of children in our classes who are English language learners. Demonstrations of motor skills need to be done correctly, and they must emphasize the part or parts the children need to pay attention to—the instep, the elbow, the shoulder, the hands—so children can clearly see how that part is to be used and how it fits into the total movement. This seems obvious, yet it is amazing to see how often teachers don't provide the children with a demonstration or fail to demonstrate slowly enough or to emphasize a part so that the demonstration is just not helpful to children. If you videotape some of your lessons, as we suggest in Chapter 7, you will be able to ascertain quickly the effectiveness of your demonstrations.

Pinpointing
There are times when we choose not to demonstrate or are unable to demonstrate a skill for the children. In these instances, pinpointing—inviting several children to do the demonstration—can be an effective technique (Graham 2008). The children are encouraged when they see that their peers can demonstrate the skill or technique. When possible, we try to select two or more children to do the pinpointing; in this way we avoid placing children who are uncomfortable performing in front of other children in a solo situation.

One Cue at a Time
Learning cues also provide students with an instructional accountability mechanism. Cues are simply short phrases or words that focus the learner on the critical elements of the skill to be practiced. If for every task presented, the last thing the teacher did was to repeat the cue(s) for the task, many students would be highly focused. Major cues are provided at the beginning of each control-level through proficiency-level task in the skill theme chapters.

Generally we focus on one cue at a time in our instruction, demonstration, and pinpointing. For example, to a class of second graders we might provide instruction and demonstrate the cue of stepping with the lead foot when batting (Chapter 26). We would then ask the children to continue the same task—batting off a tee against a wall or fence, for example—while we circulate and provide feedback.

If you can imagine this setting, you realize that the children may need several other cues. Some, for example, will not be swinging in a horizontal plane; some may not be swinging the bat appropriately on the backswing or following through. The problem, however, is that children at this age (and many adults, for that matter) can concentrate effectively on only one cue at a time. By focusing on one cue at a time, we heighten the chances that the children will learn this cue (Graham 2008; Rink 2010; Rink and Werner 1989). Once the children are actually using this cue—that is, when they are actually stepping with the lead foot as they swing—we move on to another cue. We may change the task, as suggested in the batting progression in Chapter 26, but the cue remains the same. Or in some cases, the cue remains the same for several different tasks.

Congruent Feedback

Providing specific congruent feedback about students' performance increases the accountability for learning. As the children practice a task, the teacher circulates among them, providing feedback. Again, there are many cues the teacher might provide in the form of feedback. However, we provide specific congruent feedback—that is, feedback directly related to the cues given with the task and nothing else. If a teacher provides such feedback, student performance is then more directed and focused (Belka, Conner, and Bowyer 1991; Graham 2008; Rink 2010; Rink and Werner 1989). For example, during instruction, we might ask the children to think about stepping with the lead foot as they are batting; the feedback we provide, therefore, would be about how they are (or are not) stepping with the opposite foot. We might say:

"Jackie, good step."

"Nick, don't forget to step when you swing."

"Verenda, remember to step."

"Tommy, way to step."

Interestingly, both the children and the teacher seem to benefit from this type of feedback. The children hear a consistent message—and are able to recall and apply the cue. The teacher is able to focus quickly (Chapter 11) on a specific part of a movement while moving among the children rather than attempting to analyze all of the critical elements for every child's batting swing. The feedback analysis checklist (Figure 7.1) is one tool to help you analyze the type of feedback you provide to the children, and the modified checklist in Figure 7.5 helps you analyze to whom you provide it.

Accommodating Individual Differences

We have described a process for developing the content that enables children to truly learn and benefit from physical education lessons (Rink 2010). As you know, however, the process is made even more complicated by the fact that children in our classes have different skill levels and interests. Although we have no magic solutions, we do want to suggest two techniques that can help you to accommodate individual differences within a class—that is, to match the challenge of a task with the ability of the child (Csikszentmihalyi 2000; Graham 2008). We have termed these two techniques teaching by invitation and intratask variation.

Teaching by Invitation

One of the ways a teacher can adjust for individual differences is by inviting the children to decide some parameters of a given task. The teacher makes the statement to the entire class, and each child in the class then decides in which task he or she wants to participate. Teaching by invitation provides children with choice that also increases student responsibility and ownership. The following are examples of teaching by invitation:

"You may want to continue dribbling in self-space, or you may want to begin dribbling and walking in general space."

"Working alone, or with a partner, design a sequence. . . ."

"You may want to continue batting from the tee, or you may want to work with a partner, taking turns pitching a ball to each other."

"You may want to continue striking a ball with your paddle, or you may want to try striking a shuttlecock."

"You decide how far away you want to be from the goal when you kick."

"In groups of two or three, make up a game . . . ."

If you use this technique, you will find that most of the children make intelligent decisions about the tasks in which they choose to participate. As in every instance, there will be a few children who, in your judgment, make questionable decisions. Overall, however, you will find your children will choose tasks that allow them to be successful—and yet tasks that are not too easy (Csikszentmihalyi 2000).

Intratask Variation

Teaching by invitation allows the children to make decisions about the task they prefer to work on. Intratask variation, by contrast, is a technique in which the teacher decides to extend a task for individuals or small groups in the class. The teacher bases this decision on specific knowledge of the children's abilities and interests. Typically, intratask variation is a rather private interaction between one or more children and the teacher, who makes a task easier or harder to better match the children's skill level. The following are examples of intratask variation:

"Eldridge, why don't you try striking a balloon instead of a ball?"

"José, you may want to practice dribbling behind your back and between your legs." (Other children are practicing dribbling and staying in self-space.)

"Gloria and Tanisha, why don't you two make up a partner sequence that has rolling and transferring weight in it." (Other children are practicing rolling in backward directions.)

"I would like the four of you to move over to the next field and make up a game that has kicking and dribbling with your feet in it." (Other children are practicing dribbling with their feet; these four have been playing soccer for several years and are adroit at kicking and foot-dribbling. They move to the other field and quickly begin a two-against-two soccer game.)

Unfortunately, intratask variation is not a 100 percent guaranteed panacea that will allow you to adjust tasks satisfactorily to meet the needs of every child in a class. As with most teaching techniques, intratask variation is effective with some children in some classes some of the time.

A teacher can heighten the potential success of intratask variation by explaining to the children, before using the technique, that sometimes during a lesson, various students will be asked to do different things. Understanding why this is being done—the children are already aware there is a wide range of skill levels in the class—will enable them to realize the teacher is not playing favorites but rather helping them benefit more from physical education class by adjusting tasks for children with differing abilities.

When using intratask variation, the teacher can also make the point that children at the higher skill levels—utilization and proficiency (Chapter 5)—have most likely acquired these skills because of the activities they pursue after school and on weekends. This also provides an excellent opportunity to explain that students at the utilization and proficiency levels for various skill themes have practiced those skills countless times in a variety of settings. In most physical education classes, there is just not enough practice time to attain the top two levels of the generic levels of skill proficiency (GLSP). This explanation will be especially helpful to those youngsters who may be under the mistaken impression that the more skilled youngsters in a class were born that way. They weren't! They have just had more practice.

Whatever the strategy, in order to learn, students must have a focus for the activity and be held accountable for realizing the focus. Without focus and accountability, students will lack motivation, will not learn the intended content, and will begin to behave inappropriately. This classroom learning can be achieved using multiple approaches (see Chapter 10), yet regardless of the approach, the key variables mentioned in this chapter need to be addressed.

Safety

Although teaching safety procedures could logically be included within the managerial component, it is so important that we have chosen to address it separately. We discuss it in generic terms here, but we also include specific safety aspects in each skill theme development chapter: These are coded with the safety icon ⚠.

A major responsibility of every physical education teacher is to provide students with a physically and psychologically safe learning environment (Siedentop and Tannehill 2000). You as a teacher are entrusted with the safety of students in your class. The legal terminology is *in loco parentis.* In other words, when a child is with you, you act in place of the parent. The commonly accepted definition of this type of responsibility is that while a child is in a teacher's care, the teacher should act in a reasonable and responsible manner with respect to the child's welfare and safety. Reasonable behavior has been interpreted by the courts as what one would expect of a person with ordinary intelligence, ordinary perception, ordinary memory (Koehler 1987), and specified academic and professional credentials. This means that teachers are held to the standard of the reasonably prudent "teacher" with all the pertinent credentials and experience this teacher possesses (that is, if teacher X has more than the basic knowledge, certifications, and so on, teacher X is held accountable for that knowledge). Teachers are held to the standard of the reasonably prudent teacher, not that of just any adult.

Elements of Negligence

When a teacher does not act in a reasonably prudent manner, negligence can occur. Negligence has four separate elements—duty, breach of duty, proximate cause, and injury—that all must be met to prove someone is liable.

Duty The first element is established duty. This involves the relationship that exists between a teacher and students. By virtue of being a teacher, we have a duty to the students in our classes.

Breach of Duty Duty requires that teachers maintain a certain standard of care regarding the students in their classes. A teacher is required (1) to anticipate foreseeable risk in any activity; (2) to take reasonable steps to prevent injury; (3) to provide a warning that risk is inherent in the activity; (4) to provide aid to the injured student; and (5) to prevent an increase in the severity of the injury. This standard of care is arrived at through expert testimony and other information that sets standards of practice. If an incident goes to court, the defendant's behavior will be compared to what the "reasonably prudent teacher" would have done in those circumstances to see if there was a breach of the standard of care either through an act of commission (something that was done) or an act of omission (not doing something that should have been done).This is a critical issue because all experts in a field may not always agree upon the accepted standard of care. For example, most would say that children should be warned and taught about the dangers of raising hockey sticks above the waist, but what about playing dodgeball as part of the physical education curriculum? Breach of duty, or of the standard of care, is the second element of negligence.

Proximate Cause The third element of negligence is proximate cause, which means that the teacher's behavior was the cause of the injury. An example might involve a student who has a documented medical problem that precludes participation in certain activities. The teacher requires the student to participate anyway, and the student suffers an injury directly related to the medical problem. What the teacher did was the main factor in the injury.

Injury Injury is the final element of negligence. This element requires that the injury must have occurred because of the breach of duty. For example, if a student falls from gymnastics equipment that has no mats under it and breaks a leg, an injury has occurred. If, however, a student falls under the same circumstances and no injury has occurred, then there is no case for negligence.

Areas in Which Negligence Might Occur

The four elements of negligence might occur in a variety of situations, but the three most common involve facilities and equipment, the conduct of the activity, and supervision.

Facilities and Equipment Two major areas in which facilities and equipment are subject to negligent behavior are (1) upkeep and general safety of the equipment, and (2) facilities and the appropriateness of the equipment for the child. All students have the right to participate in a safe and developmentally appropriate environment. Keeping facilities and equipment safe and in "good working order" is the obvious aspect of this domain. Standards for equipment and facilities are available from most school districts as well as the American Alliance for Health, Physical Education, Recreation and Dance (NASPE 2009). Grounds should be inspected regularly for potential hazards such as sprinkler heads, holes, rocks, and ants. If a facility or equipment needs attention, it can only be attended to if reported. Make sure the right people know what needs to be repaired and follow up on it. The less obvious aspect of this domain is that equipment should be matched to the child—that is, it should be developmentally appropriate. All equipment must be of the appropriate size and weight for the child. Thus in one class you may have multiple types of balls or rackets available to children. For example, to ask most six-year-olds or beginners of any age to use a regulation bat is not appropriate.

Supervision The teacher must be in the room or on the playground with the class and must be paying attention, and there must be enough supervisors for the participants present. This implies that you do not leave during class to do something else, even if it is to get equipment out of the equipment room. When present, teachers must actively observe the class (see Chapter 11) and be cognizant of what is occurring. If misbehavior, off-task behavior, or unsafe behavior exists, teachers have the obligation to respond to such behavior. Have all equipment out before class, and answer phone calls on breaks. In many schools, teachers going outdoors with children now carry walkie-talkies and/or cell phones for emergencies.

Conduct of Activities The conduct of the activity may be the least obvious negligence area. Four aspects are important here: (1) how children are taught to perform the skill, including proper progression; (2) how they are instructed to use equipment; (3) what safety precautions the teacher takes; and (4) whether the inherent risk is explained to the children and whether emergency medical procedures and protocols are developed. The last two aspects of safety and risk are the two that are most often teachers' focus.

Safety precautions need to be stated as part of the general instructions to the children for every activity they undertake. These can be as simple as having students wait until everyone has thrown at a target before collecting the equipment and reminding them to walk around groups when collecting stray equipment; or safety instructions can be more formal, such as posting specific safety rules for activities that involve hockey sticks. Children and parents also need to know the risks involved in physical education classes. This can be done by sending communications home at the beginning of the year so parents can inform teachers of medical conditions of which they should be aware. General safety procedures can easily be taught at the beginning of the school year by incorporating them with other gymnasium rules and routines. These safety procedures must be explained and then taught and practiced.

We've found that special safety procedures that deal with specialized equipment or unique situations are most effectively taught at the time that situation arises. Again, the procedures shouldn't be glossed over; students should thoroughly understand them before you proceed. When specific safety rules are presented and taught, it is again a good time to videotape the teaching—for students who may be absent, for those who tend to forget, or in case of legal action.

It's beneficial to explain why selected behaviors are inappropriate and why safety procedures are necessary. Explaining the possible harmful consequences of actions helps children understand the need for stated practices. As with all ongoing gymnasium rules, the consequences of breaking safety rules must be stated; they might easily be included in the general rules for behavior. The children need to understand that safety is their responsibility as well as the teacher's when activity begins. Student safety should be the first thing the teacher observes for when the children begin a task (see Chapter 11).

The first and second aspects regarding the conduct of activities—how children are taught to perform skills and how they are taught to use equipment—are equally critical. First, children need to be taught the appropriate use of all equipment in class. For example, jump ropes are for jumping over and using as nets but not for slinging around the head as they are picked up.

When equipment is not used appropriately, the risk of injury is far greater. It cannot be assumed that all children know the appropriate use of equipment.

Finally, all children are entitled to instruction that is appropriate. Proper task progressions are critically important to students' safety. A student must possess all the prerequisite skills before beginning a new task. A teacher who skips from the precontrol level to the proficiency level when students are still at the precontrol level, or from tasks to challenges without teaching critical cues, has not followed a proper progression. The teacher, in this case, is simply asking for safety and legal problems. Accurate records of lesson and unit plans allow teachers not only to establish proper progressions, but also to document them. Directions should be clear and thorough to the point that students know exactly what they are to do and how, but not to the point of giving so much information that children are confused. Critical cues need to be provided for each task given, accompanied by an unambiguous demonstration.

Students need to behave safely in a safe environment. They also need to feel safe about what they are doing in class. Students who feel comfortable about what they are doing and are willing to participate fully by experiencing appropriate task progressions tend to behave safely because they are challenged by the task at hand yet feel able to accomplish it.

This is a brief overview of some of the safety and legal issues teachers face. It is not intended as a compendium source. For more information, you may want to read *Sport, Physical Activity, and the Law* (Dougherty, Goldberger, and Carpenter 2007) or *Law for Recreation and Sport Managers* (Cotton, Wolohan, and Wilde 2007). Be sure to check with your school district regarding its safety policies and procedures.

As physical educators, we have always been conscious of safety, but in today's world of increasing legal action against teachers, we simply have to become more cautious and thorough in all that we do. To do anything less risks student injury as well as legal action.

Summary

Establishing a learning environment is essential if a teacher is to have an effective physical education program. The learning environment consists of two components: the managerial component and the instructional component. The managerial component involves all noninstructional activities, and the instructional component involves all activities designed to increase student learning. The teacher's attitude and beliefs permeate both components. The types of components that are set up are a direct reflection of the teacher's attitudes and beliefs about children, education, and physical education. Figure 8.5, which unscrambles the activities that were part of the Wordle at the beginning of this chapter, may help you to visualize the components of establishing a learning environment. Designing components that (1) involve students in decision making, (2) view children as capable and able, and (3) are consistent with clear learning expec-

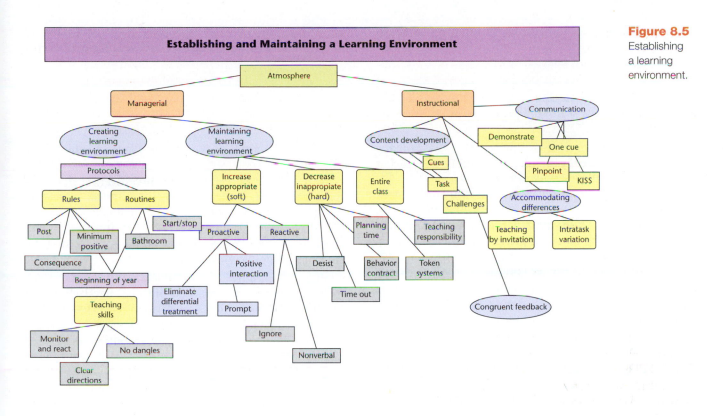

Figure 8.5
Establishing a learning environment.

tations and appropriate tasks usually creates an environment conducive to student learning and eliminates much off-task behavior. The teacher does not have to be a police officer and can really teach so children gain the skills, knowldeges, and dispositions to be active for a lifetime.

Sample Web Site

PE Central, a physical education Web site with a plethora of information on all aspects of physical education, including classroom management ideas. www.pecentral.org.

Reading Comprehension Questions

1. What is meant by the phrase, "Management is a necessary, though not sufficient, condition for learning"?
2. What are the two major components in the establishment of a learning environment, and how do they differ from each other?
3. What is discipline? How does discipline differ from establishing a learning environment?
4. How do teachers' beliefs about children impact the learning environment?
5. What is the role of atmosphere in establishing a learning environment?
6. Describe and explain the three aspects that contribute to a productive teacher–student relationship. What are your thoughts on their importance and seemingly contradictory nature?
7. What are protocols? What two aspects make up protocols, and how do they differ?

8. What are three activities you can use to teach children to listen in a physical education environment?
9. List five guidelines for establishing rules of behavior in the gymnasium.
10. What four things can a teacher do to help students learn protocols?
11. Why are the first lessons of the year so important? List five suggestions for those lessons.
12. Identify and describe three aspects of teaching protocols.
13. Define developing the content, and explain why it is an important part of teaching physical education.
14. Why is providing cues an important teaching skill for physical education teachers? What might be the result when a teacher provides no cues or does so ineffectively?

15. As a teacher, do you think you are more likely to use teaching by invitation or intratask variation? Explain your answer.

16. What are the four aspects of negligence, and in what areas of teaching are they most likely to occur?

References/Suggested Readings

Belka, D., K. Conner, and G. Bowyer, G. 1991, January. Quality and congruency of task presentations and teacher verbal feedback in preservice peer teaching episodes. Paper presented at the International Association for Physical Education in Higher Education World Congress, Atlanta.

Belka, D., and C. Short. 1991, January. Implementing a content sequencing model in physical education instruction. Paper presented at the International Association for Physical Education in Higher Education World Congress, Atlanta.

Brooks, D.M. 1985. The first day of school. *Educational Leadership* 42(8): 76–78.

Brophy, J., and C. Evertson. 1976. *Learning from teaching: A developmental perspective.* Boston: Allyn & Bacon.

Brophy, J., and T. Good. 1986. Teacher behavior and student achievement. In *Handbook of research on teaching,* 7th ed, ed. M. Wittrock, 328–75. New York: Holt, Rinehart & Winston.

Csikszentmihalyi, M. 2000. *Beyond boredom and anxiety: Experiencing flow in work and play.* San Francisco: Jossey-Bass.

Cotton, D. J., J. T. Wolohan, and T. J. Wilde. 2007. *Law for recreation and sport managers.* 4th ed. Dubuque, IA: Kendall/Hunt.

Deutsch, D. 1999. *The coaching club.* Master's thesis. University of North Dakota, Grand Forks.

Dougherty, N. J., A. S. Goldberger, and L. J. Carpenter. 2007. *Sport, physical activity, and the law.* 3rd ed. Champaign, IL: Sagamore Publications.

Doyle, W. 1979. Making managerial decisions in classrooms. In *Classroom management: Seventy-eighth yearbook of the National Society for the Study of Education,* Part 2, ed. D. L. Duke. Chicago: University of Chicago Press.

Doyle, W. 1980. Student mediating responses in teaching effectiveness. Denton: North Texas State University. (ERIC Document Reproduction Service No. ED 187 698.)

Dyson, B, (2006). Students' perspectives of physical education. In *Handbook of physical education,* ed. D. Kirk, D., Macdonald, and M. O'Sullivan, 326–46. London: Sage.

Ennis, C. 1995. Teachers' responses to noncompliant students: The realities and consequences of a negotiated curriculum. *Teaching and Teacher Education* 11(5): 445–60.

Evertson, C., E. Emmer, and M. Worsham. 2009. *Classroom management for elementary teachers.* 7th ed. Boston: Allyn & Bacon.

Fink, J., and D. Siedentop. 1989. The development of routines, rules, and expectations at the start of the school year. *Journal of Teaching in Physical* Education 8 (3): 198–221.

Galvan, C., and M. Parker. 2011. Investigating the reciprocal nature of service-learning in physical education teacher education. *Journal of Experiential Education* 34(1): 55–70.

Graham, G. 2008. *Teaching children physical education.* 3rd ed. Champaign, IL: Human Kinetics.

Graham, K. C., K. Hussey, K. Taylor, and P. Werner. 1993. A study of verbal presentations of three effective teachers [Abstract]. *Research Quarterly for Exercise and Sport* 64: 87A.

Hastie, P., and D. Siedentop. 2007. The classroom ecology paradigm. In *Handbook of physical education,* ed. D. Kirk, D. Macdonald, and M. O'Sullivan, 214–25. London: Sage.

Helion, J. 1996. If we build it, they will come: Creating an emotionally safe physical education environment. *Journal of Physical Education, Recreation and Dance* 67 (6): 40–44.

Hellison, D. 2011. *Teaching personal and social responsibility through physical activity.* 3rd ed. Champaign, IL: Human Kinetics.

Herbel, K., and M. Parker. 1995. Same story, different setting: A case study of a program for at-risk youth. Paper presented at the Northern Rocky Mountain Educational Research Convention, Jackson Hole, WY.

Jones, V., and L. Jones. 2010. *Comprehensive classroom management: Creating positive learning environments and solving problems.* 9th ed. Boston: Pearson.

Koehler, R. W. 1987. *Law, sport activity and right management.* Champaign, IL: Stipes.

Krouscas, J. 1996. No substitute for the first day of school. *Strategies* 10(1): 5–8.

Martinek, T. 1988. Confirmation of the teacher expectancy model: Student perceptions and causal attributions of teacher behavior. *Research Quarterly for Exercise and Sport* 59: 118–26.

Marzano, R. J., and J. S. Marzano. 2003. The key to classroom management. *Educational Leadership* 61(1): 6–13.

Mowling, C., K. Eider, S. Brock, and M. Rudisill. 2004. Student motivation in physical education. *Journal of Physical Education, Recreation and Dance* 75(6): 40–45.

[NASPE] National Association for Sport and Physical Education. 2004. *Moving into the future: National standards for physical education.* 2nd ed. St. Louis, MO: Mosby.

[NASPE] National Association for Sport and Physical Education. 2009. *Appropriate instructional practice guidelines for elementary school physical education.* 3rd ed. Reston, VA: National Association for Sport and Physical Education.

Parker, M., J. Kallusky, and D. Hellison. 1999. High impact, low risk: Ten strategies to teach responsibility in physical education. *Journal of Physical Education, Recreation and Dance* 70(2): 26–28.

Parker, M., and J. Stiehl. 2010. Teaching personal and social responsibility. In *Standards based curriculum development*, 2nd ed., ed. D. Tannehill and J. Lund, 163–91. Boston: Jones & Bartlett.

Rink, J. 2010. *Teaching physical education for learning*. 6th ed. New York: McGraw-Hill.

Rink, J. E., and P. H. Werner. 1989. Qualitative measures of teaching performance scale (QMTPS). In *Analyzing physical education and sport instruction*, 2nd ed., ed. P. W. Darst, D. B. Zakrasjeck, and V.H. Mancini, 269–76. Champaign, IL: Human Kinetics.

Sagor, R. 2002. Lessons from skateboarders. *Educational Leadership* 60(1): 34–38.

Siedentop, D., and D. Tannehill. 2000. *Developing teaching skills in physical education*. 4th ed. New York: McGraw-Hill.

Stiehl, J. 2011. *Course outline SES 338: Teaching diverse populations*. Greeley, CO: University of Northern Colorado, School of Sport and Exercise Science.

Stiehl, J., G. S. Morris, and C. Sinclair. 2008. *Teaching physical activity: Change, challenge, choice*. Champaign, IL: Human Kinetics.

Tousignant, M., and D. Siedentop. 1983. The analysis of task structures in physical education. *Journal of Teaching in Physical Education* 3(1): 45–57.

Ward S., and M. Parker. 2009. *Atmosphere in a positive youth development program: A youth perspective*. Presented at the annual meeting of the American Alliance of Physical Education, Recreation, and Dance, Baltimore, MD.

Xiang, P., R. McBride, and J. Guan. 2004. Children's motivation in elementary physical education: A longitudinal study. *Research Quarterly for Exercise and Sport* 75(1): 71–80.

Maintaining Appropriate Behavior

The word *freedom* can never be uttered unless accompanied hand in hand with the word *responsibility*. It is kinder to keep the lid on the school for a start, lifting it little by little, simultaneously teaching responsibility, until the time comes when the lid can be cast entirely aside and only two conditions remain—freedom and responsibility.

—Sylvia Ashton Warner

Key Concepts

- Maintaining the established learning environment is something that must be consciously cultivated.

- Appropriate behavior is not the mere absence of inappropriate behavior.

- If a learning environment is not effective, before blaming the students, assess your teaching behaviors to see if your actions have contributed to the nonfunctioning environment.

- Three hierarchical aspects are paramount to maintaining a learning environment: increasing appropriate behavior, decreasing inappropriate behavior, and dealing with whole-class problems.

- Both proactive and reactive strategies can be used to increase appropriate behavior.

- Proactive strategies include positive interaction with children, prompting correct responses, and eliminating differential treatment of students.

- Behavior problems can be classified as a nonproblem, minor problem, major problem, or escalating problem.

- Ignoring inappropriate behavior when it is inconsequential or a nonproblem, keen use of nonverbal interactions, and person-to-person dialogue are strategies that allow teachers to appropriately react to student behavior.

- To decrease inappropriate behavior, teachers can use desists, positive practice, time-outs, planning time, behavior contracts, letters to parents, and, as a last resort, can involve the principal.

- Entire class behavior can be maintained by developing personal and social responsibility, class rewards, and token systems.

- A variety of teaching strategies can be used to maintain the class environment.

Helping children learn to be accountable for their behavior is one of the least enjoyable tasks of teaching or one of the most exciting. Regardless, it is something that all teachers must do. The notion that only poor teachers have to hold children accountable is simply not accurate; it is all in how it is done that makes the difference. Holding children accountable is less likely to be a problem when effective managerial and instructional task components are in place and children have learned to take responsibility for their own actions and learning.

Consistently maintaining the environment designed for the class is second only to establishing it.

Some call this discipline, but the word *discipline* has so many varied, and mostly negative, connotations that we have chosen to avoid it. Discipline most often implies punishing some type of inappropriate behavior. That, for us, is the last resort. From our viewpoint, establishing and maintaining an environment supportive of learning is a more positive and appropriate perspective. We follow a positive approach to dealing with inappropriate behavior and attitudes that lets a teacher both create a positive atmosphere and teach students appropriate behavior for the gymnasium. In such a situation, the teacher's primary tasks are, first, to employ techniques that create the likelihood of appropriate behavior and, second, to use techniques that reduce inappropriate behavior.

We define appropriate behavior as student behavior that is consistent with the educational goals of a specific educational setting (Siedentop and Tannehill 2000) Appropriate behavior is not the mere absence of inappropriate behavior; rather, it is a set of behaviors or actions. These positive behaviors or actions must replace the inappropriate behavior.

It's normal for all teachers to be concerned about how to hold students accountable for what they are supposed to do. Our experiences with beginning and experienced teachers, as well as our own teaching experiences, suggest that most teachers ask themselves questions about responding to student behavior. The difference between so-called good teachers and poor teachers is not their concern about holding children accountable—all teachers encounter deviant and disruptive behavior and must find ways of dealing with it. Rather, successful teachers are able to minimize the amount of time they devote to dealing with inappropriate behavior and do so in a largely positive manner.

Even the teacher who develops managerial and instructional components, establishes and explains rules of behavior, prompts and provides feedback for appropriate behavior, and teaches with a critical demandingness can't be sure that a class will perform as expected. In many classes, there will be some children who find it difficult to function in a school environment, not only in physical education, but in other classes as well. Occasionally an entire class has difficulty adhering to the established behavioral boundaries.

Whether it is one, several, or most of the children who are unable to abide by the rules, your first response might be to examine your performance as a teacher. When children react in unexpected ways, you may, upon reflection, find that their reactions are justified. Children are incredibly honest; two of the top three reasons they list for misbehavior are (1) the lesson was boring or (2) they didn't think they could do the activities in the lesson, so they didn't try (Cothran and Kulinna 2007). A teacher may not want to know or believe that a lesson is a dud, but the children will let the teacher know. Occasionally it's the teacher's behavior, rather than the children's, that needs to be changed. For example, when children have problems with equipment or don't understand or hear the teacher's directions, they will participate at their own level, doing their own thing rather than ask for help. Likewise, if a task is too boring, too hard, or too easy, children will often change the task to meet their needs. Therefore it doesn't look like the task that the teacher gave, and the children will be perceived as off task.

> The class proceeded through its parody of education, following a formula validated in a thousand classrooms I have visited and countless thousands I have not. The first step in the formula is an assumption, an untested hypothesis which becomes valid merely because (and as soon as) it is assumed. Children who do not easily take the imprint of their teacher's own education and values, who are not ductile enough to be drawn wire-thin so that they may slip through traditional holes in the fabric of society—these are not "promising children" and the best that can be hoped for from them is good behavior (silence) and early withdrawal (dropout). Since silence is their most positive attribute, they should be left unmolested during the class hour so long as they practice that virtue.
>
> Perhaps worst of all the many dreadful aspects of this assumption is that the children know it. They know—and will tell you, as they told me, if they are asked—that a few of them are regarded as "good material" and the rest are nothing: "ever' time I go to her class, she make me feel like I was nothin'." Snapper, Rubbergut's half brother, said it. He said it for all the children who drown in the well of silence.
>
> —Daniel Fader, The Naked Children (1971)

If you determine that the lesson is appropriate and your performance as a teacher is satisfactory, you can then look for other causes for disruptive behavior. Try not to view disruptive behavior as a personal affront. A first step is to assess the behavior. Evertson, Emmer, and Worsham (2009) describe four possible categories of disruptive behavior: nonproblem, minor problem, major problem but limited in scope and effects, and escalating or spreading problem.

A nonproblem is a behavior that any attempt to react to it would consume too much energy and interrupt

the lesson and detract from the classroom atmosphere. A minor problem includes those things that run counter to classroom protocols but do not, when occurring infrequently, disrupt the class activities or seriously interfere with other students' learning. These behaviors are minor irritants as long as they are limited to a few students and are brief; we would not give them much attention except that, unattended, they might persist and spread. Not responding might cause an appearance of inconsistency and potentially undermine the management component, and student learning might be adversely affected. A major problem includes activities that interfere with others' learning. The occurrence may be limited to a single student or perhaps a few students not acting in concert. Major escalating problems constitute a threat to the learning environment. Table 9.1 lists examples of each type of problem.

Having assessed the behavior, you can deal with it in two phases: reacting appropriately in the short term and seeking to understand the cause in the long term. The remainder of this chapter is largely about short-term responses, as the behavior must be addressed before seeking a long-term solution. Once short-term behaviors are addressed, effective teachers

Table 9.1 Levels of Management Issues

Level	Examples
Nonproblem	• Brief periods of inattention • Short pauses while working • Standing at the back of the group while others are sitting • A little talking while others are talking • Occasionally not immediately stopping on the signal
Minor Problem	• Excessive talking during group work • Running to get equipment after being asked to walk • Excessive playing with equipment when it should be held • Inappropriate language • Interrupting • Lying
Major Problem	• Constant movement around the space • Refusal to participate • Violation of school rules • Fighting • Unsafe actions
Major Escalating Problem	• Roaming around at will; leaving the space • Constant interference with others • Blatant refusal to cooperate

will individually address long-term causes and solutions, if needed, to create a student-centered learning environment.

Comparing a referee's or an umpire's job with the teacher's need to hold children accountable places a teacher's job in perspective. Those referees that players and coaches respect share the following characteristics: they're fair, consistent, accurate, and not emotionally involved. As teachers, we should keep these good characteristics in mind as we reflect on how to help children work within our guidelines. Although a referee's job is probably less enjoyable than a player's or coach's, it's an important aspect of organized sport. Similarly, maintaining the learning environment is an important role for a teacher. In physical education, as in sports, there will be violations and infractions.

Our goal is to help children become intrinsically motivated so they can benefit from and enjoy physical activity. In some situations this motivation will occur naturally, and thus few of the techniques described will be necessary. In other teaching situations, however, many of the techniques will be needed. In either case, the goal is to use fewer and fewer of these techniques so the children participate in physical education because they like it and feel it is valuable rather than because of an external reward or motivator. Our explanation of effective techniques for helping children work within our guidelines is divided into three steps: increasing appropriate behavior, decreasing inappropriate behavior, and maintaining whole-class appropriate behavior. Remember, your action as a teacher should match the magnitude of the problem. Overreacting will soon result in a negative class atmosphere and be similar to "crying wolf"—children will cease to respond. Underreacting creates an atmosphere of physical and psychological unsafety and nonlearning.

Increasing Appropriate Behavior

When behavior doesn't conform to the expectations established for the specific setting, a teacher's first strategy would likely be to increase appropriate behavior. Six techniques teachers have found useful for increasing appropriate behavior are positive interaction, eliminating differential treatment, prompting, ignoring inappropriate behavior, nonverbal teacher interactions, and person-to-person dialogue. Most of these techniques would be considered soft skills because they are noninvasive and subtle. Three of the techniques are proactive—that is, they are to be used in the absence of

inappropriate behavior. The other three are reactive, to be used in response to inappropriate behavior.

Proactive Strategies

Teachers can use many techniques to increase the likelihood of students behaving appropriately. Many of these can be done proactively to increase the chances that appropriate behavior will prevail and that the atmosphere of the gymnasium remains positive.

Positive Interaction   As discussed in Chapter 8, one of the most powerful things a teacher can do to create an environment where students want to be is to make the gymnasium a positive place. One of the most convincing ways to create a positive environment is to interact with students positively when they behave appropriately. In essence, this approach emphasizes the positive rather than the negative. Many children who are known throughout the school as discipline problems have become accustomed to hearing nothing but negative comments about their behavior. Catching them in the act of doing something right and praising them for it can dramatically change their behavior (Siedentop and Tannehill 2000).

But praise shouldn't be contrived and meaningless, offered with no genuine feeling, as is often the case. Give praise frequently but not so profusely that it seems trivial. And give it only when a child actually displays appropriate behavior. All children are capable of receiving some type of praise—catch them being good!

This sounds like common sense, but research and our experiences have shown that this isn't the prevalent mode of operation in the gym. In 1984, Siedentop and Taggart wrote that "punitive and corrective interaction" were the most frequent forms of communication (105). Almost 20 years later, it was found that although teachers espoused a positive form of classroom management, they relied almost exclusively on rewards and punishment (Cothran, Kulinna, and Garrahy 2003). In other words, little has changed. You can stand at many gymnasium doors and hear statements such as, "I'm waiting for you!" "*Ssshh!*" "Ben, whenever you sit down, we'll start," or "Kate, carry the ball." Although these statements aren't openly negative, they in fact reinforce certain children's inappropriate behavior and ignore the appropriate behavior of a large majority of students. They are what might be called nagging behaviors. The following list includes examples of positive verbal and nonverbal interactions. For an idea of how you're doing, have a student make a simple tally of your interactions or videotape a class and critique your own behavior.

Verbal Positive Statements	Nonverbal Positive Interactions
Good	High five
Terrific	Smiling
Right	Clapping
Nice job	Thumbs up
Way to go	Winking
That's it	Pat on the back
Thank you	Shaking hands
Great	Giving an OK sign
You did it this time	Fist bumping
Beautiful	
Excellent	
Nicely done	
OK	
All right	

	Name called	Reprimand	Positive Interaction
Juan	III	I	II
Sue			
Rich	II	I	I
Jesse			
Don	ЖГ IIII	IIII	ЖГ
Billie	I		I

Figure 9.1 Chart for identifying differential treatment of students.

● *Eliminating Differential Treatment* Often a stranger can walk into a classroom and after a few minutes pick out the "discipline problems" or the "really good ones" in a group of children he or she has never seen before. Frequently these are the children whose names the teacher is constantly calling out: "Rico, are you listening?" "Sarah, sit down, please," or "Brady, that's great," "Abby, you're awesome." It is not uncommon to see the same children singled out repeatedly. Typically they are masters of their craft—they know exactly how far they can go without actually being held accountable, or conversely, they know exactly what to do to gain the teacher's praise. Because they covet adult attention, these children persist in their behavior (and as long as we reinforce their behavior by acknowledging it, they become even more skilled at it). So, avoid singling out these children whenever possible.

> *Every person needs recognition. It is expressed cogently by the lad who says, "Mother, let's play darts. I'll throw the darts and you say 'Wonderful.'"*
>
> —DALE BAUGHMAN

One way to spot differential treatment of students in your classes is to audio-record a few lessons. This can be done by placing an audio recorder in the gymnasium, attached to your arm, or in a pocket. (This observation and analysis technique is discussed further in Chapter 7.) After you've taped several lessons, listen to the tapes and record the number of times you call each child's name and the number of reprimands as well as positive comments you give to individual children.

A simple way to record your tally is to use a copy of the class roster that has three columns to the right of

the names (Figure 9.1). The first column is a tally for each time you call a child's name; the second column is a tally for each time you reprimand or interact negatively with a specific child; the third column is for tallying positive comments or interactions. After you complete your tallies, if you find that you single out the same few children and/or interact positively or negatively with a select few, you know you need to change your teaching behavior.

● *Prompting* Prompting is a teacher behavior that reminds students what is expected of them. Some teachers find themselves prompting appropriate behavior only after inappropriate behavior has occurred. However, this is not the most effective way to use prompts. Prompts should be used as a positive tool as often as possible rather than as a negative interaction. For example, it is more beneficial to say, "Remember to walk as you go to pick up equipment" than "I told you to walk!" or even "Can't you remember by now that you are supposed to walk?" Used as in the first statement, prompting is a proactive response rather than a reactive response. Remember, many of the behaviors you want students to demonstrate are learned (just like motor skills), so initially you should prompt students frequently about what behavior is appropriate; later, you will probably need to prompt only when a new or different situation arises.

Talking to Equipment

A teacher recently shared with us a creative and effective way to prompt students toward appropriate use of equipment: talking to the equipment. When a youngster finds it hard to hold equipment still or place it on the floor, the instructor simply picks up the piece of equipment and directs the appropriate behavior and his comments toward the equipment. For example, he might pick up the hockey stick and say, "I thought we agreed that you were supposed to be on the floor while I was talking. So that others can hear and I can talk, I really need you to be on the floor. Do you understand?" He says the children think he is a bit crazy, but it works.

Reactive Approaches

Interacting positively, eliminating differential treatment, and prompting are all proactive strategies for increasing appropriate behavior and thus are a means of preventing inappropriate behavior before it happens. The three strategies that follow are reactive strategies designed to increase appropriate behavior. They are intended for use after the inappropriate behavior has occurred—as a means of reacting to it. Ignoring inappropriate behavior and using nonverbal interactions and person-to-person dialogue are strategies teachers can use as responses to inappropriate behavior; each is designed to increase appropriate behavior, especially when the problem is a nonproblem or minor problem.

Ignoring Inappropriate Behavior The opposite of emphasizing appropriate behavior with positive interactions is ignoring inappropriate behavior. Many of us find that praising appropriate behavior is hard, but ignoring inappropriate behavior is even more difficult. Inappropriate behavior can be ignored as a nonproblem when it meets the following three criteria:

1. It is of short duration and is not likely to spread or persist.
2. It is a minor deviation.
3. Reacting to it would interrupt a lesson or call attention to the behavior.

Student behaviors that could be ignored in a physical education setting include occasional calling out during discussions, brief whispering, short periods of inattentiveness or nonpractice, and occasional continuation of activity after the stop signal. Unless a behavior is harmful to other students, causes a safety problem, or seriously disrupts other students, reacting to it would consume too much of your energy, interrupt your lessons constantly, and detract from your classroom climate.

To be completely effective, teachers should ignore minor inappropriate behavior and simultaneously praise appropriate behavior. Yet, when we've become accustomed to saying, "*Ssshh!*" "Hurry up!" "I'm waiting for

you to get quiet," or "Tommy!!!" it's not easy to change to phrases such as, "Jody was quiet when she heard the stop signal," "Terrific, you were ready to go in 10 seconds today," and "Jimmy, you showed thoughtfulness when you helped Jay up after he fell down." Such interactions, which can create appropriate behaviors in children, imply for many of us that the teacher is letting Tommy or the students who aren't yet quiet get away with inappropriate behavior. This is risky because the perceived implication is that our control is in jeopardy. In reality, the teacher who ignores simple inappropriate behavior while praising appropriate behavior is teaching children what desired behavior is while creating an atmosphere that is warm and conducive to learning.

There's a subtle message about what merits attention in this scenario of praising appropriate and ignoring inappropriate behavior. If a teacher instead used both sets of examples (praising appropriate behavior and reacting verbally to inappropriate behavior) described in the previous paragraph, the students would receive a message of confusion. Students would assume they could receive reinforcement and adult attention for either appropriate or inappropriate behavior.

For many of us, ignoring inappropriate behavior is uncomfortable and awkward. A good way to assess your skill in praising the good and ignoring the inappropriate is to audio-record your lessons and count the number of times you say something positive and the number of times you say something negative. Remember, even little things such as "Hurry up!" and "*Ssshh!*" count as negative interactions. Don't be surprised at what you first discover about your behavior; look at it as an opportunity to improve.

Nonverbal Teacher Interactions A number of simple nonverbal techniques are often sufficient to prompt appropriate student behavior when the behavior is a minor problem. Sometimes just the physical proximity of the teacher will solicit the desirable behavior from some students. For example, when giving directions or speaking to the class as a whole, the teacher merely stands near the student displaying inappropriate behavior. Another technique for increasing appropriate behavior is to borrow the equipment the student is using for purposes of demonstration. Finally, even less obvious actions often work. For example, simple eye contact or a signal, such as nodding the head, will redirect the student.

Person-to-Person Dialogue Another successful technique for increasing appropriate behavior with minor problems is the person-to-person dialogue. Arrange a time to meet with a child away from the class (though not immediately before or after). You might

Person-to-person dialogue allows a teacher to know students individually.

lecture, accuse, or blame a child is strong, but succumbing to this temptation is the quickest way to destroy rapport between student and teacher. If a child trusts you enough to talk candidly about personal concerns but you threaten or lecture, communication ceases. Many children—especially those who need individual attention the most—have been betrayed before, so they're likely to be sensitive and wary. Use of teacher power in this situation reinforces a child's belief that teachers are untrustworthy and that being honest only gets him or her into more trouble.

Some children never want to participate in physical education class. A person-to-person dialogue is often helpful here, as is a conference with the child's other teachers. Some children may be afraid of participating in physical activity because they've already had unsatisfactory experiences at home or on the playground. Other children may have "issues" with classmates that are easily manifested in activity-oriented settings. Still others may be unmotivated and antisocial. Regardless, if a child has a legitimate reason, we respect the child and attempt to create a satisfactory alternative. Further, if a child is unmotivated and/or antisocial, person-to-person dialogue can act as a beginning point for seeking a solution to a problem that may be beyond physical education. Transferring the child to another physical education class or arranging a one-to-one teaching situation often leads, in time, to participation with the regular class. Forcing a child to participate in physical education classes without first understanding the reason for the reluctance may not be in the child's best interests. Once you understand why a child is reluctant to participate, you can make an informed decision about the most appropriate action.

say to the child, "Robby, you don't seem to be enjoying our physical education class. I'd like you to come to my office after school today so that we can talk about it." The purpose of this meeting is to determine the reasons for the child's behavior in your class. This is not a time for a lecture; instead, it should be an open and honest conversation between teacher and student. We've found that a statement such as the following enables many children to begin a discussion of their concerns: "Robby, I'd like to talk to you about physical education class. Is there something I do that bothers you?"

This statement takes the focus off the child and places it on the teacher. Many children are quite candid about what's bothering them. Remember, this is a dialogue. Explaining to the child something about how and why you teach is constructive and often productive. Lecturing the child about behavior or threatening the child with future punishments is counterproductive. This dialogue is not teacher-to-child but person-to-person. Often the temptation to

Decreasing Inappropriate Behavior

Although our first approach in dealing with inappropriate behavior is to attempt to increase appropriate behavior, this doesn't always work. At times, with major problems or with those behaviors that may escalate into major problems, a teacher must decrease inappropriate behavior. When this is necessary, the teacher should have a repertoire of strategies—often called hard skills because they are deliberate and obvious—available. Teachers in physical education have found the following techniques useful: positive practice, desists, time-outs, planning time, behavior contracts, letters to parents, and involving the principal. Note that many of the techniques fit the psychological definition of the term *punishment*—they decrease the likelihood of an inappropriate behavior recurring by applying undesirable consequences to the behavior. To make these techniques effective, be sure that your class rules have first been established, taught, and learned. Afterward, punish the behavior and not the child; always maintain self-control without publically confronting the student. Also, any action the teacher takes to decrease inappropriate behavior should be accompanied by actions to build appropriate behavior.

Nowhere in our discussion will you find strategies that advocate physical exercise as a technique to reduce inappropriate behavior. Physical activity (sit-ups, push-ups, running laps, etc.) should never be used as a technique to hold children accountable for their behavior. Besides being deemed an inappropriate practice by professional organizations like the National Association for Sport and Physical Education (NASPE 2009), using physical activity as punishment is counterproductive to what we want to happen as a result of physical education. Our goal is for children to acquire the skills and desire to be physically active for a lifetime. Using physical activity as punishment may temporarily reduce the off-task behavior being punished, but the long-term result is often the reduction of any participation in the physical activity used as punishment. Instead of learning to love activity, children will hate activity because of its association with punishment. Following are techniques that can be used to react to inappropriate behavior in an attempt to reduce and eliminate it.

Positive Practice

Positive practice is a technique that requires the student, group, or class to practice the acceptable or desired behavior after the demonstration of an inappropriate behavior. For example, students are asked to walk and get equipment but they run instead. Most of us would remind them to walk or ignore the behavior. An acceptable way to have them learn to walk is positive practice. Stop the students and have them go back to where they started and repeat the activity of getting equipment—this time walking. You may even have them repeat it several times. Do this every time students run when you say "walk," and soon they will learn to walk.

Inappropriate Physical Education Practices

The document *Appropriate Instructional Practice Guidelines for Elementary School Physical Education* (NASPE 2009) refers to using physical exercise as punishment in the following way:

Component: Exercise as Punishment
Inappropriate Practice: Teachers use activities/exercises (e.g., run laps, perform push-ups) to punish misbehavior.

Desists

Sometimes it is impossible to ignore inappropriate behavior, especially when safety is an issue. When that is the case, one of the most common and useful ways to react to the behavior is with a desist, a verbal statement that tells a child to stop doing something. Using desists effectively can result in behavior change. Kounin (1970) established several conditions that must be present for a desist to be effective:

- A desist must be clear. "Ellen, stop doing that" isn't enough. The desist must contain exact information about what the student is doing wrong. For example, "Ellen, stop hitting the basketball with the tennis racket" is clear and specific. The student knows exactly what she is doing wrong.

- A desist must be firm. Firmness is the degree to which the teacher follows through on the desist, making sure the student knows that the teacher means what was said. Brooks (1985) found that teachers who giggled or laughed after they delivered desists weren't taken seriously. Moving a bit closer to the student, momentarily looking the student in the eyes, and keeping a straight face when delivering the desist all communicate the teacher's firmness.

- A desist must be well timed. The behavior must desist immediately before it's allowed to spread to other students and before a child forgets what was done.

- A desist must be appropriately targeted. It must be directed at the original offender, not a second or third party.

- A desist must not be harsh. Kounin found that rough desists simply upset children and weren't effective. Firmness doesn't mean harshness or punitiveness; it is simply meaning what you say.

Time-outs

A time-out is much like a penalty box in hockey. However, unlike the penalty box, our use of time-outs is designed to help children take responsibility for their own behavior and thus may differ slightly from what you have been accustomed to. During a time-out, a child, either through choice or at the teacher's request, withdraws from class until ready to return and function according to the class rules. When ready to return to class, the child simply rejoins the activity. Teach the time-out procedure with all other procedures at the beginning of the year so you can subsequently give a time-out as a standard penalty without disrupting the

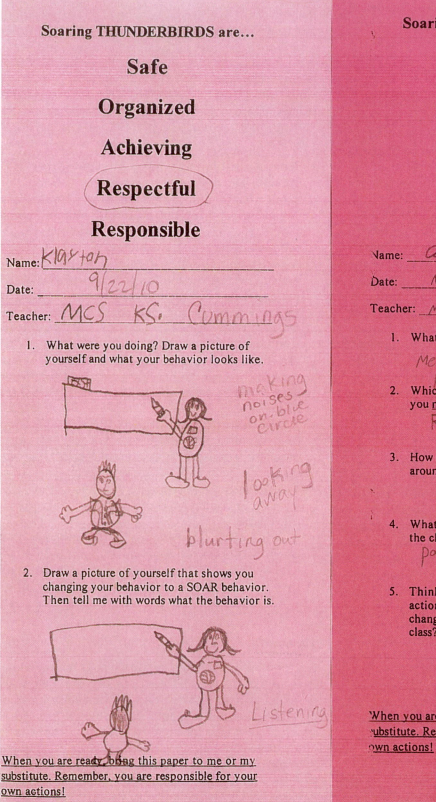

Figure 9.2 (a) Left: Time-out reflection form for lower grades. (b) Right: Time-out reflection form for upper grades.
Source: Karla Drury, Shawsheen Elementary School, Greeley, CO. Used with permission.

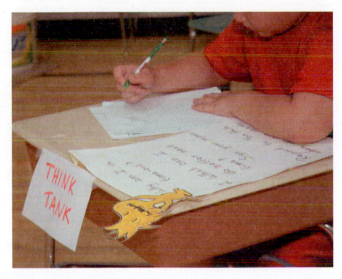

A time-out temporarily removes a child who is off task from activity.

rest of the class. Here are some other considerations for effective use of time-outs:

- The student must find physical education enjoyable; if not, the time-out may be a reward instead of a punishment.
- The time-out area should be a clearly designated place where social contact with classmates isn't possible.
- To make time-outs designed to enhance student responsibility and decision making, we advocate a four-step progressive approach. The first time a student displays a behavior that might result in a time-out, prompt him or her toward what is appropriate. The second time, ask if the student needs a time-out. (Some children are amazingly honest here.) If they elect to go to time-out, they can return when ready. The third step in the sequence is, "You need a time-out." Once again, students can return when they are ready. The fourth step is not only, "You need a time-out," but the student needs to stay there until a conversation between the teacher and the child can take place.

Some teachers have developed a version of time-out that allows students to reflect on their behavior. In these situations, students react in written format to what they did and what they should do. Younger students may draw their time-out reflections and the teacher then writes what the drawing means when talking to the child (Figure 9.2a); older students often write theirs (Figure 9.2b). While this strategy removes the child from activity for a longer amount of time, the results are that the child rarely ends up in time-out again.

Planning Time

Planning time (DeLine 1991; Horrocks 1978) is a peer-directed alternative to time-outs. It is designed for inappropriate behavior involving two students interacting with one another. When students sit alone, as in a time-out, they do not have the opportunity to discuss or resolve their problems. Planning time, by contrast, gives students who do not demonstrate appropriate behavior a chance to resolve their conflict. During planning time, students who have conflicts go to a small area of the gymnasium designated as the "planning area," where they are required to sit together and develop a resolution. To be allowed to rejoin class, they must present the teacher with a verbal (or written) plan on how to work together or how to change their behavior. In other words, No Plan, No Play!

Be aware that, as with any educational strategy, students need to be taught how to use planning time effectively. Cues and questions (Box 9-1) can be posted on the wall or on a written sheet similar to the ones used in time-out to prompt students toward appropriate behavior (Figure 9.2a and Figure 9.2b). Students can then read and review the prompts to assess the nature of their behavior and develop an alternative. Essentially, planning time allows students who are "in trouble" to get "out of trouble." As with any new technique, learning to do it takes time, but the result is a class that cooperates more and students who learn to resolve their differences.

Behavior Contracts

Have you ever tried to lose weight by making a "deal" with yourself or by rewarding yourself at the end of losing so many pounds? The same is true with some isolated children in your class: They need a written "deal" with the teacher as a prompt to make things happen. A behavior contract provides that. It is a written agreement between a student and the teacher regarding behavior in the physical education setting. Although it may seem like overkill, a contract can be done quietly, simply, and privately to provide some

Figure 9.3 Typical behavior contract.

BEHAVIOR CONTRACT

Kim Thomas and Mr. Diller agree that the following plan will be in effect for the next two weeks.

Starting date _____ Ending date _____

Kim will

1. Not interrupt other students' work by trying to knock their equipment away

2. Not disturb class by talking while the teacher is talking

3. Participate in all activities and try hard to improve her skills in throwing

Mr. Diller will

1. Give Kim individual help on throwing

2. Count one point for each day that Kim meets the three points stated above

3. Let Kim help with the physical education equipment for one week if she earns five points during the two weeks of the contract

Signed _____

_____

_____

---

students with the necessary focus to enjoy physical education and allow others to enjoy it.

The contract includes a statement of the desired behavior, the conditions (how much, for how long), and the rewards that will be earned if the behavior and the conditions are met (Siedentop and Tannehill 2000). When using a behavior contract, remember that students must have a role in defining all three aspects of the contract: behavior, conditions, and rewards. After all three have been agreed upon, it is important that both parties (sometimes a third party as a witness) sign the agreement. The student should be made aware of the importance of the agreement and, just as the teacher does, view it as a formal agreement, not to be

taken lightly. Figure 9.3 gives an example of a behavior contract with one student.

Letters to Parents

Desists, time-outs, planning time, and behavior contracts work with some children but not with others. When a child continues to misbehave and present problems, a written report to the parents can be effective in obtaining that child's cooperation. But this technique should be used only after other approaches have proved unsuccessful.

The written report lists specific behaviors (Figure 9.4). The child is to have the report signed by a parent and

ELEMENTARY SCHOOL
PHYSICAL EDUCATION BEHAVIOR REPORT

NAME _____   DATE _____

Educational research has consistently shown that when a teacher spends class time managing discipline problems, less teaching and student learning occur. Disruptive behavior, therefore, is a primary reason for poor student achievement.

   We regret to inform you that your child exhibited the following misbehavior during physical education class today:

_____ Fought with others   _____ Refused to participate

_____ Argued with others   _____ Was lazy; had no hustle or energy

_____ Mistreated equipment   _____ Was late to class

_____ Disrupted the work   _____ Was disruptive in hallway
          of others

_____ Was discourteous to others _____ Was continually off-task; did not
                                                follow teacher's directions

_____ Frequently clowned,   _____ Spoke using inappropriate language
          acting foolish and silly

_____ Talked while teacher   _____ Did not listen to
          was talking   teacher

   Teacher's Comments: _____

   _____

   _____

   Please discuss today's incident with your youngster. We are concerned about the harm your child's behavior is causing himself/herself and his/her classmates. We will keep you informed of your child's behavioral progress during the coming weeks.

   Thank you for your cooperation.

            TEACHER _____

   PARENT'S SIGNATURE _____

Figure 9.4 Behavior report for parents.

then return it to you. The report is usually followed by improvements in behavior. When that occurs, send home another report, as soon as possible, that enumerates the improvements as clearly as the earlier report catalogued the violations. This second report congratulates the child on improved behavior and, like the first one, requires a parent's signature.

   This is not to suggest that the written report to parents should be used only as a measure to decrease inappropriate behavior. The teachers of St. Andrew's Episcopal School in Austin, Texas, found that a "good letter" (Figure 9.5) was one of their most effective strategies for increasing support for the program and generating good will with parents (D. Lambdin, personal communication, July 1991). In the St. Andrew's program, a "good letter" was sent home with every deserving student during one marking period each year. The response from parents was gratifying. Many parents commented on how wonderful it was that teachers took time to let them know about good behavior.

Involving the Principal

Sending a disruptive child to the principal may or may not be successful. When you send a child to the principal, you're acknowledging—to yourself and to the child—your inability to cope with the situation. You're also placing the child in a situation you can't control.

Figure 9.5 "Good" letter for parents.

ELEMENTARY SCHOOL
PHYSICAL EDUCATION BEHAVIOR REPORT

Name _____ Date _____

Educational research has shown that when a teacher spends class time managing discipline problems, less teaching and less learning occur. Therefore, when disruptive behavior is nonexistent in a class situation, greater student achievement is likely to result.

We are glad to inform you that ____(child's name)_____ consistently exhibits the following exemplary behaviors in physical education class:

_____ Listens to the teacher   _____ Is courteous to others

_____ Is on-task, following   _____ Treats equipment with
              directions   care

_____ Is eager to participate   _____ Plays safely

Your child is doing a wonderful-terrific-dynamite job in physical education and we are proud of him/her. You are to be commended for preparing your youngster to function so well in school. We are more effective teachers because of your efforts.

Thank you for your cooperation.

TEACHER _____

Some principals are positive and helpful in working with disruptive children. Others use threats or corporal punishment, techniques likely to temporarily improve the child's behavior but permanently damage the child's enthusiasm and trust.

Only when you've tried every other possible technique to deal with behavior detrimental to the child and his or her classmates should you send that child to the principal. If you must do this, we hope your principal can help you and the child better understand each other's needs and situations so you can work together more successfully.

Maintaining Appropriate Behavior in Entire Classes

The scene: May in the Southeast, a fourth-grade class with a student teacher conducting the lesson and two cooperating teachers observing. The setting: An old school, no air-conditioning, all the windows open in the second-floor gym. The unit: Throwing and catching. The equipment: Beanbags. The task: Some version of throw-and-catch with a partner. The result: The students thought the better task would be to throw the beanbags out the windows to see if they could hit the sidewalk below. The larger result: The teacher was befuddled, unnerved, and demoralized. (This is a true story from one of the three authors of this book!)

The moral of the story: All teachers at some time experience entire classes that test their ability to maintain the preferred learning environment. At this point, two things can happen. Either you can write the class off as "bad" (it was tempting) and resign yourself to the role of a police officer trying to keep control of a group, or you can assume the role of a teacher and guide and try to find a mutually acceptable solution to the problem.

In this section we offer three approaches. The first and second, class rewards and individual rewards, are clearly behaviorally oriented and designed to remedy the problem and then find out why it existed. They are for use when nothing else seems to work. The last approach, developing personal and social responsibility, is a more detailed reiteration of establishing a learning environment and brings us back to where we started in Chapter 8. While we are not advocating that developing personal and social responsibility is a management system, we include this approach again because its use results in children who are active learners and capable partners in their educational experiences (Hellison 2011; Parker and Stiehl 2010; Stork and Sanders 2002). The personal-and-social-responsibility approach promotes children as competent decision makers, and as such, "management" becomes almost a nonissue.

Reward Systems

Rewards can reduce inappropriate behavior and help build a positive climate. The improvement occurs because children are attracted to the rewards and thus direct their behavior toward appropriate behavior and away from inappropriate behavior. If you decide to implement a reward system, consider the following guidelines:

- Check your school and district policies to see if any rewards are prohibited. For example, parties with food are not allowed in some schools, and others restrict off-campus trips.
- Make sure the rewards are attractive to the students. Successful rewards to be earned in physical education have included public recognition (name boards, photo boards, names in school newsletter), extra physical education time, free-choice time (at the end of class or the end of the week), special privileges (helping the teacher with other classes or before school), field trips, equipment use (borrowing equipment to use at home and on weekends), and t-shirts. Regardless of what reward is estab-

lished, its effectiveness is based on the children having had a part in the decision. The easiest way to do this is to ask them.

- The rewards should target the behavior you are after. If you want children to stop activity and listen when asked, then the rewards should be for those specific behaviors.
- Design a reward system in which it is not too difficult to achieve the reward (this will frustrate students) or too easy (this will lose their attention).
- Make record keeping easy so your system does not create an enormous amounts of paperwork.

One caution regarding reward systems: Research is fairly clear that extrinsic rewards can reduce intrinsic motivation (Deci and Ryan 1985). That is, if students work only for the reward, they will not be motivated to continue that same behavior when the reward is withdrawn. When using reward systems, be thoughtful about their use. No purpose is served by rewarding activities that are already motivating to students. With any reward system, the goal is to eventually withdraw the reward and have student behavior remain appropriate. Thus, when creating a reward system, also develop strategies for its eventual nonuse—for example, increasingly longer times or increasingly more displays of appropriate behavior before receiving rewards.

Two reward systems, one for a class and one for individuals, are described below.

Class Rewards With class rewards, the whole class has the opportunity to earn rewards for abiding by the class rules. The first step is to establish a reward. When an entire class does well for a day (week, month), it receives the reward. For example, if a class consistently does better than the performance standards established for management tasks over a given period of time, it receives a poster or banner to display in its room. Some teachers provide a reward for a "class of the week." We prefer, however, that rewards not be exclusionary. Every class should be able to earn a reward every week. Competition should be limited to the class against a standard, not the class against other classes.

Token Systems Time-out penalizes disruptive behavior; a token system rewards desirable behavior. A token system is a program with academic, organizational, or managerial outcomes accompanied by a system in which students can earn "tokens" that can be exchanged for various rewards (Siedentop and Tannehill 2000). The intent is to reward appropriate behavior and thereby encourage all children to behave appropriately.

The teacher initially explains to the class that a particular rule or procedure is being violated or not being accomplished as efficiently as possible. In doing this, the teacher must clearly define the behaviors to be improved. After the behaviors have been defined, rewards must be developed. This is best done with the students' input by having them rank the rewards the teacher has offered according to their desirability. The higher the ranking, the more the students will be motivated by the reward; the lower the ranking, the greater the probability it won't do much to encourage children to change their behavior.

Once the behavior has been specified and the rewards agreed upon, it must be decided how many tokens it will take to earn a certain reward. For example, 5 minutes of free time at the end of class might cost 3 tokens, whereas a t-shirt might cost 50 tokens. Just as in a store, different merchandise costs different amounts; if you don't have the money (tokens), you can't buy the reward. It is also important to specify ahead of time when the tokens can be redeemed—for example, only on Fridays.

After all aspects of the token system are in place, the project begins. For example, the teacher explains that some students aren't stopping and listening as soon as they hear the signal. Beginning today, the teacher will check off on a class list the names of the students who don't stop and listen within 5 seconds after the signal is given. Students who have less than five checks during class will earn one token.

As the project progresses, in an effort to get classes off the token system, the teacher gradually increases the number of tokens it takes to receive a reward and/or increases the length of time between token redemptions. Once children have learned to abide by the rules that are vital for the successful functioning of a large group, the token system becomes unnecessary.

Developing Personal and Social Responsibility

Because physical education largely focuses on the development of motor skills and fitness, teachers often ignore social and personal development—the very thing usually needed when an entire class seems unable to respond appropriately. Hellison (2011) states that it is usually assumed students will be under control and that cooperation will automatically result in stability. As we know, such bliss does not occur automatically.

Personal and social responsibility involves much more. In a basic sense, the concept can be defined as "personal acceptance of being answerable for our conduct concerning others, our surroundings, and ourselves" (Parker and Stiehl 2010, 165). Although these attributes occur naturally to some extent, to develop fully and appropriately they must be learned just like a motor skill. Thus they must be taught and practiced at the developmentally appropriate time and with devel-

opmentally appropriate opportunities (Brustad and Parker 2005). There is much debate about whether teaching responsibility is curriculum (what we teach) or instruction (how we teach). Regardless, the basic premises involve including all children; inviting and making use of student input; providing choice; having students practice making choices; allowing for reflection; and being student centered (Parker and Stiehl 2010). Don Hellison is the most widely known advocate for developing personal and social responsibility. In his book *Teaching Responsibility through Physical Activity* (Hellison 2011), he provides field-tested instructional strategies for fostering responsibility through physical activity (curriculum). In terms of instruction, he offers students guidelines for their behavior, outlines expectations, and invites greater participation in learning. Regarding curriculum, he identifies personal and social responsibility in terms of principles or goals: respect for the rights and feelings of others, participation and effort, self-direction, helping others, and leadership. These goals are then presented in a hierarchy of levels that represent an informal progression.

These ideas, the philosophy underlying the establishment of a learning environment presented in Chapter 8, are presented here specifically for use with classes that have a hard time accepting responsibility for their own actions. This approach is not a quick fix for class problems but rather a shift in thinking and action that permeates all activities in class. It is a philosophical approach to teaching that places the focus on creating personal and social responsibility using physical activity as the medium for all that is done. For many youngsters, this type of empowerment shifts their focus from one of fighting "the system" to actively becoming part of creating a system that works.

Through the interaction of teaching and responsibility content, students begin to develop more responsibility for themselves and their classmates' well-being. The description given here is not sufficient to implement the social responsibility model. If you are interested in implementing this approach, please see Hellison's 2011 text, *Teaching Responsibility through Physical Activity*, or the Parker and Stiehl (2010) chapter "Personal and Social Responsibility" in *Standards-Based Physical Education Curriculum Development*.

Corporal Punishment

We're unalterably opposed to corporal punishment, or physically hitting a child. Besides being against the law in 31 states (Center for Effective Discipline, 2011) and school systems (check with yours), corporal punishment, like dodgeball, powerfully indicates that it is acceptable to hit another person. For some teachers, a spanking or a paddling seems to be—inappropriately—a cathartic act that may help the teacher but is more likely to harm the child. There are times when the temptation to paddle or strike a continually misbehaving child is almost overwhelming. And yet, according to our observations, it is the same few children who receive the vast majority of the paddlings. Obviously, this shows that for many children, paddling doesn't achieve the desired result. Simultaneously, it proves to these children that physically striking another person is a legitimate alternative when no other course of action appears effective. Interestingly, many children who repeatedly receive corporal punishment are being punished for fighting or hitting others. Occasionally a first paddling achieves the desired result. But the result is only temporary and has little effect on long-term behavior; in fact, corporal punishment could become a negative reinforcer. One cannot help but wonder about the long-term impact of such an experience on a child. Use of corporal punishment is inhumane, ineffective, and an admission of failure.

Teaching Skills to Maintain a Productive Learning Environment

Near the end of Chapter 8, we talked about various teaching skills that could be used to help establish a learning environment (e.g., defining and demonstrating the desired behavior, practicing the behavior, providing feedback). Several other skills can be employed to help maintain the environment as well. One major reason beginning teachers struggle with classroom management is that they are so preoccupied with other things they simply do not see the inappropriate behavior, or if they do see it, they aren't quite sure how to approach it. The following strategies are useful in monitoring and reacting (or not reacting) to student behavior, allowing you to be consistent in what you do.

- Keep movement patterns unpredictable. Vary the way you circulate through the class during activity. Stand in various places in the gym when you give directions or speak to the whole class. In our experience, many teachers always "talk" from the same place—for example, next to the stereo system.
- Scan the class frequently to "catch students being good" and pinpoint the appropriate behavior. For example, "I like the way Nikko is holding the equipment." To scan, stop and quickly look across the class in a predetermined direction, usually right to left, at regular intervals.

- Make sure all students can see and hear you. Practice giving instructions in situations where you face the distractions, not the students—for example, students face away from the sun or other groups. Make sure you can see all students before you start.
- Provide clear and concise directions, and repeat them at least once for clarity; then ask for questions to check for understanding. For example, after providing the direction "Walk, choose a ball or beanbag to use to practice tossing and catching, and carry it to your self-space. I will know you are ready when I see you standing in your space, holding the equipment," ask a student what he is supposed to do and have him repeat it back to you.
- Separate the organization aspects of directions from the content aspects (Rink 2010). For example, for a throwing-and-catching task, you might say, "When I say 'Go,' each of you should walk, pick up a ball, and find a space on a poly spot. I will know you are ready when I see each of you on your own spot with the ball at your feet." After this organizational aspect is accomplished, then add the content: "On the signal, we will practice throwing to the wall. As you throw, concentrate on stepping forward on the opposite foot. Does everyone understand? Ready. Begin." By your separating organization from content, children are able to clearly focus on the different parts of the task.
- Maintain the quality of appearing to have eyes in the back of your head or, as some call it, "with-it-ness" (Kounin 1970).
- Attend to two tasks simultaneously. More than 40 years ago, Kounin (1970) called this skill "overlapping"; today the language could easily be "multitasking." For example, you should be able to provide feedback to one group practicing their self-designed game while at the same time being aware that one child has left the gym to use the restroom.
- Avoid dangles or issues left in midair (Kounin 1970). Statements or directions left unfinished tend to confuse students. Not knowing what to do, they make up what they think may be an appropriate response.
- Avoid flip-flopping (terminating one activity, starting another, and returning to the first) (Kounin 1970).
- Use targeting, or directing your interactions toward the appropriate students (Siedentop and Tannehill 2000).
- Display the skill of timing. As a general rule, the shorter the lag time between student action and teacher behavior, the better (Siedentop and Tannehill 2000). If, when a class is practicing balancing and

rolling, you see a student push another student off-balance, effective timing means reacting immediately to the incident rather than waiting to see if the student is pushed to the floor again.

If you practice these techniques consistently and regularly, the functioning of the gymnasium is more likely to progress in a manner that enhances learning. Inappropriate behavior problems, although they won't vanish, will be curtailed.

Summary

The key to maintaining a learning environment is the presence of appropriate behavior that supports the educational goals of the specific situation. During the time needed to establish a learning environment, behavior inappropriate for the setting may occur. When it does, the teacher should first make certain that the lesson plans are pedagogically sound. If they are, then focus on the students' behavior. It's important to understand that problems with inappropriate behavior are normal; all teachers will encounter some children who are off task.

There are two phases to managing inappropriate behavior: the immediate (short-term) response to the situation and the long-term strategy. The latter involves recognizing the need to prevent recurrence of the behavior by finding out what triggered it and developing ways of helping students learn more constructive means for dealing with inappropriate behavior. Short-term techniques give a teacher practical skills to use instantly when undesirable behavior occurs. Only after the teacher has acquired and consistently used these techniques with positive results is she or he comfortable with addressing the long-term aspects of inappropriate behavior. The techniques are simply a way of

dealing with the immediate inappropriate behavior; as a learning environment is developed and students accept the responsibility for their own behavior, such techniques should no longer be needed and can gradually be phased out.

When inappropriate behavior first occurs, the teacher should use the techniques for increasing appropriate behavior: positive interaction, eliminating differential treatment, prompting, ignoring inappropriate behavior, nonverbal teacher interactions, and person-to-person dialogue. When teachers find it necessary to decrease inappropriate behavior, successful techniques include positive practice, desists, time-outs, planning time, behavior contracts, letters to parents, and involving the principal. Remember, strategies to reduce inappropriate behavior should always be accompanied by techniques to increase appropriate behavior. At no time should physical activity or hitting a child be used as a punishment. Techniques for refocusing an entire class that is off task include class rewards, token systems, and incorporating a system for developing student responsibility. Monitoring and reacting strategies can be used to help maintain an environment conducive to learning.

Reading Comprehension Questions

1. What should your first step be when most of the students in your class are misbehaving? Why?
2. Why have we chosen not to use the word *discipline*?
3. What does it mean when we say that appropriate behavior is not the mere absence of inappropriate behavior?
4. What are the different types of problems that may occur in a class? Why is it important to differentiate the types of problems?
5. What is the first strategy for maintaining an effective learning environment in the gymnasium? What techniques can be used to accomplish this goal?
6. Why are positive interactions with students so important, especially at the beginning of the year?
7. When should you ignore inappropriate behavior?
8. What does differential treatment of children mean? How can you determine whether you are doing this?
9. What is the major point to remember in a person-to-person dialogue with a student?
10. What is the second strategy for handling inappropriate behavior in the gymnasium? What techniques can you use to accomplish this goal?
11. What are the characteristics of an effective desist?
12. What is a time-out? What points should you remember when using a time-out? When is a time-out not effective? How does planning time differ from a time-out?

13. When is a letter to parents useful? What should you include in the letter?
14. What is one strategy for dealing with an entire class that isn't able to work productively?
15. Why should physical activity not be used as punishment?
16. Why should many of the techniques discussed in this chapter not be used as the school year progresses?
17. Explain the relationship between the development of personal and social responsibility and management.

References/Suggested Readings

Brooks, D. 1985. The first day of school. *Educational Leadership* 42(8): 76–78.

Brustad, R., and M. Parker. 2005. Enhancing positive youth development through physical activity. *Psychologica* 39: 75–93.

Center for Effective Discipline. 2011. **http://www. stophitting.com**

Cothran, D., and P. Kulinna. 2007. Students' reports of misbehavior in physical education. *Research Quarterly for Exercise and Sport* 78: 216–24.

Cothran, D., P. Kulinna, and D. Garrahy. 2003. "This is kind of giving a secret away…" Student's perspectives on effective classroom management. *Teaching and Teacher Education* 19: 435–44.

Deci, E. L., and R. M. Ryan. 1985. *Intrinsic motivation and self-determination in human behavior.* New York: Plenum Press.

DeLine, J. 1991. Why can't they get along? Developing cooperative skills through physical education. *Journal of Physical Education, Recreation and Dance* 62(1): 21–26.

Evertson, C., E. Emmer, and M. Worsham. 2009. *Classroom management for elementary teachers.* 7th ed. Boston: Allyn & Bacon.

Fader, D. 1971. *The naked children.* New York: Macmillan.

Hellison, D. 2011 *Teaching responsibility through physical activity.* 3rd ed. Champaign, IL: Human Kinetics.

Horrocks, R. N. ,1978. Resolving conflict in the classroom. *Journal of Physical Education and Recreation* 48(9): 20–21.

Kounin, J. 1970. *Discipline and group management in classrooms.* New York: Holt, Rinehart & Winston.

Lavay, B. W., R. French, and H. Henderson. 2006. *Positive behavior management strategies for physical education.* 2nd ed. Champaign, IL: Human Kinetics.

[NASPE] National Association for Sport and Physical Education. 2009. *Appropriate instructional practice guidelines for elementary school physical education.* 3rd ed. Reston, VA: National Association for Sport and Physical Education.

Parker, M., and J. Stiehl. 2010. Personal and social responsibility. In *Standards-based physical education curriculum,* 2nd ed., ed. J. Lund and D. Tannehill, 163–91. Sudbury, MA: Jones & Bartlett.

Rink, J. 2010. *Teaching physical education for learning.* 6th ed. New York: McGraw-Hill.

Siedentop, D., and A. Taggart. 1984. Behavior analysis in physical education and sport. In *Focus on behavior analysis in education,* ed. W. Heward, T. Heron, B. Hill, and J. Trap-Porter. Columbus, OH: Merrill.

Siedentop, D., and D. Tannehill. 2000. *Developing teaching skills in physical education.* 4th ed. New York: McGraw-Hill.

Stork, S., and S. Sanders. 2002. Why can't students just do as they're told?! An exploration of incorrect responses. *Journal of Teaching in Physical Education* 21(2): 208–28.

Instructional Approaches

I am convinced that specific methodologies are used because of what the teacher believes about children and the process of education, not because of what he believes about course content.

—KATE BARRETT (1973)

by Gyeongmin

Key Concepts

- Instructional approaches address the issue of how content is delivered to students.

- The instructional approaches presented in this chapter range from direct to indirect instruction, and they are all designed to move students toward being more independent learners.

- When using the interactive teaching approach, the teacher influences the students' responses by telling them what to do, showing them how to practice, and directing their practice.

- The instructional approach of task teaching involves different students (often individually or in pairs) practicing different tasks at the same time.

- In peer-teaching approaches, the teacher designs and communicates the task, and students assume the roles of providing feedback and assessing.

- Guided discovery instructional approaches, either convergent or divergent, are designed to let students think and solve problems.

- In cooperative learning approaches, group interdependence and individual responsibility are promoted without compromising the integrity of motor skill learning.

- Child-designed instruction, in the form of child-designed tasks or contracts, allows children to structure their own learning.

Skill themes are most often referred to as a curricular model (Lund and Tannehill 2010), yet skill themes also embrace certain pedagogies, or ways of teaching. These ways of teaching or, as we refer to them, instructional approaches (also called teaching strategies or teaching styles), are planned interactions between the teacher and the students designed to result in the accomplishment of a specific set of learning outcomes (Byra 2006). One approach can be distinguished from another by the actions and decisions the teacher makes; the actions and decisions student makes; and the objectives that the relationship accomplishes (Mosston and Ashworth 2002). In other words, instructional approaches define the different ways a teacher organizes for the delivery of instruction—rather than what is delivered (Rink 2010; Siedentop and Tannehill 2000). This chapter focuses on six instructional approaches—interactive teaching, task teaching, guided discovery, peer teaching, cooperative learning, and child-designed instruction—that we have found to be most useful in teaching elementary school physical education. Each approach is unique in the way that content is delivered to the students and, at times, in its organizational format.

The uniqueness of the delivery of the content is centered on the degree students are involved in the decision making that takes place in a lesson. This is often referred to as the directness of instruction. Simply put, in direct instruction the teacher makes most of the decisions, whereas in indirect instruction the students share more of the decisions with the teacher.

It is easiest to view the directness of instruction as a continuum of direct to indirect. At the direct end of the continuum, the class environment involves highly active teaching; focused, goal-oriented, academic learning; structured learning activities; immediate, academically oriented feedback; and student accountability (Rink 2010). Research in education and physical education has indicated that students are more likely to learn specific content when direct instruction is used (Byra 2006).

On the other hand, indirect instruction often enhances what is known as constructivist learning and is characterized by content being presented holistically and expanding the students' role in the learning process so their thinking, feelings, and interactions are built in. In indirect instruction, individual student abilities, interests, and needs receive more attention. Indirect instruction may foster children's self-responsibility (Chen 2002), lead to more transfer of skills and the development of problem-solving abilities and other cognitive skills (Rink 2010) and affective goals. These skills, such as interaction skills, cooperation, positive interdependence, and inquiry skills (Byra 2006), result in more meaningful learning.

The obvious questions are, "Do I use direct or indirect instruction?" "Which is best?" The answer is, "It all depends." Effective teachers should be able to use both direct and indirect instruction based on a number of variables. The teacher's beliefs about the ultimate purpose of education and the lesson goal should play a vital part in the type of instruction used in a class, yet both must be tempered by other aspects. The teacher's skill and preference, the students' characteristics, the nature of the content, and the context in which the teaching is taking place (Siedentop and Tannehill 2000) all affect the directness of instruction for a certain class at a certain time.

The six approaches outlined in this chapter range from direct to indirect while serving the dual purpose of delivering the content of physical education effectively and moving children toward becoming more responsible for their own learning and interactions with others. See Box 10-1 for how instructional approaches are used in the *National Standards for Physical Education*.

Box 10-1

Instructional Approaches in the *National Standards for Physical Education*

The instructional strategy of peer teaching is referenced in the National Association for Sport and Physical Education's *National Standards for Physical Education* (NASPE 2004) as a sample performance outcome for grades K–2 under Standard 5: "Exhibits responsible personal and social behavior that respects self and others in physical activity settings." The sample performance outcome states: "Assists partner by sharing observations about skill performance during practice" (40). The approach is also cited as a grade 3–5 sample performance outcome under Standard 2: "Demonstrates understanding of movement concepts, principles, strategies, and tactics as they apply to the learning and performance of physical activities." That sample performance outcome states: "Accurately recognizes the critical elements of a catch made by a fellow student and provides feedback to that student" (23).

The use of child-designed instructional strategies is identified as a grade 6–8 sample performance outcome under Standard 1: "Demonstrates competency in motor skills and movement patterns needed to perform a variety of physical activities." The sample performance outcome states: "Designs and performs gymnastics (or dance) sequences that combine traveling, rolling, balancing, and weight transfer into smooth, flowing sequences with intentional changes in direction, speed, and flow" (18).

Your teaching skills, as well as your personal preferences, should be a major though not a controlling factor in the instructional approach you choose to use. Your comfort zone is a legitimate ingredient in how you choose to deliver content to the children. This is not to say you shouldn't ever stretch your limits, but teachers generally are more effective when they are using strategies that fit them. As teachers grow and develop, they acquire new ideas and see a need for new approaches to accomplish the goals they have set for their classes.

The characteristics of the children in your classes have a significant impact on the instructional approach you choose. How much responsibility is the class ready for? How many decisions are the students capable of sharing? Will the lesson fail if the students are allowed to choose among several activities? These are some of the other considerations a teacher must take into account. For example, if the teacher believes students should be responsible for their own decisions and should direct their own learning, then direct instruction might seem to be contradictory to the teacher's goals. But for children who have never been given the responsibility to make decisions about their own learning or have never been taught any self-direction, a child-designed program would most likely lead to chaos. Instead, the teacher might use direct instruction while giving children limited or structured choices, thus teaching them how to make responsible decisions.

Different content may lend itself to different instructional approaches. When you are teaching a basic skill, a direct instructional strategy may be the most effective. When the children are asked to design complex routines and sequences, a child-designed or guided discovery strategy may be more effective.

The environment or context in which the learning is occurring is an additional factor that influences the instructional approach used. This is especially true of facilities and equipment. If a task or lesson requires students to be spread out over a large space (such as a field), making it difficult to provide continuous feedback to and maintain verbal communication with the children, a task-teaching strategy may be appropriate. When safety is a paramount issue, as in a first experience with large apparatus in gymnastics, direct instruction may be more appropriate.

Whatever instructional approach is chosen, it should be based on careful consideration of the goals of the lesson, the teacher's skills and preferences, the children's characteristics, the content, and the context. Ultimately the approach should be based on what is best for fostering the children's learning. One approach is better than the other only for a particular situation (Table 10.1).

> *Here is Edward Bear, coming downstairs now, bump, bump, bump, on the back of his head, behind Christopher Robin. It is, as far as he knows, the only way of coming downstairs, but sometimes he feels that there really is another way, if only he could stop bumping for a moment and think of it.*
>
> —A.A. MILNE, *Winnie the Pooh* (1926)

Interactive Teaching

Interactive teaching, often referred to as direct instruction, is by far the most common approach used in physical education classes. In an effort not to confuse the notion of the directness of instruction with the name of a teaching approach, we have chosen to use the term

Table 10.1 Characteristics of Six Instructional Approaches

	Instructional Approach	Goal	Teacher Skills	Student Characteristics	Content	Context
Direct	Interactive teaching	Efficient skill learning	Clarity	Control-level learners; new students	Specific skills	Whole class
	Task teaching	Skill learning + independence	Ability to monitor multifaceted environment	Independent working skills	Already learned skills; self-assessment; product-oriented tasks	Large spaces
	Peer teaching	Skill learning + cooperation	Active monitoring	Independent working skills	Simple, clear cues; limited performance	Large spaces Large groups
	Guided discovery	Skill learning + transfer; problem solving	Questioning	Precontrol-level learners All learners with new content	Exploration Concept learning	Whole class
	Cooperative learning	Skill learning + group interdependence; individual responsibility	Ability to design meaningful tasks	Independent working skills	Complex sequences; basic skills	Groups
Indirect	Child-designed instruction	Skill learning + self-responsibility	Ability to guide and monitor	Ability to use time wisely; independent working skills	Application of learned skills	Groups

interactive teaching (Rink 2010). Interactive teaching is in the top left-hand corner of Table 10.1, thus it is a very direct style of instruction. In interactive teaching, the teacher guides the students' responses by telling them what to do, showing them how to practice, and then managing their practice. Students usually work as a whole class or in small groups. As children practice, the teacher evaluates what they are doing and provides more instruction. Each teacher decision (instruction) is based on the responses the students give to the previous task. (The ability to observe movement responses and make an instantaneous decision about the next task is a difficult skill to develop. Reflective teachers will use the observation strategies suggested in Chapter 7 to help hone this important skill.) The teacher communicates the content and controls the pacing of the lesson. Usually the entire class practices the same task or a variation of that task.

Interactive teaching is effective when the teacher's goal is to have students learn a specific skill and perform it correctly in a specific manner. For example, if your goal is to teach the underhand throw, you want children to step with the foot opposite the throwing hand, extend the arm, and follow through. At this point, interactive teaching would be an appropriate instructional choice—some children might learn the correct way of throwing without your assistance, but many would not. However, interactive teaching is not an appropriate approach for children who are at the precontrol level of skill development and are not de-

velopmentally ready to produce a mature skill pattern. These children need to explore a skill (see the guided discovery section that follows).

Interactive teaching utilizes all the components of effective teaching, but five are particularly important.

1. Initially the teacher gives the student a clear idea of what is to be learned. The teacher or a student correctly demonstrates the skill, along with the important cues. For example, the teacher who is focusing on landing from a jump emphasizes in the demonstration that for a soft, quiet landing, the ankles, hips, and knees must be flexed before landing.
2. The second aspect is to give explanations and instructions clearly and repeat the cues often. At the end of a lesson, we often ask the children to repeat the cues so we know whether we've been effective. The students' answers to the question, "What are the important things to remember when you're trying to land softly and quietly from a jump?" will tell you whether the children have really remembered your teaching cues related to soft, quiet landings.
3. Next, the teacher gives specific feedback. In our example, the children now practice flexing their knees, hips, and ankles before landing; the teacher specifically tells them how well they're flexing their knees, hips, and ankles. The teacher tells the children exactly what they are (or are not) doing correctly so they can improve. Once the children have the big idea—soft, quiet landings—the teacher helps them

Using the interactive teaching approach, this teacher can effectively communicate specific content to the class as a whole.

land softly and quietly by structuring appropriate tasks and giving them information about how well they perform. The teacher proceeds in small steps but at a brisk pace.

4. One of the most important and obvious factors in interactive teaching is often overlooked. Children need considerable opportunities for practice if they're actually going to learn to land softly and quietly. For this reason we always try to structure the learning situation so the children have plenty of practice. Most of the time we're able to arrange the environment so the children rarely, if ever, have to wait. We try to ensure all the children are active at least 60 percent of the lesson, more when possible.

5. High success rates are also important for learning, especially the basic skills. We provide tasks that allow children to be successful about 80 percent of the time. This motivates the children and allows them to grasp one skill before moving on to the next level. If children can't land softly and quietly when they jump from the floor, for example, then obviously they won't be able to land effectively when they jump from a bench or a wooden box.

Each of these components is developed and explained in more detail in Chapter 8. Box 6-1 in Chapter 6 is an example of interactive teaching.

Interactive teaching calls for a specific response, the one the teacher is looking for and helps the children to produce. Just any response is not acceptable. For example, if you want to teach the children to use opposition

when they throw overhand, you'll need to give them plenty of practice opportunities and feedback to be certain they step with the opposite foot before moving on to another aspect of the overhand throw. If you don't require the children to practice stepping with the opposite foot until the movement is overlearned, they will quickly forget the concept of opposition once the task changes. Then you'll find yourself continually reminding them, "Step with the opposite foot when you throw." The proof of this statement can be found in any high school softball class: Watch the students play a game and see how many are inefficient throwers who've never learned the concept of opposition when they throw. They were taught the concept but never to the point of learning it.

Interactive teaching works well for beginning teachers or teachers who haven't worked with a group of students for a long while. Once the teacher has established a productive learning environment, teaching by invitation or intratask variation (Chapter 8) is helpful for changing the tasks to meet individual students' needs within the interactive approach. This strategy also requires less time for organization than the other approaches, an important consideration for teachers who meet with their students only once or twice a week.

Task Teaching

As we move down the left-hand column of Table 10.1, task teaching is the first less direct instructional approach as it allows different students to practice different

Figure 10.1 Arrangement of stations (learning centers) in the teaching space.

tasks at the same time. This approach is often called station teaching and/or self-check (Mosston and Ashworth 2002). In our approach, task teaching includes both stations and task sheets. With either option, different students practice different, specified tasks, often at their own pace and gauging their performance against predesigned criteria throughout the lesson.

Stations provide several activity areas (or learning centers) in the teaching space, each with a different task, through which students rotate during the class. See Figure 10.1 for an example of arrangement of stations that could be used to practice a variety of balancing skills during one lesson. The sequence for Striking at High and Low Targets in Chapter 25 (page 510) is another example of tasks that might be used at stations.

Task sheets provide another task-teaching option that allows children to practice at their own pace. Each child is given a task sheet (Figure 10.2), which contains a progression of activities and criteria for completion. After successfully completing each task, the student records it on the task sheet with that day's date and then asks the teacher, a parent, another student, or an older child to observe the accomplishment and sign the sheet. Initially we have entire classes work on the same task sheet at the same time. As children learn to use task sheets, we let them pick from task sheets on several different skill themes. One way to use task sheets is to develop multiple task sheets for each generic level of proficiency for each skill theme and store them in a box with file dividers. Students can then choose task cards at the appropriate level of skill proficiency (C. Galvan, personal communication, 2011). Figure 10.3 provides an example of task cards for the skill theme of striking with rackets and paddles at several levels.

Task teaching provides students with a structured opportunity to work on their own or with partners, but it can create management problems. These four suggestions make task teaching more effective.

1. Explain all the stations and task sheets to the class before sending students out to practice. Tell the children what they are supposed to do and, if they are to have activities verified, who is to do the verification (teacher or another student).

2. Make sure the managerial aspects are explicit. Designate the areas in which activities are to occur or where specific stations are located. Design, explain, and teach a rotation system between stations or areas. We initially have children change stations on a signal. Once children are able to function using this strategy, they can be allowed to choose the stations at which they'd like to work (though we usually limit the number of students at any one area or station). Eventually students can rotate from one station to another at their own discretion. Post the necessary cues and directions at each station or practice area. This technique substantially reduces the time spent in providing additional instruction.

3. Check with students frequently to see how they are doing; move around the room.

4. Start slowly, with only a few (maybe three) stations or a small task sheet (maybe five items) at the end of the lesson. In our experience children enjoy working on task sheets and in stations, especially as a culminating activity, but they need guidance if this approach is going to succeed for them and you.

With task teaching, children won't all be involved in the same activity simultaneously; they and the teacher

Figure 10.2 Task sheet.
Source: Jeremy Hayes, University of Northern Colorado. Used with permission.

THROWING AND CATCHING TASK SHEET

Directions: This task sheet lists 20 tasks. Some are easy. Some are very hard. When you get to a task you cannot do, that is the one on which to spend time practicing. Don't worry about other classmates. Just try to practice so you can improve. I will help you as you practice. You may do this as partners, in a group, or by yourself. When you can do a task, write your initials beside it. For the tasks with an asterisk (*), ask the teacher to see it as well.

Your Name _____

Initials:

1. *_____ I can throw using "**Point, step, and throw**" 10 times.

2. _____ I can throw so a moving target (a classmate) can catch.

3. _____ I can throw to a target on the wall 4 times.

4. _____ I can do 10 sit-ups.

5. _____ I can throw at a target on the wall while moving.

6. *_____ I can throw 10 times to a partner.

7. _____ I can tell Mr. Hayes when my birthday is.

8. *_____ I can throw a ball off of the wall and catch it 5 times.

9. _____ I can catch a ball one handed 8 times.

10. _____ I can hit a target on the wall 7 out of 10 times.

11. _____ I can hit a target on the wall from far away 3 times.

12. _____ I can throw and hit a poster on the wall 2 times in a row.

13. _____ I can give Mr. Hayes a high-five.

14. _____ I can toss and catch a scarf in the air 20 times.

15. _____ I can do 20 jumping jacks.

16. *_____ I can catch above my head 10 times.

17. _____ I can catch below my waist 10 times.

18. _____ I can skip across the gym 2 times.

19. _____ I can throw and catch just below the ceiling 4 times in a row.

20. _____ Create your own challenge (write it in space below):

need to be ready to have more than one activity happening at the same time. Efficient task teaching demands complex organizational and managerial skills on the teacher's part. To benefit from the task-teaching approach, students need to have good independent working skills and to be able to function without close teacher supervision. Stopping when asked, rotating systematically, and not interfering with others are skills students need to practice before they can use stations effectively.

A task instructional approach works well when students are practicing skills that have already been taught, are doing self-assessment, or are performing product-oriented tasks. The approach is not effective for introducing new or complex skills. Task teaching works best with simple tasks that can be clearly and completely described and that have a clear goal—for example, "Make 10 throws that hit the target and then take a step back."

One advantage of the task-teaching approach is that it allows you to set up areas that don't require students to wait in line for turns, thus making up for limitations in space and equipment. If, for example, in a balance unit you have a limited number of balance boards and balance beams, you can design tasks for each piece of equipment and have students rotate among the stations.

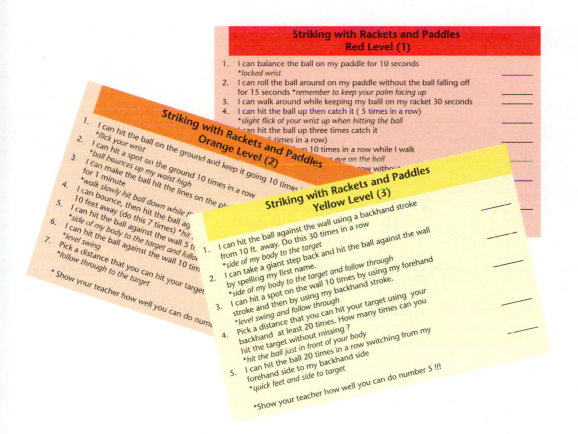

Figure 10.3 Task cards by skill level. *Source:* Christine Galvan, California State University, Long Beach.

Task-teaching instructional approaches also work well when children have to be spread out over a large space and verbal communication is difficult.

Peer Teaching

This instructional approach uses peers teamed in pairs or small groups to actively teach one another. Peer teaching provides an indirect experience that meets multiple educational goals: It provides an effective medium for children to learn a skill—they receive multiple practice opportunities, plentiful feedback, and a chance to cognitively analyze skill—and at the same time they learn to work with each other. In peer teaching, the teacher plans the tasks and communicates them to the children; the children assume the roles of providing feedback and assessing. The children and the teacher share demonstration of the skill. Often the teacher will demonstrate initially and the children, as peer teachers, will repeat the demonstration as necessary.

A simple example of peer teaching is using peers to help teach the overhand throw. The teacher might say, "For this next task you will get to teach another classmate how to throw. Each of you will get to be the player and the coach. When you are the player, you will throw five times against the wall. Your partner, the coach, will watch to see if you bring your arm way back, step forward on the opposite foot, and follow through. If you do it correctly, your coach will give you a "thumbs-up"; if you still need some practice, your coach will tell you what to correct for the next throw. After five throws, change roles. This is how it will look and sound." At this point the teacher demonstrates the entire task while providing sample feedback to the thrower. The peer assessment card for cuts and pivots while dribbling in Chapter 12 (Figure 12.9) provides an example of peer teaching.

For peer teaching to be an effective instructional approach, follow several key points:

- The skill should be simple, the cues for observation clear, and the performance easily measured.
- Post the cues either on the wall or on individual cue cards so the peer teachers can remember them.
- Start small. You might consider including one peer-teaching task in a lesson and then expand.

Children must be able to work cooperatively and independently for peer teaching to be a success. They must be responsible enough to take seriously the task of teaching another student. Children are asked to provide

Peer teaching provides the opportunity for children to analyze and teach a skill while learning to work with others.

feedback as well as analyze performance; therefore they must know the cues and what the skill looks like. The teacher's role in terms of feedback changes; instead of providing feedback to the child performing the skill, the teacher provides feedback to the coach about what he or she is seeing and saying to the performer.

Peer teaching can work with any content, but it works best when the skills are simple, there are clear criteria for observation, and the performance is limited and easily measured. For example, peer teaching works well with basic skills but is much more difficult with dynamic and tactical skills.

Children thoroughly enjoy being the teacher, but for the strategy to be successful, they must be able to both analyze skill and provide feedback—something the teacher can help them learn through her or his presentation of the task.

> *Teaching was easy. All you did was tell them and they did it.*
>
> —Fourth grader after teaching a self-designed game to another group

Guided Discovery

Guided discovery—an approach some call teaching through questions (Siedentop and Tannehill 2000), a cognitive strategy (Rink 2010), inquiry learning

(Harrison et al. 1996), or problem solving—is designed to facilitate children's critical thinking, as reflected in their movement responses (Cleland 1994), and to let them solve problems rather than copy the teacher's or another student's correct performance. Guided discovery also enhances student interest and motivation (Chen 2001). In this student-centered approach, the teacher typically gives the task by asking questions. The teacher most often describes how the task will be practiced and some way to measure success, but exactly how to perform the task is left to the child to explore and interpret. For example, the teacher may say, "From your spot on the floor, try to kick the ball to the wall both in the air and on the ground." The child knows how to practice (from the spot on the floor, kick) and a little about success (to the wall, in the air, and on the ground), but the rest is left up to the child. Guided discovery really serves as an umbrella for two different types of discovery: convergent and divergent. One asks children to find multiple answers to a task, whereas the other encourages children to find a single answer.

Convergent Inquiry

Convergent inquiry encourages children to discover the same answer(s) to a series of questions the teacher asks. The teacher guides the children toward one or more correct answers. Several educators (Doolittle and Girard 1991; Thorpe and Bunker 1989; Werner and Almond 1990) have successfully adapted this approach to teaching game skills and strategies. It is the fundamental principle underlying teaching games for understanding or the tactical approach to teaching games (Griffin, Mitchell, and Oslin 2006). Mosston (1981) suggested that children can discover ideas, similarities, dissimilarities, principles (governing rules), order or system, a particular physical activity or movement, how, why, limits (the dimensions of "how much," "how fast"), and other elements. When we want children to learn one of these elements, we often use the discovery approach to increase their involvement.

The following sequence illustrating Mosston's (1981) classic slanty rope technique is a very good example of convergent inquiry encouraging children to find ways to avoid eliminating others from activity (166).

Step 1: Ask two children to hold a rope for high jumping. Invariably they will hold the rope horizontally at a given height (for example, at hip level).

Step 2: Ask the group to jump over. Before they do so, you might want to ask the rope holders to decrease the height so that everybody can be successful.

Step 3: After everyone has cleared the height, you ask, "What shall we do now?" "Raise it!" "Raise it!" is the answer—always! (The success of the first jump motivates all to continue.)

Step 4: Ask the rope holders to raise the rope just a bit. The jumping is resumed.

Step 5: "Now what?" "Raise it!" the children will respond.

Step 6: Raising the rope two or three more times will create a new situation, a new reality. Some children will not be able to clear the height. In traditional situations, these children will be eliminated from the jumping, and only some will continue; there will be a constantly diminishing number of active participants. The realization of individual differences becomes real; the design for opportunity for all has not yet come about.

Step 7: Stop the jumping and ask the group, "What can we do with the rope so that nobody will be eliminated?" Usually one or two of the following solutions are proposed by the children: (a) Hold the rope higher at the two ends and let the rope dip in the center. (b) Slant the rope! Hold the rope high at one end and low at the other.

The effectiveness of convergent inquiry is largely dependent on the questions the teacher asks. We offer three suggestions for making the questions work successfully.

1. Formulate in advance the questions to be asked so you can determine the correct sequence of questions that will lead children to the answer you desire.
2. Ask questions in relatively small steps rather than spanning too large of a gap.
3. Wait for an answer (even 10 to 15 seconds; count to yourself) rather than becoming impatient and giving the answer. If you wait for an answer, children will really start to think and thus the learning becomes more meaningful and personal.

The Throwing to a Moving Target sequence in Chapter 23 (page 453) is an example of convergent inquiry used to teach the concepts of throwing to an open space and leading a receiver.

Divergent Inquiry

In divergent inquiry, the teacher outlines a problem and then challenges the children to find many answers. This technique encourages children to find movement alternatives. When using a divergent approach, every child will not exhibit the same movement response to a task. For example in response to the task of, "Find three different inverted balances," one child may balance with her hands and feet on the mat and down in a piked position, another child may have his head and hands and one foot on the mat with the other foot in the air, and yet another child might do a handstand. A typical divergent question will always ask for diversity; "Find at least three different ways to travel under the hoop (supported on cones) and at least three different ways to travel over the hoop."

In the divergent inquiry approach, the teacher must be careful not to impose personal values on the children's responses. The emphasis is on obtaining a variety of responses, not a single answer. For this reason, Mosston (1981) warned of two verbal behavior patterns that we try to avoid when using divergent inquiry. "You can do better than that" in response to a child's movement indicates that the teacher doesn't really value the response or that the teacher has a particular response in mind. Another counterproductive verbal behavior is a statement such as "Stop. Everyone watch Penny." After Penny finishes her movement, the teacher says, "Terrific, Penny." This teacher behavior, although perhaps innocent, suggests to students that there's a right answer and therefore encourages the children to find a correct answer (convergent) rather than searching for a variety of alternatives, the goal of divergent inquiry.

In contrast, two productive verbal behaviors might include such statements as:

"Now that you have found two ways, try to make the third one quite different."

"Stop. Everyone watch this half of the class. Good! Now, let's watch the other half. Great."

These two statements allow the teacher to provide feedback while encouraging creativity and diversity of responses.

We have found the following points helpful in our use of divergent inquiry:

- Provide feedback that encourages exploration and problem solving rather than a single right answer (see the Mosston examples above).
- Structure questions (tasks) that challenge children in small, sequential steps. These questions are based on a detailed knowledge of the content and knowing what should come next.
- Become a master at providing children with prompts—encouraging them to keep practicing by trying different ways or looking for different solutions.
- When demonstrations are used, provide multiple demonstrations of different answers to the task. If a single demonstration is used, children are likely to copy it.

The Jumping to Form a Body Shape During Flight sequence in Chapter 19 (page 332) is an example of divergent inquiry.

We've found guided discovery especially helpful for encouraging children to think on their own to discover new and different approaches to performing skills and to solve questions related to teamwork and strategy. Guided discovery is also important for those children who aren't developmentally ready to learn a mature version of a skill and simply need opportunities to explore the movement. It is often the strategy we use at the precontrol level when students are exploring a new skill. It provides children a chance to try things out without a specific focus or direction.

> Teachers have to learn how to provide transitions for their pupils. It is not possible for most young people to make choices after five or six years of being told what to do every minute they are in school. It is equally hard for them to share resources, help other students, or decide what they want to learn after years of being expected to hoard, compete, and conform. Transitional situations often have to be provided. Some students need workbooks for a while; others want to memorize times tables or have weekly spelling tests. Young people are no different from adults. When faced with new possibilities they want something old and predictable to hold onto while risking new freedom. Inexperienced teachers often make the mistake of tearing down the traditional attitudes their students have been conditioned to depend upon before the students have time to develop alternative ways of learning and dealing with school. In their impatience they become cruel to students who do not change fast enough or who resist change altogether. One just cannot legislate compassion or freedom. Teaching as a craft involves understanding how people learn; as an art it involves a sensitive balance between presenting and advocating things you believe and stepping away and encouraging your students to make their own sense of your passion and commitment.
>
> —HERBERT KOHL, *On Teaching* (1976)

Cooperative Learning

Cooperative learning is small group indirect instructional approach designed to promote group interdependence and individual responsibility while teaching content. The principles underlying the use of cooperative learning are a respect for all students coupled with a confidence in their potential for success and a belief that learning is a social process (Sapon-Shevin, Ayres, and Duncan 1994). There are three common cooperative learning formats: pairs-check, jigsaw, and co-op (Kagan 1990).

In pairs-check, children are in groups of four with two partner-pairs in each group. Each pair practices a task, teaching each other as in peer teaching. The two pairs then get together to assess each other to see if they are achieving the same outcomes, to provide further feedback, and to practice. For example, the pairs-check strategy could be used to teach dribbling with the hands. After the initial task is given, each pair works together, focusing on using the finger pads, having the knees bent, and keeping the hand on top of the ball. Then, when both members of a single pair think they have mastered the task, they come together to check the other pair. In this sense, pairs-check is much like peer teaching.

In the jigsaw format, children are usually in home groups of three or four. Each child becomes an expert on one aspect of a skill or task by working with the children who are experts from other groups. Children then return to their home group and teach their group their piece of the skill. The jigsaw format can be used quite effectively to teach activities with multiple parts and simultaneously develop interdependence.

For example, the jigsaw approach could be used when creating a simple dance routine in involving traveling, balance, and space concepts. The class is divided into home groups of four. At the beginning of class, four stations are set up—one on traveling, incorporating different levels; one with traveling in different pathways; one with twists and turns; and another with balances with different extensions. One person from each home group goes to each station and designs a sequence with her group to meet the criteria at the station. Each child then returns to his home group as an expert on that sequence and teaches it to the group. The group then puts the sequences in order to form their dance.

Co-op is a cooperative learning format in which small groups create a project with many components (Grineski 1996). Each small group is responsible for one component of the larger project. The co-op format can be used to have children create a dance sequence in which several elements are to be portrayed. For example, in the dance depicting African American heritage described in Chapter 28 (page 605), one group might develop the concept of slavery, another the concept of freedom, another the concept of strength as a people, another dispersal, another gathering, and another respect. Each group would then bring their piece to the full dance.

Posting instructions for child-designed instruction allows children to take more responsibility for their work and increases time spent in activity.

Cooperative learning works equally well with children who have highly developed responsibility skills and with children who need to team to work together. Research shows that cooperative learning has affective as well as cognitive benefits (Slavin 1990). However, to achieve such benefits, the teacher's role must change from the interactive teaching used in structured approaches to facilitation and indirect teaching. First, the teacher must be skilled in designing tasks that are meaningful to children. Second, the teacher's role regarding demonstrations and feedback shifts. As in divergent inquiry, multiple demonstrations of possible responses are needed. Feedback initially takes the form of helping groups work together to solve group issues and to answer the task, followed by skilled feedback once the groups have designed their response.

Cooperative learning strategies provide a chance for skill learning and teaching responsibility. However, we have a word of caution here. The goal of skill learning should not be sacrificed when using cooperative learning activities. The primary purpose of some cooperative learning activities, especially from adventure education, is group development and problem solving. These activities have their place and are often fun; however, they do not teach the primary content of physical education. For cooperative learning to be a viable part of physical education, it needs to integrate psychomotor, cognitive, and personal-social responsibility goals. It must provide what Rink (2010) calls a rich learning experience. The cooperative learning activity must teach a psychomotor goal while addressing the other goals.

For teachers who want to successfully use cooperative learning approaches, structure is essential. Six important guidelines help provide structure that allows student direction (Dyson 2002; Mills 2002). First, make sure you know the academic and social goals of what you want to accomplish through the cooperative learning task and communicate those goals. Second, groups need to remain small. Third, teach the children the roles they will need in the group. For example, if students need to provide feedback to others, teach them what feedback to provide. Fourth, design an assessment or accountability system (see Chapter 12) so the children are responsible for the end result or product as well as the process and there is closure to the task. Fifth, students need to learn how to communicate with each other. In other words, it is not enough to be able to provide feedback; they must learn how to deliver it so others hear it and it is not hurtful. Finally, cooperative

I recently walked into a large multipurpose room full of 30 second graders. As I sat to watch, I noticed that six very diverse activities were taking place: striking with hockey sticks in a game situation, doing pull-ups, jumping rope, shooting at targets, wall climbing, and jumping and landing using a vaulting horse. The teacher was walking around from group to group talking to the children, offering feedback and encouragement, but no instructions or managerial directions. At this point, I started to look more closely. All the children were active and on task. The noise level was productive; there was no screaming or yelling. Children were moving from activity to activity as they saw fit. Some were recording scores on wall charts. The teacher was never asked to make the decisions of a referee in the game. Children calmly retrieved stray equipment without interfering with other activities or sending the mob to chase a stray ball. These were seven-year-olds. I then asked the teacher how this situation came to be. His response: "I taught them at the beginning of the year the rules for Fridays (the designated day for choice activities), and we practiced."

learning takes time. Like any instructional format that calls for problem solving and student input, allow ample time for the children to work through the process of the task. Groups should remain together long enough to establish a working relationship.

Child-Designed Instruction

Child-designed instructional approaches are student centered, indirect approaches that allow the child to be the center of the learning activities. In these strategies the teacher serves as a guide or mentor.

Child-designed instructional approaches allow children to actively take the major responsibility for their learning. When used with careful planning and patience, these approaches empower children. Children become engaged and most often design activities appropriate to their level of development. We are committed to children designing their own experiences, although this is not always easy and is often messy. There are several child-designed strategies; child-designed tasks and contracts are the two we use most often. While older elementary students are fully capable of designing personal contracts, with structure, the use of child-designed tasks such as game, routines, and obstacle courses can begin with seven-year-olds. Child-designed games or routines ask students to create their own "game" or "routine" within

certain parameters. The game, dance, or gymnastics task is based on the skill theme being studied and allows students to apply what they have learned in a setting that matches their interests and abilities. Figure 10.4 provides an example of a checklist used with second grade, control level children to guide their creation of an obstacle course that reflected what was learned while dribbling with the feet in different speeds, with different pathways, while avoiding an object, and passing to a target. See the Self-Designed Racket Games task in Chapter 25 (page 522) for an example of a child-designed game. See Chapters 28, 29, and 30 for explicit details about how to develop child-designed activities in dance, gymnastics, and games contexts.

As children become accustomed to working on their own, the teacher can use independent contracting to make instruction more personal. A teacher who uses independent contracting is saying to the students, "I trust you to make intelligent and responsible decisions about what you need to practice."

We've used the written contract illustrated in Figure 10.5. Each child writes down the skill or activity she or he will be practicing or playing, the goal to be achieved, the time to be spent practicing each activity, and (when appropriate) the name of a practice partner. Recognizing the dynamic nature of a physical education class, we let the children change their contracts during class, provided they write down all changes. We encourage the children to save time by coming to physical education class with their contracts already completed for that day. In the final few minutes of a class, we ask the children to evaluate their accomplishments for that day.

Contracts can be used in physical education classes in a variety of ways. When you first use independent contracting, restrict each child to a single skill theme or even a certain aspect of the skill theme or unit. For example, some teachers have used contracts as a culminating activity to let students decide how they want to complete their learning on a specific topic. The sequence Throwing for Distance and Accuracy in Chapter 23 (page 454) is an example of a modified contract.

For teachers who want to try to incorporate child-designed approaches in their teaching but aren't sure where to begin, we have found the following suggestions helpful.

- Employ moderation and structure as the keys to success. Give specific directions. The results can be disastrous if you simply say, "Make up your own game; it has to include throwing and catching," or "Write a contract about what to do in physical education." We know from experience. Try to give children more specific instructions for designing activities that

Speeds:

Turtle = slow speed

Dog = medium speed

Cheetah = Fast speed

Pathways:

Straight

Curved

Zig-Zag

Avoiding an object:

Passing to a target:

Figure 10.4 Checklist for child-designed obstacle course.
Source: Jen Morse and Jesse Sirio, University of Northern Colorado.

include the exact focus of the activity and what the final product is to be, such as:

"Design beginning and ending movements for the balance, roll, balance sequence you've been practicing."

"You've been practicing five movements: leaping, spinning, sinking, exploding, and freezing. Use them in a sequence that flows together smoothly."

"We've been practicing dribbling for the past few lessons and will continue to do so for another week. Design a contract that tells what you will do each day for the first five minutes of class to practice your dribbling skills."

- Provide the managerial aspects of the task, such as how large the space can be and where; when the task should be completed; how long before they should be practicing; the maximum and minimum number of people in the group; and the equipment available.

- Check with groups often to see how they are doing (especially those who seem to be having a difficult time getting started). Move around the area. Ask questions about their activity. Prompt.

- Provide feedback while resisting telling children how to practice. Teacher responses to child-designed activities need to encourage children to stay on task while at the same time provide reinforcement for the students' decisions.

- Allow enough time. Designing instruction takes time. We usually find that it takes the majority of a lesson (and sometimes two lessons) for children to design and implement self-designed activities.

- Find ways for children to be accountable for what they are doing. A variety of assessment options—such as exit slips that ask students to explain their creation (Chapter 12), reflection on the process of the development in journals (Chapter 12), or teaching their game or routine to another group—allows children to be accountable for the learning process. These options also let children think about how much effort they put into accomplishing their independent tasks. (See Chapter 14 for more options.)

To function productively with a child-designed approach, children need to be highly motivated, self-directed, and have the skills to work independently. They need to be knowledgeable about using the time and materials available to them. The teacher must be skilled in designing the initial task—and then must let the students work on their own, making their own decisions and mistakes. This is very hard for many of us to do. Child-designed strategies work well after the basic skill has been learned. They are especially useful with dynamic situations, when children are at different skill levels, and as culminating activities.

Figure 10.5 Individual contract.
Source: Tia Ziegler, Chappelow
K-8 Magnet School, Evans, CO.

PE Class Contract

Name_____ Contract for_____, 2012

Goal for the day:
_____
_____

Things I will do to accomplish goal_____
_____

Time Allowed	Activity/Task	Equipment	Partner (if working with one)

Self Check:
Points Earned in Class_____/ 10 (5—in-class participation, 5—showing PRIDE)
Explain:

Comments:
1) How do you know you accomplished your goal or didn't accomplish it?

2) What do you need to work on during the next class?

Teacher Check:
Points Earned in Class_____/ 10 (5—in-class participation, 5—showing PRIDE)
Explain:

A Final Thought or Two

Regardless of the instructional approach used, it is important to carefully observe the children's responses to the task and make your next decision as a teacher based on what you observed. For example, suppose that while using the direct approach you have the children focus on dribbling using their finger pads, and you observe they are not doing that. The next step is to stop and redirect the task to the use of finger pads.

However, if you're using a peer-teaching approach to teach the same skill and the children are not using their finger pads, you would refocus the peer teachers on what to look for. In any case, careful observation of how children are responding to the task should guide your response and feedback to them.

To become a skillful teacher in all six instructional approaches is quite difficult and takes a lot of time to practice. While some of the indirect approaches at first appear easy, in reality they are hard. To design experiences meaningful to all students and allow them to learn what you want them to learn is complex. Yet, the use of indirect approaches takes children to a different place—one that has them become the artists of their own learning.

Summary

An instructional approach can be defined as planned interactions between the teacher and the students designed to result in accomplishing a specific set of learning outcomes. The uniqueness of each instructional approach revolves around the extent to which students are involved in the decision making that takes place in a lesson. The six instructional approaches (summarized in Table 10.1) described in this chapter range from direct to indirect instruction. One of the myriad of questions that a teacher must answer is which instructional approach to use. The answer depends on a number of factors; the primary one is the teacher's goal for a particular lesson or series of lessons.

The interactive approach is effective when students are to learn a specific skill technique. A task-teaching approach is helpful when having students practice a skill they have already learned. Peer teaching fosters cooperation and provides repeated practice and feedback for children. The guided discovery approaches stimulate thinking and students' involvement on a cognitive level. Cooperative learning develops group-relation skills, as well as stimulating cognitive involvement. Child-designed approaches encourage creativity and inventiveness; they involve children in creating their own learning experiences.

Each approach has its strengths, and each requires different student and teacher skills. Which strategy to select depends on the teacher's goals. One of the challenges reflective teachers face is analyzing both their students' and their own needs and skills and matching them with the goals of the lesson. Ideally, over a period of weeks, both the teacher and the children learn to work effectively, no matter which instructional strategy is selected.

Regardless of the approach used, the progression of the learning experience is always based on the students' response to the task they were given. Thus, the ability of the teacher to observe (Chapter 11) is critical.

Reading Comprehension Questions

1. What is the implication of the quote from Kate Barrett on the opening page of the chapter? How does it relate to the content of this chapter?
2. What is an instructional approach? How does the concept of direct or indirect instruction relate to instructional approaches? Explain the differences among the six instructional approaches presented in this chapter.
3. What criteria might the teacher use in selecting a particular instructional approach for use with a class?
4. Using the skill of punting, give examples of convergent and divergent inquiry, written in the actual form in which they would be stated.
5. Select a skill theme from one of the skill theme chapters (Chapters 16–26) and develop a task sheet similar to the one in Figure 10.2. Include at least six different tasks, ranging from precontrol through utilization levels.
6. Why do we say that an interactive approach may not be the best for children who are not developmentally ready?
7. Using the skills of throwing and catching against a defense, design a task sequence using the jigsaw cooperative learning strategy.
8. What strategies can a teacher employ to begin to use child-designed approaches for instruction? Give an example of how one strategy might be developed for a group of 11- or 12-year-olds.
9. How can different instructional approaches be used to help students meet various national standards for physical education?

References/Suggested Readings

Barrett, K. 1973. I wish I could fly: A philosophy in motion. In *Contemporary philosophy of physical education and athletics*, ed. R. Cobb and P. Lepley, 3–18. Columbus, OH: Merrill.

Byra, M. 2006. Teaching styles and inclusive pedagogies. In *The handbook of physical education*, ed. D. Kirk, D. Macdonald, and M. O'Sullivan, 449–66. Thousand Oaks, CA: Sage.

Chen, W. 2001. Description of an expert teacher's constructivist oriented teaching: Engaging students' critical thinking in creative dance. *Research Quarterly for Exercise and Sport* 72: 366–75.

Cleland, F. 1994. Young children's divergent movement ability: Study II. *Journal of Teaching in Physical Education* 13: 228–41.

Doolittle, S., and K. Girard. 1991. A dynamic approach to teaching games in elementary PE. *Journal of Physical Education, Recreation and Dance* 62(4): 57–62.

Dyson, B. 2002. The implementation of cooperative learning in an elementary physical education program. *Journal of Teaching in Physical Education* 22: 69–88.

Griffin, L., S. Mitchell, and J. Oslin. 2006. *Teaching sports concepts and skills: A tactical games approach.* 2nd ed. Champaign, IL: Human Kinetics.

Grineski, S. 1996. *Cooperative learning in physical education.* Champaign, IL: Human Kinetics.

Harrison, J., C. Blakemore, M. Buck, and T. Pellett. 1996. *Instructional strategies for secondary school physical education.* 4th ed. Dubuque, IA: Brown & Benchmark.

Kagan, S. 1990. The structural approach to cooperative learning. *Educational Leadership* 47(4): 12–16.

Kohl, H. 1976. *On teaching.* New York: Schocken.

Lund, J., and D. Tannehill. 2010. *Standards-based physical education curriculum development.* 2nd ed. Sudbury, MA: Jones & Bartlett.

Mills, B. 2002. *Enhancing learning—and more!—through cooperative learning. Idea Paper #38.* Manhattan, KS: The IDEA Center.

Milne, A.A. 1926. *Winnie the pooh.* New York: Dutton.

Mosston, M. 1981. *Teaching physical education.* 2nd ed. Columbus, OH: Merrill.

Mosston, M., and S. Ashworth. 2002. *Teaching physical education.* 5th ed. San Francisco: Benjamin Cummings.

[NASPE] National Association for Sport and Physical Education. 2004. *Moving into the future: National standards for physical education.* 2nd ed. Reston, VA: National Association for Sport and Physical Education.

Rink, J. 2010. *Teaching physical education for learning.* 6th ed. New York: McGraw-Hill.

Sapon-Shevin, M., B. Ayres, and J. Duncan, J. 1994. Cooperative learning and inclusion. In *Creativity and collaborative learning: A practical guide to empowering students and teachers*, ed. J. S. Thousand, R. A. Villa, and A. I. Nevin, 45–58. Baltimore, MD: Paul H. Brookes.

Siedentop, D., and D. Tannehill. 2000. *Developing teaching skills in physical education.* 4th ed. New York: McGraw-Hill.

Slavin, R. 1990. Research on cooperative learning: Consensus and controversy. *Educational Leadership* 47(4): 52–55.

Thorpe, R., and D. Bunker. 1989. A changing focus in games teaching. In *The place of physical education in the schools*, ed. L. Almond. London: Kogan Page.

Werner, P., and L. Almond. 1990. Models of games education. *Journal of Physical Education, Recreation and Dance* 61(4): 23–27.

Observing Student Responses

It is vital for a teacher to observe children, whatever the subject or situation. It is through observation that the successful teacher assesses the moods, attributes, needs, and potential of individuals and groups.

—E. MAULDON AND J. LAYSON (1965)

Key Concepts

- Reflective teachers are effective observers.
- Accurately analyzing classes of students in a physical activity setting is a pedagogical skill acquired through practice and experience.
- Teachers must continually assess their classes to be certain they are, and remain, safe.

Locke (1975) provided the following description of a two-minute segment of a class of 34 fourth-grade students:

Teacher is working one-on-one with a student who has an obvious neurological deficit. She wants him to sit on a beam and lift his feet from the floor. Her verbal behaviors fall into categories of reinforcement, instruction, feedback, and encouragement. She gives hands-on manual assistance. Nearby two boys are perched on the uneven bars and are keeping a group of girls off. Teacher visually monitors the situation but continues to work on the beam. At the far end of the gym a large mat propped up so that students can roll down it from a table top is slowly slipping nearer to the edge. Teacher visually monitors this but continues work on the beam. Teacher answers three individual inquiries addressed by passing students but continues as before. She glances at a group now playing follow-the-leader over the horse (this is off-task behavior) but as she does a student enters and indicates he left his milk money the previous period. Teacher nods him to the nearby office to retrieve the money and leaves the beam to stand near the uneven bars. The boys climb down at once. Teacher calls to a student to secure the slipping mat. Notes that the intruder, milk money now in hand, has paused to interact with two girls in the class and, monitoring him, moves quickly to the horse to begin a series of provocative questions designed to reestablish task focus.

After painting this picture of the complexity of teaching, Locke aptly reminds us:

That was only 120 seconds out of the 17,000 the teacher spent that day in active instruction. A great deal of detail was unobserved or unrecorded over those two minutes, and nothing in the record reflected the invisible train of thought in the teacher's mind.

That scenario provides us with glimpses of establishing a learning environment (e.g., much student choice and independence in activities); maintaining the environment (e.g., standing near students who are off task);

and developing content (e.g., providing reinforcement, instruction, feedback). It also provides us with the complexity of teaching physical education. To become a reflective (and effective) teacher who meets your student's needs, it is essential that you see and are then able to react to your students' responses, both behavioral responses and responses to learning tasks—while you are teaching. (Locke had the luxury of sitting on the sidelines and seeing when he wrote this!) There are multiple reasons to observe in the gym. In *Children Moving* we have chosen to focus on two that we deem most important—observing the children's movement responses and observing teacher actions related to effective teaching. While we treat these as two separate and distinct skills serving two different purposes, they are inextricably related to each other. There are effective teaching skills not related to observing children's movement, yet the ability to be an effective teacher without observing children's movement is impossible. Rink (2010) most poignantly communicates this when she indicates that the teaching cycle of teacher task, to children's movement response, to subsequent teacher task is at the heart of the learning process. Without acute and accurate observation of the children's movement responses, it is impossible to create appropriate follow-up tasks. Chapter 7 deals with the observation of teaching skills. In this chapter we focus on the observation of children and their movement responses.

> *Be gentle with yourself. Don't be disappointed initially if, in the relative tranquility after you've finished teaching, you find that you made some apparently obvious errors. Observation appears easy to the spectator, but the complexity of teaching and observing movement can be fully appreciated only when one assumes the role of the teacher. In time and with practice, you'll become increasingly satisfied with your ability to observe and analyze movement.*

The ability to observe—to see with understanding—is critical for a reflective teacher. It is especially critical for physical education teachers because the result of our teaching is a fleeting movement that happens in the space of only a few seconds. In contrast to math or English classes, where written products allow the teacher to provide feedback and make decisions about the next instructional move after carefully studying tangible evidence (e.g., written work), we have to make those same decisions based on a movement we may have seen once or twice. There are few permanent products as a result of our teaching. It is impossible to provide a safe environment, offer feedback to students about their performance, or make decisions about what task to present next unless you can observe and accurately determine what students are doing. Thus the teacher who designs and implements a successful physical education program must be able to observe perceptively, accurately, and continuously and then translate the information gained from the observation into usable material.

Coaches will easily and readily talk of observing their players' very detailed movements in both practice and game situations. When coaches and players with no formal training have been compared with physical education teachers on their ability to observe and analyze movement, the coaches and players scored significantly higher than the teachers, who had degrees in physical education (Hoffman 1977).

Accurate observational analysis is difficult in a nonteaching or poorly managed environment. The complexity increases considerably, however, when the teacher attempts to observe the movement and behavioral characteristics of individual children and simultaneously monitor the work of an entire class during a physical education lesson (Barrett 1977, 1979, 1983). Beginning teachers should not be dismayed by the complexity of the observation tasks; not only can the skills be learned, but they also become easier as the teacher becomes more comfortable with the content and the teaching environment.

The process of observation can be divided into two aspects: what to observe and how to observe.

- *What to observe:* This aspect includes four categories: safety, on-task behavior, class movement patterns, and individual movement patterns.
- *How to observe:* Observational techniques are generic, regardless of what is observed; they include positioning, knowing what to look for, and having an observational strategy.

The remainder of this chapter introduces you to these two aspects of observation.

What to Observe

When teaching physical education, a person is constantly bombarded by seemingly hundreds of ideas in just a few seconds. Thus we've provided a procedure that we've found valuable for observing and understanding all that goes on in our classes. Because teaching is so complex, it's important that a teacher know what to look for in a particular lesson before conducting the lesson itself. This requires planning. When we don't

plan, we often find it difficult to decide what to observe during a lesson, so our lessons lack focus or direction. It's almost as if we were just doing things with children rather than actually teaching. For this reason, when we plan, we divide our observation into four categories: (1) safety, (2) on-task behavior, (3) class movement patterns, and (4) individual movement patterns.

Safety

The teacher's initial and constant attention must always be directed toward the children's safety. This must be the first focus of any lesson. Whenever you observe an unsafe situation, remember that safety must always take priority over everything else going on in the lesson. If you have stated a task in such a way that the children are responding unsafely, stop the class, and restate the task. If equipment is unsafe or being used unwisely, stop the class to make the use of the equipment safe. We also teach the children about safety so they're able to understand and develop a respect toward potential hazards they may encounter if they aren't careful. Initially, we explain the reasons for our safety procedures to enable children to better understand and make intelligent decisions about their own safety. That's not enough, however. We need to constantly be aware of unsafe conditions. Following are several safety precautions we always keep in mind as we observe the classes. Some of these precautions are also described in Chapter 8.

- It is essential that children work independently without pushing, shoving, tripping, or otherwise interfering with other children.
- A working knowledge of self-space is obligatory. Children must work in a space a safe distance from others. When the youngsters get too close—for example, when striking with rackets—we stop the lesson and make them adjust their space.
- Depending on the surface, our children work in tennis shoes or barefoot. We don't allow stockinged feet, especially on hardwood or tile floors because they're so slippery. Children enjoy sliding, but this is a definite hazard.
- In lessons on skill themes, such as rolling, transferring weight, and balance (gymnastics context), we don't allow I Dare You and Follow the Leader games or touching and pushing.
- In lessons in which gymnastics apparatus is being used, we allow only one child on the equipment at a time unless otherwise indicated. This condition might change once the learning environment has been effectively established.

Legal liability is an increasing concern for teachers, particularly physical education teachers. We strongly encourage you to teach safety rules similar to those just described and to include the rules in the written lesson plan so they're part of a permanent record in the unfortunate event you have to document safety precautions. Most of these safety rules should be taught in the first few weeks of school (Chapter 8) and then reinforced throughout the year. Again, as you observe, make sure safety is constantly the forefront of your focus.

On-Task Behavior

Once you've determined that the environment is safe, your next focus is to decide whether children are on task. Are they actually doing what you asked them to do? For example, if you asked your class to throw and catch with a partner, are they doing so? Or are they kicking the ball, running around chasing one another? Or, more subtly, are they not working with a partner but in groups of four or five? If so, these are off-task behaviors, and you need to attend to them immediately. Stop the lesson!

There are three reasons why children may be off task:

1. The children are trying to perform the task, but it was stated unclearly. You must restate the task.
2. The task may not be appropriate for the class. The task is too hard or too easy. If it's too easy, many children will become bored and thus off task. If it's too hard, many children will become frustrated—and thus off task. Determining the students' success rate is one way to check the difficulty of the task. A guideline for the right success rate is 80 percent—in other words, the students you observe should be successful 80 percent of the time. Figure 11.1 provides an example of an observation sheet that can be used to assess task difficulty. Success at this point is defined as the use of the proper cues or the efficiency of the skills, not the result of the skill. For example, when watching a child throw, we would watch to see if the critical cues were used, not if the ball hit the target. In situations in which the task is too hard or too easy, or was not stated clearly, children will most often make up their own task. Rarely will young children come to the teacher and say, "Teacher, the task is too hard," or "Teacher, I didn't understand."
3. The children haven't yet learned to be on task. If so, you'll need to practice the appropriate behavior in physical education class. It is impossible to teach without first managing (Chapter 8). The time spent on management is well worth it later when your class is running smoothly. If you don't spend time on management early, you will find yourself constantly managing later. As the old saying goes, "An ounce of prevention is worth a pound of cure."

The reality of teaching, unfortunately, is that often a class has one or two children who tend to be off task more than others. What do you do with them? After all, their behavior interferes with your right to teach and other youngsters' right to learn. Refer to Chapters 8 and 9 for ideas about working with these students.

Class Movement Patterns

When you've determined that the class is working safely and on task, begin observing the entire class to see how students are accomplishing the task. Constantly be on the alert, however, for unsafe and off-task situations.

As you scan the entire class to see how children are moving, observe one cue at a time. Based on that, you'll make one of four decisions according to what you observe the majority of the children doing. Your choices are to (1) leave the task the same and let the students continue practicing, (2) change the task, (3) provide a cue, or (4) present a challenge to the children without changing the task. If you decide to modify the task in anyway, Chapter 6 discusses the four content development decisions in detail. We mention them here to emphasize that these decisions need to be based on what you observe, not on an arbitrary time allotment that doesn't take into account, for example, children's abilities and interests.

As part of making the decision, ask yourself if the task is really helping the students learn what they need to know (Rink 2003). If, for example, your lesson goal is to guide children to reach the National Association for Sport and Physical Education content standard such as "demonstrates understanding of concepts, principles, strategies, and tactics as they apply to the learning and performance of physical activities" (NASPE 2004, 12) and the skill you have chosen is the use of "large extensions in weight transfer," then you will want to be sure that the way the children have understood and are practicing the tasks is really leading to the use and understanding of large extensions. As if the observing the children's responses was not difficult enough, the appropriate teacher response to what is seen is even harder—especially with a class of 30 children.

Let's take another example. Say that for this lesson you've decided your second graders need practice throwing overhand and your goal is to begin to teach four characteristics of a mature throw. You select a

Figure 11.1 Practice
attempts recording sheet.

Practice Attempts Recording Sheet

Teacher: _____ *Date:* _____ *Content:* _____

Lesson Starting/Ending Time: _____ _____

Students: 1. _____ 2. _____ 3. _____

4. _____ 5. _____ 6. _____

Charting Instructions: Note each task and record the number of practice attempts provided (choose two students to observe for each task and record their total practice attempts). Indicate successful (efficient) tries by circling the tally marks for that try.

Task	# of Skill Attempts	Totals (attempts/successful attempts)
1.	Student 1:	
	Student 2:	
2.	Student 3:	
	Student 4:	
3.	Student 5:	
	Student 6:	
4.	Student 1:	
	Student 2:	
5.	Student 3:	
	Student 4:	

Totals (Student 1)

   a. # of attempts (all tasks) = _____
   b. # of successful attempts (all tasks) = _____
   c. % of attempts successful = _____
   d. Rate of attempts per minute (# of attempts/# of minutes) _____

Totals (Student 2)* (Total attempts for all students in the same manner.)

   e. # of attempts (all tasks) = _____
   f. # of successful attempts (all tasks) = _____
   g. % of attempts successful = _____
   h. Rate of attempts per minute (# of attempts/# of minutes) _____

series of tasks from Chapter 23. You also decide that your cue for this lesson will be the use of opposition—that is, that the children learn to step with the foot opposite their throwing arm. Once you've defined the task and explained the cue ("Throw the ball as hard as you can against the wall. Remember to step with the foot on the other side of your body from your throwing arm"), observe to see which children are using opposition and which ones aren't. If you observe that most of the children aren't using opposition, stop the class and remind them to use opposition (or remind children individually). You may also demonstrate the correct performance yourself or pinpoint as models several children who are using opposition. Then the children can return to their practice. Be sure to observe the children's responses to determine whether they are performing as the cue indicates. Remember, the cue (opposition) is what you actually expect the children to learn in this lesson. This cycle of teacher task/student response/teacher observation and decision about subsequent task is the heart of teaching for student learning in physical education (Rink 2010). Without the ability to observe astutely, it is impossible to teach for student learning.

Individual Movement Patterns

After observing for safety, on-task behavior, and class movement patterns, it is time to look at individuals' movement patterns. Observing individual movement patterns can yield two types of results—information that will assist a teacher in helping individual students, and information that the teacher might record on checklists and anecdotal records for future use (see Chapter 12).

Teaching children individually is something we try to do as teachers. Obviously, however, it's not an easy job. Chapter 8 describes two instructional techniques for working with individuals: teaching by invitation and intratask variation. Use of these approaches involves the ability to observe individuals and yet maintain the focus on the entire class.

We encourage teachers to focus initially on the entire class using the scanning technique described in the next section. By working with individuals too early, the teacher may lose focus on the entire class. We've seen this happen frequently with beginning teachers. The teacher becomes so involved helping an individual child that he or she loses focus on the entire class and may suddenly look up to find that a number of children are off task or that an unsafe condition has developed. This is not to suggest that teachers shouldn't work with children individually—we certainly should and do. But teachers must make sure they don't become so involved

with one child that they forget to concentrate on the whole class. As Locke's vignette at the beginning of the chapter suggests, doing so is a real challenge.

> *Recently I observed a teacher attempting to teach a child how to run and kick a stationary ball. The child was unable to adjust her run to enable herself to arrive at the ball in a proper kicking position. After each unsuccessful attempt (the ball barely moved, and the child almost appeared to step on the ball rather than kick it), the teacher would say to the child, "No, that's not it!" The child knew she had failed as she watched the ball erratically dribble away from her foot, and yet the teacher offered no prescription for improvement. Rather than stating results the student can readily observe, the successful instructor offers a prescription for practice—that is, a cue.*

When we work with individuals, we use essentially the same process we use for the entire class. We vary the task for different children (intratask variation). If you ever have an opportunity to watch a master teacher, you'll see that this teacher is constantly using intratask variation as he or she travels from child to child while remaining conscious of the entire class, safety, and on-task behavior. Now you can better understand why it's so important to spend time establishing a learning environment at the beginning of the year.

When presented separately, the four aspects or categories of observation—safety, on-task behavior, class movement patterns, and individual movement patterns—seem simple and easy to follow. When teaching, however, a teacher is rarely able to focus on any one aspect at a time. As Locke's vignette suggests, the teacher must concentrate simultaneously on the four aspects. To aid in your observation, Figure 11.2 provides a flow chart of the questions we use to guide our observation of classes. Note that the arrows between the questions go both ways, indicating that the observation focus isn't linear, but that there's a constant interplay between the questions. Note, too, that this observation may all happen within 60 seconds! Remember, whenever a new task is given, always start over with the first two questions: Are the children working safely, and are they on task?

How to Observe

Once you have decided what you want and need to observe, the next step is actually observing so that you see. As we indicated earlier, observation is a learned

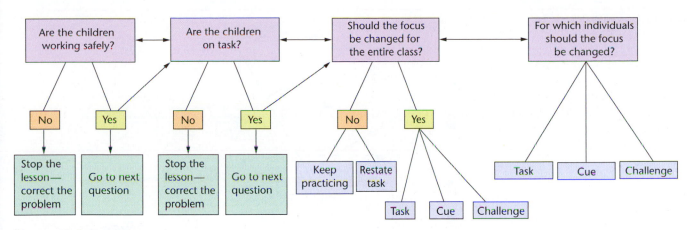

Figure 11.2 Questions reflective teachers use to guide observation.

skill that can improve with practice. Bird watching provides an apt analogy here. Non–bird watchers who see a bird might think, "There is a big bird." Novice bird watchers will say, "There is a big bird with a white head and dark body." Intermediate bird watchers, with binoculars, might note a large bird with a dark body, white head, and white on the tail. An expert, with binoculars, will identify the bird as a bald eagle. It takes practice to become an expert observer, but the result is rich and detailed information about what you have seen and hence where to proceed. Three techniques are helpful in learning to observe with insight (Rink 2010):

1. Positioning
2. Knowing in advance what you are looking for
3. Having a strategy for observing

Positioning

Positioning in the gym is essential. To return to the bird-watching analogy, if you are standing behind a tree, you might not be able to see the bird at all; if you are standing behind the bird, you might only see the tail; and if you are standing too close, you might frighten the bird. Thus positioning is important from three perspectives: being able to see, being able to see important aspects, and how you affect the learners' performance (Rink 2010).

First, for safety purposes, never spend long in a position where you are unable to observe all the students in your class. While there are a variety of techniques useful in facilitating the observation of the whole class, we have found the back-to-the-wall technique the most useful for seeing all students. Using the back-to-the-wall technique, the teacher stands outside the area in which the children are working so she or he can see the entire class. From a legal perspective, this allows for direct supervision. When the teacher enters the middle of an instructional area, he or she is unable to see part of the class (Figure 11.3) and should consequently limit the time spent in the middle. The ability to observe all that is going on, particularly with classes that are difficult to manage, is important both for effective classroom management and for comprehensive observation. Once the teacher is sure that a class is capable of working without constant monitoring, he or she can reduce the use of the back-to-the-wall technique, except when using it to observe the whole class.

Second, your position must allow you to see the critical aspects of the skill on which the lesson is focused. For example, if your lesson is focused on absorbing weight through the back of the head and shoulders and keeping the body round while rolling forward, the logical observation point would be from the child's side. If observing from the back, you would not be able to see the critical characteristics you were looking for. When teaching, be sure to choose observation positions that permit you to see what you need to see.

Finally, whether we like to admit it or not, where you stand affects children's performance. Older children tend not to work in the area immediately around where the teacher is standing, and younger children cling to the teacher. So if you always stand in the same place to give directions or observe, some children will always be where you do not have a clear view of them. Thus to be able to see better and increase on-task behavior, you should constantly move around the space and refrain from having one position that becomes your home base from which you always give directions or talk to the class.

Figure 11.3 Ineffective teacher position for observation.

The chart in Figure 11.4 allows you to assess your movement patterns. Have an observer (see Chapter 7 for possible observers) trace your movement patterns, marking an X at the start of each pathway and an O for each place you stood to give directions. You can also teach the observer to make a mark on the pathway each time you interact individually with a child.

> *The first time I taught the whole class [26 children], I had a great deal of trouble seeing individuals in the class. All I saw, no matter how hard I tried, was a mass of individuals. I couldn't see individual performances.*
>
> —FRAN MCGILLAN (as a junior in college)

Knowing What to Look For

Although being in a good position to observe is a prerequisite to observation, it does not guarantee you will see what you need to see. In order to see, you need to know what you want to see. The complexity of a dynamic environment without permanent products adds to the difficulty of this task. Filtering for the critical elements of safety and skill helps to focus your observation.

Obviously, safety is the first aspect to observe, but what makes a safe environment? The elements are usually included in class protocols—not interfering with others, following directions, and so on. You must identify what each aspect of safety looks like. For example, what does not interfering with others look like if you have asked students to "throw and catch with a partner in a space that matches your abilities"? What would be the first safety aspect to observe? For us, it would be, Are the students spread out so they do not interfere with each other? In other words, are partners not throwing across another group of partners, and do they have enough space between groups? For a different task, to "jump over a low hurdle, make a wide shape in the air, land, and roll," our first observation might be that the students were actually landing before they rolled rather than diving over the hurdle. At the same time, we might check the following: Is only one student on a mat at a time? Is there enough space between the mats? Are students pushing each other?

After safety, our focus goes to on-task behavior. For the rolling task just mentioned, this would again include whether students are jumping, landing, and rolling. (This is both a safety and an on-task focus because being off task here is unsafe.) Are students remaining at their own mats or traveling around the room? Are they simply rolling and forgetting to jump? Are they jumping but without wide body shapes?

Finally, our focus turns to the quality of students' skill. How do we decide what to look for in terms

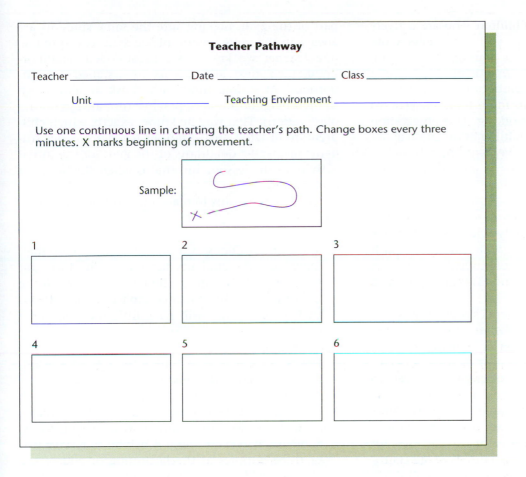

Figure 11.4 Teacher pathway observation.

---

of skill? The obvious answer is the critical aspects of the skill being taught. But there are so many of them it makes this task incredibly difficult. We have found that if we limit our observation to one cue at a time, it not only focuses our observation, but the learners as well. The easiest way we have found to accomplish this focus is to list specific cues that are the focus of your lesson on the lesson plan and to stick to them. One teacher who was having difficulty remaining faithful to the cues she had chosen actually wrote them on her hand or the inside of the drum she used as a stop/start signal to remind herself. This aspect of observation is compounded by your knowledge of the content you are teaching as well as the complexity of the task. For example, rolling forward (see Chapter 21; page 385) requires the teacher to know the cues for the forward roll (hands should be on the floor on the outside of the knees, lean forward, hike your bottom up high into the air, look back through your legs, and tip) and what they look like in practice (See Box 21-2). The task is fairly controlled, so the observation is simplified. A forward roll from a balanced position during a routine on a piece of equipment, however, requires the observer to know cues that relate to making the transition from a

balance to a roll and to performing a roll on a different surface and in a much more complex situation. As you plan lessons, identify specific cues (in the skill theme chapters, these are identified at the beginning of every task) and focus on those cues one at a time.

Strategies

Even though a teacher is in a position to observe, has planned ahead, and knows what to observe, it doesn't mean he is observing effectively. It's not unusual to become so focused on the movement or behavior of a particular individual or group that he becomes oblivious to other children within the class. The two strategies of scanning and limited selection are presented here to help you observe.

Scanning   The teacher who wants to observe the class as a whole can maintain an appropriate focus by scanning (Siedentop and Tannehill 2000). Using a left-to-right sweep, the teacher can glance at an entire class in just a few seconds and accurately assess how all the children are working. For example, if you want to determine the number of children who are actively practicing a given movement, you could quickly observe the class from left to right, counting as you scan. By comparing the number practicing a particular movement with the total number of children in the class, you can rapidly (in no more than 15 seconds) assess the way the class is working. This observation technique can be used for obtaining information about the appropriateness of the movement, the behavior of an entire class, or the behavior of individuals within the class.

Limited Selection The technique of limited selection allows you to observe only select aspects at one time. There are three ways in which we accomplish this: (1) limiting the number of students to observe; (2) limiting what we look at; and (3) limiting the area in which we observe.

Limiting the number of students simply means that you observe only a few representative students. The easiest way to limit the number of students observed while getting a representative idea of what is occurring is to choose students of different skill levels to observe and have them act as your barometer for the lesson. To do this, choose three to five students of varying skill levels prior to class; throughout that class, observe those students first to get a feel for what is occurring. (It has been fairly well substantiated that three to five students of varying skill levels are representative of the entire class.) The next time the class meets, choose three to five different students. You may want to record or mark in your records the date you observe each student until you have rotated through the entire class.

The second aspect to limit is the number of things for which you are looking. Just as we suggest giving children one cue at a time on which to focus, we suggest observing one cue at a time. For example, if students are practicing the overhand throw, you might first watch for side to the target, then opposition, then rotation, and then follow-through. Trying to observe all cues at once becomes a bit overwhelming. Limiting your observational focus also makes it easier to provide specific congruent feedback to the students, as described in Chapter 8.

Finally, similar to limiting the number of students observed is the idea of limiting the area in which you observe intently. The way many experienced teachers use this technique is to divide the gym into sections and observe only one section at a time, never trying to observe all sections during one lesson. Many teachers use this idea when making the more specific observations that lead to written records. To limit the observation area, they observe only one part of the gym, making sure the same students are always in the same section of the gym. For example, one teacher we know uses color-coded neighborhoods (or zones); all students are assigned a neighborhood. At various times he will ask students to go to their neighborhood to practice (not always during observation). That way he knows exactly which children are in what area. Another teacher has her students in specific quadrants of the gym for the initial activity of the lesson, and that is when she does her observation.

Some helpful hints to make the most of your observations are:

1. Make sure your observation has a focus. To do that, make sure the students have a specific focus for their work. This is most often evident through the use of cues. If the students don't have a focus for their practice, you will have little focus for your observation.
2. Develop a checklist.
3. Determine a manner of rating the skill—for example, "achieved," "developing," "not yet."
4. Observe the class. Remember to observe one cue at a time and to observe only the cues you have taught, even if you see other things; stick to your focus. Some teachers have found it helpful to reserve two or three minutes at the beginning or end of the class simply for observation.

Figure 11.5 is an example of a checklist for control-level dribbling. In this example, the cues for dribbling are listed across the top of the form and the children's names would be listed down the side. When asked, the children would go to their designated zone in the teaching space, and the teacher would mark with a −, ~, or + the extent to which the child demonstrated the cue. To make the observation more efficient, some teachers will only mark the children who have not received the developing stage and only observe one zone during a lesson. (Figure 12.2 is an example of a completed dribbling checklist.)

The information gathered with checklists over a period of time lends itself to a myriad of uses. The information is useful for planning future instruction, either adding additional cues or revisiting previous ones. It also provides information about where to begin when skill themes are revisited. In addition, it can be used as assessment information for the student and parents (see Chapter 12). And, while limiting allows a teacher to observe with a narrowed focus, a teacher must never lose sight of the entire class. As you watch individual movement patterns, be sure to continually scan the whole class.

Figure 11.5 Sample of a blank checklist for observing skill.

Summary

Observing—the ability to see with understanding—is a crucial skill for the reflective teacher. Successful observation can be learned and involves knowing what and how to observe. What to observe includes, first, safety, followed by on-task behavior, class movement patterns, and individual movement patterns. Although presented hierarchically, these four aspects continually interact with each other and may all be observed within a 60-second time frame. How to observe involves the positioning of the teacher, knowing what to look for, and observational strategies. Teacher positioning influences what a teacher is able to see, whom the teacher is able to see, and how the student performs a task. The teacher's knowledge of content affects the accuracy of what he or she is able to see. Two strategies, scanning and limited selection, aid teachers as they attempt to observe learners' movement responses.

Reading Comprehension Questions

1. In reflective teaching, what is the purpose of observation of student responses?

2. Why is observation in physical education so difficult?

3. In your own words, explain the key aspects of safety that a reflective teacher watches for.

4. What does off-task behavior look like? Give three examples that you remember from your physical education classes.

5. Imagine you are teaching children to kick a ball to a partner. Briefly describe what you might observe that would cause you to change the task to make it easier or harder.

6. In the same imaginary situation as the question above, describe what you might observe that would cause you to provide a kicking cue rather than to change the task.

7. Again, assuming the same teaching situation, describe what you might observe that would cause

you to provide a kicking challenge rather than changing the task or the cue.

8. If observing is the process of seeing clearly, what is the best position for observing the placement of the nonkicking foot? Why? The use of finger pads while dribbling? Why? The ball in striking with golf clubs or hockey sticks? Why? Tightness of muscles in balancing? Why?

9. How can a teacher avoid having children's performance affected by her position in class?

10. For the skill of dribbling with the feet in general space, what would you look for as a teacher?

11. If observing the cue of wide base of support while balancing, what are the three ways a teacher can limit her observation as described in this chapter?

References/Suggested Readings

Barrett, K. R. 1977. We see so much but perceive so little: Why? In *Proceedings: 1977 National Conference of the National College for Physical Education for Men and the National Association for Physical Education of College Women*. Chicago: University of Illinois, Office of Publications Services.

Barrett, K. R. 1979. Observation for teaching and coaching. *Journal of Physical Education and Recreation* 50(1): 23–25.

Barrett, K. R. 1983. A hypothetical model of observing as a teaching skill. *Journal of Teaching in Physical Education* 3(1): 22–31.

Hoffman, S. J. 1977. Toward a pedagogical kinesiology [Monograph 28]. *Quest*: 38–48.

Locke, L. F. 1975, Spring. The ecology of the gymnasium: What the tourist never sees. In *Southern Association of Physical Education for College Women Proceedings*.

Mauldon, E., and J. Layson. 1965. *Teaching gymnastics*. London: MacDonald & Evans.

[NASPE] National Association for Sport and Physical Education. 2004. *Moving into the future: National standards for physical education*. 2nd ed. Reston, VA: National Association for Sport and Physical Education.

Rink, J. E. 2003. Effective instruction in physical education. In *Student learning in physical education*, 2nd ed., ed. S. Silverman and C. Ennis, 165–86. Champaign, IL: Human Kinetics.

Rink, J. E. 2010. *Teaching physical education for learning*. 6th ed. New York: McGraw-Hill.

Siedentop, D., and D. Tannehill. 2000. *Developing teaching skills in physical education*. 4th ed. New York: McGraw-Hill.

Assessing Student Learning

The primary goal of assessment should be seen as the enhancement of learning, rather than simply the documentation of learning.

—NATIONAL ASSOCIATION FOR SPORT AND PHYSICAL EDUCATION (NASPE 2004)

You haven't taught until they've learned.

—JOHN WOODEN

Key Concepts

- Assessment is the gathering and collection of information framed by how that information is used. Assessment can be classified as assessment for learning or assessment for accountability.
- Assessment for accountability is typically large-scale standardized testing, e.g. yearly state-wide tests.
- Assessment for learning shares the following characteristics: it is linked directly to instruction; it views the student as the primary client; it is meaningful; it happens as part of instruction; and students know what they are supposed to learn ahead of time.
- Teacher observation, exit slips, student journals, homework, peer observation, self-assessment, event tasks, videotape and digital analysis, student drawings and displays, and student portfolios are all viable assessment for learning items in physical education classes.
- Holistic or analytic rubrics are used to distribute assessment criteria to students and subsequently evaluate student performance.
- Assessment should occur in cognitive, affective, and psychomotor domains of learning.
- When student achievement is reported to parents, they should be made aware of what students have learned in physical education and where students are with respect to essential learning.

(Hay 2006; Melograno 2006). Assessment information can be used in two ways: assessment for learning and assessment for accountability (Hay 2006).

While the two ways of using assessment information are not distinctly separate, they are different and serve different purposes. Assessment for accountability is most often seen in large-scale standardized testing. This type of assessment has become more commonplace within the current educational reform movement and the passage of No Child Left Behind (2001), often resulting in state-mandated assessment exams. Assessment for learning is about contextually relevant or meaningful tasks that develop higher-order knowledge and skills that can be transferred outside the classroom setting (Hay 2006). Assessment for learning focuses on the learner and assumes that assessment should provide feedback to the learner. In short you assess what you teach every day in your lessons.

Children Moving endorses assessment for learning, and this kind of assessment is much changed from the kind of assessment most of us remember. Assessment for learning is more teacher friendly and student friendly. It is the "process of determining if and to what degree a student can demonstrate, in context, his or her understanding and ability relative to identified standards of learning" (Lambert 2007, 12)—in other words, what you taught and how well was it learned—if at all. This idea of assessment contains several key pieces critical to the overall understanding of the process: what was learned; how well it was learned; and in what context the demonstration of learning took place.

This chapter is divided into three sections. The first section introduces the concept of assessing for learning or assessing what we are teaching in our lessons—often and regularly. The second section describes a process teachers follow to adapt or create assessments based on standards. The final section provides 13 examples of practical, frequently used assessments for learning.

Assessment for Learning

Many of us can vividly remember fitness tests in the fall and spring, with a few cognitive tests on rules and history thrown in during the year. But are isolated fitness scores and rules and history what we really want students to learn from our classes? Are the age-old ways of measuring that knowledge really the best way? Assessment can be defined as the gathering and collection of information framed by how that information is used

Understanding Assessment for Learning

Let's explore these ideas a bit further. The idea of demonstrating what was learned implies that the student completes some type of performance that others can evaluate. How well something is learned implies that the student's performance is evaluated against preset criteria that are known ahead of time. This performance with its evaluation criteria takes place in an authentic or real setting as far as possible. Finally, the performance, the criteria, and the setting should directly reflect a previously identified standard (goal) to be achieved. In other words, a teacher assesses what he is teaching the children. These assessments are tied directly to the objectives of the lesson plans described in Chapter 6.

A subtle but important aspect here is the "reflection of a previously identified standard or goal." Before designing any assessment item, it is critical to know what you want students to learn and how that learning contributes to the overall goal of children's physical education—becoming physically active for a lifetime. Assessment without a linked purpose is no better than no assessment at all. Three guiding questions aid in this process (adapted from Lambert 2007):

1. How does the assessment relate to your program goals, i.e. what you want your students to learn in a given period of time?
2. Are the assessments linked to one another so they gradually build into more complex, challenging assessments?
3. To what milestone or benchmark does the assessment connect, and how?

The key is that the assessments are designed to contribute to a child's learning—not just isolated events that have no personal meaning or relevance.

An example may help. Physical Education Standard 1 indicates that in order for a person to be physically active for a lifetime he should "demonstrate competency in motor skills and movement patterns needed to perform a variety of physical activities" (NASPE 2004, 11). One of the grade 3–5 sample performance outcomes is to dribble and pass a basketball to a moving receiver. This is a potential indication of learning for Standard 1 at these grade levels. A possible demonstration of the ability to dribble and pass might be to have students receive and throw a basketball pass to a partner on the move (see Chapter 24, "Dribbling and Passing with a Partner"). This would be the focus of several lessons and written in the lesson objectives (Chapter 6). The preset criteria for determining how well this ability was learned might be: (1) the student receives and passes in one motion; (2) the student passes ahead of the moving players (so the receiver does not have to stop to receive the pass); and (3) the receiving student cuts into open space to receive the pass. Students would be considered "accomplished" if they could meet all three criteria, "almost there" if two were accomplished, and "still working on it" if they could accomplish only one of the criteria. To use a "real" context, the whole class might perform the task while the teacher walks around with a checklist evaluating the criteria. This assessment might occur over several lessons as the teacher observes the children.

This assessment example has been called different things by different writers: alternative assessment, performance assessment, outcome assessment, or authentic assessment. Though each of those terms has a slightly different meaning, we have chosen to use assessment for learning to represent them all. This will makes the assessment discussion that follows much easier to follow.

> *Authentic assessment strikes me as being quite interesting. The reason for this involves my current experiences as an eighth-grade basketball coach. When choosing players for the team during tryouts, I evaluated players mostly on drills. However, I have realized that while they do quite well during drills, many of them do not utilize these skills in a game situation. Next time, I believe I will use much scrimmage time to evaluate my players.*
>
> —ANDY BARRY, sophomore physical education major and first-year basketball coach

Although assessment for learning has many distinctions that separate it from traditional assessment (e.g. fitness tests, written knowledge tests, skill tests), we have elected to focus on five characteristics:

1. Assessment and instruction are linked.
2. Assessment is learner centered.
3. Assessment is an ongoing part of teaching, not an end or an afterthought.
4. Assessment comprises meaningful tasks performed in context.
5. The criteria for assessment are known in advance.

These ideas for assessment for learning are supported by *Appropriate Instructional Practice Guidelines for Elementary School Physical Education* from the National Association for Sport and Physical Education (NASPE 2009; see Box 12-1).

Linking of Assessment and Instruction

Assessment is part of the whole learning process. It allows children and teachers not only to see that something has been learned but also to actually demonstrate it. This is critical to effective teaching. It also changes the relationship between teachers and students, as well as student outcomes. It addresses how we teach, as well as student achievement. It is said that if assessment and teaching are done well, the student should not know the difference between the two. It may be like the Friday night basketball game: Is the game an assessment of what was learned in practice during the week, or is it just another activity in which to participate?

Assessment Is Learner Centered

How many times have you been told that the purpose of a midterm exam is to help you as a student? It is much like being told that a punishment hurts

Box 12-1

Appropriate and Inappropriate Physical Education Practices

Component: Assessment

Appropriate Practice

- Formative and summative assessments are an ongoing and an integral part of the learning process for all students, including students with disabilities.
- Physical educators systematically teach and assess all domains (cognitive, affective, and physical) using a variety of assessment techniques.
- Assessments include clearly defined criteria, which are articulated to children as part of instruction prior to the assessment (e.g., a rubric is provided and explained during instruction).

Inappropriate Practice

- Assessment is rare and random and only occurs in the context of grading.
- Teachers only assess physical fitness.
- Assessments are not clearly defined and/or do not relate to program goals or objectives.
- Children are not sure what exactly is being tested/measured. They are not clear about what they are expected to do or know.
- Assessment is not multifaceted but addresses only a single performance score on fitness.

Source: National Association for Sport and Physical Education, *Appropriate instructional practice guidelines for elementary school physical education*, 3rd ed. (Reston, VA: National Association for Sport and Physical Education, 2009). Reprinted with permission.

that weren't recorded as part of your final grade? Assessment for learning is laden with those little checks. What this also means is that assessment is not grading. The primary purpose of assessment for learning is to give students information they can use to enhance learning. The secondary use of assessment for learning is for reporting or grading purposes. This "new" view of assessment requires us to change the view of assessment that has been ingrained in our thoughts our entire educational careers.

> *Because the student is the primary client of all assessment, assessment should be designed to improve performance, not just monitor it.*
>
> —GRANT WIGGINS, *Assessing Student Performance* (1993)

Assessment Is an Ongoing Process

The third characteristic of assessment for learning is that it is an ongoing process. Have you have been in a physical education or other class in which assessment was done only as a midterm and/or a final exam. This is called summative assessment. It is also an example of assessment for accountability. Did the results of these summative exams provide you, as a student, useful information you were able to use to improve your skill or knowledge? Probably not. Assessment for learning, as opposed to midterm and final exam testing, is an ongoing process. It includes both formative and summative tasks. It is a means to an end, not an end in itself. This aspect makes assessment for learning largely formative (or ongoing)—not always used for grading but brimming with feedback. Summative assessment (at the end of a term, for example) is part of assessment for learning, but it is done only after an immense amount of formative feedback. In assessment for learning, summative assessments can be considered celebrations of learning where children are given the opportunity to uniquely display all they have learned, often assessing all three learning domains simultaneously. Assessment for learning then is a planned part of the ongoing route to student learning. It should provide meaningful feedback to the learner on an ongoing basis—not only as a final exam.

Assessment Comprises Meaningful Tasks

There once was a student who was a Division I varsity soccer player. The university at which he played

your parents more than it hurts you. It may be true in your parents' or teachers' minds, but it is rarely true for you.

Assessment for learning strives to view the child or student as the person who benefits most from the assessment (remember, assessment is supposed to be a learning experience). First and foremost, assessments should provide feedback to the student that they can use and make sense of. (Failing a midterm, without feedback, simply tells you that you failed—either you didn't guess well, or the teacher didn't ask the questions you knew, or others did better than you did—it doesn't tell you how well you know something.) What would happen if a teacher provided many little checks before a test that let you know how you were doing but allowed students to "test out" of activity courses if they showed a proficiency level of skill. Proficiency was demonstrated by a series of skills tests. One of the skills tests for soccer involved kicking a ball to a wall from a certain distance a certain number of times in an allotted amount of time. The soccer player failed the skills test twice. On the third and final attempt, he failed again. As he left, he turned and said, "I can play soccer—come watch me on the field—but this has nothing to do with soccer." Today he is a professional soccer player.

That scenario is telling. The fourth characteristic of assessment for learning is to make it more meaningful and relevant. Ideally, assessment should provide students with information that will fuel their interests (Questioning 1996). A good assessment model supports students' desire to learn and improve. Assessment for learning employs tasks that make sense, are in context, and are real to the students. Assessment for learning does not ask children to demonstrate skills in situations that don't relate to what they are supposed to be learning. These real contexts may be contrived or natural, but they are as close to the actual situation in which the skill is used as possible. In other words, no more wall volleying in volleyball (since when do you get to use the wall in a volleyball game?).

Criteria for Assessment Are Known in Advance

How often have you wondered what was going to be on a test? How would you feel if you knew ahead of time what material you were going to be assessed on so you didn't have to guess what you were supposed to learn? Assessment for learning provides children with the assessment criteria (called scoring rubrics) before they actually start the learning or assessment. This is especially true with summative assessment options used for reporting to parents.

Making It Work

We hope by now you have a clearer understanding of assessment for learning. We realize all this sounds wonderful (especially if you are a college student and can get your instructors to accept it). Yet the larger question remains: How do we do this type of assessment? This is where the map analogy from Chapter 6 really helps. We have adapted the work of Lambert (2007) to help you make assessment for learning not only happen, but also work the way it should as part of learning. As you will see, it links directly to planning in Chapter 6 because assessments ask and answer the questions, "Where do we want to go?" and "How do we know if we are getting there?" Here are the four steps we suggest to make assessment for learning to succeed.

1. Be a reflective teacher. In Chapters 4 and 7 we indicated that a variety of influences need to be considered as we teach. These include our experience as a teacher, the facilities in which we work, the frequency of our class meetings, the number of students in our classes, children's attitudes toward physical education, our beliefs as a teacher, and the like. Before you begin assessing, it is critical to know what your goals are. What do you believe in? What do you want your students at your school to learn? How do you plan to guide their learning?

2. Decide on the standards or learning goals that are realistic for you to accomplish in your program. This step requires us to link our teaching and assessment to some defined end point. This endpoint or destination is the student learning outcome, the standard (or standards) we want students to be able to demonstrate. Ultimately, the standards represent the end of the school physical education journey, which is usually in high school. Therefore, it is necessary to establish checkpoints or performance outcomes along the way to determine if we are making progress toward the destination. These performance outcomes, sometimes called benchmarks, may be designed at the district level, or you may be able to design your own. Figure 12.1 gives an example of one school district's grade-level performance outcomes for the skill theme of jumping and landing. These outcomes are also reflected in the lesson objectives (Chapter 6).

Although many of us are tempted to skip the lesson objective stage, by doing so we often find ourselves on a trip to nowhere or anywhere. Rink (2010) uses the analogy of a car without a driver to describe programs that do not have defined goals. Prusak and Vincent (2005) make the point that we always encourage students to set goals and work toward achieving them. These goals serve as a starting point, a point of reference, and a place to return when things get complicated. If this is sound advice for students, it must certainly be good for teachers as well. By linking assessment to end-points, we make assessment standards-based, i.e. our lessons are focused on providing relevant learning experiences that guide students to achieve the outcomes described in the standards.

JUMPING AND LANDING PERFORMANCE INDICATORS

By the end of fifth grade students should be able to:
- Enter a long rope; jump continuously while changing levels, shape or direction and exit.
- Turn an individual rope and jump efficiently and effectively with single and/or double bounces incorporating simple tricks.
- Efficiently and effectively combine balance, weight transfer or roll, and locomotor movements into a rhythmic sequence with intentional changes of direction, speed, level and pathway, with choice of objects and/or music.
- Efficiently and effectively combine balance, weight transfer or roll, and locomotor movements into a sequence on equipment with changes of level and direction.
- Efficiently and effectively jump off equipment with turns, shapes, and different directions in the air and land safely on both feet.

By the end of fourth grade students should be able to:
- Enter, jump continuously, and exit a long jump rope.
- Turn an individual rope (individual freestyle) and jump efficiently and effectively with single and/or double bounces.
- Combine balance, weight transfer or roll, and locomotor movements (to include jumping) into a sequence with intentional changes in direction, speed, level, and pathway with choice of objects and/or music.
- Combine balance, weight transfer or roll, and locomotor movements (to include jumping) into a sequence on equipment with changes in level and direction.
- Efficiently and effectively jump with turns, shapes, and directions in the air over a low object (6–12 inches) and land safely with one and two foot landings.

By the end of third grade:
- Successfully enter a turning long jump rope and jump.
- Turn an individual jump (individual freestyle) rope and jump continuously forward and backward.
- Combine balance, weight transfer or roll, and locomotor movements (to include jumping) into a sequence using different speeds, levels and pathways.
- Efficiently and effectively jump using turns, shapes, and different directions in the air.

By the end of second grade students should be able to:
- Jump starting from a stationary position in a long jump rope.
- Turn individual jump rope overhead with multiple jumps.
- Efficiently and effectively jump and land using different body shapes and different directions in the air.

By the end of first grade students should be able to:
- Turn individual jump rope overhead with one successful jump.
- Jump and land using the five basic jumps.

Figure 12.1 Sample performance indicators: Jumping and landing.
Source: Weld Co. District 6 Schools, Greeley, CO. Used with permission.

3. Once you decide on the outcomes, the next step is to decide on the lesson content progressions that you will teach to guide your students toward attaining the selected outcomes. This content should realistically reflect your teaching situation and what you are able to accomplish. It will be influenced by number of lessons per week, geography, weather, facilities, equipment available, or even your personal comfort zone and philosophy of teaching (see Chapters 4 and 7). Your curriculum scope (Appendix) reflects these outcomes.

4. Now that you have determined your outcomes and the content that will get you there, the next step is to adopt already developed assessments (Hopple 2005; Schiemer 2000); adapt existing assessments; or develop your own assessment methods, strategies, and criteria for use in judging student learning. This step in the journey allows you to determine the progress your students are making toward attaining the performance outcomes. It requires the use of assessment items that allow students to demonstrate what they have learned using criteria that have meaning to the children. The next two sections of this chapter, "What Has Been Learned? Selecting Assessment Options" and "Assessing How Well Something Was Learned" provide multiple assessment examples you can adopt and/or adapt for assessing the progress you students are making toward your program outcomes.

If you use the National Standards for Physical Education (NASPE 2004) or your state and district standards to outline essential learning of standards or goals for all students in physical education, Step 2 above is accomplished. The skill theme and movement concept chapters in *Children Moving* (Chapters 13–26) provide content progressions designed to guide children toward meeting the standards you select. Obviously you will need to choose which content to teach and how to order it—this is your curriculum scope.

Assessment is just like instruction. It needs a plan to guide the process and to give direction and focus to the various assessment pieces. If we pursue the trip analogy from Chapter 6, Steps 1, 2, and 3 require us to choose both a destination and a means of travel. In Steps 2 and 4 we determine if we are really on the route and how we are progressing in getting there. For example, if we want to travel to Chicago by flying (destination and method) to see a Chicago Bears game, as we travel we need to check to be sure we are really on our way to Chicago by plane. At the airport, the ticket agent will check us in and reaffirm that we are going to Chicago. When we get to the gate, the sign reads "Chicago." The gate agent takes our ticket for the Chicago flight, and on the plane the pilot announces that this is the flight to Chicago. In reality, we have just experienced four assessments to make sure we are on the right route. So how will you figure out if your students are on the right route to their goal?

A variety of options exist. Although the topics of deciding on the goal and content as well as developing and teaching instructional progressions are dealt with

elsewhere in this text, they are mentioned here to reinforce how assessment is linked to instruction. The remainder of this chapter provides options for selecting and developing assessment items that meaningfully assess student learning (the "how to and in what context to assess" piece) and how to develop the criteria for use in judging the student performance (the "how well" piece). We also provide suggestions about what to do with the results.

What Has Been Learned? Selecting Assessment Options

Now that we have outlined the theory underpinning assessment for learning, in this section we are going to provide 13 assessment examples that reflective teachers are using to assess their children's progress. The first two examples, challenges and checking for understanding, are often used in every lesson taught. The next 11 assessments are more structured and typically aren't used as often.

Informal Assessments

Challenges   Many instructional tasks are in reality informal assessments. For example, throughout the skill theme chapters, challenge tasks are presented as part of the progression of tasks. Recall from Chapter 6 that challenges keep the children practicing a task without making the task harder. The challenges provide the teacher, and the children, with informal assessments about their progress. Although these tasks are designed primarily to maintain interest and focus, they also serve as a minicheck on how well a child is progressing toward a goal. The challenge task of "See how many times in a row you can hit the ball without hitting the tee or missing the ball" provides children, as well as the teacher, with feedback. If most of the class can hit the ball only once or twice, the teacher knows she needs to provide more practice before moving on. Likewise, if most of the class is successful with continuous hits and an individual student can hit the ball only once or twice, the teacher knows she needs to work with that student. Students can also measure their ability to hit in the same manner.

Checks for Understanding   The Checks for Understanding ✿ distributed throughout the skill theme chapters are also informal mini cognitive assessments. Checks for Understanding ask children to show their understanding of a particular aspect of the lesson that has been taught (Graham 2008). For example, the Check for Understanding of locomotor actions provided on page 370 of Chapter 21 would allow the teacher to informally ascertain whether children understood the differences among skipping, jumping, and hopping. Checks for Understanding can be in the form of quick questions to the entire class at the end of a lesson and may call for verbal or physical answers, a show of hands, or a simple thumbs-up or thumbs-down.

Formal Assessments

The assessment options that follow are more formal assessments. Our purpose in these assessments is to see what students have learned: Are they on the road to their goal, or have they achieved their goal? Of the multitude of assessment options available, we outline 11 here that are designed to provide feedback to the teacher as well as the student. These are broader than the challenges and the Checks for Understanding, often assessing the cognitive domain (knowledge base) and affective domain (values and feelings), as well as the psychomotor domain. With the exception of the student journal, these assessment options can provide either formative assessment to students or a summative product that can be scored for reporting. In the skill theme chapters we include suggestions (identified with the assessment icon ✓) as to when these assessments might be used. The examples show how we make assessment part of our daily teaching, not a separate entity at the end of a unit. Although we focus on a limited number of assessment options here, many more are available. We hope these suggestions will allow you to develop other options specific to your situation. When you find an assessment option that really works, we invite you to share it with us.

There are two key points to remember as you choose or design any assessment option: (1) you cannot assess content if you didn't teach it; and (2) you can't assess without a goal. The first point, to teach before assessing, is largely self-explanatory—children have to have been taught precisely what you want to assess, or the assessment won't yield information that promotes student learning. The second point, to assess with a goal, essentially says that your assessment needs to match your learning objectives as contained in your lesson plan (Chapter 6). For example, an outcome for throwing and catching at the control level might be to demonstrate the mature form of the skill in an isolated situation. When performance moves toward combining skills and skill performance in dynamic situations (utilization/proficiency), the skill will be

assessed in an environment more closely resembling the actual environment in which the skill will be used. A goal might be to throw and catch with a partner while on the move by demonstrating leading the partner at an appropriate distance. Assessment should be done in a context appropriate to the skill and assess aspects of the goal being taught—the use of throwing to lead a partner. This assumes the skill of throwing has already been mastered and assessed. Skill themes develop from the simple to the complex, or from the mastery of basic skills, to combinations of skills, to use of skills in a more complex and dynamic environment. Assessment should follow the same guidelines. Assessments at the early control level should assess the elements critical to the mature pattern in an isolated situation. As children progress to later control and early utilization levels, assessment will focus on the use of the skill in a variety of contexts and combinations. Later, utilization and proficiency-level assessments will focus on the use of the skill in changing environments. In addition, at each level of skill development, cognitive understanding needs to be assessed, as does the affective dimension of our work.

Teacher Observation

Teacher observation is the most common form of assessment used in physical education classes. It is generally employed to assess psychomotor performance but can be applied to the affective domains as well. It is highly appropriate for assessing the acquisition of critical elements of skill that together form a mature motor pattern. Figure 12.2 shows a teacher checklist used to assess the critical elements of dribbling (Standard 1, NASPE 2004). Suggestions for designing and using such checklists are included in Chapter 11, "Observing Student Responses." The key factors involved in designing checklists that yield the information you want are identifying the critical elements (or goals, at this point) and designing the checklist so that it is usable. A final hint for using checklists is to observe one cue or element at a time. Just as we teach children by using one cue at a time, we should observe one element at a time.

Exit (or Entrance) Slips

Exit slips are short written pieces given at the end (or beginning) of a lesson and designed to assess cognitive (Standard 2, NASPE 2004) and affective (personal-social) (Standard 5, NASPE 2004) goals. They are developed to assess learning outcomes specific to the lesson

Figure 12.2 Teacher observation checklist.
Source: S. Holt/Hale, *Assessing motor skills in elementary physical education:* (Reston, VA: National Association for Sport and Physical Education, 1999).

just taught. The slips, often printed on half pieces of paper, contain two or three questions or ask the student to write in some form about specific learning cues or affective goals for the lesson (Figure 12.3).

The Helping Murgatroid technique provides another format for exit slips. Following is how we use Helping Murgatroid; modify the instructions to fit your situation:

The lesson is being taught in a multipurpose room that becomes a cafeteria from 11:30 a.m. to 1:00 p.m. On one side of the room, lunch tables are permanently set up. Before beginning the lesson, the teacher places pencils and pieces of paper on the lunch tables, enough for each

child in the upcoming class. The lesson begins as normal. At some point, the teacher stops the lesson and says to the children, "Remember several weeks ago we were practicing throwing? What I want you to do now is sit at one of the lunch tables so that you each have a piece of paper and a pencil. Then I want you to write a note to your friend Murgatroid. Murgatroid is not a very good thrower. List five cues that might help Murgatroid become a better thrower. As soon as you are finished, you can return to the other side of the gym and continue working on your jumping-and-landing sequence."

Figure 12.4 provides three examples of Helping Murgatroid cues written by fifth graders. Which set

Figure 12.3 Exit slips.
Sources: Dani Schroeder, Elizabeth Devine, Grace Deputy, and Kaily Hoffman, University of Northern Colorado. Used with permission.

of responses would you be satisfied with if you were the teacher? The entire process of exit slips takes less than five minutes, but it can be enormously helpful in assessing what the children remember from past lessons.

Student Journals

Student journals, like diaries, are written records of participation, results, responses, feelings, perceptions, or reflections about actual happenings or outcomes (NASPE 1995). Student journals provide a wonderful opportunity to assess the affective domain (Standards 5 and 6, NASPE 2004) of our teaching (Cutforth and Parker 1996). Students can be asked simply to write down their feelings, or they can be asked to respond to structured questions to assess more specific goals (Figure 12.5).

Remember, the purpose of journals is for students to reflect on their feelings, growth, frustrations, joys, and successes regarding physical activity and physical education (Figures 12.6 and 12.7). Students have to feel safe in doing that. One sure way to stifle students' honesty and reflectivity is to grade journals. This is one assessment piece used almost solely as a nongraded assessment. The purpose of journals is to give students a venue for writing honestly and freely.

The use of journals and exit slips appears time consuming. (See Box 12-2 for suggestions on how to manage them.) It has been our experience that al-

though they may take some time, they yield invaluable information about what students are understanding in class and how they feel about being in physical education.

Homework

In most schools today, the time allocated to physical education does not allow for the learning we would like to help students achieve. Homework can be used to supplement in-school physical education. Essentially, homework is work a student completes outside physical education class. Some teachers use homework to enhance cognitive understanding (Standard 2, NASPE 2004); yet active homework (Smith and Claxton 2003) can be used to enhance psychomotor learning (Standard 1, NASPE 2004) and to promote physical activity (Standard 4, NASPE 2004). This homework can be fun and personalized in that it allows children to choose their own activities. Furthermore, it can produce records of student progress, process, and participation.

Figure 12.8 illustrates a homework assignment that documents regular participation in physical activity. We often ask parents to verify the work. Physical education homework is similar to reports of reading done at home, and we have found homework quite useful, especially in terms of fitness or activity participation.

1. use both hands

2. try throwing over your head

3. move your feet apart a little

4.

5.

---

1. hold the ball in one hand and when you throw step with the oposite foot.

2. follow through

3. keep your ey on the target

4. put your side to the target

5. throw hard enough to get it to the target but dont throw to hard

---

1. watch my friends first.

2. then you try.

3. then well help you throw strat.

4. then you would try.

5. then you would get it right

Figure 12.4 Sample fifth-grade responses to the question, "What cues would you suggest to help Murgatroid become a better overhand thrower?"

Teacher Question: How do you feel about today's tournament compared to the others, when you were playing with smaller teams?

Aoi: I liked the two-on-two game better than the tournament.

Justin: Bad, it's harder to win.

Dustin: It was the best tournament I played in.

Amos: It was funner than others because you [could] play the whole thing.

Beau: It sucked. Because too many people and the teams sucked and I got in a fight.

Figure 12.5 Sample journal question with student responses. *Source:* Steve Sorenson and Brad Rempel, as quoted in N. Cutforth and M. Parker, Promoting affective development in physical education: The value of journal writing, *Journal of Physical Education, Recreation, and Dance* 67, no. 7 (1996): 22. Used with permission.

Peer Observation

Peer observation of students by other students can be used to assess competence in performance of skills and demonstration of selected critical elements (Standard 1, NASPE 2004) as well as cognitive understanding of what the demonstration of a selected cue looks like (Standard 2, NASPE 2004). Peer observation is easily built into tasks by asking students to work as partners and to provide each other with selected feedback regarding performance. For example, while working on dribbling with the hands, one student can watch the other to see if the partner uses the finger pads, bends the knees, and has a staggered stance. To more fully tie assessment to instruction and learning, the partner can provide feedback (Standard 5, NASPE 2004) to the performer to help him or her improve. On a more formal basis, students can record their observations for later use by the teacher.

Children enjoy peer observations (and peer teaching), but a few key points help make the task more successful. First, define the cues clearly enough so the partner can observe and comment. Second, structure the task so the children observe only one cue at a time. Remember, doing peer observation requires practice and independent learning skills (see Chapter 10). Start

Box 12-2

Managing Journals and Exit Slips

From the teacher's perspective, managing journals and exit slips is the key to their success (or lack of it). Four guidelines may help:

- *Determine the major purpose of the journal or exit slip.* Limit the scope initially. Focus on learning cues, on behavior, or on students' thoughts about the lesson—choose one. Expand the scope when you feel comfortable.

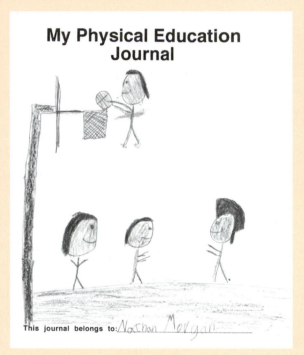

My Physical Education Journal

This journal belongs to: *Nathan Morgan*

Figure 12.6 Personalized second-grade journal cover.

- *Decide on a format for writing.* Because students are not accustomed to writing in physical education, their writing may initially be shallow and unfocused. We have therefore found it useful to give students a question to answer. As students become accustomed to writing, the level of the question may be increased to ask for more open-ended responses.
- *Organize writing procedures.* To effectively respond to journals, many teachers use journals with only two or three classes at a time and then switch to another group of classes at the end of a marking period. We have found it most effective to keep the journals in containers in the gym (or sometimes with classroom teachers) organized by class. This way you can read them when you get the chance and don't have to hunt them down. One of the best ways to encourage children to keep a journal is to let them personalize it (Figure 12.6). We have used everything from college blue books to manila folders to laminated construction paper. Usually we have students write for about three minutes at the end of class (Figure 12.7). Some teachers prefer the beginning of class if they want students to reflect on their previous journal entry before class.
- *Read and respond.* One key aspect of journals and exit slips is providing feedback to students. Teachers need to respond to student writing. Responses can be short, snappy phrases (e.g., "Good job!") or longer, probing questions. Generally, it takes less than a minute to respond to each student's entry, but the minutes add up. To manage the time, some teachers have students do journals or exit slips only once a week; others have the children do them for every lesson but review them only once a week; still others use them with selected classes only.

Figure 12.7 Fourth-grade child's class journal.

Sept. 13
Today in class we were working outside with balls and we were throwing over handed and under handed. Erin was my partner today. I had fun. but it was not. Sometimes I would catch the ball Sometimes and sometimes I would not. I throw the ball ok I guess, That is what I did today.

Sept. 14
Today in class I was working on not too much. But handspings Everybody was with me I had fun. I also worked on round off.

Sept. 15
Today in class we were working with Mats it was fun. we had to roll font and back. rolls we had to land on our feet and not fall down. I tried and I did it. Then we ran and landed in a almost falling over way, I think it was fun.

Nov. 2
Today in class we were doing all diffrent kinds of shapes. it was fun. My partner was Erin D. We worked all diffrent shapes together.

Nov. 3
Today in class we worked with beanbags. My partner was Machiel. She was not a very good worker. My other partner was going to be Corntnay, but Miss Parker put me with Machiele. It was fun (I guess).

Nov. 21
Today in class we worked on balls of anything that we wanted to do. It was fun. My partner was Corntnay.

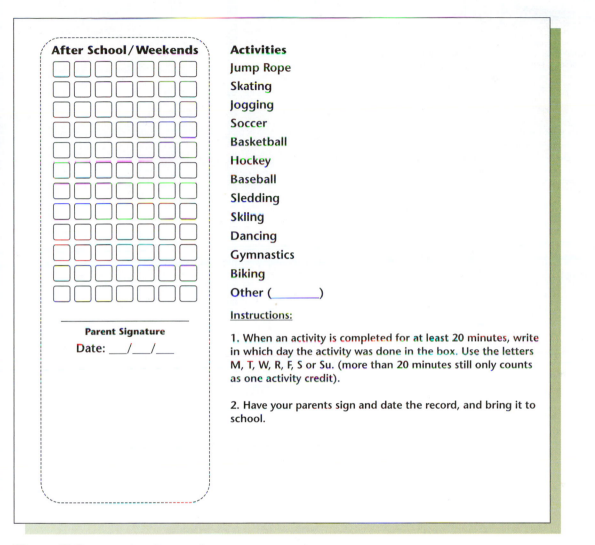

Figure 12.8 Homework assignment: fitness.
Source: M. Parker et al., Super active kids: A health related fitness program. In *Health and fitness through physical education,* ed. R. Pate and R. Hohn, 155–63. Champaign, IL: Human Kinetics, 1994.

small and simply. Figure 12.9 provides examples of peer assessments for striking with the hands (first grade) and for throwing (fourth grade).

Self-Assessment

Self-assessments can be used to assess psychomotor (Standard 1, NASPE 2004), cognitive (Standard 2, NASPE 2004), and affective (Standards 5 and 6, NASPE 2004) aspects of children's work. Although peer and teacher observations are a useful tool for assessment of the critical cues for skills, self-assessments provide a unique opportunity to evaluate larger components or application of a skill or the beginning use of a skill (Holt/Hale 1999). For exam-

ple, in the case of learning to dribble, we might ask children if they could dribble and pivot using the preferred hand, the nonpreferred hand, while walking, while traveling at a jog, without a defensive player, and with a defensive player. Figure 12.10 provides an example of a self-assessment designed to ask questions like these.

Self-assessments may be used at the end of a unit to have students assess their achievement. Alternatively, the self-assessment may be used throughout a unit as each of the components is introduced and practiced; each individual assessment is dated and provides a record of the child's achievement of the various components. In this instance, self-assessment would be an extension of a task sheet (Figure 10.2).

A

Performer Name Grant

Partner Name ~~Angela~~ Angela

Performer gets three chances for each hint. Place a smiley face in the circle if they perform the hint or an X if they don't do the hint. Be honest

Yes, performed

No, did not

Flat Palm	:)	X	:)
Extend to Target	X	X	:)
Eye on object	:)	:)	:)

A

B

Name: Jackson   Partner's Name: Nicholas

Throw, Glow and Grow!

Ready: Throwing hand should be placed by the ear with the elbow way back.

Aim: Non-throwing arm should be pointed toward target. The foot on the same side of the non-throwing arm should take a step forward to the target.

Throw: Throwing arm should be fully extended towards target. Foot on throwing side should roll onto toes and aiming arm should fall down to side.

Fill out the chart bellow. Look at the cues in the left column then circle **yes** if your partner performed the cues correctly; circle **no** if they did not perform the cues correctly.

Cues	Throw 1	Throw 2	Throw 3	Throw 4	Throw 5
Ready	(YES) NO	(YES) NO	(YES) NO	(YES) NO	(YES) NO
Aim	(YES) NO	(YES) NO	(YES) NO	YES NO	(YES) NO
Throw	(YES) NO	(YES) NO	(YES) NO	YES NO	(YES) NO

Write one thing that your partner did well (Glow).

made one

Write one thing that your partner can work on (Grow).

Pointing

B

Figure 12.9 (a) First -grade striking with hands observation sheet. (b) partner evaluation of throwing (fourth grade).
Sources: Dani Schroeder, Elizabeth Devine, Grace Deputy, and Kaily Hoffman, University of Northern Colorado. Used with permission.

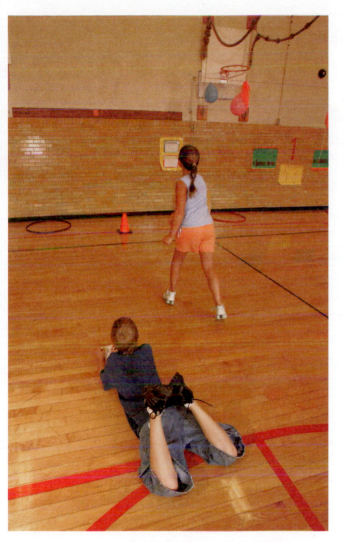

Peers can provide meaningful and relevant feedback to each other.

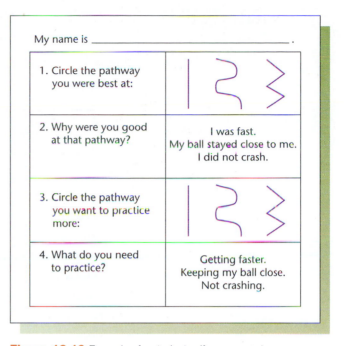

Figure 12.10 Example of a student self-assessment.
Source: Jesse Sirio and Jen Morse, University of Northern Colorado.
Used with permission.

ings may be significantly higher or lower than the teacher's observations. At this point, the self-assessment becomes an opportune place to begin discussions with individual children. Another option is to ask children directly on self-observations how they feel about performing certain skills.

Some teachers often voice concerns about children's honesty when doing self-assessments and peer assessments. We have found that children are incredibly honest when assessing their own and others' skills (they especially take the assessment of others very seriously). Some children may initially inflate scores, but if self-assessments are a regular part of instruction and children become aware of their role in the evaluation process and of the purposes of assessment, inflation is short lived (Holt/Hale 1999).

Event Tasks

Event tasks are performance tasks that can be completed in one class period or a portion of it. The task is designed broadly enough so there are multiple solutions. The task might be entirely psychomotor (Standard 1, NASPE 2004), or it may include cognitive (Standard 2, NASPE 2004) and affective (Standard 5, NASPE 2004) aspects as well. Event tasks that

Regardless of when self-assessment is used, children need to have ample opportunity to practice the various components before completing it. If it is used at the end, children should have a chance for a brief practice period before completing the assessment.

Another version of self-assessment that can be used with older children is a self-rating scale (Figure 12.11). The self-rating scale contains the same skill categories as the self-assessment, but the rating scale provides students an opportunity to assess themselves on a numerical scale. The key to this is providing descriptors for the numbers on the rating scale so children can anchor their self-assessments on clear criteria. Self-rating scales can be appropriately used for assessment before teaching as well as after.

Self-assessments can also provide a glimpse into children's feelings and attitudes. Some children's rat-

Figure 12.11 Example of a
student self-rating scale.

Dribbling and Pivoting Self-Rating

Name: _____   Homeroom: _____   Date: _____

| 1   2   3   4   5   6   7   8   9   10 |

1 – 3   I still need to practice this skill.
4 – 6   I am pretty good at this skill.
7 – 8   I am very good at this skill.
9 – 10 This is my best skill.
* This is my favorite skill.

	Rating	Comments
1. Dribbling and pivoting with preferred hand		
2. Dribbling and pivoting with other hand		
3. Dribbling and pivoting while walking		
4. Dribbling and pivoting while jogging		
5. Dribbling and pivoting at full speed		
6. Dribbling and pivoting against a cone		
7. Dribbling and pivoting against a passive defense		
8. Dribbling and pivoting against an active defense		
9. Dribbling and pivoting without breaking stride		
10. Dribbling and pivoting while keeping head up		
11. Dribbling and pivoting in a game situation		

You may add comments if you wish.

Teacher Comments:

we use frequently are self-designed games (see Chapter 30), or self-designed obstacle courses or gymnastics and dance routines (see Figure 12.12). Other tasks might be having students design a presentation for a parent-teacher conference on the skills they have been learning, or having them prepare to make a presentation to younger students on the critical pieces of a skill. Figure 12.13 shows an example of a role play used as an event task. The success of event tasks depends on the attractiveness of the task (whether it captures children's attention) and the structure the teacher provides. Event tasks require independent and group working skills. See Chapter 10 for ways to determine when children and teachers might be ready use those skills.

Videotape/Digital Pictures

Though not accessible in all schools, videotape or digital pictures are becoming less expensive and can provide a final, permanent product for gymnastics sequences, dances, or self-designed games. These formats can also let students display their knowledge and skill with respect to critical aspects of a skill. One possible task is to have students videotape or take pictures of

Figure 12.12 Self-designed obstacle course.
Source: Dani Schroeder and Elizabeth Devine, University of Northern Colorado. Used with permission.

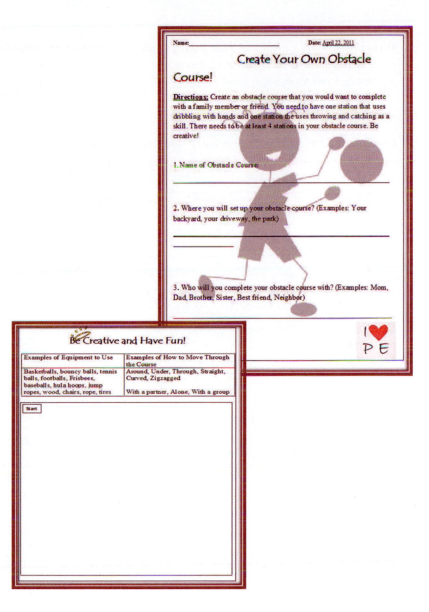

each other performing a certain skill and then analyze the critical cues for that skill. Likewise, students can videotape each other and provide color commentary (ongoing narrative as in sports announcing) regarding the performance. Another videotape assessment might require students to develop an infomercial about a certain skill or fitness activity.

For video/digital analysis to be successful, the criteria (scoring rubric; see page 192) for the task must be made explicit and a sufficient amount of time must be allotted. When they know what they are looking for, children love to watch themselves on tape. It is initially helpful to provide children with checklists (see Figure 12.2) or observation cards (see Figure 12.9) to guide their observations. Children may also combine video analysis with homework, thereby eliminating the need for multiple playback units.

Technology and Assessment

Current digital technology changes at a rapid pace; when used for observation in physical education it provides instant learning for both children and teachers. As an example, heart rate monitors and pedometers provide immediate information on physical activity levels. Flip cameras, digital still cameras, and kids' video cameras allow children and teachers to instantly view skill responses and produce permanent products that can be analyzed and shared with parents. One teacher we know uses a flip camera on a daily basis to record several children's responses in physical education; each night (while he is watching television) he sends two or three clips to parents about their child's progress. These technologies are now both relatively inexpensive and easy to use. We encourage you to incorporate them whenever possible into your teaching.

Directions: Find a group of 2 or 3 with whom you can work productively; choose one scenario card. Read your card, you will have 15 minutes to develop a role play that solves the problem on your card. When you think you are ready, I will videotape your role play. Remember, all group members must be involved in the skit; all critical elements must be explained/demonstrated; and the quality of the presentation must be first-rate—memorized, practiced, and done without prompting.

Omar is having trouble playing catch with his buds during recess. He is so scared of being hit by the ball that he turns his head whenever someone is throwing him the ball. Omar is embarrassed and ready to quit the game. How would you encourage Omar to keep playing and improve his ability to catch?

You are a group of firefighters called to a fire at an apartment building. Several small children are trapped inside and will have to jump. Absent-minded Alfred forgot to make sure the landing net was on the fire truck, so it looks like everyone is going to have to catch the children. The chief needs to instruct everyone how to catch so the children can be rescued safely.

April is having trouble throwing to her partner and is getting upset. As her partner, you want to make her feel better. You also want to help her throw better. What tip did you learn in PE that you can tell to help April throw better? What will you say to April to encourage her?

Bernice is playing flag football during physical education class and she cannot seem to catch the ball! Every time the quarterback throws to her, the football bounces off her hands. What tip did you learn in your PE class that could help Bernice? Why would you tell Bernice that it is important to keep trying?

Vladimir has just moved to the United States from Russia and is a new student to the class. Not only does he not speak English, but he has never been taught to throw overhand. You and your group must teach him to throw overhand and to try to hit a wall target. Remember, Vladimir doesn't understand English.

Figure 12.13 Example of role play used as an event task. (Note: The individual circled scenarios should be written on separate cards.)
Source: Adapted and expanded from PE Central by Jessica Segura and Cristian Sarmento, University of Northern Colorado. Used with permission.

Student Drawings

Children love to draw, and we have found drawing one of the most rewarding assessment tools. The options for student drawing are endless. Children can be asked to draw about themselves, what a sequence looks like, what a skill looks like, or what they liked best. Figure 12.14 shows a student drawing used as an assessment piece demonstrating the understanding of a critical Standard 2 (NASPE 2004) element. We also hope you have enjoyed the drawings of the children at the beginning of each chapter and hope you have wondered, as we have, what each child is trying to say about physical education. Sometimes it is obvious, and sometimes it is not—especially when the child is at the precontrol level of drawing.

Student Displays

Student displays are public displays of student work that communicate what the children have learned (Standard 2, NASPE 2004) or value (Standard 6,

NASPE 2004). These displays can take a variety of forms, from posters on which students have drawn a person displaying a skill and have labeled the cues, to photographs, to bulletin boards, to maps of where they pursue physical activity.

Portfolios

Some researchers have said that to be truly effective, assessments must not only measure current achievement but also monitor and report students' achievement over time (Wolf and White 2000). Portfolios do this. They are systematic collections of student work over time that show progress, achievement, and effort in one or more areas of learning (Melograno 2006). They may assess one or multiple learning standards and relate to a single unit, an entire school year, or students' whole elementary careers. Some have likened a portfolio to a trophy case of a child's accomplishments (Wilson and Roof 1999). Portfolios are powerful because they help students learn about

Figure 12.14 Second grader's drawing assessing the cue of using the shoelaces to kick.

their learning (Davies 2000). They provide an opportunity for students to share the responsibility for collecting proof of their learning. In addition, they provide a rich resource for reporting to both teachers and parents.

The first consideration with a portfolio is its purpose. It is quite difficult to select items without a sense of purpose. Common purposes include keeping track of progress, providing students a way to assess their own accomplishments, and determining the extent to which learning objectives have been achieved. For example, if one of the purposes of your physical education class is helping students practice a healthy lifestyle, their portfolios might include various pieces that attest to their knowledge of fitness, activities they do to stay fit, and indications of how they value fitness. Many products of the assessment options discussed in this chapter could be included in a portfolio. For example, a fitness portfolio might include some of the following artifacts: results of a health-related fitness test given at the beginning of the school year; goals set as a result of that test; activities in which the student participated to achieve the goals set; weekly homework sheets that document physical activity; a written fitness report; results of a fitness test later in the year; an indication of how well personal goals were met; and, finally, goals for the summer. The teacher may specify some items in the portfolio, but because the portfolio is a personal record, the student should be allowed and encouraged to decide which items will most strongly "make the case."

A portfolio communicates more when the reader knows why pieces have been chosen for inclusion. When children are including certain pieces, they might use categories such as "my best work," "the hardest skill I can do now," and "my most improved skill." By having criteria regarding the inclusion of items, students understand better what they are to learn and how to talk about it. Thus portfolios serve as a powerful link from instruction and assessment to learning.

The development and use of portfolios seems intimidating. Davies (2000) has the following suggestions for beginning portfolio work with children:

- Maintain a clear purpose.
- Keep the portfolio process simple. Start small.
- Remember, there is no one best way to do portfolios. Decide what is right for you and your situation.
- Include more than written work. Video or digital analysis is helpful here.
- Ask children to explain and record why they chose each piece of work.
- Ensure that children have involvement and ownership. Portfolios document their learning.

Hoerr (2000) suggests having "portfolio days" on which students share their portfolios with parents in lieu of the traditional parent-teacher conference.

> *Whenever a value is set forth which can only be attained by a few, the conditions are ripe for widespread feelings of personal inadequacy. An outstanding example in American society is the fierce competitiveness of the school system. No educational system in the world has so many examinations, or so emphasizes grades, as the American school system. Children are constantly being ranked and evaluated. The superior achievement of one child tends to debase the achievement of another.*
>
> —**MORRIS ROSENBERG,** *Society and the Adolescent Self-Image* (1965)

Assessing How Well Something Was Learned

Not all assessment items will (or need to) be scored. Any of the assessment options listed previously could be done with students and simply used to provide feedback to them. For example, the observer or teacher could give the student the peer check in Figure 12.9 with some feedback that the child needs to practice this aspect more. But some items do need to be scored for children and teachers to know to what extent the goal has been achieved. To return to our travel analogy, did we get to the Bears game or just to Chicago? Or to the Chicago airport? Or did we ever get on the plane? Remember, though, that what is assessed must match the task, what was taught, and what was expected to be learned.

Rubrics (evaluation matrices) describe varying levels of quality or achievement for a specific task. Their purpose is to guide students in the expectations for their learning, provide informative feedback about the extent to which work met the expectations, and give detailed assessment of the final product. Because rubrics ultimately guide learning, they should be shared with students in advance so students are aware of the expectations. The development of rubrics takes time, but the results make learning expectations clear, provide feedback, and support learning and the development of skills and understanding (Andrade 2000).

Writing Rubrics

There are three components to a rubric: (1) the criteria, or essential components to be assessed; (2) the steps of quality, or the rating scale; and (3) the descriptors that illustrate how each of the steps is related to the criteria.

1. *Criteria* The criteria match those asked for in a task. They are the essential elements determined necessary to achieve the specified goal. It is not necessary or feasible to include every possible element, so select ones appropriate for the level of development. For example, at the control level, the essential elements might be the critical cues of the mature motor pattern; at the proficiency level, essential elements would be the use of a variety of skills in a game situation. For students, this can often be translated into "what counts."

2. *Quality* The steps of quality, or the rating scale, identify various levels of the standard that might be achieved or various levels of competence. These can be thought of as steps or stops along the way to the final goal. These steps can be called by a variety of names—for example: 1, 2, 3, 4; "excellent," "above average," "needs improvement," "incomplete"; Junior Olympian, Bronze Medal, Silver Medal, Gold Medal; Little League, Minor League, Major League, Coach. Regardless of the scale used, it must distinguish one level of achievement from another.

3. *Descriptors* The last aspect of a rubric, descriptors illustrate or describe what the scale looks like at each level for each criterion. This is the aspect that lets children know specifically what is expected. One author (Andrade 2000) proposed the following scale: 4 = yes (I did all the aspects of the criterion); 3 = yes, but (I did X and Y criteria but didn't do Z); 2 = no, but (I didn't do X and Y criteria but did do Z); and 1 = no (I didn't do X, Y, or Z criteria). Using our travel analogy, one criterion might be getting on the right plane. The possible scale or steps might be the following: 4 = checking in at the ticket counter, going to the right gate, giving the ticket to the gate agent, and getting on the right plane; 3 = going to the right gate, giving the ticket to the agent, getting on the right plane, but not checking in at the ticket counter; 2 = giving the ticket to the gate agent and getting on the right plane, but forgetting to check in at the ticket counter and going to the wrong gate first; 1 = getting on the right plane, but not checking in, going to the wrong gate, and giving the wrong ticket to the agent; and 0 = not getting on the right plane.

Figure 12.15 illustrates a rubric written for the creation of a child designed game using the same format. These rubrics are called analytic rubrics, as performance is analyzed with respect to pieces of the whole. Analytic rubrics are time consuming but provide invaluable information for the teacher and the student (Schiemer 2000).

Rubrics can also be holistic. Holistic rubrics assess children's performance as a whole. They combine a variety of essential performance elements to determine an overall level of achievement. The result is then reflected in a single score. Holistic rubrics are easier to use and are effective in assessing large numbers of students. They use the same set of components as analytic rubrics, but all descriptors for a certain level are listed together; to achieve that level, the student must accomplish all aspects of the criteria at the level indicated. A holistic rubric for the Chicago trip might be: 4 = getting on the right plane, getting off the plane in Chicago, getting downtown, acquiring tickets for a Bears game, and attending the game; 3 = getting on the right plane, getting off in Chicago, and getting downtown, but being unable to get tickets to a Bears game; 2 = getting on the right plane and getting off in Chicago, but being unable to figure out how to get downtown or to a Bears game; 1 = getting on the right plane, but getting off at the wrong destination; and 0 = not getting on the right plane or any plane. As you can see, this assessment looks at the whole process of getting to the Bears game, not just the one

Game Creation Rubric

	3 POINTS	2 POINTS	1 POINT
Describe how to play your game	Game is well described so that you could hand your sheet to someone and they could play your game.	Game description is a little confusing and needs a little more explanation.	No game description.
Rules for the game	2–3 rules are clearly written that make sense for the game.	Only 1 rule is written and makes sense for the game.	No rules are written.
Keep Score	There is an easy scoring system used that gives points for dribbling.	Scoring system is used but it is hard to follow.	No scoring system is used.
Draw a picture	Picture clearly shows how to set up and play the game.	Picture is unclear on how to set up or play the game.	No picture is drawn.
Cue / movement Examples: (eyes up) / (start/stop)	At least one learned cue or movement is included in the game.	An incorrect cue or movement is used.	No cue or movement is used.

Total Score: _____ / 15 points

Figure 12.15 Example of an analytic rubric.

aspect of getting on the right plane. Figure 12.16 illustrates a holistic rubric for the throwing and catching role play.

Regardless of the type of rubric chosen, here are some strategies to make designing them easier:

- Look at models of well-written rubrics. In the beginning you want to adopt or adapt rubrics that others have used.
- If you are going to develop your own rubrics, start with content areas in which you have the most expertise.
- List the criteria; then relist and relist them until they don't overlap and they indicate the learning you want to see achieved.
- Have a friend review your rubric.

- Revise the draft. Be ready to write and rewrite. Creating good rubrics takes time.
- Try out the rubric with one class.
- Revise again.

Rubrics take time (and patience), but the end result clarifies student learning and your teaching. The time is well spent.

Finally, a technique that we find helps immensely with the evaluation of complex assignments that contain a variety of components, such as event tasks and portfolios, is to create an assessment checklist that designates each of the components. The teacher develops this assessment checklist in advance, showing all components of the assessment, with space for recording student data and comments. For written work such as

Figure 12.16 Holistic rubric for throwing and catching role play.

Role Playing Assessment Form

Names of Group Members:

Group Score: _____

1. _____

2. _____

Scenario/Skill: _____

Scoring Rubric

> 4. All critical elements of the skill are clearly explained/demonstrated
>   All group members are active participants in scene
>   Top-notch, professional presentation—ready for Broadway!

> 3. Most critical elements of the skill are clearly explained/demonstrated
>   All group members are active participants in scene
>   Top-notch amateur presentation—ready for center stage!

> 2. Some critical elements of the skill are clearly explained/demonstrated
>   Most group members are active participants in scene
>   Top-notch school presentation—ready for local cable TV!

> 1. Few critical elements of the skill are clearly explained/demonstrated
>   Some group members are active participants in scene
>   Could be a top-notch presentation—practicing for a school assembly!

Figure 12.17 Teacher assessment checklist for throwing and catching role play (Figure 12.13).

Throwing and Catching Role Play Assessment Slip

Date: _____

Comments:

Video completed: _____

Critical cues: _____

Group members involved: _____

_____

Quality of presentation: _____

portfolios, the assessment checklist can be stapled to the student item. This way, a teacher can simply fill out slips when projects are successful. The teacher assessment checklist in and of itself is not an assessment, but it allows you to organize and manage large assessment projects. Figure 12.17 shows an assessment checklist for the role play.

Assessing All Three Domains

We do not teach only motor skills and fitness. For us, there are clear affective and cognitive goals in our programs. Therefore we must also assess those goals. The examples provided in the previous section include assessment ideas in all three domains. Assessments for

Figure 12.18 Teacher observation affective checklist and rubric. *Source:* Adapted from Jeanette Easter and Carla Sassano, University of Northern Colorado. Used with permission.

	Respect	Self-Directed	Participation	Comments
Alicia				
Bersava				
Juan				
Miguel				
Natalia				
Jasmine				
Daisy				

Level 4 = Always   Level 3 = Mostly   Level 2 = Sometimes   Level 1 = Rarely

Rubric

Description of Cues	
Respect	Listens to others; encourages others; willingly works with anyone in class; does not disrupt the learning environment
Self-Directed	Returns equipment, stays on task (even when the teacher is not looking)
Participation	Maintains a positive attitude throughout all activities: tries new things without complaining and saying "I can't"

motor skills and fitness include homework and peer observation. Assessment of the affective domain can occur in the form of student journals or a teacher checklist (see Figure 12.18). The affective domain can be a bit tricky to assess—remember, if you want to assess something, there must be a goal, and it must be taught. Therefore, if you have affective goals, they need to be clear to students—for example, using the fingers of the hand to represent various expected responsibilities in class. Figure 12.19 provides an exit slip used to assess knowledge of the expected class responsibilities and then to have students' self-assess and goal set. The cognitive domain can be assessed through exit slips (e.g., Helping Murgatroid) or simply by checking for understanding with questions during class, identified in skill theme chapters by the Check for Understanding icon 🌼. The move to assessment for learning has provided teachers with noninvasive, instructional ways to assess all three domains.

Fitness Assessments

In Chapter 27 we discuss in depth the use of fitness assessments in physical education. We encourage you to refer to that chapter when conducting fitness assessments. The assessment of fitness should follow the same guidelines as all other learning in physical education. The potential downfall of fitness scores is that, although they are easy to collect and report, often they are not an indication of learning in physical education. As with other types of assessment, we must have taught the content of fitness with clear goals throughout the physical education program; must have used multiple formative assessments along the way; and must have provided much activity and practice. Otherwise, fitness reporting does not provide an indication of achievement in physical education. Readers sometimes think we are antifitness due to the stand we take on formal exercises/calisthenics and fitness testing for children. We believe very strongly in personal health-related fitness for children; we also believe in fitness as a process and as a product of quality physical education programs.

A Word about Assessing Movement Concepts

As you might have noticed, our discussion of assessment has largely focused on skill themes. Some might ask, "What about assessing movement concepts?" If you remember, movement concepts are always performed with a skill theme; therefore it is difficult to physically separate the skill from the concept. You will find some assessment options in the movement concept chapters, but they are largely cognitive. Cognitive understanding of the concepts (and skills) precedes application of the concepts in children's movement.

Figure 12.19 Affective exit slip. *Source:* Adapted from Emily Crisman and Justin Hagen, University of Northern Colorado. Used with permission.

> **Your Name:** *Marko*
>
> **Directions:**
>
> 1. Trace the outline of your hand in the space below
>
> *Take care of little guy*
> *Comitt to work kind*
> *Trash talk*
> *4take care of #1*
> *Creating value*
>
> *great Job* :)
>
> 2. Label each finger with the rule that it relates to.
>
> 3. What was one of the rules of the five-finger contract that you worked on today?
>
> *No Trash talk*
>
> 4. What is one rule of the five-finger contract that you need to work on next time?
>
> *Comitt to work*

Early assessment of the concepts, therefore, centers on cognitive understanding—for example, checking the class for understanding; asking for partner-to-partner recall (two students sharing key points of the lesson with each other); or using exit slips. As movement skills develop, concepts and skills are used in combination—for example, striking to send a ball to the right or left; using easy force for the drop shot; or free-flow rolling in gymnastics. While it is hard to separate the understanding of a concept from the ability to do the skill, the use and understanding of concepts can be assessed when there is a reasonable level of achievement with the skill. For example, if a child can travel at a medium speed without difficulty, the assessment of the use of pathways and changes of direction would be reasonable. However, if the child was asked to dribble a ball at the same time and the child's skill with dribbling was at the control level, you would not be able to discern the nonuse of pathways from the lack of skill in dribbling.

Assessment of Students with Disabilities

Assessment for learning offers the teacher a unique opportunity to provide feedback and guidance to the child with disabilities. Experts (Block, Lieberman, and Connor-Kuntz 1998) have strongly suggested the use of assessment for learning for children with disabilities to counteract the pitfalls of traditional assessment with them. They contend that traditional assessment is misused for determining individualized education programs (IEPs) because it has no functional relevance, doesn't help determine instructional techniques, may be inaccurate, and doesn't communicate much to parents. They claim that assessment for learning in adapted physical education allows a direct link between assessment, programming, and instruction and promotes measurement of performance in a variety of settings, including real-life functional settings. They suggest using rubrics with certain modifications to accommodate children with disabilities. First, the rubric should be extended to accommodate more levels of development. Second, rubrics within rubrics (or analytic rubrics) should be designed to accommodate specific goals included in the IEP, such as social behavior. For example, if a child is in a gymnastics unit, items can be added that include social behavior as part of the gymnastics rubric. Third, children with more severe problems may need individual rubrics. Alternative assessment, especially with the use of appropriate rubrics, may well help teachers more fully and appropriately include children with disabilities in their classes. For further information, see Block, Lieberman, and Connor-Kuntz (1998).

A second option for assessing students with disabilities is to develop a grading contract based on the student's IEP (Henderson, French, and Kinnison 2001). The grading contract lists the goals and objectives the child is to achieve in physical education. The student is evaluated based on the extent to which these goals are achieved. The objectives should be graduated so they lead to the desired goal. See Figure 12.20 for an example of a grading contract.

Annual Goals	Specific Educational Services Needed	Present Level of Performance	Person Delivering Service
Goal 1. Trevor will improve abdominal strength.	Special physical education consultant services.	Performs eight bent-leg sit-ups with assistance.	Morgan Stewart, special physical educator
Goal 2. Trevor will improve throwing skills.	Special physical education consultant services.	With a tennis ball, Trevor hits a 2'x2' target five feet away on 2 of 10 trials.	Morgan Stewart, special physical educator

Short-Term Objectives	Date Completed	Special Instructional Methods and/or Materials	Grade
Goal 1. Objectives			
1. In the gym, with assistance, Trevor will perform 10 bent-leg sit-ups.	10-21-01	mat; social praise; a performance graph	C
2. In the gym, without assistance, Trevor will perform eight bent-leg sit-ups.	11-7-01	same	B
3. In the gym, without assistance, Trevor will perform 25 bent-leg sit-ups.	Progressing; can do 21	same	A
Goal 2. Objectives			
1. With a tennis ball, Trevor will hit a 2'x2' target 5 feet away on 6 of 10 trials.	11-14-01	tennis ball and target	C
2. With a tennis ball, Trevor will hit a 2'x2' target 10 feet away on 6 of 10 trials.	11-21-01	same	B
3. With a tennis ball, Trevor will hit a 2'x2' target 20 feet away on 8 of 10 trials.	12-10-01	same	A

SIGNATURES AND TITLES OF APPROPRIATE TEAM MEMBERS: (Signatures indicate approval of this IEP)

_____   _____   _____
(Parent)   (Teacher)   (Administrator/Supervisor)

Figure 12.20 Sample grading contract.
Source: H. Henderson, R. French, and L. Kinnison, Reporting grades for students with disabilities in general physical education, *Journal of Physical Education, Recreation and Dance* 72, no. 6 (2001): 50–55.

What to Do with the Results of Assessment, or Standards-Based Summarizing and Reporting Progress

At some point, teachers are required to summarize and report children's progress to parents and others. This summative evaluation provides parents and children with an indication of what the child has learned and where he or she is with respect to essential learning in physical education. It also provides teachers with information about their program—what has been accomplished and what needs to be worked on. For physical education teachers, reporting has always been nothing short of a nightmare, however, if you have designed and collected information on an ongoing basis, these systems should allow you to report that information to parents. The two systems presented here are standards-based reporting systems because they provide both parents and children with a meaningful indication of what is being taught in physical education as well as what their child has learned.

Standards-based report cards differ from traditional report cards in that they link the learning in physical education directly to the established goals. For example, instead of simply indicating the subject area of physical education and place for a grade, they indicate the specific learning standards and or performance outcomes that children have been working on for the marking period. This new approach is more accurate because it measures each student against a stated set of criteria instead of against each other or subjective criteria. Instead of letter grades, students receive marks that show how well they have mastered selected skills. The marks might show whether the student is advanced, basic, or below basic for each standard, or they might be numbers representing whether students meet, exceed, or approach each standard. Children usually get separate marks for effort and work habits, which are important for parents to keep tabs on even if these characteristics aren't included in the assessment of the student's academic skills. Two different reporting systems are presented below as examples of standards-based report cards.

Standards-Based Reporting

Linden Elementary School. The system used at Linden Elementary School in Oak Ridge, Tennessee, consists of report cards individually designed for each grade level based on their units of study (Figures 12.21a and 12.21b) and each marking period (in this case, two per year). The skill theme and the performance outcome addressed during a specific marking period are indicated on the report card. A report of (SP) Still Practicing, (S) Satisfactory, or (M) Mastery is then entered for the performance outcome. Look closely as the fall and spring report cards differ, just as the performance outcomes addressed differed from fall to spring. This type of report card allows you to adapt the report to the various performance outcomes taught at each grade level while providing a bit more detail.

Fargo Report Card. The system designed for use by Fargo, North Dakota, schools is similar to the Linden system. Like the Linden system it provides the standard with performance outcomes addressed underneath the standard. For this system the report card remains the same for the entire school year with nonaddressed performance outcomes marked out. The assessment key clearly provides a qualitative description of the extent to which the outcome was met, while the approach to learning indicators relay important feedback about a child's approach to school that can impact learning.

Similarities Both of these reporting systems involve multiple assessments—at least two and sometimes more—for each theme studied. Often the assessments include at least one teacher observation of critical elements of the skill, one event task, and one self-assessment. While the reliability of self-assessments is often questioned, teachers using these types of systems found student self-assessment not only accurate and honest but also increased student learning while integrating instruction and assessment. The assumption is that when children think about their own learning, they attend more carefully to that learning. In addition, self-assessment helps teachers—even though they kept lots of records—find the time, energy, and ability to assess each child more accurately. Note that none of these systems reported student learning as "grades" per se: the teachers found that "grades" did not communicate much to the parents or the students.

Assessment for Accountability

While this chapter has focused on assessment for learning, the National Association for Sport and Physical Education has recently developed a document that allows for assessment for accountability. *PE Metrics: Assessing the National Standards* (NASPE 2010) provides validated and reliable assessment items for all six NASPE Standards. The assessment items in the book provide detailed information regarding how to assess various sample performance outcomes as well as validated rubrics for grades K–5.

Linden Elementary School
Fourth Grade
Physical Education Report Card Fall 2007

Homeroom: _____   Physical Educator: **S. Holt-Hale / J. Johnson**

Listed below are the major themes of study for this school year. The following codes have been used in evaluating your child's progress in skill development at the 4th grade level.

(SP) Still Practicing—practicing the skill at the fourth-grade level.
(S) Satisfactory—satisfactory progress in the development of the skill appropriate for fourth-grade level
(M) Mastery—demonstrates mastery of the skill or concept appropriate for fourth-grade level.
If no grade present, skill not assessed this semester.

Skill: Locomotors/Traveling	
Demonstrate appropriate locomotor skills in games, gymnastics, and dance	
Apply appropriate speed and endurance for one-mile run	

Skill: Dribbling	
Dribble in self-space with preferred and nonpreferred hand demonstrating mature pattern finger pads/push, opposite forward, ball at waist height)	
Dribbling and travel with control of ball and body	
Demonstrate dribbling in a group rhythmical routine or in a simple, small group game situation	

Skill: Throwing	
Overhand Throw: throw with a mature pattern in practice situations	
Throw with a two-hand bounce pass to a partner	

Skill: Catching	
Catch both large and small balls with a mature pattern, ready hands, reach & pull, hand position—thumbs in/out	
Catch a ball thrown by a partner in game situation	

Skill: Kicking		
Apply kicking through the air and punting in practice situations		
Air:	Punt:	
Identify the key components of kicking and punting pattern		

Skill: Fitness	
Complete a health-related fitness screening in the fall with a repeated evaluation in the spring	**See attached**
Design a personal fitness goal and develop an activity plan to work toward that goal	

Fitness Comments:

Skill: Jumping and Landing	
Demonstrate mastery of more advanced individual and long-jump rope skills	

Skill: Dance	
Create a dance: folk, line, square, etc.	
Utilize dance steps and movement pattern in small group and partner dance activities	

Skill: Concepts	
Demonstrate a basic understanding of the movement concepts of levels, directions, and force in games/sports, gymnastics, and dance.	

WORK HABITS: N—Needs Improvement
                    S—Satisfactory
                    E—Excellent

	Fall	Spring
Listening:		
Independent Task Completion:		
Cooperative Work with Others:		

COMMENTS:

PARENT COPY FOR:

Student: _____
Home Room Teacher: _____

Figure 12.21a Linden Elementary School Fall Fourth Grade Report Card.

Linden Elementary School

Fourth Grade
Physical Education Report Card Spring 2008

Homeroom: _____　　　Physical Educator: **S. Holt-Hale / J. Johnson**

Listed below are the major themes of study for this school year. The following codes have been used in evaluating your child's progress in skill development at the fourth-grade level.
(SP) Still Practicing—practicing the skill at the fourth-grade level.
(S) Satisfactory—satisfactory progress in the development of the skill appropriate for fourth-grade level
(M) Mastery—demonstrates mastery of the skill or concept appropriate for fourth-grade level.
If no grade present, skill not assessed this semester.

Skill	
Skill: Locomotors/Traveling	
Demonstrate appropriate locomotor skills in games, gymnastics, and dance	
Apply appropriate speed and endurance for one-mile run	
Skill: Throwing	
Overhand throw: throw with a mature pattern in practice situations	
Throw (overhand) to a partner with reasonable accuracy in game situations	
Combines dribbling and throwing for shooting baskets	
Skill: Catching	
Catch both large and small balls with a mature pattern, ready hands, reach & pull, hand position-thumbs in/out	
Catch a ball thrown by a partner in game situation	
Skill: Volley (underhand)	
Strike/volley a ball with a mature pattern: stance, open palm, control of direction and force	
Strike/volley a ball alternating hits with a partner in cooperative and competitive: wall, line, net.	
Skill: Volley (overhead)	
Volley a lightweight ball with continuous hits to the wall	
Volley a lightweight ball alternating hits with a partner over a net	
Identify the components of a mature overhead volley	
Skill: Striking with Rackets/Paddles (Sidearm pattern)	
Strike a tennis ball demonstrating selected key elements: forward/backward stance, side of target, square racket face	
Skill: Striking with Long Implements (bats, hockey sticks)	
Successfully strike a ball tossed by an adult	
Use striking skills in a small game situation	
Skill: Fitness	
Complete a health-related fitness screening in the fall with a repeated evaluation in the spring	See attached
Fitness Comments:	
«Fit_Comment»	
Skill: Balance	
Demonstrate a variety of gymnastic balances on mats and/or apparatus	
Combine balances and actions into gymnastics sequences on apparatus and/or mats	
Skill: Transferring Weight	
Safely travel onto, off of, and across gymnastics apparatus	
Combine balancing and transferring weight into sequences	
Skill: Jumping and Landing	
Perform jumping actions safely in game situations	
Demonstrate mastery of more advanced individual and long-jump rope skills	
Skill: Concepts	
Demonstrate a basic understanding of the movement concepts of levels, directions, and force in games/sports, gymnastics, and dance.	

WORK HABITS:　　N—Needs Improvement
　　　　　　　　　　　S—Satisfactory
　　　　　　　　　　　E—Excellent

	Fall	Spring
Listening:		
Independent Task Completion:		
Cooperative Work with Others:		
COMMENTS:		
PARENT COPY FOR:		
Student:		
Home Room Teacher:		

Figure 12.21b Linden Elementary School Spring Fourth Grade Report Card.
Source: From Shirley Holt/Hale. Used with permission.

FIRST GRADE LANGUAGE ARTS STANDARDS

READING PROCESS	1	2	3
Demonstrates phonemic awareness			
Uses knowledge of letter/sound relationships to decode words to determine meaning			
Uses strategies to monitor comprehension			
Reads in meaningful phrases with appropriate expression, rate & accuracy			
Retells details and events in sequence			

WRITING PROCESS	1	2	3
Understands and uses the writing process			
Produces an organized piece of writing			
Writes for a variety of purposes			

PRINCIPLES OF LANGUAGE	1	2	3
Uses the conventions of writing (parts of speech, punctuation, and capitalization)			
Uses principles of spelling in writing			

RESEARCH PROCESS AND MEDIA	1	2	3
Uses research process to answer questions			

SPEAKING AND LISTENING PROCESS	1	2	3
Practices active listening			
Formulates questions and responds appropriately in conversations			

FIRST GRADE MATH STANDARDS

NUMBER AND OPERATIONS	1	2	3
Counts, orders, identifies and writes numbers to 100			
Understands number relationships to 100			
Demonstrates understanding and fluency of basic addition and subtraction facts to 10			
Represents and explains fractions as part of a whole and part of a set			

GEOMETRIC CONCEPTS	1	2	3
Identifies geometric concepts			

DATA ANALYSIS AND PROBABILITY	1	2	3
Reads and interprets charts, graphs and diagrams			

MEASUREMENT	1	2	3
Tells time to the hour and half-hour			
Identifies and counts coins to $1.00			
Measures length to the nearest inch and foot			

ALGEBRAIC CONCEPTS	1	2	3
Identifies, sorts and classifies objects by two or more attributes			
Recognizes, extends, creates, and describes patterns			

COMMUNICATIONS & PROBLEM SOLVING	1	2	3
Solves a variety of simple problems			
Communicates thinking using mathematical language			

SCIENCE/HEALTH	1	2	3
Demonstrates and applies knowledge of key concepts			
Uses the process of inquiry in investigations			

SOCIAL STUDIES	1	2	3
Demonstrates and applies knowledge of key concepts			

VISUAL ARTS	1	2	3
Standard 1 & 2 TECHNIQUES, AND PROCESSES/STRUCTURE AND FUNCTION			
Uses grade level art vocabulary			
Standard 4 & 5 HISTORY, CULTURE and MERITS of ART			
Recognizes how animals are portrayed in art			

MUSIC	1	2	3
Standard 1 Student sings alone and with others			
Sings a three-tone melody in tune with accurate rhythm			
Standard 2 Student performs on instruments alone and with others			
Performs steady beat using body percussion and classroom instruments			
Standard 5 Students reads and writes music			
Reads and writes grade-level rhythmic and melodic patterns			
Approach to Learning: Displays a positive attitude and follows directions during music activities			

Figure 12.22 Fargo, North Dakota Public Schools Elementary Report Card. (*continued*)

Source: http://www.fargo.k12.nd.us/education/components/docmgr/default.php?sectiondetailid=2380&fileitem=1838&catfilter=ALL

Figure 12.22 (continued)

PHYSICAL EDUCATION	1	2	3
Standard 1 Students use a variety of movement forms			
Demonstrate galloping as basic locomotor skills (forward movement, step together step)			
Demonstrate hopping as basic locomotor skills (hop on right foot, hop on left foot)			
Demonstrates control in travel activities (e.g., changes directions in a safe manner, shows an awareness of objects and other people			
Standard 2 Students use movement concepts & principles in the development of motor skills			
Demonstrate the pattern of over, under, around and through to verbal/auditory cues			
Standards 3 & 4 Understand the benefits of maintaining a health-enhancing level of physical activity			
Participates in moderate to vigorous physical activity			
Identifies activities that develop flexibility (stretching toward the toes while in the sit-and reach position, moving joints through full range of motion)			
Standard 5 Students practice responsible personal and social behavior in physical activity settings			
Apply rules and procedures during physical activities (safety, equipment, following directions) and shows respect for self and others			

APPROACH TO LEARNING	1	2	3
Follows class and school rules			
Follows directions			
Respects self, others, and property			
Accepts responsibility for actions			
Participates in classroom activities			
Works cooperatively in groups			
Works independently to complete classwork			
Uses time appropriately			
Completes homework on time			
Produces and maintains quality work/writes legibly			
Keeps materials organized			

| Your child's absences/tardies negatively affect your child's progress. (Yes/No) | | | |

Assessing student work and sharing results with our students and families is an important process. Progress reports and conferences are important tools in this process. In this report we are providing you with information about the progress your child is making toward the end-of-the-year academic learning expectations. We are also giving you information on the approach to learning your child has shown. The progress your child is making in mastering the basic skills and concepts of the curriculum is evaluated according to work completed by your child, the observations of your child, and the conversations with your child about the learning.

This report is part of helping you see how your child is progressing in relation to what is expected to be learned by the end of the academic year. The conference will further explain if the progress your child currently is making is at an adequate rate to meet year end academic expectations. The conference and discussion will enhance your understanding of the progress your child is making on overall learning expectations.

Dr. Rick Buresh
Superintendent of Schools

This report is a standards-based Progress Report to give you a clear message of what your child knows, is able to do and what s/he still needs to learn in relation to state standards.

Assessment Key:
N (Novice) = Student is at a beginning level in learning this skill making minimal progress towards end of the year standards. Student's performance is inconsistent, and student needs significant guidance and support.
PP (Partially proficient) = Student is developing in the use/understanding of this skill and is progressing towards end of the year standards. Student's performance varies in accuracy/quality, and student needs additional instruction.
P (Proficient) = Student is secure in the use/understanding of this skill and has progressed to meet end of the year standards. Student's performance exhibits no major errors, and student applies concepts with accuracy/quality.

AD (Advanced Proficiency) = Student has exceeded end of the year standards. Student's performance exhibits in-depth inferences and applications that go beyond what is expected at that grade level.
NOTE: THE FOLLOWING MARKS MAY BE USED AS NEEDED:
Blacked out = Standard is not assessed district wide this marking period
* = Modified curriculum

APPROACH TO LEARNING ASSESSMENT KEY
3 = Consistently demonstrates this approach to learning
2 = Inconsistently demonstrates this approach to learning
1 = Rarely demonstrates this approach to learning. Academic progress is affected.

Grading

Standards-based report cards make grades a thing of the past. To be honest, even though we have advocated for no grades for more than 25 years, we never thought we would be able to make that statement. To many, assessment and grading are synonymous. In reality, there are subtle but significant differences between the two. Assessment involves how teachers find out what students know and can do in relation to the standards or learning goal. Grading, on the other hand, involves procedures for compiling data so an evaluation can be made for reporting to parents or others (Franklin 2002). The report systems we have shown report progress and achievement linking the content to standards and reporting student progress toward achieving the standard. We think that grades without an indication of what the standard is do not communicate meaningful information to parents or others. After all, what does an "A" say about what a child can do or has learned? We would much rather provide information that can be used as feedback and guidance.

We realize, however, that some school districts require you to grade. If that is the case, we first recommend specifying as clearly as possible what each grade means in relation to the standard (as on rubrics). Then assess exactly the same thing as specified. Translate your scales from the rubrics into grades and report to parents. For example, Fargo's rating, "novice," "partially proficient," "proficient," "advanced proficiency"—could be translated into 1, 2, 3, 4 or D, C, B, A. Remember, though, as with all assessment, there should be many assessment opportunities and options. Grades should be a result of all of these. If possible, we suggest reporting progress and achievement in ways that are the most meaningful. Grades rarely indicate such. Box 12-3 indicates appropriate and inappropriate assessment and grading practices.

Finding the Time for Assessment

Time has always been an issue in physical education. One concern many physical education teachers voice is that these assessment for learning options take time (and we have little time as it is in physical education). In recent years it has become increasingly obvious to us that physical education programs limited to one or two days a week have less impact on children than daily physical education programs (Graham, Metzler, and Webster 1991). That is true, but it has also become clear that what is not assessed is not valued (Rink and

Box 12-3

Appropriate and Inappropriate Physical Education Practices

Components: Test Procedures and Grading

Appropriate Practice

- Test results are shared privately with children and their parents/guardians as a tool for developing personal goals and strategies for developing and improving skills and health-related fitness.
- Physical educators provide regular reports of student progress to students, parents, and/or guardians using a variety of continuous, formative evaluations and assessments (e.g., heart rate monitor printouts, pedometer step sheets, skill assessments, knowledge tests, portfolios).
- Grades in physical education are based on thoughtful identified components that are aligned with course goals and national standards.
- Students know the component criteria included in their grade and the rationale for each.

Inappropriate Practice

- Individual scores are publically posted where comparisons are made between student scores.
- Parents/guardians never receive information about program content and their child's progress beyond a letter grade on a report card.
- Grades are based on a single opportunity to perform; formative assessment is not used (e.g., children receive a grade in physical education based on their scores on a standardized fitness test or the number of times they can continually jump rope).
- Teachers use subjective measures to assign grades (e.g., grades are based solely on effort, participation, and/or attitude).

Source: National Association for Sport and Physical Education, *Appropriate instructional practice guidelines for elementary school physical education*, 3rd ed. (Reston, VA: National Association for Sport and Physical Education, 2009). Reprinted with permission.

Mitchell 2002). Indeed, the marginalized status of physical education can, in part, be attributed to the lack of assessment (Hay 2006). Thus, to some extent, the future of physical education may lie in how well we can document what students learn in our classes. Remember, assessment for learning links instruction and assessment by providing meaningful learning tasks. Well-designed assessment tasks thus enhance learning.

The development of assessment items, like good teaching, takes time. No instructor who teaches several hundred children each week—as many physical education instructors do—has time to use all the assessment techniques described in this chapter. But a reflective teacher is aware of these techniques and uses them with different classes for different purposes. Perhaps you'll have one class at a time keeping logs. And you may be able to send only one written report a year to parents.

Select from the various assessment techniques those that are most appropriate; each technique provides a different type of information. For example, journals provide fascinating insights into how children are progressing in designing their own games or dances, but a checklist would be far less appropriate for that purpose. In contrast, a checklist is useful for assessing children's individual abilities in a new situation—for example, for a class of kindergarten children or during a teacher's first year in a new school. To simplify that process we encourage you to use examples you find here and to modify examples you find elsewhere. PE Central (www.pecentral.org/) is a wonderful source of possible assessment items.

Even when you narrow the assessment options to be used with your classes, time can still be an issue. For example, it's counterproductive to assess one child while the others stand in line waiting their turn. There are several ways to minimize the waiting time for children during assessment:

- Set up stations or learning centers (Chapter 10). Stay at one of the stations, and use that as the assessment station. If you plan to do this, be certain the children are familiar with the other stations so you can devote most of your time to helping with the assessments rather than explaining procedures at the other stations.
- Ask the classroom teacher (or another teacher, paraprofessional, parent, or high school student) to help with the class. The assistant can either help some children while you work with the others or supervise most of the class while you work with a few children at a time.
- Videotape the children so you can make your judgments about skill levels and progress during your planning time or after school.
- Use a digital voice recorder as you teach, and use the class list as a guide for observing each child; record your comments about the child's ability level and improvement as you move about.

- Divide the gym into sections, and have students begin each day in a home section that is consistent. Design the first task children are to do as an assessment task—for example, "Dribble with your dominant hand using the cues we have practiced." Using a teacher observation checklist, observe one or two groups each day until you have observed all children.

The recent surge of handheld computer assessment programs you can use to download results into desktop computers makes assessment much less time consuming. Many programs allow you to record "on the spot" children's scores and the results of assessment tasks and then enter them automatically into various record-keeping programs. These programs and computers have become much more affordable, accessible, and user friendly. This information changes on almost a daily basis, but we suggest you check *Using Technology in Physical Education* (Mohnsen 2010) or your district's technology department for more information on these programs.

Handheld computers (e.g., iPads, Netbooks, etc.) could easily revolutionize assessment practices because of the reduction of paperwork and increased efficiency they provide. As indicated, however, in the Chapter 27 box "Technology in Fitness/Wellness Education" (page 567), even though we encourage the use of technology to enhance your physical education program, do not confuse the increased use of technology with effective teaching.

Although it may not be possible for children to reach utilization or proficiency level in a skill such as throwing in the limited time allotted to physical education, it is realistic to expect that children can at least learn the key cues for the points we emphasize in our programs. Although that is not totally satisfactory, it does represent progress. It is encouraging to realize that even though all the children in our program are not throwing at the utilization level, they do know how to throw correctly if, and when, they choose to throw on their own. The time issue will not go away, but it is our belief that the use of time for assessment is well worth the investment. The information gathered from and provided by assessment is critical to children's learning, to instructional decisions that meet the child's needs, and to the design and maybe even to the retention of the program. The assessment movement has aligned goals and evaluation with instruction. They are no longer separate entities but pieces of the same puzzle. Assessment is an ongoing process that occurs in every lesson, simply by the nature of the tasks students do. Assessment is instruction. Assessment is simply teaching well.

Summary

Assessment can be defined as determining if and to what extent a student can demonstrate, in context, his or her understanding and ability relative to identified standards of learning. This definition alludes to three critical elements: 1) a performance of learning, 2) in a real setting, 3) against previously set standards.

Assessment also provides a direct measure of teaching effectiveness. No longer is assessment an end-of-the-unit thing; now it is an ongoing process that happens on a daily basis in physical education classes. This type of assessment is known as assessment for learning; it is directly linked with instruction, not separated from it. In this way, instruction and assessment inform the whole learning process.

Many assessment for learning options exist. The formal ones we have chosen to focus on include journals, exit slips, homework, peer observation, event tasks, video/digital analysis, student drawings, student displays, teacher observation, self-assessment, and portfolios. These assessment options can provide feedback to children, assess student learning, report progress to parents, and discover individual children's needs and interests. Standards-based report cards to children's parents are the preferred mode of reporting student progress whenever feasible.

Reading Comprehension Questions

1. What is assessment for learning? How does it differ from assessment for accountability and traditional assessment modes?
2. What are the purposes of assessment in physical education?
3. What does it mean to tie assessment to instruction and the whole learning process?
4. What are five options available for assessment for learning?
5. What is the purpose of having children keep a journal? How does the journal differ from the other assessment options?
6. What are scoring rubrics? How do they work?
7. What is the difference between assessment and grading? Why should grades be obsolete in physical education?
8. What is a standards-based report card? Provide an argument for using that type of report card as opposed to a traditional report card. Prepare your argument as if you were to present it to the superintendent.
9. Explain why assessment is necessary in children's physical education.

References/Suggested Readings

Andrade, H. 2000. Using rubrics to promote thinking and learning. *Educational Leadership* 57(5): 13–19.

Block, M., L. Lieberman, and F. Connor-Kuntz. 1998. Authentic assessment in adapted physical education. *Journal of Physical Education, Recreation and Dance* 69(3): 48–55.

Cutforth, N., and M. Parker. 1996. Promoting affective development in physical education: The value of journal writing. *Journal of Physical Education, Recreation and Dance* 67(7): 19–23.

Davies, A. 2000. Seeing the results for yourself: A portfolio primer. *Classroom Leadership* 3(5): 4–5.

Franklin, J. 2002, Spring. *Assessing assessment: Are alternative methods making the grade? Curriculum update.* Alexandria, VA: Association for Supervision and Curriculum Development.

Graham, G. 2008. *Teaching children physical education.* 3rd ed. Champaign, IL: Human Kinetics.

Graham, G., M. Metzler, and G. Webster. 1991. Specialist and classroom teacher effectiveness in children's physical education. *Journal of Teaching in Physical Education* 10(4): 321–26.

Hay, P. J. 2006. Assessment for learning in physical education. In *The handbook of physical education,* ed. D. Kirk, D. Macdonald, and M. O'Sullivan, 312–25. Thousand Oaks, CA: Sage.

Henderson, H., R. French, and L. Kinnison. 2001. Reporting grades for students with disabilities in general physical education. *Journal of Physical Education, Recreation and Dance* 72(6): 50–55.

Hoerr, T. 2000. Reporting what we respect. *Classroom Leadership* 3(5): 2–3.

Holt/Hale, S. 1999. *Assessing motor skills in elementary physical education.* Reston, VA: National Association for Sport and Physical Education.

Hopple, C. 2005. *Elementary physical education teaching & assessment.* 2nd ed. Champaign, IL: Human Kinetics.

Lambert, L. 2007. *Standards based assessment of student learning: A comprehensive approach.* 2nd ed. Reston, VA: National Association for Sport and Physical Education.

Markos, N. J. (2007). *Self- and peer assessments for elementary school physical education programs.* Reston, VA: National Association for Sport and Physical Education.

Melograno, V. J. 2006. *Professional and student portfolios for physical education.* Champaign, IL: Human Kinetics.

Mohnsen, B. 2010. *Using technology in physical education.* 7th ed. Cerritos, CA: Bonnie's Fitware, Inc.

[NASPE] National Association for Sport and Physical Education. 1995. *Moving into the future: National standards for physical education.* St. Louis, MO: Mosby.

[NASPE] National Association for Sport and Physical Education. 2004. *Moving into the future: National standards for physical education.* 2nd ed. Reston, VA: National Association for Sport and Physical Education.

[NASPE] National Association for Sport and Physical Education. 2009. *Appropriate instructional practice guidelines for elementary school physical education.* 3rd ed. Reston, VA: National Assocation for Sport and Physical Education.

[NASPE] National Association for Sport and Physical Education. 2010. *PE Metrics: Assessing the National Standards 1–6 in elementary school.* Reston, VA: National Assocation for Sport and Physical Education.

No Child Left Behind Act of 2001. Pub. L. No. 107–110, 20 U.S.C. section 6301 (2001.)

Parker, M., T. Steen, J. Whitehead, C. Pemberton, and B. Entzion. 1994. Super active kids: A health related fitness program. In *Health and fitness through physical education,* ed. R. Pate and R. Hohn, 155–63. Champaign, IL: Human Kinetics.

Prusak, K., and S. Vincent. 2005. Is your class about something? Guiding principles for physical education teachers. *Journal of Physical Education, Recreation and Dance* 76(6): 25–28.

Questioning our motives. 1996. *Education Update, Association for Supervision and Curriculum Development* 38(4): 5.

Rink, J. 2010. *Teaching physical education for learning.* 6th ed. New York: McGraw-Hill.

Rink, J., and M. Mitchell. 2002. *High stakes assessment: A journey into unknown territory.* Quest 54(3): 205–23.

Rosenberg, M. 1965. *Society and the adolescent self-image.* Princeton, NJ: Princeton University Press.

Schiemer, S. 2000. *Assessment strategies for elementary physical education.* Champaign, IL: Human Kinetics.

Smith, M. A., and D. B. Claxton. 2003. Using active homework in physical education. *Journal of Physical Education, Recreation and Dance* 75(5): 28–32.

Wiggins, G. 1993. *Assessing student performance.* San Francisco: Jossey-Bass.

Wilson, S., and K. Roof. 1999. Establishing a portfolio process for K–8 learners. *Teaching Elementary Physical Education* 10(5): 10–14.

Wolf, D., and A. White. 2000. Charting the course of student growth. *Educational Leadership* 57(5): 6–12.

PART 4

Movement Concepts Development

Lizeth

The three chapters in Part 4 explain the movement concept categories of space awareness (Chapter 13), effort (Chapter 14), and relationships (Chapter 15) and present ideas for teaching them to children. Because these are concepts rather than actual skills, *levels of skill proficiency are not discussed.* As children study space awareness, effort, and relationships, they learn to demonstrate, through movement, their understanding of the meaning of each concept. You will find many activities for each of the concepts. As a reflective teacher, you will want to make decisions about which tasks will best meet your students' needs and assist them in gaining a functional understanding of the concepts. The range of activities suggested provides a breadth of experiences related to each concept. Once children have acquired this functional understanding, the concept is used primarily as a subfocus—or an adverb— to enhance the range and quality of skill development that result from the study of the various skill themes (Part 5).

Suggested tasks are designated with the symbol **C**; challenges are designated with the symbol **T**; tasks and challenges were described in Chapter 6. In addition, you will also find suggested assessments (Chapter 12) to help you determine how well the children are understanding the concepts.

When teaching the movement concepts it's easy to forget that the purpose is to have the children actually *know* what each concept means. Imagine that one of us is going to teach a class of your second graders. Before teaching, we might ask whether your children know the space awareness concepts. If you say yes, we would assume the children can show movement of body parts and total body in self-space and/or general space when asked to do so. Or we would assume the children can travel in straight, curved, and zigzag pathways and that they can move body parts at high, medium, and low levels. "Knowing" doesn't mean the concepts were taught; knowing means the children are able to show their understanding through their movement. In other words, the children have *functional understanding.*

If one of us was going to teach a second-grade art class, we might ask the teacher whether the children know their colors. If the teacher says yes, we would assume the children know the difference between red, brown, black, orange, and so forth. We would further expect they can readily use these colors in the lesson we would teach. If the teacher says the children don't know their colors, however, we would design our lesson to help them learn their colors. *Functional understanding* means the children know and can use the concepts in their movement.

Space Awareness

Key Concepts

- Movement concepts expand the range and enrich the quality of skills in physical education.

- Movement concept categories include space awareness (location, directions, levels, pathways, extensions); effort (time, force, flow); and relationships (of body parts, with objects, with people).

- Learning experiences in the concepts chapters are designed to help children attain a functional understanding (cognitive and performance) of the concepts.

- Children need a wide breadth of experiences with each concept to achieve functional understanding.

- When movement concepts are introduced to children, the focus of the lesson is on the concept; the movement (skill) is secondary to the concept.

- Concepts become modifiers to skills as children move to higher levels of performance.

- *Levels of skill proficiency are not included for movement concepts;* they are concepts to be understood, not skills to be mastered.

- Once children understand a movement concept, it can be used in combination with other concepts and in combination with skills.

- A functional understanding of concepts must be attained before the concepts can be used in skill themes.

Box 13-1

Space Awareness in the *National Standards for Physical Education*

The movement concept of Space Awareness is referenced in the National Association for Sport and Physical Education's *National Standards for Physical Education* (NASPE 2004) under Standard 2: "Demonstrates understanding of movement concepts, principles, strategies, and tactics as they apply to the learning and performance of physical activities." The intent of the standard is facilitation of learners' ability to use cognitive information to understand and enhance motor skill acquisition and performance. At the lower-elementary level, emphasis is placed on establishing a movement vocabulary and applying introductory concepts. At the upper-elementary level, emphasis is placed on applying and generalizing the concepts to physical activity situations.

Sample performance outcomes from the *National Standards* include:

- Travels forward and sideways, changing directions quickly in response *to a signal or obstacle* using a variety of locomotor skills. (K–2)*

- Designs and performs gymnastics (or dance) sequences that combine traveling, rolling, balancing, and weight transfer into smooth, flowing sequences with intentional changes in direction, speed, and flow. (6–8)*

*Grade-level guidelines for expected student learning.

All movement occurs in space. Because children who develop a keen space sense will be better able to move safely as they travel through physical education environments, it's beneficial to focus on the concept of space awareness at the beginning of the physical education program.

Children can be made aware of the different aspects of space and then challenged to think about spatial considerations as they engage in game, gymnastics, and dance experiences. As children move their bodies in different ways through varying spatial conditions, they begin to feel and understand space in new ways. As relationships between the body and space become clear, adeptness at controlling movements in functional or expressive physical education activities is enhanced. For example, children learn to maneuver across a large span of climbing equipment, traveling around, over, and under other youngsters without bumping any of them or losing control of their own movements. See Box 13-1 for linkages between the movement concept of Space Awareness and the *National Standards for Physical Education*.

Recall from earlier chapters that the movement analysis framework consists of both movement concepts and skill themes. Space awareness—where the body moves—is one of the three categories of movement concepts (Chapter 3, Table 3.2). The space awareness categories are shaded in the movement analysis framework wheel (Figure 13.1). The position of space awareness on the wheel indicates it is a movement modifier or concept. In other words, it describes how a skill is to be performed as opposed to stating what skill is to be performed.

The space awareness section of the wheel is divided into five subcategories that delineate various concepts of space: location, directions, levels, pathways, and extensions. In turn, each of these concepts is further divided into specific components that are the working or teachable aspects of space awareness. For example, the location concept is divided into the components of general space and self-space. Study Figure 13.1 to determine all the subdivisions for each of the separate aspects of space. It helps to think of the three outermost

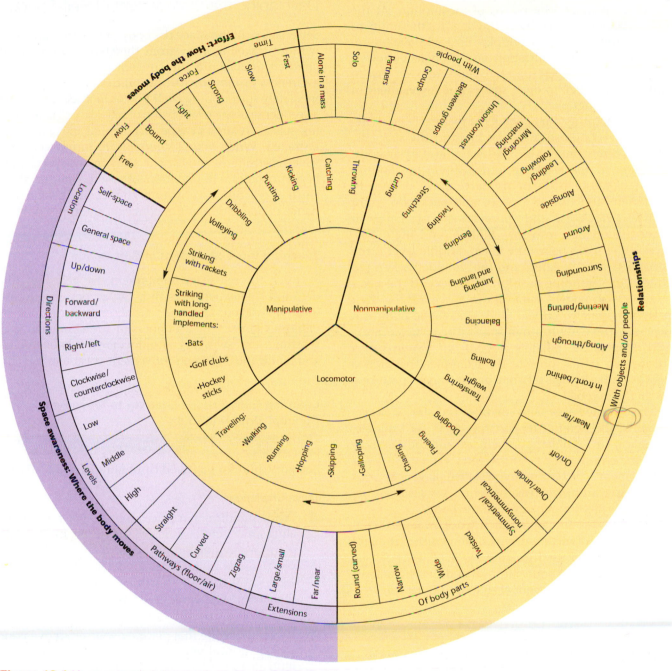

Figure 13.1 Movement analysis framework: space awareness concepts.

portions of the wheel as three levels of the same idea. The first level, or outside ring, describes the idea, the second ring gives the concepts that make up the idea, and the third ring defines the components that are found in each concept.

Activities in this section are planned as beginning tasks, not only to introduce but also to teach children the five concepts of space indicated in the second ring of the wheel. Children *must* understand these concepts before they attempt to apply them in conjunction with skill themes.

We usually begin by acquainting children with the two basic orientations of location: self-space and general space. These two ideas are crucial to all future learning; they're the foundation upon which everything else is built. Self-space is all the space the body or its parts can reach without traveling away from a starting location. General space is all the space within a room, an outdoor teaching space, or a boundary the body can penetrate by means of locomotion. At the precontrol level, space awareness denotes the ability to move throughout the work/play area without bumping others. At the utilization and proficiency levels, the ability to see open spaces, to move to open spaces, and to throw/kick to open spaces is a key element in successful games play.

The remaining four concepts of space awareness describe the relationships of the body to the space aspects of directions, levels, pathways, and extensions. *Directions* in space are the dimensional possibilities into which the body or its parts move or aim to move—up and down, forward and backward, right and left, clockwise and counterclockwise. *Levels* in space are divided into low, middle, and high. Low level is the space below the knees. Middle level is the space between the knees and the shoulders when the child is in a standing position. High level is the space above the shoulders. *Pathways* in space are the floor patterns (straight, curved, and zigzag) the body can create by traveling through space. The term *pathways* also denotes the possible floor or air patterns of a thrown or struck object—for example, the arched flight of a basketball set shot or the curved path of a pitcher's curveball.

The concept *extensions* includes the size of movements of the body or its parts in space (for example, small arm circles or large arm circles) and the distances from the center of the body the parts reach to carry out a movement. The tennis serve a skilled player performs is a far extension, whereas the tennis serve a beginner executes is often much closer to the body.

The ideas for developing each space awareness concept are stated in direct terms. Remember, though, that the method used to study each concept can be varied according to your purposes and the characteristics of the children in your class (see Chapter 10).

Developing the Concept of Location

We've found that the best way to teach the concept of *location* is to focus on its two components—self-space and general space—separately. We first teach self-space and then proceed to general space. You should repeat all the activities involved in teaching self-space and general space until it's clear the students understand the distinction between the two components, as well as the need to use space effectively.

⚠️ An understanding of self-space and general space plus starting and stopping on signal are crucial for students' safety.

Developing the Component of Self-Space

Self-space is all the space the body or its parts can reach without traveling away from the starting location. If children understand the concept of self-space, their awareness of movement possibilities in the space immediately surrounding their bodies increases. Without a keen sense of the relationship of self-space to surrounding space, children's range of potential movements is restricted. When young children are introduced to a wide repertoire of movement skills in self-space, they begin to build a foundation of nonlocomotor skills (such as twisting and turning) that can be used to enhance the development of concepts and other skills.

Teaching the Component of Self-Space

To teach the self-space component, we give the children learning experiences they can accomplish in one location, without traveling. The absence of locomotion enhances kinesthetic awareness of stretching, curling, twisting, and swinging (nonlocomotor) movements and builds the children's movement vocabularies.

Learning Experiences Leading to Movement Concept Understanding

Exploring Self-Space

Setting: Children scattered throughout general space

Tasks/Challenges:

T While standing in a place all by yourself, not traveling anywhere else, move your arms in as many places as possible around your body. Pretend that you're on an island in the middle of shark-infested waters and that all your friends are on islands of their own. You can't reach your friends on their islands, and they can't reach you. You're stranded.

T This time, while in a place by yourself, move your legs all around you. Try places that you think are difficult to get to, like behind you or way out to the side; come very close to falling off your island.

T Once you think you're very good with moving your arms and legs without leaving the space you're in, choose other parts you can move without leaving your space. Use parts you think would be really difficult to move around in your space without moving your whole body from your island. Explore your whole island.

The area that you've just explored is called *self-space*; it's like your own island or armor that travels with you wherever you go. Your self-space belongs

This young boy, appropriately challenged, is enthralled with the prospect of exploring space.

to you, and no one else is allowed in it unless you let them. Remember, too, that you're not allowed in anyone else's self-space unless they invite you.

Even with the best analogies in the world, it's sometimes difficult for children, both young and old, to understand the idea of self-space. When this happens, we've used hoops, spots, carpet squares, ropes shaped into circles, and Xs marked on the floor to help children differentiate and remember what their self-space really looks like. As soon as children properly understand what self-space is and are able to consistently remain in self-space, you can remove these prompts.

Each individual is surrounded by a self-space as he or she travels—the possible movements into space immediately surrounding the body will be the same regardless of location. But children will understand this idea most easily if they learn it while remaining stationary. Staying in one location will clarify for the children the difference between the movements possible in the space immediately surrounding the body and the movements possible when the body travels through general space.

Curling, Stretching, and Twisting in Self-Space

Setting: Children scattered throughout general space

Tasks/Challenges:

T While staying in self-space, where you can't touch anyone else, curl your body up very tightly so you look like a little ball. Now that you're curled up, begin to stretch, ever so slowly, until you're stretched as tall and wide as possible. As you stretch, remember

that you can't leave your own space. You're in your own birdcage. Slowly stretch just one arm, then the other arm. Slowly stretch only one leg, then the other leg. Don't forget to stretch your fingers and toes while you are in self-space.

T Pretend you're trying to reach the cookie jar on a shelf at the very top of your cage. Stretch as tall as you can to get it. Now, just as you have two cookies in your hand, your mother walks in. Sink very quickly back to the floor and make yourself very small in order to hide.

T This time, a big spider is on the floor of the cage, near your feet. Stretch tall; you're trying to reach the top rungs of your cage to pull yourself up out of the spider's way. Now the spider climbs to the top; shrink slowly to get away from the spider.

T Now that you've practiced your stretching and curling actions, you're going to add twisting actions to them. You want to twist your whole body, not just one part. To start, make believe the cookie jar is on the very back of the shelf, behind two boxes; as you stretch, twist your body so you can get to the cookie jar.

T Stretch toward the top of the birdcage (as you did to get away from the spider). Now pretend that suddenly you have an itch in the middle of your back. Hold on to the top of the cage with one hand and try to scratch your back with your other hand.

T Pretend you have an itch in the middle of your back that is impossible to reach. Twist your body in different directions as you attempt to reach the itch. Stretch, curl, and twist body parts in self-space to scratch the itch.

C See how many body parts you can stretch in self-space. How many different ways can you curl without moving from your self-space? Isolate different body parts for twisting in self-space.

Moving the Whole Body in Self-Space

Setting: Children scattered throughout general space

Tasks/Challenges:

T So far, all you've done in self-space is to curl, stretch, and twist; you haven't really moved your whole body using any kind of specific movement. This time, let's practice walking in place in self-space. Remember, you can't go anywhere off your island or out of your birdcage—that's all the area you have.

Other actions to practice in self-space: skipping, hopping, jumping, and turning slowly like a music box dancer.

Developing the Component of General Space

General space is all the space within a room or boundary into which an individual can move by traveling away from the original starting location (self-space).

We help the children learn different ways of traveling safely through general space by providing appropriate movement tasks. Once the children are able to travel safely (without bumping or losing control) in general space, they're ready to experience more complex tasks that include several concepts in combination, such as speed, pathways, and directions. Manipulating balls as one travels through general space is an even more difficult challenge.

Teaching the Component of General Space

The learning experiences in this section are designed to help children learn to travel safely and efficiently through general space. You can increase the complexity of the activities by focusing on the concepts of speed, pathways, and directions and on the manipulation of objects through general space. Traveling in general space is an excellent warm-up activity you can use each day; it also provides additional opportunities for practice of the various locomotor skills.

Learning Experiences Leading to Movement Concept Understanding

Exploring General Space

Setting: Children scattered throughout general space

Tasks/Challenges:

T Find a space by yourself within the boundaries of our work area. I'll know you're ready when I see you standing very still in a space where you can't touch anyone else. When I say "Go," begin to walk around the room, trying not to come near anyone else and at the same time not leaving any empty spaces in the room. On signal (*verbal signal or drumbeat*), stop very quickly right where you are. When you stop, you shouldn't be able to touch anyone else.

This area that you just moved in is called *general space*; it's all the space available for you to move in. As you move in general space, your self-space goes with you, like a bubble that surrounds you, so you're protected.

T Let's try the same activity again, but this time move a little faster through general space. Remember, as

you move and when you stop, you shouldn't be able to touch anyone else.

⚠ Increase the speed only when you observe that the children are able to travel without bumping into one another; for some classes this will take several days. Always start slowly.

T This time, instead of walking through general space, you're going to jog (*or skip, leap, hop, gallop, etc.*) through general space. Remember, always stay as far away from other people as you can. Think about visiting different places in the area, such as the corners and the middle of the area.

After you give the stop signal, you can further enhance concept development by giving the children feedback, for example:

- *Praise youngsters who stop in isolated areas.*
- *Praise youngsters who stop quickly and safely.*
- *Point out congested or vacant spaces.*
- *Praise youngsters who've avoided collisions by traveling defensively.*

🧠 Pretend you have one foot glued to the ground with sticky chewing gum; wave your arms up and down, all around. Is this movement in self-space or general space? Now travel waving your arms as you go, up and down, all around. Is this movement in self-space or general space?

Open Spaces

Setting: Children scattered throughout general space

Tasks/Challenges:

T Travel throughout general space, constantly moving to an open space. When you arrive at that open space, quickly move to another one when someone invades your open space or you see a second or a third open space.

T Travel throughout general space looking for an open space. When you see an open space, pretend you are throwing a ball to that space; then quickly travel to that space to "catch" the ball. Look for another open space, "throw," and travel again.

T Travel throughout general space looking for an open space. Each time you travel to an open space, claim that space as your own by calling "yes." Then quickly move to a new open space.

Reducing the Size of the General Space

Setting: Children scattered throughout general space facing the teacher, who is positioned at the edge of the general space. All the children will be moving within the boundaries. When you want the space to become

Spatial awareness is critical to working safely in group situations.

smaller, take a step or two toward the center of the general space—the idea is an entire wall moving forward at one time.

Tasks/Challenges:

🅣 Spread out and find a space by yourself. On the signal, begin to travel on your feet in general space, not touching anyone else. The difficult part this time will be that I'm going to keep making your space smaller as you move. For me to do that, you must always stay in front of me; I'll keep moving forward until your general space is very small.

Reducing the Size of General Space and Changing Speed

Setting: Children divided into two groups in a reduced amount of general space as in the previous activity

Tasks/Challenges:

🅣 Let's move within this reduced amount of space as if we were in a crowded city. We will begin walking at a moderate speed to avoid bumping others on the crowded streets. On signal, increase the speed of your walking as if you were in rush-hour traffic. Remember, no collisions.

🅣 Now move very slowly because the area is congested. Increase your speed again.

🅣 Group 1, stand very still in your self-space. You are the tall buildings in the city; you may be tall and wide or just tall. Group 2, walk throughout the general space without bumping other walkers or the buildings. Listen for the signal to increase or decrease your speed. (*Switch the groups after 30 seconds*.)

Dodging in General Space

Setting: Children divided into two groups: half the children on one side of the work area, half on the other side

Tasks/Challenges:

🅣 Let's practice our moving in general space in a game. The object of the game is for both groups to get to the other side of the area without touching anyone else. The difficult part is that both groups will be moving at the same time. Remember, all of you in both groups are trying to switch sides without touching anyone else. I'll watch very carefully to see if I can find anyone touching.

🅣 Now, instead of walking, you're going to gallop (*or skip, hop, jump, etc.*) to the other side.

⚠ Permit children to travel at fast speeds, such as running, only after they have mastered stopping on signal and moving with no collisions.

Traveling Over, Under, and Around Obstacles in General Space

Setting: Small obstacles (hoops and ropes on the floor, milk crates, and low benches) spread out in various places around the area

Tasks/Challenges:

🅣 Travel around the space without touching any piece of equipment or any other person. You may go over, under, or around any of the obstacles, but don't touch anyone or anything. Remember, if someone else is at a piece of equipment, go on to another one; don't wait in line.

These youngsters understand both extensions and levels as they meet and part.

From the National Standards for Physical Education

Teacher Observation

The teacher uses a checklist to assess the degree to which a class or individual students can identify a "good personal space," work in "personal space," and move in "general space" during a manipulative lesson.

Criteria for Assessment

a. Finds a personal space within general space that provides maximum room to work.
b. Stays in or returns to personal space during lesson.
c. Moves with an awareness of others as well as of space available within general space.

NASPE (1995, 7)

Space Awareness Obstacle Course

Setting: Jump ropes, wands, hoops, yardsticks, crates, and similar small equipment placed around the edge of the work area

Tasks/Challenges:

Ⓣ Today you are going to design an obstacle course for our traveling in general space. What is an obstacle course? Right; it's an area to travel through without bumping into things or going outside the boundaries. Select two or three pieces of the small equipment, and place them on the floor; you may wish to place them so they are touching or so they connect with the equipment of the person working next to you. (*Allow two to three minutes for the children to construct the obstacle course.*)

Walk throughout general space, avoiding the obstacles placed on the floor; travel without touching the equipment or any other person.

Travel in a way other than walking.

If the children have been introduced to the concept of pathways, they can design the obstacle course to show straight, curved, and zigzag pathways. Their travel can then be a combination of different locomotors and pathways—for example, walk the straight pathways, gallop the curved pathways, and jump as you travel the zigzag pathways.

Developing the Concept of Directions

Directions in space are the dimensional possibilities into which the body or its parts move or aim to move—up and down, right and left, forward and backward, clockwise and counterclockwise. There is no universally correct direction; direction is a function of the body's orientation in space. Forward and backward, for example, depend on the way a person is facing rather than a location in a room. Left and right refer to the respective sides of the body, not a certain wall or location in a gymnasium. Because the direction components of right and left (sideways) and clockwise and counterclockwise require cognitive as well as physical maturation for correct execution, it's not uncommon to find that children learn the directions forward and backward and up and down before they learn the directions right and left and clockwise and counterclockwise.

Teaching the Concept of Directions

The learning experiences in this section provide ideas for helping children understand the components of direction—forward and backward, up and down, sideways (right and left), clockwise and counterclockwise. As the children become more capable, the complexity of the tasks is increased—the children are challenged to combine two or more direction components and to move in different directions in relation to objects or people.

Learning Experiences Leading to Movement Concept Understanding

Traveling in Different Directions

Setting: Children scattered throughout general space

Tasks/Challenges:

T On the signal, walk as you usually walk, with the front of your body going first. This direction is called *forward*.

T This time, walk with your back going first. This direction is called *backward*. Sometimes going backward is hard because you have to look over your shoulder to see where you're going.

T Now walk with one side of your body going first. This direction is called *sideways*. You can move to either your right or left side. Let's practice both ways. First, move with your right side going first. When you hear the drumbeat (*if you don't have a drum, use a metal can, a baby rattle, or a party noisemaker*), change so your left side goes first.

T Skip forward, walk slowly backward, slide from side to side like an ice-skater, and jump up and down as though you were on a pogo stick.

Moving Clockwise and Counterclockwise

Setting: Children scattered throughout general space

Tasks/Challenges:

Rotation describes movement in a clockwise or counterclockwise direction. When we want children to turn, spin, or pivot, using the terms right *and* left *is inaccurate. Instead, the terms* clockwise *and* counterclockwise *indicate the appropriate direction in which to move.*

T Look down at the floor. Imagine there's a clock on the floor in front of you. Slowly turn around, turning in the direction the hands on the clock move. This direction is called clockwise. Now turn in the other direction. This direction is called counterclockwise.

T Now practice the different directions some more. See if you can spin clockwise on one foot. Now change and spin counterclockwise on the same foot.

T Swing your arms in the direction you want to spin, and see if you can spin all the way around before you stop. Swinging your arms will help you spin farther. Remember to swing in the direction you want to go.

❀ Is it easier to spin in a clockwise or a counterclockwise direction? Why do you think so? Find a partner. One of you spin or jump and turn while the other watches. See if your partner can tell you whether you were spinning (turning) in a clockwise or a counterclockwise direction. Now watch as your partner spins (turns).

T This time try jumping. Stay in your self-space, and jump and turn all the way around so you land facing the same direction you were facing when you started. Bend your knees to land in a balanced position.

T Practice turning clockwise and counterclockwise when you jump. Can you turn farther in one direction than the other?

T Now you're going to try something different. Travel in general space. When you hear one drumbeat, spin in a clockwise direction and keep traveling. When you hear two drumbeats, spin in a counterclockwise direction and keep traveling. If you hear three drumbeats, change the way you're traveling—for example, from a skip to a slide. Do you think you can remember all this? Let's see!

You can also teach and reinforce clockwise and counterclockwise when working with several of the skill themes by having the children dribble in a clockwise or counterclockwise direction, for example, or push a puck with a hockey stick in both directions.

Exploring Directions

Setting: Children scattered throughout general space

Tasks/Challenges:

T In your self-space, point with the body part named in the direction that I call out. (You can continue the list with any body part.)

With your foot, point forward.
With your elbow, point backward.
With your hip, point to the left.
With your left foot, point forward.

As you point, make sure the direction you're pointing to is very clear—so I could easily tell which way to go if you were pointing out a direction to me.

Changing Directions on Signal

Setting: Children scattered throughout general space

Tasks/Challenges:

T Now that you know the directions, move a little faster when you practice them, and mix them all up. On the signal, begin to travel in general space in a forward direction. After that, each time you hear the signal, change the direction you're moving in. For example, if you start out moving in a forward direction, the first time you hear the signal, change to a sideways direction; the next time you hear the signal, change to a backward direction; and the next time change back to a sideways direction. Remember, make your directions very clear.

While the children are waiting for the signal, have them think about how they're going to change direction.

T This time, change not only the direction of your travel, but also the locomotor movement you use—for example, gallop forward, walk backward, or slide to the right.

T This time the changes of direction are going to be a bit more difficult. They'll be in code. One beat of the drum means forward. Two beats of the drum mean sideways. Three beats of the drum mean backward. Spread out in general space in a space by yourself. When you hear the beat of the drum, begin to travel in the direction indicated by the code. When you hear the next beat of the drum, change and travel in the direction that it indicates. Listen very carefully to the drumbeats because I might try to trick you.

Turning While Moving in Different Directions

Setting: Children positioned around the perimeters of the gymnasium, facing the walls

Tasks/Challenges:

T Spread out around the outside of the room and face the wall. When you hear the drumbeat, begin to travel around the space by using a sliding pattern. As the drum beats again, turn, without stopping, to face the inside of the room—keep sliding. Each time the drum beats, change the way you're facing, and continue moving sideways. When you do this, I'm looking for turns that are smooth and slides that don't stop as you turn.

Developing the Concept of Levels

Levels are the horizontal layers in space where the body or its parts are positioned or can move.

Low level is the space below the knees, close to the floor. A stamp or twist of the foot is an action at a low level. Crawling, creeping, and rolling are locomotor actions performed at a low level.

Middle level is the space between low level and high level—the area between the knees and shoulders. Catching a thrown ball, for example, typically occurs in middle level.

High level is the space above the shoulders, toward the ceiling or the sky. Although one can't move the whole body into high level, actions such as stretching the arms up high or standing on the balls of the feet bring body parts into a high level. A jump can take much of the upper body into a high level, while part of the body remains at a middle or low level because of the pull of gravity.

Teaching the Concept of Levels

The learning experiences in this section give children movement challenges that help them learn to move the body, body parts, and objects into different levels in space.

Learning Experiences Leading to Movement Concept Understanding

Traveling and Freezing at Different Levels

Setting: Children scattered throughout general space

Tasks/Challenges:

T Spread out and find a space by yourself. On signal, begin to travel in general space. When you hear the drumbeat, stop where you are, with your whole body at a low level.

T This time, travel, and on the signal, stop with your body at low level and a body part at high level. Make it very clear which part is at a high level.

T This time, when you stop, stop with your body at a middle level. Remember, a low level means below your knees, a middle level is from about your knees to your shoulders, and a high level is above your shoulders.

Traveling with Body Parts at Different Levels

Setting: Children scattered throughout general space

Tasks/Challenges:

T Travel around general space with as many of your body parts as possible at a low level. Remember, your body parts should always be at a low level when you're traveling, not just when you freeze.

T As you travel this time, try to have as many body parts as possible at a middle level. Remember, it isn't possible to have all body parts at a middle level as you travel because your feet always have to be on the floor, but have as many parts as possible at a middle level and none at a high level.

T This time as you travel, have as many parts as possible at a high level. This activity is harder than the other two, so be very careful that all possible body parts are at a high level.

👤 Show me hands at high level, middle level, low level.

Young children enjoy exploring body parts at different levels in self-space (e.g., feet, elbows, and nose, as well as combinations of levels, such as one foot low, one foot high).

Rising and Sinking to Create Different Levels

Setting: Children scattered throughout general space

Tasks/Challenges:

T Find a space by yourself, and get into a low position you like. I'm going to beat the drum very slowly eight times. As I beat the drum, rise very slowly to the eight beats until you attain a position of stillness with as many body parts as possible at a high level. Remember, rise slowly. But also remember you have only eight beats in which to get to a high level, so judge your movement so you get there in time. After you've reached your high position, on the next eight beats slowly sink back to your low position. The sequence then goes like this: a low position; eight beats to get to a high, still position; eight beats to return to your low position. Let's try it.

Traveling While Rising and Sinking

Setting: Children scattered throughout general space

Tasks/Challenges:

T As you travel around the space this time, I'll give you drumbeats to guide your actions. The drumbeats will be in counts of four, with the accent on the first beat. Start by traveling at a low level. On the accented first

beat, quickly jump and stretch into a high level and then immediately return to a low level of travel until the next accented beat. Your movement should look like this: travel low, jump high, travel low, jump high, travel low, and so on. Make your jump very clear and as high as possible and your travel at a low level very clear. I should be able to easily tell the difference between the two levels.

Developing the Concept of Pathways

A pathway is an imaginary design that the body or its parts when moving through space create along the floor or through the air. A pathway is also the trail of an object (a ball or hockey puck) as it travels from one player to another or toward a goal.

At first, young children may have difficulty understanding the concept of pathways in space. However, a class of young children can become enthralled with the process of discovering and experimenting with the many pathways the body can travel. A teacher can plan experiences that enable youngsters to recognize pathways and to effectively use knowledge of pathways to improve control of travel. For instance, even very young children can come to understand that a curved or angular pathway is effective for avoiding collisions when traveling through a crowd.

Teaching the Concept of Pathways

Children learn to travel in straight, zigzag, and curved pathways, and in combinations of these pathways, by experiencing the activities in this section. More difficult learning experiences involve manipulating various objects in pathways and traveling in relation to others along various pathways.

Learning Experiences Leading to Movement Concept Understanding

Exploring Pathways

Setting: Tape markings on the floor similar to those shown in Figure 13.2; children scattered throughout general space

Tasks/Challenges:

T Today you're going to learn about pathways. A line that doesn't turn or twist and is always straight is called a *straight pathway*. A line that circles around is called a curved pathway. A semicircle is a *curved*

Figure 13.2 Pathways taped on the floor.

pathway. A line that looks like a lot of Zs put together is a *zigzag pathway.* Now find a space on one of the pathways marked on the floor. Travel along that pathway on your feet; be able to tell me what kind of pathway it is when I ask you.

T This time as you travel, change your direction, sometimes going forward along your pathway, sometimes sideways, and sometimes backward. Try out all directions on your pathway.

T Now change the way that you travel along your pathway. Sometimes you may want to hop, sometimes leap, sometimes run. Find at least four different ways you can travel along your pathway.

During the activity, have the children regularly change places so they're on a different pathway.

Using Pathway Maps

Setting: A card, similar to the ones shown in Figure 13.3, for each child

Figure 13.3 Pathway cards.

Tasks/Challenges:

T Take a card and find a space by yourself. Travel on your feet and follow the pathway indicated on your card. Pretend your card is a map showing the route to take to get to a new place. Keep practicing your pathway until you're very sure it's just like the one on the card and you can do it the best you can. Be able to tell me the name of the pathway you're following whenever I ask you.

T Now trade cards with someone else and practice that pathway until you think it's perfect.

Designing Pathways

Setting: Children scattered throughout general space

Tasks/Challenges:

T Pick a spot on the wall across the room from you. Remember where your spot is, and in your mind plan a pathway that will take you from where you are now to that spot. Think about it a long time so you can remember it when you start to move. When I give the signal, travel along your made-up pathway until you get to the spot you've picked out. Stop when you get there. On the next signal, travel back to the place you started from, following the same pathway you took coming over. This is similar to following a path through the woods: You can't go off the path or you'll get lost.

T Now I am *not* going to give you the signal anymore. Practice your pathway on your own until you have memorized and can repeat it exactly every time.

✔ *Student Drawing.* Asking children to draw the various pathways and label them would be an easy way to assess their understanding.

Creating Follow-the-Leader Pathways

Setting: Sets of partners scattered throughout general space

Card 1   Card 2   Card 3

Tasks/Challenges:

T Find a partner and stand in a space together. I'll know that you're ready when I see each of you standing quietly in your space. Decide which of you is going to be the leader. On the signal, the leader travels a pathway to somewhere else in the room. On the second signal, the leader stops, and the follower moves along the same pathway the leader took until the follower catches up with the leader. After doing this three times, the leader and follower switch places. The secret is for the follower to watch the leader very closely. In the beginning, the leader should not make up difficult pathways. Followers, remember to copy the leaders' pathways exactly.

√ Have each child create a pathway sequence using one straight, one curved, and one zigzag pathway in any order they choose. After they create their pathway sequences, they will draw them on paper, creating their unique design. After the child creates, practices, and memorizes the pathway sequence, a peer can watch for correct execution and order, thus assessing understanding of pathways.

Traveling Pathways and Obstacles

Setting: Half the class positioned throughout general space, the other half around the perimeter of the space

Tasks/Challenges:

T Now you're going to travel in pathways that go around, over, and under obstacles in your way. Always remember that your classmates are the obstacles, so you have to be very careful of them. You can't touch anyone else. People who are obstacles must remember to stay very still so as to not interfere with anyone who's moving. Obstacles, go find a position in a space by yourself that you can hold still. It can be any position you like—a bridge, a statue, or a balance. Those of you on the side of the space, pick a point on the other side of the room and plan a pathway to get there. Remember, your pathway can go over, under, or around any of the obstacles. Think about it and really make it different from anything you've done before.

Give the children a few seconds to plan their pathway and the obstacles time to select their position.

On the signal, follow your pathway to the point you picked on the other side of the room. Stop when you get to the point you picked. On the next signal, try to retrace your pathway until you get back to your starting position.

C Now, on your own, practice your pathway four times. Remember, avoid running into other travelers as you cross the space. Always have a clear beginning and end to your pathway.

When all have completed their pathways, have the students switch places and perform the activity. You can enhance activities such as these by asking children who are doing the activities correctly to demonstrate for the rest of the class.

Mr. Jenning's Kindergarten Class Discovers Pathways

Teacher: Boys and girls! How did we get to the physical education space today?

Children: We walked!

Teacher: Yes! And what parts of our bodies did we use?

Children: Our feet . . . our legs.

Teacher: You got it! Tell me, did we leave a trail behind us? Any footprints on the floor?

Children: No! (*Loud and laughing*)

Teacher: I don't see any either. But what if your shoes were muddy. Would we have left a trail?

Children: Yes! But Mrs. Farmer (*the principal*) sure would be mad!

Teacher: I think she would be, too! But if we did leave muddy footprints from your classroom all the way to the physical education space, what would our path look like?

Children: Long . . . Messy . . . we go by the library.

Teacher: I think you're all right. I have an idea. . . . Let's look at the whiteboard. Here's your room way over here, and this is where the physical education space is. Look at our pathway. Although we didn't leave any real footprints, we did follow a path. We follow this same pathway each time we come to the physical education space. Tell me, is our path just one straight line, or did we make any turns?

Children: We turned when we came out of the room. At the library.

Teacher: You are sharp today. Can you think of any other pathways you follow each day?

Children: We go to lunch . . . walk to school . . . down to the playground.

Teacher: We follow a lot of pathways each day. Let's see if we can have some fun with pathways today. Pick a spot somewhere on the outside edge of the room (for example, a brick, a picture), and when I say "Go," stand up and walk in a straight line to your spot and freeze. Here we go!

Following-the-Dots Pathways

Setting: A pencil plus a card with dots randomly plotted on it for each child; carpet squares (or spots) on the floor in a pattern similar to that of the dots on the card

Tasks/Challenges:

T Connect the dots on your card to form any design you like. After you've finished connecting the dots, follow the path you drew from one carpet square (spot) to the other. Make sure you know the type of pathway you've designed because I might ask you.

T Now trade maps with someone else. Follow that person's map. Decide if that pathway is different from yours.

Combining Pathways, Levels, and Directions

Setting: A task sheet, similar to that in Figure 13.4, for each child

Tasks/Challenges:

T This activity lets you combine pathways, levels, and directions. It's also a good way to test yourself. Once you think you're able to perform a challenge,

Figure 13.4 Task sheet for pathways, levels, and directions.

Name _____		Teacher _____
		Pathways, Levels, and Directions Task Sheet
Date	**Who Watched**	**Challenge**
		I can walk forward in a straight pathway.
		I can walk backward in a straight pathway.
		I can walk sideways in a straight pathway.
		I can walk forward in a curved pathway.
		I can walk backward in a curved pathway.
		I can walk forward, low, and curved.
		I can walk backward, high, and zigzag.
		I can run sideways, middle, and curved.
		I can slide backward, middle, and zigzag.
		I can
		I can
		I can
		(Make up three things you can do on your own using pathways, levels, and directions.)

have a friend watch you and sign the line on the task sheet beside the challenge. When you're finished, I'll come and check you out. You may use a friend to help you if you want extra help.

Younger children can use a smile face instead of having someone else initial the sheet.

✓ **Peer Observation.** The task sheet in Figure 13.4 would make a perfect peer observation.

Developing the Concept of Extensions in Space

Extensions in space are best understood as two separate possibilities. First, extensions are spatial relationships of body parts to the entire body. Body extremities can be held in close to the body, as in a curl, or they can be opened up, as in a stretch. Extensions are also the size of movements in space. Movements with extremities held close to the body are *small movements*, such as putting a golf ball; those with the extremities extended or opened up are *large movements*, such as driving a golf ball.

Teaching the Concept of Extensions in Space

The concept of extensions is taught through learning experiences that give children an operational understanding of the differences between large and small, as well as near and far extensions (movements).

Learning Experiences Leading to Movement Concept Understanding

Exploring Extensions

Setting: Children scattered throughout general space

Tasks/Challenges:

T Find a space by yourself. With your hands, explore all the space close to your body. Remember to not reach very far from your body; this is an extension near your body. We call it a *near* extension.

T Now, without leaving your self-space, explore all the space that is far away from your body. Try to reach as far as you can without leaving your space. Remember, explore above and behind as well as in front of you. This is called an extension that is far away from your body. We call it a *far* extension.

Traveling and Extensions

Setting: Children scattered throughout general space

Tasks/Challenges:

T Travel around the room. When you hear the drumbeat, stop in a position where your body reaches as far into space as possible. Be very sure that all possible body parts are as far away from the center of your body as you can get them.

T This time as you travel, when you hear the drumbeat, stop with all body parts as close to your body as possible. Remember, keep all your body parts as close to yourself as you can.

T Now try traveling with change. When you hear the drumbeat, jump high into the air, extending your arms and legs as far away from your body as possible. When you land, hold a position very still, with all body parts very close to the center of your body. Really try to make a clear difference between the far and near extensions.

Changing from One Extension to Another

Setting: Children scattered throughout general space

Tasks/Challenges:

T Find a space by yourself, and get into a tight position you like. I'll beat the drum six times, in slow beats. On the first six beats, gradually extend all body parts far away from your body. On the next six beats, slowly move to your tight, curled position. The movement then goes like this: first a tight, curled position; on six beats, slowly move to a spread-out position; on the next six beats, slowly move back to a near extension. Try to make your extensions very clear. We'll practice this activity a number of times so you can work on doing your best.

Using Extensions and Imagery

Setting: Children scattered throughout general space

Tasks/Challenges:

T As you travel around general space, pretend you're carrying an object you don't want anyone to see or that you're trying to hide or protect something, such as a baby bird, a million-dollar jewel, or a lot of money. As you walk, think very carefully about how you would actually carry the object you've chosen.

T Now, instead of having an object you want to hide, you have one you're proud of and want to show off—maybe a trophy you just won. How would you carry it? Go!

❋ In which activity did you use a near or small extension? In which activity did you use a large or far extension?

To create this group balance, these youngsters need to understand personal space, extensions, and levels.

Applying the Space Awareness Concepts

Location (self-space and general space) is often the appropriate beginning concept for children who have had little experience in formal physical education classes. One of the important skills children need to develop early is the ability to occupy an area or to travel in an area while maintaining awareness of others. An understanding of self-space and general space is helpful when learning these skills.

The concepts of directions, levels, and pathways are usually introduced after children have developed the ability to differentiate self-space from general space. Until the children actually acquire a functional understanding of directions, levels, and pathways, the observational focus is primarily on the concept rather than on correct performance of a particular skill. For example, if you ask the children to throw so that the ball starts off at a high level, you're less interested in the actual mechanics of throwing than in the child's ability to release the ball at a high level. Once you're confident that the children are able to apply the concepts, you can focus more on appropriate skill technique.

Most children take a longer time to grasp right and left, air pathways, and extensions. Thus, it's wise to introduce the other concepts and components to children before focusing on these.

The ability to understand the notion of right and left is related to cognitive maturation. Some children will need more time and more practice opportunities than others to master left and right. Many children easily acquire cognitive understanding of the concepts of extensions and air pathways for objects, but most require a certain degree of skill before they can express these ideas in movements. Children with immature throwing and kicking patterns, for example, have difficulty propelling objects so they travel in different (but intended) air pathways. Children with immature striking or catching patterns are unable to consistently catch or strike an object far from or near to the body.

If you wait until children have developed the skills related to these concepts, you'll find they grasp the concepts more easily than if you try to teach the concepts and then the skills. There's no universally successful sequence for introducing these concepts and their components. The reflective teacher uses all available information and makes judgments about the most appropriate time, sequence, and duration for introducing and studying the concepts of space awareness and the application of the concepts to specific skill-practice situations. Sample lesson plans for teaching the movement concepts can be found in *On the Move,* a collection of lesson plans designed to accompany *Children Moving*.

Reading Comprehension Questions

1. What is the primary reason for focusing on space awareness at the beginning of a physical education program?
2. What does the term *space awareness* mean? What are the characteristics of someone who is "aware of space"?
3. Why is space awareness so important for children at the precontrol level?
4. Why is an understanding of open spaces important for proficiency and utilization movers?

5. What directions in space are studied in this program? Why do children find some directions more difficult than others to understand?

6. Distinguish the three levels of space from each other.

7. List the three types of pathways an individual might travel. Explain the difference between a floor pathway and an air pathway.

8. Give two examples each of a far extension and a near extension.

9. Why do we have children study self-space while stationary rather than traveling?

10. What does it look like when children are able to travel safely in general space?

11. Using the movement analysis wheel, manipulate it to show space awareness in relation to locomotor, manipulative, and nonmanipulative skills. Identify two skills for each category that space awareness can modify, and write a sample task for each.

References/Suggested Readings

Holt/Hale, S. 2012. *On the move: Lesson plans to accompany Children Moving*. 9th ed. New York: McGraw-Hill.

[NASPE] National Association for Sport and Physical Education. 1995. *Moving into the future: National standards for physical education*. St. Louis, MO: Mosby.

[NASPE] National Association for Sport and Physical Education. 2004. *Moving into the future: National standards for physical education*. 2nd ed. Reston, VA: National Association for Sport and Physical Education.

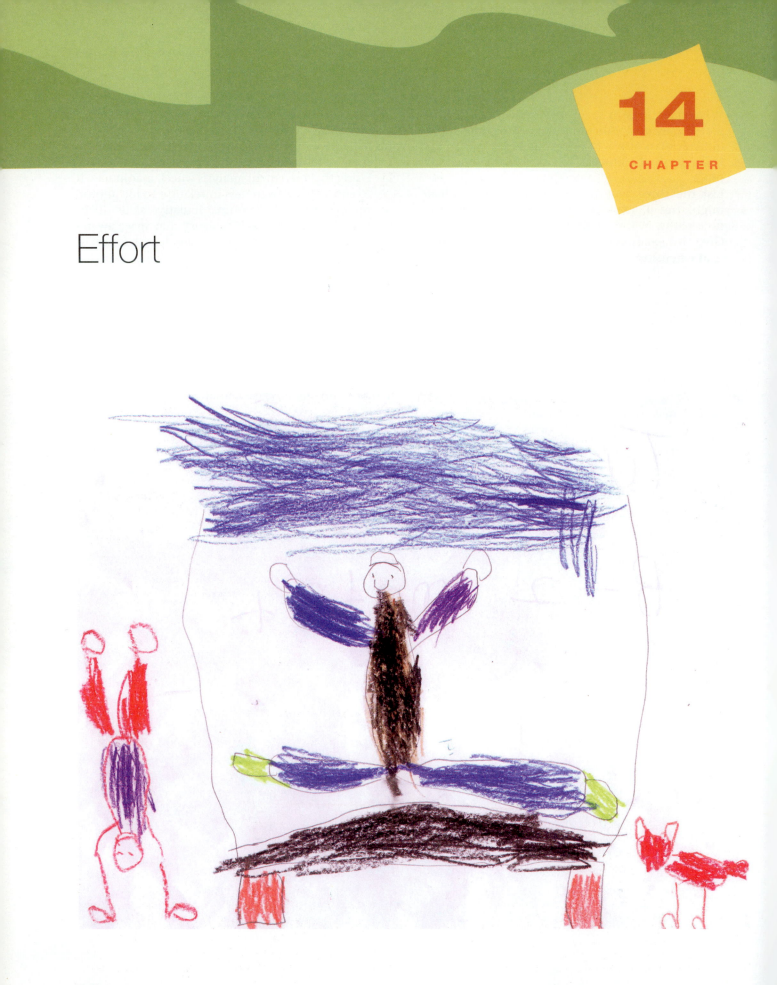

Effort

This chapter explains and provides multiple learning experiences for the movement concept category of effort. (See Table 3.2 in Chapter 3 for a full listing of the movement concepts taught in elementary school physical education.) Remember, we first provide experiences for children to attain a functional understanding of the movement concepts. When they have this understanding, the concepts are then used to enhance the skill themes—adverbs to enrich action verbs.

Too often teachers make no conscious, planned attempt to help children understand the effort concepts of time, force, and flow and the application of these concepts to specific skills.* Many teachers don't feel comfortable teaching these concepts, which are vague and abstract. It is not like teaching a child to strike a ball with a paddle, in which the objective of striking is obvious and the result easily perceived. Despite many teachers' hesitancy to undertake teaching effort concepts, there is agreement that an applied understanding of these concepts is essential in skill development, from beginning through advanced levels. See Box 14-1 for linkages between the movement concepts of Effort and the *National Standards for Physical Education.*

The effort concepts define how the body moves. The category is divided into three concepts—time, force, and flow—that are defined by observable characteristics that can be taught to children. Figure 14.1 conceptualizes this idea and puts it into perspective with the other movement concepts and skill themes. The effort category is in the shaded portion of the framework. The outside ring identifies the category, the second ring identifies the concepts, and the third ring defines the three components.

Highly skilled (proficiency level) movers have developed an internalized, reflexive knowledge of the proper amount and degree of time, force, and flow. They're able to adjust the quality of movements in relation to the demands of a situation—harder or softer, faster or slower, bound or free.

We begin to teach effort concepts to children by providing experiences to help them understand the contrasts of fast-slow, strong-light, and bound-free. Once the children have grasped the differences between the extremes, we focus on the concepts as they apply to specific skills (such as throwing, striking, and transferring weight) and in different situations (for example,

---

*Some movement analysis frameworks include direct and flexible space as effort qualities of movement. In our teaching, however, we use them so infrequently we've chosen not to include them in the discussion of the qualities of movement.

Box 14-1

Effort in the *National Standards for Physical Education*

The movement concept of Effort is referenced in the National Association for Sport and Physical Education's *National Standards for Physical Education* (NASPE 2004) under Standard 2: "Demonstrates understanding of movement concepts, principles, strategies, and tactics as they apply to the learning and performance of physical activities." The intent of the standard is to facilitate learners' ability to use cognitive information to understand and enhance motor skill acquisition and performance. At the lower-elementary level, emphasis is placed on establishing a movement vocabulary and applying introductory concepts. At the upper-elementary level, emphasis is placed on applying and generalizing the concepts to physical activity situations.

Sample performance outcomes from the *National Standards* include:

- Demonstrates clear contrasts between slow and fast movement when skipping (or hopping, galloping, sliding, etc.) (K–2)*
- Develops and refines a gymnastics sequence (or creative dance sequence) demonstrating smooth transitions (3–5)*
- Designs and performs gymnastics (or dance) sequences that combine traveling, rolling, balancing, and weight transfer into smooth, flowing sequences with intentional changes in direction, speed, and flow (6–8)*

*Grade-level guidelines for expected student learning.

---

to assist in the expression of an idea or to accomplish a particular strategy). As children become more skillful, we focus on the gradations among the extremes. To illustrate, initially we might ask children to travel rapidly and slowly. As children develop the ability to differentiate between the extremes, we focus more on the movement possibilities that occur between the extremes—faster, slower, accelerating, decelerating, sudden changes of speed.

Many activities in this chapter use imagery to help children distinguish among different concepts of effort. It's important to keep in mind that the focus is on the movement qualities of the various images rather than on the images themselves. For example, when we say "Move like a hippo," we're not asking the children to pretend to be hippos; we're using this task to help the children envision a slow, lumbering movement.

Figure 14.1 Movement analysis framework: effort concepts.

Box 14-2 and Chapter 28 contain additional information about the appropriate use of imagery in teaching movement.

Developing the Concept of Time

Time to a young child is the tick-tock of a grandfather clock, the cuckoo clock on the wall, or the numbers racing by on a digital timepiece. When spoken of in relation to movement, time is fast—being able to run like the wind; being the fastest in the class; zip, dash, zoom.

In physical education, speed is often the measure of success; therefore children often have difficulty comprehending slowness and seeing the importance of this rate of movement in their activities. Yet the performer executing a walkover on the balance beam grasps the idea of slowness, as does the leaping dancer who seems to remain suspended in the air

Box 14-2

Imagery and Movement

Much has been said about imagery and movement, specifically related to dance. We've all had the experience of asking children to "show a flower growing," only to discover that instead of exploring the movement possibilities available, the children were pretending to be flowers. Herein lies the pitfall of imagery: Concept development isn't pretending; it's understanding.

To be beneficial, teaching movement concepts and ultimately dance must begin with children learning a movement vocabulary and then relating it to other ideas (much like the development of movement skills before relating them to game play). This notion implies we must talk about movement first and use images to lead to an understanding or enhancement of that movement. It precludes moving or dancing "about" something (anger, fear, excitement, horses, etc.) or pretending to be something (a piece of fruit, a cowboy, a flower, an airplane, etc.).

Mary Joyce (1994) developed three useful phases regarding dance and imagery that can be easily applied to any creative movement:

1. Images that lead to movement: "Make your back curved like a banana."
2. Images that arise from movement: "You're in a curved shape. What else do you know that is curved?"
3. Images as a basis for movement: "What kind of movement might a banana do?"

Always remember to talk about the movement first and the image second.

---

while the hands and arms express a certain feeling or emotion.

Changes in the timing of a movement usually occur without forethought as children adapt to different situations—speeding up or slowing down to maintain possession, to avoid being tagged, to get in open space and receive a pass. Many movements and specific skills dictate the rate of movement. A handspring is done quickly, but a back walkover is performed slowly. In some activities, the child is free to assess a situation and then perform a skill at the best rate. For example, a movement executed quickly in dance or gymnastics elicits feelings of power and speed; the same movement executed slowly expresses the ultimate in control.

We begin teaching the concept of time to young children by contrasting extremes. Gradually we ad-

vance to work that focuses on degrees of speed along a continuum—the ability to execute movements at varying speeds for the purpose of adapting, changing, or creating a situation.

Teaching the Concept of Time

The learning experiences that follow are designed to help children develop a functional understanding of time by contrasting fast and slow actions of the total body and body parts, as well as by focusing on acceleration-deceleration. *When the children are traveling fast, try to keep the activity period short to avoid undue fatigue.*

Learning Experiences Leading to Movement Concept Understanding

Exploring Time

Setting: Children scattered throughout general space

Tasks/Challenges:

T Find a space by yourself. Without leaving your space, move with the drumbeat. The beat will be very loud and quick to begin with, so you'll want your movements to be very sharp and quick. The trick to having very quick actions is to make them very short; something that's really quick can't go on for very long. This action is called a *sudden* movement.

T This time the drumbeat will be slower and longer. Try to move your whole body as slowly as the drumbeats, much like a balloon floating through the air or a feather being dropped from a high building. Think about moving every part of your body slowly, not just your arms but your head, shoulders, back, stomach, legs, everything. This action is called a *sustained* movement.

Using Different Speeds in Self-Space

Setting: Children scattered throughout general space

Tasks/Challenges:

T In a space by yourself, bring your hands together very slowly, as if to catch an insect that might try to fly away. At the very last moment before your hands are going to touch, quickly separate them as if you're surprised to find out that the insect is a bee. When you do your slow movements, remember to make them very slow but to always keep your hands moving; make your quick movements so quick that they're like flashes of lightning.

These young children are enjoying the sensation of running—a fast movement.

Slowness is necessary for travel at low level.

C Let's try those movements five more times. You can bring your hands together any way you want as long as you do so slowly, and then quickly take them away any way you want. Remember, make your slow and quick movements as clear as they can be. Five times. Go.

T Now, on your own, find other body parts you can bring together slowly and then quickly pull apart. Try to find at least three combinations. Practice each movement so the difference between fast and slow is very clear.

This activity is more difficult than it sounds because it asks for extremes of a movement. You can have children practice this activity over and over; always ask for faster and slower actions than the children previously exhibited.

Moving at Different Speeds

Setting: Children scattered throughout general space

Tasks/Challenges:

T On the signal, move as fast as you can, but remain in self-space; on the next signal, freeze in a balanced position that you can hold very still. Remember, try to go as fast as you can, but you must be able to stop on the signal without falling over.

T Now, on the start signal, move as slowly as you can in self-space. Try to move very slowly, but always keep moving. On the stop signal, freeze in a balanced position. Remember, stay in your self-space.

T Your first movement was at a fast speed; your second, at a slow speed. Could you tell the difference? Again, you're going to practice both fast and slow speeds. Try to make the movements very clear so I can really tell the difference between them. As you move, I'll call out "Fast" or "Slow," and you change your speed accordingly. So if I call out "Slow," move very slowly, and if I call out "Fast," move fast. Listen very carefully because I might try to trick you. Make your fast really fast and your slow really slow.

Once the children demonstrate an understanding of speed in self-space, you can transfer these same tasks to traveling in general space.

Traveling and Freezing by Using Changes in Time

Setting: Children scattered throughout general space

Tasks/Challenges:

T This time, begin your traveling with a quick explosion of speed, and keep going at a fast speed; then freeze very quickly in a balanced position. The movement should be like this: Begin really fast as if you've been shot out of a cannon; then move fast as if you're running from someone; then freeze quickly as if someone has surprised you and you can't move. Make each segment of your traveling very clear so that I can tell when you change from one part to the other. I'll give you the start signal; then you're on your own.

T Now that you've practiced sudden starts, traveling fast, and then freezing, you're going to make up a sequence using those speeds. Choose one sudden-start, fast-travel, and freeze position you really like, and practice it until you can do it smoothly and with control. Each of the three parts should be very clear and very different from one another. After you think the sequence is really good, practice it three more times. Remember, start and end in the same place each time. Your three movements should look the same every time, as if they had been videotaped.

T Now begin very slowly, as a car does on a cold morning. As you warm up, gradually increase your speed until you're moving fast. Then freeze suddenly. The sequence should look like this: a slow start, a gradual increase to fast speed, then a freeze. This is different from your last traveling action, so make that difference very clear.

C Now make up a sequence that includes a slow start that gradually increases to a fast speed and suddenly freezes. Practice the sequence until you're

---

Box 14-3

Designing Sequences

Helping children learn how to design movement sequences is much like helping them learn how to design their own games (see Chapter 30). Following are several tips we've found helpful when beginning to have children design sequences.

- It takes time.
- Structure the sequence into a simple form that is easily remembered—for example, a starting shape, a middle moving phase based on a specific aspect of movement, an ending shape.
- Practice the starting and ending shapes separately before adding the middle movement.
- Initially, provide a beginning signal, some time to practice (20–25 seconds), and then an ending signal.
- During the first stages, prompt the children during the movement aspect about exactly what movements need to be included (change of level, speed, etc.).
- Have children repeat their sequence several times. The middle movement aspect may vary slightly each time, but the beginning and end should remain constant.
- Hold the children accountable for what they've created—for example, divide the class in half and have them present their sequence to their half; present their sequence to another person; or write it down.

As the children's ability to design sequences increases, you can gradually relax some of these guidelines, but we've found these steps useful for both the students and the teacher when children first begin to create movement sequences.

Source: Adapted from Mary Joyce, *First steps in teaching creative dance to children*, 3rd ed. (Palo Alto, CA: Mayfield, 1994).

---

ready to show someone else, who, after seeing it, should be able to tell you what the three parts were.

Children often equate slowness with heavy, jerky, stiff actions rather than with graceful movement. Examples of animals with slow, graceful movements can be useful here. Box 14-3 also contains hints for helping children learn to design movement sequences.

Combining Imagery and Time

Setting: Children scattered throughout general space

Tasks/Challenges:

T This time you're going to practice traveling the way different things that move fast or slowly move. Remember, you aren't really trying to act like the things you're pretending to be; you're just trying to move at the speed they move. Let's practice one movement. On the signal, move as a turtle would move. Think carefully about it—a turtle moves very slowly. Now try moving as fast as a rabbit. Go really quickly.

T How does a well-tuned race car move? Let's try to go as fast as a race car can. There's only one thing different about this race car: It goes so fast it can't make any noise. So go as fast as a silent race car. Change your race car to an old jalopy trying to go uphill; the car is really tired and old, so remember that it goes very slowly.

Some classes enjoy and can accept the responsibility for making the sounds of race cars and jalopies. You'll have to use your judgment about whether to encourage the sounds, which can be either productive or detrimental, depending on the circumstances.

T Now pretend the carnival is in town and you're going to go with your friends tonight to ride all the rides and eat all your favorite foods. How excited are you? Really let your excitement show as you go home from school. Try it. Now, instead of going to the carnival, you're going home, and you know you'll be in trouble because your mom told you not to take anymore cookies from the cookie jar, and you got caught taking the last two.

T You're the fastest sprinter in the Olympics and you're in the starting blocks waiting for the gun to go off. Go. Now you're a distance runner just about to start a 10-mile race; you have a long way to go, and you don't want to wear yourself out.

T You're a mouse running from a cat. Now you're a hippopotamus with a full stomach trying to run.

※ Show me fast movement with your fingers. Show me slow movement with your fingers. Show me slow jogging, fast running.

Differentiating Among Time Words

Setting: Children scattered throughout general space

Tasks/Challenges:

T Show me the differences between the words *dash*, *waddle*, *dart*, and *crawl*. First, dash. Go. Now, waddle. Go. Now, dart. Go. Next, crawl. Remember, change speeds with each word so the speeds are very clear.

T Let's try them again. Listen very carefully because I'm going to start calling them out faster, and you'll have to change quickly from one to the other.

Other pairs of words can be used to elicit changes in time: creep/explode, pop/sneak, gallop/totter, slither/stride. *See Box 14-4 for other action words that can be used in teaching the various effort concepts.*

Combining Sport Skills and Time

Setting: Children scattered throughout general space

Tasks/Challenges:

T Before beginning, I want you to think of your favorite sports person. Be sure you can tell me who it is when I ask because this is important. After you decide who your favorite person is, choose one action she or he performs that you really like. For example, if you choose a famous football quarterback, you might pick "throwing the bomb" as your favorite action. Think carefully to pick your person and action.

T Now, on the signal, you'll perform the action you chose as if it were on video set at a fast speed—in a fast motion instead of slow motion. Repeat your fast-motion action four times, each time making the motion faster.

T Now do the same action as if it were in slow motion, just like instant replays. Make sure there's a clear difference between your fast and slow motions. I should be able to tell just from watching which motions are fast and which ones are slow.

Continually Changing in Time While Traveling

Setting: Children scattered throughout general space

Tasks/Challenges:

T As you're standing in your self-space, pick a point across the room you want to focus on. All the traveling you do will be directed toward that point. On the signal, slowly begin to travel around the point you've chosen, much like a lion stalking its prey. Gradually increase your speed so you're traveling at your maximum speed. Just before you reach the spot you've chosen, slow down, slowly circle, then suddenly pounce. The differences in the speeds at which you travel should be very clear. Thus, your sequence should go like this: Pick a point to focus on, start slowly circling toward that point, gradually pick up speed until you're going really fast, then gradually slow down and suddenly pounce toward your spot.

C Now that you have the idea, pick a new spot and practice your circling routine five times so it's very good. Try to make it the best you can because we're going to show some of them to the class. Slow

Box 14-4

Action Words

When you're teaching the effort concepts, action words help elicit many of the responses desired. For the exercise to be productive as well as exciting, students need to have more than a few common words repeated over and over. Here are some possibilities.

Single Action Words

Traveling Actions

Run	Hop	Creep
Dash	Skate	Sneak
Dart	Jump	Slither
Skip	Bounce	Crawl
Gallop	Slide	Step
Stamp	Kick	Stride
Whirl	Spin	Shuffle
Waddle	Totter	

Nontraveling Actions

Flick	Squeeze	Contract	Dangle
Jerk	Compress	Fold	Jab
Twitch	Explode	Splatter	Slash
Writhe	Spread	Punch	Chop
Stab	Tense	Pull	Saw
Grip	Relax	Press	Drip
Release	Push	Lower	Drag

Stopping Actions

Pause	Collapse
Stop	Slide
Freeze	Flop
Anchor	Crumble

Sinking Actions

Melt	Spin	Screw
Flop	Turn	Hammer
Drop	Slink	Spread
Collapse	Squash	Deflate
Pounce	Shrink	Crumple

Rising Actions

Evaporate	Spin	Swell
Float	Pop	Inflate
Rise	Grow	Lift
Turn	Blossom	Gyrate

Vibratory Actions

Shake	Wriggle
Rattle	Squirm
Vibrate	Snake
Whisk	
Tumble	

Sentences of Action Words

Run—freeze—skip	Slither—inflate—explode	Rise (turn)—twitch—skip
Dart—collapse—pop	Squeeze—jump—release	Gallop—stamp—screw
Grow—spin—deflate	Creep—pounce—explode	Jump—freeze—jab
Writhe—jerk—pop	Skip—pause—flop	Chop—whirl—slash

Descriptive Words (for use with action words)

Droopy	Excited	Light	Springy	Spikey	Square
Tired	Heavy	Tense	Carefree	Sharp	Angular
Happy	Strong	Floppy	Carefully	Rounded	Curvy
Greedy	Loving	Gentle	Fierce	Soft	Hard
Prickly	Spongy	Big	Small	Enormous	Tiny
Bubbling	Nervous	Unsure	Confident	Bold	Afraid

Nonsense Words

Snickersnack	Spelunk	Krinkle	Blump
Gallumph	Brip	Siczac	Crickcrock
Cavort	Bruttle-brattle	Swoosh	Snap-crackle
Flip-flop	Achoo	Kerumph	Wheezey
Grunch	Hic-up	Squizzog	

Source: David Docherty, *Education through the dance experience* (Bellingham, WA: Educational Designs and Consultants, 1975). Used with permission from the author.

should be really slow, fast really fast, and the pounce as quick as lightning.

To help clarify this activity, choose three or four children who are successfully completing it to demonstrate (they can all demonstrate at the same time). Reinforce the notions of gradually increasing speed and the sudden contrast of the pounce.

Developing the Concept of Force

Force is the contrast of muscular tensions. The extremes are strong and light, but there are obvious gradations between the extremes. Just as *speed* to a young child is "as fast as you can go," *force* often means trying to bat a ball as hard as possible, whether the situation calls for a bunt or an outfield placement. A preschooler is likely to use the same degree of force to throw a ball 3 feet as to throw it 10 yards.

We usually introduce the concept of force by combining it with a skill that has been developed to the control level, preferably to the utilization level. For example, think of the child at a precontrol level who is learning to strike a moving ball. The youngster is so fully concentrating attention on making contact with the ball that the concept of force is an unnecessary and probably confusing thought. Hard and easy hits can come later, once the child is able to hit a ball consistently.

A dancer exemplifies the qualities of strong and light movement while expressing aggression, strength, and power; the gymnast exemplifies the qualities in floor and apparatus routines while combining firm and fine actions and balancing in a demonstration of muscular control and strength.

Teaching the Concept of Force

This section provides suggestions for helping children to understand the concept of force. The learning experiences presented help youngsters develop a functional understanding of the strong (firm) and light (fine) actions of body parts and of the entire body. *Actions of concentrated movement and muscular tensions are very tiring; keep the activity periods short.*

Learning Experiences Leading to Movement Concept Understanding

Exploring Force

Setting: Children scattered throughout general space

Tasks/Challenges:

🅣 In your own space, with your whole body, make a statue that shows how strong you are. (A strong

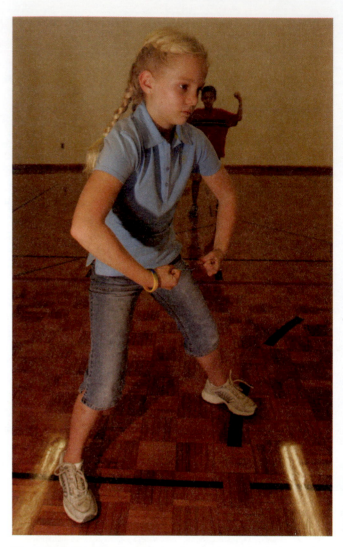

Young children's attempts at strong shapes show a beginning understanding of the concept of force.

force is also called "heavy" or "firm.") Now practice the activity again, but think about making every muscle in your body strong, even your head, neck, stomach, back, hands, and feet.

🅣 Now make a statue that is very light, such as a ghost would be. Your statue should be so light it would blow away if a strong wind came along. This is called a light force. Try a light shape again, such as a leaf floating through the wind.

🅣 When I beat the drum, change from a strong to a light statue and then back.

Traveling and Changing Force Qualities

Setting: Children scattered throughout general space

Tasks/Challenges:

T This time you're going to travel around the whole space. But as you travel, try to be as strong as you can be. You're an indestructible and all-powerful force; make all your body parts strong.

T Now, as you travel, make yourself as light as can be, just as if you were floating away. All your muscles should be loose, not tight at all; make your entire body light.

Using Imagery and Force

Setting: Children scattered throughout general space

Tasks/Challenges:

T This time you're going to use different images you know to help you understand the force qualities. On the signal, think of yourself as a pat of butter left out on a hot day. All day long you sit in the hot sun, all weak and melted. Then suddenly someone puts you in the refrigerator, and in a little while you feel strong and solid again. Remember, make it clear with your whole body what it's like to be weak, and then make it clear with your whole body when you're strong again.

The imagery sequences you design provide experiences in extreme contrasts. Focus on the degrees along the continuum (the subtle changes) in conjunction with the actual skill, such as jumping and landing or balancing.

J **Exit Slip.** This is an appropriate time to use an exit slip to check students' understanding of the concept of force.

Showing Contrasts of Force

Setting: Children scattered throughout general space

Tasks/Challenges:

T Now you're going to show the force differences in your movements. On the signal I'll call out an idea; you show me what the idea looks like by moving either strong or light. Make it very clear which you are: strong or light.

Young children often equate the concept of strong force with the concept of size. Be careful not to pair all imagery examples as such—for example, big-firm or small-fine.
Ideas:

1. **Frosty the Snowman.** You're going to show the life of Frosty the Snowman. First you're a single snowflake falling through the air; then you're several snowflakes that are beginning to stick together to make a shape; now you're the solid, sturdy snowman that can't be knocked over; and finally you're the snowman melting slowly as the sun comes out.

2. **Punch/flick.** Now we're going to use words to help us tell the difference between strong and light movements. The first two words are *punch* and *flick*. I'll give you a story, and you make the movements that go with it. One movement should be strong, the other light. Make each movement very clear. Pretending that you're a boxer, punch your opponent as hard as you can. Now, just flick a fly off your mother's freshly baked chocolate cake.

3. **Creep/pounce.** The words *creep* and *pounce* can help us learn strong and light movements. Let's try it. You're playing hide-and-seek; creep very quietly from your hiding place so no one will see or hear you. Now, you're creeping up to catch your runaway kitten. You've found her and are ready to pounce and grab her before she runs away again. Ready, pounce. Oops, you missed.

✿ Which movement was strong and which was light?

4. **Sneak/scare.** This time you're going to show light and strong actions when I use the words *sneak* and *scare*. Let's pretend your brother has a note from his girlfriend. You want to know what it says, so you sneak up behind him to find out. You can't read over his shoulder, so you figure if you scare him, he'll drop the note and run. Go. You need to sneak, then scare.

5. **Float/collapse.** Have you ever seen a hang glider? It's like a big kite that floats through the air, but a person is floating with it, just as if he or she were attached to a kite. You're now a hang glider sailing over the mountains. Go. Oh, no—all the wind suddenly died; your hang glider is crashing to the ground. You just collapse as you hit the ground.

6. **Glide/stomp.** You're a very good skater, and today you go rollerblading. You are gliding along, having a grand time. Now something sticks to your skate; you don't fall, but you have to stomp your skate really hard to try to get the object off. Clearly show the difference between your light and strong movements.

7. **Raindrop/thunderstorm.** You're a raindrop in a gentle spring rain that makes all the flowers bloom and the grass turn its greenest green. Now you're a raindrop in a bad summer thunderstorm—you know, a storm where the wind blows so hard you think the trees will fall down and the sky turns very dark. Remember, make it very clear which raindrop is strong and which one is light.

8. **Friends/foes.** Now you're going to show strong and light as you greet your friend and then as you

meet an enemy. Pretend you're walking down the street and see an old friend. How would you greet her? Now play as if you've just seen the biggest bully in the school. How would you greet him?

Which force was light? Which one was strong?

9. *Ant/rock.* Imagine what an ant trying to lift a rock feels like. Try hard; you're the only hope of the rock getting off the ground. Now you're a strong person trying to lift the same rock the ant lifted. How are your actions different?

10. *Olympic weight lifter.* You're an Olympic weight lifter going for the gold medal; this is the heaviest weight you've ever lifted. As you pretend, remember to keep your entire body strong. Even show in your face that you're strong. Now you're lifting a five-pound bag of flour. How easy is it for you? Make your whole body light as you show this action. All your muscles should be loose as if they're hardly being used at all.

Developing the Concept of Flow

Watch a very young child running down a hill. The actions are unstoppable, almost out of control, until the child reaches the bottom. A batter's swing at a baseball, the smash a tennis player executes, a gymnast's giant swing on the high bar—all these are examples of *free flow* in movement. It seems that the performer is lost in the movement; the movement, not the performer, seems to control the situation.

Bound actions are stoppable, cautious, and restrained. The performer is in control at all times. Pushing a heavy object, traveling an angular pathway while trying to stay within boundaries, executing a slow cartwheel with a pause for a handstand before traveling on are all examples of *bound flow*.

Teaching the Concept of Flow

This section provides learning experiences designed to help children understand and demonstrate the difference between free flow and bound flow. The activities encompass a variety of movements important for both skill performance and safety. *Music can greatly enhance the feel of bound and free flow.*

Learning Experiences Leading to Movement Concept Understanding

Traveling and Flow

Setting: Children scattered throughout general space

Tasks/Challenges:

T On the signal, travel around the room and pause the instant you hear the stop signal. I'm really looking for stops that happen suddenly, without you taking any extra steps. Freeze in your tracks. This kind of movement—jerky and with lots of stops—is said to have *bound flow.* In other words, it doesn't flow very smoothly.

Children tend to anticipate the teacher's signals. Make stop signals close together and frequent so this activity will be successful.

T This time as you travel around the space, pretend you're completely free, like an eagle soaring high, or a really happy person who has no cares in the world. Make your traveling seem as if it has no end; it could just keep going and going. This type of movement is said to have *free flow;* it doesn't stop, much like a balloon or cloud floating in the air.

Eliciting Flow Qualities

Setting: Children scattered throughout general space

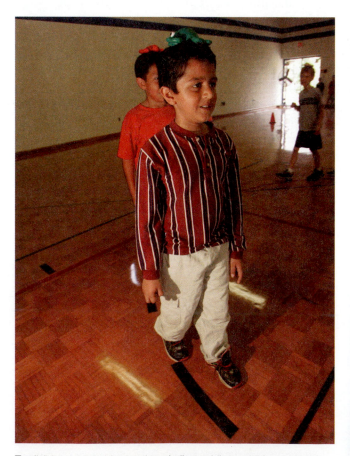

To elicit bound flow, the teacher challenged these children to travel while balancing beanbags on their heads.

Tasks/Challenges:

T This time I'm going to give you some actions to help you practice bound flow. Pretend to do each action I tell you, always showing the bound flow of what you're doing. Remember, bound flow can be stopped and is generally slow and sometimes jerky.

1. Press the floor with your hands and feet as you move. Make sure you keep a bound flow throughout the whole motion.
2. Pretend you're pushing a heavy box.
3. Now carry a glass of milk that is too full without spilling any of it.
4. Play as if you're pulling from the bottom of a well a full bucket of water on a pulley.

T Now I'll give you some actions that require free flow. Free flow can be more difficult than bound flow, so really concentrate on making your movements seem as if they could go on forever. Make it very clear these are free movements and unstoppable.

1. Pretend to flick away a fly.
2. This time you're really mad at your brother. Slash your arms through the air to show how really mad you are.
3. You're cooking bacon on the stove, and the grease starts to spatter; jerk your head and arms away so you won't get burned.

T This next action will combine free and bound flow. Raise your arm high above your head with bound flow, stoppable at any moment. Let your arm fall freely downward in an unstoppable action.

✿ Which movement is unstoppable—bound or free? Which movement is stoppable at any time—bound or free?

✓ *Student Display.* Flow is a difficult concept for students to understand. A useful assessment is having children bring in magazine pictures that illustrate the various qualities in action and then creating a student display labeling the qualities.

Following Flow Sentences

Setting: Children scattered throughout general space

Tasks/Challenges:

T On the board are a number of sentences. The first one says, "Walk, run, jump." On the signal, begin to travel, using the sentence as your guide. The words are clear; the commas mean to pause or hesitate, and the periods mean to stop. Make it very clear where your pauses are and when you stop. Repeat the action of the sentence three times.

Other possible sentences: "Walk, sneak, pounce." "Leap, stamp, twist." "Creep, hop, flop."

T What you just did was an example of bound flow. Now you're going to turn the same thing into free flow. This time, on the signal, you're going to follow the same sentences but without the punctuation marks—in other words, no commas and no periods or no pauses or stops. So you'll start at the beginning of the sentence and keep going all the way through; no one should know when you're going to change to the next action. Your action should just flow smoothly, one action leading to the next. When you get to the end of a sentence, just start over again. On the signal, let's start with the first sentence.

Children enjoy using interpretations of different punctuation marks, such as the exclamation point and question mark, as different ending shapes.

C Now that you're so good at the sentences, you're going to make up one of your own. On the board is a list of words. (Such words as walk, shrink, gallop, skip, explode, jump, roll, and hop are good to use.) Choose three of the words, and make your sentence. Put punctuation in because punctuation is the key to when you stop or pause. Practice your sentence five times with the punctuation in it; then practice it five times without punctuation. Practice it very carefully because we'll show some of the sentences to the class. It should be obvious when the punctuation is and isn't in the sentence.

Practicing Flow Sequences

Setting: Children scattered throughout general space

Tasks/Challenges:

T This time, there are two columns of words on the board but no punctuation. You're going to join the words together to make a sequence. The first column of words reads *melt, inflate, slither, shrink*. On the signal, practice the words in the order you see them. It is your choice when to change from one word to the next. Go.

   Now, do the second column of words: *jump, spin, stride, pop*.

✿ Which sequence gave you a bound feeling? Which one a free feeling?

C Now go back and practice each sequence three times, making it very clear each time which one is bound and which one is free.

Using Flow for Movement Conversations

Setting: Children with partners, scattered throughout general space

Tasks/Challenges:

Children beginning sequence work often need guidance in restricting the length of the sequence; generally two or three actions are appropriate for the initial sequence.

T Now you're going to work with and talk to your partner. The only catch is that neither of you can use your voice to talk. You're going to talk with your body. One of you needs to be bound flow and the other one free flow; go ahead and decide that now. Ready? This is how you'll talk: The partner who is bound flow will talk about being imprisoned and not being allowed to go out to see the world; the partner who is free flow will talk about how wonderful it is to roam and explore and run up and down the hills; in other words, what it's like to be free. Now, one of you start; with your body, talk about your aspect. Keep your sentence very short. As you move, your partner listens or watches. After you make your statement, stop; your partner then answers with a statement, and you listen. When your partner finishes, you again provide an answer. The whole conversation should go back and forth until each of you has moved five times.

C After you've completed the conversation once, go back and practice it twice more so that it's very clear who is free flow and who is bound flow. I know this is a bit hard to understand, so let me go over it one more time. You and your partner are going to talk about bound and free flow with your body actions, not your voices. Just as in any conversation, it's a give and take situation. One of you will make a short body action sentence, and then the other one will answer. Each of you gets to talk five times, and then it ends. After you've finished once, go back and practice two more times. Remember, two people can't talk at once, so listen when your partner is talking. "Still" is the word.

It really helps to find at least one twosome (ideally more) doing the activity correctly and have them demonstrate. Be patient; the task will take time if the children are to really develop their conversations. Children should switch roles after sufficient time to practice the other aspect of flow.

Combining Time, Force, and Flow

Setting: Children scattered throughout general space

Tasks/Challenges:

T The task sheet (Figure 14.2) for today will allow you to practice combining the concepts of time, force,

and flow. After you practice each challenge so you feel it's as clear as you can make it, find a friend to watch you. If the friend feels you've done the challenge correctly, she or he signs her or his name in the blank; if not, you'll have to go back and practice some more. I'll walk around the class, and at any time I can ask you to show me any challenge you've marked off. If you have any questions, ask me.

✓ *Self-Assessment.* The task sheet in Figure 14.2 could easily serve as a self-assessment of the effort concepts by changing "Who watched" to "I still need practice" or "I'm good" or "I need help."

See Chapter 12 for more information on developing student self-assessments.

Applying the Effort Concepts

We focus on concepts until the children have learned the basic terminology related to the effort qualities of movement. When the children are able to accurately demonstrate the differences between the extremes of each concept, we no longer focus on the concept. Instead, we focus on how the concept relates to the performance of a particular skill: fast dribble, fluid roll, or light gallop. We want the children to learn the effort concepts so they can apply the concepts to actual skill-learning situations.

The ability to use gradations of movement qualities distinguishes the inept performer from the skilled one, the sloppy movement from the polished one. An individual can learn to execute the basic requirements of a cartwheel, for example, so it can be recognized as a cartwheel. But when that cartwheel is executed in a ragged, uneven, uncontrolled manner, it is clearly and easily distinguishable from a cartwheel performed by an experienced, trained gymnast. We teach children to apply the qualities of movement to their skill performances to help them become skillful movers.

Generally, the concept of time (fast-slow) is easier for children to grasp than either the concept of force (strong-light) or the concept of flow (bound-free). For this reason, you may need to focus more on force and flow than on time. Time can be studied as an applied concept—fast and slow skips, rolling fast and rolling slowly, accelerated and decelerated change of levels—before force or flow. The difference is that in teaching a concept, our observational focus is primarily on the children's ability to understand and apply the effort concepts. In contrast, when we use a concept as a subfocus, we know the children already understand the concept from previous lessons, and therefore our teaching focus is primarily on the skill and how it can be executed by using varying movements.

Name _____ Teacher _____

Time, Force, and Flow Task Sheet

Date	Who Watched	Challenge
		Find three body parts that you can move at a slow speed.
		Find three body parts (different from the ones in the first challenge) that you can move at a fast speed.
		Find four ways to move while showing free and light qualities.
		Find two movements that you can first make strong and slow and then make light and fast.
		Find any movement you want that combines two aspects of the effort concept (**time:** fast-slow, **force:** strong-light, **flow:** bound-free). After you finish, write down your movements and the concepts they included. Movement Concept _____ _____ _____ _____ _____ _____ _____ _____

Figure 14.2 Task sheet for time, force, and flow.

Reading Comprehension Questions

1. How is a movement performed fast different from the same movement performed slowly?

2. How is a movement executed with strong force different from the same movement performed with light force?

3. How is a movement performed with bound flow different from the same movement performed with free flow?

4. Initially, the extremes, rather than the gradations, of the effort concepts are emphasized. Why?

5. When is slowness an important concept? List several movements.

6. What does the term *acceleration-deceleration* mean? Answer by using examples from the text or from your own experiences.

7. What does focusing on the movement quality of an image rather than on the image itself mean? This statement will help you: "Imagine the floor is covered with peanut butter 6 inches deep." Why is this focus important?

8. When do you change from focusing on the effort concept to focusing on how the concept relates to the performance of a particular skill?
9. What is the purpose of teaching children to apply the qualities of movement to their skill performances?

10. Using the movement analysis wheel, manipulate the wheel to show an effort concept in relation to locomotor, manipulative, and nonmanipulative skills. Identify two skills for each category that an effort concept can modify, and write a sample task for each.

References/Suggested Readings

Joyce, M. 1994. *First steps in teaching creative dance to children.* 3rd ed. Palo Alto, CA: Mayfield.

[NASPE] National Association for Sport and Physical Education. 2004. *Moving into the future: National standards for physical education.* 2nd ed. Reston, VA: National Association for Sport and Physical Education.

Relationships

Relationships is the third, and last, of the three movement concept chapters (Table 3.2). This chapter focuses on the myriad relationships in our lives. The first part of the chapter emphasizes the relationship of one body part to another. These categories are typically taught to young children as they begin to learn the names of body parts and how they work with each other to form balances and shapes. They also learn about traveling on a variety of body parts.

The second part of the chapter focuses on ideas for teaching the relationship with different objects as they travel over, under, around, and through benches and hoops in a variety of ways. While we understand concepts like along, close to, and far away, these are new to young children. For example, we understand that the concept of matching parts in a balance can be a real test for the young child to figure out which parts match and which do not. There are numerous suggestions in this chapter for teaching young children these concepts.

The final section of the chapter, relationships with people, is far more difficult to learn. These relationship concepts are emphasized throughout the school years and throughout adulthood, albeit in different contexts. If you watch a professional team sport, for example, a major emphasis is continually on maintaining a relationship with others—those on your own team and your opponents too. Are you familiar with "Xs" and "Os," the shorthand coaches use to diagram plays in team sports? Using these letters, the coach is trying to tell the team where players need to be in relationship to others on the team.

Initially, as you will see, we start teaching children to work alone in mass (without interfering with other children) and gradually progress to working with groups and eventually between groups. Working with others in groups (teams) to design a dance or gymnastics sequence, however, is not an easy process to learn as you well know. The relationship between groups (as in basketball or soccer) is even more complicated and difficult to learn. This why we wait until the children are ready for the relationship concepts of working with groups until they are older. If you are an experienced teacher, you understand that some children find it very difficult to share with others and work as a team—one of the many challenges of teaching.

As you know, however, the concept of relationships is important not only in physical education classes but also in everyday life. Driving to and from work in an automobile, maneuvering through an aisle crowded with people in a supermarket, or walking in a crowd—

all these activities involve complex, dynamic relationships. And each relationship involves several contextual variables (bodies, body parts, and objects) in simultaneous interaction.

Figure 15.1 revisits the wheel (movement analysis framework) introduced in Chapter 3 (Figure 3.1) and emphasizes the relationship concepts. Notice that almost half of the movement concept categories on the wheel are in relationships.

As explained at the beginning of this chapter, we typically begin with the simplest relationships for children to understand—the self-relationships. Because so many young children are still at the "I" stage, the initial lessons focus on naming and identifying body parts and their relationship to one another, followed by body part shapes. As the children develop an applied (functional) understanding of the relationships between body parts, we shift the emphasis to moving in relation to different objects and to one another. In preschool settings, many of the relationship concepts will be new to children. In the primary grades, however, some of these concepts will simply be a review for the children, and therefore the lessons can progress more rapidly. The third category of concepts, relationships with others, is typically combined with the study of other concepts and skill themes. Initially, the focus is on working with partners; when the children develop the social and physical maturity needed to collaborate with three or four others, we're able to include tasks that require them to work in groups.

When teaching the relationship concepts, it's easy to forget that the purpose is to have the children actually understand and be able to demonstrate each of the relationship concepts. Imagine that one of the authors of *Children Moving*, Dr. Melissa Parker, came to your school to teach a class of your second graders. Before teaching, she might ask whether your children have been taught the relationship concepts. If you say yes, she would assume, for example, that the children can demonstrate the difference between a symmetrical shape and a nonsymmetrical shape when asked to do so. "Knowing" doesn't mean the concepts were taught; knowing means the children can demonstrate their understanding through their movements. In other words, the children have a functional understanding—they are able to demonstrate the concepts. So Dr. Parker might quickly review these symmetrical and nonsymmetrical shapes and then begin to focus on using these shapes as children travel and stop and in balances. Now we want to share our ideas for how to teach the relationship concepts to your class(es).

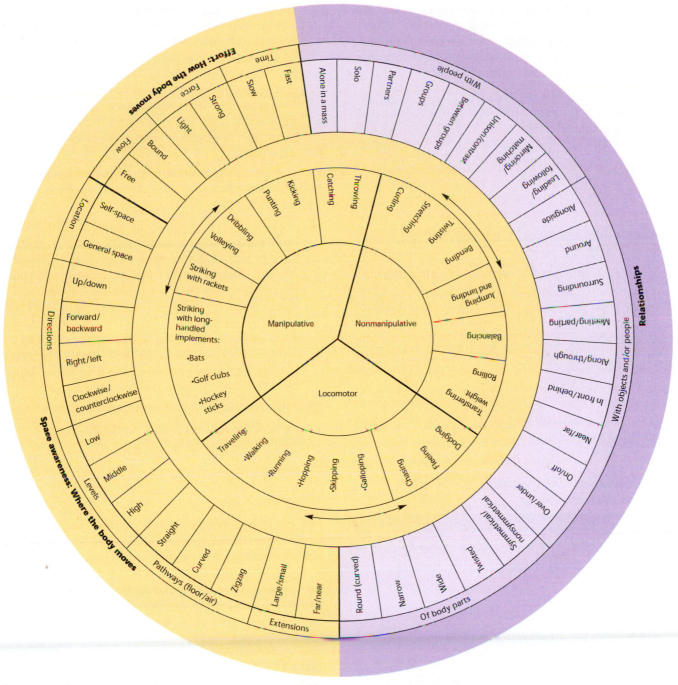

Figure 15.1 Movement analysis framework: relationship concepts.

Developing the Concept of the Relationships of Body Parts

Before children, especially preschool children, can focus on the relationships between body parts, they need to be able to identify specific body parts. Thus it's essential for each child to acquire a functional vocabu-lary of body part names. Examples of tasks that can be used in teaching this vocabulary include:

- Point to the ceiling with the elbow (knee, nose).
- Touch the floor with the wrist (waist, stomach).
- Travel around the room and, on the signal, stop and touch heels (shoulders, heads) with another person.

Once the children have learned the names of the body parts, lessons focus on making shapes (round, narrow, wide, twisted, symmetrical, and nonsymmetrical) and using body parts in relation to one another. For example, we might ask children to:

- Travel and stop in a twisted shape.
- Change slowly from a symmetrical to a nonsymmetrical shape.
- Make a wide shape during a jump.
- Try to find three different ways to get their feet higher than their heads.

Teaching the Concept of the Relationships of Body Parts

This initial section provides activities for teaching children to identify and use different body parts and how different body parts can relate to one another. Tasks for teaching the concepts of various body shapes and body part shapes also are presented. You can use any body parts for the activities given here, but with the tasks that require balancing, be careful not to use parts that will elicit balances that may be too complex for some students. For example, when using parts such as the hands, make it clear that other parts can be used in conjunction with them.

Learning Experiences Leading to Movement Concept Understanding

Identifying Body Parts

Setting: Children in self-space, on a carpet square, or on an X on the floor

Tasks/Challenges:

T I'm going to call out different body parts. Touch the body parts I call out as quickly as possible when you hear them. Remember, pay close attention to what I'm saying because I may start to go faster or try to trick you. Ready? Remember, touch each body part as I call it out.

Body parts might include nose, arm, chin, ankle, ear, foot, elbow, temple, wrist, neck, shoulder, eyebrow, eye, teeth, cheek, leg, forehead, knee, thumb, mouth, side, hip, lip, earlobe.

T This time, instead of just touching a body part as I name it, you'll have to touch whatever hand I call out to the different body parts I call out. This activity will be harder because you'll have to remember which is your right and which is your left. For example, if I say "Right hand to left knee," touch

your right hand to your left knee. Try to do this as quickly as possible, but be careful in deciding what body parts to use. Just to help you out, let's review right and left. Raise your right hand. (Check to see that students are correct.) Ready? Let's try it. If this is new to the children, you may want to provide each of them with a thick rubber band around the right wrist, a sticker, or some other technique, to help them distinguish their right hand from their left hand.

Body parts can include left hand to right knee, right hand to left elbow, left hand to left shoulder, right hand to left knee, left hand to left foot.

T This time you're going to play a game with finding body parts, similar to Simon Says, except you don't have to sit out if you miss. Here's how to play. I'll call out, "Simon says to touch your toes," and you'll touch your toes. But if I don't say "Simon says," then you aren't supposed to do it. So if I just say "Touch your toes," you aren't supposed to touch your toes because Simon didn't say to do it. Pay attention because the game will start to go very quickly. Remember, I'm watching to see if you touch the right parts and how quickly you can do it.

T This time, instead of touching your hands to different body parts, you're going to touch two different body parts together. For example, I'll call out "Knee to elbow," and you'll touch your knee to your elbow. You'll have to think hard on this one. Ready? I'm looking to see if you can get the correct different parts together.

Possible body part combinations include knee to elbow, hands to waist, head to knees, foot to shoulder, knee to foot, elbow to wrist, back of wrist to back of knee.

Balancing While Using Different Body Parts

Setting: Each child on a poly spot or carpet square, or inside a hoop

Tasks/Challenges:

T Find a poly spot for yourself, and sit on it. I'll know that you're all ready when I see everyone seated on their own poly spot. This time when I call out a body part, put that body part on the poly spot and make a shape with the rest of your body, leaving the one part that I called out on the spot. So if I call out "Elbow," put your elbow on the spot, and then make a shape with the rest of your body. When you make your shape, be sure to hold it very still so I can see what part is on the spot and what your shape looks like. Ready? Let's try it.

These young children explore the various ways their arm can move in relationship to their bodies.

T Shapes that you hold very still are called balances, almost like statues. Let's try this activity again; make your balances and shapes very clear and still.

T Now you're going to balance on different numbers of body parts. I'll call out a number of parts; you balance by touching that number to the floor. Count your parts touching the floor very carefully because I'll be coming around and asking you how many parts are on the floor and which parts they are.

Four parts
Three parts
More than four parts
Two parts
One part

For each number, offer suggestions or hints, or identify several students to pinpoint the possible combination of parts. Also mix up the order in which the parts are called out.

Freezing on Different Body Parts

Setting: Children scattered in general space

Tasks/Challenges:

T You're going to travel around the space on your feet. When you hear the stop signal, touch the body part I call out to the floor. So if I call out "Elbow" as you stop, touch your elbow to the floor. As you move, be very careful to stay in a space by yourself, so you don't touch anyone when you're trying to touch different body parts to the floor. This activity will start to go very fast, so touch the parts to the floor as quickly as possible, and make it very clear which part is touching the floor.

Body parts can include arm, ankle, foot, leg, side, hip.

T When you travel this time, instead of touching body parts to the floor, touch the body parts I call out to the same parts of another person. So if I call out "Heels," stop, touch your heels to the heels of one other person, and then freeze. As you do this, make the touching parts very clear; don't just stand beside the other person. To be safe, make sure as you touch that you stop first and then touch easily so no one gets hurt. The idea is to quickly and easily touch and then be ready to go again. Ready?

Body parts can include wrist, shoulder, forehead, knee, thumb, arm, ankle, foot, elbow, leg, side, back.

Traveling on Different Body Parts

Setting: Children scattered in general space

Tasks/Challenges:

T This time, instead of balancing on different body parts, you're going to travel on different body parts. What body parts do we usually travel on? Let's start with the feet just to get warmed up. Make sure to travel in all the space and to stay on your feet. Let's start by walking.

T Now try something a little different: the hands and feet. Remember to travel with your hands and feet both touching the floor at some time. Ready? Make sure you actually go someplace, and be careful of others.

T This time you're going to make up your own way of traveling using different body parts (not your feet). As you do this, make sure that I can tell from just looking at you what body parts you're using for traveling; you should be using different body parts to move around the room. Be very careful to watch where you're going and not touch anyone else.

Balancing on Matching and Nonmatching Parts

Setting: Each child in a personal space

Tasks/Challenges:

Ⓣ This time, instead of balancing on a certain number of parts, you're going to balance on parts that are alike and parts that are different. Parts that are alike are called matching parts. What parts do you have that are matching or alike? *(Children respond "Hands," "Feet," etc.)* Good; let's try to balance on some of those parts. First let's try an easy one: the feet. Now, how about the knees? Think up one of your own. Make sure that the parts you use are matching parts.

Ⓣ Now pick one set of matching parts; make up a balance you like and practice it until you can hold it very still for at least three seconds. Be sure you know the name of the matching parts you're balancing on because I'll come around and ask some of you, just to make sure.

Ⓣ This time you're going to balance on different parts. Different parts are parts that don't match each other; they aren't alike. What are some possible combinations of different parts? *(Children respond "Knee and elbow," "Back and hands," etc.)* Let's try some. First, try the seat and the feet. Now try the shoulders and the elbows. What about the knees and the elbows? Now, make up one combination on your own.

Ⓒ Now pick one set of different parts and make up your own balance. Practice your balance until you can hold it very still. See if you can hold it perfectly still until I count to three alligators. *(Children enjoy fun ways to challenge themselves; you can make up your own terms to challenge the children to*

Freeze in a low, wide shape.

hold their balances for several seconds, e.g., the name of your state, the name of a team, foods, etc.) Be sure the different parts you're using are very clear because I might ask you what they are.

Round, Narrow, Wide, and Twisted Body Shapes

Setting: Each child in self-space

Tasks/Challenges:

Ⓣ Today you're going to learn about different shapes you can make with your bodies. Everyone find a self-space so you can't touch anyone else. The first shape you're going to make is a pretzel. All of you try to make a pretzel out of your body; hold very still. This shape is called a twisted shape.

Ⓣ Now make a different twisted shape on your own. As you do so, make sure your whole body is twisted, not just your arms and legs. Try to twist your stomach, too.

Ⓣ The next shape is a circle. Try to make your whole body look like a circle. This is called a round shape.

Ⓣ Now try to make up a different round shape by yourself. Make sure your whole body is making the round shape and that it is very round. Remember, round things have no bumps in them.

Ⓣ This time you're going to make a skinny shape. Try to make your body as skinny as possible, so skinny that if you turned sideways, no one would be able to see you. This is called a narrow shape.

Ⓣ Find another narrow shape by yourself. Make it as skinny as possible, as if you were trying to hide.

Ⓣ What do you think the opposite of narrow is? *Wide,* right. Make your body as wide as possible.

Ⓣ Try another wide shape by yourself. Remember, get as wide as possible, as if you were trying to stop someone from getting around you.

Ⓒ This time pick your favorite kind of shape, and make it, holding it very still. I'm going to come around and guess which type of shape it is, so make your shape as clear as possible. Your shape should be wide, narrow, round, or twisted.

Ⓣ Things are going to be a little harder this time. Still staying in your own space, you're going to make a wide shape. Then, when I give the signal, change your wide shape to a narrow shape, and hold it very still. The difference between the wide and narrow shape should be very clear. Make a wide shape, and hold it. Now change that wide shape to a narrow shape.

T Try it again—another wide shape; change to a narrow.

T Now, a third.

C This time pick the shape you liked the most, and practice it until it changes very easily from wide to narrow. Work on it until it's your best and both shapes are very clear.

T You thought the last activity was hard? This one is even harder! Think you can do it? You're going to change from a twisted shape to a round shape. So make your twisted shape. Got it? On the signal, change that twisted shape to a round shape.

T Now, let's try a different twisted to round shape. Go.

T And a third twisted to round shape. Make sure your twisted shape is really twisted and your round shape is very round. I should be able to easily tell the difference between the two shapes.

C Now, pick your favorite round and twisted shape. Practice your favorite one so your move from twisted to round is smooth (not jerky) and your shapes are so clear the principal could easily tell the difference if she walked in.

Changing from One Body Shape to Another

Setting: Children in self-space moving to a drumbeat

Tasks/Challenges:

T You'll really need to be in a good self-space for this activity, so make sure you're as far away from everyone else as you can be. Again you're going to change from one shape to another, but I'm going to give you drumbeats to help. You're going to move from a round shape to a wide shape, but instead of just doing it on your own, you'll have six drumbeats to get from the round shape to the wide shape, and then six beats to get back to your round shape. Listen now while I give you the drumbeats. Does everyone understand? You'll start in a round shape and on the six beats of the drum open to a wide shape. You'll hold your wide shape very still, and then on the next six beats of the drum you'll return to your round shape. Let's try it. Find your round shape.

T Let's try it again; this time find different round and wide shapes.

T Now, let's do a third set of shapes.

C You're now going to practice one set of shapes four more times so you can make it really good. Pick your favorite shapes. Remember as you move to

make each shape very clear, and make sure the movement goes with the drumbeats.

Pinpoint two or three children who are succeeding with the activity, and ask them if they'd like to show it to the class.

T You're going to make the shapes a little different this time. Instead of opening up on six beats and closing on six, you're going to open up on one quick beat and then close slowly on six. So the sequence will now go like this: Start in a round shape; on the drumbeat, quickly open up to a wide shape, and hold it still; then on the next six drumbeats, slowly return to your round shape. Remember, open from the round to the wide shape very, very quickly, as if you were a flash of lightning.

Pinpoint several children to show the activity to the rest of the class.

C Now practice your favorite shapes four times. Remember not only to make the quick shape sudden and the slow shape sustained, but also to make your round and wide shapes very clear. To look really good, remember to hold the beginning and the end very still so we all know when you started and when you finished.

Traveling and Freezing in Different Body Shapes

Setting: Children traveling in general space

Tasks/Challenges:

T Instead of making shapes in your self-space, this time you're going to travel around the space and on the signal stop and quickly make the shape I call out. For example, if you're traveling and I call out "Twisted," on the signal, make a twisted shape. As you make your shapes, be sure they're very clear so I can easily tell what they are. If I can't tell what they are, I'll have to ask you. As you travel, be careful of your classmates.

T Now, as you stop to make your shape, try to do it as quickly as possible, almost as if you just froze in that shape when you stopped. Remember, frozen shapes don't fall over.

Making Symmetrical and Nonsymmetrical Shapes

Setting: Children in self-space

Tasks/Challenges:

T You've already learned about wide, narrow, round, and twisted shapes. This time you're going to learn about two different kinds of shapes. The words describing these shapes are hard, so listen carefully.

First, find a body shape that looks exactly alike on both sides of your body; in other words, if you were divided in half, both sides of you would look alike. This is called a symmetrical shape.

T Try making a symmetrical shape. Remember, both sides of your body must look exactly alike.

T Now find a shape in which the two sides of your body don't look alike. In other words, if you were cut in half, each side would have a different shape. We call this a nonsymmetrical shape.

T Make another nonsymmetrical shape. Remember, both sides must be different.

T Since you now know the difference between symmetrical and nonsymmetrical, let's find three more balances of each shape. First do symmetrical; remember, both sides are alike. When I beat the drum, change from one symmetrical shape to the next one. Try to make each of your balances very clear so I can tell without thinking what kind of shape it is.

T Now do nonsymmetrical shapes. Find three more nonsymmetrical shapes. Try to make the sides of your body as different as possible so no one could possibly confuse your shape with a symmetrical one. Change each time you hear the drumbeat.

C Once you've found three more nonsymmetrical shapes, practice your favorite one five extra times so you can show it to the whole class. (Half the class demonstrates their favorite nonsymmetrical shape, and then the other half shows their favorite nonsymmetrical shape.)

✓ *Event Task.* This would be an appropriate time to use an event task to determine if students are able to make different body shapes. A possible task might be the following:

You and a partner are going to make up a routine. It will consist of three shapes. In each of the shapes, you and your partner should match—you should look exactly alike. Here are three shapes:

1. Symmetrical, narrow shape
2. Twisted shape
3. Nonsymmetrical wide shape

Start with the first shape and hold it for three seconds (crocodiles, elephants, hamburgers, your city or state). When I say change (or beat the drum), change to the second shape. Hold it for three seconds, and then change to the third shape and hold that one for three seconds.

Creating Postcard Sculptures

Setting: Museum postcards of statues, one postcard for every child. Photos laminated from magazines can also

be used for this task so children are clear on the terms *statue* or *sculpture*. Children love to play the roles of statues and sculptors but tend to get silly during this activity. Remind them they need to respect their partners. Also caution them to place others only in shapes they can hold without too much difficulty so no one gets hurt. This may not work for some of your classes if they have yet to learn to work successfully with a partner.

Tasks/Challenges:

T You're going to pretend you're sculptors who are creating great statues. To do this you'll need a partner. When I say "Go," find a partner, and sit beside him or her. I'll know you're ready when I see everyone seated beside a partner. Each set of partners has two postcards (photos) of statues; you're going to form each other into these statues. Decide which partner will be the sculptor first; the other partner is a ball of clay in a round shape in low level. The sculptor then decides which statue to make the partner into. First, form the statue by gently guiding your partner (the ball of clay) into the shape just as it is on the card. Remember, balls of clay cannot talk, so you need to guide them into the shape you want, not tell them.

Once you are satisfied with your sculpture, if it's symmetrical, change it to nonsymmetrical; if it's nonsymmetrical, make it symmetrical. Mold each statue very carefully, and be sure you can tell me which statue is symmetrical and which is nonsymmetrical. After you make your statue, trade places with your partner; now you will become the ball of clay and your partner will become the sculptor.

T This time you're going to design your own statues. You'll still need your partner. Go ahead and decide which of you is to be the sculptor and the ball of clay first. Make your first statue symmetrical. The statue stays "frozen" until the signal. At the signal, move to someone else's statue and redesign it to suit yourself. On the next signal, move to another new statue and redesign it. Keep doing this until you're told to change. When you hear the change signal, find your partner and now you will become the ball of clay.

Let's practice once. Form your partner into a symmetrical statue. (Allow at least one minute.) Now, move to another statue and remake it, still into a symmetrical shape. Do you have the hang of it? *(Select several children for demonstration.)* Go to the next statue.

T Now trade places with the statue you've just made. The activity changes a little this time; you're going to create nonsymmetrical statues. Ready? Without moving to a new place, form a nonsymmetrical statue out of your partner.

T Change to a new statue, and then change this statue to a nonsymmetrical shape. Remember: Nonsymmetrical means that both sides of the body are very different from each other.

T Change one more time. Make this your best statue yet.

If you have access to a digital camera, the postcard sculptures are excellent photo opportunities. They also can be used on a bulletin board with actual sculpture photographs next to them. This project can be especially interesting in combination with the study of European countries.

Creating Body Shapes in the Air

Setting: Boxes, benches, and/or low beams set up around the space. *(Figure 15.2 shows a typical equipment setup.)*

Tasks/Challenges:

T Now you're going to combine all the different kinds of body shapes you've practiced so far. What you're going to do may be hard, but it'll be fun. Remember, as you work, all the rules for gymnastics apply. (See Chapters 8 and 29 for establishing an environment for learning and for the rules of a gymnastics environment.) Three or four of you will be at a piece of equipment at once. One at a time, you'll each jump off the equipment and make a shape in the air. Each time you jump, try to

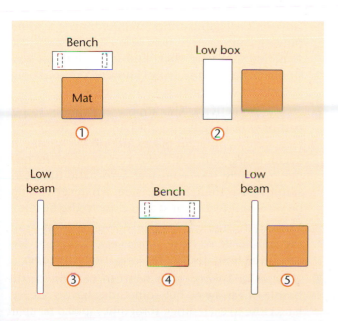

Figure 15.2 Equipment set up for creating body shapes in the air.

make that shape in the air. Let's start with a wide shape. Make sure you land on your feet after the jump and don't crash to the ground. See if you can hold your landing as still as a statue when you land for two seconds.

After a while, change to narrow, twisted, round, symmetrical, and nonsymmetrical shapes.

T Now that you've been through all the shapes separately, you may practice them in any order you wish. Make the shapes so clear that I don't have to ask you what they are. Remember to land on your feet.

Developing the Concept of the Relationships with Objects

Some concepts are studied in relation to objects; others have more meaning when they're practiced in relation to people. The concepts of *on* and *off, along, through, over, under, around,* and *surrounding* apply primarily to relationships with objects. The concepts of *near* and *far, in front, behind,* and *alongside* are generally studied as person-to-person relationships. Because objects are more predictable (less dynamic) than children, however, we first focus on the concept of relationships with objects and then on relationships with people.

Children frequently identify a lesson by the equipment used in the lesson rather than the movement concept. For example, after a lesson in which hoops were used to study the concepts of traveling over, under, and through, children might say, "Hey, that was fun! Are we going to play with hoops again tomorrow?" In time, however, children begin to understand and use the terminology we use. For instance, a child might say, "It's easier to go over and under the hoop than to go through the hoop."

Within the context of a game or a dance lesson, specific terms are classified as objects. In dance, for example, wands, streamers, newspapers, or scarves are considered objects. Goals, boundaries, nets, and targets are objects with which the child learns relationship concepts within a game context. See Box 15-1 for information from the National Standards on relationships.

Teaching the Concept of the Relationships with Objects

The activities in this section are designed to enhance the children's awareness of and ability to function effectively in relation to some of the objects (equipment) used in a variety of physical activity contexts.

Box 15-1

Relationships in the *National Standards for Physical Education*

The movement concept of relationships is defined, with sample performance outcomes, in the National Association for Sport and Physical Education's *National Standards for Physical Education* (2004) in Standards 1 and 2. Sample performance outcomes for relationships are:

- Discovers how to balance on different body parts, at different levels, becoming like a "statue" while making symmetrical and nonsymmetrical shapes." (Standard 1, Grades K–2, 16).
- Identifies correctly body planes (i.e., front, back, side). (Standard 2, Grades K–2, 22).
- Identifies correctly various body parts (e.g., knees, foot, arm, palm). (Standard 2, Grades K–2, 22).

Learning Experiences Leading to Movement Concept Understanding

Traveling Over, Close to, Far Away, Inside

Setting: A hoop or a rope for each child

Tasks/Challenges:

T To warm up, travel over your hoop (rope) in any way you want to. As you travel, make sure you actually go over the equipment, not around it.

T This time as you travel over your equipment, try to stay as close to it as possible. Try to keep as much of your body as possible close to the equipment, not just one body part.

T Now, instead of being close to the equipment, try to have as many body parts as possible as far away from the equipment as possible. Only the parts that are really used to support your body should be near the equipment. Make sure your whole body is as far away as possible, not just the upper parts of your body.

T The activity is a little harder now. Start on the outside of your equipment, put your weight down on your hands inside the hoop (or a circle made with a rope), and then continue to travel over the equipment. Make sure you shift your weight to your hands inside the hoop (rope) at some point.

T These are all relationships your body can have to equipment or other people. We can go over things, we can be close to things, we can be far away from things, or we can go inside things. Practice all four

of these relationships on your own: over, close to, far away, and inside. See if you can find three different ways to do each relationship—for example, three different ways to go over your rope. Be sure you know which concept you're practicing, because I'll come around and ask you.

If you say you're going to come around and ask the children questions or see their work, do it! Otherwise, the children may soon stop believing you.

Traveling Over, Under, Close to, and Far Away from Equipment

Setting: A rope inserted into two cones so the middle is 12–18 inches off the ground, hurdle, or other object that the children can travel over and under (Figure 15.3)—one for each child in the class, scattered throughout the space

Tasks/Challenges:

T To begin, travel *over* the rope (hurdle) any way you can; you can jump, use your hands and feet, or use only your hands. Whatever you do, make sure you can land on your feet on the other side without falling down. This is called going over an object. Sometimes when we try to go over an object, we cheat and actually go around the side of it. Make very, very sure you really do go over and not around.

T Now, instead of going over the hurdle, you're going to go under it. This will be hard because the hurdle (rope) isn't very far off the ground. You'll really have to scrunch up. Try to do it without upsetting the hurdle.

T Now, let's try going under in different ways. Sometimes go under feet first, sometimes head first, sometimes on your back, and sometimes on your stomach. Be careful; always know where your body is, even those parts that you can't see.

T One more activity. This time you're going to put part of your weight on your hands and bring your feet down in different places around the hurdle. To begin, bring your feet down very close to the hurdle. You may take your feet across the hurdle or simply leave them on one side; whatever you do, be sure your feet come down close to the hurdle.

T Now try bringing your feet down far away from the hurdle. Make sure that every time your feet touch the floor, they're far away from the rope.

T Now, as you work, your feet can be close to the hurdle or far away, but sometimes have your feet land close to each other, sometimes spread far apart from each other. Be able to tell me if your feet are

Figure 15.3 Construction of hurdles. Hurdles can be made from plastic bleach or milk jugs and rolled newspaper held together with masking tape. A more permanent type of hurdle can be made from wood and dowel rods.*

Rolled newspaper

Plastic bleach or milk jugs

Blocks may be made from wood, if desired.
Step 1. Obtain 4" x 4" square stock. Sand all surfaces smooth.

Step 2. Square pencil lines around stock at 12" or 24" increments.

Leave 1½" of waste at both ends

Step 3. Drill 1" or ¾" holes at right angles to each other.

Step 4. Saw blocks. Sand ends smooth after sawing.

*Prior to constructing homemade equipment we recommend you be certain that teacher-made equipment is permitted in your school and/or school district.

close together or far apart when I ask you. Remember, close together means almost so close that nothing could get between, and far apart means spread out so much that a person could crawl through.

Onto/Off Concepts

Setting: Low boxes or benches, scattered throughout the space

Tasks/Challenges:

T You're now going to learn two more types of relationships: *onto* and *off*. I think you probably already know what these two concepts mean, but let's practice them just to make sure. Find at least three different ways to get onto and three different ways to get off your piece of equipment. I'm really looking for very different ways to get onto and off the equipment—as long as they are safe and you are being careful.

C After you find three different ways, practice your favorite way four extra times, so that you can show it to the class. Make it really special.

T I'm going to make the activity a little harder this time by combining different types of relationships. When I say "Go," each of you get a hoop and place it on the floor beside your box. Travel into the hoop before you travel onto and off the box or bench. So your sequence will involve three different relationships: into, on, and off. Find three different ways to do this. Make them very different from each other. Go.

Pinpoint several children who are doing the activity correctly or have found very creative ways to accomplish the activity to demonstrate their actions for the rest of the class. Be sure to use a variety of students so the rest of the class has a number of different creative ideas to base their work on.

T Now you're going to make up a sequence of the relationships you practiced with the box and hoop. You must include the concepts of *off, onto,* and *into* in your sequence. You can start with any of the three. Once you find a sequence you really like, practice it until you can do it from memory and it looks the same each time.

Over, Under, Around, In Front Of, and Behind Concepts

Setting: A streamer, such as one used in rhythmic gymnastics, for each child; paper and pencils. You can make streamers from 2-inch-wide crepe paper or from surveyors' tape cut into 4- to 10-foot lengths. Index cards and pencils.

Tasks/Challenges:

T Just to warm up, practice moving your streamer anywhere around your body. Remember, always try to keep the streamer in the air. To do this, you'll have to keep the streamer moving all the time; you can't let it stop, or it'll touch the floor.

T Now that you know how to keep the streamer in the air, try to make it go over, under, around, in front of, and behind different body parts, such as your head, legs, and trunk. *(You will ask the children to do these one at a time—e.g., over, then under, then around.)* Try to keep the streamer moving at all times.

T Now you're going to pretend you're Olympic gymnasts. Make up a sequence in which your streamer goes over, under, around, in front of, and behind two different body parts—for example, over your head and over an arm. After you make up a sequence you like, practice it until it looks the same each time and you can do it from memory. It's very important that you remember exactly what you did because we're going to do something really special with it. It may help to say each concept out loud as you do your sequence.

T Do you remember your sequence? Now you're going to write it down on a card and exchange the card with a friend. Your friend will try to do your sequence, and you will try to do your friend's sequence just by reading the directions on the card, so make it very clear which parts you went over, under, around, in front of, and behind.

C Now practice your friend's sequence until you think you've learned it perfectly. When you think you're ready, ask your friend to watch you do the sequence. In a few minutes I'll ask for volunteers to show routines that clearly have all five of these concepts.

This series of activities is also very good for developing the concept of free flow (smooth rather than jerky, halting movements). You will find it works best to gradually combine the concepts—for example, over, then under, then over and under together, and so on.

Traveling Along Equipment

Setting: Low balance beams, benches, or ropes on the floor set up around the room

Tasks/Challenges:

T So far we've practiced the relationships of on, off, over, in front of, *under, around,* and *behind.* Now we're going to learn the relationship of *along.* At your piece of equipment, each of you, one at a time, should travel along the beam or bench by walking. Make sure you travel from one end of the beam or bench to the other. This relationship of along means being on a piece of equipment and traveling from one part of it to another.

If it's easy for you to walk on the beam, try some other ways. Try a slide. If you need help keeping your balance, spread your arms out to either side.

As children progress with learning how to travel on or along equipment, you can increase the complexity of the activities by changing the locomotor pattern required for traveling. Patterns can include hopping, skipping, running, or fun movements like waddling. Before you change the pattern, be sure the children are able to advance safely to the next pattern. In other words, don't have them run on the balance beam before they can keep their balance at a fast walk.

T This time, we're going to be funny by combining two different relationships while you travel along the bench. Have some of your weight on the bench and some on the floor. For example, have one hand and foot on the bench and one hand and foot on the floor, or have both your feet on the bench and both your hands on the floor. The idea is to place part of your weight on the equipment and part on the floor. Make sure I can tell where your weight really is.

C Make up one way you like to travel with part of your weight on the floor and part on the bench, and practice it so you can show the class. Try to give your movement a name.

Traveling Through Obstacles

Setting: Hoops on foam supports

Tasks/Challenges:

T So far we have practiced traveling over, under, around, in front of, behind, and along. Now we are going to practice traveling *through* obstacles. Look around the area. You will see hoops standing up straight on foam supports. See if you can travel through the hoops without touching the sides.

Can you travel through the hoop without touching it?

Moving in relationship to a rolling hoop is a fascinating challenge for the skilled child.

Start going through at a slow speed. If that is easy, gradually go through at a faster speed.

T If you can travel through the obstacle without knocking it down or touching it at a fast speed, then try going through it in a backward direction—slowly at first and then faster and faster.

C See if you can go through the hoop three times without touching it in a forward direction at a fast speed. See if you can travel through three times in a backward direction without touching the obstacle.

T This game is called rolling hoops. You may work alone or with a partner. The object is to travel through a rolling hoop without touching it so the hoop keeps rolling after you travel through it. If you work with a partner, ask your partner to roll the hoop slowly or to make it spin by throwing it so the hoop spins back to the thrower. Try to go through the hoop when it changes direction and starts back to the thrower.

✓ *Teacher Observation.* **The following task might be** used with a teacher observation to assess children's ability to use the concepts of *over, into, out of, around,* and *along.*

I am going to ask you to travel in relationship to a hoop and do five things.

1. Travel over the hoop. (It's OK if you just travel over part of the hoop.)
2. Travel into the hoop.
3. Travel out of the hoop.
4. Travel around the hoop.

5. Travel along the hoop. (Don't worry if you fall off sometimes; just keep trying.)

I will call out each relationship. Don't start the next one until I ask you to change. Sometimes you will keep moving. Sometimes you will stop after the movement is done.

Remember, cognitive understanding precedes the ability to perform. If children are having difficulty "doing" the concepts, you may want to assess their cognitive understanding. For example, can they verbally explain the difference between around *and* along?

Going Over and Under the Obstacle Course

Setting: An obstacle course made by placing elastic or regular ropes at various heights around the room. Chairs, volleyball standards, and benches can be used to anchor the ropes.

Tasks/Challenges:

T You can see that the whole room is now a giant maze. Your task is to go through the maze by going over or under the ropes. Everyone can move at once, but be sure to not touch anyone else as you find your way through the maze. You can start at different places on the maze, but everyone needs to move in the same direction.

T Now that you've gone through the maze at least once, I'm going to make the activity harder. This time, try to go over some of the high ropes that you went under, and go under some of the low ropes that you went over. Be very careful not to touch anyone else, and try not to touch the ropes.

C This will take a lot of concentration—pretend the ropes are electric fences that will zap you if you touch them.

This is a good initial activity because you can set it up before class and then have the children help you take it down if you don't want to use it for the entire class. Children really enjoy this activity.

Using Partners as Obstacles

Setting: Partners in a self-space

Throughout this series of tasks, emphasize that the children move in relationship to their partners without touching them. Sometimes a partner will need to create a nonsymmetrical shape, with some body parts at a low level to allow a partner to travel over her. Hint to the teacher—these tasks and challenges assume the children have learned to work successfully with a partner. If they are not ready to do so, these tasks will probably not be effective. This is probably best for intermediate grade children.

Tasks/Challenges:

T Things are going to change a little this time. Instead of using equipment as obstacles, you're going to use partners. To warm up, partner 1 freezes in any shape he or she likes and can hold still. Partner 2 tries to find as many ways as possible to go over, under, around, and through the shape, without touching partner 1. When partner 2 has found two different ways to do each of the four movements (over, under, around, and through), she changes places with partner 1. Partner 2 now freezes in a shape, and partner 1 goes over, under, around, and through the shape.

T Now partner 1 makes a low-level, nonsymmetrical shape and holds it while partner 2 finds three ways to go over that shape without touching it. Make sure you're actually going over the shape, not around it. After you've found three ways to go over the shape, trade places with your partner and repeat the exercise.

T To make things a bit harder, this time as you cross the low-level nonsymmetrical shape, try to match it. So if your partner is in a small, round shape, you want to be in a small, round shape in the air as you cross over your partner. Your partner on the floor makes three different shapes and then switches. I'll be watching to see how closely the two shapes match each other.

T This time, instead of matching, you're going to try to look the opposite as you cross. So if your partner is in a round, curled shape, you want to be in a wide, spread-out shape. After you do this three times, trade places.

T Let's make the activity even more difficult. Partner 1 forms a shape, and partner 2 crosses the shape. Partner 2 now makes a shape for partner 1. Partners keep taking turns making shapes and crossing them. Every time you cross a shape, you immediately stop and form a shape for your partner to cross. Let's try it. Each partner should make three shapes and then stop. Remember, do not touch your partner.

T Let's work on making the movement smoother so it flows together well. This time, cross the shape, and smoothly and immediately go into your shape as if you just flowed into it. The person getting up should begin movement as soon as her or his shape has been crossed. Partners should perform as if they can read each other's mind and are continually changing places.

It may help to plan your shapes ahead of time. Talk about your shapes first so you know exactly what you're going to do. Remember, you must go over your partner, not around.

T This will be the hardest activity yet. Each set of partners should mark off their own space. No one else can travel in this space, and the partners can't travel out of it. This is very important, so do it now. You must be able to show me the boundaries to your space when I ask. You may use ropes, cones, lines, or benches to mark your space.

Now that you have your space, here's what you'll be doing. Both of you will be traveling on your feet in your space. Suddenly, one of you will stop and make a low-level shape; when this happens, the other person quickly travels over the shape, and then both of you continue traveling. Do this again, with the other partner making the shape. The whole movement is split-second and unpredictable. No one knows when a shape will be made, and it is barely made before it's crossed. The action goes like this: Both of you travel, one of you stops and makes a low-level shape, the other one crosses the shape, and you keep moving. The object is to perform this movement three times without breaking the flow of the movement or touching each other. Let's give it a try.

The secret to this task is to react as soon as you see your partner beginning to make a shape. You have to anticipate, somewhat like making an interception in football. Try again and see if you can move more smoothly, with fewer breaks and jerks.

Developing the Concept of the Relationships with People

The third category in relationships is relationships with others. As stated at the beginning of the chapter, this is the hardest relationship to learn and is one that is truly important throughout a lifetime. When teaching youngsters about relationships with people, we focus on five related relationships: alone in a mass, solo, partners, groups, and between groups. These relationships can occur in a variety of ways: Each child dribbles a ball in general space (alone in a mass); one child demonstrates a sequence before an entire class (solo); a child mirrors or matches the movement of a partner or partners; children meet or part in a dance with a group to express an idea (groups); and individuals work with others as a team to accomplish a task against another team (between groups).

Alone in a Mass

We use the term *alone in a mass* to describe those times when all children move simultaneously, with no intent of observing one another. It's frequently seen in lessons that use a problem-solving or guided discovery approach (Chapter 10). The children are indirectly relating to one another as they move throughout general space. In contrast to a solo relationship (explained in the next section), the children practice independently, even though they're surrounded by classmates. A child is alone in a mass when dribbling his or her own ball through general space or when an entire class is running simultaneously to a predetermined location.

Solo

A solo relationship exists between an individual and an audience. Examples are the pitcher on a baseball team, a featured performer in a ballet, and a gymnast—or a child who is being pinpointed by a teacher (Chapter 8). Because some children experience unpleasant pressure or tension when they're the center of attention, we make solo performances voluntary rather than mandatory. This is particularly important for the poorly skilled child, who often feels increased tension and pressure when asked to perform in front of an audience. For this reason, we always try to pinpoint two or more children simultaneously (Chapter 8). Some children, however, enjoy the challenge of solo performances and actually seem to do better when watched by a group. The feeling experienced when moving and being observed by others is an interesting phenomenon and one

we want children to explore but in a safe, nonthreatening environment. In all classes we discourage the children from laughing at or negatively criticizing the other children's performances.

Partners

Most primary-grade children will be able to work cooperatively with a partner to explore different relationships. In every class, however, there may be a few children who are not yet developmentally ready to cooperate with a partner—especially if you are asking them to share equipment. Examples of partner relationships include two dancers moving in synchronization to express harmony or peace, two people paddling a canoe, and two synchronized swimmers performing a routine together. Relationship concepts introduced as children work with partners (or groups) include:

- Meeting and parting—traveling toward or away from a partner
- Unison and contrast—both partners intentionally do the same thing (unison), or they intentionally do the same thing in different ways (contrast)
- Leading and following—one partner leads; the other follows
- Matching—partners are side by side and attempt to duplicate one another's movements instantaneously (to make the same movement at the same time)
- Mirroring—partners face one another and form the reverse reproduction of the partner's movements, as if looking in a mirror

Groups

Group cooperative relationships occur when more than two children work together for a common purpose. These relationships include children working together to express an emotion in dance, to design a game or a sequence, or as a team trying to keep a ball from touching the floor but without catching it.

As the size of the group increases, so, too, does the complexity of the relationship. A partner relationship involves being aware of one other child; a successful group relationship necessitates an awareness of two or more children. The difficulty of decision making also increases proportionately with the size of the group. The concepts of meeting and parting, unison and contrast, and leading and following all become increasingly challenging as the size of a group increases. Group relationships are typically focused on in game situations—for example, a play in basketball, spacing on a soccer field. When coaches are drawing their Xs and Os, they are describing group relationships.

Working with a partner increases the fun of an activity for many children.

Between Groups

A between-group relationship occurs when two or more children relate to two or more children. It's the most complex of relationships because it involves not only being aware of one's own group, but having a responsibility to relate to another group. This relationship is extremely challenging, as demonstrated by the wide appeal of sports that match one team against another. We keep intergroup relationships small (two to three on a side) and try to allow choices about whether or not to participate in an intergroup relationship.

Between-group relationships can be competitive (working with a group to outmaneuver another group) or collaborative (two groups striving for a common goal). We usually begin with collaborative relationships and provide children the opportunity to choose competitive activities.

Teaching the Concept of the Relationships with People

The following activities are designed to improve children's ability to function successfully with other individuals and groups in a variety of situations.

Learning Experiences Leading to Movement Concept Understanding

Matching

Setting: Partners in a self-space

Tasks/Challenges:

🔵 Stand alongside a partner. Partner 1 should make a shape, and partner 2 should try to copy it exactly.

Try to make the shapes so alike that you look like twins. After making five different shapes, partners should change places, with partner 2 now making the shapes while partner 1 copies them. Work hard to make the shapes exactly alike.

🔵 These types of shapes are said to match; they look alike as much as possible. Now you're going to make matching balances a little harder by playing follow the leader. On the signal, partner 1 leads by traveling; partner 2 follows. When I beat the drum, you both stop, and the follower, partner 2, matches the balance the leader, partner 1, makes. As you make your shapes, try to match exactly what your partner does. Your whole body should do this, not just your trunk. Be sure when you're the leader that you make a shape your partner can actually do—not one that's too hard. After four shapes we will switch the leader and the follower.

Traveling and Matching

Setting: Partners traveling in general space

Tasks/Challenges:

🔵 Now you'll perform matching actions while traveling instead of being still. With your partner, make up five different ways you can travel and then perform the movements side by side at the exact same time, as if you're both part of a marching band that does everything alike. Skipping and hopping are two of the ways you might want to try. Practice doing the movements together so you do them at exactly the same time. It may help to count to yourselves as you move. When I beat the drum, switch to a different way of traveling (e.g., from skipping to hopping).

Children try to match their partner as they make nonsymmetrical balances.

Mirroring

Setting: Partners in a self-space

Tasks/Challenges:

T This time you're going to try something a little different. Face your partner; partner 1 will be the leader and partner 2 the follower. The leader will make a balance, and the follower will then make the same balance, only opposite. For example, if partner 1 uses her right arm to do something, partner 2 uses his left arm—just like looking in a mirror. Make five statues, and then trade places. Hold each statue for two elephants (count one elephant, two elephants) before moving to the next statue. Work very hard to make every part of the statue the exact opposite of what you see. These types of actions are called *mirroring* actions because it is like looking in a mirror.

Matching and Mirroring

Setting: Partners in a self-space

Tasks/Challenges:

T This activity tests how well you understand the difference between mirroring and matching. With your partner, make a matching balance. On the signal, change that balance so you mirror each other.

It helps to have two partners that are doing the activity correctly pinpoint it for the class so you are sure they understand the task.

T With your partner, now try to find three more balances that you can change from matching to mirroring. I'm going to come around as you practice and ask to see at least one of your combinations, so be sure you know the difference. If you have questions, ask now.

T This time, the activity will be harder. Instead of copying a still statue your partner makes, you're going to mirror your partner's movements. It will be just like looking in a mirror when you brush your hair. Remember, this is still in your own space and there's no traveling. So if your partner moves his or her left arm down, you move your right arm down. Make four moves and change leaders. This is hard. Think about it.

T This time, try to tell a story with your mirroring actions, such as a baby first seeing herself in the mirror, your mother putting on her makeup, or your father shaving. Practice your story until you can do it the same way three times in a row. Then we'll have the class try to guess what you're saying.

Traveling Alongside/Following

Setting: Traveling in general space with a partner

Tasks/Challenges:

T In many of our other lessons you were practicing another type of relationship when you followed your partner around the space: leading and following. Now let's try traveling alongside (next to) your partner. One person is still the leader and the other the follower, but you both move as if you were a team of horses: beside each other. Switch leaders when I give the signal. This activity is harder than leading and following, so you have to watch very closely what your partner does. Start out with slow walking, and you can get faster gradually. Once you get the hang of it, try to find fun, different ways to travel.

T Now try to speed it up a little. Watch carefully. Try to follow exactly.

Children try to match each other's rocking motions.

The leader must be aware of the follower's capabilities so that the leader challenges the partner but doesn't frustrate the partner with movements that are too difficult.

Following with a Group

Setting: Traveling in general space with a group

Tasks/Challenges:

🅣 This time, you're going to try another type of following: from behind, with four or five of you in a group. The first person in line is the first leader and leads the group all over the room. Start with walking. Then when you hear the drum (or tambourine), the first person goes to the end of the line, and the second person becomes the leader and travels in a different way—for example, if the first leader hops, the second leader might gallop; this change continues until everyone has had a chance to lead. The activity is just like follow the leader. Remember, no touching. Can your group come up with five different ways to travel?

🅣 This time you're going to make the activity even harder. I'm not going to give you the signal to change anymore. Your group will have to make up its own change signal—maybe a hand clap or a whistle. You'll start as you did before, with the first person leading. Then at some time, the second person in line will give the change signal and at the same time start traveling a new way. When this happens, the whole line starts to follow the new leader, and the old leader goes to the back of the line. The hard part is that you're going to do this without stopping the movement; try to always keep moving. Keep going until everyone has had a chance to be the leader. Remember, the second person in line always gives the change signal.

Meeting/Parting

Setting: Partners working in self- and general space

Tasks/Challenges:

🅣 Now you're going to work with partners again. Find a different partner. First you and your new partner are going to work only with your hands while sitting in a self-space, facing each other. Very slowly, try to bring your hands as close to your partner's as you can without touching them. As soon as your hands are close, pull them as far away as you can without moving your body.

🅣 This relationship is called *meeting and parting*. To make it a little easier, I'm going to give you a drumbeat to go by. On the six slow counts of the drum, bring your hands as close as possible without touching them, and freeze. Then, on the sudden loud beat, quickly pull your hands as far away as possible, as if you don't want them to touch poison.

🅣 Now try meeting and parting with your whole body. Stand up and move a few feet apart. Use the six slow drumbeats to walk as close together as possible without touching, and then freeze. On the sudden beat, quickly move back to where you started. The secret is to walk away quickly, as if you were a flash of lightning, and then freeze very still.

🅣 The activity will be harder this time. You'll still have the same partner, but you will be traveling around the room without your partner. When you hear the drumbeat, quickly come toward your partner and freeze very close to each other in a matching shape, just for a few seconds, and then begin your traveling again. Do this every time you hear the signal. The secret is to always know where your partner is. Maintain eye contact but also watch for others.

(T) This time, as you and your partner meet on the sound of the signal, come together as if you're greeting a friend you haven't seen in a long time; then, as you get right up to each other, you realize that you really don't know the person and quickly move away. It could be really funny.

Forming Cooperative and Collaborative Relationships

Setting: Groups of four traveling, throwing, and catching balls or beanbags in a large space. This idea works well if a lined field (such as a football field) is available and the children can follow the lines as guides. It also assumes that the children are at least at the control level of catching. These tasks would not succeed for most primary grades.

Tasks/Challenges:

(T) So far, all our relationships with people involved how we moved with those people. In your group of three, you're going to travel in a line spread out across the field (gym) toward the other side. As you travel, throw the ball (beanbag) back and forth to each other, always trying to stay the same distance apart. Imagine a marching band moving across the field but throwing a ball as they move. The secret is that the receivers move slightly ahead of but not toward the passers, and the passers throw the ball ahead of the receivers so they don't have to stop walking to catch it. This type of relationship is called a *cooperative relationship* because everybody has to work together to make it work.

When children begin to work with others in collaborative and competitive situations involving a manipulative skill (e.g., throwing and catching), the skill level tends to deteriorate briefly if they're concentrating on the relationship. This should be expected and explained.

(T) Now you're going to change the cooperative relationship a little. You're still going to work with your group of three to move the ball across the field (gym) while staying the same distance apart, but one person is going to try to steal the ball while it is in the air coming toward you. It will be really hard to resist the temptation to go close to your own players to try to help them, but remember you have two goals: to stay away from your teammates and to not let the other person steal the ball. It really does help to stay away from the other people on your team.

This is called a collaborative relationship because you have to work with the people on your team to keep the other person from getting the ball. Let me give you a few more hints on how to make such a relationship work really well. First, when it's your turn to receive the ball, move slightly in front of the passer so the passer can easily throw the ball to you. Second, pass before the defender gets close to you; when you're free to pass, don't wait until the defender is so close that you're forced to pass.

You may want to make the choice of having a defender optional because for some children it will be enough of a challenge to try to throw, catch, and travel at the same time with a defender.

Meeting and Parting in a Cooperative Group

Setting: Groups of three or four in general space

Tasks/Challenges:

(T) This time, instead of meeting and parting with a partner, you're going to meet and part with a small group. Your group forms a group shape (e.g., circle, square, triangle)—Remember, be close but not touching. Then on the signal, suddenly leave, as if you're in a hurry, but take only a few steps and then freeze into a shape you like. On the next signal, slowly come back to your group and form the same group shape with which you started. To repeat, start with a group shape, on the signal quickly leave and form a shape of your own, and on the next signal return to the first group shape—almost as if someone was playing a movie forward, backward, forward, backward.

(C) Let's work on this activity with one series you really like. Practice it so it works out the same each time. This will involve hard thinking. It may help to count your steps so you know exactly how far to move. It also helps not to laugh too much. Who knows, you could be stars!

Performing Solo

Setting: Groups of six, each group with a foam ball and cones to define an area for each group; pencil and paper for each child

Tasks/Challenges:

(T) You're going to play a bunch of small tag games—only six people in a group. Start with two people as taggers. When you get tagged, do not sit out, but become a tagger, so in the end there will be many taggers and one person in the middle. When you finish one game, just start another one. The last two players left in the middle are the first taggers in the next game. Remember, think about what it's like to be left in the middle.

After the youngsters have played the game, you have an excellent opportunity to briefly discuss the feelings of being in a solo relationship when each child is the center of attention. Point out that some people (probably the highly skilled) like being solo, but others (probably the less skilled) prefer to not be solo.

It is important to determine children's understanding of relationships. Either of the following ideas will allow you to do that rather quickly:

- *Exit slip.* Ask children to draw a symmetrical shape and a nonsymmetrical shape.
- *Homework.* Ask children to find an example of a shape (e.g., wide, narrow, round, or twisted) in a magazine or newspaper. Ask them to label the shape.

Applying the Concept of Relationships

The concept of relationships with objects and people is a beginning theme in the dance and gymnastics areas as the children are taught the concepts of *over*, *under*, *around*, *through*, *along*, and *onto*. This is explained further in Chapters 28 and 29. At this time, however, focus is on whether the child understands the concept rather than on how she is doing the skill. For example, you could observe whether a child was actually jumping symmetrically over a hurdle rather than whether she was crossing without knocking it over or using correct form. Once you're sure the child understands the concept, then in later grades you will focus on the cues (critical components) related to successful jumping. Once a particular concept has been learned, it can also be used for expressive purposes in dance.

We don't introduce the concept of relationships with objects in the games area until children have reached at least the control level for the manipulative skills (e.g., throwing, kicking) (Chapter 5). Children must learn to manipulate objects alone before they can reasonably be expected to manipulate them in relation to objects or people. If children are given tasks involving manipulative skills and relationships too early, they become frustrated and bored.

The concept of relationships with others is the last concept we introduce. Socially, children enjoy working near other children at a very young age (parallel play), but often physically and cognitively they aren't able to function effectively in relationship to others. For example, children at the precontrol level don't possess enough skill to be able to consistently work with a partner throwing and catching a ball. Therefore, it's best not to deal with relationships with others as a concept until the children's fundamental motor skills are adequate and they've matured enough socially so their abilities are enhanced when they work with other children. There are no magical ages or times for introducing the different relationship concepts. Each teacher must reflect on information about the environment, the children, the skill, and personal ability to determine the best time for introducing the concept of relationships. Typically, however, the concepts are introduced in the early primary grades and then revisited when the children are practicing various skill themes.

Competition

We were not sure where to discuss competition within the skill theme approach, so we chose to place it at the end of the relationship chapter because most competitive situations involve relationships—between individuals, partners, or groups. The National Association for Sport and Physical Education (2009) suggests that requiring students to compete in games in which there are "winners and losers" is an inappropriate practice for elementary school physical education, especially when there are rewards for winning and losing in class games. Traditionally, however, physical education classes have consisted of a plethora of team sports, especially at the secondary level.

We are not opposed to competition! However, we are opposed to requiring youngsters to compete in games against their will. When youngsters, or adults for that matter, choose not to compete, it is often because they do not have the prerequisite skills (are at the precontrol or control level) or prefer not to be placed in situations that are potentially humiliating or embarrassing. This is hard for many to understand, especially physical education majors, many of whom were varsity athletes and thrive on competitive situations. An emphasis on winning creates an intense emotional involvement that can produce disturbing feelings in some children.

In the skill theme approach, if competition is involved, it is often deemphasized by the teacher, and you will not find games pitting one half of a class against another. However, you will find many ideas for small-sided games and opportunities for youngsters to design their own games (Chapter 30). When youngsters play small-sided games, they have a choice to keep score or not. (We often find they intend to keep score but forget to do so after a few minutes into the game.) In the skill theme approach, we try to help youngsters to understand that it's acceptable to choose not to keep score.

Finally, we need to realize there are many opportunities for youngsters to participate in competitive situations outside of physical education. By the time many youngsters are in third grade, they have already been on softball, basketball, soccer, or swim teams, or have participated in other types of competitive situations. Thus competition is not new for most youngsters. When teachers can help children to place competition in perspective and understand the strong feelings associated with winning and losing, they need to do so. The major purpose of the skill theme approach, however, is to encourage youngsters to develop motor skill proficiency and positive attitudes toward physical activity. Although some youngsters thrive in competitive situations, others do not. For this reason, in the skill theme approach we present competition as a choice, not as a requirement.

Reading Comprehension Questions

1. List three tasks you might use when teaching children each of the three relationship categories in this chapter—body parts, relationships with objects, and relationships with people (total of nine tasks).
2. What does the term *functional understanding* mean?
3. Today you made symmetrical and nonsymmetrical shapes when you were in class, studying, or eating lunch. Briefly describe what you were doing when you made your symmetrical shapes and when you made your nonsymmetrial shapes. For example, "When I was taking a nap I was in a. . . ."
4. We recommend that you teach the concept of relationships with objects before teaching relationships with people. Why?
5. Briefly describe one example of when you prefer to be in a solo relationship as defined in this chapter. Then describe one example when you prefer not to be in a solo relationship. It may help to refer to the generic levels of skill proficiency (GLSP) from Chapter 5 for your explanation.
6. We recommend that solo performances and intergroup experiences be voluntary, not required. Why?
7. Explain the difference between mirroring and matching. Use one example from the book and one example from something you did yesterday.
8. Pick a team sport you are familiar with. Use the wheel (movement analysis framework) (Figure 15.1) to indicate how five of the 22 relationship concepts are used when playing that game at the varsity or professional level.

References/Suggested Readings

[NASPE] National Association for Sport and Physical Education. 2004. *Moving into the future: National standards for physical education.* 2nd ed. St. Louis, MO: Mosby.

[NASPE] National Association for Sport and Physical Education. 2009. *Appropriate practices for elementary school physical education.* Reston, VA: National Association for Sport and Physical Education.

Skill Theme Development

Chapters 16 to 26 discuss the content of the skill themes we focus on in our physical education programs. The chapters are ordered in the progression used to organize the yearly plan (discussed in Chapter 6). Each chapter begins with an introduction to the skill theme; the introduction includes a discussion of the skill theme's characteristics and how the theme can be applied to teaching children. It's tempting to skip the introduction and get to the actual lesson ideas, but we recommend that you carefully read the introduction so you'll be able to adapt the skill theme to your particular needs. Obviously you'll change some of the ideas; an understanding of the skill as taught to children will help you make these adaptations.

Each skill theme chapter is arranged in a logical progression, from precontrol through proficiency levels as explained in Chapter 5. Precontrol experiences are designed for exploration of the skill; experiences at the control, utilization, and proficiency levels are designed to lead youngsters in the skill development of the particular theme. This progression is accompanied by what we call a progression spiral, which outlines the content of each skill theme. Each line in the spiral corresponds to a section in the chapter that explains how to develop that idea. The progressions are presented as a series of tasks (not lessons) that you will be able to develop based on the skill level and abilities of your classes.

The skill theme chapters are based on the generic levels of skill development, not on chronological age or grade level progressions. While many of the skill themes may be mastered at the precontrol or control levels in elementary school, they will not be mastered at the utilization or proficiency levels where children are asked to apply the skill in more complex contexts. Therefore practice at these levels will need to continue in middle school and even into high school physical education. The development of competency requires time and guided practice of skills; placing students into physical activity situations before the competent skill base is developed results in failure and frustration which thus does not lead to a lifetime of physical activity.

(Reflective of the National Standards of Physical Education and the philosophy of Children Moving, the development of competency in skills and movement patterns must precede participation in sports and physical activity.)

263

Each series of tasks begins by describing the space and equipment you will need. At the precontrol level, children are exploring a movement, and therefore cues are not provided. At the next three generic skill levels, however, cues are provided before the actual task(s). You are reminded that it is probably most effective to focus on only one of these cues at a time. The reason we provide several at the beginning of the series of tasks is to allow you to observe your children to determine which cue will be the most appropriate for them. At times when it was not logical or safe to omit a cue from a task, we have included some cues within the tasks. When this occurs, the cue is in bold print. Following the cues are one or more suggested tasks (designated with the symbol **T**) and also challenges (designated with the symbol **C**). As you recall, tasks, cues, and challenges were described in Chapter 6. In addition, you will find suggested assessments (Chapter 12) to help you determine how well the children are understanding the concepts and skills you are teaching.

Finally, we encourage you to adapt the suggested progressions and implied methodologies to suit your students' needs and your teaching goals. Our suggestions are certainly not prescriptions. Reflect on your situation and your students, and design the curriculum for your children.

Key Concepts

- Skill themes are fundamental movements modified into more specialized patterns in which activities of increasing complexity are built.

- Skill themes include: manipulative (kicking and punting; throwing and catching; volleying and dibbling; striking with rackets, paddles, and long-handled implements); nonmanipulative (rolling, balancing transferring weight, jumping and landing, stretching, curling, bending and twisting); and locomotor skills (traveling, chasing, fleeing, and dodging).

- Learning experiences in the skill theme chapters are designed to assist children in moving from precontrol to control to utilization to proficiency levels of skill.

- Children need multiple and recurring experiences with each skill to become competent movers.

- When skill themes are introduced, the initial tasks allow children to explore the skill (precontrol). Tasks then focus on helping children produce the correct skill in nonchanging environments (control). This is followed by combining skills in dynamic situations (utilization), and finally the use of skills in a variety of changing environments (proficiency).

- It is only after the skill can be produced consistently that it is made more complex with the addition of movement concepts.

- As children gain increasing competency with skills, the skills are applied in games, dance, and gymnastics environments.

Traveling

Children are first capable of changing the location of their bodies at about three months of age, when they turn over from their backs onto their stomachs. Unless seriously handicapped, they'll soon begin to crawl, then creep. At about one year, they'll take their first step. And by the time they enter school, they'll exhibit relatively mature walking and running patterns. Unlike other skills—such as throwing, catching, and striking—the basic locomotor patterns develop naturally in most children.

Most school-age youngsters, therefore, are beyond the precontrol level in walking and running. Nevertheless, the teacher's first task is to evaluate traveling performance to ensure that any youngsters who exhibit severely immature or inefficient patterns will receive remedial assistance. See key observation points on pages 267–270.

Most children attain a mature walking pattern through experience. Verbal cues from the teacher, plus modeling the correct pattern, will help children with inefficiencies. Continued deviations (e.g., toes turned out or in) signal the need for a thorough physical examination by a pediatrician.

Similarly, it's important to ascertain how many students can perform the fundamental locomotor skills that emerge from the walk-run pattern: hopping, leaping, sliding, galloping, and skipping. Young children need much practice of each skill when the skills are introduced, and they also need distributed practice of the locomotor skills throughout the primary grades. Young children inexperienced in different locomotor skills may not be able to give the correct locomotor response to a verbal command because they often lack cognitive understanding rather than motor performance. We've found that modeling is the best way for young children to learn these skills; the children follow the example of the teacher and other children who've mastered the skill. It's also important to name the locomotor skill each time you or others demonstrate it to the children.

By approximately age eight, we expect children to be able to execute the locomotor skills of hopping, leaping, sliding, galloping, and skipping in response to a verbal command. This expectation implies that children recognize the word and the action it represents and that they've mastered the skill. After mastery of the locomotor skills, traveling occurs as combinations of skill themes, in a game, dance, or gymnastics context. See Box 16-1 for linkages between the skill theme of Traveling and the *National Standards for Physical Education*.

Box 16-1

The Skill of Traveling in the *National Standards for Physical Education*

The movement skill of traveling is referenced in the National Association for Sport and Physical Education's *National Standards for Physical Education* (NASPE 2004) under Standard 1: "Demonstrates competency in motor skills and movement patterns needed to perform a variety of physical activities." The intent of the standard is developing the physical skills needed to enjoy participation in physical activities, with the mastery of movement fundamentals as the foundation for continued skill acquisition. At the lower-elementary level, students achieve mature forms of the basic locomotor skills and vary the manner in which these skills are performed in relation to changing conditions and expectations. At the upper-elementary level, students demonstrate locomotor skills for performance outcomes, using locomotor skills in dynamic and complex environments, and in combinations.

Sample performance outcomes from the *National Standards* include:

- Skips (or hops, gallops, slides, etc.) using mature form (K–2)*
- Performs a basic tinikling step (3–5)*
- Performs a variety of simple folk and square dances (6–8)*
- Designs and performs gymnastics (or dance) sequences that combine traveling, rolling, balancing, and weight transfer into smooth, flowing sequences with intentional changes in direction, speed, and flow (6–8)*

*Grade-level guidelines for expected student learning.

Fundamental Locomotor Skills

Walking

Walking is a process of alternately losing balance and recovering it while moving forward in an upright position. While moving forward, the body should display little up-and-down or side-to-side movement. The arms and legs move in opposition. A mature walking pattern looks smooth and is accomplished easily.

When assessing the walking pattern of young children, look for the following inefficiencies:

- Bouncy walk—too much vertical push
- Excessive swing of the arms away from the sides
- Failure to swing the arms at the shoulders
- Feet held too close together so the entire body looks jerky as the child walks

Box 16-2

Key Observation Points: Running Pattern

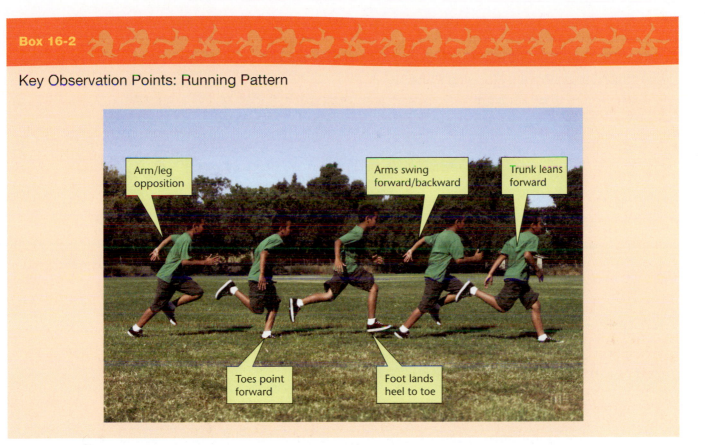

- Feet held too far apart—duck walk
- Toes turned out
- Toes turned in—pigeon-toed
- Head too far forward—body leaning forward before the lead foot touches the ground

Running

During the earliest stage of running (at about 24 months), a child's new speed produces precarious balance. The child makes exaggerated leg movements. In particular, the knee of the recovery leg swings outward and then around and forward in preparation for the support phase. This knee action is accompanied by the foot of the recovery leg toeing out. These exaggerated movements gradually disappear as the legs become longer and stronger.

Most school-age youngsters are able to run at a relatively fast speed and are fairly successful at changing direction while running. In a mature running pattern (observed when the children are attempting to run at maximum velocity), each leg goes through a support phase and a recovery phase, and the full sequence produces two periods of nonsupport. The essentials of the mature running pattern are as follows (Wickstrom 1977, 37–57):

- The trunk maintains a slight forward lean throughout the stride pattern.
- Both arms swing through a large arc and in synchronized opposition to the leg action.
- The support foot contacts the ground approximately flat and nearly under the center of gravity.
- The knee of the support leg bends slightly after the foot has made contact with the ground.
- Extension of the support leg at the hip, knee, and ankle propels the body forward and upward into the nonsupport phase.
- The recovery knee swings forward quickly to a high knee raise, and simultaneously the lower leg flexes, bringing the heel close to the buttock.

Use the critical elements in Boxes 16-2 thru 16-7 to assess the locomotor patterns. The illustrations of "correct" patterns will help you answer the questions you should ask yourself as you evaluate a youngster's performance.

Hopping

A hop is a springing action from one foot, in any direction, to a landing on the same foot (Box 16-3). The

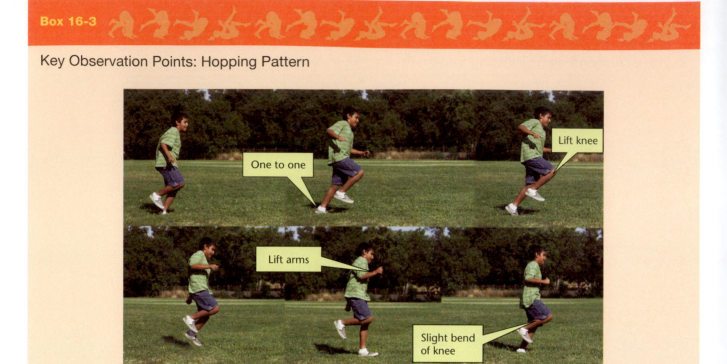

Box 16-3

Key Observation Points: Hopping Pattern

knee seldom straightens fully; the work of the ankle joint is primarily what accomplishes the push into the air and the absorption of the landing shock.

Leaping

A leap is an extension of a run—greater force is used to produce a higher dimension than a run (Box 16-4). A one-foot takeoff propels the body upward to a landing on the opposite foot. Arm opposition is the same as for the run. There's an emphasis on body extension for height or for distance. Upon touching the floor, the landing leg bends to absorb the force of the body.

Sliding

A slide is a combination of a step and a run. The lead step is quickly followed by the free foot closing to replace the supporting foot (Box 16-5). The lead foot quickly springs from the floor into a direction of intended travel. The weight is primarily on the balls of the feet. The sequence is repeated for the desired distance. The same foot always leads in a slide, producing an uneven rhythm: step-close, step-close, step-close.

Galloping

A gallop is an exaggerated slide in a forward direction. (Box 16-6). The lead leg lifts and bends and then thrusts forward to support the weight. The rear foot quickly closes to replace the supporting leg as the lead leg springs up into its lifted and bent position. The rhythm is uneven, the same as that of a slide.

Skipping

A skip is a combination of a step and a hop, first on one foot and then on the other foot (Box 16-7). The pattern has the alternation and opposition of the walk plus the same-sided one-foot hop. The skip has an uneven rhythm.

Young children love to move; they run, jump, leap, hop, skip: They move! Children run in games at recess; they chase, dodge, and flee for the pure joy of movement. They run, slide, leap, and jump in basketball, soccer, and football. They gallop, skip, jump, and leap in dance. They run, jump, and leap in gymnastics. The skills of traveling are critical for children's success in dance, gymnastics, and games. The progression spiral on page 271 shows the development of the skill theme of traveling at the precontrol, control, utilization, and proficiency levels.

Box 16-4

Key Observation Points: Leaping Pattern

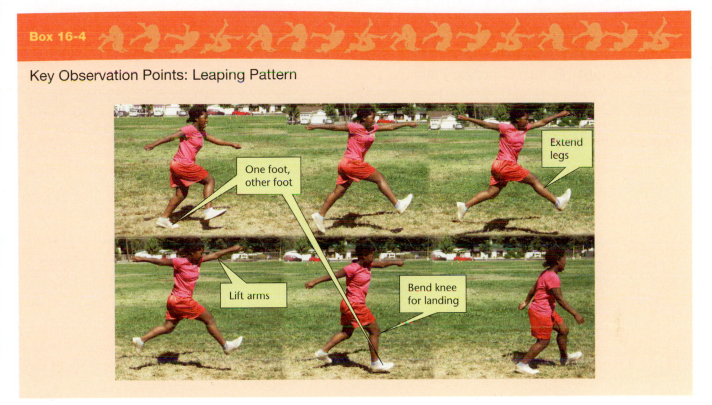

Box 16-5

Key Observation Points: Sliding Pattern

Box 16-6

Key Observation Points: Galloping Pattern

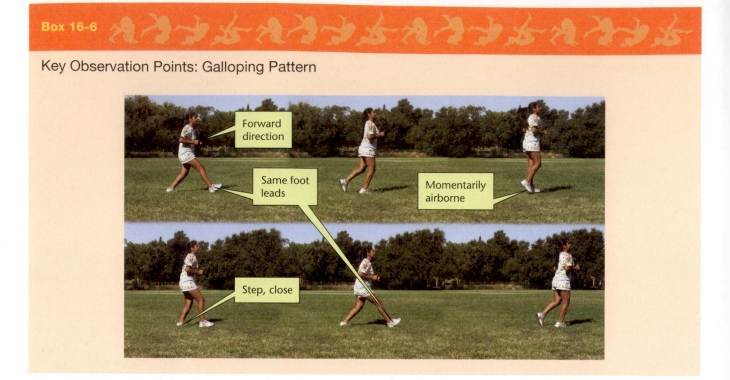

Forward direction

Same foot leads

Momentarily airborne

Step, close

Box 16-7

Key Observation Points: Skipping Pattern

Step, hop

Alternating feet

Lift knee

Swing arms

Momentarily airborne

Skill Theme Development Progression

Traveling

Proficiency Level

Traveling in gymnastics
Traveling in games and sports
Performing rhythmical patterns: tinikling
Body shapes and group travel: A study in form
Traveling with shapes and actions: A story without words

Utilization Level

Traveling in bound and free flow
Traveling to tell a story: The fountain of youth dance
Performing rhythmical patterns
Meeting and parting while traveling with a partner
Shadowing a partner's travel
Traveling with a partner: changing speed and direction
Traveling with a partner: copying locomotors and directions
Traveling with a partner: matching pathways

Control Level

Combination locomotors
Traveling in slow-motion: The sports dance
Traveling with changes in speed: A dance of water, steam,
    and ice
Changing speeds to music
Traveling using different directions, levels, pathways,
    and locations
Traveling at different speeds
Locomotors and rhythm: The follow-me dance
Locomotors with directions and pathways: The locomotors
    dance
Traveling in different pathways
Slidestepping
Traveling in different directions
Traveling an obstacle course
Traveling with music
Traveling in confined spaces
Moving to rhythms
Performing locomotor sequences
Traveling to open spaces
Running
Leaping
Skipping
Hopping
Galloping
Sliding
Traveling with different locomotor patterns

Precontrol Level

Traveling among wide and narrow shapes
Traveling through rope pathways
Traveling with imagery
Traveling in different ways
Traveling with different locomotor movements
Traveling in general space

Precontrol Level (GLSP): Activities for Exploration

Activities at the precontrol level are designed to introduce children to the fundamental locomotor patterns and help them explore the skill of traveling. Children learn to travel without bumping others; they experience traveling with different locomotor movements and traveling on body parts other than their feet.

Traveling in General Space

Setting: Children scattered throughout general space

Tasks/Challenges:

T On the signal, travel any way you wish in general space. Avoid colliding with others, and stop without falling when you hear the drum.

T Change to a different way to travel. Some of you are hopping; some are galloping; most are running. Travel throughout general space any way except running. Watch out for others as you travel.

T See how many different ways you can travel on your feet, sometimes traveling on one foot, sometimes on two feet, sometimes on one foot and then the other.

C Show me three different ways you can travel on your feet.

Traveling with Different Locomotor Movements

Setting: Children scattered throughout general space

Tasks/Challenges:

T When we explored different ways to travel, some of you were hopping, some were walking, some were galloping. Let's explore the different locomotor skills as we travel in general space. Travel throughout general space with your favorite locomotor movement; I will name the ones I see: walking, running, galloping. . . .

T Travel throughout general space with a hop, staying on one foot. Switch to the other foot after several hops so you will not become tired and lose your balance.

T Travel throughout general space with a jump, two feet to two feet. Make some of your jumps small and low, some of them long, some of them high in the air.

T Travel throughout general space with a gallop, one foot always staying in front of the other. Can you gallop backward?

T Travel throughout general space with a run, always looking for the open spaces. Remember, stop on the signal without falling down.

This child explores traveling pathways.

C Thus far, you have traveled by hopping, jumping, galloping, and running; you were already very good at walking. Of those five locomotor actions, choose your favorite three and practice them as if you were going to teach them to someone who does not know how to do them—perfection!

Traveling in Different Ways

Setting: Children scattered throughout general space

Tasks/Challenges:

T Travel throughout general space on two feet. On the signal, change the way you are traveling, yet remain on your feet.

C How many different ways can you travel on your feet?

T Travel throughout general space on two feet and two hands; travel forward, backward, sideways on your feet and hands.

T Travel throughout general space on body parts other than your feet. How many different combinations of body parts can you use for travel?

Traveling with Imagery

Setting: Children scattered throughout general space

Tasks/Challenges:

T Travel throughout general space like a rabbit, jumping from two feet to two feet; travel like a frog, jumping from pad to pad.

T Travel throughout general space, walking as if in sticky mud or a sea of peanut butter.

T Walk like a robot. March like a soldier.

T Travel throughout general space like a large elephant. Will your steps be heavy or light?

T Travel like a tall giraffe with your head above the clouds.

T Run quietly like deer through the forest.

T Slither like a snake. Crawl like an inchworm, then like a snail.

The imagery of animals for movement is almost endless. Always remind children of the movement with a simple lead question, such as "How does a giraffe move?"

Traveling Through Rope Pathways

Setting: An obstacle course of marker cones and ropes on the floor to form varying pathways of different widths for travel (Figure 16.1)

Tasks/Challenges:

T On the signal, travel around the cones and between the rope boundaries without touching them. I will time you for 30 seconds. Try to finish with a perfect score—no touches.

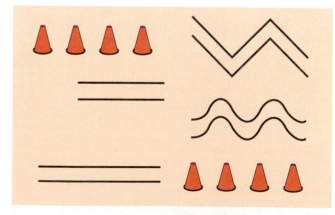

Figure 16.1 Rope pathways as an obstacle course.

These children are enjoying traveling at a low level.

C Challenge yourself to travel throughout the obstacle course three times with no collisions with others or the items in the course.

Traveling Among Wide and Narrow Shapes

Setting: Children with partners, scattered throughout general space

Tasks/Challenges:

T Stand in your self-space, stretching in all directions to be sure you have a clear self-space; it is not important that you be near your partner. Partners A, stand in your self-space, extending your arms to make a very large, wide shape. Partners B, travel throughout general space with any locomotor pattern you wish; avoid touching anyone traveling or a stationary wide shape. Have partners switch travel and stationary activities after one or two -minutes of travel.

T Partners B, stand in your self-space with a tall, narrow shape. Partners A, run throughout general space with no collisions; always look for open spaces as you travel. Switch activities after one or two minutes.

Control Level (GLSP): Learning Experiences Leading to Skill Development

Control-level experiences are designed to help children master the basic locomotor skills and expand their traveling abilities. Mastery of the basic locomotor skills is the primary focus for beginning control level experiences. Following mastery of the locomotors, the learning experiences focus on using different traveling patterns with movement concepts, traveling rhythmically and traveling expressively to create new dances.

A note about cues: Although several cues are listed for many of the learning experiences, it's important to focus on only one cue at a time. This way, the children can really concentrate on that cue. Once you provide feedback to the children and observe that most have learned a cue, it's time to focus on another one.

Traveling with Different Locomotor Patterns

Setting: Children scattered throughout general space

Cues	
Heads Up	(Keep your head up for good balance and to avoid collisions with others.)
Balanced Stops	(Spread your feet apart and lower your hips slightly to maintain your balance when you stop.)

Tasks/Challenges:

T On signal, travel any way you wish in general space. Avoid colliding with others, and stop without falling when you hear the drum.

Sliding

Cues

Side to Target (Point your shoulder to the wall or your target as you move.)

Step, Chase (The back foot tries to catch the lead foot with each step . . . but never does.)

Spring, Spring (Make light, "springy" actions as you travel.)

Task/Challenges:

T Raise your right arm and point toward the far side of the blacktop (gymnasium). On the signal, use a slidestep to travel across the area. When your left foot almost touches your right foot, step again quickly to the side with your right foot.

T Slide across the area like a dancer, arms extended to the side and your body stretched upward as you "leap."

T Slide like a basketball player with your knees bent, hips lowered, and arms extended in front.

Galloping

Cues

Same Foot Forward (Keep the same foot in front as you gallop.)

Step, Chase (The back foot tries to catch the front foot with each step . . . but never does.)

Tasks/Challenges:

T On the signal, gallop in general space, keeping the same foot in front throughout the action.

T Now lead with the other foot as you gallop.

Hopping

Cues

One to One (Up and down on one foot/the same foot.)

Arms Out (Keep your arms out for good balance.)

Up, Up, Light, Light (Make light, quick actions as you hop.)

Tasks/Challenges:

T Hop on one foot five times, and then hop on your other foot five times. Continue to alternate hopping on your right foot and then your left foot until you hear the signal to stop.

Skipping

Cues

Step, Hop (Step forward on one foot and then hop on the same foot with an uneven rhythm.)

A clap or drum beat of the uneven rhythm will be helpful to the children.

Lift Your Knees (Lift your knees, swing your arms . . . step, hop.)

Keep It Moving (Keep moving; don't stop.)

Tasks/Challenges:

T Now that you can hop and gallop, try skipping. Skip throughout general space until you hear the signal to stop.

Developmentally, children progress from a gallop to a skip only on the dominant side, then to a mature skipping pattern.

Leaping

Cues

One to One (Take off on one foot and land on the other foot.)

Soft Landings (Bend your knee and hip as you land for a cushioned landing.)

Arms Up . . . Stretch (Lift your arms; stretch your arms and legs as you leap.)

Tasks/Challenges:

T We did leaping when we worked on jumping and landing. Who can remember what a leap is? Right, it's taking off on one foot and landing on the other, with the body airborne between the takeoff and landing. Travel in general space by running. After running three steps, leap high in the air, and when you land, continue to run. Your travel will be this: Run, run, run, leap; run, run, run, leap. Remember to land softly by bending your knee.

T I'm going to number you off in 1s and 2s. The 1s will be spread throughout general space, standing with your arms stretched high over your heads. On signal, the 2s will run throughout general space, leaping high in the air each time you pass a 1 standing with arms stretched high. Try to leap so high in the air that you are higher than the stretched arms of the 1s. On signal, the 2s will stand with arms stretched high, and the 1s will run and leap.

Keep the activity short in duration with a focus on leaping. Repeat several times for endurance.

A When children are running and leaping, a reminder for sufficient space and awareness of others is important to avoid airborne and landing collisions.

Running

Cue

Light on Your Feet (Make light, buoyant landings for quick steps.)

Tasks/Challenges:

T Now that you can move without bumping others and stop on signal, try running throughout general space. Cover as much area as you can. Be sure your entire foot contacts the floor, not just your toes.

As you observe children running, ask yourself the following questions. Provide individual cues as needed for deviations.

- *Does the knee of the child's recovery leg swing forward and backward rather than outward, around, and then forward?*
- *Do the child's arms move forward and backward in opposition to the legs without crossing the midline?*
- *Do the child's arms stay close to the body throughout the action?*
- *Does the child's trunk lean slightly forward?*

Assessment Example

From the *National Standards for Physical Education*

Teacher Observation

The student will be asked to travel through general space with a steady run and, upon a designated signal, perform the next locomotor action announced by the teacher (e.g., walk, hop, gallop). Upon observing the

student's performance, the teacher marks on a checklist mastery of the various critical elements (e.g., arm swing, balance, foot placement).

Criteria for Assessment

a. Demonstrates selected critical elements of locomotor skills.
b. Responds with correct locomotor skill as named by teacher.

NASPE (1995, 6)

Assessment Example

From the *National Standards of Physical Education*

Event Task

Students will perform a "Dance of Locomotors" in which they travel in different ways through general space. Upon hearing a designated signal from the teacher, students will change to the locomotor pattern named by the teacher. Repeat the dance, but this time upon the signal to change locomotor pattern the students will respond by selecting any locomotor pattern they desire. The teacher should encourage creative modes of travel.

Criteria for Assessment

a. Demonstrates a variety of locomotor skills.
b. Identifies and models locomotor movements shown by the teacher.
c. Exhibits correct locomotor skill when the skill is named by the teacher.

NASPE (1995, 7)

Traveling to Open Spaces

Setting: Children scattered throughout general space

Cues

Heads Up (Keep your head up for good balance and to avoid collisions with others.)

Balanced Stops (Spread your feet apart and lower your hips slightly to maintain your balance when you stop.)

Tasks/Challenges:

T In your self-space, look around the work space. Do you see open spaces that no one has taken as his or her space? On the signal, run to that open space. When you arrive, stop and look for another open space; run to that space.

Traveling in general space lets children practice finding open spaces.

T Travel throughout general space, always looking for the open spaces. This time you will only pause at an open space long enough to see your next open space.

C I will time you for 60 seconds of travel. Your task is to travel throughout general space always looking for and moving to open spaces with no collisions.

Performing Locomotor Sequences

Setting: Index cards with a sequence of locomotor movements written on them—for example, "Walk, hop, gallop"—one sequence card per child

Cues	
Heads Up	(Keep your head up for good balance and to avoid collisions with others.)
Pause and Go	(Pause momentarily; then continue your locomotor movement.)
Balanced Stops	(Spread your feet apart and lower your hips slightly to maintain your balance when you stop.)

Tasks/Challenges:

T Think of your favorite locomotor movement that you've practiced. On signal, use that movement to travel in general space. I should be able to identify the locomotor movement by watching you travel.

T There are cards spread around the wall. When I say "Go," get a card and bring it back to your space. Go. Read your card. Each card contains a movement sentence: three locomotor movements separated by commas. What does a comma mean in your reading? Right—pause. After each locomotor movement, you'll pause. Your sequence will be travel, pause; travel, pause; travel, stop. Practice your movement sentence until you can do it the same way three times.

Children whose reading level reflects ways to end a sentence enjoy stopping with an image of a period, an exclamation, or a question mark.

Assessment Example

From the *National Standards of Physical Education*

Event Task

Students are asked to design and practice a movement sequence of three different locomotor skills. Following the practice period, students demonstrate their movement sequence for the class.

Criteria for Assessment

a. Demonstrates three different locomotor movements.
b. Demonstrates mature pattern of each locomotor skill.
c. Demonstrates smooth transitions between locomotor patterns.

NASPE (1995, 19)

Moving to Rhythms

Setting: Children scattered throughout general space

Cues	
Heads Up	(Keep your head up for good balance and to avoid collisions with others.)
Pause and Go	(Pause momentarily; then continue your locomotor movement.)

Traveling while manipulating an object is used in a game setting.

Tasks/Challenges:

T Listen to the drumbeat. I'll beat a cadence of one, two, three, four, and then you'll clap the same. Listen. (Beat drum four times in even rhythm.) Now clap. Walking and running are both even rhythms. Let's try again. Listen; then clap.

T Let's walk the rhythm of the beat. Listen to the speed. (Beat four times in even rhythm, slowly.) Ready? Walk as I beat the drum. Clap as you walk.

T You'll need to walk more quickly or slowly now, depending on the beat of the drum. I'll pause between each segment so you can hear the change in tempo.

T Now run to the beat of the drum. It's an even rhythm but a faster speed. Be sure you listen for the beat. Ready, go.

Traveling in Confined Spaces

Setting: Large marker cones designating general space for travel; children scattered throughout this space

Cues	
Heads Up	(Keep your head up for good balance and to avoid collisions with others.)
Open Spaces	(Look for open spaces as you travel.)
Speed Check	(Slow your speed slightly to avoid others.)

Tasks/Challenges:

T For today's class, the area inside the cones is your city, and you cannot go out of the city until class is over. Travel throughout the city in any locomotor pattern you wish.

T This time, the city has begun to shrink and will keep doing so—so watch the cones. Begin to move the cones closer in as the children become more adept at moving without bumping into each other or falling down.

Traveling with Music

Setting: Children scattered throughout general space; music with appropriate even and uneven beats for different locomotor movements; hoops, one per child, at the edge of the space

Cues	
Heads Up	(Keep your head up for good balance and to avoid collisions with others.)
Balanced Stops	(Spread your feet apart and lower your hips slightly to maintain your balance when you stop.)

Tasks/Challenges:

T Walk, skip, gallop, or hop throughout general space without touching anyone else. Remember, you may have to move to the right or left to avoid bumping into someone else. When I give the signal, stop quickly with both your feet on the floor.

T I've selected music for each of our locomotor movements. The first is for skipping. Listen to the beat. Is it an even or uneven rhythm? Right, skipping is an uneven rhythm. Begin skipping when you hear the music. Stop when the music stops.

T Now listen to the music for the gallop; it's also uneven. (Pause, play music.) Ready? Gallop.

T The music for hopping is short and quick. Clap the rhythm. Is it even or uneven? Hop on one foot to the music.

T I've saved your favorite locomotor movement until last. What is it? Running. Run quietly so you'll hear the music stop.

Children tend to practice only their favorite locomotor skill when the task is open. We find it helps to specify each skill in addition to "your choice" or "your favorite."

T This is a game like musical chairs, except that you are never out. When the music begins, travel throughout general space using the traveling action that I call out. When the music stops, find a space inside a hoop as quickly as possible. Each time I will remove some of the hoops. The trick is that someone must be in every hoop, but any number of people can be inside the hoops as the number of hoops decreases.

Traveling an Obstacle Course

Setting: An obstacle course of hoops, bamboo poles, low beams, and other items (Figure 16.2)

Cues	
Heads Up	(Keep your head up for good balance and to avoid collisions with others.)
Pause, Look, Go	(Pause momentarily to avoid others who are also moving.)

Tasks/Challenges:

T You've worked on various locomotor skills and on moving with control. Using a combination of a hop, skip, gallop, leap, walk, and slide, move through the obstacle course without touching other people, the hoops, or the bamboo poles.

Traveling in Different Directions

Setting: Children scattered throughout general space

Cues	
Heads Up	(Keep your head up for good balance and to avoid collisions with others.)
Hips over Feet	(Keep your body centered over your feet for good balance and quick changes of direction.)

Tasks/Challenges:

T You have learned six directions. Let's name them together: forward, backward, right, left, up, and down. This time as you walk, run, or hop, change directions as you travel.

T Begin walking forward. On the signal, change directions and walk backward. Exaggerate your movements so you look like a toy soldier or robot.

T On the signal, run in a forward direction. When you hear the drum, slow your speed, and run to the side or backward. Take only a few steps; then continue running forward.

Figure 16.2 An obstacle course.

T Pretend you're going to draw a square with one foot. Hop forward, backward, to the right, and to the left to draw your square.

C This time, we will really see how well you can travel in different directions. I will call out a traveling action and a number. If the number is even, travel forward; if it is odd, travel backward.

Remember, do this task only with students who know the difference between odd and even numbers. It can be quite embarrassing for students not to know how to travel because of their math skills.

Slidestepping

Setting: Children scattered throughout general space

Cues	
Heads Up	(Keep your head up for good balance and to avoid collisions with others.)
Hips over Feet	(Keep your body centered over your feet for good balance and quick changes of direction.)

Tasks/Challenges:

T Use a sliding action (a slidestep) to travel toward the far end of the field. On the signal, change the direction of your slidestep.

T Using the slidestep, travel eight steps to the right, then eight steps to the left. Stop and balance on one foot. Repeat eight steps to the left, eight steps to the right. Stop and balance in a wide shape. This combination of travel and balances is the ingredients of the folk dance "Seven Jumps." Many folk dances use this slidestep.

C In a small group of four, six, or eight persons, use a combination of slidesteps and balances to create your own version of "Seven Jumps." Practice with your group until you are ready to show the dance to the class. We will then videotape the dances for your portfolios.

√ *Videotape/Digital Analysis.* With the establishment of criteria, video is an excellent means for assessing children's work. *Refer to Chapter 12 for details on checklists for use in observing critical cues.*

Traveling in Different Pathways

Setting: Children scattered throughout general space

Cues	
Heads Up	(Keep your head up for good balance and to avoid collisions with others.)
Hips over Feet	(Keep your body centered over your feet for good balance with changes in direction and/or pathways.)

Tasks/Challenges:

T A while ago you learned three different pathways. Who remembers what they were? That's right: straight, curved, and zigzag. This time, change your pathway as you travel. Begin by walking in a straight pathway. On the signal, change to a curved pathway. Exaggerate your movements so the pathway is really quite curved.

T This time, practice traveling in a zigzag pathway. Remember, zigzag looks like the letter Z; make really sharp angles.

T On the signal, begin traveling in a straight path. You may use any form of traveling you wish. When you hear the drum, change to another pathway. The next time you hear the drum, change your pathway again.

T This will be a test of how well you can travel using the different pathways. The game is like follow the leader. When I say "Go," find a partner whose skill in traveling is about the same as yours. Go. Now, the shorter one of you will be the first leader. You are to travel using any traveling action you like and as many different pathways as possible. The follower will try to copy your every move. But don't make it so hard that your follower can't possibly keep up with you. Make it a fun game. When you hear the signal, you must be able to stop without falling over or touching each other. After three times as a leader, switch positions.

Locomotors with Directions and Pathways: The Locomotors Dance

Setting: Class divided into groups of five to eight persons; paper and pencil for each group

Cues	
Heads Up	(Keep your head up for good balance and to avoid collisions with others.)
Hips over Feet	(Keep your body centered over your feet for good balance with changes in direction and/or pathways.)

Tasks/Challenges:

🅣 You have practiced hopping, skipping, galloping, sliding, leaping, and running. You have traveled in different directions and pathways. In your group, combine the locomotors with directions and pathways to create a dance of locomotors. You will need to decide:

- The amount of space you'll need
- Changes in leaders (with a special signal for changes)
- Which locomotors and what directions and pathways

When you have created your dance, record it on paper, and practice it several times; then we will watch them. The criteria for observation will be correct execution of the locomotors, cooperative work with your group, and creative ideas in the dance.

✔ *Event Tasks.* Children's dance projects can serve as events tasks and provide excellent assessments of student learning. *See Chapter 12 for establishing criteria and designing rubric guidelines.*

Locomotors and Rhythm: The Follow-Me Dance

Setting: Instrumental music with a strong beat (e.g., hoedown or country music); children scattered throughout general space, facing the teacher

Cues	
Heads Up	(Keep your head up for good balance and to avoid collisions with others.)
Hips over Feet	(Keep your body centered over your feet for good balance and quick changes of direction.)
Balanced Stops	(Spread your feet apart and lower your hips slightly to maintain your balance when you stop.)

Tasks/Challenges:

🅣 We're going to practice our locomotor skills today; we'll combine the skills with rhythm and keeping the beat in self-space. This is called Follow Me, country-western style. Spread throughout general space, facing me. I'll move to the right, the left, forward, and backward. You'll mirror my direction. So if I go left, you go right; if I go forward, you go backward. I'll hop, jump, gallop, slide, walk, and move in other ways. After each locomotor phrase, you'll stop in self-space and do such things as touch your hands to your heels, nod your

head forward and backward, cross your knees as in a Charleston, and so on. You only need to watch and follow me.

Keep all activities in a count of eight—for example, eight slides to the left, eight slides to the right, stop, touch hands to heels in time with the music; one, two, three, four, five, six, seven, eight; gallop forward eight steps, gallop backward eight steps, stop, clap hands in time with the music: one, two, three, four, five, six, seven, eight.

Traveling at Different Speeds

Setting: Sheets of newspapers stacked at the edge of the gymnasium; children scattered throughout general space

Cues	
Heads Up	(Keep your head up for good balance and to avoid collisions with others.)
Pause and Go	(Check your speed slightly to avoid others.)

Tasks/Challenges:

🅣 Each of you will need one sheet of newspaper. After you get your sheet, unfold it and place it against your chest, holding it at your shoulders. At the signal, begin running; you'll no longer have to hold your newspaper. What will happen to the newspaper when you stop running? Ready, go.

🅣 Try running at different speeds, sometimes very fast, sometimes very slowly, to see if the paper will stay up.

Traveling Using Different Directions, Levels, Pathways, and Locations

Setting: Several sets of task cards: one set that names single locomotor actions (e.g., walk, run, or hop); a second set that names different directions; a third set that names different levels; a fourth set that names different locations (general and self-space); and a final set that names different pathways. It is helpful to color-code the different sets.

Cues	
Heads Up	(Keep your head up for good balance and to avoid collisions with others.)
Hips over Feet	(Keep your body centered over your feet for good balance with changes in direction and/or pathways.)

Tasks/Challenges:

T Choose a card from each color (stack), and return to your self-space. You are going to travel using the directions on the cards you have. For example, if your cards say "Walk," "Backward," "Low," and "General Space," you walk backward at a low level in general space.

T This time, change one card of the same color with the person next to you. Now move according to the new directions.

The combinations here are endless. You could trade as many cards as you like until the children have practiced a multitude of combinations.

C With the last set of cards that you have, practice the action until you think it is so clear that anyone could figure it out just by watching you. (Give children time to practice.) Now, when I say "Go," choose a partner whom you can work with well. Go. Show your partner your sequence, and see whether he or she can guess what your cards said. Now, switch: Watch your partner's sequence, and you guess.

✓ *Peer Assessment.* Sharing sequences with partners can be an excellent peer assessment. *See Chapter 12 for establishing criteria and designing rubrics.*

Changing Speeds to Music

Setting: Recordings of music with increasing and decreasing speeds; children scattered throughout general space

Cues

Heads Up	(Keep your head up for good balance and to avoid collisions with others.)
Speed Check	(Slow your speed slightly to avoid others.)
Balanced Stops	(Spread your feet apart and lower your hips slightly to maintain your balance when you stop.)

Tasks/Challenges:

T Listen to the music; it will start slowly and gradually increase in speed to a faster tempo. Do you think you can run with a gradual increase and decrease in your speed? Match your running speed with the music. Begin slowly, and gradually increase to your fastest speed; as the music begins to slow, decrease your speed to a jogging pace.

Traveling with Changes in Speed: A Dance of Water, Steam, and Ice

Setting: Children scattered throughout general space

Cues

Pause and Go	(Pause between actions to emphasize changes.)
Exaggerate	(Exaggerate movements and shapes for emphasis.)

Tasks/Challenges:

T Let's think about how water changes form as the temperature changes. At normal temperature, water is a liquid whose molecules are moving at a medium speed. As the temperature increases, the water molecules move faster and faster until the water is transformed into steam. As the temperature decreases, the molecules move more and more slowly until they finally freeze, forming ice. Let's put this story into a creative dance. As I tell the story, you'll travel with changes in speed as the molecules increase their speed, decrease their speed, and freeze.

Traveling in Slow-Motion: The Sports Dance

Setting: Children scattered throughout general space

Cues

Pause and Go	(Pause between actions to emphasize changes.)
Exaggerate	(Exaggerate movements and shapes for emphasis.)

Tasks/Challenges:

T Think about how the players move when a film is shown in slow motion or when the sports announcer replays a special segment from a game. I want each of you to think of your favorite moment in a sport. Is it when the quarterback breaks away to run for a touchdown, or was it when you scored the winning soccer goal? Perhaps it was the throw of the javelin at the Olympics or the relay team running at the track meet. Decide what kind of locomotor movement would portray your favorite moment. Combine your movements as in a slow-motion replay. How would you begin—in what position? How will the replay end? Practice the segment until you can do it three times the same way, just like a replay. Remember, it's slow motion. We'll look at the movements when you're ready.

Box 16-8

The Grapevine Step

The grapevine step is used in many line dances, as well as in intermediate folk dances; it may be done to the right or to the left. Children enjoy combining it with forward and backward steps and turns to create new dances.

Cue: Front, Side, Back, Side

Count 1: Cross right foot over in front of left foot.
Count 2: Step to left on left foot.
Count 3: Cross right foot behind left foot.
Count 4: Step to left on left foot.

The Grapevine Step

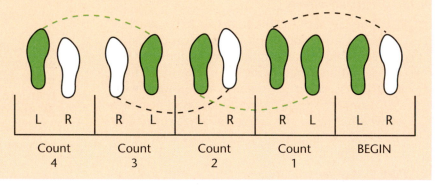

L R	R L	L R	R L	L R
Count 4	Count 3	Count 2	Count 1	BEGIN

Other ideas for creative dance and travel include walking through a thick jungle, walking through a completely dark and haunted house, walking on the ledge of a 10-story building, traveling across a high wire on a windy day, traveling during an earthquake.

Combination Locomotors

Line dances, as well as traditional folk and square dances, are combinations of locomotor skills and nonlocomotor body actions. Although there are excellent resources available for the teaching of such dances (see Chapter 28, Box 28-3), we encourage our students—and you as teachers—to create new line, square, and folk dances. See Boxes 16-8 and 16-9.

Utilization Level (GLSP): Learning Experiences Leading to Skill Development

At the utilization level children combine travel with other skills and concepts in preparation for their application in the contexts of dance, game, and gymnastics. Most of the tasks focus on traveling with a variety of movement concepts and traveling with partners and in small group situations., e.g., matching traveling pathways with a partner, maintaining position beside

or behind a partner while traveling and changing speeds, and the exaggeration of actions for expressive movements.

A note about cues: Although several cues are listed for many of the learning experiences, it's important to focus on only one cue at a time. This way, the children can really concentrate on that cue. Once you provide feedback to the children and observe that most have learned a cue, it's time to focus on another one.

Traveling with a Partner: Matching Pathways

Setting: Sets of partners scattered throughout general space

Cue

Heads Up (Keep your head up for good balance and to avoid collisions with others.)

Tasks/Challenges:

Ⓣ Stand back to back with a partner. When I say "Go," each partner travels in the direction he or she is facing. That is, each of you travels away from your partner. When you hear the drum, stop, turn around, and return to your partner with the exact

Box 16-9

The Margie Dance

Description

This dance was choreographed as an attribute to Margie Hanson for her contributions to children's dance and physical education.

Music

"I'd Like to Teach the World to Sing," Metromedia KMD1051.

Formation

Lines

Counts and Steps

1–2—Introduction, sway with body or hands.
3–4—Hands in air and sway to the right, left, right, and left.
5–8—Walk to right and give a high-five greeting on step 8.
1–4—Walk to left and give a high-five greeting on step 4.
5–8—Hands in air and sway to the right, left, right, and left.
1–4—Join and raise hands.
5–8—Lower hands.
1–4—"Thank you" in sign language (see illustration), two times.
5–8—"I love you" in sign language (hold two middle fingers down and keep pinky, index finger, and thumb up) and raise hands.

Repeat dance three more times. At the end, hug your neighbors in this world and give them some N and Gs, which means tell them some nice and good things.

"Thank you" in sign language

Source: J.C. Bennett and P.C. Riemer, *Rhythmic activities and dance* (Champaign, IL: Human Kinetics, 2006), pp. 111–12. With permission from John P. Bennett.

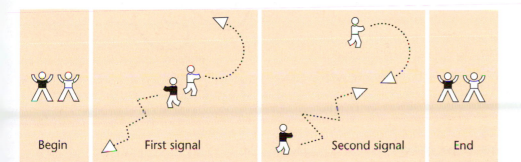

| Begin | First signal | Second signal | End |

Figure 16.3 Traveling in pathways away from and toward a partner.

pattern and locomotor movements you used before (Figure 16.3). Return at the same speed you used to travel away from your partner.

Earlier you learned there are three pathways. (See Chapter 13, "Space Awareness.") What are they? *(Ask for answers.)* All patterns are made up of those pathways or combinations of those pathways. This time as you travel away from your partner, be aware of the pathways you use. On your return, copy the same pathways.

Stand beside your partner. This time as you travel, use a slidestep to move away from your partner. Remember, return using the same pathway.

Select a partner, and decide who is to be the first leader. When the follower says "Go," the leader travels across the field with a combination of

Box 16-10

Designing Floor Patterns for Dance

The floor patterns created in dance experiences and the loco-motor movements used are important components of creative dance. The patterns created as the dancer moves can tell a story, set a mood, or portray an idea. The various ways of travel used in dance and the patterns created aren't accidental; they're planned and carefully designed. When designing the travel pattern of a dance, teacher and children can focus upon the following concerns:

- What idea stimulated the dance? Was it a music selection? An action movie? A wiggly snake?
- What qualities are inherent in the theme of the dance or the music selection? Is the tempo slow, moderate, or fast? Is the rhythm even or uneven? Is the music harmonious? Vibrant? Mellow?
- What pathway best expresses the feelings or emotions you sense? Advancing, attacking? Retreating? Collapsing? Gathering? Departing? Wavy? Angular, jagged?

It's a good idea to have the children keep notes and diagram their pathways as they design them, for several reasons. First, they will clearly visualize what the floor pattern looks like and be better able to evaluate its suitability for the dance. Second, children usually use several classes to put together a completed dance and often fail to remember ideas they had in earlier classes. Third, when children finish a dance, they can add the written work to their portfolios.

It's often beneficial to post several examples of pathways around the room on the walls, to give children an idea of what's expected. Another effective teaching aid is to post drawings of locomotor skills and positions of stillness that the children have experienced. Rather than trying to diagram a sequence from memory, youngsters can look at these posters and select movements to incorporate along their floor patterns.

Zigzag path   Straight path

Curved path

straight, curved, and zigzag pathways. When the leader stops, the follower then travels the same pattern. The other partner then designs the pattern. (For tips on helping children learn to design floor patterns for dance, see Box 16-10)

Traveling with a Partner: Copying Locomotors and Directions

Setting: Music, such as "Dueling Banjos," that features copy phrases; sets of partners scattered throughout general space

Cue

Heads Up (Keep your head up for good balance and to avoid collisions with others.)

Tasks/Challenges:

T Earlier this year you practiced traveling with a partner, copying pathways. This time you will copy not only pathways with your partner, but also locomotors and directions in a dance called "The Copy Cat." For your beginning, you may choose to stand beside or behind your partner.

Partner A will travel away from partner B as the first phrase of music plays; partner B will then travel with the exact pattern and locomotor. The dance continues as one partner leads and the other copies. Listen to the phrases of the music to time the length of your travel.

✓ *Event Task.* Creative dance projects provide event tasks that are excellent assessments of children's work. The above task could easily be made into an event task by having students write out their dance and perform it for someone else. *See Chapter 12 for the development of rubrics to accompany event tasks.*

Traveling with a Partner: Changing Speed and Direction

Setting: Sets of partners scattered throughout general space

> **Cues**
>
> **Heads Up** (Keep your head up for good balance and to avoid collisions with others.)
>
> **On Your Toes** (Keep your weight on the balls of your feet for quickness.)

Tasks/Challenges:

T Stand facing a partner approximately 3 feet apart: One of you is the leader; the other is the follower. The leader slides to the right or left, changing directions quickly. The follower tries to stay directly across from the leader at all times. I'll give the signal every 60 seconds for you both to switch positions. *Note that by adding dribbling a ball and defensive arm position to this pattern, we form an offensive–defensive drill in basketball.*

Shadowing a Partner's Travel

Setting: Sets of partners scattered throughout general space

> **Cues**
>
> **Heads Up** (Keep your head up for good balance and to avoid collisions with others.)
>
> **On Your Toes** (Keep your weight on the balls of your feet for quickness.)

Tasks/Challenges:

T Choose a partner whose speed and ability to change directions are very similar to yours. Partner 1 stands approximately 2 feet behind partner 2. When I say "Go," partner 2 travels quickly, changing directions with sharp turns to the right and to the left; partner 1 attempts to stay within an arm's distance at all times. When you hear the drumbeat, stop without colliding or losing your balance. Partner 1 now stands in front, ready to be the new leader. Keep your eyes on your partner's waist when you're the follower.

Meeting and Parting While Traveling with a Partner

Setting: Sets of partners scattered throughout general space

> **Cue**
>
> **Heads Up** (Keep your head up for good balance and to avoid collisions with others.)

Tasks/Challenges:

T This task is called Leapin' Lizards. On the signal, you are to travel throughout the general space. On the cue "Leapin' Lizards," find a partner as quickly as possible, travel side by side for a few steps, then leap in unison and split up to continue traveling using the new pattern I call out. The next time you hear the signal, find a new partner, travel and do two leaps, then split to travel in a new way. We will continue until the number of leaps gets to five.

T This time, instead of partners, find a group of three whenever you hear the cue. Make sure all of you leap at the same time. With a larger group it is harder to coordinate your leaps. It might help if one person calls out "One, two, three, leap."

Performing Rhythmical Patterns

Setting: Hoops, one per child, scattered throughout general space

> **Cues**
>
> **Heads Up** (Keep your head up for good balance.)
>
> **Soft Landings** (Bend your knees for a soft landing.)

Tasks/Challenges:

T Jump in and out of your hoop with a four-four rhythm: two jumps in, two jumps out, or three jumps in, one jump out. Maintain an even tempo by clapping the four counts as you jump.

I'll clap the rhythm I want you to use for your jumps: one, two, three, four. Let's all clap the rhythm together before we begin our jumps. (Group practices with teacher as leader.)

C Practice until you can match the rhythm three times with no mistakes.

T Try your jumping pattern in and out of the hoop with the music. Remember, you may choose a three-one or a two-two pattern in and out.

Folk/Cultural Dances

Folk/cultural dances are combinations of locomotors—combinations into specific steps, changes in directions, and partner/group formations. See Chapter 28, "Teaching Dance," for the teaching of folk/cultural dance in elementary physical education.

Traveling to Tell a Story: The Fountain of Youth Dance

Setting: Children scattered throughout general space

Cue

Exaggerate (Exaggerate your actions and gestures for expression.)

Tasks/Challenges:

T Using combinations of locomotor movements, body language, and gestures, tell the story of an old, old person who discovers the Fountain of Youth. Let me set the stage for you. An old, old person is walking down the street. The person feels weary, tired, without enough energy to hold his or her head high. While walking down the street, the oldster sees a bottle in a gutter. An examination of the bottle reveals the words Fountain of Youth Juice. Puzzled, hesitant, yet desperate, the oldster takes a drink and then a few more. The transformation begins. The old person is changed into an ecstatic youth who dances merrily down the street. Think of the following as you prepare your dance:

What type of movements would the old person use? Jerky or smooth? Slow or fast?
What body posture and what hand gestures would the old person assume?
How would the oldster approach the bottle?
Would the transformation occur quickly or be rather slowly executed?

How would you contrast the oldster's movements with those of the ecstatic youth: type of travel, speed, level, gestures?

Dance that tells a story can easily become only pantomime. Children will need guidance in avoiding exactly replicating gestures and using more total body movement and space.

Traveling in Bound and Free Flow

Setting: Children scattered throughout general space

Cues

Exaggerate (Exaggerate your actions and gestures for expression.)
Free Flow (Unstoppable from beginning to end.)
Bound Flow (Jerky; stoppable at any moment.)

Tasks/Challenges:

T Here are two additional ideas for short dance phrases based on imaginary situations. First, a rag doll comes to life for a brief time. One interpretation is that the rag doll slowly comes to life with jerky, uncoordinated (bound) movements, falls over, and has trouble gaining control and balance; the doll gradually improves and is then running and leaping, turning in the air (free), and enjoying life. Then the doll suddenly stops, slowly walks back to the starting location, sits and sighs, freezes, and is a doll once again.

T Second, a balloon filled with helium escapes from the hands of its owner, floats across the sky, leaks, and falls back to earth.

These types of dance experiences are often short, culminating the practice of travel patterns. Discuss with children the travel qualities and movement concepts (space awareness, effort) appropriate for each activity. Each dance should have a clear beginning, rise to a climax, and then wind down to a conclusion.

Proficiency Level (GLSP): Learning Experiences Leading to Skill Development

At the proficiency level, learning experiences are designed to encourage youngsters to use their travel skills and knowledge of travel patterns in combination with other skills to design and perform dances, gymnastics routines, and strategic game maneuvers.

In games, they use effective travel skills and strategic pathways, reacting quickly to a batted ball by charging forward, to the left or right, to collect a ground ball and throw accurately to a teammate; using fakes and quick changes of direction to lose an opponent while dribbling;

running a planned pass pattern to receive a ball a team-mate throws. See Chapters 22–26.

In gymnastics, they combine travel patterns with the skills of jumping and landing, balancing, and transferring weight to create gymnastics sequences on the floor and on apparatus. See Chapters 18–21.

In dance, experiences become increasingly complex with the number of movement concepts, the combinations of locomotor patterns, the use of space, shapes and nonlocomotor actions.

A note about cues: Tasks are more complex at the proficiency level, typically requiring children to coordinate several movements simultaneously in a dynamic context. A list of cues is provided to assist the children in being more successful in the learning experience. The challenge for the teacher is in determining which cue will be most beneficial for each child . . . and when. Thus careful observation and critical reflection are important as you watch the children move and then decide which cue will be the most helpful to move each learner to a higher skill level.

Traveling with Shapes and Actions: A Story Without Words

Setting: Class divided into two groups

Tasks/Challenges:

T Dance can be a story without words. You're going to tell the story of primitive tribes through shapes and actions. (Show children cave drawings of tribal dances.) Use your imagination as you look at the drawings. How do you think these people lived? What was their work? What was home like for them—did they have a home? Now let's put your ideas into movement terms. At what level would the people move? Would their movements be flowing or sustained, jerky or smooth?

Your dance will tell the story of two primitive tribes. Part 1 of your dance will show how the people live as a group. Show through your movements and gestures the life of a person in a primitive tribe. Part 2 of your dance will portray the two tribes discovering each other, their fear of the unknown, and their battle to defend their territory. In Part 2, each group begins with the movements portraying preparation for battle. The battle will consist of approach, attack (with no contact), and a retreat.

The following questions will help you design your movements for this dance story:

- Will your travel be fast or slow when preparing for battle, approaching the enemy, retreating from the battle?
- How can your gestures best represent the punching, jabbing, kicking, slashing actions of battle?
- Will your travel be low, with angular actions, or high and smooth?
- As you retreat from battle, how will your travel show caution, fear, injury?

Body Shapes and Group Travel: A Study in Form

Setting: Class divided into two groups

Tasks/Challenges:

T Dance doesn't always tell a story. Sometimes dance is a study in form—the shapes we can make with our bodies, the spatial patterns we create as a group. Group 1 will represent tradition. Use your body shapes and group travel to show the characteristics of tradition—for example, a firm, solid shape, such as a square group, formed by the identical and simultaneous group movements; use of a small amount of space; and firm, sustained quality—control at all times.

Group 2 will represent the forces of change. The characteristics of change include individualized shapes, travel in different directions, use of a large amount of space, and a variety of movements. Working together as a group, design a dance that combines at least five shapes and three locomotor patterns to portray the characteristics of your group.

When we look at the tradition group, we should see oneness, sturdiness, caution; the shapes and actions of the change group should portray individuality, risk taking, and freedom.

√ *Videotape.* Videotaping dances for future analysis, accompanied by a written description with established criteria and rubric, would be an excellent summative assessment.

Performing Rhythmical Patterns: Tinikling

Setting: Sets of tinikling poles, approximately 12 feet in length, either made from bamboo poles or purchased commercially. Each set of poles will accommodate four children—two for tapping the poles and two for jumping (Figure 16.4). In its traditional form, tinikling is performed with a 3/4 rhythm, with the poles tapping "out, out, in" and the dancers performing "in, in, out." We have found a 4/4 rhythm to be much easier for children first learning the activity.

Cues	
Weight Balanced over Poles	(Keep your shoulders and hips over the poles.)
Feet In, In, Out, Out	(Your feet go inside, inside the poles, then outside, outside the poles.)

Figure 16.4 Basic tinikling setup.

Tasks/Challenges:

T Tinikling is a rhythmical activity that involves coordinated stepping, hopping, and jumping actions with the tapping of long bamboo poles. In the beginning position, the bamboo poles are approximately 2 feet apart; they're tapped down on the floor twice: tap, tap. The poles are then brought together for two counts: tap, tap. This pattern is repeated: apart, apart, together, together. This opening and closing position is maintained while dancers step or jump in and out without touching the poles. Let's do the action of the poles with our hands; clap the rhythm with me: out, out, in, in. (Demonstrate with your hands apart, apart, together, together.) This is the action of the bamboo poles for all our tinikling skills: out, out, in, in.

T Divide into groups of four. Two people clap the 4/4 rhythm; the other two people practice the tapping action with the poles.

We find it helps to tape the ends of the poles where the children grip them to prevent the bamboo poles from cracking and pinching the children's fingers.

T You now know how to clap the 4/4 rhythm and to tap the bamboo poles to that rhythm. Now you'll learn the basic single-step pattern.

Stand on your left foot; hop two times on your left foot. Step on your right foot between the lines; transfer your weight to your left foot between the lines. Hop on your right foot two times outside the lines. Repeat the action to the left. Clap the 4/4 beat as you hop.

Figure 16.5 shows the single-step pattern. Have the children stand outside the parallel tape lines on the floor. Their right sides should be toward the tape lines.

Count 1—Hop on left foot outside poles

Count 2—Hop again on left foot outside poles

Count 3—Hop on right foot between poles

Count 4—Hop again on right foot between poles

Count 1—Hop on left foot outside poles (other side)

Count 2—Hop again on left foot outside poles

Count 3—Hop on right foot between poles

Count 4—Hop again on right foot between poles

Figure 16.5 Tinikling: single-step pattern.

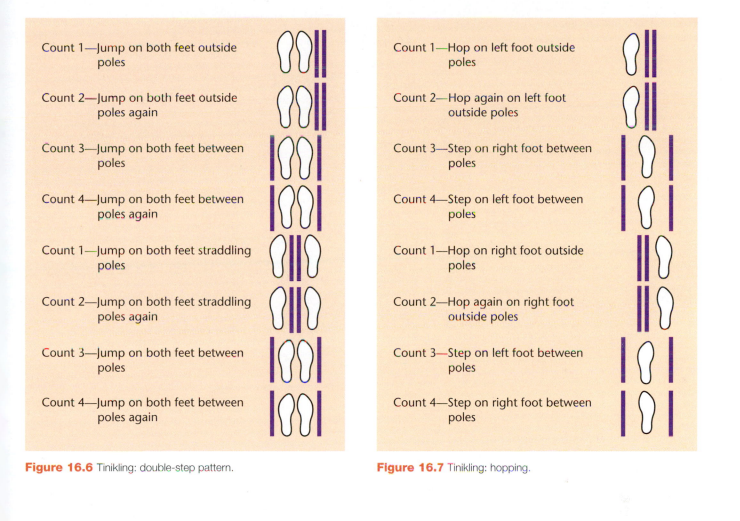

Figure 16.6 Tinikling: double-step pattern.

Figure 16.7 Tinikling: hopping.

C Practice until you can perform the pattern four times with no mistakes. You'll then be ready to practice the single-step pattern with two people tapping the poles. Remember, your feet go in, in, out, out while the poles go out, out, in, in.

T After you feel comfortable with the single-step pattern, try the double-step or the hopping pattern (Figures 16.6 and 16.7). When you're really good, you can create a new pattern with a four-four or three-four beat.

Students with advanced tinikling skills enjoy the action with four poles—two poles crossed over two poles—and the combination of basic tinikling actions with gymnastics stunts—for example, cartwheels and walkovers between the poles as they move apart.

Traveling in Games and Sports

The ability to travel in games is often what separates the skilled player from the average player. Many children can throw and catch accurately and with control while they're stationary, but they regress to a precontrol level when travel is added. Thus, traveling is an important part of the utilization and proficiency sections of the games skills chapters. Games-related tasks that incorporate traveling are discussed in Chapter 17, "Chasing, Fleeing, and Dodging," and in Chapters 22 through 26: "Kicking and Punting," "Throwing and Catching," "Volleying and Dribbling," "Striking with Rackets and Paddles," and "Striking with Long-Handled Implements," respectively.

Traveling in Gymnastics

Traveling in gymnastics supplies the buildup of force necessary for step and spring takeoffs when transferring weight on mats and onto equipment, as well as for many Olympic stunts (Figure 16.8). The floor patterns the travel creates form an important component of gymnastics routines. Travel in relation to gymnastics is discussed in Chapters 19, 20, and 21: "Jumping and Landing," "Balancing," and "Transferring Weight and Rolling," respectively.

Figure 16.8 Children's travel patterns in gymnastics.

Leah, Missy, Heather, Sheri

1. Curved to start
   - come up and cartwheel one at a time
2. Turn and Roll.
3. Turn and ½ split
4. Get up and cartwheel
5. Neal down and roll
6. Jump up - Run and Leap.
7. Run - cartwheel - Run
8. Run a little and Leap
9. End two go out 10 steps and turn
   Cartwheel into pair - Curl-up and end.

Reading Comprehension Questions

1. What components of traveling are taught in a program of physical education for children?
2. What does "naturally developing skill" mean? List two examples.
3. List the fundamental locomotor skills. Why are these skills important for children?
4. Describe a mature running pattern. Do all children have mature running patterns? Do all adults? Explain.
5. What are the differences between a hop, a leap, a slide, and a gallop?
6. Describe how travel is studied at the proficiency level in games, gymnastics, and dance.
7. What is tinikling?

References/Suggested Readings

Bennett, J. P., and P. C. Riemer. 2006. *Rhythmic activities and dance*, 111–12. Champaign, IL: Human Kinetics. Used with permission from John P. Bennett.

[NASPE] National Association for Sport and Physical Education. 1995. *Moving into the future: National standards for physical education*. St. Louis, MO: Mosby.

[NASPE] National Association for Sport and Physical Education. 2004. *Moving into the future: National standards for physical education*. 2nd ed. Reston, VA: National Association for Sport and Physical Education.

Wickstrom, R. L. 1977. *Fundamental motor patterns*. 2nd ed. Philadelphia: Lea & Febiger.

Chasing, Fleeing, and Dodging

Since ancient times, children have delighted in countless chasing, fleeing, and dodging games. These games all challenge children to evade a chasing player through dodging and fleeing. Such sports as basketball, hockey, soccer, and football are simply more elaborate forms of these games using the same elements. Physical education programs can build on the innate pleasure children experience from playing these games. By providing a variety of challenging tasks and game situations, a teacher can help youngsters develop chasing, fleeing, and dodging skills (see our skill progression development on this page).

Skill Theme Development Progression

Chasing, Fleeing, Dodging

Proficiency Level

Self-designed chasing, fleeing, and dodging game
Dodging while manipulating an object in an invasion gamelike situation
Using team strategy for chasing, fleeing, and dodging in an invasion gamelike situation
Dodging in a target gamelike situation
Dodging in a gamelike situation
Chasing and fleeing in an invasion gamelike situation
Chasing and dodging simultaneously
Dodging while maintaining possession of an object
Continual fleeing and chasing with a large group

Utilization Level

Dodging while manipulating an object
Dodging in a dynamic situation
Dodging and chasing one person in a mass
Dodging semistationary obstacles
Dodging and faking moves to avoid a chaser
Dodging stationary obstacles

Control Level

Fleeing a chaser
Overtaking a fleeing person
Dodging with quick changes of direction
Dodging the obstacles
Fleeing from a partner
Dodging in response to a signal

Precontrol Level

Make-believe chase
Traveling to dodge
Traveling to flee
Moving obstacles

Experience suggests that it's best to focus on chasing, fleeing, and dodging skills after children have developed a working understanding of space awareness concepts and have mastered fundamental traveling skills. In reality, chasing, fleeing, and dodging are an advanced combination of traveling skills combined with the refined use of effort, space, and relationship concepts and often requiring the manipulation of an object. Therefore the use of chasing, fleeing, and dodging will often appear in the traveling chapter (Chapter 16) and the manipulative skill themes (Chapters 22–26). In this chapter our purpose is to focus on the skills in some isolation before applying them in more complex situations.

Chasing, fleeing, and dodging tasks and games using these skills are best played outdoors in large, grassy areas. Refer to Box 17-1 for linkages between the skill theme of chasing, fleeing, and dodging and *National Standards for Physical Education.*

Chasing

Chasing is traveling quickly to overtake or tag a fleeing person. In many game situations, the fleeing player is given a head start and allowed time to run away before the chaser can begin traveling. The fleeing player tries to avoid being caught or tagged. Thus the chaser needs to be able to run at full speed and to react quickly to changes in the direction of the fleeing player's travel.

Fleeing

Fleeing may be considered the antithesis of chasing as it involves traveling quickly away from a pursuing person or object. In most game situations, the fleeing person tries to keep as much distance as possible between himself or herself and the chaser. When the pursuer does close in, the fleeing player uses any maneuver possible to avoid being tagged—the fleeing person dodges, changes direction quickly, or runs full speed. This continual demand on the fleeing player to react quickly to emerging, uncertain situations is what makes tag games such thrilling activities for children.

Dodging

Dodging is the skill of quickly moving the body in a direction other than the original line of movement. This includes any maneuver a person undertakes to avoid being touched by a chasing person. Dodging may occur while a person is fleeing or stationary. Effective dodging actions include quick fakes, twisting, and stretching.

Levels of Skill Proficiency

We've found that most school-age children are familiar with a variety of tag and dodging games. But some youngsters whose chasing, fleeing, and dodging skills are at the precontrol or control level of proficiency have limited success in playing these games; that is, although many children can chase, flee, and dodge, they can't perform these skills effectively in dynamic game situations. In a game of tag, for instance, the child doing the chasing is often unable to overtake or tag any of the fleeing players and quickly tires of playing the game. In their classic study of children's games, Iona and Peter Opie (1969) noted that chasing games were often plagued with arguments and ended prematurely in heated disputes.

Many utilization and proficiency-level activities incorporate dynamic and often gamelike tasks in the development of chasing, fleeing, and dodging skills. Because of the nature of the skills themselves, the use of dynamic gamelike activities may be more prevalent here than with other skill themes, and the tasks may initially look and sound more like "traditional" games. Look closely beyond the name. All the tasks involve small-sided groups in reduced spaces and are designed to help children develop and subsequently apply the skills of chasing, fleeing, and dodging. The tasks should be used as an integral part of the lesson, after the prerequisite skills are developed, not just as an activity to do. As noted, many of these experiences involve the use of groups. The groups recommended here are of small sizes and can usually be designed by having children form their own groups. See Box 8-4 (in Chapter 8) for tips on partner and group formation.

Children are inherently attracted to chasing, fleeing, and dodging activities, and it is easy for us and the children to get caught up in the excitement and lose sight of the quality of the movement. Children can't continue these intense activities for long periods without tiring, which is almost always accompanied by a deterioration in quality. It is best to pursue these skills for short periods.

A note about dodgeball, which was actually included in the first edition of *Children Moving*. Over the past 30 years our knowledge of child growth and development has expanded exponentially, and as a result, practices have changed. Consequently, we eliminated all dodgeball activities from the development of dodging skills. A number of factors influenced this decision. From a psychological perspective, we believe that throwing an object at another person, with the intent of hitting the person, subtly supports violence and goes against all that we know and believe about appropriate practice (NASPE 2009; Williams 1992; see Box 17-2). From a safety standpoint, the risk of detached retinas, as well as other serious head injuries, is extreme in dodgeball (regardless of the type of ball used). From a transfer perspective, we know of no sport that utilizes the skill of throwing at a human being. From a legal perspective, many states have already banned dodgeball from schools (check yours).

If you are a physical education major reading this book, you are probably thinking, "I loved dodgeball"

Box 17-2

Dodgeball in *Appropriate Instructional Practice Guidelines for Elementary School Physical Education*

Appropriate Instructional Practice Guidelines for Elementary School Physical Education, under the safety aspect of the learning environment, identifies dodgeball as an inappropriate practice. Their statement, "Human target games (dodgeball) and/or drills that allow aggressive behavior to other students are permitted," **reflects what should not happen in physical education classes.** The appropriate practice is, "Activities are selected carefully to ensure that they match students' ability and are safe for all students, regardless of ability level."

Source: National Association for Sport and Physical Education, *Appropriate instructional practice guidelines for elementary school physical education*, 3rd ed. (Reston, VA: National Association for Sport and Physical Education, 2009), 10.

and that it was "really fun." For you it was because you were the skilled player. If you are an elementary education major reading this, you are probably joyous that it has been eliminated. It is important to remember that physical education is for all students, not just the skilled. There are aspects of dodgeball we all like—the intrigue, the fast pace, the challenge—and we encourage you to redesign activities to keep these aspects while removing the aspects that are counterproductive. For more information about redesigned games, see Chapter 30, "Teaching Games," or *Teaching Physical Activity: Change, Challenge, Choice* by Jim Stiehl, Don Morris, and Christina Sinclair (2007).

Precontrol Level (GLSP): Activities for Exploration

In school situations in which preschool youngsters' opportunities to play with other children are limited; a teacher may need to provide precontrol-level chasing, fleeing, and dodging activities. These activities are designed to help children explore the skills of chasing, fleeing, and dodging in simple situations, such as:

- Running as fast as possible from one location to another
- Traveling around a room and changing the direction of travel quickly when a signal is sounded
- When a signal is given, quickly performing a designated dodging maneuver
- Running as fast as possible away from a partner; on the signal, running quickly toward a partner

Before beginning any practice with this theme, children should be at the control level of traveling and have had ample practice with space awareness.

⚠ When working with chasing, fleeing, and dodging activities that involve a finish line, be certain the line is far away from any obstructions. This precaution allows the children to run through the finish line at full speed safely.

Moving Obstacles

Setting: Children scattered in general space

Tasks/Challenges:

Ⓣ At the signal, travel in general space. Make sure you look up so you can avoid collisions with others.

Ⓣ This time make your travel faster but still avoid others.

Have half the children move to one side of the room and half to the other.

Ⓣ On the signal, both lines will try to walk to the opposite side of the room without touching anyone else.

Ⓣ This time, travel with three body parts touching the floor. Still no touching.

Ⓣ Now you will cross the space using different levels. Everyone who has blue eyes will travel with his or her body parts high in the air; those with brown eyes should travel at a low level; those with green or gray eyes, at a medium level.

Ⓣ This time you can choose any way you wish to travel, but go at a medium speed.

Ⓣ Try jogging or running, if you feel ready.

Ⓒ You have 10 points to start; subtract 1 point for every collision. Try to end with all 10 points.

Begin slowly. Have children walk. Gradually increase speed as you observe the children traveling competently and without collisions.

⚠ Because of the exciting nature of chasing, fleeing, and dodging activities, children's speed tends to increase, sometimes to unsafe levels. Monitor the speed of activities, always reminding children that they must be able to stop and change directions without falling. They should be able to tag someone without pushing.

Traveling to Flee

Setting: All children spread out in a space (an outside grassy space is best) about 20 yards by 20 yards

Tasks/Challenges:

Ⓣ You've all played games in which you had to run away from someone who was chasing you. This time you are going to have an imaginary chaser. On the signal, practice fleeing from your chaser by walking very quickly. On the next signal, stop. Remember, everyone is moving, so look up.

Ⓣ This time, practice fleeing your chaser by running.

Ⓒ How fast can you move to get away from your chaser?

Traveling to Dodge

Setting: Carpet squares or spots, hoops, milk jugs, or ropes spread out on the floor as obstacles

Tasks/Challenges:

Ⓣ On the signal, travel around the general space without touching anyone else or any of the objects on the floor. Be sure to keep your head up so you can avoid collisions.

C How many different ways can you find to avoid the obstacles?

T This time try to go as fast as you can with no collisions and avoiding all the objects.

Make-Believe Chase

Setting: Children spread out in general space

Tasks/Challenges:

T On the signal, try to catch your make-believe partner. Your partner is very quick, so you will really have to work hard to catch him or her. Remember, everyone is chasing, so look up to avoid collisions.

T This time, you will chase your dog, which got off its leash. You want to catch your dog before it gets to the street.

★ What are the differences among chasing, fleeing, and dodging?

Control Level: (GLSP) Learning Experiences Leading to Skill Development

Children who can competently perform a variety of quick, dodging maneuvers while running fast are at the control level. Challenging control-level tasks have children keep their eyes focused on a target child and react quickly to that child's movements by chasing, fleeing from, or dodging the target child. Such tasks include:

- Staying as close as possible to a fleeing, dodging partner
- Chasing after a person who has been given a slight head start and is fleeing
- Trying to run across a field while dodging one or more chasers

These learning experiences are designed to allow children to practice chasing, fleeing, and dodging in relatively static situations. Often chasing, fleeing, and dodging are combined with only a single other variable.

A note about cues: Although several cues are listed for many of the learning experiences, it's important to focus on only one cue at a time. This way, the children can concentrate on that cue. Once you provide feedback to the children and observe that most have learned a cue, it's time to focus on another one.

Dodging in Response to a Signal

Setting: Children scattered in general space

> **Cues**
>
> **Fake**   (Step/lean one way; go the other.)
> **Split Second** (Make your moves quicker than the speed of light.)

Tasks/Challenges:

T Now you're going to become really sneaky. As you travel throughout the general space, when you hear the signal, pretend you are going in one direction and then quickly change and go in a different direction.

T This time, whenever you hear the signal, try not to let anyone know which direction you'll travel; try to fake them out.

T Now, instead of me giving you the signal, you'll fake on your own. Whenever you come to another person, pretend you're going to go one way, but go another. Really try to confuse the other person so he or she doesn't know where you'll be going. Make your move quickly once you decide which way you're going.

C See if you can travel and dodge for 20 seconds without colliding with anyone.

Fleeing from a Partner

Setting: Partners about 10 feet apart

> **Cue**
>
> **Split Second** (Make your moves quicker than the speed of light.)

Tasks/Challenges:

T Face your partner. On the signal, walk slowly toward each other until you are as close as you can be without touching. Then, quickly jump back as if you're scared, and walk backward to your starting position, keeping a close watch on your partner.

T This time, you're going to do the activity a little differently because you seldom would move slowly to get away from someone. Try to move a little quicker and faster as you flee or go away from your partner. Just remember: Don't go so fast that you fall down.

T Now, instead of walking away from your partner, try jogging.

Dodging the Obstacles

Setting: Low- and medium-height objects placed around the room as obstacles

Cues

Split Second	(Make your moves quicker than the speed of light.)
Change Speed	(Use changes of speed to avoid the obstacles.)
Change Direction	(Use changes of direction to avoid the obstacles.)

Tasks/Challenges:

T On the signal, travel around the general space without touching anyone else or any of the obstacles on the floor. Everything is poison. Be sure to watch for other people as well as the objects.

T This time try to move through the area a little faster.

C I will time you for 30 seconds. See if you can travel for that long with no touches.

Children never seem to tire of this task, regardless of their skill level. As the children's skill levels increase, decrease the space between obstacles or use more obstacles to increase the complexity of the task.

Dodging with Quick Changes of Direction

Setting: Children scattered in general space

Cues

Fake	(Step/lean one way; go the other.)
Split Second	(Make your moves quicker than the speed of light.)

Tasks/Challenges:

T This is very similar to what you practiced before. Travel around in the general space. When you come close to someone, get as close as possible, and then quickly dodge away and look for another person to approach. There should be a clear burst of speed as you dodge away from the person—as if you're trying to escape. Remember, watch out for others.

T Dodging with speed as you did is called darting. This time practice getting as close to the person you approach as you can before quickly darting away. Make the dart very clear.

C Practice until you can make five darts in a row without having to stop.

Overtaking a Fleeing Person

Setting: Partners scattered in general space

Cues

Runner

Split Second	(Make your moves quicker than the speed of light.)
Fake	(Step/lean one way; go the other.)
Change Direction	(Use changes of direction to avoid the chaser.)

Chaser

Watch the Hips	(Watch the hips of the runner to tell his or her next move.)

Tasks/Challenges:

T In this task you are going to try and catch your partner, who has a head start. On the first signal, the front partner darts away from the back partner. After 3 seconds, another signal is sounded, and the second partner, who has remained still, chases after the first partner, trying to tag him or her before I blow the stop whistle in 20 seconds. For the next round, switch places. You must always stay inside the boundaries. So the activity goes like this: Stand together. On the first signal, partner 1 takes off running. On the second signal, partner 2 takes off and tries to catch partner 1 before I blow the whistle in 20 seconds.

T Let's go again. Remember, never give up, even if the runner keeps getting away. See if you can use all the moves you know.

This task is appropriate when the children have learned to travel in general space without bumping into one another. Initially, children can perform this task more easily (and safely) in large areas because they're able to focus more on their partners and less on avoiding other children.

✓ *Exit Slip.* This is an appropriate time to use an exit slip (Chapter 12) to assess whether the children know the difference among chasing, fleeing, and dodging and the cues associated with each.

Fleeing a Chaser

Setting: Five people in a group *(see Figure 17.1 for setup)*

Cues

Fleers

Split Second	(Make your moves quicker than the speed of light.)
Fake	(Step/lean one way; go the other.)
Dart	(Use quick changes of direction to avoid the chaser.)

Chaser

Watch the Hips	(Watch the hips of the runner to tell his or her next move.)

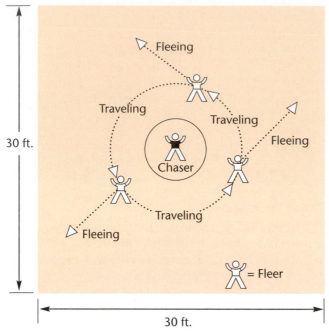

Figure 17.1 Setup for fleeing a chaser.

Tasks/Challenges:

T This task is designed to let you practice fleeing from a chaser. There will be five people in a group—one chaser and four fleers. The chaser, who is in the middle circle in a squat position, tells the fleers how to travel. The fleers then travel inside the box

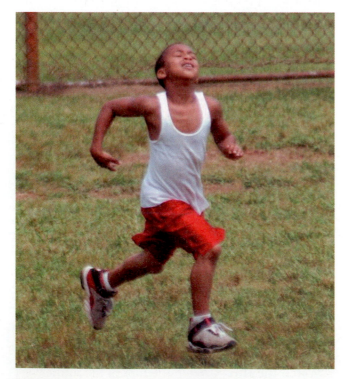

Fleeing a chaser always provides a challenge for youngsters.

and not in the center circle. When the chaser gets to his or her feet, all the fleers run toward the outside of the square, trying not to get tagged. A fleer who is tagged helps the chaser the next time. When all the fleers are caught, the last fleer caught becomes the new chaser. Chasers, be sure to change the traveling action each time.

This task requires multiple groups playing at once; be sure there is ample space between groups so the fleeing children do not disrupt others. Mark the boundaries clearly.

✓ **Teacher Observation.** Each of the preceding tasks is an opportune place for teacher observation of the use of critical cues for skills of chasing, fleeing, and dodging before moving on to more dynamic settings. See Chapters 11 and 12 for the development of observation checklists and assessment items.

Utilization Level: (GLSP) Learning Experiences Leading to Skill Development

When children can effectively dodge a chasing person and can react quickly and accurately to others' swift, darting movements, they're ready for utilization-level activities. Now the youngsters' chasing, fleeing, and dodging skills enable them to enjoy testing their abilities in ever-changing and complex environments. Challenging activities include the following:

- The players of one group flee and/or dodge the players of an opposing group while controlling an object (such as a football, flying disc, or basketball).
- One group chases the members of an opposing group but, instead of fleeing their chasers, tries to run past and dodge them without being touched. Children at the utilization level are ready to test their skills in increasingly complex and gamelike situations. In these experiences, children will have to fake and dodge quickly in reaction to the deceptive movements of others.

A note about cues: Although several cues are listed for many of the learning experiences, it's important to focus on only one cue at a time. That way, the children can really concentrate on that cue. Once you provide feedback to the children and observe that most have learned a cue, it's time to focus on another one.

Dodging Stationary Obstacles

Setting: Groups of six: three taggers, three dodgers, each group with a space about 10 feet by 20 feet; spots on the floor to indicate where the taggers are to stand

Cues

Split Second (Make your moves quicker than the speed of light.)
Fake (Step/lean one way; go the other.)
Dart (Use quick changes of direction to avoid the obstacles.)

Tasks/Challenges:

T This task will give you a chance to practice your dodging skills. Three people in each group are taggers and the others are dodgers. Taggers stand with both feet on a spot. The dodgers start on one side of the space and try to get to the other side of the space without being tagged. After five runs, switch places. If you get tagged, try to figure out how to avoid being tagged the next time.

T Now the activity gets a little harder. If you're tagged, you must freeze right where you're tagged and become a tagger. Dodgers, this will get really hard at the end, so be on your toes.

✓ *Videotape/digital analysis.* Videotaping students chasing, fleeing, and dodging in this activity would be an appropriate way to assess their use of chasing, fleeing, and dodging in a more complex situation. Students can assess themselves in relation to the critical cues.

Dodging and Faking Moves to Avoid a Chaser

Setting: Groups of six, each with a space about the size of a quarter of a basketball court

Cues

Dodgers
Split Second (Make your moves quicker than the speed of light.)
Fake (Step/lean one way; go the other.)
Dart/Change Speed (Use quick changes of direction and speed to avoid the chaser.)
Chasers
Watch the Hips (Watch the hips of the runner to tell his or her next move.)
Teamwork (Decide your plan for catching together.)

Tasks/Challenges:

T This chasing-and-fleeing task will really make you work hard. You can't be slow; if you are, you'll be caught. Make sure you know where your boundaries are. Two people will start out as chasers—you decide who they'll be. The other four are dodgers. On the signal, the chasers have 1 minute to try to catch all the runners. If tagged, a dodger has to freeze and then count to 10 out loud before starting to run again. The object is for the chasers to catch all the dodgers at the same time. After the first minute, change chasers and play again. Remember, the chasers have to try to catch everyone, and no one can go outside the boundaries.

⚠ When children tag one another, they can be quite rough, sometimes knocking others over. Here are two rules that have helped us: (1) A tag is only a touch, not a slap or hit. (2) All tags must be on the shoulders or below.

Dodging Semistationary Obstacles

Setting: Class divided into groups of about 10 to 14, each group in a space about 20 feet by 20 feet; tape or spots on the floor approximately an arm's length apart to designate where the members of one group must place their feet (Figure 17.2)

Cues

Split Second (Make your moves quicker than the speed of light.)
Fake (Step/lean one way; go the other.)
Dart (Use quick changes of direction to avoid the obstacles.)

Tasks/Challenges:

T To do this activity, half of your group will be taggers, and you must stand on the marks on the floor. One foot must always stay on the mark; you can move the other foot to reach in different directions. The other half of you are dodgers. You'll begin at this end of the room and try to travel through the taggers without being touched. After the dodgers make it to the other side of the room, return around the outside of the room, and keep trying to get through the taggers until you hear the stop signal. On the stop signal, switch places.

T This time, things are going to be a little harder for the taggers. Instead of just tagging the dodgers, the taggers have to tag the left knees of the dodgers with their right hands.

Figure 17.2 Setup for dodging semistationary objects.

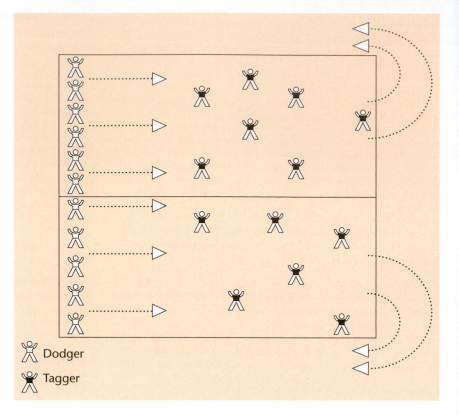

🧍 Dodger

🧍 Tagger

You can change these directions to several combinations of body parts—for example, right hand–right knee; left hand–right knee; left hand–right elbow.

T This time, let's make it harder for the dodgers. Taggers can now move one foot to tag. The other foot has to be on the mark.

Dodging and Chasing One Person in a Mass

Setting: Partners spread apart on a field

Cues	
Dodgers	
Split Second	(Make your moves quicker than the speed of light.)
Fake	(Step/lean one way; go the other.)
Dart/Change Speed	(Use quick changes of direction and speed to avoid the chaser.)
Chasers	
Watch the Hips	(Watch the hips of the runner to tell his or her next move.)

Tasks/Challenges:

T For this task, you and your partner are on opposite teams. One of you is a tagger; the other one is a dodger. On the signal, the taggers will spread out inside the boundaries, and the dodgers will line up on this side of the field. On the next signal, the dodgers will try to get to the other side of the field without being touched by their partners, the taggers. The trick is that each dodger can be tagged only by his or her partner. When the dodgers get to the other side, they return to the starting line by going around the outside of the field and continue to travel across the space until they hear the stop signal. On the stop signal, trade places with your partners.

T This time I'm going to decrease the space to half the size it was. Ready? Go again.

C Can you stay untagged until the signal sounds?

✓ *Peer Observation.* This would be an appropriate opportunity for a peer observation assessment. Two sets of partners could be paired. One set would participate and the other set would observe. The observers would have an index card with the critical cues listed and a space for names and would assess whether the participants used the cues. After five tries, the observers and participants would switch places. See Chapter 12 for the development of peer observation checklists and scoring rubrics.

Bombardment

In some school yards we've observed classes of children playing a game popularly called Bombardment, Killer, or Murder Ball. As these names imply, the game can be dangerous. Typically, a class is divided into two teams, with a middle line separating each team. Each team throws a hard ball in an attempt to strike players on the opposing team; the teams often throw from close range and toward an unsuspecting child. We don't support this activity. There are many other dodging-type experiences you can plan that are safer, allow more children to participate, and are more apt to result in skill development.

Dodging in a Dynamic Situation

Setting: Groups of 10: 8 runners and 2 chasers; a space about 30 feet by 30 feet, preferably grass

Cues	
Dodgers	
Split Second	(Make your moves quicker than the speed of light.)
Fake	(Step/lean one way; go the other.)
Dart/Change Speed	(Use quick changes of direction and speed to avoid the chaser.)
Chasers	
Watch the Hips	(Watch the hips of the runner to tell his or her next move.)
Teamwork	(Decide your plan for catching together.)

Tasks/Challenges:

T This is a tag activity. The object, if you are a tagger, is to tag the runners on the named body part or, if you're a runner, to avoid being tagged on the named body part. Chasers, try to touch the runners on the body part I call out. Any runners you tag must freeze. The tagged runners can be unfrozen if they're tagged by a free runner on a body part other than the tagged part. The taggers will have 1 minute to try to catch all the runners.

At the end of 1 minute, start again with two new taggers. You must stay inside your boundaries. "Shoulders"—Go.

Dodging While Manipulating an Object

Setting: Multiple circle areas about 10 feet in diameter marked off on the floor or the pavement; two or three, one of whom is trying to take the ball away, children occupying each circle

Children should be at the utilization level in dribbling before attempting this task.

Cues	
Dodgers	
Protect the Ball	(Keep your body between the ball and the other players.)
Fake	(Step/lean one way; go the other.)
Dart/Change Speed	(Use quick changes of direction and speed to avoid the chaser.)

Tasks/Challenges:

T The object of this task is to dribble a ball while protecting it from someone else. Here's how it works. Each of you in your circle will be dribbling a ball. There will be one defender trying to take the ball away from you. As you dribble, try to use fakes and changes of speed to get away from the defender. If your ball gets knocked out, just go get it and start again.

Proficiency Level: (GLSP) Learning Experiences Leading to Skill Development

Children at the proficiency level are ready to use their skillful chasing, fleeing, and dodging abilities in a variety of complex and ever-changing, gamelike situations. Both the chasers and the fleeing, dodging players are skilled. At times, the chaser gets the target; at other times, the fleeing, dodging player escapes. Advanced chasing, fleeing, and dodging skills are evident in invasion (see Chapter 30 for more on invasion-type games) situations such as the following:

- A player in a running invasion game darts quickly past the defense, dodging around the players who are chasing him.
- A player in a foot dribble invasion activity advances the ball past a defensive player by faking one way and then traveling quickly in the opposite direction.

- A defensive player in a running invasion game runs 20 to 30 yards to overtake an offensive runner heading for a score.
- In a hand dribbling invasion game, a player races down court to score although a defensive player is chasing right behind.

In elementary school settings, children at the proficiency level enjoy playing teacher- and student-designed games in which chasing, fleeing, and dodging are the primary movements. Although some activities are included here, when children are at the proficiency level of chasing, fleeing, and dodging, they are in actuality using those skills in combination with manipulative skills. Thus appropriate activities would also be game-like proficiency-level manipulative activities in which chasing, fleeing, and dodging skills lend the strategic dynamics to the game. See proficiency-level tasks in the manipulative skill theme chapters (Chapters 22–26).

A note about cues at the proficiency level: At the proficiency level, tasks are more complex, typically requiring children to coordinate several movements simultaneously in a dynamic context. A list of cues is provided to assist the children in being more successful in the learning experience. The challenge for the teacher is in determining which cue will be most beneficial for each child . . . and when. Thus, careful observation and critical reflection become very important as you watch the children move and then decide which cue will be the most helpful to move each learner to a higher skill level.

Continual Fleeing and Chasing with a Large Group

Setting: Children scattered throughout the space: three taggers (with colored armbands); the rest, dodgers

Note: The complexity of this task—as with most chasing, fleeing, and dodging tasks—can be increased or decreased by increasing or decreasing the space available or changing the size of the group. Smaller groups and smaller spaces increase the difficulty for the dodgers; larger groups and larger spaces increase the difficulty for the chasers.

Cues	
Dodgers	
Split Second	(Make your moves quicker than the speed of light.)
Fake	(Step/lean one way; go the other.)
Dart/Change Speed	(Use quick changes of direction and speed to avoid the chaser.)

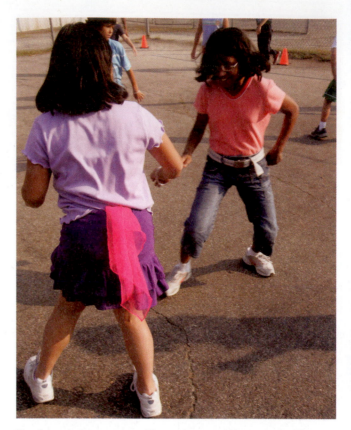

Practicing dodging moves with a partner would be an appropriate control-level task.

Chasers	
Watch the Hips	(Watch the hips of the runner to tell his or her next move.)
Teamwork	(Decide your plan for catching together.)

Tasks/Challenges:

Ⓣ This task is very much like freeze tag, except that when you are tagged, you must freeze with your legs wide apart and your hands clasped to your head. You can then be "freed" by any free player crawling through your legs. There will be three taggers, each with a colored armband.

Note: It is virtually impossible for the taggers to catch all the dodgers, so set a time for play (e.g., 1 to 2 minutes) and switch taggers.

✿ How did you use teamwork to catch the runners?

Dodging While Maintaining Possession of an Object

Setting: For each child, a rumble rhumba (Figure 17.3) and a beanbag; first put partners in a space about 10

Figure 17.3 To make a rumble rhumba, you'll need a 1-gallon plastic jug (e.g., an empty milk or water container), 1 yard of clothesline cord, and duct tape. Cut the bottom inch from the jug, and make two holes on either side of the handle. Then run a length of clothesline through the holes, and tie the jug (open end up) around the waist. Cover the cut edges with duct tape.*
*Prior to constructing equipment, we recommend you check with school administration to be certain that district policy permits homemade equipment.

feet by feet and then alone using the space approximately the size of the entire gym

Tasks/Challenges:

T For this task, you will need a rumble rhumba tied around your waist with one beanbag in it (Figure 17.4). You and your partner should find a space where you are not close to other groups. When I say "Go," you will try to snatch the beanbag from your partner's rumble without having yours snatched. If you snatch the beanbag, simply give it back to your partner. The other rules are (1) you can take a beanbag only from a rumble, not your partner's hands; (2) you can't protect your rumble with your hands; and (3) you can't touch your partner. Remember, stay in your own space.

T This time the task becomes harder. You now can travel over the entire space and try to snatch anyone's beanbag. If you snatch a beanbag, this time

Figure 17.4 Rumble rhumba in position around the waist.

it goes in your rumble. The same rules of (1) only taking a beanbag from a rumble, not someone's hands, (2) not protecting your rumble with your hands, and (3) not touching anyone still apply.

C How many points can you get? Score one point for each beanbag you snatch; subtract five points if yours is taken.

In many primitive tribal games, the tribes believed that the chaser was evil, magic, or diseased and that the chaser's touch was contagious. Although today's games are a far cry from fleeing possible death, one has a hard time believing otherwise when observing the intensity and all-out effort children display when fleeing a chaser!

Chasing and Dodging Simultaneously

Setting: Start with partners in a space about 5 feet by 5 feet; then increase the group size to about six and the space to about 20 feet by 20 feet; enough flag belts or scarves (of two colors) for all the youngsters

Cues	
Dodgers	
Split Second	(Make your moves quicker than the speed of light.)
Fake	(Step/lean one way; go the other.)
Dart/Change Speed	(Use quick changes of direction and speed to avoid the chaser.)
Chasers	
Watch the Hips	(Watch the hips of the runner to tell his or her next move.)

Tasks/Challenges:

T Each partner should have on a flag belt or scarf tucked into his or her waist. In your space your task will be to try to grab the flag from your partner. If you grab it, give it back and start again. Remember, you cannot protect your flag with your hands, and you cannot touch the other person.

T This task pits each player against every other player. The object is to snatch the flag from another player's belt without losing your own flag and while staying within the designated boundaries. If your flag is pulled off, another player can put it back on and you can keep playing. You can't put your own flag back on. You've really got to watch all the other players and move to stay out of their way. Remember all the turning, twisting, and jumping dodges.

C How many points can you accumulate? Score one point for every flag you take; subtract three points for every time your flag is taken.

T Now form a group of six. Each group of six should divide into two groups of three, each group having a different-colored flag belt. Find a space about 20 feet by 20 feet. You will now work as a team, and your task is to try and grab the flags of the other group. If you get them all, return them and start over again.

Chasing and Fleeing in an Invasion Gamelike Situation

Setting: Small groups of four to six, each with a ball; enough flag belts or scarves (of two colors) for all the youngsters; a space about 20 yards by 10 yards

Cues	
Offense	
Toward Goal	(Always move toward your goal.)
Fake	(Step/lean one way; go the other.)
Dart/Change Speed	(Use quick changes of direction and speed to avoid the chaser.)
Defense	
Watch the Hips	(Watch the hips of the runner to tell his or her next move.)
Teamwork	(Decide your plan for catching together.)

Tasks/Challenges:

C One group will start with the ball. On the signal, a player on the group with the ball (group 1) tries to pass or run the ball from its goal line to the other group's goal line without the ball touching the ground or group 2 grabbing the flag of the player with the ball. If a flag is grabbed, the ball touches the ground, or the goal line is crossed, the other group gets the ball.

✓ *Videotape/Digital Analysis.* The above task, with established criteria and a rubric, provides a wonderful opportunity for video analysis of the use of the critical elements in a dynamic situation. Each group could do its own analysis.

Dodging in a Gamelike Situation

Setting: A large marked-off area containing hoops as safety bases (Figure 17.5); groups of no more than five

Cues	
Dodgers	
Split Second	(Make your moves quicker than the speed of light.)
Fake	(Step/lean one way; go the other.)
Dart/Change Speed	(Use quick changes of direction and speed to avoid the chaser.)
Chasers	
Watch the Hips	(Watch the hips of the runner to tell his or her next move.)
Teamwork	(Decide your plan for catching together.)

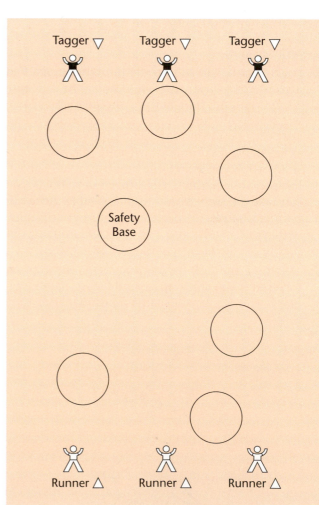

Figure 17.5 Setup for dodging in a gamelike situation.

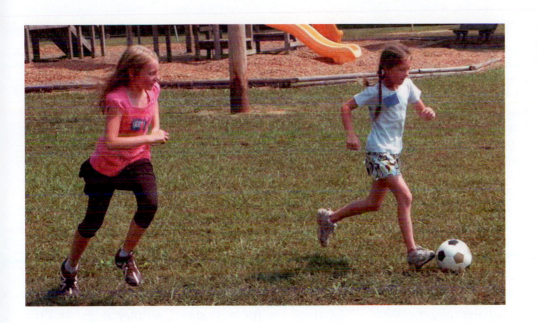

Invasion gamelike experiences involve constant chasing and fleeing.

Tasks/Challenges:

T The object of this task is for a group of runners to cross the space without being touched by the other group, who are taggers. The runners begin at one end of the space; the taggers begin at the other end. On the signal, the runners try to cross the space without being tagged; the taggers try to stop any runners from getting across the space. The runners are safe—can't be tagged—when they're in any of the hoops. The runners have about 1 minute to cross the space. After two turns, you'll switch places. The safety bases will help, but use them wisely—only as a last resort when you're about to be tagged. Don't just stand in them the whole time.

You have used teamwork before to catch runners. How does the teamwork in this game differ? What teamwork strategies did you use here?

Dodging in a Target Gamelike Situation

Setting: A marked-off square playing area initially about 10 feet by 10 feet and later about 20 feet by 20 feet with a hoop in its center and a beanbag inside the hoop (Figure 17.6); first in partners and then in groups of about five

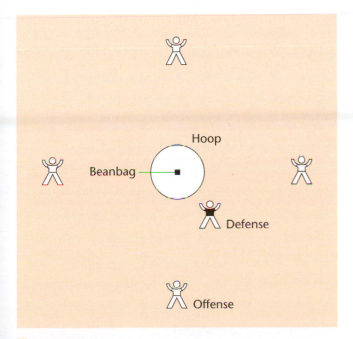

Figure 17.6 Setup for dodging in a target gamelike situation.

Cues

Offense

Split Second	(Make your moves quicker than the speed of light.)
Fake	(Step/lean one way; go the other.)
Dart/Change Speed	(Use quick changes of direction and speed to avoid the chaser.)
Heads and Shoulders Up	(As you bend to retrieve an object, be sure to keep your head and shoulders up and to bend at the knees.)

Defense

Watch the Hips	(Watch the hips of the runner to tell his or her next move.)

Tasks/Challenges:

T To begin this task, you and your partner will need one hoop and one beanbag in a space about 10 feet by 10 feet. Place the beanbag inside the hoop. One of you will be offense and the other, defense. Do you remember what offense and defense are? The defensive player will try to protect the beanbag from the offensive player, who is trying to grab it out of the hoop. No one can step inside the hoop. If the offense gets it, just put it back in the hoop and start again. I will tell you when to change roles.

! This is a task children love, but much attention needs to be paid to their keeping their heads and shoulders up as they try to retrieve the beanbag. If children are dodging with their heads down, the likelihood increases that heads will collide.

T The task now gets harder. There are now four offensive players and one defensive player. Make your square a little bigger and be sure to mark your boundaries. The object stays the same—try to get the beanbag or protect it. I will tell you when to switch positions.

C Now we will make a game of it. On the signal, the offense will have 2 minutes in which to retrieve the beanbag from inside the hoop and get it to the outside of the square without being touched by the defense. If the offense gets the beanbag to the outside or the 2-minute limit is reached, play starts over again, and a new defender tries to protect the treasure. No one can go inside the hoop.

✓ *Event Task.* A likely assessment option would be to have each group write out the strategy the members plan to use in the game. After the game is over, they can analyze how well it worked and what they will need to practice next time to be more effective. This plan can then serve as the initial activity in the next lesson.

Using Team Strategy for Chasing, Fleeing, and Dodging in an Invasion Gamelike Situation

Setting: Groups of eight, four players in each group, each group with matching colored flags of a different color from those of the opposing group; a flag belt with two flags on it for each group member

Cues	
Dodgers	
Split Second	(Make your moves quicker than the speed of light.)
Fake	(Step/lean one way; go the other.)

Dart/Change Speed	(Use quick changes of direction and speed to avoid the chaser.)
Chasers	
Watch the Hips	(Watch the hips of the runner to tell his or her next move.)
Teamwork	(Decide your plan for catching together.)

Tasks/Challenges:

T The object of this task is to see how many of the other group's flags you can get without losing your own. One group begins at each end of the space. On the signal, both teams move into the playing area, and each group tries to snatch as many flags as possible from the other group's belts while preventing the other group from stealing their own flags. On the next signal, all play stops, and the teams return to their sidelines and count how many flags they were able to steal.

✓ *Journal.* For a journal entry at this point, you might ask children how they feel about their chasing, fleeing, and dodging abilities.

Dodging While Manipulating an Object in an Invasion Gamelike Situation

Setting: This activity requires utilization-level skills in the manipulative activity you choose to use. It can be done with virtually any manipulative skill; the most common are dribbling and passing with the hands or feet, throwing and catching, or striking with a hockey stick. Whatever skill you choose, you will need one ball per group and appropriate other equipment. Even-numbered groups of six to eight.

Cues	
Offense	
Split Second	(Make your moves quicker than the speed of light.)
Fake	(Step/lean one way; go the other.)
Dart/Change Speed	(Use quick changes of direction and speed to avoid the chaser.)
Defense	
Watch the Hips	(Watch the hips of the runner to tell his or her next move.)
Teamwork	(Decide your plan for catching together.)
Play the Ball	(Force the pass by playing the ball first.)

Tasks/Challenges:

T This task is like Keep-Away. There will be equal numbers on each team. You must clearly mark your boundaries, which can be no larger than half a basketball court. The object is for your group to keep the ball away from the other group. Here are the rules:

1. A ball can be stolen only on a pass; it cannot be taken when someone else has control of it.
2. No one can hold onto the ball longer than 5 seconds before passing it.
3. There can be no direct hand-offs; the ball must be passed.
4. If the ball goes out of bounds, it belongs to the other group.

T We are going to change the game a little this time. You will keep your same teams, but each group will be trying to score by getting the ball across a goal line. All you have to do is get the ball across the line; the trick is that you cannot throw it across the goal line until you are in the striking zone marked on the floor (Figure 17.7). The difference between this game and the last one is that now you should be moving in one direction, not all over.

Figure 17.7 Goal line for Dodging While Manipulating an Object in an Invasion Gamelike Situation.

Self-Designed Chasing, Fleeing, and Dodging Game

Note: This task is an example of a student-designed instructional approach.

Setting: This activity requires utilization level skills in the manipulative activity used if youngsters choose a manipulative activity. Even-numbered groups of six to eight. Equipment depends on the game created.

Cues

Appropriate to the game

Tasks/Challenges:

T Today you're going to combine all that you've practiced into a game. You'll make up your games yourselves. In your groups, make up a game that involves chasing, fleeing, and dodging. You can use equipment or not; it's your choice. You can have whatever rules you want as long as you include these three:

1. The game must involve chasing, fleeing, and dodging.
2. Everyone in your group must be playing at the same time.
3. You cannot throw an object at another person.

In other words, nobody sits out and waits for a turn, and no one gets hit. Remember, groups of no more than six; chasing, fleeing, and dodging; and everybody plays. Go.

T After you've made up your rules and started to play your game, make sure you know your rules so you can tell somebody else how to play your game. At the end of class, I'll ask you to write down your game.

✓ *Event Task.* An appropriate assessment task at this point would be to have children write down how to play their games and then share the games with others. See Chapter 12 for more assessment examples.

Reading Comprehension Questions

1. List the differences among chasing, fleeing, and dodging.
2. Describe three effective dodging movements.
3. What are the characteristics of each of the four levels of skill proficiency for chasing, fleeing, and dodging?

4. Rank the following tasks by placing the number 1 in front of the easiest (most basic), the number 2 in front of the next more difficult level, and so on.
   ( ) A defensive player in a football-type game pursues an offensive runner.

( ) You travel around the room. On a signal, you change directions as quickly as possible.

( ) You stay as close as you can to your partner, who'll try to get away from you.

( ) One group chases the members of an opposing group.

5. What is a fake? Give several examples of when a fake might be used.

6. Why do you use large areas when introducing the chasing, fleeing, and dodging skills?

7. Why have we eliminated dodgeball activities from the development of dodging skills?

8. What are some important cues to give when you're teaching fleeing? List at least three.

9. When a child is tagged during a tag game, what is one alternative to eliminating the child until a new game begins?

10. Killer (also called Bombardment) is a game that has been played for years in elementary schools. What is our reason for not recommending it?

11. What are two strategies for offense and two for defense that apply when chasing, fleeing, and dodging while manipulating an object?

References/Suggested Readings

[NASPE] National Association for Sport and Physical Education. 2004. *Moving into the future: National standards for physical education.* 2nd ed. Reston, VA: National Association for Sport and Physical Education.

[NASPE] National Association for Sport and Physical Education. 2009. *Appropriate instructional practice guidelines for elementary school physical education.* 3rd ed. Reston, VA: National Association for Sport and Physical Education.

Opie, I., and P. Opie. 1969. *Children's games in street and playground.* New York: Oxford University Press.

Stiehl, J., D. Morris, and C. Sinclair. 2007. *Teaching physical activity: Change, challenge, choice.* Champaign, IL: Human Kinetics.

Williams, N. 1992. The physical education hall of shame. *Journal of Physical Education, Recreation and Dance* 63(6): 57–60.

Bending, Stretching, Curling, and Twisting

By Meghan Wampler

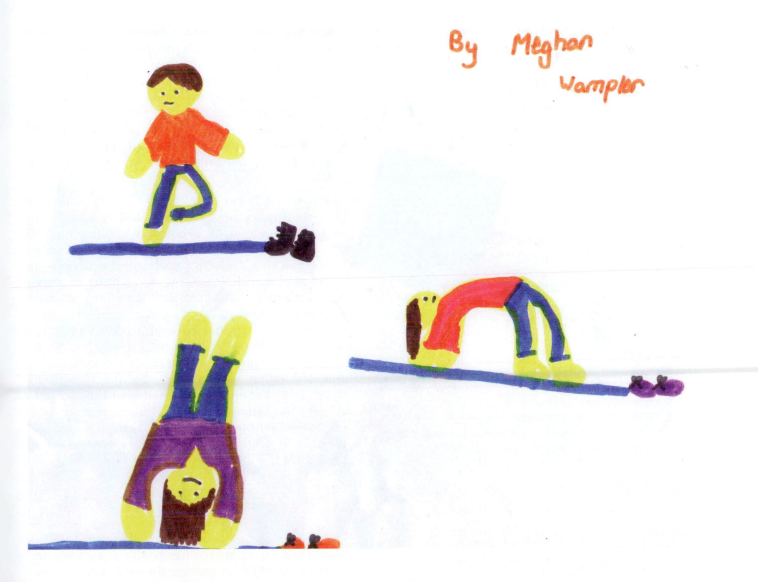

The professional baseball player hitting a line drive across third base, the high school swimmer performing a pike dive, the college basketball player reaching the extra inch to gain possession

Progression Spiral— Bending, Stretching, Twisting, Curling

Proficiency

In combination with other skill themes in complex and
dynamic games, dance, and gymnastics settings

Utilization

Stretching, curling, bending, and twisting against multiple
opponents
Stretching, curling, bending, and twisting against an opponent
Stretching to catch against an opponent
Stretch, catch, release
Stretching to catch with a partner while traveling
Transferring weight to hands and forming a bridge
Transferring weight onto hands and twisting

Control

Balancing on apparatus with body actions
Stretching, curling, and twisting into weight transfers
Twisting for placement when batting
Twisting while striking a tossed ball
Twisting while striking with a bat
Twisting to catch a ball with a partner
Stretching for the jump ball
Stretching to catch a ball with a partner
Catching with a stretch and curl
Jumping sequences with twisting, curling, and stretching
A dance of stretching, bending, twisting and curling
Jumping while twisting, curling, and stretching
Traveling and jumping while twisting, curling, and stretching
Bending, stretching, twisting, curling in mime
Balancing with bends, stretches, twists, and curls

Precontrol

Stretching and curling
Stretching, body shapes, and locomotion
Twisting in self-space
Bending body parts
Curling to roll
Curling in self-space
Stretching in self-space

of the rebound, the ballet dancer leaping as he travels across the stage, the Olympic gymnast performing an aerial roll, the rock climber reaching for the next hold—all are executing skills from a foundation of body actions—twisting, bending, stretching, and curling. Stretching, curling, bending, and twisting are the core of the advanced skills of gymnastics, dance, and sports. The ability to integrate them in the execution of the skill often delineates the difference between the average and the proficient athlete. We begin teaching the difference between these body actions with young children and, throughout our program, combine them with other skill themes to enhance the quality of their movement. The definitions of each action follow.

- *Stretching* is the extension of body parts away from the trunk and/or the stretching of the trunk itself.
- *Bending* is the creation of angles—of body parts and/or the trunk to produce a pike position of the trunk, angles of body parts.
- *Twisting* is the rotation of the trunk or body parts around a stationary axis. Arms, legs, the head, and the trunk can perform the twisting action.
- *Curling* involves the spine. The trunk can curl; body parts cannot. The spine can curl forward into a tight curved shape, slightly to either side, or even backward.

When children are introduced to the body actions of stretching, curling, twisting, and bending, they explore the action in isolation, e.g., stretching in self-space at different levels, sometimes slowly, sometimes quickly. Exploring each of the actions in isolation is then followed by the addition of traveling, the action combined with other skill themes, such as stretching to catch a ball at high level. After mastery of the action in combination with other skills and concepts, the student is ready for the dynamic environments of games/sports, gymnastics, and dance that require quick decisions regarding which body action is appropriate and the ability to execute the action correctly. The progression spiral on this page shows bending, stretching, curling, and twisting at each level of skill development, from precontrol to proficiency.

Experiences at the precontrol are designed to introduce children to stretching, bending, curling, and twisting. As children explore the body actions, they become aware of the stretching, curling, twisting, and bending, the difference between each of the actions, and the correct vocabulary for each action.

Stretching in Self-Space

Setting: Children scattered throughout general space

Tasks/Challenges:

T In your self-space explore stretching body parts as far as possible. Stretch your legs, your arms, your finger, and your toes.

T Lie flat on the floor and stretch your entire body, even your trunk, to be a tall as possible, as wide as possible. Now try tall and wide; really stretch.

T Let's try the same stretching action while in a sitting position.

T Now explore stretching while standing in your self-space.

Curling in Self-Space

Setting: A mat, space on a mat, or a carpet square in a grassy area for each child; children positioned so they will not rock into each other (Figure 21.5)

Tasks/Challenges:

T In your self-space curl like a playground ball, a roly-poly bug, the letter C.

T Explore curling while lying on the floor. How many different ways can you curl? What body part is always involved in the curling action? Right, the spine is always involved in the curling action.

T Sitting in your self-space, explore curling—forward with arms and legs tucked tightly to the trunk. Can you curl to the side? Arch the spine slowly backward? Which direction is best for the curling action? Right, curling for the letter O is a forward action of the spin.

Standing in your self-space, slowly curl the spine forward being careful not to lose your balance. Remember, curl the spine so I can see the curve when I look at you. Now explore curling to the side and ever so slowly backward. That one is very difficult.

T On your mat try to find as many ways as possible to curl your body so it is round. Three different ways would be good.

Curling to Roll

Setting: A mat for every child or two, or a large grassy space; children positioned so that they do not roll into each other

Tasks/Challenges:

T Can you make your body like a ball? How many ways can your ball move around your space? Remember, only round balls roll.

Bending Body Parts

Setting: Children scattered throughout general space

Tasks/Challenges:

T Explore bending body parts while in your self-space. How many body parts can bend? Fingers, wrists, elbows, knees, ankles. Create very sharp angles as you bend body parts.

T Create contrasting shapes as you bend opposite body parts, i.e., fingers of left hand versus fingers of right hand; left arm versus right arm. I will play some electronic music as you create your Dance of Bending Parts.

T Standing in your self-space, bend forward at the waist, creating a 90-degree angle with your body. This is called the *pike position* in gymnastics and in diving. We may use it later in our rolling activities.

Twisting in Self-Space

Setting: Children scattered throughout general space

Tasks/Challenges:

T Stand in your self-space with your feet "stuck" to the floor. Rotate your trunk clockwise without moving your feet. This is a twisting action. Now twist the trunk counterclockwise. Remember, keep your feet firmly planted—no movement.

T Extend your arms outward to the side. Rotate your arms in a forward motion. Rotate them in a backward motion. Twist one arm forward and the other backward; reverse the twisting action. Cross your arms in front of you. Is this a twisting action? No, the body part must rotate for the twisting action.

T Sitting in your self-space, twist one leg toward the body. Twist both legs inward. Twist body legs outward. What body parts can twist? Arms, legs, and trunk. Remember one part is stuck like glue; it remains still while other parts perform the twisting/rotating action.

T Sitting or lying down in your self-space, begin to twist different body parts until you look like a pretzel. How many different body parts can you twist? Create a really unique pretzel. When everyone has completed their twisting, we will freeze in a Portrait of Pretzels. Ready, begin.

A child at the precontrol or control level of twisting is likely to twist body parts without twisting the torso.

Stretching, Body Shapes, and Locomotion

Setting: Children with partners, scattered throughout general space

Tasks/Challenges:

T Stand in your self-space, stretching in all directions to be sure you have a clear self-space; it is not important that you be near your partner. Partners A, stand in your self-space, stretching your arms to make a very large, wide shape. Partners B, travel throughout general space with any locomotor pattern you wish; avoid touching anyone traveling or standing in a wide shape.

Have partners switch travel and stationary activities after one or two minutes of travel.

T Partners B, stand in your self-space twisting to form a tall, narrow shape. Partners A, run through-

out general space with no collisions; always look for open spaces as you travel.

Switch activities after one or two minutes.

Stretching and Curling

Setting: Children scattered through general space

Tasks/Challenges (Taken from *On the Move*):

T In your self-space bring your arms and legs close to your body, curling into a tight ball. On the 8-count signal, slowly stretch your arms and legs away from your body. On the 8th count, you should be fully extended, even fingers and toes. On signal, quickly curl the body back into a tight ball.

T How many of you have ever seen a tiny bug called a roly-poly? What special thing does this bug do? Yes, it curls into a tight ball to protect itself from possible danger. When everything is safe, the roly-poly bug uncurls and stretches out, ready to crawl. That is exactly what you are going to do. Pretend to be roly-poly bugs crawling in general space. When I come close to you/when I enter your self-space, quickly curl into a tight ball. When I move away, stretch your arms, your legs, your total body, and begin moving again. Remember, the curling action is quick; the stretching action is a slow extension.

Control Level (GLSP): Learning Experiences Leading to Skill Development

At the control level children begin combining the stretching, curling, twisting, and bending actions with the skills of traveling, catching, jumping, striking, rolling, etc. The children will need to be at the control level (nearing mastery) of the combined skill before the body action is added to the learning experience. The combined skills will be developed in isolation at this level of skill development.

A note about cues: Although several cues are listed for many of the learning experiences, it's important to focus on only one cue at a time. This way, the children can really concentrate on that cue. Once you provide feedback to the children and observe that most have learned a cue, it's time to focus on another one.

Balancing with Bends, Stretches, Twists, and Curls

Setting: Children scattered in self-space with sufficient mat space to work safely

Cues:

Stillness	(No wiggles, no wobbles. Hold the balance very still.)
Extend	(Extend body parts with tight muscles.)
Curl the Spine	(Curve the spine forward, to the right, to the left.)
Sharp Angles	(Bend body parts, bend at the waist for clear, sharp angles.)
Pretzels	(Twist the trunk, the legs, the arms, and the neck.)

Tasks/Challenges:

T Standing on one foot, stretch the free leg and both arms to create a balance.

T Sitting on your mat, stretch body parts to create a balance. Create balances on different bases of support by stretching free body parts.

T Create balances by curling your spine. How many different bases of support can you use for curling into balances?

T Create balances by twisting the trunk and/or body parts. See how many different ways you can twist into balances.

T Standing on your mat, bend forward creating a 90-degree angle with your body. Using this balance as the beginning, create balances by twisting, curling, and stretching.

C Create a 4-part sequence by stretching into balances. Remember, hold each balance very still for 3 seconds before stretching into the next one. (Repeat with curling, bending, twisting action.)

Through using both stretching and bending, this balance is both stable and unique.

C You have really created a large number of balances today by stretching, curling, bending, and twisting. Of all the balances you have completed today, choose one that shows stretching into the balance, one that shows curling into the balance, one for the twisting action, and one for bending. Remember, I am watching for the action; the balance is the ending of the stretching, bending, etc.

Bending, Stretching, Twisting, and Curling in Mime

Setting: Children scattered in general space

Cues

Extend	(Extend body parts with tight muscles.)
Curl the spine	(Curve the spine forward, to the right, to the left.)
Sharp Angles	(Bend body parts, bend at the waist for clear, sharp angles.)
Pretzels	(Twist the trunk, the legs, the arms, and the neck.)

Tasks/Challenges:

T Have you ever seen a mime? They tell a story without ever speaking; in fact, they never speak. They use their bodies to convey emotions and express feelings. Today we are going to use the body actions of stretching, curling, twisting, and bending to express feelings, to tell a story. You may travel, but only a short distance in relation to your "spot," your chosen self-space. Begin with bending stretching, curling, and twisting, really exaggerating the action. The music will set the tempo for the movements.

C After you have explored a variety of stretching, twisting, curling, and bending actions, think of an emotion you wish to express, a simple story of two to three sentences you wish to convey. Now combine the actions to complete that sequence. When you are ready, you may be the Mime on the Street Corner.

Traveling and Jumping While Twisting, Curling, and Stretching

Setting: Children scattered throughout general space

Cues

Extend	(Extend body parts with tight muscles.)
Curl the Spine	(Curve the spine forward, to the right, to the left.)
Pretzels	(Twist the trunk, the legs, the arms, and the neck.)

Tasks/Challenges:

T As you travel around the room, make the kind of jump that I've called out each time you hear the drumbeat. The jump may simply be stretched, or it may be bent, curled, or twisted. You'll have to be alert to what I'm saying as well as watching out for others.

Jumping Sequences with Twisting, Curling, and Stretching

Setting: Children scattered throughout general space, each with a hurdle or a rope in a shape on the floor

Cues	
Extend	(Extend body parts with tight muscles.)
Curl the Spine	(Curve the spine forward, to the right, to the left.)
Pretzels	(Twist the trunk, the legs, the arms, and the neck.)

Tasks/Challenges:

T Jump over your equipment, and stretch while you're in the air. A stretch shape means your arms and legs are away from your body—and you can be skinny or wide. Remember, make all the parts of your body stretched, not just one part. Practice your stretch until it's as stretched as it can be.

C Now think of five more stretches you can make while you're in the air. Practice all the stretches until they're the best you can do. I'll come and ask each of you to show me your best stretch, so be ready. Remember not to fall over on your landings; your feet should stick as if you had glue on them. What kind of landings will you need?

T This time you're going to jump using twists in the air. A twist means that you will make your body like a pretzel. Remember as you jump to make your whole body twist in the air; not just a few parts of your body. Practice your shape until it's as twisted as it can be.

A Remind children they need to be able to land on their feet and not "crash" after doing twists in the air.

C Now that you know what a twist is, think of five more twists you can make when you jump. Let them be really different, even weird. Practice all the twists until they're the best you can do. I'm going to ask some of you to show your twists, so work hard.

Pinpoint several children who are using different twists in the air.

T This time, you're going to learn some harder moves. First, you're going to make bent shapes with body parts in the air. A *bent* shape has sharp angles like this. *(Be sure to demonstrate here.)* At your equipment, practice making body parts bent while you are in the air.

C Create five more jumps with bent parts.

T This time you're going to jump while curling your body. In a curled jump, your body has a C shape. Remember, absorb force when you land by bending your knees.

C Create five curled jumps you can do in the air.

A Students should attempt running, jumping, and different body actions while airborne only after they have demonstrated safe landings in self-space—absorbing the force by bending the knees and landing in a balanced position without falling forward.

A Dance of Bending, Stretching, Twisting, and Curling

Setting: Partners scattered in general space

Cues	
Extend	(Extend body parts with tight muscles.)
Curl the Spine	(Curve the spine forward, to the right, to the left.)
Sharp Angles	(Bend body parts, bend at the waist for clear, sharp angles.)
Pretzels	(Twist the trunk, the legs, the arms, and the neck.)

Tasks/Challenges:

T Begin your dance facing your partner. The movements of your dance will be opposites, for example, if partner A stretches to the left, partner B will stretch to the opposite side. If partner B stretches high in the air, partner A will stretch arms toward the floor. If partner B bends arms and fingers inward, partner B will bend arms and fingers outward. One curls to the right; one curls to the left. One twists clockwise, one twists counterclockwise. Explore the possibilities of stretching, curling, twisting, and bending. Begin facing your partner, and then try standing side by side or one behind the other. Use the bending, stretching curling, twisting actions we have practiced to create a dance of Opposite Matches.

T When you are comfortable with creating opposites that match in body action, vary the speed of the movement—sometimes slowly, sometimes very quickly. Now for the really difficult part: Can you create a sequence of 4 opposite matches that are timed exactly together?

Performing Jumping Sequences with Bending, Twisting, Curling, and Stretching

Setting: Note cards with various twisting, curling, stretching sequences written on them, each sequence containing at least four body actions; children scattered throughout general space, each with a sequence card

Cues	
Extend	(Extend body parts with tight muscles.)
Curl the Spine	(Curve the spine forward, to the right, to the left.)
Sharp Angles	(Bend body parts, bend at the waist for clear, sharp angles.)
Pretzels	(Twist the trunk, the legs, the arms, and the neck.)

Tasks/Challenges:

T On your card are listed four body actions. You're going to make up a sequence of jumps that shows those body actions in the air. To do this, you'll first travel a bit and then jump, showing the first body action; then you'll travel again and jump and show the second body action listed; you'll travel again and jump using the third body action; you'll travel one more time and jump showing the last body action. So your sequence should be like this: Travel, jump; travel, jump; travel, jump; travel, jump, freeze. Repeat the sequence enough times so you can do it the same way each time. Memorize it. When it's memorized, show the sequence to a friend. Remember, use buoyant landings between jumps and a yielding landing after your last jump.

Catching with a Stretch and Curl

Setting: Children scattered in general space, each with a ball for catching

Cues	
Extend	(Reach toward the ceiling/sky as you stretch to catch.)
Reach and Pull	(Reach to catch the ball, then pull it in as the body curls around it.)

Tasks/Challenges:

T In your self-space toss the ball above your head, stretch to catch the ball, and then curl around the ball as if protecting an opponent from getting the ball. Toss the ball higher so you must really stretch to catch. Don't forget the curl.

T Stand approximately 6 to 8 feet from the wall. Toss the ball to the wall and jump to catch it high above your head. Stretch your arms really high.

Stretching to Catch a Ball with a Partner

Setting: Children with partners, sufficient space to throw and catch; a variety of balls for catching

Cues	
Reach and Pull	(Reach to catch the ball, then pull it to your belly button.)
Extend	(Reach toward the ceiling/sky as you stretch to catch.)

Tasks/Challenges:

T Stand approximately 10 feet from your partner. Toss the ball above your partner's head, just out of reach so the person must jump to catch. Catching partner, stretch your arms really high toward the ceiling to catch the ball. Remember, pull the ball in toward the body as if protecting it.

T Toss the ball to your partner's side so he or she must stretch to catch. Catcher, keep one foot firmly planted as you extend to the opposite side to catch. Let's make it easy. Catcher, keep your left foot still; extend to your right side for the catch. Thrower, toss the ball to your partner's right side, just beyond the person's reach so he or she must extend for the catch. After 5 tosses, switch the toss to the opposite side.

T When you are successful at the stretch and catch, the thrower will mix up the throws, some to your left side and some to your right side. Don't forget to switch position so each person is the catcher and each is the thrower.

T Pretend you are the second baseperson in the softball game. Keep one foot firmly planted "on the base" and stretch to catch—high, to the right, to the left. Maybe even stretch at low level!

T Try the stretch and catch with different types of balls of different shapes and sizes—football, softball, basketball—stretching to catch will be important in each game/sport.

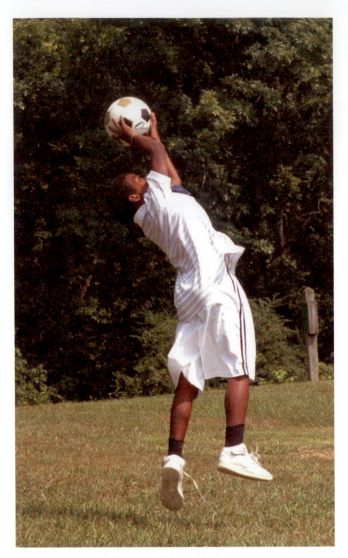

This youngster uses complete stretching of the body to catch.

Stretching for the Jump Ball

Setting: Class divided into groups of three, each person in each group approximately the same height

> **Cues**
>
> **Extend** (Stretch really high toward the ceiling/sky as you reach to tap the ball.)

Tasks/Challenges:

T Partners A and B stand facing each other, approximately 6 inches apart; partner C is going to toss the ball above your heads, beyond your reach like the referee in a basketball game. Jump high in the air, extend your arm really high to tap the ball as if sending it to a teammate. Remember, tap the ball; don't catch it. You are trying to jump higher and

stretch farther than your partner. After five tries, switch positions so the next person is the referee tossing the ball.

Twisting to Catch a Ball with a Partner

Setting: Partners scattered in general space with sufficient space for travel, a variety of balls for catching

> **Cues**
>
> **Over the Shoulder** (Look backward over your shoulder to see the ball.)

Tasks/Challenges:

T Stand beside your partner. Partner A, with the ball, will give the signal for partner B to begin running away from the starting position. When partner A hears the special signal, he or she will twist the head, looking back over the shoulder, to catch the ball. Continue travel to the opposite side of the gymnasium/playing area. Hint: In the beginning partner A will tell you which shoulder he or she is going to throw to so you will know which way to twist.

T When you are successful at twisting, catching, and continuing your travel, the throwing partner will no longer tell you in advance which way to twist. That will be determined by which shoulder the ball is traveling toward. Remember, it is a twisting action, not a full turn.

Twisting While Striking with a Bat

Setting: Partners positioned in open space with sufficient space for striking a ball; whiffle ball and batting tee for each set of partners

> **Cues**
>
> **Watch the Ball** (Watch the ball until your bat makes contact.)
>
> **Twist the Trunk** (Twist your upper body to send the ball to left field [right-handed batter].)
> (Twist your upper body to send the ball to right field [left-handed batter].)

Tasks/Challenges:

T Partner A in position for batting. Remember the things we learned when striking with a bat, such as position of the feet, grip of the bat. On signal, strike the ball sending it far into the "outfield."

Partner B will retrieve the ball and run it back to home plate and then return to the pitcher's position. Remember, wait for the signal for batting. Hint: I will know everyone is ready when I see each batter in position and each fielder in the pitcher's position. Switch positions after five hits.

How many of you were successful at sending the ball to right (left) field? What is the key for successful direction?

Twisting While Striking a Tossed Ball

Setting: Class divided into groups of three (batter, pitcher, outfielder) with sufficient space for striking a ball; whiffle ball and bat for each group

Cues	
Watch the Ball	(Watch the ball until your bat makes contact.)
Twist the Trunk	(Twist your upper body to send the ball to left field [right-handed batter].)
	(Twist your upper body to send the ball to right field [left-handed batter].)

Tasks/Challenges:

T Partner A is in position for batting, partner B is in position as the pitcher, and partner C is in the outfield. Partner A remember all the cues we learned for successful striking. Partner B will toss the ball underhanded for a successful hit. Partner C will be ready to catch/retrieve the ball after you hit.

T Your challenge is to strike the ball so it travels to the outfield—even for a homerun. Remember, wait for the signal for batting and retrieving. After five hits, we will rotate positions so everyone practices as the batter, the pitcher, and the outfielder.

Twisting for Placement when Batting

Setting: Class divided into groups of three (batter, pitcher, outfielder) with sufficient space for striking a ball; whiffle ball, bat, and batting tee for each group

Cues	
Watch the Ball	(Watch the ball until your bat makes contact.)
Ready Twist	(Twist your upper body in preparation for hitting the ball.)

Twist the Trunk	(Twist your upper body to send the ball to left field [right-handed batter].)
	(Twist your upper body to send the ball to right field [left-handed batter].)

Tasks/Challenges:

T Partner A is in position for batting, partner B is in position as the pitcher, and partner C is in the outfield. Partner A, remember all the cues we learned for successful striking. Partner B and partner C will be ready to catch/retrieve the ball after you hit. Partner A will be batting off the tee. This will allow you to concentrate fully on the direction of the hit. Your challenge is to strike the ball so it travels to the outfield—even for a homerun. Practice hitting the ball so it travels straight forward over the pitcher, sometimes to the left (right) field. Remember, wait for signal for batting and retrieving. After five hits, we will rotate positions so everyone practices as the batter, the pitcher, and the outfielder.

T When you are successful at sending the ball forward and to the right (left), tell your partners where you are going to hit the ball before you hit it. What is the difference in the twisting action for hitting forward and hitting to the right (left) field?

T When you are ready, you may have partner B toss the ball to you for the hit. (Repeat the tasks with a partner tossing the ball.)

Striking a ball with a bat requires twisting actions at the beginning and end of the swing.

Stretching, Curling, and Twisting into Weight Transfers

Setting: Small mats and/or carpet squares scattered throughout general space

Cues	
Extend	(Extend body parts with tight muscles.)
Curl the Spine	(Curve the spine forward, to the right, to the left.)
Pretzels	(Twist the trunk, the legs, the arms, and the neck.)

Tasks/Challenges:

🅣 Balance on one foot. Bend at the waist, extending your arms forward and your free leg backward. Stretch your arms forward until you are off balance; then transfer your weight to your hands and next to your curled back to roll forward out of the balance.

⚠ Children should demonstrate a mastery of rolling forward with a rounded back before they attempt this task.

🅣 Balance on your knees and one hand. Extend your free arm under your body, twisting your trunk until your weight transfers to your shoulder and new bases of support. Twist gently into the new balance.

🅣 Balance in a shoulder stand with your weight on your shoulders, upper arms, and head, stretching your legs toward the ceiling. Twist your legs and trunk, bringing your feet to the mat behind you in a new balance.

These girls demonstrate the result of curling to form a partner balance.

🅣 Balance on your chosen base of support. Twist until you are momentarily off balance; transfer your weight onto a new base of support.

🅣 Balance on your chosen base again. Use different stretching, curling, and twisting actions to transfer onto new bases of support.

Balancing on Apparatus with Body Actions

Setting: Variety of gymnastics equipment (tables, benches, beams) with sufficient mats and space for children to work safely

Cues	
Stillness	(No wiggles, no wobbles. Hold the balance very still.)
Extend	(Extend body parts with tight muscles.)
Curl the Spine	(Curve the spine forward, backward, to the right, to the left.)
Sharp Angles	(Bend body parts, bend at the waist for clear, sharp angles.)
Pretzels	(Twist the trunk, the legs, the arms, and the neck.)

Tasks/Challenges:

🅣 Remember when we worked on balances that followed stretching curling, bending, and stretching? Today we are going to try stretching, twisting, bending, curling into balances on equipment. You may choose to be on the bench (beam, table) or to be partially supported by the bench, i.e., on the mat beside the bench. Explore the actions we practiced earlier of stretching into a balance. Some of the balances may be easier on or beside the equipment; some may be more difficult. Remember, slow stretching into the balance. (Repeat for each of the body actions.)

Depending on the length of time between balancing on the mats and the equipment, you may need to repeat each of the above tasks.

⚠ *Emphasize safety, body control, and stillness]*

Utilization (GLSP): Learning Experiences Leading to Skill Development

Experiences at the utilization level are designed for children to experience the body actions in combinations in dynamic skills. The skills practiced in isolation at the control level are now put into the unpredictable environment of game situations, more advanced gymnastics routines, and the choreography of dance.

A note about cues: Although several cues are listed for many of the learning experiences, it's important to focus on only one cue at a time. That way, the children can really concentrate on that cue. Once you provide feedback to the children and observe that most have learned a cue, it's time to focus on another one.

Transferring Weight to Hands and Twisting

Setting: Large gymnastics mats throughout general space, with sufficient room for children to work safely on transfers

Cues

Pretzels (Twist the trunk, the legs, the arms, and the neck.)

Tasks/Challenges:

T Transfer your weight to your hands, twist your body a half turn, and bring your feet to the floor so you are facing in the opposite direction.

T While balanced on your hands, slowly walk on your hands a half turn to face in the opposite direction.

Transferring Weight to Hands and Forming a Bridge

Setting: Large gymnastics mats throughout general space

Cues

Curl the Spine (Curve the spine forward, backward, to the right, to the left.)

Strong Muscles (Strong arms and shoulders for supporting weight on hands.)

Tight Muscles (Tighten the abdominals for control.)

Tasks/Challenges:

T Using a step action, transfer your weight to your hands with sufficient force to continue the forward motion. Your feet should remain in the step-like stance as they move upward over your hands. Just before your feet contact the floor, bring them together, and bend your knees slightly. You will then balance in a bridge with your feet and hands supporting your weight. Keep your legs in the step-like stance throughout the transfer.

T As your feet contact the surface, push with your hands to continue your transfer to a standing position. This transfer without a pause is a walkover.

Stretching to Catch with a Partner While Traveling

Setting: Partner scattered throughout general space, a variety of balls for catching

Cues

Reach and Pull (Reach to catch the ball, then pull it in as the body curls around it.)

Open Spaces (Open spaces for the catcher.)

Tasks/Challenges:

T You and your partner will be traveling throughout general space, avoiding collisions with others. Throw the ball to your partner so it is above the person's head, just out of reach. Catcher, stretch high in the air for the catch, travel, and then throw to your partner. Remember, you are both traveling; all throws must be above the head so the catcher is stretched.

Stretch, Catch, Release

Setting: Partners scattered throughout general space; a variety of balls for catching

Cues

Reach and Pull (Reach to catch the ball, pull it in to the body, then release for the throw.)

Control (Gain control of the ball and body before the throw.)

Open Spaces (Open spaces for the catcher.)

Tasks/Challenges:

T This time when you and your partner are traveling, throwing, and catching, you will receive the ball at high level, travel 1-2-3-4-5, and then throw to your partner. This is a pretty quick release; don't forget to pull the ball into the body before you throw.

T Can you reduce the count to 1-2-3 and then release the ball for the throw? Remember, the throw must reach your partner at high level.

T In a game situation the count for the throw will vary, sometimes more, sometimes less, often determined by the position of your partner. Travel and throw to an "open" partner. Receiver, remember open spaces for a good catch.

Stretching to Catch Against an Opponent

Setting: Class divided into groups of three, with a variety of balls for catching.

⚠ Sufficient space for children to travel safely.

Cues

Receiver	(Open spaces for catching.)
Thrower	(High-level throws to stretch partner.)
Be Aware	(Be aware of others traveling, throwing, and catching.)

Tasks/Challenges:

Ⓣ Partners A and B will be traveling and throwing to each other. Partner C will be trying to intercept the throw, to gain possession of the ball. If partner C successfully makes an interception, return the ball to partners A and B; I will give the signal for changing positions in 30 seconds or so.

Ⓣ Remember, the throw and catch must be at high level—stretch for the catch. Increase the distance of your throws. Change the speed of your traveling.

Stretching, Curling, Bending, and Twisting against an Opponent

Setting: Class divided into groups of three, with a variety of balls for catching. Sufficient space for children to travel safely.

Cues

Receiver	(Open spaces for catching.)
Be Aware	(Be aware of others traveling, throwing, and catching.)

Tasks/Challenges:

Ⓣ Thus far, we have focused on stretching to catch, and stretching to intercept the ball. Now we will put stretching, curling, twisting, and bending into the game. Partners A and B will be traveling and throwing to each other. Partner C will be trying to intercept the throw, to gain possession of the ball. If partner C successfully makes an interception, return the ball to partners A and B; I will give the signal for changing positions in 30 seconds or so. The throw can now be at high level, to the side, even at low level. Receiver, you must now be ready to stretch, to twist, even to bend for the catch. Receiver, remember to curl momentarily to protect the ball before traveling.

Ⓣ Increase the distance of your throws. Change the speed of your traveling.

Stretching, Curling, Bending, and Twisting Against Multiple Opponents

Setting: Class divided into groups of four, with a variety of balls for catching.

⚠ Sufficient space for children to travel safely.

Cues

Receiver	(Open spaces for catching.)
Be Aware	(Be aware of others traveling, throwing, and catching.)

Tasks/Challenges:

Ⓒ Today we are going to use all the skills we have learned of throwing and catching while traveling, combined with stretching, bending, twisting, and curling in a game of two versus two, an old-fashioned game of Keep-Away. We call it an old-fashioned game because your parents probably played this game at recess when they were in elementary school. However, they were not as skilled as you; they had not learned the actions for stretching, twisting, bending, curling, and how to use them in the game.

Ⓣ Your game will be two partners throwing and catching (offense), two partners trying to intercept (defense). Receiver, look for the open space and move quickly to receive the pass. Interceptors, try to close the open space. Remember to momentarily curl the body/bend the arms to pull the ball close after the catch. If you are successful at an interception, give the ball back to the offense; I will give the signal for the switch of offense and defense.

✳ *After a couple of switches, with teams being both offense and defense, pull the class together to discuss the body actions used in combination with the throwing and catching. Guided self-assessment works really well and moves the game to a higher level of play.*

Proficiency Level: (GLSP) Learning Experiences Leading to Skill Development

There are two reasons you will not find a series of proficiency-level tasks for bending, stretching, twisting, and curling in this chapter. First, children at the proficiency level of bending, stretching, twisting, and curling almost always use these skills in conjunction other skills—not in isolation. You will notice that bending, stretching, twisting, and curling are included in many of the other skill theme chapters in combination with that skill theme.

Second, at the utilization and proficiency levels, the actions are used in game, dance, and gymnastics settings that are beyond the scope of most physical education programs, e.g., gymnastic clubs competitions, little league, and ballet or yoga classes. This is the primary reason these actions are so important to learn in the elementary years—so they can lead to successful and enjoyable participation in a range of sports and physical activities as adolescents and adults.

Reading Comprehension Questions

1. Use your own terms, not the ones at the beginning of the chapter, to distinguish between the actions of bending, stretching, curling, and twisting.
2. Young children often cross their arms and/or legs and think they are twisting. What would you say to help them understand the concept of twisting?
3. Make a table that has four rows and four columns. Label the columns *bending*, *stretching*, *twisting*, and *curling*. Pick four activities, or sports, you like and list them in the four rows. Then indicate how bending, stretching, twisting, and curling (the columns) are used in each the sports or activities you have listed (the rows).
4. Why are proficiency-level tasks not included for bending, stretching, twisting, and curling?
5. Imagine a parent asks you why you are teaching bending, stretching, twisting, and curling in your program. Write the response you might give—in 25 words or less.

References/Suggested Readings

Holt/Hale, S. 2012. *On the move: Lesson plans to accompany Children Moving*. New York: McGraw-Hill.

Jumping and Landing

Christopher Whi

Jumping is a locomotor pattern in which the body propels itself off the floor or apparatus into a momentary period of flight. As an isolated maneuver or in combination with other basic patterns, jumping—particularly the flight phase, when the body is unsupported in the air—is a fascinating body action.

A jump is performed for one of two reasons: (1) to raise the body vertically (straight up) for height or (2) to raise the body with a forward momentum to travel over a distance. Children who learn to jump effectively for height and distance are prepared for a multitude of game, dance, and gymnastics activities in which the performer needs to be a skilled jumper. See Box 19-1 for linkages of the skill theme of jumping and landing to the *National Standards for Physical Education.*

Fundamental Jumping Patterns

Wickstrom (1977, 63) suggested that children are developmentally capable of performing a jumping action when they're approximately 24 months old. He described the types of jumps preschool children achieve in terms of progressive difficulty:

Jump down from one foot to the other

Jump up from two feet to two feet

Jump down from two feet to two feet

Run and jump from one foot to the other

Jump forward from two feet to two feet

Jump down from one foot to two feet

Run and jump forward from one foot to two feet

Jump over object from two feet to two feet

Jump from one foot to same foot rhythmically

Box 19-1

Jumping and Landing in the *National Standards for Physical Education*

The skill theme of jumping and landing is referenced in the National Association for Sport and Physical Education's *National Standards for Physical Education* (NASPE 2004) as a sample performance outcome, across the third- to fifth-grade range, under Standard 1: "Demonstrates competency in motor skills and movement patterns needed to perform a variety of physical activities." The standard speaks of children developing mature forms in the basic skills and performing those skills in changing conditions and in combinations. The sample performance outcome states that a child "jumps vertically to a height of 9 inches and lands using mature form" (17).

It's safe to assume that within an average class of young children, some will be incapable of performing one or more of these jumping tasks. Initial observations will probably reveal a wide range of jumping abilities. Typically, kindergarten students are at the precontrol level. Their jumps usually achieve little height or distance, and they jump on two feet to ensure they maintain their balance. Children at this level seem to be jumping merely to enjoy the sensation of momentarily losing contact with the ground and the challenge of maintaining balance upon landing. A teacher can build on this natural fascination by providing learning activities that progressively lead children toward the mature performance of jumping and landing in different dance, game, and gymnastics situations.

The basketball player with mastery of jumping for height secures the rebound from a missed shot, a pass from a teammate. The football player with that extra inch on the jump receives the pass or captures the interception. The split-step in tennis, the jump-stop in basketball, and the preparatory two-one jump prior to the spike in volleyball all stem from mastery of the basic patterns of jumping. The two-foot takeoff in preparation for vaulting, aerials, and mounts onto gymnastics apparatus; the dancer suspended in flight; the elite basketball player who appears suspended in time following a leap—all are executing skills from the theme of jumping and landing. See our progression spiral on page 325 for the development of jumping and landing from precontrol to proficiency levels.

The fundamental jumping pattern consists of the following five basic variations:

1. Two-foot takeoff to a one-foot landing
2. Two-foot takeoff to a two-foot landing
3. One-foot takeoff to a landing on the same foot (hop)
4. One-foot takeoff to a landing on the other foot (leap)
5. One-foot takeoff to a two-foot landing

However, the specific actions of the body in performing a jump vary according to the purpose or intention—for example, jumping to catch or jumping to dismount from apparatus.

When we begin to focus on jumping, we have children think of the skill as three successive phases:

1. **Takeoff:** Actions of the body as it's propelled off the ground
2. **Flight:** Actions of the body while it's off the ground and in the air
3. **Landing:** Actions of the body as it reestablishes contact with the ground

The photo sequences in Boxes 19-2 and 19-3 show the "correct" forms for the takeoff, flight, and landing phases of jumping and landing. Box 19-2 illustrates the critical elements for jumping for height; Box 19-3 shows the critical elements for jumping for distance.

Key Observation Points: Jumping for Height

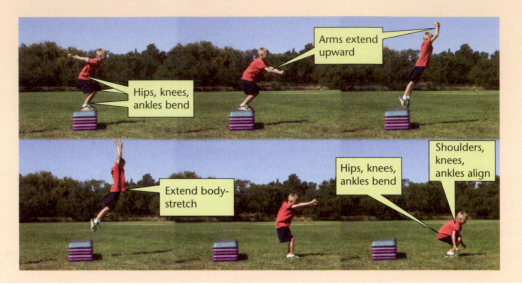

Key Observation Points: Jumping for Distance

Skill Theme Development Progression

Jumping and Landing

Proficiency Level

Jumping hurdles
Jumping, dancing, and imagery
Jumping as part of a dance creation
Jumping with a springboard
Jumping with a partner to match actions
Jumping with a partner to mirror actions

Utilization Level

Jumping to an accented beat
Throwing and catching while jumping
Jumping on a bench
Jumping to throw
Jumping to catch

Control Level

Jumping and landing task sheet
Jump, Squash, TaDa
Jumping on and off equipment using buoyant and
    yielding landings
Jumping over equipment using buoyant landings
Performing jumping sequences and making body shapes
Traveling, jumping, and body shapes
Jumping to form a body shape during flight
Jumping using buoyant and yielding landings
Jumping a self-turned rope
Jumping a turned rope
Jumping in rhythmical sequences
Jumping rhythmically
Jumping over low obstacles: hurdles
Jumping over low obstacles: hoops
Jumping for height
Standing long jump
Jumping and landing: basic patterns

Precontrol Level

Jumping over a swinging rope
Jumping for height
Jumping for distance
Jumping and landing: different patterns

Young children are challenged by the task of propelling the body off the ground for a momentary period of being airborne.

In the beginning we have children focus on the take-off and the landing phases of jumping. As they experiment with different takeoff and landing combinations, they begin to sense which take-off procedures result in the highest jumps as opposed to which result in the longest jumps. They find that actions of the legs, arms, torso, and head during the flight phase influence the trajectory of the jump. They come to recognize the unique giving action of the ankles, knees, and hips in absorbing the shock of landing. Actions during the flight phase of jumping are introduced only after children can achieve momentary suspension of the body in flight and have control of their bodies for balanced landings. A mature pattern of jumping and landing signals children are now ready for combining jumping with other skills and maneuvers while in the air. As is true with the learning of each new skill, guided practice is extremely important—practice that often extends beyond elementary physical education into middle school physical education and the specific jumping skills for sports, gymnastics, and dance.

The following activities are designed for exploration of jumping. Through these activities children will begin to discover different types of jumps as well as jumps that take them high and jumps that take them far.

Jumping and Landing: Different Patterns

Setting: Ropes (one per child) placed around the edge of the teaching area

Tasks/Challenges:

T At the edge of our working space are ropes. Select a rope and place it in a straight line in your self-space. Jump over the rope, and land on the other side without falling down.

T Explore different ways to jump over your rope, sometimes taking off on one foot and landing on two, sometimes taking off on two feet and landing on two.

A It is important to stress from the beginning that children land on their feet when jumping, not fall to the floor when they land.

T Jump high in the air as you travel over your rope.

T Stand at one end of your rope with a foot on either side of it. See if you can jump the distance of your rope.

A Before children jump distances over ropes, conduct a safety check to be sure each child has sufficient space for landing safely after the jump, with no collisions with another child.

T Arrange your rope in a shape different from a straight line—for example, a circle or a rectangle. Jump into the shape and out the other side. Jump across your new rope shape.

Jumping for Distance

Setting: Ropes (one per child) placed around the edge of the teaching area; strips of masking tape (one per child) on the wall

Tasks/Challenges:

T Place your rope on the floor away from others. Jump over your rope, landing as far from your rope as possible.

T Place your piece of masking tape on the floor. Lie down with your feet touching the tape, and place the rope by the top of your head. If you have trouble, ask a friend to help. The distance from the rope to the tape is how tall you are. Standing behind your rope, try to jump your height.

A Remember, land on your feet.

C Can you jump even farther than your height?

Jumping for Height

Setting: Streamers hung at various heights from a rope stretched along the work area

Tasks/Challenges:

T Jump to see if you can touch the streamers hanging from the rope.

T Run and jump to touch the streamers.

Jumping over a Swinging Rope

Setting: Class divided into groups of threes, each group with a "long" rope

Tasks/Challenges:

T In your groups of three, you are going to take turns jumping over a swinging rope. Two of you will gently swing the rope while the third person jumps. After 5 jumps, trade places.

C Practice for 10 jumps without a mistake.

At the control level, we encourage children to practice both long and high jumps until their landings are balanced and controlled with the goal being a mature pattern of jumping and landing. Children begin to explore the flight phase of the jump; they discover the world of jumping rope. They are challenged with jumping and landing as they relate to dance, gymnastics, and game skills.

A note about cues: Although several cues are listed for many of the learning experiences, it's important to focus on only one cue at a time. This way, the children can really concentrate on that cue. Once you provide feedback to the children and observe that most have learned a cue, it's time to focus on another one.

Jumping and Landing: Basic Patterns

Setting: Ropes (one per child) placed around the edge of the teaching area

Cue

Squash (Bend your knees to absorb the force and maintain balance when you land.)

Running and jumping combine skill and spatial awareness.

Tasks/Challenges:

T When we first worked on jumping, you explored different ways to jump over your rope—just for fun. Place your rope in a straight line on the floor; choose three of your favorites from those different types of jumps and practice jumping over your rope, landing each time in a balanced position without falling down. Bend your knees when you land so your landings are very quiet.

T Jump over your rope, taking off on two feet and landing on two feet.

T Position yourself approximately 10 feet from your rope. Approach your rope with a series of running steps; jump over your rope, taking off on one foot and landing on two feet.

⚠ Teach the children to conduct a safety check before they begin any jumping that involves an approach to assure sufficient space for landing safely with no collisions.

T Using a series of running steps to approach your rope, take off on one foot and land on the opposite foot on the other side of your rope. Taking off on one foot and landing on the opposite foot is called a leap.

T Change the shape of your rope from a straight line to a circle, rectangle, or triangle. Standing just outside the rope shape, take off on one foot and jump inside your shape, landing on the same foot. What locomotor action did you just do with this jump? A hop. Hop into and out of your rope.

✓ ***Peer Observation.*** Peer observation of the different jumping patterns would be beneficial at this point. *Review Chapter 12 for specific examples of assessments.*

Standing Long Jump

Setting: Ropes (one per child) placed around the edge of the work area; large color/panel gymnastics mats; strips of masking tape (one per child) on the wall

Cues	
Squash	(Bend your knees to absorb the force and maintain balance when you land.)
Swing Forward	(Swing your arms forcefully forward for maximum distance.)

Tasks/Challenges:

T Stand at one end of your rope with the rope between your feet. Bend your knees and swing your arms in preparation for the jump. Taking off on two feet and landing on two, jump forward as far as you can, trying to jump the full length of your rope.

T Remember when you practiced jumping your height by placing a piece of masking tape on the floor at the place of your feet and your rope on the floor the distance from your feet to your head? Try that jump again, taking off on two feet and landing on two feet. If you jump farther than your height, move the tape to where your heels first land.

Jumping at high level varies as children practice the skill.

T Standing at one end of the mat, jump as far as you can toward the other end of the mat. Count your score by the number of panels you jumped over. **Remember, bend your knees and swing your arms in preparation for the jump, then swing your arms forward for a really far jump.** Keeping your arms stretched forward will also keep you from falling backward when you land!

The three tasks just described work well in station format for practice of the two-foot to two-foot standing jump.

Jumping for Height

Setting: Balloons suspended at various heights from a stretched rope; milk crates, or low boxes (packed with newspaper) at large gymnastics mats

Cues	
Squash	(Bend your knees to absorb the force and maintain balance when you land.)
Swing Upward	(Swing your arms upward for good height.)

Tasks/Challenges:

T Scatter throughout general space and jump high in the air, returning to the floor in your same self-space. Take off on two feet and land on two feet.

T Jump high in the air, taking off on two feet and landing on two feet. Swing your arms upward; this will help you jump higher.

T Positioned around the work area are milk crates and boxes stuffed with newspaper on large gymnastics mats. Standing on the box or crate, jump high in the air and land on two feet on the mat in front of the box or crate. **Remember, swing your arms upward, reaching for the sky, to gain maximum height on your jump.**

T Travel throughout general space; on the signal, jump high in the air by taking off on one foot and landing on the opposite foot. This is the leap we practiced earlier; swing your arms upward as you jump to stay airborne as long as possible.

T Positioned around the work area are balloons suspended from stretched ropes. Using a two-foot takeoff and a two-foot landing, jump to touch the balloons like a basketball player trying to tap the ball on the jump.

T Approach the balloon with a series of running steps using a one-foot takeoff and a two-foot landing to jump for the balloon. Which type of jump gives you more height: a two-foot takeoff or a one-foot takeoff? A standing jump or a running approach to the jump?

Assessment Example

From the *National Standards for Physical Education*

Teacher Observation

Students are requested to demonstrate the skills introduced in class as the teacher observes their performance and records the satisfactory use of the critical elements of the skills on a checklist.

Criteria for Assessment

a. Demonstrates critical elements of the selected skills (jumping and landing) over several trials.

NASPE (1995, 18–19)

Jumping over Low Obstacles: Hoops

Setting: Hoops (one per child) scattered throughout the teaching area

Cues	
Squash	(Bend your knees to absorb the force and maintain balance when you land.)
Swing Upward	(Swing your arms upward for good height.)
Swing Forward	(Swing your arms forcefully forward for maximum distance.)

Tasks/Challenges:

T Jump over your hoop. As your feet touch the ground, freeze your body perfectly still; this means you must bend your ankles, knees, and hips as you land. **Think of your feet sinking into the floor as if the floor were a sponge.**

T Practice jumping over your hoop with two-foot takeoffs and landings until you can land without falling three times in a row. Can you then do the same three perfect landings with a one-foot takeoff and a two-foot landing?

T Travel throughout general space, leaping over hoops. **Remember to extend your arms up for good height as you leap.**

Jumping over Low Obstacles: Hurdles

Setting: One hurdle (cones and rolled newspaper or rope) per child

Cues	
Squash	(Bend your knees to absorb the force and maintain balance when you land.)
Swing Upward	(Swing your arms upward for good height.)

Tasks/Challenges:

T Standing just behind your hurdle, jump over it using a two-foot takeoff and a two-foot landing. Try to be really high when you cross the top—**push with your toes; reach for the sky.**

T Now as you jump over the hurdle, try to use the different types of jumps you have learned. Try the easiest ones first and then the most difficult ones.

C Practice each jump until you can do it three times with a soft landing and without touching the crosspiece.

T Stand approximately 6 feet behind your hurdle. Approach the hurdle with quick, running steps. Jump over your hurdle using a one-foot takeoff and a two-foot landing.

T When you can clear the hurdle without touching the crossbar and land without falling down, approach the bar with quick, running steps. Jump over the bar using a one-foot takeoff and then land on the opposite foot; continue with a few quick, running steps before you stop. Wow! You look ready for the Olympics.

Jumping Rhythmically

Setting: Carpet squares/spots scattered throughout general space; a recording of the sounds of tools and machines; a recording of "Pop Goes the Weasel"

Cues	
Spring, Spring	(Quick, springy landings for the fast beat.)
High Jumps, Full Squash	(Full squash following the high jumps.)
Heads Up	(Keep your head and shoulders up for good balance.)

Tasks/Challenges:

T Standing on your carpet square/spot, jump while keeping beat with the drum. You'll have to listen carefully because the drumbeat will change at different times. **To do this without losing the beat, take little jumps so your feet barely leave the floor.** In other words, you'll be almost bouncing on your toes.

For the next task, play music with the sounds of tools and machines. (Children enjoy electronic/synthesizer music.)

T This time, instead of a drumbeat, you'll hear the sounds of different machines and tools you're familiar with. Staying on your carpet square, take little jumps, keeping time with the tool and machine sounds you hear. The sounds will change often, so be alert, and take little bouncy jumps on your toes.

T Again, the drumbeat will guide your jumps. As you hear the slow beat, take big, high jumps. When you hear the quick beat, take small jumps. This maneuver involves careful listening, so be prepared to change at any time. Make sure your jumps are clearly big on the slow beats and really little on the fast beats; adjust the height of your jump for fast (low) and slow (high).

Place the carpet squares/spots in a circle with approximately 6 to 8 inches between each carpet/spot.

T Let's combine our jumping and rhythmic response to "Pop Goes the Weasel." Select a carpet square/spot and stand on it without moving it from the circle. We will stay on our squares/spots, our self-space, during the verse of the song. Follow the leader (me) during that portion as we do self-space actions—stretching, twisting, clapping, tapping, jogging in place, and so forth. When we come to the "Pop" in the song, jump from your square/spot to the next one—clockwise around the circle. Be ready for new nonlocomotor actions in self-space when you land.

Choose a new leader for the self-space actions after each jump. Younger students enjoy singing "Pop Goes the Weasel" along with or instead of the recording.

The folk dance "Jump Jim Joe" is an excellent activity for the practice of rhythmical jumping. Young children enjoy the repetitive nature of the jumping in the dance.

Jumping in Rhythmical Sequences

Setting: Children scattered throughout general space

Cues	
Spring, Squash	(Springy landings to continue travel; full squash to stop.)
Heads Up	(Keep your head and shoulders up for good balance.)
Swing Upward	(Swing your arms upward for good height.)

Tasks/Challenges:

T This time, you're going to travel and then jump and travel again, always keeping the same rhythm. To begin, you'll all practice the same travel jump pattern, which will go like this: Run, run, run,

leap/run, run, run, leap. As you move, all of you will say together, "Run, run, run, leap," so you can stay together. Let's practice saying that and keeping the same tempo before beginning to move. (Practice saying the phrase in tempo.) As you jump and run this time, remember to stay with the voices; everyone should be jumping at the same time if you're all together.

T Now instead of saying the phrase, you're going to clap it as you go. You'll have to remember what to do on your own.

T Now that you can follow the phrase I designed for you, you're going to make up your own and follow it. Your phrase should contain three traveling actions followed by one jumping pattern. You should repeat the sequence three times before coming to a stop. Practice the whole thing until you think it's the best you can do. As you begin, it helps to say to yourself what you're supposed to be doing, just as you did in the previous activity. When you think you know it, try clapping instead of saying it. When you're really good, practice doing it with no noise at all. Remember: three traveling actions followed by one jumping action, repeated three times. Keep the same rhythm throughout each part of the sequence. *(Pinpoint several children who've created an interesting sequence—they don't have to be the most skilled children in the class.)*

Jumping a Turned Rope

Setting: Class divided into groups of two or three, each group with one long rope. If the children are in groups of two, attach one end of the rope to a post, pole, or chair. Mark a box on the floor at the center of the rope for the jumper and an X on the floor where the turner or turners stand.

Cues	
Jumpers	
Heads Up	(Keep your head and shoulders up for good balance.)
Jump, Jump	(Small, springy jumps with very little height.)
Turners	
One, Two, Three	(Swing the rope back and forth before the first swing over the head, counting "One, two, three"; this will help the jumper be ready.)
Smooth Turns	(Turn the rope with large, smooth swings.)

Tasks/Challenges:

T At your ropes, two people will turn and one person will try to jump. Jumpers should try to stay in the box marked on the floors as you jump. After 10 jumps, trade positions.

T When you can successfully jump the rope by starting in the middle, try to start from the outside: run in and jump. Turners: Turn the rope so it turns toward the jumper—the front-door approach. Jumpers: Start your run as soon as the rope touches the floor.

C Create a new rhyme as you jump the long rope. *Record the children's rhymes in a booklet of "Jump Rope Rhymes."*

Jumping a Self-Turned Rope

Setting: Ropes of different lengths so each child has a personal rope of the proper length

Cues	
Heads Up	(Keep your head and shoulders up for good balance.)
Jump, Jump	(Small, springy jumps with very little height.)

Tasks/Challenges:

T Practice jumping your rope by turning it over your head. Some of you will find that jumping forward is easier; others will find that jumping the rope as it turns backward is easier. Be sure you try jumping both ways.

T If you're having trouble, bring the rope over your head, stop it on the floor in front of your feet, and then jump over the rope. As you become successful, go a little faster, and don't let the rope stop so much. As you practice, you will find yourself stopping the rope less.

T When you become successful at jumping in one direction (forward or backward) without missing, try jumping in the other direction.

C Set a goal for yourself of the number of jumps you want to make without a mistake.

T Try jumping with the different types of jumps we have learned—two feet to two feet, one foot to the other foot, two feet to one foot, and so forth.

Jumping Using Buoyant and Yielding Landings

Setting: Children scattered throughout general space; paper and pencil available outside the work area

Jumping rope is a favorite children's pastime.

Cues	
Yielding Landings	(Bend your knees to absorb the force when you land, as if sinking into the floor.)
Buoyant Landings	(Bend your knees as you land; then spring up quickly.)
Swing Upward	(Swing your arms upward for good height.)
Heads Up	(Keep your head and shoulders up for good balance.)

Tasks/Challenges:

T Jump three times in a row on two feet, pausing between each jump. This is called a yielding landing.

T This time, jump three times in a row using a two-foot takeoff and a two-foot landing without pausing between each jump. This is a buoyant landing. **Spring up quickly after each jump.**

T Now, jump twice in a row, the first time with a buoyant landing and the second time with a yielding landing. Make sure your landings are clearly different so I can tell which one you're doing simply by watching.

T This time on the signal, jump high, turn in the air, land balanced, and freeze. Again, use yielding landings.

T Now, jump high, turn in the air, and upon landing collapse to the floor, curl, and freeze. **Remember, use your arms to help you turn in the air.**

T Try this one: Jump high, turn in the air, and upon landing collapse to the floor, curl, and freeze for an instant—and then quickly resume traveling. Make your moves very smooth so they really go together and you know exactly what you're doing and what comes next. Use your arms to help you get up in the air. Strive for a yielding landing.

C So far I've made up all your jumping and traveling patterns. On your piece of paper *(pass out paper to the youngsters)*, write down a jumping/traveling pattern that you would like to do yourself. After you've written it down, practice it until it goes smoothly and you know it by heart. Make sure you always begin and end in the same place, which is one way you know you're doing the same thing each time. I should be able to tell what you're doing and the type of landing by watching you. If I can't, I'll ask you.

Jumping to Form a Body Shape During Flight

Setting: Children scattered throughout general space, each with a hurdle or a rope in a shape on the floor

Cues	
Yielding Landings	(Bend your knees to absorb the force when you land, as if sinking into the floor.)
Swing Upward	(Swing your arms upward for good height.)
Heads Up	(Keep your head and shoulders up for good balance.)

Tasks/Challenges:

T Jump over your equipment, and form a narrow body shape while you're in the air. A narrow body

The sensation of jumping delights young children.

shape is very thin. Remember, make all the parts of your body narrow, not just one part. Practice your shape until it's as narrow as it can be.

C Now think of five more narrow body shapes you can make while you're in the air. Practice all the shapes until they're the best you can do. I'll come and ask each of you to show me your best shape, so be ready. **Remember not to fall over on your landings; your feet should stick as if you had**

glue on them. What kind of landings will you need?

T This time you're going to jump using wide body shapes in the air. A wide shape is very big and spread out, like a wall. **Remember as you jump to make your whole body wide in the air by stretching your arms and legs outward from your body.** Practice your shape until it's as wide as it can be.

A Feet need to return to shoulder-width for a safe landing; remind the children not to land with the legs stretched in a wide shape.

C Now that you know what a wide shape is, think of five more wide shapes you can make when you jump. Let them be really different, even weird. Practice all the shapes until they're the best you can do. I'm going to ask some of you to show your wide shapes, so work hard.

Pinpoint several children who are using wide shapes.

T This time, you're going to learn some new names for body shapes. First, you're going to make symmetrical shapes in the air. A symmetrical shape looks exactly alike on both sides. For example, if I were to cut you in half from head to toe, you would look the same on each side. At your equipment, practice making a symmetrical shape in the air. Be sure the two sides of your body look exactly alike.

C Create five more symmetrical shapes with your jumps.

T This time you're going to do nonsymmetrical jumps. In a nonsymmetrical jump, the two sides of your body look really different. So if I were to cut you in half, one arm might be up in the air and the other one out to the side, or one leg might be going forward and the other one backward. In other words, one side shouldn't look like the other one. In your space, create a nonsymmetrical jump. **Remember, absorb force when you land by bending your knees.**

C Create five nonsymmetrical jumps you can do in the air.

T Try to do wide symmetrical jumps. Find three you really like, and practice them.

T Now try to find three narrow symmetrical jumps. After you do that, find three wide nonsymmetrical jumps and three narrow nonsymmetrical jumps. I'm going to ask some of you to show your jumps to the class, so make them the best that they can be.

T Approach your hurdle or rope shape with a series of running steps. Jump in the air, making a wide

shape. **Land in a balanced position without falling down.**

T Try your other shapes in the air combined with your short running approach.

A Students should attempt running, jumping, and making shapes while airborne only after they have demonstrated safe landings in self-space—absorbing the force by bending the knees and landing in a balanced position without falling forward.

Traveling, Jumping, and Body Shapes

Setting: Children scattered throughout general space

Cues	
Buoyant Landings	(Bend your knees as you land; then spring up quickly.)
Swing Upward	(Swing your arms upward for good height.)
Heads Up	(Keep your head and shoulders up for good balance.)

Tasks/Challenges:

T As you travel around the room, make the kind of jump I've called out each time you hear the drumbeat. The jump may simply be wide, or it may be narrow and nonsymmetrical. You'll have to be alert to what I'm saying as well as watching out for others. We'll use buoyant landings so we can be ready to travel again. Remember, make your shapes as clear as you possibly can.

Performing Jumping Sequences and Making Body Shapes

Setting: Note cards with various body-shape sequences written on them, each sequence containing at least four different body shapes (e.g., wide; wide symmetrical; narrow nonsymmetrical; narrow); children scattered throughout general space, each with a sequence card.

Cues	
Buoyant Landings	(Bend your knees as you land; then spring up quickly.)
Yielding Landings	(Bend your knees to absorb the force when you land, as if sinking into the floor.)
Swing Upward	(Swing your arms upward for good height.)
Heads Up	(Keep your head and shoulders up for good balance.)

Tasks/Challenges:

T On your card are listed four body shapes. You're going to make up a sequence of jumps that shows those body shapes in the air. To do this, you'll first travel a bit and then jump, showing the first body shape; then you'll travel again and jump and show the second body shape listed; you'll travel again and jump using the third body shape; you'll travel one more time and jump showing the last body shape. So your sequence should be like this: Travel, jump; travel, jump; travel, jump; travel, jump, freeze. Repeat the sequence enough times so you can do it the same way each time. Memorize it. When it's memorized, show the sequence to a friend. **Remember, use buoyant landings between jumps and a yielding landing after your last jump.**

Jumping over Equipment Using Buoyant Landings

Setting: Pairs of hurdles around the room, spaced so children can jump the first and then the second hurdle

Cues	
Buoyant Landings	(Bend your knees as you land; then spring up quickly.)
Yielding Landings	(Bend your knees to absorb the force when you land, as if sinking into the floor.)
Heads Up	(Keep your head and shoulders up for good balance.)

Tasks/Challenges:

T Earlier in our work, you practiced taking off on one foot and landing on the opposite foot, as in a leap. This is the action you use to clear a hurdle. Approach the first hurdle with quick, running steps; jump over the first hurdle with the one-foot to one-foot action; use a buoyant landing to continue your travel and jump over the second hurdle.

C Practice this activity until you seem to just pop over the first and then the second hurdle.

Jumping On and Off Equipment Using Buoyant and Yielding Landings

Setting: Boxes, low benches, milk crates, and other low equipment around the room

Cues	
Buoyant Landings	(Bend your knees as you land; then spring up quickly.)
Yielding Landings	(Bend your knees to absorb the force when you land, as if sinking into the floor.)
Heads Up	(Keep your head and shoulders up for good balance.)

Tasks/Challenges:

T Jump onto a piece of equipment, and use a buoyant landing to quickly spring off with another jump to the floor. **You should barely touch the equipment before you are off again and back to the floor, almost as if you were on a springboard—no stopping between jumps.**

T This time, jump onto the piece of equipment using a yielding landing, hold still on top of the equipment a couple of seconds, then jump to the floor with another yielding landing. **Remember, on this jump, your knees should really bend, and you should be able to hold still when you finish.**

T Try jumping onto the equipment with the different jumps we have learned—two feet to two feet, one foot to two feet, and so on. Sometimes use a buoyant landing on the equipment so you can quickly jump off; sometimes use a yielding landing on the equipment, pausing before you jump off. Always use a yielding landing on two feet when you jump off the equipment to the floor.

✺ Which landing is used for a quick, springy action to continue movement? Which landing is used for landing and holding still?

Assessment Example

From the *National Standards for Physical Education*

Videotape
Students are asked to skip, gallop, and jump off a low box. A camera is set up in one corner of the gym to record their performance. Each student is asked to go in front of the camera and perform the specified movement patterns. The teacher uses a checklist to assess the extent to which mature and skilled patterns have been attained.

Criteria for Assessment
a. Exhibits mature form for each of the movement patterns.
b. Demonstrates consistent and smooth performance.

NASPE (1995, 19)

Jump, Squash, TaDa

Setting: Low benches, low balance beam, folded mats positioned throughout general space; children divided into groups for stations

Cues

Squash	(Bend your knees to absorb the force and maintain balance when you land.)
Swing Upward	(Swing your arms upward for good height.)
Heads Up	(Keep your head and shoulders up for good balance.)

Tasks/Challenges:

T Have you ever watched gymnasts perform a stunt and then extend their arms high above their heads? Why do you think they do this movement? They do it to regain balance and proper body alignment after the gymnastics action. In the cartoon *Calvin and Hobbes*, Calvin called this recovery the "TaDa" of gymnastics, the recovery to a balanced position no matter what has happened during the movement. Let's add that action to our jumping and landing work today. Jump from your mat (bench, beam) with a two-foot takeoff and a two-foot landing. Jump for maximum height, squash into a balanced position, then stretch your body upward, extending your arms to the sky as you say "TaDa."

T Jump off your mat (bench, beam) with a quarter turn in the air. Land in a balanced position; recover with a full extension. **Don't forget the TaDa!**

T When a friend gives you a thumbs-up for a good landing on your quarter turn, you may want to try a one-half turn. Practice turning your body clockwise and counterclockwise.

T Jump off the mat (bench, beam), make a shape in the air, land in a balanced position, and recover with a full gymnastics extension.

T Combine jumping off the low equipment, landing, and rolling in a gymnastics sequence; finish your sequence by returning to a standing TaDa.

⚠ Use the previous task only if children have mastered rolling from Chapter 21 or in combination with work from that chapter.

See Chapter 21 for additional combination tasks, as well as for transferring off low apparatus.

Jumping and Landing Task Sheet

Setting: A jumping and landing task sheet (similar to the example in Figure 19.1) for each child

Cues

Buoyant Landings	(Bend your knees as you land, then spring up quickly.)
Yielding Landings	(Bend your knees to absorb the force when you land, as if sinking into the floor.)
Heads Up	(Keep your head and shoulders up for good balance.)
Swing Upward	(Swing your arms upward for good height on the jump.)
Swing Forward	(Swing your arms forcefully forward for maximum distance.)

Select cues appropriate to the tasks on the sheet (e.g., jumping forward, jumping upward, jumping and continuing action, jumping/landing with a stop of movement).

Tasks/Challenges:

C This task sheet lets you test the jumping skills you've practiced so far. Whenever you've practiced a challenge and think you can do it correctly, ask a friend to watch you. If your friend thinks you've done the challenge well, the friend signs her or his name on the sheet next to the challenge.

Utilization Level (GLSP): Learning Experiences Leading to Skill Development

Experiences at the utilization level provide contexts in which children use jumping and landing in combination with other movements. They are challenged to combine jumping with throwing and catching in both static and dynamic situations. They combine jumping and landing with the gymnastics skills of balancing and transferring weight. They explore the complexity of rhythm with accented beats.

A note about cues: Although several cues are listed for many of the learning experiences, it's important to focus on only one cue at a time. This way, the children can really concentrate on that cue. Once you provide feedback to the children and observe that most have learned a cue, it's time to focus on another one.

Figure 19.1 Task sheet for jumping and landing.

Name _____	Teacher _____

Jumping Task Sheet

Verification	Challenge
	I can jump starting on two feet and landing on two feet.
	I can jump from two feet to one foot.
	I can jump from one foot to the other foot.
	I can hop from one foot to the same foot.
	I can jump from one foot to two feet.
	I can jump, turn in the air, and land without falling.
	I can jump off a box and land without falling.
	I can jump off a box, turn in the air, and land without falling.
	I can run and jump over a hurdle and land without falling.
	I can turn a jump rope myself and jump 15 times without missing.
	I can
	I can
	I can

Jumping to Catch

Setting: Low benches, chairs, or milk crates scattered throughout general space; sets of partners with beanbags, plastic balls, foam footballs, tennis balls

Cues

Yielding Landings	(Bend your knees to absorb the force when you land, as if sinking into the floor.)
Swing Upward	(Swing your arms upward for a full extension and added height on the jump.)

Tasks/Challenges:

T One partner stands on the low bench (chair, milk crate) and then jumps from the bench to catch the ball the other partner tosses. Catch the ball while in the air. After three jumps, switch catcher–thrower positions with your partner. Hint for the thrower: Stand close and begin the toss as soon as your partner begins to jump.

For the next task, clear the general space of benches, crates, and other obstacles.

T Pairs, scatter throughout general space. See how many times you can jump and catch without a mistake; count your score only if you catch the ball before you land. After three trials, switch thrower/catcher as you did earlier.

T When the activity becomes easy for you and your partner, try throwing the ball so your partner has to reach to the left or to the right to make the catch.

T Throw the ball so your partner is forced off the ground to catch it; this means you have to throw the ball to a point above where the catch will actually be made. This is a high-level catch—feet off the floor, arms extended above the head. Throwers: It helps to pick a spot on the wall (tree, telephone pole) above and behind your partner to aim at.

T Try both one- and two-foot takeoffs.

T Switch with your partner after five throws. You are now the catcher; your partner will throw the ball above your head, so you must jump for the catch.

T When you are confident throwing and catching while jumping, you and your partner can add a new element—traveling. Practice running, jumping, and catching in the air. For the two of you to do this task well, your partner will need to make a good throw. At first, run and jump from right to left; then, run and jump from left to right.

T When you are able to make at least three catches in a row, run away from the thrower—that is, start close to and run away from your partner, as you might in a football game.

Jumping to Throw

Setting: Low benches, chairs, or milk crates throughout general space; sets of partners with whiffle balls, tennis balls, footballs

Cues	
Yielding Landings	(Bend your knees to absorb the force when you land, as if sinking into the floor.)
Vertical Jumps	(Jump upward, not outward, to throw.)

Tasks/Challenges:

T Stand 10 to 12 feet from your partner. Jump from the bench (chair, crate) and throw the ball to your partner before you land. Try to throw the ball so your partner can catch it easily. Switch with your partner after four jumps/throws.

Clear the general space of benches, crates, and other obstacles.

T Pick a target, such as a target on the wall (or a basketball backstop, a hoop, or a stationary partner). Jump and throw the ball to the target.

Catching at a high level combines jumping and stretching.

T When you hit the target five times in a row, move farther away from the target. It counts as a successful throw only if you hit the target and make your throw while in the air.

T As this activity gets easier, try running, jumping, and throwing to the target.

Jumping on a Bench

Setting: Low benches scattered throughout the work area

Cue	
Squash	(Bend your knees to absorb the force and maintain balance when you land.)

Tasks/Challenges:

T You will work one at a time on the bench. Travel to the middle of the bench; jump upward, taking off and landing on two feet on the bench. **Focus your eyes on the end of the bench.**

T When you're able to do this activity several times without falling off, practice landing on only one foot. Hold your balance on the bench before your other foot comes down on the bench. Try to hold your balance for 2 or 3 seconds.

C Design a sequence along the bench that includes at least two different jumps. For example, hop on one foot along the bench, jump and turn so you land facing the opposite direction, and travel back to the start using small leaps. At first, your jumps won't be very high, but as you get better, you'll want to make them higher. Practice your sequence until you can do it three times in a row without falling off.

Jumping onto a bench challenges utilization-level children

When you observe that children are competent and comfortable with different types of jumps on the bench, they may progress to low and medium balance beams. This is an excellent opportunity for intratask variation.

Throwing and Catching While Jumping

Setting: A court, its boundaries marked with a rope or a net (size of court is determined by space available; the larger the court, the more difficult the game)

Cues	
Buoyant Landings	(Bend your knees as you land; then spring up quickly—to throw or travel.)
Yielding Landings	(Bend your knees to absorb the force, and sink into a balanced position.)

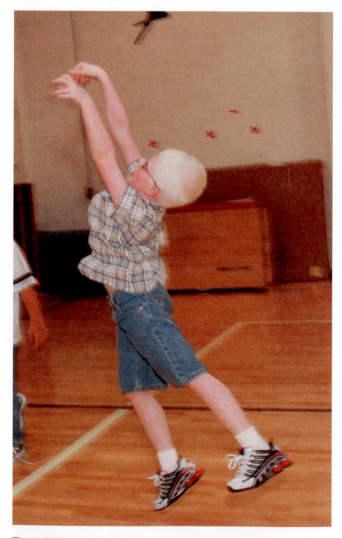

The skill of jumping is important to success in games, dance, and gymnastics.

Tasks/Challenges:

T The game you're going to play will give you a chance to practice throwing and catching while jumping. The object is to have the ball touch the floor on the opposite side of the net. Here are the rules:

1. There are three players on a team.
2. There is one team on each side of the rope (or net).
3. A player must be off the floor when the ball is thrown or caught.
4. At least two players on your team must touch the ball before it is thrown back over the rope (net).
5. Points are scored when the ball lands out of bounds, the ball hits the floor inbounds, or a player throws or catches the ball while that player's feet are touching the ground.

This game can also be played cooperatively: Both teams work together to see how many times the ball can cross the rope or net without breaking any of the rules. A point is scored each time the ball crosses the net. A good score to aim for is 10 throws in a row over the net without breaking a rule.

Jumping to an Accented Beat

Setting: Children scattered throughout general space, each with a hoop

Cue

Buoyant Landings (Bend your knees; then spring up quickly to travel.)

Tasks/Challenges:

T When I beat the drum, jump into and out of your hoop each time you hear the drumbeat.

T Now take off on two feet, and land on two feet. As the drumbeat gets faster, be ready to jump by having your knees bent and your arms flexed. Try to land on only the balls of your feet, which means your heels won't touch the ground.

T Take off on one foot, and land on the same foot.

T Try to keep up with the beat—it's going to get faster and faster. When one leg gets tired, change to the other leg.

T Listen as I beat the drum. The first beat is louder than the others. This is called an accented beat. Use one- or two-foot takeoffs and landings, but jump on only the accented beat. The first beat will be accented; the next three beats will be unaccented.

Proficiency Level (GLSP): Learning Experiences Leading to Skill Development

At the proficiency level, dynamic dance, game, and gymnastics experiences are designed to help youngsters use, refine, and enjoy their jumping abilities. At this level children almost always jump in relation to objects or other people (or both) and use jumping for both expressive and functional purposes. Jumping is now infused into the skill themes of games. It is an integral part of gymnastics routines, both with and without apparatus. It is a major component of all styles of dance and a key element in choreography.

A note about cues: At the proficiency level, tasks are more complex, typically requiring children to coordinate several movements simultaneously in a dynamic context. A list of cues is provided to assist the children in being more successful in the learning experience. The challenge for the teacher is in determining which cue will be most beneficial for each child . . . and when. Thus careful observation and critical reflection become very important as you watch the children move and then decide which cue will be the most helpful to move each learner to a higher skill level.

Jumping with a Partner to Mirror Actions

Setting: Two pieces of equipment (benches, tables, or vaulting boxes) about 15 feet apart, with a large mat on the floor between; children with partners

Cues

Yielding Landings (Bend your knees to absorb the force, and sink into a balanced position.)
Buoyant Landings (Bend your knees as you land; then spring up quickly.)
Heads Up (Keep your head and shoulders up for good balance.)

Tasks/Challenges:

T You and your partner are going to mirror each other's jumps. Mirroring means you face each other and copy the other's movements, as if you were looking in a mirror. Therefore, if your partner uses the left arm, you'll use your right arm. To start, decide which of you will be the first leader. The leader makes up the first jump and shows it to the partner. Then you both face each other and do that jump at the same time, mirroring each other exactly. This activity will be hard at first because you'll have to take off at the same time, jump the same height, and do everything exactly together. Start with some easy jumps and then go to harder ones. Each person takes three turns as leader and then switches. Again, make your jumps look like a reflection of your partner's. **Don't forget: Yielding and buoyant landings will be part of the mirror action.**

Pinpoint several pairs who are mirroring jumps accurately.

T As you get better at mirroring your partner, you may want to include such actions as gesturing in the air, turning in the air, or rolling after landing. **This will really take a lot of work; you may want to count out everything before you do it.**

Jumping with a Partner to Match Actions

Setting: Two pieces of equipment (benches, tables, or vaulting boxes) about 15 feet apart, with a large mat on the floor between; children with partners

Cues	
Travel, Jumps, and Landings	(Everything must match your partner—travel, jumps, and landings.)
Heads Up	(Keep your head and shoulders up for good balance.)

Tasks/Challenges:

T Now that you've become very good at mirroring a partner's actions and jumps, you're going to try matching jumps. Matching means you do the same thing at the same time; thus if you're facing your partner, your actions look the opposite of your partner's. If you use your right leg, then your partner must also use the right leg. Again, decide which of you will be the first leader. The leader makes a jump and faces the partner; the two of you then match jumps. Take three turns as leader, and then switch. Start with easy jumps. **Counting will help you match starting each jump.**

T Once you've become quite good at matching jumps with your partner while facing each other and standing still, try this: Travel a short distance together, and then, at a set point, do matching jumps in the air. This activity will be hard. You must pick a starting point, count exactly how many steps you'll travel before you jump, and then jump and land. First, by yourself, practice the traveling by itself and then the jump by itself; then, combine the traveling and jumping. Finally, try to do the task with your partner. The sequence is this: Travel, jump, land, freeze—all movements exactly

matching those of your partner. You two should look like twins.

T To the sequence you just made up, add a second traveling action and a second jump.

Jumping with a Springboard

Setting: Springboards positioned throughout the work space with sufficient large mats for safe landings

Cues	
Push	(Push hard with your feet and legs as you contact the board.)
Swing Upward	(Swing your arms upward for good height.)
Squash	(Bend your knees and spread your feet for a stable, soft landing.)

Tasks/Challenges:

T Using the nearest springboard, run and jump, using a two-foot landing/takeoff on the board; spring up high and land on two feet on the mat.

T As you become good at going off the springboard and landing without falling over, add a turn in the air as you jump so you end up facing the place where you started. **Remember, bend your knees and spread your feet apart when you land.**

T When you're able to do this activity, try a complete 360-degree turn in the air before you land. To get all the way around, you'll have to throw your arms up and around in the direction you want to turn.

Jumping as Part of a Dance Creation

Setting: Children divided into small groups, no more than four per group

Cues
Individual cues as needed

Tasks/Challenges:

T Now you're going to use jumps to make up a dance. The main actions of the dance will all use different jumps. First, think of a theme for your dance, such as a battle scene. If you use that idea, your jumps will contain such gestures as punching, slashing, jabbing, protecting, and retreating.

As a group, think of what you want your dance to say. Once you've decided the theme, try to put together a series of jumps that express that idea.

You'll be using your jumps and other movements to tell a story. It may be that you all move at the same time, or that two of you move and then the other two move. Your dance needs to have a definite beginning and a definite ending, with at least six different jumps in the middle. Try to make the dance look really professional. This will take a while to do; I'll be available to help each group as you work. Toward the end of class, we'll show the dances to the rest of the class.

Jumping, Dancing, and Imagery

Setting: Children divided into small groups, no more than four per group

> **Cues**
>
> Individual cues as needed

Tasks/Challenges:

T Jumps can be used to create a dance about the things around you (the flight of a bird, leaves in the wind, etc.). This time, you're going to create a dance that uses one of these things as its main idea. Jumps will communicate that idea to your audience. You must decide in your group what natural thing you would like to communicate in a dance using jumps.

After you've decided, begin to develop your dance, keeping the following ideas in mind:

- The actions you're demonstrating should clearly portray your theme.
- The starting location of each person should be clear.
- The dance should rise to a climax and then wind down to a conclusion.
- The jumps and gestures you're using to communicate your ideas should be the most effective ones you can create.
- The pathways used in the dance should be clear.

At the end of class, you may show your dance to the class.

Jumping Hurdles

Setting: A series of hurdles set up throughout the work area, with sufficient space between for children to run between, jumping over each; stopwatches at starting line (optional)

> **Cues**
>
> **Foot to Foot** (Opposite: one foot to the other foot.)
>
> **Extend** (Front leg upward and forward.)
>
> **Heads Up** (Keep your head and shoulders up for good balance.)

Tasks/Challenges:

T In this activity you'll be *hurdling,* which is sprinting over barriers, called hurdles, placed along the way. Begin behind the first hurdle, and run to the end of the line of hurdles. Each time you come to a hurdle, jump it and keep going. Run to the end of the line, come back to the first hurdle, and start again. Start your jump *before* you reach the hurdle by extending your front leg upward and forward. Try to get over the hurdles by barely clearing them rather than jumping really high over them. You need a horizontal rather than a high vertical jump for hurdles.

Use low barriers at first so youngsters can focus on proper technique without worrying about clearing the obstacles. Once children begin to exhibit quality hurdling actions, you can gradually increase the height of the barriers. Milk crates spread apart with bamboo poles supported between them are satisfactory barriers.

C As you feel you're getting better at hurdling, time yourself and see if you can improve each time. You can use one of the stopwatches available at the starting line of each row of hurdles.

For transferring weight over apparatus (vaulting box), see Chapter 21.

Reading Comprehension Questions

1. Name the two basic reasons for performing jumps.
2. What are the three phases of a jump?
3. List in order of difficulty the different takeoff and landing patterns for jumping.
4. What does a precontrol jump look like?
5. How does jumping and landing differ at each of the Generic Levels of Skill Proficiency?
6. What is the focus of the jumping and landing activities for the control and proficiency levels?

7. Describe a low obstacle children can safely practice jumping over.
8. What is the difference between a buoyant landing and a yielding landing?
9. Describe a sequence for teaching young children to jump rope.

10. Describe how jumping is used in (1) gymnastics, (2) games/sports, and (3) dance. Give a specific example of jumping in each of these content areas.

References/Suggested Readings

Holt/Hale, S. A. 2012. *On the move: Lesson plans to accompany* Children Moving. 9th ed. New York: McGraw-Hill.

[NASPE] National Association for Sport and Physical Education. 1995. *Moving into the future: National standards for physical education.* St. Louis, MO: Mosby.

[NASPE] National Association for Sport and Physical Education. 2004. *Moving into the future: National standards for*

physical education. 2nd ed. Reston, VA: National Association for Sport and Physical Education.

Wickstrom, R. L. 1977. *Fundamental motor patterns.* 2nd ed. Philadelphia: Lea & Febiger.

20
CHAPTER

Balancing

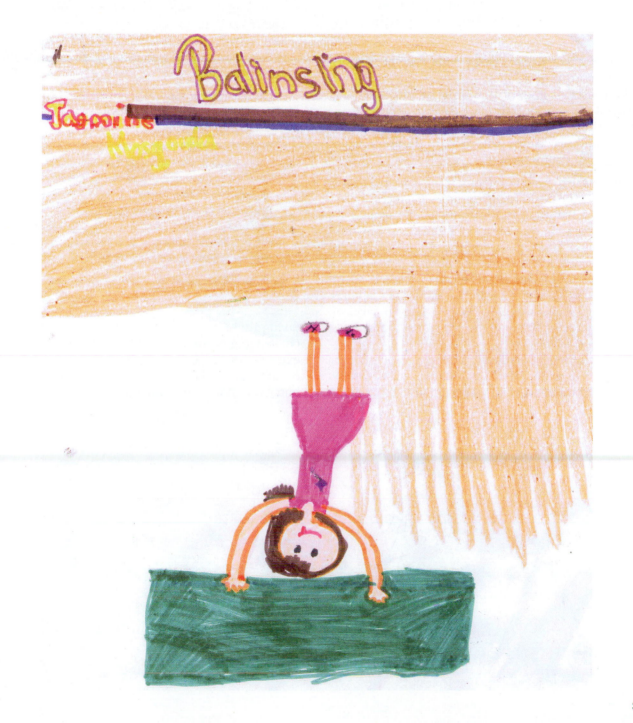

Merriam Webster's Collegiate Dictionary, 11th edition, defines *balance* as "stability produced by even distribution of weight on each side of the vertical axis" and as "an aesthetically pleasing integration of elements." There's no extraneous motion, no flagrant waving of arms to maintain position, no near topple or wobble from side to side. The center of gravity is clearly over the base of support.

The elementary school child attempting to do a headstand, walk a beam, ride a skateboard, or use in-line skates encounters different types of static and dynamic balance challenges. Among the key teaching concepts in providing balance experiences are the following:

- It's easier to balance over a wide base of support than a narrow base.
- The center of gravity should be aligned over the base of support for stationary balance (Figure 20.1).
- Extensions to one side of the body beyond the base of support necessitate extensions in the opposite direction for counterbalance.

Static balance involves maintaining a desired shape in a stationary position; gymnastics balances, headstands, and handstands are examples. Dynamic balance involves maintaining an on-balance position while moving, starting, or stopping. Dynamic balance occurs in weight transference, jumping, throwing, catching, and all forms of travel. Balance as a concept is discussed in Chapters 16, 19, 21, and 23 as it applies to learning specific skills. See Box 20-1 for linkages of the skill theme of balancing to the *National Standards for Physical Education*.

Young children sporadically achieve balance; it's often more coincidental than intentional. The very young child attempting to stand upright, the toddler

Balancing in the *National Standards for Physical Education*

The skill theme of balancing is referenced in the National Association for Sport and Physical Education's *National Standards for Physical Education* (NASPE 2004) under Standard 1: "Demonstrates competency in motor skills and movement patterns needed to perform a variety of physical activities." The standard speaks of children demonstrating control in traveling, weight bearing, and balance activities on a variety of body parts, and being able to participate with skill in gymnastics.

Sample performance outcomes from the *National Standards* include:

- Discovers how to balance on different body parts, at different levels, becoming "like" a statue while making symmetrical and nonsymmetrical shapes (K–2)*
- Balances with control on a variety of objects (e.g., balance board, large apparatus, skates) (3–5)*
- Develops and refines a gymnastics sequence demonstrating smooth transitions (3–5)*
- Designs and performs gymnastics sequences that combine traveling, rolling, balancing, and weight transfer into smooth, flowing sequences with intentional changes in direction, speed, and flow (6–8)*

*Grade-level guidelines for expected student learning.

taking those first steps, the youngsters in our classes challenging themselves as they attempt new balance experiences—all are attempting to master stability, i.e., balance. The balance is momentary as the child calls out, "Watch me" and immediately loses balance. The

Figure 20.1 Center of gravity over base of support.

momentary balance is the incentive for continued practice, both for the beginner and the advanced; the momentary mastery provides both the reward and the challenge.

The skill theme of balance must be taught in a safe environment. (See Chapter 29 for the establishment of procedures for working on gymnastics skills, working with and along side others, as well as on apparatus.) With the establishment of procedures for activity, the selection of developmentally appropriate tasks, and the use of intratask variation, the skill theme of balance provides challenging activities for all children.

We tend to think of balance as a gymnastics skill, and while extremely important in gymnastics, balance is an important skill for everyday activities as well as sports. Carrying a heavy backpack while drinking from a water bottle and walking down a flight of stairs, performing the sharp turns of marching band drill while playing the musical selection on the chosen instrument, maintaining a hold on the family dog while walking on an icy street—all are tasks that require balance. The seemingly effortless execution of a punt, the heading of the soccer ball, the dodging of a tag in baseball, the twists and turns of skateboarding, the aerials of snowboarding—all of these require a solid foundation of balance and its continued application into sports. Balance does not reach completion with maintaining a headstand for 3 seconds. The study of balance continues into middle school and high school physical education. The progression spiral for the skill theme of balance at the precontrol, control, utilization, and proficiency levels of skill development is found on this page.

Precontrol Level (GLSP): Activities for Exploration

Activities at the precontrol level are designed to provide exploration of the concept of balance. As children explore the concept of balance, they begin to maintain simple stationary balances and to stop in balanced positions while traveling.

Balancing on Different Bases of Support

Setting: Carpet squares or small mats placed throughout general space, with sufficient room between them for children to work without bumping others

Tasks/Challenges:

Ⓣ Balance on different bases of support on your mat. Your base of support is the body parts holding you in the balance. See how many body parts can be bases of support. Hold each balance as you count

Skill Theme Development Progression
Balancing

Proficiency Level

Performing apparatus sequences that combine stationary balances and traveling with movement concepts
Transferring off equipment with weight on hands
Balancing on hanging ropes
Balancing while supporting the weight of a partner

Utilization Level

Performing sequences that combine stationary balances and traveling on mats
Performing inverted balances on equipment
Traveling into and out of balances by rolling
Moving out of and into balances by stretching, curling, and twisting
Balancing on crates

Control Level

Balance boards
Balancing on stilts
Balancing sequence
Traveling while balanced
Traveling on large apparatus
Stationary balances on equipment
Traveling and stopping in balanced positions
Doing kickups
Alignment of body parts
Performing inverted balances
Balances and shapes: The Gymnastics Dance
Balancing in different body shapes
Balancing symmetrically and nonsymmetrically
Counterbalance
Tightening the gymnastics muscles
Balancing on different bases of support

Precontrol Level

Balancing on boards
Traveling on low gymnastics equipment
Traveling and stopping in balanced positions
Balancing in different body shapes
Balancing on a wide base of support
Balancing on different bases of support

to yourself 3 seconds: "one thousand one, one thousand two. . . ."

Ⓣ Try different combinations of body parts as you create your balances.

(T) Let's list all the body parts you've used as bases of support for your balances. *(List on board or flip chart as students give responses.)* Do you see some body parts listed as bases of support that you didn't try? Take a few minutes to try all the combinations.

(⚠) Some children will watch others in class, often the more skilled students, and attempt to copy their balances. This can result in injury to the less skilled. A reminder to the group and/or to the less confident students of what the teacher is looking for eliminates this potential problem.

(T) Now I'll name the body parts I want to be the bases of support. First, hand(s) and feet. Be creative in your balance. Although you're all using the same base of support, the gymnastics balances may be very different.

Additional exploration: feet and head, knees and elbows, stomach, base of spine, and shoulders in combination with other body parts.

(⚠) Sometimes children attempt to balance on body parts that aren't appropriate for supporting weight. Don't let youngsters balance in unsafe positions that could result in stress or injury.

(C) Balance on your favorite bases of support, holding the balance very still. Let's pretend I am going to take a photo of the balance—no wiggles, no wobbles.

(✓) **Exit Slip.** Young children enjoy labeling on a large stick figure the body parts that can serve as bases of support. *Refer to Chapter 12, "Assessing Student Learning," for the use of exit slips in physical education.*

Balancing on a Wide Base of Support

Setting: Carpet squares or small mats placed throughout general space with sufficient room between them for children to work without bumping others

Tasks/Challenges:

(T) Create a four-part balance on your hands and lower legs; have your hands under your shoulders and your legs approximately the same distance apart as the width of your hips. This wide base of support creates a very stable balance.

(T) Move your hands toward each other and your legs toward each other until they touch. Do you feel stable now? Could I push you over?

(T) Explore the concept of wide to narrow balances with different bases of support: hands and feet, knees and elbows.

Balancing in Different Body Shapes

Setting: Carpet squares or small mats placed throughout general space, with sufficient room between them for children to work without bumping others

Tasks/Challenges:

(T) Create a gymnastics balance on a wide base of support. Create a wide body shape by extending free body parts outward from your trunk (free body parts are those you're not using as bases of support).

(T) Create a narrow-shape gymnastics balance on your base of spine—long and thin like a piece of spaghetti. Keep all free body parts close to your trunk.

(T) Create a curled-shape gymnastics balance on your chosen base of support. Free body parts can be tucked close to the body, or they may be added to the curled shape by bending them in the curve.

(T) Create a twisted-shape gymnastics balance. Use your two feet as your base of support and twist your body like a pretzel.

Traveling and Stopping in Balanced Positions

Setting: Children scattered throughout general space

Tasks/Challenges:

(T) Travel through general space any way you choose. On the signal, stop and create a gymnastics balance with two feet and two hands touching the floor.

Additional exploration: two feet and one hand, base of spine, two knees and one hand.

(T) Travel again, but this time balance on three body parts when you hear the signal. Think which three parts you're going to use before traveling. Ready? Go.

Additional exploration: four body parts, five body parts, two body parts.

Traveling on Low Gymnastics Equipment

Setting: Jump ropes; low balance beams; 2-by-4-inch planks; low, narrow benches; tape pathways arranged on the floor (Figure 20.2)

Tasks/Challenges:

(T) Travel on the different pieces of equipment without losing your balance and falling off.

Additional exploration: travel backward; travel with your arms above your head; walk with a beanbag on your head.

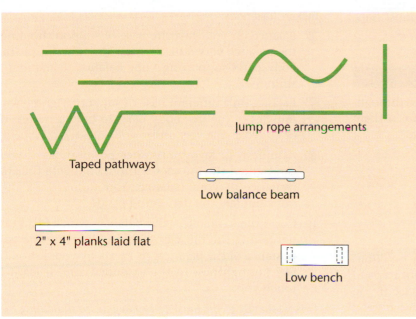

Figure 20.2 Equipment arrangement for traveling.*

Taped pathways

Jump rope arrangements

Low balance beam

2" x 4" planks laid flat

Low bench

*Prior to constructing homemade equipment we recommend you be certain that teacher-made equipment is permitted in your school and/or school district.

Balancing on Boards

Setting: Square, rectangle, and circular balance boards arranged as a station for the study of balance (Figure 20.3)

Tasks/Challenges:

T Balance on a balance board without falling off or letting the edges of the board touch the ground. You may want a partner to stand in front of the balance board to help when you first step up; place your hands on the partner's shoulders for support.

T Explore standing with your feet shoulder-width apart and with your feet close together. Which gives you better balance on the board?

Control Level (GLSP): Learning Experiences Leading to Skill Development

Learning experiences at the control level focus on maintaining the stillness and control of a balance. Children balance on increasingly smaller bases of support while holding the body in inverted positions, and in stationary balances on apparatus. These experiences begin to provide the ingredients for a movement repertoire of balances that may be included in sequences involving traveling and other balances. Several tasks explored at the precontrol level will be repeated at the control level, with the focus on refinement cues.

A note about cues: Although several cues are listed for many of the learning experiences, it's important to focus on only one cue at a time. This way, the children can really concentrate on that cue. Once you provide

Figure 20.3 Construction of balance boards of various shapes.*
*Prior to constructing homemade equipment we recommend you be certain that teacher-made equipment is permitted in your school and/or school district.

feedback to the children and observe that most have learned a cue, it's time to focus on another one.

Balancing on Different Bases of Support

Setting: Carpet squares or small mats scattered throughout general space with sufficient room between them for children to work without bumping others

> **Cue**
>
> **Stillness** (No wiggles, no wobbles—hold perfectly still for 3 seconds.)

Tasks/Challenges:

T Earlier in the year we explored balancing on different bases of support. Balance on different bases of support on your mat or carpet square. See if you can remember which body parts can serve as good bases for gymnastic balances.

T Listed on the board (flip chart) are the body parts that serve as bases of support. I will call out the combination of body parts; you create the balance with that base—for example, feet and hands. What other body parts can you use with your feet to create a good base for gymnastic balances?

T Create balances using the following combination of bases: head and hands, head and knees, head and feet; elbows and knees; elbows, feet, and head; stomach only; base of spine only; shoulders, upper arms/elbows, and head.

T Create balances by adding your chosen base or bases to the following: feet and head and elbows.

C From all the balances you have practiced, choose three of your favorites, each showing a different combination of body parts as bases of support. Practice until you can hold each balance 3 seconds without moving or losing your balance. When you are ready, show your balances to a partner, who will give you a thumbs-up if you hold the balance stationary for 3 seconds.

Tightening the Gymnastics Muscles

Setting: Carpet squares and/or small mats scattered throughout general space, with sufficient room between them for children to work without collisions

> **Cues**
>
> **Stillness** (No wiggles, no wobbles—hold perfectly still for 3 seconds.)
> **Tight Muscles** (Muscular tension is the key to holding the balance.)

Tasks/Challenges:

T Balance on your favorite base of support, holding the balance very still. Tighten the muscles of the body parts supporting your balance to maintain stillness.

T Balance on a different base of support. Tighten the muscles of the free body parts to hold a stretched or curled shape very still.

T Assume your favorite balance position. See if you can tighten the muscles without changing the appearance of your balance. You should look the same but feel the tightening inside.

C Continue to practice your balances with a focus on tightening the muscles without changing the appearance of the balance. As I walk by you, I should feel the tightness in the extended arm or leg if I touch you.

This tightening of the muscles is a key factor in holding the balance very still without extraneous movement and in maintaining the position.

Counterbalance

Setting: Carpet squares or small mats scattered throughout general space, with sufficient room between them for children to work safely

> **Cues**
>
> **Stillness** (No wiggles, no wobbles for 3 seconds.)
> **Tight Muscles** (Muscular tension is the key to holding the balance.)
> **Extensions** (Extend free body parts for stability in your balance.)

Tasks/Challenges:

T Balance on one foot. Extend your arms and free leg, holding the balance very stationary. Repeat the balance, extending the arms but not the leg. Which balance is easier to maintain? Right, the one with arms and free leg extended in opposite directions. This is the concept of counterbalance. Extensions to one side of the body necessitate extensions in the opposite direction.

T Balance on your base of spine. Extend free body parts to one side only; repeat with the extension in the opposite direction.

T Explore balances on different bases of support, extending your body parts in different directions from your body for counterbalance.

Balancing Symmetrically and Nonsymmetrically

Setting: Carpet squares and/or small mats scattered throughout general space, with sufficient room between them for children to work safely

Cues	
Tight Muscles	(Muscular tension is the key to holding the balance.)
Extensions	(Extend free body parts for stability in your balance.)
Smooth Transitions	(Move slowly from one balance to the next for a smooth transition.)

Tasks/Challenges:

T Balance on your base of spine, with arms and legs extended outward. Create exactly the same shape on both sides of your body. This is called a symmetrical shape; both sides of the body look the same.

T Keeping the same base of support, change your free body parts, still creating a symmetrical shape.

T Balance on your chosen base of support. Create a symmetrical shape. Now change to a nonsymmetrical shape—the sides look different—while balanced on that same base.

T Balance on your shoulders, back of head, and arms. Create a symmetrical shape with your legs. Change to a nonsymmetrical shape and then back to a symmetrical one.

T Repeat this three-part symmetrical, nonsymmetrical, symmetrical sequence; slowly change your legs into the different shapes. This smoothness in transition is an important component of gymnastics.

Assessment Example

From the *National Standards for Physical Education*

Peer Observation

Students are asked to work on balancing on different bases of support (e.g., two hands and one foot, hands and knees, headstand). Students should balance in four different positions, two using symmetrical shapes and two using asymmetrical shapes. Students are asked to draw their favorite symmetrical and asymmetrical balances on paper, labeling S and A, respectively. Students now select a partner who will observe their balances and then indicate on the paper: (1) if the drawn figures were labeled correctly and (2) if the balances were held still for 3 seconds.

Criteria for Assessment

a. Completes four balances—two symmetrical and two asymmetrical.

b. Correctly labels balances S and A.

c. Maintains stillness in balance for 3 seconds.

d. Observer correctly assesses the appropriateness of the labels and the extent to which the performer was still.

NASPE (1995, 19)

Balancing in Different Body Shapes

Setting: Small mats and/or carpet squares scattered throughout general space, with sufficient room between them for children to work safely

Cues	
Tight Muscles	(Muscular tension is the key to holding the balance.)
Extensions	(Extend free body parts for stability in your balance.)
Smooth Transitions	(Move slowly from one balance to the next for a smooth transition.)

Tasks/Challenges:

T Remember when we explored basic body shapes for physical education? Who can name the four shapes? Wide, curled, twisted, narrow—that's right. Let's create balances that show each of those shapes. Now that you have learned to balance on different bases of support, try to have a different base of support for each of your balances.

T Let's focus on wide-shape balances. Create wide-shape balances with different bases of support. Remember, extensions of arms and legs away from the body create wide shapes.

C I'm going to put on some background music for a few minutes. Create three balances that show wide shapes; each balance is to have a different base of support. Challenge yourself with a level of difficulty that tests your skills. When the music stops, we will look at the balances.

T Now let's create gymnastics balances that show narrow shapes. Remember, we create narrow-shape balances by holding body parts close to each other. How many different narrow balances can you create?

T Create a narrow balance on your base of spine. **Stretch your legs and arms to counterbalance.**

T Create two new narrow balances, one at a low level, the other at medium level.

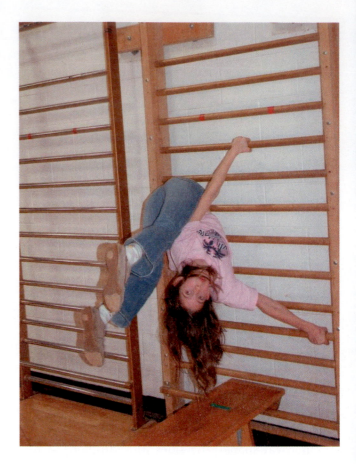

These youngsters maintain stillness in symmetrical and nonsymmetrical balances

T You can create a curled (round) shape by curling your spine forward or arching your spine backward. Free body parts may be tucked close to the body, or they may be added to the curled image by bending in the curve. Create a curled gymnastics balance on your chosen base of support.

T Create a curled-shape gymnastics balance in which the spine curls forward; slowly change into a curled-shape balance with your spine arched backward.

T Stand in a balanced position, with both feet as bases of support for your weight. Create a twisted shape by turning your body to the right or the left without moving your feet. Now balance, using your left foot and the lower portion of your right leg as bases of support. Create a twisted shape from this base.

T Create twisted shapes by rotating your trunk, arms, legs, neck, ankles, and wrists while balanced on different bases of support.

T Balance on three body parts. Create a twisted shape by rotating free body parts—for example, arms, legs, trunk, neck. Create two more twisted-shape balances on various bases of support.

C Think of all the balances you have created today. They represent four shapes: wide, narrow, curled, twisted. Review the balances you did; choose your favorite balance for each shape. On each signal, show me your favorite wide-, narrow-, curled-, and twisted-shape balance. **Concentrate on holding each perfectly still and moving smoothly from balance to balance.**

✓ *Peer Observation.* Peer observation of body shapes and balances would be appropriate here. A possible task would be to have students, using stick figures, draw each of the four balances, one representing each of the four shapes. Have them label the body shape of each figure, then exchange papers with a neighbor, who will be the "gymnastics judge" (Figure 20.4).

Refer to Chapter 12, "Assessing Student Learning," for the use of peer observation as assessment.

C Working in groups of four, create a balance statue in which each person partially supports another. Each person should represent one of the four basic shapes; wide, narrow, curled, and twisted. After you make the body-shape statue, convert it to a movable monster by moving as a unit in either self-space or general space.

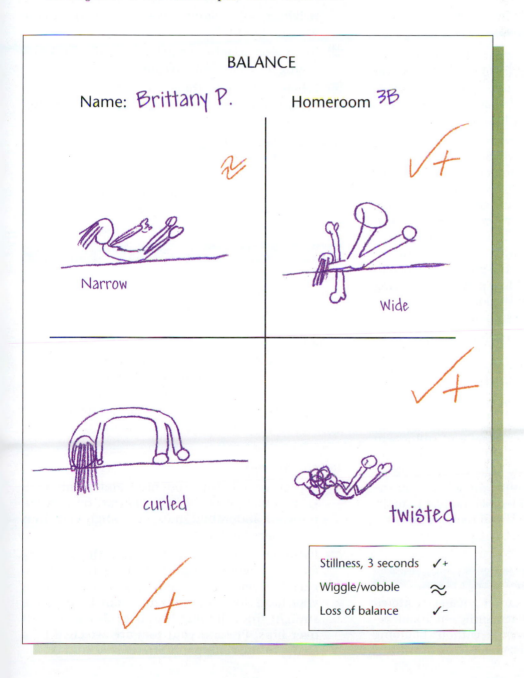

Figure 20.4 Student balance drawings and peer assessment results.

BALANCE

Name: Brittany P.   Homeroom 3B

Narrow

Wide

curled

twisted

Stillness, 3 seconds	✓+
Wiggle/wobble	≈
Loss of balance	✓–

Balances and Shapes: The Gymnastics Dance

Setting: Children scattered throughout general space, in groups of 6–8 per group.

> **Cues**
>
> **Tight Muscles**   (Muscular tension is the key to holding the balance.)
> **Extensions**   (Extend free body parts for stability in your balance.)
> **Smooth Transitions**   (Move slowly from one balance to the next for a smooth transition.)

Tasks/Challenges:

T Let's create a gymnastics dance that focuses on body shapes and balance. I will select one person in each group to form a statue by holding a gymnastics balance with a wide base of support. You will need to hold your wide balance as others come and go.

T Each person in the group will add to the statue by making a wide, narrow, curled or twisted shape. When I touch you, move slowly toward the "statue," connect by touching the statue with one body part, and then make a wide, narrow, curled, or twisted shape. (Move among the children, touching individuals to move to the central statue; continue until everyone in the group has added to the statue by touching the first person and making a shape.) That looks really good; the shapes are clear, and the balances are stationary.

T On signal (drumbeat, tambourine), begin to move slowly from the original wide-shape balance that was the first one created without disturbing others in the group. Use a locomotor movement or a turning action to move from the group.

T As I touch you, move slowly back into the large balance statue, with clear shapes and stillness in your balance. On signal, move away again, forming an individual statue by yourself with a different base of support and different shape from the one you used before. (Remember a touch to move toward the main statue, a signal to move away.)

Performing Inverted Balances

Setting: Small mats and/or carpet squares scattered throughout general space, with sufficient room between them for children to work without bumping others

> **Cues**
>
> **Tight Muscles**   (Tighten your abdominal muscles to hold the inverted balance—stretch toward the sky!)
> **Equal Weight**   (Take weight equally on all body parts that are bases of support.)

Tasks/Challenges:

T Balance with your head and two feet as your base of support.

A When performing an inverted balance involving the head, it's important to distribute the body weight equally among all body parts serving as the base of support.

T Balance on your head and hands, with your knees resting on your elbows (Figure 20.5).

T When performing these inverted balances, concentrate on taking your weight equally on the following bases:
- Head and knees
- Head, hands, one foot
- Back of head, shoulders, arm

T Explore other inverted balances that you can safely hold for 3 seconds (Figure 20.6).

Alignment of Body Parts

Setting: Small mats and/or carpet squares scattered throughout general space, with sufficient room between them for children to work safely

> **Cues**
>
> **Tight Muscles**   (Tighten your abdominal muscles to hold the inverted balance—stretch toward the sky!)
> **Alignment**   (Toes over knees, over hips, over shoulders to form a straight line.)

Tasks/Challenges:

T Repeat your balance on head and hands with knees resting on elbows. **Concentrate on tightening your abdominal muscles to align your hips over your shoulders.**

T Balance on your head and hands, with your trunk and legs extended toward the ceiling. Form a triangular base with your weight equally distributed on your head and hands. **Stretch your body like a straight line, aligning hips over shoulders, feet over hips. Pretend your toes are attached by a string to the ceiling. . . . Stretch.**

Figure 20.5 Inverted balance on head and hands.

Setting: Large gymnastics mats and/or small mats that will not slip, scattered throughout general space, with sufficient room between them for children to work safely

Cues	
Tight Muscles	(Tighten your abdominal muscles to hold the inverted balance—stretch toward the sky!)
Alignment	(Toes over knees, over hips, over shoulders to form a straight line.)

⚠ Teach children to roll safely out of an off-balance head-and-hands position by pushing with the hands, tucking the chin, and curling the back.

Tasks/Challenges:

🅣 Place one foot in front of the other (front-back stance); lean forward, and place your hands on the floor shoulder-width apart, fingers pointing forward. Using your back leg as a lever, kick your leg upward so your weight is supported on your hands only.

🅒 Practice counting seconds as you balance on your hands.

With practice, the success rate for balancing on hands is very high, but practice must be massed and distributed.

⚠ Teach the children to come safely out of an off-balance weight-on-hands position by twisting the trunk slightly to bring the feet down in a new place.

Doing Kickups

Spotting

The question of spotting—physically assisting a child with a skill—often arises with gymnastics. Spotting is seldom used in educational gymnastics because it often encourages or forces children to attempt a skill before they are ready. See Chapter 29 for a more complete discussion on the use of spotting.

Figure 20.6 Other inverted balances

Traveling and Stopping in Balanced Positions

Setting: Children scattered throughout general space

Cues	
Stillness	(Hold your balance perfectly still—no wiggles, no wobbles.)
Tight Muscles	(Muscular tension is the key to holding the balance.)
Extensions	(Extend free body parts for stability in your balance.)

Tasks/Challenges:

T We worked earlier on traveling through general space and creating a gymnastics balance when we stopped. Let's review those skills: Travel through general space any way you choose. On the signal, stop and create a gymnastics balance with two hands and one foot touching the floor.

T This time, change your way of traveling. If you ran before, skip or gallop through general space. On the signal, stop and create a balance with four body parts as bases of support. Think of the four parts you will choose before traveling.

T Repeat the travel, stop, balance sequence with different combinations of body parts as bases of support and different ways to travel.

C Remember the balance you created with four bases of support? Think of the balance you created with two bases. Now you are going to make a sequence of two travels and two stationary balances. Your sequence will be this: Travel, stop and balance on four bases; travel, stop and balance on two bases of support. I'll give the signal for travel each time. You will decide the ways you are going to travel; use the balances you just practiced. We will practice several times so you can repeat the travel, balance sequence exactly the same way each time.

C After you have completed your two-part sequence and feel good about your travel and balances, create a larger sequence by adding other ways to travel and additional balances—for example, three bases, five bases. How about going from five bases of support to one base, with travel between the balances? Remember, there are ways to travel other than on your feet.

Stationary Balances on Equipment

Setting: Various pieces of gymnastics apparatus arranged throughout general space: low tables, boxes, benches, climbing frames, low balance beams. (*See Figures 20.7 and 20.8 for plans for constructing balance beams and balance benches.*)

Cues	
Stillness	(Hold your balance perfectly still—no wiggles, no wobbles.)
Tight Muscles	(Muscular tension is the key to holding the balance.)
Extensions	(Extend free body parts for stability in your balance.)

Maintaining stillness while balancing on different body parts is important before balancing on equipment.

Figure 20.7 Construction of a balance beam.*

*Prior to constructing homemade equipment we recommend you be certain that teacher-made equipment is permitted in your school and/or school district.

⚠ Extended edges and bases/supports of gymnastics apparatus sometimes need extra padding to assure safety and prevention of injury.

Tasks/Challenges:

T Earlier in the year we explored traveling safely on gymnastics equipment. Select the piece of apparatus you want to begin working on; spend a few minutes exploring the apparatus until you are comfortable on this new surface and height. Travel forward and backward on the apparatus. Try some of the balances you did on the floor/mat surface on the apparatus.

T Perform your balances at different places on the apparatus: on the top, near one end, in the middle, on a low rung, underneath. Try some balances with a combination of bases on the floor and on the apparatus.

T Balance on your hands only on the low bench, low beam, or crate. The chart on the wall (Figure 20.9) will provide examples of balances that do not require you to be inverted when you balance hands-only on the equipment.

T Create a balance on the apparatus; then move slowly to another part of the apparatus for your second balance. Can you create a combination of travel and three different balances?

T After you create three balances on the first piece of apparatus, move to another piece of gymnastics apparatus and create balances on that one. You may be able to repeat balances from before, or you may need to create balances on different bases of support to suit the different apparatus. Continue rotating to the various pieces of apparatus until you've created three balances on each piece of apparatus.

When children first begin this type of gymnastics, they may not be able to move independently from apparatus to apparatus. We have found it best in the beginning to assign the children to groups and rotate the stations.

Figure 20.8 Construction of a balance bench.*

*Prior to constructing homemade equipment we recommend you be certain that teacher-made equipment is permitted in your school and/or school district.

Figure 20.9 Noninverted hands-only balances on apparatus.

T Create combinations of balances and travel on each of the pieces of apparatus.

T Choose your favorite piece of apparatus for a sequence. Create a sequence of four balances and four different ways to travel on that apparatus. Select different combinations of body parts as your bases of support, and be creative in your ways to travel on the apparatus. Don't forget different levels and directions as you create your sequence.

✓ *Portfolio.* Sequences provide a good opportunity for portfolio use. Have students record their sequences on paper using stick-figure drawings and writing; place the sequences in their portfolios. Make sure you let students know you will return to this work later in the year, possibly when you work on approaches and dismounts from apparatus.

⚠ Permit the children to attempt balances on apparatus only after they can safely hold the balances for 3 to 5 seconds on the floor or mats.

Traveling on Large Apparatus

Setting: Large apparatus—benches, tables, beams, commercial gymnastics equipment—arranged in open space

Cues

Eyes Forward (Focus on a spot on the wall or the end of the beam, keeping your head up for good balance.)

Extensions (Extend your arms for good balance as you travel.)

Tasks/Challenges:

T Travel forward and backward on the large apparatus. **Focus your eyes on something stationary to help maintain your balance as you travel.**

T Sometimes travel with your center of gravity close to the apparatus—that is, lower your hips. Sometimes travel with your center of gravity high—for example, walk on your tiptoes with your body stretched toward the ceiling.

T Walk forward the length of the beam or bench; make a half turn, and walk forward again. The secret to the turn is to take your weight on the balls of your feet and then pivot and quickly drop your heels so they make contact with the beam.

T Practice turning both clockwise and counterclockwise while traveling forward and backward.

T Walk to the center of the apparatus, and lower your hips into a squat position. Execute your turn in this low-level position.

Traveling While Balanced

Setting: Large apparatus—benches, tables, beams, commercial gymnastics equipment—arranged in open space

Cues

Eyes Forward (Remember to focus your eyes on something stationary when you travel.)

Extensions (Extend your arms for good balance when doing your locomotors.)

Tasks/Challenges:

T Travel on the apparatus using a series of gallops, hops, or skipping steps. You'll probably want very little height when you perform these skills on the apparatus.

T Travel across the apparatus on four body parts.

T If you are comfortable doing forward rolls on the mats, try rolling slowly forward across the

Traveling on equipment while balanced requires a constant point of focus.

apparatus. **Pretend you are executing the skill in slow motion; tighten your abdominal muscles for control.**

Ⓐ Students should perform rolling on apparatus only after demonstrating mastery of the rolls on the floor or mats.

Ⓒ Perform the tasks on each piece of apparatus.

Ⓣ Add changes in directions and levels to your locomotors on the apparatus.

Balancing Sequence

Setting: Large apparatus—benches, tables, beams, commercial gymnastics equipment—arranged in open space

Cues	
Eyes Forward	(Remember to focus your eyes on something stationary when you travel.)
Smooth Transitions	(Move smoothly between balances and travels.)

Note: Individuals, sometimes classes, may need reminders of earlier cues—for example, Stillness, Extensions, Tight Muscles.

Tasks/Challenges:

Ⓣ Remember those balances you created on apparatus earlier in the year? You recorded them on paper and placed them in your portfolios. We are now going to revisit that lesson to create a sequence of traveling and balancing on your favorite piece of appara-

tus. Your task will be to design a sequence of traveling and balancing on one piece of equipment. You will choose either sequence A or sequence B.

Sequence A: Create a sequence of traveling combined with balancing on different bases of support. Your sequence must contain three balances with different bases and at least two travels.

Sequence B: Create a sequence of traveling combined with balancing in the basic body shapes. Your sequence must contain the four basic shapes—wide, narrow, curled, twisted—and at least three travels.

Practice your sequence on the floor and then on the apparatus. When you have the sequence memorized, let a friend watch it to see if:

- The bases of support are clear.
- The balances are stationary.
- The travels are smooth.

Ⓣ You have refined your sequence nicely, with a friend giving pointers. Now we need to add the beginning shape and the ending of the sequence. Begin your sequence on the apparatus positioned in what you wish to be your starting shape. The beginning shape you choose will be determined by your first action: travel or balance. Think of the level you need, and the direction, as well as the shape.

Ⓣ Now that you have a beginning shape, let's focus on the ending of your sequence. Earlier in the year we studied jumping and landing—jumping for height and landing safely. We will review those skills, and then you can select the type of jump/land action with which you want to end your sequence. *Review jumping off apparatus (Chapter 19) with the children, emphasizing safe landings and body shapes in the air.*

C On the assignment table you will find the forms for sequence A or B. The paper is divided into four parts: beginning shape, travel and balances, dismount, and ending shape. Using stick figures to represent your balances, write/draw your sequence, remembering the number of balances needed for the sequence. When you can repeat the sequence without referring to your paper, ask a friend to watch it.

✔ *Peer Observation.* Your friend will be your "refinement coach" giving you pointers to make your sequence even better. The "coach" will observe your sequence for the following cues: stillness (3 seconds for each balance with no wiggles, no wobbles); tight muscles (muscular tension that holds body parts perfectly still); extensions (pointed toes, stretched arms and legs). After the friend watches your "dress rehearsal," come to me for your final assessment.

✔ *Event Task.* The above task can easily become an event task assessment of children's work. *Specifics for development of criteria and rubrics can be found in Chapter 12, "Assessing Student Learning."*

At the control level, youngsters are challenged to create matching nonsymmetrical balances.

Balancing on Stilts

Setting: Several stations in general space at which children can experience/practice dynamic balance; tin can stilts (*see* Figure 20.10) for instructions for making them) at some of the stations; wooden stilts (*see* Figure 20.11) at others; marker cones placed around the general space

Cue

Heads Up (Eyes focused forward, shoulders erect.)

Children first experiencing this type of dynamic balance can develop confidence on tin can stilts before progressing to regular stilts.

T Walk forward on the tin can stilts. You'll have to take smaller steps than you would when walking normally.

T Walk backward.

T Walk around the marker cones.

T After you've mastered walking on the tin can stilts, you're ready for the higher wooden stilts. It's easier to mount the stilts from an elevated position, such as from a step or chair.

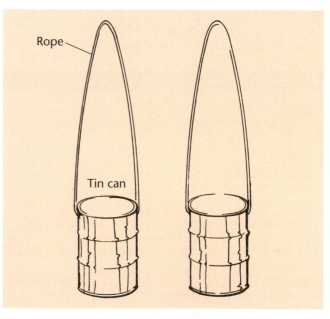

Figure 20.10 Construction of tin can stilts from discarded rope and large cans from the school cafeteria. To create, (1) cut two holes in the top sides of the cans and (2) string rope through the holes and tie it together inside each can. To use the stilts, children put each foot on a can and pull on the rope with their hands.*

*Prior to constructing homemade equipment we recommend you be certain that teacher-made equipment is permitted in your school and/or school district.

*Prior to constructing homemade equipment we recommend you be certain that teacher-made equipment is permitted in your school and/or school district.

Figure 20.11 Construction of wooden stilts. (Each board makes one set of stilts.)*
Directions:
1. Cut 12 inches from one end of the board.
2. Cut the 12-inch board in half.
3. Cut the 6-inch board diagonally in half for the steps.
4. Cut the remaining 7-foot board lengthwise to make two 2-inch by 7-foot poles.
5. Nail or bolt the steps to the poles.

(T) Walk forward, backward, and sideways.

(T) Walk around the marker cones.

(T) Shift your weight to one stilt; lift your other leg, and swing it around.

Balance Boards

Setting: Balance boards set up as one of several stations at which children can experience static and dynamic balance

Cues

Heads Up   (Eyes focused forward, shoulders erect.)
Extensions (Extend arms to the sides for
                good balance.)

Tasks/Challenges:

(T) Remember when we did balances on boards earlier in the year? You practiced balancing on the different boards and learned that a wide base of support—feet shoulder-width apart—created a more stable balance on the boards, as in all balances. Practice your balance skills on the boards. Try to maintain your balance, without partner support, for several seconds.

(T) When you can stand on the board for 5 seconds without the support of your partner and without losing your balance, you're ready to try the tasks written on the chart:

1. Slowly move your arms above your head. What happens to your center of gravity? (Right—it moves upward.)

2. Slowly move from a standing to a squat or low-curl position. Which is more stable? Why is the low position more stable? (When working on large apparatus, remember that we're better balanced when the center of gravity is low.)

3. Catch a ball thrown by your partner; toss the ball to your partner.

Write additional tasks on flip charts or task cards near the balance board. Balance board activities can also be recorded on a task sheet (see Figure 20.12).

Utilization Level (GLSP): Learning Experiences Leading to Skill Development

Learning experiences at the utilization level combine balancing and transferring weight for a contrast in stillness and action. Children experience balancing in dynamic environments and transferring weight into and out of balances. Gymnastics sequences that involve skills and concepts, transfers and stillness, are particularly important and valuable. Children make decisions about the combination of movements and select and invent ways for one balance or action to move smoothly into another.

A note about cues: Although several cues are listed for many of the learning experiences, it's important to focus on only one cue at a time. This way, the children can really concentrate on that cue. Once you provide feedback to the children and observe that most have learned a cue, it's time to focus on another one.

Figure 20.12 Task sheet for balance board activities. Younger children enjoy drawing the smile face for completed tasks; older children can record the date of successful completion.

Name _Melissa_

Homeroom _4b_

Balance Board Task Sheet

Draw a smile face beside those activities you can successfully complete.

I am able to:

__☺__ Balance on the board standing on two feet

__☺__ Sit in a balance position on the board

_____ Change from a standing to a sitting position on the board without losing balance

_____ Raise my hands high above my head while standing on the board

_____ Balance on the board standing on one foot

_____ Catch a ball tossed to me by a friend

_____ Toss a ball to a friend without losing my balance

New ideas by me:

_____ clap my hands 3 times

_____

_____

Balancing on Crates

Setting: Milk crates and boxes (stuffed with newspaper or packing materials and taped closed so they will support a child's weight) positioned throughout general space, with sufficient room between for children to work safely

Cues

Tight Muscles	(Muscular tension is the key to holding the balance.)
Extensions	(Extend free body parts for balance/counterbalance.)
Alignment	(Position yourself over your base of support or extend free body parts for counterbalance.)

Tasks/Challenges:

🅣 In our previous work on balance, you explored balancing on different bases of support and in different shapes. You practiced holding balances stationary while performing them on mats, on low equipment, and on large apparatus. Review your balances on different bases of support on the crate or box. Many of the balances that were easy for you to perform on the mat or the low equipment will be more difficult on the crate or box because of the added height and the size of the surface.

🅣 Create a series of balances without ever leaving the surface of the crate or box. Transferring from one balance to the next will now be a major part of the sequence.

T Create a sequence of balances on your crate or box that includes an approach to the crate, a transfer onto the crate, a series of balances on the crate, and a dismount from the crate. You may choose to focus on either bases of support or different shapes.

Select tasks from Chapter 21, "Transferring Weight and Rolling," for a review of approaches to and dismounts from low equipment.

T Select a partner to work with for a sequence on the crates. Explore matching symmetrical and non-symmetrical balances on the crates or boxes. You may choose to work side by side to match shapes, or face to face to mirror shapes.

C Design a partner sequence of symmetrical and nonsymmetrical balances on the crates or boxes. Your sequence must contain the following:

- Three symmetrical and two nonsymmetrical balances
- A minimum of three different bases of support
- An approach to the crates or boxes and a dismount

Your sequence should represent a double image. Not only will your balances match those of your partner, but also the transitions between them will be the same action and the same speed.

✓ *Videotape.* The children's sequences provide an excellent means of assessing their gymnastics skills. A possible idea is to have partners videotape their completed sequence. Both partners can then evaluate the sequence using the guidelines discussed in class. After the initial evaluation, children may make changes in the sequence. *Refer to Chapter 12, "Assessing Student Learning," for examples of videotape analysis and assessment.*

Moving out of and into Balances by Stretching, Curling, and Twisting

Setting: Sufficient mats for children to work safely without bumping others as they practice

Cues	
Line of Gravity	(Extending beyond your line of gravity will make you lose your balance unless you have an extension for counterbalance.)
Smooth Transitions	(Move smoothly through the transition from balance to balance.)

Tasks/Challenges:

T Balance on a very narrow base of support. Stretch your free body parts in one direction away from the base. When you begin to lose your balance, you have moved just beyond the "line of gravity." At the moment of moving beyond the line of gravity—of moving off balance—transfer your weight to a new base of support.

T Balance on one foot. Stretch forward until you are off balance; transfer your weight to your hands and feet in a new balance.

T Balance on favorite bases of support. Extend free body parts with a stretching action to move into a new balance.

T Balance on your head and hands with knees on elbows as in a three-point stand or tripod. Push with your hands, tuck your head, and curl your back to roll out of the balance. Make a new stationary balance after the rolling action.

T Explore curling your spine to roll out of different balances until you find three balances in which you can use the curling action to get out of and into a new balance.

Extensions provide aesthetic appeal as well as good balances.

T Balance on the base of your spine only, as in a V-seat. After you have held the balance very still, twist your trunk until the action moves you off balance and into a new balance with a different base of support.

T Balance on two hands and one foot, with the free leg extended. Twist your trunk and the free leg until you transfer to a new balance on hands and feet.

C Practice balances with different bases of support and moving out of the balance by stretching, curling, or twisting. When you are comfortable with one of each, put them together in a sequence as follows: balance, stretching action into new balance, curling action into new balance, twisting action into new balance. Your sequence will include four stationary balances and three transitions.

Additional balances with stretching, curling, and twisting actions can be found in Chapter 21, "Transferring Weight and Rolling."

Traveling into and out of Balances by Rolling

Setting: Sufficient mats for children to balance and roll without bumping into others as they practice

Cues	
Stillness and Action	(Remember to hold your balance perfectly still for 3 seconds; then move smoothly through the rolling action.)
Rounded Body	(Keep your back round and your chin tucked for a good roll.)

Tasks/Challenges:

T Rock backward into a shoulder stand; hold the balance for 3 seconds, and then roll either forward or backward.

Children functioning at the utilization level in balancing should also have mastered rolling forward and backward.

T Balance in a headstand for 3 seconds; then, press with your hands, and roll forward.

T Balance with your weight on your hands, slowly lower yourself to the mat, and roll forward. **Remember to tuck your chin and curl your back.**

T Transfer your weight from your feet to your hands; pause in the handstand; then make a quarter turn, and transfer your weight back to your feet.

Performing Inverted Balances on Equipment

Setting: Boxes or crates, benches, and/or low tables arranged for balancing, with sufficient mats around them for children to work safely

Cues	
Tight Muscles	(Remember to tighten the abdominal muscles plus free body parts for stillness in your balances.)
Alignment	(Position yourself over your base of support or extend free body parts for counterbalance.)

Tasks/Challenges:

T Balancing in an inverted position on a piece of apparatus is quite different from balancing on the mats or the floor. The position of your hands is often quite different, and the surface is much smaller. Perform the balances until you are quite comfortable and skilled with them on the low equipment before you attempt them on the higher, more narrow apparatus (Figure 20.13).

T Balance on your shoulders, back of your head, and arms. Stretch your legs upward.

T Balance on your head and hands in a tripod position.

T Balance on your head and hands with your legs extended toward the ceiling.

T Balance on your hands only in an inverted balance.

T While balanced on your hands only, turn slightly, and bring your feet down to the floor beside the beam, bench, or crate. This is the safety skill you will need when you become overbalanced.

T Perform your inverted balance on the larger pieces of apparatus—vaulting box, balance beam, climbing frames.

A Inverted balances on apparatus should be attempted only after children show mastery of the balances on the floor or mats. Always have a mat area available for children to use to practice before performing their balances on apparatus.

A Position yourself at the station where children are doing inverted balances; be sure you maintain a visual scan of the entire class.

Performing Sequences That Combine Stationary Balances and Traveling on Mats

Setting: A floor gymnastics area designed using available mats

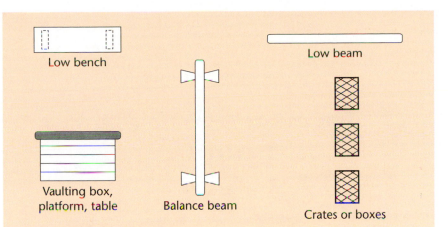

Figure 20.13 Low equipment for inverted balances.

Low bench

Low beam

Vaulting box, platform, table

Balance beam

Crates or boxes

Cues

Stillness in Balances	(Tighten the muscles to hold the balance very still.)
Smooth Transitions	(Make transitions between balances very smooth, whether they're fast or slow.)
Extensions	(Extend free body parts for aesthetic appeal as well as good balance.)
Alignment	(Position yourself over your base of support or extend free body parts for counterbalance.)

Tasks/Challenges:

Ⓣ Create a sequence that combines stationary balances and travel. As with an Olympic-style gymnastics routine, design your sequence to cover the length of the mat, as well as each corner. Your sequence must include the following:

- A minimum of six balances, each with a different base of support
- A minimum of three travels, with a change in direction and level
- At least two inverted balances
- A beginning and an ending shape

Ⓣ Add contrasts in time of actions—some fast, some slow—and changes in force—some powerful movements, some delicate—to add interest to your sequence.

Ⓒ Tomorrow we're going to practice the routines to music. If you like, bring a recording of music from home, or you may select from those we have. You will then practice your routine with the music until you can repeat it three times exactly the same way. *(See Figure 20.14 for an example of a routine.)*

✓ Gymnastics routines are excellent projects for assessment of children's gymnastic skills and their understanding of the critical cues. *Refer to Chapter 12, "Assessing Student Learning," for guidelines for developing criteria and rubrics.*

Proficiency Level (GLSP): Learning Experiences Leading to Skill Development

At the proficiency level, balance is studied on the floor and on various pieces of apparatus in combination with movement concepts to express contrast in power, stillness, and excitement in sequences. Children are encouraged to perfect the flow of their movements from one position to another and to develop their use of focus and full extensions.

Although often not readily available, such activities as unicycling, skating, skateboarding, snowboarding, skiing, and surfing are challenging dynamic balancing experiences for children at the proficiency level. Sometimes these experiences can be provided during field trips or after-school programs.

A note about cues: At the proficiency level, tasks are more complex, typically requiring children to coordinate several movements simultaneously in a dynamic context. A list of cues is provided to assist the children in being more successful in the learning experience. The challenge for the teacher is in determining which cue will be most beneficial for each child . . . and when. Thus careful observation and critical reflection become very important as you watch the children move and then decide which cue will be the most helpful to move each learner to a higher skill level.

Balancing While Supporting the Weight of a Partner

Setting: Sufficient mats for children to work safely without bumping others

Figure 20.14 Child's sequence to music, showing use of rolling; weight transfer; balance; and concepts of narrow, wide, curled, and directions.

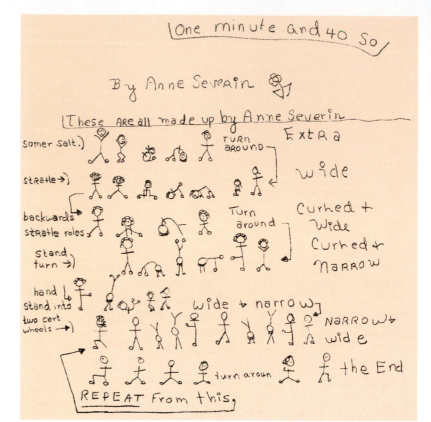

<table>
<tr><td colspan="2">

Cues

Wide Base   (A wide base of support provides greater stability.)

Extensions   (Extensions beyond the line of gravity require extensions in the opposite direction for counterbalance.)

</td></tr>
</table>

Tasks/Challenges:

T Working with your partner, create a balance that shows one wide and one narrow shape. You and your partner must be helping each other by partially supporting each other's weight.

T Create different balances with your partner in which you are partially supporting each other's weight. If you and your partner are not the same weight, which of you will be the supporting partner?

Partners of similar size enjoy experimenting with each being the base for the balances and/or equally supporting each other. If partners are not the same weight, assist the children in understanding the important role of the base partner.

T Create a balance in which the base partner is supporting the weight of the top partner, who is in an inverted position.

⚠ *Base partner.* Your bases of support—for example, your arms and legs—should be no farther apart than the width of your hips and shoulders. *Top partner:* Make sure you put your weight over your partner's arms and hips, never in the middle of the back, which is unsupported.

C Create two new balances supporting your partner's weight (Figure 20.15). You will need to make decisions based on the weight of both partners: Will you partially support each other, or will one of you totally support the other? Draw your two balances on a sheet of paper, and post them at the partner balance center.

The combination of partner/group balancing, tumbling, and dance has evolved into an activity called Acrosport. Groups perform routines of supportive dynamic and static balances connected by tension balance positions.

Balancing on Hanging Ropes

Setting: Hanging ropes with sufficient mats below for children to work safely

<table>
<tr><td>

Cue

Tight Muscles   (Tighten your muscles to support body weight and maintain balance on ropes.)

</td></tr>
</table>

Tasks/Challenges:

T On a hanging rope, support your weight with both hands, then your hands and legs, and finally one hand. Create each of the basic shapes—wide, narrow, curled, twisted—with your free body parts (Figure 20.16). Perform your balances on the hanging ropes with your head upward.

T Create a series of symmetrical and nonsymmetrical shapes while supporting your weight on the rope.

⚠ Permit inverted balances on the hanging ropes at low height and only for children with sufficient upper-arm/shoulder strength.

Tasks/Challenges:

T Balance momentarily on your hands on the apparatus, make a quarter turn, and transfer your weight from your hands to your feet on the mat. **Remember the cues for safety as you land.**

T Practice this skill on the floor and on the low apparatus to be sure you can turn to the right or to the left.

⚠ Be sure students have mastered this skill on the floor or mats and on low apparatus before they attempt it on higher, narrower apparatus.

Transferring off Equipment with Weight on Hands

Setting: Gymnastics apparatus positioned throughout general space, with sufficient mats for children to work safely

Cues	
Alignment	(Feet over hips, over shoulders, over hands for a straight-line weight on hands.)
Tight Muscles	(Muscular tension is the key to holding the balance.)

Performing Apparatus Sequences That Combine Stationary Balances and Traveling with Movement Concepts

Setting: Gymnastics apparatus positioned throughout general space, with sufficient mats and spacing for children to work safely

Cues	
Individual cues as needed	

Balances can be performed alone, with a partner, or in a group.

Tasks/Challenges:

T Select a piece of equipment that will be your choice for your final gymnastics project. Your assignment will be to design a sequence combining stationary balances and travel in relation to that piece of apparatus. The sequence must include the following:

1. An approach to the apparatus and a mount onto the apparatus
2. A series of stationary balances and travels on the apparatus
3. A dismount from the apparatus

You can add excitement and interest to your sequence with:

- Contrasts in fast and slow actions
- Turning, twisting, curling actions
- Changes in levels and directions
- Combinations of slow, controlled movements and quick, sharp movements
- Inverted balances and actions

Practice your sequence as if you were preparing for the Olympics. When you have completed and timed it with your music, show it to a friend and then to me. We will videotape the sequence for inclusion in your portfolio.

T Select a grouping of three to four pieces of gymnastics apparatus for your final project. Design a sequence that combines stationary balances and travel in relation to each piece of apparatus, as well as travel between the pieces of apparatus. The sequence must include the following:

1. An approach to the first pieces of apparatus and a mount onto the apparatus
2. A series of stationary balances and travels on the apparatus
3. A dismount from the apparatus
4. Travel to the next piece of apparatus
5. A series of balances and travels on that apparatus

Figure 20.16 Head-up balances on hanging ropes.

6. A repeat of Steps 4 and 5 until you have visited each of the three (or four) pieces of apparatus in the grouping
7. A dismount and ending shape

Remember, excitement and interest are added to your sequence with changes and contrasts in movement concepts. (See listing above.) Also, grouping the apparatus and traveling between them frees the inner spirit for creativity, as dance and gymnastics are combined for your final project.

✓ *Portfolio. It is good to provide portfolio opportunities as an option for students. As an example, you might tell students the following:* Practice your sequence as if you were preparing for a gymnastics competition or a recital. When you have completed and timed it with your music, show it to a friend and then to me. If you wish, we will then videotape the sequence for inclusion in your portfolio as your self-expression in gymnastics. *Refer to Chapter 12, "Assessing Student Learning," for the use of portfolios for assessment in physical education.*

Reading Comprehension Questions

1. In your own words, define *balancing*. Be sure to include the meanings of *base of support* and *center of gravity*.
2. Draw or diagram (stick figures are best) the three key teaching concepts that are emphasized in providing balance experiences.
3. What is the difference between a static balance and a dynamic balance?
4. What are the characteristics of balancing for each of the skill levels? For example, what does a pre-control-level balance look like?
5. List three concepts or skills typically used as subthemes with balance.
6. Why are muscular tension, counterbalance, and alignment of body parts important in teaching gymnastics for children?
7. List five different pieces of equipment that children can use to practice balancing. Include a task you might use with each piece of equipment.
8. Educational gymnastics does not require Olympic-style apparatus. List or diagram four pieces of non-Olympic gymnastics equipment that can be used for balancing. List three tasks for your balance study on the equipment.
9. What does *inverted balance* mean?
10. Why are jumping and landing studied in conjunction with balances on apparatus?
11. How is transfer of weight typically combined with balancing to present challenging tasks to children at the utilization and proficiency levels?

References/Suggested Readings

[NASPE] National Association for Sport and Physical Education. 1995. *Moving into the future: National standards for physical education.* St. Louis, MO: Mosby.

[NASPE] National Association for Sport and Physical Education. 2004. *Moving into the future: National standards for physical education.* 2nd ed. Reston, VA: National Association for Sport and Physical Education.

Transferring Weight and Rolling

Gymnastics By Isabella

Transferring Weight

To travel—walking, running, leaping, rolling, stepping, springing, sliding—is to transfer weight on hands, on feet, on different body parts. The infant creeping on trunk and elbows is transferring weight, as is the toddler shifting weight from side to side during the beginning phase of walking unassisted, the gymnast performing a walkover, the Russian dancer executing a series of rapid mule kicks, the athlete poised to shift her weight to fake an opponent, and the dancer collapsing to the floor in an expression of grace and control. Locomotion is transfer of weight.

The most common form of transferring weight is from foot to foot. In its simplest form, this is walking. At an advanced level—and when combined with the stretching, curling, and twisting actions of layouts and with full-body twists—it demands extraordinary kinesthetic awareness, muscular strength, and control. While we have chosen to develop transferring weight and rolling separately in this chapter, rolling is simply one form of transferring weight, and often the two ideas are developed simultaneously. See Box 21-1 for linkages of the skill theme of transferring weight to the *National Standards for Physical Education.*

Young children come to us with control of their bodies in the basic forms of locomotion, i.e., transferring weight. They are fascinated with exploring transferring weight in different ways, e.g., on their hands, on their backs, stretched, curled and twisted. This fascination with the skill of transferring weight leads to a world of exciting challenges as children defy gravity and gain control of their bodies. Our task as teachers is to capture this fascination with the skill and lead the children to higher levels of skill development, expanding the child's realm of possibilities while maintaining safety. The progression in our teaching of gymnastics is from mats on the floor to low apparatus with a large surface to higher apparatus with a narrow surface.

The skill theme of transferring weight must be taught in a safe environment. (See Chapter 29 for the establishment of procedures for working on gymnastics skills, working with and alongside others, as well as on apparatus.) With the establishment of procedures for activity, the selection of developmentally appropriate tasks, and the use of intratask variation, the skill theme of transferring weight provides exciting, challenging activities for all children.

While transferring weight is inherent in all forms of locomotion and therefore a component of all skill themes, we have chosen to focus this chapter on transferring weight as it applies to gymnastics. Children are fascinated with the challenge of transferring weight, balancing on head, walking on hands with twists and turns. Gymnasts expand those skills with round-offs; aerials; vaulting; transfers while on large apparatus; and dismounts with twisting, curling, stretching actions while in flight. Olympic gymnasts build upon the transference skills with increased time in flight, more complex combinations of twisting, curling, and twisting actions on mats and apparatus. At this level, transferring weight, balance, and dance come together to create routines in hopes of the "Perfect 10."

Our progression spiral on page 370 presents the full spectrum of transferring weight, from the precontrol level to the proficiency level of skill development. Alternative ways of further developing the ideas are discussed in Chapter 10.

Box 21-1

The Skills of Transferring Weight and Rolling in the *National Standards for Physical Education*

The movement skill of transferring weight is referenced in the National Association for Sport and Physical Education's *National Standards for Physical Education* (NASPE 2004) under Standard 1: "Demonstrates competency in motor skills and movement patterns needed to perform a variety of physical activities."

Sample performance outcomes from the *National Standards* include:

- Develops and refines a gymnastics sequence demonstrating smooth transitions (3–5)*
- Designs and performs gymnastics sequences that combine traveling, rolling, balancing, and weight transfer into smooth, flowing sequences with intentional changes in direction, speed, and flow (6–8)*

*Grade-level guidelines for expected student learning.

Precontrol Level (GLSP): Activities for Exploration of Transferring Weight

Tasks at the precontrol level are designed for the exploration of transferring weight to different body parts and in relation to gymnastics equipment. Through this exploration children will begin to develop an awareness of the body parts best suited for transferring weight and control of their bodies as they transfer weight in different ways.

Skill Theme Development Progression

Transferring Weight

Proficiency Level

Club gymnastics
Olympic-style transfers

Utilization Level

Combining weight transfer and balances into sequences on
    mats and apparatus
Combining skills on mats
Transferring weight on bars
Transferring weight to hands on low apparatus
Transferring weight by rolling (bench, box, or table)
Transferring weight along apparatus
Transferring weight over apparatus (vaulting box)
Transferring weight onto bars (parallel bars, climbing frame)
Transferring weight to head and hands on apparatus (box,
    beam, table)
Transferring weight onto large apparatus
Transferring weight to hands and forming a bridge
Transferring weight to hands and twisting
Transferring weight to hands: walking

Control Level

Transferring weight to hands by stepping: cartwheels
Maintaining transfer from feet to hands
Transferring onto low apparatus
Traveling over low apparatus
Making spring/step takeoffs with sequences
Transferring off low apparatus (bench, crate, or low table)
Performing spring/step takeoffs onto crates and/or benches
Performing spring/step takeoffs
Transfers with stretching, curling, and twisting
Transferring weight from feet to combinations of body parts
Transferring weight with a rolling action
Transferring weight to hands across mats

Precontrol Level

Transferring weight onto and off equipment
Transferring weight to hands momentarily
Transferring weight with a rocking action
Locomotor actions

Locomotor Actions

Setting: Children scattered throughout general space

Tasks/Challenges:

Ⓣ All locomotor movements are actions of transferring weight. When you walk, hop, skip, or gallop,
you transfer your weight from foot to foot. Let's review some of the locomotor movements. Travel throughout general space with a skip or gallop.

Ⓣ Travel with a jump—two feet to two feet.

Ⓣ Hop on one foot. Do you transfer weight to different body parts when you hop? No, you move on one foot only.

Additional exploration:

Ⓣ Travel and jump high in the air like a basketball player.

Ⓣ Travel and jump over a brook; a large, flat rock; a puddle. This jump is sometimes called a leap—taking off on one foot and landing on the other.

Ⓣ Explore other ways to travel throughout general space, transferring weight from foot to foot; twirl, spin, slide. . . .

Ⓣ Explore traveling on body parts other than your feet: slither, crawl, walk like a crab. . . .

🜚 When you skip, you transfer weight from what body part to what body part? When you jump, you transfer from what to what? What is the difference between a jump and a hop?

Transferring Weight with a Rocking Action

Setting: Individual mats and/or carpet squares throughout general space, with sufficient room between them for children to work safely

Tasks/Challenges:

Ⓣ Squat on your feet with your back rounded like an egg. Transfer your weight from your feet to your back with a rocking action.

Ⓣ Transfer your weight from your feet to your rounded back, and return to your feet with the rocking action.

Ⓣ Give the rocking action a little extra effort, transferring your weight from feet to rounded back, to feet, and then returning to a standing position.

Transferring Weight to Hands Momentarily

Setting: Large gymnastics mats and/or small mats that will not slide as children transfer weight, scattered throughout general space

Tasks/Challenges:

Ⓣ Transfer your weight from your feet to your hands to your feet, momentarily taking your weight on your hands only.

Wedge mats or folded or rolled mats may be easier for children just beginning to take weight on their hands and/or for

those uncomfortable with transfer from standing position to mat on floor.

Transferring Weight onto and off Equipment

Setting: Low gymnastics equipment—benches, tables, balance beams, and so on—scattered throughout general space

⚠ Carefully examine all equipment to be used for gymnastics in elementary school physical education. Extended edges of gymnastics equipment and bases/supports of apparatus sometimes need extra padding to assure safety and prevention of injury for children.

Tasks/Challenges:

The focus for exploration of equipment at the precontrol level is safety—getting on and off equipment with personal safety and without creating an unsafe situation for others.

Control Level (GLSP): Learning Experiences Leading to Skill Development in Transferring Weight

Tasks at the control level are designed to help children transfer their weight to specific body parts—feet to back, to hands, to head and hands—as they balance, as they travel, and in relation to gymnastics apparatus. Control of their bodies, i.e., safety throughout the weight transfer, is the goal at the control level.

A note about cues: Although several cues are listed for many of the learning experiences, it's important to focus on only one cue at a time. This way, the children can really concentrate on that cue. Once you provide feedback to the children and observe that most have learned a cue, it's time to focus on another one.

Transferring Weight to Hands Across Mats

Setting: Small mats (carpet squares or ropes stretched on the floor) scattered throughout general space with sufficient room between for children to work safely

Cues	
Strong Muscles	(Strong arms and shoulders— no collapse.)
Stretch Your Legs	(Extend your legs upward— stretch to the sky.)

Tasks/Challenges:

Ⓣ When we were exploring transferring weight, you practiced taking your weight on your hands and

bringing your feet to the floor at the same place. Practice taking your weight on your hands and bringing your feet down safely at a new place—to the right or the left of their original place.

Ⓣ Now you are going to transfer your weight from your feet to your hands to travel across your mat or rope. Begin at one end of your mat (carpet square or rope), transfer your weight to your hands, and bring your feet down on the other side. You will travel across your mat by transferring your weight from feet to hands to feet.

You may want to begin in a squat position with your feet on the floor and your hands on the other side of the rope or carpet square, or relatively close to your feet on the mat. Transfer your weight to your hands and bring your feet down a short distance away—just over the rope or carpet square.

Ⓒ When you are comfortable taking your weight on your hands a longer time and you are landing safely, kick your legs higher in the air to remain on your hands even longer. **Stretch your legs as you kick them higher.**

Ⓣ Stand at the side of your mat (square, rope) in a front-back stance. Extend your arms upward. Step forward with your lead foot, and transfer your weight to your hands. Bring your feet to the floor on the opposite side of your mat (square, rope). If you stretch your trunk and legs as you transfer your weight to one hand and then the other, you will begin to do a cartwheel.

Transferring Weight with a Rolling Action

Setting: Small mats and/or carpet squares scattered throughout general space

Cues	
Rounded Back	(Keep your back rounded, body curled for a good roll.)
Push with Your Hands	(Remember, push with your hands so your head does not get stuck when you roll.)

Tasks/Challenges:

Ⓣ Remember when you did the rocking action by transferring your weight from your feet to your rounded back? We are going to use that action now for a roll. Transfer your weight from your feet to your rounded back. As you rock back to your shoulders, push with your hands to roll backward across the mat. Remember, push hard with your hands so your neck doesn't get stuck.

If this is the children's first experience with rolling, follow the teaching progression for rolling in the second half of this chapter. If this is a revisitation, review the progression carefully with the children.

Rolling backward is a weight-transfer skill. What body part do you transfer to in a backward roll? Feet to what?

Think of the forward roll. When you do a forward roll, you transfer your weight from your feet to what? What is the critical cue for rolling? Now travel across your mat, transferring your weight, as in a forward roll.

Peer Observation. After successfully completing transfers of weight with a forward or a backward roll, maintaining a rounded back, a friend could then observe the roll. That person should then record the date and initial the roll on a gymnastics checklist in children's portfolios. *Refer to Chapter 12, "Assessing Student Learning," for more on the use of peer observation for assessment in physical education.*

Forward and backward rolls should always be optional for children; insisting that students perform specific rolls can result in serious neck injuries.

Transferring Weight from Feet to Combinations of Body Parts

Setting: Small mats and/or carpet squares scattered throughout general space, with sufficient room between them for children to safely transfer weight

Cues	
Strong Muscles	(Strong arms and shoulders for the transfer to hands—no collapse.)
Rounded Back	(Curl your back and body for all rolling skills.)
Stretch Your Legs	(Extend your legs upward, as if there is a string attached to your legs, pulling them to the sky.)

Tasks/Challenges:

Transfer your weight from your feet to other combinations of body parts as you travel across your mat or carpet square. Always return to your feet (Figure 21.1).

Transfers with Stretching, Curling, and Twisting

Setting: Small mats and/or carpet squares scattered throughout general space

Cues	
Smooth Transitions	(Move smoothly through the transition from balance to off balance to balance.)
Tight Muscles	(Tighten your abdominal muscles as you transfer weight for control of the action.)

Tasks/Challenges:

Balance on one foot. Bend at the waist, extending your arms forward and your free leg backward. Stretch your arms forward until you are off balance; then transfer your weight to your hands and next to your curled back to roll forward out of the balance.

Children should demonstrate a mastery of rolling forward with a rounded back before they attempt this task.

Balance on your knees and one hand. Extend your free arm under your body, twisting your trunk until your weight transfers to your shoulder and new bases of support. Twist gently into the new balance.

Balance in a shoulder stand with your weight on your shoulders, upper arms, and head, stretching your legs toward the ceiling. Twist your legs and trunk, bringing your feet to the mat behind you in a new balance.

Balance on your chosen base of support. Twist until you are momentarily off balance; transfer your weight onto a new base of support.

Balance on your chosen base again. Use different stretching, curling, and twisting actions to transfer onto new bases of support.

Performing Spring/Step Takeoffs

Before practicing spring and step takeoffs in weight transfer, children should be at the control level of jumping and landing (Chapter 19).

Setting: Large gymnastics mats throughout general space

Cues	
Heads Up	(Keep your head and shoulders erect for a balanced landing.)
Soft Landings	(Bend your knees on landing to absorb the force.)

Figure 21.1 Transfer of weight from feet to other body parts.

Tasks/Challenges:

T Approach your gymnastics mat from a distance of 10 to 12 feet. Just before you reach the mat, use a two-foot takeoff to spring high in the air; land softly in the center of the mat. The spring takeoff in gymnastics is very similar to the approach on the diving board.

The spring takeoff is used for gymnastics skills requiring power—for example, mounts onto beams and parallel bars, handsprings, and vaulting. It is a jump for height; that is why the arms are extended upward. It is also the takeoff used for a basketball jump ball or rebound.

T Approach the mat, spring off your two feet, make a quarter turn, and land in a balanced position. Now try the turn in the opposite direction.

T When you are comfortable with the quarter turn, try a half turn. Remember, practice both clockwise and counterclockwise turns.

T Approach the mat from the distance of 10 to 12 feet. Using a step takeoff, land on your two feet in the center of the mat.

The step takeoff is the takeoff used for gymnastics skills requiring slow control. Who can give some examples of those? Right, walkovers and cartwheels. It is also the takeoff needed for a layup in basketball.

Performing Spring/Step Takeoffs onto Crates and/or Benches

Setting: Milk crates positioned against large gymnastics mats

⚠ Place the crates against mats to prevent them from sliding.

⚠ If there is any danger of crates sliding during the activity, have partners work together with one holding the crate steady as the other practices transfers onto the crate.

Cues

Heads Up (Keep your head and shoulders erect for a balanced landing.)

Easy On (Slowly absorb weight on crate—with control.)

Tasks/Challenges:

T Approach the crate or bench from a distance of 10 to 15 feet. Using either a spring or a step takeoff, land in a balanced position on the crate.

C Practice each takeoff until you can transfer your weight onto the crate or bench in a balanced position three times.

T Approach the crate or bench, use a spring takeoff, and transfer your weight to your feet and hands on the crate or bench. **Remember, take your weight momentarily on your hands and then softly lower your body to the crate or bench.**

T Approach the crate or bench, use a step takeoff, and transfer your weight momentarily to your hands only on the crate or bench. Remember, strong arms for weight on hands.

Transferring off Low Apparatus (Bench, Crate, or Low Table)

Setting: Benches, crates, and/or low tables surrounded by mats and positioned throughout general space

⚠ Place the crates against mats to prevent them from sliding.

⚠ If there is any danger of crates sliding during the activity, have partners work together with one holding the crate steady as the other practices transfers off the crate.

Cues

Rounded Back (Keep your back rounded, body curled with chin tucked for a good roll.)

Soft Landings (Bend your knees on landing to absorb the force.)

Tasks/Challenges:

T Transfer your weight off the bench or crate by assuming a kneeling position, placing your hands on the mat, slowly lowering your weight to the mat, and rolling forward.

⚠ Transferring off apparatus by rolling should be introduced only after children have mastered rolling on the floor or mats.

T Transfer your weight off the bench or low table with a jump. Make a wide body shape by extending your arms and legs while in the air. Land in a balanced position on two feet on the mat. **Remember, keep your head and shoulders erect as you jump.**

T Transfer off the bench or low table with a jump, making curled, narrow, and twisted shapes while in the air, and then each time land in your balanced position.

T Transfer off the bench or low table with a jump, turning in the air so you land facing in a different direction. Remember, twist your shoulders in the direction you wish to turn.

T When you are comfortable with a quarter turn, try to execute a half turn in the air so you land facing in a different direction.

Revisit/review "Jumping to Form a Body Shape During Flight" in Chapter 19 (page 332) for additional tasks. Although specific tasks for transferring weight with large apparatus aren't listed until the utilization level, children at the precontrol and control levels need exploration time on large apparatus to become familiar with the equipment and to gain confidence moving on it.

Making Spring/Step Takeoffs with Sequences

Setting: Benches, crates, and/or low tables surrounded by mats

Cues

Soft Landings (Absorb the force; land softly on and off the equipment.)

Smooth Transitions (Move with control from balance, to transfer, to balance. . . .)

Rounded Back (Remember, a curled body with chin tucked for all rolls.)

Children should be able to tell you the critical cues for the skills and demonstrate the individual skills before combining skills in sequences.

Tasks/Challenges:

T Approach the bench (crate, table), and use either a step or a spring takeoff to transfer onto it. Decide what body parts are going to serve as your first bases of support before you begin; this will determine whether you use a step or a spring takeoff.

T Create a series of four balances by transferring your weight to different body parts on the bench (crate, table).

Figure 21.2 Equipment setups for transfer of weight when traveling over low apparatus.

Review "Balancing on Different Bases of Support" (page 345), "Balancing in Different Body Shapes" (page 346), and "Balancing Symmetrically and Nonsymmetrically" (page 349) in Chapter 20.

T Transfer off the bench (crate, table) in one of the following ways: (1) jumping and turning, (2) jumping and making a shape while in the air, (3) rolling, or (4) using a transfer that you have created.

A Have the student tell you if the transfer off the low apparatus includes inversion or weight on hands; if so, be sure the student demonstrates mastery on the floor or mats before attempting a transfer off the low apparatus.

Traveling over Low Apparatus

Setting: Milk crates, benches, low tables, hurdles, and milk-jug/rolled-newspaper or dowel-rod "hurdles" throughout general space (Figure 21.2)

Cues

Strong Muscles	(Strong arms and shoulders—no collapse.)
Stretch Your Legs	(Extend your legs upward—stretch to the sky.)

Tasks/Challenges:

T Travel over the various pieces of low equipment by transferring your weight from your feet to your hands to your feet. At the hurdles and the newspaper or dowel rods, place your hands on the mat on the other side of the hurdle or rod, and then transfer your weight over, landing on your feet. At the benches and milk crates, place your hands on the equipment, take your weight on your hands only, and land on your feet on the opposite side of the equipment.

T As you become comfortable taking your weight on your hands, kick higher toward the ceiling, stretching your legs and trunk.

Transferring onto Low Apparatus

Setting: Benches, crates, and/or low tables surrounded by mats in general space

Cues

Strong Muscles	(Strong arms and shoulders for transfer onto hands.)
Soft Landings	(Absorb the force on feet and/or hands and lower body gently onto apparatus.)

Tasks/Challenges:

T Use the benches (crates, low tables) to practice transferring your weight onto equipment. Transfer your weight from your feet to your hands on the equipment by springing off your two feet and landing on your hands and feet. Take your weight momentarily on your hands, then softly lower to your feet; don't jump onto the equipment.

T Using your spring takeoff, transfer your weight to your hands and knees on the apparatus. Yes, you still take your weight momentarily on your hands only.

Traveling over, under, and through apparatus builds youngsters' skills in transferring weight to a variety of body parts as well as their comfort with the equipment.

T Use a front-back stance and step into the transfer, momentarily taking your weight on your hands only on the equipment, then lowering your total body onto additional body parts. Be sure your hands are firmly planted on the equipment so you won't slip when you transfer to hands-only.

Maintaining Transfer from Feet to Hands

Setting: Large gymnastics mats scattered throughout general space, with sufficient room between them for children to work safely

Cues	
Strong Muscles	(Strong arms and shoulders to take weight on hands.)
Stretch to the Sky	(Stretch your trunk and legs upward.)
Alignment	(Feet over hips, over shoulders, over hands—in a straight line.)

Tasks/Challenges:

T Transfer your weight from your feet to your hands to your feet, momentarily taking your weight on your hands only. Reach downward, not forward, with your hands. **Stretch your legs toward the ceiling and tighten your stomach muscles to maintain your balance.**

You may want to begin in a squat position with your hands and feet touching the floor. Transfer your weight to your hands by kicking your feet in the air.

Use a step action to transfer your weight to your hands; try to have your shoulders directly over your hands when you kick your legs up.

T When you are comfortable with your feet being just a few inches off the floor, begin to kick your feet higher in the air.

C Practice until you can balance for 3 seconds on your hands. Transfer your weight back to your feet in their original position each time.

A Teach children in the practice stages of taking weight on hands to twist the trunk, doing a quarter turn and bringing feet down to the floor safely, if they begin to overbalance. This prevents falling on the back in the event of an overbalance.

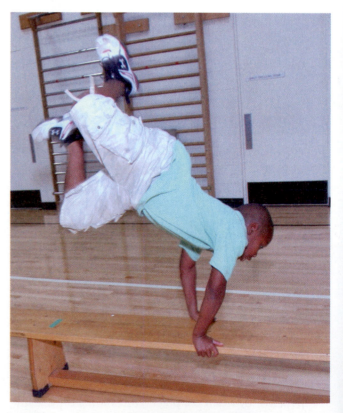

This student practices transferring off apparatus, taking weight on hands.

✓ *Journal.* This is an opportune time to have children record in their journals the date on which they successfully took their weight on their hands for 3 seconds. Have them describe the feeling of "weight on hands." *Refer to Chapter 12, "Assessing Student Learning," for the use of journals in physical education.*

Transfer of weight, combined with balance and apparatus, is a utilization level task.

Transferring Weight to Hands by Stepping: Cartwheels

Setting: Large gymnastics mats throughout general space, with sufficient room between them for children to work safely

---

Cues

Strong Muscles	(Strong arms and shoulders to take weight on hands.)
Stretch	(Stretch your trunk and legs toward the sky—legs straight.)

Tasks/Challenges:

T Using a step action, alternate transferring your weight to your feet and to your hands, returning to your feet in a step action, as in a cartwheel. Your weight transfers momentarily from one foot to the other foot, to one hand, to the other hand, to the foot, to the other foot.

T Experiment with beginning the cartwheel by facing the mat or by standing sideways with one shoulder toward the mat. You may choose either starting position.

T As you feel comfortable with the foot-foot-hand-hand-foot-foot transfer, try to make a straight pathway with your feet and hands along the mat.

T Practice leading first with your right and then with your left side so you can do a cartwheel in either direction.

C Practice until you can perform your cartwheel in a straight line three times.

✓ *Portfolio.* Achievements in weight transference are exciting for children. When they can perform a cartwheel in a straight line, with legs fully stretched in the air, have a partner assess the skill. Have them record the date on a gymnastics checklist in their portfolios. *Refer to Chapter 12, "Assessing Student Learning," for guidelines on assessment.*

T Transfer your weight to your hands, as in the cartwheel. While you are balanced in the inverted position, bring your feet together, twist a half turn, and bring your feet down quickly to face in the opposite direction; this is a round-off.

Children won't master gymnastics tasks in only one or two 30-minute lessons. A station format plus revisitation (see Chapter 10) provides opportunities for distributed practice of skills.

Utilization Level (GLSP): Learning Experiences Leading to Skill Development in Transferring Weight

Children at the utilization level of transferring weight learn to transfer their weight to their hands for longer periods of time and in combinations with stretching, curling, and twisting actions. Tasks are designed to teach children to transfer weight onto, over, and off large apparatus. The tasks also emphasize the development of more complex sequences involving transferring weight.

A note about cues: Although several cues are listed for many of the learning experiences, it's important to focus on only one cue at a time. This way, the children can really concentrate on that cue. Once you provide feedback to the children and observe that most have learned a cue, it's time to focus on another one.

Transferring Weight to Hands: Walking

Setting: Large gymnastics mats throughout general space, with sufficient room between them for children to work safely on transfers

Cues

Strong Muscles	(Strong arms and shoulders for weight on hands.)
Stretch	(Stretch your trunk and legs toward the sky—legs straight.)
Alignment	(Feet over hips, over shoulders, over hands—in a straight line.)

Tasks/Challenges:

T When you are confident and comfortable balancing on your hands for 3 seconds, try walking on your hands.

⚠ Children should attempt walking on their hands only if they have sufficient upper-body strength to support weight in the inverted position for several seconds and can move into and out of a balance on their hands only with control.

Transferring Weight to Hands and Twisting

Setting: Large gymnastics mats throughout general space, with sufficient room between them for children to work safely on transfers

Cues

Strong Muscles	(Strong arms and shoulders for weight on hands.)
Stretch	(Stretch your trunk and legs toward the sky—legs straight.)
Alignment	(Feet over hips, over shoulders, over hands—in a straight line.)

Tasks/Challenges:

T Transfer your weight to your hands, twist your body a half turn, and bring your feet to the floor so you are facing in the opposite direction.

T While balanced on your hands, slowly walk on your hands a half turn to face in the opposite direction.

Transferring Weight to Hands and Forming a Bridge

Setting: Large gymnastics mats throughout general space

Cues

Strong Muscles	(Strong arms and shoulders for supporting weight on hands.)
Tight Muscles	(Tighten the abdominals for control.)
Extend	(Stretch from your fingertips to your toes as you transfer from feet to hands to feet.)

Tasks/Challenges:

T Using a step action, transfer your weight to your hands with sufficient force to continue the forward motion. Your feet should remain in the step-like stance as they move upward over your hands. Just before your feet contact the floor, bring them together, and bend your knees slightly. You will then balance in a "bridge" with your feet and hands supporting your weight. Keep your legs in the step-like stance throughout the transfer.

T As your feet contact the surface, push with your hands to continue your transfer to a standing position. This transfer without a pause is a walkover.

Transferring Weight onto Large Apparatus

Setting: Large apparatus—benches, tables, vaulting boxes, balance beams, parallel bars, large climbing frames—placed around the gym. *Many transfers at the utilization and proficiency levels of transferring weight are specific to particular pieces of apparatus; the name of the apparatus appears in parentheses following the task title.*

Cues

Heads Up	(Keep your head and shoulders erect as you approach the apparatus.)
Soft Landings	(Absorb the force on your feet and/or hands and lower your body slowly to the apparatus.)

Tasks/Challenges:

T Transferring weight onto large apparatus in gymnastics usually includes an approach to build momentum, a spring or step takeoff, and the transfer onto the apparatus. Approach the apparatus from about 15 feet. Using a spring takeoff, transfer your weight from your feet on the floor to your feet and hands on the apparatus (box, beam, table). **Remember, you will need a spring takeoff for power and/or height; a step takeoff is a slower way to transfer weight.**

Figure 21.3 Tuck, wolf, and straddle positions on large apparatus following spring takeoffs.

T Transfer your weight to your feet and hands with your body curled in a tuck position. *(Model.)*

T Transfer your weight to your feet and hands with legs extended in a straddle position. *(Model.)*

T Transfer your weight to your feet and hands in a "wolf" position: one knee bent, one leg straight (Figure 21.3) *(Model.)*

T Approach the apparatus from the sides as well as the front. Practice both spring and step takeoffs to transfer your weight to various body parts on the apparatus. **Remember, you will need a spring takeoff for power and/or height; a step takeoff is a slower way to transfer weight.**

Many of the control-level tasks for transferring weight onto and off low apparatus can be repeated for large apparatus. This is good practice because it enables children to adjust comfortably to the increased height and narrower surface of large apparatus.

> **Transferring Weight to Head and Hands on Apparatus (Box, Beam, Table)**

Setting: Large apparatus placed throughout general space, with sufficient mats for children to work safely

Cues

Heads Up	(Keep your head and shoulders erect as you approach the apparatus.)
Strong Muscles	(Strong arm and shoulder muscles to support weight on the apparatus.)
Soft Landings	(Absorb the force on your feet and/or hands and lower your body slowly to the apparatus.)

Tasks/Challenges:

T Approach the apparatus, and use a spring takeoff to transfer your weight to your hands and head on the apparatus. Push hard with your legs on the takeoff for sufficient height and time for the transfer, taking your weight first on your hands only and then gently, with control, on your head and hands.

⚠ Have the children approach the box, beam, or table from the end rather than the side for this transfer to head and hands. This allows sufficient space for rolling across the apparatus if they overbalance.

⚠ Teach the children to roll slowly across the apparatus if they overbalance on the head-and-hands transfer; teach them to transfer weight back to their feet on the floor if they do not have sufficient push to move into the inverted position on the apparatus.

Transferring Weight onto Bars (Parallel Bars, Climbing Frame)

Setting: Large apparatus placed throughout general space, with sufficient mats surrounding for safety

Cues	
Heads Up	(Keep your head and shoulders erect as you approach the apparatus.)
Strong Muscles	(Strong arm and shoulder muscles to support weight on the apparatus.)
Soft Landings	(Absorb the force on your feet and/or hands and lower your body slowly to the apparatus.)

Tasks/Challenges:

T Standing under the apparatus, use a spring takeoff to transfer your weight to your hands on a high bar. Hanging on the bar, pull up with your arms as you swing your legs over a lower bar and balance in a sitting position.

T Approach the apparatus with a series of steps. Using a spring takeoff, grasp the bar with your hands and jump up. Push really hard with your arms to lift your body above the bar; balance with your hands and upper thighs on the bar. Swing a leg over the bar so you can straddle the bar.

T Approach the apparatus with a series of steps. As you step under the bar, grasp it with your hands, and kick your rear leg forcefully upward to bring your hips to the bar. Keeping your arms bent and pulling your body close to the bar, assume a pike position by bending at the hips. The momentum of the leg kick will cause your body to circle the bar. Balance on your hands and upper thighs on the bar.

C You have now practiced jumping into a hip mount and doing a hip circle with the body in a pike position. Practice these skills until you master them. Then add them to your gymnastics checklist in your portfolio.

T Approach the apparatus from the back, front, and side; practice both spring and step takeoffs to transfer your weight to various body parts on the apparatus.

Transferring Weight over Apparatus (Vaulting Box)

Setting: Vaulting boxes, with sufficient mats for safety, in general space

Cues	
Heads Up	(Keep your head and shoulders erect as you approach the apparatus.)
Strong Muscles	(Strong arm and shoulder muscles to support weight on the apparatus.)
Soft Landings	(Bend your knees for a controlled landing.)

Tasks/Challenges:

⚠ Position yourself at the vaulting station when children are transferring weight over the apparatus. As a spotter, you should not help the children perform the skill, but you can help prevent serious injury from a fall. Because spotting techniques differ for each skill, you should consult a gymnastics text or certified gymnastics coach before attempting to spot students in specific gymnastics tasks.

T Approach the vaulting box with light running steps, keeping your weight on the balls of your feet. Using a spring takeoff, plant your hands firmly on the box, shoulder-width apart. Travel over the vaulting box, landing on your two feet on the mat.

T Now transfer over the box by placing your hands shoulder-width apart on the apparatus, bringing your legs up between your arms in a tuck or curled position. Pause momentarily on the box in this curled shape; then jump forward to the mat.

T Push harder with your hands this time to bring your body into a curled position, and push yourself over the box without pausing in the tuck position on top of the box.

⚠ Children should attempt vaulting over the box with a curled, straddle, or wolf vault only after they have mastered transferring onto the apparatus with these techniques.

T Transfer over the vaulting box by bringing your feet and legs together, stretched to one side, as you cross over the box. Place your hands shoulder-width apart on the box, and shift your weight to one hand as you swing your legs over the box. Push off from the vaulting box with the supporting hand, landing on two feet with your back to the vaulting box. This is called *a flank* vault. That spring takeoff we practiced earlier becomes increasingly important as you work on mounts onto and transfers over large apparatus.

Transfer of weight on low equipment precedes the use of high equipment.

T Transfer your weight onto the vaulting box in a wide shape by placing your hands shoulder-width apart and stretching your legs to either side of the box, supporting your weight momentarily on your feet and hands. From a standing position on the vaulting box, transfer your weight to your feet by jumping to the mat. You will need a really strong takeoff to gain the height for this transfer.

T Transfer your weight over the vaulting box by taking your weight on your hands, shoulder-width apart, and bringing your feet over the box in the stretched, wide shape. Keep your head and shoulders erect to prevent losing your balance. This is called a *straddle* vault. Do not attempt this vault without the spotter (teacher or qualified adult) at the station.

⚠ Always have the children tell you which vault they are attempting and whether they are stopping on top or transferring over before they begin their approach. This allows you to be ready for the proper spotting of that skill.

Transferring Weight Along Apparatus

Setting: Stationary bar, tables and benches of various heights, vaulting boxes, balance beam, a stage

Many of the gymnastics skills learned on the floor and on low equipment can also be performed on large apparatus. Before children try them on a large apparatus, they should review the skills on the floor or mats, then on the low equipment, concentrating on the skill and its critical elements.

Transferring Weight by Rolling (Bench, Box, or Table)

Setting: Benches, vaulting boxes, and/or tables of various heights, surrounded by sufficient mats for children to work safely

Cues	
Rounded Back	(Keep your back curled, chin tucked for a good roll.)
Control	(Tight muscles, slow-motion action for control throughout the roll.)

Tasks/Challenges:

⚠ Remind children to position themselves at one end of the bench, box, or table to start the roll so they will have enough surface to complete the rolling action.

T Transfer your weight to your feet and hands on the bench, box, or table, with your back curled. Place your thumbs and the sides of your palms on top of the bench or box, with your hands and fingers on the sides of the apparatus. (Although this position is quite different from that used for rolling on mats, it provides a steady grip and constant awareness of the width of the surface.) Tuck your head, and slowly roll forward across the apparatus.

T Transfer your weight to your feet and hands with a curled back. Slowly transfer to your curled back and hands for rolling backward across the bench, box, or table. Extend your hands above your head to hold onto the sides of the box or bench; place your head to one side, and roll backward over one shoulder.

T Roll backward on the apparatus by transferring your weight from your curled back to one bent knee with one leg extended. This backward transfer is often easier when balancing on the small surface.

A Permit students to transfer weight by rolling across the apparatus only after they have demonstrated sustained control of the rolling action on the low apparatus. They should be able to stop the movement at any point in the rolling action.

Transferring Weight to Hands on Low Apparatus

Setting: Tape lines on the gym floor, with sufficient space between them for children to work safely; low benches surrounded by mats

Cues	
Strong Muscles	(Strong arms and shoulders to take weight on hands.)
Stretch	(Stretch your trunk and legs toward the sky—legs straight.)
Muscular Tension	(Maintain tension through arms, trunk, and legs for full extension—stretched for cartwheels, arched for walkovers.)

Tasks/Challenges:

T Practice a cartwheel on a tape line on the floor until you can do it perfectly three times. Now transfer your weight from your feet to your hands in a cartwheel on the low bench.

Teaching by invitation or intratask variation (Chapter 6) is very effective when working with transferring weight on apparatus. Permit only those children who are clearly ready to do so to practice inverted weight transference along apparatus.

T Transfer your weight from your feet to your hands, as in a walkover, on the bench.

T Transfer your weight from your feet to your hands, slowly execute a half turn, and bring your feet down on the apparatus surface facing the opposite direction.

A Teach children to push with their hands to move the body away from the bench and to transfer weight to their feet on the floor if they feel off balance or unable to complete the transfer after inverting.

C Create three ways to transfer your weight while moving along the apparatus. Consider changes in levels and directions of travel. Diagram and/or describe your transfers on paper. Show your three transfers to a friend; ask the friend to give you pointers to make your transfers even better.

✓ *Peer Observation.* Children working together, as in the preceding task, can be an excellent type of assessment. *Refer to Chapter 12, "Assessing Student Learning," for more information on peer assessment.*

Transferring Weight on Bars

Setting: Parallel bars and/or large climbing frame, with sufficient mats surrounding

Cues	
Strong Grip	(Maintain a strong grip on the bars to work safely.)
Strong Muscles	(Strong arm and shoulder muscles to maintain control on the bars.)

Tasks/Challenges:

T Transfer your weight to different body parts as you move from bar to bar on the parallels or other climbing apparatus. Make some of your transfers very slowly; make others very quickly.

T Circle the bar with your body curled, in a pike position.

T Use twisting actions to move your body off balance and into the transfer.

Combining Skills on Mats

Setting: Large gymnastics mats in general space, with sufficient room between them for children to work safely

Cues
Individual cues as needed

Tasks/Challenges:

T Travel the length of your mat, transferring your weight from your feet to other body parts, in various combinations to create a sequence. For example:

- Perform slow movements and then very quick movements for contrast.
- Do movements that show strength and then movements that demonstrate slowness and smooth control.
- Perform twisting, turning actions—for example, a round-off, weight on your hands, a 360-degree turn on your hands.

- Travel the length of your mat, combining a balance, a jump, a roll, and a hands/feet action.
- Travel the length of your mat, transferring your weight from your feet to your hands, followed by a roll and an ending balance.

Combining Weight Transfer and Balances into Sequences on Mats and Apparatus

Setting: Large and small gymnastics apparatus, the large apparatus positioned in general space

Cues

Individual cues as needed

Tasks/Challenges:

Gymnastics routines on mats and apparatus are combinations of weight transfers and balance. Children at the utilization and proficiency levels of balance and weight transfer are ready for sequences involving combinations of skills and travel. Figure 21.4 gives an example of an assignment, plus guidelines for completing it.

Figure 21.4 Sample assignment for utilization- or proficiency-level weight-transfer and balance sequence.

Name _____

Final Project: Gymnastics

Grade 6: (a) mat sequence, (b) equipment sequence

Alone; with a partner: mirror, side by side

1. Beginning
    A. Approach:
        distance, starting point, pathway
        walk, run, leap, roll, walkover, cartwheel
        other _____
    B. Takeoff:
        spring, step
2. Development of sequence: Mix in any order for interest.
    A. Balances:
        minimum of four body shapes/four different bases of support
    B. Actions:
        minimum of three
        stretch, curl, twist, turn
    C. Transfers:
        movement
        feet to hand, back, head/hands
        (headstands, cartwheels, rolls, etc.)
    D. Inversion:
        minimum of two
3. Ending shape or dismount
    A. Music selection: ninety seconds
    B. On back side of page, list the progression of section 2; illustrate it if you wish.

Assessment Example

From the National Standards for Physical Education

Event Task

As the final project in gymnastics, students are to design a 90-second routine for either mats or apparatus. They may choose to work alone or with a partner; the partner relationship may be mirror or side by side. The routine must include an approach, development, and ending shape or dismount. The development portion of the routine must include the following: a minimum of four balances of different shapes and bases of support, a minimum of three locomotor and/or non-locomotor actions, weight transfer, and at least two inversions. The selection of music for the routine is a student decision. The routine is to be diagrammed or written on paper and practiced until the sequence is memorized in its entirety. The routine will be videotaped for inclusion in student portfolios.

Criteria for Assessment

a. Routine includes all necessary components: approach, balances, weight transfers, inversion, dismount (ending shape).
b. Routine matches music in length.
c. Demonstrates changes in tempo in routine.
d. Selects balances and weight transfers that can be correctly performed (i.e., skills matched to personal gymnastic ability).
e. Maintains stillness in balances.
f. Displays creativity in routine design.
g. Transitions between movements are smooth.

NASPE (1995, 47–48)

Proficiency Level (GLSP): Learning Experiences Leading to Skill Development in Transferring Weight

Tasks at the proficiency level focus on increasing the horizontal and/or vertical distance of the weight transfer, as well as the intricate maneuvers (twisting and curling actions) that the body and its parts perform as weight is transferred from and received by different body parts. Examples include hands-only vaulting; performing stretching and twisting actions while airborne; and dismounting from apparatus by transferring weight from hands to feet combined with aerial twists, turns, and curls.

Activities at this level use specific gymnastics equipment and more closely resemble Olympic-style stunts. These skills are most often learned through club gymnastics. We do not teach them to the total class because very few children attain this level of performance. For those children who are ready to learn these skills or already proficient in these tasks, we provide individual teaching or coaching (see Chapter 29).

Rolling

Rolling is the act of transferring weight to adjacent body parts around a central axis. Children find the sensations of rolling—dizziness, loss of perception, and not knowing where they are or how they'll finish a roll—intriguing and perplexing. So children love to roll. As they become adept at rolling, the fascination of traveling upside down is augmented by the pleasure of being able to roll in different directions and at various speeds. Whether recovering after falling off a skateboard or bicycle or participating in formal gymnastics settings, children who master the skill theme of rolling are able to participate comfortably and safely in activities that involve being off balance and falling because they possess sufficient recovery techniques. In physical education classes, rolling is generally dealt with in a gymnastics context, as transference of weight providing children a fluid way to connect different balancing actions and to change direction and/or speed in a dynamic, unpredictable situation. In addition, safety through rolling is introduced early to help children avoid crashing to the floor when they lose their balance. In dance and games, rolling is dealt with briefly to increase the children's range of movement and to enhance expressive abilities (see the progression spiral on page 386).

You will notice that no proficiency level is included in the progression spiral for rolling. Children proficient in rolling enjoy rolling over high equipment and aerial rolls. They also combine rolling as a means of weight transfer between various forms of balance and other forms of weight transference. At this level, children are capable of difficult and sophisticated rolls, but because of safety considerations, the teacher's skills, equipment requirements, and the student–teacher ratio of physical education classes, we do not teach them. Such rolls as dive rolls; rolls along high, narrow equipment; and rolls from aerial positions are better left to club gymnastics.

The key observation points in Box 21-2 show the correct form for rolling. Carefully observe to see that:

- The arms and hands receive the body evenly at the beginning of the roll so the child does not roll to one side.
- The head slides through as the weight shifts from the hands to the upper back.
- The arms leave the mat as soon as the shoulders touch.
- The body stays tightly throughout the roll.
- The roll ends on the feet.
- The feet are parallel on landing and not crossed.

As with any weight-bearing activity, it is critical to give careful consideration to each child's physical maturity and skill. Before they're ready to attempt traditional

Box 21-2

Key Observation Points: Rolling Pattern

Hips raised

Hands on mat

Head slides through

Body tight and round

Comes to feet

forward and backward rolls, children *must be able to support their body weight with their arms.* We believe that children should not be forced to do any specific forward or backward roll. We are especially concerned about asking children to do traditional backward and forward rolls when they haven't yet developed the strength they need to protect themselves from back and neck injuries. Thus, we have provided illustrations of the hand and body positions for a variety of rolls.

Finally, while children love the sensation of rolling, it is an activity that cannot be done for extended periods. In an effort to maintain the quality of the skill and to prevent off-task behavior because children are too dizzy, we have often found it more productive to focus on rolling for only part of a lesson. Thus, especially in the early stages of rolling, children are able to recover between practices of rolling.

When introducing the skill of rolling, we prefer to have one mat for each child. When we don't have a mat for each child, we use as many mats as possible. We've found that a good ground rule for any rolling situation is to have only one child at a time on the mat. This does not mean the other children must stand in line and wait; they can stand around the mat and roll, in turn, as soon as the mat is empty. (See Figure 21.5 for a class setup that maximizes rolling opportunities

for each child.) Sometimes we set up learning centers to prevent long waits in line. Grassy areas or carpeting can also serve as appropriate areas for practicing rolling. When children roll on or over equipment, we make sure the surrounding area is covered with mats. When teaching rolling, it is especially important to employ the back-to-the-wall observational technique discussed in Chapter 11.

Precontrol Level (GLSP): Activities for Exploration of Rolling

The precontrol level of rolling is characterized by exploration of various ways in which the body is able to be round. This exploration includes rocking actions from the head to feet on the back and stomach. At this level, children are challenged when asked to perform actions such as rocking back and forth like a rocking chair or rolling in a stretched position like a log. Rocking in a ball-like position, in preparation for rolling, is also explored at this level. When a child first begins to roll, the arms and hands are of little use. The child may get over, but the whole body usually uncurls in the middle of the roll, and the child lands sitting down.

Skill Theme Development Progression

Rolling

Proficiency Level

Club gymnastics

Utilization Level

Rolling, catching, and throwing
Rolling and striking
Rolling to meet and part
Rolling and balancing on equipment
Rolling onto low equipment
Rolling while throwing, and catching
Rolling to express an idea
Rolling, balancing, and rolling
Traveling and rolling between pieces of equipment
Rolling off low equipment
Rolling on low equipment
Rolling over low hurdles
Rolling, jumping, and traveling in relationship to others
Rolling and traveling quickly

Control Level

Rolling while traveling, jumping, and landing
Rolling, levels, directions, and jumping
Rolling after jumping over equipment and landing
Rolling after jumping from different heights
Rolling after jumping for height and landing
Rolling after jumping off equipment and landing
Rolling using different directions and speeds
Linking rolls
Rolling from different directions and positions
Rolling in different directions
Rolling backward
Handclasp backward roll
Back shoulder roll
Rolling at different speeds
Rolling from different positions
Rocking backward over the shoulders
Rolling forward
Rocking backward
Rolling sideways over a shoulder
Rolling sideways on different body parts
Rolling in a long, narrow position (log roll)
Rocking to match a partner

Precontrol Level

Curling to roll
Rolling sideways
Rocking on different body parts
Making curled shapes

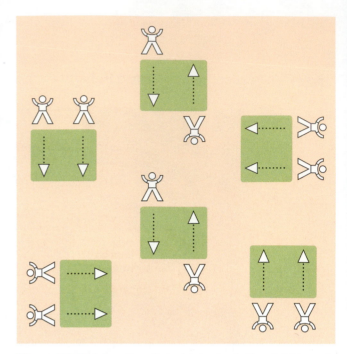

Figure 21.5 Mat positions that minimize the likelihood children will rock or roll into each other.

Making Curled Shapes

Setting: A mat, space on a mat, or a carpet square in a grassy area for each child; children positioned so they will not rock into each other (Figure 21.5)

Tasks/Challenges:

Ⓣ On your mat try to find as many ways as possible to curl your body so it is round. Three different ways would be good.

Rocking on Different Body Parts

Setting: A mat, space on a mat, or a carpet square in a grassy area for each child; children positioned so they will not rock into each other

Tasks/Challenges:

Ⓣ In self-space, you're going to pretend to be a rocking horse. But this rocking horse can do special things. First, you want to find out what it is like to rock on your back. To rock on your back, you must make your back round because flat things can't rock.

Ⓣ Now your special rocking horse is going to try to rock on its stomach. Remember, make your stomach round so you can rock smoothly.

Ⓣ Now you are going to try to do what no rocking horse has ever done: You are going to try to rock on your side. Can you make your side round? Try it.

T Your rocking horse is just getting warmed up, so let's see if it can go faster. See if you can rock so fast on your back that it takes you up to your feet.

T Now see if you can keep rocking on your back without stopping, almost as if you can't stop. If it helps, use your hands and arms.

Rolling Sideways

Setting: A mat for every child or two or a large grassy space; children positioned so they do not roll into each other

Tasks/Challenges:

T Now we are going to try something different: rolling sideways like a log. Try to roll slow and fast.

T Can you find another way to roll sideways? Maybe like an egg?

Curling to Roll

Setting: A mat for every child or two or a large grassy space; children positioned so they do not roll into each other

Tasks/Challenges:

T Can you make your body like a ball? How many ways can your ball move around your space? Remember, only round balls roll.

Rolling and Equipment

Many people are hesitant to teach gymnastics due to a perceived lack of equipment. Many people are hesitant to teaching rolling due to a perceived lack of mats. The surface needed for most fundamental rolling activities only needs to be large enough to cushion the head and upper back.

Control Level (GLSP): Learning Experiences Leading to Skill Development in Rolling

At the control level, children become capable of controlling their bodies while rolling. They learn to roll in different directions using their arms and hands to push while the body stays curled and from different positions so they're able to perform other movements safely and use rolling as a response to a fall. Children also practice rolling as a conclusion to jumping and landing. Emphasis at this level is on control and the ability to roll in various situations. Rolls are performed as floor activities, and rolling is developed as a safety skill.

A note about cues: Although several cues are listed for many of the learning experiences, it's important to focus on only one cue at a time. This way, the children can really concentrate on that cue. Once you provide feedback to the children and observe that most have learned a cue, it's time to focus on another one.

Rocking to Match a Partner

Setting: Partners side by side on a mat or in a grassy area, with enough space between them so that they do not hit each other

Cue

C Bodies (Curve your body like the letter C to rock.)

Tasks/Challenges:

T To warm up a bit, practice rocking back and forth on your mat. See if you can make your rocks very smooth.

T This time you are going to play a game called Twin Rockers. You and your partner will be side by side. On the signal, you'll start to rock on your back. The challenge is to rock the same way and at the same time as your partner so you look like twins.

T This time, rock on your stomach.

C Now see if you and your partner can develop two other Twin Rockers. Practice them until you can do them so they match exactly.

Rolling in a Long, Narrow Position (Log Roll)

Setting: A mat (no larger than 4 feet by 6 feet) for every child or two or a large, grassy space; children positioned so they do not roll into each other

Cues

Stretch Arms (Stretch your arms above your head.)
Straight Body (Straighten your body.)
Feet Together (Bring your feet tight together.)

Tasks/Challenges:

T On your mat make your body long and skinny with your arms over your head. You could call this a log or pencil. See if you can roll to the right and to the left in this position. Practice until you can go both ways just as smoothly.

T This time try to make your log roll go in a straight line, still keeping your body position. Try to go from one end of your mat to the other without rolling off.

T Try changing the speed of your log roll: Sometimes roll slowly as if you were rolling on flat land and sometimes move quickly as if rolling downhill.

T If you feel comfortable doing your roll with your hands over your head, try to do it with your arms at your sides.

C Try to make a sequence of rolls in this narrow position—for example, one slow to the right, two quickly to the left, one slow to the right, and then repeat the sequence. Be sure to stay in your space or on your mat.

✓ *Portfolio.* Children can write their sequences out, date them, and include them in their portfolios as an assessment task.

Rolling Sideways on Different Body Parts

Setting: A mat for every child or two or a large grassy space; children positioned so that they do not roll into each other

> **Cues**
>
> **C Bodies**   (Curve your body like the letter C to roll.)
>
> **Hold Knees** (Hold your knees together, either from the outside or from the inside out; *see* Figure 21.6.)

Tasks/Challenges:

T This time try to roll sideways like an egg in a curled position. Practice rolling this egg in different directions—sometimes left, sometimes right.

Figure 21.6 Arm positions for keeping ankles and knees together while rolling sideways on different body parts.

T Try rolling on different body parts—shoulder, back, even upper legs.

T In your space or on your mat, practice using the egg roll to travel. Can you roll around the whole space?

T Roll at different speeds around your space or mat.

Rolling Sideways over a Shoulder

Setting: A mat for every child or two or a large grassy space; children positioned so they do not roll into each other

> **Cues**
>
> **Drop** (Drop one shoulder to the mat.)
> **Tuck** (Tuck the elbow and knee of the dropped shoulder under.)
> **Roll** (Roll over.)

Tasks/Challenges:

T This time we are going to roll over a shoulder. To do that you need to start on your hands and knees, drop one shoulder to the mat, tuck your elbow and knee under your body, and roll over. Your roll should take you back up to your hands and knees. *(Demonstrate the roll.)* Let's all do it together this first time. Ready? Hands and knees, drop, tuck, roll. Good.

T Practice the roll on your own. **Say the cues out loud as you go to help you remember the process.** Do one roll across your mat, get up, and try another one. You know you are really good when you can come up to your hands and knees each time.

T Once you feel comfortable rolling in one direction, try dropping the other shoulder and rolling that way.

C See if you can do three rolls in each direction that stay round throughout the whole roll.

T If you feel really good about rolling on your shoulder from your hands and knees, you may want to try it from a squatting position. The cues are the same; just the starting position changes. *(If this task is worded in this way, it is "teaching by invitation," allowing children to progress at their own speed. See Chapter 8 for more about this concept.)*

✓ *Children's Drawing.* This would be a wonderful time to use children's drawings of rocking and rolling to assess their knowledge of the critical elements. *See Chapter 12 for the development of children's drawings as assessment items.*

Rocking Backward

Setting: Each child with a space at a mat or in a large grassy area; children positioned so they do not roll into one another; music conducive to rocking and a CD player

Cues	
C Back	(Round your back like the letter C.)
Tuck	(Tuck your chin to your chest.)
Knees to Chest	(Pull your knees to your chest and hold.)

Tasks/Challenges:

T Remember when we explored rocking horses and did Twin Rockers? This time we are going to try a back rocker. Start by squatting down with your back to the mat, place your fingers on the floor, slowly transfer your weight backward to the mat, and, as your back reaches the mat, tuck your chin in, bring your knees to your chest, wrap your arms around them, and rock backward until your head touches the mat. Rock forward to your starting position. Watch me as I show you. (Demonstrate.) Squat, lower, tuck, knees, rock.

T Practice the back rocker on your own. Don't ever go over your head. See how smoothly you can make the rock.

T As you rock, try to come back up to your feet at the end. What does it take to do this?

C See if you can keep your back rocker going for as long as I play the music. (Play music in increasingly longer intervals, beginning with about 5 to 10 seconds.)

✳ What does it look like when body parts are round? Show me.

Rolling Forward

Setting: Each child with a space at a mat or in a large grassy area; children positioned so they do not roll into one another

Cues	
Hands	(Your hands should be on the floor on the outside of your knees.)
Lean	(Lean forward.)
Hike	(Hike your bottom up high into the air.)
Look	(Look back through your legs.)
Tip	(Tip over; place the top of your shoulders on the mat.)

⚠ We do not force children to do a specific roll. Some may still prefer to roll over their shoulder at this point. If so, we place the emphasis on being round and staying in control. Gradually, we encourage children to move to positions higher than their hands and knees—for example, squatting—and to start the roll from there.

Tasks/Challenges:

T Now we are going to try rolling forward. This roll goes over your head. To do it, begin in a squat position, lean forward, hike your seat up in the air, look through your legs, and tip over. Everyone watch me do it once. (Demonstrate.) Now, let's do it together on the cues: Hands, lean, hike, look, tip.

T Now practice on your own. Practice once across your mat. **Say the cues as you roll so you don't forget them.** Get up and go again.

C See if you can do three rolls that stay round all the way.

T When you can stay round all the way through the roll, you may want to try to return to a standing position after the roll. The starting position is the same.

Bubble Gum = Head Down

Getting children to keep their heads down is often difficult when they are first learning to roll. Two hints we have seen used are asking children to think of bubble gum connecting their chin and chest or having children hold a beanbag with their chin to their chest. Both ideas work.

Cues	
C Back	(Round your back like the letter C.)
Tuck	(Tuck your chin to your chest.)
Hike	(Hike your bottom up high into the air.)
Push	(Push off with your legs and make sure your weight is on your arms so your shoulders and back touch the mat in a very controlled way. The top of your head should not touch the mat. Imagine there is paint on the top of your head; try not to get any on the mat.)

✳ Have children touch the back of their heads with their hand so you know they can distinguish between the back and top of their heads.

Figure 21.7 Hand positions on forward roll.

⚠ Children should not be forced to roll over their heads if they cannot support their body weight with their hands or are uncomfortable with the roll.

Tasks/Challenges:

Ⓣ Now we are going to try a forward roll. Squat down at your mat and place your hands on the mat just to the outside of your knees. Make your back really round like the letter C. Tuck your chin all the way down to your chest. Hike your bottom way up in the air. Push with your arms and roll. Watch me while I show you how it will look. *(Demonstrate.)* Practice once with me all together as we say the steps: Hands (Figure 21.7), C, tuck, hike, push, and roll.

Point of Contact

There is some debate regarding the point of contact on the forward roll. Some prefer the shoulders and back; others indicate the back of the head. In our research we have found both. (We advocate the shoulders.) Regardless of which point of contact is used, several key points ensure the safety of the skill: (1) the weight is held by the arms, not the neck and head; (2) the body parts are in a round position and stay that way throughout the roll; and (3) the transference of weight occurs under control so there is no sudden crunching of weight onto any body part.

⚠ Some children may be more comfortable doing a shoulder roll. Encourage them to concentrate on roundness and tucking, while gradually trying to

Smaller mats are adequate for introducing children to rolling; larger mats can be used for rolling in sequences and in relation to apparatus.

get them to raise their starting position farther off the ground to kneeling or squatting.

T Now practice on your own. Do one roll, get up, and start again. Roll straight across the mat. Say the cues aloud as you practice so you won't forget them.

C See if you can do three forward rolls that stay round from beginning to end. Remember, stop and reset yourself between the rolls.

T If you feel really good about your forward roll, try to come up to your feet at the end.

C See if you can do five forward rolls that the Olympic judges would give a "10."

✳ What parts of your body have to be round to roll forward? Show me.

Figure 21.8 Handclasp position for rocking over the shoulders.

Inclined Surfaces

For many children it is easier to learn to roll forward on an inclined surface. To do this, use a wedge mat approximately 10 inches high at the top tapering to 2 inches high at the bottom, and at least 30 inches long and 18 inches wide. You will need a box for children to stand on at the top of the mat. With this task, be sure that children start their rolls from a squatting position. The cues remain the same.

Rocking Backward over the Shoulders

Setting: Each child with a space at a mat or in a large grassy area; children positioned so they do not roll into one another

Cues

C Back	(Round your back like the letter C.)
Hands Behind Head	(Clasp your hands behind your head with your elbows sticking out to the sides; *see* Figure 21.8.)

Tasks/Challenges:

T Start by squatting down with your back to the mat; clasp your hands behind your head with your elbows out as far as possible; slowly transfer your weight backward to the mat; as your back slowly reaches the mat, tuck your chin in, bring your knees to your chest, and rock backward as far as possible until your weight is on your elbows. Rock forward to your starting position. Watch me

as I show you. *(Demonstrate.)* Practice it once with me: Squat, clasp, lower, tuck, knees, rock.

T When you feel comfortable bringing your weight back on your elbows, challenge yourself a little more—try to make your feet touch the mat over your head. Then rock back to the starting position.

C Try to do five rocks in which your feet touch the mat over your head.

Rolling from Different Positions

Setting: Each child with a space to roll on a mat or grassy area

Cues

Round Body	(Round your back and tuck your chin for a good roll.)
Strong Muscles	(Use strong arms and shoulders to transfer weight slowly to the roll.)

Tasks/Challenges:

T So far you have been starting your rolls from a low position, close to the mat. Now we are going to try starting your rolls from different positions. The first position we will try may be easier than the low position you have been using. It is called a straddle position. Watch me as I show you. *(Demonstrate.)*

Stand behind your mat with your feet wide apart; stretch your hands to the ceiling. Now put your hands on the mat almost between your feet (don't reach forward), tuck your chin to your chest, and roll forward. You will land sitting down. As with all rolls, keep your back rounded. Let's practice one together as we say the steps out loud:

feet apart, stretch arms, hands on mat, tuck chin, slowly roll.

T Practice the straddle roll on your own until you can do it slowly and smoothly.

T Now that you can roll from the squatting position and the straddle position, see if you can find other positions from which to roll. You may want to try your knees, standing, one leg, and one arm. **Each time, remember to use strong muscles to lower slowly to the mat.** Try to find four different starting positions.

C Choose the starting position you like most. See if you can do four rolls from that position that stay rounded, and lower slowly to the mat. When you think you can, ask a friend to watch you and give a thumbs-up for each roll that you do correctly.

Rolling at Different Speeds

Setting: Each child with a space to roll on a mat or grassy area without rolling into each other

Cues	
Round Body	(Round your back and tuck your chin and knees for a good roll.)
Arms	(Your arms are your brakes and accelerator for these rolls.)

Tasks/Challenges:

T Do you remember when you worked on traveling at different speeds? Now you are going to roll at different speeds. Sometimes you will roll fast, sometimes you will roll slowly, and sometimes you will roll at a medium speed. Now practice doing rolls at different speeds. Your speed should be so clear that I can tell which speed it is just by watching. I shouldn't have to ask you.

C Now I am really going to give you a challenge. I'll call out a speed, and you roll at that speed. I'll be watching to see if you really roll at the speed I call out.

Back Shoulder Roll

Setting: Each child with a space at a mat or in a large grassy area; children positioned so they do not roll into one another

Cues	
Round Body	(Round your back and tuck your chin and knees for a good roll.)
Arm to Side	(Keep the arm of the shoulder you are going to roll over out to the side of your body.)
Head to Side	(Tuck your head to one side as you go over.)

Tasks/Challenges:

T We are going to try rolling backward over a shoulder with our hands on the mat to push. Watch me as I show you what it looks like. *(Demonstrate.)* Squat with your back to the mat with your hands on the floor in front of you, push with your hands and rock backward to the mat, bring the arm of the shoulder you are going to roll over out to the side of your body and the other arm back over your head, tuck your head to one side, push with your arms, and roll over that shoulder. Let's practice one together as we say the steps: Squat, hands in front, push and rock back, arm to side, tuck head, roll (Figure 21.9).

T Now practice the back shoulder roll on your own, **each time saying the steps so you don't forget them.**

T When you feel good about going over one shoulder, try to tuck your head the other way and go over that shoulder.

C Try to do four backward rolls that stay round all the way through. When you think you can do it, raise your hand and ask me to come watch, or have a friend watch.

✿ What parts of your body have to be round to roll backward over your shoulder? Show me.

Figure 21.9 Hand and head positions for rolling backward over a shoulder.

Handclasp Backward Roll

Setting: Each child with a space at a mat or in a large grassy area; children positioned so that they do not roll into one another

Cues

Round Body	(Round your back and tuck your chin and knees for a good roll.)
Hands Behind Head	(Clasp your hands behind the base of your head.)

Tasks/Challenges:

Ⓣ Now we're going to practice rolling backward. It will be almost like when we did the rocking action with our hands behind our head, except this time we will try to roll over. Watch me as I show you what it looks like. *(Demonstrate.)* Squat with your back to the mat, clasp your hands behind the base of your head with your elbows sticking out to the sides, sit down quickly, tuck your knees and chin to your chest, and roll completely backward. Your weight should be on your elbows. Let's practice one together while I say the steps out loud: Squat, clasp, sit, tuck, roll.

Ⓣ Practice the backward roll this way on your own. Remember, one roll at a time. **Stay round.**

⚠ If children cannot roll over backward, allow them to practice rocking back and forth with the elbows out. In no case should anyone apply force to a child's hips to attempt to help the child get over.

Rolling Backward

⚠ Children should not attempt to roll backward with the traditional backward roll until they can support their bodies with their arms. Until then, have them practice with their hands clasped at the base of their heads or have them do a shoulder roll.

⚠ Force should **never** be applied to the hips to help a child get over.

Setting: Each child with a space at a mat or in a large grassy area; children positioned so they do not roll into one another

Cues

Mickey Mouse Ears	(Hands back by shoulders, fingers pointing toward shoulders, thumbs near ears.)
Tight Ball	(Keep a tight, round shape all the way through the roll.)
Push	(Push with your arms all the way through the roll.)

Tasks/Challenges:

Ⓣ Now you are going to do a backward roll that goes over your head and uses your arms to push. This combines the two backward rolls you have done before. Watch me as I show you what this one looks like. *(Demonstrate.)* Start from a squatting position, place your hands on the floor in front of you, push and rock backward, tuck your knees and chin tight to your chest, bring your hands to your shoulders and make Mickey Mouse ears, push with both arms, and roll over your head. Let's do it together. Squat, hands in front, push, rock back, tuck, hands to shoulders, push, and roll. Practice rolling backward (Figure 21.10).

Ⓣ Practice on your own. **Remember to say the hints as you roll.**

When trying to roll backward, children often get stuck and roll no farther, usually because they:

- Make a flat rather than a round shape (knees move away from the chin), so they find it virtually impossible to roll
- Fail to place their hands in the proper position and thus are unable to push with the force needed to complete the roll

Figure 21.10 Hand positions for rolling backward.

Figure 21.11 Peer Observation for Rolling Backward

My Name is: _____	I Watched: _____	
Did your partner say the cues?	Yes 👍	Needs Help 👎
Did your partner use Mickey Mouse ears?	Yes 👍	Needs Help 👎
Did your partner keep a tight ball?	Yes 👍	Needs Help 👎
Did your partner push with his or her arms?	Yes 👍	Needs Help 👎

Practicing to overcome these two critical errors will enable children to roll backward.

C Do two backward rolls that stay tight and round. When you can do them, yell, "Yes!" Remember, stop in between the rolls to get set again.

T A little more practice with the backward roll: This time, try to roll so you can land on your feet instead of your knees at the end of the roll.

This is a good time to use teaching by invitation or intratask variation (Chapter 8) to let children practice the rolls they need to work on.

T This time, you are going to practice your backward rolls with a partner. Your partner will be your coach. He or she will watch and tell you if you have followed all the hints for the backward roll: tight ball, Mickey Mouse ears, push, and land on feet. After three tries, switch places.

Peer Observation. This task works well as a peer observation opportunity, even with young children, provided the cues are simple and clear. It also gives children an opportunity to take responsibility for helping someone else learn. See Figure 21.11 for a possible peer observation sheet.

Rolling in Different Directions

Setting: Multiple large mats scattered around the area with ample space between them; each child with a space at a mat

Cues	
Round Body	(Round your back and tuck your chin and knees for a good roll.)
Three Directions	(Make sure you roll backward, sideways, and forward.)

Tasks/Challenges:

T You have practiced rolls that went sideways, forward, and backward. Now you are going to put all three together. Practice rolls from all three directions—one roll at a time. Remember as you work that only one of you rolls on the mat at a time; however, as soon as the person ahead of you finishes, you can roll. I shouldn't see anyone standing in line, just rolling from all places around the mat.

T This time I am going to add one more thing to what I would like to see. Each time you roll, try to end up on your feet, not your knees or your seat.

T Decide which roll is the hardest for you to do. Practice that roll until you feel it is as good as your others.

Rolling from Different Directions and Positions

Setting: Each child with a space on a mat or grassy area to roll

Cues	
Round Body	(Round your back and tuck your chin and knees for a good roll.)
Strong Muscles	(Use strong arms and shoulders to transfer weight slowly to the roll.)

Tasks/Challenges:

T We are going to combine two things you have done: rolling in different directions and rolling from different positions. There are many combinations. Why not start by rolling forward from a standing position? You can use any version of forward, backward, and sideways rolls you want.

T Next roll backward from a sitting position.

T Now roll sideways from a squatting position.

T On your own, practice as many ways to roll as you can think of. You should always be able to tell me the direction of your roll and the position you are starting from.

C Now that you've practiced on your own, find three different direction/position combinations you like, and practice them until they are very smooth and flowing. Be able to tell me what position and direction you are using.

✓ *Exit Slip.* This would be an appropriate time to use an exit slip (see Chapter 12) that asks the children to record the three combinations of rolls used and react to the difficulty they had in making the sequence flow together.

Multiple Rolls

⚠ Having children do multiple (more than two) rolls in a row is not helpful—and can be dangerous. When more than two rolls are asked for in a sequence, some other movement or a balance should come between them.

Linking Rolls

Setting: A large mat or a soft grassy space for each child to roll, or multiple large mats scattered around the area with ample space in between them

Cues	
Round Body	(Round your back and tuck your chin and knees for a good roll.)
Strong Muscles	(Use strong arms and shoulders to control your body from one roll to the next.)
Smooth Transfer	(Pause between rolls.)

Tasks/Challenges:

T Now you get a chance to do what you have wanted to do for a long time: more than one roll at a time. First, practice by doing two forward rolls in a row. When you can do two smoothly, balance, and try two more. To make the links look good, the transfer between rolls should be smooth. To make it smooth, pause for a second and then go into your next roll. Use only a pause, not a stop.

T When you feel comfortable doing forward rolls, try two backward rolls.

T Try sideways rolls: one, then a pause, then two.

T This time we are going to put together a sequence of three different rolls. For starters, try forward, backward, forward. There should be one pause or balance in your sequence.

C Now make up your own sequence. It should have three or four rolls, pauses, and two directions. When you can do your sequence really well, ask a friend to watch. See if your partner can name the sequence of rolls. Then watch your partner's sequence and name the rolls.

Rolling Using Different Directions and Speeds

Setting: Each child with a space on a mat or grassy area to roll; two bags—one containing index cards with a speed category on each card and the other containing index cards with a direction on each card; the number of cards in each bag should equal or exceed the number of children in the class; paper and pencil for each child

Cues	
Round Body	(Round your back and tuck your chin and knees for a good roll.)
Arms	(Your arms are your brakes and accelerator.)

Tasks/Challenges:

T Here's another combination—directions and speeds. This means, for example, that sometimes you will roll backward at a fast speed and sometimes at a slow speed. Practice on your own using all three speeds—fast, medium, and slow—combined with all three directions—forward, backward, sideways. That makes nine different ways you can roll; practice all of them.

T Now you are going to draw your speeds and directions out of a bag. On the signal, one at a time come and draw one card from each bag. One card will have a direction on it, and the other card will have a speed on it. The two cards together will give you the direction and speed you are to practice.

T Now for the hardest rolling task yet. Imagine you are in the Olympics and you are going to do a rolling sequence that combines directions and speeds. Let's start with this sequence: forward, fast; pause, backward, slow; forward, fast. The sequence is written on the board in case you forget.

C Now make up your own combination. Practice it until it flows together well. When you finish, write it down. You can use the example on the board as a guide to tell you how to write it. Practice your combination three more times.

✓ *Portfolio.* The previous task can be used as an assessment task by having children record the sequence as an entry in their portfolios. This is also an opportune time to use a live or videotaped teacher/peer observation checklist to assess the critical elements of rolling.

Rolling After Jumping Off Equipment and Landing

Setting: A low box, milk crate, or low step aerobics platform placed against every mat the children are using for rolling

You can sometimes get milk crates from the local dairy. Low boxes can be made by filling soft-drink cases (24-can

size) with flat newspapers and taping the outside of the boxes shut securely. Place crates, boxes, or platforms against the mat so they won't slide. If you are still worried about crates sliding, children can work in partners with one partner holding the crate and the other one jumping.*

Cues	
Jump, Land, Roll	(Jump; land on your feet; then roll.)
Strong Muscles	(Use strong muscles to lower slowly to the roll.)
Round Body	(Round your back and tuck your chin and knees for a good roll.)

The cues for the following tasks focus largely on rolling, not on jumping and landing. This assumes children have already mastered jumping and landing. If they crash when they land or do not use soft landings, you will want to revisit jumping and landing (Chapter 19) before progressing.

⚠ The first observation you need to make after children begin this task is whether they are landing on their feet before they roll. Quite often, children begin dive-rolling here. If they do, stop the task immediately, and refocus or provide another demonstration that shows the correct way.

Tasks/Challenges:

T You're now going to jump off a box (crate), land with your knees bending as your feet contact the floor, and then roll. There's a box (crate) at the end of your mat. One at a time, jump off the box (crate), land on your feet, and then roll. Go slowly at first until you get the hang of it. Always be sure to land on your feet. The next person can go as soon as the person in front gets off the mat. Don't rush, but go quickly.

⚠ Make sure children jump up, not out. When they jump out, they push against the box or crate, sending it sliding across the floor, which causes them to fall.

T It's getting harder. This time, change the direction of your jump. Sometimes jump backward, sometimes sideways, and sometimes forward; then roll in any direction you want. If you aren't sure about

---

*Prior to constructing equipment, we recommend you check with school administration to be certain that district policy permits homemade equipment.

jumping backward, just try stepping off until you get used to it.

T We're going to change the activity again. This time, you'll still jump off in different directions, but you'll roll in the same direction as the jump. So if you jump sideways, you roll sideways; if you jump backward, you roll backward.

✳ What does it mean to land before you roll?

Rolling After Jumping for Height and Landing

Setting: A low box or milk crate placed against every mat the children are using for rolling

Cues	
Jump, Land, Roll	(Jump, land on feet with knees bending on contact with the floor, then roll.)
Strong Muscles	(Use strong muscles to lower slowly to the roll.)
Round Body	(Round your back and tuck your chin and knees for a good roll.)

Tasks/Challenges:

T This time, instead of changing directions, you're going to practice jumping higher off the boxes (crates), still landing, and rolling. Do you remem-

ber when we worked on jumping? What do you do to make your jump go higher? **Right—you bend your knees and throw your arms up as if you were reaching for the sky.** To warm up, just practice jumping high off the box (crate) and landing on your feet. If you fall on the landing, you know you're jumping too high.

T Now add a roll after your jump and landing. Everything should be in control. If you're falling on your landing or crashing into your roll, you'll know you're jumping too high. Try it: High jump, land, and roll.

T So far, most of what I've been seeing are jumps, lands, and rolls in forward directions. Go back and add different directions to your high jumps.

Jumping backward from the equipment is difficult for some children as well as scary. Have the youngsters first step backward if they're hesitant or fearful.

⚠ Permit children to jump backward only to a height they can control when they land. They should be able to land on their feet, on balance, absorbing their weight.

Rolling After Jumping from Different Heights

Setting: Boxes and benches of varying heights at stations around the room (Figure 21.12); arrows pointing from station to station on the floor; children in groups of four; mats at each station

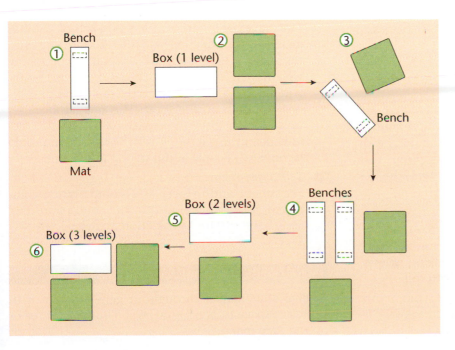

Figure 21.12 Stations to facilitate jumping from different heights, landing, and rolling.

Cues

Jump, Land, Roll	(Jump, land on your feet with knees bending on contact with the floor, and then roll.)
Strong Muscles	(Use strong muscles to lower slowly to the roll.)
Round Body	(Round your back and tuck your chin and knees for a good roll.)

Tasks/Challenges:

T We're working at stations for this task, which will give you practice jumping from objects of different heights. This is how the activity works. There will be four of you at each station. On the signal, you'll begin to practice jumping, landing, and rolling from the equipment at your station. On the next signal, stop, rotate to the station the arrow on the floor points to, and then start all over again. Remember, you're practicing jumping, landing, and rolling from the equipment that's at your station.

Rolling After Jumping over Equipment and Landing

Setting: A hurdle set up at the end of each mat; see Chapter 15 (Figure 15.3) for hurdle construction details

Cues

Jump, Land, Roll	(Jump, land on your feet with knees bending on contact with the floor, and then roll.)
Strong Muscles	(Use strong muscles to lower slowly to the roll.)
Round Body	(Round your back and tuck your chin and knees for a good roll.)

⚠ The hurdle should be only as high as children are able to jump over without difficulty and land in control (see Chapter 19). The hurdle should be an obstacle to cross, not a challenge to jump. Our hurdles are no higher than about 8 to 12 inches and may be as low as 3 to 4 inches.

Tasks/Challenges:

T Your task now is to jump over the hurdle, land, and roll. Remember, just as in jumping off objects, you must land on your feet before you roll.

T This time, change the direction of your jump. Sometimes try to jump sideways and backward as well as forward.

T Now change the direction of your roll after the jump to match the direction of the jump. So if you jump backward, roll backward. **Controlled jumps and round rolls are our goal.**

T You can also change the speed of the jump and of the roll. This time, practice mixing up the speeds of the jump and roll. In other words, you might mix a slow-motion jump with a fast roll or combine a fast jump and a fast roll. Make whatever speeds you use very clear.

☀ What does it mean to have controlled jumps? What do they look like?

Rolling, Levels, Directions, and Jumping

Setting: A jumping and rolling space for each child and several spaces that include boxes; a task sheet (Figure 21.13) for each child

Cues

Jump, Land, Roll	(Jump, land on your feet with knees bending on contact with the floor, and then roll.)
Strong Muscles	(Use strong muscles to lower slowly to the roll.)
Round Body	(Round your back and tuck your chin and knees for a good roll.)

Tasks/Challenges:

C Today I'll give you the chance to test yourself and see how well you can do the rolls you've been practicing. I'll also give you time to practice the rolls that have been hardest for you. Each of you has a task sheet. Your challenge is to do all the tasks on the sheet. When you think you can do something well, have a friend watch you; if the friend thinks you did the challenge correctly, the friend puts his or her initials on the sheet. The area has been set up so there's space to practice each challenge. Remember, at the stations with boxes, there should be only two people at the station at one time.

☑ *Self-assessment.* This task can serve as a self-assessment and/or peer assessment. When completed, it can be included in the child's portfolio. See Chapter 10 for information on developing task sheets.

Rolling While Traveling, Jumping, and Landing

Setting: Mats spread throughout general space with sufficient space between for travel. Groups of three or four at each mat.

Figure 21.13 Task sheet for
Rolling

Name _____   Teacher _____

Rolling Task Sheet

Friend's Check-off	Challenge
	I can roll forward, coming up to my feet.
	I can roll sideways, coming up to my feet.
	I can roll backward, coming up to my feet.
	I can jump, land, and roll forward.
	I can jump, land, and roll sideways.
	I can jump, land, and roll backward.
	I can jump over an obstacle, land, and roll, coming back to my feet.
	I can jump, land, change directions, and roll.
	I can jump, twist in the air, land, and roll without falling down.
	I can jump off a box, land, and roll without falling down.
	I can jump off a box in different directions, land, and roll.
	I can jump off a low box, make different body shapes in the air, land, and roll.
	I can jump off a box, twist in the air, land, and roll without falling down.
	I can . . . (make up your own sequence)

Cues

Jump, Land, Roll	(Jump, land on your feet with your knees bending on contact with the floor, and then roll.)
Strong Muscles	(Use strong muscles to lower slowly to the roll.)
Round Body	(Round your back and tuck your chin and knees for a good roll.)

Tasks/Challenges:

T Now you're going to use only the mats, but you're going to jump, land, and roll at your mats all on your own. Practice jumping, landing, and rolling in different directions at your mat. Remember, you can start or end at any place around the mat, so there should be no lines.

T This time, begin to travel around the outside of the mat. When the mat is empty, take a little jump, land, and roll. You'll almost be jumping from a moving position, but not quite. You'll travel, jump, pause, and roll, so you really come to a short stop before you roll. If you crash, you're going too fast. There should only be one person on the mat at a time.

T Here's a new challenge. Instead of just jumping this time, try jumping over the corners of the mat; then, land and roll. Remember, practice all the different jumps you learned: one foot to the other, one to the same, two to one, one to two, and two to two.

T Now I'll challenge you even further. As you jump the corners of the mat, add a twist or turn in the air before you land. You still have to land on your feet before you roll.

Utilization Level (GLSP): Learning Experiences Leading to Skill Development in Rolling

At the utilization level, children no longer focus on rolling as an isolated skill but concentrate on using rolling for other purposes. Children develop the ability to combine rolling with manipulative skills, such as catching and throwing and as an expressive form. Much of their rolling at this level is directed toward its use as a form of weight transfer between balances. In addition, rolling is used to transfer weight onto, from, and over large apparatus.

At this level rolling is most often used not as an isolated skill but as an act of weight transference, so many tasks at the utilization level of rolling are included in the earlier weight transference section of this chapter. When that occurs, reference is provided.

A note about cues: Although several cues are listed for many of the learning experiences, it's important to focus on only one cue at a time. This way, the children can really concentrate on that cue. Once you provide feedback to the children and observe that most have learned a cue, it's time to focus on another one.

Rolling and Traveling Quickly

Setting: Mats spread out throughout the space; three or four children at a mat

Cues	
Jump, Land, Roll	(Jump, land on your feet with your knees bending on contact with the floor, and then roll.)
Strong Muscles	(Use strong muscles to lower slowly to the roll.)
Round Body	(Round your back and tuck your chin and knees for a good roll.)

Two tips:

1. If students are not able to safely decide who is to roll when, specify the order in which they'll roll before they begin.

2. This is an exhausting task; if children are really doing it well, they usually can't continue it for a long time.

Tasks/Challenges:

T This is a game called Busy Mat. It'll really give you a workout, so get ready. The object of the game is to have someone always rolling on the mat while the others are traveling around the outside of the mat. As soon as one person finishes rolling, another person should start. The timing should be split-second. Everyone should always be moving, either on the outside by jumping and landing, or on the mat by rolling. Let's do a practice round.

Rolling, Jumping, and Traveling in Relationship to Others

Setting: Mats spread out throughout the space; three or four children at a mat

Cues	
Off Balance	(Be slightly off balance toward the mat as you land.)
Strong Muscles	(Use strong arms and shoulders to smoothly lower to the roll.)
Round Body	(Round your back and tuck your chin and knees for a good roll.)

Tasks/Challenges:

T Now you're going to practice making your jumps, landings, and rolls more professional. We could call them touch-and-go rolls. So far you've been coming to a clear stop after landing and before rolling. Now you're going to roll with no hesitation. Your feet should barely touch the floor before you're into the roll. Your roll just flows, but your feet still have to hit the floor before you roll. **To do this, you'll really have to bend your knees on landing, let your arms absorb your weight, and make sure your shoulders are round.**

T Practice making your jumps so you land **a little off balance right before you move into the roll.** You are trying to make it as smooth as possible, as if to save yourself from crashing. No stopping—touch and go.

T Make sure you sometimes change the direction of your land and roll, making it backward or sideways as well as forward, and still keeping your touch-and-go actions.

Aerial Rolls

Because of safety considerations, the student–teacher ratio, the varied student skill level, and the high skill level required to teach and spot aerial rolls, we feel that they are best left to the private setting. To explain this to the students who are capable of such tasks, we simply say that we don't have the facilities to practice the rolls and don't want to encourage the children who aren't ready to try them. The more skilled students can instead use physical education class for refining their skills or helping others. We do not advocate teaching aerial or dive rolls in physical education classes.

Rolling over Low Hurdles

Setting: A low hurdle at each mat

🔺 The height of the hurdle should be low enough so children can put their hands on the ground on the other side with no effort. Hurdles may be as low as 3 to 4 inches and no higher than 10 to 12 inches. Hands must be on the floor before the feet leave the floor.

Cues

Strong Muscles	(Use strong arms and shoulders to slowly lower into the roll.)
Round Body	(Round your back and tuck your chin and knees for a good roll.)
Hands on Floor	(Start with your hands on the floor on the other side of the hurdle.)

Tasks/Challenges:

Ⓣ Place your hands on the mat on the other side of the hurdle and try to roll over the hurdle without touching it. **You really have to raise your bottom in the air and push off with your legs. Remember, tuck your head to keep your body round. As you do this, make sure your arms really give when your feet leave the floor. Bending your arms a little as you push off helps you let yourself down softly.**

Rolling on Low Equipment

(See Transferring Weight by Rolling [Bench, Box, or Table] on page 381.)

🔺 Rolling on equipment should be introduced only after children have mastered rolling on the floor or mats.

Setting: Low, wide benches around the room with mats under them

🔺 At this point, the equipment should be low and wide, not more than 18 inches off the floor.

Cues

Round Back	(Round your back and tuck your chin and knees for a good roll.)
Control	(Tight muscles, slow-motion action for control throughout the roll.)

Tasks/Challenges:

Ⓣ At your piece of equipment, get on it in any way you like, and practice rolling on the top of it, lengthwise; then get off in any way you like. **To do this, place your thumbs and the sides of your palms on the top of the bench, with your hands and fingers on the side of the bench.** Although this position is very different from the one you use for rolling on mats, it provides a steady base on equipment. Tuck your head and slowly roll forward on the equipment. If you fall off a lot, you may want to go to a wider piece of equipment.

Ⓣ As you practice now, try to make your rolls very smooth.

Ⓣ Now try to roll backward by transferring your weight very slowly to a rounded back. **Extend your hands above your head to hold on to the sides of the equipment, place your head to one side, and roll slowly over your shoulder.**

Ⓒ Now you're going to make up a sequence using all you've practiced. First figure out how you want to get on the equipment; you don't have to get on by rolling. When you're on the equipment, roll along the equipment, get off any way, and roll after your dismount. The sequence will go like this: Get on, roll along, get off, roll on the mat. Practice on your own until your sequence looks the same each time you do it.

Practice your sequence three more times just to make sure it's really in your memory. When you finish, write it down (Figure 21.14).

Rolling off Low Equipment

Setting: Low boxes and benches, scattered throughout the space; mats around and under each piece of equipment. Children must be able to reach the mat from the equipment.

Sofia M.

Bench

walk on — roll forwards
slide off and roll

backwards

Figure 21.14 Child's rolling sequence.

Cues

Round Body   (Keep your back round and tuck your chin and knees for a good roll.)

Strong Muscles (Use strong arms and shoulders to lower slowly into the roll.)

Tasks/Challenges:

T Assume a kneeling position at the end of your piece of equipment, place your hands on the mat, slowly lower your weight to the mat, and roll forward.

T Once you feel comfortable with one piece of equipment, try another one.

A This task should be preceded by the task of rolling over low hurdles. To do this activity safely, children must be able to absorb their body weight with their arms.

✱ What is the key to rolling off equipment safely?

Traveling and Rolling Between Pieces of Equipment

Setting: Two pieces of low, wide equipment placed about 2 to 3 feet apart at each station; mats under, around, and between all equipment

---

Cues

Round Body   (Keep your body round and tuck your chin and knees for a good roll.)

Control   (Use tight, strong muscles to roll slowly.)

Tasks/Challenges:

T This next activity is similar to others you have done. As you can see, there are two pieces of equipment at each station. Your task now is to get on the first piece of equipment, roll one way on it, travel to the second piece of equipment without touching the floor, roll a different way on the equipment, jump to get off, and roll on the mat. The sequence goes like this: Get on, roll, travel across, roll another way, jump off, roll. Practice these ideas.

C Now pick one sequence you really like, and practice it until it's smooth and fluid. There should be no breaks, and you shouldn't have to stop and think about what comes next. Make sure you land on your feet after you jump off and before you roll.

✓ *Video/Digital Analysis.* As children develop sequences using selected skills, the videotaping of their sequences provides an excellent opportunity for videotaped assessment. As children watch the video for the first time, have them write down the moves they used to develop the sequence. When they watch for the second time, have them assess their execution of those skills in relation to the critical cues.

Rolling, Balancing, and Rolling

(See also Traveling into and out of Balances by Rolling on page 362 of Chapter 20, "Balancing.")

Setting: Mats around the room large enough for children to roll and balance

---

Cues

Round Body   (Keep your body round and tuck your chin and knees for a good roll.)

Control   (Tight, strong muscles to roll slowly.)

Tasks/Challenges:

T You worked on balancing before; now you're going to combine balancing and rolling. At your mat, practice rolling forward into a symmetrical balance. Try to roll right into the balance so there's no pause between the roll and the balance.

T This time try to focus on the connection between the roll and the balance. **Instead of stopping after the roll and before the balance, see if you can roll right into the balance.**

T Most of you are balancing on very stable body parts, such as knees and hands. This time, try some body parts that aren't quite so stable and see if you can still balance.

T Now try rolls from different directions—backward and sideways—and still roll straight into the balance. Hold the balance still. **Shifting some of your weight backward, just as you balance, might make your balances a little easier.**

Rolling to Express an Idea

Setting: A soft, grassy area; children in pairs

Cue	
Round Body	(Keep your back round and tuck your chin and knees for a good roll.)

Tasks/Challenges:

C This time you're going to roll to express an idea. You're going to pretend and tell a story by rolling. The first thing you're going to tell is "being scared." Here's how it works. Your partner will come close to you and pretend to scare you, without using words. You're so scared that you fall down and roll backward trying to get away. Make sure your roll really shows that you're afraid; it should be a very stiff roll. After two turns, switch places with your partner.

C You're going to tell a desert story this time. Have any of you seen those old Westerns on television where tumbleweeds go blowing across the desert, with nothing stopping them? Well, you're going to be a tumbleweed, just blowing and rolling all over the desert. Remember, a tumbleweed is loose and bouncy as the wind just bumps it along.

T Instead of being a loose piece of tumbleweed, this time you're going to be a seed. The wind is blowing you all over; you're bouncing all around. Suddenly, the wind stops and you sprout roots and start to grow. When you start to grow, remember the ideas we talked about earlier about rising and spreading. Your sequence goes like this: The wind blows you around, the wind stops, you send out roots and grow into a big tree or flower.

Rolling While Throwing and Catching

Setting: A soft grassy area (or if done inside, a very large mat [like a wrestling mat] or a space completely covered with smaller mats); children in pairs; a variety of objects (beanbags, flying discs, balls) for each set of partners to throw and catch

Cues	
Tuck Shoulder	(Tuck your shoulder so it is round.)
Round Body	(Round your back and tuck your chin and knees for a good roll.)

Tasks/Challenges:

T With your partner, throw and catch the beanbag. Throw so your partner has to really stretch to catch the beanbag. **Remember to make your partner stretch: you have to throw at a point away from your partner.**

T Now that you're stretching to catch, as soon as you catch the beanbag, roll in the direction you had to stretch to catch the beanbag. Keep the beanbag in your hand as you roll. Remember the whole sequence: Stretch to catch, catch, and then roll.

T Now, for just a little while, practice throwing and catching the beanbag to yourself. Throw to yourself so you have to jump to catch the beanbag in an off-balance position and then roll to break the fall from being off balance. The hardest part is throwing so that you force yourself to be in an off-balance position.

T Now go back to working with your partner. Try the same task. Throw so your partner has to first catch the beanbag in an off-balance position and then roll after catching it. Catchers, make sure you're really off balance and have to roll to recover your balance or so you won't be hurt. Throwers, really force the catchers off balance when they catch.

T Once you feel comfortable with a beanbag, try using another object, such as a flying disc or football.

Successful throwing and catching with partners depends on throwers' ability to force the catchers to be off balance or to move to catch. Before exposing children to these ideas, make sure they're at the utilization level of throwing and catching.

Spotting

The question of spotting—physically assisting a child with a skill—often arises with gymnastics programs. While the skill of spotting can be taught and learned, it isn't used often in educational gymnastics programs as it often encourages or forces children to attempt a skill before they are ready. See Chapter 29 for a more complete discussion on the use of spotting.

Rolling onto Low Equipment

Setting: Benches or low boxes with mats surrounding them

Cues	
Round Body	(Round your back and tuck your chin and knees for a good roll.)
Control	(Tight muscles, slow-motion action for control throughout the roll.)

Tasks/Challenges:

T Use a roll to get onto your piece of equipment. Stand at the end of the equipment. **Place your thumb and the sides of your palms on the top of the equipment and your hands and fingers on the sides of the equipment; then slowly lower into a forward roll to get on the equipment.** Get off in any way you like.

T Now I'm going to add to your task. Roll onto the equipment, travel any way you want while on the equipment, jump to get off, land, and roll. Again, make sure you're actually using a roll to get onto the equipment.

Rolling and Balancing on Equipment

Setting: Benches and beams spread throughout the room, with mats surrounding all the equipment

Cues	
Round Body	(Round your back and tuck your chin and knees for a good roll.)
Control	(Tight muscles, slow-motion action for control throughout the roll.)
Stillness	(Keep balances motionless.)

Tasks/Challenges:

T At your equipment, practice mounting the equipment, balancing on it, rolling out of the balance, and dismounting. Make sure your rolls out of the balances are going in the direction that seems natural for the balance, not necessarily the easiest way for you.

T Now, keep the same balances, but for each balance find at least one more roll, going in a different direction than the first roll. Thus, you should have two rolls out of each balance, each roll going in a different direction.

C See if you can develop five balances and rolls you can do so they are smooth and round.

✓ *Student Display.* A fun assessment project at the utilization level is for students to develop a poster or bulletin board that displays how rolling is used in sports other than gymnastics. *See Chapter 12 for the development of scoring rubrics to accompany such a project.*

Rolling to Meet and Part

Setting: Groups of five; a large grassy area or wrestling mats

Cues	
Smoothness	(Make your rolls flow smoothly into and out of each other.)
Planned Pauses	(Be sure any stops in your routine are on purpose.)

Tasks/Challenges:

T You're going to work with the idea of meeting and parting. There will be five people in each group. Start by spreading apart from one another and coming together by traveling on your feet. When you get together, make any group shape you want and hold it still for a few seconds. Next, each of you leaves your group by rolling away and freezing in a shape by yourself. You need to plan your rolls so all of you come together at the same time to form the group shape, and you know exactly when to roll away.

C Practice your routine until you can repeat it three times in a row, always doing it the same way. When you've done that, we will show the routines to the rest of the class.

✓ *Video/Digital Analysis.* Videotaping routines provides an excellent assessment option for seeing if children can both use the rolling cues and incorporate them with smoothness to express an idea. Either teachers or peers could use a checklist to assess the tape.

Rolling and Striking

Setting: A large grassy area; a plastic ball or training volleyball or the like for each person; children by themselves initially and then in pairs

Cues	
Tuck Shoulder	(Tuck your shoulder so it is rounded.)
Round Body	(Round your back and tuck your chin and knees for a good roll.)

Tasks/Challenges:

T In a space by yourself, strike a plastic ball with any body part so you fall off balance when you strike and have to roll in the direction that you're falling. Make sure you really strike the ball before you roll, and roll in the direction you're falling, not some other direction.

T Try to strike the ball so you have to roll in directions other than forward, such as backward or sideways.

T Now work with a partner. The partner throws the ball to you; you try to strike the ball back to your partner, roll, and be ready for the next throw. The thrower should always throw the ball so the striker really has to reach for it. After five strikes, change places.

Catching, Throwing, and Rolling

Setting: A large grassy area; partners; one ball or beanbag per pair

Cues

Tuck Shoulder (Tuck your shoulder so it is rounded.)
Round Body (Round your back and tuck your chin and knees for a good roll.)

Tasks/Challenges:

T This is a really tough task. Your partner will throw you a ball so you have to stretch and roll to catch it. Your job is to try to throw the ball back to your partner as you begin the roll. **The secret is to keep your eyes open and try to catch with your throwing hand.** Remember, you must throw as you begin the roll, not after you've rolled. After five times, switch places.

Proficiency Level: Learning Experiences Leading to Skill Development in Rolling

At the proficiency level, children enjoy aerial rolls that defy gravity and intricate combinations of rolls with other movements. Because of time limitations, equipment requirements, safety aspects, and the normal student–teacher ratio, we do not teach skills at this level. However, if you have students who have progressed to this level and enjoy the sensation these types of movements produce, encourage them to pursue out-of-school gymnastics clubs. These organizations allow children to increase their skill level beyond what we can do in a class setting.

Reading Comprehension Questions

1. List several examples of weight transfer.
2. What is the most common example of weight transfer?
3. Children at the precontrol, control, utilization, and proficiency levels are ready for what types of weight-transfer experiences?
4. Which relationship concepts are typically used as a subfocus in the study of weight transfer?
5. What does the question "Do the feet come down with control?" mean?
6. What are weight-transfer tasks at the utilization level designed to do?
7. What is the difference between a spring takeoff and a step takeoff? What is the purpose of each in gymnastics?
8. Define rolling and rocking.
9. How is rolling used in dance and in games?
10. In what way is rolling a safety skill?
11. What are the characteristics of rolling for each of the four skill levels? For example, what does a control-level roll look like?
12. What is our position on spotting? Why?
13. What problems does a child usually encounter when rolling backward?
14. What are the safety issues of backward rolls? When should children be allowed to practice backward rolls?
15. Identify three key safety points you would observe when teaching rolling.
16. Why don't we advocate teaching aerial rolls in physical education class?

References

[NASPE] National Association for Sport and Physical Education. 1995. *Moving into the future: National standards for physical education.* St. Louis, MO: Mosby.

[NASPE] National Association for Sport and Physical Education. 2004. *Moving into the future: National standards for physical education.* 2nd ed. Reston, VA: National Association for Sport and Physical Education.

Kicking and Punting

A young boy kicking a stone along the sidewalk as he walks home from school, a neighborhood game of kick the can, kickball on the school playground at recess, an aspiring athlete practicing the soccer dribble, and the professional punter—all are executing a similar movement: the kick. This movement requires accuracy, body control, point of contact, force, and direction. Some children seem to perform the kick with intense concentration; others, effortlessly.

We try to give children a variety of opportunities to practice kicking so they'll develop a foundation of kicking skills they can use in different situations. For young children the challenge is simply making contact with the ball; at the advanced level the challenge is participation in dynamic group activities combining the skill of kicking with other skills and movement concepts. See Box 22-1 for linkages of the skill theme of kicking and punting to the *National Standards for Physical Education.*

Kicking

Children come to us with a range of kicking abilities. Some have been involved in youth sports at a very early age; some come from families where outdoor play activities have provided rich experiences in

Skill Theme Development Progression
Kicking

Proficiency Level

Playing Cone Soccer
Playing Alley Soccer
Playing Soccer Keep-Away
Playing Mini Soccer
Kicking at a moving target
Kicking at small stationary targets

Utilization Level

Playing two-on-one soccer
Passing to a partner in general space
Kicking to a traveling partner
Kicking to a partner from various angles
Tap/dribble and kick: playing soccer golf
Playing one-on-one soccer
Traveling and kicking for a goal
Performing a continuous tap/dribble and change
   of direction
Changing directions: tap/dribble

Control Level

Tap/dribble: control of ball and body
Dribbling around stationary obstacles
Tap/dribble: Traveling in pathways
Tap/dribble: Starting and stopping
Tapping the ball along the ground (Soccer Dribble)
Kicking to a partner
Kicking a rolling ball from a stationary position
Kicking to targets
Kicking to a distance zone
Kicking for distance
Kicking in the air
Kicking on the ground

Precontrol Level

Tapping the ball
Approaching a stationary ball and kicking
Kicking at large targets
Kicking a stationary ball from a stationary position

Box 22-1

Kicking and Punting in the *National Standards for Physical Education*

The skill theme of kicking and punting is referenced in the National Association for Sport and Physical Education's *National Standards for Physical Education* (NASPE 2004) under Standard 1: "Demonstrates competency in motor skills and movement patterns needed to perform a variety of physical activities." The standard speaks of younger children demonstrating progress toward achieving mature form in the more complex manipulative skills, such as the foot dribble, and achieving mature form in the less complex manipulative skills. Older children then use the skills in dynamic and complex environments, and in combinations.

A sample performance outcome from the *National Standards:*

- Taps the ball from foot to foot, shifting weight and balancing the body on the nondribbling foot, while in one location, i.e., not moving (K–2)*

*Grade-level guidelines for expected student learning.

manipulative skills. The critical elements of kicking (Box 22-2) will assist you in the selection of appropriate tasks as you observe the kicking action of children.

Whether involved in a kickball game at recess, a pick-up game of soccer in the neighborhood, or being selected as the punter for the high school football team, the skills of kicking and punting are important for

Box 22-2

Key Observation Points: Kicking a Stationary Ball in the Air

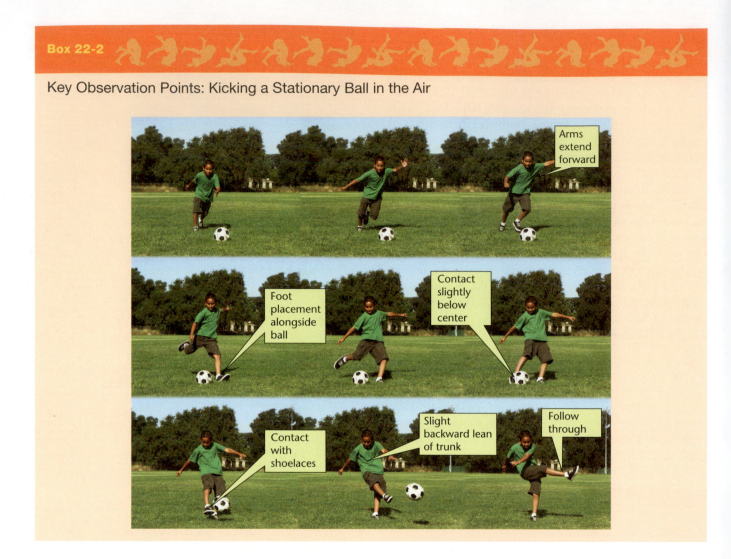

successful physical activity within and beyond the school day. The skills of the tap/dribble and all its combinations are in the sport of soccer from beginning to advanced levels. The punt increases in accuracy, distance, and placement as the youngster advances from mastery of the skill to punting in football and soccer. The entire spectrum of kicking experiences, from precontrol through proficiency, is represented in our progression spiral on page 407. The tasks are stated in terms that imply a direct approach (see Chapter 10), but teachers are encouraged to vary the approach according to the purpose of the lesson and the characteristics of the class.

Precontrol Level (GLSP): Activities for Exploration of Kicking

At the precontrol level children are challenged to make contact with a stationary ball and with the gentle tap/tap of kicking a ball from foot to foot.

Kicking a Stationary Ball from a Stationary Position

Setting: A variety of plastic, foam, and rubber balls for kicking, placed around the gymnasium approximately 10 feet from the wall

Tasks/Challenges:

T Stand behind a kicking ball. Kick the ball really hard so it travels to the wall.

C Practice until you can kick the ball three times in a row to the wall.

T Practice kicking with one foot and then with the other foot.

T Practice kicking the ball, making it go sometimes along the ground, sometimes in the air.

🌟 What determines whether the ball travels along the ground or in the air?

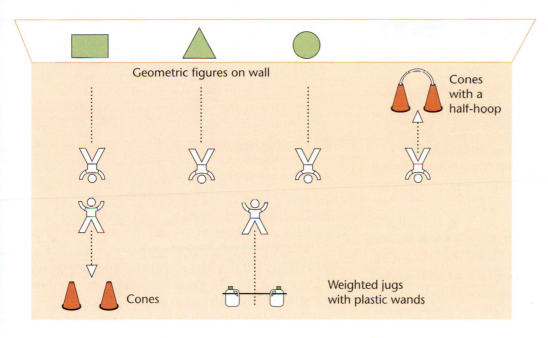

Figure 22.1 Target arrangement for kicking at large targets.

T Move outdoors and practice your kicking in an open space for maximum distance.

Kicking at Large Targets

Setting: Large targets on the wall at low level; freestanding targets placed 4 to 5 feet from the wall (Figure 22.1); a variety of plastic, foam, and rubber balls for kicking

Tasks/Challenges:

T Stand behind your kicking ball. Kick the ball toward the target, trying to hit it.

T Try kicking at the different types of targets. Which is your favorite? Which is your best for accuracy?

T Choose your favorite target; stand 8 feet away from the target and kick. When you can hit the target two times in a row, take a giant step backward and try from that distance.

Approaching a Stationary Ball and Kicking

Setting: Balls for kicking, placed around the gymnasium approximately 10 feet from the wall (Figure 22.2)

Tasks/Challenges:

T Stand 3 to 4 feet behind the kicking ball. Approach the ball and kick it forward to the wall.

T Alternate kicking with your right foot and your left foot so you will be skilled at using either foot.

C Practice until you can successfully approach and kick to the wall three times. Success equals foot contacting the ball, and ball contacting the wall.

Figure 22.2 Arrangement for the approach and kick of a stationary ball.

Tapping the Ball

Setting: Children scattered throughout general space, with foam balls at their feet

Tasks/Challenges:

T Gently tap the ball from one foot to the other, using the inside of your foot.

T On the signal, begin tapping the ball from foot to foot; continue until you hear the signal to stop.

C I will time you for 30 seconds. Try to continue tapping between your feet for the full amount of time.

T Walk through general space, tapping the ball from foot to foot—left, right, left, right—as you go. Keep the ball between your feet throughout the travel.

T Walk through general space, tapping the ball from foot to foot, avoiding collisions with others. This means you must control for the tap and control for no collisions.

After a couple of years, the 8 1/2-inch inexpensive plastic balls become partially deflated. These half-life plastic balls are excellent for kicking, especially indoors. We mark them with a large K so children know which balls are for kicking, which ones for dribbling. Playground balls and kickballs can also be partially deflated for beginning practice and for use indoors.

Control Level (GLSP): Learning Experiences Leading to Skill Development in Kicking

At the control level, children focus on consistently contacting the ball, with a goal of a mature kicking pattern. Experiences include kicking for accuracy, kicking in different directions, and partner relationships.

A note about cues: Although several cues are listed for many of the learning experiences, it's important to focus on only one cue at a time. This way, the children can really concentrate on that cue. Once you provide feedback to the children and observe that most have learned a cue, it's time to focus on another one.

Kicking on the Ground

Setting: A variety of balls for kicking—foam, plastic, rubber—placed around the gymnasium approximately 10 feet from the wall (see Figure 22.2)

Cues	
Shoelaces	(Contact the ball with the top of your foot—not your toes.)
Behind the Ball	(Contact the ball directly behind center for travel forward at a low level.)
Beside the Ball	(Place your nonkicking foot beside the ball.)

Tasks/Challenges:

T When we were exploring kicking, you kicked balls that were positioned on the ground with you standing behind them. You also kicked balls placed on the ground with you running to the ball. Practice kicking the ball to the wall from both starting positions.

T Kick the ball hard so it hits the wall with enough force to rebound back to you.

Place a series of 2-inch tape markers on the walls of the gym approximately 3 feet above the floor.

T Kick the ball so it hits the wall below the tape line. Remember, contact the ball directly behind center so it will travel at a low level.

T Practice your kicking with both your right and your left foot. In game situations, you need to be skilled with both feet.

C Practice kicking with each foot until you can kick three times in a row with each foot, the ball contacting the wall below the tape line.

T The balls for kicking are scattered around the edge of the gymnasium. Begin traveling in general space, avoiding collisions with others or the balls on the floor. On the signal, approach the ball nearest you and kick it toward the wall. Quickly retrieve the ball you kicked and place it 10 to 12 feet from the wall. You are now ready to move again. Ready? Travel in general space. Remember to listen for the signal to kick.

✓ *Exit Slip.* This would be an excellent time for an exit slip to assess student understanding of the critical cues for kicking. The exit slip might be a drawing of a shoe with directions for the child to circle the part of the foot that should be used for contact on the ball; a verbal statement, "shoelaces" versus "toes," to a partner or the teacher; or a whisper to the teacher as each child exits the gymnasium.

Kicking in the Air

Setting: A variety of balls for kicking—foam, plastic, rubber—placed around the gymnasium approximately 10 feet from the wall (see Figure 22.2)

Cues	
Shoelaces	(Contact the ball with the top of your foot—not your toes.)
Under the Ball	(Contact the ball below center for travel upward through the air.)
Step-Hop	(Step-hop on your nonkicking leg to complete a running approach.)

The skill of kicking improves with practice.

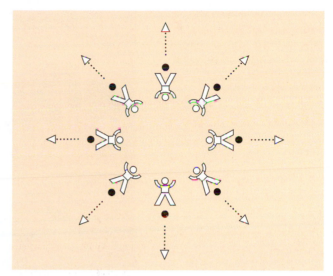

Figure 22.3 Circular pattern for distance kicking.

Cues	
Shoelaces	(Contact the ball with the top of your foot—not your toes.)
Behind the Ball	(Contact the ball directly behind center for travel at a low level, along the ground.)
Under the Ball	(Contact the ball below center for travel upward through the air.)
Step-Hop	(Step-hop on your nonkicking leg to complete the running approach.)

Tasks/Challenges:

T When we were exploring kicking, you kicked balls that were positioned on the ground with you standing behind them, and you kicked balls placed on the ground with you running to the ball. Practice kicking the ball to the wall from both starting positions.

T Assume a starting position 5 to 6 feet behind the ball. Approach the ball for the kick; immediately after you kick the ball, take a small hop on your nonkicking leg, and then step forward in the direction of the kick. This step-hop checks your forward momentum.

T Practice your kicking with the step-hop, sending the ball through the air so it contacts the wall above the tape line.

C Practice kicking through the air until you can successfully complete the aerial kick five times.

Kicking for Distance

Setting: Balls for kicking placed in a large circle on the playground (Figure 22.3); children positioned inside the circle, facing outward

Tasks/Challenges:

T Stand inside the circle, just behind a ball, facing away from the center of the circle. You are going to practice kicking along the ground and in the air. There's enough room for you to kick as hard as you wish. Practice your first series of kicks standing just behind the ball—no running approach. Kick the ball so it travels along the ground at low level. After you kick, retrieve the ball and quickly bring it back to your starting place for the next kick.

T Now kick the ball with your nonpreferred foot. Does the ball travel as far?

T Kick the ball with your preferred foot, sending it through the air. Remember, stand just behind the ball for the kick.

✿ What is the key for sending the ball along the ground? In the air? Where on the foot do you make contact for each kick?

T Place the ball on the ground, and take three or four steps back from the ball. Approach the ball

As they practice, children will discover that the force required to kick a ball for accuracy is initially different form that required to kick a ball for distance.

Figure 22.4 Numbered distance zones.

with three or four running steps, and then kick the ball along the ground (and in the air). Don't forget the step-hop on the nonkicking leg as you make contact.

C Practice kicking both along the ground and through the air. Challenge yourself to kick farther each time. Can you attain that distance both along the ground and in the air?

Numbering the balls 1, 2, 3, 4, and so forth, eliminates confusion about which ball belongs to which child.

Kicking to a Distance Zone

ing: Marker cones or plastic milk cartons placed at   t intervals across the playground, numbered

consecutively so the children can see the numbers from the kicking line (Figure 22.4)

Cues	
Shoelaces	(Contact the ball with the top of your foot—not your toes.)
Under the Ball	(Contact the ball below center for travel upward through the air.)
Step-Hop	(Step-hop on your nonkicking leg to complete a running approach.)

Tasks/Challenges:

T Place the ball you are going to use at the kicking line. Approach the ball from about 5 to 6 feet. Kick

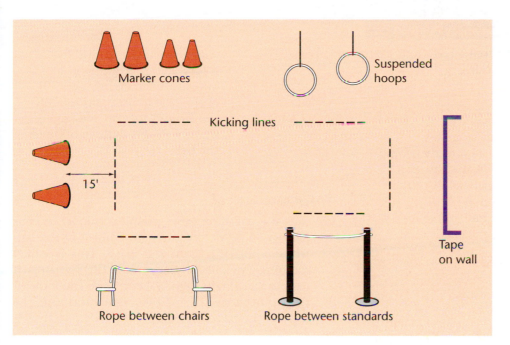

Figure 22.5 Targets for kicking.

the ball so it travels as far as possible through the air. Note the number of the zone in which the ball first contacts the ground. Kick five times, trying to improve your distance.

C Try to kick the ball so it lands in the same zone three times in a row.

Kicking to Targets

Setting: A series of targets of different heights arranged throughout the gymnasium (Figure 22.5); a variety of balls for kicking

Cues

Shoelaces	(Contact the ball with the top of your foot—not your toes.)
Under the Ball	(Contact the ball below the center for travel upward through the air.)
Behind the Ball	(Contact the ball directly behind center for travel at a low level, along the ground.)
Watch the Ball	(Focus on the ball, not the target, until the ball leaves your foot.)

Tasks/Challenges:

T Spaced around the gym are targets for kicking—suspended hoops, marker cones to kick between and to hit, ropes hung between chairs for kicking over, tape squares on the wall.

I'll assign you to a station; at that station, practice kicking at the target. Place the ball at the kicking line. Approach the kicking line with two or three steps before you make contact. After your turn, retrieve the ball and return to your group to wait your next turn. Continue practicing at your station until the signal is given to change to another kicking station. You may need to adjust your force when you're kicking to hit a target.

Here's what you'll do at the different stations. At the hoops, kick the ball through the circle. At the large and small marker cones, kick the ball hard enough to make the cone fall over. At the rope between the chairs and the rope stretched between the standards, kick the ball so it travels over the rope. At the marker goals, kick the ball along the ground between the cones. At the tape square, kick the ball so it touches the wall inside the square.

Weighted jugs, cones, or tape marks on the wall can serve as goals. Vary the width of the goal according to individual abilities.

J *Peer Observation.* Station practice provides an opportune time for peer observation of critical cues. Designate one station, for example, marker cones, and have partners observe each other kicking for travel along the ground. When partners are observing for a critical cue, such as contact behind the ball or on shoelaces, remind the observers of their focus; accuracy of the kick is not what is being assessed. *See Chapter 12, "Assessing Student Learning," for development and recording of peer observation.*

Kicking a Rolling Ball from a Stationary Position

Setting: Partners positioned 10 to 12 feet from each other, each pair with a ball for kicking

Cues

Shoelaces	(Contact the ball with the top of your foot—not your toes.)
Behind the Ball	(Contact the ball directly behind center for travel at a low level.)
Under the Ball	(Contact the ball below center for travel through the air.)
Watch the Ball	(Focus on the ball, not your partner, until the ball leaves your foot.)

Tasks/Challenges:

T Partner 1: Roll the ball along the ground to partner 2. Partner 2: Kick the ball so it travels back to partner 1. Kick only hard enough for the ball to travel to your partner.

T Practice the kick along the ground with both your right foot and your left foot.

T Practice the kick through the air to your partner. Sometimes in game situations you want to kick along the ground; sometimes you need to kick in the air.

C Practice until you can kick the ball along the ground five times to your partner so your partner does not have to move from self-space to retrieve the ball—five times with the left foot, five times with the right.

C Can you meet the challenge of kicking the ball through the air so your partner does not have to move to retrieve it? Give it a try!

Kicking to a Partner

Setting: Partners facing each other, 15 to 20 feet apart, each pair with a ball for kicking

Cues

Sender

Shoelaces	(Contact the ball with the top of your foot—not your toes.)
Behind the Ball	(Contact the ball directly behind center for travel at low level, along the ground.)
Watch the Ball	(Focus on the ball, not your partner, as you kick and as you receive.)

Receiver

Trap	(Gain control of the ball by rotating your nonsupport leg outward/knee slightly bent, raising the nonsupport foot off the ground/toes up, and giving slightly to absorb the motion of the ball.)

Tasks/Challenges:

T Kick the ball along the ground (or floor) to your partner so he or she can gain control of the ball without moving from self-space. This is called trapping the ball. To trap, rotate the nonsupport leg outward/knee slightly bent, raise the foot off the ground/toes up, and give slightly to absorb the force of the traveling ball.

T Practice sending and receiving—kicking and trapping—with your partner. Always gain control of (trap) the ball before kicking it back to your partner.

C Practice until you can kick five times to your partner so he or she can trap without moving from self-space.

T When you are comfortable with your skill and can kick accurately five times, take a large step backward and repeat the task. Practice at different distances to determine your maximum distance for accuracy with your partner.

Tapping the Ball along the Ground (Soccer Dribble)

Setting: Children scattered throughout general space, with plastic (foam, rubber) balls for kicking; listening position is one foot resting on the ball

Cues

Tap, Tap	(Gently tap the ball so it stays within 3 to 4 feet of you at all times.)
Inside of Foot	(Tap the ball with the inside of your foot—left and right.)
Open Spaces	(Look for open spaces as you travel.)

Tasks/Challenges:

T When we were exploring kicking, you practiced tapping the ball between your feet, inside to inside. Practice that skill of gently tapping back and forth.

T On the signal, begin traveling through general space, tapping the ball with the inside of your foot. When you hear the signal, quickly rotate the nonsupport leg slightly outward, raise the foot off the ground, and give to absorb the force of the moving ball—trap the ball.

T Alternate tapping on your right foot and then your left foot; turn your feet out like a duck.

C On the signal, begin traveling in general space, tapping the ball in the soccer dribble. Try to travel and tap with alternate feet and without letting the ball get away from you or colliding with another person. Ready? Tap, tap . . . open spaces.

C Now dribble in general space. See if you can keep it up for 30 seconds without colliding ball to ball or person to person.

As the children improve, you can increase the time to 45 seconds and then to 1 minute.

T Begin traveling in general space, dribbling the soccer ball as you go. Gradually increase your speed, keeping the ball within 3 to 4 feet of you at all times. Increase and decrease the speed of your travel, adjusting the force of your kick as you increase and decrease the speed.

C I will time you again for a 30-second dribble. Challenge yourself to dribble at your personal maximum speed—with soccer ball and using body control.

✓ *Teacher Observation.* Teacher observation of critical cues in a dynamic, noncompetitive setting is important at this point. *See Chapters 11 and 12 for teacher observation examples.*

Tap/Dribble: Starting and Stopping

Setting: Children scattered throughout general space, each with a ball for kicking

Cues	
Tap, Tap	(Gently tap the ball so it stays within 3 to 4 feet of you at all times.)
Inside of Foot	(Tap the ball with the inside of your foot—left and right.)
Trap	(Gain control of the ball by rotating the leg outward/knees slightly bent, raising the foot/toes up, giving to absorb the force.)

Tasks/Challenges:

T Begin dribbling in general space. When you hear the signal, quickly trap the ball. Maintain a balanced,

ready position (weight centered over support leg) so you can move again quickly. Ready? Begin.

This activity provides practice in stopping the ball quickly. Frequent signals will be needed: 10 seconds of dribbling, stop; 30 seconds of dribbling, stop. . . .

T Travel through general space, dribbling as you go. Each time you meet another person, trap the ball quickly, execute a quarter turn, and continue dribbling. The ability to stop and start quickly is an important offensive skill that helps you maintain control of the ball and avoid your opponents.

C Test your dribbling and trapping skills with this 2-minute activity: On the signal, begin dribbling in general space. Each time you hear the drum or meet another person, trap the ball, execute a quarter turn, and continue dribbling. Your goal is to stop-start for 2 minutes without losing control of the ball or bumping another person or ball. The signal at the end of the 2 minutes will be a double drumbeat. Look for the open spaces.

Tap/Dribble: Traveling in Pathways

Setting: Various pathways taped on the floor or spray-painted on the grass; children scattered throughout general space, each with a ball for kicking

Cues	
Tap, Tap	(Gently tap the ball so it stays within 3 to 4 feet of you at all times.)
Inside/Outside	(Use both the inside of your foot and the outside of your foot—left and right—to tap the soccer ball.)

Tasks/Challenges:

T On the ground are straight, curved, and zigzag pathways. Travel through the formations using the soccer dribble, traveling at a speed you can control—no collisions, no loss of the ball. Be sure to travel all the pathways.

T As you tap/dribble the different pathways, you begin to discover that the inside of the foot is perhaps not always the best surface to use for the tap/dribble. Practice the tap/dribble with the outside of your foot as well as the inside. **Keep the tap gentle—with control.**

Dribbling Around Stationary Obstacles

Setting: Marker cones and/or milk jugs positioned throughout general space; a kicking ball for each child

Cues

Tap, Tap	(Gently tap the ball so it stays within 3 to 4 feet of you at all times.)
Inside/Outside	(Use both the inside of your foot and the outside of your foot—left and right—to tap the soccer ball.)
Heads Up	(Keep your head up to avoid collisions—people, obstacles, soccer balls.)

Tasks/Challenges:

T Tap/dribble the ball throughout general space, alternating contact with your right foot and your left foot. Avoid bumping into the cones (jugs) with either the ball or your body. Travel in zigzag and curved pathways to avoid the obstacles. Your visual range must now include the ball you're dribbling, other people, the balls they're using, and the obstacles.

T Tap/dribble in general space. Each time you approach an obstacle, trap the ball, execute a quarter turn to either the right or the left, and continue dribbling.

T Vary the speed of your travel—sometimes approach a cone (jug) very quickly, sometimes slowly.

T Tap/dribble in general space. As you near a cone (jug), tap the ball gently with the inside of your right foot, passing the ball to the left of the cone (jug). Quickly continue the dribble.

T Tap/dribble in general space. As you near a cone (jug), tap the ball gently with the inside of your left foot, passing the ball to the right of the cone (jug).

T Tap/dribble in general space. As you near the cone (jug), tap the ball gently with the outside of your right foot, passing the ball to the right of the cone (jug).

T Tap/dribble in general space. As you near a cone (jug), tap the ball gently with the outside of your left foot, passing the ball to the left of the cone (jug).

C This time as you practice dribbling, trapping, and turning, pretend you have 100 points. If the ball you are dribbling contacts a cone (jug), subtract 10 points from your score. If you have a collision with another person, subtract 25 points. Try to complete your practice with 100 points!

Tap/Dribble: Control of Ball and Body

Setting: Marker cones and/or milk jugs positioned throughout general space; a kicking ball for each child

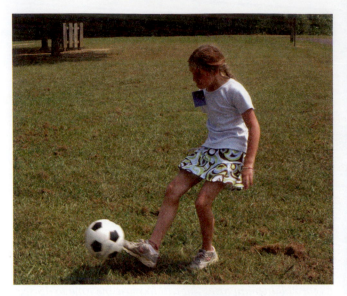

Kicking a moving ball requires visual focus and concentration.

Cues

Tap, Tap	(Gently tap the ball so it stays within 3 to 4 feet of you at all times.)
Inside/ Outside	(Use both the inside of your foot and the outside of your foot—left and right—to tap the soccer ball.)
Heads Up	(Keep your head up to avoid collisions—people, obstacles, soccer balls.)

Tasks/Challenges:

T Thus far in our tap/dribble study, you've practiced dribbling with control, trapping the ball, avoiding obstacles, changing the speed of your travel, and tapping the ball to the right or the left, as in passing. The game of Keeping It Perfect: Zero, Zero will give you a chance to test these skills.

Each of you has a perfect score of zero. The object of the game is to still have the perfect score at the end of the 2 minutes of activity. On the signal, begin to tap/dribble in general space. You may travel at any speed you choose, increasing and decreasing your speed as you wish. When you hear the drum, trap the ball quickly; I'll give a verbal "Go" for you to continue.

You earn negative points if you:

- Don't trap the ball within 2 seconds of the drumbeat (−1)
- Bump into another person or the ball they're dribbling (−1)
- Bump into a marker cone (−1)

The key is control. Ready? Go.

You can use this activity to focus on specific skills. For example, in the first 2 minutes, children are to travel in general space (control); in the second 2 minutes, they are to travel in each area of the gymnasium (speed); in the third 2 minutes, they are to zigzag around as many cones as possible (passing, accuracy).

At the end of each 2 minutes, stop, rest, and calculate your scores. Remember, a perfect score is zero.

Utilization Level (GLSP): Learning Experiences Leading to Skill Development in Kicking

At the utilization level, experiences are designed for applying kicking skills in unpredictable situations of increasing complexity. Performing skills on the move and in relation to an opponent are important challenges. A great degree of accuracy and control is the goal at this level.

A note about cues: Although several cues are listed for many of the learning experiences, it's important to focus on only one cue at a time. This way, the children can really concentrate on that cue. Once you provide feedback to the children and observe that most have learned a cue, it's time to focus on another one.

Changing Directions: Tap/Dribble

Setting: Children scattered throughout general space, each with a ball for kicking.

Cues	
Tap, Tap	(Gently tap the ball so it is always within your control—no more than 3 to 4 feet from you—even with increased speed.)
Middle of Ball	(Contact directly behind the middle of the ball, using the insides, outsides, and heels of your feet for the dribble.)

Tasks/Challenges:

T Begin traveling in general space, tapping the ball 3 to 4 feet in front of you as you go. When you are comfortable with your control of the dribble, tap the ball ahead of you, run quickly beyond the ball, tap it gently with your heel, quickly turn, and continue the dribble. Be sure you run beyond the ball to tap the front of it; contact on top of the ball will cause you to fall.

Performing a Continuous Tap/Dribble and Change of Direction

Setting: Children scattered throughout general space

Cues	
Tap/Tap	(Tap the ball with control so it stays within 3 to 4 feet of you at all times.)
Inside/Outside/ Heels of Feet	(Tap the ball with different parts of your feet as you dribble.)
Heads Up	(Keep your head up to avoid collisions—people, soccer balls.)

Tasks/Challenges:

T You learned to change the direction of the ball by tapping it to the right or left with the inside or outside of your foot. And you just learned one method of changing direction front to back. Travel within the boundaries of our work area using changes of direction to avoid contact with others and to avoid crossing the outside boundaries. Your task is continuous dribbling. Ready? Begin.

T Approach a boundary quickly; use the heel tap to change the direction of the dribble at the last moment to prevent crossing the boundary.

T Purposely approach some other students; use a pass to the right or left to avoid contact with them.

C Challenge yourself by increasing your speed to the maximum rate you can travel with a controlled dribble and frequent changes of direction.

✓ *Videotape.* As children begin combining skills, videotaping their practice provides an excellent opportunity for self-assessment. Have them watch the video and code the number of skills they included in their practice, for example, inside of foot, outside of foot, trapping with heel. As they watch the video clip the second time, have them assess their execution of those skills relative to the critical cues.

Traveling and Kicking for a Goal

Setting: Hoops or milk jugs scattered throughout general space; marker cones for goals (Figure 22.6)

Cues	
Behind the Ball	(Contact the ball directly behind center for travel along the ground.)
Gentle Taps/ Hard Kicks	(Gently tap the ball for the dribble; kick hard for the goal.)

Figure 22.6 Setup for combination dribble and kick with varying degrees of force.

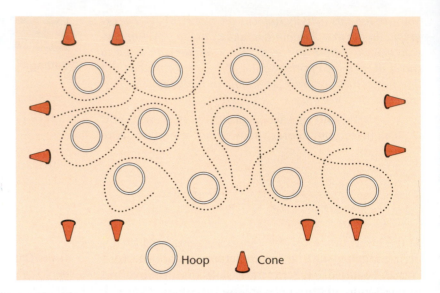

Hoop   Cone

Dribbling in open space allows children to focus on kicking and their relationship to others.

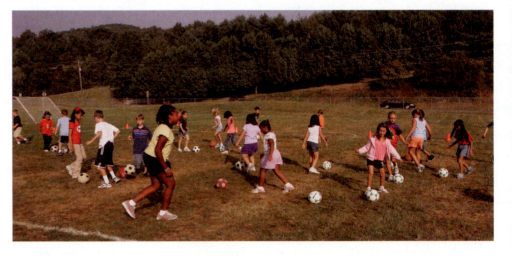

Tasks/Challenges:

ⓣ Travel at your own speed and tap the ball while avoiding obstacles and other people. On the signal, travel quickly to an open space, and kick for the goal. Retrieve the ball; begin dribbling again, listening for the signal to kick for the goal.

ⓣ Practice dribbling around obstacles and kicking for the goal on your own; I won't give the signal for the kick.

Playing One-on-One Soccer

Setting: Sets of partners in general space; kicking balls; marker cones (milk jugs) for goals

Cues	
Gentle Taps/ Hard Kicks	(Gently tap the ball for the dribble; kick hard for the goal.)

Heads Up	(Keep your head up to avoid collisions—people, soccer balls.)
Inside/Outside/ Heels of Feet	(Tap the ball with different parts of your feet as you travel.)
Offense	(Open Spaces . . . Look for Them, Move to Them)
Defense	(Trap or Tap to Gain Possession)

Tasks/Challenges:

ⓣ Select a partner whose tap/dribble skills are very similar to your skills. Cooperatively decide the boundaries for your area; a small area provides more practice. Partner 1 begins to travel and dribble the soccer ball within that area; partner 2 attempts to gain possession of the ball by using the feet to trap the ball or tap it away. Follow these rules:

1. Contact the ball, not the person.
2. Gain possession of the ball; don't kick it away.

3. If you gain possession of the ball, begin your dribble as the offensive player; your partner will be the defense.

If partners are unmatched in skill, give a signal for the change from offense to defense. That is, each time partner 2 gains possession of the ball, that person will give it back to partner 1, who continues to tap/dribble until the signal to switch positions is given.

T Within your area, set up two marker cones (milk jugs) as a goal. Partner 1 will tap/dribble until within scoring range (10 to 12 feet of the goal) and then kick for the goal. Partner 2 will attempt to gain possession of the ball using the feet only. After each kick for the goal, switch positions.

C You may want to design a game using the skills of the soccer dribble and kicking for the goal. Work cooperatively with your partner to decide the rules of the game, scoring, boundaries. Can you think of a name for your game? (See Chapter 30.)

Tap/Dribble and Kick: Playing Soccer Golf

Setting: Obstacle course arrangement (Figure 22.7); a kicking ball for each child

Cues	
Behind the Ball	(Contact the ball directly behind center for travel along the ground.)
Under the Ball	(Contact the ball slightly below center for travel upward through the air.)
Gentle Taps/ Hard Kicks	(Gently tap the ball for the dribble; kick hard for the goal.)

Tasks/Challenges:

T The game of Soccer Golf involves the skills of dribbling in pathways, kicking for a goal, and kicking over a low height. The playground is arranged as a golf course. Your task is to complete the course with the fewest number of kicks. There are boxes to dribble around, zones to zigzag through, hoops to kick into, and poles to kick over. Count your kicks as you proceed through the course. When you finish the course, begin again, trying to lower your score.

To decrease waiting time, have the children begin at different holes on the course rather than having everyone start at the first hole.

Kicking to a Partner from Various Angles

Setting: Partners positioned 15 to 20 feet from each other, each pair with a kicking ball

Cues	
Behind the Ball	(Contact the ball directly behind center for travel along the ground.)
Foot, Not Toes	(Kick the ball with the inside or the outside of your foot, not with your toes.)
Kick Hard	(Kick the ball with enough force to send it to your partner.)

Tasks/Challenges:

T Review the skill of kicking along the ground (the floor) so your partner can trap the ball without moving. When you are comfortable with the kick, take three to four steps to the right so you are at an

Figure 22.7 Soccer Golf course arrangement.

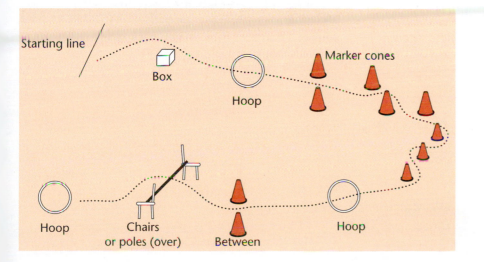

angle to your partner. Kick the ball from this position so it travels directly to your partner. Kick with the inside of your right foot and the outside of your left foot until you can kick four out of five times directly to your partner with each foot.

T Move to the left three to four steps from your original position. Kick the ball to your partner from this angle. Practice the kick with the inside of your left foot and the outside of your right foot. Then practice with the outside of your left foot and the inside of your right foot.

T Position yourself at different angles in relation to your partner, and practice kicking to your partner from these positions. The ability to kick at different angles is important in passing the ball to teammates and in kicking for a goal in games.

Kicking to a Traveling Partner

Setting: Sets of partners at one end of the playing field (gymnasium) approximately 15 feet from each other; one partner with the ball for kicking (Figure 22.8)

Cues	
Behind the Ball	(Contact the ball directly behind center for travel along the ground.)
Inside of Foot	(Kick the ball with the inside of your foot, not with your toes.)
Kick Hard	(Kick the ball with enough force to send it to your partner.)
Sender	
Ahead of Partner	(Kick beyond your partner.)
Receiver	
On the Move	(Don't stop and wait for the ball.)

Tasks/Challenges:

T Travel the length of the playing field (gymnasium) passing the ball to each other as you travel.

Figure 22.8 Kicking to a traveling partner.

Remember, pass to your partner while you are on the move; don't stop to execute the kick.

T Pass the ball *ahead* of your partner so he or she can continue traveling, rather than having to stop to receive the pass.

The second set of partners may begin their travel/pass when the partners in front of them are one-third the distance of the field (gymnasium), or you may signal when each set of partners is to begin traveling.

Passing to a Partner in General Space

Setting: Sets of partners in general space, each set with a ball for kicking

Cues	
Heads Up	(Keep your head up to avoid collisions—people, soccer balls.)
Pass at an Angle	(Use the inside/outside of your feet [right/left] to send the ball to your partner.)
Pass to the Open Space	(Kick the ball to the open space ahead of your partner.)

Tasks/Challenges:

T Travel in general space, dribbling and passing to your partner. All other players will be traveling and passing at the same time, so it is important that you be aware of others and of passing to open spaces. Ready? Begin.

T Challenge yourself always to pass the ball ahead of your partner—to the open space. If you are successful, your partner will never have to stop to receive the pass. Try for five successful completions: open space, partner on the move.

Playing Two-on-One Soccer

Setting: Groups of three in general space; marker cones for goals; balls for kicking

Cues

Pass at an Angle	(Use the inside/outside of your feet [right/left] to send the ball to your partner.)
Pass to the Open Space	(Kick the ball to the open space ahead of your partner.)
Gentle Taps/ Hard Kicks	(Gently tap the ball for the dribble; kick hard to pass and to make a goal.)

Tasks/Challenges:

T Form groups of three; two of you will be offensive players, and one of you will be a defensive player. The two offensive players will tap/dribble and pass to each other within the boundaries of your soccer area. The defensive player will attempt to gain possession of the ball by intercepting passes or tapping the ball away on the dribble.

The offensive team will have possession of the ball for 2 minutes. See how many goals you can score within that interval; remember, there is no goalie! The offensive team must execute at least two passes before attempting a kick for the goal. At the end of each 2 minutes, I will give the signal for the defensive player to rotate to offense and one offensive player to rotate to defense, thus changing the two-on-one teams.

Proficiency Level (GLSP): Learning Experiences Leading to Skill Development in Kicking

At the proficiency level, experiences are designed to give children opportunities to use the skill of kicking in group games and for learning the strategy of offensive/defensive participation. Children play self-designed games, or the teacher chooses the games. These games involve relationships made increasingly complex by the number of players and types of strategies required.

A note about cues: At the proficiency level, tasks are more complex, typically requiring children to coordinate several movements simultaneously in a dynamic context. A list of cues is provided to assist the children in being more successful in the learning experience. The challenge for the teacher is in determining which cue will be most beneficial for each child . . . and when. Thus, careful observation and critical reflection become very important as you watch the children move and then decide which cue will be the most helpful to move each learner to a higher skill level.

Angles and Open Spaces

Kicking (passing) at angles and kicking (passing) to the open space are two of the most critical skills for game play. They provide the bridge between skill mastery in a static situation and successful skill execution in a dynamic environment.

Kicking at Small Stationary Targets

Setting: Sets of marker cones 6 feet apart to serve as targets; a line for kicking 15 to 20 feet from each target (Figure 22.9)

Cues

Individual cues as needed

Tasks/Challenges:

T Each person will have 10 kicks at the goal; mentally record your personal score. After each person has kicked 10 times, move the cones closer together until they are 3 feet apart. Now kick 10 times at this target. Compare this score with your score for the 6-foot target.

T Position yourself at an angle facing the target. Repeat the tasks, kicking at an angle rather than in a direct line to the target. Compare your scores to your direct-line kicks.

C Set a personal goal for successful kicks. Practice to meet that goal for both direct and angle kicks.

√ *Teacher Observation.* At the utilization and proficiency levels, children's kicking should show mature

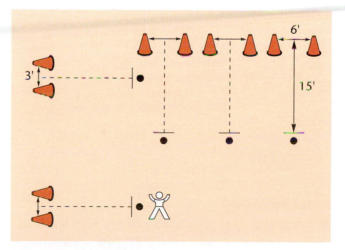

Figure 22.9 Kicking at small targets.

patterns as well as accuracy. Checklists for recording accuracy scores can also include analysis of errors and correction cues. *See Chapter 12 for the development of observation checklists.*

Kicking at a Moving Target

Setting: Hoops suspended from a rope hanging from a frame, wall bars, or outdoor playground equipment (partners may also hold hoop for each other)

> **Cue**
>
> **Ahead of the Target** (Kick the ball to the open space just beyond the moving target.)

Tasks/Challenges:

T Partner 1 starts the suspended hoop swinging or moves back and forth, holding the hoop in the hand. Partner 2, approximately 10 to 12 feet away, kicks the ball at the moving target, attempting to kick the ball through the hoop. After five trials, partners change places.

This learning experience reinforces kicking to the open space and kicking at angles, which were introduced earlier. Remind children to kick the ball to the space where the hoop will swing, not to the space where the hoop is when they execute the kick, thus the concepts of angle and open-space target!

Playing Mini Soccer

Setting: Milk jugs and marker cones as boundaries; children in groups of four, six, or eight

> **Cues**
>
> *Offensive*
> **Pass at an Angle**
> **to Teammates**
> **Pass to Open Space** (Pass ahead of the receiver.)
> **Body Between Ball**   (Keep your body between
> **and Opponent**   the ball and the defender at
>   all times; quickly switch the
>   tap/dribble to the outside
>   foot.)
>
> *Defensive*
> **Tap or Trap**

Tasks/Challenges:

T With your group, design a game of Mini Soccer using the skills we have been practicing. Cooperatively decide the rules, scoring, and the boundaries. I will place only one limitation on the game: Each member of the offensive team must dribble the ball before making a kick for the goal.

✓ *Journal.* After children are involved in a dynamic kicking/dribbling situation involving combining of skills, have them reflect on their play with a journal entry. *See Chapter 12, "Assessing Student Learning," for journal entry guidelines.*

Playing Soccer Keep-Away

Setting: Children in teams of three to six; large open space

> **Cues**
>
> *Offensive*
> **Pass at an Angle**
> **to Teammates**
> **Pass to Open Space** (Pass ahead of the receiver.)
> **Body between Ball**
> **and Opponent**
> *Defensive*
> **Close the**   (Move quickly to close the
> **Open Spaces**   open spaces.)

Tasks/Challenges:

T The object of Soccer Keep-Away is to keep the ball away from your opponents using the tap/dribble and passing skills you have been practicing. There is no kicking for the goal, only passing and dribbling in the game. To begin the game, one person throws the ball (two hands, overhead) in from the sideline. Play continues with the ball being dribbled and passed as the other team attempts to gain possession by trapping, intercepting, or gaining control of the dribble. At the end of each 3 minutes of play, I will signal for the other team to execute the throw-in to begin a new game.

Alley Soccer and Cone Soccer (below) are proficiency-level games that demand combinations of skills. Because it is rare for all the students in a class to be ready for this type of game at the same time, some children will benefit from practicing different types of kicking while others are playing the game (see Chapter 30).

Playing Alley Soccer

Setting: A playing field divided into five equal alleys (Figure 22.10); marker-cone goals 6 feet apart at each end of the field; six-member teams

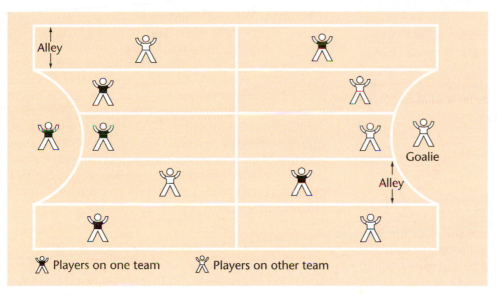

Figure 22.10 Alley Soccer.

Cues

Offensive
**Pass at an Angle
to Teammates
Pass to Open Space
Body Between Ball
and Opponent**
Defensive
Close the Open Spaces (Move quickly to close
the open spaces.)

Cues

Offensive
**Kick at an Angle to Teammates
Pass to Open Space
Gentle Taps to Dribble/Hard Kicks to the Target
Body Between Ball and Opponent**
Defensive
Close the Open Spaces

Tasks/Challenges:

T Alley Soccer is an activity that uses dribbling, passing, and kicking for a goal. Each team has six players—one player for each alley plus a goalie. Players may travel the length of their alley but can't cross into another alley. Your task is to dribble, avoid the opponent in your alley, pass to teammates, and kick for the goal. At regular intervals, I'll give the signal to rotate alleys; this rotation will allow each of you to play each position.

Playing Cone Soccer

Setting: A marker cone placed at either end of the playing area with a circle (spray paint or marking dust) 10 feet in diameter surrounding each cone (Figure 22.11); teams of two to six members

Tasks/Challenges:

T Cone Soccer emphasizes dribbling, passing, and kicking for accuracy. The object of the game is to kick the ball, knock over the other team's cone, and protect your own cone. No one is allowed inside the circle to kick or to defend. If one team makes

Figure 22.11 Cone Soccer. Dimensions of the playing area may be adjusted to the size of the available area and the number of players.

body contact, the other team gets a free kick on the spot; everyone must be 3 feet away for the free kick.

A good way to form teams for equal skill is to ask children to select a partner and then place the selected partners on opposite teams. We have found when given this choice, children select partners with very similar skill to their own, i.e., highly skilled with highly skilled, etc.

Punting

Punting is a form of kicking: A ball is released from the hands and kicked while it is in the air. This is a difficult skill for children to master. Because the punt involves a complex coordination of body movements—moving the body forward, dropping the ball accurately, and kicking it before it reaches the ground—we have found it best to introduce the punt after children have practiced other types of kicking.

When children first try to punt, they toss the ball up and then "kick" it with a knee or leg rather than the foot. Often the novice punter will contact the ball after it bounces. We give children at the precontrol level round, lightweight balls and balloons, challenging them to contact the "ball" with the foot before it touches the ground. As children advance in their ability to punt, they are challenged with accuracy and placement, as well as dynamic situations such as might occur in football or rugby. The critical elements of punting (Box 22-3) will assist you in the selection of appropriate tasks for children as you observe their punting. Ideas for varying the contexts in which punting skills can be practiced at the precontrol, control, utilization, and proficiency levels are presented in our progression spiral on page 425.

Precontrol Level (GLSP): Activities for Exploration of Punting

At the precontrol level, children explore punting different types of lightweight balls, sometimes with a bounce before contact, sometimes contacting the ball before it touches the ground. At this level we are not concerned with mastery but with children enjoying a variety of experiences as an introduction to the skill of punting.

Box 22-3

Key Observation Points: Punting

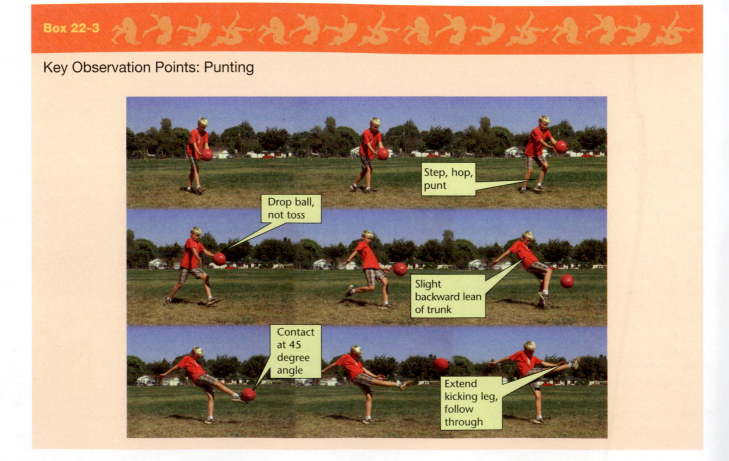

Drop ball, not toss

Step, hop, punt

Slight backward lean of trunk

Contact at 45 degree angle

Extend kicking leg, follow through

This child practices punting, a difficult skill for youngsters to master.

Tasks/Challenges:

T Stand behind the kicking line, holding the ball in both hands. Drop the ball and kick it to the wall, making contact before the ball touches the floor. This drop-kick action is called a punt.

Children who are having difficulty with the drop-kick action can benefit from practicing punting with a balloon. This helps them understand the concept of dropping—rather than tossing—the object to be punted.

Dropping, Bouncing, and Kicking Lightweight Balls

Setting: Lightweight balls (plastic, foam) positioned around the perimeter of the gym, approximately 15 feet from the wall

Tasks/Challenges:

T Drop the ball to the floor. After the first bounce, contact the ball with your shoelaces, sending it to the wall.

T Try the kick with your right foot and with your left foot to determine which is your preferred foot.

C With your preferred foot, drop and kick the ball after the bounce five times. Repeat several times to determine your personal best.

Dropping and Punting

Setting: Kicking balls (plastic, foam) positioned around the perimeter of the gym, approximately 15 feet from the wall

Control Level (GLSP): Learning Experiences Leading to Skill Development in Punting

At the control level, children need experiences to develop consistency in contacting the ball for the punt, with the goal of a mature punting pattern. After children can consistently make contact, they are provided opportunities to punt different types of balls, to increase distance on the punt, and to improve accuracy, reinforcing execution of the mature punting pattern.

A note about cues: Although several cues are listed for many of the learning experiences, it's important to focus on only one cue at a time. This way, the children can really concentrate on that cue. Once you provide feedback to the children and observe that most have learned a cue, it's time to focus on another one.

Punting for Consistency

Setting: Lightweight balls for punting placed around the perimeter of the gym, approximately 20 feet from the wall

Cues	
Shoelaces	(Contact the ball with the top of your foot—not your toes.)
Eyes on the Ball	(Watch the ball until it contacts your foot.)
Drop	(Drop the ball for the punt; don't toss it upward.)

Tasks/Challenges:

T When we worked on punting earlier, you punted just for fun. Sometimes the ball went through the air, sometimes backward over your head, and sometimes nowhere! Today we will begin to practice punting so we can consistently kick the ball forward through the air. Stand behind the ball, holding it in both your hands at waist height. Take a small step on your nonkicking leg, then extend your kicking foot for contact on the shoelaces. Drop the ball as you swing your kicking leg forward; contact the ball just before it touches the floor (ground).

T Punt the ball five times. How many times did you contact the ball before it touched the floor (ground)? Continue your practice until you make three or more contacts.

T Good, you are now consistently contacting the ball before it touches the floor (ground). Now let's focus on the ball consistently traveling forward when you punt. Continue your practice with sets of five punts; mentally record how many times in each set you are successful at punting with your shoelaces and sending the ball forward to the wall.

Punting over Low Ropes

Setting: Ropes suspended between standards or across chairs at a height of 4 to 6 feet; lightweight balls for punting

Cues	
Extend	(Extend your foot to contact the ball with your shoelaces, not your toes.)
Eyes on the Ball	(Watch the ball until it contacts your foot.)
Drop	(Drop the ball for the punt; don't toss it upward.)

Tasks/Challenges:

T Stand approximately 10 feet behind the rope. Punt the ball so it travels over the rope. Retrieve the ball and punt from the opposite side of the rope.

C Give yourself a point each time you are successful at punting the ball over the rope. How many points can you make out of 10 trials?

✓ *Teacher Observation.* Before children incorporate skills into dynamic situations, observation of critical cues is very important. A teacher observation checklist is useful here.

Punting with an Approach

Setting: Lightweight balls for punting, placed around the perimeter of the gym, approximately 20 feet from the wall. *If indoor space is not sufficient for this task, move the class outside and punt away from the circle; see Figure 22.3.*

Cues	
Nonstop Approach	(Take a few running steps; then punt without stopping your forward momentum.)
Step-Hop	(Make your last step before contact a step-hop on your nonkicking leg so you'll be airborne for the punt.)

Tasks/Challenges:

T Take a series of quick steps forward. As your kicking leg moves back to front for the contact with the ball, hop slightly on your supporting leg so you are actually airborne for the contact. Quickly straighten your kicking leg at the moment of contact. *(Demonstrate or ask a child to demonstrate the step-hop action.)*

T Continue to practice the approach and punt. As you become more comfortable with the step-hop action, you will probably want to lean slightly backward as you kick to counterbalance the forceful swing of your kicking leg.

C Practice until you can punt successfully three times in a row. When I watch your punting action, I should see the following:

1. A series of quick steps
2. Your body airborne for contact
3. The ball being dropped, not tossed
4. The top of your foot (your shoelaces) making contact with the ball

Punting Different Types of Balls

Setting: A variety of balls for punting—plastic, foam, deflated rubber, Nerf footballs—placed around an outdoor teaching area

Cues

Extend	(Extend your foot to contact the ball with your shoelaces, not your toes.)
Eyes on the Ball	(Watch the ball until it contacts your foot.)
Drop	(Drop the ball for the punt; don't toss it upward.)
Step-Hop	(Make your last step before contact a step-hop on your nonkicking leg so you'll be airborne for the punt.)

Tasks/Challenges:

T Scattered around the practice area are punting balls of different types and sizes. Practice punting with each type of ball using your running approach and airborne action for the kick.

C Practice with each type of ball until you can punt successfully three out of five times.

T Select a football for punting. What is very different about this ball? Yes, all the others are round. Hold the football with one end facing the direction in which the ball is to travel; all your other actions are the same as for punting other types of balls. Compare how well you're able to punt the football with your success with the other types of balls.

When footballs are added to the selection, some children may want to practice punting only with the footballs; encourage the children to practice punting with each type of ball.

Punting for Distance

Setting: A variety of balls for punting; colored jugs for use as markers; children positioned at one end of an outdoor practice area

Cues

Extend	(Extend your foot and your kicking leg for a really good punt.)
Step-Hop	(Make your last step before contact a step-hop on your nonkicking leg so you'll be airborne for the punt.)
Kick Hard	(Kick hard to send the ball really far.)

Tasks/Challenges:

T Take a series of running steps, and punt the ball as far as possible. Place a colored jug at the spot where

the ball first touches the ground, and then try to punt beyond that spot. Remember, making the ball travel at a 45-degree angle when you punt it gives you the best distance. **To achieve that angle, extend your foot and contact the ball just before it touches the ground.**

Continue to practice your punting, trying to extend your distance with each punt. Each time you better your distance, move your marker to that spot. **Straightening your kicking leg when you contact the ball will increase your power for distance.**

When a new factor (distance) is added, children may modify their kicking patterns. Some may need verbal cues as they practice.

Using Punting Zones

Setting: Colored tape, spray paint, marker cones, or colored streamers to mark a series of target zones, each approximately 15 feet in length (Figure 22.12); a variety of balls for punting (target zones may be numbered, color-coded, or named for states, professional teams, etc.)

Cues

Extend	(Extend your foot and your kicking leg for a really good punt.)
Step-Hop	(Make your last step before contact a step-hop on your nonkicking leg so you'll be airborne for the punt.)
Nonstop Approach	(Take a few running steps; then punt without stopping your forward momentum.)

Tasks/Challenges:

T Approach the kicking line with a series of running steps; punt the ball for maximum distance. Mentally note the zone the ball first lands in. Retrieve the ball and be ready for another turn.

A key component in punting for distance is practice. Keeping the same distances and codes (colors, names) for zones permits children to check themselves against their best during previous lessons.

Punting for Accuracy

Setting: Colored tape, spray paint, marker cones, or colored streamers to mark a series of target zones, each approximately 15 feet in length (see Figure 22.12); a variety of balls for punting

Figure 22.12 Punting zones.

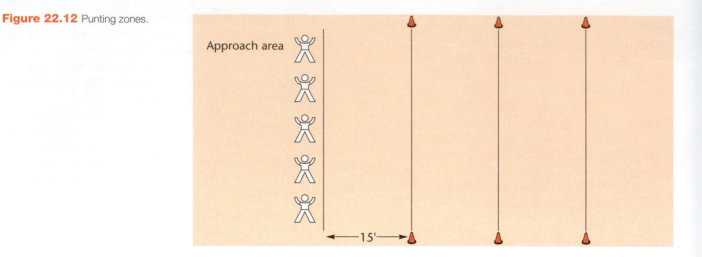

Approach area

←—15'—→

Cues

Extend　(Extend your foot and your kicking leg for a really good punt.)

Step-Hop　(Make your last step before contact a step-hop so you'll be airborne for the punt.)

Hard Kick,　(Use a hard kick for maximum
Soft Kick　distance, a soft kick for shorter distances.)

Tasks/Challenges:

Ⓣ We previously used the target zones in punting for distance. Now we will use them to focus on accuracy—making the ball land within a particular area. Practice punting with a running approach to review the skill and to determine the zone that is your best distance. Try to punt the ball consistently to that zone.

Ⓒ Punt the ball five times attempting to make it land within the same zone each time.

Ⓣ Punt the ball so it lands within the first target zone. To do that you must adjust the amount of force behind the kick.

Ⓣ Choose a zone midway between the first target zone and your best distance. Punt the ball so it lands within that target zone.

Ⓒ Select three zones as your targets. Practice until you can successfully punt three out of five balls into each of those zones.

Ⓣ Repeat the process for your three selected zones using each type of ball—foam, deflated rubber, soccer ball, football. Compare your accuracy with the different types of balls.

Being able to adjust force to kick a shorter distance is an important punting skill for playing games and one that does not come easily for children. Encourage them to select zones of varying distances, not just their maximum.

Punting for Height

Setting: Colored tape, spray paint, marker cones, or colored streamers to mark a series of target zones, each approximately 15 feet in length (see Figure 22.12); a variety of balls for punting.

Cues

Under the Ball　(Contact the ball below center to send it upward and forward.)

Eyes on the Ball　(Watch the ball until it contacts your foot.)

Kick Hard　(Make a firm step-hop and swing of leg for good height.)

Tasks/Challenges:

Ⓣ Sometimes in a game you want the ball to travel in a high aerial path rather than at a 45-degree angle so you can adjust the forward distance of the punt. What did we learn earlier about contacting a ball to send it upward rather than forward? Right, contact must be made directly underneath the ball for travel upward. You will also get more height on the punt if you contact the ball closer to waist height. Take a series of small steps, then punt the ball so it travels as high as possible.

Ⓣ Punt the ball high in the air; see if you can catch it before it touches the ground.

⚠ Because of the hazard of running to catch while looking up, this task must be done in a large

Figure 22.13 Punting at angles.

outdoor field space. If such a space is not available, some children can practice punting for height while others practice punting for distance.

T Select one of the first three target zones as your target area. Punt the ball so it travels in a high aerial path to that zone.

Children highly skilled in punting for accuracy will enjoy the challenge of smaller targets, such as hoops.

What makes the difference between the ball traveling in a very high aerial path versus a 45-degree angle for distance?

Utilization Level (GLSP): Learning Experiences Leading to Skill Development in Punting

At the utilization level, we provide punting experiences in dynamic situations. This encourages children to use punting skills in combination with other factors, such as time and accuracy. To stress relationships with a partner, focus on punting so a partner can catch the ball or on punting shortly after receiving a pass from a partner.

A note about cues: Although several cues are listed for many of the learning experiences, it's important to focus on only one cue at a time. This way, the children can really concentrate on that cue. Once you provide feedback to the children and observe that most have learned a cue, it's time to focus on another one.

Punting at Angles

Setting: Spray paint, marker dust, or milk jugs to mark target zones divided by width and length (Figure 22.13); lightweight balls for punting

Cues

Extend to Target (Extend your kicking foot and leg toward the target, to the right or left.)

Individuals and/or classes may need reminders of earlier cues (e.g., Eyes on the Ball, Drop, Step-Hop).

Tasks/Challenges:

T Practice punting into the different target zones—to the right and to the left of where you're standing.

T Select a target zone, and practice until you can consistently punt the ball into that zone. Then select a zone on the opposite side.

C Practice until you can select a target zone, tell a partner which one you've chosen, and then punt three out of five balls into that zone. How about five out of five?

Punting to a Partner

Setting: Colored tape, spray paint, marker cones, or streamers to mark target zones, each approximately 15 feet long; partners, each pair with a lightweight ball for punting (Figure 22.14)

Cues

Eyes on the Ball	(Watch the ball—not your partner—until it contacts your foot.)
Step-Hop	(Make your last step before contact a step-hop so you'll be airborne for the punt.)
Adjust	(Adjust your power to match the distance your partner is from you.)

Figure 22.14 Punting to a partner.

Tasks/Challenges:

(T) Using the target zones as a measure of distance, tell your partner where to stand for the two of you to punt to each other; choose a distance at which both of you have been successful. Punt the ball so your partner can catch it without moving more than a couple of steps.

(T) Punt so your partner can catch without moving from self-space.

(T) From behind the kicking line, practice punting to your partner in each of the target zones: near/far, right/left angles.

(T) Punt some balls high and lofty, others at a 45-degree angle.

Receiving a Pass, Then Punting

Setting: Partners scattered throughout general space in an outdoor area; a variety of balls for punting—playground balls, soccer balls, footballs

Cues

Eyes on the Ball (Watch the ball, not your partner.)

Step-Hop-Punt (Take a couple of steps only; then punt.)

Tasks/Challenges:

(T) Select a partner with whom you can work well independently. Separate to a distance at which you can both throw and catch successfully. Partner 1 throws the ball to partner 2; partner 2 receives the ball and then quickly takes a couple of steps and punts the ball across the playing field. Your goal is to punt as quickly, yet correctly, as possible. Alternate positions as passer and punter.

(A) With children throwing, catching, and punting, space awareness can be a safety factor. Organize this activity with all passes and punts traveling in the same direction—across the playing area or end to end, not in multiple directions.

Punting Within a Limited Time

Setting: Partners scattered throughout general space in an outdoor area; a variety of balls for punting—playground balls, soccer balls, footballs

Cues

Eyes on the Ball (Watch the ball, not your partner.)

Step-Hop-Punt (Take a couple of steps only; then punt.)

Tasks/Challenges:

(T) Partner 2 throws the ball to partner 1. As soon as partner 1 receives the pass, partner 2 begins to count "one alligator, two alligators, three alligators." After receiving the pass, partner 1 punts it across the playing field as quickly as possible

Approach circle

Punter

Flight of pass

Passer and rusher

Figure 22.15 Punting quickly: Rush the circle.

passer runs toward the circle, trying to reach the circle before the punter can kick the ball. The punter punts the ball as quickly as possible when he or she receives the pass. In other words, the punter tries to punt the ball before the passer reaches the circle.

At this level of punting and kicking combined with throwing and catching, some children will enjoy developing point systems and minigames for each task. Others will continue to enjoy practicing the skill in the dynamic environment.

trying to complete the punt before partner 2 counts "three alligators." Partner 1 retrieves the ball and switches positions with partner 2. Follow all the proper steps, even though you're punting quickly.

Videotape. It would be beneficial to videotape a game situation containing a punt with added pressure. Use self-analysis or peer analysis or both of the execution of the punt. To structure the observation, provide the children with lead questions: Was the punt as well executed as it was when you were not rushed by a partner? What makes the difference? Should there be a difference in the execution? What cue do you consider most critical for success in this situation? Why?

Punting Quickly: Rush the Circle

Setting: A spray-paint or marker-dust circle drawn on a field, with a diameter of 10 feet or larger, and a passing line approximately 15 feet from the edge of the circle (Figure 22.15); children with partners; a variety of balls for punting—playground balls, soccer balls, footballs

Cues

Eyes on the Ball (Watch the ball, not your partner.)

Step-Hop-Punt (Take a couple of steps only; then punt.)

Tasks/Challenges:

Select a partner whose throwing and catching skills are similar to yours. The punter will be positioned inside the circle; the passer will be approximately 20 feet away, behind the passing line. The passer throws the ball from behind the passing line. When the punter receives the catch, the

Punting experiences at the proficiency level lead to the ability to punt accurately and for distance in dynamic and unpredictable situations. The relationships are more complex. Emphasis is on punting while traveling and on working with others in game situations.

A note about cues: At the proficiency level, tasks are more complex, typically requiring children to coordinate several movements simultaneously in a dynamic context. A list of cues is provided to assist the children in being more successful in the learning experience. The challenge for the teacher is in determining which cue will be most beneficial for each child . . . and when. Thus, careful observation and critical reflection become very important as you watch the children move and then decide which cue will be the most helpful to move each learner to a higher skill level.

Receiving and Punting Against Opponents

Setting: Groups of three, each group with a ball for punting

Cues

Focus on the ball, not your opponents. Drop—don't toss—the ball, even under pressure. Remember the approach, even with opponents. Individual cues as needed

Tasks/Challenges:

Working in groups of three, two partners will assume the offensive positions of passer and punter. The other player will be the defense, attempting to block the punt. *Offense:* Partner 1 (the passer) throws the ball to partner 2 (the punter) from a distance of about 20 feet. Partner 2 punts the ball down the playing field. *Defense:* Rush the punter, starting from the 20-foot distance at which the passer is standing, to tag the punter before the punter releases the kick. You can't begin the rush until the punter receives the pass.

Alternate positions until each person has been the punter, the passer, the defense.

Punting While Traveling

Setting: Spray paint, marker dust, or milk jugs to mark distance zones approximately 15 feet in length; a variety of balls for punting

Cues	
Nonstop Approach	(Take a few running steps; then punt without stopping your forward momentum.)
Step-Hop	(Make your last step before contact a step-hop on your nonkicking leg so you'll be airborne for the punt, even with a longer approach.)

Tasks/Challenges:

T Run with the ball the distance to two target zones, then quickly punt the ball. Focus on accuracy of contacting the ball for forward travel.

T Focus on making the ball land accurately in a specific zone.

T Focus on punting for maximum distance.

Punting for Distance and Accuracy: Punt Over

Setting: Spray paint or marker dust to mark target zones, approximately 10 feet in length; teams of four or six players; a choice of football or playground ball for each team

Cues
Individual cues as needed

Tasks/Challenges:

T The object of the game Punt-Over is to punt the ball over your opponents so it lands in the end zone. You can play it in groups of four or six. Here are the basic rules:

1. Play begins with the punting team in their first zone; one person punts the ball toward the opposite end zone.
2. If the opponents catch the ball, they advance forward one zone before they punt.
3. If the opponents retrieve the ball short of the end zone, they punt from that spot.
4. The game consists of alternate punts; the number of points awarded for landing in the end zone corresponds to the zone from which the ball was punted (Figure 22.16).

The groups decide cooperatively:

1. If the defensive team catches the ball on the punt, can they run to the opposite end zone to score?
2. Can members of the opposite team rush the punter after the punter has received the pass?

Figure 22.16 Punting for distance and accuracy: Punt-Over.

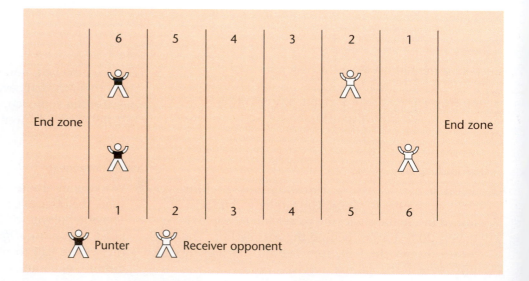

Reading Comprehension Questions

1. What is the difference between a kick and a punt?
2. What is a mature kicking pattern? What is a mature punting pattern?
3. What kicking tasks lead to the development of a mature kicking pattern?
4. Describe appropriate kicking tasks for each of the four levels of skill proficiency.
5. At the precontrol level, why do you number the balls?
6. Where does a child's foot need to contact the ball so it travels into the air? Along the ground?
7. What experiences do children have at each of the four skill levels when they're learning to punt a ball?
8. What is the outcome when a child makes contact with the ball too soon in a punt? What happens when the child makes contact too late?
9. How is the tap/dribble of soccer different from a regular kick?
10. List the kicking skills needed for success in soccer.

References/Suggested Readings

[NASPE] National Association for Sport and Physical Education. 2004. *Moving into the future: National standards for physical education.* 2nd ed. Reston, VA: National Association for Sport and Physical Education.

Wickstrom, R. L. 1977. *Fundamental motor patterns.* 2nd ed. Philadelphia: Lea & Febiger.

Throwing and Catching

Throwing and catching go together just as nicely as soup and a sandwich. The two skills, however, are opposite in movement focus and unusually difficult for young children to master. It is important that they master these skills, however, as they are necessary for enjoyable participation in neighborhood games and backyard catch as well as possible participation in sports like softball, basketball, and ultimate Frisbee, to name a few.

Although throwing and catching are complementary, we've learned that children have limited success in combining throwing and catching in game situations unless each skill has been given specific attention and developed in appropriate practice situations. It is important that the teacher be certain children can throw and catch with relative success before progressing to the utilization and proficiency levels. Activities at those levels—throwing to a running partner or trying to prevent an opponent from catching a ball—require mature throwing and catching skills. Too often teachers neglect catching, feeling it isn't that important. But as anyone who has ever watched a professional baseball game knows, catching is a skill that often determines whether a game is won or lost. Refer to Box 23-1 for linkages of the skill theme of throwing and catching to the *National Standards for Physical Education.*

Throwing

Throwing is a basic movement pattern performed to propel an object away from the body. Although throwing style (overhand, underhand, sidearm) and purpose may vary, the basic pattern and cues remains consistent.

Box 23-1

Throwing and Catching in the *National Standards for Physical Education*

The skill theme of throwing and catching is referenced in the National Association for Physical Education's *National Standards for Physical Education* (NASPE 2004) under Standard 1: "Demonstrates competency in motor skills and movement patterns needed to perform a variety of physical activities." The standard speaks of the child learning the skills as simple closed skills, developing a mature motor pattern, and increasing the variety and versatility of the action.

Sample performance outcomes for throwing and catching include:

- Drops a ball and catches it at the peak of the bounce (K–2)*
- Throws a ball underhand using mature form (e.g., places feet together and shoulders square to target, swings throwing arm straight back, shifts weight forward by stepping onto the opposite foot, rolls ball off fingers, and finishes with throwing arm outstretched toward target) (K–2)*
- Catches a fly ball using mature form (e.g., has eyes on ball, moves to position, reaches with hands, catches with hands only rather than trapping the ball, bends elbows to pull ball into chest to absorb force) (3–5)*
- Throws a ball overhand and hits a target on the wall (6-foot square centered 4 feet above the ground) from a distance of 40 feet (3–5)*
- Throws a ball overhand to a partner 15 yards away using mature form (e.g., turns side to target, uses T-position [ball held close to and behind ear], rotates hips and chest toward target, twists, releases, follows through across body) after fielding a ball (3–5)*

The skill theme of throwing and catching is also referenced under Standard 2: "Demonstrates understanding of movement concepts, principles, strategies, and tactics as they apply to the learning and performance of physical activities." This standard speaks of the child identifying the characteristics of a quality movement pattern and safety.

The sample performance outcomes state:

- Recognizes appropriate safety practices in general space by throwing balls only when others are not in the direct line of the throw (K–2)*
- Corrects movement errors in response to corrective feedback (e.g., remember to twist your tummy when throwing the ball) (K–2)*
- Accurately recognizes the critical elements of a catch made by a fellow student and provides feedback to that student (3–5)*

The skill theme of throwing and catching is further referenced under Standard 3: "Participates regularly in physical activity." In this standard, throwing and catching are used in nonschool settings.

The sample performance outcome states:

- Participates in a variety of activities that involve the manipulation of objects in and outside of physical education class (e.g., tossing ball, juggling) (K–2)*

*Grade-level guidelines for expected student learning.

Box 23-2

Key Observation Points: Throwing

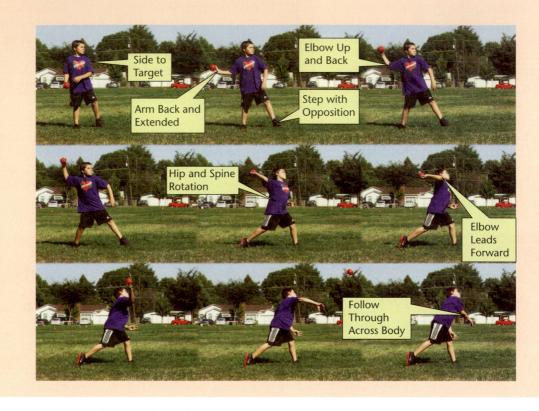

When we begin to focus on throwing, we have children think of it in three phases: preparation, throw, and follow-through. The preparation phase builds momentum for the throw; the throw is the actual release of the object; and the follow-through is to maintain control and balance while using up the momentum of the throw.

The photo sequence in Box 23-2 show the correct for form for the overhand throw.

The control level cues of throwing—arm way back, step with opposite foot, and follow-through—are designed to elicit this throwing pattern.

In the elementary school setting, a wide range of throwing abilities among a class will be observed. To initially assess children's generic level of skill proficiency (Chapter 5), it is best to ask them to throw small or medium-sized objects, such as beanbags or yarn balls, hard and fast to open space or the wall. At this point, the teacher can observe for significant developmental characteristics; after making a gross assessment of the students' development in throwing, there is a basis for structuring appropriate instructional tasks for the class as a whole and designing intratask variations (Chapter 10) for those who might benefit from them. (See our progression spiral for throwing and catching activities on page 437.)

When children begin throwing at a target or a partner (often at the control level), they frequently begin to focus primarily on hitting a target and regress to inefficient throwing patterns. What they are actually doing is using a pattern that allows them to be accurate—a pattern in which they control as many segments as possible and thus use as few body parts as possible. They have adapted their skill level to the task. Asking children to use a mature throwing pattern when throwing at a close or small target is an inappropriate request for the task. Generally, longer throws (or hard throws) to a large target elicit mature throwing patterns. Therefore, it is a good idea to vary the distance of the throw, sometimes fostering success at hitting the target, other times enhancing the development of a mature throwing pattern by having the children throw far or hard.

Throwing and Catching

Proficiency Level

Throwing and catching while using simple offense and defense in a small-sided invasion game
Throwing, catching, and dribbling in a small-sided invasion game
Throwing and catching with a football in a small-sided invasion game
Throwing and catching with a flying disc in a small-sided invasion game
Throwing and catching in a small-sided keep-away type invasion game
Throwing at a stationary object while being defended
Throwing and catching in a small-sided invasion game
Throwing to avoid a defender
Throwing and catching in a field, run, and score game-like situation
Throwing and catching a flying disc in different places around the body with a partner

Utilization Level

Throwing while in the air
Catching to throw quickly to a target
Catching to throw quickly to a partner
Throwing flying discs at targets
Throwing at a target from different distances
Throwing for distance and accuracy
Throwing to a moving target
Throwing to make a partner move to catch
Throwing on the move
Throwing and catching while traveling
Moving to catch

Control Level

Catching off a bounce
Throwing and catching over a net with a partner
Throwing and catching with a partner
Throwing for distance
Throwing a ball against a wall and catching the rebound
Catching off the fly
Catching with a scoop
Throwing a flying disc
Throwing backhand to a target
Throwing to high targets
Throwing underhand to targets: hoops
Throwing underhand to targets: jugs
Throwing overhand at a low stationary target
Throwing overhand at a high stationary target
Catching in different places around the body
Throwing an object to different levels and catching it
Bouncing a ball to self and catching it
All three throwing patterns: over, under, and side
Throwing sidearm
Throwing overhand
Throwing underhand

Precontrol Level

Tossing to self and catching
Drop–Catch
Catching from a skilled thrower
Catching a rolling ball
Throwing at a large target
Throwing a yarn ball against the wall

Catching

Catching is the receiving and controlling of an object by the body or its parts. Initially, a young child's reaction to an oncoming object is to fend it off, to protect self—often by using the whole body rather than the arms and hands. Typically, a ball bounces against the young child's chest as the remainder of the body scrambles to surround it and still maintain equilibrium.

Children's catching abilities, like their throwing skills, vary immensely. Until children can catch on a consistent basis in static situations, they generally have an easier time and experience more success when soft, textured, relatively large balls are used. Initially, the teacher who plans learning sessions in which young children use such as objects as beanbags, foam balls, or yarn balls can observe for the developmental characteristics of catching. (See the photo sequence for catching in Box 23-3 as a guide.) To determine children's generic level of skill proficiency in catching, have them catch a soft, larger-sized object that is thrown easily and consistently.

The progression spiral for throwing and catching (page 437) has activities the teacher can expand while leading children from the precontrol to the proficiency level. Initially, children need experiences that let them explore the whole action of catching—trying to accurately manipulate their arms and hands into a position to receive an object. At this level, it is important to note that children are often also at the precontrol level of throwing and thus have difficulty throwing an object accurately to themselves or to a partner, and an inaccurate throw is difficult to catch. Consequently, we have found it helpful to find ways to minimize throwing inaccuracy. We often teach the skill of throwing before catching. More skilled throwers, such as older children or parents and grandparents serving as teacher aides, can gently and accurately throw a ball to children whose throwing skills are still inconsistent. In addition, children can work as partners. For example, one child stands on a chair with a ball held in an outstretched hand and drops the ball to the partner, who is positioned directly below, ready to catch.

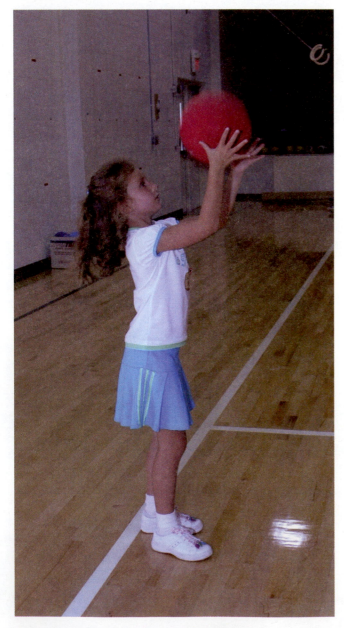

Young children use extreme concentration to catch.

Targets for Throwing

A student teacher once embellished Throwing at a Large Target (page 439) with his own creativeness. It was Halloween, so on the target he painted the school, a full moon, corn stalks, and other autumn scenes. The children certainly threw hard to try to hit the target once there was a little colored paint and a semblance of a drawing at which to aim! You don't have to be an artist—a little tempera paint, a little imagination, and a good story to tell the children are all that it takes.

Precontrol Level (GLSP): Activities for Exploration

For children at the precontrol level, the tasks are designed to provide exploration of a multitude of throwing and catching experiences. Many of the throwing experiences are designed to elicit distance throws, which force children to use a more mature throwing pattern. With catching, emphasis is placed on catching throws made directly to the child and on throwing in static situations, to enable success.

Box 23-3

Key Observation Points: Catching

Watch | Reach | Pull

Throwing a Yarn Ball Against the Wall

Setting: Spots about 10 feet from the wall, one square for each child; one yarn ball per child *(see Figure 23.1 for construction of a yarn ball)*

Tasks/Challenges:

T Throw the ball against the wall as hard as you can. Use the hand you hold your pencil with.

C Practice until you can hit the wall three times in a row.

Wind yarn around doughnuts until center hole is filled.

Two cardboard doughnuts

Figure 23.1 Construction of a yarn ball.*
1. Cut two "doughnuts"—rings made from cardboard—with a diameter 1 inch larger than you want the diameter of the yarn ball to be. The center hole of each doughnut should be about 1 inch in diameter.
2. Cut several 10-foot lengths of yarn. Rug yarn is excellent, but any heavy yarn will do. A 1-ounce skein will make two 3-inch balls.
3. Place one doughnut on top of the other. Wind yarn around each doughnut (through the hole and around the circle) until the cardboard is covered and each hole is full of yarn.
4. Slip scissors between the doughnuts at the outer edge, and cut the yarn all the way around.
5. Slip nylon string between the doughnuts, making a circle around the yarn in the middle. Pull tight, and then make a strong knot.
6. Pull the doughnuts off, and fluff the ball. You can trim any longer strands of yarn to make a smoother, rounder ball.

*Prior to constructing equipment, we recommend you check with school administration to be certain that district policy permits homemade equipment.

T Practice throwing the ball with your other hand—the one you do not hold your pencil with.

T This time move three steps farther away from the wall and try to hit the wall.

T See how many different ways you can throw—sometimes overhand, sometimes underhand, and sometimes from the side of your body.

Throwing at a Large Target

Setting: Several large targets suspended in various places around the room; several balls or beanbags for each child; spaces marked on the floor about 10 feet from each target for four children to throw at each target. (For the large targets, old sheets work well. Attach the top of the sheet to a broom or dowel stick, and weight the bottom with heavy washers. Attach a rope to both ends of the rod at the top of the sheet, and then hang the rope from basketball goals or rafters.)

Tasks/Challenges:

T Now you have a target at which to aim. This kind of target will soak up your ball; your ball won't come bouncing back to you. Your job is to throw at the target as hard as you can and try to make the target move. Throw all the balls you have, then bring them back and start again. Remember, do not get your balls until everyone at your target has thrown and do not throw until everyone is back to the throwing space.

T When you can make the target move three times in a row, take one giant step backward and try again.

T Move back to your starting position, and try to make the target move by throwing with your other hand.

T When you can make the target move three times, take a giant step backward and try again.

T Move back to your first spot and try to throw a different way than you threw the first time. Practice that throw about 15 times.

For children at the precontrol level, the emphasis is on providing many throwing experiences. Varying the context too early (for example, placing children in gamelike situations) causes children to use immature throwing patterns in an attempt to achieve the called-for results.

Catching a Rolling Ball

Setting: Partners about 5 feet apart; one large plastic or rubber ball per pair

Tasks/Challenges:

T With your partner, you're going to practice catching the ball. You should be seated facing each other, with your legs like a V. One of you rolls the ball to the other, and the other one of you catches it with your hands. The second partner then rolls the ball back to the first.

T When the two of you can make five catches in a row, both of you should move backward a little and try again.

C See if the two of you can make 10 catches without missing.

Catching from a Skilled Thrower

Setting: A skilled thrower (older students, classroom teacher, parents, or grandparents) partnered with each child; one light, medium- to large-sized ball per pair

This activity is a wonderful way to directly involve others in the physical education program. It serves as a great public relations activity.

Tasks/Challenges:

T For this task you have a "big" partner. You and your partner will stand about 4 to 5 feet apart in your own space. Your big partner will throw the ball to you so you can practice catching. When you catch the ball, throw it back to your big partner so he or she can throw it to you again.

T After you can make five catches in a row from your partner, take one giant step backward. When you can make five more catches, take another giant step backward.

Drop–Catch

Setting: A stable chair (one that will not move or collapse) for every pair of partners; one light, medium- to large-sized ball per pair

Tasks/Challenges:

T This is a fun task. One of you will stand on the chair and hold the ball in your hands with your arms straight out from your body. The other one of you will stand close to the chair where your hands and arms can be under the ball. The partner on the chair drops the ball, and the other partner catches it. After five turns, switch places.

C Say one letter of your name every time you catch. See if you can spell your name before missing.

Tossing to Self and Catching

Setting: Self-space; a yarn ball, beanbag, or lightweight ball for every child

Tasks/Challenges:

T In a space by yourself, you're going to practice tossing and catching by yourself. Toss the ball

At the control level, remind youngsters to concentrate on the catching cues: Eyes on Ball, Reach, Pull It In.

(beanbag) very close to your body, close enough so the ball (beanbag) doesn't go very high over your head or very far out from your stomach. Catch it.

T When you can toss and catch the ball (beanbag) five times in a row, keeping it very close to your body, then toss it just a little farther away and see if you can still catch it.

C This is your challenge for the day. See if you can toss and catch the ball (beanbag) 10 times in a row without moving more than one step from your space.

Control Level (GLSP): Learning Experiences Leading to Skill Development

Children at the control level still need practice developing mature throwing and catching patterns, yet they are also ready to focus on more complex learning experiences that still allow them to throw and catch in static situations. Therefore we expose children to various contexts so they use throwing actions in different but relatively static situations that are designed to help children learn to throw for accuracy and with varying degrees of force, and to throw a variety of objects.

Children at the control level of catching need opportunities to develop the skills used when catching with the right and left hands, on either side of the body, and at various levels. For example, they are challenged by catching at different levels, catching at different places around their bodies, and using either hand to catch.

A note about cues: Although several cues are listed for many of the learning experiences, it's important to focus on only one cue at a time. This way, the children can really concentrate on that cue. Once you provide feedback to the children and observe that most have learned a cue, it's time to focus on another one.

> *Reed and Sophie, both 5 years old, were playing a game in which they threw a ball under their legs to knock over a pile of tin cans. Reed placed his head a bit too far under his legs and inadvertently fell into a forward roll as he released the ball. With an expression of sheer excitement, Reed announced that he had discovered the "flip throw."*

Throwing Underhand

Setting: Tape marks or spots on the floor about 15 feet from the wall; one ball per child

Cues

Face Wall	(Your body should be looking at the wall.)
Arm Way Back	(Your throwing arm should come back behind your seat.)
Step with Opposite Foot	(Step forward on the foot opposite the hand you are using to throw.)
Follow Through	(Make your arm follow your throw straight to the wall.)

Make sure to demonstrate the throw.

Tasks/Challenges:

T This time, instead of throwing overhand, you are going to practice throwing almost as if you were bowling. You are going to throw to the wall, just like before. This is called an *underhand throw.*

T Move back three steps, and practice again.

T Move back to your first spot, and try to throw with the other hand.

T Again, move back, and try to throw with the hand you don't write with.

Throwing Overhand

Setting: Tape marks or spots on the floor about 15 feet from the wall; one ball per child; children alone at first and later with a partner

Cues

Side to Target	(Make sure the side of your body away from the hand you are throwing with is toward the wall; if you were to walk straight ahead, you would walk along the wall, not toward it.)
Arm Way Back	(Bring your throwing arm way back so your elbow is almost above your ear and your hand is behind your head.)
Step with Opposite Foot	(Step forward on the foot opposite the hand you are using to throw with.)
Follow Through	(After you throw, make your arm follow the ball. Your hand should end up almost at your knee.)

Tip: It is useful to demonstrate these cues. After the children understand them, it is easy to reduce them to one-word cues: Side, Arm, Step, Follow.

Some children have a hard time remembering which foot to step with to achieve opposition. To help these children, place an old wrist sweatband around the appropriate foot as a reminder to step with the opposite foot. You can also use a large loose-fitting rubber band; some teachers have children take off one shoe to illustrate this point.

Tasks/Challenges:

T At your own mark, practice throwing at the wall. Throw the ball overhand as hard as you can. **Remember, in an overhand throw, your arm comes above your shoulder.**

T This time move three steps farther away from the wall and practice overhand throwing.

T Move back to your first spot and try to throw with your other hand—the one you don't write with.

T This time you will have a partner, who is your coach. You throw three times, with your favorite hand, and your partner has to tell you if you used each of the cues: Side, Arm, Step, Follow. The partner gives you a thumbs-up if you did them all or a thumbs-down if you didn't. If you didn't use the cues, the partner tells you which part to practice, and you practice that two times. Then switch places.

Throwing Sidearm

Setting: Tape marks or spots on the floor about 15 feet from the wall; one ball per child

Cues	
Face Wall	(Your body should be looking straight at the wall.)
Arm Way Back	(Your throwing arm should come back sideways, behind your back.)
Step with Opposite Foot	(Step forward on the foot opposite the hand you are using to throw.)
Follow Through	(Make your arm follow your throw across your body.)

Demonstrate the throw.

Tasks/Challenges:

T Now you are going to try another throw. Instead of throwing overhand or underhand, you are going to throw from the side. This is called a *sidearm throw.* To do this, ring your arm around from the side of your body. You would use a throw like this to throw a flying disc. Remember, it's not a fling. **Let loose of the ball just as your hand faces straight at the wall.**

T After you can hit the wall eight times in a row, move back one giant step. Try again.

☼ Which way should your body face when you are throwing overhand? Underhand? Sidearmed?

All Three Throwing Patterns: Over, Under, and Side

Setting: Tape marks or spots on the floor about 15 feet from the wall; one ball per child

Cues	
Face Wall/Side or to Wall	(Remember, depending upon your throw, your body should be looking straight at the wall or be turned sideways to it.)
Arm Way Back	(Your throwing arm should come way back behind your back, head, or seat depending upon the throw.)
Step with Opposite Foot	(Step forward on the foot opposite the hand you are using to throw.)
Follow Through	(Follow your throw.)

Tasks/Challenges:

T Now that you know the names for the three different kinds of throws, you're going to practice the throws on your own. You can practice them in any order you want, but make sure you practice each one at least 15 times.

T Here's some more practice. Pick out the throw you're having the most trouble with. Practice only that throw until you can hit the wall 10 times in a row. After you can hit the wall 10 times with the throw you found the most difficult, pick another throw you're having trouble with, and practice it until you can hit the wall 10 times in a row.

T When you can hit the wall 10 times in a row with all three throws, take three giant steps backward and try again.

✓ *Exit Slip.* This would be a good time to include a Helping Murgatroid (see Chapter 12) exit slip that has children explain to Murgatroid how to throw correctly.

Bouncing a Ball to Self and Catching It

Setting: Self-space; a playground ball (or tennis ball if you want to increase the complexity of the task) for each child

Cues	
Hands	(Always use your hands—not your arms or stomach—to catch.)
Watch the Ball	(Your eyes should be on the ball. You should see the ball as it comes into your hands.)

Tasks/Challenges:

T You're going to practice catching this time so you can get used to catching a ball that's coming down toward you. In your own space, bounce the playground ball (tennis ball) so it barely goes over your head, and try to catch it as it comes down, before it hits the floor.

T If you can catch the ball six times in a row, bouncing it the way you have been, try bouncing it a little higher and still catching it using only your hands. If you have to use your body to catch the ball, you know you're bouncing the ball too high.

Throwing an Object to Different Levels and Catching It

Setting: Self-space; a beanbag or yarn ball for each child

Cues	
Watch the Ball	(Keep your eyes on the ball; see it come into your hands.)
Reach	(Reach to meet the ball; don't wait for it to come to your hands.)
Pull It In	(Pull the ball toward you so your catches are soft and quiet; give with the ball.)

Tasks/Challenges:

T This task is to give you more practice catching. In your own space, throw the beanbag (yarn ball) up in the air and catch it. To warm up, throw the object at about head level.

T Now that you're warmed up, practice throwing the object about arm's length above your head and catching it. This makes catching a little more difficult because there's more force involved.

T Once you're able to catch the object 10 times in a row using soft, quiet catches, you're ready to throw it a little higher still, maybe 5 feet over your head. Always remember, you must still be able to catch quietly at each level you throw to. If you can't, then you know you're throwing too high and need to bring the throw down a little.

Catching in Different Places Around the Body

Setting: Self-space; a beanbag or yarn ball for each child

Cues	
Watch the Ball	(Keep your eyes on the ball; see it come into your hands.)
Reach	(Reach to meet the ball; don't wait for it to come to your hands.)
Pull It In	(Pull the ball toward you so your catches are soft and quiet; give with the ball.)

Tasks/Challenges:

T You practiced catching an object that goes to different heights; now you're going to practice catching an object that goes to different places around your body. Standing in your own space, throw the beanbag (yarn ball) so you have to reach in different places around your body to catch it. This may mean catching it to the sides sometimes, or behind your head. See how many different places you can find to catch the beanbag (ball) from without leaving your self-space.

C Most of us don't like to practice places that are really hard. This time as you practice, pick out two places that you tried to catch and had the hardest time with. Practice those two places until you can catch the beanbag (yarn ball) four out of five times.

Staying in Self-Space and Catching

While many tasks ask that youngsters throw and catch in self-space, if they are pushing themselves to really accomplish the task, the balls and beanbags will often force them out of their self-space. This is the nature of the task and necessary for skill development, so it is important that they be taught how to retrieve objects when they enter someone else's space and to return to their space to resume practice.

T This time practice your same catches in new places around your body. **Always try to make sure the catches are as quiet as possible.**

T I'm going to make this task a little harder still. It's easy to catch the beanbag (ball) when it's fairly close to your body, but now I want you to practice catching the beanbag (ball) so you have to reach to catch it. Really stretch so you feel you're almost going to fall over. It helps to think of keeping one foot glued in place all the time. You stretch from that glued foot—the foot can't move.

T As you're stretching to catch, don't forget to keep trying to catch in different places. So the task should be like this: Stretch and reach to catch in different places around your body.

The child's success with the previous tasks depends a great deal on the child's ability to throw so she or he has to stretch. It helps to practice stretching without the throw or simply throwing away from the body. If the students aren't catching on as you think they should, see if the reason is the throw.

Throwing Overhand at a High Stationary Target

Setting: Targets about 5 or 6 feet high on the wall, one for each student (paper plates with pictures on them make good targets), a spot for each child (to help maintain their spacing); a ball for each child.

When drawing targets for children to throw at, we do not draw faces on the targets. Putting faces on targets subtly reinforces the idea of throwing at people, a violent concept we do not support in physical education programs.

More Targets for Throwing

Two student teachers came up with a great target for Throwing Overhand at a Stationary Target. They partially filled self-tie plastic kitchen trash bags with old aluminum cans. On the outside of each bag they drew a target and then inserted a coat hanger in the top of each bag, closed it, taped it for reinforcement, and hung each one from various things in the gym. The children loved it—the targets were big and made noise when they were hit. The cleanup was much simpler than with plates, more than one child could work at a target, and the targets were reusable.

Cues	
Eyes on Target	(Your eyes should be on the target all the time.)
Side, Arm, Step, Follow	(Don't forget the cues for throwing—always use them.)

Tasks/Challenges:

T This time you're going to throw at targets. You'll have to keep your eyes on the target. Each of you has a target in your own space. See how often you can hit it.

T When you can hit your target three times in a row, take a giant step backward and try from that distance.

This same task can be changed for underhand throwing by lowering the targets to 2 to 3 feet from the floor. The second cue would change from Side to Face, Arm, Step, Follow.

Assessment Example

From the National Standards for Physical Education

Peer Observation

Using an appropriate size ball, students practice throwing at a target on the wall, alternating with a partner in five-throw turns. The students should be instructed to concentrate on the critical elements of throwing as taught by the instructor (i.e., ready position, arm preparation, opposite side to the target, step with leg opposite the throwing arm, follow-through, accuracy of throw). After each bout of five throws the partner gives feedback on one of the critical elements by drawing a smiley face on a score sheet each time the element was employed as instructed. Note changes in performance with subsequent five-throw bouts.

Throwing at a large target challenges youngsters at the control level.

Criteria for Assessment

a. Recognizes critical elements of basic movement pattern.

b. Adjusts conditions for success following feedback.

NASPE (1995, 20)

Throwing Overhand at a Low Stationary Target

Setting: Partners, one ball or beanbag per pair; institutional food cans stacked on benches or other objects (or on the floor) to form a can target for each pair; spots as starting points

Children love this activity because of the noise. Beware of the noise level of the cans, especially if you have a tile floor.

Cues	
Eyes on Target	(Your eyes should be on the target all the time.)
Side, Arm, Step, Follow	(Always use the throwing cues.)

Tasks/Challenges:

T With a partner, you're going to practice throwing at the tin cans stacked in front of you. Stand behind your spot as you throw. To start, one of you is the thrower, one of you the stacker. The stacker stands far enough behind the cans so as not to get hit if the thrower hits the cans but close enough to pick them up quickly if they topple. After six throws, trade places. The secret is in the stacking: the faster you stack, the faster the game goes.

T If you can knock the cans over two times in a row, move your spot back three giant steps and try throwing from the new distance.

When practicing throwing at targets, we always try to have a throwing area for each child or group or pair of partners to maximize the number of throwing opportunities.

Throwing Underhand to Targets: Jugs

Setting: Partners, each with a target on the floor (such as several 2-liter plastic bottles, weighted with sand or dirt or plastic bowling pins) and a 4- to 6-inch playground ball

Cues	
Eyes on Target	(Your eyes should be on the target all the time.)
Face, Arm, Step, Follow	(Don't forget the cues for throwing—always use them.)

Tasks/Challenges:

T With a partner, you're going to practice throwing at targets on the ground by using an underhand throw that rolls along the floor. One of you is the setter; the other is the bowler. Using an underhand throw, roll the ball and try to knock the pins over. The setter will set the pins up again and roll the ball back to you. This is like bowling. After five turns, trade places.

T If you knock the pins over twice in a row, move one giant step back and try again.

Throwing Underhand to Targets: Hoops

Setting: Partners with a hoop (on the floor between them) and a beanbag for each pair. Tape marks on the floor at various places around the hoop.

Cues	
Eyes on Target	(Your eyes should be on the target all the time.)
Face, Arm, Step, Follow	(Don't forget the cues for throwing—always use them.)

Tasks/Challenges:

T This time you're going to practice throwing so your beanbag lands in the hoop that's in the middle of your space on the floor. Throw the beanbag so it lands inside the hoop. Move one giant step back each time the beanbag lands in the hoop. Your partner will collect the beanbag and throw it back to you. After five throws, switch places. **Remember, the best way to do this is to throw underhand.**

C A game you can play is called Around the World. Start in one place and try to hit the hoop. If you hit the hoop from that place, move to the next spot, and try to hit the hoop from there. You can keep adding new spots to throw from as you get better.

Assessment Example

From the National Standards for Physical Education

Peer Observation

Students are given a task of practicing the underhand throw at a target with a partner. Students may choose the type and size of ball, distance from the target (enough distance to produce a throw and not a toss), and the height of the target. Partners assist each other by marking a score sheet for accuracy for each of five throws. Partners change roles after five throws. Take as many turns as time allows.

Figure 23.2 Hoops suspended from rope as targets.

Criteria for Assessment

a. Chooses appropriate ball and placement of target for personal competence.
b. Records partner's performance accurately and honestly.
c. Assists partner by speaking politely and taking turns.
d. Assumes personal responsibility for the results of the activity.

NASPE (1995, 27)

Throwing to High Targets

Setting: Partners, with a beanbag or ball for each pair; ropes with hoops attached strung across the space (Figure 23.2) at different heights as targets: some at chest height, others above the heads

Cues	
Eyes on Target	(Your eyes should be on the target all the time.)
Side, Arm, Step, Follow	(Don't forget the cues for throwing—always use them.)

Tasks/Challenges:

T You're going to be aiming at a high target or goal—the hoops. This task will give you good practice for basketball later. Decide how far away from your goal you want to stand. Use your overhand throw for this task.

C This time you're going to test yourself. Pick a place to stand, and see how many throws in a row you can put through the hoop. When you make 8 out of 10 goals, move to a new spot and try for 8 out of 10 goals again.

Throwing Backhand to a Target

Setting: Individuals or partners; sticks (similar to horseshoe stakes) in the ground and plastic deck rings for each child

Cues	
Eyes on Target	(Your eyes should be on the target all the time.)
Throwing Side to Target	(The side of the arm you throw with should be facing the target.)
Arm Way Across Body	(Instead of bringing it to the back, bring the arm you throw with way across your body.)
Step with Same Foot	(This is one of the few times you step toward the target with the foot on the same side as the arm you're throwing with.)
Follow Through	(Make your arm follow your throw toward the target.)

Tasks/Challenges:

T Try to throw the ring so it goes over your stick. This activity is a little different from anything you've done before, so start very close. The throwing action is also different; instead of throwing overhand or underhand, you're actually throwing sort of backward—sidearm using a flick of your wrist away from your body toward the stick. *(The teacher or a skilled child should demonstrate the throw.)*

T If you can ring the stick six times in a row from where you're standing, move back a couple of steps and try it again.

Throwing a Flying Disc

Setting: Partners; one flying disc per pair

Cues	
Eyes on Target	(Your eyes should be on the target all the time.)
Throwing Side to Target	(The side of the arm you throw with should be facing the target.)
Arm Way Across Body	(Instead of bringing it to the back, bring the arm you throw with way across your body.)
Step with Same Foot	(This is one of the few times you step toward the target with the foot on the same the arm you're throwing with.)
Follow Through	(Make your arm follow your throw toward the target.)

Tasks/Challenges:

T Now you get to practice throwing a flying disc. The action involved is similar to the one you just did with the ring: a flick of the wrist to make the flying disc fly. (*A demonstration is essential here.*) Practice throwing the flying disc toward your partner, and have your partner throw it back to you. Don't worry about aiming—just try to throw to the general area where your partner is. You'll know you're getting better when the flying disc flies flat (not tilted) each time you throw it.

T Now try to throw the flying disc so it goes fairly close to your partner. Start off pretty close together, and slowly move farther apart as you improve.

Catching with a Scoop

Setting: Individuals alone at first, and then partners; a plastic scoop (Figure 23.3) for each child

Cues

Watch the Bag	(Keep your eyes on the bag; see it come into your hands.)
Reach	(Reach to meet the bag; don't wait for it to come to your scoop.)
Pull It In	(Pull the scoop toward you so your catches are soft and quiet—give with the bag.)

Tasks/Challenges:

T In your self-space, practice throwing the beanbag up with your hand and catching it in the scoop. To be a good catch, the beanbag must stay in the scoop and not bounce out.

T Now your partner will throw the beanbag to you, and you'll catch it with the scoop. The partner shouldn't be very far away to begin. After seven throws, trade places.

T The way you reach and pull in with the scoop as you catch the beanbag has changed a little now that a partner is throwing to you. **Instead of**

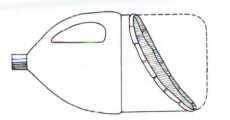

Figure 23.3 Plastic scoop. You can make scoops for throwing and catching by cutting the end and part of the side from large plastic jugs that have grip-type handles. For protection, place tape over the cut edges.*

*Prior to constructing equipment, we recommend you check with school administration to be certain that district policy permits homemade equipment

reaching up and pulling down, as you did when you caught from a throw you made yourself, you have to reach out and pull back.

☺ Why is it so important to "watch, reach, and pull it in" when catching with a scoop?

Catching off the Fly

Setting: Large space; groups of three or four; one playground ball and one beanbag per group

Cues

Watch, Reach, Pull	(Watch the ball, reach for it, and pull it in.)
Get Behind	(As the beanbag comes toward you, position your body so you are behind the beanbag, not to the side of it.)

Tasks/Challenges:

T This task could be called Flying Beanbag Catch (Humphries, Lovdahl, and Ashy 2002). We are going to practice catching a beanbag on a hop. This is like baseball players catching a baseball on a bounce. To do this, one person puts the beanbag

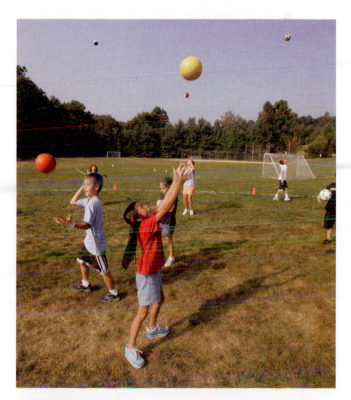

Intratask variation can be used to adjust the catching task to different children's skill levels.

on the ball and drops the ball. *(A demonstration would be good here.)* When the beanbag "flies" off the ball, the closest person to it catches it. Switch "droppers" after five turns.

C How many flying beanbags can you catch in a row?

Throwing a Ball Against a Wall and Catching the Rebound

Setting: A wall with enough space so the children can spread out and not be in each other's way as they throw; spots as helpful reminders of self-space; one tennis ball per child; a line on the wall 3 feet above ground and one on the ground 10 feet from the wall

Cues	
Throwing	
Eyes on Target	(Your eyes should be on the target all the time.)
Side, Arm, Step, Follow	(Don't forget the cues for throwing—always use them.)
Catching	
Watch, Reach, Pull	(Watch the ball, reach for it, and pull it in.)
Get Behind	(As the ball bounces off the wall, position your body so you're behind the ball, not to the side of it.)
Thumbs/Little Fingers	(When you catch over your head, make sure your thumbs are together; if the catch is low, make sure your little fingers are together.)

Tasks/Challenges:

T At your spot, throw the ball against the wall, let it bounce on the ground on the return, and catch it.

T **As you practice this time, try to catch the ball at stomach or chest level.**

T As you practice now, sometimes throw the ball hard and sometimes soft so you have to move forward and backward to catch it.

T To make it a little harder, now try to catch the ball without letting it bounce.

T Now throw from behind the line on the ground so the ball hits the wall above the line on the wall. Catch the ball as it rebounds before it hits the ground. Give it a try.

C We'll make a game out of it this time. I'll time you for 1 minute. Count to yourself how many times you can hit the wall above the line and catch the ball in the air on the rebound. Remember the number because we'll do it again so you can try to improve your score.

Assessment Example

From the National Standards for Physical Education

Peer Observation

Have partners observe the preparatory phase of a designated skill in an attempt to ascertain the correct use of critical elements. For example, student A will throw a ball toward a target five times using the overhand pattern while student B observes the performance, focusing on a single critical element during the preparatory phase (e.g., opposite foot forward, side to target, arm pulled way back). The observing student gives a thumbs-up if the critical element is correct; if incorrect, the observing student tells what is needed to improve the movement.

Criteria for Assessment

a. Thrower displays the critical element that is the focus of the observation.
b. Observer makes an accurate judgment on the performance.

NASPE (1995, 33)

Throwing for Distance

Setting: Partners in a large outdoor field, each pair with a bucket of about 10 tennis balls; beanbags to mark where the balls land (often you can get old tennis balls from parents who play tennis. Send parents a note at the beginning of the year asking tennis players to save old tennis balls; collect them regularly. It doesn't take long to accumulate more balls than you need.)

Cues	
Side to Target	(Turn your hips and upper body toward your throwing hand when you pull it back in preparation to throw.)
Arm Way Back	(Pull your throwing arm way back before you begin the throw.)
Step	(Step forward on the foot opposite the hand throwing the ball.)
Follow Through	(Follow through toward the target, ending at your knees.)

Tasks/Challenges:

T You're going to practice throwing long distances—like playing the outfield in baseball. Throw each tennis ball as far as you can. With markers, your partner will mark your farthest throw and collect the balls. Each time, try to beat your last throw. After you've thrown all the balls you have, trade places with your partner.

Baseball Gloves

A baseball glove is an implement that can be used to catch an object, but generally we prefer not to use gloves in our program. When children bring their own gloves to school, there are problems. Many children prefer to not share their gloves with children who don't have gloves. We also have a hard time justifying the expense of purchasing gloves for a physical education program. In the schools we've taught in, we've always wanted other equipment that needs to be purchased and is more important than baseball gloves. However, if you do have some gloves, you may want to create a task teaching experience (see Chapter 10) that provides for the use of gloves.

Throwing and Catching with a Partner

Setting: Partners about 10 feet apart; one ball (varying the object used to throw and catch increases or decreases the complexity of this task) per pair

Cues

Throwing

Eyes on Target (Your eyes should be on the target all the time.)

Face, Arm, Step, Follow (Don't forget the cues for throwing—always use them.)

Catching

Watch, Reach, Pull (Watch the ball, reach for it, and pull it in.)

Get Behind (As the ball comes toward you, position your body so you're behind the ball, not to the side of it.)

Thumbs/Little Fingers (When you catch over your head, make sure your thumbs are together; if the catch is low, make sure your little fingers are together.)

Tasks/Challenges:

T Throw the ball so your partner doesn't have to move to catch it. You'll probably want to start with an underhand throw.

T If you and your partner can make 10 throws and catches from the place where you are now without missing, then both of you move back two giant steps and practice from there. Do the same thing as before: Make good throws so your partner doesn't have to move more than a step in either direction to catch.

T Try to make sympathetic throws. These are throws that have enough force to get to your partner but are not so strong your partner can't catch them.

C From wherever you are standing, see how many throws and catches you can make without a miss. To count, the ball must be caught, not just batted back to your partner.

C This time we'll play a game called One Step, which goes like this: Each time you and your partner make a catch, both of you move back one giant step; if you miss, you both move toward each other one giant step.

T Change and use an overhand throw. First, just practice back and forth. When you can make 10 in a row, move back two giant steps.

If children are relatively close to one another, don't expect mature throwing patterns. As the distance between the partners increases, you should start observing more mature patterns.

Assessment Example

From the National Standards for Physical Education

Event Task

Have the students pretend that Rapunzel recently enrolled in your school. She knows nothing about catching a ball. Students are asked to explain what Rapunzel needs to know to catch a ball thrown to her from the front at about chest height. Instruct the students to imagine themselves practicing with Rapunzel and providing feedback after each attempted catch. Have them imagine looking for critical elements (ready position, hand and arm position, eye contact, and absorption of force).

Criteria for Assessment

a. Identifies critical elements of catching.
b. Uses appropriate feedback to improve performance.
NASPE (1995, 21)

Throwing and Catching over a Net with a Partner

Setting: Partners; nets or ropes between two chairs at various heights, enough for one per pair; beanbags and yarn balls

Cues

Throwing

Eyes on Target	(Your eyes should be on the target all the time.)
Face, Arm, Step, Follow	(Don't forget the cues for throwing—always use them.)

Catching

Watch, Reach, Pull	(Watch the ball, reach for it, and pull it in.)
Get Behind	(As the ball comes toward you, position your body so you're behind the ball, not to the side of it.)
Thumbs/Little Fingers	(When you catch over your head, make sure your thumbs are together; if the catch is low, make sure your little fingers are together.)

Tasks/Challenges:

T With your partner, choose a net (rope) that you want to practice throwing and catching over and a beanbag or a yarn ball. After you've chosen your net (rope), begin throwing underhand and catching. Try to throw so the throw has an arch on it and

---

Accommodating Different Skill Levels

Teachers often ask, "How do I accommodate different skill levels in one class?" More specifically, "How do I do this with little equipment?" We've found the best way is to vary the major task using intratask variation or teaching by invitation for individual children according to their needs (see Chapter 8 for more on these concepts). Often you can reduce or increase the complexity of the task without substantially changing the equipment used.

Consider the task of throwing a ball to a partner so the partner is fully extended to catch. You can reduce the complexity of this task by changing the equipment from a ball to a beanbag or by having the partner use an outstretched arm as the target. Then, by changing the task so the throw forces the partner to take a step to catch the ball, you increase the complexity of the same task.

You can make such changes by moving from group to group, observing, and modifying accordingly. In this way, the entire class is then practicing variations of the same task.

---

your partner doesn't have to move more than one step in either direction to catch the beanbag or ball.

C See how many throws and catches you and your partner can make without missing. Watch the object closely. Use sympathetic throws.

T If you are really good with the underhand throws over the net, change to overhand throws.

C See if you and your partner can get 20 overhand throws and catches in a row without missing.

Catching off a Bounce

Setting: Partners, each pair with a playground ball and a bench or table

Cues

Throwing

Eyes on Target and Bench (Table)	(Your eyes should see your partner and the bench [table] at the same time—they are both targets.)

Catching

Watch, Reach, Pull	(Watch the ball, reach for it, and pull it in.)
Get Behind	(As the ball comes toward you, position your body so you're behind the ball, not to the side of it.)
Thumbs/Little Fingers	(When you catch over your head, make sure your thumbs are together; if the catch is low, make sure your little fingers are together.)

Tasks/Challenges:

T Let's call this Bench Bounce Catch. You will need to bounce the ball on your side of the bench (table) so it travels over the bench (table) and your partner catches it. Your partner shouldn't have to move more than one step in either direction to catch the ball. Remember, the ball should bounce on the floor on your side of the bench, not on the bench itself.

T As you bounce the ball over the bench (table), sometimes bounce it with one hand and sometimes with two hands.

C Try to keep the ball going back and forth as long as you can, using the bounce throw over the bench (table). To do this you will have to remember your quick feet. Remember, this is a throw and catch, not a volley across the bench.

Once the children are able to perform smooth throwing and catching actions in a variety of static contexts, they're ready for utilization-level experiences. At this level, children are given tasks that encourage refinement of skills and begin to use the skills in dynamic, unpredictable situations. Throwing tasks at the utilization level are designed to help children learn to throw while traveling, to throw accurately at moving targets, and to jump to throw. Catching experiences include catching while traveling, while in the air, and in gamelike activities that require the ability to catch while moving in relationship to various objects and/or people.

At the utilization level, children profit from stretching and/or jumping to catch.

A note about cues: Although several cues are listed for many of the learning experiences, it's important to focus on only one cue at a time. This way, the children can really concentrate on that cue. Once you provide feedback to the children and observe that most have learned a cue, it's time to focus on another one.

Moving to Catch

Setting: Individuals in self-space with a lot of extra space around each one; one ball per person

Cues	
Throwing	
Away, But Close	(Throw away from your body so that you have to move, but don't throw so far that you can't catch the ball.)
Catching	
Under or Behind Ball	(Move to a position that puts you under or behind the ball, not to the side)
Watch, Reach, Pull	(As always, watch the ball, reach for it, and pull it in.)

Tasks/Challenges:

T You're going to practice throwing so you have to move to catch. Each of you has to be in your own self-space with much space around you so you don't run into others. To begin, toss the ball so you have to move just one step to catch it—put the ball just barely out of your reach. This is a skill often used in football and basketball.

T Practice throwing and catching in all places around your body: forward, backward, and sideways.

T I see some people catching at the same place; try to catch at different places, especially toward the back of your body.

Setting: A large area (a full-size gymnasium or, preferably, outdoors in a large, open space)

Tasks/Challenges:

T This task will take a lot of concentration on your part, not only to catch the ball, but to make sure you do not run into or hurt others. It's fun, but it must be done with a great deal of safety. You practiced moving one or two steps to catch the ball; now you are going to practice moving a long way to catch. Throw the ball away from you so you have to move several steps to catch it. Make the catch; then throw again so you have to move to catch the ball. Your throws should always be catchable. In other words, don't throw so far that there is absolutely no way that you could possibly catch the ball. Start out with throws that make you move only a few steps, and then try longer throws. **Remember, if at all possible, you should be under and behind the ball when you catch it.**

T After each successful catch, see if you can throw the ball a little farther the next time. In other words, see how far you can really move to make the catch.

✓ *Teacher Observation.* This would be an excellent time to use a teacher observation checklist (videotape or live) of the critical catching elements developed at the control level. You know real learning has occurred if the children are able to catch in the dynamic situations of the utilization level using the cues.

Throwing and Catching While Traveling

Setting: Individuals in self-space with a lot of extra space around each one; one ball or beanbag per person

Cues	
No Stopping	(Both the throws and the catches should be on the move, with no stops.)
Throwing	
Away, But Not Too Far	(Throw away from your body so that you have to move, but not so far that you can't catch the ball.)
Catching	
Under or Behind Ball	(Move to a position that puts you under or behind the ball, not to the side.)
Watch, Reach, Pull	(As always, watch the ball, reach for it, and pull it in.)

Tasks/Challenges:

T You practiced throwing that made you move to catch, but you were standing still when you threw. Now you are going to throw and catch while moving. To begin, toss the ball into the air and catch it while you walk around the space. You must be very careful while you do this and use two sets of eyes: one to watch the ball and

one to watch out for other people so you don't run into them.

⚠ Mastery of space awareness—moving in relation to others—is a prerequisite to this activity.

T If you can catch the ball almost all the time when you are walking and throwing and catching, try slowly jogging as you travel. Always watch closely so you don't collide with others.

Throwing on the Move

Setting: A large space; partners; relatively large, stationary targets (a hoop hanging from a basket, a tire hanging from a tree, a target placed on a backstop) for each pair; one ball or beanbag per pair

Cues	
Straight Pathway	(The ball should travel in a straight pathway, not curved or arched.)
No Stopping	(The throws should be on the move, with no stops.)

Tasks/Challenges:

T With a partner, you're going to practice throwing at a target while running. Run across in front of your target, and try to throw the ball through or into your target. Your partner will give the ball back to you so you can throw again. After four throws, trade places.

Throwing and catching different objects increase children's physical activity options.

(T) Sometimes when people perform this task, they tend to run, stop, and then throw. **What you really want to be doing is throwing as you run, so the throw just seems to flow out of the run and you keep running afterward.** This time, have your partner watch you closely as you run and throw. Your partner's task is to tell you whether you stop and throw or throw on the run. Sometimes it is hard to feel what we are actually doing; partners make good observers.

Throwing to Make a Partner Move to Catch

Setting: A large space; partners; one ball or beanbag per pair

Cues

Throwing

Throw Beyond	(Throw beyond your partner. Pick a spot just beyond your partner and aim for it.)
Catching	
React Quickly	(As soon as the ball leaves the thrower's hand, move to the spot to catch.)
Watch, Reach, Pull	(Watch the ball, reach for it, and pull it in.)

Tasks/Challenges:

(T) With your partner, throw back and forth so your partner has to stretch or move a few steps to catch. The idea is not to make your partner miss but to force your partner to really stretch or move to catch so he or she can practice difficult catches.

Assessment Example

From the National Standards for Physical Education

Event Task

Students are requested to design a game of throwing and catching for one or two persons to play. The game must include the underhand throwing skill that has been taught in class. Students write a description of the game so students in another class could, after reading the information, play the game. They are also asked to describe how the critical elements of the skill might change when used in different conditions.

Criteria for Assessment

a. Game incorporates use of underhand throwing and catching skills.

b. Description of game adequately identifies needed skills and critical elements of each.

c. Description accurately describes how critical elements might change under varying conditions.

NASPE (1995, 35)

Throwing to a Moving Target

Setting: A large space; partners; one ball per pair

Cues

Throwing

Lead the Receiver	(Throw to an open space just in front of the catcher.)
Catching	
Know Where to Go	(Know where the throw is supposed to go and run toward that spot.)
Watch Passer, Then Ball	(Watch the passer as you start to run, and then after the ball is thrown, track it all the way into your hands.)

Tasks/Challenges:

This task is an example of a convergent guided discovery instructional approach.

(T) We are going to practice throwing the ball to your partner, who is moving. Your ultimate goal is to throw so your partner doesn't have to stop moving or turn around to catch the ball. The thrower should remain still; the catcher jogs away from the thrower. After six tries, trade places. *(Call the class together and ask where the ball should be so the catcher can keep moving. There will be multiple responses that include: to them and in front of them.)*

(T) Let's practice again. This time try to throw the ball to the receiver. Take five turns and trade places. *(Gather the class. How did that work? Could the catcher catch without having to stop? The answer is almost always no. What should we do? Throw the ball in front of the catcher.)*

(T) This time try to throw the ball in front of the catcher. After five tries, switch places. *(Ask the class, Was the catcher able to catch without stopping? Usual answer: Sometimes. Why? Our timing was off. Sometimes it went in front, and sometimes it didn't. How could we help that? Throw to a place in front of the catcher that both of us decide on.)*

(T) This time practice throwing to a place the two of you decide on. Seven times each and switch. *(How did that work?)*

T Instead of your partner running away from you, change so your partner is running across in front of you. **As before, you still throw the ball to a space in front of the runner; the runner is simply coming from a different direction.** Decide ahead of time where you are going to try to give the runner the ball. *(A similar line of questioning can be used here, if needed.)*

T There's one more way to practice this idea. This time the runner must be coming toward the thrower. **Again, target a space in front of the runner so the runner doesn't have to stop and turn around to catch the ball.**

T Until now, each set of partners decided where the catch was to be made. Now practice without deciding ahead of time where you'll throw the ball. This means the thrower will have to be very accurate with the throws, and the catcher will have to be always on the alert to catch the ball whenever and wherever it goes.

Assessment Example

From the National Standards for Physical Education

Teacher Observation/Observational Record

Students are asked to receive and send a basketball pass to a partner on the move. The teacher observes the passing and uses a checklist to annotate the performance.

Criteria for Assessment

a. Receives the pass and sends it in one motion.
b. Passes ahead of the moving player (receiver does not have to stop).
c. Receiving student cuts into a space to receive the pass.

NASPE (1995, 32)

Throwing for Distance and Accuracy

Setting: A large space; partners; one ball per pair

Cues	
Watch the Target	(Look at your partner the whole time.)
Side, Arm, Step, Follow	(For long throws you really have to do all of these.)
Almost Straight	(The ball should travel in a pathway that is almost halfway between the ground and straight up in the air—at about a 45-degree angle.)

Shooting a basketball is a version of throwing at a target.

Tasks/Challenges:

T The object of this task is to practice throwing and catching accurately to someone far away. You and your partner need to start throwing about 10 yards apart. Throw so your partner doesn't have to move to catch the ball. You want the ball to go straight to your partner.

T If you can throw successfully 10 times to your partner 10 yards away, each of you back up two giant steps and try again. Each time you can successfully make 10 throws, back up another two giant steps. Try to find your maximum distance.

✓ *Exit Slip.* This is a wonderful place to use an exit slip that asks each group of partners to evaluate the throwing and catching and plan an initial activity for the next class that will let students practice what they need to work on.

Shooting Baskets

In addition to throwing and catching in relation to others, the game of basketball involves a specific type of throwing at a target—shooting a basket. When children are first learning the skill of shooting baskets, the following cues will be helpful:

Preparation

- Keep eyes focused on the goal.
- Bend the knees.
- Keep elbows close to the body, not extended outward from the body.
- Place hands behind the ball, fingers (not palms) touching the ball.

Release

- Push the ball upward from the chest toward the basket.
- Extend legs as arms extend toward the target.
- Arch the ball upward and over the front rim of the basket.

Throwing at a Target from Different Distances

Setting: A large space; stationary targets in various places (against baseball backstops, trees, or playground apparatus) around the space

Cues

Watch the Target	(Look at the target the whole time.)
Side, Arm, Step, Follow	(For long throws you really have to do all of these.)
Almost Straight	(The ball should travel in a pathway that is almost halfway between the ground and straight up in the air—at about a 45-degree angle.)

Tasks/Challenges:

T The task is now to try to hit the target from far away. Start close enough so you know you can hit the target. When you hit it three times, back up about five steps and throw again. After five successful throws, back up again.

C See how far you can get and still hit the target.

C See how many throws out of 10 you can make right to the target.

Throwing Discs at Targets

Setting: A flying disc for each student; a flying disc golf course: Use hoops tied between two chairs or hoops suspended from trees as targets. The distance and angle of the targets from the starting lines can vary, depending on the amount of space available and the skill of the students. Trees, playground apparatus, fences, or backstops can be used as obstacles to throw over and around.

Cues

Watch Target	(Always look at the target.)
Throwing Side to Target	(The side of the arm you throw with should be facing the target.)
Arm Way Across Body	(Instead of bringing it to the back, bring the arm you throw with way across your body.)
Step with Same Foot	(This is one of the few times that you step toward the target with the foot on the same side as the arm you're throwing with.)
Follow Through	(Make your arm follow your throw toward the target.)

Tasks/Challenges:

T The name of this game could be Disc Golf. The object is to throw the disc for distance, and often around obstacles, eventually placing it through a target hoop. You want to use as few throws as possible. Here are the rules:

1. All players make their first throw from behind the starting line.
2. Players make the second throw and all throws after that from the landing spot of the previous throw. Players are allowed to take one step in throwing.
3. Players count how many throws were needed to place the disc through the hoop.

Assessment Example

From the National Standards for Physical Education

Self-Assessment/Check List

Following a period of working on throwing different types of objects (flying discs, footballs, deck tennis rings), students are asked to identify the number of different objects they have thrown and the types of throwing patterns they have used with these objects. They are also asked to do a self-assessment of their throwing performance using a check list provided by the teacher.

Criteria for Assessment

a. Recognizes difference in various types of throws.
b. Compares and contrasts throwing of different objects for different purposes.
c. Analyzes personal throwing skills accurately.

NASPE (1995, 47)

Lacrosse Sticks

The use of small lacrosse sticks is an exciting way to extend the skill theme of throwing and catching. Virtually all tasks in this chapter could be repeated with lacrosse sticks. The cues for the static throw would be:

Throw
Dominant (throwing) hand at the top of the stick; nondominant hand at bottom of stick
Nonthrowing shoulder toward target; throwing hand above shoulder
Step forward on opposite foot
Follow-through across body

Catch
Watch the ball into the pocket
Reach for the ball
Give or cradle the ball to reduce force

Catching to Throw Quickly to a Partner

Setting: Partners; one ball or beanbag per pair

Cues	
Move and Face	(Move toward the approaching ball and begin to face the direction you are to throw.) *It is helpful to demonstrate this cue.*
Flow	(The catch and the throw should flow together; simply move directly into the throw.)

Tasks/Challenges:

T Sometimes it is necessary to throw very quickly after you catch the ball, much as baseball players do when they are trying to make a double play. With your partner you are going to practice throwing quickly after catching. Your partner will throw the ball to you; you throw it back as quickly as pos-

sible, like a hot potato. The throw to your partner needs to be accurate as well as quick. To begin, one of you practices quick throws; the other one simply makes the first throw and is a target. After seven throws, switch places.

T When most of the throws go directly to your partner, back up a few steps and try the task again.

T Now, to make the task even harder, try to catch the ball with one hand and throw it with the same hand. This is almost as if you don't really want to hold the ball—as if you need to get rid of the ball quickly. You may want to use a beanbag for this task.

Catching to Throw Quickly to a Target

Setting: Partners; fairly large (2-by-2-feet) targets spread around the area

Cues	
Move and Face	(Move toward the approaching ball and begin to face the direction you are to throw.) *It is helpful to demonstrate this cue.*
Flow	(The catch and the throw should flow together; simply move directly into the throw.)

Tasks/Challenges:

T With your partner, you're going to practice catching and throwing quickly to a target. This skill is used, for example, in the game of team handball. Your partner throws you the ball; you catch it and quickly throw it to the target. You're trying for a quick throw so no one can block your shot. After six times, switch places.

C See how many times out of 10 you can hit the target. **Remember, quick throws only**; ones that stop don't count. Your partner is the judge.

Many of the throwing and catching skills at the utilization level can be transformed into gamelike situations for children. Some children at this level enjoy practicing in non-game contexts, whereas others are interested in practicing only if the skill is used in a gamelike situation. Generally, these are the children who continually want to know, "When do we get to play the game?"

Throwing While in the Air

Setting: A large grassy space; partners; one ball or beanbag per pair

Cues	
Face Target	(When you are in the air, your upper body should be facing the target.)
Follow	(Follow through to the target.)
Throw in Air	(Be in the air when you throw; don't jump, land, and then throw.)

Tasks/Challenges:

T Sometimes when you throw you need to be in the air. This type of throwing is harder than throwing when you're on the ground. To start, run a few steps, jump in the air, and throw the ball to your partner while you're in the air. Make the throw as accurate as possible.

T Often when people practice this task they aren't in the air when they think they are. Sometimes people run, throw, and then jump; sometimes they run, jump, land, and then throw. It's hard to tell exactly what you're doing without some help, so your partner's job is to watch you very carefully to see if you're really in the air as you throw. For now, your partner takes the place of the teacher—your partner must tell you exactly what he or she saw.

Proficiency Level: Learning Experiences Leading to Skill Development

Children are at the proficiency level of throwing and catching when they are able to throw and catch effectively in unpredictable, dynamic contexts. They are ready to practice throwing and catching as it's used in the relatively complex and changing environments in combination with other skills in gamelike situations. Experiences at the proficiency level include throwing and catching in relation to an opponent who attempts to prevent the throw or the catch. These tasks foster development of consistent degrees of accuracy and distance in throwing. Children learn to catch a variety of objects while traveling rapidly and suddenly changing direction and level.

Many of the activities at the proficiency level resemble traditional games. Yet they are designed to enhance skill development. Thus they are all designed to be played in small groups with multiple games being played at once. They are not designed to be played with large groups, for if we played with large groups, many students would be waiting and not participating. Strategies for achieving maximum activity in game settings are included in Chapter 30

A note about cues: At the proficiency level, tasks are more complex, typically requiring children to coordinate several movements simultaneously in a dynamic context. A list of cues is provided to assist the children in being more successful in the learning experiences. The challenge is in determining which cue will be most beneficial for each child . . . and when. Thus careful observation and critical reflection become very important as you watch the children move and then decide which cue will be the most helpful to move each learner to a higher level.

Throwing and Catching a Flying Disc in Different Places Around the Body with a Partner

Setting: A large space; partners; one flying disc per pair

Cues	
Catching	
Behind and Under	(Move so you are behind and under the disc when you catch it.)
Watch, Reach, Pull	(Watch the disc, reach for it, and pull it in to your body.)
Throwing	
Throw Away	(Pick a spot just barely out of your partner's reach and aim for it.)

Tasks/Challenges:

C The object of this activity is to throw the flying disc so your partner has to stretch to catch it. The scoring is this: If the flying disc is caught, that counts as one point. If the body is stretched a long way while reaching to catch the flying disc, that counts as three points. I'm going to throw a few to Mary. Let's watch to see how many points she'll get for each of her catches. (*Select a skilled catcher and throw, or have someone else throw the flying disc so the catcher has to stretch to make the catch.*)

C You may want to change the way you score the game. You can work together to see how many points you can make; or you may want to play against your partner. Remember, though, you'll have to make good throws if your partner is going to have a chance.

Throwing and Catching in a Field, Run, and Score Gamelike Situation

Setting: Two teams, four players each; four bases as in baseball; one ball

Cues

Watch Target	(Your eyes should always watch the target. This time it is the catcher's chest.)
Move and Face	(Move toward the approaching ball and begin to face the direction you are to throw.)
Flow	(The catch and the throw should flow together; simply move directly into the throw.)

Tasks/Challenges:

Ⓣ The object in this situation is to throw a ball around the bases twice before a runner can circle the bases once. Here are the rules:

1. The fielding team places a player at each base—first, second, third, and home plate.

2. The player at home plate (the catcher) begins with the ball. On the signal, two runners try to run the bases before the fielders throw the ball to each base twice.

3. If the runners travel the bases before the fielders throw and catch the ball twice, they score a run. If all the fielders throw and catch twice before the runners circle the bases, it's an out.

4. After three outs or when all runners have had a chance to run the bases twice, the teams switch roles.

Adjust the distance between the bases according to the throwers' ability and the runners' speed.

A Thematic Approach to Games

Almond (1986) proposed a thematic approach to classifying games that is now used in Tactical Games approach (Griffin, Mitchell, and Oslin, 2006). The approach, which classifies games according to conditions, goals, and tactics used to play the game versus individual sports, parallels the notion of skill themes, and we have chosen to use it here. Striking and fielding games involve games in which an object is struck into a space defended by players with accuracy and force so the striker can run between two points. Invasion games involve two groups invading the other's space to score, and net/wall games include those activities that require striking an object into court space so an opponent cannot return it. We have chosen to use these designations as they allow more options for youngsters without "trapping" them (or us) into preconceived notions of traditional games and allow for more conceptual transfer.

Throwing to Avoid a Defender

Setting: A 15-by-15-foot space; groups of three; one ball or beanbag per group

Cues

Throwing	
Lead the Receiver	(Throw to an open space just in front of the catcher.)
Quick	(Make your throw quickly, as soon as you know the receiver is open.)
Catching	
Move to Open Space	(Move to a space that is at an angle from the thrower.)
Watch Passer, Then Ball	(Watch the passer as you start to run, and then after the ball is thrown, track it all the way into your hands.)
Intercepting	
Hips	(To tell where a person is going to move, watch the hips or the belly button.)
Play the Ball	(Always go after the person with the ball—to force the person to pass it.)

It is very helpful to children to demonstrate the concept of moving away from the thrower at an angle of about 45 degrees (Figure 23.4).

Tip: When playing against a defense, the concept of catching changes to being able to catch while outmaneuvering the opponent. We assume that children at this point have mastered space awareness and dodging. The ability to move to an open space at an angle (approximately 45 degrees) away from the thrower is initially very difficult to understand. To get students to move away from the passer at an appropriate angle, a skilled soccer coach once provided these cues: *See the Passer, See the Ball, See as Much of the Field as Possible.* You may want to try using them.

Tasks/Challenges:

Ⓣ In this task, you'll practice throwing to someone against a defense. One of you is the thrower, one is the receiver, and the other one is the interceptor. Thrower, your job is to get the ball to the receiver. **Use quick moves, and get rid of the ball when you have a chance. Receiver, move to an open space to catch the ball. Interceptor, make them throw the ball, but don't forget that you are not**

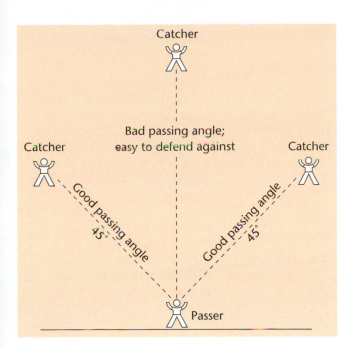

Figure 23.4 Passing angles for throwing against a defense.

allowed to touch the receiver or the thrower. After five throws, change places.

What is one strategy you can use to throw successfully when being defended? What can the catcher do to be successful in catching? What can you do to intercept the ball?

Throwing and Catching in a Small-Sided Invasion Game

Setting: Self-determined space; cones for markers; groups of three; one ball

Cues

Throwing

Lead the Receiver	(Throw to an open space just in front of the catcher.)
Quick	(Make your throw quickly, as soon as you know the receiver is open.)

Catching

Move to Open Space	(Move to a space that is at an angle from the thrower.)
Watch Passer, Then Ball	(Watch the passer as you start to run, and then after the ball is thrown, track it all the way into your hands.)

Intercepting

Hips	(To tell where a person is going to move, watch the hips or the belly button.)
Play the Ball	(Always go after the person with the ball—to force the person to pass it.)

Tasks/Challenges:

T This is really a Keep-Away-like game. One of you will be trying to take the ball away from the other two. Here are the rules:

1. Decide your boundaries and mark them off with cones.
2. You can only catch the ball in the air.
3. If you get the ball, trade places with the person who threw it.
4. You may run with the ball, but you can't keep it for longer than 5 seconds.

Throwing at a Stationary Object While Being Defended

Setting: Groups of six; six pins and one ball (Figure 23.5)

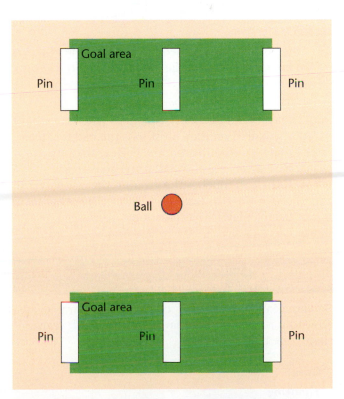

Figure 23.5 Setup for throwing at a stationary target while being defended.

Cues

Throwing

Lead the Receiver	(Throw to an open space just in front of the catcher.)
Quick	(Make your throw quickly, as soon as you know the receiver is open.)

Catching

Move to Open Space	(Move to a space that is at an angle from the thrower.)
Watch Passer, Then Ball	(Watch the passer as you start to run, and then after the ball is thrown, track it all the way into your hands.)

Intercepting

Hips	(To tell where a person is going to move, watch the hips or the belly button.)
Play the Ball	(Always go after the person with the ball—to force the person to pass it.)

Tasks/Challenges:

Ⓒ This task could be called Hit the Pin; the object is to knock over one of the other team's pin. Here are the rules:

1. There are three players on each side.
2. Players can take only two steps when they have the ball; then they must pass the ball to a teammate or shoot (throw the ball) at the pin.
3. No players are allowed in the goal area.
4. If the ball touches the ground, the last player to touch the ball loses possession. The other team begins play at that location.

Throwing and Catching in a Small-Sided Keep-Away Type Invasion Game

Setting: Half a basketball court or comparable area around a basket or large target on the wall; teams of three; one ball per court

Cues

Throwing

Lead the Receiver	(Throw to an open space just in front of the catcher.)

Cues

Quick	(Make your throw quickly, as soon as you know the receiver is open.)

Catching

Move to Open Space	(Move to a space that is at an angle from the thrower.)
Watch Passer, Then Ball	(Watch the passer as you start to run, and then after the ball is thrown, track it all the way into your hands.)

Intercepting

Hips	(To tell where a person is going to move, watch the hips or the belly button.)
Play the Ball	(Always go after the person with the ball—to force the person to pass it.)

Tasks/Challenges:

Ⓒ This is like a basketball game with one exception: It is all throwing and catching—no dribbling. Here are the rules:

1. When a player has the ball, the player must shoot it to the basket (or target) or pass it to a teammate. No dribbling or steps are allowed.
2. Every player must touch the ball before a shot.

Have the children focus on traveling, with changes in direction, when they don't have the ball. When they receive the ball, have them focus on getting rid of it quickly—to a teammate or toward the goal.

Throwing and Catching with a Flying Disc in a Small-Sided Invasion Game

Setting: Playing field *(see Figure 23.6 for set up)*; teams of two to four; one flying disc (alternatives: a ball or a beanbag)

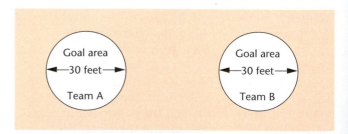

Figure 23.6 Setup for throwing and catching with a flying disc in a small-sided invasion game. There are no boundaries other than the two goal areas, each of which is 30 feet in diameter. Generally, the farther apart the goal areas can be placed, the more interesting the game is.

Cues

Throwing

Lead the Receiver (Throw to an open space just in front of the catcher.)

Quick (Make your throw quickly, as soon as you know the receiver is open.)

Catching

Move to Open Space (Move to a space that is at an angle from the thrower.)

Watch Passer, Then Ball (Watch the passer as you start to run, and then after the flying disc is thrown, track it all the way into your hands.)

Intercepting

Hips (To tell where a person is going to move, watch the hips or the belly button.)

Play the Ball (Always go after the person with the ball—to force the person to pass it.)

Tasks/Challenges:

C This task is like modified ultimate flying disc. The object is to catch the flying disc in the other team's goal area. Here are the rules:

1. When a player has the flying disc, he or she can take no more than three steps before passing it to a teammate.
2. A point is scored when a player catches the flying disc in the opposing team's goal area.
3. If the flying disc touches the ground, the team that touched the flying disc last loses possession. The opposing team puts the flying disc in play from that location. There is no out-of-bounds.
4. The flying disc can only be intercepted in the air. It can't be taken from someone's hands.

As you observe, you may see a need to stop the game and ask the children to practice throwing to a partner who's traveling or to reduce the difficulty by having the children practice two against two or two against one. The emphasis needs to be on leading the partner with the throw.

T To make the game a little harder, this time you always have to throw to a partner who is moving.

T To make the game a little easier, play two versus two or two against one.

Throwing and Catching with a Football in a Small-Sided Invasion Game

Setting: A large space with goals on each end, about 20 yards from midfield (size of the field depends somewhat on the type of ball being used; children must be able to throw the football into the other team's goal area); teams of two; a foam football

Cues

Throwing

Lead the Receiver (Throw to an open space just in front of the catcher.)

Quick (Make your throw quickly, as soon as you know the receiver is open.)

Catching

Move to Open Space (Move to a space that is at an angle from the thrower.)

Watch Passer, Then Ball (Watch the passer as you start to run, and then after the ball is thrown track it all the way into your hands.)

Intercepting

Hips (To tell where a person is going to move, watch the hips or the belly button.)

Play the Ball (Always go after the person with the ball—to force the person to pass it.)

Tasks/Challenges:

T This football game has just throwing and catching, no running with the foam football. You and your partner are a team. You try to throw the ball to your partner, who's being guarded by someone on the other team. Here are the rules:

1. Each team has four chances to throw and catch the ball in an attempt to move the ball from their goal line to the opposing team's goal area.
2. When on offense, one player is the thrower. He or she may not move forward. The thrower tries to accurately throw the ball downfield to her or his teammate, the receiver.
3. When on defense, one player tries to stay with the receiver to block or intercept the ball. The other player remains at the location where the play starts. That player counts aloud, "One alligator, two alligators," up to "five alligators," and then rushes the thrower, trying to touch the thrower or block the thrower's pass.
4. A play is over when the ball touches the ground or when a defensive player touches the offensive player who has possession of the ball.

Throwing, Catching, and Dribbling in a Small-Sided Invasion Game

Setting: A large open space (*see* Figure 23.7 *for setup*); teams of three or four; a 5-inch playground ball or team handball

Figure 23.7 Setup for throwing, catching, and dribbling in a small-sided invasion game. Goals can be made of stacked tires; semicircles can be spray-painted on the ground.

Cues

Throwing

Lead the Receiver	(Throw to an open space just in front of the catcher.)
Quick	(Make your throw quickly, as soon as you know the receiver is open.)

Catching

Move to Open Space	(Move to a space that is at an angle from the thrower.)
Watch Passer, Then Ball	(Watch the passer as you start to run, and then after the ball is thrown, track it all the way into your hands.)

Intercepting

Hips	(To tell where a person is going to move, watch the hips or the belly button.)
Play the Ball	(Always go after the person with the ball—to force the person to pass it.)

Tasks/Challenges:

T This game is a little like soccer because there's a goalie, but you throw the ball rather than kick it. The object is to throw the ball through the other team's goal. Here are the rules:

1. Players must stay out of the semicircle.
2. The goalie must stay in the semicircle. She or he tries to collect the ball to prevent it from going through the goal.
3. A player who has the ball can bounce it, pass it to a teammate, or throw it toward the goal. Once a player stops bouncing the ball, he or she must pass or shoot it; she or he can no longer dribble it.

Throwing and Catching While Using Simple Offense and Defense in a Small-Sided Invasion Game

Setting: A large open space (*see* Figure 23.8 *for setup*); teams of three; any type of ball or beanbag

Cues

Throwing

Lead the Receiver	(Throw to an open space just in front of the catcher.)
Quick	(Make your throw quickly as soon as you know the receiver is open.)

Catching

Move to Open Space	(Move to a space that is at an angle from the thrower.)
Watch Passer, Then Ball	(Watch the passer as you start to run, and then after the ball is thrown, track it all the way into your hands.)

Intercepting

Hips	(To tell where a person is going to move, watch the hips or the belly button.)
Play the Ball	(Always go after the person with the ball—to force the person to pass it.)

Tasks/Challenges:

T This game is a little like football. The object is to pass a ball to someone on your team who's in the other team's goal area. It helps to decide the type of pathways the receivers will be running before each play: straight, curved, or zigzag. Here are the rules:

1. The quarterback must remain behind the line spray-painted across the middle of the field. No defensive player may cross the line.

Figure 23.8 Setup for throwing and catching while using simple offense and defense in a small-sided invasion game. Adjust the dimensions of the field according to the children's ability.

2. The offensive team has three plays or attempts to have successful pass completions. Then the teams switch roles.

3. A point is scored each time a receiver catches the ball. Two points are scored when a receiver catches the ball in the end zone.

4. After each play, the ball is again placed at midfield.

5. No player may purposely bump or block another.

6. All players rotate to different positions after each play.

Assessment Example

From the National Standards for Physical Education

Journal

Students are asked to perform a self-assessment of their progress on throwing different types of objects (e.g., flying disc, football, softball, deck tennis rings) and record this information in their journal. Moreover, they should describe the differences and similarities in throwing these objects and discuss which objects were easy/difficult to throw.

Criteria for Assessment

a. Correctly identifies personal status on the use of critical elements of throwing.

b. Identifies differences and similarities that occur when applying principles of throwing different objects.

c. Describes which objects they found easy/difficult to throw.

NASPE (1995, 49)

Reading Comprehension Questions

1. Name the three styles of throwing. What type of task encourages children to practice overhand throws?

2. What does hip and spine rotation mean when throwing a ball?

3. What issues exist when children begin to throw at targets? Design a task that will alleviate the issues created by throwing at a target and illicit a mature throw.

4. What does throwing in a static context mean? Describe an example of a task that includes throwing in a static context and an example of a task that includes throwing in a dynamic context.

5. Why do we focus on throwing before catching?

6. Name two characteristics of an individual at the utilization level in catching.

7. What does tracking a ball mean? How can a teacher tell if a child is tracking a ball appropriately?

8. Rank the following tasks by placing the number 1 in front of the easiest (most basic) task, the number 2 in front of the next more difficult task, and so on.

   ( ) Throw and catch while using simple offense and defense in a small-sided invasion game.

   ( ) Toss up a beanbag and try to catch it with a plastic scoop.

   ( ) While running, throw a ball to a partner who's also running.

   ( ) Toss a yarn ball high in the air so you have to travel to catch it.

   ( ) Throw and catch with a partner.

9. What four cues do we use to remind children about the correct way of throwing a ball overhand? Explain the meaning of each cue.

10. What three cues do we use to remind children about the correct way of catching a ball? Explain the meaning of each cue.

References/Suggested Readings

Almond, L. 1986. Reflecting on themes: A games classification. In *Rethinking games teaching,* ed. R. Thorpe, D. Bunker, and L. Almond, 71–72. Loughborough, England: University of Technology.

Griffin, L., S. Mitchell, and J. Oslin. 2006. *Teaching sports concepts and skills: A tactical games approach.* 2nd ed. Champaign, IL: Human Kinetics.

Humphries, C., P. Lovdahl, and M. Ashy. 2002. Elementary physical education and the National Standards. *Journal of Physical Education, Recreation and Dance* 73(5): 42–45.

[NASPE] National Association for Sport and Physical Education. 1995. *Moving into the future: National standards for physical education.* St. Louis, MO: Mosby.

[NASPE] National Association for Sport and Physical Education. 2004. *Moving into the future: National standards for physical education.* 2nd ed. Reston, VA: National Association for Sport and Physical Education.

Young, D. B., and J. Langdon. 2011. *Moving to success.* Greenville, SC: DBY Publications.

Volleying and Dribbling

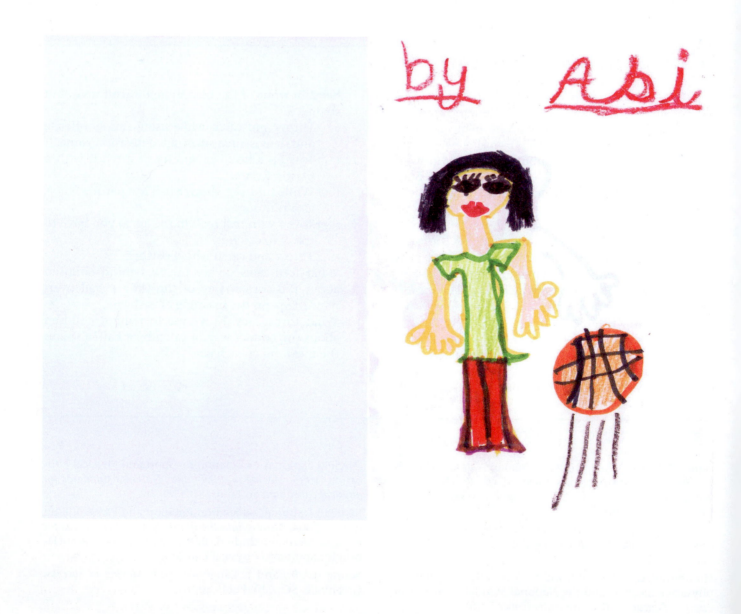

by Abi

The word *volley* brings images of a high net, two teams, and the sport of volleyball, but the skill of volleying is much broader, as proved constantly by children's creative games. Games designed by youngsters, games of different cultures, and innovative equipment have opened our eyes as teachers to volleybirds, foot bags, bamboo balls, and balzacs, as well as to Don't Bounce Count, Power, and Hand Bumping. Volleying is no longer limited to volleyball; dribbling is no longer confined to basketball.

Volleying

For our purposes, we define *volleying* as striking or giving impetus to an object by using a variety of body parts—for example, hands, arms, head, or knees. Dribbling is a subdivision of volleying. Although our discussion here is divided into two separate sections—volleying and dribbling—when teaching, you may choose to develop dribbling and volleying together. Volleying and dribbling are almost exclusively game skills and are used in such sports as soccer, volleyball, handball, basketball, and speedball. See Box 24-1 for linkages of the skill theme of volleying to the *National Standards for Physical Education*.

Children at the precontrol level of volleying are still struggling to achieve the hand–eye coordination required to contact a ball. They are rarely able to intentionally direct the flight of a ball when contact is made. Therefore at this level we provide a variety of activities for the exploration of volleying—balloons and lightweight balls to maximize visual tracking and success.

As the children are able to continuously strike the ball, challenges are presented with overhead and underhand patterns, volleying with different body parts,

Box 24-1

Volleying in the *National Standards for Physical Education*

The skill theme of volleying is referenced in the National Association for Sport and Physical Education's *National Standards for Physical Education* (NASPE 2004) under Standard 1: "Demonstrates competency in motor skills and movement patterns needed to perform a variety of physical activities." The standard speaks of the child's showing progress toward achieving mature form in manipulative skills (grades K–2)* and using the skills in dynamic and complex environments (grades 3–5).

*Grade-level guidelines for expected student learning.

Skill Theme Development Progression

Volleying

Proficiency Level

Volleying Game: Modified Teacher Designed Game
Volleying in a line formation
Striking downward with force
Volleying with different body parts while traveling

Utilization Level

Volleying over a high net (underhand pattern)
Volleying three-on-three
Volleying continuously to a partner
Volleying over a high net (overhead pattern)
Volleying to the wall—varying levels, force, and body position
Volleying with a volleybird
Volleying from head to foot: Aerial Soccer
Volleying with the foot
Volleying a ball continuously with different body parts
Volleying game: child-designed

Control Level

Obstacle-Course Volley
Volleying with a bounce
Cooperative volleys (overhead pattern)
Volleying to a partner (overhead pattern)
Volleying a ball upward (overhead pattern)
Volleying to the wall (overhead pattern)
Volleying over a low net (underhand pattern)
Volleying for direction and accuracy: Four Square, Two Square
Volleying for accuracy (underhand pattern)
Volleying a ball to a partner (underhand pattern)
Volleying a ball to the wall (underhand pattern)
Volleying a ball upward with the forearms
Volleying a ball upward (underhand pattern)
Volleying a ball noncontinuously with different body parts

Precontrol Level

Volleying lightweight objects
Volleying with different body parts
Volleying a balloon forward
Volleying balloons in the air

and volleying in a variety of contexts. Our goal is twofold: a mature pattern of volleying and expanding the repertoire of volleying skills for children, e.g., low nets, high nets, handball, four-square, foot bags, bamboo balls, and volleyball.

Give a child a ball, balloon, a volleybird, a foot bag—and they begin to bounce it on the ground/floor.

If it will not bounce, they immediately begin to volley in the air—sometimes upward, sometimes forward—with the hand, the head, the thigh, the foot. Thus volleying is the skill of striking with a body part; dribbling and kicking are forms of volleying. For our purposes dribbling and volleying are separated within this chapter; kicking and punting are in Chapter 22. Volleying for children is seen in the original playground games of Keep Away and Four Square. Volleying with a flat surface is Hand Ball; volleying with "crab fingers" is Volleyball. All of these stem from the skill theme of volleying.

Volleying is a major skill in many of our game situations. Efficient striking patterns are generally the last of the fundamental manipulative patterns to develop because of the fine perceptual and motor adjustments the child must make. Once the child does begin to strike an object, the range of possible activities is enormous. Our progression spiral for volleying (page 465) indicates activities and experiences at various levels, from precontrol through proficiency. The text ideas include suggestions for children at the different levels, and a range of activities and experiences within each level, stated directly. Remember, though, we encourage you to modify the suggested organizational structure to satisfy your objectives (see Chapter 10).

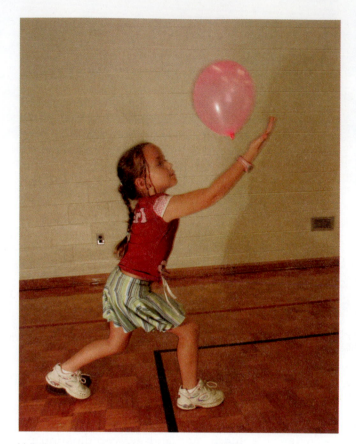

Volleying an object requires visual tracking.

Precontrol Level (GLSP): Activities for Exploration

At the precontrol level, children need a variety of activities involving the skill of volleying. As with all skills involving sending and/or receiving an object, they will need to watch the object as it approaches (and contacts) the hand or body part used for the volley. At this exploration level, variety is the focus; contact is the measure of success.

Volleying Balloons in the Air

Setting: Children scattered throughout general space, each with an inflated balloon and a carpet square (or poly spot) to designate self-space

Tasks/Challenges:

T Strike the balloon upward with your open palm so it stays in the air. Try to keep the balloon from touching the floor.

T Strike the balloon high above your head. Practice striking with both your right and your left hand so you will be equally good with each hand.

C See if you can volley the balloon 10 times without letting it touch the floor.

T Volley the balloon in the air, staying close to your carpet square or spot.

C As you volley in the self-space of your carpet square or poly spot, say one letter of the alphabet for each volley. Can you get to Z?

Volleying a Balloon Forward

Setting: Children scattered throughout general space, each with an inflated balloon

Tasks/Challenges:

T Strike your balloon in the air so it travels forward as you walk through general space.

T Strike your balloon so it travels forward as you walk in curved pathways. Can you travel in zigzag pathways as you volley the balloon?

C Travel across the gymnasium (blacktop area) as you volley the balloon forward. Can you complete your volley/travel without letting the balloon touch the ground?

✱ Where on the balloon is contact made for it to travel upward? Where is contact made for the balloon to travel forward?

Volleying with Different Body Parts

Setting: Children scattered throughout general space, each with an inflated balloon

Tasks/Challenges:

T Keep the balloon in the air by striking it with different body parts. How many different body parts can you use to volley the balloon upward?

T Volley the balloon upward by striking it with your head, then your hand. Try a combination of hand, elbow, head. Try alternate volleys from foot to hand.

C Count how many times you can volley the balloon before it touches the floor. Don't use the same body part two times in a row.

T Let's try a combination of more than two body parts. Volley the balloon with these body parts: hand, head, knee, elbow.

C Make your own combination of volleys using different body parts. You may choose a two-, three-, or four-body-part sequence.

Volleying Lightweight Objects

Setting: Children scattered throughout general space; a variety of lightweight objects for exploration of the volley—beach balls, lightweight plastic balls, balloons, foam balls, newspaper balls, and so forth

Tasks/Challenges:

T You have been exploring volleying with balloons—striking them upward in self-space and forward while walking slowly through general space. Now we will try the volley with different types of lightweight balls. Select the ball (or balloon) of your choice and volley it upward in your self-space. On the signal, you will exchange that ball or balloon for a different type (rotate each 2 to 3 minutes until the children have volleyed with each type of ball or balloon).

T When you begin to volley with some of the balls, you may wish to let the ball bounce after each volley; the skill then becomes "volley, bounce, volley, bounce. . . ." Remember, strike the ball upward when you volley.

T Let's try one more exploration: This time the sequence will be "volley, bounce, catch; volley, bounce, catch. . . ." Are you discovering that some types of balls are better for the volley; that some require volley, bounce; and that others require volley, bounce, catch?

As children become more skilled, they enjoy volleying with a small group.

T Count the number of times you can volley the ball or balloon before it touches the ground. Repeat the task for a second trial; remember to count your score. After two tries, switch to a different type of ball or a balloon. Which did you like best? Which one was easiest? Which gave you the highest score?

C Choose your favorite type of ball or balloon to volley. Choose your type of volley: continuous volley; volley, bounce, volley, bounce; or volley, bounce, catch. See how many times you can complete your volley sequence without a mistake.

Volleying with Lightweight Objects

At the precontrol and control levels, volleying activities are best done with larger, lightweight objects, such as beach balls, balloons, or inexpensive plastic balls. They float slowly, providing more time for visual tracking. This allows children time to move under the object and volley it without the fear that accompanies heavier objects.

Most equipment companies have also developed a large lightweight volleyball that provides an excellent progression from the very lightweight objects. These "trainer" balls are lighter in weight and larger, yet their flight is true; children at the utilization and proficiency levels of volleying are challenged by the trainers. None of these objects works outside well on windy days, however.

Control Level (GLSP): Learning Experiences Leading to Skill Development

At the control level, children learn an underhand and an overhead volley. They volley with different body parts, volley in relation to other people, and with a variety of objects. Children at this level still find that it helps to let the ball bounce between volleys so they can gain control of the volley; they will eliminate the bounce when they are ready to do so.

A note about cues: Although several cues are listed for many of the learning experiences, it's important to focus on only one cue at a time. This way, the children can really concentrate on that cue. Once you provide feedback to the children and observe that most have learned a cue, it's time to focus on another one.

Volleying a Ball Noncontinuously with Different Body Parts

Setting: Children scattered throughout general space, each with a lightweight ball (beach ball, foam ball, plastic ball)

Cues

Flat Surface	(Keep the striking surface—your leg, foot, hand—as flat as possible for contact.)
Extend to Target	(Extend upward as you contact the ball.)

Tasks/Challenges:

T Strike the ball upward with different body parts: foot, elbow, upper thigh, shoulder, head, hand. Catch the ball after each volley.

T Of the body parts you used for the volley, which parts can provide a flat surface for the volley? This time as you volley the ball upward, contact the ball with the flattest surface possible—foot, upper thigh, hand. Where is the contact surface for a head volley?

C Practice until you can do three single volleys, with a catch after each, without moving from your self-space. Practice with your foot, thigh, hand, head.

T Try your body-part volleys with a beach ball, a foam ball, a plastic ball. When you are comfortable with the upward volley, you may wish to try the skill with a playground ball or soccer ball.

Volleying a Ball Upward (Underhand Pattern)

Setting: Children scattered throughout general space, each with a beach ball, a foam ball, or an 8-inch plastic ball

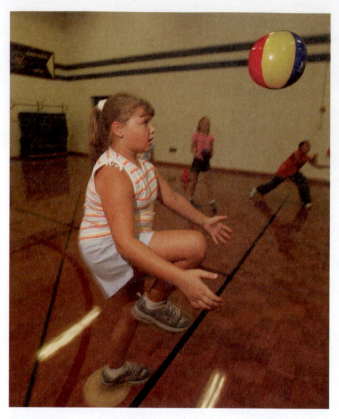

This youngster experiments with using the flat surface of the thigh to volley.

Cues

Flat Surface	(Extend your hand with your palm flat, like a pancake.)
Extend to Target	(Extend your hand upward on contact.)
Quick Feet	(Move your feet quickly to always be in position to volley the ball upward.)

Tasks/Challenges:

T Strike the ball with your hand, palm flat, so it travels directly upward. Where on the ball will you need to make contact if you want the ball to travel in a straight pathway upward?

T Volley the ball directly upward so you can catch it without moving from your self-space.

T Volley the ball directly upward a distance of 4 to 5 feet above your head.

C Practice until you can do this underhand volley five times, never leaving your space.

T Volley the ball upward continuously. Move your feet quickly to always be in position directly under the ball.

C Record your personal best for today by counting the number of consecutive volleys you can complete without a mistake.

✓ *Peer Observation.* This is an excellent time for a peer observation of critical cues, for example, "flat surface for volley," "quick feet to be in position under the ball." Peer assessment can also include verbal recall of cues and peer feedback for improvement. *See Chapter 12, "Assessing Student Learning," for development of peer observations.*

Volleying a Ball Upward with the Forearms

Setting: Children scattered throughout general space, each with a lightweight ball

Cues

Flat Surface	(Extend your arms forward, forearms together, to create a flat surface.)
Extend to Target	(Extend your arms upward on contact.)
Quick Feet	(Move your feet quickly to always be in position to volley the ball upward.)

Tasks/Challenges:

T Toss the ball slightly upward. Quickly extend your arms, bringing your forearms together to form a flat surface. Volley the ball upward above your head so it returns to you. Catch the ball after each volley. In volleyball this is called a *bump.*

T Toss the ball, and then volley (bump) it upward two times before you catch it again.

T How many volleys (bumps) can you do without a mistake?

Volleying a Ball to the Wall (Underhand Pattern)

Setting: Children spaced around the perimeter of the gymnasium, facing the wall at a distance of about 6 feet; a lightweight plastic ball for each child

Cues

Flat Surface	(Keep your palm flat, like a pancake.)
Extend to Target	(Extend your legs, body, striking arm toward the wall.)
Quick Feet	(Move your feet quickly to always be in position behind the ball.)

Tasks/Challenges:

T Bounce the ball one time, then strike it with your open palm, underhand volley, so it travels to the wall. As the ball rebounds from the wall, let it bounce one time and then catch it (Figure 24.1). **Where on the ball do you need to make contact for it to travel forward to the wall? Right, slightly below center and behind the ball.**

Select two children who are using the correct pattern to demonstrate for the class.

C Practice until you can execute the drop-hit-bounce pattern three times. Remember, catch after each sequence.

T Using the underhand action, strike the ball with your open palm so the ball contacts the wall 3 to 4 feet above the floor. Continue the volley after each bounce. The pattern will be this: volley, bounce; volley, bounce. . . . The ball will not always come back exactly to you; **move your feet**

Figure 24.1 Underhand striking pattern.
1. Hold ball in one hand, with feet in front-back stance.
2. Let ball bounce once. Bring hitting arm back so it's ready to hit.
3. As ball bounces back, hit it from underneath with open palm and with body extending forward.

quickly to be in position to extend toward the target as you volley.

C Count the number of volleys you can make without a mistake. A mistake is two bounces on the rebound or a volley that hits the ceiling.

T Practice the volley with each hand. When the ball comes to your right side, contact it with your right hand; when it rebounds to your left side, use your left hand.

T You have been practicing volleying to the wall by yourself. Now you are going to add a partner. The rules are the same, except after you volley the ball, your partner will take the next hit. You will be alternating volleys. **Now your quick feet will really be important!**

C See how many times you and your partner can volley without missing.

✓ *Peer Observation.* Partner work provides an opportune time for children to observe/assess the critical cues—for example, Flat Surface, Extend to Target. *See Chapter 12 for development of peer assessments.*

Volleying to a Partner (Underhand Pattern)

Setting: Sets of partners scattered throughout general space; tape line on floor between each set

Cues	
Flat Surface	(Keep your palm flat, like a pancake.)
Extend to Target	(Extend your legs, body, striking arm toward the target.)
Quick Feet	(Move your feet quickly to always be in position behind the ball.)

Tasks/Challenges:

T You'll be practicing underhand hits with your partner. Stand approximately 3 feet from the tape line and face your partner across the line. Using the underhand action, strike the ball so it crosses the line and bounces on the other side. Your partner will then volley the ball back to you so it bounces on your side.

T Practice striking the ball with each hand so you will be skilled with your right and your left hand.

C Cooperate with your partner to see how many times you can strike the ball back and forth over the line. Set a personal goal for your volleys over the line.

Volleying for Accuracy (Underhand Pattern)

Setting: Children with partners/three hoops and one lightweight ball for each group; arrange two of the hoops across from each other; place the third hoop in the middle (Figure 24.2)

Cues	
Flat Surface	(Keep your palm flat, like a pancake.)
Extend to Target	(Extend your legs, body, striking arm toward the target.)
Control	(Adjust your force to control the volley.)

Tasks/Challenges:

T You have been practicing the underhand volley, striking the ball to the wall and over a line. Today you will practice striking the ball to send it to a partner; however, the ball must bounce inside the middle hoop on its way to the partner! Remember, we are practicing the underhand pattern; that is the skill you must use in your game.

Volley the ball through the center hoop. You need to stay in your hoop, and you can volley the ball only after it bounces in the center hoop coming from your partner.

C See how many times you can keep the ball going without missing.

Volleying for Direction and Accuracy: Four Square, Two Square

Setting: Children's choice: Some children in groups of four (Four Square); others in groups of two (Two Square); squares marked off on the floor for the games (Figure 24.3)

Cues	
Flat Surface	(Keep your palm flat, like a pancake.)
Extend to Target	(Extend your legs, body, striking arm toward the target.)

Figure 24.2 Setup for Volleying to a Partner (Hoop Volley).

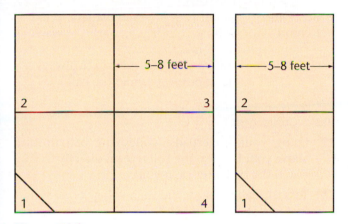

Figure 24.3 Four Square and Two Square courts.

Quick Feet	(Move your feet quickly to always be in position behind the ball.)

Tasks/Challenges:

T Stand outside your assigned square. Serve the ball by dropping it and hitting it underhand after the bounce. The server can hit the ball to any of the other three courts (Four Square). The player receiving the ball must keep it in play by striking the ball with an underhand hit to any square. Play continues until one player fails to return the ball or commits a fault. Faults include hitting the ball sidearm or overhand, stepping in another square to play the ball, catching the ball, and letting the ball touch any part of the body other than the hands. After each mistake, rotate positions and servers. (Use two squares for a two-person game.)

T Play your game cooperatively by counting the number of volleys made by your group before a mistake. Hit the ball so the person will be in the best position to contact it.

T Play the game competitively by changing force and angles of travel for the ball; however, the volley must be underhand—no sides, no overs. **The receiver will really need quick feet to move into position for the volley.**

✓ *Teacher Observation.* Game play provides an excellent setting for teacher observation of critical cues in dynamic situations, that is, alternative assessment. *See Chapter 11, "Observing Student Responses," and Chapter 12, "Assessing Student Learning," for examples.*

Volleying over a Low Net (Underhand Pattern)

Setting: Partners; nets at varying heights (lower standard nets or improvise nets from ropes (Figure 24.4) throughout the gym; one lightweight ball for each pair

Cues	
Flat Surface	(Keep your palm flat, like a pancake.)
Extend to Target	(Extend your legs, body, striking arm toward the target.)
Quick Feet	(Move your feet quickly to always be in position behind the ball.)

Tasks/Challenges:

T You have practiced the underhand volley against the wall and over a line on the floor. Now you are ready to use the same skill to send the ball over a net to a partner. The server bounces the ball one time and then sends it over the net with the underhand volley. The partner returns the volley after the ball bounces one time.

C When you are ready, keep a collective score of how many volleys you and your partner can do before making a mistake.

T Slant your net from high to low, and repeat the skill, volleying the ball over the net at differing heights.

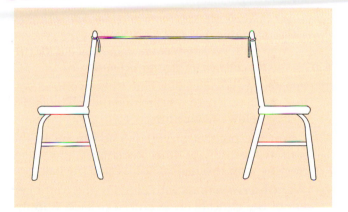

Figure 24.4 Construction of a net. Suspend a rope between two chairs.

T Practice varying the force with which and the angles at which you volley the ball to your partner. Remember, the ball must bounce one time on each side before the contact.

C Based on your scores from the collective game, set a personal goal and see if you and your partner can attain that goal for the underhand volley over the net. Remember, volley the ball so your partner will always be in the best position for the return.

T Challenge your partner to a competitive game of volleys over the net. Add to the challenge with changes in force and angles; however, the hit must be the underhand volley you have practiced.

Volleying to the Wall (Overhead Pattern)

Setting: Lines taped on the wall at heights of 5 to 7 feet; a lightweight ball or beach ball for each child

Cues	
Crab Fingers	(Curl your fingers for contact on the pads.)
Bend and Extend	(Bend your knees in preparation; extend your legs and arms upward on contact.)
Quick Feet	(Move your feet quickly to be in position behind and under the ball for contact.)

Tasks/Challenges:

T Stand approximately 4 feet from the wall at the tape height you choose. Toss the ball slightly in front and above your head, then volley it to the wall with both hands. Catch the ball after the volley and begin again.

Select two children who are contacting the ball with their fingerpads and using their legs for the force of the volley to demonstrate the key concepts of the skill. Point out the critical cues to the children as they are demonstrated.

C Practice until you can execute three overhead volleys to the wall without catching the ball or letting it drop below the tape line.

C Count the number of volleys you can hit to the wall above the tape line. Remember, the volley must be with two hands; don't catch the ball.

✓ *Peer Observation.* As with all skills, the continued use of the critical cues is crucial to success in dynamic situations. A peer observation assessment of critical cues with appropriate feedback for improvement would be useful here.

Volleying a Ball Upward (Overhead Pattern)

Setting: Children scattered throughout general space, each with either a beach ball or a lightweight plastic ball

Cues	
Crab Fingers	(Curl your fingers for contact on the pads.)
Bend and Extend	(Bend your knees in preparation; extend your legs and arms upward on contact.)
Quick Feet	(Move your feet quickly to always be in position under the ball.)

Tasks/Challenges:

T Using your fingerpads, volley the ball upward above your head so the ball returns directly to you. Catch the ball after each volley.

T Toss the ball upward, and then volley it one time 2 to 3 feet above your head.

T Toss and then volley the ball upward two times before you catch it.

C How many times can you volley the ball before it touches the ground?

T Toss and then volley the ball from medium level: Let the ball drop until it's 3 to 4 feet from the floor; then volley. This really requires you to bend your knees!

C Now that you know how to volley the ball at a lower level, count the number of times you can volley before the ball touches the floor.

Volleying to a Partner (Overhead Pattern)

Setting: Sets of partners scattered throughout general space; one lightweight ball for each set of partners

Cues	
Crab Fingers	(Curl your fingers for contact on the pads.)
Bend and Extend	(Bend the knees in preparation; extend the legs and arms upward on contact.)
Quick Feet	(Move your feet quickly to always be in position under the ball.)

Tasks/Challenges:

T Stand 3 to 4 feet from your partner. Using the overhead skill you just learned, volley the ball back and forth to your partner. Each of you gets two hits on your side: Volley the ball first to yourself for control and then to your partner.

T When you are comfortable with two volleys per side, try doing the task with only one hit per side.

C On the signal, begin your partner volleys. I will time you for 30 seconds. Try to continue without a mistake for the entire time . . . and beyond!

Cooperative Volleys (Overhead Pattern)

Setting: Groups of four or five children (the smaller the group, the more participation/practice of the skill each child gets); a lightweight ball (or a volleyball trainer—a larger, lightweight volleyball) for each group

> **Cues**
>
> **Crab Fingers** (Curl your fingers for contact on the pads.)
> **Bend and Extend** (Bend the knees in preparation; extend the legs and arms upward on contact.)
> **Quick Feet** (Move your feet quickly to always be in position under the ball.)

Tasks/Challenges:

T The object of the game Keep It Up is to see how many times your team can volley the ball before it touches the ground. There are only two rules: A player cannot hit the ball twice in a row, and the hit must be the overhead volley. Practice several times; then count your team volleys.

T Continue your cooperative volleys with your team, this time calling out the volley number as you contact the ball.

T This time as your group plays Keep It Up, be sure each person in the group does a volley before anyone takes a second turn.

C As a group, set a goal for the number of volleys you wish to attain, then play the game to see if you can reach that number without a mistake.

Keep It Up can be played with the forehand volley or with a combination of the forehand volley and the overhead volley.

✓ Teacher Observation. Cooperative games provide an opportune time for teacher observation of critical cues. *See Chapters 11 and 12 for development of teacher observation assessments.*

Volleying with a Bounce

Setting: Children in teams of equal numbers (three or four per team) on either side of a low net; a lightweight ball that will bounce

> **Cues**
>
> **Bend and Extend** (Bend the knees in preparation; extend the legs and arms upward on contact.)
> **Quick Feet** (Move your feet quickly to always be in position under the ball.)

Tasks/Challenges:

T A player begins the game by bouncing the ball one time and striking it over the net with an underhand serve (much like the underhand volley action). The receiving team may let the ball bounce one time before hitting it back (or may volley the ball with no bounce). Only one bounce is permitted before the ball is volleyed back over the net; however, any number of players may volley the ball before it crosses the net. You may use either the overhead volley or the forearm volley. The serving team scores a point when the receiving team fails to return the ball over the net within bounds or when the ball bounces more than one time.

Obstacle-Course Volley

Setting: Prior setup. (See Figure 24.5 for an example of a volley obstacle course.) Once the course is ready, the class pretty much runs itself. Challenges in the obstacle course can require a student to use a number of different volleying skills. It may be helpful to provide a number of different objects to volley in order to allow for differences in skill development.

Tasks/Challenges:

T Work your way through the course, following the instructions at each station. (This activity was adapted from Mustain 1990.)

Utilization Level (GLSP): Learning Experiences Leading to Skill Development

For continuing skill development in volleying, children must develop consistency and accuracy. They should be able to use various body parts to volley and move in relationship to other people and objects. Strategic placement skills in a relatively stable situation are developed at the utilization level.

A note about cues: Although several cues are listed for many of the learning experiences, it's important to focus on only one cue at a time. This way, the children

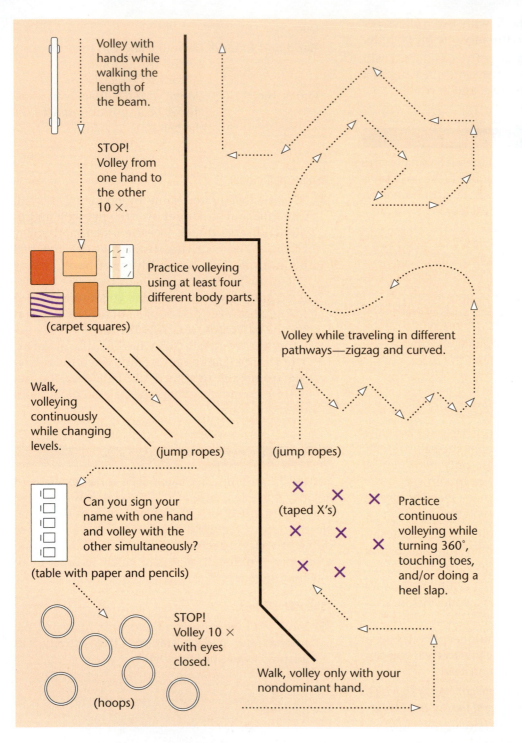

Volley with hands while walking the length of the beam.

STOP! Volley from one hand to the other 10 ×.

Practice volleying using at least four different body parts.

(carpet squares)

Walk, volleying continuously while changing levels.

(jump ropes)

Can you sign your name with one hand and volley with the other simultaneously?

(table with paper and pencils)

STOP! Volley 10 × with eyes closed.

(hoops)

Volley while traveling in different pathways—zigzag and curved.

(jump ropes)

(taped X's)

Practice continuous volleying while turning 360°, touching toes, and/or doing a heel slap.

Walk, volley only with your nondominant hand.

Figure 24.5 Setup for Obstacle-Course Volley. *Source:* Adapted from Wendy Mustain, A manual of elementary physical education skill theme activities for physical education specialists to use in collaboration with classroom teachers. Unpublished master's project, Virginia Polytechnic Institute and State University, Blacksburg. Used with permission.

can really concentrate on that cue. Once you provide feedback to the children and observe that most have learned a cue, it's time to focus on another one.

Volleying Game: Child-Designed

Setting: A variety of lightweight balls; paper and pencils for children to record their games

Cues

Flat Surface	(For underhand volley: Keep your palms flat, like a pancake.)
Extend to Target	(Extend your legs, body, striking arm toward the target.)
Quick Feet	(Move your feet quickly to always be in position under the ball.)

Tasks/Challenges:

T Earlier in our work you practiced striking the ball against the wall and over a line using the underhand volley—striking with an open palm. You are very good at that volley. Today you will use that skill in a game situation. Your task is to design an original game for two partners or a small group to provide practice of the underhand volley in a dynamic, on-the-move situation. You can design your game so it can be played against the wall or over a line on the floor. **Remember, the focus is the underhand volley; your game must use that skill.** You will need to decide the following:

- Will your game be against the wall or over a line?
- Will the game be cooperative or competitive?
- Will you keep score?
- How does a player score a point?
- Will the game be played with a partner or in a small group?
- What are the boundaries?
- What are the rules?

Record your game on a piece of paper so you can refer to it later and others in the class can learn how to play it. You may give your game a name if you wish (Figure 24.6).

Children not experienced in designing games will need more direction from the teacher and fewer opportunities to make decisions; for example, the teacher decides whether the game is against the wall or over a line and whether the game is cooperative or competitive. See Chapter 30 for more on child-designed games.

Striking a Ball Continuously with Different Body Parts

Setting: Children scattered throughout general space, each with an object suitable for the volley—plastic ball, soccer ball, playground ball, foot bag

Cues	
Flat Surface	(Keep the body part as flat as possible for contact.)
Bend and Extend	(Bend your knees to be in position for the head volley; extend upward on contact.)
Quick Feet	(Move your feet quickly to always be in position under the object.)

Tasks/Challenges:

T Volley the ball (foot bag) from your thigh to your foot by striking it with your upper thigh and then with the top of your foot. Catch the ball (foot bag) after the volley from your foot.

T Practice with your right leg and foot as well as with your left. You want to be equally skilled with both.

T When you are comfortable with the volley from your thigh to your foot (three times with no mistakes), add your head: In other words, volley the ball (foot bag) from your head—this is called heading in soccer—to your thigh to your foot, or from your head to your foot to your thigh.

T Now choose any three body parts to keep the ball (foot bag) going. See if you can keep it going from part to part without letting it touch the ground.

C This time you are going to see how well you can use different body parts for consecutive volleys. Choose the three body parts with which you like to volley. Try to keep the ball (foot bag) going with your three parts. Can you keep it going for 15 seconds? Thirty seconds? Sixty seconds?

What Is a Foot Bag?

A very popular game that has made a resurgence in the past few years is foot bag. Foot bags are small leather-covered (or crocheted) beanbag-type balls. The game requires a great deal of skill but delights children and adults for hours. Children at the utilization and proficiency levels will enjoy using a foot bag at times instead of a ball. Foot bags are relatively inexpensive and are great on the playground or field trips.

Volleying with the Foot

Setting: Children scattered throughout general space, with access to beach balls, plastic balls, and/or playground balls

Cue	
Flat Surface	(Make the inside, outside, top of your foot as flat as possible for the contact.)

Tasks/Challenges:

T Volley the beach ball with your foot, keeping the ball in the air for several contacts. Use the inside, outside, and top of your foot and your heel to send the ball upward.

T If consecutive volleys with the beach ball are easy, try the plastic or the playground ball.

C On the signal, begin your foot volley. I'll give the count each 10 seconds; keep the ball in the air as long as possible.

Hand Bumping

Object

You start out with ten points. And you try not to lose them.

You drop the ball and hit it.

Ember U., Maryh.

Name (of game): Don't Bounce Count ✓+
Name (of maker): Melanie Gillespi
Rules 1. Your ball moves in the wall
then *bounce once on the ground*
then hit...
2. You try not to earn points
3. When your ball bounces
   more than once you gain
   a point
4. When you get 21 points
   you lose.
5. You try not to
   get 21 points to win!
6. always keep the ball
   moving

Pomer

John Davis Peter Wiegand

We hit agensts the Wall. and let the Ball Bonch Onench, and the ather Parson hits it Agent the Wall

Figure 24.6 Child-designed games over a line (Hand Bumping) and against the wall (Don't Bounce Count; Pomer).

Volleying from Head to Foot: Aerial Soccer

Setting: Children scattered throughout general space, with 6-inch woven bamboo balls (or balls similar in texture, size, and weight)

Cues	
Flat Surface	(Make the foot surface as flat as possible for the contact.)
Bend and Extend	(Bend the knees to be in position for the head volley; extend the legs and body upward on contact.)
Quick Feet	(Move your feet quickly to always be in position for a good volley.)

Tasks/Challenges:

Ⓣ Practice your skills of heading, foot volleys, aerial kicks, and foot-to-head volleys with the bamboo ball. When you feel comfortable with the individual skills of Aerial Soccer and can keep the ball aloft for at least 10 seconds, you can play a game of Aerial Soccer with a partner or in a small group. The ball must stay aloft at all times. You will need to decide the following:

- Is the game to be cooperative or competitive?
- How many will be in the group? (Not more than six—three-on-three.)
- Will you play in self-space or travel in general space?
- What boundaries do you need?

This game was observed at Regent's Park in London, England. It's exciting for observers to watch and challenging for highly skilled soccer players.

Volleying with a Volleybird

Volleybirds are flat-bottomed shuttlecocks that have been used in Taiwan for centuries. The volleybirds are volleyed with different body parts, including hands, thighs, the instep of the foot, and the inside and outside of the foot. The volleybirds are flat bottomed, so they can also be caught on different body parts. Young children find these relatively slow moving and brightly colored "birds" very attractive.

Setting: Children scattered in general space, each with a volleybird

Cues	
Flat Surface	(Make your hand, thigh, foot surface as flat as possible for the contact.)
Quick Feet	(Move your feet quickly to always be in position for the volley—under the volleybird.)

Tasks/Challenges:

T See how many times in a row you can strike the volleybird before it touches the ground. Start with one hand; then try your other hand. Other body parts you can use are your thigh, the instep of your foot, or the inside or outside of your foot.

C Make up a sequence that uses three different body parts. See if you can repeat the sequence without a miss.

Striking to the Wall—Varying Levels, Force, and Body Position

Setting: Lines marked on the wall at heights of 3 and 7 feet; a variety of balls for a combination of volleying and bouncing (plastic balls, playground balls)

Cues	
Flat Surface	(Flat/open palm for contact.)
Extend to Target	(Extend your legs, striking arm, and body toward the target.)
Quick Feet	(Move your feet quickly into position for the volley.)

Tasks/Challenges:

T Strike the ball to the wall between the 3- and 7-foot tape marks so the ball contacts the wall at different levels. Strike the ball so it sometimes hits the wall at a high level, just below the 7-foot mark, and sometimes at a low level, just above the 3-foot mark.

T Vary your striking action; sometimes use an underhand strike, sometimes an overhead one.

T Vary the amount of force you use when hitting the ball. Sometimes hit the ball hard so it rebounds far from the wall; sometimes use just enough force to get the ball within the tape zones. How will the ball rebound this time? Right—close to the wall.

T Strike the ball from different positions in relation to your body. Contact the ball while it's high over your head, close to the floor, on your right side, on your left side. Being able to contact the ball from different positions is important in game situations when you don't always have enough time to get in position.

T With a partner, play handball. Your target is the area between the 3- and 7-foot tape marks. Try to strike the plastic (playground) ball to the wall so your partner can't return the shot. Challenge your partner to a game of 15 points.

Each time you select a partner, both of you should agree on the rules, including the outside boundaries, type of hits, how to keep score, and number of bounces permitted on the rebound. Possible rules include alternating hits and hitting the ball to a certain space on the wall.

T With a group of two or four, play Hand Corner Ball. (See Figure 24.7 for court setup.) The rules are these:

1. It can be a singles or a doubles game.
2. You serve by dropping the ball and underhand-volleying it against the wall.
3. The ball must contact the wall above the 18-inch line and rebound back into one of the three activity zones.
4. Volleying alternates between teams. In doubles play, it also alternates between players. So, if player 1 on team A serves and player 1 on team B returns it, player 2 on team A takes the next volley.

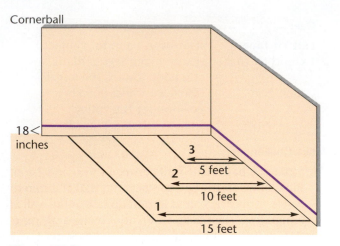

Figure 24.7 Setup for Hand Corner Ball.

5. If a team is unable to return the ball, the other team earns the number of points of the zone in which the ball landed.
6. A game is 15 points.

✓ *Videotape/Digital Analysis.* Game play at the utilization and proficiency levels provides an excellent opportunity for videotaping or digital picture analysis of performance and student self-assessment. Students assess themselves in authentic settings in relation to the critical cues of skills performed in dynamic environments.

Volleying over a High Net (Overhead Pattern)

Setting: Nets at a no greater than 7-foot height; a variety of beach balls, 8-inch plastic balls, and volleyball trainers

Cues	
Crab Fingers	(Curl your fingers for contact on the pads.)
Bend and Extend	(Bend your knees in preparation; extend your legs and arms on contact.)
Quick Feet	(Move your feet quickly to be in position under and behind the ball.)

Tasks/Challenges:

T Select a partner; stand on either side of the net, and face each other. Partner 1 tosses the ball over the net; partner 2 volleys the ball back over the net to partner 1 with the two-hand overhead hit. Partner 1 catches the ball and then tosses again. After 10 tries, partner 2 tosses, and partner 1 volleys.

T Volley the ball so your partner can catch it without moving from self-space.

T For this task, you will need four people, two on each side of the net. One of you will be on the court, and the other waits behind the end line. The activity is almost the same as the last one, with one exception: After you hit the ball, you run off the court, and the person behind comes up to return the shot. Then, that person runs off the court, and you come back on (Figure 24.8). The game goes very quickly, so you must be ready to move as soon as your partner hits the ball.

T Now that you understand the basics of the activity, let's make one change: You may choose to let the ball bounce on your side and then use a forearm volley, or you may choose to take the volley before the bounce with an overhead volley. **Remember the cue for the forearm volley—Flat Surface with Forearms.**

Volleying Continuously to a Partner

Setting: Nets at no greater than 7-foot height; a variety of beach balls, 8-inch plastic balls, and volleyball trainers

Cues	
Crab Fingers	(Curl your fingers for contact on the pads.)
Bend and Extend	(Bend your knees in preparation; extend your legs and arms on contact.)
Quick Feet	(Move your feet quickly to be in position under and behind the ball.)

Figure 24.8 Two-person running volley.

Tasks/Challenges:

T Partner 1 tosses the ball slightly above the head, then volleys the ball over the net to partner 2. Partner 2 volleys the ball back over the net. Continue to volley, using the overhead volley for balls at both high and medium levels.

C Set a personal best goal with your partner. See if you can attain that goal. Give your partner your best volley each time.

The above tasks/challenges can be used for continuous volleys with the underhand volley (the bump) or a combination of overhead and underhand volleys. Review with the children the differences between the critical cues for the overhead and the underhand volleys.

Volleying Three-on-Three

Setting: Children in groups of six, with three on each side of the net (Figure 24.9)

Cues	
Crab Fingers	(Curl your fingers for contact on the pads.)
Bend and Extend	(Bend your knees in preparation; extend your legs and arms on contact.)
Quick Feet	(Move your feet quickly to be in ready position for the ball.)

Tasks/Challenges:

T Use only the overhand volley to hit the ball in the air three times on your side of the net. On the third contact, volley the ball over the net to the other team. Each team volleys the ball three times, sending it over the net on the third hit. A different player makes each one of the three hits.

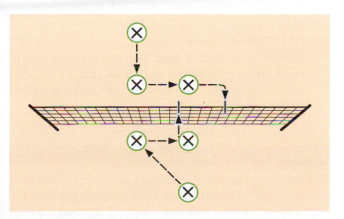

Figure 24.9 Three-on-three volleys: two patterns.

T Rotate positions, so you hit the ball from different places.

C Work cooperatively to keep the ball in the air as long as possible. Remember: three hits per side, one hit per person.

T Challenge the other team to a three-on-three game. Rather than cooperating to keep the ball in the air, use strategies to outscore the other team. Rather than just hitting the ball over the net, direct it to a certain location; vary the amount of force on the volley, sometimes sending it just over the net, sometimes sending it deep into the court. A point is scored when the ball hits the floor or lands out of bounds.

Volleying over a High Net (Underhand Pattern)

Setting: Lines marked on the wall 7 feet from the floor; nets at a no greater than 7-foot height; plastic balls and volleyball trainers

Cues	
Watch the Ball	(Watch the ball until the striking arm contacts it.)
Extend to Target	(Extend the striking arm toward the target—over the net.)

Tasks/Challenges:

T You learned the underhand action of striking the ball with your open palm, swinging your arm forward/backward, stepping forward on your opposite foot, and contacting the ball slightly below center and back. Now you're going to modify that skill slightly for the underhand action of a volleyball serve. Stand 10 to 15 feet from the wall; serve the ball to the wall; your target is the area just above the 7-foot tape line. *(Model)*

Distance from the wall/net for the service is determined by the children's skill; modify the distance for success, gradually increasing the challenge.

T I'll walk around and observe the underhand action of your serve. When it's correct and you feel successful, select a partner for practice over the net. Partner 1 stands 10 to 15 feet from the net and serves the ball over the net. Partner 2 retrieves the ball and then serves it back over the net.

T After you feel successful serving over the net, your partner will select a position on the court and stand in that spot. Serve the ball away from your partner so your partner can't catch the ball without moving from self-space.

The last task may seem a bit backward from "what has always been done." It is. When children begin by "serving" to a partner, they tend to do the same thing in a game situation—the exact opposite response from the one required. This way, we get them to practice serving to an open space early on.

> For children at the proficiency level of volleying with a ball who are interested in progressing to a teacher designed game with volleyball skills, USA Volleyball provides developmentally appropriate, school based educational programs. See USA Volleyball School Programs (http//usavolleyball.org) for more information about these programs.

Proficiency Level (GLSP): Learning Experiences Leading to Skill Development

Children at the proficiency level should be able to move consistently and accurately in relation to others and to react effectively to increasingly dynamic and unpredictable situations. They can simultaneously focus on volleying and on the game activity around them.

A note about cues: At the proficiency level, tasks are more complex, typically requiring children to coordinate several movements simultaneously in a dynamic context. A list of cues is provided to assist the children in being more successful in the learning experience. The challenge for the teacher is in determining which cue will be most beneficial for each child . . . and when. Thus careful observation and critical reflection become very important as you watch the children move and then decide which cue will be the most helpful to move each learner to a higher skill level.

Striking with Different Body Parts While Traveling

Setting: A variety of lightweight balls: 8-inch plastic, foam, volleyball trainers

Cue	
Quick Feet	(Move your feet quickly to always be in position to volley the ball.)

Tasks/Challenges:

Ⓣ Travel the length of the gym, volleying the ball with different body parts as you go. Don't catch the ball at any time, and don't let it touch the floor.

Ⓣ Select a partner. Travel throughout general space, volleying the ball back and forth with different body parts. Both of you should always be moving.

Ⓣ This time as you travel and volley with your partner, vary the level of the volley—sometimes high, sometimes medium level. **Remember, Flat Surface, Quick Feet.**

Striking Downward with Force

Setting: Tape lines on the wall at about 7 and 2 feet from the floor; a variety of lightweight balls for individual practice

Cues	
Quick Feet	(Move your feet quickly to always be in position to volley the ball; transfer your weight forward as you volley.)
Up, Up, Up, Down Soft, Soft, Soft, Hard!	(Volley the ball up, up, up, down; soft, soft, soft, hard.)

Tasks/Challenges:

Ⓣ Standing 10 to 12 feet from the wall, begin volleying the ball between the tape lines, using the underhand pattern; you may or may not include a bounce with the volleys. After several volleys, strike the ball on top so it travels downward to the wall, contacting the wall just above the 2-foot tape line. Contact the ball with your hand slightly cupped. *(Demonstrate.)*

Ⓣ Practice a pattern of three underhand volleys followed by a downward hit with force.

Ⓣ Challenge a partner to a handball game against the wall. Throughout the game, use a combination of forceful downward hits and underhand volleys.

Ⓣ Challenge the same partner to a competitive Two Square game over a line. Use the forceful downward striking to create situations that move your partner/opponent out of position, making a good return more difficult.

Volleying in a Line Formation

Setting: Tape marks on the wall at a height of about 7 feet; groups of four, each in a line formation facing the wall and 3 to 4 feet from it; a variety of lightweight balls (8-inch plastic, Nerf, volleyball trainers)

Cues

Crab Fingers	(Curl your fingers for contact on the pads.)
Quick Feet	(Always keep your feet on the move to be in position for the volley.)
Bend and Extend	(Bend the knees in preparation; extend the arms, legs, and body toward the target on contact.)

Tasks/Challenges:

Ⓣ The first person in your line volleys the ball to the wall so it contacts the wall above the tape line; then that person moves quickly to the back of the line. The second person volleys the ball to the wall, moves quickly to the back, and so on. The objective is to keep the volley going. Don't let the ball touch the floor or touch the wall below the tape mark.

Ⓒ Count the number of volleys your team can complete without a mistake.

Ⓣ Continue the line volley, with each person calling "mine" just before he or she contacts the ball.

Ⓣ Remaining in your group of four, face another group, with approximately 10 feet between the two leaders. Team members line up behind the leaders. One leader tosses the ball to the leader of the other team; that leader then volleys the ball back and quickly moves to the end of the line. This game is very similar to the volley against the wall: Each person volleys and then moves to the end of the line. The objective is to keep the volley going between the teams.

Volleying Game: Modified Teacher Designed Game

Setting: Teams of four or six, depending on space available *(place an equal number of children with comparable skills on each team; the size of the court and the height of the net are determined by the players' skill)* a beach ball, plastic ball, or oversized volleyball

Cues

Quick Feet	(Always keep on the move to be in position for the volley.)
Bend and Extend	(Bend the knees and arms in preparation; extend the arms, legs, and body toward the target on contact.)

Offense	
Open Space	(Hit to the open space.)
Defense	
Ready	(Bent knees, ready hands.)

Tasks/Challenges:

Ⓣ The game begins with a serve from the back boundary line; you will have two chances to serve the ball successfully over the net. In a regulation volleyball game, the ball may be hit only three times on a side; we'll decide as a class if we want three hits per side or unlimited. *(Discuss; vote.)* Getting unlimited hits per side increases the volley practice and the overall physical engagement in the game. Here are the guidelines for play:

1. You can contact the ball only one time and then someone else must volley the ball before you volley again.
2. Remember, you score a point only if your team is serving.
3. A serve that touches the net is no good; a ball in play is good even though it touches the net.
4. Although this is not an official rule, try to use the skills you learned, such as the two-hand volley. Use one hand only for the serve.

The purpose of the game today is to practice the overhead and forearm skills of volleying we have learned. We will rotate positions so everyone plays each spot on the court.

Dribbling

Give children balls that bounce and what happens? More often than not, they bounce them. *Dribbling* is striking or bouncing downward, generally with the hands. An important skill theme to develop, dribbling most often leads to participation in the traditional sport of basketball whether in recreational pick-up games or more organized competition. Dribbling also plays a prominent role in team handball, speedball, and netball. Yet, because its possible uses are endless, we focus on it as one aspect of volleying (or striking) rather than as a sport-specific skill. Children enjoy working with bouncing and dribbling skills and will spend many hours practicing the finest details. Remember, though, that dribbling, as a skill—like volleying upward—is one of the last fundamental skills to develop because it requires fine hand–eye coordination and the control of two objects that do not come to rest. Our progression spiral for dribbling appears on the page. Dribbling a ball on the floor or ground, as in soccer, could have been included in this chapter, but because it's also a kicking skill, we have included it in the kicking and punting discussion (Chapter 22). Refer to Box 24-2 for linkages of the skill theme of dribbling to the *National Standards for Physical Education (NASPE, 2004)*

Skill Theme Development Progression

Dribbling

Proficiency Level

Child-designed invasion games
Dribble/Pass Keep-Away
Dribbling and throwing at a target
Child-designed dribbling/passing routines
Maintaining possession while dribbling and passing
Dribbling while dodging
Dribble Tag
Dribbling against opponents: Moving defenders
Dribbling against opponents: Stationary defenders

Utilization Level

Dribbling against an opponent: One-on-one
Dribbling and passing with a partner
Mirroring and matching while dribbling
Dribbling around stationary obstacles in limited space
Dribbling around stationary obstacles in general space
Dribbling while stopping, starting, and turning (pivots and fakes)
Dribbling in different pathways
Dribbling in general space while changing directions
Dribbling and changing speed of travel

Control Level

Dribbling, traveling, and switching hands
Dribbling and traveling
Dribbling while changing directions in self-space
Dribbling in different places around the body while stationary
Dribbling with the body in different positions
Dribbling while switching hands
Dribbling and looking
Dribbling at different levels
Continuous dribbling
Dribbling in self-space

Precontrol Level

Dribbling and walking
Bouncing a ball down (dribbling) continuously
Bouncing a ball down and catching it

Box 24-2

Dribbling in the *National Standards for Physical Education*

The skill theme of dribbling is referenced in the National Association for Physical Education's *National Standards for Physical Education* (NASPE 2004) under Standard 1: "Demonstrates competency in motor and movement patterns needed to perform a variety of physical activities." The standard speaks of the child developing the mature motor skill in isolation and in combination with other actions and being able to use the skill in a dynamic situation.

Sample performance outcomes include:

- Drops a ball and catches it at the peak of the bounce (K–2)*
- Dribbles and passes a basketball to a moving receiver (3–5)*
- Dribbles a ball while preventing an opponent from stealing the ball (6–8)*

*Grade-level guidelines for expected student learning.

Precontrol Level (GLSP): Activities for the Exploration of Dribbling

At the precontrol level, children explore dribbling from a stationary position with a ball that has a good deal of bounce; they also explore walking and dribbling. We want children to strike down a ball repeatedly without losing the ball from self-space. When the children are able to do this, we add limited dribbling while walking. Relatively light balls—8-inch rubber playground balls or rubber basketballs—that bounce true (i.e., they aren't lopsided) are best for introducing children to dribbling. Be careful when inflating balls: Too much air equals too much bounce for control.

Bouncing a Ball Down and Catching It

Setting: Children scattered in general space, each with a ball

Tasks/Challenges:

Ⓣ Bounce the ball down in front of you so it comes straight back up to you. Catch it when it comes up.

Ⓣ Try bouncing the ball with two hands.

Ⓣ Now try bouncing with one hand.

Ⓣ Try bouncing with the other hand.

It is difficult for children at the precontrol level to dribble continuously.

Bouncing a Ball Down (Dribbling) Continuously

Setting: Children scattered in general space, each with a ball

Tasks/Challenges:

T Bounce the ball with both hands so it keeps going. This bounce that keeps going is called a dribble.

T Try dribbling the ball with one hand.

T Now try the other hand.

C Can you bounce three times in a row?

T Try changing from one hand to the other.

Dribbling and Walking

Setting: Children scattered in general space, each with a ball

Tasks/Challenges:

T Bounce the ball with two hands and catch as you walk forward slowly.

T Try bouncing the ball with one hand while you walk forward slowly.

C See if you can take three steps without losing the ball.

Control Level: (GLSP) Learning Experiences Leading to Skill Development in Dribbling

At the control level, children are introduced to varying their dribble while at the same time learning to use the nondominant hand. They'll also be able to dribble in different places around their bodies and dribble and travel while varying both direction and pathway. Some tasks very similar to those suggested for the precontrol level are repeated at the control level for continued practice and added skill development.

A note about cues: Although several cues are listed for many of the learning experiences, it's important to focus on only one cue at a time. This way, the children can really concentrate on that cue. Once you provide feedback to the children and observe that most have learned a cue, it's time to focus on another one.

Dribbling in Self Space

Setting: Children scattered throughout general space, each with a ball

Cues	
Fingerpads	(Remember to use the soft parts of your fingers.)
Knees Bent	(As you dribble, bend your knees a little, keeping your back straight, just like you are sitting down a little.)
Hand on Top of Ball	(Make sure your hand touches the ball almost on its top.)
Forward–Backward Stance	(The foot of the hand you are not dribbling with should be a little in front; see Figure 24.10.)

Tasks/Challenges:

T Dribble the ball with one hand.

T Dribble the ball with the other hand.

C Count the number of times you can dribble without losing control.

T On the signal, begin dribbling with one hand. Continue dribbling until the signal is given to stop.

Figure 24.10 Correct hand and body position for dribbling a ball.

Have children repeat each task with their nondominant hand throughout all levels of the skill. The proficient dribbler is equally skilled with each hand.

Continuous Dribbling

Setting: Children scattered in general space, each with a ball (either a smaller basketball or a playground ball)

Cues	
Fingerpads	(Use the soft parts of your fingers near the end to dribble, not the very ends.) *(Demonstrate.)*
Knees Bent	(As you dribble, bend your knees a little, keeping your back straight, just like you are sitting down a little.)
Hand on Top of Ball	(Make sure your hand touches the ball almost on its top.)

Tasks/Challenges:

T Remember when you bounced a ball down so it came back up to you and then pushed it down again so the bounce continued? This continuous bounce is called a dribble. Practice dribbling now.

C Practice until you can dribble the ball five times without losing control of it.

C Say one letter of the alphabet for each time you dribble. Can you get to Z?

Tip: Children tend to dribble either with the whole palm or with the ends of the fingers. Besides using the term fingerpads, we have also found it useful to put chalk or tape on the fingerpads to help children learn the correct part of their fingers to use.

✿ Point to which parts of your fingers are used for dribbling.

From the National Standards for Physical Education

Student Drawing

Students are provided with a drawing of a handprint and are asked to color the portion of the hand used in mature dribbling. Students may also be asked to draw an entire person dribbling to show the overall critical elements of this movement task.

Criteria for Assessment

a. Correctly identifies position of hand used in mature dribbling.
b. Identifies the critical elements of dribbling.

NASPE (1995, 20–21)

Dribbling at Different Levels

Setting: Children scattered throughout general space, each with a ball

Cues	
Knees Bent	(Make sure that your knees are bent just slightly.)
Firm, Flexible Wrists	(Make sure that your wrists are strong and bendable.)
Hand on Top of Ball	(Make sure your hand touches the ball almost on its top.)

Tip: The preceding cues focus on the skill of dribbling. At the same time it is necessary to check to see if children are also dribbling at the appropriate level. The cues would then change to high, medium, and low.

Tasks/Challenges:

T Staying in self-space, dribble the ball with your preferred hand. Continue dribbling until you hear the signal to stop.

T Dribble the ball at a low level so it bounces only to your knees. Keep your body in a standing position; don't kneel or squat to the floor.

T Dribble the ball so it rebounds to a level between your waist and your knees. This medium-level dribble is the one most often used in games and the one we will concentrate on throughout our work.

T On the signal, begin dribbling the ball at waist level. Continue dribbling until you hear the drumbeat. Stay in your self-space.

✿ How do the cues for dribbling change at the different levels?

Dribbling and Looking

Setting: Children scattered in general space, alone at first and later with partners, each child with a ball for dribbling

> **Cue**
>
> **Look Up** (You may want to find a spot on the wall to look at to help you look up. Just glance down at the ball sometimes to check on it.)

Tasks/Challenges:

T Begin dribbling the ball, then raise your head and continue dribbling without looking at the ball. Your peripheral vision enables you to look straight ahead and still see the ball. Your peripheral vision is your ability to see things at the edges of your field of vision and straight ahead at the same time. This is extremely important in a game involving dribbling.

T For this task you will need a partner, and each one of you will need a ball. Face your partner; decide which one of you will be the first leader. The leader starts dribbling at any level he or she wants; the partner must follow by dribbling at any other level than the level at which the leader is dribbling. For example, if the leader is dribbling at a high level, the partner can dribble at a low or a medium level. The leader can change levels after three dribbles at the same level. Use quick changes of level to try to fake your partner. When you hear the signal (about 30 seconds), change leaders. How many times before the signal can you catch your partner dribbling at the same level as you are?

✓ *Peer Observation.* Dribbling at the control level lends itself to partner assessment. Check cards (index cards with the critical cues listed) can be used. The observer calls out how the partner is to dribble (e.g., low and right-handed) and then checks off the critical cues that are used. Any combination of movement concepts can be combined with dribbling. *See Chapter 12 for examples of peer observation cards.*

Dribbling While Switching Hands

Setting: Children scattered in general space, each with a ball for dribbling

> **Cue**
>
> **Hand to Side of Ball** (Keep your hand a little behind and to the outside of the ball.)

Figure 24.11 Changing hands while dribbling.

Tasks/Challenges:

T Begin dribbling with your preferred hand. After several dribbles, switch to the other hand and continue dribbling. Don't catch the ball; simply switch from dribbling with one hand to dribbling with the other.

T Begin dribbling with your preferred hand. Dribble five times, and then switch to your other hand. Continue to switch after five dribbles per hand. **One change here from the regular dribbling hints: Instead of having your hand directly on top of the ball, it is helpful to push the ball from the side when you want to change dribbling hands** (Figure 24.11).

C On the signal, begin dribbling with your preferred hand. Each time you hear the drumbeat, switch hands. Continue to dribble and switch hands on each drumbeat until you hear the signal to stop.

✱ When switching hands while dribbling, how does your hand position on the ball change?

Dribbling with the Body in Different Positions

Setting: Children scattered in general space, each with a ball

> **Cues**
>
> **Firm, Flexible Wrists** (Remember the strong, bendable wrists we used before—they are really important now.)
>
> **Ball: Side and Front** (Keep the ball a little in front of your body and out to the side.)

Tasks/Challenges:

T Assume a kneeling position. Balance on one knee and one foot, with your body at a low level. Dribble with one hand while you maintain the balanced position.

T Dribble while in a squat or tuck position, balanced on both feet at a low level.

C Balance in different positions, dribbling with one hand. Create three different positions in which you can dribble with either your right or left hand.

T Begin dribbling in a standing position. Continue to dribble as you change your position to a low level— a kneeling or squatting position. Continue changing body positions while maintaining the dribble.

Choose several children to demonstrate the combinations of body positions they assume while dribbling.

Dribbling in Different Places Around the Body While Stationary

Setting: Children scattered in general space, each with a ball for dribbling

Cues	
Ball Close to Body	(Remember, the ball should be close to your body so you don't lose it.)
Firm, Flexible Wrists	(Your wrists have to be really strong and bendable for this dribbling—floppy will not work.)

Tasks/Challenges:

T Standing in self-space, dribble the ball in different places around your body: on your right, on your left, behind your legs. **As you dribble, remember to keep the ball close to your body.**

T Begin dribbling with your right hand; after several dribbles, bounce the ball under your right leg from back to front, and continue the dribble with your left hand. **The hand position will be like that for switching hands, a little to the side of the ball.**

T Practice the skill from right to left and from left to right until you can execute it in both directions.

T Dribble the ball directly in front of your body; bounce the ball between your legs from front to back. **You will need to twist your body to recover the dribble in the back.**

T Can you dribble the ball from back to front?

C Put together a dribbling sequence of all the ways you can dribble in self-space: in front, to the side, in back, around your body, between your legs. Remember, change levels as you go and to find different positions balanced on different parts.

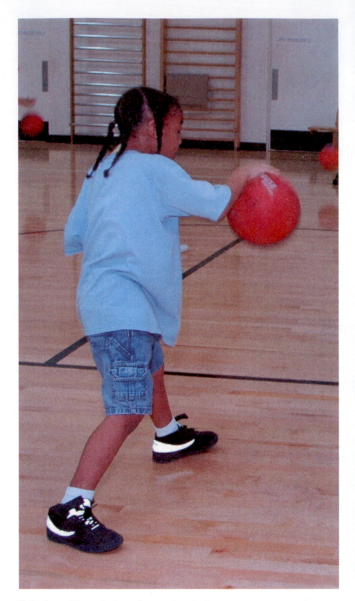

Dribbling with control requires concentration.

J **Exit Slip.** This might be a good time to include an exit slip to assess students' knowledge of different positions, places around the body, and levels, as well as a self-assessment of skill. A possible exit slip could ask children to write out the dribbling sequence they performed, indicating which positions were easy and which they will want to practice in the future.

Dribble While Changing Directions in Self-Space

Setting: Children arranged in a scattered formation, about 3 to 4 feet apart, all facing the same direction (Figure 24.12); teacher at the front of the group, facing the children

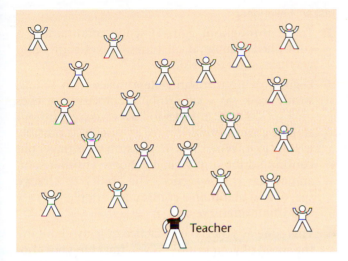

Figure 24.12 Formation for practicing dribbling and moving in directions the teacher suggests.

Cues

Hand Position   (The hand positions we used before are important here. If you want to go to the side, your hand is on the side; to go forward, hand behind; to go backward, hand in front.)

Slide   (Especially when going sideways, be sure to slide your feet; don't cross them.)

Tasks/Challenges:

T Begin dribbling in self-space, keeping your head up, eyes focused on me. On the first signal, I'll point to your left; dribble with your right hand as you sidestep to your left. When you hear the next signal, stop your travel but continue to dribble. I'll then point forward; travel backward as you dribble. Stop on the signal. Each time the signal is given, change the direction of your travel: right, left, forward, backward.

Children need both verbal and visual directional signs as well as audible signals (via drumbeat or whistle) for change of directions. The children will mirror your visual cues.

Dribbling and Traveling

Setting: Children scattered throughout general space, each with a ball

Cue

Hand a Little Behind   (For walking and
the Ball   dribbling, your hand
position changes: Keep
your hand just a little
behind the ball.)

Tasks/Challenges:

T This time start dribbling in self-space. After a few dribbles take two steps, then stop and dribble two times in self-space, then take two more steps, then stop and dribble twice. Keep traveling in general space like this until you hear the stop signal. **As you dribble, push the ball slightly forward.**

Tip: This task works well when children are first learning to travel and dribble because they are able to regain control of the ball if they are close to losing it. You can gradually increase the number of steps and decrease the stationary dribbles as the skill level increases.

T Begin dribbling and walking in general space. When you hear the drumbeat, stop in self-space and continue dribbling. The second drumbeat is the signal to travel again. The pattern is this: drumbeat, travel with dribble, drumbeat, stop with continued dribble, . . .

C Each of you has 100 points. On the signal, begin traveling in general space. If you lose control of the ball, subtract 10 points; if you collide with another person, subtract 25 points. I'll time you for 60 seconds; try to keep all 100 points. Ready? Begin.

Another way to do the challenge is to have it as "keep it zero." Each person has no points, and you add points rather than subtract. It works well if children's subtraction skills aren't as developed as their addition skills.

J *Teacher Observation.* At this point, when children are beginning to combine skills and practice them in more dynamic situations, it is appropriate to use a teacher checklist or observation to assess youngsters' continued use of the critical cues.

Dribbling, Traveling, and Switching Hands

Setting: Children scattered in general space, each with a ball

Cues

Hand Behind and   (Your hand position changes
to Side of Ball   just a little: Keep your hand
a little behind and to the
outside of the ball; see
Figure 24.11.)

| Look Up | (Remember to look at other people's faces as you dribble and just sneak glances at the ball.) |

Tasks/Challenges:

🅣 Start dribbling with your favorite hand while walking. On the signal, without stopping, change the dribbling to the other hand and keep walking.

🅣 Begin dribbling in general space; each time you meet someone, switch hands, and continue to travel and dribble.

👤✳ We have now practiced three different hand positions on the ball. Where should your hand be for stationary dribbling? Where should it be for dribbling while traveling? Where should it be for switching from one hand to the other?

Utilization Level (GLSP): Learning Experiences Leading to Skill Development in Dribbling

At the utilization level, children enjoy focusing on traveling while dribbling and on incorporating traveling into dynamic gamelike situations by combining the skills of throwing, catching, dodging, and dribbling; the complexity of the dribbling is increased by providing children with situations in which they must dribble with either hand, without looking at the ball.

A note about cues: Although several cues are listed for many of the learning experiences, it's important to focus on only one cue at a time. This way, the children can really concentrate on that cue. Once you provide feedback to the children and observe that most have learned a cue, it's time to focus on another one.

Dribbling and Changing Speed of Travel

Setting: Children scattered in general space (alone at first and later with partners), each child with a ball

Cues	
Look Up	(Remember to look at faces.)
Ball Low	(Dribble the ball only as high as your waist.)

Tip: You may also need to refocus on speeds here. If so, the cues would be fast, medium, and slow. (See Chapter 13.)

Tasks/Challenges:

🅣 Travel throughout general space, maintaining a controlled dribble at all times. Travel sometimes very fast, sometimes slowly.

🅣 Begin moving through general space with a slow, steady walk. As you're dribbling, focus your eyes on a spot on the floor 15 to 20 feet away. Without stopping your dribble, move as quickly as possible to that spot. When you arrive, stop your travel but continue dribbling. Visually choose another spot, and repeat the sequence. The ability to change speeds and maintain a continuous dribble is a very important offensive skill in basketball.

🅣 This time as you travel, practice quickly changing the speed of your dribble as you travel to your chosen point. It will be as if you have almost invisible stops and starts along the way. Slow down and speed up, changing the speed of travel in mid-dribble.

🅣 Stand beside a partner whose dribbling skill is very similar to yours. Partner 1 begins the travel/dribble throughout space, changing from fast to slow speeds at will. Partner 2 attempts to stay beside partner 1 at all times. Both of you will dribble continuously. When the signal is given, rest for 10 seconds. Then partner 2 becomes the leader.

Dribbling in General Space While Changing Directions

Setting: Children scattered throughout general space, each with a ball for dribbling

Cues	
Hand Position	(The hand positions we used before are important here. If you want to go to the side, your hand is on the side; to go forward, hand behind; to go backward, hand in front.)
Slide	(Especially when going sideways, be sure to slide your feet; don't cross them.)

Tasks/Challenges:

🅣 Dribble throughout general space, changing directions as you go: travel forward, backward, to the right, to the left. Travel slowly when you first begin the travel/dribble with a change of direction. Maintain the dribble during all your direction changes; don't stop and start again.

Figure 24.13 Dribbling in a curved or zigzag pathway.

Traveling backward and dribbling isn't easy because the ball must move toward the body and often hits the feet. Children should develop this direction last and should be made aware of the difficulty of dribbling backward.

T Begin dribbling in general space, traveling in a forward direction. Each time you hear the drumbeat, quickly change the direction of your travel and continue the travel/dribble.

Dribbling in Different Pathways

Setting: Children scattered in general space (alone at first, then with a partner), each with a ball

Cues	
Ball Close	(It is important to keep the ball close to your body, within half an arm's length.)
Ball on Outside	(In a curved or a zigzag pathway, keep the ball on the outside of the curve, the wide side.) *(Demonstrate; see Figure 24.13.)*

Tasks/Challenges:

T Dribble throughout general space, traveling in straight, curved, and zigzag pathways.

T Travel in a straight pathway as you dribble. Each time you meet another person or hear the drum, turn quickly to your right or left and continue to travel/dribble in a straight pathway.

T Follow the straight lines on the gym floor (or playground) as you travel/dribble.

T Travel in a series of curved pathways as you dribble. **If you curve to the left, dribble with your right hand; if you curve to the right, dribble with your left hand. Always keep the ball on the outside of the curve.**

T Travel/dribble throughout general space, quickly moving from side to side in a zigzag pathway. Make sure the ball changes hands each time you move from side to side.

T Travel/dribble in a straight pathway. On the signal, quickly zigzag to miss an imaginary opponent and then continue dribbling in a straight pathway.

T Stand approximately 3 feet behind a partner; each of you has a basketball (playground ball). Partner 1 (in front) travels/dribbles throughout general space, changing pathways. Partner 2 (in back) attempts to stay 3 feet behind the lead partner at all times. *(Give each partner several chances to be the leader.)*

C Design a traveling/dribbling strategy to move from the center of the gym (or outside blacktop) to the end line. Design the strategy using combinations of pathways to outwit imaginary opponents. Practice the traveling/dribbling strategy until you can do it three times exactly the same way. After you are done, draw and write out your strategy (Figure 24.14).

✿ If I were to place three opponents in your way, could you still execute your plan?

Setting: The gym set up with four or more "vacation spots" around the space. Each vacation spot should be designated with a large cone, a laminated picture of the vacation spot (e.g., Rocky Mountains #1, Disney World #2, Statue of Liberty #3, Joshua Tree National Park #4) and envelopes for each group with questions in them. For example:

Envelope #1: Make up a name for your group that you all agree on!

Envelope #2: Make up a group cheer that you all agree on. At your final vacation spot, you have to shout your group cheer as loudly as possible. Example: *1, 2, 3, Go Tigers! Give me a T, give me an I, give me a G, give me an E, give me an R, give me an S! What's that spell? TIGERS!*

Envelope #3: Introduce yourself and your group name to the teacher! Example: Hi! My name is _____. Our group name is _____.

Envelope #4: Write down one nice thing about somebody in your group on a note card.

Figure 24.14 A child's dribbling pathway map.

Kelley Reynolds
to Miss Parker

First I went fourd then zizzaz then fourd again Backwards curve finish.

Start.

Ziggag

Backwards

curve

Children in four or more groups (note the number of groups and the number of vacation spots should be the same). Number groups 1 through 4.

C Your group is going on a vacation around the United States. Each group will start at the vacation spot that matches your group number. Your group must dribble with your hands using curved or zigzag pathways to get to the next vacation spot. Each group member must use the same pathway to reach the vacation spot, and you must follow the person in front of you. Once you have arrived at your new vacation spot, find the envelope with your group number on it, open the envelope, and follow the directions found inside the envelope. Before your group can continue to the next vacation spot, you will need to complete the directions found in your group's envelope and draw the pathway your group is going to use to get to the next vacation spot. Your group must travel over the star in the middle of the map before reaching your next vacation spot.

(This task was created by Jerod Dean and Brian Gerwig, University of Northern Colorado, Greeley, Colorado.)

✓ *Event Task.* The above task can easily be used as a formative or summative assessment.

Dribbling While Stopping, Starting, and Turning (Pivots and Fakes)

Setting: Children scattered in general space, each with a ball

Cues	
Ball Close	(It is important to keep the ball close to your body, within half an arm's length.)
Forward–Backward Stance	(When you stop, your feet should be about 18 inches apart, with the foot opposite the hand you are dribbling with forward.)

Tasks/Challenges:

T Begin dribbling in general space. Travel slowly at first, and then gradually increase your speed until you are moving quickly while maintaining your dribble. On the signal, quickly stop both your travel and the dribble.

T Begin dribbling throughout general space. On the signal, stop quickly in a forward–backward stance, maintaining the dribble. Pivot by reversing the way you are facing; turn on the balls of your feet. Continue your travel/dribble. **To pivot, turn backward on the foot toward the ball hand. Remember, the ball changes hands as you turn.**

T Choose a point across the gym. Begin dribbling in general space, moving toward your point. Every time you come to a line on the floor, stop, fake as if you are going to change pathways, and keep going. **To use a fake, come to a stop, quickly take a step with one foot as if you are going to change pathways, and then keep going in the same pathway.** It may be easier if you pretend there is an imaginary defender in your way who you have to get around. When you reach your point, choose another one and keep going.

T This time, as you travel to your point, sometimes fake and sometimes change pathways. **Remember, in a game you are trying to outsmart a defender.**

Dribbling Around Stationary Obstacles in General Space

Setting: Marker cones or milk jugs placed randomly (not in a line) throughout general space (spots do not work well because children can go over them) with varying space between the cones or jugs (place some 3 feet apart, others 5 to 6 feet apart)

Cue
Body, Ball, Cone (Remember, the cone [jug] is your opponent. Protect the ball by putting your body between the cone [jug] and the ball.)

Tasks/Challenges:

T Travel/dribble throughout general space, dribbling around the obstacles.

C See if you can dribble 60 seconds without bumping into an obstacle or another person—**Heads Up.**

Dribbling Around Stationary Obstacles in Limited Space

Setting: The floor or blacktop divided into a series of alleys with colored tape; children in groups, one group per alley

Tasks/Challenges:

T One person in your group will be the dribbler; that person will stand at the end of the alley. The others in your group should arrange themselves in a zigzag

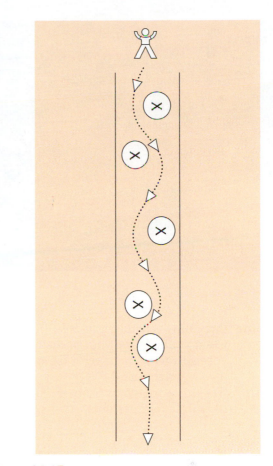

Figure 24.15 Dribbling around stationary obstacles in general space.

obstacle pattern in your alley (Figure 24.15). The dribbler attempts to dribble the length of the alley, avoiding the obstacles and staying within the side boundaries. The obstacles try to gain possession of the ball. Obstacles can stretch and pivot, but one foot must remain glued in place at all times. Obstacles can touch only the ball, not the dribbler.

The difficulty of this task can be increased or decreased by adjusting the width of the alley or by changing the alley to a square and spreading the obstacles out.

Mirroring and Matching While Dribbling

(See Chapter 15, "Relationships," for a discussion of mirroring and matching.)

Setting: Partners of approximately the same skill level facing each other about 3 to 4 feet apart

Cues
Mirroring (Remember, mirroring is like looking in a mirror. If your partner uses the left hand, you use your right hand.)

Dribbling at the precontrol and control levels requires an awareness of space.

Matching (Matching is harder than mirroring when you're facing your partner. If your partner uses the right hand, you use your right hand.)

Look Up (For this activity it is really important to look at your partner.)

Tasks/Challenges:

T Face your partner. The partner whose name comes first in the alphabet is the first leader. The leader starts dribbling, and the follower has to mirror the actions of the leader. Remember, don't make it too hard on your partner. On the signal (about 45 seconds), change leaders.

T Now that you have gotten to be so good, try matching your partner's actions. **Remember, if your partner works with the left hand, you will use your left hand.**

T This one is really hard. The leader can now travel in general space. The follower must try to copy exactly what the leader does. This is matching again.

Dribbling and Passing with a Partner

Setting: Partners, facing the same direction, about 10 feet apart at one side of the gymnasium or blacktop; one partner with a basketball for dribbling and passing

Cues

Receiver Slightly Ahead of Passer (The receiver should be ahead of the passer by about four or five steps.)

Lead Receiver (Pass the ball to the open space just in front of the receiver so he or she doesn't have to back up to catch it.)

No Stopping (Both the passer and the receiver should always be moving to the other side; never stop moving forward.)

Smooth Transition (Pick up the ball to pass in one motion without having to stop; receive the ball from the pass to the dribble in one motion.)

Tasks/Challenges:

T The object of this task is to practice passing while moving forward. You and your partner are traveling in the same direction. Your job is to move across the space to the other line. Partner 1 will dribble three or four times and then pass to partner 2, who has been traveling forward. Partner 2 receives the pass, dribbles as he or she travels forward, and then passes back to partner 1. Partners continue to travel/dribble the length of the space.

Setting: Partners about 15 feet apart, scattered throughout general space, each pair with a ball

Tasks/Challenges:

T On the signal, begin traveling, dribbling, and passing to your partner. (*Allow about 2 minutes of activity, and then let the children rest for 10 seconds. Repeat.*)

Dribbling Against an Opponent: One-on-One

Before beginning tasks that involve offense and defense, students should be skilled with the space awareness and dodging tasks that ask them to use the offensive and defensive skills of moving into open space; avoiding other persons; and using fakes, stops and starts, pivots, and other avoidance skills without manipulating equipment. (See Chapter 13, "Space Awareness," and Chapter 17, "Chasing, Fleeing, and Dodging.") Children need to have polished these skills before they are asked to use them while manipulating equipment.

One key to this task—and to other initial tasks involving offense and defense—is to clearly define the boundaries of the space the students are to use. A small space gives an advantage to the defense; a large space provides an offensive advantage. Similarly, a long, narrow space gives the advantage to the defense; a wider space helps the offense. Initial tasks should generally favor the offense.

Setting: Partners facing each other, scattered throughout general space, each pair with a ball

Cues	
Offense	
Look Up	(You have to be able to see your partner to avoid him or her.)
Move to Goal	(Always move to your end line.)
Ball, Body, Defense	(Keep your body between the ball and your defense.)
Defense	
Body Between Offense and Goal	(Keep yourself between your partner and where he or she is trying to go. Your back should be to the partner's goal.)
Watch Hips	(Just like dodging, watch the hips or belly button if you want to know where your partner will move next.)
Stay About Two or Three Feet Away	(If you get too close, your partner can go right by you.)

Tasks/Challenges:

Ⓣ Select a partner who dribbles while traveling as well as or slightly better than you do. On the signal, partner 1 begins dribbling while traveling toward the end line; partner 2 (facing partner 1) attempts to gain possession of the ball by tapping it away. Neither partner should foul the other by bumping, pushing away, or reaching in. Partner 1 attempts to keep possession of the ball for 30 seconds; if partner 2 gets the ball, he or she gives it back. At the end of 30 seconds, partner 2 will dribble and partner 1 will try to take the ball away. Begin.

✓ *Videotape/Digital Analysis.* Videotaping or taking digital pictures and subsequent self-assessment of the use of the critical cues is essential when youngsters start to use skills in dynamic, changing situations. Students could be provided with a self-assessment checklist and view the video or pictures with their partner to analyze "film" as coaches do.

Proficiency Level (GLSP): Learning Experiences Leading to Skill Development

Children at the proficiency level seem to dribble without thinking about it; dribbling seems to be almost automatic. They're able to change direction, speed, and pathway at will. They're challenged by situations that involve other children as partners or as opponents who make the situation increasingly unpredictable. They enjoy dribbling in larger groups with more complex relationships and the excitement of strategy development.

A note about cues: At the proficiency level, tasks are more complex, typically requiring children to coordinate several movements simultaneously in a dynamic context. A list of cues is provided to assist the children in being more successful in the learning experiences. The challenge is in determining which cue will be most beneficial for each child . . . and when. Thus careful observation and critical reflection become very important as you watch the children move and then decide which cue will be the most helpful to move each learner to a higher level.

Dribbling Against Opponents: Stationary Defenders

Setting: Children divided into two equal groups, one group with playground balls for dribbling; initially, a fairly open space; later, to increase the complexity of the task, a reduced amount of space

Cues	
Offense	
Look Up	(Remember to look up to see where your opponents are.)
Use Fakes	(You'll need to use all the fakes we learned before—stopping and starting, changing speeds, changing directions—here.)

*The cues at this level assume mastery of basic dribbling skills; hence, they are really cues about **how to use the dribble and how to stop the dribble.** Many of the cues are taken from the concepts of space awareness and chasing, fleeing, and dodging. If needed, return to and reinforce the dribbling cues and practice the basic offensive and defensive moves, but increasingly move toward children being able to use these skills in gamelike situations.*

Tasks/Challenges:

T Students without balls are the obstacles; you can spread out anywhere in the space. Your job is to try to steal the balls as the other group dribbles across the space. The only rules are you may not touch an offensive player, and one foot must always remain "glued" to your spot. In other words, you can step with one foot, but you cannot move from your spot. On the signal, the offense will begin dribbling from one end line and try to get to the other side without losing the ball. If the defense (the obstacles) gets a ball, just give it back. We'll trade places after three tries.

When the activity is a game situation with competing skills, it is best if you ask children to form groups with those "whose skill level is about the same as theirs," or if you divide the children into groups so that groups have relatively equal skill levels.

Dribbling Against Opponents: Moving Defenders

Setting: Children divided into two groups on opposite sidelines of the gym or blacktop; one group with playground balls or basketballs

Cues

Offense

Look Up	(Remember to look up to see where your opponents are.)
Use Fakes	(You'll need to use all the fakes we learned before—stopping and starting, changing speeds, changing directions.)

Defense

Watch Hips and Ball	(The best way to tell where the dribbler is going is to look at the hips or belly button and at the same time watch the ball.)
Slap Up	(If you really want to knock the ball loose, slap from the bottom up.)

Tasks/Challenges:

T Each team stands on opposite sidelines of the gym (blacktop) and faces each other. Each member of team A has a playground ball for dribbling. On the signal, team A players begin dribbling toward the opposite sideline. Team B, without the playground balls, begins moving forward, trying to take away the balls. If a team B player gains possession of the ball, that player dribbles toward the opposite sideline. When the players from team A or team B make it over their goal line, they stay there until all the balls are behind one sideline. Team B is then given all the playground balls, and the task begins again.

☑ ***Teacher Observation.*** As children begin to play in dynamic situations, it is essential that teachers continue to assess their use of the critical cues as they pertain to that situation. Any of the tasks at this level would allow for that. See Chapter 12 for the development of a teacher observation checklist.

Dribble Tag

Setting: Each child with a playground ball for dribbling; two or three children designated "it" wearing identifying jerseys if possible

Cues

Look Up	(Remember, look up to see where your opponents are.)
Use Fakes	(You'll need to use all the fakes we learned before—stopping and starting, changing speeds, changing directions.)

Tasks/Challenges:

C On the signal, everyone with a ball will begin dribbling in general space. The players who are "it" will try to tag you as you're traveling and dribbling. You're caught if:

1. You're tagged by an "it."
2. You lose control of the ball.

If you're caught, stand and hold the ball above your head. You'll be free to travel if a player who is dribbling touches you. Each 2 minutes, we'll rest for 10 seconds while I choose new people to be "it."

A way to make this activity more complex is to have the taggers not have to dribble. This small change calls for a significant increase in dribbling skills and more closely resembles basketball gamelike activities. Just remember the heightened level of dribbling skill needed.

Dribbling While Dodging

Setting: Children, each with a basketball or a playground ball and a flag tucked in the waist

Cues

Look Up	(Remember, look up to see where your opponents are.)
Use Fakes	(You'll need to use all the fakes we learned before—stopping and starting, changing speeds, changing directions.)
Ball, Body, Defense	(Remember, protect the ball by keeping your body between the ball and the defense.)

Tasks/Challenges:

Ⓣ You will need a partner of about your same ability level for this task. You will need to establish clear boundaries for your area, about 10 feet square. Start by facing each other and dribbling. The object is to keep dribbling and pull your partner's flag. See how many times you can pull your partner's flag in 2 minutes.

⚡ What is one hint for not losing control of the ball in this activity?

Maintaining Possession While Dribbling and Passing

Setting: A clearly defined space (the complexity of the task is increased or decreased depending upon the size of the space; initially, a larger space gives the advantage to the offense); groups of three

Cues

Offense

Move to Open Space	(When you don't have the ball, move to an open space at an angle to the passer; *see Chapter 23 for a detailed explanation of this idea.*)
Lead the Receiver	(Throw to an open space in front of the receiver.)

Defense

Go After the Ball	(Go after the person with the ball; otherwise he or she doesn't have to throw it.)
Hustle	(Move quickly when the ball changes players.)

Tasks/Challenges:

Ⓣ Working in your group of three, two of you will dribble and pass while the third player tries to steal the ball. We'll rotate the interceptor every 2 minutes. Remember, you must either be dribbling or passing the ball. You may not hold it; no touching.

Child-Designed Dribbling/Passing Routines

This task is an example of a child-designed instructional approach. See Chapter 10 for more ideas on child-designed tasks.

Setting: Groups of four to six; a space about 15 feet square; any number of basketballs; music and CD players (optional)

Cues

The cues for this task are dependent upon what you want students to include in the routine. Some possibilities:

Pathways	(In your routine be sure to include at least two different pathways: straight, curved, zigzag.)
Dribbling	(The dribbling part of your routine needs to include different levels of dribbling and dribbling in different places around the body.)
Passing	(Your routine might also include passing.)

Tasks/Challenges:

Ⓒ Put together a series of dribbling and passing skills in a fancy routine—kind of like a basketball warm-up drill. Design the floor pattern, ways to travel, individual tricks, and partner or group skills. Practice your routine until you have it memorized and in time with the music.

✓ *Videotape/Digital Analysis.* Routines such as this are good places to use videotape or digital pictures for observation and assessment. The videotaping or picture taking also adds incentive for students to perform well and do their best. Remember, design your scoring rubrics ahead of time so students know what is expected of their performance.

Dribbling and Throwing at a Target

Setting: Four-foot-square targets marked with colored tape on the wall at one end of or the sides of the gym, approximately 7 feet above the floor; each child with a ball at first, then later with partners and a shared ball

Cues	
No Stopping	(Pick up your dribble and throw to the target without coming to a complete stop.)
Watch the Target	(To increase your accuracy, watch the target.)

Tasks/Challenges:

(T) Beginning at the center of the gymnasium, travel/dribble toward the wall with the target on it. When you're within 12 feet of the target, throw the ball, trying to hit the wall within the target square. Collect the ball, quickly move to the side, and return to midcourt.

(T) Select a partner who will serve as defense. Partner 1 dribbles toward the wall and attempts to score by hitting the target; partner 2 tries to gain possession of the ball on the dribble or block the throw to the target. Change partner roles after each try.

(T) Practice the dribble/target activity with an offensive partner. Combine dribbling and passing to a partner as you travel toward the target. Alternate the throw to the target between partners.

(✓) ***Event Task.*** By having partners join with another set of partners for a two-on-two game of dribbling, passing, and throwing at a target, you can create a self-designed game to be used as an event task. *(See Chapter 12 for how to design a scoring rubric to use with self-designed games.)*

Tip: *Place targets around the walls as space allows. Place targets on both sides and on end walls to provide maximum activity.*

Dribble/Pass Keep-Away

Setting: Groups of four in a space about one-quarter the size of a basketball court (or smaller)

Cues	
Offense	
Don't Pass Until the Defense Commits	(Until the defense plays defense on you, there is no need to pass. You might as well keep moving and dribbling the ball.)
Receiver Move to an Open Space	(Move to an open space at an angle to the passer.)
Stay Away from the Passer	(Wherever you go, your defense goes with you. If you stay close to the passer, everyone stays together and the passer has nowhere to throw.)
Defense	
First Player Ball; Second Player Receiver	(Play defense on the person with the ball first; then play defense on the receiver.)
Go After the Ball	(Make the passer throw the ball.)

Tasks/Challenges:

(T) In your group, two of you will dribble and pass while the other two try to gain possession of the ball either by intercepting the pass or by stealing the ball on the dribble. Remember, on defense you cannot touch the other player. When you walk, you must dribble the basketball.

Child-Designed Invasion Game

This task is an example of a child-designed instructional approach. See Chapter 30 for more ideas on child-designed games.

Setting: Groups of no more than three; half-court or short basketball court with lowered baskets

Cues	
Offense	
Don't Pass Until the Defense Commits	(Until the defense plays defense on you, there is no need to pass. You might as well keep moving and dribbling the ball.)
Receiver Move to an Open Space	(Move to an open space at an angle to the passer.)
Stay Away from the Passer	(Wherever you go, your defense goes with you. If you stay close to the passer, everyone stays together and the passer has nowhere to throw.)
Defense	
Go After Ball	(Force the pass by pressuring the player with the ball.)
Ball, Body, Basket	(Keep your body between the basket and the offensive player.)
Hustle Back	(After a score, run back down the court.)

Tasks/Challenges:

C If you are comfortable with your skills of dribbling, passing, and throwing at a target, you may want to play a small-group basketball-type game. The maximum number of players on a team is three. The one rule I have is that every player must touch the ball before a shot is made. Match the skills on your team so the game will be a challenge for everyone; it's no fun if the score is a runaway.

✓ *Event Task.* At this point, it is helpful to have students think about their skill as well as doing it. Before beginning team play, have students think of all the skills needed for being successful in basketball: spatial awareness, throwing, catching, traveling, dodging, dribbling, shooting at a target. Within each group, discuss what a person needs to be able to do with each skill to be successful in basketball.

Reading Comprehension Questions

1. Discuss the difference between volleying and dribbling.
2. Name four body parts that can be used to volley a ball.
3. What is the primary focus of the tasks at the precontrol level of volleying? What is the teacher trying to accomplish before moving on to the control level?
4. List four different types of balls that can be used to practice volleying at the precontrol level.
5. What does the phrase "strike the ball with a level body part" mean? What does the phrase "meeting the ball" mean?
6. Rank the following tasks by placing the number 1 in front of the easiest (most basic) task, the number 2 in front of the next more difficult task, and so on.
   ( ) Volleying a ball to different levels
   ( ) Volleying a ball with two hands
   ( ) Volleying a ball to outwit an opponent
   ( ) Volleying a balloon
   ( ) Volleying a ball to a partner
7. Explain the meaning of the phrase "the location of the hit determines the direction of travel."
8. Give two examples of dynamic and unpredictable situations related to the skill of volleying.
9. What characterizes each of the four skill levels of dribbling?
10. What does it mean to keep one's hands firm and flexible as opposed to flat and stiff when dribbling?
11. How can you teach a child to use the fingerpads while dribbling?
12. How does the size of the space affect dribbling skills that are used in offensive and defensive situations?
13. How do the cues for dribbling and volleying change at the proficiency level?

References/Suggested Readings

Kessel, J. 2005. Starting an elementary program off right. http://usavolleyball.org.

Mustain, W. 1990. A manual of elementary physical education skill theme activities for physical education specialists to use in collaboration with classroom teachers. Unpublished master's project, Virginia Polytechnic Institute and State University, Blacksburg.

[NASPE] National Association for Sport and Physical Education. 1995. *Moving into the future: National standards for physical education.* St. Louis, MO: Mosby.

[NASPE] National Association for Sport and Physical Education. 2004. *Moving into the future: National standards for physical education.* 2nd ed. Reston, VA: National Association for Sport and Physical Education.

Striking with Rackets and Paddles

Ello Rumann

Tennis, racquetball, badminton, table tennis, and squash—What do they all have in common? They are all activities in which people can participate for a lifetime, and they all stem from the skill theme of striking with a racket or paddle. Participation in lifelong physical activity requires both confidence and competence in the activity to be performed. Mastery of striking with rackets and paddles helps develop skills that provide a viable option for youth and adults to be physically active for a lifetime.

Yet, striking with rackets and paddles, as well as striking with long-handled implements (Chapter 26), is one of the last skills that children develop. There are three basic reasons: (1) children don't refine or develop visual tracking until the later elementary school years, (2) hand–eye coordination at greater distances from the body is more difficult, and (3) most often in striking situations with rackets and paddles there are two objects in motion at once—the paddle and the object being struck.

Striking with these implements, however, is a skill children enjoy and can be taught at younger ages with a few simple equipment modifications. Because of the complexities of striking, we teach the skill of striking with rackets and paddles after children have been introduced to the skill of striking with body parts, specifically the hand (see Chapter 24); because the difficulty of striking with an implement increases with the length of the implement, we teach the sidearm pattern of striking with rackets and paddles before striking with long-handled implements in a horizontal plane (Chapter 26). If you are teaching in a program where children only have physical education once or twice a week, mastery of the skill theme of striking with rackets and paddles may be acquired at the precontrol or control levels, but children will still need practice at these levels as well as utilization and proficiency levels in middle school before being introduced to the regulation games associated with them. If children do not achieve mastery at the utilization and proficiency levels before introduction to the sport, they will be unsuccessful when they have to use the skill in dynamic situations and thus likely to end their participation in activities that involve striking with rackets and paddles. The end result: Activities that involve striking with rackets and paddles will be eliminated from their list of possibilities of being physically active for a lifetime.

Children learning to strike with a racket or paddle must coordinate many familiar skills into one new ones. They must learn to accurately toss or drop the object to be contacted, visually track the object while they're traveling to an appropriate location, and contact the

Skill Theme Development Progression

Striking with Rackets and Paddles

Proficiency Level

Child-designed racket games
Group striking across a net
Team striking across a net
Aerial striking over a net
Partner striking across a net
Striking to and from different places
Striking at angles to two walls with a partner
Striking to one wall with a partner

Utilization Level

Striking upward in a dynamic situation
Striking in various aerial pathways in dynamic situations
Striking continuously upward with a group
Striking overhead over a net
Striking overhead
Striking to different places around a partner
Hitting cooperatively and continuously with a partner
Hitting from different places

Control Level

Striking continuously over and through a target
Striking a ball rebounding from a wall
Striking an object to send it over a net
Striking through a target
Striking to different places
Striking at high and low targets
Striking backhand to the wall
Striking forehand to the wall
Striking for hoops (varying the distance)
Striking for distance (varying the force)
Striking to wall targets
Striking to self on both sides of the body
Striking Up, Down, and Forward
Striking forward against a wall
Striking Up and Down
Striking Up
Striking Down

Precontrol Level

Upward Bound
Hit the wall
Striking a suspended ball
Balloon strike (lightweight paddle)
Paddle balance

Box 25-1

Key Observation Points: Striking with Rackets and Paddles

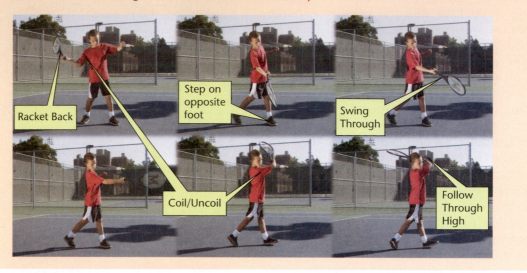

Racket Back

Step on opposite foot

Swing Through

Coil/Uncoil

Follow Through High

Box 25-2

Striking with Rackets and Paddles in the *National Standards for Physical Education*

The skill theme of striking with rackets and paddles is referenced in the National Association for Sport and Physical Education's *National Standards for Physical Education* (NASPE 2004) under Standard 2: "Demonstrates understanding of movement concepts, principles, strategies, and tactics as they apply to the learning and performance of physical activities." This standard speaks of the child's recognizing and applying the concept of an appropriate grip to the striking action and the correct biomechanics of the striking action. The sample performance outcome states: "Identifies and demonstrates key elements of a proper grip when holding a racket to perform a forehand strike (3–5).*

*Grade-level guideline for expected student learning.

object at exactly the right moment. And simultaneously, they must adjust to the weight and length of the implement. A successful striker must coordinate all these variables. When teaching children to strike it is important to observe that:

- There is a step forward on the foot opposite the striking arm
- In preparation for the strike, the weight is shifted to the back foot and the racket is drawn back

- The body trunk rotates to the back and the hips and trunk are cocked
- As the strike begins in quick succession, the weight shifts to the front foot, the body rotates forward, and the racket is swung in a full arc around the body

The key observation points in Box 25-1 illustrate correct sidearm striking with rackets and paddles.

Our skill theme progression presents ideas for developing the skill of striking with rackets and paddles from the precontrol through the proficiency levels. Refer to Box 25-2 for linkages of the skill theme of striking with rackets and paddles to the *National Standards for Physical Education*.

Precontrol Level (GLSP): Activities for Exploration

Children at the precontrol level struggle just to make contact between the implement and the object and are truly excited when they do—regardless of where the object goes. At this level, we provide exploratory activities using short-handled, lightweight implements to contact balls, shuttlecocks, and other objects. These objects are often suspended from ropes at various heights to make the task easier.

We recommend balloons at the precontrol level because the flight of a balloon is longer and slower than that of a ball, and the child therefore has more time for visual tracking. Heavier balloons, although a bit more expensive, are more durable than inexpensive, lightweight balloons. They also tend to be less erratic during flight and consequently are easier for children to strike successfully. Before using balloons, be sure to check with your school about any latex restrictions that may be in place.

⚠ Striking is one skill theme in which safety plays an important role. Be sure to include wrist strings or guards on all rackets and paddles (and have children use them), and provide ample space for children to strike and move safely around one another.

Paddle Balance

Setting: A paddle and a balloon, beanbag, and ball for each child. *Foam paddles are best because they are lightweight and easy to control.*

Tasks/Challenges:

Ⓣ You're going to practice a new skill now. Try to balance the balloon on the paddle. **As you do this, try to keep the balloon in the middle of the paddle.**

Ⓣ If you are having a little trouble with the balloon on the paddle, you may want to try balancing a beanbag on the paddle.

Ⓣ The balloon was fairly easy to balance, but this time we are going to make the task a little harder. Instead of a balloon, try to balance a ball on your paddle. Try to keep the ball on your paddle as long as you can.

Ⓣ If you are really good at keeping the ball on your paddle so it doesn't fall off very often, try rolling the ball around on the paddle while still keeping it on the paddle. At times you will really have to do some fast work to keep the ball on the paddle.

Ⓒ I will time you. See if you can keep your object on the paddle for 15 seconds. Ready? Go.

Ⓣ This time we are going to try something even harder. Choose the object you like best. Try to walk around your self-space and balance the object on your paddle at the same time.

Volleybirds or petecas (badminton shuttlecocks with flat bottoms; see Chapter 24) also work well with children at the precontrol level. The youngsters learn to keep the paddle flat as they walk around carrying the volleybird or peteca on the paddle.

Balloon Strike (Lightweight Paddle)

Setting: A nylon-hose (Figure 25.1) or foam paddle and a balloon for each child; a spot or other way of defining self-space for each child. When children first begin striking balloons with paddles, tie the balloon with string to the paddle handle. This saves much chasing time and makes it easier for the children to remain in self-space.

Tasks/Challenges:

Ⓣ In your own space with your paddle and balloon, strike the balloon up in the air. Do one hit, then catch, and start again. Find out how to make the balloon go in the air.

Ⓣ Now try to strike the balloon more than once— maybe twice—then catch.

Ⓒ How many times can you strike the balloon, keeping it in the air without missing it or moving from your space? Five would be a really good number.

Ⓣ So far, you've tried to stay still in your own space while you were striking the balloon. This time try and move around in your self-space.

Ⓣ Now we are going to try to walk while striking the balloon. Go slowly and look where you are going so you don't hit others. To be safe, the balloon should be close to you.

Figure 25.1 Construction of nylon-hose paddles. Lightweight paddles can be made from old coat hangers, nylon socks (or stockings), and tape.*

*Prior to constructing equipment we recommend you check with school administration to be certain that district policy permits homemade equipment.

This young girl is practicing balancing a ball on a paddle as a prerequisite to striking.

At the park, I noticed a girl named Sarah. Her older brothers were busy playing street hockey and tennis (on the tennis courts). She was about six and, being ignored by her brothers, was in her own world. The boys had left a tennis racket and a ball lying aside. She picked them up, held the racket somewhere in the middle of the handle, and began to try to hit the ball. It took four tries before she even made contact, and the ball rolled away into the grass. It didn't matter; you could tell by the smile on her face that she was delighted. She ran after the ball, picked it up and (after a few attempts) hit it again, and was again off to chase it. Her game took her on a journey all over the park and continued for 20 minutes or so. Then she proudly walked over to her mother and declared, "I can play tennis!"

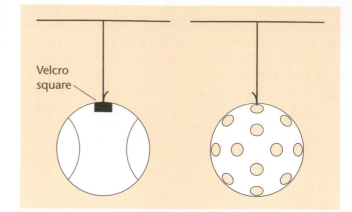

Figure 25.2 Suspending balls on strings. Glue a hook-and-loop tape square to a string and another to a tennis ball to enable the ball to drop from the string when the ball is struck, or knot string or elastic into the holes of a plastic whiffle ball. Balls can be hung from climbing apparatus, from traveling rings, and between vertical game standards, and they can be attached to walls in the corners of the gym.*

*Prior to constructing equipment we recommend you check with school administration to be certain that district policy permits homemade equipment.

Striking a Suspended Ball

Setting: A ball suspended from a string (Figure 25.2) and a paddle for each child; for the first task, suspend the balls above shoulder height; place spots or other markings on the floor behind each ball

Tasks/Challenges:

T In your own space you have a ball hanging from a string. Try to strike the ball forward while standing on your spot. After each strike be sure to stop the ball before you try to hit it again.

Setting: Balls lowered to waist height; spots moved to a position beside the suspended balls

Tasks/Challenges:

T Things have changed a little this time. Now your spot is beside the ball. Again, try to strike the ball from your spot so it travels straight forward—as in baseball. Be sure to stop the ball after each hit.

C You have been striking the ball fairly well. This time, if you strike the ball well, yell, "Whacko!" If you miss, just start again.

At this point, children should be striking on their preferred side. When the children begin to strike consistently, challenge them to strike on the opposite side of their bodies (for example, backhand).

By allowing children the choice of striking implement and type of object to strike, children are able to adapt the task to their ability.

Hit the Wall

Setting: A foam or wooden paddle and a foam ball, Nerf tennis ball, or volleybird for each child; spots on the floor about 5 feet away from the wall to identify self-space

Tasks/Challenges:

T At your spot, strike the ball so it travels to the wall. Just try for one hit at a time. Remember, if the ball goes away from you, collect it and bring it back to your spot before striking again.

T Try hitting the ball on both sides of your body.

C Try for five single hits; if you can do five, try seven.

Upward Bound

Setting: A wooden, foam, or plexiglass paddle (Figure 25.3); a shuttlecock or volleybird and a lightweight ball; a spot or some way to define self-space for each child

Tasks/Challenges:

T This time try striking the shuttlecock (volleybird) upward. Drop the object, and try to strike it so it goes straight up.

T Once you are comfortable with one hit, try to hit the shuttlecock (volleybird) more than once before catching it.

C Try to hit the shuttlecock (volleybird) four times in a row.

T Trade in your shuttlecock (volleybird) for a ball. Try to hit the ball up in the air. **Remember, one hit and catch it; then hit again.**

T Try to strike the ball up more than once—maybe twice—and then catch it.

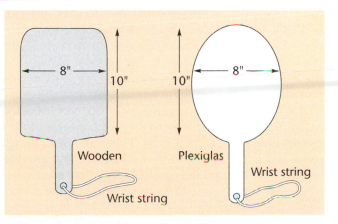

Figure 25.3 Construction of short-handled paddles. Short-handled paddles can be cut with a jigsaw from 1/2-inch finished plywood or from 1/4-inch plexiglass. Sand plywood edges until they're smooth, and wrap the handles with fiberglass tape.* *Each paddle should have a wrist string for safety.*

*Prior to constructing equipment we recommend you check with school administration to be certain that district policy permits homemade equipment.

Paddles and Safety

Although wooden and plexiglass paddles are very good for learning to strike, they do present a safety problem. Paddles made of foam—with both short and long handles—are available. We prefer foam paddles whenever the children are working in close spaces or in groups.

Control Level (GLSP): Learning Experiences Leading to Skill Development

When children are able to strike a ball consistently in precontrol level contexts, they're ready for control-level experiences, which include contacting a rebounding ball a number of times in succession, sending the object in a desired direction, and varying the force of the contact. Experiences at this level are designed to help children go beyond just contacting the ball. Children now learn to control the direction, force, and aerial pathway of an object. One of the first cues we give children when beginning striking activities is "watch the ball." This is hard for many youngsters because so much else is going on around them. To help children focus on the ball, paint a bright dot or letter on it, and direct their concentration toward that mark.

At the control level we also introduce children to a variety of striking implements and to objects with various surfaces, lengths, and types and degrees of bounce, including table tennis paddles, racquetball rackets, paddleball paddles, badminton rackets, short-handled tennis rackets, paddleballs, Nerf tennis balls, tennis balls, racquetballs, rubber balls, shuttlecocks, petecas, and table tennis balls. This allows teachers to help children choose the equipment that best meets their needs. We also introduce children to the sidearm pattern. (At the utilization and proficiency levels, we continue to provide a variety of striking implements and objects.)

A note about cues: Although several cues are listed for many of the learning experiences, it's important to focus on only one cue at a time. This way, the children can really concentrate on that cue. Once you provide feedback to the children and observe that most have learned a cue, it's time to focus on another one.

Nerf Tennis Balls

Recently equipment companies have developed a Nerf tennis ball. These balls come in a variety of sizes—some slightly larger than a regular tennis ball—and have a density that facilitates striking. We have found they are more effective for use with rackets and paddles than dead tennis balls.

Equipment Modifications

Visual tracking is a skill that is not refined until the later elementary grades; therefore striking, unless modified, is a difficult skill theme for children. A few simple equipment modifications allow young children to experience success in tracking. The use of large, slow-moving, easy-to-see objects, such as balloons or beach balls, makes tracking easier. The use of lightweight, short-handled, easily maneuverable rackets compensates for the developing hand–eye coordination and limited arm strength and endurance. The basic guideline to follow is that the equipment should not hamper the movement pattern; if it does, modify the equipment.

Striking Down

Setting: A wooden paddle, a dead tennis ball or foam ball, and a spot or some way to define self-space for each child

Cues	
Flat Paddle	(Keep your paddle flat as a board.)
Watch the Ball	(Keep your eyes on the ball all the time.) *It's helpful to paint a dot on the ball so children have something on which to focus.*

Tasks/Challenges:

T In your own space strike the ball down with your paddle. See if you can keep it going without a miss. **Remember, if the ball starts to get away, just catch it and start over again.**

T Once you can keep the ball going five times or more in a row without leaving your space, see if you can strike the ball so it stays below your waist.

C How many down strikes can you get in a row without having to leave your self-space? These strikes don't have to be below your waist. Ready? Go.

Modifying the Task

The difficulty of all striking tasks can be increased or decreased by changing the object being struck. We most often start with shuttlecocks or volleybirds and progress to foam balls and dead tennis balls or Nerf tennis balls. We tend to stay away from "live" tennis balls because they encourage children to "hit hard" rather than use the correct pattern and move to receive the ball. Adjust the equipment for each task as appropriate for your children.

Even the youngest children are fascinated with striking.

Striking Up

Setting: A wooden paddle, a dead tennis ball or a foam ball, and a spot or some way to define self-space for each child

> **Cues**
>
> **Flat Paddle** (Keep your paddle flat as a board.)
> **Stiff Wrist** (Keep your wrist tight; don't let it flop around.)
> **Watch the Ball** (Keep your eyes on the ball all the time.) *It's helpful to paint a dot on the ball so children have something on which to focus.*

Tasks/Challenges:

T Now let's see if you can stay in your self-space and keep the ball going, but hit it up so it doesn't touch the floor. If you need to let it bounce every so often to gain control, that is OK.

T Can you hit the ball up so it goes above your head every time and still stay in self-space?

C Every time the paddle hits the ball, say one letter of your name. Can you spell your first name? Your last name? Your best friend's name? **Remember, each time you miss, you have to start spelling the word over again.**

* Show me what a flat paddle looks like.

Striking Up and Down

Setting: A foam or wooden paddle, a dead tennis ball or a foam ball, and a spot or some way to define self-space for each child

> **Cues**
>
> **Flat Paddle** (Keep your paddle flat as a board.)
> **Stiff Wrist** (Keep your wrist tight; don't let it flop around.)
> **Watch the Ball** (Keep your eyes on the ball all the time.)

Tasks/Challenges:

T Now let's see if you can still stay in self-space and keep the ball going. One time bounce it off the floor, and the next time hit it into the air.

C Let's make up a sequence. For example, your sequence might be: up once, down once, up twice, down twice, up three times, down three times, and then start over. Practice until you can do your sequence two times in a row.

T Can you hit the ball up and down while walking around your self-space—without losing control of the ball?

C Try to do your sequence while you walk around in self-space.

T If that was easy, you might want to try skipping, or sliding, or galloping in self-space as you strike the ball.

T This time it becomes harder. We are going to walk in general space while striking the ball. Walk very slowly while you continue to strike the ball. For safety, be sure to look where you are going. If you think you are going to lose control of the ball, stand still for a second and catch the ball or let it bounce on the floor until you get control back; then keep going. If you do lose your ball, walk and pick it up, and start again.

▲ When children begin moving and striking simultaneously, they tend to concentrate so much on the striking they forget to watch out for others and for rolling balls. Besides reminding them to watch out, conduct these tasks in the largest possible space, preferably outdoors.

✓ *Student Drawing.* This would be a great time to have students draw a picture of themselves striking up and striking down to assess their knowledge of the critical cues of flat paddle and stiff wrist.

Striking Cues

The skill of striking with rackets and paddles is complex and has a number of critical cues associated with it. These cues include, for the underarm striking pattern:

Slanted Paddle	Follow Through
Paddle Way Back	Watch the Ball
Opposite Foot	

For the sidearm pattern, cues include:

Paddle Way Back	Opposite Foot
Side to Target	Follow Through
Flat Paddle	Watch the Ball
Firm Wrist	Low to High

We have elected to highlight only some of these cues with various tasks throughout the remainder of the chapter. Feel free to interchange the cues that will best meet your students' needs with those we have selected.

Striking Forward Against a Wall

Setting: A shuttlecock, a foam ball or a dead tennis ball, and a paddle for each child; children about 5 feet from the wall, with spots to remind them of their self-space

Cues	
Paddle Way Back	(Start the paddle back behind your hips.)
Opposite Foot	(Just as in throwing, step forward on the foot opposite the arm you are using to strike.)
Slanted Paddle	(For this hit, keep the paddle face flat, but slant it just slightly toward the ceiling so the ball will go to the wall.)

The slight angle (slant) of the paddle face is critical here. It is helpful to demonstrate the subtle difference between it and a flat paddle and what the skill looks like.

Tasks/Challenges:

T Facing the wall and at your own spot, drop the shuttlecock and try to strike it so it goes straight ahead—forward toward the wall. **This strike is a little like an underhand throw—you are actually striking the shuttlecock from slightly underneath, not from the side.**

T Now trade in your shuttlecock for a ball. This will be a little harder, but it's the same idea. Try to strike the ball with the paddle so it goes straight forward toward the wall. You may want to let the ball bounce first before you hit it. Remember, just one hit at a time. Drop, hit, catch—then go again.

C Practice until you can hit the ball so it travels to the wall five times.

C Ask the person beside you to watch you strike the ball. Your neighbor will give you a point if you step forward on the opposite foot as you hit. You'll get a second point if you swing the paddle underhand, not sidearm or overhead. Practice with your neighbor watching for a few minutes; then watch your neighbor.

✓ *Peer Observation.* The preceding task could easily be turned into a peer assessment of critical cues by using a peer observation card. See Figure 12.9, page 186.

Striking Up, Down, and Forward

Setting: Four stations set up (see Figure 25.4), with children divided equally among the stations; at stations 1 and 3, foam balls or dead tennis balls and paddles for every child; at station 2, balloons and paddles for each

Figure 25.4 Station setup for ups, downs, and forwards.

child; at station 4, yarn balls and paddles for each child, as well as seven hoops in a cloverleaf pattern for each pair

Cues

Stations 1, 2, and 3

Flat Paddle	(Keep your paddle flat as a board.)
Stiff Wrist	(Keep your wrist tight; don't let it flop around.)
Watch the Ball	(Keep your eyes on the ball all the time.)

Station 4

Paddle Way Back	(Start the paddle back behind your hips.)
Opposite Foot	(Just as in throwing, step forward on the foot opposite the arm you are using to strike.)
Slanted Paddle	(For this hit, keep the paddle face flat, but slant it just slightly toward the ceiling so the ball will go to the hoops.)

Tasks/Challenges:

T The stations today provide a chance to practice all the striking activities we have been doing. Some are just practice; others are challenges. Do your best. Change on the signal.

Station 1: How many downward hits can you do with no mistakes? Count them.

Station 2: Travel across the gym, striking the balloon upward as you go.

Station 3: Can you do five single upward hits without moving from self-space? Try continuous hits.

Station 4: Strike the ball so it travels forward and lands in a hoop. Each time you are successful, increase your distance by taking one giant step backward. One partner can strike and the other can collect the balls. Switch every five strikes.

✓ *Self-Assessment.* The preceding task could easily be turned into a self-assessment by having children record on cards how they did at each station.

Striking to Self on Both Sides of the Body

Setting: A wooden or foam paddle, a dead tennis ball or foam ball, and a spot or other way to define self-space for each child

Cues

Flat Paddle	(Keep your paddle flat as a board.)
Stiff Wrist	(Keep your wrist tight, don't let it flop around.)
Watch the Ball	(Keep your eyes on the ball at all times.)

Tasks/Challenges:

T In tennis, racquetball, or badminton, players use both sides of the paddle. Let's try this. Keep hitting the ball up. Try to hit the ball with one side of the paddle, then the other.

T If that is easy, see if you can use both sides of the paddle and both sides of the body. Try to not always strike the ball when it is right in front of you.

T Can you make a rainbow with the ball? Hit it on one side of your body and then the other so the ball travels in a rainbow shape. Remember, if you miss the ball and have to chase it, go back to your self-space before you start striking again.

C How many rainbows can you make? Each time the ball goes over your head, it counts as one. Five rainbows without a miss would be excellent!

Striking to Wall Targets

Setting: A wooden paddle and tennis ball for each student; 12- to 20-inch circles about 6 feet up on the wall in a scattered pattern

Cues

Paddle Way Back	(Start the paddle back behind your hips.)
Opposite Foot	(Just as in throwing, step forward on the foot opposite the arm you are using to strike.)
Slanted Paddle	(For this hit, keep the paddle face flat, but slant it just slightly toward the ceiling so the ball will go to the wall.)

Tasks/Challenges:

T Find a spot about 10 feet from the wall in front of a circle. Strike the ball to the wall, trying to hit the circle. Remember, this is a back-to-front swing—like an underhand throw. **If you are doing it correctly, your arm will almost brush your hip on the way forward.**

T For the next five hits, freeze your follow-through. **Check to see if you have the opposite foot forward and your arm extended, with the racket face slanted slightly toward the ceiling.**

C When you think you can do five perfect hits with opposition and slanted racket facing the target, raise your hand and I will come to observe or a friend can observe for you.

T Try to send the ball to the wall so it touches within 2 to 3 inches of the target.

C Can you come that close five times?

T Take a giant step backward. Strike the ball so it contacts the wall at the height of the target.

T When you are successful in hitting the target six times, take another giant step backward.

T Move back to your first space closest to the wall. See if you can use an underhand strike to make the ball drop just in front of the wall.

T When you can successfully drop the shot just in front of the wall, take a giant step backward and try the drop shot from the longer distance.

C Pick your favorite distance. Count how many times you can hit the target without a mistake. How many times can you drop the ball just in front of the wall?

🧠 How does the paddle face differ when striking to the wall from when striking up or down?

Striking for Distance (Varying the Force)

Setting: Outdoors on a large field (so children can work safely without hitting one another); children all facing the same way, either in a line or away from the center of a circle; a paddle and a variety of objects to strike for each child; objects (spots or cones) for use as markers

Cues	
Opposite Foot	(Just as in throwing, step forward on the foot opposite the arm you are using to strike.)
Slanted Paddle	(For this hit, keep the paddle face flat, but slant it just slightly toward the ceiling so the ball will go to the target. Use less slant for longer hits.)
Low to High	(Follow through low to high.)

Tasks/Challenges:

T Standing on the line, all facing the same direction so you won't hit anyone else, practice striking the objects, changing the amount of force you use for hitting. Sometimes use a lot of force, sometimes not very much force. Each time, make sure you use the proper underarm swing and follow through, no matter what amount of force you use. Use up all your objects and then go collect them.

C This time you're going to play a game with yourself. First, strike an object as far as possible. Take a marker, and mark the place where your object fell. Be sure you can see the mark from the striking line. Now try to hit an object to halfway between the striking line and your far object. Practice until you feel as if you've really figured out just exactly the right amount of force to use. Then see if you can hit the middle spot three times in a row.

T After you've done this task three times in a row, hit another object as far as you can, mark it, and try the same thing all over again.

Striking for Hoops (Varying the Distance)

Setting: Partners; a wooden paddle and a variety of objects to hit for each child; a hoop to serve as a target for each pair

Cues	
Opposite Foot	(Just as in throwing, step forward on the foot opposite the arm you are using to strike.)
Slanted Paddle	(For this hit, keep the paddle face flat, but slant it just slightly toward the ceiling so the ball will go to the target. Use less slant for longer hits.)
Low to High	(Follow through low to high.)

Tasks/Challenges:

T Place your hoop on the ground. One partner will be the hitter; the other, the catcher. The hitter strikes the object so it lands in the hoop—that is, it hits the target. First, stay close, and then after you can hit the target three times, move back a few steps and try again. Your partner will keep the objects from going all over the place. After you take six hits, switch places with your partner for six hits and then switch back.

C Now you're going to make a game out of striking into hoops. Place three hoops on the floor, one about 3 feet away from you, one 6 feet away, and one 10 feet away. One partner will try to strike so the object lands in each hoop; the other partner will collect the object after the hits. Then the partners switch places. You can make up any other rules you wish, but you both need to practice striking into all three hoops.

✓ *Teacher or Student Observation.* This task lends itself well to a teacher or student observation checklist on the use of the critical cues for striking at various distances. *See Chapter 12 for the development of checklists.*

Forehand grip   Backhand grip

Figure 25.5 Examples of forehand and backhand grips.

Striking Forehand to the Wall

Setting: A paddle and ball for each child; marks or spots to define self-space; large Xs placed about 3 feet high on the wall in front of each space

Cues

Flat Paddle	(Keep your paddle flat as a board.)
Stiff Wrist	(Keep your wrist tight; don't let it flop around.)
Side to Wall	(Keep to the wall the side opposite the arm you're using to hit.)
Opposite Foot	(Just as in throwing, step forward on the foot opposite the arm you are using to strike.)

An additional cue sometimes needed with the sidearm pattern is to keep the elbow away from the side. We use that cue as necessary with individuals or groups of children.

Tasks/Challenges:

T Until now you have used an underhand pattern to strike the ball. Now we are going to learn a new pattern: the sidearm pattern, similar to what is used in tennis and racquetball. **This time your side is to the wall and your paddle is flat.** This is called the forehand, and you will use the forehand grip (Figure 25.5). Practice striking the ball to the wall from a mark on the floor using the sidearm pattern. Remember, these are single hits—drop, hit, and catch, and go again.

C Practice until you can hit the ball so it travels to the wall five times.

T After you can hit the wall five times, take one giant step backward and try from that distance. When you can hit the wall five times, move backward again.

T Return to your first spot, and try to hit the X on the wall in front of your space. When you can make five hits, move backward again.

C Pick your favorite distance. How many times can you hit the target without missing?

With the forehand and backhand grips, we demonstrate the grip before the task, observe the children's grips as they practice, and provide feedback as necessary. We do not spend a lot of time teaching the grip.

Striking Backhand to the Wall

Setting: Partners; a paddle and a ball for each child; marks or spots to define self-space; large Xs placed about 3 feet high on the wall in front of each space

Cues

Flat Paddle	(Keep your paddle flat toward the wall all the time.)
Stiff Wrist	(Keep your wrist tight; don't let it flop around.)
Watch the Ball	(Keep your eyes on the ball all the time. Watch it hit the paddle.)
Same Foot/ Same Shoulder	(Just as in throwing a flying disc, step forward on the same foot. The shoulder of the arm you are using to strike should be toward the wall.)

Tasks/Challenges:

T This is also a sidearm pattern, but from the other side of your body. In tennis it is called the backhand, and you will use the backhand grip (Figure 25.5). It is the same as the forehand, except the side of your body with the striking arm is to the wall, and you step forward on the same foot as your striking arm. You reach across your body to hit. With a partner find a space at the wall, one partner will drop the ball while the other one strikes and hits to the wall after the bounce. After every five hits, switch roles. *(Demonstrate this as the partner needs to drop so the hitting partner can hit backhand.)*

T By yourself now, start with a strike on the forehand side and hit so the ball comes to your backhand. After that, try to hit on the backhand side as much as you can. Let the ball bounce before striking it back to the wall. You may catch it and start over each time or hit continuously.

C Practice until you can hit the ball so it travels to the wall five times.

T After you can hit the wall five times, take one giant step backward and try from that distance. When you can hit the wall five times, move backward again.

T Return to your first spot, and try to hit the X on the wall in front of your space. When you can make five hits, move backward again.

C Pick your favorite distance. How many times can you hit the target without missing?

Striking at High and Low Targets

Setting: A paddle and a ball for each child; four stations (see Figure 25.6 for set up). At stations 1 and 2: spots marked on the floor about 6 and 10 feet from the wall; targets on the wall in front of each space about 3 feet high. At station 3: spots marked on the floor about 10 feet from the wall; targets on the wall about 6 feet high (see Figure 25.7). At station 4: hoops on the floor against the wall; spots marked in various places around the hoops about 3, 6, 10, and 15 feet away. *This sequence of activities is an example of task teaching.*

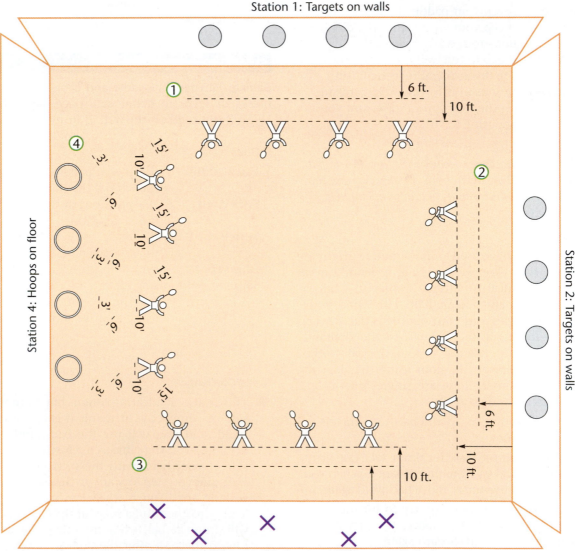

Figure 25.6 Station setup for striking at high and low targets.

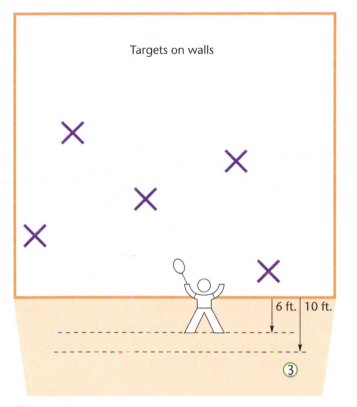

Figure 25.7 Target design for striking at high and low targets, station 3. *The Xs on the wall should be large enough to be hit easily.*

Cues

Paddle Face	(Your paddle will be slightly slanted or flat depending on which striking pattern you use.)
Stiff Wrist	(Keep your wrist tight; don't let it flop around.)
Watch the Ball	(Keep your eyes on the ball all the time. Watch it hit the paddle.)
Opposite Foot/ Same Foot	(Step forward on the opposite foot for the forehand; the same foot for the backhand.)

Auditory Feedback

Place a metal gong, small bells, loose plastic jugs, or similar sound-producing objects on a wall as targets. Young children enjoy the auditory feedback when contact is made.

Task/Challenges:

Ⓣ You have practiced both underhand and sidearm striking patterns. You can use them both, but one is better for some things, and the other is better for

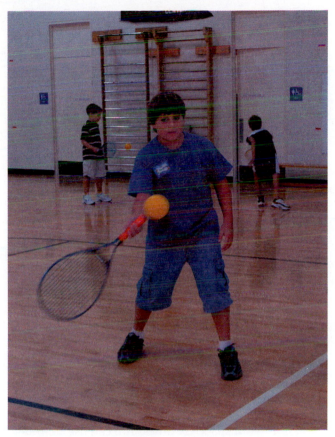

Children at the control level benefit from striking a ball rebounding from the wall.

other things. The underhand pattern works best when you want to send the ball to high places or make it drop low. The sidearm pattern works when you want the ball to go in a more straightforward route. Now you will get a chance to mix them up. At each station you will have to decide which striking pattern is best to use. See if you can figure out each station. I will tell you that at station 2 you have to use the backhand.

Station 1: Try to hit the target as many times as you can. When you hit the target six times, move backward to the next mark.

Station 2: Try to hit the target with a backhand pattern. What is the highest number of times you can hit the wall from each spot?

Station 3: Pick out one X on the target and see if you can hit it five times; then choose another X, and another, and finally the last X. When you can hit all of them five times, move backward one step.

Station 4: From each of the marks on the floor, see if you can drop the ball into the hoop.

✓ *Exit Slip.* It would be appropriate here to use an exit slip to assess the children's understanding of the various striking patterns, their cues, and their uses. *See Chapter 12 for examples.*

Striking to Different Places

Setting: A paddle and a ball for each child; marks or spots to define self-space; large Xs about 3 feet high on the wall in front of each space

Cues	
Paddle Face	(Your paddle will be slightly slanted or flat depending on which striking pattern you use.)
Low to High	(Follow through low to high.)
Watch the Ball	(Keep your eyes on the ball all the time. Watch it hit the paddle.)
Opposite Foot	(Just as in throwing, step forward on the foot opposite the arm you are using to strike.)

Tasks/Challenges:

T This time, instead of trying to hit the X, pretend the target is your opponent. Try to hit a space about 2 feet to the right of the X. Practice until you can hit your space six times. You can use an underhand or a sidearm pattern.

T Now practice trying to hit a space to the left of the X. Again, practice until you can hit the space six times.

T This time, practice doing one hit to the right, the next hit to the left, and the next hit to the X. See if you can repeat your pattern five times.

C Ask the person next to you to be your partner. You will call out where you are going to hit before the strike. Your partner gives a thumbs-up if you hit where you called out or a thumbs-down if you didn't. After eight hits, trade places.

✓ *Peer Observation.* The previous task is a great peer observation assessment task. *See Chapter 12 for more information on peer assessments.*

Striking Through a Target

Setting: A hoop suspended at about shoulder height for each group of two; a paddle for each child; one ball per group

Cues	
Paddle Face	(Your paddle will be flat or slightly slanted depending on which striking pattern you use.)

Watch Ball/ Watch Target	(Keep your eyes on the ball all the time: See it hit the paddle; see it go to the target. Watch the target out of the corner of your eye.)
Opposite Foot/ Same Foot	(Step forward on the opposite foot for the forehand; the same foot for the backhand.)

Tasks/Challenges:

T At your hoop, one of you will bounce the ball on the floor and then try to strike it through the hoop. The partner will catch the ball and return it to the striker. After 10 strikes, change places.

T Now that you've practiced by first letting the ball bounce, try it without letting the ball bounce. In other words, just drop the ball, hit it before it hits the ground, and try to make it go through the hoop.

C Since you are so good at this, why don't we make it a game? How many hits in a row can you and your partner combined get?

Striking an Object to Send It over a Net

Setting: A net (or a rope between two chairs) about 2 to 3 feet high for each group of partners; a paddle for each child; one ball per group

⚠ When striking with a partner, children tend to forget their own space and often unknowingly encroach on the space of other groups, risking collisions. Therefore, for this task and all tasks that involve striking to a partner, have children clearly define their space with lines or spots.

Cues	
Paddle Face	(Your paddle will be flat or slightly slanted depending on which pattern you use.)
Watch Ball/ Watch Target	(Keep your eyes on the ball all the time: See it hit the paddle; see it go to the target. Watch the target out of the corner of your eye.)
Opposite Foot/ Same Foot	(Step forward on the opposite foot for the forehand; the same foot for the backhand.)

Tasks/Challenges:

T With one partner on either side of the net, partner 1 strikes the ball across the net. Partner 2, instead of hitting the ball back, will catch it and throw it back to partner 1. After 10 hits, change roles. It helps to bounce the ball on the floor once before you hit it across the net.

T This time, use three different striking patterns to hit the ball across the net: forehand swing, backhand swing, and underhand swing. Take 10 practices with one swing, and then switch; take 10 practices with another swing, and then switch; take 10 practices with the third swing, and then switch. Ready? Three different ways of striking, 10 practices each.

T You can practice any way of striking you want this time, but try to pick a spot on the opposite side of the net and hit the ball to that spot, as if you were aiming for a target. Ten practices each, then switch.

Many teachers hesitate to teach striking over nets due to a lack of equipment. A simple solution so children in every group have their own net to work over is to suspend a rope between two chairs. This way you can set up nets of different heights and lengths at various places around the space. Let children set up their "own nets" in their "own space" for increased responsibility and more effective use of space.

Striking a Ball Rebounding from a Wall

Setting: Wall space, with a line marked about 3 feet up the wall and a line marked on the ground 6 to 8 feet from the wall; a paddle and a ball for each child

Striking Safely

To be accomplished both safely and effectively, striking activities require a great deal of space. Unfortunately, many indoor facilities in elementary schools don't have such spaces available. If this is true at your school and there aren't any outdoor alternatives, you can have two activities going simultaneously in the space available. Some children can carry out striking activities against the walls while other children carry out activities that require less space, such as balancing or weight transference, in the center of the space or on a stage area.

Cues

Quick Feet	(As the ball returns, you want to be behind it and a little to the side. You will have to move quickly to get there.)
Watch the Ball	(Keep your eyes on the ball all the time. See it hit the paddle; see it go to the wall.)

Bend Knees	(You want to contact the ball at about your waist. You'll have to bend your knees to do this.)

Tasks/Challenges:

T Now you're going to have a chance to strike the ball against a wall. In your space, about 6 feet from the wall, practice striking the ball against the wall with a forehand strike and the forehand grip (Figure 25.5). **When you hit the ball, you should be slightly behind and about an arm's length to the side of the ball.**

C Here comes the challenge. See how many times you can strike the ball against the wall and let the ball bounce only once before hitting it again. If you miss, just start counting over.

T Now the activity will be a little harder for you. Hit the ball to different places on the wall, always trying to be ready to hit it when it comes back to you. **In other words, you'll have to figure out where the ball is coming when it bounces off the wall and be behind it so you can hit it again. Remember, hit different places on the wall.**

C This time, the challenge is really hard. You need to see how many times in a row you can hit the ball above the line on the wall. The ball can bounce only once on the ground between hits. Ready? Go.

T This time, you can do what you've wanted to do for a long time: Hit the ball as hard as you can. But there are some rules. First, the ball must land behind the line marked on the ground; second, you're allowed only one bounce to hit the ball back. This prevents you from hitting the ball so hard you can't get to it.

A When allowing children to strike the ball as hard as they can, make sure they are spread far apart and clearly understand the rules for retrieving a ball that has gone into another person's space.

※ When do you use a forehand grip and swing? A backhand grip and swing?

Striking Continuously Over and Through a Target

Setting: A hoop, hoop stand, two paddles, and a ball for each set of partners

Cues

Quick Feet	(As the ball returns, you want to be behind it and a little to the side. You will have to move quickly to get there.)

| Watch the Ball | (Keep your eyes on the ball all the time. See it hit the paddle; see it go over the hoop.) |
| Bend Knees | (You want to contact the ball at about your waist. You'll have to bend your knees to do this.) |

Tasks/Challenges:

C Now you'll play a game with your partner using all you have learned. Set up the hoop on the hoop stand on the center line of your area. Hit the ball back and forth over the hoop, letting the ball bounce on your side before hitting it back. After five hits over the hoop, the receiver must hit the ball through the hoop so it goes to the partner's side. If the hit through the hoop is good, play continues for another five "overs" and one "through." If the "through" is not good, the five "overs" start over again.

Utilization Level (GLSP): Learning Experiences Leading to Skill Development

Children at the utilization level are able to contact a ball repeatedly without a miss (bouncing it up or down with a paddle or racket) and send a ball or other object various distances and in different directions. Experiences at this level enable children to strike with an implement, not as an invariant skill, but in dynamic environments that involve partners and striking from different positions in relation to the body. These children are now ready to apply striking skills in dynamic situations, such as moving into various positions to contact an object at different places around the body and returning shots to a partner.

A note about cues: Although several cues are listed for many of the learning experiences, it's important to focus on only one cue at a time. This way, the children can really concentrate on that cue. Once you provide feedback to the children and observe that most have learned a cue, it's time to focus on another one.

Hitting from Different Places

Setting: A space about 10 feet by 10 feet; partners, each with a paddle; one ball per group

| Cues | |
| Watch the Ball | (Keep your eyes on the ball all the time. See it hit the paddle; see your partner hit it.) |

Bend Knees	(You want to contact the ball at about your waist. You'll have to bend your knees to do this.)
Side to Target	(Whether you strike forehand or backhand, your side should face your partner.)
Get Home	(Return to a position in the center and near the back of your space after each hit. This is called home. It will take quick feet to get there.)

Tasks/Challenges:

T This time, your partner is going to throw rather than hit to you. Partner 1 will throw the ball to partner 2 so it bounces once before it reaches partner 2. Partner 2—the hitting partner—then tries to hit the ball straight back to partner 1—the thrower—regardless of where the ball has been sent. Partner 1 then catches the ball and throws to a new place. After 10 throws, switch places. The first time, always throw the ball to your partner's right side. The next time, always throw it to your partner's left side.

T This time, don't let your partner know to which side you're going to throw the ball. **Hitters, as soon as you see the ball leave the thrower's hand, adjust your position so you can return the ball.** Throw 10 times, and change.

In the beginning stages of striking a ball sent by a partner, children benefit from having the ball tossed consistently to their preferred or nonpreferred side. This way they can progress to adjusting the preparatory stage according to the direction of the oncoming ball.

✓ *Peer Observation.* This is an excellent time for a student observation of the critical cues practiced at the control level. True learning occurs when children can use the cues correctly in dynamic, unpredictable situations. *See Chapter 12 for assessment examples.*

Hitting Cooperatively and Continuously with a Partner

Setting: A space about 10 feet by 10 feet; partners, each with a paddle and one ball

Cues	
Get Home	(Return to a position in the center and near the back of your space after each hit. This is called home. It will take quick feet to get there.)
Watch the Ball	(Keep your eyes on the ball all the time. See it hit the paddle; see your partner hit it.)

Striking activities require well-defined spaces.

Bend Knees	(You want to contact the ball at about your waist. You'll have to bend your knees to do this.)

Tasks/Challenges:

T With your partner, in a space by yourselves, see if you can strike the ball back and forth to each other. The ball should bounce in the middle, but remember to get ready to hit the ball again after each hit.

C Set a personal-best goal with your partner for the number of hits you can get without missing. See if you can attain your goal. Give your partner your best hit each time.

T Make sure you and your partner practice hitting on both sides of your body.

Tip: The preceding task can be used with any of the striking patterns or a combination of patterns. You may need to remind children about the cue differences for sidearm and underhand striking.

❀ Where is home position when hitting with a partner?

Striking to Different Places Around a Partner

Setting: A space about 10 feet by 20 feet for each set of partners; two paddles and a ball

Cues	
Get Home	(Return to a position in the center and near the back of your space after each hit. It will take quick feet to get there.)

Cues	
Watch the Ball	(Keep your eyes on the ball all the time. See it hit the paddle; see your partner hit it.)
Low to High	(Follow through low to high in the direction you want the ball to go.)

Tasks/Challenges:

T With your partner, strike the ball back and forth, each time hitting to the alternate side of your partner's body. In other words, once you will hit to your partner's left and the next time to your partner's right. Try to keep the ball going for as long as possible. *(Have skilled students demonstrate what it looks like to hit to alternate sides.)*

C As you practice now, see how long you can keep the ball going, but almost try to make your partner miss.

Striking Overhead

Setting: A wall space, with a line marked on the wall about 3 feet from the floor, a spot marked on the ground about 10 feet from the wall, and a paddle and a ball for each child

Cues	
Toss	(Toss the ball just barely above the top of the paddle.)
Reach and Stretch	(When you hit the ball, reach and stretch as high as possible.)
Flat and Down	(Your paddle should be flat and facing slightly downward and forward as you strike the ball.)

Demonstrate the skill of striking overhead.

Tasks/Challenges:

T Stand on your spot, about 10 feet from the wall. Toss the ball higher than your racket can reach in the air and then stretch to hit the ball when it's at its highest point. In other words, throw the ball up, and when it reaches the very top of the throw—the point where it won't go up any farther and hasn't started to come down—hit it so it goes against the wall. Don't try to hit the ball back when it bounces off the wall; just catch it and start over.

T Now that you've caught on to this idea, try to make the ball go down so it hits the wall near the line, about 3 feet above the floor. **To make it go down like that, the face of your racket must point slightly down as you hit the ball. Give it a try. Remember, watch the ball contact the racket so you can see what you're doing.**

T This time, try to strike overhead again, but have the ball strike the wall just above the line. **Watch your racket contact the ball so you can tell which direction your racket face is pointed.**

☑ *Exit Slip or Self-Assessment.* After this task, an exit slip or self-assessment would be an appropriate way to see how students feel about their ability to strike in overhead fashion. Questions on an exit slip might include a recall of the cues or a Helping Murgatroid question. A self-assessment might ask how well they did with each of the cues. *See Chapter 12 for further information on both of these techniques.*

Striking Overhead over a Net

Setting: Balls, a paddle, and a net 2 to 3 feet high for each set of partners

Cues	
Toss	(Toss the ball just barely above the top of the paddle.)
Reach and Stretch	(When you hit the ball, reach and stretch as high as possible.)
Flat and Down	(Your paddle should be flat and facing slightly down and forward as you strike the ball.)

Tasks/Challenges:

T You're going to practice hitting overhead again. Stand at the back of your court area, with your partner on the other side of the net. The partner with a paddle and some balls throws a ball in the air just above her or his reach, including the reach of the paddle, and then hits the ball down and over the net. This is like a tennis serve, only everything is smaller. The nonhitting partner should collect all the balls as they're hit. After 10 times, switch places.

T As you begin to hit more balls over the net and in the court, start to try to hit the ball a little harder. But don't attempt this until you can get 10 hits in a row over the net and into the court.

⚠ Whenever children are striking over a net, always have them clearly define the boundaries of their striking area so they don't interfere with others.

Striking Continuously Upward with a Group

Setting: Groups of three; a paddle for each player; one ball for each group

Cues	
Flat Paddle	(Keep your paddle flat as a board.)
Watch Ball/ Watch Players	(Always watch the ball. Watch the other players and the space out of the corner of your eye.)
Quick Feet	(It will take quick feet to get behind and under the ball.)

Tasks/Challenges:

C You need to clearly define the boundaries of your space; they should be approximately 8 to 10 feet apart. Your task is to keep the ball moving by striking it to each player without losing control. Bounces are allowed if you want them, but you do not have to use them. There is no set order in which you have to hit. See how long you can keep the ball going without losing control.

Setting: Groups of three, each group with one ball, three paddles, and five hoops; a space (see Figure 25.8 for set up)

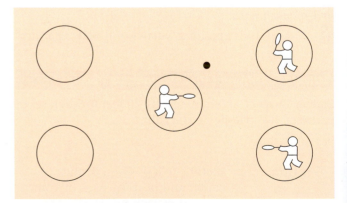

Figure 25.8 Setup for striking continuously upward with a group.

Tasks/Challenges:

C This is a game that will let you practice striking in the air. The person in the center hoop begins by striking the ball in the air to a person in one of the other hoops. That person receives the ball, strikes it twice to himself or herself, and sends it back to the middle person, who also has to strike it twice before sending it to the other outside person. That outside person has to strike three times to himself, before sending it back to the middle, where it is struck three times. This continues until the middle person has to strike seven times to himself or herself. Just to make it harder, the outside people, after striking the ball, have to move to one of the empty hoops. If anyone misses, the whole group starts over again. We will change middle hitters after seven hits or 3 minutes.

Striking in Various Aerial Pathways in Dynamic Situations

Setting: Different-colored pieces of yarn suspended one above the other—at 3 feet, 6 feet, and 10 feet—for use as nets (Figure 25.9); partners, each with a paddle; one shuttlecock, volleybird, or peteca per group

Cues

Slanted Paddle (Your paddle needs to have a flat face that is slanted upward.)

Low to High (Follow through low to high toward the string you are trying to go over.)

Get Home (After each hit, move back to your center back position to get ready to hit again.)

Tasks/Challenges:

T Using a shuttlecock (volleybird) and an underarm swing, try to make the object go over the lowest piece of yarn. After five tries, switch with your partner.

T Now try the middle piece of yarn. Do this five times each, then switch.

T Now the highest piece. For this one, you're really going to have to use a big underarm swing to get the object over the net.

C This task will be difficult. Try to keep the shuttlecock (volleybird) going with your partner, but this time, on the first hit, make it go over the low piece of yarn; on the next hit, make it go over the middle piece; on the third hit, make it go over the top piece. Then start over and reverse the order. Practice until you can do the sequence one time all the way through.

Striking Upward in a Dynamic Situation

Setting: Group of up to five people, each with a paddle; one ball per group

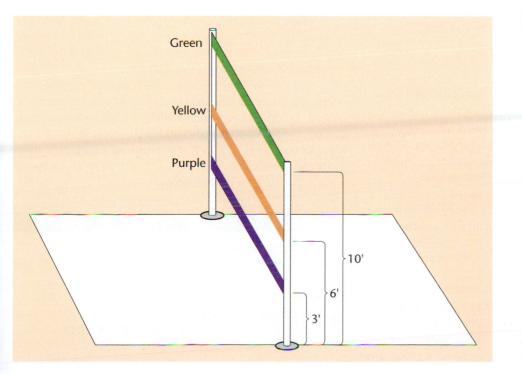

Figure 25.9 Setup for aerial pathways.

Green

Yellow

Purple

10'

6'

3'

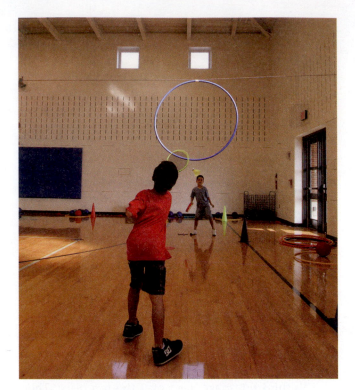

Striking using various aerial pathways provides challenges for utilization-level children.

Cues

Flat Paddle	(Keep your paddle flat as a board.)
Watch Ball/	(Always watch the ball; watch the
Watch Players	other players and the space out of the corner of your eye.)
Quick Feet	(It will take quick feet to get behind and under the ball.)

Tasks/Challenges:

C You are going to strike in a gamelike situation. Here are the rules:

1. One person stands in the middle of a circle.
2. The person in the middle hits the ball with a paddle straight up in the air and calls out the name of another person in the group.
3. The person whose name is called out must run to the middle of the circle, hit the ball up in the air before it bounces, and call out another student's name.
4. The caller takes the place of the person whose name was called out.

⚠ This is an exciting task for youngsters, and they often lose track of where they are in space. Constant safety reminders may be necessary.

The type of racket used can increase the complexity of any striking situation. A light, short-handled racket is the easiest

for a child to master; a heavy, long-handled racket is the most difficult. As children begin to master the skills of striking with rackets, we gradually change the type of racket used to make the task more difficult.

<h3>Proficiency Level (GLSP): Learning Experiences Leading to Skill Development</h3>

When the children have attained the proficiency level, they demonstrate a mature pattern of striking: the ability to control both body and implement while traveling and to select the most effective type of striking when responding to a partner.

Experiences at this level encourage children to enjoy the challenge of striking with short-handled implements in gamelike situations. These experiences involve partner or opponent relationships, spatial strategy, and the varied use of effort qualities. Because of the gamelike nature of the tasks, it can be quite tricky to keep these activities developmentally appropriate, especially in terms of active participation for all children. There are several solutions here. Set up multiple courts around the gym. The courts may be odd sizes, but they should allow for maximum participation. Another option is to have stations, several that offer gamelike activities and several that have practice opportunities that require less setup and space. Finally, you could have peer assessment opportunities in which half the members of a small group will play and half will observe; then switch. Regardless of the solution, please remember that gamelike activities should be appropriate for all children. See Chapter 30 for more information on game options in physical education.

A note about cues: At the proficiency level, tasks are more complex, typically requiring children to coordinate several movements simultaneously in a dynamic context. A list of cues is provided to assist the children in being more successful in the learning experiences. The challenge is in determining which cue will be most beneficial for each child . . . and when. Thus, careful observation and critical reflection become very important as you watch the children move and then decide which cue will be the most helpful to move each learner to a higher level.

<h3>Striking to One Wall with a Partner</h3>

Setting: Two children per group, each with a paddle; one ball per group; court (see the set up in Figure 25.10)

Cues

Get Home	(Return to a position in the center and near the back of your space after each hit.)

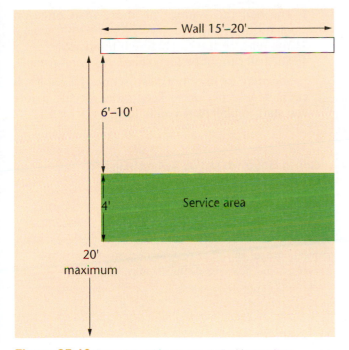

Figure 25.10 Setup for striking to one wall with a partner.

| **Watch the Ball** | (Keep your eyes on the ball all the time. See it hit the paddle; see it hit the wall; see your partner hit it.) |
| **Mix 'Em Up** | (It's time to use all your different strikes: to different spots on the wall and soft and hard strikes.) |

Tasks/Challenges:

Ⓒ The objective of this task is to hit the ball against a wall so your opponent is unable to return it. Here are the rules:

1. You may score only when you serve.
2. The ball may be returned either after one bounce or before the bounce.
3. To make your partner miss, you must use placement, not force. All shots should be of a force that is playable.

The courts are marked on the floor. To start play, partner 1 serves the ball against the wall, and partner 2 tries to return it. Each time partner 1 hits the ball, partner 2 tries to return it. You can play cooperatively—seeing how long you can keep the rally going—or competitively—accumulating points when you make your opponent miss. The choice is yours.

Striking at Angles to Two Walls with a Partner

Setting: Two people per group, each with a paddle; one ball per court; court (see the set up in Figure 25.11)

Cues	
Get Home	(Return to a position in the center and near the back of your space after each hit.)
Watch the Ball	(Keep your eyes on the ball all the time. See it hit the paddle; see it hit the wall; see your partner hit it.)
Mix 'Em Up	(It's time to use all your different strikes: to different spots on the wall and soft and hard strikes.)

Tasks/Challenges:

Ⓒ This activity is very much like the last one you played, except it's played in a corner instead of just flat against the wall. The same rules apply as when you hit against the wall: There are two players; you can play cooperatively or competitively; and the ball is hit either after one bounce or before it bounces. And ball placement should cause someone to miss, not force. Go ahead and get used to playing in the corner.

For a more advanced game of striking at angles to two walls with a partner, see Striking to the Wall—Varying Levels, Force, and Body Position in Chapter 24 (page 477).

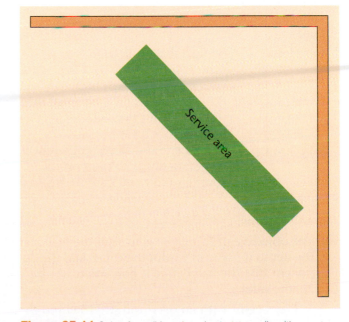

Figure 25.11 Setup for striking at angles to two walls with a partner.

Striking to and from Different Places

Setting: Four square courts, each about 15 by 15 feet, labeled A, B, C, and D; groups of four students, with paddles and a ball

Cues	
Ready Position	(Keep your weight on the balls of your feet, with your knees slightly bent.)
Paddle inFront	(To be ready, hold your paddle in front of your body about waist high.)
Back of Square	(Stay near the back of the square so you can move forward.)

Tasks/Challenges:

C This task is like Four Square. Here's how it works:

1. Square A starts the game.
2. You must hit the ball to another square.
3. The ball can't be hit to the person who hit it to you.
4. You must hit the ball after its first bounce.
5. The person who misses the ball goes to square D, and everyone else moves up a square.
6. All strikes must be underhand.

Partner Striking Across a Net

Setting: Partners; a low net on a surface that allows the ball to bounce, with a marked-off court at each net area for each pair

Cues	
Get Home	(Return to a position in the center and near the back of your space after each hit.)
Watch the Ball	(Keep your eyes on the ball all the time. See it hit the paddle; see your partner hit it.)
Mix 'Em Up	(It's time to use all your different strikes: to different spots on the court and soft and hard strikes.)

Tasks/Challenges:

C The objective of this game is to send the ball over the net so it bounces within the court, and the opponent hits the ball before it bounces twice. Here are the rules:

1. Play begins with an overhead strike behind the end line.

2. The ball can bounce no more than once on each side of the net.
3. You may hit the ball before it bounces.
4. The ball cannot be hit so hard it is unreturnable.

You may or may not keep score; the choice is yours. If you decide to keep score, decide before you start to play how you'll do so.

Going Beyond: USTA School-Based Programs

For those interested in progressing to longer-handled rackets the United States Tennis Association has developmentally appropriate school-based educational programs that offer curricular as well as equipment support. See http://tennis.teamusa.org/resources/coaches/usta-school-tennis-for-physical-educators for more information about these programs.

Aerial Striking over a Net

Setting: Solid rackets, paddles, or badminton rackets; shuttlecocks, tennis balls, or volleybirds; one net (between children's shoulder and head height) for each set of partners; a marked-off court at each net with a serving line (Figure 25.12)

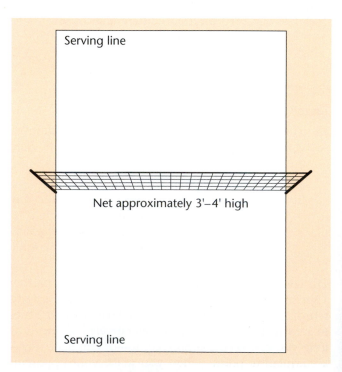

Figure 25.12 Court setup for aerial net games.

Cues

Get Home	(Return to a position in the center and near the back of your space after each hit.)
Watch the Ball	(Keep your eyes on the ball all the time. See it hit the paddle; see your partner hit it.)
Mix 'Em Up	(It's time to use all your different strikes: to different spots on the court and soft and hard strikes.)

Tasks/Challenges:

C The objective of this aerial net game is to send the object over the net so the opponent can return it before it touches the floor. Here are the rules:

1. Play begins with an underhand strike behind the serve line.
2. Aerial strikes continue until the object touches the floor or goes out of bounds.
3. If you like, you can make up your own way of changing serves and keeping points.

Aerial net games using a shuttlecock can be played with regular tambourines, with old ones that are discarded from rhythm bands because the jingles have been lost, or with tambourines with rubberized heads. Children enjoy the sound made when the shuttlecock strikes the tambourine.

Team Striking Across a Net

Setting: Groups of four with Nerf tennis balls, paddles, and a net; a court of four equal squares, with a net running down the center

Cues

Get Home	(Return to a position in the center and near the back of your space after each hit.)
Watch the Ball	(Keep your eyes on the ball all the time. See it hit the paddle; see your opponents hit it.)
Mix 'Em Up	(It's time to use all your different strikes: to different spots on the court and soft and hard strikes.)
Cover Space	(You want to block all the space on the court. One player usually plays near the net, and one back. When one moves, the other must adjust.)

Tasks/Challenges:

T This task is like a miniversion of tennis or pickleball doubles. Here's how you play:

1. There are two people on each team.
2. Team A serves underhand and diagonally to team B.
3. The two teams hit the ball back and forth across the net until one team misses.
4. When the team serving misses, the other team takes over serving.
5. When the receiving team misses, the serving team keeps serving.
6. The serve always begins in the back right-hand corner behind the line, alternates to the back left-hand corner on every consecutive serve, and then back to the right.
7. The ball may be hit before it bounces or after one bounce.
8. The ball cannot be hit so hard that it is not returnable.

✓ *Homework.* At this point in learning to strike, you might give children a homework assignment to observe a tennis match in person or on television and analyze how one player uses the strategies of getting home, watching the ball, mixing up shots, and covering space.

Group Striking Across a Net

Setting: Groups of six, with badminton rackets or paddles, shuttlecocks, and a net

Cues

Quick Feet	(Move quickly to get behind and under the shuttlecock.)
Close to Net	(One player should be close to the net for the last hit.)
Get Home	(After each hit, move back to your position on the court so the space is covered.)

Tasks/Challenges:

C You're going to strike across a net with a team. Here are the rules:

1. There are three players on each side.
2. A player near the back of the court serves underhand to the other side of the net. The opponents hit the shuttlecock twice on their side of the net and then return it over the net.
3. The shuttlecock must be hit twice by two different players on each side of the net before it's returned.
4. The shuttlecock must be hit before it touches the ground.
5. When the serving team misses, the other team scores.
6. Keep score any way you want or not at all.

⚠ The preceding activity is an enjoyable game, but the use of long-handled rackets requires enough room to allow children to strike without hitting each other. Play the game in a space at least the size of a regulation volleyball court.

Self-Designed Racket Games

This task is an example of a child-designed instructional approach. See Chapter 10 for more ideas on child-designed tasks.

Setting: Depends on the game; groups of four or fewer, each child with an appropriate racket or paddle of choice

Cues

Appropriate to the game

Tasks/Challenges:

Ⓒ Today you're going to combine all that you've practiced into a game. You'll make up your games yourselves. In your groups, make up a game that involves striking with a racket. You can have whatever rules you want as long as you include these two: (1) The game must involve striking with rackets, and (2) everyone in your group must be playing at the same time. In other words, nobody sits out and waits for a turn. Remember, groups of no more than four, striking with rackets, and everybody plays. Go.

After you've made up your rules and started to play your game, make sure you know your rules so you can tell somebody else how to play your game. At the end of class, I'll ask you to write down your game.

✔ *Event Task.* An appropriate assessment task at this point would be to have children write down how to play their games and then share the games with others. See Chapter 12 for more assessment examples.

Reading Comprehension Questions

1. Why is striking with rackets or paddles one of the last and most difficult skills to develop?
2. Students at the precontrol level benefit from striking an object suspended from a string. Describe three different ways to suspend objects.
3. What types of striking implements and objects are recommended for students at the precontrol level?
4. How does a teacher know when a child is ready to be challenged to strike the ball on the opposite side of the body (i.e., backhand)?
5. Describe the position of a child's arms and feet when the child is striking with a racket or paddle.
6. What characterizes each of the four generic levels of skill proficiency of striking with rackets and paddles?
7. What does a flat paddle look like? What does a slanted paddle face look like? What happens when an object is struck with a paddle held in each position?
8. What does it look like when children run around the ball instead of striking the ball on the opposite side of the body? Describe a task that would help them learn to not run around the ball.
9. A child swings a racket so it remains at waist level throughout the swing. What direction does the ball travel if the child strikes the ball too early in the swing? Too late in the swing?
10. Design six tasks related to striking with rackets or paddles. Rank them in order from the easiest to the hardest. Be certain to include at least one task from each skill level. Use a different striking implement or object for each task.
11. Name the major safety cue regarding striking.

References/Suggested Readings

[NASPE] National Association for Sport and Physical Education. 2004. *Moving into the future: National standards for physical education.* 2nd ed. Reston, VA: National Association for Sport and Physical Education.

Wickstrom, R. L. 1977. *Fundamental motor patterns.* 2nd ed. Philadelphia: Lea & Febiger.

Wickstrom, R. L. 1983. *Fundamental motor patterns.* 3rd ed. Philadelphia: Lea & Febiger.

Striking with Long-Handled Implements

By Lindy Mutter

The skill theme of striking is used in many games—from 4th of July backyard softball to baseball, golf, and hockey. We have divided striking into various skill themes: kicking and punting, volleying and dribbling, striking with rackets, and striking with long-handled implements. While this division allows us to cover in some detail the gamut of striking activities, the basic purpose in all striking is the same—giving impetus to an object with a hit, punch, or tap—although often the specific motion and the equipment differ.

Like the transferring weight and rolling and volleying and dribbling, we have subdivided striking activities in this chapter to more fully cover the striking activities that use long-handled implements. In three separate sections, this chapter focuses on one striking action that uses swings in a horizontal plane (batting) and two striking actions that use vertical (hockey-type and golf-type actions) planes. The implements used to accomplish these swings vary from bats to hockey sticks to golf clubs to Pilo-Polo sticks—yet all issue the underlying challenge of coordinating hands and eyes when striking with a long implement. Because vertical and horizontal swings have distinctive characteristics, key observation points for each are presented separately. Both swings involve striking away from the body, but the motor skills differ in relation to the purpose of the task.

We don't introduce children to striking with long-handled implements so they'll become experts at golf, baseball, or hockey. We provide children opportunities to practice striking patterns they're likely to use in a variety of contexts throughout their lives. This rationale can be fully appreciated when watching an adult trying to strike with a long-handled implement. If that individual has had no previous experience with a particular striking pattern, the results can be disastrous. Frustration will result, and ultimately the person may abandon the sport. Our emphasis is on giving children a variety of movement opportunities rather than on perfecting the technical aspects of a particular swing. Specific opportunities to refine and perfect different swings are provided at the secondary level or in private instruction.

Most long-handled implements are designed for adults. Because children aren't "regulation size," they find it difficult to manipulate implements of official size, length, and weight, so we use lightweight plastic implements in our programs, or we make implements that match the sizes of the children. This prevents the children from learning poor habits when they try to use equipment that is too heavy or too long. The equipment should never inhibit the mature striking pattern.

Generally, striking is the last fundamental motor pattern learned because of the complexity of the hand–eye coordination involved. Within this skill theme, there are also multiple levels of complexity. Actions that require striking a stationary ball (as in golf) are easier than actions that require the striking of a moving object (as in hockey). Both of these actions are less complex than striking a pitched ball with a bat. In the latter action, both objects are moving and never come to rest. In all cases, children may possess a mature striking pattern before they're able to consistently make contact with the ball.

Striking with Long-Handled Implements—Hockey Sticks

Think about it: Where would you find adults (or children for that matter) striking with a hockey stick–type implement except in hockey? What about polo? Hurling? Pilo Polo? Roller hockey? Croquet? All these activities require an object on the ground to be struck with a stick, and there are sure to be many more. Because the striking possibilities are endless, we focus on it as a generic skill rather than as a sport-specific skill. Remember, though, that striking as a skill is one of the last fundamental skills to develop because it requires fine hand–eye coordination and the control of two objects that do not come to rest. Our progression spiral for striking with a hockey stick appears on page 525. Striking with a golf club could have been included with striking with a hockey stick, but due to its specialized nature we have included it in a separate section later in this chapter.

A swing with a hockey stick–type implement uses a vertical arc—referred to as an underhand swinging pattern because in many ways it resembles the movement used to throw a ball underhand. As children learn to strike in a vertical pattern, watch for the following characteristics:

- The child's weight is shifted to the back foot.
- The hips and trunk rotate away from the ball.
- The implement is raised up and behind the back shoulder with the arms firm and the wrists cocked at the top of the backswing, and both knees remain bent.
- The weight shifts to the forward foot as the swing begins.
- Hips and spine rotate forward, forearm swings downward, and back arm and wrists uncock.
- Arms stay straight throughout the swing.

In addition, dribbling (stick handling) is also included as an underhand pattern. We have developed most of the tasks that utilize an underhand striking pattern around the shortened hockey-type swing because that is the action most often developed in elementary physical education, in our experience. Numerous implements can be substituted for hockey sticks (see the "Implements for Underhand Striking" box). See our skill theme progression for striking with hockey sticks for skill development ideas from precontrol through proficiency levels.

Skill Theme Development Progression

Striking with Long-Handled Implements— Hockey

Proficiency Level

Small-sided hockey invasion game
Keep-Away
Striking to dodge an opponent

Utilization Level

Two-on-one hockey
Keeping It Moving
Passing and receiving on the move
Striking from a stationary position to a moving target
One-on-one hockey
Traveling and striking for a goal
Pathways, speeds, and directions
Performing a continuous dribble and change of direction
Dribbling and changing directions backward
Striking to small targets

Control Level

Striking while dodging stationary obstacles
Striking to targets
Traveling and striking while changing pathways
Traveling and changing speeds
Traveling, stopping, and controlling the ball
Traveling slowly while striking a ball
Striking to a stationary partner
Striking to a target (Around the World)
Striking to targets
Striking for distance
Striking a stationary ball on the ground

Precontrol Level

Traveling slowly while striking a ball
Striking (dribbling) a ball in self-space
Striking to large targets
Striking a stationary ball

Before the children begin swinging bats, golf clubs, or hockey sticks, you will need to define clear zones and spaces where the swing may occur—and where it cannot. Use ropes, cones, hoops, and other equipment to provide a hitting zone (that is, an area for *each child* clearly defined by ropes or cones or spray paint if you are outside). For striking with bats and golf clubs, you will also need to define a "no-enter zone" so the children who are not swinging do not accidentally run into a bat or golf club. It is also important to teach children that when they hear the phrase "safety check" they should check around them to make they are in their own space. Chapter 8 becomes very important here—the children need to listen and follow your instructions so that no one gets injured.

Precontrol Level (GLSP): Activities for Exploration

Activities at the precontrol level ask children to explore all varieties of striking with long-handled implements. At this level, a chopping, downward swing is typical for any striking pattern. Children struggle just to make contact between the ball and the striking instrument. Therefore we give children activities that let them explore striking with the added length that comes with hockey sticks—and the greater demands that length places on their hand–eye coordination. Due to the difficulty of the skill, tasks are developed using large objects to be struck. Children explore striking stationary objects, and they begin to develop the ability to control a ball while traveling.

All activities at this level need to be done with balls of various sizes. For beginners, yarn balls or large plastic balls are easier because they're larger and/or don't roll as fast as other balls. For tasks that involve traveling, plastic pucks are easier to control initially if the lesson is being taught on a smooth wood or tile floor.

Striking a Stationary Ball

Setting: Preferably a large outdoor space (but can be adapted for an indoor space); plastic field hockey stick (see Figure 26.1) for each child (short-handled and long-handled street hockey sticks aren't appropriate); a variety of foam and plastic balls and pucks; each child in his or her individual striking zones defined by ropes or cones, facing a wall or an object that will block the ball

Tasks/Challenges:

T Stand beside your ball and strike it so it travels to the wall. Hit it hard so it goes all the way to the wall. Make sure to stop the ball when it comes back before you hit it again.

1. Dowel rod   Hose

2.   Coat hanger wire

3., 4.   Nail

5.   Tape

Figure 26.1 Construction of a hockey stick (design by Tom Trimble, University of Georgia).*

Materials
   Hardwood dowel rod, 5/8- by-39-inch
   Garden hose or rubber tubing
   5/8 inch (inside diameter)
   Roll of electrical or adhesive tape (one roll is enough for at least 12 sticks)
   Two flat-headed nails, 5/8 inch
   Coat hanger

Directions
1. Cut an 18-inch piece of the garden hose and slip it approximately 3½ inches onto the dowel.
2. Insert a piece of coat hanger wire into the hose so it butts up against the bottom of the dowel and extends almost to the end of the hose.
3. Bend the hose so the ends meet on the dowel rod. Form the hose at whatever angle you desire.
4. Use two nails to secure the hose to the dowel. One of the two nails can be used to attach the bottom portion of the hose, bent in half, to the top portion.
5. Use tape to further support the hose or the dowel.

*Prior to constructing equipment we recommend you check with school administration to be certain that district policy permits homemade equipment.

C Practice until you can hit the wall three times in a row.

T Practice hitting from both sides of your body. Each time, try to make the ball go to the wall.

T Try striking the ball so it sometimes goes along the floor and sometimes in the air. What makes it go in the air? On the ground?

T Trade in the ball for another kind of ball or a puck. Try all the different things with your new piece of equipment.

T Now move behind your ball. Try striking it to the wall from that position.

C Practice until you can get the ball or puck to the wall three times.

T If you are outside, practice striking the ball as far as you can. Practice strikes from the back and from the side. Which position do you like best?

Striking to Large Targets

Setting: A plastic hockey stick and a foam or plastic ball or puck for each child; a large target marked on the wall within 6 inches of the floor for each child; children about 6 feet from the target and at least 5 feet apart with individual striking zones marked with cones or ropes. The target needs to be far enough away (and high enough) so the children need to make a full, forceful swing to reach the target. If the target is placed too close, the children will not practice the mature swing that is the purpose of this task. Swinging for accuracy is taught later in the striking with long-handled-implement progression.

Tasks/Challenges:

T Stand to the side of the ball. Strike the ball toward the target, trying to hit the target.

C Your challenge is to see how many times in a row you can hit the target in front of you. Remember, stop the ball each time it comes back to you before hitting it again.

T When you can hit the target three times in a row, move back one giant step and try again.

Striking (Dribbling) a Ball in Self-Space

Setting: Children in self-space, each with a hoop, a hockey stick, and a foam or plastic ball or puck

Tasks/Challenges:

T In your own space inside the hoop, use the hockey stick to gently move the ball around in as many ways as possible. Don't leave your self-space.

T On the signal, begin striking the ball in your own space, and keep striking until you hear the signal to stop. Remember, stay in your own space. Do not travel.

C I will time you for 15 seconds. Try to keep your strikes going for the whole time.

Traveling Slowly While Striking a Ball

Setting: A hockey stick and a foam or plastic ball or puck for each child

Tasks/Challenges:

T This time, instead of staying in your own space, you are going to travel using all the space. Begin by walking throughout general space, tapping the ball as you did in self-space. The ball must always be very close to your stick.

T This time as you are walking, try to avoid running into others. This means you will have to keep the ball very close.

Implements for Underhand Striking

Although we have associated hockey with tasks that use an underhand striking action, other sports also use the underhand swing pattern. Several striking implements may be substituted for hockey sticks or golf clubs; many times, these alternatives may be more appropriate. Pilo-Polo sticks are lighter and softer than hockey sticks. Short-handled broomball sticks provide a wider striking surface but unfortunately are available only in certain areas of the country. Substitution of either of these implements not only may reduce the complexity of the task, but also can take the focus away from a single sport.

Modified equipment allows for swings with golf clubs to be practiced indoors.

Control Level: Learning Experiences Leading to Skill Development

At the control level, children begin to develop mature striking patterns that are used in increasingly complex contexts. They can be challenged with tasks that require them to include one or two other variables besides striking, such as traveling while striking or tapping an object along the ground combined with changing direction and/or speed.

A note about cues: Although several cues are listed for many of the learning experiences, it's important to focus on only one cue at a time. This way, the children can really concentrate on that cue. Once you provide feedback to the children and observe that most have learned a cue, it's time to focus on another one.

Striking a Stationary Ball on the Ground

Setting: Preferably a large outdoor space (but can be adapted for an indoor space); a plastic field hockey stick (short-handled or long-handled street hockey sticks aren't appropriate) and a plastic or foam ball for

each child; each child in his or her individual striking zones defined by ropes or cones, facing a wall or an object that will block the ball; at least 5 feet between children

Cues	
Arms Way Back	(With both hands on the stick, bring your arms way back as you swing.)
Watch the Ball	(Keep your eyes on the ball all the time.)
Knees Bent	(Keep your knees bent throughout the swing.)
Sweep Low	(Swing the stick forward sweeping the stick to make contact with the ball.)

Tasks/Challenges:

T When we explored striking with hockey sticks, you practiced hitting the ball to the wall by standing beside it and behind it and having it travel on

Figure 26.2 Hockey stick grip.

the ground. Using a full swing, practice striking the ball, standing beside it so it travels to the wall.

T As you practice, bring your backswing way back over your shoulders. Follow through so your arms end above your other shoulder—a full swing.

T Practice the same swing, but use a hockey grip (Figure 26.2); start the backswing below your waist and end below your waist. An easy way to help it end below your waist is to turn your wrists over on the follow-through. This is called a short swing.

T Using both swings—full and short—strike the ball to the wall with enough force so it comes back to you. Which swing sends the ball harder?

T Practice standing behind the ball and hitting.

T From that position, try to strike the ball with enough force so it rebounds back to you off the wall.

C Practice striking the ball against the wall until you can hit the wall three times in a row from each starting position.

T Stand behind the ball. In this position, most of you have been hitting the ball from the preferred side of your body. That is called your *forehand*. This time we are going to practice hitting the ball from the non-preferred side of your body. You don't change your hands; instead you use the back side of the stick to do it. Try to hit the ball to the wall this way.

T Practice hitting the ball hard enough so it rebounds back to you.

C Again try for three hits in a row that are hard enough so the ball comes back to you.

Which Swing?

The underhand swing patterns can be confusing. There is the side-to-the-target swing characteristic of passes that are intended to make the struck object travel a long distance; some swings have short backswings, some longer, some are made on the move, and some are made while stationary. In interactive settings—games like hockey, broomball, and Pilo Polo—it is unsafe for the swing to come above the waist on either the backswing or the follow-through. Also, to complicate matters, in hockey-type situations, there is also an underhand striking pattern that requires the passer to face the target. This striking action is used for most short (10 yards or less) passing situations using both a forehand and a backhand action. Given the space restrictions of physical education classes, especially when they are taught inside, this underhand swing is most frequently used. Thus, at the precontrol and control levels, we have children practice swings from both the side and the back. Other than the starting position in relation to the ball, the swings have the same critical cues. As children learn to use each swing, they will naturally select the one that fits the situation.

Striking for Distance

Setting: Markers of various colors (to be used for measuring) or zones at various distances from where the children are hitting; a plastic striking implement and five or six foam, plastic, or whiffle balls for each child; children positioned in a circle in the center of a field or playground, facing out each in his or her individual striking zones defined by ropes or cones

Cues	
Arms Way Back	(Bring your arms way back as you swing.)
Watch the Ball	(Keep your eyes on the ball all the time.)
Knees Bent	(Keep your knees bent throughout the swing.)
Behind the Ball	(Contact directly behind the ball to make it travel on the ground or low.)
Under the Ball	(Contact the ball below its center so it will travel upward through the air.)

Tasks/Challenges:

T Stand facing the outside of the circle, making sure there is enough space between you and the people next to you so you can all swing your sticks without hitting one another. First, we are going to practice striking along the ground and in the air. There's enough room to strike as hard as you like.

Practice your first strikes from behind the ball so the ball travels along the ground. Use your forehand strike and hockey grip. After you hit all the balls, wait for the signal, then go get yours and quickly bring them back to your starting place for the next hits.

(T) This time, try your backhand strike—along the ground. Does the ball travel as far with your backhand?

(T) Move beside the ball. Hit the ball as far as you can.

(✳) Which starting position sends the ball farther? In "face-the-target" position, which sends it farther—forehand or backhand?

(T) This time we are going to stand beside the ball. Practice hitting the ball so it travels through the air.

(C) Practice striking both on the ground and through the air. Before each strike, call out loud "air" or "ground." Challenge yourself to be able to do the strike you called out.

(✳) What is the key for sending the ball through the air? On the ground?

(T) Now see with each of your strikes if you can hit the ball farther each time. The markers on the field will help you remember how far you hit the ball each time. Each time, see if you can hit the ball a little farther than the last time. Practice air and ground strikes—all from the side.

(C) Can you hit the ball so it lands in the same zone three times?

Striking to Targets

Setting: Plastic hockey stick or other implement and a foam or plastic ball for each child; in front of each child, a target on the floor next to the wall marked with cones or spots about 4 feet apart and tape marks on the floor in front of each target at about 6 feet, 10 feet, and 12 feet; each child in his or her individual striking zone defined by ropes or cones

Cues	
Step	(Step forward on the opposite [front] foot.)
Watch the Ball	(Keep your eyes on the ball all the time.)
Knees Bent	(Keep your knees bent throughout the swing.)
Follow Through	(Follow through toward the target with your stick.)

Safety with Hockey Sticks

There is much concern over the use of hockey sticks and the teaching of related skills in the elementary school. With the increased popularity of street and ice hockey, hockey sticks are being raised above the shoulders on both the backswing and the follow-through. Because elementary school physical education classes are usually crowded, raised hockey sticks can cause injuries. We've successfully reduced the chance of such injuries by not letting youngsters raise their hockey sticks higher than their waists on *any* stroke. This restriction doesn't significantly alter the striking action; in fact, it encourages the correct field hockey striking action while providing a much safer environment for learning skills involving striking with hockey sticks.

Tasks/Challenges:

(T) Starting from behind the ball at the closest mark, try to strike the ball so it goes between the two cones.

(T) Practice sending the ball between the cones from your forehand and backhand sides.

(C) Practice striking until you can hit the ball between the cones five times from each side. Remember, stop the ball each time it comes back to you before hitting it again.

(T) When you can hit the target five times in a row without missing from the closest mark, move back to the next mark. When you can hit the target from that spot five times without missing, move back again. If you hit the target four times and then miss, start your counting over. Practice from both the forehand and backhand sides.

(T) Now start back at your closest spot and strike to the target from a starting position standing beside your ball.

(⚠) With this task, make sure that students are spread well apart, that they stop the ball completely on its return, and that they move in front of others only when no one is striking.

Striking to a Target (Around the World)

Setting: Targets, with five tape marks in a semicircle on the floor in front of each; three or fewer students per target; a hockey stick or other striking implement and ball or puck for each child

Note: This task is also appropriate as one of a series of stations.

Cues

Watch the Ball	(Keep your eyes on the ball until it leaves your stick.)
Knees Bent	(Keep your knees bent throughout the swing.)
Step	(Step forward on the opposite [front] foot.)
Follow Through	(Follow through toward the target with your stick.)

Tasks/Challenges:

T This time, the striking is going to be a game. Have you ever played Around the World in basketball? This game is going to be Around the World in striking. As you see, there are five tape marks on the floor in front of you. You must hit the ball to the target from each tape mark. Strike from behind the ball. You can start on either side.

T When you make it through once, go back and hit from each mark using the backhand strike.

T Start over, striking from beside the ball.

✓ *Teacher Observation.* This task lends itself easily to a teacher observation of the critical cues of striking with hockey sticks: Watch the Ball, Step, and Follow Through. *See Chapter 12 for the development of a teacher observation checklist.*

Striking to a Stationary Partner

Setting: Partners about 6 to 7 feet apart, each with a hockey stick; one ball or puck per group. Each striking zones defined by ropes or cones

Cues

Sending

Watch the Ball	(Keep your eyes on the ball at all times.)
Knees Bent	(Keep your knees bent throughout the swing.)
Step	(Step forward on the opposite foot.)
Follow Through	(Follow through toward your partner with your stick.)

Receiving

Give	(Relax your grip and move your stick back a little just as the ball hits your stick, to absorb the force.)
Watch the Ball	(Keep your eyes on the ball all the time.)

Tasks/Challenges:

T Strike the ball (puck) back and forth to your partner. Hit straight to your partner so she or he doesn't have to move. You hit the ball to your partner; your partner stops the ball completely still and then hits it back. Remember, strike easily so your partner is able to stop the ball.

T Before you worked with a partner, you practiced hitting the ball (puck) to different places. Now you're going to do that with your partner, and your partner is going to be a target for you to aim at. The partner who is to receive the ball will put his or her hockey stick out in one place and hold it still; the partner hitting the ball will use the stick as a target and try to hit it without the receiving partner moving the stick. Remember, stop the ball every time before returning it. Change roles each time.

C With your partner, see how many times you can hit the ball (puck) back and forth without a miss. Remember, you must stop the ball before you return it to your partner. If you miss, just start counting all over. If you get to 10, let me know.

T After you hit the ball (puck) successfully to your partner 10 times and your partner is able to stop the ball, move back two steps each and start again. When you're successful 10 times in a row, move back again.

T This will make it a little harder: Move back to your close position. After you pass the ball this time, move to a new space and stand still. The receiver must control the ball (puck), look to see where you are, and then pass. Each time after someone passes, move to a new space, stop, and then receive the ball.

C Now see how many times you can keep this up without missing.

We must have seen at least 26 ways children can curve the blades of hockey sticks. Having the children keep the blade straight ensures two things: (1) The puck (ball) has a greater chance of staying on the floor, and (2) your hockey sticks last a lot longer.

Traveling Slowly While Striking a Ball

Setting: A hockey stick and a tennis ball or puck for each child

Cues

Light Taps	(Use light taps to keep the ball close to your stick.)

Passing to a partner is a task appropriate at the control level.

Hands Apart	(Move your hands 8 to 10 inches apart to control the ball better.)
Ball in Front	(Keep the ball slightly in front of your body on the same side on which you are dribbling.)

Tasks/Challenges:

T Before, we practiced moving around the entire space while striking a ball with the hockey stick. Let's practice again—this is called dribbling or stick-handling. To begin, go slowly. Your task is to travel around the entire space while striking the ball and not touching anyone else.

T This time as you move around the room, I'm going to hold up different numbers of fingers. Tell me how many fingers I'm holding up. You'll have to look often because I'll change the number of fingers often and try to trick you.

C You have 50 points. Your task is to keep all your points. Move around the room dribbling the ball. Every time you lose the ball, subtract 5 points. See how many points you have at the stop signal.

Traveling, Stopping, and Controlling the Ball

Setting: A plastic hockey stick and a ball for each child

Cues	
Give	(Relax your grip and bring your stick back a little to absorb the force when trying to stop the ball.) *A demonstration is helpful here.*

Light Taps	(Use light taps to keep the ball close to your stick.)
Hands Apart	(Move your hands 8 to 10 inches apart to control the ball better.)

Tasks/Challenges:

T Before, you practiced traveling around the room keeping the ball close to you. This time, you're going to do the same thing, but with something added. Whenever you hear the signal, stop the ball, using only your stick, and wait for the signal to go again.

T This time, try going a little faster and doing the same thing. Move around the space, striking the ball with your hockey stick. On the signal, stop the ball and wait for the "Go" signal. I'll know you can really do this if I always see the ball close to the stick and all the balls stopped on the signal, without your having to chase them all over the room.

T Now I am going to change the task a little. Again, you should move around the entire space striking the ball. But this time, on the signal, instead of stopping the ball, stand still and keep moving the ball in your self-space until you hear the signal to travel again. This is called controlling the ball. You'll know you're really good at this when, as soon as you hear the signal, you can stop and start moving the ball in your self-space without first having to chase the ball across the room.

C This time, the stopping will be like a game. When I say "Stop," I'll start counting backward from 10. When all the balls have stopped, I'll stop counting. Your goal is to get me to stop counting before I get to zero.

T You're going to play a little game with the stopping this time. Every time you come near another person, stop or control the ball and then start again. It's as if you don't want anyone to come near your ball, so you are going to protect it—and the only way you can protect it is by controlling it in your self-space or stopping it.

❂ Why should you control the ball or puck before you send it back? What do you have to do to control it?

Traveling and Changing Speeds

Setting: A striking implement and a ball or puck for each child

> **Cues**
>
> **Light Taps**   (Use light taps to keep the ball close to your stick.)
> **Hands Apart** (Move your hands 8 to 10 inches apart to control the ball better.)
> **Ball in Front** (Keep the ball slightly in front of your body on the same side on which you are dribbling.)

Tasks/Challenges:

T One of the important things in games that use dribbling or stick-handling is the ability to change the speed at which you are traveling while you dribble. Travel in general space, and change your speed as you go. It should be easy for me to tell which speed you are using.

T This time I will call out speeds as you travel. See if you can match every speed I call out.

T Now you will practice using different speeds with a partner. It is like follow the leader. You will follow a partner, dribbling in general space. The first partner starts and travels, changing the speed of the travel often. The second partner follows, always trying to travel at the same speed as the first partner. On the signal, switch places.

Traveling and Striking While Changing Pathways

Setting: A hockey stick and ball or puck for each child; various pathways (the more, the better) taped or marked on the floor

> **Cues**
>
> **Light Taps**   (Use light taps to keep the ball close to your stick.)

> **Hands Apart** (Move your hands 8 to 10 inches apart to control the ball better.)
> **Ball in Front** (Keep the ball slightly in front of your body on the same side on which you are dribbling.)

Tasks/Challenges:

T You're going to practice something new this time: changes in pathways. Do you remember pathways: straight, curved, and zigzag? Again, you're going to move around the entire space, but whenever you come to a pathway on the floor, try to follow it exactly. Once you finish one pathway, travel to another and follow it. As you follow the pathways, be sure you're striking the ball, not pushing it along.

T Something very different happens when you follow a zigzag pathway. What is it? That's right—you have to move your stick from one side of the ball to the other, like moving the ball in self-space to keep control of it. Practice zigzag pathways on your own. Remember, every time you come to a zig or a zag, you have to move your stick to the other side of the ball.

T This time, we are going to practice striking while traveling in different pathways with a partner. You're going to play follow the leader. The leader travels in different pathways—curved, straight, and zigzag—as the follower tries to stay close behind, copying the exact pathways the leader

Traveling, stopping, and controlling an object with a hockey stick takes an acute awareness of others.

makes. Leaders: As you begin, make easy pathways. The object is not to lose your partner but to practice striking while traveling in different pathways. On the signal, change positions as leaders and followers.

T This time, the following is going to be a little harder. Instead of staying right behind the leader, the follower is going to watch while the leader moves in a short pathway sequence. When the leader stops and freezes, the follower moves, copying the pathway of the leader until she or he catches up with the leader. When the follower catches up, the leader takes off again. This is a bit like a game of cat and mouse: Just as soon as you think you've caught someone, the person slips away again. As you move, remember that the purpose of this task is to practice different pathways, so include them in your movements. After five turns as a leader, switch places.

C This is the real pathway test. By yourself, make up a sequence of traveling and striking that involves four changes of pathways. Practice your sequence until you can do it from memory three times without stopping. Each time the sequence should look the same. Then we'll all share the sequences.

√ *Student Drawing.* This task lends itself to a perfect opportunity for student drawing. Have youngsters draw the pathway sequence and label the pathways used.

Striking to Targets

Setting: A hockey stick, a ball, and three targets (plastic milk bottles, 2-liter soda bottles, or tennis ball cans) placed against a wall or fence for each child; each child's individual striking zone defined by ropes or cones

Cues	
Face Target	(Always face your upper body to the target.)
Step	(Step forward on the opposite foot toward the target.)
Follow Through	(Follow through with your stick toward the target.)

Tasks/Challenges:

T This time you'll practice striking from the same place each time, but trying to hit one of three different targets. Take a minute and practice striking at the three targets in front of you.

C Now you're going to see how many points you can score in 2 minutes. You get one point if you hit a target and three points if you hit the particular target you call out ahead of time.

√ *Student Display.* Have students either draw or collect pictures of people striking to different targets that indicate the use of the cues of facing the target, stepping into the hit, and following through. The pictures could then be displayed on a bulletin board to indicate the diverse targets that exist and how the cues are the same.

Striking While Dodging Stationary Obstacles

Setting: An obstacle course of cones and hoops or other equipment; a hockey stick and a ball for each child

Cues	
Light Taps	(Use light taps to keep the ball close to your stick.)
Both Sides of Stick	(Use both sides of the stick to dribble around the obstacle.)
Look Up	(Look up as you travel so you can see the obstacles.)

Tasks/Challenges:

T You've traveled while dodging objects. This time, you're going to travel and dodge objects while striking a ball with a hockey stick. Your task is to travel throughout the space, striking the ball with the hockey stick. Try not to let the ball get away from you. Don't touch any of the obstacles or other people. Freeze on the signal, and have the ball with you.

T As practice for looking up, we're going to play the counting game again. I'll keep holding up a different number of fingers, and you tell me how many I'm holding up while you're striking the ball around the space.

T Dribble or stick-handle in general space. Each time you come to an obstacle, control the ball, execute a quarter turn to the right or left, and continue dribbling.

T You've all been going at fairly slow speeds. This isn't always good in game situations, so you're going to practice going at different speeds. Sometimes approach an obstacle very quickly, sometimes slowly. Make the change clear. The rules are still the same: No touching, and you must be able to stop on the signal and have the ball with you.

T Dribble in general space. As you near an obstacle, use both sides of your stick to dribble past the obstacle; then quickly continue regular dribbling. Sometimes go to the right and sometimes to the left.

C What you have just learned are called dodges. This time as you practice dodging, pretend you have 100 points. If the ball you are dribbling touches a cone, subtract 10 points from your score. If you have a collision with another person, subtract 25 points. Try to complete your practice with 100 points!

At the utilization level, children are able to control a ball in the space around them and strike consistently with the appropriate striking pattern. We challenge them to use their striking skills in more dynamic and unpredictable situations.

A note about cues: Although several cues are listed for many of the learning experiences, it's important to focus on only one cue at a time. This way, the children can really concentrate on that cue. Once you provide feedback to the children and observe that most have learned a cue, it's time to focus on another one.

Striking to Small Targets

Setting: Pins (2-liter soft-drink bottles or lightweight plastic bowling pins), a ball, and a hockey stick for every two children; a marked lane leading away from the pins, as for a bowling alley

Cues	
Eyes on Target	(Watch the target at all times.)
Step	(Step forward on the opposite foot.)
Follow Through	(Follow through toward the target with your stick.)

Tasks/Challenges:

C This game is called Hockey Bowl. Your task is to strike the ball from behind the line and see how many pins you can knock down. After three hits, or when all the pins have been knocked down (whichever happens first), trade places.

T The first time you can knock down all the pins three times in a row, move back three steps and try it again. If you still want to make the task harder, take away some of the pins so you have a smaller target.

Dribbling and Changing Directions Backward

Setting: Children scattered throughout general space, each with a hockey stick and ball

Cues	
Light Taps	(Use light taps to keep the ball close to your stick.)
Back of Stick	(Use the back side of the stick to bring the ball backward.)
Pull Back	(Quickly pull the ball toward you.)

Tasks/Challenges:

T Travel in general space, dribbling the ball 2 to 3 feet in front of you as you go. **When you are comfortable with your control of the dribble, dribble the ball ahead of you; quickly put your stick in front of the ball; tap the ball lightly with the back of your stick, pulling it toward you; quickly turn and continue the dribble.**

⚠ As hard as we try, somehow, at some time, hockey sticks and balls/pucks seem to get raised higher than they should, especially in dynamic situations. In fact, the most serious accident I've ever had while teaching involved a hockey stick and an eye. Therefore, we advocate wearing eye guards, especially in dynamic hockey situations.

Performing a Continuous Dribble and Change of Direction

Setting: Children scattered throughout general space, each with a hockey stick and ball

Cues	
Light Taps	(Use light taps to keep the ball close to your stick.)
Both Sides of Stick	(Use both sides of the stick to dribble when you go around an obstacle.)
Heads Up	(Look up to avoid collisions.)

Tasks/Challenges:

T You learned to change the direction of the ball by dribbling it to your right and left with both sides of the stick. You have just learned one method of changing direction from front to back. Travel within the space, using changes of direction to avoid collisions with others. Your task is continuous dribbling.

T Approach a line quickly; use the "pull back" with the stick to change the direction of the dribble at the last moment, to keep from crossing the line.

T Dribble as close as you can to another person without touching him or her and quickly use a move to the right or left to dodge him or her.

T Gradually increase the speed of your travel to determine the maximum rate you can travel with a controlled dribble and frequent changes of direction.

> *A while ago I was at a party where the hosts set up a croquet game. Adults and children alike were intrigued, and, bingo, I realized: This is a striking game! Do you remember it? Croquet is a fun activity to add to physical education class as a special treat and ties together the ideas of striking at targets and varying force and distance really well. No croquet sets, you say? You'll be amazed how many families have croquet sets at home that they're willing to let you use (or sometimes even give to you). I just acquired an antique croquet set that was on its way to Goodwill. Give croquet a try sometime!*

Pathways, Speeds, and Directions

Note: This task is an example of a task teaching instructional approach. See Chapter 10 for more ideas on task teaching ideas.

Setting: A hockey stick and ball for each child

Cues	
Light Taps	(Use light taps to keep the ball close to your stick.)
Both Sides of Stick	(Use both sides of the stick to dribble when you go around an obstacle.)
Heads Up	(Look up to avoid collisions.)

Tasks/Challenges:

C This is a self-testing task. The task sheet (Figure 26.3) lets you assess your traveling and striking in different directions, pathways, and speeds. Practice the tasks one by one. When you think you can do a task well, have a partner watch you. If your partner thinks you did the task successfully, the partner signs the sheet. I'll check to see how you're progressing.

✓ *Peer Observation.* The preceding challenge is a wonderful peer observation assessment. With the date recorded, it provides an indication of when students accomplished the skill.

Traveling and Striking for a Goal

Setting: Cones scattered throughout general space; markers for goals around the outside boundary; a hockey stick and ball for each child

Cues	
Face Goal	(Your upper body must face the goal as you hit to it.)
Light Taps/Hard Strikes	(Light taps to dribble the ball; strike hard at the goal.)
Follow Through	(Follow through toward the goal with your stick.)

Tasks/Challenges:

T Travel at your own speed and dribble or stick-handle the ball while avoiding the obstacles and other people. On the signal, travel quickly toward an open space, and strike for the goal. Retrieve your ball; begin dribbling again, listening for the signal to strike for the goal.

T Practice dribbling around the obstacles and striking for the goal on your own; I won't give the signal.

It's a challenge to try to keep the puck away from a partner while dribbling it.

Figure 26.3 Task sheet for striking.

Name _____ Class _____

Task Sheet for Striking

Observer's Name	Task
	I can strike a ball with a hockey stick in a straight pathway, keeping the ball close to the stick.
	I can strike a ball with a hockey stick in a curved pathway, keeping the ball close to the stick.
	I can strike a ball with a hockey stick in a zigzag pathway, keeping the ball close to the stick.
	I can strike a ball with a hockey stick around four cones set up about four feet apart, keeping the ball close to the stick.
	I can strike a ball with a hockey stick through the cones while running, keeping the ball close to the stick.
	I can strike a ball with a hockey stick while traveling sideways.
	I can make up a sequence including two pathways, two changes in speed, and two different directions. I have written my sequence below.
	Sequence:

One-on-One Hockey

Setting: Partners in general space, each with hockey sticks, a ball, and markers for a goal

Cues

Light Taps/	(Light taps to dribble the ball;
Hard Strikes	strike hard at the goal.)
Heads Up	(Look up to avoid collisions.)
Dodges	(Use stopping/starting, both sides of the stick, and turns to avoid your partner.)

Tasks/Challenges:

Ⓣ Select a partner whose dribbling or stick-handling skills are about the same as yours. Cooperatively decide the boundaries for your area; a small area provides more practice. One of you begins to dribble the ball within the area; the other one tries to gain possession of the ball by using the stick to steal the ball. Follow these rules:

1. You can only contact the ball, not the person.
2. Be sure to gain possession of the ball; don't slap it away.

3. If you gain possession, begin dribbling as the offensive player; your partner is now defense.

If partners are unmatched in skill, provide a signal to change from offense to defense. Players stay on offense or defense until they hear the signal.

T Within your area, set up two markers as a goal. The first partner will dribble until within scoring range (10 to 12 feet) and then shoot for a goal. The second partner will attempt to gain possession of the ball, using only the stick. After each strike for goal, switch positions.

C Design your own game using the skills of stickhandling and shooting for the goal. Work with your partner to decide the rules of the game, scoring, and boundaries. Can you think of a name for your game?

√ *Peer Observation.* After students have a chance to play their one-on-one games for a while, a peer observation would be appropriate. Have another pair of partners observe for the use of the cues of Light Taps/Hard Strikes, Heads Up, and Dodges. After a designated time, the observers and players switch roles.

✹ When playing one-on-one hockey, how can you steal the ball and not hit the other player's legs with the hockey stick?

Striking from a Stationary Position to a Moving Target

Setting: Partners, each pair with two hockey sticks and a ball; a large enough space (about 10 feet by 10 yards) to send and receive the ball on the run

Cues

Lead Receiver	(Pass the ball to an open space in front of the receiver.)
Angles	(Your receiver should always be to the side and in front of you.)
Heads Up	(Always look up so you can see where your receiver is.)

Tasks/Challenges:

T You practiced striking the ball to a partner before, but then you were always standing still. When you're in a real game, how often are you able to pass to a partner who is standing still? Not very often. You're going to practice striking to a partner who is moving. One of you will be the passer, and the other the receiver. The passer stands still and

the receiver starts to run downfield, away from the passer at an angle. When the receiver is about 5 yards away, the passer sends the ball. The receiver should collect the ball on the run and then keep going for a few more steps. Take five turns, and then switch positions.

T You've been passing to the same side so far. Now try passing to the other side so the receiver has to receive with the backhand. This will seem awkward at first, but stick with it. Pass 10 times, and then switch.

Passing and Receiving on the Move

Setting: A large, grassy outdoor area; children in pairs, with one ball for each pair and a hockey stick for each child

Cues

Lead Receiver	(Pass the ball to an open space in front of the receiver.)
Angles	(Your receiver should always be to the side and in front of you.)
Heads Up	(Always look up so you can see where your receiver is.)

Tasks/Challenges:

T Travel in the same direction as your partner, side by side, about 20 feet apart. As you're traveling, pass the ball back and forth using the hockey stick. The key is that you both must always be moving forward. When you get to the end of your area, turn around and come back.

T Now travel with your partner in general space, dribbling and passing. All the other players will be doing the same thing, so it's important that you are aware of others and of passing to open spaces. Go.

C Challenge yourself to always pass the ball ahead of your partner—to the open space. If you are successful, your partner will never have to stop to receive the pass. Try for five successful completions: open space, no stopping.

Keeping It Moving

Setting: Four cones marking a space 5 yards by 5 yards; four children per group, each group with four hockey sticks and a ball or puck

Cues	
Lead Receiver	(Pass the ball to an open space in front of the receiver.)
Angles	(Your receiver should always be to the side of and in front of you.)
Heads Up	(Always look up so you can see where your receiver is.)

Tasks/Challenges:

C This time you're going to play a game called Keeping It Moving. One person begins by passing the ball to another player. That player passes it to someone else, and so on. The object is to never let the ball stop moving and never let it go out of bounds.

Two-on-One Hockey

Setting: Children in groups of three, each group with sticks, a ball, and cones to use as goals

Cues	
Offense	
Lead Receiver	(Strike the ball to an open space ahead of your receiver.)
Light Taps/ Hard Strikes	(Light taps to dribble the ball; strike hard at the goal.)
Angles	(The receiver should be in an open space at an angle to and in front of the passer.)
Defense	
Play the Ball	(Make your first move to the player with the ball.)

Tasks/Challenges:

C In your group, two of you will be the offensive players, and one will be the defensive player. The two offensive players will pass and dribble to each other within the boundaries of your area. The defensive player will attempt to gain possession of the ball by intercepting passes or tapping the ball away on the dribble.

Each team will have possession of the ball for 2 minutes. See how many goals you can score in that time. The offensive team must execute at least two passes before attempting a goal.

Proficiency Level: Learning Experiences Leading to Skill Development

When children reach the proficiency level, many possess mature striking patterns, and striking becomes a skill that can be used in complex, unpredictable, gamelike situations. At this point, children are able to incorporate previous experiences into situations that involve strategic and split-second decisions. At this level, children are given situations that facilitate development of the ability to strike with implements while focusing on the strategy and outcome of the action and on their skill. The focus at this level is the attainment of consistency and accuracy while standing still or moving. Cues are focused on the use of the skill rather than on the skill itself.

As with other skill themes, at the proficiency level, many appropriate activities call for the use of striking skills in a gamelike situation. It can be quite tricky to keep these activities developmentally appropriate, especially in terms of active participation for all children. There are several solutions here. One is to set up multiple playing areas around the space. Another option is to have stations, several of which offer gamelike activities, and several of which have practice opportunities that require less space and setup. Finally, you could have peer assessment opportunities; within small groups, half will play and half observe, and then they switch. Regardless of the solution, all game-type activities should be appropriate for all children. See Chapter 30 for more information on game options in physical education.

A note about cues: At the proficiency level, tasks are more complex, typically requiring children to coordinate several movements simultaneously in a dynamic context. A list of cues is provided to assist the children in being more successful in the learning experiences. The challenge is in determining which cue will be most beneficial for each child . . . and when. Thus careful observation and critical reflection become very important as you watch the children move and then decide which cue will be the most helpful to move each learner to a higher level.

Important points for the following activities: Before beginning tasks that involve offense and defense, students should be skilled in the space awareness and dodging tasks that ask them to master the offensive and defensive skills of moving into open space; avoiding other persons; and using fakes, stops and starts, pivots, and other avoidance skills without manipulating equipment. (See Chapter 13, "Space Awareness," and Chapter 17, "Chasing, Fleeing, and Dodging.") Children need to have mastered these skills before they are asked to use them while manipulating equipment.

One key to these tasks—and to other initial tasks involving offense and defense—is to clearly define the boundaries of the space the students are to use. A small space gives an advantage to the defense; a large space provides an offensive advantage. Similarly, a long, narrow space gives the advantage to the defense; a wider space helps the offense. Initial tasks generally favor the offense.

Children dribbling

Children as obstacles ·········· Pathways made by children dribbling

Figure 26.4 Arrangement for dribbling and dodging activity.

Striking to Dodge an Opponent

Setting: A group of 10 or fewer children, several with hockey sticks and balls; the others positioned as obstacles, holding hockey sticks in their hands and wearing blue armbands or other identifying clothing (Figure 26.4)

Cues	
Heads Up	(Always look up to avoid collisions.)
Dodges	(Use stopping/starting, both sides of the stick, changes of speed, and turns to avoid obstacles.)
Lead Receiver	(Pass to an open space ahead of the receiver.)
Angles	(The receiver should be in an open space to the side and in front of the passer.)

Tasks/Challenges:

T This is a dodging game. We've played games like this before but without equipment. To begin, those of you wearing blue will be the obstacles; the rest of you will be dodgers. Obstacles, find a self-space and stand there. Dodgers, try to cross the room without coming near an obstacle. The obstacles have the right to steal the ball if it comes within their area. Their area is that space they can reach while keeping one foot glued to the floor. The dodgers' goal is to get to the other end of the space without having the ball stolen. The group gets five tries and then switches places.

C We're going to change the game a little this time. Instead of all the dodgers having their own balls,

they're going to have only one ball. Their job is then to get the ball to the other end, as a team. The obstacles still have the same rule: They can take the ball only when it comes into their area. After four tries, switch places.

T Now that you have the idea, let's form groups of six. Two people are dodgers; four are obstacles. Switch every time so you all get a turn.

✓ *Teacher Observation.* At this point children should be demonstrating their ability to use skills and strategies to avoid other players. A teacher observation of the use of the cues of Heads Up, Dodges, Lead Receiver, and Angles would be appropriate before advancing to more complex tasks.

Keep-Away

Setting: Groups of four: three players on the outside standing about 20 feet apart and one in the middle; each player with a hockey stick; one ball or puck per group

Cues	
Offense	
Don't Pass Until the Defense Commits	(Hold on to the ball until the defense makes you pass by coming close to you.)
Receivers to Open Space	(Receivers should move to an open space at an angle from the passer.)
Stay Away from Passer	(Receivers shouldn't go close to the passer.)
Defense	
Play the Ball	(Play defense on the person with the ball.)

Tasks/Challenges:

T This is like Keep-Away, except that it's played with hockey sticks. There will be four in a group: three on the outside standing about 20 feet apart, and one in the middle. The three on the outside pass the ball back and forth; the one in the middle tries to intercept the pass. After eight successful passes or four interceptions, trade places. You must stay in the boundaries of your space. There is no contact.

√ *Video/Digital Analysis.* As children learn to play in dynamic situations, it helps them immensely to watch their own performance and analyze the use of the offensive and defensive cues.

Small-Sided Hockey Invasion Game

Setting: Groups of four or six, two or three players on each team; hockey sticks for every player; one ball or puck per group; milk crates, cones, or boxes for goals; a space at least 20 feet by 15 feet

Cues	
Offense	
Don't Pass Until the Defense Commits	(Hold on to the ball until the defense makes you pass by coming close to you.)
Receivers to Open Space	(Receivers should move to an open space at an angle from the passer.)
Stay Away from Passer	(Receivers shouldn't go close to the passer.)
Defense	
Ball First; Player Second	(First play defense on the person with the ball; then cover the receivers.)
Hustle Back	(When you lose the ball to the offense, hurry back on defense.)

Tasks/Challenges:

C This game is called Mini Hockey. The objective is to strike the ball into the opponent's goal. Here are the rules:

1. The players on the teams decide the boundaries and width of the goal. There should be one goal on each end of the space. Use milk crates, cones, or boxes for the goals.
2. One team gets the ball first.
3. The ball can be stolen only on the pass.
4. No contact.

5. Everyone must be playing—no standing around.
6. Make up your own form of scoring (if you want to keep score).
7. Make up any more rules you need.

We're going to change the game a little this time. Instead of one goal on each end of the field, there will be two.

Striking with Long-Handled Implements—Bats

If only everyone could enjoy 4th of July softball! The skill theme of batting can lead to that as well as participation in games in more traditional sports like

---

Skill Theme Development Progression

Striking with Long-Handled Implements—Bats

Proficiency Level

One-Base Baseball
Six-player striking and fielding in a gamelike situation
Directing the pathway, distance, and speed of an object

Utilization Level

Batting, combining distance and placement
Striking a pitched object varying the distance
Hitting to open spaces
Directing the placement of an object
Grounders and flies

Control Level

Striking a pitched ball
Striking a self-tossed ball to different distances
Throwing a ball in the air and striking it
Hit and Run
Hitting a stationary ball from different places
Striking suspended objects
Striking a stationary ball for distance
Level swings
Striking a stationary ball

Precontrol Level

Striking off batting tees

Box 26-1

Key Observation Points: Side-Armed Striking Pattern (Batting)

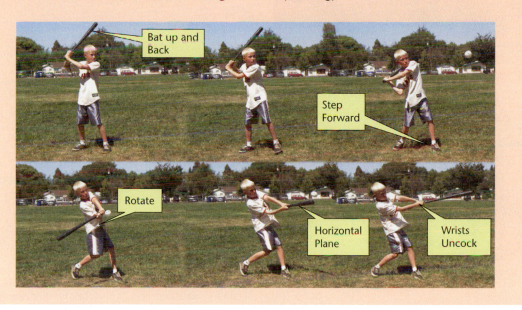

Bat up and Back

Step Forward

Rotate

Horizontal Plane

Wrists Uncock

baseball and a myriad of "made-up" games. A sidearm pattern is used when striking a ball with a bat to keep the bat at the same distance from the ground and in a horizontal plane throughout the swing. We have identified the equipment used as a bat, though you could easily substitute a tennis racket or a badminton racket. See Box 26-1 for the correct form for striking sidearm. Remember, striking a pitched ball with a bat is one of the last skills that children develop. Our progression spiral for striking with bats provides activities that will lead to skill development.

Precontrol Level (GLSP): Activities for Exploration

Activities at the precontrol level ask children to explore all varieties of striking with bats. At this level, a chopping, downward swing is typical for any striking pattern. Children struggle just to make contact between the ball and the striking instrument. Therefore we give children activities that let them explore striking with the added length that comes with bats—and the greater demands that length places on their hand–eye coordination. Due to the difficulty of the skill, tasks are developed using large objects to be struck.

All activities at this level need to be done with balls of various sizes. For beginners, large plastic balls are easier because they're larger and move more slowly.

Implements for Batting

While we refer generically to bats in this chapter, there are a variety of "bats" that may be used and that, at times, may be more appropriate as well as more challenging for youngsters. These "bats" may include traditional plastic bats, large plastic bats, flat-sided plastic bats, and cricket bats.

Striking Off a Batting Tee

Setting: Preferably outside in a large open space; for at least every two children (but preferably for every child) a box containing five plastic balls or beach balls, a bat, and a batting tee (Figure 26.5). Each individual striking zones defined by ropes or cones.

Tasks/Challenges:

T This time, you're going to hit a big ball off a tee with a plastic bat. Stand to the side of the tee so you are batting to the field. Now line up facing the same way, so you won't hit one another. Hit all the balls in your box, and then wait until I give the signal before collecting them. Remember: Hit hard.

T Practice hitting until you can hit the ball three times in a row.

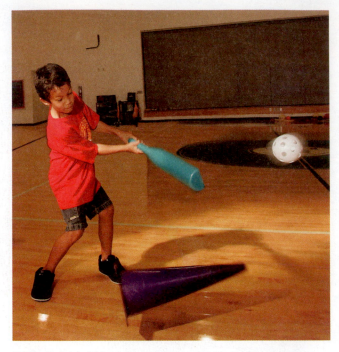

Batting tees let children at precontrol and control skill levels practice independently.

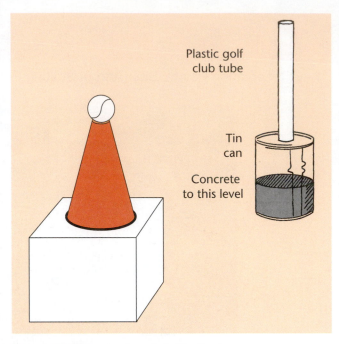

Figure 26.5 Construction of a batting tee.*
The easiest way to make a batting tee is to use a large (36-inch) traffic cone, which is high enough for young children. Increase the height by placing the traffic cone on a cardboard box. A batting tee can also be made out of a tin can and a plastic tube.

Materials
   Large tin can (available from the school cafeteria)
   Plastic golf club tube (obtained from a sporting goods store)
   Sack of ready-mixed concrete (1/10 to 1/8)

Directions
1. Place the golf club tube into the tin can.
2. Add water to the concrete mix, and fill the tin can approximately half full.
3. After a few minutes, when the concrete begins to harden, make sure the golf club tube is not leaning to the side. Once the concrete dries, the batting tee is ready to use.

You can vary the heights of the batting tees by shortening the plastic golf club tubes before inserting them into the cans. We try to have batting tees of three different heights.

*Prior to constructing equipment we recommend you check with school administration to be certain that district policy permits homemade equipment.

T Now see how far you can hit the ball.
Batting tees are helpful for children at the precontrol level who are unable to strike a moving ball and for children at the control level who are practicing ball placement.

Control Level: Learning Experiences Leading to Skill Development

At the control level, children begin to develop mature striking patterns used in increasingly complex contexts. They can be challenged with tasks that require them to include one or two other variables besides striking such as striking a pitched ball for distance.

A note about cues: Although several cues are listed for many of the learning experiences, it's important to focus on only one cue at a time. This way, the children can really concentrate on that cue. Once you provide feedback to the children and observe that most have learned a cue, it's time to focus on another one.

Striking a Stationary Ball

Setting: Preferably a large, open, outdoor space big enough for every child to hit against a backstop or a wall; children about 15 feet from the backstop or wall with their individual striking zones defined by ropes or cones (or place a line on the ground about 15 feet from the batting positions for children to hit over); a box of about five balls (large, light plastic or beach balls, and whiffle balls), bats, and batting tees for each child or pair of children.

Cues

Side to the Field (Turn your side to the target or field.)

A New Cue

The idea of shifting weight forward on a batting swing has long been accepted. Recently an accomplished softball coach told us a new (and probably more effective) cue for this. Instead of telling children to step forward or shift their weight, tell them, "Picture a shoe with the laces tied, facing upward as usual. As the hips rotate and the weight shifts during the swing, the back foot should roll so the laces almost face the ground." This not only forces the rotation of the hips but automatically causes the weight shift.

Bat Back	(Bring the bat way back over your shoulder so it sticks up like a toothpick.)
Watch the Ball	(Keep your eyes on the ball all the time.)
Level	(Extend your arms to swing flat as a pancake.)
Rotate and Shift	(Roll over the shoelaces of your back foot.)

Tasks/Challenges:

T When we explored striking, you practiced hitting a ball off a tee. We're going to practice that again. Stand about a bat's length away and to the side of your batting tee. **Take a batting grip** (Figure 26.6). (If you are having a hard time remembering which hand to put where on the bat, an easy way to remember is that the bottom hand on the bat is the same side as facing the field—so if your left side

faces the field, your left hand is the bottom hand on the bat.) **Bring your bat back over your shoulder so it sticks up like a toothpick, extend your arms all the way so you have a level swing, shift your weight forward, rotate your hips, and hit.** Let's practice five times without hitting the ball. Just swing and say the cues out loud.

T Now practice striking off the tee. Use a plastic ball or a beach ball. **If you are batting the ball correctly, your swing will follow through over your other shoulder.**

T Practice until you can hit the plastic ball 10 times in a row off the tee.

T When you can hit the plastic ball 10 times in a row, trade it in for a whiffle ball. Now practice with that ball.

T Hit the ball so hard that it goes in the air to the wall (over the line).

T Practice hitting with the bat until you can hit five times in a row so the ball hits the wall (lands over the line).

Increasing the size of the ball reduces the complexity of the task. Increasing the size of the bat does the same thing. Some teachers also use soap bubbles for children to practice striking. One partner blows bubbles; the other gets to swing away, trying to pop the bubbles as they fall. It works!

What is the most important cue for making contact with the ball? What is one hint that will help you do this?

Level Swings

Setting: Ropes suspended from the ceiling or a line hung across the room to about children's shoulder height (Figure 26.7); batting tees and bats for each child. Individual striking zones defined by ropes or cones.

Cues	
Side to the Field	(Turn your side to the target or field.)
Bat Back	(Bring the bat way back over your shoulder so your back elbow is level with your shoulder.)
Watch the Ball	(Keep your eyes on the ball all the time.)
Level	(Extend your arms to swing flat as a pancake.)
Rotate and Shift	(Roll over the shoelaces of your back foot.)

Figure 26.6 Batting grip.

Figure 26.7 Setup for level swings.

Suspended ropes

Rope hanging over

Strike zone

Batting tee

Tasks/Challenges:

T Place your batting tee directly under your rope. The tee should come up to your knees. The area between the end of the rope and the top of your tee is your strike zone. Step up to the tee and swing. There is no ball for this task. Your swing should go through the strike zone without touching the rope or the tee.

T Practice until you can get three strikes in a row through the strike zone without touching the rope or the tee.

T Now both raise the tee and lower the rope 1 inch. Take swings through this strike zone. Again, practice until you can get three. Then make the strike zone smaller again.

✓ *Teacher Observation.* At this point it is appropriate to conduct a teacher observation of the use of the critical cues for batting before proceeding to a more complex use of the skill.

Striking a Stationary Ball for Distance

Setting: Partners, each pair with a batting tee, three whiffle balls, and a bat; batters in a circle in the middle of the playground facing out with individual striking zones defined by ropes or cones (Figure 26.8); fielders about 30 feet (or whatever is appropriate) in front of their partner; marker cones or zones at 10-foot intervals around the center circle

Cues	
Watch the Ball	(Keep your eyes on the ball all the time.)
Bat Back	(Bring the bat way back over your shoulder so your back elbow is level with your shoulder.)
Side to the Field	(Turn your side to the target or field.)

Level	(Extend your arms to swing flat as a pancake.)
Rotate and Shift	(Roll over the shoelaces of your back foot.)

Tasks/Challenges:

T Stand inside the circle about a bat's length away from your tee with your side to the field. You are going to practice batting the ball in the air. There's enough room to hit as hard as you like. Your partner will collect the balls. After three hits, trade places. Remember, watch the ball.

T This time, have your partner stand where your ball landed. Try to hit the next ball farther. The partner moves to that spot. Try again to hit farther than the previous hit. After three hits, trade places with your partner.

T Bat the ball as far as possible. Remember the zone in which the ball first lands. Bat three times, each time trying to improve your distance. Trade places.

T Try to bat the ball so it lands in the same zone three times.

Striking Suspended Objects—Bats

Setting: Whiffle balls suspended about waist height from strings (see Figure 25.2) around the practice area; a bat for each child and individual striking zones defined by ropes or cones

Cues	
Side to the Field	(Turn your side to the target or field.)
Bat Back	(Bring the bat way back over your shoulder so it sticks up like a toothpick.)

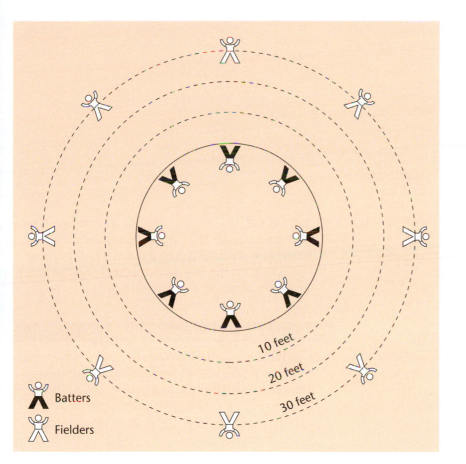

Figure 26.8 Setup for striking a stationary ball for distance.

10 feet
20 feet
30 feet

Batters

Fielders

Watch the Ball	(Keep your eyes on the ball all the time.)
Level	(Extend your arms to swing flat as a pancake.)
Rotate and Shift	(Roll over the shoelaces of your back foot.)

How does rolling over your shoelaces help you bat?

Tasks/Challenges:

T This task is a little harder than the last one. Instead of hitting balls that don't move from batting tees, you're going to hit balls that are hanging from strings. Stand to the side of the ball about a bat's length away. Practice hitting the ball. Remember, stop the ball still before you hit it again.

T Practice batting until you can hit five balls in a row without missing.

C Now the game changes a little. See how many times you can strike the ball in a row without missing.

Hitting a Stationary Ball from Different Places

Setting: A batting tee, ball, and bat for each child or pair of children; place the tee so the balls are batted

Balls suspended on strings give youngsters the opportunity to practice swinging level.

into a fence or wall, mark individual striking zones with ropes or cones or have the partner field balls; mark a home plate in the batting area

Cues	
Bat Back	(Bring the bat way back over your shoulder so it sticks up like a toothpick.)
Watch the Ball	(Keep your eyes on the ball all the time.)
Side to the Field	(Turn your side to the target or field.)
Level	(Extend your arms to swing flat as a pancake.)
Rotate and Shift	(Roll over the shoelaces of your back foot.)

Tasks/Challenges:

T Place the batting tee so the ball is on the inside corner of home plate at your knees. Hit five balls as hard as you can from this position. Switch places.

T Move the tee to the inside corner with the ball chest high. Make five hits as hard as you can. Switch.

T Move the tee to the outside corner, knee high. Go again.

T Now try the outside corner, chest high. Five and switch.

Hit and Run

Setting: Partners with individual striking zones defined by ropes or cones; ball, bat, batting tee, and spot (set up as in Figure 26.9)

Cues	
Bat Back	(Bring the bat way back over your shoulder so it sticks up like a toothpick.)
Watch the Ball	(Keep your eyes on the ball all the time.)
Side to the Field	(Turn your side to the target or field.)
Level	(Extend your arms to swing flat as a pancake.)
Rotate and Shift	(Roll over the shoelaces of your back foot.)

Tasks/Challenges:

T Partner A stands at the batting tee; partner B, on the spot about 15 feet away. Partner A strikes the

Figure 26.9 Setup for Hit and Run.
Source: S. Holt/Hale, *On the move: Lesson plans to accompany Children Moving*, 9th ed. (New York: McGraw-Hill, 2013).

ball off the tee, hitting it as far as possible. Then partner A runs to the carpet square and back to the batting tee. Partner B collects the ball and runs and replaces it on the tee. Switch places after each hit. Be careful: Both of you are running.

Throwing a Ball in the Air and Striking It

Setting: Preferably a large outdoor space, where children can bat against a wall or fence; large round targets on the wall; a plastic bat and a ball for each child and individual striking zones defined by ropes or cones

For this task and beginning tasks that involve hitting a pitched ball, sock balls work quite well. They won't travel too far, allowing children to focus on the swing. To make a sock ball, stuff an old sock with other socks and tie off. Cut off the tail.

Cues	
Bat Back	(Bring the bat way back over your shoulder so it sticks up like a toothpick.)
Watch the Ball	(Keep your eyes on the ball all the time.)
Side to the Field	(Turn your side to the target or field.)
Level	(Extend your arms to swing flat as a pancake.)
Rotate and Shift	(Roll over the shoelaces of your back foot.)

Tasks/Challenges:

T You're going to practice hitting a ball you throw into the air yourself. In your own space facing the wall (fence) and about 10 feet from it, toss a ball up into the air and then hit it with the bat. You must have both your hands on the bat when you hit the ball, so you'll have to work quickly. *(Demonstrate.)*

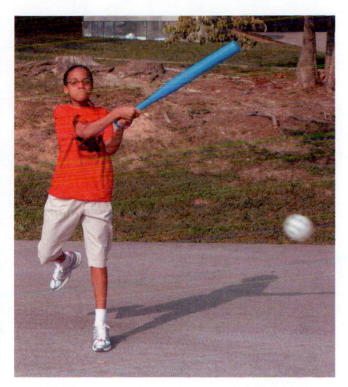

Striking a pitched ball is much more complex than striking off a tee; regression in the execution of the strike is to be expected.

T Now practice trying to hit the large circle on the wall.

T Score 5 points for every ball that hits the target; 3 points for every ball that hits the wall but misses the target; and 1 point for every ball you hit that doesn't hit the wall. Try to get to 21 points.

Striking a Self-Tossed Ball to Different Distances

Setting: Lines marked on a field for distance measurement; a number of whiffle (or tennis) balls and a plastic bat for each child; each child's individual striking zones defined by ropes or cones

Cues

Bat Back	(Bring the bat way back over your shoulder so it sticks up like a toothpick.)
Watch the Ball	(Keep your eyes on the ball all the time.)
Side to the Field	(Turn your side to the target or field.)
Level	(Extend your arms to swing flat as a pancake.)
Rotate and Shift	(Roll over the shoelaces of your back foot.)

Figure 26.10 "Neat feet" for a right-handed striking action. You can easily make "neat feet" by painting them in the correct position on a rubber mat. Challenge the children to move the left foot to the position of the dotted foot as they swing.

Tasks/Challenges:

T Now we're going to add something you worked on before: striking to different distances. This involves using different amounts of force to hit the ball. There are a lot of lines on the field; you can use them to judge how far you hit the ball. Each time you hit a ball, see how far you can make it go. If you hit it over one line one time, try to hit it over the next line the next time you hit.

T Pick out a line you know you can hit the ball past. Try to hit the ball past that line five times in a row. After you've practiced at one line, pick another line and try again.

Striking a Pitched Ball

Setting: A large outdoor space, marked as follows: a pitcher's square and a batting box for each group of two, each batter's box marked with "neat feet" in the correct batting position (Figure 26.10); a skilled thrower (older student, classroom teacher, parent, or grandparent) as a partner for each child; one plastic or sock ball and a bat for each pair

Cues

Bat Back	(Bring the bat way back over your shoulder so it sticks up like a toothpick.)
Watch the Ball	(Keep your eyes on the ball all the time.)
Side to the Field	(Turn your side to the target or field.)
Level	(Extend your arms to swing flat as a pancake.)
Rotate and Shift	(Roll over the shoelaces of your back foot.)

Tasks/Challenges:

T Before, you hit a ball off a batting tee or from a self-toss. This time you're going to practice batting

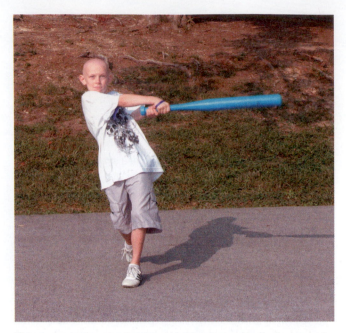

This youngster has clearly rotated his hips forward by "rolling over his back shoelaces."

a ball that's pitched by a "big" partner. Your big partner will be the pitcher, and you will get to bat all the time. Your partner stands on the pitcher's square and pitches the ball to you. You stand on the batter's square and try to hit the ball. The batter's square has a secret help in it: pictures of feet that show you exactly where to stand so you have the best chance of hitting the ball. Just try to hit the ball; it doesn't have to go far.

T Each time you bat, your big partner will give you a thumbs-up if you do everything correctly. If you miss a cue, he or she will tell you so you can use it for the next swing. *Note: Pitches from skilled throwers enhance the learning of batting skills.*

C Try to hit five balls in a row.

T *Homework.* The same task of striking pitched balls could be done as a homework assignment. The assignment could be in the form of a task card that includes the cues and asks a parent, grandparent, or older brother or sister to pitch 20 balls to the child. The parent would check on every fifth throw whether the cues were used.

Utilization Level (GLSP): Learning Experiences Leading to Skill Development

At the utilization level, children are able to control a ball in the space around them and strike consistently with the appropriate striking pattern. We challenge

them to use their striking skills in more dynamic and unpredictable situations.

A note about cues: Although several cues are listed for many of the learning experiences, it's important to focus on only one cue at a time. This way, the children can really concentrate on that cue. Once you provide feedback to the children and observe that most have learned a cue, it's time to focus on another one.

Grounders and Flies

Setting: Groups of three or four: one batter and one pitcher per group, the rest are fielders; a space large enough for all groups to bat without interfering with the others and marked with cones or ropes

Cues	
Under the Ball	(Hit the ball slightly below its center for a fly ball.)
Behind the Ball	(Hit directly behind the ball for a line drive.)
Over the Ball	(Hit near the top of the ball for a grounder.)

Tasks/Challenges:

T So far you have practiced hitting from behind the ball. This usually makes the ball travel in a straight aerial pathway—a line drive. Yet, there are times when you will need to hit balls high, and other times when you will need to hit grounders. That is what we will practice first—grounders. Hit the pitches so they hit the ground about 6 to 10 yards away. After five hits, switch places.

T The next practice will be for fly balls. Practice hitting these pitches so they don't hit the ground until past the baseline. They should go higher in the air than a line drive.

T Do you remember the game where the pitcher told the batter which field the batter was to hit the ball to? This game is similar, but here the pitcher calls out line drive, pop fly, or grounder, and the batter has to hit that kind of ball. After five hits, switch places.

C This time the batter calls out the type of hit before the ball is pitched. The batter gets one point for each hit that goes the way it was called. Try for four points—out of five pitches.

Assessment Example

From the National Standards for Physical Education

Event Task

Students are placed in groups of five or six members and are asked to role-play the following scenario: The city Little League coach has asked your group to serve as assistant coaches this season. Specifically, the coach wants you to do a presentation of either (a) throwing and catching or (b) striking with a bat for a bunt versus a home run. Within each group, students should prepare a demonstration to include an oral presentation of the various skills, explaining the variation of each and demonstrating the skills. Each person within the group must be part of the presentation. Each group will present their mini-demonstrations to the class.

Criteria for Assessment

a. Demonstrates the skill correctly.
b. Compares and/or contrasts variations within the skills.
c. Presentation is organized and interesting.

NASPE (1995, 47)

Directing the Placement of an Object

Setting: Partners, each pair with a batting tee, a bat, a cone, a hoop, and a ball; each pair with enough space to bat for distance and marked with cones or ropes. (See Figure 26.11 for setup.)

> **Cue**
>
> **Front Foot to Target** (Change your stance so your front foot points toward your target.)

Tasks/Challenges:

T Before, you practiced hitting the ball different distances; this time, you're going to practice hitting the ball to different places. To start, one person will be at bat, and the partner will be in left field. The batter first tries to hit five balls to left field,

aiming for her or his partner. If everything works correctly, the partner shouldn't have to move very far to catch the balls. After the first five hits, the partner moves to center field, and the batter tries to hit the next five balls to right field. Then switch places. You'll know you're really good when your partner doesn't have to move to catch the balls.

T This time, the fielder is going to make it harder. After every hit, the fielder moves to a new position, and the batter tries to hit the ball exactly to the fielder. The fielder can choose any place to go. After 10 hits, trade places.

T Now that you've gotten the hang of placing the ball, you're going to try to hit where the fielder isn't. In softball, you want to be able to hit to open spaces so you can get on base. Hit three balls off the tee, trying to send them to different places in the field. The fielder will collect them. After three hits, trade places.

C As you hit the three balls this time, call out where the hit will go. You get one point for every hit that goes where you indicated. Try for a perfect three.

T Now, you get to run as well. Bat the ball. As soon as you bat the ball, run around the cone and try to get home before the fielder has the ball in the hoop. After three hits, trade places.

Note: Either through teaching by invitation or intertask variation (Chapter 10), the difficulty of this task could be increased by striking a pitched ball.

Hitting to Open Spaces

Setting: A large outdoor area; children in groups of three or four, each group with a bat and a ball and individual striking zone defined by ropes or cones

> **Cue**
>
> **Front Foot to Target** (Change your stance so your front foot points toward your target.)

Tasks/Challenges:

T You're going to practice hitting a pitched ball and try to make it go to open spaces. One of the fielders will become the pitcher. All pitches must be easy so they can be hit. The batter will try to hit the outfield and have the ball hit the ground before the fielder can touch it. After 10 hits, switch places.

C You get one point for every ball that hits the ground untouched. Try for six points. Every 10 hits, trade places.

Figure 26.11 Setup for directing the placement of an object.

Striking a Pitched Object Varying the Distance

Setting: A large outdoor space; groups of three or four with a bat in an individual striking zone defined by ropes or cones, and five balls

Cues	
Full Swing	(Swing quickly all the way through to send the ball a long way.)
Medium Swing	(Swing at a medium speed all the way through to send the ball a shorter distance.)

Tasks/Challenges:

T This time, you're going to practice hitting a pitched ball different distances. To begin, one of you will pitch, one will hit, and others are fielders. Batter, your task is sometimes to hit the ball short so it lands near the pitcher and at other times to hit it long so it goes to the outfield. Try to decide ahead of time where you want the ball to go, and then hit it there.

T Now, to show how good you are, call out where the ball is going—a short or a long distance—before you hit it. Do this 10 times, and then switch places.

T This task is a little different from the last one. Instead of the batter calling out where the ball is to go, the pitcher calls out where the ball is to be hit. Change places after five hits.

Batting, Combining Distance and Placement

Setting: A large open space where children can bat balls safely in their individual striking zones defined by ropes or cones; bases marked in a diamond pattern; children in groups of four or five

Cues	
Front Foot to Target	(Your front foot should be pointed to your target.)
Full Swing	(Swing quickly all the way through for hits that go a long way.)
Medium Swing	(Swing at a medium speed for shorter hits.)

Tasks/Challenges:

T In your group, one of you will be the pitcher, one of you the batter, and the rest fielders. You're now

going to combine hitting for distances and hitting to open spaces. The pitcher will pitch 10 balls to the batter, who tries to hit the balls to where no one is standing. Some hits need to be short and others long, but all hits should be to empty spaces.

T This is a pretend baseball game. You are at bat; you get five swings. You will try to place each of the hits to advance the make-believe base runners. Your first two hits should be short, near the pitcher or third base. Your third swing is for a hit and run—try to place a ground ball between second and third so a runner could advance to second. Your fourth hit should move the runner to third—so hit a grounder between first and second. Your last swing is to score the run—hit a long fly ball to the outfield.

T *Homework.* Students at this point can profit from watching skilled players. An appropriate homework assignment would be to watch a baseball game (live or on television) and record all the places to which two selected players hit the ball (e.g., left field, bunt down third-base line).

Proficiency Level (GLPS): Learning Experiences Leading to Skill Development

When children reach the proficiency level, many possess mature striking patterns, and striking becomes a skill that can be used in complex, unpredictable, gamelike situations. At this point, children are able to incorporate previous experiences into situations that involve strategic and split-second decisions. At this level, children are given situations that facilitate development of the ability to strike with implements while focusing on the strategy and outcome of the action and on their skill. The focus at this level is the attainment of consistency and accuracy. Cues are focused on the use of the skill rather than on the skill itself.

As with other skill themes, at the proficiency level, many appropriate activities call for the use of striking skills in a gamelike situation. It can be quite tricky to keep these activities developmentally appropriate, especially in terms of active participation for all children. There are several solutions here. One is to set up multiple playing areas around the space. Another option is to have stations, several of which offer gamelike activities, and several of which have practice opportunities that require less space and setup. Finally, you could have peer assessment opportunities; within small groups, half will play and half observe, and then they switch. Regardless of the solution, all game-type activities should be appropriate for all children. See Chapter 30 for more information on game options in physical education.

A note about cues: At the proficiency level, tasks are more complex, typically requiring children to coordinate several movements simultaneously in a dynamic context. A list of cues is provided to assist the children in being more successful in the learning experiences. The challenge is in determining which cue will be most beneficial for each child . . . and when. Thus careful observation and critical reflection become very important as you watch the children move and then decide which cue will be the most helpful to move each learner to a higher level.

Directing the Pathway, Distance, and Speed of an Object

Setting: Groups of five: one batter, one pitcher, and three fielders; one plastic bat and ball per group; a space large enough for groups to bat without interfering with other groups marked with ropes or cones

Cues	
Quick Swing	(Quick swing = long.)
Medium Swing	(Swing at a medium speed all the way through to send the ball a shorter distance.)
Below, Over, Behind the Ball	(Below = fly ball; over = ground ball; behind = line drive.)

Tasks/Challenges:

Ⓣ For this task you will use a plastic bat and ball. Here are the rules:

1. There are five people in a group: one batter, one pitcher, and three fielders.
2. Before the pitcher pitches the ball, she calls out the type of hit and the placement. The batter has to hit the ball the way the pitcher calls it.
3. Change batters after five hits.
4. Each player keeps his or her own score—one point for every ball that was hit as the pitcher called it.

Six-Player Striking and Fielding in a Gamelike Situation

Setting: Groups of six players, three-person teams; bases as in softball, but with the distance between each reduced to make the game challenging for the group; one bat, ball, and tee per group; sufficient space so children can bat without interfering with one another with each field marked with cones or ropes

Cues	
Batters	
Hit to Open Spaces	(Always hit to open spaces.)
Fielders	
Throw Quickly	(Throw the ball as soon as you get it.)
Have a Plan	(Know where the runners are; plan where to throw the ball.)

Tasks/Challenges:

Ⓣ This game involves the skills of striking, throwing, and catching. The objective is to place a batted ball, catch and throw, and run bases. Here are the rules:

1. There are three players on each team.
2. The batter strikes the ball from the tee and tries to run the bases.
3. The fielders try to catch or collect the ball and throw it to one another so all three players catch the ball before the batter finishes running the bases.
4. Each player on a team bats, and then the teams switch places.

During the class, we focus on each child's individual improvements rather than on class or individual competition. Many children (and faculty!) enjoy voluntary tournaments after school or at lunch.

Assessment Example

From the National Standards for Physical Education

Student Report

Partners videotape each other while striking a ball resting on a batting tee (five times) and while striking a ball thrown by a pitcher (five times). They review the tape with their partner and self-assess according to criteria presented to them in class. Based on this information they write a description of one or more of the following: the critical elements of batting; the consistency of their movement patterns; the differences in cues available when striking from a tee (closed skill) versus striking a pitched ball (open skill); and practice suggestions for improvement in each skill.

Criteria for Assessment

a. Accurately describes the criteria for good batting.
b. Accurately assesses their own consistency of performance.
c. Accurately identifies cues available in open or closed skills.

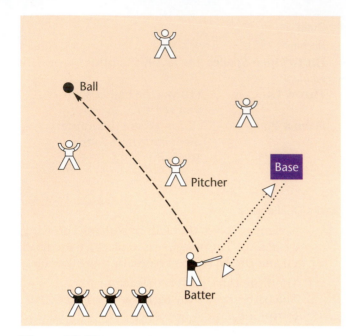

Figure 26.12 Setup for One-Base Baseball.

d. Selects appropriate practice options based on the difference between the two skills.

NASPE (1995, 48–49)

One-Base Baseball

Setting: Groups of six or eight, three- or four-person teams; one base, one bat, and one ball per group; a field set up (see Figure 26.12) marked with ropes or cones

Cues	
Batters	
Hit to Open Spaces	(Always hit to open spaces.)
Fielders	
Throw Quickly	(Throw the ball as soon as you get it.)
Have a Plan	(Know where the runners are; plan where to throw the ball.)

Tasks/Challenges:

T You're going to play One-Base Baseball. The objective is to get to the base and back before the pitcher gets the ball. Here are the rules:

1. Each team has three or four people.
2. The batter bats and then tries to run to the base and back to home plate before the pitcher gets the ball again.
3. Each person on a team bats, and then the teams trade places.

Striking with Long-Handled Implements—Golf Clubs

Hitting a golf ball and actually having it travel where it is intended never fail to excite the player. The golf swing is unique to golf but can be used in a variety of circumstances from playing 18 holes of regulation golf, to three par courses, to the "back nine," to the driving range, or even putt-putt. Wherever and whatever, golf requires the use of swing in a vertical plane to strike a stationary ball. Our skill development progression spiral provides basic activities for learning to use a golf swing from precontrol to utilization.

Precontrol Level (GLSP): Activities for Exploration

Activities at the precontrol level ask children to explore striking with golf clubs. At this level, a chopping, downward swing is typical for any striking pattern. Children struggle just to make contact between the ball and the striking instrument. Therefore we give children activities that let them explore striking with the added length that comes with golf clubs—and the greater demands that length places on their hand–eye coordination. Due to the difficulty of the skill, tasks are developed using large objects to be struck.

Skill Theme Development Progression

Striking with Long-Handled Implements— Golf

Proficiency Level

Box Golf
Whiffle Ball Golf

Utilization Level

Playing Hoop Golf
Putting

Control Level

Striking to varying distances
Striking a ball so it travels in the air: Air Ball

Precontrol Level

First swings

First Swings Golf

Setting: If possible set up individual striking areas for each child defined by ropes and cones. If you do not have enough clubs for each child then define an area safely behind the children who are striking with golf clubs for their partners to stand a safe distance away. You will need to use your critical demandingness (Chapter 8) to be certain they remain in their zones and do not change until you give them the command to do so. If you are using partners switch, when you give the command, every 5 swings. Hoops for each child.

Tasks/Challenges

T Do you see the hoops in front of you? See if you can hit the ball into or past the hoop? (Hoops placed about 10 yards in front of the children who are striking).

T *(After all the children have had 20–30 swings, move the hoops to different distances—some closer, some farther away).* Now aim for different hoops—but remember to try to hit the ball so it goes past the hoop.

Note: At the precontrol level the children are just discovering the sensations associated with striking a ball with a golf club. So provide them with plenty of opportunities to swing the club before you start teaching them the cues that will lead to better golf swings.

Figure 26.13 Golf club grip.

use ropes in cones, hurdles, chairs to make a target to hit over about three feet high.

Cues	
Stance	(Feet shoulder width apart, knees bent.)
Grip	(Thumbs pointing slightly to the sides—one o'clock and eleven o'clock for right handers—not straight down the shaft; all fingers touching.) (Figure 26.13)
Circle Swing	(Turn shoulders away from the target and toward the target)

Setting: Children in their individual striking zones defined by ropes and cones. Ideally a club for each child and plenty of foam or whiffle balls. If you use partners be sure to define a zone that the children who are not swinging a club must remain inside of so they do not accidentally run into someone swinging a club.

Tasks/Challenges:

T Do you see the line (rope, chairs, hurdles) in front of you? It is about three feet high. We are going to practice hitting balls over this line. To do so you will need to get the ball into the air. To do this you will need to keep your knees bent throughout the swing. Go ahead and start hitting.

C Try to send the ball in the air so it hits above the mark (over the hurdle) three times in a row. If you do, tell the teacher your favorite golfer—or if you don't know a golfer, your favorite kind of ice cream.

Control Level: (GLSP) Learning Experiences Leading to Skill Development

At the control level, children begin to develop mature striking patterns that are used in increasingly complex contexts. They can be challenged with tasks that require them to include one or two other variables besides striking such as striking a golf ball for distance.

A note about cues: Although several cues are listed for many of the learning experiences, it's important to focus on only one cue at a time. This way, the children can really concentrate on that cue. Once you provide feedback to the children and observe that most have learned a cue, it's time to focus on another one

Striking so the Ball Travels in the Air: Air Balls

Setting: Plastic golf clubs and foam or whiffle balls; striking zones defined with ropes and/or cones; children about 10 feet from the wall; marks on the wall about 3 feet off the floor in inside. If outside you can

Striking to Varying Distances

Setting: Preferably a large outdoor space; a golf club and a bucket of plastic balls for each child; all children facing the same direction in their individual striking zones defined by ropes and cones, with at least 6 feet between them; large buckets or other targets at various distances from the children who are striking

Cues

Setup   (Legs form an A, arms and shaft of the club form a Y. Knees bent.)

Full Swing (Shoulders turn away from the target, club sweeps low and then shoulders turn back toward the target.)

Tasks/Challenges:

T Use the golf grip (Figure 26.13). You're going to be practicing a golf swing. Let's practice first without the ball. Stand to the side of the make-believe ball, side to the target (field), and take a full backswing, bend your knees, swing, and follow through. Make five practice swings and then start hitting balls. Remember, only swing in your individual striking zone.

Cue

Circle Swing (Turn your shoulders away from the target and then toward the target to hit the ball as far as you can.)

Tasks/Challenges:

T There are markers (buckets, hoops) on the field to help you judge the length of your hits. Hit the ball, and then try to hit the next ball farther. Try to find your maximum distance. If working in partners switch after 10–15 swings. Be sure the partners remain in their own zone when they are not hitting

C Every time you hit the ball longer then you have before, jump in the air three times and say "YES!"

Putting

Note: This task can be used at the utilization and proficiency levels also.

Setting: Inside in a gym or on a carpeted surface. Each child has a putter, a ball, and a plastic cup. Use a poly spot or carpet square to mark a distance about 5 feet

from the cup. Set up as many stations as you can—cup, putter, ball for each child, and poly spot.

Cues

Grip   (Both thumbs straight down the shaft.)
Wrists (Stiff, as if in a cast.)
Swing   (Like a pendulum, back and through.)

Tasks/Challenges:

T Today we are going to practice golf putting. Look around the gym and you will see holes set up. Each hole has a putter, a ball for each of you, a cup and a starting spot (carpet square or poly spot). Your goal is to putt the ball so it goes into the cup in as few strokes as possible. A perfect score would be a 1. Remember not to swing your putter—but just use it for the putting stroke, which is much shorter than the full swing.

T Begin by putting into your own cup. Demonstrate and remind them of the cues as they practice—one cue at a time.

C Now we are going to play a game. You are going to play three times (holes) into your own cup. See how few putts you can take for the three holes. What would a perfect score be? Right: a three.

T Now look around the gym and you will see that the holes are numbered (on the cups and by the poly spots). This time you are going to start at your hole and then process to the next number hole. So if the number on your cup is 5, you will start there; once the ball is in the cup you will go to the next highest number. When you finish putting at hole number 30 (the highest hole), you will go to hole 1.

C On the scorecard I have provided, use the pencil to write down your score for each hole. How many putts did it take you to go through the entire course? A good score would be two putts a hole. So if there are 15 holes, a score of 30 would be a good score. (*Note: This score will depend on the GLSP of the children and also the distance from cup to cup. Higher-skilled children will be challenged by setting a lower target score and/or moving the cups a further distance from the starting point*).

Utilization Level (GLSP): Learning Experiences Leading to Skill Development

At the utilization level, children are able to control a ball in the space around them and strike consistently with the appropriate striking pattern. We challenge them to use their striking skills in more dynamic and unpredictable situations.

A note about cues: Although several cues are listed for many of the learning experiences, it's important to focus on only one cue at a time. This way, the children can really concentrate on that cue. Once you provide feedback to the children and observe that most have learned a cue, it's time to focus on another one.

Playing Hoop Golf

Setting: A plastic golf club and ball for each child. Children can share clubs if there are not enough. You will need to designate a hitting zone and a standing zone for the partners—one hits, the other one stands on a poly spot a safe distance from the tee (cone). Only introduce this task if the students in the class have learned to work safely and follow directions (Chapter 8).

Cues	
Grip	(Thumbs pointing slightly to the sides—one o'clock and eleven o'clock for right handers—not straight down the shaft; all fingers touching.) (Figure 26.13)
Stance	(Legs form an A, arms and shaft of the club form a Y. Knees bent.)
Swing	(Shoulders turn away from the target, club sweeps low making a circle, and then shoulders turn back toward the target.)

Tasks/Challenges:

T The starting point for each hole is a tee. The "hole" is a hoop. The object is to strike the ball into the hoop in as few strokes as possible. If you are hitting your ball too far, don't turn your shoulders as much. If you want to hit it farther, turn your shoulders farther.

C Play the hole 3 times. Each time you hit the ball counts as one until the ball stops inside the hoop. What is your score for three holes? A perfect score would be...? Right: a three. Now I want you to switch to a different hole and tee (and hoop). Play the hole three times. Is your score better or worse than the score on the last hole you played?

T Now find a partner. Play the same hole. What is your total score between the two of you? Remember to count each hit (stroke). Now can you and partner make an even better score? If your total score is two, then you need to move the hoop further away.

T Now you and your partner can join up with two other partners. You can play for a total score (all four of you) and see if you can improve. Or you may want to play a game where you and your partner try to make a lower score then your opponents. Remember, you have to count each swing—even if you miss the ball.

Proficiency Level: (GLSP) Learning Experiences Leading to Skill Development

When children reach the proficiency level, many possess mature striking patterns, and striking becomes a skill that can be used in complex, unpredictable, game-like situations. At this point, children are able to incorporate previous experiences into situations that involve strategic and split-second decisions. At this level, children are given situations that facilitate development of the ability to strike with implements while focusing on the strategy and outcome of the action and on their skill. The focus at this level is the attainment of consistency and accuracy. Cues are focused on the use of the skill rather than on the skill itself.

A note about cues: At the proficiency level, tasks are more complex, typically requiring children to coordinate several movements simultaneously in a dynamic context. A list of cues is provided to assist the children in being more successful in the learning experiences. The challenge is in determining which cue will be most beneficial for each child . . . and when. Thus careful observation and critical reflection become very important as you watch the children move and then decide which cue will be the most helpful to move each learner to a higher level.

Whiffle Ball Golf

Setting: A Whiffle Ball Golf course (Figure 26.14); a golf club and whiffle ball for each child. Cones or large balls mark the tees.

This task can be adapted for use with control or utilization level classes.

Cues	
Grip–Grip	(Thumbs pointing slightly to the sides [one o'clock and eleven o'clock for right-handers]—not straight down the shaft; all fingers touching.) (Figure 26.13)
Stance	(Legs form an A, arms and shaft of the club form a Y. Knees bent.)
Full Swing	(Shoulders turn away from the target, club sweeps low and then shoulders turn back toward the target.)

Figure 26.14 Whiffle Ball Golf course.

Tasks/Challenges:

T The game you're going to play is Whiffle Ball Golf. It's played just as regular golf is played. The objective of the game is to get the ball to land in the hoop with as few strokes as possible. Each of you will start at the hole I assign you and then go to the next higher numbered hole. Each hole has a tee area from which to start: This area is marked with big rubber balls to guarantee that everyone starts from the same place. When you get to hole 9 (or however many holes you set up), go to hole 1. Keep score by counting the shots it takes you to go around the entire course.

C You may want to have the children play alone or with (or against) a partner. You may also want to have two partners play the course challenging another pair for the lowest score.

Box Golf

Setting: Boxes of various heights set up throughout the entire space. A tee that marks the starting point; a golf club and a ball for each child. As always you will have to be clear about where the children stand to swing the club and where children who are not hitting need to stand (inside a hoop, for example, several feet from the tee where the child is swinging the club). *Note: This is an appropriate task-teaching station instructional approach as well as an example of a child designed instructional approach. (See Chapter 10 for more information on these teaching approaches.)*

Cues

Knees Remain Bent	(Remember, keep your knees slightly bent as you swing.)
Hinge and Hold	(Make an L with your arms as you swing back, swing low, and try to hold the L in your arms on the follow-through.) *(You want the children to avoid scooping the ball when their hands get ahead of the ball and "top" the ball.)*
Follow-Through	(Swing all the way through and over your shoulder.)

Tasks/Challenges:

T Can you land the ball in your box? If you can land it in the box three times in a row, move your tee one giant step away from the box and try again.

T Design your own box golf game. You may have up to three players in a group. When you are finished, write down the rules for the game. *(See Chapter 30 for details about how to help children design their own games.)* Do you want to give different points for hitting the box and for making the ball stop inside the box? How many swings will each of you get?

✓ *Event Task.* The written self-designed game is an appropriate assessment task to be included in a child's portfolio.

Reading Comprehension Questions

1. What basic action is used in striking with any long-handled implement?
2. What is a sidearm pattern? What is an underhand swinging pattern? Which swings are used with which implements?
3. What is the purpose of introducing children to striking with long-handled implements?
4. What can be the long-term result when children try to swing implements that are too heavy or too long?
5. Describe the correct form for striking a ball with a bat? See if you can find a group of children playing baseball (or softball). Do their forms match those in the photo sequence (Box 26-1)?
6. How does the idea of "roll over shoelaces" to enhance the cue of "rotate and shift" promote a mature striking pattern?
7. Why do we recommend that children initially practice striking using yarn or plastic balls?
8. Describe two examples, one for bats and one for hockey sticks, of contexts that are unpredictable or changing.
9. In using a hockey stick to handle a ball, what do the terms *give* and *control* mean?
10. Find a picture from a magazine (or other media) that illustrates what the cue of "Legs form an A, arms and shaft of the club form a Y" looks like in the set up for a golf swing. Label the A and the Y.
11. List three safety cues for striking with long-handled implements.

References Suggested Readings

Holt/Hale, S. 2010. *On the move: Lesson plans to accompany Children Moving*. 8th ed. New York: McGraw-Hill.

National Association for Sport and Physical Education. 1995. *Moving into the future: National standards for physical education*. St. Louis, MO: Mosby.

Wickstrom, R. L. 1970. *Fundamental motor patterns*. 2nd ed. Philadelphia: Lea & Febiger.

Wickstrom, R. L. 1983. *Fundamental motor patterns*. 3rd ed. Philadelphia: Lea & Febiger.

World Golf Association. 2008. *The First Tee National School Program curriculum manual*. 2nd ed. http://www.thefirsttee.org for The First Tee National School Program trainings.

Skill Theme Application

Now that we have introduced you to the movement concepts and skill themes in the previous section, we want to focus on their application in different contexts in physical education. Chapter 27 defines fitness for children, revisits the differences between physical activity and physical education, and discusses the role of the physical education teacher as the physical activity director for the school. The chapter describes how health-related fitness concepts are interwoven throughout our lessons and provides numerous examples of ways children can increase their physical activity and improve fitness both within and beyond the school day.

Chapters 28, 29, and 30 discuss how dance, gymnastics, and games, respectively, are developed in the skill theme approach. You will not, however, find a series of rules for games, steps for dance, or specific gymnastics stunts in these chapters. To do so would violate the very premise on which *Children Moving* is based—children have different needs and interests! Thus these three chapters are designed so that the skill themes and movement concepts most associated with games, dance, and educational gymnastics are combined and developed in that context. For example, Chapter 29, "Teaching Gymnastics," links the skill themes of jumping and landing, balancing, and transferring weight and the actions of bending, stretching, twisting and curling in gymnastics settings. The three chapters on dance, games, and gymnastics each focus on predesigned and child-designed curriculum experiences, with child-designed experiences being the underlying focus of all our work in *Children Moving* (see Chapter 13).

Chapter 31, "Adapting the Content for Diverse Learners," provides an overview of the philosophy of inclusion and focuses on ways teachers can adapt both their teaching and their curricular content to maximize learning and participation for all children in physical education. The richness of diversity is addressed through the concepts of changes, challenges, and choices.

The final chapter in this part—Chapter 32, "Integrating the Skill Theme Approach Across the Curriculum"—offers valuable insights into classroom teachers and physical education teachers working together to develop integrated, or interdisciplinary, learning experiences for children.

Teaching Physical Fitness, Physical Activity, and Wellness

Intelligence and skill can only function at the peak of their capacity when the body is healthy and strong.

—JOHN F. KENNEDY

Key Concepts

- The focus of fitness in elementary school physical education has shifted from strenuous exercise programs to physical activity as a preventive for disease and a formula for good health.
- Physical fitness has shifted from skills-related/athletic to health-related fitness.
- Physical fitness for youngsters centers around understanding the health-related fitness components and concepts of fitness, and appreciating the importance of being physically active.
- The purpose of fitness assessment is to identify areas of concern and assist youngsters in establishing personal fitness goals; fitness assessment should never be used for assigning grades to children.
- Physical fitness is a product of movement that provides children with skills, confidence, and enjoyment.
- Physical fitness becomes a process, maintained through a physically active lifestyle that begins in childhood.
- Physical activity is a leading indicator of the health of children and adults.
- Wellness encompasses emotional, mental, spiritual, social, and environmental well-being as well as fitness.
- The concepts of wellness are partners with fitness and physical activity for a healthy lifestyle.

The goal of physical fitness is a healthy individual. The goal of physical education is children who become and remain physically active for a lifetime. Wellness encompasses physical, emotional, mental, spiritual interpersonal/social and environmental well-being, with the goal of a healthy, productive lifestyle. Thus the goals of fitness, physical education, and wellness are intertwined. This chapter focuses on physical activity as the medium for the development of fitness in children, the relationship of wellness to physical education, and physical education as the priority venue for wellness and fitness in children.

Physical Activity

The importance of physical activity is evidenced with its inclusion in *Healthy People 2020* (USDHHS 2010), reports from the Surgeon General (USDHHS 1999), and the *National Standards for Physical Education* (NASPE 2004a). *Healthy People 2020* identified physical activity as one of the leading indicators that most greatly affects health for individuals and communities. The Surgeon General's report speaks of the development of an active lifestyle, with physical inactivity portrayed as hazardous to health. NASPE's physical education standards devote one of the six standards to regular participation in physical activity.

Physical activity is now recognized as a preventive for disease and a formula for good health (Shephard 2005; Strong et al. 2005; Watts 2005; Welk and Blair 2000). Childhood obesity and preventive degenerative diseases have reached epidemic proportions in the United States. The health risks of obesity can be largely managed through physical activity. The health risks of degenerative diseases, appearing in children as early as age eight, can be prevented through daily physical activity.

The obesity and degenerative diseases epidemic presents the following:

- Young children predicted to not outlive their parents (Katz 2004)
- Childhood obesity that has more than tripled in the last two decades (USDHHS 2010)
- Health care costs related to obesity exceeding $147 billion per year (Obama 2011)
- One in three children, born in 2000 and beyond, who will develop type 2 diabetes (McConnaughey 2003)

Obesity is a health issue, an emotional issue, and a social issue. Here are some of the facts we know relating to obesity:

- Ninety percent of our children are born healthy and are genetically predisposed to lead normal lifestyles (Seffrin 2010)
- Birth weight has not changed significantly in more than 300 years (Seffrin 2010)
- Obesity in children between the ages of 6 and 11 is highest among ethnic minorities (Forster-Scott, 2007)
- Culture plays a significant role in attitudes toward exercise, food and nutrition, and body image (Peralta 2003)
- Inactivity is both a contributing cause of excess weight and a consequence of being overweight (Welk and Joens-Matre 2007)
- Obese children feel alienated and isolated

For children struggling with being overweight, the emphasis should be on good health rather than on weight loss. A positive focus contributes to emotional wellness and self-esteem as well as increased physical activity. Excellent resources are *Real Kids Come in All Sizes* (Kater 2004) and *Supersized P.E.* (Trout and Kahan 2008).

Physical Inactivity

Physical inactivity is a health issue, an environmental issue, and an emotional issue. As a health issue, we now know inactivity is a contributing factor in children being overweight and obese. Inactivity has a direct link to degenerative diseases; more than 40 years ago the term *hypokinetic* was used to describe diseases associated with a lack of physical activity (Corbin et al. 2008). Decreases in physical activity have been linked to increased television time, video games, and computers—that is, increases in sedentary time. Less outdoor play, due to a variety of reasons, has also contributed to the increase in physical inactivity. A drive through any neighborhood provides a very vivid visual of the decrease in children's physical activity.

> *Hypokinetic diseases are those diseases or conditions associated with lack of physical activity or too little regular exercise.*
>
> —CORBIN ET AL. 2008

Physical inactivity increases with age; girls are less active than boys. Minority children are less likely to be active, with the highest rate of physical inactivity among minority females. The percentage of physically inactive minority females who become less active as they grow into adolescence is of clinical and public health significance (Crespo 2005). Self-confidence and self-esteem are consistently mentioned as important predictors of physical activity, or lack of activity, in both boys and girls, increasing in importance as children reach upper elementary school. Self-confidence is linked as a protective factor against obesity and depression (Dunton et al. 2006). Confidence in self breeds increased activity; a lack of confidence breeds a lack of activity leading to less activity and increased weight gain. The negative cycle: Inactivity leads to more inactivity, to obesity and degenerative disease, to low self-esteem and fear of failure, and thus to increased inactivity. The positive cycle: Physical activity leads to more activity, serves as a preventive for obesity and degenerative disease, and increases self-esteem and emotional, as well as physical, health.

Enjoyment and skill development are the two key factors children and adolescents give as reasons to engage in and maintain programs of physical activity (Bengoechea et.al. 2010; Gao, Lodewyk, and Zhang 2009; Lohman, Going, and Metcalfe 2004). Perceived competence of that skill development greatly affects participation in physical activity (Davison et al. 2006; Fairclough and Stratton 2006). It is important for us as teachers to remember the word is *perceived*. Children may be very capable of successful participation in a variety of activities but do not view themselves as having the skills for success. Very young children think they are very skilled, capable of conquering the highest climbing wall, shooting at the tallest basket, and performing at the highest level on all measures of physical ability. As children progress through elementary school, this perception begins to match against the reality of the performance and the comparison to others, which all too often results in a decrease in perceived competence and confidence that leads to a decrease in willingness to participate and a decrease in the joy in doing so. Our task as teachers is to provide developmentally appropriate activities, in a "differentiated, inclusive learning environment" (Dunton et al. 2006) to assure children's enjoyment, confidence, and competence in physical activity (Ennis, 2010).

Let's Move

In February, 2011, first lady, Michelle Obama announced a national goal of solving the challenge of childhood obesity. The Let's Move campaign (www.letsmove.gov) is a collaborative effort of public and private sectors—families, schools, and communities—that focuses on better nutrition and increased physical activity.

Let's Move in School

In support of Let's Move, NASPE has launched the Let's Move in School initiative (www.letsmoveinschool.org) to educate youth about the benefits of a physically active lifestyle and to ensure that every school provides opportunities for quality physical education and physical activity. Let's Move in School provides tools to support school-based physical education and comprehensive physical activity programs—integrated classroom activities, physical activity breaks, recess, before- and after-school programs, sports, and walk-to, bike-to school programs.

Both Let's Move and Let's Move in School place a heavy emphasis on the collaborative efforts of schools, families, communities, and corporate America. It does indeed take a village to raise a physically active, healthy child.

Guidelines for Physical Activity

The importance of establishing physical activity habits in childhood is supported in the research. Habits established early in life tend to remain into adulthood, thus becoming lifestyle. The recommendations for children's physical activity are included in the *Physical Activity Guidelines for Americans* (USDHHS 2008).

Key guidelines for children and adolescents are as follows:

- Children and adolescents should do 60 minutes or more of physical activity daily.
- Aerobic: Most of the 60 or more minutes a day should be either moderate- or vigorous-intensity aerobic physical activity and should include vigorous-intensity physical activity at least three days a week.
- Muscle-strengthening: As part of their 60 or more minutes of daily physical activity, children and adolescents should include muscle-strengthening physical activity at least three days of the week.
- Bone-strengthening: As part of their 60 or more minutes of daily physical activity, children and adolescents should include bone-strengthening physical activity at least three days of the week.
- It is important to encourage young people to participate in physical activities that are appropriate for their age, that are enjoyable, and that offer variety. The *Physical Activity Guidelines for Americans* (USDHHS 2008) provides toolkits for schools, families, and communities to support physical activity for children and adolescents, ages 6–17.

One of the most reliable predictors for lifelong physical activity is the power of early physical activity experiences (Ennis 2010). Youth who are regularly active tend to be active as adults, and thus have a better chance of a healthy adulthood. That activity should be developmentally appropriate, enjoyable, and contribute to the child's skillfulness in physical activities. Figure 27.1 provides examples of moderate- and vigorous-intensity activities as well as muscle- and bone-strengthening activities for children.

Key concepts from the *Physical Activity Guidelines* include:

- Aerobic activities increase cardiorespiratory fitness.
- Vigorous activity comes in short bursts for children, accumulated through the day.
- Vigorous-intensity activities are important as they cause more improvement in cardiorespiratory fitness.
- Bone-strengthening is especially important for children; the majority of peak bone mass is obtained by the end of adolescence.
- Children do not need formal muscle-strengthening programs, e.g., lifting weights.
- Children doing moderate-intensity activities will notice their hearts are beating faster than normal and they are breathing harder.
- Children doing vigorous-intensity activities will feel their hearts beating much faster than normal and they will breathe much harder than normal.

Figure 27.1 Sample Activities for Children (pre-adolescents)

Type of Physical Activity	Children
Moderate–intensity aerobic	• Active recreation, such as hiking, skateboarding, rollerblading • Bicycle riding • Brisk walking
Vigorous–intensity aerobic	• Active games involving running and chasing, such as tag • Bicycle riding • Jumping rope • Martial arts, such as karate • Running • Sports such as soccer, ice or field hockey, basketball, swimming, tennis • Cross-country skiing
Muscle-strengthening	• Games such as tug-of-war • Modified push-ups (with knees on the floor) • Resistance exercises using body weight or resistance bands • Rope or tree climbing • Sit-ups (curl-ups or crunches) • Swinging on playground equipment/bars
Bone-strengthening	• Games such as hopscotch • Hopping, skipping, jumping • Jumping rope • Running • Sports such as gymnastics, basketball, volleyball, tennis

Source: U.S. Department of Health and Human Services, *Physical activity guidelines for Americans* (U.S. Department of Health and Human Services: 2008).

- A variety of activities is important to reduce the risk of overtraining or injury.
- Physical activity is important for children with disabilities; when possible/appropriate, the *Guidelines* should be met.

The *Physical Activity Guidelines* are based on children's needs and developmental characteristics; the guidelines focus on developmentally appropriate physical activity, skill development, and fitness through activity. Physical education provides the tools; physical activity provides the arena for good health and fitness development.

With the recommendations of 60 minutes or more of physical activity per day for children, the importance of physical education and recess becomes increasingly apparent. It is through physical education that the skills for activity are developed. It is through recess that play as physical activity is fostered, social interaction in activity is "tested," and confidence in physical activity is increased. Given the skills learned in physical education and the potential positive interaction on the playground, children gain competence and confidence in themselves, thus engaging in more physical activity.

Physical Activity In and Beyond the School Day

With only 12 percent of elementary schools in the nation offering daily physical education (NASPE 2010), and with recess decreasing to provide more time for classroom academics, it is readily apparent that, in most situations in our elementary schools today, we cannot meet the recommendations for 60 minutes or more of daily physical activity. Thus programs before and after school, in school, and at home are essential to successful promotion of daily physical activity. Lee and Solomon (2007) term this the "whole-school approach," involving all school clients—students, physical education specialist, classroom teachers, and parents—in the promotion of physical activity for children.

In-School Activities

With many school programs not affording children daily physical education, activities beyond the gymnasium are critical for meeting the guidelines for physical activity daily, as well as for establishing the pattern for a lifetime of daily participation. In-school activities include before- and after-school activities, daily recess, physical activity breaks during the school day provided by the classroom teacher, and educational television/PBS or child-designed activity/exercise programs. Examples of in-school programs to provide physical activity include:

- Jump rope clubs organized at different skill and interest levels. These clubs are organized for full participation by all students, in comparison to a jump rope team with selected students.
- Jogging/walking clubs with an emphasis on jogging or walking for distance, as opposed to running for speed. These clubs can focus on total miles completed for each student, matching the miles of a friend/parent/community volunteer on a hiking trail, or walking/jogging across the state.
- *Kid Fit and Fun,* age-appropriate activities for classroom breaks locally produced by PBS/educational television. Upper-elementary students can produce in-school programs to promote physical activity using students, parents, and community volunteers.

Pedometers

Pedometers can be excellent instruments for increasing children's awareness of their physical activity level. Wearing pedometers during recess and after school/at home will assist children in assessing their individual levels of activity and the amount of cumulative activity they attain in a given time period and in different environments (e.g., on the playground, in organized sports, in free play).

Children enjoy charting their steps for "A Walk Across America," calculating the miles (and steps) to various destinations within the state, or climbing Mt. Everest. Classroom teachers appreciate the reinforcements of mathematics and geography lessons. It is important to remember that 10,000 steps as a daily goal is a target number of steps set for adults. It is a goal that is too high for sedentary individuals or those with chronic diseases. It is a number that is low for many children during an average day; their goal is 12,000. If pedometers are used to motivate children for increased physical activity, it is important to set personal goals after establishing baseline steps for the child, specific health goals, and sustainability of the goal for that child in a routine day (Tudor-Locke 2002).

Pedometers allow children to calculate the amount of activity they receive and to set goals for the future.

www.mhhe.com/graham9e

- *Take10!,* an integration of physical activity and academics for classroom teachers. Ten minutes of physical activity supporting academics are provided for elementary school children, arranged by grade levels, K–5. (see www.take10.net).
- "Challenges," lesson plans to promote active participation and skill development with minimum teacher supervision at recess, found in *On the Move: Lesson Plans to Accompany Children Moving* (Holt/Hale 2012).
- The Centers for Disease Control and Prevention (CDC) BAM! (Body and Mind) Web site offers interactive activities for students and teachers linked to national standards for health and science; designed for students ages 9–13 (www.bam.gov).
- The CDC's VERB! (It's What You Do) Web site offers physical activity ideas and resources for students ages 9–13, parents, and teachers (www.cdc.gov/youthcampaign).
- The American Heart Association's What Moves U campaign offers activities for Pre-K through upper elementary students, organized by grade levels, focused on nutrition and physical activity; their Balance It Out program offers activities for elementary focused on nutrition (www.heart.org).

See References/Suggested Readings at the end of this chapter for additional Web site listings.

Thomas Jefferson introduced pedometers to America. They came into the commercial market in Japan in 1965 under the name of manpo-meter (manpo in Japanese means 10,000 steps).

—HATANO AND TUDOR-LOCKE (2001)

Physical activity leads to fitness and wellness.

Outside-of-School Activities

The decrease in physical activity is an environmental issue. We are seeing a lack of play spaces, safety concerns for children at play, fewer children riding bikes or walking to school, and fewer neighborhood schools within walking distance for children. Opportunities for physical activity beyond the school setting are important for the children we teach, for their parents, and for the communities that collectively are our present and our future.

Fitness clubs, physical activity clubs, and playgrounds provide additional physical activity for youngsters and involve their families in the physical activity. Awards systems often give double points for parental

participation. Family physical activity nights, fitness fairs, and fitness/health checks bring families together to participate in physical activity, as well as to learn the current information on physical activity, fitness, nutrition, and good health.

Saturday activities such as "Bark in the Park," which invites you to bring along your dog for the activities, and "Play with Mr. J," scheduled playtime with the physical education teacher Mr. J, bring students and parents to school playgrounds and community parks for informal physical activity. School playgrounds become community parks as children and adults play together in an environment that is emotionally safe and fosters confidence and competence. Remembering that parents are the number one influence in the lives of elementary-age children, what better way to establish the habits and instill the importance of physical activity for good health?

The development of skill promotes increased physical activity; increased physical activity promotes increased fitness.

Technology in Fitness/Wellness Education

The world of technology relative to fitness/wellness education has exploded in recent years. Fitness technology now includes electronic portfolios and heart rate monitors for upper-elementary students, equipment for fitness/wellness labs, interactive video games, the storage and analysis of fitness data for both students and teachers, and a wealth of information via the Internet. Jogging/walking club members can now connect with other students around the world charting mileage and comparing adventures. The list of Internet resources is almost limitless in fitness, nutrition, and other areas of wellness. We encourage you as physical education teachers to explore the use of technology in your teaching of physical education; however, we caution you to use technology to enhance your program of physical education, not as a substitute for quality teaching.

Physical Activity Director

With quality programs of physical education and daily programs of physical activity both inside and outside the school, we can meet the recommendation of 60 minutes or more of daily physical activity for children. A commitment from everyone—students, parents, classroom teachers, and the physical education specialist—is critical to attaining the goal. We as teachers must believe we can make a difference in the lives of children, that we can have a positive effect on

children's present and their future of attaining and maintaining physical activity and good health.

While everyone in the school needs to be united in the goal of daily physical activity for all children, it is the physical education teacher's role to take the lead, to design and/or coordinate the programs of physical activity. Our role as teachers expands to include not just our physical education curriculum, but also programs of physical activity in our schools, homes, and communities. The physical education teacher thus becomes the school's "Physical Activity Director" as well as the teacher of physical education, designing comprehensive programs of physical activity for both within and beyond the school day.

Physical Activity Beyond Physical Education

- A before-school activity program*
- Family Fun and Wellness Education nights*
- A before-school coed dance program*
- A town-wide exercise program for students, families, dignitaries, and friends*
- Fitness homework calendars*
- A Run/Walk Club at recess*
- Nonelimination games, physical activity choices for recess
- Integrated movement/academics activities for classroom
- Classroom activity breaks

*Susan Donovan, Director of Physical Activity and Physical Education Specialist, Guiteras Elementary School

Active Schools

With the physical education specialist as director of physical activity and a school committed to meeting the recommended requirement of physical activity for good health, schools can become "Active Schools" designed to maximize school-based opportunities for reinforcing the relevance and value of physical activity for all children (Fox, Cooper, and McKenna 2005). We as physical education teachers, in collaboration with classroom teachers, parents, and community leaders, can design and promote our schools as Active Schools with the following strategies:

- Develop "safe routes" for walking and riding bikes to school.
- Develop and maintain safe, developmentally appropriate playgrounds at school and in the community.
- Permit access to the gymnasiums and school playground after school hours and on weekends.
- Work with classroom teachers to incorporate physical activity breaks during the day and "active" lessons.
- Mark outdoor paved surfaces for game play.
- Adopt a policy of daily recess for all children (NASPE 2001).
- Promote the value of physical education and the importance of physical activity in each school newsletter.
- Ensure safe play during recess, both physically and emotionally.
- Market the school as being healthy, active, and safe.

Physical Fitness for Children

Quality physical education contributes to increased physical activity, improved self-concept, increased self-efficacy, improved motor skills, increased enjoyment, increased motivation, and a reduction in sedentary behavior (LeMasurier and Corbin 2006). Competence in motor skills/early motor skills proficiency is related to the health-related aspects of fitness and to fitness in adolescence and beyond (Stodden et al. 2009; Barnett, et al. 2010). Physical activity is a preventive to degenerative diseases and obesity. With the importance of physical education and physical activity well documented in the research, what then is the role of physical fitness for children? What is the role of physical fitness in our physical education programs?

For some teachers, fitness is the focus of physical education, with the curriculum devoted almost entirely to activities that promote specific areas of physical fitness. For some teachers, a segment of every class is devoted to fitness, with a specific number of minutes targeting a fitness component. For some teachers, every physical education class begins with exercises. We as the authors of *Children Moving* believe that fitness is a product of a quality physical education program, a process that is ongoing as children move and learn in our gymnasiums and on our playgrounds.

Physical Fitness and the *National Standards for Physical Education*

Standard 3: Participates regularly in physical activity

Standard 4: Achieves and maintains a health-enhancing level of physical fitness

The National Standards for Physical Education (NASPE 2004a) recognize the importance of physical fitness for children, with an emphasis at the elementary level on the learning of skills, knowledge, and behaviors that will enable children to be physically active now and in their adult years. The focus for children in the early elementary years is the enjoyment of activity: positive participation in physical education on the playgrounds of school and community and in active play. As children grow and mature, the focus is on an awareness of fitness concepts and their importance, coupled with the development of skills and knowledge for regular participation in meaningful activity. In the *National Standards*, fitness is viewed as a product of a physically active lifestyle; a physically active lifestyle is the product of movement competency and knowledge gained through the *process* of positive participation in physical activity.

History of Physical Fitness

The first alarm on children's physical fitness was sounded in the mid-1950s in response to a comparison of fitness levels of American and European children. The Kraus-Weber test battery had a significant impact on physical education programs in schools, resulting in increased emphasis on exercises to improve physical fitness in children and youth and fitness as the major curricular focus for physical education.

The second alarm on children's fitness was sounded with the linkage of physical fitness in childhood to the prevention of cardiorespiratory and coronary disease in adults, as well as of the degenerative diseases of hypertension and diabetes. The result was a curricular shift to health-related fitness and a renewed emphasis on activities to boost fitness components. The alarm sounding today focuses on children's lack of physical activity and the increase in overweight and obese children.

The importance of physical activity as a preventive for disease and a formula for good health places the emphasis of physical fitness on a broad range of health-enhancing physical activities. Physical fitness then is a product of movement that provides children with confidence, skills, and enjoyment. Through quality physical education, fitness becomes a process, attained and maintained through health-related physical activity. Physical fitness as a process, a part of a quality program of physical education, is inherent throughout *Children Moving*. It is the philosophy the authors have held since the idea of fitness for children was first introduced in the text more than 25 years ago.

Physical Fitness: A Definition

Physical fitness is the capacity of the heart, blood vessels, lungs, and muscles to function at optimum efficiency. In previous years, fitness was defined as the capacity to carry out the day's activities without undue fatigue. Automation, increased leisure time, and changes in lifestyles following the Industrial Revolution meant this criterion was no longer sufficient. Optimum efficiency is the key. Physical fitness is now defined as the body's ability to function efficiently and effectively in work and leisure activities, to be healthy, to resist hypokinetic diseases, and to meet emergency situations (Corbin et al. 2008).

Physical fitness in the past focused on skill-related components associated with athletic performance; fitness today centers around factors pertaining to a *healthy lifestyle*. The components of health-related fitness are muscular strength and endurance, flexibility, aerobic fitness, and body composition.

Concepts of Physical Fitness

Fitness concepts in elementary physical education center around children's understanding of fitness, an awareness of the linkage of fitness to good health, and a working knowledge of activities that promote a healthy level of fitness:

Physical Fitness   It is important that teachers help children understand these critical concepts about physical fitness:

- It's OK for your heart to beat rapidly when you run and play.
- Sweat is a good thing.
- The heart is a muscle; it gets stronger with physical activity and exercise.
- Body size does not determine fitness; physical fitness is not bulky muscles.

- Good exercise and physical activity habits begin in childhood.
- Exercise and physical activity should be a daily habit, like brushing your teeth.
- Fitness doesn't just happen; you prepare and practice.
- Athletic fitness is different from health-related fitness.
- Fitness has several components, and a truly physically fit person is healthy in each area.
- To develop a specific fitness component—for example, muscular strength—you must do exercises and activities targeted for that component.

In addition, the following are important concepts for teachers to remember:

- An emphasis on conditioning for sports is not appropriate at the elementary-school-age level.
- The principle of overload (muscles and bones) can be accomplished through activity for young children.
- Given the opportunity to be active, children will do so.
- Because physical activity participation declines as boys and girls reach adolescence, teaching the concepts and behaviors of fitness in the elementary school years is critically important.

Health-Related Fitness   Fitness concepts for each of the components of health-related fitness center on children's understanding of that component, its linkage to good health, and activities that promote that area of health-related fitness. Here we highlight concepts associated with muscular strength, endurance, flexibility, aerobic fitness, and body composition as they relate to elementary school children.

Muscular Strength and Endurance   The following are important concepts for teachers to remember:

- Activities that require children to move and lift their body weight, as opposed to forced exercise and conditioning, are desirable at the elementary school level.
- Weight training is not appropriate for elementary students.
- Lack of upper-body muscular strength can be very discouraging for children; therefore, focus on praise for progress.

Flexibility   Children should understand these critical concepts about flexibility:

- You must continue to exercise to maintain flexibility.
- Stretching should be done slowly, without bouncing.
- Stretching and/or gentle activity before activity will help prevent injury in vigorous physical activity.

Aerobic Fitness   Children should understand these important concepts about aerobic fitness:

- The heart is a muscle that benefits from exercise, as do other muscles.
- Endurance running is not sprinting; pacing is important for endurance activities.
- Being on an athletic team doesn't automatically increase your aerobic fitness; active participation is necessary.

In addition, teachers should remember that participation in continuous aerobic activities of long duration is not desirable for elementary-school-age children.

Body Composition   The important concepts to remember about body composition are:

- A certain amount of body fat is needed for good health.
- Body weight and body composition are not the same.
- A good balance of body fat and lean tissue is attained by good nutrition and physical activity.
- Body composition is affected by heredity, nutrition, and lifestyle.

FITT for Children

The principles of fitness training (frequency, intensity, time, and type) must be used with caution when working with children. They accept what adults say, especially teachers and coaches they respect, quite literally. If we say 8 push-ups are good for arm strength, but 50 will be even better, their goal is 50 push-ups each and every day. If we say run until you feel the pain, they will run to the point of collapse. Figure 27.2 presents the FITT guidelines as they apply to aerobic fitness for youngsters, ages 5–12.

   The principles of fitness training when applied to children can best be stated as fun, intrinsic motivation, and the 2 Cs: competence and confidence (Corbin, 1986). Pain is not the name of the game in fitness for children. If fitness activities are fun and if children experience success, they will be intrinsically motivated to be physically active. They will be motivated to improve themselves. Children who participate in developmentally appropriate physical education will develop confidence in themselves as they develop competence in physical education skills. This combination of competence and confidence motivates children to adopt lifestyles that include moderate to vigorous activity on a regular basis. Our task as physical education teachers is to provide programs that give children confidence, skills, and enjoyment; in doing so we provide (1) fitness for the present and (2) a desire

Figure 27.2 FITT Guidelines Applied to Aerobic Fitness

	Children (5–12 years)
Frequency	• Developmentally appropriate physical activity on all or most days of the week. • Several bouts of physical activity lasting 15 min or more daily.
Intensity	• Mixture of moderate and vigorous intermittent activity. • Moderate includes low-intensity games (hopscotch, Four Square), low-activity positions (goalie, outfielders), some chores, and yard work. • Vigorous includes games involving running or chasing and playing sports.
Time	• Accumulate at least 60 min, and up to several hours, of activity. • Up to 50% of minutes should be accumulated in bouts of 15 min or more.
Type	• Do a variety of activities: play games, ride a bike, jump rope, hike, different sports. • Continuous activity should not be expected for most children.

Source: Adapted from National Association for Sport and Physical Education, *Physical education for lifelong fitness*, 3rd ed., ed. S. F. Ayers and M. J. Sariscsany (Campaign, IL: Human Kinetics, 2011); National Association for Sport and Physical Education, *Physical activity for children ages 5-12: A statement of guidelines*, 2nd ed. (National Association for Sport and Physical Education: Reston, VA, 2004b).

to continue physical activity, which results in fitness for the future.

Fitness in the Physical Education Curriculum

Research has shown that children can be trained and coached in the components of fitness if (1) exercises are maintained at a rate of intensity high enough to produce the desired results and (2) diversified physical education programs are replaced with programs of just physical fitness a minimum of three times per week. Both these concepts, however, are in direct opposition to our beliefs about activity programs for children.

   Programs of strenuous calisthenics for children can result in "winning the battle but losing the war." We may develop fitness in children for the period of time they're under our control, but the negative feelings associated with the forced exercise/activity often lead to negative feelings toward activity and exercise that continue into adulthood.

> *Although a carefully designed weight-training program is appropriate for adolescents, experts recommend that children lift weights only under the careful supervision of a qualified teacher or trainer who has an extensive background in pediatric strength training (CSMF 2008). We do not recommend weight training as part of an elementary school physical education program.*

We try to present moderate to vigorous activity as an enjoyable experience so children develop a positive attitude toward an active lifestyle. We also try to provide children and their parents with sufficient knowledge of fitness and training concepts to be wise consumers of commercial fitness items, packaged programs, and health spas. As teachers, we can help children and their parents choose sports and activities for enjoyment of physical activity and fostering fitness. Fitness is a personal matter; its goal is self-improvement toward healthy living. Within our elementary physical education curriculum we can teach basic concepts of fitness, design our lessons to promote physical activity, and help children build a repertoire of skills for their personal use. The skill themes, Chapters 16–26, are rich in physical activities that develop the components of fitness, such as "Traveling with a Partner: Changing Speed and Direction" (Chapter 16), "Locomotors and Rhythm: The Follow-Me Dance" (Chapter 16), "Chasing and Dodging Simultaneously" (Chapter 17), Stretching, Curling, Twisting Actions (Chapter 18), "Stretching to Catch Against an Opponent" (Chapter 18), "Jumping Rhythmically" (Chapter 19), "Transferring Weight to Hands" (Chapter 21), "Transferring Weight Onto, Off Of, and Over Apparatus" (Chapter 21).

An example of the integration of skill themes and fitness was observed in a fourth-grade physical education class. The theme was dribbling; the movement concept was pathways. The lesson began with a brief discussion of heart rate and the children counting their pulse before activity began. On the music signal, the children began dribbling in different pathways (marked with tape on the floor). When the music stopped the children went to a nearby station where an upside-down cup had a fitness activity taped inside, such as "Do high-five push-ups with your partner in the position of your choice." When the music began, cups were returned to their original position and the dribbling in pathways resumed. Each time the music stopped, the children found another cup for the fitness

activity. The children counted their pulse (older children, the target heart rate zone) several times during the class. The class culminated with a discussion of the various activities and changes in heart rate.

> *The use of calisthenics is unacceptable in children's physical education. Formal exercises are unrelated to child life situations and have very little, if any, carryover value.*
>
> —Neilson and Van Hagen (1935)

The Teaching of Fitness Concepts

Teaching fitness concepts involves a series of lessons, distributed throughout the year, that are designed to focus on a fitness concept or health-related fitness component. For example, the concept of physical fitness is chosen as the theme for a lesson in physical education. The concept is introduced with a brief discussion of children's perceptions of a physically fit person: What does a physically fit person look like? Do you know one? How do you know he or she is physically fit? Stations, various activity areas set up around the teaching space, provide active participation, targeting each of the health-related fitness components. Children working with partners discuss and answer questions regarding the activity and its contribution to fitness.

Following participation at each of the stations, younger children draw a picture to illustrate a physically fit person; older youngsters write two or three sentences in their journals describing what it means to be physically fit. The lesson concludes with children's responses to a definition of physical fitness. Lesson plans for introducing fitness components and examples of concept lessons may be found in *On the Move* (Holt/Hale 2012), the collection of lesson plans designed to accompany *Children Moving*. In addition to the focus lessons, support activities are provided for classroom teachers, bulletin boards highlight the concept, linkage cues are given during instructional physical education, and the concept is revisited and/or expanded throughout the year.

In teaching the importance of physical activity and health-related fitness, it is our goal that children will learn the following concepts and internalize them as guides in making decisions relative to their health and well-being:

Physical Activity

- Be active at recess; don't just walk or sit and talk with your friends.
- Be active at home; go outside, run and play.

- The experts recommend 60 minutes or more of physical activity every day.
- Sweat that results from physical activity is good sweat.
- The heart beats faster when we run; that is a good thing.
- Physical activity leads to good health; a healthy person has less risk of certain diseases.
- Physical activity and good nutrition are the keys to a healthy weight.

Physical Fitness

- You don't need formal exercise or a fitness club membership to be fit.
- The heart is a muscle; it gets stronger by running, swimming, playing hard.
- You have to work the arms for strong arm muscles; you have to work the legs for strong leg muscles… and the heart…it's the same.
- Gentle stretching, no bouncing, is important prior to and after playing in sports, running long distances, and hiking.
- Being physically active and fit will help me be better in sports and help prevent soreness and injury when I play hard.
- I am happier…I am healthier…I sleep better…I even do better in school…when I am physically active and fit.

Teaching fitness in physical education also includes planning all instructional lessons to maximize active participation, and reflection on the overall fitness of classes and individual children. In addition to instructional physical education, teaching fitness to children includes providing opportunities for physical activity during and beyond the school day. Finally, teaching health-related fitness involves assisting those youngsters below the healthy range of fitness in the design of personal programs to meet their needs.

Assessing Physical Fitness

The components of fitness are assessed with a battery of tests designed to measure a child's performance on each component. Fitness assessment may be conducted with a commercial packaged assessment program, with a teacher-designed test, or by children choosing from a "menu" with several assessments for each component. The two most widely used commercial assessments for physical fitness are the President's Challenge and Fitnessgram. Further information on the specifics of each test, awards systems, and so forth can be obtained by contacting the President's Council on Fitness, Sports, and Nutrition (President's Challenge) or The Cooper

Simple playground activities lead to fitness.

RTI for Fitness and Health

Response to Intervention for Fitness and Health (RTI) is a program of interventions for students who are struggling in the general education curriculum. RTI consists of tiers of intervention progressing from additional support within the general program, to additional small group interventions, to individualized services including parents and professionals to address the child's needs. RTI for Fitness and Health provides a system of assessing children's fitness and nutritional needs, decisions based on physical activity and nutritional reports, Body Mass Index (BMI) scores, and health-related fitness scores. The three-tier approach for intervention is designed to provide the additional support within and beyond the school day to assist the child in becoming a healthy, physically active youngster. (For further information contact dauenhauer@mail.utexas.edu)

Institute (Fitnessgram). The President's Challenge is a norm referenced test, with norms established by testing a large number of boys and girls at each age level. Fitnessgram is a criterion reference test, with criteria established for health fitness—that is, the score is the level needed for good health. See Box 27-1 for contact information.

Box 27-1

Physical Fitness Test Packages

Additional information concerning specific physical fitness packages, national norms, awards programs, and so on may be obtained from the following sources:

Fitnessgram

Developed by:
The Cooper Institute
www.cooperinstitute.org

Distributed by:
Human Kinetics
P.O. Box 5076-5076
Champaign, IL 61825
www.humankinetics.com

President's Challenge

Developed by:
President's Council on Fitness, Sports and Nutrition
www.presidentschallenge.org

Distributed by:
The President's Challenge
501 N. Morton Street, Suite 203
Bloomington, IN 47404
www.presidentschallenge.org

Physical fitness assessments can be used to culminate a unit, to motivate students, as diagnostic screening instruments, and/or as an ongoing process throughout the year. Physical fitness assessment is part of the overall fitness education for children, providing information on their levels of health-related fitness, ways to measure the components of fitness, and the linkage between physical activity and improvements in fitness. We strongly advocate using physical fitness assessments for screening purposes and as an ongoing process. Fitness assessments should never be used to assign a grade in physical education. Young children should not be formally evaluated with a fitness test. We recommend not recording test scores of children below the fourth grade. Younger children can take the

test as an educational experience, but the characteristics of young children do not promote maximum effort and extended concentration on a subject that is of more interest to the teacher than to them.

Whether the physical fitness assessment is used as a screening tool in the fall, as a culminating experience for children, or as an ongoing process, it should be an educational endeavor. Each test item should be carefully explained, emphasizing the particular component being tested. All too often, children do poorly on an assessment because they do not understand the directions. Sufficient time should be allowed for practice so children understand the proper techniques and stretch their muscles. The purpose of the test is to motivate the children to do their personal best, not to trick them.

If the physical fitness assessment is to be used as a diagnostic tool, administer the test in early fall. You can then use the test results to help develop yearly plans, assist youngsters in establishing personal fitness goals, and plan remedial programs for individual students. We recommend that children who have extremely low scores be given remedial fitness programs—individualized education programs (IEPs)—for their area(s) of weakness. The physical education teacher can counsel these students individually on ways to improve fitness through physical activity. Programs of activity and exercise can be designed for use at home, and parents can become active participants with their child.

Children with extremely low scores reflecting an area of fitness that is of concern can benefit from experiences in a school fitness lab, activities to do at home to focus on a particular fitness component, and family activities to promote fitness and physical activity for everyone. Schools with available space and staffing can create a fitness/wellness lab to which children can come for physical activity and exercise designed for their areas of weakness. Working on their personal fitness plans, under the supervision of a trained volunteer and/or the physical education teacher, children follow their prescribed programs of activity, record the activity in their fitness logs, and describe feelings via journal entries. At-home "prescriptions" can be written, for which children complete the activities along with their parents. A monthly calendar can be provided for the child to code (with color, star, or sticker) at the completion of the activity each day. We have found the at-home prescriptions to be an excellent introduction to family fitness as parents and children take part in the activities together. Examples of prescription activities and exercises for flexibility, muscular strength, and cardiovascular fitness as well as family fitness activities can be found in Appendixes 27A and 27B at the end of this chapter.

After the Assessment

What is important in fitness assessment for children is not the test itself, but what is done after the test is completed. Fitness assessment should be an educational experience for the child, the parents, and the teacher. Simply sending home scores on a report card or at the end of the semester is of very little benefit to anyone. The recording of scores should be done in a manner that provides ownership to children, is personal and private for each individual, and assists children in setting fitness goals. Children can be active participants in recording their fitness scores following test completion. Scores may be recorded with computer programs or with teacher/child-designed activity sheets, both providing interactive participation for the children. With commercial programs, students enter their test scores in the computer program and receive the print-out of physical fitness assessment; some commercial programs also provide suggestions for improvement in low score areas.

At Linden Elementary School, we have found the children enjoy recording their fitness scores with bar graphs and bright colors. A simple graph can be designed listing test items (Figure 27.3). After the health fitness screening in the fall, each child is provided his

Figure 27.3 Personal fitness profile.

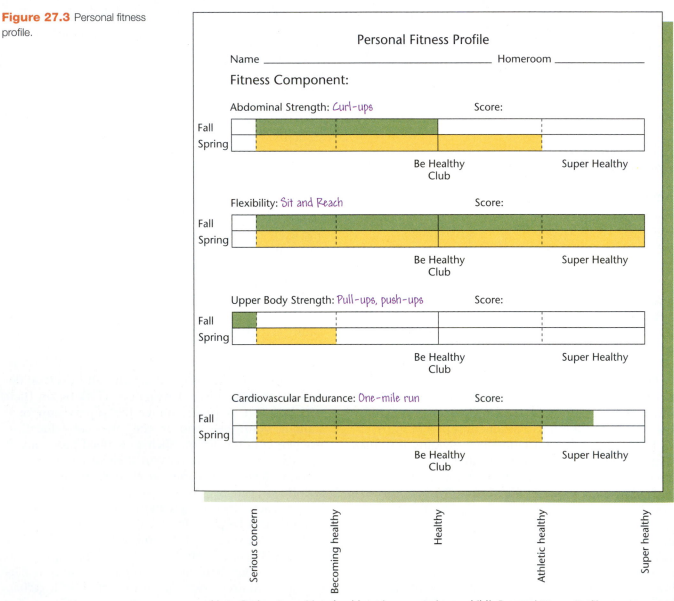

Note: Body composition should not be reported on a child's Personal Fitness Profile.

or her scores from the assessment. Using a highlighter, the child colors in the portion of the bar corresponding to the score for each test item—upper bar for fall scores. Completion of the graph provides a visual representation for the child of the areas of fitness in the health fitness range, those above, and those needing remediation. When the children have recorded their scores and reflected on the assessment results, they can write in their journals their feelings about their test results and record their personal fitness goals for the year. When the fitness assessment is repeated in the spring, each child again colors the portion of the bar corresponding to spring scores (lower bar for spring scores), using a different color highlighter. A comparison of fall and spring scores shows changes in fitness and progress toward personal goals established in the fall. *Note:* A simple turning of the paper reveals for each child a bar graph of the year's fitness assessments and opportunity for an integrated mathematics lesson.

The focus of elementary physical education is the child; the focus of physical fitness should also be the child. No child should be asked to give more than his or her personal best. Scores from the assessment test are personal; they are not to be compared with other children's scores. We recommend the following guidelines for the assessment of children's physical fitness:

- Develop an assessment tool that meets your needs: times per week you see the children for physical education, entry-level fitness for children, class size, your goals for fitness.
- Assist the children in setting their personal fitness goals. Following the fall screening and graphing of scores, have the children record in their journals their personal goals for the year. Young children often need teacher assistance in setting realistic goals. All too often the school athlete is the measure of success for children. Instead, goals should be based on a reflection of assessments and increments of success.
- Praise children's accomplishments at the lower end of the spectrum, as well as those at the high-performance level. (In the fall, the class cheered Molly's efforts on the mile run [21:00 minutes]; in the spring, they cheered her accomplishments [16:34 minutes].)

Jonathan, a large fourth-grader, was not looking forward to the one-mile run for spring fitness testing. On the day of testing, his mother appeared on the jogging track to encourage him as he began his laps. He completed his mile run in 13:35 minutes. During the last week of school, fourth-graders were asked to write in their journals about their favorite activity in

physical education—the favorite of all the things they had done during the year. Jonathan's favorite: the one-mile run! Enjoyment and a secure environment are keys to physical activity and fitness for children.

As teachers, we need to remember:

- The purpose of fitness assessment is to determine those areas that are below the desired range for good health.
- Factors such as chronological age, maturation, and heredity influence scores on a fitness test.
- The goal of fitness assessment is a healthy level of physical fitness.

Appropriate and inappropriate practices with regard to physical fitness and fitness testing are summarized in Box 27-2.

A Final Thought on Fitness

The goal of physical fitness for children is to enable them to develop health and activity habits that will become lifestyles. The two most important factors in attaining this goal at the elementary school level are (1) enjoyment of physical activity and (2) mastery of the basic skills of physical education that will enable them to participate successfully in physical activities that promote fitness. Only if physical activity and fitness are fun will children pursue them outside the time they are with us in physical education. Therefore we focus on the teaching and learning of skills, knowledge, and behaviors that will enable children to value physical activity and be physically active today, tomorrow, and throughout their adult lives.

If we at the elementary level can provide enjoyment in activity, a solid cognitive base of the importance of fitness for good health, and the skills with which to be active, we will have made tremendous strides in children having the competence, confidence, and acceptance of the personal responsibility for their fitness as adolescents and young adults.

Wellness for Children

Physical activity, physical education, and fitness come together in the concept of wellness—the child's total well-being. The dimensions of wellness for children translate into mental/emotional health; personal and social responsibility; personal safety (bicycle, auto, water, and fire); nonabuse of drugs, alcohol, and tobacco; and nutrition, as well as physical activity and fitness.

Box 27-2

Appropriate and Inappropriate Physical-Education Practices

Component: Developing Health-Related Fitness

Appropriate Practice

- The health-related component of fitness is the focus on fitness activities. Skill-related components of fitness are emphasized in their relation to skill development.
- The teacher helps students interpret and use assessment data for setting goals and helping to develop a lifelong fitness plan.

Inappropriate Practice

- Fitness activities are random and unrelated to lifelong learning benefits. Physical fitness activity consists of mass exercises following a designated leader or standard routine.
- The teacher conducts the fitness assessment but never uses results to set goals or to design a personal fitness plan.

Component: Fitness Testing

Appropriate Practice

- Physical educators use fitness assessment as part of the ongoing process of helping students understand, enjoy, improve, and/or maintain their physical fitness and well-being (e.g., students set goals for improvement and they are revisited during the school year).
- As part of an ongoing program of physical education, students are physically prepared in each fitness component so they can safely complete the assessments.

Inappropriate Practice

- Teachers use fitness test results to assign a grade.
- Students are required to run a mile without appropriate conditioning or acclimatization.

Source: National Association for Sport and Physical Education, *Appropriate instructional practice guidelines for elementary school physical education* (Reston, VA: National Association for Sport and Physical Education, 2009).

All the dimensions of wellness are critical to a child's well-being. Crisis in any dimension leads to a breakdown in that child's optimum health. The total package comes to school; the total package comes to physical education each time a child enters our class. Our task is teaching the skills of physical education while not neglecting any dimensions of the total child. This focus on the total child often adds to the curriculum for teachers of elementary physical education as they are asked to address health, safety, and nutrition as well as physical education, physical activity, and fitness. Collaboration with classroom teachers and integration of concepts/benchmarks within the curriculum will preserve quality time for teaching the skills of physical education.

Mental and Emotional Health

Emotional security ranks second only to food and shelter in the individual's most basic needs. The need to be loved and accepted moves quickly to the top for children as the basic needs of food and shelter are met. What happens in the life of children at home, on the way to school, at breakfast, and in the classroom affects their emotional health in the gymnasium. Emotional health affects their learning. What happens in our gymnasiums and on our playgrounds affects the child's emotional health in the classroom, for the day, and beyond the school day.

The foundation of young children's emotional health is self-esteem—how worthy and valuable they consider themselves (Anspaugh and Ezell 2004). We as teachers play a critical role in how children view themselves. Our reactions to their skill or lack of skill, our reaction to their mistakes and sometimes loss of control greatly affect their view of themselves. Children's opinions of themselves are established early and are very fragile. A quick, negative response can have a lasting effect on a child. Children with a strong sense of worth and importance are free to develop their potential, better able to resolve personal and interpersonal conflicts, and free to establish their independence and self-expression.

As teachers we need to remember:

- Acceptance of children, even on their worst days, is critical.
- What happens in elementary school affects children throughout life.
- The most important influences in young children's lives are their parents; the most powerful influences at age 11 and older are their peers.
- Perception of self may or may not match reality; perception of self greatly affects self-esteem.

R. M. Page and T. S. Page (1993) offer the following suggestions to foster a positive climate for emotional wellness:

- Quickly learn the names of students, call them by name, and show respect for each child.

- Be sensitive to diverse cultures, ethnicities, and races; strive to view children from their perspectives rather than your own.
- Expect students to be competent, capable, and eager to learn … and they will.
- Create an atmosphere in which children feel at ease.
- Arrange for a high ratio of successes to failures.

We are teachers of children; our interactions with them, our actions, and our language affect not just the moment, but their lives.

Personal and Social Responsibility

The gymnasiums and playgrounds of our schools provide a rich environment for the development of personal and social responsibility. The physical activity setting provides a miniworld of emotional, interactive situations. Within this world of competition and cooperation, success and failure, and fast-moving action, children make a multitude of decisions on a daily basis. The development of personal and social responsibility—and its importance to the future of our society—is a reminder that we are teachers of children, not just teachers of skills, sequences, games, and dances.

Personal and social responsibility stem from acceptance of two basic concepts:

- I will respect myself and others.
- I am responsible for myself, my actions, and my behavior.

Responsible adults develop from responsible children who have had opportunities to make decisions, to experience success and failure, to be accepted, and to accept others. Acceptance of self and others leads to respect for self and others and to personal and social responsibility.

Safety (Bicycle, Auto, Fire, Water) The concepts of safety relative to helmets and safe riding of bicycles, rollerblades, and skateboards; the buckling of seat belts at all times when riding in automobiles; and water safety for swimming and recreational outings/sports are all matters of personal responsibility. Each of these areas of personal responsibility and safety presents excellent opportunities for collaborative endeavors with community agencies as schools and agencies come together to present programs, sponsor community events, and provide hands-on demonstrations of safety for children. Again, we cannot assume that young children know the safety concepts for each of these areas; they must be taught by responsible, caring adults. We do know that when learned at an early age, the lessons of "helmets, seat belts, and life jackets" become habits for a lifetime.

Fire Safety Should Be a Part of All Elementary School Curriculums

The concept of fire safety can be addressed via a school assembly and hands-on activities conducted by the local fire department personnel. We have found fire fighters eager to come to the schools; they bring trucks and ladders for demonstrations, provide active participation in "stop, drop, and roll" and "stay low," and teach the basic critical emergency response, "911."

Drug, Alcohol, and Tobacco Abuse With children experimenting with drugs, alcohol, and tobacco at increasingly younger ages, it is never too early to educate them on the risks of use and dangers of substance abuse. We can no longer pretend that drug and alcohol use and abuse are limited to older adolescents and young adults. Nor can we pretend that abuse and overdose happen only somewhere else. Elementary-school-age children are experimenting with drugs and alcohol. No socioeconomic level is immune to substance abuse.

Physical educators serve a key role for children in the area of substance abuse. With daily reports of professional athletes and media celebrities involved in substance abuse, children receive a confusing message regarding the dangers of drugs and the consequences of use. We can provide positive role models and clear, consistent messages regarding abstinence. Responsible decisions/personal responsibility begin with a solid knowledge base provided by adults that are respected and viewed as important in a child's life. We as teachers are second only to parents in the potential influence we have on young children.

Much research and thought have been given to the reasons individuals use drugs. Two of those reasons are boredom and low self-esteem. A youngster actively involved in physical activity and sports is an active youngster. A youngster involved in a quality physical education program develops the skills for successful participation in a variety of sports and physical activities. A solid movement-skills base provides a positive self-image in this important area for children. Thus physical education has the potential to contribute directly to a healthy, drug-free world for children.

Nutrition

The importance of nutrition as a contributor to a child's well-being cannot be overestimated. Nutrition contributes to cognitive learning in the classroom and in the gymnasium. Nutrition contributes to a child's physical development and to his or her physical activity. Lack of good nutrition contributes to obesity and numerous health problems.

A number of factors have contributed to the existing state of poor nutrition among school-age children in the United States. A large number of children are responsible for their own meals, especially breakfast and after-school snacks. Children do not choose fruits and vegetables as a favorite snack; young children do not have the knowledge or skills to prepare healthy meals or snacks. For many children, the foods needed for good nutrition are not available in their homes. Thus, by choice and by circumstance, many children are the victims of poor nutrition.

Busier schedules and more fast-food meals have also contributed to a decrease in good nutrition for America's families. A positive increase in physical activity—that is, organized sports, dance, and gymnastics clubs for children—has been coupled with a decrease in family meals at home. All too often the quickest meal is one from a drive-through, one that is high in fat and low in the balance of nutrients needed for good health.

Although elementary-age children may not be interested in nutrition for good health (after all, they are immortal), we have found they are very interested in nutrition as it relates to running, jumping, throwing, and being a better athlete. Thus the appeal of athletics opens the door to educating children about the importance of eating fruits and vegetables, decreasing fats, attaining healthy body weight, and maintaining a balance of physical activity and nutrition as a daily pattern, a childhood pattern that becomes a lifestyle for wellness.

MyPlate

Children at the elementary level need an understanding of nutrition, the contribution of the major essential nutrients to building and maintaining healthy bodies, and the role of nutrition in overall good health.

My Plate (Figure 27.4) has been designed for easy understanding of food portions and the relationship of the food groups. Children easily visualize the plate and are quick to educate their parents on the recommended portions. MyPlate (www.choosemyplate.gov) includes suggestions for increasing physical activity and interactive games and projects for teachers, children, and families. The role of nutrition in achieving and maintaining good health was recognized in 2011 by the President's Council on Physical Fitness and Sports (PCPFS), which was renamed the President's Council on Fitness, Sports & Nutrition.

Figure 27.4 MyPlate.
Source: www.choosemyplate.gov

As children approach puberty, the balance between exercise and nutrition in maintaining proper body weight becomes very important for both boys and girls; however, for young children the emphasis on the balance is for good health. Lessons on teaching nutrition as a wellness concept and its linkage to physical activity and good health can be found in *On the Move, Lesson Plans to Accompany Children Moving* (Holt/Hale 2012).

The Good Health Balance

Physical activity and good nutrition are the essential ingredients for the body's good health balance. Envision a young child first learning to walk a balance beam; the arms are extended outward on either side of the body for good balance. If neither arm is extended or if the extension is only on one side, the child's balance is in jeopardy. In adults we speak of the match between caloric intake and daily energy expenditure—that is, energy balance. In children we call it *the good health balance* (Graham, Holt/Hale, and Parker 2006).

Adults in the United States have a tremendous mismatch between caloric intake and energy expenditure, the results of which are the obesity epidemic and the health risks associated with obesity. A combination of larger food portions, more readily available food, a lack of knowledge regarding portion sizes and number of servings within containers, and the abundance of high-fat, high-calorie food mean energy expenditure—that

The good health balance.

is, physical activity—must increase. However, advances in technology and automation have created just the opposite—an environment that supports less physical activity. The same mismatch exists for children. We as teachers must take the lead in creating the good health balance for children—a balance of daily physical activity and good nutrition that leads to children becoming, and remaining, physically active for a lifetime.

The balance of physical activity and nutrition are not new concepts. Coordinated School Health was established by the CDC in 1998 to promote student health and wellness by "putting it all together to help students grow strong and healthy." Two of the eight components of Coordinated School Health are nutrition and physical education. The Child Nutrition and WIC (Women, Infants, and Children) Reauthorization Act of 2004 mandated that all school districts receiving federal monies for food services establish wellness policies regarding nutrition and physical activity. Both Coordinated School Health and the Child Nutrition Act emphasize school-based wellness councils composed of teachers, parents, and community leaders and collaboration to promote wellness for children. Physical education teachers can and should be vital members of each.

A Final Note on Wellness

Many elementary and middle schools are "community centers for learning." Hours are extended to include adult education, physical activity in gymnasiums, nutrition classes for parents, and in many schools a health service center. District educational administrators and community leaders, recognizing the importance of wellness, are working together to provide optimal learning communities for children and their families. Physical education professionals are regarded as leaders in these endeavors. Our task is to embrace the challenge and assist all children in reaching their potential in all areas of learning and development—wellness for all children.

Summary

Physical activity is a preventive for disease and a formula for good health. Physical activity and fitness are products of competence and confidence in the skills of physical education. The *Physical Activity Guidelines for Americans* provide the framework for the daily amounts and types of activity children need.

Physical fitness is the capacity of the heart, blood vessels, lungs, and muscles to function at optimum efficiency in work, in leisure activities, and in emergency situations. In previous years, fitness was defined as the capacity to carry out the day's activities without undue fatigue; we are now recognizing that this condition may not be sufficient for healthy hearts and lungs. Optimum efficiency is the key. That efficiency also includes resistance to hypokinetic diseases.

Fitness is a process and the product of a physically active lifestyle; a physically active lifestyle is the product of movement competency and knowledge gained through the process of positive participation in physical education and physical activity.

Physical fitness for children includes a health-related screening each fall, setting individual goals, a cognitive understanding of the components of fitness, and moderate to vigorous activity on a regular basis. It involves the physical education specialist, the classroom teacher, the child, and the parent(s). Physical fitness can be incorporated into the theme of study, added to the lesson as a group activity, and increased through before- and after-school programs. The focus of physical fitness for the elementary school child is the development of a positive attitude toward an active lifestyle, a knowledge of the concepts of fitness, and an understanding of how to attain and maintain personal fitness.

Physical activity, nutrition, and physical education culminate in well-being for children, i.e., wellness. Wellness is optimal health and well-being (physical, emotional, mental, spiritual, interpersonal/social, and environmental well-being).

Sample Web Sites for Physical Activity and Nutrition

After *School Physical Activity.* Activities to promote group participation and physical activity, sponsored by the San Diego County Office of Education and the California Department of Education; designed for grades 4–8; www.afterschoolpa.com

Alliance for a Healthier Generation. A national initiative to combat childhood obesity with strategies for schools, homes, doctors' offices and the community; www.healthiergeneration.org

Body Venture. An educational exhibit for nutrition and physical activity, sponsored by the Kansas Department of Education; designed for grades K–5; www.bodyventure.org

Brain Breaks. Guides to integrating physical activity and academics, sponsored by the Michigan Department of Education; designed for grades K–6; www.emc.cmich.edu/BrainBreaks

CircusFit. Physical activity and nutrition activities for youngsters, parents, and families, sponsored by Ringling Bros. and Barnum & Bailey; www.circusfit.com

Fit, Healthy, and Ready to Learn. Guidelines for promoting good health, nutrition, and physical activity, available from the National Association of State Boards of Education bookstore; www.nasbe.org

Nation at Risk. A statistical sourcebook on obesity, physical activity, and nutrition; www.heart.org

Physical Best. A standards-based program to assist physical educators in teaching health-related fitness education, sponsored by the National Association for Sport and Physical Education; workshops, resources, fitness testing for children grades K–12; www.aahperd.org/naspe/physicalbest

School Health Index. A self-assessment and planning guide to assist schools and wellness committees/councils in the analysis of physical activity and nutrition, sponsored by the CDC, linked to the Coordinated School Health components; www.cdc.gov

Walking Works for Schools. A walking program for schools, sponsored by BlueCross BlueShield of Tennessee, the Governor's Council on Physical Fitness, and the Tennessee Association for Health, Physical Education, Recreation and Dance; www.walkingworksforschoolstn.com

Web Sites with Emphasis on Nutrition for Teachers, Children, and Parents

ABC for Fitness. A physical activity program for children with five- to six-minute activity bursts for the classroom; www.davidkatzmd.com/abcforfitness.aspx

Dole SuperKids. A focus on nutrition for children, families, teachers, and school food services via games, songs, and activities for children; http://www.dole.com/DoleHTMLSuperKids/tabid/1173/Default.aspx

KidsHealth. All about children's health, including nutrition, wellness, and fitness; www.kidshealth.org

Nutrition Detectives. Teaching children to make healthy choices regarding nutrition; www.davidkatzmd.com/nutritiondetectives.aspx

Reading Comprehension Questions

1. Why is physical inactivity called an environmental, an emotional, and a health issue?
2. Why is physical activity termed a preventive for disease and a formula for good health?
3. Design a program of physical activity beyond physical education classes for elementary-age children.

4. Define physical fitness. Why can we no longer define the level of fitness as the capacity to carry out the day's activities without undue fatigue?

5. What is the difference between health-related and skill-related fitness?

6. Why do we emphasize health-related fitness in our programs?

7. What is the focus of fitness at the elementary school level?

8. Discuss the linkage of physical activity to physical fitness and wellness. Why is this relationship so important to children in our elementary schools?

9. Describe the options for physical fitness assessment for children.

10. Why do the authors of *Children Moving* not recommend testing of children for fitness below the fourth grade?

11. What is meant by the term *good health balance*? Why is it important for children?

12. How do the FITT guidelines affect the fitness for children?

13. Give two examples of tasks/challenges from the skill themes to illustrate each FITT guideline.

14. What is meant by the term *Active Schools*? Design a collaborative project for working with community leaders, the parent–teacher organization, or local agencies to increase physical activity for children.

15. Define wellness. What are the components of wellness for children at the elementary school level?

16. Choose one wellness component. Design a strategy for working with the classroom teacher to teach that component. Include in your action plan the integrating of the component into physical education.

References/Suggested Readings

Anspaugh, D. J., and G. Ezell. 2004. *Teaching today's health.* 7th ed. San Francisco: Benjamin Cummings.

Barnett, L. M., E. van Beurden, P. J. Morgan, L. O. Brooks, and J. R. Beard. 2010. Gender differences in motor skill proficiency form childhood to adolescence: A longitudinal study. *Research Quarterly for Exercise and Sport* 81(2): 162–70.

Bengoechea, E. G., C. M. Sabiston, R. Ahmed, and M. Farnoush. 2010 Exploring links to unorganized and organized physical activity during adolescence: The role of gender, socioeconomic status, weight status, and enjoyment of physical education. *Research Quarterly for Exercise and Sport* 81(1): 7–16.

[CDC] Centers for Disease Control and Prevention. 2003. Prevalence of physical activity, including lifestyle activities among adults—United States, 2000–2001. *Morbidity and Mortality Weekly Report* 52(32): 764–69.

Corbin, C. B., W. R. Corbin, G. J. Welk, and K. A. Welk, 2008. *Concepts of fitness and wellness: A comprehensive lifestyle approach.* 7th ed. New York: McGraw-Hill.

Corbin, D. B., 1986. Fitness is for children: Developing lifetime fitness. *Journal of Physical Education, Recreation and Dance* 57(5), 82–84.

Crespo, C .J. 2005. Physical activity in minority populations: Overcoming a public health challenge. *PCPFS Research Digest* 6(2).

[CSMF] Council on Sports Medicine and Fitness. 2008. Strength training by children and adolescents: A policy statement. *Pediatrics* 121: 835–40.

Dauenhauer, B. 2010. *Applying response to intervention to preventive school health.* AAHPERD convention. Indianapolis, IN.

Davison, K. K., D. S. Downs, and L. L. Birch. 2006. Pathways linking perceived athletic competence and parental support at age 9 years to girls' physical activity at age 11 years. *Research Quarterly for Exercise and Sport* 77(1): 23–31.

Dunton, G. F., M. Schneider, D. J. Graham, and D. M. Cooper 2006. Physical activity, fitness, and physical self-concept in adolescent females. *Pediatric Exercise Science* 18(2): 240–51.

Ennis, C. D. 2010. On their own: Preparing students for a lifetime. *Journal of Physical Education, Recreation and Dance* 81(5): 17–22.

Fairclough, S., and G. Stratton. 2006. Physical activity, fitness, and affective responses of normal-weight and overweight adolescents during physical education. *Pediatric Exercise Science* 18(1): 53–63.

Forster-Scott, L. 2007. Sociological factors affecting childhood obesity. *Journal of Physical Education, Recreation and Dance* 78(8): 29–30, 47.

Fox, K. R., A. Cooper, and J. McKenna. 2005. The school and promotion of children's health-enhancing physical activity: Perspectives from the United Kingdom. *Journal of Teaching in Physical Education* 23(4): 338–58.

Gao, A., K. R. Lodewyk, and T. Zhang. 2009. The role of ability beliefs and incentives in middle school students' intention, cardiovascular fitness, and effort. *Journal of Teaching in Physical Education* (28): 3–20.

Graham, G., S. Holt/Hale, and M. Parker. 2006. *Children moving: A reflective approach to teaching physical education.* 8th ed. New York: McGraw-Hill.

Hatano, Y., and C. Tudor-Locke. 2001. *Pedometer-assessed physical activity: Measurement and motivations.* Paper presented at the American College of Sports Medicine Meeting, Baltimore, MD.

Holt/Hale, S. A. 2012. *On the move: Lesson plans to accompany Children Moving.* 9th ed. New York: McGraw-Hill.

Kane, M. 2004. *Kid fit and fun*. Knoxville, TN: East Tennessee Public Communications.

Kater, K. J. 2004. *Real kids come in all sizes: Ten essential lessons to build your child's body esteem*. New York: Broadway Books.

Kater, K. J. 2005. *Healthy body image: Teaching kids to eat and love their bodies too!* 2nd ed. Seattle: National Eating Disorders Association. Available from www.bodyimage.org.

Katz, D. 2004. How we grew so big. *Time Magazine* 163: 23.

Kennedy, J. F. 1960. The soft American. *Sports Illustrated* 13: 15.

Lee, A., and M. Solomon. 2007. School programs to increase physical activity. *Journal of Physical Education, Recreation and Dance* 78(5): 22–24.

LeMasurier, G., and C. B. Corbin. 2006. Top 10 reasons for quality physical education. *Journal of Physical Education, Recreation and Dance* 77 (6): 44–53.

Lohman, T. G., S. B. Going, and L. Metcalfe. 2004. Seeing ourselves through the obesity epidemic. *PCPFS Research Digest* 5 (3): 1–6.

McConnaughey, J. 2003. CDC diabetes warning for children. Associated Press, June 16.

[NASPE] National Association for Sport and Physical Education. 2001. *Recess in elementary schools: A position paper from the National Association for Sport and Physical Education*. Reston, VA: National Association for Sport and Physical Education.

[NASPE] National Association for Sport and Physical Education. 2004a. *Moving into the future: National standards for physical education*. 2nd ed. St. Louis, MO: Mosby.

[NASPE] National Association for Sport and Physical Education. 2004b. *Physical education for children ages 5–12: A statement of guidelines*. 2nd ed. Reston, VA: National Association for Sport and Physical Education.

[NASPE] National Association for Sport and Physical Education. 2009. Appropriate instructional practice guidelines for elementary school physical education. Reston, VA: National Association for Sport and Physical Education.

[NASPE] National Association for Sport and Physical Education. 2010. *Shape of the nation report: Status of physical education in the USA*. Reston, VA: National Association for Sport and Physical Education.

[NASPE] National Association for Sport and Physical Education. 2011a. *Physical best activity guide: Elementary level*. 3rd ed., ed. L .L. Borsdorf and L. A. Boeyink. Champaign, IL: Human Kinetics.

[NASPE] National Association for Sport and Physical Education. 2011b. *Physical education for lifelong fitness*. 3rd ed, ed. S. F. Ayers and M. J. Sariscsany. Champaign, IL: Human Kinetics.

Neilson, N. P., and W. Van Hagen. 1935. *Physical education for elementary schools*. New York: A.S. Barnes.

Obama, M. 2011. *Let's move: America's move to raise a healthier generation of kids*. Press Release. www.letsmove.gov.

Page, R. M., and T. S. Page. 1993. *Fostering emotional well-being in the classroom*. Boston: Jones & Bartlett.

Peralta, R. L. 2003. Thinking sociologically about sources of obesity in the United States. *Gender Issues* 21(3): 5–16.

Rink, J. E ., T. J. Hall, and L. H. Williams 2010. *Schoolwide physical activity*. Champaign, IL: Human Kinetics.

Seffrin, J. R. 2010. *Address to the American Alliance for Health, Physical Education, Recreation and Dance*, Indianapolis, IN., March.

Shephard, R .J. 2005. The obesity epidemic: A challenge to pediatric work physiologists? *Pediatric Exercise Science* 17(1): 3–17.

Stodden, D., S. Langendorfer, and M.A. Roberton 2009. The association between motor skill competence and physical fitness in young adults. *Research Quarterly for Exercise and Sport* 80(2): 223–29.

Strong, W.B. et al. 2005. Evidence based physical activity for school-age youth. *Journal of Pediatrics* 146: 732–37.

Trout, J., and D. Kahan 2008. *Supersized P.E.: A comprehensive guidebook for teaching overweight students*. Reston, VA: National Association for Sport and Physical Education.

Tudor-Locke, C. 2002. Taking steps toward increased physical activity: Using pedometers to measure and motivate. *PCPFS Research Digest* 3(17): 1–6.

[USDHHS] U.S. Department of Health and Human Services. 1999. *Physical activity and health: A report of the Surgeon General*. Atlanta.

[USDHHS] U.S. Department of Health and Human Services. 2000. *Promoting better health for young people through physical activity and sports*. Silver Springs, MD: Centers for Disease Control and Prevention.

[USDHHS] U.S. Department of Health and Human Services. 2008. *Physical activity guidelines for Americans*. www.health.gov/paguidelines.

[USDHHS] U.S. Department of Health and Human Services. 2010. *Healthy people 2020: Improving the health of Americans*. www.healthypeople.gov

Watts, K., et al. 2005. Exercise training in obese children and adolescents. *Sports Medicine* 35(5): 375–92.

Weathers, W. 1983. *Physical fitness activity program for health-related physical fitness test*. Special projects report. Murfreesboro: Middle Tennessee State University, Department of Physical Education.

Welk, G. J., and S. N. Blair. 2000. Physical activity protects against the health risks of obesity. *Research Digest* 3(12): 1–8.

Welk, G. J., and R. Joens-Matre. 2007. The effect of weight on self-concept, and psychosocial correlates of physical activity in youth. *Journal of Physical Education, Recreation and Dance* 78(8): 43–47.

Appendix 27A: Family Fitness Activities

Strength and Endurance Activities

Wake-up Time

- Before getting out of bed, tighten all the muscles in your body, rest your muscles, then tighten them again—hard! Can you tighten one part of your body at a time?

Getting Ready

- While you're wringing out the washcloth, squeeze and twist it as hard as you can. What does this movement strengthen?
- After putting on your shoes, lift both your feet and legs up and down from a sitting position. How many times can you do this without stopping? Can you hold both legs in the air for 30 seconds?

Going to School

- Hold a heavy book in one hand and see how many times you can lift it up and down by bending your elbow. Try lifting the book while keeping your arm straight.

- On the bus, put your feet underneath the seat in front of you and tighten your leg muscles to make them straight and stiff.

Studying

- Hold the sides of your chair and pull as hard as you can, but don't bend your back.
- How hard can you push down on the desk with your hand and arm? Push and hold for 30 seconds.

Television Time

- Lie on your side, and lift one leg up and down in the air. Can you do each leg for a whole commercial?
- Lie on your back with knees bent, feet flat on the floor, and arms at your sides. Tighten your abdominal muscles and raise your arms, shoulders, and head slightly off the floor. Hold that position for a couple of seconds.
- Lie on your back. Place a pillow between your knees and try to curl up in a ball so your nose touches the knees. How many times can you do this during one commercial?

Flexibility Activities

Wake-up Time

- Stretch all your body in all different directions; then wiggle like Jell-O on a plate.
- Lie on your stomach, and then reach back and grab your feet with your hands. Try to make a bowl shape with your body by raising up your chest and legs and rocking on your stomach.

Going to School

- Keep one arm straight, and swing it in a big circle from the front of your body to the back. Hold on tight to your books.
- Shake your leg each time you take a step. If you're wearing long socks, try to shake them down to your ankles. The vibration of the skin and muscles will help loosen you up.

Studying

- Hold your hands together behind your chair, keeping your arms straight. Can you feel which muscles are being stretched?
- Let your head fall to one shoulder, and then roll it around to the other shoulder. Be limp, but don't fall asleep.

In the Kitchen or Den

- Stand about 3 feet from the kitchen counter or a table. Lean toward it, holding on to the edge of the counter or table. Can you keep your legs straight and your feet flat on the floor?

Television Time

- Sit on the floor and pull your feet up to your body with the bottoms of your feet together. Hold on to your feet; then use your elbows to push your knees to the floor. Next, try to touch your chest to your feet. What do you feel stretching this time?

Family Time

- Sit facing a partner with your legs spread apart and your feet touching your partner's feet. (If you're doing this exercise with your father or mother, your feet may touch only their ankles because their legs are much longer.) Hold hands; one partner leans back and slowly pulls the other partner so he or she is stretching. Take turns stretching your partner.

Cardiovascular Activities

Wake-up Time

- Before getting out of bed, lie on your back and kick your legs up in the air. Keep kicking them as fast and as long as possible, or move them in a circular motion, as if you were riding a bicycle.

Getting Ready

- Stand in front of the mirror and pretend you're boxing with yourself. How quickly can you swing and punch? How long?

Going to School

- Walk, skip, ride a bicycle, or even jog to school or the bus stop.
- If you ride in a car pool, run to the car before mom or dad gets there, and then count the number of times you can jump up and down before she or he arrives.

Family Time

- Put on some upbeat music and dance. See who can move around the most, longest, and best.

Appendix 27B: Prescriptions for Fitness

Activities/Exercises for Abdominal Strength and Endurance

Wall Push   Stand with your back against a wall, your feet only a few inches from the wall. Your knees should be slightly bent, with your arms at the sides of your body. Pull in your abdomen and press your shoulders, small of back, and buttocks against the wall. Hold the position for 5 seconds.

Untimed Sit-ups   Lie flat on your back with your knees bent and your arms crossed on your chest. Gradually perform sit-ups.

Sit-up variations:

- Extend your arms forward. Shake your hands and arms as you curl up.
- Extend your arms forward. Clap your hands on the floor as you curl back to the mat.

Finger Walk   Lie flat on your back with your knees bent in the sit-up position. Extend your arms at your sides. Walk your fingers forward on the mat in the direction of your feet as you tighten your stomach muscles and raise your shoulders slightly off the mat. Gently lower your shoulders to the mat and repeat.

Activities/Exercises for Upper-Body Strength and Endurance

Flexed-Arm Hang   In a pull-up position, palms facing forward, chin above the bar (Figure 27.5), hold the position for 5 to 8 seconds without letting your chin touch the bar or drop below the bar. When holding for 8 seconds feels comfortable, increase the duration to 15 seconds.

Figure 27.5 Correct position for flexed-arm hang.

⚠ The flexed-arm hang should not be held for extended periods because of the possibility of elbow injury and/or extreme muscular fatigue.

Reverse Pull-ups   Hold the bar as in the flexed-arm position, chin above the bar, palms either forward or reversed. Slowly lower your weight to a hanging position by straightening your arms.

Walking Hands   Assume a push-up position with your body fully extended and your hands on the floor behind a line or tape mark (Figure 27.6). Walk your hands forward and backward over the line as you count 1-2-3-4; aim for 60 counts. Variation: Time for 60 seconds.

Figure 27.6 Weight on hands improves upper-body strength.

Figure 27.7 Correct position for pillow push-ups.

Figure 27.8 Correct position for belly-ups.

Figure 27.9 Student performing the inner-thigh stretch on the right leg.

Figure 27.10 The lying knee-pull exercise.

Pillow Push-ups In a push-up position (Figure 27.7), hands shoulder-width apart, fingers forward, slowly lower your body toward the floor until your chest gently touches the pillow. Straighten your arms to raise your body back to starting position. We have found that children have a fear of crashing to the floor when attempting a push-up. Placing the pillow under the chest eliminates this fear. You may begin with a modified push-up—knees bent—if you wish; when you are confident and ready, switch to the regular position—legs straight.

Belly-ups Sit on the floor with legs extended forward, arms at the side, hands flat on the floor, with your fingers pointing away from your body (Figure 27.8). Raise your hips, extending your body—straight like a board. Bend your elbows to slowly lower your body toward the floor; do not allow your buttocks to touch the floor. Return to the extended starting position by pushing your body upward. Bending the elbows to lower the body is the key to building the arm muscles.

Activities/Exercises for Shoulders, Lower Back, and Hamstring Flexibility

Trunk and Shoulder Extensions Slowly extend both your arms overhead as high as possible and hold them for 10 seconds. Gently lower arms; repeat extension.

Trunk and Shoulder Rotation With your right arm at shoulder level, look and slowly turn to your left; hold 10 seconds. Repeat the movement in the opposite direction.

Inner-Thigh Stretch Sit on the floor with your legs spread apart and extended. Slowly lean forward with one arm on each side of one leg and hold the position (Figure 27.9). Repeat the exercise on the other leg.

Lying Knee Pull Lie flat on your back with your legs extended and arms straight at your sides. Bring your left knee to your chest, grabbing under the knee with both your hands (Figure 27.10). Pull and hold your knee for 5 seconds. Repeat the exercise with your right leg. Remember, keep your extended leg straight and on the floor.

Teaching Dance

One of the great values in the education of children comes from the experience of making their own forms to express, to communicate, to enjoy. Each child is unique in his individualism and in his environment. He needs a chance to say what he is, how he feels, what his world means to him.

—RUTH L. MURRAY

Key Concepts

- Dance experiences should give children freedom in movement, confidence in their movement, and most important, an enjoyment of dance.

- Dance experiences for children include predesigned (rhythmic experiences, folk/cultural, ethnic, and square dances); and child-designed (creative rhythmic experiences and expressive dance).

- Rhythmic experiences for children are designed to assist them in becoming competent and confident in recognizing and moving to internal and external rhythms.

- Folk, ethnic, and square dances can be studied in their authentic form as the cultural dances of a society, or they can be studied for their composition/component parts leading to children's creation of new dances.

- The focus of expressive dance is performing movements to communicate a message, to express feelings and emotions through movement.

- Props and imagery can be helpful to the youngster insecure in dance, redirecting the child's attention and reducing self-consciousness; however, the focus of the dance should progress quickly to the child and his or her movement.

For many teachers dance may be the most difficult teaching area, for the same reason that teaching games is the easiest. Most teachers have an extensive background in games playing, but few teachers have experience as dancers. And most of us do teach best what we know best. Because of their limited background in dance, many teachers omit dance or have only a few dance experiences in their programs. Others shy away from teaching dance, unsure of children's reactions and fearing a negative response from the class. Yet one need only teach Theresa Cone's Spaghetti Dance (2005, 103–106) to realize that the dance is as much fun for the teacher as for the children actively involved in spaghetti that "moves in a box, jumps in boiling water, and slithers down a wall."

None of the authors of this book is a dancer, yet each of us has learned to provide children exciting, interesting, and educational dance experiences. In fact, dance has become one of the most enjoyable areas for most of us to teach because of the children's enthusiasm and excitement about dance. We're convinced that individuals who've had a minimum of formal training in dance can learn to teach it successfully.

The Purpose of Dance in Elementary School

One key to providing children with successful dance experiences is to develop an understanding of dance and its purpose in an educational program. When we teach games, our purpose isn't to produce varsity athletes. Similarly, when we teach dance, our purpose isn't to train children to become professional dancers. Few, if any, physical education teachers have the expertise to train professional dancers, and not all children want to dance professionally. Dance experiences in physical education classes are designed to provide children with:

- An introduction to using their bodies to express feelings and attitudes about themselves and others
- A sense of self-satisfaction that can be derived from effectively using one's body as an instrument of expression
- Enjoyment and appreciation of dance as a worthwhile experience for all, not for just a few
- An appreciation of dance as an art medium that can have value for both the participant and the spectator
- The ability to interpret and move to different rhythms

When children begin school, many are still in tune with their bodies as instruments of expression (Box 28-1). The task of the teacher of young children is not so much to teach them how to use their bodies as instruments of expression but to enhance the expressive abilities that young children's bodies already possess. Sue Stinson (1988) refers to it as rediscovering the magic deep inside and using the magic to transform movement into dance. By helping children at an early age to become aware of how they use their bodies for expressive purposes, we can help each child avoid a mind–body dichotomy. We're able to help children develop an increasing awareness of their bodies as instruments for the expression of feelings and ideas. See Box 28-2 for information on dance in the *National Standards for Physical Education*.

Dance Experiences

Dance experiences for children can be classified into two types: pre-designed and child designed. Predesigned dance experiences include rhythmic experiences, folk/cultural, ethnic, or square dances in which the teacher makes the decisions and selects or creates the rhythmic experience or dance. Many of these dances have been taught for years and passed on from generation to generation. In folk/cultural dances, children are taught

Box 28-1

The Movement Movement

When we are children, most of us can run and tumble and roll in the grass. We can yell and laugh and cry. We can sing our inner songs and dance our personal dances. Our feelings are visible in our actions. When we're unhappy, we stomp and mope. When we're happy, we turn cartwheels and splash in puddles. Our imaginations have a direct line to our arms and legs. We can take giant steps and be giants. We can flap our arms and they will fly us away over houses and mountains. We can do all of this and more, for a while.

And then, somewhere between 5 and 20, we stop.

We stop running just for the fun of it. We stop letting out the shouts and belly laughs. We stop looking at the treetops and start walking the city sidewalks staring at the pavement. We begin, somewhere along the line, to "keep a stiff upper lip," to put "starch" in our spines, to speak softly and when spoken to. Our behavior becomes "acceptable" and, in the process, we are cut off bit by bit from ourselves and therefore from each other. If my impulses can't get through to me, how can I possibly share them with you? As we lose touch with our bodies, our heads take over and begin to monitor our actions, to restrict our responses until the simple interaction of children becomes an elaborate and inaccurate communication system between brain A and brain B.

Jules Feiffer pictures one of these disconnected, clever heads floating around complaining about its headless, funny-looking, malfunctioning body. "It's lucky," Feiffer's head says, "that I need my body to carry my head around . . . otherwise . . . out it would go."

Too drastic.

We can fit our heads back onto our bodies. We can rediscover the links between the headbone and the toebones. We can regain the freedom to spread our arms out wide; to run and shout without feeling awkward or embarrassed. We can learn to fall down, jump up, and bend over without breaking. We can unlock the sounds of our sadness and our joy. We can tune in to the beat of our pulse and stamp our feet to our inborn sense of rhythm. We can explore the sounds and the gestures of our feelings and our dreams. We can reclaim our bodies and our voices; free them to rediscover our inherent sense of balance and design, and use them to show each other who we are and what we hope to be.

Source: Ken Jenkins, The movement movement, *California Living: The Magazine of the San Francisco Sunday Examiner and Chronicle*, January 25, 1976, 19. Used with permission.

Box 28-2

Dance and the *National Standards for Physical Education*

The National Association for Sport and Physical Education's *National Standards for Physical Education* (NASPE 2004) link to dance in the content statement "physical activity for health, enjoyment, challenge, self-expression, and/or social interaction," as well as with "competency in motor skills and movement patterns" and the "understanding of movement concepts as they apply to the learning and performance of physical activities."

Sample performance outcomes from the *National Standards* include:

- Performs a simple dance step in keeping with a specific tempo (K–2)*
- Demonstrates clear contrasts between slow and fast movement when skipping, hopping, galloping, sliding, etc. (K–2)*
- Demonstrates a smooth transition between locomotor skills in time to music (K–2)*
- Performs a basic tinikling step to 3/4 time (3–5)*
- Develops and refines a creative dance sequence demonstrating smooth transitions (3–5)*
- Demonstrates correct pattern for the polka step (3–5)*
- Performs a variety of simple folk and square dances (6–8)*
- Designs and performs gymnastics (or dance) sequences that combine traveling, rolling, balancing, and weight transfer into smooth, flowing sequences with intentional changes in direction, speed, and flow (6–8)*

*Grade-level guidelines for expected student learning.

The teacher challenges a class to rhythmic movement at a high level.

dances that are part of a society's heritage. The teaching of these dances may be coordinated with classroom studies—for example, the culture of Greece or the pioneer period of American history (Chapter 32). Child-designed dance experiences, in contrast, are invented or created by the children. We divide them into creative (rhythmic) experiences and expressive dance. In rhythmic experiences, children learn about different rhythms; they develop an awareness of rhythm and the ability to move in relation to various beats. In expressive dance, children express feelings and ideas through movement. Whereas traditional folk dance and group rhythmic experiences often call for a correct response, there are no right or wrong answers in expressive dance. Children are asked to provide interpretations or responses to a particular problem or situation. Individual responses are encouraged; diversity is valued.

Before learning structured (predesigned) dance forms, children need experiences in locomotor movements and responses to rhythm. They need to move about in free space before they are asked to move within the set formations of circles, squares, and such. They need to move freely in response to their own internal rhythm before moving to music. For these reasons, our primary focus in dance for young children is on rhythmic experiences and expressive dance.

Predesigned Dance Experiences

Rhythmic Experiences   Rhythmic experiences for children are designed to assist them in becoming competent and confident in recognizing and moving to rhythm. Children respond to the beat and the tempo of an external rhythm; they walk, skip, and gallop to their internal rhythm and to external rhythms. At the precontrol level, the rhythmic experiences are chosen to reinforce the movement concepts and themes the children are already studying. They may move body parts (head, feet, knees) to a simple beat played on a drum, tambourine, or wood block. After experiencing the locomotor movements freely at their own tempo, children may be asked to walk three beats in one direction and change directions on the fourth beat. In this combination of skill (walking) and movement concept (direction), children are now matching the tempo of their movements to that imposed by the external beat. Figure 28.1 illustrates several rhythmic instruments that can be used to provide the beat. Children may echo the beat by moving body parts or swinging the total body at fast or slow tempo to match a verbal rhythm. Moving body parts in self-space in accompaniment to a beat enhances children's body awareness.

Cultural Dance and Rhythms

The Opening Ceremonies from the 2008 Summer Olympics in Beijing provide children with a view of elite rhythmic experiences and dance reflective of the Chinese culture. (www.olympic.org)

Figure 28.1 Easy-to-make rhythm instruments.*

DRUMS

Tin can drum

Remove the top and bottom on any size tin can. Cut two circles, about an inch larger in diameter than the tin can, from an inner tube. Punch about six small holes around the edge of each rubber circle. Place one circle over each end of the can. Tighten by lacing strong string or nylon cord through the holes. Bells or bottle caps may be added for additional sound.

Bleach (or milk) jug drum

Screw top of jug and secure with tape or glue. Hit with dowel rod. The children can decorate the jug with paint or colored tape.

CLACKER

Cut two pieces of board to the same size. Drill holes in one end of each board and join the boards with nylon cord or wire. The children can decorate the boards.

SHAKERS

Tube shaker

Cover one end of an empty paper towel tube with heavy paper or aluminum foil. Fill with small round stones or dried beans. Then cover the other end. The children can decorate the shaker.

Pie pan shaker

Place small round stones or dried beans in an aluminum pie pan. Staple another pie pan of the same diameter onto the top of the first pan.

Balloon shaker

Pour sand, rice, beans, or a combination of these ingredients into a balloon. Partially inflate the balloon and tie the end.

Cup shaker

Partially fill a paper or plastic cup with small stones, beans, or bottle caps. Tape another cup on top of the filled cup.

Once the children are able to move (1) to their internal tempo and (2) to an external beat imposed by the teacher's voice or a simple instrument (e.g., a drum, shaker, clacker), music is introduced. The music should have a steady beat; although it provides the beat for the movements, it should accompany, not dominate, the children's movements.

Once children have grasped the basic concepts of rhythm and are able to respond correctly to different beats, they enjoy the addition of a manipulative to the rhythmic experiences. Streamers, scarves, cardboard pizza circles, Lummi sticks, and playground balls are examples of equipment that we have discovered enhance rhythmic experiences for children. Initial activities focus on individual responses to rhythm. Following this exploration phase, teacher-designed routines are used to elicit a group response to a given rhythm. These control-level experiences are designed to involve the children in working together as a group, responding correctly to the rhythm, and remembering a sequence of movements and/or actions to be performed.

*Prior to constructing equipment we recommend you check with school administration to be certain that district policy permits homemade equipment.

routines are excellent for promoting physical education at assemblies, parent–teacher association/organization (PTA/PTO) programs, and community functions (see Chapter 33).

The amount of time a teacher can spend on rhythmic group routines depends to a great extent on how often physical education is scheduled. When physical education classes meet only twice a week, for example, more time is spent on mastery of the basic skills involved in the rhythmic experiences—rope jumping, ball handling, and such.

Children at the utilization and proficiency levels focus on creating new Lummi stick routines, designing individual and partner jump rope routines, and using ball-handling skills in routines to music, like the activity making up fancy dribbling/passing routines (chapter 24, page 495). At this point rhythmic experiences transition from predesigned to child designed, with children creating the routines. Children at these levels of rhythmic experiences combine various movement qualities and patterns with their manipulative skills—for example, floor patterns, directions, levels, phrases, and variations in rhythm, such as double time, half time, and so on.

It isn't sufficient for the teacher to say, "Today we're going to design a jump rope routine. Find a partner and get started." Children need guidance in the transition from predesigned/teacher-directed to child-designed experiences. As teachers, we provide a template for the routine. We tell the children the limitations we're imposing, such as the number of persons in a group, the length of the routine, the minimum number of skills to be included, and the music to be used (if this is a teacher decision). Children also need to know the

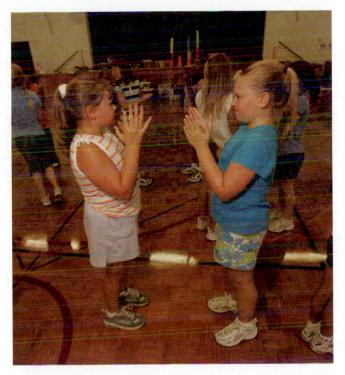

These youngsters enjoy matching rhythms.

Teacher-designed routines for Lummi sticks, Chinese ribbons, jump ropes, and parachutes can be found in Appendix 28A at the end of this chapter; a group routine for ball gymnastics can be found in *On the Move: Lesson Plans to Accompany Children Moving* (Holt/Hale 2012).

Most of the ideas for our teacher-designed routines come from observing children during their exploration of the manipulative, listening to the music, and matching action to tempo and beat. Rhythmic group

For these partners, jumping rope becomes a creative rhythmic experience.

necessary inclusions in the routine that are to be group decisions—for example, directions, pathways, floor patterns, and levels, as well as basic skills to be performed. If the teacher selects the music, there is maximum participation by the children during class because all can practice to the same music. If each group of children selects the music, the variety of music is greater, but practice time is limited.

One of the most difficult parts of child-designed rhythmic experiences is the time factor—that is, the matching of the length of the routine to the length of the music. Children often need guidance in choosing whether to add skills, repeat phrases, or repeat the entire routine.

Folk/Cultural and Ethnic Dances   Folk/cultural, ethnic, and square dances (line and country) are the cultural dances of a society, the cultural heritage of a people. Cultural dances range from simple to very complex; some are designed for partner and group formation, while others have a focus on individual creativity. Folk and square dances involve a series of actions with one or more of the following: a stated progression, verses and a chorus, locomotor and nonlocomotor actions, formations, changes in directions, right and left discrimination, and designated music. Ethnic dances have a combination of locomotor and nonlocomotor actions, often with a focus on individual creativity and a range of rhythmic and musical selection.

When children are first introduced to dance, it is important that they feel free to move, that they are confident in their movement, and, most important, that they enjoy the dance. This is especially true for folk/cultural dance, with its definite formations and progressions. With these goals in mind, the following guidelines will be beneficial when introducing children to structured dance forms (Weikart 1997, 2006):

- Start with free-space movement; allow students to move about the room with no set formation. Then proceed to simple circle and line dances with no changes in direction.
- Provide multiple opportunities for students to practice locomotor and nonlocomotor sequences in different combinations to a variety of music.
- Begin with dances that require neither partners nor holding hands.
- Choose dances that do not specify the use of the right or left foot.
- Choose dances that do not require complex footwork, rhythms, or changes in direction.
- Select music with a strong underlying beat; the musical phrases should be distinct and in groupings of 8 or 16 beats, with no resting beats.

- Select dances with a repetition of sequences; sequences should be short and uncomplicated.
- Choose dances that can be easily modified for beginners. For example, Kinderpolka and Jump Jim Joe (Box 28-3) are dances with partners that can easily be modified for introduction with no partners.

When children participate in the folk/cultural, ethnic, and square dance as an integrated study of a culture, the dances are performed in their traditional form with attention to maintaining the authenticity of the dance. This is also true when cultural dances are performed for a PTA/PTO program or school assembly for parents and community. The dance is representative of the culture, and as such is often demonstrated with children in the costumes of that culture. The focus is a demonstration of the enjoyment of dance from different cultures and dance as part of the heritage of the people.

When we have children participate in folk/cultural or ethnic dances as a study in dance, we often approach them differently. We may change the formation of the dance from circle to line or scattered. We may change the way partners are selected, or do the dance without partners. We may change the travel patterns or actions

---

Box 28-3

Traditional Folk/Cultural Dances

Here are some examples of beginning and intermediate folk dances appropriate for elementary-school-age children with no previous dance experience:

Beginning Dances

Seven Jumps (Denmark)

Jump Jim Joe (United States)

Kinderpolka (Germany)

Cshebogar (Hungary)

Scattered Square Dance (United States)

Intermediate Dances

Greensleeves (England)

Teton Mountain Stomp (United States)

Virginia Reel (United States)

Gustav's Skol (Sweden)

Kavelis (Lithuania)

LaRaspa (Mexico)

Troika (Russia)

Mayim! Mayim! (Israel)

of the dance. We may combine components of different dances or combine types of dances. These dances, usually teacher designed, still have set travel patterns and actions, repetition of sequences, and correct responses to rhythm. The focus is the study of dance, the enjoyment of participation in dance, and the freedom of movement and confidence in that movement.

When older children, who have acquired competence in rhythm and movement, study dances from different countries, they carry out a variety of locomotor and nonlocomotor actions to music. They learn formations for dances, moving to musical phrases, repetition of pattern, and so on. They're able to analyze the dances according to spatial awareness, effort qualities, and relationships. Based on the patterns of movement, formations, and specific steps they have learned, upper elementary and middle school students use the dance skills and concepts to create new dances. This creation of new dances moves students from predesigned to child-designed dance and provides them avenues for self-expression and creativity. Dance for many children is their sport; they excel in its creation and performance, "for enjoyment, self-expression, and/or social interaction" (NASPE 2004). Many cultural/ethnic dances are created as young people, alone and with others, choreograph their dance moves and rhythmic expressions.

With the richness of diversity increasing in our schools (Chapter 31), it is important that we as teachers recognize the diversity within our classes, the wealth of ethnic and cultural dances the children bring to us, and the appreciation for dance and cultures that can be gained by learning from each other. Dance provides the platform to learn about one's own culture, maintain a cultural connection, or learn about different cultures (Ward 2007).

Box 28-4 provides additional information about folk/cultural dances.

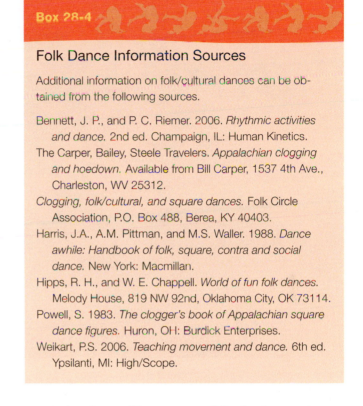

Box 28-4

Folk Dance Information Sources

Additional information on folk/cultural dances can be obtained from the following sources.

Bennett, J. P., and P. C. Riemer. 2006. *Rhythmic activities and dance.* 2nd ed. Champaign, IL: Human Kinetics.

The Carper, Bailey, Steele Travelers. *Appalachian clogging and hoedown.* Available from Bill Carper, 1537 4th Ave., Charleston, WV 25312.

Clogging, folk/cultural, and square dances. Folk Circle Association, P.O. Box 488, Berea, KY 40403.

Harris, J.A., A.M. Pittman, and M.S. Waller. 1988. *Dance awhile: Handbook of folk, square, contra and social dance.* New York: Macmillan.

Hipps, R. H., and W. E. Chappell. *World of fun folk dances.* Melody House, 819 NW 92nd, Oklahoma City, OK 73114.

Powell, S. 1983. *The clogger's book of Appalachian square dance figures.* Huron, OH: Burdick Enterprises.

Weikart, P.S. 2006. *Teaching movement and dance.* 6th ed. Ypsilanti, MI: High/Scope.

expressive dance. The content of rhythmic experiences is the content of creative rhythmic experiences. What separates the two is the focus of the lesson. Creative and rhythmic experiences in dance aren't separated in our programs at the early stages. In fact, it isn't uncommon for us to switch the focus several times during a lesson, sometimes focusing on the rhythm of the movement, other times focusing on the expressive qualities of the movement. When concentrating on rhythmic experiences, the primary focus is on the children's ability to move to the rhythm. In contrast, creative rhythmic experiences are intended to provoke creativity and expression. Creative rhythmic experiences for children are designed to evoke the expressiveness and lack of body inhibition so characteristic of the young child.

Technology and Dance

There are a multitude of electronic gaming devices (e.g., X-Box 360 Connect, Play Station 3, Wii, Trazer, Dance Dance Revolution [DDR]) with "dance" applications. These programs provide an exciting venue for children to refine and apply the skill themes associated with dance (and fitness) in after- or before-school programs, in-school activity breaks, or at home.

Rapping

One of the earliest forms of rhythmic accompaniment for young children is their own voices. Observe preschoolers at play, and you will hear them talking and singing as they move. The popular pastime of rapping is a rhythmic expression of voice and actions. Its popularity is confirmed with a quick browse of YouTube. Children should be encouraged to use the human voice to accompany their rhythmic and expressive dance experiences as appropriate.

Child-Designed Dance Experiences

Creative Experiences Child-designed dance experiences include creative rhythmic experiences and

Dance experiences provide movement and joy for children.

Expressive Dance   The focus in expressive dance is not on executing a particular movement, but on performing the movement so it communicates the message the child intends. Once children are able to perform the movement efficiently, they can begin to experiment with different qualities of the movement. For example, turning actions combined with the concept of time: slow, hesitant turns or fast, sudden turns are two possibilities. Eventually these qualities of turning can be used to express inner feelings. Slow, hesitant turns might be used to depict sadness or uncertainty; sudden,

quick turns could be used to express anger, frustration, or perhaps joy. Turning, by itself, communicates little. It's the quality of the turn that communicates a message, just as it's the quality of any movement that is expressive. This is the reason it's so important to give children a movement vocabulary if they're to become expressive movers.

The movement framework, depicting the interaction of skill themes and movement concepts (Chapter 3), is used as the foundation for expressive dance experiences for children. The majority of locomotor skills within the skill theme of traveling (walking, running, hopping, skipping, and galloping); the nonmanipulative skills of rolling, balancing, transferring weight, jumping and landing; and the actions of stretching, curling, bending, twisting and turning are used in expressive dance. Virtually all the movement concepts (Chapter 3) are used to heighten and expand the child's ability to express feeling and emotion through movement (see Table 28.1).

At the precontrol level, experiences are designed to help children develop awareness of movement by focusing on fundamental body actions and traveling skills. Stretching, curling, bending, twisting and skipping, galloping, and leaping are movements frequently used with precontrol children. Initially it's a good idea to focus on giving children opportunities to explore a wide range of movement possibilities. Once this has been accomplished, we shift the emphasis to the spatial quality of the movements by introducing the movement concepts. For example, we might have the children do a complete, full stretch or a very tight curl, and use the movement concepts of effort to enhance the children's awareness of the potential of movement. The primary emphasis, however, is still on the movement rather than on than the body's expressive or communicative possibilities.

Table 28.1 Overview of the Content and Rationale of Teaching Expressive Dance to Children

We Want Children to Acquire:	By Learning a Movement Vocabulary of:	That Can Be Used to Express Emotions and Thoughts Such As:	Stimulated by Catalysts Such As:
An ability to use their bodies as a means of expression	Movement concepts	Friendship	Sounds
	Space awareness	Warmth	Music
The sense of self-satisfaction that can be derived through	Effort	Anger	Poetry
	Relationships	Unhappiness	Art
expressive movement	Skill themes	Peace	History
An enjoyment and appreciation of dance	Locomotor	Hostility	Motion pictures
	Nonmanipulative	Joy	Personal experiences
An ability to interpret and move to different rhythms		Satisfaction	
		Harmony	

Source: Adapted from K. R. Barrett, Educational dance, *Physical education for children: A focus on the teaching process,* ed. B. Logsdon, K. Barrett, M. Ammons, M. Broer, L. Halverson, R. McGee, and M. Roberton (Philadelphia: Lea & Febiger, 1984).

Box 28-5

Books as Prompts for Creative Dance

The following serve as excellent examples of the many books available as prompts for young children's experiences in creative dance:

Andreae, G. *Giraffes can't dance*. 2001. New York: Orchard Books.

Appelt, K. *Bats around the clock*. 2000. New York: Scholastic.

Appelt, K. *Bat jamboree*. 1997. New York: Scholastic.

Bond, F. *Tumble bumble*. 1997. Cambridge, MA: Barefoot Books.

Carle, E. *From head to toe*. 1997. New York: HarperCollins.

Marzollo, J. *Pretend you're a cat*. 1990. New York: Scholastic.

Pandell, K. *Animal action*. 1996. New York: Scholastic.

Ryder, J. *Night gliders*. 1996. Mahwah, NJ: Bridgewater Books/Troll Communications.

Steinberg, D. *The turkey ball*. 2005. New York: Penguin Young Readers Group.

Tankard, J. *Grumpy bird*. 2007. New York: Scholastic.

Walsh, E. S. *Hop jump*. 1993. San Diego: Harcourt Brace.

Books are excellent "prompts" for creative dance for young children at the precontrol level, providing the story to be read or told by the teacher as the children respond with their individual interpretations via movements and movement concepts. The listing of appropriate books is endless. See Box 28-5 for examples. We have found the book fair at elementary schools to be a rich source of developmentally appropriate, inexpensive books for children. If you are fortunate, the PTA/PTO will post a "wish list" for teachers, and most books you request will be donated to the physical education program.

At the control level, we begin to clarify for children the expressive and communicative aspects of movement. The focus now centers more on the effort and relationship concepts (Chapters 14 and 15). Box 28-6 describes the effort and relationship concepts used for expressive dance. Through these concepts, movement is explored as a tool for expressing an idea, attitude, or feeling. Movement is no longer studied primarily as an entity in and of itself; it's viewed as a medium of expression. We challenge the children to structure their movements to an imposed beat or rhythmic pattern, or have them verbalize how their movements feel and describe their emotional reactions to classmates' expressive movements.

The following creative dance experiences and ideas for creative dance development are some of the examples to be found in *On the Move: Lesson Plans to Accompany Children Moving* (Holt/Hale 2012): The Amoebae; Colors, Shapes and Actions; Dance of Locomotors; Karate Dancing; Matching Jumps and Shapes; Shadow Dancing; Partner Statues; and People in Motion.

Children at the utilization level have learned to efficiently perform the movements studied at the precontrol level and to modify the movements intentionally by focusing on different movement concepts. At this level, children can begin to structure their communicative movements into organized forms. This structuring is often termed *sequencing* or *phrasing*.

It's usually a good idea to narrow the focus of a sequence or phrase to one, two, or at most three skills and concepts. When youngsters at this level are given too many possibilities, they're often unable to decide where to begin. The ability to move, however, combined with a working knowledge of movement concepts, enables pupils to elicit varying and qualitative responses to a single challenge.

Dance making—structuring several sequences or phrases into a whole—is the focus at the proficiency level. The idea behind a dance can be stimulated by an infinite variety of sources, such as machines, natural phenomena (flowers, snowflakes), sculpture, music, poetry, or painting. Dance making involves both design and evaluation.

A Story Without Words (Primitive Tribes), page 287, A Study in Form (Tradition Versus Change), page 287, and From Slavery to Freedom, Appendix 28-B are examples of child-designed dances at the utilization and proficiency levels. Additional stems for child-designed dances can be found in the skill themes of jumping and landing, traveling, and balancing.

Design of Dance

We've found it valuable to have children at the utilization and proficiency levels of creative dance view the dance-making process as composed of the following procedures:

1. Selection of the purpose, idea, or theme of a dance
2. Identification of appropriate movements and movement concepts to express the intended idea, feeling, or theme
3. Design of a powerful opening statement for the dance
4. Design of a series of actions rising to a climax
5. Design of the portion of the dance that is to be the climax or peak of the action
6. Design of the concluding statement of the dance

Box 28-6

Expressive and Communicative Activities

Time

- Travel or gesture in slow motion.
- Travel to an externally imposed beat or rhythmic pattern, such as a handclap or drumbeat.
- Rise and sink suddenly or slowly.

Flow

- Combine two travel skills, such as running and leaping, always moving smoothly.
- Display hesitant, jerky, mechanical flow to create the illusion of being a robot.
- Feel and observe the differences in combining a step with a turn, first with smooth, continuous flow, then with pauses (stillnesses) interspersed between each step and turn.

Force

- Travel or perform nonlocomotor actions to a strong beat.
- Travel or perform nonlocomotor actions to light, gentle, delicate music.
- Freeze in a strong, dramatic pose.

Relationships

- Experience the sensation of matching, mirroring, or shadowing the movements of a partner.
- Explore the expressive possibilities of group formations—for example, sculpture for the city park, or a mountain range.
- Experience the feeling of contrasting the movements of a partner—for example, as one partner rises the other sinks, or one partner travels in a geometric path (square) while the other travels in a random path.

The possibilities for dance making are infinite. Dances can center around contrasting movement concepts, telling a story, interpreting a theme, reflecting a poem, or portraying emotions and ideas. A Study in Form: Tradition Versus Change is an example of an expressive dance designed to portray emotions. It is an abstract dance contrasting tradition with the forces of change. One group arranges itself as a solid square facing in one direction. Symmetrical movements prevail; actions are firm, sustained. The other group is scattered widely, facing in random directions. Nonsymmetrical movements, free use of space, and variety are used.

The story of Rosa Parks and her refusal to ride in the "back of the bus" led children to create a dance portraying the struggles of African Americans during slavery, their freedom from slavery, the struggles after emancipation, and their strengths as individuals and as a people united. From Slavery to Freedom is an expressive dance based on the theme of freedom and the journey of a people to freedom centered around a study of Alex Haley's historical novel *Roots*.

Hailstones and Halibut Bones: Adventures in Color (O'Neill 1961) was the inspiration for the expressive dance Colors, Shapes, and Actions in *On the Move*. In O'Neill's book of poetry, colors are portrayed as objects, feelings, space, relationships, and abstract entities. As is true with many prompts for expressive dance, this one is suitable for children of all ages, the complexity of the dance design determined by past experiences in expressive dance. For example, red to young

children is playground balls, paint that splatters when spilled, fire, and rubber bands. Red to older children is anger, fierce battle scenes, and courage. For children at the precontrol and control levels, we found it best to discuss the colors, their shapes and actions, and then select one color for the class to use as the prompt for their dances. For the older children, after reading a selection of the poetry, the children were free within their groups to determine the color that would be the focus of their dance. Creative dances ranged from simple combinations of actions and shapes for younger children to group interpretations for older children that included all six steps of the design process.

Evaluation of Dance Making

The process of dance making, from simple sequences to complex choreography, is one of exploration and refinement. The evaluation of dance making is a continual process. Children need to be satisfied with the process and the product. Evaluation examines all movement skills and concepts the teacher and children have incorporated into the dance. Considerations include the following:

- Beginning location and pathway of each youngster— how the children choose to locate themselves at the beginning of the dance and the pathway they choose to express various feelings
- Selection of traveling skills (leaping, skipping) and the quality with which they're performed—whether

Youngsters explore the expressive possibilities of partner formation.

the children are using a variety of traveling skills and executing them clearly and precisely as intended, with the desired impact

- Flow of the dance—how the parts of the dance are connected to give a unity of expression
- Relationship of the children to one another—whether the children are reacting to one another with sensitivity and whether the timing, strength, and speed of their responses are appropriate

Dance and rhythmic activities provide a rich environment for fostering positive social interaction and respect for differences among people. As youngsters actively participate in dances from different cultures, they expand their understanding of others and broaden their cultural world. As they cooperate in dance making and the creation of rhythmic routines, they develop cooperative skills and respect for others.

Responsible social behavior, understanding and respect for others, and positive social interaction are important for all children (NASPE 2004).

The Process of Teaching Dance

Teaching expressive dance is different from teaching functional* movements. A functional (predesigned) movement is performed correctly or incorrectly, and the teacher's task is to guide the child toward an appropriate execution. Dance movements, performed to express an idea or emotion, are more difficult to define clearly, and so the teacher's task is different.

Because the child is trying to express a feeling or an idea, observation and feedback are also more complex. In games and gymnastics, the purpose of a movement is obvious; this isn't true in expressive dance. When teaching dance, the teacher initially encourages, expands, and embellishes rather than correcting or refining. As the teacher comes to know the children and understand them as individuals, and as the children begin to trust the teacher, the children will seek sensitive and supportive feedback from the teacher. Remember, though, that human expression is very fragile and easily misinterpreted. Nothing stifles expression more quickly than insensitivity or lack of understanding. The teacher of expressive dance needs to be constantly aware of how easily creativity is threatened. The incident described in Box 28-7 illustrates how fragile a child's creativity is.

You don't have to be a dancer to be a successful teacher of children's dance. The following ideas may be helpful for those teachers unsure of their ability to teach dance, unsure of their students' reactions, yet searching for ways to develop effective programs of expressive dance.

Don't Call It Dance!

Children who've had little exposure to expressive dance experiences often react negatively to the prospect of studying dance. Children in the upper grades have been known to express their hostility to the idea with groans, frowns, sighs, and even emphatic refusals to participate. This resistance can be understood when you realize that too often children in the upper elementary grades have had few opportunities to move creatively. Too often even those few opportunities have been poorly presented. Children have been forced, for

---

*A functional skill is a fundamental motor or object control skill with a predetermined result and the mechanics of proper execution, e.g., running, skipping, throwing, catching.

Box 28-7

The Awful Beginning: A True Story, Unfortunately

I looked across the desk at my big girl. She'd come for help in planning her semester schedule.

"Look," I said, "you have some electives. Why don't you take a course or two for fun? You've worked hard and really should take something outside your major that will be pleasurable."

"Like what?" she asked.

My eyes scanned the college schedule of courses. "Like Dr. Mann's Creative Writing or Dr. Camp's Painting for Beginners or something like that."

She threw back her head and laughed. "Who me? Paint or write? Good grief, Dad, you ought to know better than that!"

"And this," I thought, "is the awful ending."

It was not always like this. I remembered an early golden September day when I went to my garage studio and gathered together my easel, paintbrushes, and watercolors. I sensed someone was watching me and looked up from my activity to see her framed in silhouette in the doorway. The breeze and the sun tiptoed in the gold of her curls. Her wide blue eyes asked the question, "Whatcha doin'?"

"I'm going to the meadow to paint," I said. "Want to come along?"

"Oh, yes." She bounced on her toes in anticipation.

"Well, go tell Mommy and get your paints." She was off but returned in no time carrying the caddy I had made to hold her jars of paint and her assortment of brushes.

"Paper?" she asked.

"Yes, I have plenty of paper. Let's go."

She ran down the hill before me, pushing aside the long soft grasses of the meadow. I watched closely for fear of losing her golden top in the tops of the goldenrod. She found a deserted meadowlark's nest and we stopped to wonder at it. A rabbit scurried from under our feet. Around us yellow daisies and goldenrod nodded in friendly greeting. Above, the sky was in infinite blue. Beyond the meadow, the lake slapped itself to match the blue of the sky.

On the lake, a single white sailboat tipped joyously in the breeze. My daughter looked up and saw it. "Here!" she said.

Trusting her wisdom as I always did, I set up our easels. While I deliberated over choice of subject and color, she had

no such problem. She painted with abandonment and concentration and I left her alone, asking no questions, making no suggestions, simply recognizing uncontaminated creative drive at work.

Before I had really begun, she pulled a painting off her easel.

"There!" she said. "Want to see?" I nodded.

I cannot describe the sense of wonder that flooded over me as I viewed her work. It was all there—that golden September day. She had captured the sunlight in her spilled yellows, the lake in her choppy, uneven strokes of blue, the trees in her long, fresh strokes of green. And through it all, there was a sense of scudding ships and the joyousness of wind that I experience when I sail, the tilting and swaying of the deck, the pitching of the mast. It was a beautiful and wondrous thing and I envied her ability to interpret so honestly, so uninhibitedly, so freshly.

"Are you going to give it a name?" I suggested.

"Yep! Sailboats!" she responded, as she taped another sheet of paper to the easel.

There wasn't a single sailboat in the picture.

She began school the following week. One dreary November day she came into my study with a sheet of paper in her hand.

"Daddy," she asked, "will you help me draw a sailboat?"

"Me? Help you draw a sailboat?"

My eyes turned to the wall where her golden September painting hung in a frame I had made for it.

"Me? Help you draw a picture of a sailboat? Why, sweetheart, I could never paint a picture like the one over there. Why don't you paint one of your own?"

Her blue eyes looked troubled.

"But, Daddy, Miss Ellis doesn't like my kind of painting."

She held up her sheet of paper in the middle of which was a dittoed triangle.

"Miss Ellis wants us to make a sailboat out of this."

And that was the awful beginning!

—James A. Smith

Source: James A. Smith, The awful beginning, *Today's Education*, April 1972. (Used with permission.)

example, to participate in uninteresting, unstructured forms of dance that had no purpose or reason for involvement that was apparent to the children.

When that happens, children turn away from the joy of dance instead of becoming excited about creative movement. For this reason, we recommend that you involve the children in enjoyable, challenging movement experiences without labeling the lesson as dance. People in Motion—an integrated project of art, music, and physical education with a focus on sport and physical activity—is one example of this type of movement experience/dance (see *On the Move*, Holt/Hale 2012, for details). As the youngsters become comfortable with dance and their awareness of dance as exciting and stimulating grows, the stigma attached to the word *dance* will disappear.

Begin Gradually

The class's first experiences with expressive dance need not last for an entire class session. A few minutes at the beginning or end of a class are often sufficient to introduce creative movement concepts—and simultaneously build your confidence as a teacher of creative dance. A short creative dance activity at the beginning of class can serve as a review of a concept related to the skill theme for the day—for example, twisting and turning actions in Karate Dancing (dance) before their use in the skill theme of balance (gymnastics). A short creative dance activity at the conclusion of an active lesson can also be effective. While the children lie on the floor, eyes closed, ask them to move only their fingers (or toes, arms, legs, elbows) to the music. Short segments of lively music are most effective. The children, whose eyes are closed, are less inhibited; the teacher, whose eyes are open, sees the creative dance potential that seems to be an inborn characteristic of the young child. At Linden Elementary School in Oak Ridge, Tennessee, almost all lessons designed for primary children include A Moment of Dance—a few minutes, usually at the beginning of the lesson, for self-space and/or general space dance activity.

Start with a Cooperative Class

Some classes are more agreeable to work with than others. Select a class that is generally cooperative as the first one to which you'll teach expressive dance. You don't need to start dance programs with all your classes at the same time. Instead, pick one class that you feel comfortable with. As your confidence builds, start dance programs in other classes. Use the first class as a testing ground for your ideas.

Use Props

Expressive dancers derive great pleasure and satisfaction from focusing on how they can move their bodies. In contrast, immature dancers often feel insecure when asked to focus on how they're moving. Props can serve as catalysts, redirecting the child's attention and so reducing self-consciousness. The use of such props as scarves, newspapers, balloons, dowel rods, stretch nylon, and even shadows can effectively divert the attention of uncertain children from their bodies. For example, when attempting to duplicate the light, airy movements made by a floating sheet of newspaper, the child focuses attention on moving as the newspaper does, rather than on trying to travel lightly. As confidence builds, the children gradually focus their attention on their own movements.

Imagery

Imagery is the use of a creative stimulus as a catalyst for movement. Many people believe, inaccurately, that imagery provides the content of dance. The content of expressive dance is movement; imagery is a helper. Asking children to use imagery as the content of expressive dance is similar to asking children to write a story when they have a vocabulary of only 50 words. One or two extraordinarily intelligent pupils might do well. Most, however, would fail miserably because they hadn't yet acquired the tools needed for successful story writing.

The same principle can be applied to expressive dance. Children must be provided with the tools of dance, the ability to use a variety of movements effectively. Only when children have developed these skills can they successfully combine the movements into dances that express what they want to communicate. Movement vocabularies, however, aren't acquired through imagery, as the following example illustrates.

A teacher focusing on the concept of slow, heavy movement may ask children to travel as if the floor were coated with 6 inches of peanut butter. But using the peanut butter image without first teaching the concept of slow and heavy travel is of little value. Children who are adept at such movements at the beginning of the class will remain adept. Those individuals who were unable to travel slowly and heavily might move in the desired manner when stimulated by the image of a peanut butter floor, but they won't have acquired a functional understanding of slow, heavy movement as a concept that can be transferred to other movement situations. In short, imagery can be useful as a reinforcer for certain movements, but imagery by itself doesn't enhance the quality of children's expressive movement.

Start with Exciting Movement Experiences

Fast, vigorous, large movements are attractive and appealing to young children. A lesson that focuses on running, leaping into the air, landing, and rolling evokes the exuberance associated with speed and flight. Gradually the teacher can begin to focus on the quality of the leaps, the effectiveness of the landings, and the use of gestures while in flight.

Dance to the Music

One of the most devastating experiences for poorly skilled or less confident children occurs when a teacher plays some music and simply says, "Today is a dance lesson. Go ahead and dance to the music." This can be a terrifying task for youngsters with no background or confidence in creative movement and no vocabulary of functional movements. The challenge "Move to the music" may be appropriate later, when children put together the movements they have acquired, but it is not appropriate in the early stages of teaching expressive dance to children.

A Final Thought

One instructor's initial attempts at teaching expressive dance are still vivid. He recalled teaching to a second-grade class an entire lesson that focused on running, jumping, and turning to different rhythms. Afterward he remarked to a friend that it was the best workout the children had experienced the entire year and added that he was going to teach another lesson because of the physical fitness benefits. After another lesson was received as enthusiastically as the first, he was struck with the realization that the reason the children had been so actively involved was that they were totally immersed in the exciting atmosphere that was generated by exploring fast and slow turns, and acceleration and deceleration leading into jumps. The children loved expressive dance.

The physical education instructor who doesn't offer creative movement experiences is being professionally irresponsible. You may be more qualified to teach gymnastics or games, but you'll always be teaching some children who might eventually choose creative/expressive dance as their primary form of physical activity. Depriving children of opportunities to experience creative movement is no more acceptable than eliminating all opportunities to practice throwing and catching. You may have to devote much time and work to developing a successful program. But any teacher, even one who has little background in expressive dance, can provide children with effective creative movement experiences.

Summary

Teachers who lack experience and educational background in dance find it difficult to teach dance to children. But any teacher who's willing to try new and possibly unfamiliar ideas can learn to successfully teach children's dance. Children look forward to and enjoy dance experiences that are presented appropriately.

Dance for children includes both predesigned (rhythmic experiences, folk/cultural, ethnic and square dances) and child-designed dance (creative rhythmic experiences and expressive dance). Because of the ages and abilities of children in elementary schools, we've found expressive dance to be the most successful. Expressive dance is also consistent with the nature and characteristics of young children, who are already adept at fantasizing and expressing their thoughts and feelings through movement.

The content of expressive dance is derived from the movement concepts and the majority of locomotor and nonmanipulative skill themes. The initial emphasis is on executing particular movements. As children

learn to perform these skills efficiently, the emphasis shifts to varying the quality with which the movement is executed.

Children should have both rhythmic and expressive dance experiences. In rhythmic experiences, the focus is on moving in relation to different rhythmic beats. In contrast, expressive dance experiences focus on interpretation by children as they expand their movement vocabulary for communicating feelings and moods.

Through a process of trial and error, we've discovered numerous techniques that help make dance lessons for children both interesting and educational. For example, we suggest that teachers initially avoid the word *dance* because it has negative connotations for some children. Inexperienced dance teachers may find it helps to begin by teaching dance to one cooperative class. Using props and designing vigorous, action-packed lessons are also strategies that help excite children about dance.

Reading Comprehension Questions

1. What should dance in the elementary school provide for children?
2. What are the two types of dance experiences for children? Where does each form fit into a curriculum, and why?
3. What skill themes and movement concepts generally appear in expressive dance content?
4. Name three settings for cultural dance in the elementary school. Choose a folk, ethnic, square, or country dance and describe its development in each of the three settings.
5. What is the focus of expressive dance?
6. What is the role of imagery in dance? What must children possess before they can effectively use imagery?
7. What is the primary focus of expressive dance? How does the purpose of expressive dance differ at each skill progression level?
8. What is sequencing?
9. What is dance making? What procedures must be included in dance making?
10. How can you evaluate dance making?
11. Choose a theme for an expressive dance for children. Outline the dance to show beginning and ending shapes, locomotor movements, travel pathways, and concepts that express the theme.
12. What cues do the authors give for starting to teach expressive dance?

References/Suggested Readings

Barrett, K. R. 1984. Educational dance. In *Physical education for children: A focus on the teaching process*, ed. B. Logsdon, K. Barrett, M. Ammons, M. Broer, L. Halverson, R. McGee, and M. Roberton. Philadelphia: Lea & Febiger.

Bennett, J. P., and P. C. Riemer. 2006. *Rhythmic activities and dance*. 2nd ed. Champaign, IL: Human Kinetics.

Boorman, J. 1969. *Creative dance in the first three grades*. New York: McKay.*

Carroll, J., and P. Lofthouse. 1969. *Creative dance for boys*. London: MacDonald & Evans.*

Cone, T., and S. Cone. 2005. *Teaching children dance*. 2nd ed. Champaign, IL: Human Kinetics.

Davis, J. 1995. Laban movement analysis: A key to individualizing children's dance. *Journal of Physical Education, Recreation and Dance* 66(2): 31–33.

Fleming, G. A. 1976. *Creative rhythmic movement*. Englewood Cliffs, NJ: Prentice Hall.*

Fleming, G. A., ed. 1981. *Children's dance*. Reston, VA: American Alliance for Health, Physical Education, Recreation and Dance.

Holt/Hale, S. 2012. *On the move: Lesson plans to accompany Children Moving*. 9th ed. New York: McGraw-Hill.

Joyce, M. 1993. *Dance technique for children*. New York: McGraw-Hill.

Joyce, M. 1994. *First steps in teaching creative dance*. 3rd ed. New York: McGraw-Hill.

McGreevy-Nichols, S., H. Scheff, and M. Sprague. 2005. *Building dances: A guide to putting movements together*. 2nd ed. Champaign, IL: Human Kinetics.

[NASPE] National Association for Sport and Physical Education. 1992. *Outcomes of quality physical education programs*. Reston, VA: National Association for Sport and Physical Education.

[NASPE] National Association for Sport and Physical Education. 2004. *Moving into the future: National standards for physical education*. 2nd ed. Reston, VA: National Association for Sport and Physical Education.

O'Neill, M. 1961. *Hailstones and halibut bones*. New York: Doubleday.

Russell, J. 1975. *Creative movement and dance for children*. Boston: Plays.*

Slater, W. 1974. *Teaching modern educational dance*. London: MacDonald & Evans.*

Smith, J. A. 1972. The awful beginning. *Today's Education* 61(4): 56.

Stinson, S. 1988. *Dance for young children: Finding the magic in movement*. Reston, VA: American Alliance for Health, Physical Education, Recreation and Dance.

Stinson, S. W. 1993. Voices from schools: The significance of relationship to public school dance students. *Journal of Physical Education, Recreation and Dance* 64(5): 52–56.

Ward, S. A. 2007. Why we all should learn to dance: Reflecting on the African cultural heritage. *Journal of Physical Education, Recreation and Dance* 78(5): 3–5, 47.

Weikart, P. S. 1997. *Teaching folk dance: Successful steps*. Ypsilanti, MI: High Scope Press.

Weikart, P. S. 2006. *Teaching movement and dance*. 6th ed. Ypsilanti, MI: High Scope Press.

Willis, C. M. 1995a. Creative dance education: Establishing a positive learning environment. *Journal of Physical Education, Recreation and Dance* 66(4): 16–20.

Willis, C. M. 1995b. Creative dance: How to increase parent and teacher awareness. *Journal of Physical Education, Recreation and Dance* 66(5): 48–53.

*The skills/movement concepts foundation for creative dance for children.

Appendix 28A Teacher-Designed Rhythmic Routines

Lummi Sticks

Lummi sticks for elementary-age children are usually 12 inches long and 1 inch in diameter. They may be made from rolled newspaper sealed with tape or cut from broom and mop handles or dowel rods. We have found it best to have children practice with the paper sticks until they master the basic patterns. Each child needs two sticks. The routine that follows is designed in two parts. First, children learn the basic patterns without tossing the sticks; then they work with a partner to add tossing and catching the sticks in the rhythm of the pattern.

Basic Patterns

Pattern 1: Hold sticks together vertically, one in each hand. Tap sticks down, tap sticks together, extend right hand forward. Tap down, tap sticks together, extend left hand forward. Repeat entire pattern two times.

Pattern 2: Hold sticks vertically, one in each hand. Tap both sticks down, tap them together, extend right hand, extend left hand. Repeat pattern four times.

Pattern 3: Hold sticks horizontally, with front tips extending toward the floor. Touch the edge of the sticks to the floor, and then half-flip the sticks, catching the sticks in your hands. Hold sticks vertically for one count. Repeat pattern 2. Touch edge of sticks to floor; half-flip the sticks, hold sticks one count. Then repeat pattern 2: Tap down, tap sticks together, extend right hand, extend left hand. Repeat entire pattern four times.

Pattern 4: Hold sticks horizontally on each side of your body. Touch the edge of each stick on the floor, and then half-flip the sticks. Bring sticks in front of you and perform pattern 3: Side touch, flip; front touch, flip; tap down, tap together, extend right hand, extend left hand. Repeat entire pattern four times.

Pattern 5: Hold sticks horizontally on each side of your body. Touch side front, side back, side front. Bring the sticks in front of your body; touch front, cross your arms over, touch on opposite side, uncross arms and touch. Repeat pattern 2: Side, touch front, back, front; front, side, cross, side. Tap down, tap together, extend right hand, extend left hand. Repeat entire pattern four times.

Tossing to a Partner
Children sit facing a partner, approximately 3 feet from the partner. Patterns are the same basic patterns, except that instead of an

Student-designed Lummi stick routine, to be performed with a partner.

extension of the arm, the stick is tossed to the partner, who catches it.

Chinese Ribbons/Streamers

Chinese ribbons or streamers for elementary school students are 8 to 12 feet long and made of plastic. Crepe paper can be used, but it doesn't withstand children's practice or rough handling. Streamers can be made by attaching the plastic to a 12-inch dowel rod with either an eyelet and screw or a swivel hook and nylon fishing line.

In time with the music, the streamers are twirled in front of the body, to the side, or over the head. The following patterns represent a combination of skills suited for control level. Routines become more advanced as locomotor skills are added.

Pattern 1: Side circles—right side, left side

Pattern 2: Front circles

Pattern 3: Figure 8s—in front of the body

Pattern 4: Helicopter—circles overhead

Pattern 5: Lasso—front circles near the floor

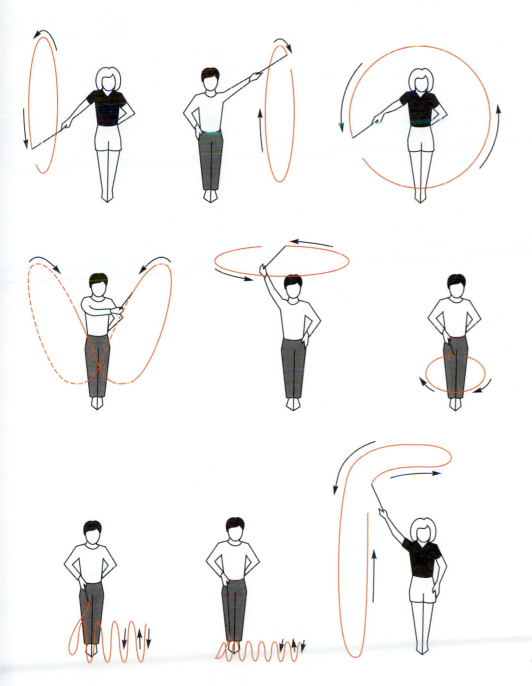

Chinese ribbon patterns.

Pattern 6: Walk the Dog—waist-high vertical movements in front, to the sides

Pattern 7: Snake—forward, backward movements near the floor, in front, to the sides

Pattern 8: Mountain Peaks—slow vertical movements, high to low levels

The ribbon routines of rhythmic gymnastics in the Olympics are examples of this skill at the proficiency level. Visuals and educational materials relating to rhythmic gymnastics are available from the U.S. Olympic Committee (www.olympic.org).

Musical Parachute

Parachute routines are combinations of locomotor and nonlocomotor actions. Sample skills include:

Waves: Shaking the parachute up and down

Umbrella: Raising the parachute high overhead

Mountain: Bringing the umbrella down to touch the edges on the floor

Merry-go-round: Locomotor actions moving the parachute clockwise and counterclockwise

Floating cloud: Umbrella with release of the parachute

Mushroom: Inflating the umbrella and moving forward to a mushroom shape

Music that is flowing, smooth, and expressive with a strong underlying beat is good for parachute routines. The best music is a song with meaningful lyrics and expressive movements in the format of the music. Routines should be easy to understand and perform, with creative movements and shapes that flow and change with the music. We have found it best to begin with instrumental music; words can be a distraction to the routine directions. After the students have mastered the routine, the music can be either instrumental or vocal.

The following routine is designed for students whose skills are at the control level and is done to the music "Pop Goes the Weasel":

Children sit around the parachute and face clockwise. They hold the parachute in their right hands. The children are numbered 1 and 2, with 2 being behind 1, who is the partner.

Start the introductory music ("Pop Goes the Weasel"). The children stand up on the first "pop," still holding the parachute with their right hands only.

The children march clockwise in time with the music until they hear "Pop Goes the Weasel," at which point the 1s let go of the parachute and walk under the chute and behind their partners. Now the 2s are in front.

Students march clockwise. On the next "pop," the 2s let go of the chute and go under the chute and behind their partners. Now the 1s are in front again.

Children now skip clockwise. On the "pop," the 1s go under the chute and behind their partners.

The children continue skipping. On the "pop," the 2s go under the chute and behind their partners.

Students now face the center of the circle, holding the parachute with both their hands. Using the slidestep, they travel clockwise. On the "pop," children stop, then repeat the slidestep counterclockwise. They stop again, raise the parachute high in the air, and bring it back to the tuck position; they don't let go of the chute.

Students wait for the next "pop," at which point they raise the parachute high in the air, walk forward three steps, and then pull the parachute down behind them so they're "in the cave."

Students wait quietly in the cave. When they hear the final "pop," they come out of the cave.

Jump Rope

Jump rope routines at the control level should be relatively short and include only the basic jumps that everyone in class can do. As a rhythmic experience, a group jump rope routine involves executing the jump rope skills correctly, staying in rhythm with the music, and staying in time with others in the group.

Music that has a strong beat and generates energy is best for jump rope routines. The following is an example of a group jump rope routine for children at the control level; it is designed for 4/4 rhythm:

The children place their ropes in a V shape on the floor, so they can stand inside the V and jump outside the V.

Start with a 6-count introductory phrase. Then have the children execute six double jumping jacks. Starting inside the V, they clap thighs twice and clap hands above head twice. They jump outside the V as they clap overhead, inside the V as they clap thighs: out, out, in, in.

The children then pick up their ropes and step over the rope so it is behind them, ready for the first skill (4 counts).

They jump the rope using two-foot jumps eight times.

Next, they hold both handles of the rope in their right hands and execute eight double-side swings. They turn the ropes in a forward circle on each side of their bodies.

Then they open the ropes and jump 12 times, using the step-jump skill.

Children again hold handles in their right hands. This time, they twirl the rope overhead like a helicopter (16 counts).

Finally, they quickly place the ropes in a V on the floor and stand inside (4 counts). Then they execute six double jumping jacks.

Children Designing Their Own Dance: A Description of a Process

One goal in teaching dance is to work with children so they learn to design dances to express feelings or thoughts that are important to them. This description of the process of creating a dance tells how one teacher worked with a group of upper-grade children, assisting them to create their own dance. The description is intended to reveal the process of creating dances; it isn't presented as a predesigned dance to be taught to other children.

Background

The population of the community in which the children in this class lived was predominantly black. The eight children in this group wished to create a dance that expressed pride and respect for their African American heritage.

We began by using several methods to develop an outline for the dance:

- One student wrote a short paper describing what he considered the most important events in the miniseries *Roots*.
- The school media special list provided several sources of information. Individual students read and outlined these sources for the remainder of the group.
- Several students interviewed teachers and classmates about their family backgrounds. They also asked people to describe what emotions they had about their heritage.

Without question, *Roots* had the biggest influence in determining the students' conception of black history. The pride and courage of Kunta Kinte and his descendants were the qualities the children wanted most to exhibit in their dance.

An Outline of the Dance

After gathering and reviewing this information, we discussed a sequential outline for the dance. It was agreed that:

1. We'd begin by depicting, in some way, the period of slavery.
2. The arrival of freedom would be expressed. Interestingly, the children didn't want this portion of the dance to be happy or exhilarating, for several reasons. They felt that blacks were always free, despite slavery, that many freedoms were long in coming, and that the struggle for equality continues today.
3. Upon arrival of freedom, it was important to display the pride and courage of African Americans in overcoming many injustices, both as individuals and as a people.
4. The conclusion of the dance would be spiritual, exhibiting respect and thankfulness to God for blessing a cherished people.

Creation of the Dance

Children focused on each section of the dance before putting it all together. For each portion the youngsters needed to decide upon and write down the following:

1. Beginning location of each dancer
2. Sequential travel pathway of each dancer or of the entire group

Travel Pattern for "Freedom"

Travel pathways
   Random: Dancers weaving in, out, and around one another
Qualities
   Smooth, wavy, uncertain, looking to others for help
Actions
   Wavy gesturing of arms, held upward for protection or reaching out
   Slow stepping, with changes in direction and levels

(*continued*)

Appendix 28B (*continued*)

3. Expressive qualities they intended to exhibit in their movements
4. Sequence of specific gestures and travel skills incorporated to express desired qualities

Once the group could perform one section to the teacher's and their own satisfaction, work began on the next phase of the dance.

Slavery

After discussing the accumulated information, the children agreed to begin the dance by exhibiting the qualities and actions of field slaves laboring under a hot sun.

Freedom

This phase of the dance was the most difficult for the children. After experimenting with several ideas, the youngsters asked if they could select music to serve as background for the dance. They thought that if they had appropriate music as a stimulus, they would be able to solve their dilemmas. After listening to several cuts from the *Roots* soundtrack, the children unanimously agreed that the words and slow pulse of the song "Many Rains Ago (Oluwa)" was perfect for their purposes.

They decided to express freedom by simply putting down their tools and slowly and smoothly beginning to interweave with one another, making eye contact with others for the first time. This was intended to express changed circumstances in which they were free and proud but still struggling. During this

phase, the youngsters' facial features exhibited fear and uncertainty about the future. The travel pattern was random.

Gathering Together: Strength as a People

To express their solidarity and pride as a people, the children's random travel began to be directed toward the center of the room where they gathered one by one, grasped one another's hands tightly, and formed a strong, unified statue.

From this point the youngsters were able to complete their dance with little teacher suggestion or intervention.

Dispersing: Strength as Individuals

Youngsters dispersed from center stage with new vigor and traveled along definite travel patterns.

Gathering Again: Strength, Pride, Confidence

Children leaped to the center of the room, where suddenly and simultaneously they clasped hands with one another overhead and formed a statue.

Respect and Thankfulness to God

From the statue position, youngsters slowly bowed and traveled to semicircle formation. Slowly they dropped to their knees, and then slowly they raised their hands and heads upward.

Conclusion: We Are Strong and Proud

Youngsters slowly bent to curled position. . . . Suddenly and simultaneously they rose on knees to grasp one another's hands to form a statue as a final statement of strength and pride.

Travel Pattern for "Gathering Again: Strength, Pride, Confidence"

Travel pathways
    All dancers suddenly and simultaneously gather in the middle with a run, leap, and turn
Qualities
    Strong, confident, proud, smooth, and fluent
Actions
    Smooth, fluent leap and landing when dancers grasp each other's hands overhead and freeze into a stillness

Teaching Gymnastics

If gymnastics is to be for everyone, including the handicapped child, then all children cannot be asked to do the same gymnastic movement at the same time, in exactly the same way, for clearly some children are going to be underchallenged and some are going to be overchallenged.

—ANDREA BOUCHER (1978)

Key Concepts

- The form of gymnastics described in *Children Moving* is called educational gymnastics.

- Educational gymnastics focuses on children challenging themselves to maneuver their bodies effectively against the force of gravity with challenges appropriate for each child and his or her skill level.

- In contrast, Olympic-style/artistic gymnastics centers on defined stunts performed the same way by all children with a goal of formal competition.

- The skill themes of balance, transferring weight, and rolling, in combination with jumping/landing, traveling, and the actions of bending, stretching, curling, twisting, are the major skill themes used in educational gymnastics contexts.

- Educational gymnastics includes floor experiences and apparatus experiences.

- Educational gymnastics apparatus includes tables, benches, beams, bars, vaulting boxes, and playground apparatus.

- Children should never be forced into attempting a gymnastics skill or activity; the teacher's knowledge of individual students and selection of developmentally appropriate activities are critical for positive learning experiences and safety.

The skill themes of balancing and transferring weight, coupled with jumping/landing and traveling, and bending, stretching, curling, twisting, form the foundation of educational gymnastics. As stated earlier in the text, skill themes and movement concepts form the curricular base for elementary physical education, with dance, educational gymnastics, and games/sports skills as the contexts, or settings, through which these skills and concepts are explored, mastered, and applied. The development and mastery of skills would be of little value if left in isolation, without infusion into games, gymnastics, and dance. This chapter integrates the skills of traveling, jumping and landing, balancing, and transferring weight, as well as the concepts of space awareness, effort, and relationships, into the content area of educational gymnastics.

The Nature of Gymnastics

The self-testing nature of gymnastics is challenging to children. They constantly ask themselves, "Can I balance in this position without falling? Can I walk this curb? Can I stand on my head? Can I climb this tree and hang by my arms?" These self-testing challenges meet the criteria of effective teaching/learning in several ways.

First, children receive immediate feedback regarding the skill: "Yes, I can do a headstand," or "No, I am still losing my balance." Second, the feedback is personal and not dependent on others; children do not have to rely on others to determine whether they are successful at the task. Third, the self-challenging tasks of gymnastics are a natural part of children's world; their environment, coupled with their curiosity and love of movement, creates multiple opportunities for climbing, hanging, supporting weight on different body parts, balancing, rolling, and so on. Finally, the self-testing nature of gymnastics permits younger children who are still in the egocentric stage of development to participate fully and successfully in a personal challenge without the necessity of team play or cooperative work with other children.

Children are exposed to advanced, competitive gymnastics through television coverage of the Olympics, as well as by watching local club gymnasts on the playgrounds and in their neighborhoods. Children without a background of gymnastics experiences often enter our gymnasiums saying, "I can't do those things" or asking, "Will we do back handsprings today?" Our task is to present gymnastics for children in a way that is both challenging and appropriate for all students in our classes. The skills covered in the earlier chapters on balancing and transferring weight and rolling, along with those of jumping and landing, and locomotion, are the skills in educational gymnastics that are appropriate for elementary physical education.

To children, the self-testing, risk-taking nature of gymnastics brings excitement; to the teacher, it brings the challenge of creating a safe environment. We as teachers must always be sure the equipment arrangement, class organization, and selection of tasks maximize safety for our students. There must be a match between student and task, with intratask variation to allow for individual differences. The skills must progress from simple to complex, and the students must master each task before moving to the more complex. The teacher must never require that all students perform the same task. Performance of a certain skill must never be linked to a "grade" in physical education. The gymnastics tasks presented must be challenging to the less skilled, yet not boring to the highly skilled; tasks that are too easy or too difficult can lead to boredom and frustration. As a result, children may create their own agenda and an unsafe environment for learning in gymnastics. Finally, the mastery of gymnastics skills

Young children enjoy the challenge of balancing on different body parts.

Moving in relation to apparatus is part of educational gymnastics.

is a slow process and must not be rushed by us as teachers or by our students. *These considerations are critically important to creating a safe learning environment for all children.*

Gymnastics in Elementary School

Gymnastics can be divided into two types: predesigned and child-designed. Predesigned gymnastics is artistic gymnastics, the gymnastics of Olympic competition. Olympic-style gymnastics centers on specialized stunts or skills, with all students performing the same way, and on training for formal gymnastics competition. Educational gymnastics is child-designed gymnastics. In educational gymnastics, we provide experiences to teach children to maneuver their bodies effectively against the force of gravity with balance and transferring weight challenges matched to individual skill levels and in appropriate floor and apparatus environments. All gymnastics within *Children Moving* is child-designed gymnastics/educational gymnastics.

The Purpose of Gymnastics

The purpose of educational gymnastics as taught in physical education is to provide our students with a foundation of gymnastics experiences that increase their skills and introduce them to the types of activities characteristic of gymnastics. The *National Standards for Physical Education* (NASPE 2004) support the inclusion of educational gymnastics in elementary physical education. See Box 29-1 for the sample outcomes specific to gymnastics in the elementary school curriculum contained in the National Standards.

The specialization of skills for competitive, Olympic-style/artistic gymnastics is reserved for club gymnastics and after-school programs with trained gymnastics specialists and coaches. These programs provide the training needed for specialization in specific stunts, required routines, and advanced aerial skills. Children interested in Olympic-style/artistic gymnastics or advanced work beyond the level of educational gymnastics can enroll in programs sponsored by youth agencies or private clubs. Some schools offer after-school programs for students who want additional practice in gymnastics.

Specializing in and teaching Olympic-style/artistic gymnastics in physical education class can educate a few students, but the majority will be left behind, and the risk of injury for the less skilled students will increase. Educational gymnastics programs are designed to assist all children, regardless of ability, to improve

Box 29-1

Educational Gymnastics and the *National Standards for Physical Education*

The National Association for Sport and Physical Education's *National Standards for Physical Education* (NASPE 2004) cites the following performance outcomes for educational gymnastics in elementary physical education:

- Discovers how to balance on different body parts, at different levels, becoming "like" a statue while making symmetrical and nonsymmetrical shapes (K–2)*
- Balances with control on a variety of objects, such as large apparatus (3–5)*
- Develops and refines a gymnastics sequence demonstrating smooth transitions (3–5)*
- Designs and performs gymnastics sequences that combine traveling, rolling, balancing, and weight transfer into smooth, flowing sequences with intentional changes in direction, speed, and flow (6–8)*

*Grade-level guidelines for expected student learning.

Box 29-2

Appropriate and Inappropriate Physical Education Practices

Educational Gymnastics

Appropriate Practice

- Educational gymnastic lessons develop skills appropriate to the children's abilities and confidence in balancing, rolling, jumping, landing, climbing, and transferring weight.
- Children practice on apparatus designed to match their gymnastic abilities and confidence.

Inappropriate Practice

- Teachers require all students to perform the same predetermined stunts and routines while the rest of the class sits and watches.
- Predetermined stunts require extensive teacher direction and spotting because they're too difficult for many of the children.

Source: National Association for Sport and Physical Education, *Appropriate instructional practice guidelines for elementary school physical education,* 3rd ed. (Reston, VA: National Association for Sport and Physical Education, 2009).

their gymnastics skills—to become better able to control their bodies in the variety of planned and unplanned encounters they will have, as children and as adults, with the force of gravity (Box 29-2).

Do we exclude Olympic stunts from our curriculum? Not at all. Children at the utilization and proficiency levels who have a background in gymnastics experiences and the proper body control often use Olympic stunts as a response to a gymnastics task. When children use a handstand, walkover, or cartwheel, for example, the maneuver should be identified as such. With children who do have a background in gymnastics, we discuss the stunts they have chosen in response to the task given. We decide whether the response is appropriate for physical education class or best reserved for club gymnastics; for example, we consider whether the stunt requires a spotter and whether the other children will be tempted to imitate a stunt beyond their capabilities that could result in injury.

An example may help to clarify this point. If we ask the children in a class to "transfer their weight from their feet to their hands to their feet," there are a variety of ways to do this. Some children might do a cartwheel or even a handspring. Others may simply place their hands on the grass and lift their feet only a few inches from the ground. Both are "correct" responses! If you ask the entire class to do a cartwheel, those children who are unable to do so may feel as if they have

failed. In contrast, the "gymnasts" in the class would be bored if they were asked to only lift their feet a few inches from the ground. If you understand this example, then you understand the theory underpinning educational gymnastics. In either instance the teacher's guidance is very important. As teachers, we can assess the child's skill level and the difficulty of the stunt. If these match, we can give the verbal cues and/or assistance to enable the children to learn a skill correctly and safely.

The Content of Educational Gymnastics

The content of educational gymnastics derives from the skill themes of balancing, transferring weight, and rolling in combination with jumping/landing, and traveling. The specifics of these themes, as well as appropriate challenges for children, are found in Chapters 16, 19, 20, and 21. The content also includes such movement concepts as directions, levels, pathways, time, shapes, and the actions of stretching, curling, and twisting (Chapters 13, 14, 15, 18). These movement concepts and actions are incorporated into the gymnastics themes only after children have experienced them in isolation and/or in games and dance. For example, children do not study twisting into and out of balances before they have an understanding of the action of twisting.

Before studying a skill theme in educational gymnastics, children need to understand the concept of balance in gymnastics—maintaining stillness in a position and holding that position for 3 to 5 seconds. Many children can take weight on their hands momentarily or balance in a headstand for 1 to 2 seconds but cannot hold the position stationary for 5 seconds. Children need early experiences in aligning body parts for balance and in tightening the muscles to maintain balance as prerequisites to skill themes in educational gymnastics. Children often fall out of inverted balances because the body parts are not properly aligned over the base of support and muscular tension is not sufficient to hold the proper alignment. Introductory and review lessons focusing on these fundamental skills will contribute to a safer environment in which students experience balance and weight transference activities and will also enhance mastery in gymnastics learning experiences.

Educational gymnastics is divided into floor experiences and apparatus experiences. Floor experiences are movements executed on grass, mats, or carpeting that don't require equipment to enhance the challenge. Apparatus experiences involve moving in relation to one or several pieces of equipment (tables, benches, beam, bars, vaulting boxes, and playground apparatus). Although apparatus adds excitement to gymnastics, children can experience challenging, rewarding work in educational gymnastics with floor experiences only.

Even in a program rich in gymnastics apparatus, children should spend a large amount of time on floor/mat experiences before they begin work on apparatus. Balancing, transferring weight, and rolling activities should be mastered on mats and carpet squares before they are attempted on low or high gymnastics apparatus. Many of the movements performed on the floor will be replicated on apparatus, but the height and narrowness of the surfaces will increase the difficulty of the task. Students begin apparatus work on low, larger surfaces—that is, crates/boxes, low beams, and benches—before they work on higher, narrower pieces of apparatus.

Floor Experiences

Children at the precontrol level in educational gymnastics explore balancing on different body parts as bases of support, balancing on wide bases, and balancing in different shapes. They learn to curve their bodies into rounded shapes and to maintain the rounded shape for rocking/rolling. They also learn to transfer weight safely on and off equipment and apparatus.

Exploring basic shapes on apparatus follows balances on the floor/mats.

Control-level experiences include rolling from different positions and in different directions. Inverted balances are introduced, with a strong emphasis on alignment of body parts and muscular tension to maintain balance. The concept of stillness is studied in combination with weight-transfer actions and as a contrast to rolling. Beginning at the control level, children are challenged with combinations of skills and the combination of skills and concepts—for example, moving from a two-part balance into a three-part balance on new bases of support or balancing in a wide body shape at different levels.

Floor experiences for children are designed to lead children from exploration of balances and transferring weight, to control of their bodies in these self-imposed challenges, to application of the skills in gymnastics sequences. Children are introduced to sequences at the control level. Beginning-level sequences may be as simple as a beginning shape, followed by three balances on different bases of support and an ending shape. As children become more competent in gymnastics and more confident in the process, sequences become increasingly complex, with combinations of transfer actions and stillness, movement concepts, and transitions. These sequences still include a beginning and an ending shape.

More advanced and increasingly complex sequences of movements are enjoyable and challenging to children at the utilization level who have developed control over movements executed singularly. Gymnastics sequences include stretching, curling, twisting, and/or rolling actions as transitions between balances, as well as combinations of balances, weight-transfer actions, and traveling. Movement concepts and variations of a concept (e.g., changes in levels, variations in speed) are incorporated in the sequences.

Maintaining weight on hands, exploring the state of being "almost off" balance, and taking part or all of a partner's weight are appropriate proficiency-level tasks for children in educational gymnastics. Students at this level enjoy focusing on the quality of movement execution in gymnastics. The concepts of acceleration and deceleration, strong and light, bound and free are added to sequences. Matching or mirroring a partner's movements, repeating sequences of several gymnastics movements, and experiences that involve several students supporting one another's weight are all proficiency-level gymnastics floor experiences.

Apparatus Experiences

Once children demonstrate control of their bodies in educational gymnastics floor experiences, have an understanding of safety in gymnastics, and understand the concept of sequences, we introduce them to experiences on apparatus. Balance beams, parallel bars, side horses, vaulting boxes, and still rings are Olympic/artistic gymnastics equipment. Some elementary schools have this official gymnastics apparatus, but many elementary school programs use benches, tables, chairs, hoops, the edge of a stage, climbing ropes, and climbing frames to provide gymnastics experiences on apparatus. Unofficial equipment is often more compatible with the children's abilities, and children have fewer preconceived notions about what is expected when they practice movements on an unfamiliar or nontraditional piece of equipment.

You can introduce the children to a piece of apparatus by encouraging them to explore the equipment and to discover safe ways to get on and off it. Children at the precontrol level can start by walking along a low beam or bench, jumping from a chair or low table, hanging from a climbing rope at a low height, or traveling along a climbing frame. Obstacle courses designed from available equipment—tables, benches, chairs, hoops, ropes—are also challenging to children at this level as they learn the concepts of under, over, along, and through. Some children will immediately begin to explore the apparatus; other children will be more cautious. Never force any child onto a piece of apparatus.

Children at the control level, while continuing to explore apparatus, can begin to focus on different ways to move in relation to the equipment. They can try different ways of traveling along a beam, hanging from a bar or rope, jumping from a table or chair, or traveling from side to side on a climbing frame. They can balance on different bases of support and combine traveling with stationary balances on apparatus. Sequence work at the control level might include transferring weight onto the apparatus, balancing and traveling on the apparatus, and traveling off the apparatus. Skills that were mastered during the floor experiences present a new challenge to children as they attempt them on various pieces of gymnastics apparatus.

Children at the utilization level can try different ways to get onto equipment, vaulting over equipment, and forming shapes in flight while moving from apparatus to the floor. Apparatus experiences that involve supporting weight on different body parts, transferring weight on equipment, nonsymmetrical balances, and inverted balances are also appropriate for children at this level.

When children reach the proficiency level, they should continue to focus on increasingly demanding balances, shapes, ways of traveling, and ways of supporting body weight. As with gymnastics experiences on the floor that lead from exploration to mastery to

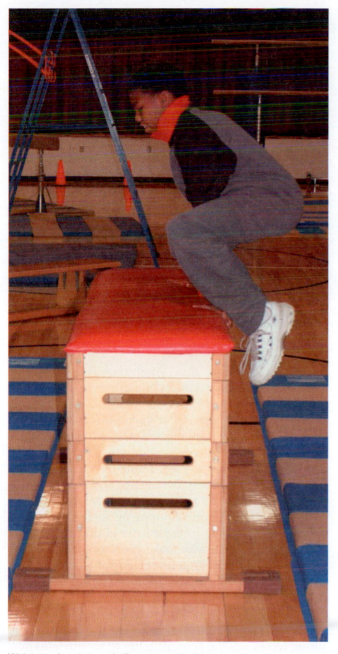

Weight on hands is a challenge on apparatus.

application, children on gymnastics apparatus progress from exploration and safety on apparatus to control of their bodies and mastery of skills to application in sequences. Educational gymnastics sequences at the utilization and proficiency levels demonstrate mastery of advanced skills, complex combinations of skills and concepts, and individual and/or partner creativity.

From the beginning, children should be encouraged to focus on the quality of their movements and to be creative and versatile in their sequence composition. The educational gymnastic sequence is the child's ex-

pression of self—a portrayal of self in gymnastics showing skills and concepts that flow together smoothly and fluently.

Series of lessons that demonstrate the progression of educational gymnastics from floor/mat experiences to low apparatus to higher, narrower apparatus can be found in *On the Move: Lesson Plans to Accompany Children Moving* (Holt/Hale 2010) under the skill themes of jumping and landing, balancing, and transferring weight.

Recording Sequences

A sequence in gymnastics can be compared to a recital piece in music. Once the children have learned the skills, they are to memorize and then repeat them in exactly the same order with exactly the same balances and actions. This is one of the most difficult parts of sequencing for children. They enjoy creating but not memorizing for repetition. Recording the sequences with paper and pencil helps children retain them. The children may record their gymnastics sequences with drawings and stick figures. We call them stick figures; the art teacher calls them pictographs. We have found several approaches to recording gymnastic sequences: You as a teacher may develop a method of recording sequences that will be used in all your gymnastics classes. The children may create their individual notation systems, or each class may devise a system of notation for balances and actions. With a strong emphasis on the creativity and the children's individual uniqueness, we enjoy the children each creating their individual notation systems.

Outdoor Play Equipment as Gymnastics Apparatus

Outdoor playground equipment can serve as gymnastics apparatus in schools that have no indoor equipment or indoor physical education facility and as an additional avenue of exploration for children who've experienced indoor gymnastics. Children at the pre-control and control levels can focus on body control on various pieces of equipment. Children at the utilization and proficiency levels will be challenged by the complexity of structure, the number of bars, the distance between bars, and the variety of levels on playground equipment. Horizontal ladders, parallel bars, jungle gyms, monkey bars, and telephone pole balance beams can be used for rolling, balancing, and transferring weight on apparatus. (See Chapters 20 and 21 for these activities.)

Very often the key to successfully teaching gymnastics on the playground is the positioning of the

Rolling on a bench is a challenge for this utilization student.

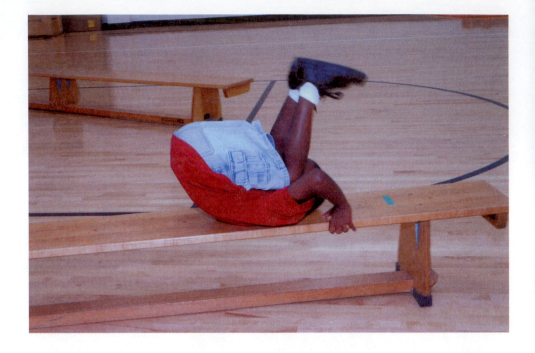

playground equipment: grouping versus isolated pieces of equipment. If the playground equipment is grouped, several pieces can easily accommodate a class of 25 to 30 children. But if the playground arrangement is such that instruction of the group as well as individuals on various apparatus isn't possible, cable spools and milk crates can be added to supplement large apparatus.

Children's work on playground apparatus should begin with a study of the proper use of the equipment—the acceptable and unacceptable activities on the apparatus—and correct ways of getting on and off the apparatus. Early in the school year, let the children explore the various pieces of apparatus; this will lead to questions from the children and class discussions about what is permitted during both physical education class and recess. Any safety rules needed should be developed cooperatively by teacher and students; the rules may vary for younger and older children.

The use of playground equipment in physical education class will lead to increased use of that equipment during recess, which may make classroom teachers uncomfortable with children on the equipment. However, a booklet of the rules established for physical education class and for recess will help the classroom teacher be more at ease. The use of apparatus during physical education can be very different from the use of apparatus during recess; it's our responsibility to be sure children understand the difference.

The Process of Teaching Educational Gymnastics

Teaching gymnastics is different from teaching either dance or games because of the self-testing nature of gymnastics and because apparatus is used. Successful educational gymnastics teachers are able to match interesting and challenging tasks to the children's ability levels. This is a teaching skill learned only with time and practice.

These youngsters enjoy creating matching balances.

Some teachers avoid gymnastics because they are concerned about the children's safety and are afraid that children might be injured; some administrators are hesitant to include gymnastics in the curriculum for the same reasons. Injury is always a possibility in physical education classes. When the focus is on educational gymnastics (as opposed to Olympic-style stunts) and when the experiences are presented sequentially and in an appropriate environment, gymnastics is no more dangerous than other physical education activities. The following ideas relating to the learning environment and the teaching of educational gymnastics help create successful and safe experiences for children. Taken together, these suggestions, along with the safety emphasis icon (⚠), will help establish a safe learning environment for teaching educational gymnastics.

The Learning Environment

From the initial lessons, children learn spatial awareness of their movements and the movements of others. They are taught not to interfere with others attempting their gymnastics work, either by touching or talking to them. Concentration on the task is essential in gymnastics.

An appropriate learning environment in gymnastics emphasizes safety throughout. Encourage the children to be responsible for their own safety. Stress that if they don't think they can do something, they should either not do it or ask you for help. Games of I Dare You and Follow the Leader are inappropriate in gymnastics classes. Remember, following the progression outlined in the spirals for gymnastics skills, and mastering a skill before attempting the next, are critical for safety. Gymnastics classes are not the place for off-task behavior; being off task in games and/or dance may result in inappropriate behavior, but off-task behavior in gymnastics can lead to injury. When we encourage children to be responsible for themselves, they will rely less on us and more on themselves to determine what is appropriate. Acceptance of responsibility and self-reliance are goals of physical education; they are major goals in teaching gymnastics.

Gymnastics Equipment

Gymnastics apparatus is heavy, cumbersome, and difficult for one person to move. In some situations, gymnastics would never be taught if the teacher had to move the gymnastics equipment alone. Children can be taught to move gymnastics equipment correctly during the first few lessons in which the apparatus is used. Once they learn to maneuver the apparatus safely and efficiently, the children can set up or take down a gymnastics environment in a short time. The

Children are encouraged to be responsible for themselves and their own safety.

following guidelines should be used when children move gymnastics apparatus:

- An adequate number of children (as determined by the teacher) must be present before equipment can be moved.
- Children are to lift the equipment together and lower it together, being careful of toes and fingers.
- Each piece of apparatus has its own storage space to which it is to be returned.

Moving gymnastics apparatus correctly is as important a part of the children's learning in educational gymnastics as working safely on the apparatus. Taking the time during the initial lessons to teach them the proper procedure will help create a safe environment for gymnastics and increase valuable instructional time in subsequent lessons.

Stations

Initial gymnastics lessons for children at the precontrol level focus on floor experiences with large-group instruction. During this time, the children learn how to control their bodies when balancing, transferring weight, and rolling; they also learn about safety in gymnastics and working independently. After children demonstrate the ability to work safely and independently, allowing the class to work at stations (learning centers) can be a most efficient method of providing maximum participation on gymnastics apparatus. The stations are set up in different parts of the teaching area (see Chapter 10), with groups working on the same or different skills on the various pieces of equipment. Sample tasks include jumping from a low table or chair onto a mat, landing, and rolling; traveling different

ways along a bench or beam; climbing a rope; practicing taking weight on hands; and traveling onto and off a table.

This method of organization allows the use of various pieces of equipment and eliminates long lines. Tasks for the stations can be written on poster boards and taped to the wall near each station. This increases practice time: The children can read the directions and begin work immediately. The number of stations and complexity of the setup are guided by answers to the following considerations:

- How many stations will the total available space accommodate?
- Are there enough mats to place under and around each piece of equipment?
- Is the space surrounding the station adequate for the children to practice getting off the equipment—for example, jumping, landing, and rolling—safely?
- Is the space between the stations sufficient to allow the children to work without interfering with those at the adjoining station?
- Does the setup provide the teacher the freedom to move throughout the learning environment, giving individual assistance as needed?

Safety Check

Teach children very early in gymnastics to do a "Safety Check" before they begin work at any station: mats correctly placed under equipment, adequate space surrounding the equipment. In the beginning, stop the class frequently and ask the children to do a "Safety Check," visually scanning the working area for space and equipment safety.

Transferring weight from feet to hands is a control-level skill that can later be used in gymnastics routines.

Varying the Task

When all the children in a class are expected to perform the same skill the same way, two things are likely to happen. Many of the children in the class will be bored because they can already perform the task successfully. Some of the children will be frightened because the task is too difficult for them, and they know it. When you offer children some choices about how they'll perform a task, each child can select an appropriate level of activity. For example, it's unlikely that all the children in a particular class will be able to do a handstand. Some children may not be strong enough to support all their body weight on their hands; some won't be able to land safely if they lose their balance. Instead of telling the entire class to do a handstand, you could tell the children to find a way to place some or all of their weight on their hands. An instruction that allows for individual differences in ability affords all children an opportunity for success. Intratask variation and teaching by invitation (Chapter 10) are important tools for safety and appropriate challenges in gymnastics.

Safety Rules

Rules for working safely on mats and apparatus should be explained, demonstrated, and enforced very carefully. We suggest posting the rules where the children can see them as they work. (See Chapter 8, "Establishing an Environment for Learning," for additional suggestions.)

Club Gymnasts

Some of the children in your classes may be studying gymnastics independently, perhaps in a club or recreation program. Most of the club gymnasts are more skilled than the other children—many are at the proficiency level in many skills. Their skills in gymnastics may exceed your teaching knowledge and ability in this area. Because you're responsible for the safety of all the children, the activities of these club gymnasts may cause you some uneasiness.

If you explain your concern to these children, you'll find they appreciate your candor. Tell these young gymnasts you're working to learn about the movements they're practicing. Assure them that once you're skilled enough to help them practice appropriately and safely, you'll be delighted to have them resume practice in class.

This approach makes it clear you aren't criticizing but instead are respecting their proficiency. Students will, in turn, respect you for acknowledging your limitations and seeking their cooperation, and teacher–student rapport will be enhanced.

The other children will look to the club gymnasts as models and sources for new ideas. The presence of club gymnasts in a gymnastics class results in an interesting blend of child-created gymnastics skills and Olympic/artistic gymnastics skills, providing an interesting dimension to gymnastics lessons.

Spotting

Spotting—the practice of physically assisting children as they perform a movement—isn't commonly used in educational gymnastics classes. Children who depend on such help are likely to be unsure and even afraid unless a teacher is nearby. And, conversely, spotting encourages children to attempt movements they may not be ready for. We've observed a number of programs, including our own, in which children have progressed to a relatively high level of skill proficiency without any spotting. Even though we do not "spot" children when they are performing skills in educational gymnastics, we strongly believe in safety for all children in the gymnastics setting. Throughout the skill themes for gymnastics (Chapters 16, 19–21), you will have noted the safety icon (⚠) emphasizing safety tips for the teacher.

Demonstrating

Some teachers feel that because they aren't skilled gymnasts themselves, they won't be able to teach gymnastics effectively. Certainly a thorough background in a teaching area is an asset in teaching. But even teachers who aren't skilled gymnasts can provide children with appropriate gymnastics experiences. In educational gymnastics, the instructor doesn't need to be able to demonstrate a skill correctly because the children are never expected to perform the same skill the same way. If you want to give children additional ideas or to emphasize a particular movement quality or concept, you can invite some of the more proficient children to demonstrate for the rest of the class. This technique has the added advantage of reinforcing those children who are working especially well.

The Little Gymnast

Come with us, now, to a very nice place where little children swing on rings.

Where laughter is king—and happiness queen—and everyone likes who they are.

On a little green island called Mercer, in a big blue Washington lake surrounded by trees, is a wonderful building assembled by people who think it's important for children to play. And learn. And find out what they can do.

The building is called the Jewish Community Center, and children come from miles around to follow a Pied Piper of a man named Robin West.

Robin grew up in South Africa and then went to college at the University of Saskatchewan in Canada. Now he teaches movement, tumbling, and gymnastics to hundreds of boys and girls in the United States. One of his favorite classes is "kiddie gymnastics," for little gymnasts, four to six.

Most four-year-olds already know how to run, jump, and play when they come to their very first day of kiddie gymnastics. But in no time at all, Robin can open their eyes to hundreds of new ways to move, swing, roll, bend, and balance their bodies with success.

"Success for everyone" is the motto in kiddie gymnastics. It's such a simple motto—so easy to follow—that sometimes even Robin and the children's parents must stop to remind themselves of its magic.

A child is a butterfly in the wind. Some can fly higher than others; but each one flies the best way it can. Why compare one against the other? Each one is different. Each one is special. Each one is beautiful.

In kiddie gymnastics, everyone flies and nobody fails. There's plenty of praise for the attempt well-tried. To balance on a beam for the very first time is discovery. To be praised and applauded for the very same motion is joy.

In just a few short weeks the children in Robin's class have learned to move with a confidence, poise, and imagination that surprises and pleases both themselves and their parents.

But they've also learned something else along the way. You can see it in their eyes when they tug so gently on Robin's bushy black beard. You can see it in the way they lie on their backsides and stare at the ceiling and giggle. It's as if they've learned something deep and exciting about themselves.

"I'm me . . . I'm special . . . I can try."

"If I make a mistake, it's all right. I'll start over . . . I'll learn . . . I'll get better."

"Look at my friend. I'm helping him stand on his head. He's special, too."

"We're good. We're children. We're okay."

—Dan Zadra

Source: Dan Zadra, The little gymnast, *Young Athlete Magazine* (June 1976), 8. Reprinted with permission.

A Final Thought

Teaching educational gymnastics is, in the beginning, perhaps more difficult than teaching Olympic-style/artistic gymnastics. In Olympic gymnastics, the desired outcomes are clear—the teacher wants the children to learn to execute predetermined skills in specific ways. In educational gymnastics, the skills to be learned aren't predetermined, nor are they to be executed in one correct way. Instead, the teacher helps the children to improve their abilities to move in relation to the force of gravity, to learn self-confidence and self-reliance in interpreting tasks and determining the best ways to execute skills. Often it's more difficult for a teacher to share decisions with children than it is for the teacher to make the decisions. You'll find, however, that the process of sharing decisions in educational gymnastics can be exciting for you, the teacher, and rewarding for the children, regardless of their gymnastics abilities.

Summary

Because of the self-testing nature of gymnastics, most children are fascinated by the challenge of attempting to defy the force of gravity. It's important to distinguish educational gymnastics from Olympic/artistic gymnastics. Child-designed, educational gymnastics focuses on enhancing each child's ability to maneuver the body more effectively against the force of gravity. Predesigned, Olympic gymnastics empha-sizes the learning of specific gymnastics stunts, usually for the purpose of entering individual or team competition.

Many gymnastics movements are learned on the floor (mats) first and then practiced on apparatus. Gymnastics apparatus can be purchased, or equipment available in schools—such as tables, chairs, and benches—can be adapted to serve the same purposes.

Because of the increased likelihood of injury in gymnastics, it's important to establish an appropriate learning environment so children avoid games like Follow the Leader or I Dare You. Gymnastics tasks can be presented in ways that allow for individual differences, and this should be done so children aren't tempted to try movements they aren't ready for.

Reading Comprehension Questions

1. Why do children find balancing, transferring weight, and supporting weight on different body parts fascinating skills?
2. What is the difference in predesigned and child-designed gymnastics?
3. What are the purposes of Olympic/artistic gymnastics and educational gymnastics?
4. Why do we choose educational gymnastics for children in our physical education programs?
5. What are the two types of experiences in educational gymnastics? Describe each type.
6. What activities are taught at the different levels of skill proficiency for both types of educational gymnastics experiences?
7. How are children introduced to equipment?
8. Why are equipment arrangement, class organization, and selection of tasks extremely important in the teaching of educational gymnastics? Explain the significance of each in establishing the learning environment.
9. Why is it important to vary the task in gymnastics?
10. Why is teaching Olympic/artistic gymnastics somewhat easier than teaching educational gymnastics?

References/Suggested Readings

Boucher, A. 1978. Educational gymnastics is for everyone. *Journal of Physical Education and Recreation* 49(7): 48–50.

Cameron, W. McD., and P. Pleasance. 1971. *Education in movement—gymnastics*. Oxford, England: Basil Blackwell.*

Carroll, M. E., and D. R. Garner. 1984. *Gymnastics 7–11: A lesson-by-lesson approach*. London: Falmer Press.*

Holbrook, J. 1974. *Movement activity in gymnastics*. Boston: Plays.*

Holt/Hale, S. 2010. *On the move: Lesson plans to accompany Children Moving*. 8th ed. New York: McGraw-Hill.

Mauldon, E., and J. Layson. 1965, 1979. *Teaching gymnastics*. London: MacDonald & Evans.*

Morison, R. 1969. *A movement approach to educational gymnastics*. London: Dent.*

[NASPE] National Association for Sport and Physical Education. 2004. *Moving in the future: National standards for physical education*. 2nd ed. Reston, VA: National Association for Sport and Physical Education.

[NASPE] National Association for Sport and Physical Education. 2009. *Appropriate instructional practice guidelines for elementary school physical education*. 3rd ed. Reston, VA: National Association for Sport and Physical Education.

Nilges, L. M. 1997. Stages of content development in educational gymnastics. *Journal of Physical Education, Recreation and Dance* 68(3): 50–55.

Nilges, L. M. 1999. Refining skill in educational gymnastics: Seeing quality through variety. *Journal of Physical Education, Recreation and Dance* 70(3): 43–48.

Trevor, M. D. 1985. *The development of gymnastics skills*. Oxford, England: Basil Blackwell.

Werner, P. H. 2004. *Teaching children gymnastics: A developmentally appropriate approach*. 2nd ed. Champaign, IL: Human Kinetics.

Williams, J. 1974. *Themes for educational gymnastics*. London: Lepus Books.*

Zadra, D. 1976. The little gymnast. *Young Athlete Magazine* (June): 8.

*The foundation of educational gymnastics for children.

Teaching Games

The game is not sacred; children are.

—Jim Stiehl

Megan c.

Key Concepts

- The purpose of educational games in the elementary curriculum is for youngsters to become versatile, adaptable, and skillful games players in meaningful game situations.

- Games and sports are different; sports (in their institutionalized form) are inappropriate for children in physical education classes—games are appropriate.

- The content of games is largely based on the manipulative skills themes.

- Skill themes are applied to the context of games in three phases: invariant game skill experiences, dynamic game-like experiences, and games-playing experiences.

- In the invariant game skill phase, the focus is practicing isolated skills in an unchanging situation and the "game" takes the form of self-testing challenge activities.

- The dynamic game-like phase includes using skills in a changing (open) environment, combining skills, and developing tactics.

- The games-playing phase can be predesigned or child-designed and involve playing games that conform to all that is known about appropriate practices in physical education.

- Predesigned games playing experiences include: ready-made games, modified ready-made games, teacher-designed games. Child-designed games playing experiences include teacher/child-designed games and games designed by children.

- The process of teaching games-playing experiences includes whether or not the teacher should officiate, what to call the game, whether the game should be cooperative or competitive, what size and variety of equipment should be used, when to give feedback, what size the groups should be, and whether the game is truly a learning experience.

Initially in the skill theme approach, we focus on children acquiring the building blocks, the fundamentals of movement that provide the foundation for a lifetime of enjoyable physical activity. Over time, these movement fundamentals are studied and practiced in different contexts and settings. Traveling in straight, curved, and zig-zag pathways while dribbling a ball becomes the means to scoring a goal in either soccer or basketball, for example. The manipulative skill themes and movement concepts combined with the locomotor skill themes of traveling, chasing, fleeing, and dodging are largely applied in the context of games. As such, it is not the game that is important, but the application of skill themes in game settings. The "game" allows children to apply the skills they have learned in a dynamic environment. Our goal, then, is to provide games experiences for children in a way that is both challenging and appropriate for all students in our classes.

You might ask at this point, why include this chapter here since the types of experiences presented in this chapter are included in the skill theme chapters? What we have done in this chapter is let you see how the tasks, cues, and challenges presented in the skill theme chapters can be appropriately and developmentally used in the context of games so that children can apply the skills they have learned. The notion that children must do boring "practice" tasks before "playing the game" is exactly what skill themes is *not* about. Our thinking is that children should apply their newly acquired skills in developmentally appropriate activities throughout their learning. This chapter is designed to link the skill themes to the richness of game possibilities.

The Nature of Games

Games always seem to take us back. They take us back to our own childhood, when we played for hours on the school playground, in the streets, and in our neighborhood backyards. We played our made-up games; we played games with names like Red Rover and dodgeball that we had learned somewhere, and we played games that were called by "real" names such as baseball and football. Our games playing is steeped in tradition. And tradition can be good or bad. It is good when it enables us to pass on the best of what games have to offer—friendship, skill practice, teamwork, camaraderie, and the sheer excitement of playing.

Yet all too often, games playing seems to be the content area that traps us in the negative aspects of our tradition. We are trapped by the same tradition that brought us joy, trapped into thinking that what gave us excitement and satisfaction will also bring excitement and satisfaction to all of today's children. That entrapment lets us forget how we were usually the highly skilled players and how even we changed those games. We become so ingrained in the tradition that we forget how we made constant adjustments to all our games to make them "our own" and to meet our needs and the needs of others.

We made the games fit us rather than fitting ourselves to the games. Rarely, if ever, did we play on regulation fields with regulation equipment with the "right" number of players or by any rules other than our own. We had bricks for bases, four players on a baseball team, imaginary runners, and no gloves, and we played with whatever bat and ball we could find. We didn't have people sit out—they were all our friends. Yet somehow when we teach games to children, we tend to get caught in the rules we learned later in life, rules we played by as teenagers and adults. Our challenge is to help all children enjoy playing games that are theirs, not ours, and to help prepare them to want to play games forever—whatever those games may be. Our challenge is to make the games playing experience fit the child. Thus you will not find "games" in this chapter or in the skill theme chapters, but you will find experiences that allow children to apply their skills in a variety of developmentally appropriate games-playing situations.

Sports and games are different. The concept of a game holds a very different connotation for children than it does for adults. Children tend to view games as play-like, challenging, vigorous, skillful, and having rules. These activities may or may not look like adult versions of sports. Sports are designed primarily for adults, have standardized rules and procedures, and require a level of technical expertise to which children will never aspire. Games use the same basic skills as many sports but lack the standardized rules and procedures. Quite often, children call their game activities by names similar to those of standardized sports, and their games may use equipment similar to that of standardized sports; however, the "game" is quite different.

Games content occupies a large percentage of what is taught in many elementary physical education programs. Sport content should not. Sports happen after school. Games happen in school. Games may look like sports at times, but they are not. At no point in the elementary school curriculum should we see games being played with full-fledged sports rules. Never should there be full-sided teams, regulation rules, regulation fields, and children waiting their turns. We should see small-sided teams, modified fields, rules that don't stop the flow of the activity, and all children playing all the time. Never should the teacher be the pitcher. Understanding the difference between games and sports is critical to the reflective elementary school teacher: Games are appropriate elementary school content; sports in their common form are not. So what purpose should games serve?

So What's Wrong with Playing the Game?

This question invariably arises. And yes, there are multiple answers. Here are just a few:

- The actual time a child is involved in activity is minimal.
- The game is not appropriate for all children in the class—in terms of physical, psychological, or skill readiness.
- The equipment is not appropriate for all children.
- Children are eliminated from play (and these are the children who need to play the most).
- Children are spotlighted for their lack of skill (or their skillfulness).
- Winners and losers rate one child or group of children better than the others.
- When teams are chosen some children are publicly humiliated.
- The game is often just played to play a game; it is not linked to skill development.

The list can go on. For a more extensive discussion of the inappropriateness of playing "*the* game" see Neil Williams's "Hall of Shame" articles in *Journal of Physical Education, Recreation and Dance* (1992; 1994; 1996).

The Purpose of Games in the Elementary School

Our view of games is what can be called educational games (Rink 2008). The main focus of educational games is the development of skill and using it to play against an opponent (Department of Education and Science 1972). Educational games can be grouped in a variety of ways. Most often they are grouped by either the skill used or the tactics involved. If grouped by tactics, games are commonly classified as invasion, net, target, striking/fielding, and individual games (Almond 1986; Mauldon and Redfern 1969; Mitchell, Oslin, and Griffin 2003; Rink 2008). Alternatively, we develop games around the skill theme used, with the hope that those skills are then later customized for use in invasion, net, target, or striking games. The purpose of games in the elementary school is not to have youngsters' games participation confined to a few adult inventions with restricted, highly specialized skills, but to have children become versatile, adaptable, and skillful games players in meaningful game situations. Games experiences should help children apply the cognitive, affective, and psychomotor skills they have acquired in an effort to become competent and knowledgeable games players. Our responsibility is to provide experiences that allow this to happen and are appropriate for all children. As a result of participating in physical education games experiences, children should be excited about participating in games-playing activities on their own. Our purpose is not to develop elite athletes.

The National Association for Sport and Physical Education's *National Standards for Physical Education* (NASPE 2004) support the inclusion of games in elementary physical education. Box 30-1 lists the sample performance indicators specific to games in the elementary school curriculum.

In addition, *Appropriate Instructional Practice Guidelines for Elementary School Physical Education* (NASPE 2009) provides a useful analysis of the appropriateness of games in different situations. It is our responsibility as physical educators to teach developmentally appropriate games (Box 30-2).

So how do we teach games appropriate to the elementary school child? Essentially, there are two pieces to the elementary games puzzle: how skill themes are linked to games play (what is taught) and how it is taught (the process). The two are inextricably linked, but for clarity they are developed separately here.

Skill Themes in the Context of Games

The primary skill themes used in games are the manipulative themes combined with traveling, chasing, fleeing, and dodging. These themes are then integrated with almost every possible movement concept. For example, a player is asked to run while dribbling a ball, using changes in speed and direction to dodge an opponent, all the while being aware of where two other teammates and opponents are. Dance reconfigures skill themes and movement concepts into expressive movements; gymnastics uses skill themes to defy gravity; but games situations require players both to combine skills themes and use them tactically to outsmart and outplay an opponent. This requirement assumes ongoing tactical decision making. It is precisely these constructs that make it the most difficult to teach well. Thus, although many of us are most comfortable and familiar with games context, and although a game tends to be self-propelling once students grasp the basic concepts, the game context is complex and takes the same care in planning as gymnastics and dance.

We have found it easiest to think of applying the skill themes in the context of games in three phases: (1) invariant skill development, (2) dynamic game-like skill development, and (3) games playing. Games playing can be either predesigned or child designed. Historically, our teaching has largely been limited to the invariant skill development phase and then immediately moves to the games-playing phase. The middle phase, dynamic game-like skill development, which focuses on the combination of skills and acquisition of tactics, has often been omitted. We have done little to help children learn how to combine skills or learn tactics. The bottom line is this: Just because a skill is linked to a context area (games, dance, or gymnastics), this doesn't mean that by acquiring the skill one can use it appropriately in games, dance, or gymnastics settings. Teaching throwing and catching is one thing; learning how to throw and catch in a game situation is another. And although we talk about tactics, we haven't taught them (and children haven't learned them). We have now realized we need experiences

---

Box 30-1

Games and the *National Standards for Physical Education*

The diverse and personally meaningful nature of games is referenced in the National Association for Sport and Physical Education's *National Standards for Physical Education* (NASPE 2004) as sample performance outcomes under Standards 2, 3, 4, and 6.

The performance outcomes for Standard 2—"Demonstrates understanding of movement concepts, principles, strategies, and tactics as they apply to the learning and performance of physical activities"—state:

- Designs a new game incorporating at least two motor skills, rules, and strategies (3–5)*

The performance outcomes for Standard 3—"Participates regularly in physical activity"—state:

- Participates in organized sport activities provided through local community programs (3–5)*
- Participates in an intramural sports program provided by the school (3–5)*

The performance outcome for Standard 4—"Achieves and maintains a health-enhancing level of physical fitness"—states:

- Participates in a variety of games that increase breathing and heart rate (K–2)*

The performance outcome for Standard 5—"Exhibits responsible personal and social behavior that respects self and others in physical activity settings"—states:

- Takes seriously the role of teaching an activity or skill to his or her team (3–5)*

The performance outcome for Standard 6—"Values physical activity for health, enjoyment, challenge, self-expression, and/or social interaction"—states:

- Develops a dance (or game) that is personally interesting (3–5)*

*Grade-level guidelines for expected student learning.

Box 30-2

Appropriate and Inappropriate Physical Education Practices

Component: Productive Learning Experiences

Appropriate Practice

- Teachers select, design, sequence, and modify games to maximize the attainment of specific learning, fitness/skill enhancement, and enjoyment.
- Teachers modify the rules, regulations, equipment, and playing space to facilitate learning by children of varying abilities or to focus learning on particular games or skills components.

Inappropriate Practice

- Teachers use games with no obvious learning purpose or goal other than to keep children "busy, happy, and good."

Component: Maximizing Participation

Appropriate Practice

- Physical educators use small-sided games (1 v. 1; 2 v. 2; etc.) or mini-activities that allow students ample opportunity to participate.

Inappropriate Practice

- The teacher consistently uses only one ball for most activities that involve playing with a ball (e.g., soccer, softball). In game situations, most players rarely touch the ball.

Component: Competition and Cooperation

Appropriate Practice

- Physical educators develop learning experiences that assist students to understand the nature and the different kinds of competition. For example, the students may elect to keep score or play for skill practice in selected situations.
- Physical educators create a mastery learning environment that encourages students to compete against previous personal performances or against a criterion score. Children are given the opportunity to choose their competitive environment.

Inappropriate Practice

- Students are required to always keep score and participate in activities that publicly identify students as winners or losers (e.g., relay races, elimination tag).
- Teachers focus on the production of full-scale competition and limited skill instruction (e.g., teachers play 11 v. 11 soccer instead of modifying the game to 2 v. 2).

Source: National Association for Sport and Physical Education, *Appropriate instructional practice guidelines for elementary school physical education*, 3rd ed. (Reston, VA: National Association for Sport and Physical Education, 2009).

with all phases as an integrated whole (Griffin, Mitchell, and Oslin 2006; Rink 2010). Some skill development results from playing games, but game playing isn't the most efficient way for all children to improve the motor skills used in games. Thus it's useful to distinguish lessons in which the primary purpose is to improve skills (invariant and dynamic game-like skill phases) from lessons in which the primary purpose is to develop enthusiasm for and a playing knowledge of a variety of games (games-playing phase).

One implication teachers often draw from these three phases is that until children become exceedingly proficient at the dynamic game-like skill development phase and approach the proficiency level of skill development, they shouldn't play games. This contention is only partially true. Children should have games-playing experiences on a continuous basis, and instruction in skill and tactics should grow out of that play (Griffin, Mitchell, and Oslin 2006; Rink 2010). Isolating skill development and keeping children in invariant games-

playing experiences over a long period of time is just as inappropriate as teaching games playing before children possess the prerequisite skills. There is no clear line of demarcation for moving from one phase to another—it depends on students' development level. Children cannot reach high levels of skill (utilization or proficiency) without also being able to use that skill tactically. Similarly, children can only advance so far in the use of tactics before their skill level limits what they can choose to do (Rink 2010). Thus the phase of games experience offered is constantly changing, depending on what is to be taught and students' level.

A broad rule might be that children at the precontrol and early control levels of development are in the invariant skill-development phase (remember, youngsters will most often think of the challenges used in this phase as games) because they are trying to master a skill. Players at control and utilization levels are in the dynamic game-like phase. Utilization- and proficiency-level players will find games-playing challenges exciting and engaging. This does not mean you never return to invariant game skill phase (think of how many Olympic-caliber athletes practice basic skills for hours daily); it means you can gradually make the invariant skills more complex so they approach an increasingly open situation. As with the dynamic game-like phase, as students become more proficient players, you gradually extend the challenges used in the games playing phase to make it more complex while ensuring it remains developmentally appropriate.

The instructor who teaches children to play games successfully and effectively creates a variety of learning opportunities and situations in which children combine skills into game-like situations, as well as situations in which children play games and in which they practice skills. The children in such programs acquire a foundation of movement skills that enables them to participate successfully in a broad variety of games and sports. Once children have acquired the prerequisite game skills, sport becomes an attractive leisure-time alternative for them throughout their lives.

Invariant Game Skill Development Phase

The invariant skill development phase essentially involves practice of the isolated skills used in games in relatively closed or unchanging situations. In this phase experiences really don't look like games at all to adults—they look like skill development, which is what they are. The "games" focus is the potential use of the skill in the games-playing phase that will emerge later. The "game" experience here is that of a self-testing or challenge activity.

Learning experiences during the invariant skill development phase allow the students to gain control of an object using a specific motor pattern (Rink 2010). The experience is structured so the task is as identical as possible each time—the experience is invariant in that the child isn't required to predict the flight of a ball or the movement of an opponent, for example. At this point, refinement is the major emphasis (Belka 2000). For example, the task progression of Continuous Dribbling (Chapter 24, page 484) is an example of an invariant skill development experience. The challenges of, "Practice until you can dribble the ball five times without losing control of it" and "Say one letter of the alphabet for each time you dribble. Can you get to Z?" are perceived as "games" for the children performing them.

Such experiences are appropriate for a child who is at the precontrol or control level of skill proficiency and who would have difficulty executing a skill in a dynamic or open situation. As a child's proficiency in a skill increases, you can increase the difficulty of the tasks while retaining the relative predictability of the skill. For example, when a child is learning to throw a ball to hit a stationary target, you can increase the distance to the target. If the child is learning to run and leap over a low obstacle, increase the height of the obstacle.

When a child who isn't able to perform a basic skill consistently (precontrol level) is placed in a game that requires that skill and the ability to perform it in a dynamic or changing situation, the results are often counterproductive. A child in that situation often fails and becomes frustrated because of continuing inability to execute the prerequisite movements of the game. The child may then become a self-proclaimed, permanently terminated games player or a teenager or adult who vows to never again play in a game situation. And the other children are frustrated when an unskilled player interrupts the flow and their enjoyment of the game.

Trying to roll a ball through a target is an example of invariant game experience.

Dynamic Game-like Skill Development Phase

The second phase of applying skill themes in the context of games provides children with dynamic game-like experiences. These experiences may look and feel like games to children, but they are designed to teach the use of basic skills in a changing environment, combinations of skills, and simple offensive and defensive strategies. During these experiences, "games" are almost always small sided with restricted rules (two passes before a shot; no more than three dribbles before a pass) and limited space. They have clear learning goals and are permeated by stops and starts to refine skill and provide cues. In the beginning they are often cooperative; they develop into competitive games when children no longer find cooperative experiences challenging.

For example, the task of "Maintaining Possession While Dribbling and Passing" (Chapter 24, page 495) would be a dynamic game-like skill development experience. The task states that: "working in your group of three, two of you will dribble and pass while the third player tries to steal the ball. We'll rotate the interceptor every 2 minutes. Remember, you must either be dribbling or passing the ball. You may not hold it; no touching."

The children completing this task would view it as a game, while the purpose would be the development of passing and dribbling skills against a defender. The implication is that as the child slowly becomes more adept at using a motor skill or combination of motor skills, the child is simultaneously learning games-playing tactics to accompany the skill.

These three different and equally important aspects—the use of skills in a changing environment, the use of combinations of skills, and the development of game tactics—like games experiences themselves, are developmental but not hierarchical. In actual practice they intermingle greatly. Teaching skills in an open environment and teaching combinations of skills, as well as tactics, are critical to children learning to be competent games players. Yet it is precisely these experiences that are usually omitted.

Skills in an Open Environment

Research suggests that a child has little chance of actually being able to use basic skills in a changing or dynamic (game) environment unless he or she has first practiced them in an open, changing, and dynamic situation (Rovegno et al. 1995; Schmidt 1977). The skill acquired by a child who throws and catches a yarn ball may transfer minimally to the skill of throwing and catching used in, for example, baseball or basketball. For this reason, as soon as a child displays a minimum level of mastery in an invariant situation, it is necessary to create open situations that are progressively and increasingly complex and in which skills are used in combination as they occur in games-playing situations. For example, shooting a basket with no opposition is a skill different from shooting a basket after stopping a dribble or while being guarded by an opponent.

Young children's games rarely have game-playing qualities.

Combinations of Skills

When children are involved in dynamic game-like experiences, they need to be exposed to many experiences that relate to a variety of types of games. The infinite combinations of and linkages between skills has to be taught (Belka 2004a). Skill combinations might include dribbling and passing, shooting off a pass, receiving a pass and dribbling, receiving a pass and passing, and the like. Practicing skills in combinations is a critical and often neglected aspect of learning how to play games. It is critical because it is the transition between the two skills that makes the combination skillful and effective. To make the transition well, preparation for performing the second skill must occur while the first skill is being performed. For example, when young players are learning receiving and passing with the feet, they commonly receive the ball, stop, move into position to pass, and then pass. The skilled player moves the ball into position to pass as he or she is receiving it and passes without stopping. The difference is the transition. For players to be successful in games situations, they have to learn the transitions after they learn the skills. The focus at this point is on the transition, not on the two isolated skills. Tasks and cues can be developed that focus on the transition. For example, in the dribbling and passing scenario below, the task might be to pass in a moving triangle. Cues might be step into the pass as the ball is received and not to stop.

Tactics

The third critical and often neglected aspect that occurs in dynamic games skill experiences is learning offensive and defensive tactics that allow players to use the skills they have learned to outwit others. At this point, children shouldn't have to devote their attention to controlling objects. They should already know to how to do a skill; their focus is now on when to use that skill. Thus, it is wise to teach tactics when children's skills are at the utilization level. Tactics, like basic skills, can be taught and cued. One example might be learning to create space in an invasion-type activity using dribbling with the feet. In a two-on-two situation, students can play a game-like activity that asks them to provide a 45-degree passing angle for their partner. The focus is on the angle for passing and when to pass rather than the pass itself. As with skills, it is best to learn these activities in less complex situations first, then gradually increase the complexity. For example, the idea of passing angles can first be learned with no defense, then with a passive defense or in a two-on-one situation, and then with an aggressive defense. Complexity can be increased by adding play-

ers, boundaries, or scoring. The key aspect here is to add complexity very gradually. The utilization- and proficiency-level activities described in the manipulative skill theme chapters contain cues for simple offensive and defensive tactics.

During these experiences, many teachers use inquiry teaching to teach tactics (Doolittle and Girard 1991; Griffin, Mitchell, and Oslin 2006; Mitchell, Oslin, and Griffin 2003). For example, in a one-on-one situation of striking over a net, you are trying to teach the idea of hitting to open spaces and covering space. Children already can keep the ball going back and forth to each other. A teacher may stop the lesson and ask, "Where do you have to hit to make your opponent miss?" Answer: "Open space" (most often phrased as "where they are not"). "Where do you have to be to prevent your partner from having a lot of open space to which to hit?" Answer: "Home" (middle of court just behind center). Then the teacher sends them back to practice doing those things, even giving them points for doing those things. Tactics can also be taught through direct instruction, but it lends itself well to the inquiry approach as it is a cognitive concept as well as a physical ability.

> ### Tactic or Strategy—What Is the Difference?
>
> Tactics can be defined as an understanding of what to do during game-play situations or the problems players need to solve to be successful in game play (Mitchell, Oslin, and Griffin 2003). Tactics generally involve how to score and how to prevent scoring from occurring. Strategy, on the other hand, is an overall game plan and would include the use of a variety of tactics.

Games-Playing Phase

Unlike the two previous phases in which experiences were characterized by starts and stops, in the games-playing phase experiences are somewhat different as they allow children to focus on gaining knowledge and enthusiasm for playing a developmentally appropriate game while using the skills and tactics previously learned. The enjoyment and satisfaction derived from playing games frequently are products of playing a game without interruption. This does not mean the teacher does nothing during games-playing experiences. Observe the types of skill work that children need as they're playing games, and focus on those needs during later classes. Remember, games-playing

Dribbling a ball past a defender into a goal is a dynamic game-like skill experience.

Nettie Wilson (1976) conducted a study to determine the number of throwing, catching, and kicking opportunities in the game of kickball as played by third- and fourth-grade children under the direction of a classroom teacher. Her findings include the following:

- Less than half of the game was actually spent using the criterion skills.
- The average number of catches attempted in the kickball games was slightly more than two—35 percent of the children never caught the ball. Of the children who didn't catch the ball, 83 percent were girls.
- The average number of throws made in the kickball games, excluding those made by the pitcher and catcher, was slightly more than one—52 percent of the children never threw the ball at all during the entire game, and 67 percent of those who never threw the ball were girls.

experiences don't occur in every lesson; they are only a part of the total physical education program.

We have divided games playing experiences into predesigned experiences and child-designed experiences. Each has its own inherent strengths and weaknesses.

Predesigned Games-Playing Experiences

There are three types of predesigned games-playing experiences: ready-made, modified ready-made, and teacher designed.

Ready-Made Games   Ready-made games are those described in textbooks or learned in methods classes and taught to children without modification. The textbooks imply that such games will be appropriate, as well as interesting, for children. Brownies and Fairies; Duck, Duck, Goose; Red Rover; Four Square; and Steal the Bacon are well-known ready-made games.

Ready-made games are easy to teach because they require little preparation or teaching skill. The teacher selects a game and explains it to the children. When the children understand the game, they start to play, and the game continues until the lesson ends or the teacher changes the activity.

It has been our experience that few ready-made games are appropriate for all the children in a class. A few skilled children often dominate such games, whereas others are minimally involved, both physically and emotionally. Some (Belka 2004b) say these games should be discarded. However, you may occasionally encounter a situation in which a particular ready-made game is appropriate for a class or group of children. Usually, though, you'll find that although

many of the ideas in a ready-made game are worthwhile, you have to extensively modify the structure of the game to the abilities and interests of different children (Belka 2004b).

Modified Ready-Made Games   Modifying ready-made games requires greater planning and organizing ability. Yet by modifying a ready-made game, you can do much to make the game more appropriate for a particular class.

Both Rink (2010) and Stiehl, Morris, and Sinclair (2008) provide useful ideas for modifying ready-made games. The teacher can change the rules (e.g., allow two tries instead of only one); the equipment used (e.g., larger and lighter); the number of players involved (generally, it's best to decrease the number); the playing area (e.g., larger or smaller); or the skills involved (e.g., throwing instead of striking). Many teachers modify

When I first started teaching, I was looking for games that were recommended for first-grade children and did not require a great deal of game skill. Brownies and Fairies, a simple running and chasing game, was prescribed in one text as appropriate for six-year-olds. The first time the game was played, two children fell down and bloodied their knees when they tried to run in a crowd of children. They could run by themselves without falling. But when they were placed in a dynamic situation that involved both running and dodging, they were unsuccessful. They probably forgot that experience many years ago—once their knees healed. I haven't.

one aspect of the game at a time until it provides an experience appropriate for the children's skill level (see Table 30.1). The task of Volleying Game: Modified Teacher Designed Game in Chapter 24 (page 481) is an example of a modified ready-made game. A good rule to follow is to change or eliminate anything that impedes or slows the flow of a game.

During the lesson, you may use the same teaching skills required to teach a ready-made game—explaining the game and intervening only when that's necessary to keep the game going. Evaluating the game is more complex. You'll have to decide, after observing the children, whether the game should be modified further or is satisfactory as currently structured.

Teacher-Designed Games Sometimes a teacher can't find a ready-made game appropriate for a particular class, and modifications of ready-made games don't seem effective. In such a situation, the teacher may design a game that satisfies a specific goal. Designing a game places a greater demand on a teacher's creative abilities than do either of the game lesson structures already discussed.

The teacher needs to understand the children's skill abilities and interests and be able to use this knowledge to design a game form that the children will find interesting and enjoyable. For example, a teacher could design a game to focus on striking a ball with a bat. The object would be to strike a pitched ball and then run around a cone and back before the other players catch or collect the ball and touch the home base with the ball. If the children used rather narrow

boundaries and played in small groups, they would get more striking, throwing, and catching opportunities than the standardized nine-per-side version of softball provides. The teacher could design the game to be played by two teams or design it so each child goes back "to the field" once she or he hits the ball and runs around the cone. Punting for Distance and Accuracy: Punt-Over (see Chapter 22, page 432) is an example of a teacher-designed game. Once you've created the game, the teaching skills used are virtually identical to the skills needed to teach a modification of a prede-signed game.

Child-Designed Games

Each of the three game lesson structures in prede-signed games places the responsibility for selecting or designing a game on the teacher. One advantage of these games structures is that the children spend most of the time—once the game has been explained and organized—playing the game. But the children don't contribute to the design of the game, nor do they have anything to say about whether they would like to continue playing the game as is or change the game to make it better. The previous three game designs are direct instructional approaches; the following two child-designed game structures, by contrast, involve the children in the design of the game. They would be classified as inquiry or child-designed approaches and require more advanced teaching skills. (See Chapter 10 for a discussion of instructional approaches and the skills necessary to use each.)

Table 30.1 Game Aspects That Can Be Modified

Aspect	Possible Changes			
Players	Reduce the number of players	Increase the number of players	Mix skill levels	Combine like skill levels
Purpose	To practice skill	To practice combined skills	To practice strategy	To play games
Player Movement	Restrict the movement of some players	Allow some players to move		
Equipment	Use smaller equipment	Use larger equipment	Use lighter equipment	Use heavier equipment	Use more (or less) equipment
Organization	Define the organization— circle, etc.	Let the organization be random		
Space	Increase the space	Decrease the space	Make the space long and narrow	Make the space short and wide
Rules	Omit rules that restrict the flow	Add rules to enhance opportunities		
Skills	Reduce the number of skills involved			

Child-designed games include those designed by the teacher and children working together and those designed by the children with teacher support and structure.

Teacher/Child-Designed Games

When the children and the teacher design a game together, the teacher presents the purpose of the game and the restrictions. The children and the teacher then work cooperatively to decide the rules, scoring, and equipment to be used. The whole class plays in small groups.

You'll find it's wise to stipulate that once the game has begun, only the team with the ball (or the advantage) can stop play to suggest a change. (Unless the children are restrained by this rule, they're likely to stop the game and suggest a change every time the other team gains an advantage.) After a brief discussion of the proposed change, the class or group votes, with the majority decision prevailing. If a rule needs to be made to ensure safety, offer solutions to be voted on or ask the children to propose a solution.

One example of a teacher/child-designed game is Magladry Ball, which the children named after their school. The teacher was concerned about the children's inability to travel and pass a ball or other object to a teammate who was also traveling, particularly when an opponent attempted to intercept or prevent the pass from being made. After describing the purpose of the game, the teacher imposed two restrictions: Children couldn't touch each other; and once the ball (object) touched the ground, it was automatically in the possession of the team that didn't touch it immediately before the object hit the ground. The object of the game was to throw the ball (beanbag, flying disc) through a hoop suspended from a goal post by a rope at either end of a field. Once the game began, children made decisions about how long one child could remain in possession of the ball (object); what type of ball (object) to play the game with; boundaries, violations, and penalties; and scoring.

Teacher/child-designed games evolve slowly, and you may spend several lessons creating games children are excited about and enjoy playing. Once the time and effort to create a game have been spent, the children will want to have opportunities to play it.

The instructor in a teacher/child-designed game serves as a facilitator, enhancing and expanding ideas rather than imposing personal ideas on the children. The teacher helps the children modify the games, offers suggestions, and manages a group of charged-up children who are eager to get the game going again.

This isn't an easy task, and it often takes some time to master this approach.

Games Designed by Children

The underlying assumption of ready-made games, modified ready-made games, teacher designed games, and teacher/child-designed games is that the entire class is playing the same game, in small groups. In child-designed games, however, we assume that many games are being played simultaneously and that few, if any, are identical. Such an environment is a far more complex one in which to teach (Rovegno and Bandhauer 1994). The teacher is assisting groups of children to develop different games and is also responsible for observing a number of different games and assisting or staying away when appropriate.

Games designed by children have some definite advantages. Children in groups of similar skill ability (given a choice, children typically choose to be with others of similar ability) are allowed to design games that are interesting and exciting to them. These may be cooperative or competitive, active or passive, depending on the children's intent.

Initially, children need help in creating their own games. Teachers who've met with success in using child-designed games have found that in the beginning it's helpful to suggest a structure for the game—that is, the purposes, boundaries, and rules (Rovegno and Bandhauer 1994). For example, the teacher may say, "Make up your own striking game. There may be up to four people in the group. All of you must play at once; there's to be no waiting in line. And the space can be no larger than 15 feet by 15 feet." The teacher can also help the children organize the game by asking them to identify their rules, either verbally or in writing (Figure 30.1). Three child-designed games for volleying and dribbling are illustrated in Figure 24.6 (page 476).

As children learn to make decisions about their games, you can decrease the amount of imposed structure. If children are to make significant and worthwhile decisions about their game, you must stay out of as many decisions as possible; this is just as important as providing proper initial guidance. Even if you're certain some idea won't work, it's no longer your role to tell them so (except in the case of safety). They'll find out soon enough.

You may consider it a disadvantage that some children take a great deal of time to create games. Children who've had little experience in creating their own games may spend as much as half of a lesson seriously working out the way they want a game to be played, perhaps without ever actually playing the game. But you'll find that as students gradually

Gym

Our group plays soccer. Our Rules are: If the ball hits the curb and bounces in it's still in play. But if the ball hits the curb and bounces over it is out of play. There are three people on each team. Two people on each team go out on the field and try to score. The other two people stay back and play goalie. The goalie is the only person that can use his hands If the ball hits the (goal post) cone and bounces in it is good. But if the ball hits the cone and and bounces out it is No good. We use one soccer ball and four cones The game starts off when a person on any team drops the ball and its in play. The object of the game is to score on your opponent.

Figure 30.1 Example of a child-designed game—sixth grade.

become more adept at creating games, playing time increases substantially.

Most children enjoy participating in the creation of their own games. But the children must be ready— they must be able to function successfully in a small group (two or three is an appropriate number) when

I would like to contrast the richness of children's natural play with the stultifying rigidity of play that is organized by adults. No better example can be found than that of the Little League, for what boys, left to their own devices, would ever invent such a thing? How could they make such a boneheaded error as to equate competition with play? Think of the ordinary games of boys—in sandlots, fields, parks, even stickball in the street. They are expansive and diverse, alternately intense and gay, and are filled with events of all kinds. Between innings the boys throw themselves on the grass. They'll wrestle, do handstands, turn somersaults. They hurl twigs and stones at nearby trees, and yell at the birds that sail by. A confident player will make up dance steps as he stops a slow grounder. If an outfielder is bored, he does not stand there pulling up his pants and thumping his glove, but plays with the bugs in the grass, looks at the clouds. . . . There is almost always a dog on the field, and no part of the competition is gayer or more intense than that between the boys and the dog, who when he succeeds in snapping up their ball, leads them off in a serpentine line that is all laughter and shouts, the dog looking back over his shoulder and trotting with stiff legs, until finally he is captured and flattens his ears as they take back their ball. No one has forgotten the score or who was at bat. The game goes on. The game goes on until darkness ends it, and the winners can hardly be distinguished from the losers, for by then everyone is fumbling the ball and giggling and flopping on the grass.

—GEORGE DENNISON, *The Lives of Children* (1969)

Children enjoy playing a self-created game.

Box 30-3

Helping Children Create Their Own Games

1. Limit group size to six or less.
2. Provide structure:

   - Identify the equipment that can be used.
   - Identify the skills and movements to be included.
   - Identify the space each group may use and have them mark the space.

3. Allow adequate time:

   - Provide time for thinking and creativity, but then indicate a time needed to start play.
   - Provide time for "sorting out" the game as they play.
   - Provide time for playing.

4. Create accountability:

   - Have children name their game.
   - Have children identify the rules.
   - Have children teach others.
   - See if children are able to and want to play the game another day.
   - Have children write their game down.

playing a game they know before they can begin to design games (see Chapter 10 for more detail on the skills a teacher and the children need in order to implement child-designed activities). Some teachers, even of younger children, can use child-designed games from the time they begin teaching and have exciting, successful lessons. But when a teacher—even one who believes in the philosophy represented by child-designed games—tries to have children design their own games before the children (and the teacher) are ready, the outcome can be a disaster. Helping children design their own games is skill in-and-of itself. We have learned from experience (the hard way) that just telling children to make up their own game without any structure or guidance leads to chaos and an unproductive experience. Start with the design you think is most appropriate to a class and situation, and proceed from there. See Box 30-3 for suggestions on helping children create their own games.

The ecology of the particular teaching situation determines which game design is best. When selecting a games-playing lesson design for a class, consider the purpose for playing the game, the skills required, the children's interests and abilities, the playing area and equipment available, and your skills as a teacher. We try very carefully to match the skills required in games-playing phase to the children's skills. Nothing is as counterproductive as having children participate in games for which they don't possess the prerequisite skills. The teacher who has closely assessed the children's skill level can discover and/or design well-matched games-playing situations to ensure the children's success and pleasure.

The Process of Teaching Games-Playing

The type of experience selected for a class during the game-playing phase is the first critical aspect with respect to the process of teaching games. The fundamental instructional pieces discussed in the following paragraphs, however, are paramount to making the type of game selected "work" for a group. If your choice of game is perfect for a class and then the instructional aspects contradict your game choice, the class climate negates the content.

It is hard to modify the content without modifying the instruction, yet we have seen it done. It is our thought that for the games playing to be effective, instruction has to be modified as well. Teaching games-playing experiences that meet children's developmental needs is not as simple as it initially appears. For many of us, game playing is so intertwined with deeply imbedded sport experiences that it is difficult to "see differently." To see differently we must focus on the type of games-playing experience we choose, the equipment used, what we call the game, the number of players involved, our role as an official or teacher, when to provide feedback, whether the game should be cooperative or competitive, and the whether the experience is truly a learning experience. It is only then that we truly start to look at the child first and the game second.

Games Equipment   The equipment used to play games most certainly affects the quality and difficulty of the game (Graham 2008). Large, regulation-size sports equipment slows the play and promotes the use of incorrect skills. In recent years, equipment manufacturers have begun to design equipment for children: foam paddles, balls, and hockey sticks are three examples. Smaller, lighter, more colorful balls that don't hurt reduce the fear of catching. Basketball goals that can be adjusted to multiple heights (not just one or two) allow all children to be able to shoot at an appropriate basket. The bottom line is this: Adult equipment is almost always inappropriate for elementary school children. Make sure the equipment matches the child.

> *A true game is one that frees the spirit—the true game is the one that arises from the players themselves.*
>
> —PETER OPIE AND IONA OPIE, *Children's Games in Street and Playground* (1969)

The Name of the Game By calling a game by the name of the sport its skills are usually associated with, we effectively limit children's options. The skilled children think they have to play by the rules of the sport, and the unskilled unconsciously evaluate themselves against some external standard, whether or not they really know much about the sport. As a result, some children are disenfranchised and others are frustrated. We have found children are much more creative and open in their games playing if we refer to the experience by a new name or by the name of the skill. This is why in the index you will find games linked to the skill theme they are used to develop but not listed separately by their name.

Group Size To many, there is a "right" number of players for a game. Because of our conscious or unconscious sport orientation, the "right" number of players is often the number of players associated with the sport in which the skill is most commonly used. And because predesigned games are usually designed for entire classes, they often call for 15, 20, or more players. Rarely does either of the preceding scenarios contain the "right" number of players for games appropriate to the elementary school setting. Games experiences should never involve more players than can be active at any one time, or so many that the flow of the game is slowed. We have found this usually means four to six (and maybe eight) players as a maximum in any games experience. Choose the "right" number of players for the children's experience—some have even said the "right" group size is equal to the grade level, e.g., a group size of four for fourth grade. The small group size we recommend implies that more than one game will be played simultaneously. Having several games going on at one time, however, can be uncomfortable for many of us. If this is true for you, we suggest you begin slowly. Start with a class you are confident with, and have only two games play concurrently. As you feel more confident, gradually add more games. Amazingly, more games actually decreases many potential management problems. Because more children are actively and appropriately involved in playing and are spending less time waiting or otherwise unengaged, the amount of off-task behavior is substantially reduced.

To Ref or Not to Ref? We do not believe in officiating children's games. Officiating does several things that detract from the ultimate value of the games-playing experience. First, officiating places the responsibility for coming to decisions about the process of the game on the teacher, taking away all responsibility and decision making from the children. The end result is that they can "blame the teacher" for what happened and avoid learning to cooperate and decide for themselves. Second, officiating takes the teacher out of the teaching role and limits the teacher's ability to provide feedback and instruction—our primary goal. Third, a teacher can only be in one place. If we officiate, only one game can be occurring; this means that all the children aren't active and that more than likely we have created an inappropriate games environment.

We have been very successful in letting children "call" their own games. They not only adapt the rules to fit their situation but also develop decision-making and cooperation skills. The flow of the game is also generally more continuous; they stop only when they need to.

Provide Feedback or Not? Take your cue from the children in determining when to provide feedback. A lull in the game, a water break, the end of class, or other natural interruption provides an opportunity to check with the children and offer guidance if needed. Try not to stop or interfere in the children's games to

THE FAMILY CIRCUS.   **By Bil Keane**

6-28
Copyright 1978.
The Register and Tribune
Syndicate, Inc.

"We made it up ourselves. You don't need nine guys on a team, or grownups, or uniforms. . . . It's like baseball, only better!"

teach skills, unless the game has become unsatisfying and boring because of lack of ability. Adults prefer not to be interrupted during a game, even by someone who wants to provide feedback. Children share this feeling, and teachers must respect it if they want to create positive attitudes toward games.

Cooperative or Competitive? Score or No Score? Much has been written about cooperative games versus competitive games. Competition is not inherently bad for children; inappropriate competition is. Children should never be forced to compete against another child until they are ready, and all children are not ready at the same time. Therefore to have an entire class playing by the same rules of competition disenfranchises many children. We have found two guidelines that work for us. First, let children choose whether or not they want to be in a competitive situation. If there are multiple small-sided games occurring simultaneously, then some could be competitive and some cooperative. Second, cooperative experiences always precede competitive experiences. It is only when cooperative experiences are no longer challenging that competitive experiences are appropriate (Rink 2010). Children, when left to their own devices, almost always follow this maxim.

Cooperation and competition also impact several other aspects of physical education classes. Research clearly indicates that children learn best in a mastery climate focusing on cooperation, hard work, learning, and task mastery (Biddle 1999; Standage, Duda, and

Ntoumanis 2003). On the other hand, learning is diminished in classes where children are compared to each other, where there is a focus on competition between children, and where mistakes are punished. In addition, there is recent evidence that during cooperative, nonelimination games, children accrue more moderate and vigorous physical activity than in elimination games (Bruggeman et al. 2008).

Learning Experience or Not?

Judy Rink (2010) suggests four criteria for a physical education experience designed for learning outcomes: (1) the experience has the potential to improve motor skills; (2) there is maximum participation for all children; (3) the experience is at the appropriate experiential level of all children; and (4) there is the possibility of integrating cognitive, psychomotor, and affective learning. We suggest that these criteria are good ones to use in assessing the games-playing experiences designed and implemented in our programs. If our games-playing experiences do not meet these criteria, they should probably be modified.

After-School Sport Programs

Many children in your classes may be participating in various sport programs. Often these children are very skilled—many are at the proficiency level of the skills involved in their sport—and so provide an interesting dimension to games lessons. We have found that by using small groups for games playing experiences, intratask variation, and teaching by invitation, these students can be challenged in our classes just as any other student can be. For example, if students are allowed to design their own game, they can (and will) make it more or less competitive to meet their needs.

Child Development and Games

The research on child development (Piaget 1962) and the development of reasoning (Kohlberg and Mayer 1972) further supports placing children in game situations designed to accommodate their skills, interests, and abilities. For moral and social development and growth to occur, a motivation to change must exist. This motivation requires both developmental readiness and opportunity (Brustad and Parker 2005). Game situations provide an attractive opportunity for children to develop their social skills and reasoning when the situations are developmentally appropriate. Before the age of 8, children are in the egocentric stage. They have a personal conception of reality; the world centers

---

Competition/Cooperation

Some children love to compete; others prefer (and seem to learn better in) games that encourage cooperation. We attempt to respect each child's preference by giving choices and trying never to place an entire class in a competitive situation. Instead, we let children choose between two or more games or ask them to make up their own games. The teachers heighten or lessen the degree of competition. Teachers who constantly shout out the score, post team win-and-loss records, and reward the winners (thereby punishing the losers) place an emphasis on competition for which some children aren't ready. If you don't believe us, talk to the thousands of adults who were unskilled as children and yet were placed in highly competitive situations. They can describe, in vivid detail, the feelings of being picked last, shouted at for dropping a ball, and ridiculed for "letting the team down." Such distasteful experiences usually have lasting and negative influences on the individual's willingness to participate in sports.

around self. There's no sense of obligation to rules, no desire to check for accuracy. "I" am right at all times. Whatever meets the needs at the present time is what is true. Following rules is fine if it serves the purpose at the time. The concept of cheating doesn't exist because rules constantly change to fit the child's needs. At this stage, the child feels that everyone completely understands him or her and is in agreement with what the child wants. Imagine placing 25 youngsters in a traditional group game when each child thinks he or she is completely understood and in agreement with all!

Piaget (1962) described the game play of the young child (from the child's viewpoint) as a situation in which everyone plays the game as each understands it, with no concern for "checking" on others. Nobody loses and everybody wins at the same time because the purpose is to have fun (Piaget and Inhelder 1969).

Children between 8 and 11 have a strong social need. To be a part of the group, to belong, is extremely important to children in the upper elementary years. In the early phases of this stage, however, children still have strong egocentric tendencies. Group interaction is desired, but they also desire to cling to the comfortable self-centered view. The earlier "absolute" view is now confronted with the viewpoints of others, viewpoints perhaps not in agreement with one's own. How many children do we see get upset and leave the game when things don't go their way or when they're asked to sacrifice themselves for the good of the team? Cooperative game situations with small groups of children can facilitate establishing the child as a member of the group and foster acceptance of differing points of view.

Students entering the higher level of cognitive development, ages 11 and above, begin to create strategies and mentally test their abilities. They enjoy group activity and respect the physical and mental skills of others in the game situation. The game no longer rules the group; the game is made for the use of the group—to be adapted as needed.

A Final Thought

Much has been written about the inappropriateness of adult versions of sports for children (Orlick and Zitzelsberger 1996; Smoll and Smith 1996). The child who seeks sport experiences can find them outside the school. Most communities in the United States offer adequate sports at the middle and high school levels, in after-school programs, and in programs sponsored by youth agencies.

Tyson-Martin (1999) has challenged us to refocus, recycle, reorganize, and restructure games for children. It seems an appropriate challenge to take. Physical educators have a responsibility to provide instruction for all children, to help them become skillful games players who enjoy participating in games and are eager to play games on their own time. We must do more than produce a few good athletes. In a successful physical education program, all the children improve their games-playing skills and are eager and excited about playing games. The purpose of this chapter has been to provide an overview of the teaching of games in the elementary school. See Box 30-4 for more resources on children's games.

Box 30-4

Resources for the Teaching of Children's Games

Belka, D. 2000. Developing competent games players. *Teaching Elementary Physical Education* 11(3): 6–7.

Belka, D. 2004a. Combining and sequencing games skills. *Journal of Physical Education, Recreation and Dance* 75(4): 23–27.

Belka, D. 2004b. Substituting developmental for traditional games in elementary physical education. *Teaching Elementary Physical Education* 15(4): 21–24.

Doolittle, S., and K. Girard. 1991. A dynamic approach to teaching games in elementary physical education. *Journal of Physical Education, Recreation and Dance* 62(4): 57–62.

Hastie, P. (2010). *Student-designed games.* Champaign, IL: Human Kinetics.

Mauldon, E., and H. Redfern. 1969. *Games teaching.* London: MacDonald and Evans.

Mitchell, S., J. Oslin, and L. Griffin. 2003. *Sport foundations for elementary physical education: A tactical games approach.* Champaign, IL: Human Kinetics.

Stiehl, J., G. S. Morris, and C. Sinclair. 2008. *Teaching physical activity: Change, challenge, choice.* Champaign, IL: Human Kinetics.

Todorovich, J. R., J. P. Fox, S. Ryan, and S. W. Todorovich, S. W. 2008. A dynamic-rules game for teaching striking-and fielding game tactics. *Journal of Physical Education, Recreation, and Dance* 79(5), 26–33.

Summary

Because games playing is the context with which we are most comfortable, we find games easier to teach than dance or gymnastics. This deceptive ease, however, is an educationally unacceptable rationale for curricular decision making. Games in the elementary school allow children to become versatile, adaptable, and skillful games players in meaningful game situations. Thus teachers need to provide children with developmentally appropriate experiences that lead to the acquisition of games-playing skills. In the context of games, skill themes are developed in three phases: (1) invariant skill development, (2) dynamic game-like skill development, and (3) games playing. The invariant games phase focuses on skill acquisition in a predictable, closed environment in which the movement is essentially the same each time. The dynamic game-like skill development phase requires children to use skills in a changing environment and to use combinations of skills and tactics in situations that resemble those found in games-playing experiences. The games-playing phase is designed to expose children to the joy and satisfaction that can be found in games. In these experiences children use skill and tactics in an attempt to outwit an opponent. This phase is divided into pre-designed games and child designed games. The pre-designed games include ready-made games, modified ready-made games, and teacher designed games, while child-designed games incorporate both teacher/child designed games and games designed by children.

Several variables affect the process of teaching games to children. The type of game selected can influence the success of the experience. Other factors to be considered when teaching games to children are the equipment used, the number of children in the game, the role of the teacher as an official, whether the game is cooperative or competitive, when to provide feedback, the name of the game, and whether the game provides the opportunity to learn.

The role of games in elementary physical education is to provide all children the chance to be successful in playing in dynamic, unpredictable situations that challenge them to outwit their opponents. It is the teacher's responsibility to design game experiences that meet the needs of all students.

Reading Comprehension Questions

1. What is meant by the statement, "It is not the game that is important but the use of skills in game settings"?
2. What is the purpose of educational games in the elementary school? How does that differ from more traditional approaches to games?
3. How can games be classified, and what classification is used here?
4. What are the characteristics of developmentally appropriate and inappropriate games for children? Identify one activity that you know is appropriate and one that is inappropriate.
5. Skill themes in games are developed through three phases. How does each phase differ and provide an example from one of the skill theme chapters.
6. What happens when we place children in dynamic situations before they're ready?
7. When is it appropriate to move children from the invariant skill development phase to a dynamic game-like skill development phase? Why is such movement necessary?
8. How is the role of the teacher different between the dynamic skill-development phase and the games-playing phase?
9. What is the difference between predesigned games and child-designed games? From your own experience identify a game that fits each category.
10. Using the ready-made predesigned game you identified in the previous question, modify it into a game that is more appropriate for a class of 25 control-level children.
11. How would you go about helping children design a striking with paddles game?
12. What factors should be taken into account in the process of teaching in the games-playing phase?
13. Why do we recommend small group sizes and multiple games in physical education class?

References/Suggested Readings

Almond, L. 1986. Reflecting on themes: A games classification. In *Rethinking games teaching*, ed. R. Thorpe, D. Bunker, and L. Almond, 71–72. Loughborough, England: University of Technology.

Belka, D. 2000. Developing competent games players. *Teaching Elementary Physical Education* 11(3): 6–7.

Belka, D. 2004a. Combining and sequencing games skills. *Journal of Physical Education, Recreation and Dance* 75(4): 23–27.

Belka, D. 2004b. Substituting developmental for traditional games in elementary physical education. *Teaching Elementary Physical Education* 15(4): 21–24.

Biddle, S. 1999. The motivation of pupils in physical education. In *Learning and teaching in physical education*, ed. C. Hardy and M. Mawer, 105–25. Philadelphia: Falmer Press.

Bruggeman, K., D. Dzewaltowski, T. Behrens, and A. Jager. 2008. The effects of elimination and non-elimination games on physical activity and psychosocial responses in children. Paper presented at the Annual Meeting of the American College of Sports Medicine. Indianapolis, IN.

Brustad, R., and M. Parker. 2005. Enhancing positive youth development through sport and physical activity. *Psychologia* 39: 75–93.

Dennison, G. 1969. *The lives of children.* New York: Random House.

Department of Education and Science. 1972. *Movement: Physical education in the primary years.* London: Her Majesty's Stationery Office.

Doolittle, S., and K. Girard. 1991. A dynamic approach to teaching games in elementary physical education. *Journal of Physical Education, Recreation and Dance* 62(4): 57–62.

Graham, G. 2008. *Teaching children physical education: Becoming a master teacher.* 3rd ed. Champaign, IL: Human Kinetics.

Griffin, L., S. Mitchell, and J. Oslin. 2006. *Teaching sports concepts and skills: A tactical games approach.* 2nd ed. Champaign, IL: Human Kinetics.

Kolhberg, L., and R. Mayer. 1972. Development as the aim of education. *Harvard Educational Review* 42(4): 449–96.

Mauldon, E., and H. Redfern. 1969. *Games teaching.* London: MacDonald and Evans.

Mitchell, S., J. Oslin, and L. Griffin. 2003. *Sport foundations for elementary physical education: A tactical games approach.* Champaign, IL: Human Kinetics.

[NASPE] National Association for Sport and Physical Education. 2004. *Moving into the future: National standards for physical education.* 2nd ed. Reston, VA: National Association for Sport and Physical Education.

[NASPE] National Association for Sport and Physical Education. 2009. *Appropriate instructional practice guidelines for elementary physical education.* 3rd ed. Reston, VA: National Association for Sport and Physical Education.

Opie, P., and I. Opie. 1969. *Children's games in street and playground.* New York: Oxford University Press.

Orlick, T. D., and L. Zitzelsberger. 1996. Enhancing children's sport experiences. In *Children and youth in sport: A biopsychosocial perspective*, ed. R. E. Smith and F. L. Smoll, 330–37. New York: McGraw-Hill.

Piaget, J. 1962. *Play, dreams, and imitation in childhood.* New York: Norton.

Piaget, J., and B. Inhelder. 1969. *The psychology of the child.* New York: Basic Books.

Rink, J. 2008. *Designing the physical education curriculum.* New York: McGraw-Hill.

Rink, J. 2010. *Teaching physical education for learning.* 6th ed. New York: McGraw-Hill.

Rovegno, I., and D. Bandhauer. 1994. Child-designed games: Experience changes teachers' conceptions. *Journal of Physical Education, Recreation and Dance* 65(6): 60–63.

Rovegno, I., R. Skonie, T. Charpenel, and J. Sieving. 1995. Learning to teach critical thinking through child-designed games. *Teaching Elementary Physical Education* 6(1): 6–7, 15.

Schmidt, R. 1977. Schema theory: Implications for movement education. *Motor Skills: Theory into Practice* 2: 36–48.

Smoll, F. L., and R.E. Smith. 1996. Competitive anxiety: Sources, consequences, and intervention strategies. In *Children and youth in sport: A biopsychosocial perspective*, ed. R. E. Smith and F. L. Smoll, 359–80. New York: McGraw-Hill.

Standage, M., J. Duda, and N. Ntoumanis. 2003. A model of contextual motivation in physical education: Using constructs from self-determination and achievement goal theories to predict physical activity intentions. *Journal of Educational Psychology* 95(1): 97–110.

Stiehl, J., G. S. Morris, and C. Sinclair. 2008. *Teaching physical activity: Change, challenge, choice.* Champaign, IL: Human Kinetics.

Tyson-Martin, L. 1999. The four "Rs" of enhancing elementary games instruction. *Journal of Physical Education, Recreation and Dance* 70(7): 36–40.

Williams, N. 1992. The physical education hall of shame. *Journal of Physical Education, Recreation and Dance* 63(6): 57–60.

Williams, N. 1994. The physical education hall of shame: Part II. *Journal of Physical Education, Recreation and Dance* 65(2): 17–20.

Williams, N. 1996. The physical education hall of shame: Part III: Inappropriate teaching practices. *Journal of Physical Education, Recreation and Dance* 67(8): 45–48.

Wilson, N. 1976. The frequency and patterns of selected motor skills by third- and fourth-grade girls and boys in the game of kickball. Unpublished master's project, University of Georgia, Athens.

Adapting the Content for Diverse Learners

Movement is learning; movement is life. No matter how disabled a child, movement can make a difference in his/her life. Movement can help a child become oneself. If a child can move, he/she can become more a master of the environment rather than being controlled by it.

—Jane R. Evans (1980)

Key Concepts

- With recent increases in the diversity of America's school-children, physical education teachers must be prepared to provide a quality physical education experience to students with a wide variety of abilities, needs, and interests.

- Inclusion is the philosophy that diverse learners—including those with differences in mental and physical ability, skill level, fitness levels, gender, culture, language, religion, class, and physical characteristics—are able to learn and to develop skills in the regular physical education program.

- It is physical education teachers' responsibility to learn about the unique needs of each diverse learner and the implications for physical education.

- By changing basic activity components and providing students choice among appropriate tasks, the teacher can challenge all students in ways that provide maximum opportunities for learning and development of their personal potential.

- Physical education is a direct, required service for all children with disabilities under the Individuals with Disabilities Education Act (IDEA) of 1990.

- The physical education teacher is a critical member of the IEP Team and should be in attendance at all meetings that involve students he or she teaches in physical education.

- It is at the IEP Team meeting that goals are established for the child with disabilities and the environment most conducive to meeting those goals is identified.

- A top-down ecological model provides the template for successful inclusion of children with disabilities: determine critical skills, analyze the existing program, and design modifications.

- Zero exclusion is the standard for all children in physical education.

As a group of second graders enters the gym for class on the first day of school, Mrs. Thomas, the physical education teacher, notices one child rolling his wheelchair through the door and hears two other children speaking an unfamiliar language. Mrs. Thomas's heart begins to beat a little faster, and even though she has several years of teaching experience, she feels a rush of self-doubt and begins to question her ability to meet the needs of all her students.

Although this may seem like an unusually diverse group, it is more common now than ever before to find physical education classes across the country with increasingly diverse groups of students. In addition to more than 6 million special education students, approximately 45 percent of the total public school population is minority students (NCES 2010). By the year 2020, more than two-thirds of the school population will be African American, Asian, Hispanic, or Native American, with Hispanic youths representing over 20 percent of the total 5- to 17-year-old population (Meece and Kurtz-Costes 2001). Furthermore, physical education teachers are working with more children at low levels of fitness than in years past because of increased levels of obesity among American youths (AOA 2010). Although finding ways to meet the needs of all students in physical education can bring both joy and challenge for everyone involved, to make a difference we must commit ourselves to providing a physical education experience in which all children can be successful.

This chapter provides strategies to help physical education teachers meet the needs of the increasingly diverse population of children entering American schools. *Diversity* is defined as the differences that exist among people (Chappelle and Bigman 1998). For the purposes of this chapter, diversity includes not only differences in mental and physical ability, but also differences in skill levels, fitness levels, gender, culture, language, religion, class, and physical characteristics. Our goal is for all students to experience a sense of empowerment and competence in physical education that leads to lifetime participation in physical activity. Therefore we will first define the philosophy of inclusion and examine ways children can be different from one another. Then we shift the focus to ways children are alike and ways to include all students.

Inclusion Expanded

Traditionally, in terms of physical education, inclusion has meant that students with disabilities are placed in regular physical education programs (Block 2000). However, to better represent the wide variety of student abilities, needs, and interests resulting from the increased diversity of America's schoolchildren, and because teachers today are faced with more than teaching children with special needs, we have expanded our philosophy of inclusion. It is time to support diverse learners, in all their variety of forms, through a broadened conceptualization of inclusion.

Inclusion is a philosophy that says all children can learn and all children want to learn. It involves teachers creating a healthy learning climate in which all children feel physically and emotionally safe, successful, motivated, and connected to others and have a sense of ownership/autonomy (Stiehl, Morris, and Sinclair 2008).

In an inclusive environment, the question is not whether children are smart, but *how* they are smart. The question is not whether they can develop skills in physical education, but *how* they can develop their skills. Perhaps Tomlinson (2003) put it best when she explained that it is all in how you frame the question. Rather than asking, "What labels do my students have?" instead ask, "What are their particular interests and needs?" Rather than asking, "What are my students' deficits?" instead ask, "What are their strengths?" Rather than asking, "How do I remediate students?" instead ask, "What can I do to ensure that each student works to the highest level of thought and production possible?" Instead of asking, "How can I motivate these students?" instead ask, "What releases the motivation born in all humans?" As a whole, these questions capture the essence of inclusion. Discovering children's abilities and helping them learn what they are good at is critical to their success. Inclusion identifies and nurtures each student's unique abilities, recognizing that all children do better when the emphasis is on strengths (Oberti 1993). Remember, "There are no real disabilities, but only different abilities" (T. Shriver in Block 2007, xi).

Physical education programs that include diverse learners have the same basic goals and objectives as any other quality program. However, strategies are used to support program goals while taking into consideration participant needs, interests, abilities, and skill and fitness levels. These strategies may include implementation of modified tasks, assistance for a child as needed, and/or support for the teacher, such as in-service training, working with a translator, or team teaching with an adapted physical education teacher. Inclusion does not mean placement of all children in the general physical education setting with no assistance and support for the teacher. However, inclusion does mean creating conditions so the children's needs are met and program outcomes are achieved.

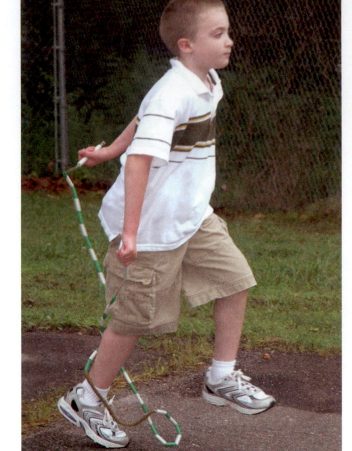

The individualization of instruction leads to success for all children.

Inclusion begins with a teacher willing to accept all children; a teacher open and responsive to individuals and the unique needs of each; a teacher who celebrates children's strengths and adjusts, accommodates, and modifies to provide maximum learning for each child. Before learning specific strategies for including diverse learners, it is important to first focus on ways the children may be different. The better informed we are about the diversity of our children, the better we will be able to teach the child using strategies we will discuss later in the chapter. Diversity and the philosophy of inclusion, beyond children with disabilities, include overweight children, cultural differences, gender equity, religious differences, and children of poverty.

Overweight Children

As mentioned in Chapter 27, childhood obesity rates have reached epidemic proportions. In fact, obesity among children has more than tripled in the last two decades; one in five children is overweight (AOA 2010). Obese children and adolescents are more likely to be overweight or obese as adults; overweight adults are at increased risk for heart disease, high blood pressure, stroke, diabetes, some types of cancer, and gallbladder disease. Also, being overweight during childhood, and particularly adolescence, is related to increased risk of asthma, type 2 diabetes, hypertension, orthopedic complications, and sleep apnea. Psychosocial effects such as developing a negative body image and being subjected to weight-related teasing, jokes, and potentially hurtful comments by peers and family can have a profound effect on children (AOA 2010).

Today's youth are considered the most inactive generation in history. Physical education teachers can help overweight children build healthy bodies and establish healthy lifestyles by teaching them ways to include physical activity in their daily lives (Chapter 27). Physical educators can play an important role in the treatment and prevention of overweight children by giving them the skills and confidence they need to participate in physical activity for a lifetime and educating children about the importance of health-related fitness concepts as outlined in Chapter 27.

To help children increase their physical activity levels, it is important to know the factors that influence physical activity levels among children. The National Association for Sport and Physical Education (NASPE 2011) lists the following factors:

Biological Factors
- Boys are generally more active than girls.
- Physical activity declines between the ages of 6 and 18.
- Obese children prefer low-intensity activities, and obese children with obese parents view endurance activities more negatively than do lean children with lean parents.

- Only 20 percent of the variation in a person's physical activity is explained by genetics.

Psychological Factors
- If children value an activity and feel competent and satisfied while performing it, they are more likely to engage in the activity.
- For children to persist at an activity, they must feel competent and confident in their ability to reach a specific goal (self-efficacy).

Social Factors
- Parents and siblings influence young children's physical activity behaviors.
- In adolescence, peers are more likely to have a greater influence on physical activity levels.
- Enthusiastic and knowledgeable physical education teachers and coaches are more likely to influence their students' enjoyment of physical activity.

Environmental Factors
- Because of safety concerns in many neighborhoods, children engage in indoor activities such as watching television, reading, or playing video games.
- Transportation can also be a barrier to participating in group activities.

Specific implications for teaching overweight children include the following:

- Emphasize enjoyable participation in a variety of physical activities.
- Create a psychologically safe climate where children feel successful and have choices of activities to help them reach goals.
- Help children develop the knowledge, attitudes, and skills they need to adopt and maintain physically active lifestyles.
- Keep all or most children active at the same time so no one feels pressure to perform alone in front of peers because overweight children often have low skill levels and would consider this humiliating.
- Use short bouts of high-intensity activities throughout the class period. Knowing the higher level of intensity will not last long can help motivate less fit children.
- Use heart rate monitors with older students to help them determine when they reach their target heart rate (THR) zone. Overweight students often push themselves well beyond the THR, thinking this is what exercise feels like, when in reality they can get the full benefits of exercise by participating at a much lower and thus more comfortable intensity level.

- Modify activities so students have choices related to intensity (see "Creating Conditions for Inclusion" later in this chapter).
- Allow children to set individual goals related to their own skill and fitness improvement.
- Emphasize self-improvement and personal bests instead of comparing children to each other.

Cultural Differences

Culture serves as the fabric of one's being and includes language, beliefs, attitudes, and patterns of communication (Tiedt and Tiedt 1990). The 2010 census shows the United States is more ethnically, racially, culturally, and linguistically diverse than ever before. Today the national portrait is being increasingly enriched with Asian, Hispanic, and multiracial people. A monolingual, English-speaking physical education teacher is increasingly likely to face the challenge of teaching young children whose languages and backgrounds are completely unfamiliar (Harrison, Russell, and Burden 2010). Often in this situation even the most well-meaning educators inadvertently reinforce children's conflicting feelings about their own culture and the majority culture (Cummins 1992). To become more culturally responsive and reflective teachers (Chapter 4), we must use the cultural knowledge, prior experiences, and learning style preferences of children from diverse cultures to make learning more appropriate and effective for them. Culturally responsive teaching is teaching to and through the strengths of these students (Gay 2000).

The teacher plays a critical role in the success at school of children from diverse cultures. Minority students are often empowered or disabled as a direct result of their interactions with educators (Cummins 1992). The extent that each of the following characteristics is implemented in the school setting can directly affect the success of minority students:

- Minority students' language and culture are incorporated into the school program.
- Minority community participation is encouraged as an integral component of children's education.
- Instruction is used to motivate children to use language actively to generate their own knowledge. (Cummins 1992)

Implications for building a culturally responsive instructional approach in physical education include the following (Sparks 1994):

- ***Build trust.*** A class climate perceived as trusting and accepting is important. One way we can build trust is by sharing information about ourselves and our own cultural backgrounds. This helps children begin to make connections with us that develop the foundation for trust. Learning students' names and how to pronounce them correctly in their native language indicates we are interested and want to get to know them as individuals. Physical education offers a perfect setting for breaking social barriers through cooperative and competitive as well as group and individual physical activities. Each of these serves as a way to strengthen the bond between teacher and students.
- ***Become culturally literate.*** Learn about the children's cultural background. This includes learning about traditions, communication styles, or social values of diverse cultures. We can increase our cultural literacy by observing children outside of the school setting, getting to know their families, making home visits, and allowing children to share cultural experiences in the curriculum. In addition, when children's home language is encouraged, they get a sense of acceptance of themselves and their cultural backgrounds. Challenge yourself to learn and use greetings in many languages, and never hesitate to ask children how to say basic expressions. This validates the children and shows them that teachers, like the children themselves, struggle with new languages.
- ***Use a variety of teaching methods.*** Become aware of the children's learning styles. Some cultures use more visual cues, while others prefer tactile or auditory cues for learning. Physical education offers many opportunities for explanation and demonstration of skills. Peer teaching (Chapter 10) allows children to assist each other in learning.
- ***Promote critical thinking.*** Although critical thinking and problem solving are important for all children, they can be especially helpful to children from diverse cultures. Critical thinking empowers children to make their own decisions rather than always looking to others for answers. This can help build self-esteem and confidence. Developing original routines, creating games (Chapter 30), and using mental imagery are techniques that will challenge children to think critically in physical education.
- ***Provide effective feedback.*** Make all feedback concrete and specific. It is also a good idea to demonstrate what you mean when giving corrective feedback. Be sure all children regardless of color, gender, or ethnic origin receive feedback that is positive, specific, and of equal quality. Chapter 7 gives specific information on providing student feedback.
- ***Analyze instructional materials.*** Be sure that all instructional materials include perspectives from

different cultural groups rather than just the majority group within the class. Use materials that represent diverse cultural groups and are not discriminatory based on race, ethnicity, religion, or gender. Use the rich heritage of physical activity and sport that has evolved from cultures throughout the world to highlight unique contributions.

- *Establish positive home and community relations.* Create positive relationships with parents early in the year. This can be done through visiting the home, making phone calls, inviting parents to come to physical education classes to see what their child is learning, or simply sending home a letter introducing yourself to parents. Remember, many parents do not read English. For example, in many regions of the United States, it is best to send home materials in English and Spanish (this is required in some school districts). Seek out resources in the school district to help with translation of materials. Children love having parents come to school to speak to the class, demonstrate a skill, or do an interactive activity.

To effectively build a culturally responsive environment, we as teachers of physical education must value the richness of diversity in our gymnasiums, in our classrooms, and on our playgrounds. We must foster positive attitudes toward diversity in our classes and promote an environment in which all children can be successful. The goal of inclusion is not to make differences invisible, but to create a classroom, a gymnasium, a society in which all children and their families feel welcomed and valued. (Sapon-Shevin, 2008)

Gender Equity

In 1972, the United States Congress passed Title IX of the Education Amendments, mandating gender equity in all educational institutions receiving federal funding. One of the intentions of Title IX was to provide equal opportunity for physical education instruction to all students. Title IX also mandated coeducational classes, which may begin the process of providing gender equity but does not ensure an equitable environment or equal opportunities for boys and girls in our classes. When equipment is assigned to boys and to girls rather than by choice, when boys demonstrate skills more often than girls and their questions are more frequently answered, gender bias exists in our gymnasiums.

Many teachers treat children differently based on gender without even realizing it. To develop gender fairness, physical education teachers must create an environment in which both sexes feel safe to explore

and develop their abilities in sport and physical activity. Title IX provided the foundation for change, but we as teachers are the key to assuring its implementation. Implications for creating a more gender-equitable environment as outlined by Napper-Owen (1994) include:

- *Student grouping* Use categories such as their birth date, number of pets, color of clothing, or favorite foods, rather than gender.
- *Individualized instruction* Group students for instruction by ability levels to ensure more individualized instruction.
- *Feedback* Provide an equal amount of quality feedback to all students.
- *Student helpers* Ask equal numbers of boys and girls to demonstrate skills, help with equipment, and answer questions in class.
- *Student names* Call all students by their first name.
- *Inclusive language* Use inclusive language, such as "base player," "player-to-player defense," "straight-leg push-ups," "modified push-ups" (rather than "boys' push-ups" and "girls' push-ups"), and "you" rather than "you guys."
- *Activities* Teach nontraditional activities.
- *Teaching materials* Use teaching materials that show both boys and girls in traditional and nontraditional roles.
- *Modification of activities* Modify activities for maximum participation by all students. A great way to increase awareness of gender equity is to videotape a lesson and count how often boys and girls answer questions, participate in activity, receive feedback, and demonstrate skills. Chapter 11 provides additional suggestions for checking gender equity awareness.

Religious Differences

The First Amendment to the U.S. Constitution granted freedom of religion to all people more than 200 years ago. Today parents from diverse religious backgrounds entrust the education of their children to the teachers in public schools. Therefore it is important for schools to be places where religion and religious conviction are treated with fairness and respect. Public schools uphold the First Amendment when they protect the religious liberty rights of students of all faiths or none. Because of the confusion that has surrounded the topic of religion in public schools across the years, this is perhaps easier said than done. One of the best ways to respect the religious rights of all children is for teachers and administrators to work closely with parents and community members to know, understand, and appreciate religious differences. Kahan (2003) provides helpful information for physical educators based on current understanding of the law:

- **Lesson content** Children who object to lesson content on the grounds of religious beliefs should be excused without punishment.
- **Absences** Schools are advised but not obligated to set calendars around various religious holidays; they are required, however, to provide opportunities for students who are absent for religious reasons to make up missed work without any adverse consequences.
- **Dress and physical contact** Children whose dress reflects their religious views or modesty should be allowed to wear such clothing. For example, Muslim girls should be allowed to wear a hijab over their hair and long pants under their shorts, and Sikh boys should be allowed to wear turbans. In addition, observance of clothing customs and rules regulating physical contact and modesty may prevent some students from participating in activities such as swimming and dance.
- **Religious symbols** Religious symbols may be used as teaching aids (e.g., cross, crèche, menorah); however, religious symbols should not be used as seasonal decorations. Exercise restraint, plan inclusively, and consider the context of displays. For example, a bulletin board with a winter scene of snow, snowmen, presents, holly, menorahs, Christmas trees, and Kwanzaa candles may evoke general seasonal feelings and not perceptions of endorsing any single religion and would therefore be acceptable.
- **Holiday lessons** Special lessons or treats prepared for the observance of holidays occurring during the

school year such as Halloween, Thanksgiving, Valentine's Day, and St. Patrick's Day have indirect roots in religious events, people, and symbols and therefore may not suit the religious beliefs of all children.

Overall, teaching children in one of the most religiously diverse countries in the world requires additional planning, communication, and flexibility.

Children of Poverty

The ever-widening gap between socioeconomic levels in the United States has resulted in a tremendously large group of children with special needs. Approximately 44 percent of all public school children are eligible for free or reduced lunch (NCES 2010). These are the children of poverty. For some families the poverty is situational, created by a loss of jobs, divorce, illness, death, and other variables beyond the control of the children or parents in the family. For other families the poverty is generational, existing for such a long period of time that neither the children nor the adults in the family have ever known nonpoverty conditions. Children of poverty live in apartments, in houses, in shelters, on the streets, and in automobiles. They live with single parents, with multiple families, and with no parents. They exist in all ethnic groups. What they have in common is poverty—an existence below that necessary for meeting the basic needs of food, clothing, and shelter, an existence void of the basic components of wellness.

Children of poverty:

- Have higher rates of lead poisoning
- Have poorer vision and poorer oral hygiene
- Have more asthma and more exposure to smoke
- Have poorer nutrition and less adequate pediatric care
- Go to bed hungry or ill fed more often
- Have families who relocate more frequently and must change schools several times within a single year
- Watch more television and have less access to adults who can read to them or talk to them in intellectually stimulating, enriching ways

The social class differences in academic potential exist by the time children are three years old. Children of poverty enter kindergarten with academic delays and cognitive experiential deficiencies. Many come to us with developmental delays and motor deficiencies. The belief that children of low socioeconomic status are naturally very skilled in sports and the belief that excellence in sport will provide the avenue to success, security, and the fulfillment of all dreams are two of the misconceptions for these children. They are skilled

---

Cultural Heritage

Acknowledging the legitimacy of the cultural heritages of different ethnic groups can begin with A, B, C, D:

Architecture: What are the places of religious/cultural importance? What are the places of worship called?

Books: What books tell the history of the culture? Who are the leading authors of the culture? Where are the key teachings of that religion kept?

Cities: Where are the key cities of that culture? What are the cities of importance for that religion?

Days: What dates are important in that culture? What days are celebrated in that religion?

Adapted from L. M. Cruz and S. C. Petersen, 2011.

in physical education, as in academics, only if they have had the experiences for readiness in those skills, the nurturing of caring adults, and good health to overcome the environmental variables acting negatively upon that health.

Our task as teachers of children of poverty is the same as our task for all children:

- To provide physically, emotionally safe environments for learning
- To assure that each child feels loved and feels worthy
- To provide hope for a significant future

We must believe that all children are capable of success (Tipps 2006) and empower them with the tools for success—in physical education, in the classroom, and beyond their years in school—and believe in their ability to achieve that success.

Children with Special Needs

People with disabilities are the largest minority group in the United States (Block 2007). More than 50 percent of students with disabilities are from backgrounds "other than white" (USDE 2007). Diversity and disabilities cannot be ignored in our schools or in our society.

Public Law 94-142 (the Education for All Handicapped Children Act of 1975) and the Individuals with Disabilities Education Act of 1990 and 2004 (IDEA) guarantee all children with disabilities from ages 3 to 22 a free and appropriate education in the least restrictive environment. That education includes physical education as a direct service—one that must be provided for all students. IDEA defines physical education as the development of physical and motor fitness; fundamental motor skills and patterns; and skills in aquatics, dance, games, and sports. IDEA further states that, to the maximum extent appropriate, children with disabilities are to be educated together with children without disabilities—that is, in their home school, in the classroom, and in the gymnasium that would be theirs if they had no disabilities.

Early interpretations of "least restrictive environment" led to the mainstreaming of children with disabilities for art, music, and physical education and to a somewhat limited exposure to the classroom environment of their peers, with the remainder of the day spent in a "special ed" classroom. Parents of children with disabilities voiced concern at this separate but equal approach to education at the same time that research was questioning the benefits of the approach. There was strong concern about the negative (and once affixed, everlasting) label of special education. Thus began the gradual move from mainstreaming to a philosophy of inclusion. With very few exceptions, the education of children with disabilities is done in the general program of physical education (PL 105-17, IDEA Amendments, 1997; PL 108-446, IDEA, 2004).

Children with disabilities can successfully participate in physical education.

Natural Proportions

During the early days of mainstreaming, children with disabilities were often grouped together and placed in one general physical education class, resulting in the class increasing in number by as many as 5 to 10 children with special needs. "Natural proportions" is the recommended principle to match the philosophy of inclusion and maximize learning for all students (Block 2007). The principle of natural proportions means the normal ratio of persons with disabilities will be the guideline for the placement of children with disabilities in general classes. With approximately 10 to 15 percent of the school-age population having disabilities, a general elementary physical education class of 20 to 25 youngsters would have 2 to 3 children with disabilities. The principle of natural proportions creates a physical education environment that promotes success and positive experiences for all children.

Physical Activity and Fitness

Children with disabilities tend to be less physically active than children without disabilities. This is due to a number of factors: the nature of the disability itself, overprotective parents, and a lack of recreational and play facilities accessible for those with disabilities. Yet physical activity is extremely important for children with disabilities. Through physical activity, skills are developed for recreational use throughout life. In a physical activity environment, social skills are learned and practiced, and self-confidence for social interaction is enhanced. Through physical activity, fitness is improved. Better fitness brings increased muscle tone for those prone to being less mobile; muscle tone brings better posture, more control of manipulatives,

Box 31-1

Physical Fitness Test Package for Students with Disabilities

Additional information concerning specific physical fitness assessment for students with disabilities may be obtained from the following source:

Brockport Physical Fitness Test Manual (1999), by
J. Winnick and F. Short.
Human Kinetics
P.O. Box 5076
Champaign, IL 61825-5075
www.humankinetics.com

and thus increased independence. A health-enhancing level of fitness is important for all children.

Many children with disabilities can participate in the regular fitness assessment program. However, for some boys and girls, modifications in assessment will be necessary. Box 31-1 provides information relative to fitness assessments designed especially for students with disabilities.

Disabilities, Impairments, and Disorders

Disabilities, impairments, and disorders include visual and hearing impairments; a number of physical disabilities; health-related disorders; emotional, behavior, and social disorders; and intellectual and learning disabilities. Each child with a disability, impairment, or disorder has unique needs; successful inclusion, participation, and learning are our goals for each child.

Visual Impairments

The two categories of visual impairment are blindness and partial sight. Impairments range from blindness to blurred/distorted vision, tunnel vision, and the ability to see out of the corners of the eyes only. Children with serious visual impairments may exhibit the following characteristics:

- Self-stimulating mannerisms—for example, stamping feet, rocking, clicking fingers, and turning the head from side to side—often due to boredom and lack of external stimulus
- Awkward, clumsy total-body movements and poor motor skills from lack of experience and limited sensory information
- Poor posture due to lack of visual modeling
- Developmental lag of at least one year, often due to lack of stimulus and/or overprotective parents
- Lack of fitness and a tendency toward being overweight because of sedentary lifestyle
- Difficulty dealing with abstractions and a limited conception of the "whole"
- Difficulty in conceptualizing boundaries

The child with severe visual impairments needs auditory and tactile stimulation. As teachers, we need to encourage this child to venture beyond the known environment, to explore the gymnasium and the playground. We need to promote social interaction with peers as well as adults, and to maximize learning through all the senses. Learning goals for children with serious visual impairments focus on attention to sensory abilities, spatial awareness, and mobility. Visually impaired children need the maximum use of their proprioceptive, auditory, haptic, and spatial perceptions.

For visually impaired children, proprioceptive perception is important for maintaining balance. Body awareness and proprioceptive perception can be increased through activities that focus on the identification of body parts and awareness of the relationship of body parts to each other and of the body part's position in space. Children can be asked to move individual body parts when the body part is named and to perform certain movements with the isolated body part, for example, swing or tap (Chapters 13, 15). Teachers can increase proprioceptive awareness by adding small weights to body parts and then instructing children to move the parts. The gymnastics skills of balancing on different body parts and in different positions also help this development.

Ron, a child blind since birth, was mainstreamed into a physical education class. The class was studying balance—balance on different bases of support and balance in inverted positions (Chapter 20). Ron was working independently in the space defined by the boundaries of his gymnastics mat. Suddenly he cried aloud; the entire class stopped and turned in his direction. Nothing was wrong; Ron was experiencing for the first time the change in body position and perception that accompanies being balanced in an inverted position on the hands only. Ron apologized for disturbing the class, and activity continued. During sharing time at the end of the class, Ron shared his feelings of the experience and his enthusiasm for more gymnastics.

The senses are also used to establish spatial awareness. Children who are blind have difficulty perceiving the relationship of objects in space and the spatial relationship of themselves to objects. Lateral and directional activities, such as identification of left and right sides; movement away from self—left, right, up, down, front, back; and positioning of self in relation to equipment (for example, a table or a chair) help develop this perception in children without the visual sense. Auditory cues help these children determine distance in space. Sound-emitting devices can be placed on stationary equipment and the equipment used with a partner to help measure distance, location in space, and pathways of travel. Young children can face sounds made at different locations and thus determine near and far. Older children can follow a bike rider by the sound of cardboard on the spokes or copy the pathway of a partner by changes in intensity of the sound.

One of the greatest disabilities of visually impaired children is lack of mobility. A mobility training program in the gymnasium, as well as in the outdoor play area, increases the child's independence and thus the ability and desire to participate fully. Three-dimensional models of both the indoor and outdoor physical education environments, including permanent equipment, give visually impaired children the concrete, hands-on experience to develop a conception of the whole and the ability to move within the physical education space. The mobility training should also include a peer-guided tour of the environment and time for personal exploration of the environment, including full use of tactile and auditory senses. The blind child should be free to walk, crawl, and touch the gymnasium without the embarrassment of a class of onlookers; the teacher, parent, or a trusted adult should be present to answer questions and ensure safety.

The inclusion of visually impaired children in physical education classes has implications for the teacher, the environment, and the physical education equipment. Specific implications for the teacher include the following:

- Teach with manual guidance accompanied by verbal directions.
- Remember, the visually impaired child relies heavily on tactile perception. Manually guiding the visually impaired child can serve as the demonstration of the skill for other children, thus benefiting the group as well as the individual.
- Provide specific and immediate feedback. For profitable feedback, the teacher must thoroughly analyze movement skills and provide the verbal cues for correcting deviations.
- Use peer teaching to assist with the manual guidance and verbal feedback.
- Involve visually impaired children in small-group and partner activities rather than large-group situations.
- Avoid activities that involve throwing and catching with fast speed and travel.
- Progress from simple tasks in gymnastics and games to sequentially more difficult tasks to develop motor skill and cognitive complexity.
- Involve all children in the world of creative movement experiences and dance. Creative dance comes from the inner self; it is born of the senses. Vision is necessary only for the observer.

Adaptations in the environment include:

- Ensure the gymnasium is well lighted to help the child with residual vision.
- Vary the texture of the boundaries for game areas—dirt/grass for the play area, sand for the surrounding area.
- Make pathways between targets or bases 3 to 4 feet wide and of a different texture.

- Keep the outdoor teaching area and the gymnasium well organized and consistent. Introduce new equipment to visually impaired children by means of three-dimensional models.
- Provide tactile markings on the floor as a reference for teaching stations, the center for teacher directions, water fountains, and so on.
- Place guide ropes across the gymnasium or playground to permit the practice of locomotor skills and freedom of travel. Tie a series of knots in the ropes to signal the approach of the boundary.

The inclusion of visually impaired children may necessitate such special equipment as:

- Brightly colored balls and objects for children with limited vision
- Sponge and foam balls for projectile activities
- Protection for the eyes; eyeglasses
- Audible beep balls for tracking and location
- Battery-powered electronic sound devices within large marker cones to serve as bases
- A large gymnastics mat to serve as "personal space" for balancing and transferring of weight activities

Contact the American Foundation for the Blind (www.afb.org) for catalogs of special equipment.

We expect children with visual disabilities to participate to their fullest potential in physical education and try not to let the child use the disability as an excuse to withdraw from activity and social interaction. Game situations that involve constant contact with the participants require the least adaptation. When new activities are introduced, having children with visual disabilities play in slow motion will help their orientation to the play environment and the rules. The use of the buddy system also helps these children participate in traveling activities. Note, however, that although young children naturally hold hands with partners, they need to know the correct way to assist a visually impaired person. That is, the visually impaired person should grasp the guide's upper arm above the elbow, thus permitting the nonsighted person to maintain a sense of control rather than being led as if helpless.

Falls, scratches, and bruises are a part of physical education for children with serious visual impairments. Visually impaired children need to be permitted to recover on their own, to maintain their dignity, and to attain maximum independence. The teacher must discuss with all members of the class the danger of being overprotective. With the exception of ball-handling/striking activities, the visually impaired child can function quite independently in physical education classes. Following orientation and mobility training, the teacher's task is simply to help the child develop skills and a belief in self.

Hearing Impairments

The term *hearing impairment* refers to hearing loss that can range from mild to profound. The disability includes those who have trouble hearing normal speech and those who can't understand even amplified speech. The term *deaf* is rarely used to classify a hearing impairment; most individuals labeled deaf have some level of hearing are able to understand speech with the help of amplification or by hearing combined with watching the speaker's lips, facial expressions, and gestures. The danger of labeling a child deaf is that it may cause peers to stop interacting with the child and may actually make the child functionally deaf as an adult.

The social domain is the greatest problem for children with serious hearing loss. The hearing-impaired young child doesn't engage in play experiences with other children; speech, if present, is garbled and communication quite limited. Hearing-impaired children don't understand their role in the play experience and often withdraw, thus denying themselves the social interaction and development of motor skills that accompany play for young children. As children's games become more complex, the hearing-impaired child is likely to be left out of the activities. Rules are developed as the game is played; instructions are shouted in the midst of play. Without special assistance, the hearing-impaired child is unable to comprehend all the intricacies of the game. Thus the child fails to develop the social skills learned through group interaction in play. Withdrawal from activity causes a developmental lag in motor skills.

The frustration of being unable to communicate, to be understood by others, and to express emotions in socially accepted ways often leads children with serious hearing impairments to express their emotions through physical means. Aggressive behavior is often the means of expressing negative emotions. Additional characteristics of a child with a serious hearing impairment may include:

- Slow development of inner and expressive language, which often leads others to mistake the child as intellectually disabled
- Poor pronunciation; garbled speech
- Absence of laughter
- Difficulty in dealing with abstractions due to slowness in developing inner language
- Hyperactive appearance because of constant movement to maintain visual contact
- Lack of good balance in some hearing-impaired children caused by inner-ear damage
- Shuffling gait resulting from not hearing the sound of movement

We strongly recommend a course in sign language for teachers with hearing-impaired children in their classroom or gymnasium. Think of how much better the hearing-impaired child will feel when greeted the first day of physical education by a teacher she or he can communicate with!

Most children with hearing impairments function quite well in the regular physical education program. As a rule, adaptations in equipment or environment won't be necessary. However, the physical education teacher needs to modify certain aspects of teaching:

• Position yourself so the child with a serious hearing impairment can read your lips; be conscious of not turning your back when speaking; and be close enough for lip reading.

• Face the sun when outdoors so that the hearing-impaired child doesn't have to face the sun.

• Let the hearing-impaired child move freely in the teaching environment so he or she can always be in the best position for hearing.

• Visually and manually demonstrate skills; don't rely on verbal directions alone.

• Remember, the hearing-impaired child can't read lips or hear a whistle across the playing field or gymnasium; accompany the auditory sound with large hand signals.

• Learn the basic sign language needed for communication. Figure 31.1 provides specific signs for physical education and basic communication.

Hearing-impaired children with a developmental lag in motor skills need additional physical education to develop the motor skills and movement patterns

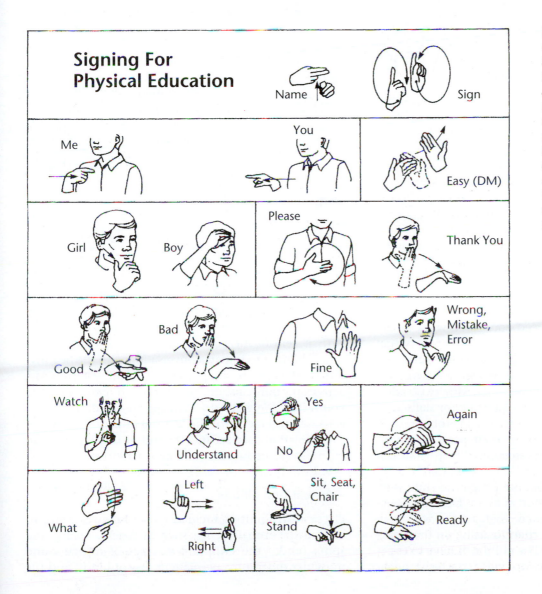

Figure 31.1 Signing for physical education.
Source: From C. B. Eichstaedt, Signing for physical education, *Journal of Physical Education, Recreation and Dance* 19, no. 5 (1978): 20–21. Used with permission from the *Journal of Physical Education, Recreation and Dance,* a publication of the American Alliance for Health, Physical Education, Recreation and Dance, 1900 Association Drive, Reston, VA 20191.

Figure 31.1 Continued

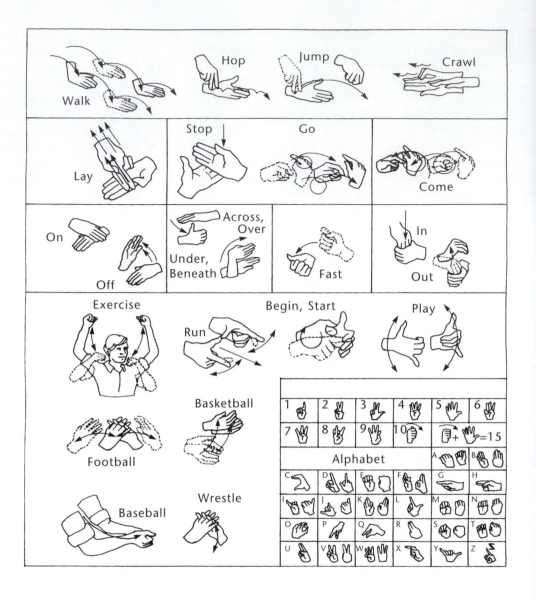

needed for successful participation in the regular program. Those with balance problems and vertigo due to damage to the inner ear need additional work in the area of balance to develop maximum use of the visual and kinesthetic cues for balancing activities. Tumbling activities with rotation and climbing to heights on large apparatus should be done only with close adult supervision. Children who have poor motor skills and/or difficulty with balance are very conscious of how their abilities compare with those of their peers; a private place to practice can help overcome self-consciousness in attempting skills.

Like many children with disabilities, the child with a serious hearing impairment may be less skilled because of a lack of experience. As teachers, we try to maximize strengths rather than focusing on the weakness, the inability to hear. The child will have to experience success in activities to build the self-esteem

needed for eager participation and social interaction. The directions and simple activities the class can grasp easily may have to be carefully explained to the child with a serious hearing impairment. Encourage the other children to initiate conversation with the hearing-impaired child to help the child understand class activities, but caution them not to patronize the youngster. We need to educate all children in our classes to interact with the hearing impaired, to accept their less-than-perfect speech, and to involve them in both physical education and play activities.

Physical Disabilities

Physical disabilities include conditions resulting in orthopedic impairments, such as cerebral palsy and spina bifida, the crippling diseases of arthritis and muscular dystrophy, permanent loss of limbs, and the temporary disabilities caused by fractures. Other related health factors that can mean limited or restricted physical education for children include hemophilia, severe burns, congenital heart defects, and respiratory disorders.

Each child with a physical disability has different physical and motor capabilities, so the learning goals must be designed to meet individual needs. The child's physical education program will include two aspects: (1) the exercises and activities to meet specific needs and develop motor skills and (2) any adaptations in the regular program of physical education. The following procedure is recommended when planning the program for children with physical disabilities:

1. Identify the child's clinical condition.
2. Determine what activities would be contraindicated based on medical recommendation.
3. Determine functional motor skills needed.
4. Select activities that will develop desired motor skills.
5. Adapt the physical education environment and equipment as needed to provide the program.

It's important to remember the program will be designed in consultation with a physician and a physical therapist. As teachers of physical education, we aren't expected to make a clinical diagnosis or to prescribe a program of individualized remedial exercises without the assistance of trained medical professionals. The professionals familiar with the child's medical history will be valuable consultants to the team developing the child's program (Box 31-2).

Cerebral Palsy Perhaps the most misunderstood of all children with disabilities are those with cerebral

---

Box 31-2

What Do I Say? What Do I Do? Tips for Times with Children Who Have Disabilities

- Act naturally. Be you. We often have a tendency to either ignore a disabled child or overattend. Like Goldilocks, pick the amount of attention that is "just right."
- Assume the child is bright. Talk as you would to any child until you are told to do otherwise. It is better to "talk up" to someone than to talk down.
- Talk to the *child,* not to the attendant, parent, or teacher.
- Establish eye contact. This may mean sitting down, comfortably half-kneeling, or moving to one side (if the child cannot look straight ahead). Avoid standing behind the wheelchair and talking. Many children rely on facial cues, gestures, and clear hearing to understand all that you are saying.
- Avoid simple yes/no questions. They make for dull, one-sided conversation—for anyone! Instead, ask about family, friends, activities. Don't ask, "Did you enjoy the circus?" but rather, "What did you see at the circus?" "Whom did you go with?" and "Tell me about the elephants."
- Wait for replies . . . patiently. Repeating a question too soon may interrupt a child who is attempting to formulate an answer.
- Keep conversation about a child's wheelchair to a minimum, not because it is insulting (it isn't), but because often it is all people find to talk about (e.g., "I bet you can zoom around in that thing! I wish I had one. How fast does it go? Can I ride? How long do the batteries last?"). A little wheelchair talk is OK, but move to other topics that are more interesting to the child.

- It is fine to use phrases like "I have to run now" to a child in a wheelchair, or "I see" to a child who is blind.
- Many children cannot help drooling. Saliva won't kill you. Don't be hesitant to wipe someone's mouth (with their permission) or hold a hand that is wet.
- Yes, touching is OK. Holding hands, hugging, or a pat on the back is appropriate if it is something you would do with any child. A pat on the head is typically considered a condescending gesture. Appropriateness is the key. Keep in mind that some children are too affectionate and need to learn proper social interaction.
- Roughhousing is great—provided you get clearance (ask the parents). Being "thrown around" is part of growing up!
- Ask permission before you help a child. Ask the parents, too, if they are present—but ask the child first.
- When lifting children, first show them and then tell them where they will be set down.
- A child with a disability can misbehave just like any other child. Not to mince words: They can be snotty. Or they can be nice. Don't let yourself become so tolerant that you allow clearly unacceptable behavior.
- Don't feel as if everything you have to say needs to be funny or light. Serious topics are welcomed. Some children appreciate a break from laughing because they cannot control that response very well.

Source: Dave Taylor, *Project Active Newsletter* 12, no. 1 (1991), ed. Joe Karp, Northshore School District, Bothell, WA. Used with permission.

palsy. Because of the language and auditory disabilities and the lack of muscular control that often accompany cerebral palsy, the child is often labeled intellectually disabled. Social acceptance and recognition of strengths are major obstacles for children with cerebral palsy. Cerebral palsy is a neurological impairment caused by incomplete development of, or injury to, the central nervous system due to prenatal factors, injuries during birth, or postnatal conditions such as a serious childhood disease with a high fever or a head injury. Characteristics associated with cerebral palsy include:

- Disabilities in visual, auditory, and perceptual development and in speech
- Lack of concentration, distractability, overexcitability, and hyperactivity causing underachievement and poor behavior
- Poor coordination and lack of balance, resulting in awkward movements and frequent falls
- Difficulty in coordinating eye movements
- Tendency toward seizures

The lack of coordination associated with cerebral palsy results in a delay in motor control. The child with cerebral palsy will benefit from the breakdown of skills to basic components and sequential presentation of those components. Due to either restricted or extraneous movements, the child with cerebral palsy expends a great deal of energy when performing physical activity; a decrease in endurance may result. The physical education program for a child with cerebral palsy should concentrate on perceptual motor activities—locomotor patterns, balance, response to rhythm, development of ocular control, and form perception—as well as the development of skills for successful participation.

For some children with cerebral palsy, the only effect is a slight speech impairment; others have a total inability to control body movements. The physical education teacher will benefit from extensive reading concerning the type of cerebral palsy and from discussion with the physical therapist concerning special needs and the adaptation of equipment and activities for maximum participation.

Spina Bifida   Spina bifida is a congenital condition in which the bony elements of the spine don't close properly during development in the womb. In mild cases of spina bifida, the only effects may be weak muscles and deviations in posture. Because spina bifida causes paralysis in the legs and a loss of sensation in the lower limbs, children with mild spina bifida benefit from weight-bearing activities to stimulate bone growth and circulation in the lower limbs, as well as from exercises/activities to develop muscular strength in the upper body.

Children with spina bifida have normal intelligence; they have the same play and social needs as all children. Adaptations in physical education will be those needed to accommodate their mode of transportation—that is, crutches or a wheelchair. In addition to the areas of need noted above, it is necessary for children with spina bifida to develop skills for participation with their peers in physical education and skills for lifetime sports and activities in which they can be successful.

Like many children with disabilities, children with spina bifida benefit from the socialization inherent in physical education, in addition to learning and developing skills. Guiding this growth is perhaps the greatest contribution we as physical educators can make in educating children with disabilities.

Muscular Dystrophy   Childhood muscular dystrophy begins between the ages of two and six. Muscular dystrophy is a progressive disease that affects the voluntary muscles—for example, legs and arms; involuntary

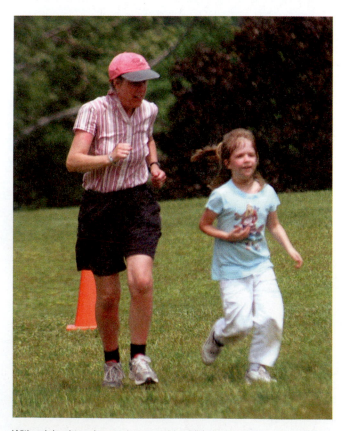

With minimal teacher assistance, this child participates successfully in the physical education program.

muscles, such as the diaphragm, aren't affected. First affected are the muscles involved in walking and standing; the child with muscular dystrophy will begin to have difficulty maintaining posture, getting up from a chair, or walking up stairs. The degenerative nature of the disease causes the general deterioration of the muscle tissue and a replacement of muscle with fat. Thus the young child with muscular dystrophy initially appears quite healthy as the legs and arms maintain or increase in size.

The child with muscular dystrophy has a tendency to tire easily. Fine manual dexterity is gradually lost, and the progressive weakening of the muscles causes adverse postural changes. The learning goals for the child with muscular dystrophy should concentrate on exercises to strengthen the muscles involved in the basic tasks of daily living, walking patterns, posture control, and stretching of contractures. However, these exercises must be selected in consultation with the child's physician. The child with muscular dystrophy should be kept actively involved in physical education to the extent the condition permits; inactivity only increases the atrophy of the muscles. Adaptations will be necessary as the child becomes dependent on crutches, braces, or a wheelchair.

Health-Related Disorders

Although not normally thought of as physical disabilities, several other health-related disorders can affect a child's full participation in physical education. The following disorders may require temporary adaptations in the child's environment or limitations in physical activity: juvenile arthritis, asthma, diabetes, heart defects, sickle-cell anemia, severe burns, and respiratory disorders. The physical educator should review health records early in the school year, making note of any conditions that require monitoring and/or temporary adaptations. Open communication with the child's parents, rapport with the child, and an understanding of the particular disorder and its effects will result in maximum participation for the child as well as trust among you, the parents, and— most important—the child.

Asthma Children are being affected in increasing numbers by asthma, an allergic reaction that results in wheezing, coughing, tightening of the airways, and accumulation of mucus in the bronchial tubes. An asthmatic attack can be triggered by allergens, upper respiratory infections, or even robust laughing. The most common conditions we see in physical education are reactions to changes in the weather (especially cold weather) and to strenuous exercise (e.g., the distance run for fitness assessment).

All too often in the past, physical educators treated lightly the asthmatic child who had a note, an excuse from running, or a request for adaptation in activity. Asthma is a serious health problem for millions of children. Failure to attend to the condition can result in serious and sometimes life-threatening consequences for the child.

The following suggestions will be helpful in ensuring maximum, healthy participation for children with asthma:

- Scan health records in the fall, noting children with asthma and/or serious allergies.
- Code your daily record system for individual reminders.
- Notify children with asthma or allergies and/or their parents before a day of especially vigorous activity.
- Encourage extra hydration during vigorous and/or prolonged physical activity.
- Ask the child before the activity if he or she brought an inhaler to physical education class.
- Consult with the parents of children with serious asthmatic conditions for any special safeguards or procedures.
- On days when adaptation is necessary, make needed modifications to provide maximum participation.

Diabetes Another health disorder that necessitates our attention is type 1 (insulin-dependent) diabetes. Although we may experience only one or two children with diabetes in our years of teaching, the child with diabetes requires our having a thorough understanding of the disorder, an awareness of the warning signs of low blood sugar, and the knowledge to instigate immediate emergency procedures.

The goal for a child with diabetes is to make the diabetes fit into daily life, as opposed to daily life fitting into the diabetes treatment plan. Children with diabetes can be expected to participate fully in physical education. If their physical education is scheduled before lunch or in the late afternoon, a snack may be advised in anticipation of the physical activity. On days of especially strenuous activity (e.g., the distance run for fitness assessment), the parents may provide an extra snack. Children with diabetes react emotionally as well as physically to daily insulin, ketone checks, and a routine different from that of their friends. Confidence in self and acceptance by peers are very important for these children. Success in movement skills extends beyond the gymnasium to aid feelings of self-worth and social acceptance.

Intellectual Disabilities

The term *intellectual disabilities* refers to intellectual functioning that is significantly below average, accompanied by deficits in adaptive behavior. Children with intellectual disabilities have problems of maturation, learning, and/or social adjustment, which, to different degrees, result in a degree of independence or social responsibility lower than that expected for their age. These characteristics manifest themselves during the early developmental periods of life.

The physical skills of many children with mild or moderate intellectual disability are average and above; the difficulties center around comprehending the instructions and following through to complete the assignment. The youngster with intellectual disabilities can more easily understand and follow directions if we remember the following:

- Keep verbal directions to a minimum; when possible use both visual and verbal instructions.
- Communicate in a direct, simple, and meaningful manner.
- Present tasks within the child's current level of physical skills.
- Structure the environment for focus on tasks and a minimum of distractions.
- Maintain a routine so the child knows what to expect.
- Provide repetition of experiences for overlearning.
- Minimize the number of variables to which the child must attend; simplify the task.
- Present the lesson in short segments; restate the task at regular intervals.
- Reinforce strengths with frequent praise; minimize weaknesses.

Children with intellectual disabilities can perform simple gymnastics sequences and rhythmical routines and participate in skill development activities. The teacher's attentiveness to task presentation and lesson design will result in better learning, not just for children with cognitive deficits, but for all students.

Many children with intellectual disabilities are lacking in areas of verbal expression and social interaction. Physical education classes can provide excellent opportunities for growth in both these areas. The following suggestions will help foster personal

Teacher

I will know you.
I will touch you and hold you
And smell and taste and listen
To the noises that you make—and the words, if any.

I will know you.
Each atom of your small, lonely
Aching, raging, hurting being
Will be known to me
Before I try to teach you.
Before I try to teach
I must first reach you.

And then, when I have come to know you, intimately,
I will insist, gently, gradually, but insist
That you know me.
And later, that you trust me
And then yourself.

Now, knowing each other, we will begin to know the world—
The seasons, the trees, animals, food, the other children,
The printed word, books,
The knowledge of what has gone before and been recorded.

Then as surely as I moved toward you
I will move away.
As I once insisted on being close to you,
Demanding entrance into your half wild world
Of fear and fantasy, refusing you aloneness.

So now, I move away.
As your words come and your walk quickens,
As you laugh out loud
Or read clearly and with understanding,
I stand behind you—no longer close—
Available, but no longer vital to you.

And you—you grow!
You are! You will become!

And I, the teacher,
I turn, with pride in you,
Toward my next child.

Mary MacCracken

Source: In Touch 1, no. 6 (July 1978). Used with permission from the National Mental Health Association.

and social growth for the child with intellectual disabilities:

- Engage the child in conversation. Ask questions; encourage a response.
- Be an attentive listener; listen when the child speaks.
- Create opportunities for cooperative activities that actively involve the child.
- Recognize achievements; share them with the whole class so they can appreciate and share in the child's accomplishment.
- Encourage verbal expression of feelings.

Just as we as teachers must take an active role in interacting socially and verbally with children with intellectual disabilities, we must also teach their fellow students to do the same. The child's initial response to another child's attempts at conversation or group participation may be silence; children with intellectual disabilities may be unsure of themselves or not understand. Remind the other children to repeat the question or to reach out with a touch to include the child with disabilities in the group.

Emotional Disturbance and Behavior Disorders

In increasing numbers, children come to us with behavior disabilities: emotionally disturbed, behavior disordered, hyperactive, distractive, aggressive, impulsive, and socially unacceptable. Some may have been diagnosed with attention deficit disorder (ADD) or attention deficit hyperactivity disorder (ADHD). Children classified as emotionally disturbed or behavior disordered have deficiencies in at least one of the following: characteristics that facilitate learning, characteristics that promote interpersonal relationships, and characteristics that foster appropriate behavior under normal conditions. What classifies children with these characteristics as emotionally disturbed/behavior disordered is the persistence of the behavior, its severity, and its adverse effects on educational performance.

The role of the teacher is to control the learning environment while helping the child gain control. The following guidelines have implications for teachers of physical education:

- Provide a sense of order, structure, and dependability in the learning environment.
- Teach the child that verbal responses to frustration and conflict are acceptable but that physical aggression is not.
- Make it clear to the child that he or she is accepted even when the behavior is unacceptable.
- Establish short-range, achievable goals geared to the child's current level of functioning.

- Convey your expectations through your conduct and consistent messages.
- Avoid overreacting to extreme behavior; an emotional response from the teacher is counterproductive.
- Remember, what works for one child with emotional disturbance or behavior disorders may not work for another.

Physical activity has been shown to have a positive influence on children with behavior disorders or disruptive behaviors. These children benefit from physical education programs that emphasize fitness, balance, and basic movement; many have great difficulty with competitive games and sports. Because of their behavior, these children's past experiences in physical education have included less activity, more "time-out," and less skill development than other students have experienced. The development of basic skills may require attention. Programs such as Hellison's responsibility model (Chapter 8) and programs with a cooperative rather than a highly competitive focus have been found to positively influence the development of personal and social responsibility for these at-risk students.

Social Interaction Disorders/Autism Spectrum Disorder

Children with social interaction disorders or pervasive developmental disorders include those with autism, Asperger syndrome, and Rett's disorder. Although each disorder has its unique characteristics and varying degrees of severity, common to all are severe impairment of communication and/or social interaction skills and the presence of repetitive behaviors. These children appear extremely shy, often withdrawn into their own world. The indoor and outdoor environments of physical education can be a nightmare with loud sounds, an abundance of visual stimuli, and constantly changing activity. Very often their recourse is to withdraw to the inner world of self-movement (stimming) and self-talk or to wander aimlessly in the midst of the physical activity/instruction/play. Motor skills are often below the level of their peers.

Children with social interaction disorders can more easily function as members of our physical education classes if we remember:

- Changes in routine and transitions in activity are very difficult for these children.
- Visual cues are much more effective than auditory.
- Motor performance tests often underrepresent ability because of the child's failure to respond to auditory directions.
- Skills should be developed in contexts (i.e., functional patterns), not as isolated skills.

Major goals for children with social interaction disorders are appropriate social behaviors and social/verbal interactions. The physical education environment is rich in opportunities for this development. For these children, such skills must be taught and consistently reinforced.

Appropriate nonverbal and verbal social skills do not develop naturally, nor do the children learn them from modeling others. As with all children with disabilities, each child with a social interaction disorder is unique; each disorder is unique to that child. Close communication with the child's consultant on the multidisciplinary team will be invaluable as you work toward the short- and long-range goals of the individualized education program.

Disability Awareness

Children who have mild or moderate intellectual disabilities, learning disabilities, or emotional disturbances but whose physical appearance does not manifest the disability are sometimes the least accepted by their peers. The class has the same expectations of them as of the nondisabled, and the class can become frustrated when the child with disabilities does not behave or respond as expected. The class response is usually due to the students' lack of awareness of the disability or knowledge of its characteristics. We as teachers must educate our students regarding specific disabilities. We must answer their questions, increase their awareness of the disability, and thus increase their understanding and acceptance of all children.

Learning Disabilities

A specific learning disability is a disorder in one or more of the basic processes involved in understanding or using language. According to the U.S. Department of Health and Human Services, the disability may manifest itself as an imperfect ability to listen, think, speak, write, spell, or do mathematical calculations. Children with learning disabilities have normal intelligence but, unlike other children, are unable to perform academically within the normal IQ range. Children with learning disabilities are typically characterized by hyperactive behavior, short attention span, impulsiveness, poor self-concept, and often a delay in play development.

The motor skills of children with learning disabilities are difficult to categorize. Some children with learning disabilities experience no motor delays; others demonstrate a number of delays. The most common difficulties include visual-motor coordination,

fine motor coordination, bilateral coordination, and balance. In the past, learning goals for children with learning disabilities focused on perceptual-motor development; more recently the focus has been on sensory integration. Selection of the activities for meeting learning goals must be based on assessment of the child's deficiencies. Not all learning-disabled children have motor/perceptual delays; not all have the same deficiencies.

Children with learning disabilities can be expected to participate fully in all physical education activities. Slight teaching modifications may be needed for individual students:

- To reduce hyperactive tendencies, prepare the lesson with several short activities in mind rather than one lengthy period of concentration.
- Give clear, brief instructions; ask the child to repeat the directions before beginning the activity.
- Use small learning steps, and praise the child's efforts and accomplishments. Remember, the attitude of the learning-disabled child is "I can't."
- Use a positive behavior modification program if needed to increase appropriate and decrease inappropriate behavior (Chapters 8 and 9).
- End the lesson with a brief relaxation period.

Teaching children with learning disabilities can be a most rewarding experience (see Box 31-3). Teachers can help the youngsters develop socialization skills, motor skills many didn't know existed, and self-confidence. We believe children with disabilities can benefit from physical education and from integration with others.

Atlantoaxial Subluxation

A number of children with Down syndrome have a condition called *atlantoaxial subluxation*, a maladjustment of the cervical vertebrae in the neck. Because of the possibility of serious injury, people with atlantoaxial subluxation should not participate in any activities that place stress on the head and neck muscles. Down syndrome children with atlantoaxial subluxation should not be actively involved in inverted balances, rolling activities, or other gymnastics actions that could place stress on the head and neck.

Remedial Physical Education

Although many children with disabilities have average or above-average physical skills, others have physical skills that are far below average because of a lack of experience or as a secondary characteristic of the

Box 31-3

Examples of Items and Choices in Activity Categories

Grouping	Movements	Equipment	Conditions	Organizational Pattern
Age	**Locomotor:** Power walk, push wheel chair, run, skip, hop, gallop, grapevine	Nets, walls, rackets, bats, scarves, ropes, music, hoops, toss rings, discs, scoops, sticks, skates, bicycles, heart rate monitors, spots, mats, wedges, balance beams, volley birds, climbing harness	One bounce, using a wedge, four beats, lower net, all must hit, three-step rule, using two points of balance, may run to first or third base, until music stops, without using feet, within boundaries	Scattered, in lines, in rows, with a partner, in corners, back to back, elbow to elbow with two people, against wall, across from your group
Coed				
Mixed skill levels				
Similar skill	**Nonmanipulative:** Turn, twist, roll, balance, stretch			
Season of birthday (fall/spring)				
Favorite movies	**Manipulative:** Throw, catch, volley, dribble, strike, kick			
Favorite fruit				
Clothing colors	**(See the wheel in Chapter 13 for more)**			
By drawing numbers or cards	**Other:** To music, to the beat of a tambourine			

Creating Choices for Each Category

You may want to combine with another group or keep your current group.	You can throw or hit the ball over the line to start the rally with your partner.	You may choose a large hula hoop or a smaller one (a larger hula hoop is easier to twirl around the waist than a smaller one).	You may choose to let the ball bounce once per side or use a no-bounce rule.	You may choose to work with a partner or alone.
	You can choose to roll, step, or jump over the rope.	You may choose to raise or lower the net height. You may also decide to hit over a line on the floor.	For the first four beats of music you can either do four quick single jumps side to side or do two double-count jumps, one on the right, one on the left.	

Source: G. S. D. Morris and J. Stiehl, *Changing kids' games,* 2nd ed. (Champaign, IL: Human Kinetics, 1999).

disabling condition. For some children with disabilities, the small-group physical education class can provide the "extra" practice they need to succeed in the general physical education class. For these children, the remedial physical education class provides the environment for learning the basic skills of physical education that will enable them to participate successfully in the gymnasium and on the playground.

The content of the remedial physical education class centers around three areas of physical/motor skill development. The first area of concentration is mobility, balance, and muscular strength—hopping, jumping, and running; stepping onto a low platform or climbing the first rung of a ladder; walking a low balance beam or bench; and grasping a bar and lifting the body off the floor, taking weight on hands and feet.

These areas contribute not only to success in physical education but also to greater independence throughout life.

The second area of concentration is physical fitness. Although the child's flexibility is often very good, muscular strength—both abdominal and upper body—and cardiovascular endurance may be extremely poor. See Box 31-2 for fitness relative to students with disabilities. The third content area is the basic manipulative skills of physical education—throwing, catching, dribbling, kicking, and so forth. Children who succeed in these three content areas will participate meaningfully in physical education, attain greater personal independence, and improve their recreational/leisure skills on the school playground and beyond.

Early testing of the motor skills of the children in the remedial physical education class will help the teacher develop the educational program for each child. This program should be based on the child's present level of functioning and include goals for the year. Although evaluation is ongoing, motor skills tests should be conducted at least by midyear and again in the spring. Records of activities and achievements can be kept in simple chart form. Remember, progress for these children is often very slow and is measured in small increments; charting their progress will help you recognize and praise achievements.

Resources: See Web sites pertinent to specific disabilities, impairments, and disorders at the end of this chapter.

RTI in Physical Education

Response to Intervention (RTI) is a program of interventions for students who are struggling in the general education curriculum. RTI consists of tiers of intervention progressing from additional support within the general program, to additional small-group interventions, to individualized services including parents and professionals to address the child's needs. The program relies heavily on assessment, data driven decisions, and research based interventions (Stephens, et.al. 2010). RTI in physical education provides a system of assessing students based on established benchmarks and providing the additional support within and beyond the school day to assist the child in becoming competent, confident, and joyful in physical activity. (See Chapter 27 for RTI designed for health-related fitness and physical activity.)

Creating Conditions for Inclusion

The question that still remains is, How do you create an inclusive environment where all students meet program goals through maximum learning and participation? At this point, the idea of meeting the needs of so many different learners may feel overwhelming. However, rather than focusing on student differences, the purpose of this section is to provide strategies for creating five universal conditions needed to maximize student learning and participation: Students need to feel competent, to belong, to feel useful, to have a sense of ownership, and to feel optimistic (Sagor 2002).

Kids are sacred; activities or learning tasks are not. If the learning tasks or activities you choose to teach do not align with program goals or meet these five basic needs of all learners, you have three options: (1) continue to use the activity the way it has always been done and thus not meet the children's needs; (2) stop using the activity entirely and miss the benefits of the activity; or (3) give the activity a make-over—modify it by accentuating the positive features and minimizing or eliminating the negative or inappropriate features (Stiehl, Morris, and Sinclair 2008). The third option allows you to modify activities in ways that meet needs specific to your own setting. Stiehl and his coauthors point out that the three keys to making successful and effective modifications are (1) change, (2) challenge, and (3) choice.

Change

A teacher must be willing to make changes when learning tasks or activities do not meet the needs of all learners. All activities are made up of basic categories that can be changed (Box 31-3). These categories can include **grouping** (how learners are grouped—e.g., individually, in pairs, small groups, coed); **organizational pattern** (how learners are arranged—e.g., circle, lines, scattered, in designated zones); **equipment** (any objects, materials, or props—e.g., music, hoops, task cards, ropes, balls); **movements** (e.g., crawl, walk, crab walk, strike); and **conditions** (e.g., three minutes, without hands, until everyone stops, four turns, or with blindfold); (Stiehl, Morris, and Sinclair 2008). See Chapter 30 for additional strategies for changing games play for children.

Simple changes across such categories can make almost any activity more inclusive. When teaching students at the precontrol level to catch by having them learn to stop a rolling ball (Chapter 23), simply change the equipment from a regular plastic ball to a larger, slow-moving, sound-emitting ball so visually impaired students can also learn to catch a rolling ball.

Changes can also alter the nature of student participation. For example, many students enjoy and even beg at times to play elimination games (activities that involve eliminating other students in order to win, which are not promoted or included in *Children Moving*). This creates a situation where the more skilled students are allowed to dominate the activity while less skilled students, who actually need more practice, are sitting on the side and often feeling quite discouraged. A traditional game of Four Square is an elimination game. In the traditional game, a student who misses by not being able to return the ball to an opponent is out of the game. The game becomes nonelimination by changing the elimination rule to having students count how many in a row they can hit without missing, making the game a cooperative activity, or by having students earn as many individual points as they can in a given time period (two minutes). These simple rule changes exemplify best practices in physical education by maximizing participation for all students.

Challenge

Changes across each of the categories in Box 31-3 also can be made to challenge all students at an appropriate level. It is important to monitor the success of students closely. Children engaged in learning a new skill should be successful approximately 80 percent of the time; otherwise, consider modifying the task so it becomes more or less difficult. (See Chapter 6 for more on student success rates.) When a group of diverse learners is learning a skill, it is not unusual for a task to challenge some children at an appropriate level while others seem almost bored with the task, and still others are frustrated because the task is too difficult. To challenge all students at a more appropriate level, the teacher needs to utilize intratask variation (Chapter 6). Intratask variation is a technique in which the teacher decides to modify a task for individuals or small groups within the class; it is a private interaction between one or more students and the teacher. The following are examples of intratask variation for the activity traveling to flee (Chapter 17).

The task is for students to spread out in space and, on signal, to flee from an imaginary chaser by walking quickly.

1. Intratask variation used to make the activity more inclusive for a visually impaired student:

   "John, I would like you to use this guide rope (place rope in the visually impaired student's hand) to practice moving away from your imaginary chaser." The guide rope extends across the gym or playground to permit the practice of locomotor skills and freedom of travel. Tie a series of knots in the ropes to signal the approach of boundaries. Other children are spread out in space and practice fleeing an imaginary chaser by walking quickly.

2. Intratask variation to make the task more inclusive for several very skilled students:

   "See if the three of you can flee an imaginary chaser while avoiding the hoops on the ground." Other children continue original task.

3. Intratask variation for a less fit student:

   "Sue, you can move away from the chaser slowly until you feel ready to walk quickly again."

Choice

When modifying activities to meet the needs of all students, choice is the key (Stiehl, Morris and Sinclair 2008). Offering children choice among appropriate challenges (or tasks) not only creates a more inclusive environment, but also empowers children by allowing them to make decisions about how they want to participate. When students have choices, they are much more likely to participate. This becomes increasingly important for children in upper-elementary school and middle school. One way to offer students choice is through teaching by invitation (Chapter 6). Unlike intratask variation, teaching by invitation allows students to decide what task they prefer to work on. The following are examples of ways to give children choices:

1. "Choose one of the objects in the hoops and keep the object from touching the ground by hitting it up using an underhand motion." Place a variety of objects in hoops around the play area. Suggestions: Large bright items such as balloons and beach balls are slow moving and easy to see, and therefore may be appropriate for less-skilled students. Medium-size, softer items such as a volleyball trainer or an inexpensive plastic ball may offer more challenge for others. Students may also find it motivating to use a less traditional item such as a Volleybird just to try something new.

2. Station teaching or learning centers are popular instructional approaches among physical education teachers. A typical lesson may involve asking students to perform an exercise at each of several fitness stations. Jim Stiehl, a teacher of diverse learners, advises if you want to ensure that students fail, provide only one way to do something. This one-size-fits-all approach in fitness stations means requiring that everyone perform the same thing at each station. To avoid this outcome, set up each station to represent a health-related fitness component such as muscular fitness, cardiovascular fitness, and flexibility or body composition. At each station place three color-coded plates (red, white, and blue). Tell students that red represents the most difficult task, white represents the medium-level task, and blue represents the easiest task. Then place pictures and/or descriptions of exercises under each plate. At each station, students can choose to perform the red, white, or blue exercise or a combination of all three. For example, at a flexibility station, the exercise under the red plate (most difficult) might be, "While sitting, touch your toes with both hands and hold for 10 seconds"; under the white plate (medium difficulty), "While sitting, see if you can touch your toes with both hands for 5 seconds"; and for the blue plate (easiest), "While sitting, see if you can touch your knees with both hands and hold for 10 seconds." Another set of plates may

include red: straight-leg push-ups; white: modified push-ups (bend knees); blue: wall push-ups.

3. It is also important to break ourselves of thinking that games, dance, and gymnastic activities must be done "the way they have always been done" or even done according to their names. For example, when playing a modified striking and fielding game, a student with a disability came to bat and told the pitcher (a preservice teacher) that he could not bat but could kick, so he wanted the pitch rolled to him. Amazingly, the idea of not participating because he was unable to bat never crossed this student's mind. Instead he quickly thought of a modification and insisted he could play as long as he had the choice to kick a larger ball rather than hitting a small ball. Less-skilled students then created their own adaptation by asking to have the larger foam ball tossed to them so they could hit it with the bat. Choice can be offered to students within the same activity by keeping an open mind about how a game or activity must be played and by allowing student input.

To create more inclusive physical activity environments, physical education teachers must make deliberate attempts to provide choices. Karl Rohnke (1989) reminds us to always offer choices because a coerced player is no longer a player. Choice encourages participation, accommodates diversity, and empowers students to make responsible decisions about their own participation (Stiehl, Morris, and Sinclair 2008). A quality, caring teacher will always struggle to meet all students' needs. However, by structuring the environment in ways that provide choice, students can make decisions about what works best for them. Using the concepts of change, challenge, and choice will enable us as teachers to create or modify any activity to better meet learners' needs and achieve program goals.

Meeting the Needs of Children with Disabilities

Meeting the needs of the child with disabilities is a joint effort of school professionals, parents, and professionals from related services. The physical education teacher is a critical member of the professional staff planning for and implementing the program for a child with disabilities.

The IEP Team

The appropriate education—both placement and curriculum—for each student with disabilities is determined by an IEP Team. The Team is composed of all those involved in providing an appropriate education for the child: the classroom teacher, special educators (physical education), parents, and professionals from related services. Following an educational assessment by the school psychologist and other professionals as needed, the IEP Team designs the educational program for the child; identifies support services needed and services to be secured from outside agencies; and establishes the educational goals to be attained within the given school year.

Because physical education is a direct service for all children with disabilities, the physical education teacher is a vital member of the IEP Team. As a member of the Team, the physical education specialist provides information about how the identified disability will

Physical activity is just as exciting to children with disabilities as it is for those without disabilities.

affect the child's performance in the existing program of physical education; the child's performance in physical fitness and basic motor skills and patterns of physical education; and the support services needed to meet this child's unique needs and facilitate maximum learning in physical education.

It is the *responsibility* of the physical education professional to provide input into the IEP meeting for each child with disabilities. While physical education schedules do not always provide an "open" time during the IEP meeting, your input is essential for every child with an IEP; that input can be with your presence at the meeting or with a written report.

During the IEP Team meeting, short- and long-term goals are written for all areas of the child's learning, including physical education, and the environment most conducive to meeting those goals is identified. As the physical education professional on the Team, your input is needed to establish the short- and long-term goals relative to physical education and to identify the environment most conducive to meeting those goals. Physical education options may include full inclusion, inclusion with a teacher assistant, or remedial physical education in addition to the regular program. The goal of the last is assistance in specified areas for better functioning/performance in the regular physical education program.

Individualized Education Program

Education for a child diagnosed with disabilities is formulated through the individualized education program. Generally, the IEP is limited to curricular areas of special education and related services—instruction designed to meet the child's unique needs and the related services necessary to help the child achieve maximum success. The IEP includes:

- A statement of the present level of the child's functioning
- Annual goals
- Short-term instructional objectives with timelines
- An explanation of the extent to which the child will not participate in the regular educational setting (physical education program)
- Special services to be provided, including their duration and extent
- Support services needed—personnel and equipment
- Plan for evaluation of annual goals

For some students with disabilities, full participation in physical education is possible; therefore the IEP will not address physical education. For other students, full participation is possible with support services, that is, personnel and/or equipment; these services will be identified in the IEP. For still other students, the development of skills for successful participation will require modification within the physical education curriculum, perhaps an alternative when an activity is not appropriate or is contraindicated. This alternative may be participation in another physical education class or work on a short-term physical education goal from the IEP within the class setting. *Zero exclusion* (Weber, 2009) is the basic concept of physical education for all children with disabilities.

Even at the elementary level, physical education for children with disabilities should focus on the development of functional and motor skills that lead to physical activity and successful recreational participation. Short- and long-term goals for the child in physical education will center around the skills needed for meaningful participation in physical education, the remediation of deficient motor skills and fitness components, and the skills needed for successful participation in physical activities at recess and in after-school play/recreational activities.

The IEP is a projection of what professionals and the parents think the child can accomplish. If the annual goals are inappropriate, the IEP Team reassesses the child's curriculum and formulates new goals better suited to the child's needs.

Least Restrictive Environment

The least restrictive environment is the educational setting that is most appropriate and most enabling for the child with disabilities. To the maximum extent appropriate, children with disabilities are to be educated with nondisabled students—thus the philosophy of inclusion.

Legal reasons aside, there are sound educational reasons for educating children with disabilities in the least restrictive environment. Research has shown that placing these youngsters with nondisabled children yields positive benefits in behavior and life skills. Educators have long agreed on the effectiveness of peer modeling in academics and skill acquisition among children. Furthermore, the inclusive classroom and gymnasium more closely mirror the real world than does the classroom or physical education setting that consists entirely of children with disabilities. Most of the students with disabilities we see in our public schools will reside and work within our communities and participate in community activities. The least restrictive, more enabling educational environment should give students with disabilities the same opportunities to learn, to develop personal potential, and to interact and mature socially that all other students receive.

The Ecological Model of Inclusion

After the IEP has been written, it's the responsibility of all teachers working with the child with disabilities to implement what is written in the program. It is the responsibility of the physical education teacher to design instruction and to modify both teaching and curriculum to meet the short- and long-term goals written for physical education within the environment deemed least restrictive by the IEP. Implementation actually begins with the IEP itself—the long- and short-term goals for the child with disabilities. When planning for inclusion, we suggest using a top-down ecological model* (Block 2007), as follows.

Step 1: Determine the critical skills the child with disabilities will need to be successful in the present— in physical education, on the playground—and in future recreational settings. Observe the child's homeroom at recess. What activities do the children choose to participate in during this time? What skills are needed for the child with disabilities to successfully participate in activities at recess? What are the skills he or she will need to be successful in the physical education program? What are the skills needed for successful participation in recreational activities outside the school setting? These are the skills that should be contained within the goals for physical education for the child with disabilities.

Step 2: Analyze the existing physical education program to match the existing program to the long- and short-term goals of the student's IEP. Are the skills taught within the general physical education program consistent with the needs of the child with disabilities? What existing activities within the program will benefit the child? What activities are not appropriate for this child? An analysis of the existing curriculum will reveal areas of match between goals and existing program and areas in which modifications are needed. Ask yourself the following questions: Where are modifications needed? What modifications are needed in instruction (Chapter 10)? What modifications are needed in curriculum (Chapters 28–30)?

Step 3: Design modifications in your teaching and curriculum to meet the needs of the child with disabilities. Planning for inclusion in physical education permits the child with disabilities to be physically

educated along with his or her peers. Implementation of the IEP will be much easier and learning much greater with planning for this special child and with the design of a developmentally appropriate program of physical education.

Whether the IEP specifies full inclusion, inclusion with support services, or inclusion plus a remedial program, we can no longer be content with letting the child with disabilities serve only as the scorekeeper. Neither can we accept "token" participation. Our task is to design the program to develop each child's skills in gymnastics, games, and dance, and to provide opportunities for these students to reach the goals established for them.

Adaptations in tasks will permit any child to participate, to achieve, and to develop skills commensurate with personal ability. With an understanding of basic concepts, an awareness of the children's needs, and knowledge of how to adapt the environment and the curriculum, the teacher can create an enabling environment for children with special needs. Children with disabilities can function in an elementary physical education environment that allows individual response and fosters performance at the individual's skill level and that is taught by teachers who observe, reflect, and make changes in light of children's needs.

Essential Elements of Inclusion Programs

- A full continuum of placement options and services. Placement and services must be determined for each student by a team that includes all stakeholders and must be specified in the individualized education program.
- Appropriate professional development, as part of normal work activity, for all educators and support staff associated with such programs.
- Adequate time, as part of the normal school day, to engage in coordinated and collaborative planning on behalf of all students.
- Class sizes that are responsive to student needs.
- Staff and technical assistance that are specifically appropriate to student and teacher needs.

Source: NEA Today (July 1996). (Washington, DC: National Education Association).

*A top-down ecological model implies that planning is based on the skills students need to achieve to be successful in the future, chronological age-appropriate activities that will lead to the development of functional skills for physical activity. We plan for the skills they need now and in their next school setting.

Implementing Inclusion

Even with a strong belief in the philosophy of inclusion, initial attempts at implementation are often accompanied with feelings of apprehension. Can I meet the needs of this child with disabilities? Can I meet the needs of all the children in my class? The following strategies will assist in implementing inclusion:

Prepare yourself
- Learn everything you can about the disability. Contact your nearest medical library; the librarians will be happy to provide information for you. Search the Internet; the search will be limited only by the time you can devote to the learning.
- Get to know the child and his or her family. Visit with the child in the home environment. Invite the parents to school to observe a physical education class. Let the family and the child get to know you. Discussion will be much easier if the child and the parents are comfortable with you as the teacher.

Prepare the class
- Discuss the disability in general terms with the class that the child with disabilities will be attending.
- Tell the class about the child—his or her likes and dislikes, his or her strengths. Discuss things the class can do to help the child in physical education—things to help, not hinder, the child.

Become an *active* member of the IEP Team
- You are the expert in terms of the child's motor functioning and skill level. You are the key in the design of goals for motor development and appropriate placement for the child. You are critical to the discussion of assistance needed for the child in physical education.

Plan for success
- Using the ecological model described above, make the following decisions in your daily planning: Is this lesson appropriate for the child with disabilities? What modifications need to be made in the tasks presented for the child with disabilities? Is this a lesson that is not appropriate, and if so, what goals from the IEP can be the alternative activities for the lesson?
- The "ecological model" approach to planning plus participation in the remedial physical education class will greatly facilitate positive, successful physical education for the child with disabilities and for the teacher.

Most important, remember, inclusion is a philosophy that reflects a belief that all children, regardless of abilities or disabilities, are educated within the same environment (Block 2007). It is a physical education environment where each and every child has his or her needs met. It is an environment where all children are accepted, all are valued, an environment in which

we design, adapt, and modify experiences on a daily basis to maximize individual learning.

A Final Thought

If we are to become teachers of all children—children of diversity, children with disabilities—we must be aware of and move beyond our individual biases, beyond our preconceived expectations of students and their potential (Timken 2005). We must value the richness of diversity and be responsive to the cultures, needs, interests, and abilities of the children we teach. We must know our students and know them well.

As we strive to provide maximum opportunities for learning and development of personal potential in all children, may the following student request be our inspiration:

Please, my teacher, open up your . . .
> ***Heart*** to ***care*** ever more deeply for us;
> ***mind*** to ***think*** ever more creatively about ways of helping us learn;
> ***mouth*** to ***seek*** fresh ideas and feedback (including from us!); and
> ***classroom*** to ***join*** colleagues and parents in a thriving community
> where as teacher, parents and children together
> we strive to reach our potential.
> ***okay?***
> —*Ronald F. Ferguson, August 2003*

Sample Web Sites for Disabilities, Impairments, and Disorders

Attention-Deficit/Hyperactivity Disorder

Attention Deficit Disorder Association: www.add.org

Children and Adults with Attention Deficit/Hyperactivity Disorder: www.chadd.org

National Resource Center on ADHD: www.help4adhd.org

National Institute of Mental Health (Deficit Disorder): www.nimh.nih.gov/

Autism, Asperger Syndrome

Autism Research Institute: http://autism.com

Autism Society: www.autism-society.org

Life Journey Through Autism: An Educator's Guide to Asperger Syndrome: www.aspergersyndrome.org/ www.researchautism.org

National Institute of Neurological Disorders (Asperger Syndrome): www.ninds.nih.gov/

Sample Web Sites for Disabilities, Impairments, and Disorders (*Continued*)

Blindness and Visual Impairments

American Foundation for the Blind: www.afb.org

Cerebral Palsy

MyChild with Cerebral Palsy: www.cerebralpalsy.org

Hearing Impairments

National Institute of Child Health and Human Development (Deafness and Other Communication Disorders): www.nichd.nih.gov

Strategies for Teaching Students with Hearing Impairments: www.as.wvu.edu/~scidis/hearing.html

Developmental Disabilities

National Institute of Child Health and Human Development (Developmental Disabilities): www.nichd.nih.gov/

About Developmental Disabilities (Developmental Disabilities): www.cdc.gov

Diabetes

Safe at School (Living with Diabetes/For Parents & Kids/Safe at School): www.diabetes.org

Learning Disabilities

Learning Disabilities Association of America: www.ldanatl.org

National Center for Learning Disabilities: www.ncld.org

Tourette Syndrome

National Tourette Syndrome Association: http://tsa-usa.org

Summary

Diversity in the United States is steadily increasing. Diversity is defined as differences that exist among people. Physical education teachers must be prepared to teach all students, including those with differences in mental and physical ability, skill level, fitness level, gender, culture, language, class, and physical characteristics. It is time to support diverse learners through a broadened conceptualization of inclusion that goes beyond accommodating students with special needs.

Inclusion does not mean sitting on the sidelines keeping score. Inclusion involves teachers in creating a healthy learning climate where all children feel safe, successful, motivated, and connected to others and have a sense of ownership. When learning tasks or activities do not meet these basic needs of all learners, modifications must be made.

The concepts of change, challenge, and choice provide structure for making these modifications. Changes can be made to any task or activity across five categories: grouping, movements, equipment, conditions, and organizational pattern. Teachers should make changes across these categories in order to challenge all students at the appropriate level. Another strategy for meeting the needs of diverse learners is to create conditions that allow students choice among appropriate tasks or challenges.

In addition to developing strategies for modifying learning tasks, we should learn about the many ways students can be different. This includes learning about culturally responsive teaching, gender equity, religious differences, children of poverty, teaching overweight children, and teaching children with mental and physical disabilities. When a student with a disability or who speaks another language enters our classroom, we should educate ourselves about their unique needs through extensive reading, as well as communicating with qualified professionals, parents, and community members.

When working with diverse students, it is important to know that integrating children with special needs into regular educational settings is no longer a choice for teachers and administrators. The Individuals with Disabilities Education Act of 1990 guarantees each child with a disability a free and appropriate education in the least restrictive environment. The individualized education program (IEP) Team determines the placement that constitutes the least restrictive environment.

The child's educational program, including annual goals, support services, and any special services, is written into the IEP. The IEP includes physical education as a direct service for all children with disabilities.

We need to educate all children concerning individual differences and to orient them to the world of diversity. By promoting the acceptance of all individuals and presenting a curriculum that focuses on the development of skills commensurate with ability, we can promote the acceptance of all children as contributing members of physical education classes. Zero exclusion is the standard for all children in physical education; nothing less is acceptable.

Reading Comprehension Questions

1. Define diversity and provide three specific examples of diversity in physical education.
2. Explain the term *inclusion expanded*.
3. Explain what culturally responsive teaching is. Use two specific examples of things a physical educator might do to become a more culturally responsive teacher.
4. Describe three ways a teacher can create a more gender-equitable environment.
5. Explain the purpose(s) or reasons for modifying activities.
6. Name three categories that can be used to change activities. For each category list one modification that could be made to decrease the difficulty of a task, and one modification that could be made to increase the difficulty of a task.
7. Explain how choice can be used to accommodate individual differences in physical education. Be sure to include a specific example in your answer.

8. What is the Individuals with Disabilities Education Act? What is its impact on physical education?
9. What is an IEP Team? What is its function? Who serves on the Team?
10. Why is the physical education teacher an important member of the multidisciplinary team?
11. What is an individualized education program? What does it include?
12. What are the three steps in planning for inclusion? Why is this planning important for inclusion of a child with disabilities in physical education?
13. Choose one physically disabling condition and explain its implications for physical education. Discuss the adaptations involved in physical education for this child—adaptations for the child, adaptations for the whole class, and adaptations for the teacher.

References/Suggested Readings

American Association for Physical Activity and Recreation. 2003. *Physical education for infants, children, and youth with disabilities: A position statement.* Reston, VA: American Association for Physical Activity and Recreation.

[AOA] American Obesity Association, 2010. Childhood overweight. www.obesity.org (accessed August 25, 2010).

Association for Supervision and Curriculum Development. 2003. Teaching all students. *Educational Leadership* 61(2).

Auxier, D., J. Pyfer, L. Zittel, and K. Roth. 2010. *Principles and methods of adapted physical education and recreation.* New York: McGraw-Hill.

Block, M. E. 2000. *A teacher's guide to including students with disabilities in regular physical education.* 2nd ed. Baltimore: Brookes.

Block, M. E. 2007. *A teacher's guide to including students with disabilities in general physical education.* 3rd ed. Baltimore: Brookes.

Chappelle, S., and L. Bigman, with F. Hillyer. 1998. *Diversity in action.* Hamilton, MA: Project Adventure.

Cummins, J. 1992. The empowerment of Indian students. In *Teaching American Indian students,* ed. J. Reyhnor, 3–12. Norman: University of Oklahoma.

Cruz, L. M. and S. C. Peterson 2011. Teaching diverse students: How to avoid marginalizing difference. *Journal of Physical Education, Recreation and Dance* 82(6): 21–28.

[DOE] Department of Education. 2011. Creating equal opportunities for children and youth with disabilities to participate in physical education and extracurricular athletics. http://www2.ed.gov (accessed August 25, 2011).

Eichstaedt, C. B. 1978. Signing for physical education, *Journal of Physical Education, Recreation and Dance* 19(5): 20–21.

Evans, J. R. 1980. *They have to be carefully taught: A handbook for parents and teachers of young children with handicapping conditions.* Reston, VA: American Alliance for Health, Physical Education, Recreation and Dance.

Gay, G. 2000. *Culturally responsive teaching: Theory, research, and practice.* New York: Teachers College Press.

Harrison, L., R. L. Russell, and J. Burden. 2010. Physical education teachers' cultural competency. *Journal of Teaching in Physical Education* 29(2): 184–96.

Kahan, D. 2003. Religious boundaries in public school physical activity settings (law review). *Journal of Physical Education, Recreation and Dance* 74(1): 11–13.

MacCracken, M. 1978, July. Teacher. *In Touch* 1 (6).

Meece, J. L., and B. Kurtz-Costes. 2001. The schooling of ethnic minority children and youth. *Educational Psychologist* 36(1): 1–7

Morris, G. S. D., and J. Stiehl. 1999. *Changing kids' games.* 2nd ed. Champaign, IL: Human Kinetics.

Napper-Owen, G. E. 1994. Equality in the elementary gymnasium. *Strategies* 8(3): 23–26.

[NASPE] National Association for Sport and Physical Education. 2011. *Physical education for lifelong fitness: The physical best teachers guide.* 3rd ed. Champaign, IL: Human Kinetics.

[NCES] National Center of Educational Statistics. 2010. Digest of educational statistics. Washington, DC: U.S. Department of Education. http://www.NCES.ed.gov (accessed August 25, 2011).

National Education Association. 1996, July. *NEA Today.* Washington, DC: National Education Association.

Oberti, C. 1993. Inclusion: A parent's perspective. *Exceptional Parent* 23(7): 18–21.

Rohnke, K. 1989. *Cowstails and cobras II: A guide to games, initiatives, ropes courses and adventure curriculum.* Dubuque, IA: Kendall/Hunt.

Sagor, R. 2002. Lessons from skateboarders. *Educational Leadership* 60(1): 34–37.

Sapon-Shevin, M. 2008. Learning in an inclusive community. *Educational Leadership* 66(1):49–53.

Sherrill, C. 2004. *Adapted physical activity, recreation, and sport.* 6th ed. New York: McGraw-Hill.

Sparks, W. G. III. 1994. Culturally responsive pedagogy: A framework for addressing multicultural issues. *Journal of Physical Education, Recreation and Dance* 65(9): 33–36, 61.

Stephens, T. L., L. Silliman-French, L. Kinnison, and R. French (2010). Implementation of a response-to-intervention system in general physical education. *Journal of Physical Education, Recreation and Dance* 81(9): 47–53.

Stiehl, J., G. S. D. Morris, and C. Sinclair. 2008. *Change, challenge, choice: Creating strategies that include everyone.* Champaign, IL: Human Kinetics.

Taylor, David. 1991. *Project Active Newsletter* 12(1).

Tiedt, P. L., and I. M. Tredt. 1990. *Multicultural teaching: A handbook of activities, information, and resources.* Boston: Allyn & Bacon.

Timken, G. L. 2005. Teaching all kids: Valuing students through culturally responsive and inclusive practice. In *Standards-based physical education curriculum development,* ed. J. Lund and D. Tannehill, 78–97. Boston: Jones & Bartlett.

Tipps, C. R. 2006. Kids at hope: All children are capable of success—No exceptions! *Journal of Physical Education, Recreation and Dance* 77(1): 24–26.

Tomlinson, C. A. 2003. Deciding to teach them all. *Educational Leadership* 61(2): 7–11.

[USDE] U.S. Department of Education, Office of Special Education Programs, Data Analysis System. 2007. Report of children with disabilities receiving special education under Part B of the Individuals with Disabilities Education Act.

Weber, M. C. 2009. Special education law: Challenges old and new. *Phi Delta Kappan* 90(10): 728–32.

Winnick. J. P., and F. X. Short. 1999. *The Brockport physical-fitness test manual.* Champaign, IL: Human Kinetics.

Integrating the Skill Theme Approach Across the Curriculum

When asked what I teach, I like to respond "children."

—JOHN HICHWA (1998)

Key Concepts

- Interdisciplinary learning connects content from at least two subject areas in an attempt to promote learning in both subjects.

- Making connections between the cognitive and psycho-motor domains and between content areas, such as mathematics and reading, is motivating to children and helps them see connections in what they are learning.

- When integrating lessons, we cannot lose sight of the educational goals we want to accomplish in our physical education programs, but we can effectively reinforce important concepts taught in other subject areas across the curriculum.

- Three approaches—content linkage, shared integration, and the thematic unit—all connect curricular content from at least two subject areas.

- For successful integration, we need knowledge of and an appreciation for other subject area content and an under-standing of the scope and sequence of the subjects being integrated.

- Recent research suggests there is a connection between physical activity and academic performance.

By now you have a thorough understanding of the skill theme approach, why it is important, and how teachers are implementing it in their programs. One advantage of the skill theme approach is that it provides numerous opportunities for teachers to focus on concepts being taught in the classroom while students also work to improve their motor skills and physical fitness. This concept of integrated learn-ing experiences, or *interdisciplinary learning*, has gained impetus in the past few years, and we believe it will continue to be recognized as a powerful way to help children make connections and learn.

This chapter will help you better understand how to integrate physical education concepts and skills with those from other subject areas throughout the elemen-tary curriculum. Three approaches to integrating skills and concepts are discussed—the content linkage ap-proach, the shared integration approach, and the the-matic unit approach. Examples from different content areas are used to illustrate how these approaches work.

The chapter ends with a review of recent literature that makes the connection between physical activity and successful performance in the classroom, includ-ing research suggesting an important link between movement and brain function. Both the connection between physical education and other areas of school curriculum and the connection between physical ac-tivity and academic performance reinforce the impor-tance of an effective physical education program in all elementary schools.

Connecting Physical Education and the Classroom Curriculum Through Interdisciplinary Learning

Any time we can make learning more relevant and per-sonally meaningful to the child's life, it has a more profound effect and will be remembered longer (Roberts and Kellough 2006). For some children, especially those that are kinesthetic learners (Gardner 2006), the connections are best made through movement.

Defining Interdisciplinary Learning

A major thrust in curriculum development in schools today is the integration of subject content across the curriculum (Wood 2009). "Interdisciplinary learning is an educational process in which two or more subject areas are integrated with the goal of fostering enhanced learning in each subject area" (Cone et al. 1998). Inte-gration helps kids make sense of what they know as it pertains to them and their world. The terms *interdisci-plinary* and *integration* are usually considered synony-mous and will be used interchangeably in this chapter.

Integration enhances learning by:

- Reinforcing curriculum content in a variety of edu-cational settings
- Encouraging children to transfer what is learned in one setting or situation to new settings and situa-tions, adding meaning to what is being learned
- Providing children with multiple opportunities to practice particular skills and concepts
- Encouraging children to better understand and to see the connectedness of what they are learning and how it relates to their own world

Interdisciplinary Learning and Quality Physical Education

The National Association for Sport and Physical Educa-tion (NASPE) developed a document outlining criteria for schools to follow to ensure a quality learning en-vironment for students in physical education. This document, entitled *Opportunity to Learn: Guidelines for Elementary School Physical Education* (NASPE 2010), was written to complement the content-focused National Standards for Physical Education (NASPE 1995), and it

As part of health class, students are learning about nutrition and physical activity.

directly addresses the importance of interdisciplinary learning experiences. The criteria for providing an adequate learning environment for children related to physical education are listed in Box 32-1. The criteria clearly focus on a combined effort by both the physical education teacher and the classroom teacher to provide physical activity opportunities throughout the school day and to foster cognitive development through movement experiences.

Integrating Physical Education and Other Curricula Content

Physical education as part of an integrated curriculum can work in two ways—integrating core subject-matter content into the physical education lesson, or integrating physical education skills and concepts into other curriculum areas in the classroom. (See Table 32.1.) Any type of integrative curriculum most likely will encourage a new sense of respect and increased interest between teachers about their subject areas. One physical education teacher who integrated an orienteering unit into the math and science core curriculum in an elementary classroom said he felt rewarded by gaining respect from the other teachers in the school who then saw him as a more significant contributor to the overall school curriculum (Placek 1992).

As a result of the connections among learning domains and between subject-specific information sets that integration allows, children often see the knowledge gained as having more importance in the real-life context. For example, students who are normally

---

Box 32-1

Opportunity to Learn: Guidelines for Elementary School Physical Education

- 2.7 The curriculum integrates kinesthetic experiences that reinforce math concepts, language arts, social studies, science, and health.
- 2.10 The curriculum gives students opportunities to develop critical thinking skills.
- 7.6 Physical education teachers are provided planning time for interdisciplinary work and program development so that they can meet with other classroom teachers and/or specialists in other disciplines.
- 8.8. Physical education teachers are encouraged to engage in cross-curriculum projects to ensure active participation in joint technology projects.

Source: National Association for Sport and Physical Education, *Opportunities to learn: Guidelines for elementary physical education: A position statement from the National Association for Sport and Physical Education* (Reston, VA: National Association for Sport and Physical Education, 2010).

Table 32.1 Example of Two-Directional Integration Between Physical Education and Science

Physical Education	integrated ⟶ into	Science	Plan a hike through a nearby part to identify trees, flowers, and other plants
Science	integrated ⟶ into	Physical Education	Children use different locomotor movements to travel through a large replica of the heart on the gym floor to show the pathway of blood flow

unenthusiastic about physical education may be motivated by the integrative activities that allow them success in both the cognitive and psychomotor domains, such as learning to swim while studying water in science. By the same token, students who excel in physical activities but are less interested in other subject areas may find an interesting connection that motivates them to learn other subject-specific content. One example might be the student who is struggling with reading but is excited to complete a reading assignment about a famous hockey player while learning the skill of striking with a hockey stick in physical education class. In either case, the integrative approach increases the potential for motivating children to learn.

Physical education and physical activity can be integrated with any other content area in the curriculum, including math, reading/language arts, social studies, science, health, technology, music, and art. Integration examples are provided throughout this chapter as a guide in helping teachers develop integrated lesson ideas for connecting physical education/activity and any other subject-specific standard.

Benefits of Integration

It is important to understand why integrating subject areas is worthwhile and to reflect on the benefits of integration for both physical education and other subject content areas. Following are some of the most notable benefits—from both the physical education class and the classroom perspectives.

Benefits of Integrating Other Subject Skills/Concepts into the Physical Education Class

- Children learn best by seeing connections in what they are learning. For most children, physical education is fun! A quality physical education program helps them to become proficient in many skills, and most elementary children are innately inclined to be physically active at every given opportunity. Kinesthetic learning of other subject content often helps children grasp concepts in language arts, science, and math that they might otherwise struggle with in a more inert classroom environment.
- Some children who are not as proficient in motor skills and movement but who excel academically will find the connection between the cognitive and psychomotor domains and between the two content areas to be motivating and enjoyable.
- When the physical education environment is used to reinforce other academic skills and concepts, physical education has a newfound importance to other teachers and administrators in the school. Even though the importance of the physical education program goals should be recognized foremost by the school, when teachers work together to help students succeed on standardized tests their efforts are applauded.

Web Sites for Integrated Lesson Ideas

The following Web sites are excellent resources for specific examples of lesson ideas that integrate physical activity in core academic areas in the elementary curriculum.

Active Academics (www.activeacademics.org). More than 150 active learning ideas designed to incorporate movement with grade-appropriate standards in reading, language arts, math, science, and health; includes ideas for short activity breaks in the regular K–5 classroom.

Eat Smart Move More North Carolina: Energizers for Elementary School (www.eatsmartmovemorenc.com/Energizers/Elementary.html). A collection of short activities integrating physical activity with academic concepts; developed by East Carolina University in conjunction with the North Carolina Department of Public Instruction; designed for elementary school classroom teachers.

PE Central (www.pecentral.org). More than 180 integrated lesson ideas submitted by teachers that connect physical activity and academic content; for use in the classroom or on a large play area.

Benefits of Integrating Physical Activity in the Regular Classroom

- It is recommended that children be physically active at least 60 minutes a day (IOM 2005; NASPE 2004). Schools should strive to meet as much of this time recommendation as possible during the school day. As outlined in the new national campaign, Let's Move in School, a comprehensive school physical activity program encourages physical activity opportunities throughout the school day, in addition to a quality physical education program (cross-laterally classroom physical activity breaks not only contribute to increased daily physical activity time, but also have been shown to improve classroom attentiveness and behavior (Mahar et al. 2006)).

- By integrating physical education skills and concepts with other subject areas, children are able to simultaneously practice motor, language arts, and math skills, for example, while also gaining the benefits of being physically active. In addition, short activity breaks every 20 to 30 minutes help children to concentrate more and be ready to learn.

- Children love to move! For children, movement is a critical means of communication, expression, and learning. The active rather than passive involvement in learning that movement allows often makes children more excited and motivated to learn. (See Box 32-2.)

Box 32-2

Gardner's Theory of Multiple Intelligences

According to Howard Gardner's Theory of Multiple Intelligences, we have at least eight types of intelligences—linguistic, logical-mathematical, spatial, bodily-kinesthetic, musical, interpersonal, intrapersonal, and naturalistic. His premise is that humans possess all of these intelligences to some degree, but we are gifted more in some than others. We learn best when given opportunities for them to interact and work to solve problems in a naturalistic setting.

Gardner's view of intelligence supports the interdisciplinary approach to learning. He encourages educators to look at different learning styles of children, and to help connect learning while focusing on the particular intelligences individuals possess. Many children are kinesthetic learners—they learn best through movement—however, they all too often are expected to sit passively for hours in desks in classrooms. Classroom teachers should strive to focus on all of the eight intelligences, including bodily-kinesthetic, while physical education teachers can take the opportunity to help children expand as many intelligences as possible through integrated learning experiences in the physical education setting.

Source: Howard Gardner, *Multiple intelligence: New horizons in theory and practice* (New York: Basic Books, 2006); T. Armstrong, *Multiple intelligences in the classroom* (Alexandria, VA: Association for Supervision and Curriculum Development, 2009).

Important Considerations

Before deciding to use the interdisciplinary approach in your program, there are some important considerations to ponder. For successful integration, you should have knowledge of and an appreciation for other subject area content, be prepared to put forth more effort, and always keep your goals in mind.

Reciprocal Respect for Subject Content

Integrating physical education and other subject content is not always easy. Physical educators will have to alter the way they think about physical education. They will have to become familiar with developmentally appropriate content in other subject areas in order to promote real learning. The classroom teachers and administrators will have to see physical activity and physical education skills as important components of a child's education, and see physical educators as viable contributors to the overall education of the child.

Standards-Based Instruction

Before planning interdisciplinary learning activities for your children, you (and any other collaborating teacher) should identify standards for each discipline, determine the assessment to be used to show what students know or can do at the end of the lesson(s), and then plan the appropriate activities and tasks. As with all standards-based curricula, the learning goals, activities, and assessments should align with each other.

Extra Effort

Developing effective interdisciplinary learning experiences, as with any curricular innovation, requires effort and time. You may have to rearrange the order of your teaching to coincide with the lesson concept or theme the classroom teacher is teaching, and vice versa. Some learning experiences will be successful; others may not. Be prepared to reflect on the learning experience, make changes, and try again.

Your Goals One challenge of interdisciplinary teaching is not to lose sight of the educational goals and objectives you want to accomplish as you plan integration activities with other subject areas. Always assess the potential benefits of the proposed integrative activity or unit, and if educational goals and objectives are not met, then it should not be considered a worthwhile endeavor. Remember, it is through the physical education program that children learn to perform locomotor, nonmanipulative, and manipulative movements proficiently, which will enhance their interdisciplinary learning.

The Process of Teaching Using an Interdisciplinary Learning Approach

A variety of interdisciplinary models have been introduced over the years. As we gain experience in integrating lessons, we typically develop and name our own models that guide us. We have chosen three approaches to discuss in this book that we hope will give you a general understanding of subject integration from simple to more complex. Other models and a more detailed breakdown of the approaches we are discussing here can be found in the related literature recommendations.

The three approaches—**content linkage, shared integration**, and **thematic unit**—all combine the teaching of skills and concepts from at least two subject areas. The content linkage approach can be used by one teacher independently, while the shared integration approach and the thematic unit approach both require a collaborative effort between at least two teachers from different subject areas in the school curriculum.

Content Linkage Approach

The *content linkage approach* is used by one teacher to connect content from at least two subject areas. One content area may be the primary focus of the lesson, but skills/concepts from another subject area enhance the learning experience and provide practice opportunities for learning the skills/concepts in the other subject area. Physical education teachers can find ways to reinforce classroom content without jeopardizing their primary focus of teaching skill themes, movement concepts, and fitness concepts using the content linkage approach. For example, the physical education teacher teaching a kindergarten class might reinforce the math concept of counting from 1 to 30 while focusing on traveling to pick up beanbags to transport across the gym.

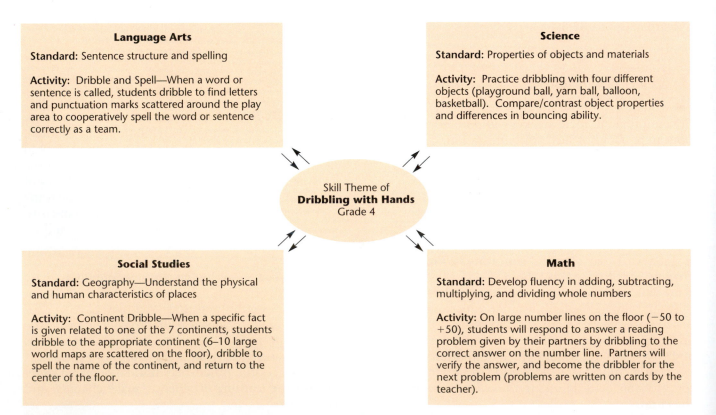

Language Arts

Standard: Sentence structure and spelling

Activity: Dribble and Spell—When a word or sentence is called, students dribble to find letters and punctuation marks scattered around the play area to cooperatively spell the word or sentence correctly as a team.

Science

Standard: Properties of objects and materials

Activity: Practice dribbling with four different objects (playground ball, yarn ball, balloon, basketball). Compare/contrast object properties and differences in bouncing ability.

Skill Theme of
Dribbling with Hands
Grade 4

Social Studies

Standard: Geography—Understand the physical and human characteristics of places

Activity: Continent Dribble—When a specific fact is given related to one of the 7 continents, students dribble to the appropriate continent (6–10 large world maps are scattered on the floor), dribble to spell the name of the continent, and return to the center of the floor.

Math

Standard: Develop fluency in adding, subtracting, multiplying, and dividing whole numbers

Activity: On large number lines on the floor (−50 to +50), students will respond to answer a reading problem given by their partners by dribbling to the correct answer on the number line. Partners will verify the answer, and become the dribbler for the next problem (problems are written on cards by the teacher).

Figure 32.1 Examples of other subject content integrated with the skill theme of dribbling.

Have a large map of the United States painted on the play area, or use four to six large maps taped to the floor. Activities that incorporate traveling, space awareness, and/or other manipulative skills can be used to identify states by names, facts, relationships, etc.

Task Example: On each state, place tokens with the state names. Students on teams of three will answer questions posed by the teacher by sending a team member to the correct state to get a token (i.e., state bordering West Virginia that begins with a P). After 10 questions, check for correct number of tokens for each group.

Other examples are depicted in Figure 32.1, which shows how content-specific skills for fourth graders might be integrated in the physical education curriculum while focusing on practicing the skill theme of dribbling with hands.

Likewise, classroom teachers can use movement to teach specific concepts in subject areas throughout the curriculum. For example, a classroom teacher who is teaching a language arts spelling lesson might have her fourth graders throwing and catching a ball with a partner while spelling a specific word or group of words. A more detailed example is shown in Figure 32.2, illustrating how math content for second graders might be taught through movement and the reinforcement of physical education concepts.

Shared Integration Approach

Another strategy for connecting more than one subject-specific content area is the shared integration model. In this approach, two teachers work together to provide a lesson or multiple lessons that focus on shared concepts from the two distinct disciplines. (For a comparison between this approach and the content linkage approach, see Table 32.2.) This type of lesson integration can be used readily in both the classroom and the physical education setting to reinforce skills and concepts. When teachers work together to teach and reinforce related skills from two or more subject areas, it helps integrate the cognitive, affective, and psychomotor domains of learning.

An example of shared integration is a lesson activity in Box 32-3 called "Stepping Across the U.S.," for fourth or fifth grades. This activity reinforces three physical education goals—teaching children about (1) the importance of physical activity, (2) what activities

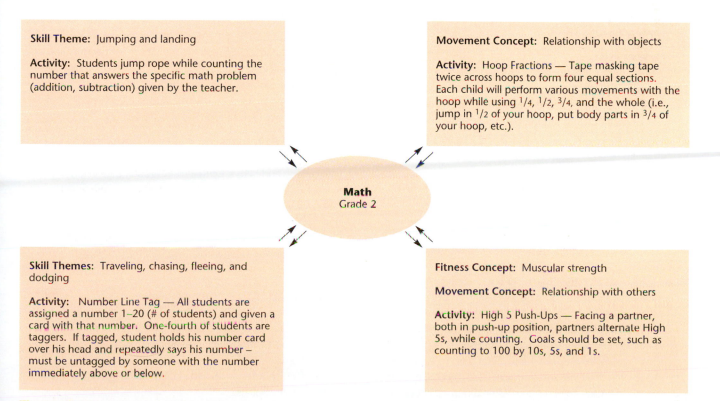

Skill Theme: Jumping and landing

Activity: Students jump rope while counting the number that answers the specific math problem (addition, subtraction) given by the teacher.

Movement Concept: Relationship with objects

Activity: Hoop Fractions — Tape masking tape twice across hoops to form four equal sections. Each child will perform various movements with the hoop while using $1/4$, $1/2$, $3/4$, and the whole (i.e., jump in $1/2$ of your hoop, put body parts in $3/4$ of your hoop, etc.).

Math
Grade 2

Skill Themes: Traveling, chasing, fleeing, and dodging

Activity: Number Line Tag — All students are assigned a number 1–20 (# of students) and given a card with that number. One-fourth of students are taggers. If tagged, student holds his number card over his head and repeatedly says his number – must be untagged by someone with the number immediately above or below.

Fitness Concept: Muscular strength

Movement Concept: Relationship with others

Activity: High 5 Push-Ups — Facing a partner, both in push-up position, partners alternate High 5s, while counting. Goals should be set, such as counting to 100 by 10s, 5s, and 1s.

Figure 32.2 Examples of reinforcing math concepts through skill themes and movement concepts.

Table 32.2 Comparing Integrated Approaches

Comparison of Content Linkage and Shared Integration				
Approach	Number of Subject Areas	Number of Teachers Needed	Time	Focus
Content linkage	2 or more	1	Usually during 1 lesson	Primary focus on 1 content area, with another subject area used to enhance
Shared integration	2 or more	2 or more	Could be for 1 lesson, but often extends over a longer period	Equal focus on shared concepts from two distinct disciplines

promote more movement and therefore more pedometer steps, and (3) the amount of physical activity needed to reach a set goal during each day. In addition, the learning experiences reinforce the social studies concepts of geography—location, distance, and facts about the states across the country. It could also be used to practice the math skills of estimation and comparison. This lesson would require both the physical education teacher and the classroom teacher to work together to equally reinforce these concepts.

Box 32-3

Example of a Shared Integration Learning Experience

Stepping Across the U.S.

Grade level: 4–5

PE skill/concept focus: Fitness and wellness concepts

PE content standard: Exhibits a physically active lifestyle

Social studies skill/concept focus: Geography—U.S. states

Social studies content standard: Understands the physical and human characteristics of places

Math skill/concept focus: Convert steps to miles, estimate, compare stats, add class miles/steps

Math content standard: Computes fluently and makes reasonable estimates

Materials needed: Pedometers for each child, paper logs or daily access to **PE Central Log It** (www.peclogit.org), maps for classroom and gym to track class progress, state facts, flags, etc.

Description of activity: Children are given a pedometer by the physical education teacher to be worn on weekdays for 3 consecutive weeks. The classroom teacher has the students log their steps each day on paper logs, or at **PE Central Log It** (www.peclogit.org). Students convert steps to miles using the conversion of 2,000 steps = 1 mile. Total class miles are calculated each day, and the class moves across the U.S. map according to the miles accumulated. When a new state capital is reached, both the classroom teacher and the physical education teacher will reinforce state facts such as the state seal; flag; bird; flower; animal; and the location, area, and population of the state, etc. Daily or weekly goals can be set, and estimation and comparisons can be taught. The physical education teacher should instruct students to set daily goals, to identify activities that promote the most physical movement by monitoring steps after specific activities, and to participate in physical activity outside of school.

Note: Using **PE Central Log It** to record pedometer steps allows students to record their steps daily, compare their stats with others, and take a "virtual hike" around the United States. When a new state is reached, students are able to see state information online, as well as see how many miles their class must log to travel to the next state. Individual goal setting is built into the Web site, and students earn certificates for reaching daily goals. Teachers must register their classes online.

Assessments:

- Check written logs for math accuracy in converting steps to miles, calculating total steps/mile, totaling and averaging group steps/mile, setting reasonable daily goals, and meeting them.
- Student worksheets should identify states traveled and list their state capitals.

Developing an Integrated Learning Experience

Once you have chosen a class or grade level with which you wish to teach an integrated lesson(s) using the content linkage approach, you will first need to review the grade-specific content scope and sequence and the state standards for the integrated subject and compare those with your own. Then choose the concepts/skills for each subject you wish to integrate, and you are ready to design an appropriate learning experience that focuses on the chosen concepts. (Use the format applied to the "Stepping Across the U.S." lesson as a guide.) Before implementing your lesson, share it with a teacher(s) of the other content area for awareness and feedback. After teaching the lesson, assess the success of the learning experience.

For the shared integration approach, both teachers should share program scope and sequence and standards and identify targeted standards, discuss possible integration experiences and assessment strategies, and decide which skills/concepts will be targeted. Together, write an appropriate lesson experience(s) that equally focuses on at least one skill/concept from each of the subject areas being integrated. Decide on the implementation date so lessons can be adjusted, if necessary.

Criteria for Integrated Lesson Development

When preparing and implementing learning experiences using either the content linkage approach or the shared integration approach, ask yourself the following questions. Does the integrated lesson:

- Provide developmentally and instructionally appropriate tasks (for grade, for individual children)?
- Focus on a skill theme, movement concept, and/or fitness concept that is consistent with the program scope and sequence?

Box 32-4

Examples of Integrating Reading/Literacy and Physical Education

Making connections between books and movement can help enhance reading comprehension and promote physical activity. Here are some examples:

Grade: K

Book: *The Silly Tail Book* (Marc Brown)
Lesson Idea: Read the story and discuss the different kinds of tails that jungle animals have. As the teacher pulls different tails from the bag, the children identify the animal to which it belongs, and then move through the jungle (classroom or cones on the gym floor) as that animal would move (e.g., elephant, giraffe, snake, panther, monkey, etc.). *Source:* Debra Williamson, Concord University, Athens, WV.

Grade: 1

Book: *Stellaluna* (Janell Cannon)
Lesson Idea: Have children recollect the beginning of the story when the baby bat, Stellaluna, is knocked from her mother's safe grasp by an angry owl one night while looking for food. In Stellaluna Steal Tag, four taggers (owls) try to tag mother bats carrying their young (a beanbag). If tagged, owls take the baby bats to the "baby bat bin," and they are rescued by their mother as she travels in various pathways to the bin. *Source:* www.activeacademics.org—Dorothy Reynolds, creator.

Grade: 1–2

Book: *Going on a Bear Hunt* (Rosen and Oxenbury)

Lesson Idea: After reading the book to the students, read again, this time allowing children to "act out" the story as the children and their father go through the tall grass, over the river, through the mud, etc. *Source:* www.activeacademics.org.

Grade: 2–3

Book: *Brand New Kid* (Katie Couric)
Lesson Idea: After reading the book about a boy who comes to a new school and is not readily accepted by his classmates, the children can discuss how his soccer skills impressed one of his classmates and helped her encourage others to accept him. Children can practice soccer dribbling skills like Lazlo and discuss ways to make others feel less lonely and less scared in any kind of "scary" situation. *Source:* www.activeacademics.org.

Grade: 4–5

Book: *Backyard Birding for Kids* (Fran Lee)
Lesson Idea: This book will help teach children to appreciate birds and will help them to identify birds through sight and song. It identifies birds common to the city, the woodlands, the country, the wetlands, the seashore, and the desert. Helping children learn to appreciate birds can lead to an outdoor hobby of birdwatching. If appropriate at your school, take your class on a "mini field trip" around campus to look for birds, and to begin a birdwatching journal. Assign children birdwatching walks outside of school (with a family member) to add more birds to their journals. *Source:* www.activeacademics.org.

- Reinforce specific content standard(s) in all subject area(s) being integrated, and is it consistent with the specific program scope and sequence for that grade?
- Include assessment strategies for assessing student learning in both subject areas?

Thematic Unit Approach

In the third approach to content integration, the thematic unit approach, teachers overlap the content across the curriculum over a set period while focusing on one theme. Many educators believe that integrating subjects such as physical education, art, and music with the core subject areas of math, science, social studies, and language arts using a thematic approach should be considered in school curriculums (Roberts and Kellough 2006; Wood 2009).

Evaul (1980) and others recommended the thematic approach in physical education years ago by suggesting that developmental themes such as cooperation, courage, independence, and responsibility be used as themes for organizing the physical education curriculum. Now, the interdisciplinary thematic unit approach is being incorporated in many elementary school curriculums to help connect student learning across a number of subject areas, including physical education. Thematic units can be planned and implemented by one teacher with his or her students, but to include subject areas across the curriculum, most teachers work together as a team to plan and implement learning experiences centered around a theme or topic over a specific period. A thematic unit of instruction might be a one-week study, or it might focus on a theme on an ongoing basis over many weeks. An example of a theme that might be used to connect different subject content in a kindergarten class is "The Jungle." Young children are interested in and intrigued by animals. This theme could easily incorporate lessons related to jungle animals, including characteristics of different types of animals, the jungle habitat, math concepts such as measuring and comparing (i.e., elephant foot to human foot), and many of the movement concepts (space awareness, relationships, and effort).

Included in this chapter are two examples of how thematic units can be developed to include a variety of subject areas, including physical education, connected through a theme. The thematic unit "Recreation in (Your State)" in Table 32.3 focuses on the study

Table 32.3 Thematic Unit: Recreation in (Your State) (Grades 5–6)

Overview: This thematic unit focuses on the study of recreational areas in your state. Learning activities include students working in groups to study and report on a specific recreational area, preparing a budget associated with participating in the recreational opportunity, and practicing motor and fitness skills necessary for successful participation in the physical activities of that area.

Social Studies	Math	Science	Language Arts	Physical Education	Health
Locate recreation opportunities throughout the state on the map; research each park or recreational area; determine distance from home area to each recreational area; study economy of the area; in a group, prepare a PSA or commercial to promote the area and its recreational opportunities.	Choose a recreational area that the class will visit; prepare a budget for a trip to the area, including cost of the trip (transportation, lodging, meals, fees), equipment, clothing, and any other costs associated with participating in the physical activity.	Decide what muscles need to be developed to prepare to participate in the physical activity.	Prepare a group report and poster about one recreational area in the state; use the Internet to read specific information about the recreational area you will visit.	Choose one recreational sport (e.g., snow skiing) and discuss and practice the motor skills and fitness levels necessary to enjoy participating in the sport.	Determine benefits of the physical activity; determine preferences; set personal goals—proper diet and activity; learn and practice basic first aid.

Culminating event: Plan a field trip to one of the recreational areas in the state, and participate in recreational opportunities in that area; utilize prepared budget, and apply the knowledge of the area and the physical activity.

Parental and community involvement: Parents join in on the trip, help organize and make arrangements for the trip; community resources that will be utilized are local recreation agencies, which will provide informational pamphlets, and clothing/equipment catalogs or retailers.

Source: B. McCracken, *It's not just gym anymore* (Champaign, IL: Human Kinetics, 2001).

Table 32.4 Thematic Unit: The Wild Wild West (Grade 4)

Overview: This thematic unit focuses on the westward expansion of America during the 19th century. The unit connects content in social studies, language arts, fine arts, and physical education.

Social Studies	Language Arts	Physical Education	Fine Arts
Map making of the U.S., locating landmarks and cities that travelers would see traveling west	"Wild West" theme folders to include a vocabulary list, daily journal entries as a frontiersperson, and other related activities	Introduction to orienteering—map reading, compass reading	Art: Begin to create a quilt and discuss the history of quilt making
Identify famous people involved in the settlement of the Old West; hardships of the early settlers	*How the Settlers Lived* by George and Ellen Laycock	Complete an orienteering activity, using landmarks that represent the Old West	Art: Incorporate *The Quilt Story* by Tony Johnston
The Oregon Trail computer software (The Learning Co. Inc.) takes you on an educational adventure	Prepare and rehearse oral presentations on various aspects of the Wild West	Participate in simple folk and square dances representative of that period	Music: Video musical *Oklahoma*—socializing aspects and time period comparisons

Culminating event: The Wild Wild West Celebration will conclude the thematic unit, with demonstrations of quilting, square dancing, story-telling, and oral presentations by the students. Displays of student work will be shown. Parents will be invited and all will be invited to wear period clothes and bring period items to share, such as old hats, pictures, lanterns, and other unique items.

Parental and community involvement: Parents are invited to be guest storytellers, observers, and participants in the final celebration. They are asked to help with their child's period costume. Local media are invited to attend the culminating event.

Source: Developed by Brenda Cannon, Kevin Hutchinson, Rick Spreeder, and Shannon Owen, Concord University, Athens, WV.

of recreational areas in a state and incorporates six subject areas that revolve around the theme. The "Wild Wild West" thematic unit in Table 32.4 is based on the westward expansion of America and incorporates four content areas. These examples illustrate only an overview of the partial unit but will help you see how learning across subject areas can be interconnected and how children might better "connect" their learning in ways that are more meaningful to their everyday experiences.

What Is a Culminating Event?

An effective thematic unit includes a culminating event or finale that will bring closure to the unit. The culminating event should provide an opportunity for students to demonstrate their "connected" knowledge, through written, oral, and/or movement presentations. It allows students to share what they have learned in different and individual ways. Examples are individual/class presentations to parents or other students in the school, field trips, and class projects.

Tips for Developing an Interdisciplinary Thematic Unit

1. Choose a theme, together with your students, that is motivating to them and that can incorporate skills/concepts from a variety of subject areas. If you are working with another teacher, include him or her in the theme selection process.
2. Inform school administrators and other teachers of your intent, and ask for their support and assistance. (Team teaching may require special planning time; outside speakers may be asked to come into the classroom; field trips may be planned, etc.)
3. Form a teaching team of interested teachers from other content areas. The team will:
   - Share content materials and brainstorm ideas for the unit.
   - Develop an overview of the unit, goals, instructional objectives, and final assessment.
   - Develop the theme-based learning experiences that meet subject areas content standards and those of the thematic unit, including a culminating event, assessment strategies, and timelines.

Pedometers can be used to teach important concepts in mathematics.

4. Inform parents and seek parental involvement. For example, parents may be asked to assist their children with special projects, bring expertise on a particular topic to the class, join the students for a special presentation, and so forth.

5. Locate instructional resources for the unit, including community resources. For example, if you are planning a unit around the theme of "Heart Health," you might have a pediatric cardiologist speak to the class, take children to a local park to explore physical activity possibilities, organize a field trip to the grocery store to analyze food selections, and have local athletes come to talk with the children about tobacco avoidance.

6. Implement the interdisciplinary thematic unit and assess the success of the unit (student learning).

Understanding the Scope and Sequence of Subject Area Content

For teachers to effectively integrate subject area content, they must be knowledgeable in the scope and sequence of the subjects being integrated.) In their text *Interdisciplinary Teaching Through Physical Education*, Cone et al. (1998) have reviewed textbooks and projects in the content areas of math, language arts, social studies, science, and the arts and have compiled

a scope and sequence for each area in grades K–6. They have given us permission to reprint their work in Table 32.5 to help you better understand the skills/concepts taught at each grade level in math. *Interdisciplinary Teaching Through Physical Education* also offers many suggestions in each subject area for active learning experiences that would be helpful to any physical education teacher planning interdisciplinary learning experiences.

Integrating physical education concepts with learning in other subjects in the school curriculum can be considered a viable approach to help physical education teachers enhance what is being learned in other subject areas and to help classroom teachers promote healthy lifestyles and physical activity. But clearly, it is the teachers that make integration work. If teachers recognize the contributions each field of study can make to the others, and strive to make connections between the subject areas, then student learning can be enhanced in new ways. Children benefit from seeing teachers working together to focus different subject areas on a common theme and reinforce what they are learning across the curriculum.

The Connection Between Physical Activity and Academic Performance

Educational reform movements of the last decade, including the No Child Left Behind (NCLB) Act of 2001, placed increased emphasis on math and reading for all grades, and schools and teachers are being held more accountable for adequate student progress toward achievement of state standards in the core subjects (NCLB 2002). With high-stakes testing programs taking precedence across the nation, some administrators are tempted to reduce, or even eliminate, physical education as a solution to improve test scores. Recent evidence suggests this is ill advised. In fact, students who have regular physical education, are more physically fit, and have more opportunities to be physically active may do better in school than those who are deprived of these valuable experiences.

Finding State and National Content Standards

An excellent source for locating national and state content standards in all subject areas is www.education-world.com/standards.

Table 32.5 Example of Scope and Sequence of Mathematical Concepts Taught in Elementary Schools

Concept	Grade						
	K	1	2	3	4	5	6
Numbers	x	x	x	x	x	x	x
Meaning of numbers 1–12	x						
Meaning of numbers through 99		x					
Meaning of numbers through 999				x			
Meaning of addition and subtraction		x					
Addition and subtraction computation				x			
Meaning of numbers through 100,000					x		
Meaning of multiplication and division					x		
Meaning of numbers through 1,000,000						x	
Multiplication and division computation						x	
Meaning of decimals through hundredths						x	
Meaning of decimals through thousandths							x
Meaning of addition and subtraction of fractions and decimals							x
Number theory							x
Meaning of multiplication and division of fractions and decimals							x
Integers and ratios							x
Percents							x
Measuring and graphing	x	x	x	x	x	x	x
Geometry	x	x	x	x	x	x	x
Patterns and functions	x	x	x	x	x	x	x
Probability and statistics	x	x	x	x	x	x	x
Logic		x	x	x	x	x	x
Algebra			x	x	x	x	x

Source: Reprinted, by permission from T. P. Cone, P. Werner, S. L. Cone, and A. M. Woods, *Interdisciplinary teaching through physical education* (Champaign, IL: Human Kinetics, 1998), p. 70.

What the Research Suggests: Physical Activity, Fitness, and Physical Education

In recent studies, researchers have focused on the connection between physical activity, physical fitness, and/or physical education and academic performance. One of the first studies to get national attention related to a positive relationship between academic performance and fitness levels was conducted by the California Department of Education (CDE 2004) (Figure 33.1). The study matched scores on the Fitnessgram test with reading and math scores on the Stanford Achievement Test (SAT-9) of 353,000 students in fifth grade. Although this study did not show evidence that improving physical fitness causes academic achievement to improve, or vice versa, it did provide support for the assumption, held by many, that there is a positive relationship between students' level of fitness and their academic achievement. A meta-analysis by Sibley and Etnier in 2003 examined the results of 44 studies related to physical activity and cognition in children. The results of their study found that there is, indeed, a significant positive relationship between children's physical activity level and their cognitive functioning and support the argument that physical education could affect students' academic performance. A recent study by the Centers for Disease Control and Prevention examined the association between time spent in physical education and academic achievement. The longitudinal study of K–5 students showed a significant correlation between academic achievement and higher amounts of physical education for girls (Carlson et al. 2008). Other researchers have also found compelling evidence that supports the relationship between physical activity and enhanced learning in the classroom, including:

- Integrating physical activity within the elementary curricula had a positive influence on fluid intelligence and academic achievement of third grade students (Reed et al. 2010)

- Preadolescents scored a full grade level higher in reading comprehension after a 20-minute bout of moderate treadmill walking than after a 20-minute sedentary period (Hillman et al. 2009)
- In a group of diverse, urban school children, the odds of passing academic achievement tests in both math and English increased as the number of fitness tests passed increased (Chomitz et al. 2009)
- Children in the third and fifth grades who scored better on the aerobic fitness and the BMI (body mass index) components of a fitness test tended to have higher standardized test scores in reading and math (Castelli et al. 2007).
- Children who participated in four times as much physical activity per day as previously reported, through exposure to a designated 14-week physical education program, showed improvements in fitness, classroom behavior, and academic performance (IOM 2005).
- Allocating less time for physical education, art, and music did not relate to higher standardized test scores (Graham et al. 2002).
- Allocating twice as many minutes per week to physical education for a control group did not show it interfered with standardized reading or math scores (Sallis et al. 1999).
- Increased physical activity time during the school day led to higher test scores in math (Shephard 1997).
- An intense school physical activity program had a positive effect on math, reading, and writing test scores (Symons et al. 1997).
- Canadian children who spent an extra hour a day in physical education class performed higher on exams than their less active counterparts (Hannaford 1995).

The obesity epidemic currently plaguing our nation focuses increased interest on the physical activity levels of children. As school administrators begin to be held accountable for the amount of physical activity time provided for children during the school day, this body of research will become increasingly important to support daily physical education.

Neuroscientists and brain researchers are compiling another compelling body of evidence related to the importance of movement and optimal brain function.

What the Research Suggests: Brain-Based Learning

Brain researchers believe that exercise contributes to optimal brain functioning and optimal learning, and the evidence is mounting to make their case over the last two decades. In 1995, Carla Hannaford in her book *Smart Moves* cited a meta-analysis of 13 studies that found exercise to be a stimulant for brain development. In *Learning with the Body in Mind* (2000), author Eric Jensen reported that:

- Vigorous daily physical exercise can promote new brain cell growth.
- Exercise and aerobic conditioning may help improve memory and strengthen other areas of the brain.
- Downtime, such as recess, is necessary for children to learn. It allows for the "strengthening of synaptic connections in the brain that solidify prior learning" (66).
- Exercise of longer durations creates more cognitive boosts.

Dr. John Ratey, author of *Spark: The Revolutionary New Science of Exercise and the Brain* (2008) is the latest to draw together emerging findings from science and educational research that correlates physical activity and brain functioning. Dr. Ratey connects physical activity to improving attention (including attention deficit/hyperactivity disorder [ADHD]), reducing anxiety and depression, and in general, optimizing the brain for learning.

Hannaford, Jensen, and Ratey all support the need for quality physical education programs in all schools, and additional physical activity time throughout the day for all children, to promote learning and therefore increase student achievement. Integrating physical activities with the core subjects helps students engage both their bodies and their brains in learning, as suggested in the brain research. The skill theme approach readily lends itself to "brain activities" and to promoting both cognitive and psychomotor learning.

The skill theme approach emphasizes many of the concepts that brain researchers say are so important to brain development and learning. Skills such as balancing, tracking, moving cross-laterally, and moving rhythmically are all included within the movement concepts and skill themes. (Some examples of brain-enhancing activities are included in Box 32-5.) In addition, Prigge (2002) suggests other ways we can increase "brain power" through physical education programs. These ideas include:

- *Using music.* Research on music and learning has shown that music improves learning and memory and increases optimum functioning.
- *Teaching personal goal setting.* Goal-setting skills help students to "think smart."
- *Reinforcing good eating habits.* To "eat smart," students should always eat breakfast, consume sugar and carbohydrates in moderation, and increase fruit and vegetable intake.

Box 32-5

Examples of Brain-Enhancing Activities

Tracking activities help prepare the eye muscles for reading. An example is following the flow of a scarf, a bubble, or a feather as it falls to the ground, or tracking a balloon as it is struck with a racket from one side of the body to the other.

Cross-lateral movements enable the brain to cross the midsection from the right side across the center to the left side, which is important for allowing the brain to be ready to read and write. Examples of cross-lateral activities include basic scarf juggling, elephant walks, windmills, and rhythm ribbons.

Rhythmic movements such as tapping rhythms, moving body parts to the beat, moving equipment to the beat, and marching are all ways to stimulate the frontal lobes and can potentially enrich language development.

- *Reinforcing water consumption.* Children should drink plenty of water throughout the day to avoid dehydration and less-than-optimal learning.
- *Remembering the importance of first and last.* We remember most what is presented first and last. Have powerful beginnings, present new information early, and always review during lesson closure.
- *Having fun.* Laughter lowers stress and contributes to a relaxed learning environment.

A Final Thought

In concluding this chapter, we would like to reemphasize that the goals of physical education, as expressed in national and state standards, must take top priority because they make such an important contribution to youngsters' overall health and well-being. It is possible, however, to accomplish these goals and simultaneously reinforce the concepts being taught in the classroom and included on the high-stakes tests that have become so important in recent years. It also makes sense for us to ensure that we include "brain activities" that neuroscientists are telling us help with learning. In addition, the integration of physical activity in the classroom helps to get classroom teachers involved and accountable for their role in providing physical activity opportunities for children throughout the school day. This increased activity time can potentially lead to better health, better academic performance, and better motor skill levels.

Striving to meet the National Standards for Physical Education, which focus on physical activity and the development of a healthy lifestyle, is certainly a responsibility that should be considered by all those involved in educating children in the school setting, not only the physical education teachers. Because most children love to move and often learn best through kinesthetic experiences, physical education readily lends itself to interdisciplinary learning.

Summary

Interdisciplinary or *integrated teaching* are terms used to describe teaching subject matter from two different disciplines within the same lesson, thereby promoting learning in both subjects simultaneously and, when physical education is involved, making connections between the psychomotor and cognitive domains. Three approaches to interdisciplinary learning are described in the chapter—content linkage, shared integration, and thematic units. It is important that the teacher have a mastery of the subjects to be taught if the lessons (units) are going to be effective and maximize learning. The chapter also includes overviews of research related to the relationships between academic performance, optimal brain functioning, and human movement and physical fitness.

Reading Comprehension Questions

1. Define *interdisciplinary learning*. What are some advantages of using this approach to teaching/learning?
2. How does integration enhance learning?
3. How does the skill theme approach support interdisciplinary learning?
4. Describe and discuss three unique benefits for both classroom teachers and physical educators for integrating physical education with other subject areas.
5. Identify three approaches to integration discussed in this chapter. What are the characteristics of each? How are they alike/different?

6. What are some examples of two-directional integration between physical education and math? Language Arts? Social Studies? Science?
7. Briefly describe an integrated learning experience using both the content linkage approach and the shared integration approach.

8. Briefly describe a thematic unit overview that includes at least three subject areas for a primary or intermediate grade.
9. Briefly summarize key points made in the recent literature about the connection between physical education and academic performance.

References/Suggested Readings

Active Living Research. Active education: Physical activity, physical education, and academic performance. Research brief. 2009. **http://www.activelivingresearch .org/files/Active_Ed_Summer2009.pdf.**

Armstrong, T. 2009. *Multiple intelligences in the classroom.* 3rd ed. Alexandria, VA: Association for Supervision and Curriculum Development.

Blaydes, J. 2002. Advocacy: A case for daily quality physical education. **http://www.actionbasedlearning.com.**

[CDE] California Department of Education. 2004. A study of the relationship between physical fitness and academic achievement in California using 2004 test results. **http://www.cde.ca.gov/ta/tg/pf/documents/2004 pftresults.doc.**

Carlson, S., J. Fulton, S. Lee, L. Maynard, D. Brown, H. Kohl, and W. Dietz. 2008. Physical education and academic achievement in elementary school: Data from the Early Childhood Longitudinal Study. *American Journal of Public Health* 98(4): 721–27.

Castelli, D., C. Hillman, S. Buck, and H. Erwin. 2007. Physical fitness and academic achievement in third- and fifth-grade students. *Journal of Sport and Exercise Psychology* 29: 287–88.

Chomitz, V. R., M. M. Slining, R. J. McGowan, S. E. Mitchell, G. F. Dawson, and K. A. Hacker. 2009. Is there a relationship between physical fitness and academic achievement? Positive results from public school children in the northeastern United States. *Journal of School Health* 79: 30–37.

Clancy, M. 2006. *Active bodies, active brains.* Champaign, IL: Human Kinetics.

Cone, T., P. Werner, S. L. Cone, and A. Woods. 1998. *Interdisciplinary teaching through physical education.* Champaign, IL: Human Kinetics Publishing.

Elliott, E., and S. Sanders. 2002. Keeping children moving: Promoting physical activity throughout the curriculum. Teacher Source, PBS. **http://www.pbs.org/teachers/ earlychildhood/articles/physical.html.**

Evaul, T. 1980. Organizing centers for the 1980s. *Journal of Physical Education, Recreation and Dance* 51(7): 51–54.

Fingon, J. 2011, March/April. Integrating children's books and literacy into physical education curriculum. *Strategies:* 10–13.

Gardner, H. 2006. *Multiple intelligence: New horizons in theory and practice.* New York: Basic Books.

Graham, G., J. M. Wilkins, S. Westfall, S. Parker, R. Fraser, and M. Tembo. 2002. The effects of high-stakes testing on elementary school art, music and physical education. *Journal of Health, Physical Education, Recreation and Dance* 73(8): 51–54.

Hannaford, C. 1995. *Smart moves: Why learning is not all in your head.* Arlington, VA: Great Ocean Publishers.

Hichwa, J. 1998. *Right fielders are people too.* Champaign, IL: Human Kinetics.

Hillman, C., M. Pontifex, L. Raine, D. Castelli, E. Hall, and A. Kramer. 2009. The effect of acute treadmill walking on cognitive control and academic achievement in preadolescent children. *Neuroscience* 159: 1044–54.

[IOM] Institute of Medicine. 2005. *Preventing childhood obesity: Health in the balance.* Washington, DC: National Academies Press.

Jensen, E. 2000. *Learning with the body in mind.* San Diego, CA: The Brain Store.

Mahar, M., S. Murphy, D. Rowe, J. Golder, A. Shields, and T. Raedeke. 2006. Effects of a classroom-based program on physical activity and on-task behavior. *Medicine and Science in Sport and Exercise* 38(12), 286–94.

McCracken, B. 2001. *It's not just gym anymore.* Champaign, IL: Human Kinetics.

[NASPE] National Association for Sport and Physical Education. 1995. *Moving into the future: National standards for physical education.* Reston, VA: National Association for Sport and Physical Education.

[NASPE] National Association for Sport and Physical Education. 2nd ed. 2004. *Physical activity for children: A statement of guidelines for children ages 5–12.* Reston, VA: National Association for Sport and Physical Education.

[NASPE] National Association for Sport and Physical Education. 2009. *Comprehensive school physical activity programs.* Reston, VA: National Association for Sport and Physical Education.

[NASPE] National Association for Sport and Physical Education. 2010. *Opportunities to learn: Guidelines for elementary physical education: A position statement of the National Association for Sport and Physical Education.* Reston, VA: National Association for Sport and Physical Education.

[NCLB] No Child Left Behind. 2002. U.S. Department of Education. **http://www.nclb.gov.**

Placek, J. 1992. Rethinking middle school physical education curriculum: An integrated, thematic approach. *Quest* 44: 330–41.

Prigge, D. 2002. 20 ways to promote brain-based teaching and learning. *Intervention in School and Clinic* 37(4): 237–41.

Ratey, J., with E. Hagerman. 2008. *Spark: The revolutionary new science of exercise and the brain.* New York: Little, Brown.

Reed, J., G. Einstein, E. Hahn, S. Hooker, V. Gross, and J. Kravitz. 2010. Examining the impact of integrating physical activity on fluid intelligence and academic performance in an elementary school setting: A preliminary investigation. *Journal of Physical Activity and Health* 9: 343–51.

Roberts, P., and R. Kellough. 2006. *A guide for developing interdisciplinary thematic units.* Upper Saddle River, NJ: Prentice Hall.

Sallis, J., T. McKenzie, B. Kolody, M. Lewis, S. Marshall, and P. Rosengard. 1999. Effects of health-related physical education on academic achievement: Project SPARK. *Research Quarterly for Exercise and Sport* 70(2): 127–34.

Shephard, R. 1997. Curricular physical activity and academic performance. *Pediatric Exercise Science* 9: 113–26.

Sibley, B., and J. Etnier. 2003. The relationship between physical activity and cognition in children: A meta-analysis. *Pediatric Exercise Science* 15(3): 243–56.

Symons, C., B. Cinelli, T. James, and P. Groff. 1997. Bridging student health risks and academic achievement through comprehensive school health programs. *Journal of School Health* 67(6): 220–27.

[USDHHS CDC] US Department of Health and Human Services, Centers for Disease Control and Prevention. 2010. *The association between school-based physical activity, including physical education, and academic performance.* Atlanta: US Department of Health and Human Services, Centers for Disease Control and Prevention.

Wood, K. E. 2009. *Interdisciplinary instruction for all learners K–8: A practical guide.* 4th ed. Upper Saddle River, NJ: Merrill Prentice Hall.

The Future

Our last two chapters emphasize future directions in physical education. Chapter 33, "Building Support for Your Program," describes how teachers can work with seven different populations to gain support for their physical education programs. We offer practical ideas for working with other teachers in the school, the principal, parents, the school board, legislators, the children themselves, and the community at large.

Chapter 34, "Physical Education for Tomorrow's Children," is in many ways our favorite. We end the book by focusing on the future, presenting some of our thoughts. We hope our ideas will encourage you to dream too.

Building Support for Your Program

Many parents, students, teachers, and administrators do not know how physical education contributes to an individual's growth. The lack of a public relations plan can result in an absence of communication between the physical educator and the public, thereby hampering the growth of the physical education program.

—MICHAEL TENOSCHOK AND STEVE SANDERS (1984)

Physical education has undergone major changes in the past decade. So have its consumers. In order for physical education to be viewed as an integral part of the educational process, more attention must be paid to the marketing of tangible and intangible benefits.

—ALLISON MCFARLAND (2001)

Key Concepts

- Successful teachers, in addition to everything else they are asked to do, must also successfully market or build support for their programs.

- Physical education programs need to be marketed to several populations—school and district administrators, other teachers in a school, parents, the school board, the community at large, and legislators.

- Teachers who create positive, enjoyable, and productive programs are building support with their most important population—the children they teach.

When the first edition of *Children Moving* was published in 1980, there was a need to convince parents that regular physical activity was important for their children. Since the publication of the Surgeon General's report in 1996 (USDHHS 1996) documenting the scientific evidence of the value of physical activity, there is an increasing understanding of the benefits that accrue to those who are physically active (www.americanheart.org). Thus the role of the physical educator today is to convince the seven populations described that quality physical education programs can lead to a lifetime of enjoyable participation in physical activity (Stodden et al. 2008).

Most teachers need support from a variety of sources to develop the type of programs they want for their children. This is especially true in physical education, for two reasons. First, even with the scientific evidence about the value of physical activity for children and adults (CDC 2011), many continue to regard physical education as less important than other subjects, such as reading and math. Second, physical education is a relatively expensive program to conduct because of the necessary equipment involved. (It's important, however, that we continually remind others that physical education is for every child in the school—for the entire five or six years they are in attendance.)

While we wish it wasn't necessary to convince these various populations of the value of a quality physical education program, this becomes an important and necessary part of the job today. Notice that we continue to use the term "quality physical education." Unfortunately many of the populations you are working with may have experienced a different type of program than the one we have been describing in this text and described by NASPE (2011). Thus, it's necessary to cultivate support from the various segments of a school community who have the potential to be allies in our quest for improved programs. The seven related populations we have identified who need to be aware of and supportive of our program are: the school administration, especially the principal; other teachers in the school; parents; the school board; the community at large; legislators, in some instances; and the children.

This chapter discusses ideas for building support within each of these seven populations. However, note that it's important that a teacher first build as good of a physical education program as possible with the support that is currently available. Even with limited resources, it's possible to begin a good program, and this is a necessary first step because much of the work that will go toward building more support involves opening the program to administrators, parents, and the community in general. Obviously, if the program doesn't get off to a good start, you won't want visitors.

Once the program is off to a reasonable start, however, the teacher can invite observers to visit the classes. It may take months before the program is ready; the learning environment has to be established first, with the children and teacher working together comfortably, before visitors are welcome. Once the teacher is ready, the principal and other teachers in the school will probably be the first visitors. You might want to consider your answers to the questions in Box 33-1 as you begin to build support for your program.

The principal is an important component of a quality physical education program.

Box 33-1

Building Support Through Social Media

Facebook, Twitter, and other social media have the potential for informing parents, colleagues, and the administration about many of the good things you are doing in your program. We have several suggestions for using social media in a school setting.

- Before using any social media, be sure to discuss it with your principal, especially if you are going to be the first teacher at your school to incorporate it to promote your program.

- It would be wise to set up separate accounts for use at your school. For example, use a different Facebook account than the one you use with your friends. While the parents and children you teach might be interested in seeing pictures of what you and your friends did on Saturday night, it is probably not a good idea.

- Some of the parents and children at your school may want to "friend" you on Facebook. The decision to become their "friends" should be made cautiously and should probably be discussed with your principal. Remember, you are a teacher, and a professional, not their buddy.

- Social media is a great opportunity to let others know what you are doing in your program and to remind them of upcoming events. Do it wisely, however. Several postings a day is probably too many.

The Principal

Principals are critical in building support for your program (Giles-Brown 1993). Many principals, through no fault of their own, however, know very little about quality physical education programs—especially the approach we're advocating in *Children Moving*. Thus, it's important not to take for granted that the principal knows and understands the program you're trying to develop (Schneider 1992). We suggest the following ideas for working with your principal. The ideas aren't arranged in order of implementation, and we don't suggest they all need to be done. We've simply listed practical suggestions you may find helpful for your school.

- Invite your principal to observe the skill theme approach at a nearby school with you. Sit with your principal, and be certain that he or she focuses on the aspects of the program that are critical to the growth of your own program, e.g., equipment, class size. Be certain to schedule a visit with the principal at the school you're observing so the two administrators can discuss their programs and your principal can ask questions.

- If you are new to a school, or you are changing your program, invite your principal to a class or two that is beginning to work the way you intend. Be certain to follow up this visit so you can answer any questions that may have arisen. Some administrators, for example, are unaccustomed to seeing every child with a ball and may be concerned about the "chaotic" appearance of a class that differs from their experiences in which there was only one ball for an entire class—and most children were waiting in lines.

- If you're able to obtain videotapes of other skill theme teachers, invite your principal to view one of the tapes with you. Be sure to comment on the critical aspects of the program and relate them to your needs. Remember, the principal is busy, so you may want him or her to watch only certain key features, not the entire videotape. There are also videos of parts of lessons on PE Central (www.pecentral.org) that will provide an insight into quality teaching, and the equipment needed.

- Occasionally give your principal a copy of an article or book you think is particularly well done and relevant to your program. Be certain to discuss the document after your principal has had a chance to read it. This is especially important if, for example, you're teaching 12 classes a day and you're able to locate a publication that recommends 9 classes a day as a complete load for a physical education specialist. We recommend the publication by the National Association for Physical Education and Sport, *Appropriate Practices for Elementary School Physical Education* (NASPE 2009). It provides important guidelines written in an easy-to-understand format. It can be obtained from the Web site for the National Association for Sport and Physical Education (http://www.aahperd.org/naspe/). Also be sure to share overviews of the 1996 Surgeon General's report (USDHHS 1996), the *National Standards for Physical Education* (NASPE 2004), and your state standards with your principal. Another good source of information for you, and your principal, is PE Links 4U (www.pelinks4u.org).

- Be on the lookout for research that you can use to support the importance of physical education, especially if your principal is feeling pressure to increase test scores in reading, math, and science. For example, one study that surveyed Virginia elementary school principals found that allocating less time for art, music, and physical education did not correlate with higher reading and math scores in elementary schools (Graham

Figure 33.1 Fitnessgrams scores and SAT 9 reading and math scores for 353,000 fifth-grade California children.
Source: California Department of Education. 2002. The relationship of reading, math, and physical fitness scores in 5th, 7th, and 9th grade children. http://www.cahperd.org.

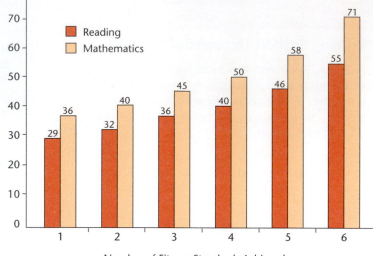

2001 Grade 5 SAT 9 and Physical Fitness

et al. 2002). Another study of 353,000 fifth graders discovered a positive relationship between physical fitness and reading and math scores (Grissom, 2005) (Figure 33.1). You may also want to share a copy of the book *Spark* by a Harvard professor about the important relationship between exercise, the brain, and academic achievement (Ratey 2008).

Try to avoid falling into the trap of thinking your principal really doesn't like your program, or physical education in general, if she isn't initially enthusiastic. It takes some principals several years to become active supporters of your program. In fact, we've worked with principals who took several months to find time to come view our programs. Eventually, however, they did support our program and came to view it as an asset to the school.

Teachers in the School

As you build your program, it's important that other teachers in the school understand and support your efforts. You'll certainly want to invite these teachers to observe your classes. Some of the ideas you use with your principal can also be used with your colleagues. Physical education specialists also find the following ideas helpful:

- Develop a thematic approach (Ward 1999) to an integrated curriculum in which the entire school or a certain grade level focuses on an idea or theme as suggested in the last chapter. With this approach, content in all disciplines is centered around the same selected theme. This is quite a natural fit for music, art, and physical education, but it can also be used in a total-school or grade-level approach. (See

Holt/Hale 2010 and Cone et al. 1998 for more information on integrating curriculum.) Remember, when developing an integrated curriculum, content should be integrated in a manner that does not compromise physical education content, force integration, or sacrifice the existing curriculum.

- On a smaller scale, work in conjunction with a classroom teacher on certain projects (Chapter 32). Child-designed games, for example, provide marvelous opportunities for writing, math, and art projects. Expressive dance is an excellent catalyst for creative writing.
- If you require your students to keep student logs or do written assignments (Chapter 12), some classroom teachers will provide class time for students to do the writing immediately after physical education class (Stevens 1994).
- Arrange for several of the primary grades to view the last 10 minutes of an intermediate grade's lesson to show the younger children the progress the older children have made. This motivates the younger children, encourages the older children, and provides some extra physical education for the younger children who attend the minishow.
- When a class has done a particularly good job on a physical education project, it's a treat for the classroom teacher to share in the children's efforts. Invite him or her to observe the last 10 minutes of a class while the children demonstrate their progress—for example, child-designed games or gymnastics sequences. This also has the added incentive of encouraging the classroom teacher to observe your physical education program.
- When feasible, try to eat with other teachers in the lunchroom. This not only helps to fight isolation,

but also develops rapport and helps them see you as a caring person and a professional.

The classroom teacher's support of the physical education specialist is important. Classroom teachers who understand that physical education is educational, not simply recess, will be less likely to keep children "in" to complete math or reading assignments. They also respect the fact that the physical education program has certain time limits, so make sure their children arrive on time and are ready to return to the classroom on schedule. This may seem to be a minor point, but it can be a source of considerable friction when all the teachers in a school aren't working together to provide the best possible program for children. When teachers understand the value and quality of a physical education program, their support is easier to obtain.

Parents

The physical education teacher must be sure to establish administrator and colleague support before beginning a major program to cultivate enthusiasm among parents. Parent support is important, but it's not enough without the assistance of the principal and the other teachers. If "internal" support doesn't exist, a principal might feel you're going "over her head" by appealing to parents, which can be disastrous for a new program. Once the administration understands your program and its needs, in many instances the principal will encourage you to generate parent support. And parent support can be especially helpful in obtaining funds that aren't available in the school's budget. There are many ideas for generating support among parents. Try a few of the following one year, a few the next year. Be sure to adapt the suggestions to match the needs and interests of parents in your community.

- Attend PTA/PTO meetings regularly, even if you aren't required to. Try not to sit in the back corner with the other teachers; take the time to meet some of the parents—introduce yourself, tell them what you teach, and invite them to observe your classes. This isn't necessarily the most enjoyable part of building a program, but it certainly can be a major factor in creating support.

- If you're invited to do a presentation for the parents' group, try to involve as many children as possible to ensure a large turnout for your program. Be certain to include children at all skill levels, not only the utilization- and proficiency-level youngsters—and if possible, relate your program to the 1996 Surgeon General's report (USDHHS 1996) and your state standards. You will also find short videos on PE

Central (www.pecentral.org) that illustrate quality programs of physical education that are appropriate for parents and administrators and school board members.

- Send a letter home at the beginning of the year. Tell parents about your program and the general rules the children will be expected to follow (for example, shoes for physical education class). Invite parents to visit. Include an e-mail address so parents can contact you if they have questions about the program or your policies.

- Many elementary schools today have a Web site for the school. If your school has one, be sure to take advantage of the opportunity and keep it up to date (Figure 33.2). Include items such as community programs of interest, books and articles to read, special accomplishments of the children, upcoming television programs of interest, and future programs you've scheduled. Also include a brief sketch of what you've been working on in physical education and suggest activities for the parents and the children to do together—for example, include the directions from this text for making a nylon-hose racket or golf club, and suggest several activities for the parents to do with their children. Be careful to proofread before you submit it so there aren't any spelling or grammatical errors.

- Bulletin boards are a great way to let parents know about your program. If you don't have the skills to make attractive bulletin boards, try trading with another teacher—for example, one week of bus duty for one bulletin board. In many communities there are retail stores for teachers that have very attractive bulletin board letters, pictures, backgrounds, and so on, that even the least skilled person can use to make an appealing bulletin board. Written student assessments, illustrated with their drawings, make appealing bulletin boards. PE Central features ideas for bulletin boards and links to other Web sites that contain tips for creating interesting and appealing bulletin boards at www.pecentral.org/websites/bulletinboardsites.html.

- Send a "good news" note home with the children, which informs the parents of their children's accomplishments in physical education class. Design and print a supply of notes at the beginning of the year so it won't take long to send several every week (Figure 33.3). These notes are particularly effective for the children who work hard but rarely get noticed.

- Some teachers use positive phone calls to communicate with parents about the program. A positive phone call is just a brief phone call to tell a parent how pleased the teacher is about the child's progress (attitude, effort) in physical education. It doesn't take

Figure 33.2 Example of a physical education newsletter. *Source:* S. Diller, Newsletters make parents and professionals take note, *Strategies* 8(1): 18–20.

The Physical Education Quarterly Report

While some schools view physical education merely as a good break time for teachers or a time for students to blow off a little steam, this is not true for us at Davis. Physical Education is a necessary and integral part of the total curriculum and is viewed with the same seriousness as any other subject matter. One of my primary goals is to provide each student with specific instruction to enable them to become more skillful movers. As students become more proficient in the various motor skills taught in class, I hope that they will enjoy using these skills on a regular basis. Medical and exercise science research indicates that regular physical activity contributes to a healthier and more enjoyable lifestyle while decreasing the incidence and seriousness of various illnesses and diseases. This report will help you know more about the activities in which your child has been instructed this last quarter of the school year.

Space

The second grade students began the school year by reviewing the spatial awareness concepts related to safe, efficient movement. Some of these concepts included moving in personal and general space where students attempt to move either alone or among others without interfering with the others' movements. Additional space concepts included movement at different levels (low, medium, and high), in different directions (forward, backward, sideways, up, and down), and in pathways (straight, curved, and zigzag). A proper understanding and use of these movement concepts permit children to move more safely and effectively in all settings. Games like "Bridges & Boulders," "High-Five Freeze Tag," and "Octopus" made this learning a lot of fun for everyone. Ask your second grader how to play these games and which one they enjoyed the most.

Throwing and Catching

The students also worked on tossing, the underhand throw, the overhand throw, and catching. To help students learn these skills, we use learning cues, key words that help students remember how to perform a skill. Learning cues can also be used to prompt students when they are practicing these skills. The learning cues for the underhand throw are:

- arm back
- step (on opposite foot)
- swing, and
- throw (the ball toward target)

The cues for the overhand throw are:

- cock (arm back in ready position, elbow out)
- step (on opposite foot)
- twist (upper body in direction of throw), and
- throw (the ball toward target)

To put these steps together into a smooth progressive action was not easy, but a lot of practice helped!

The learning cues for catching are:

- watch (the ball)
- reach (for the ball)
- grab, and
- give (with the ball to absorb the ball's force and slow it down)

Students participated in various activities to further develop throwing and catching for accuracy, distance, and with partners. "Throw and Go" and "Bombs Away" were two of the most popular games. Play these games with your students; you will have fun.

Jump Rope & Kicking

We are currently refining and extending jump rope skills during the warm-up portion of class. We work on kicking skills for the remainder of the lesson. The kicking skills students are learning are most related to soccer, such as dribbling (with the feet) trapping, juggling (thigh and foot), and kicking with various amounts of force using the instep.

The Best

As teachers and parents, we want the very best for our students. One thing we desire most is for our students to be healthy, to enjoy the benefits of good health throughout their entire lives. You can help them establish healthy levels of physical activity and support the physical education program by encouraging your children to view physical education as a place to learn, to have a serious learning aptitude, to always try their best, and to practice at home to facilitate the learning process and insure success.

Our own example is one of the most important influencing factors in the lifestyle habits passed on to our children. We must take care of ourselves. Take time to go outside and play with your children—play ball or tag, jump rope, go roller skating. These are all fun ways to stay fit and show your children that good health is in many ways a matter of what you do, as well as what you do not do.

Feel free to contact me if you would like to know more about our program. Thanks for your support!

Scott Diller, Physical Educator
Davis Elementary School

long, but the fact that the teacher takes the time to make the call means much to the parent. In many instances it's also unexpected because most phone calls from the school tend to be negative. Challenge yourself to make two good phone calls a week.

- Pete Tamm, a physical education teacher at Michael McCoy Elementary School in Orlando, Florida, wrote letters to his students (Tamm 1993). During a three-year period he averaged more than 1,000 letters a year to his children. Figure 33.4 contains several examples of his letters.

- Several nights a year hold an open house for parents and the children. The children must have adults with them to gain admittance. At the open house, equipment is available, and the children show the adults what they've been practicing in physical education. Other ideas include mother–daughter, father–son, mother–son, and so forth, open houses. Some teachers hold these open houses on Saturday mornings because many of the parents work nights. If you schedule the open houses informally, parents are free to spend a few minutes or an hour, depending upon their schedule. The PE Central Challenge (www.pecentral.org) is another popular event for a parents' night.

- Once a year schedule a parent work evening in which parents can help build, repair, and paint equipment for the physical education program. The

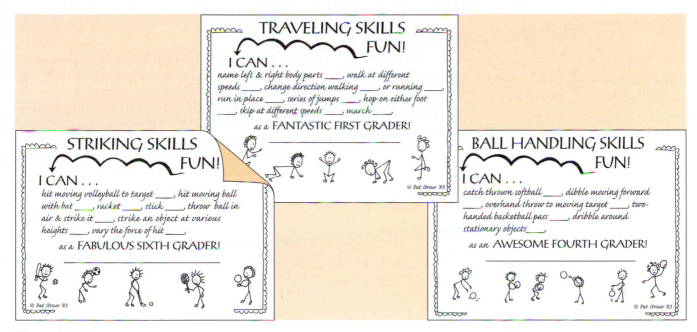

Figure 33.3 Examples of "good news" notes. Reprinted with permission.

January 14, 1996

Chris,

You designed an interesting kicking game. The goal was to kick the ball across the other person's line. Thanks for sharing your idea.

It's a game other students will want to try.

Mr. Tamm

September 23, 1997

Jodie,

You and Lee had a very interesting idea. The two of you combined your rubber band strands with the tininkling poles. That made the tininkling pole dance even more interesting.

Thanks for sharing your idea.

Mr. Tamm

March 3, 1997

Kim,

I could tell by the expression on your face that you were proud of your new jump rope record. You increased your record from 20 jumps to 107 jumps.

Terrific!

Mr. Tamm

June 9, 1997

Tracy,

When you met your goal of 30 sit-ups I could tell you were pleased with your effort. You should be.

Keep up the good work.

Mr. Tamm

Figure 33.4 Letters to students.
Source: P. Tamm, Dear physical educator: Writing letters makes a difference, *Strategies* 6, no. 8 (1993).

advantage of such an evening is that it gives parents an understanding of the need for physical education equipment. Make sure the evening is well organized; two hours is adequate.

- Walking is so popular today that parents may enjoy a family walk once the children have built up their ability to walk (or run) a limited distance. It's important to explain that it isn't a race but just a chance to get together and run. A local celebrity walker makes an appropriate guest for such an event.

- Schedule a speaker for parents only. For example, you might invite a child psychologist, a medical doctor, a former athlete. Be certain that you've heard the speaker personally—don't trust someone else's opinion. The speaker has to be worthwhile if the parents are going to enjoy and benefit from the talk. The entire program should run a maximum of

Box 33-2

Why Should My Child Take Physical Education?

As you consider ways to build support for your program, it helps to formulate answers to the questions that a parent (administrator, board member) might ask:

- Why should my children take physical education?
- What benefits is he or she gaining from participating in your program?

Today we are able to suggest that quality physical education has the potential to lead youngsters to a lifetime of physical activity. Every parent wants these benefits, outlined by the Centers for Disease Control and Prevention (CDC), for their children. There is scientific evidence suggesting that regular participation in physical activity:

- Reduces the risk of dying prematurely
- Reduces the risk of dying from heart disease
- Reduces the risk of developing diabetes
- Reduces the risk of developing high blood pressure
- Helps reduce blood pressure in people who already have high blood pressure
- Reduces the risk of developing colon cancer
- Reduces feelings of depression and anxiety
- Helps control weight
- Helps build and maintain healthy bones, muscles, and joints
- Helps older adults become stronger and better able to move about without falling
- Promotes psychological well-being (CDC 2011)

Other good resources are the National Association for Sport and Physical Education (www.naspeinfo.org) and the American Heart Association (www.americanheart.org). The CDC Web site (www.cdc.gov) is especially good if you are searching for PowerPoint slides about the obesity epidemic to share with parents.

60 minutes. Make sure the speaker understands the difference between physical education and physical activity.

- Invite parents with special skills—for example, a mountain climber, dancer, self-defense expert, or triathlete—to visit your physical education classes and discuss their sport.
- Report cards can also be used as a way to advocate for your program. Obviously you will need to design the report card with this in mind so it communicates the progress a child is making but also educates the parents about your program (Sims & Dowd, 2010).

The School Board

Another obviously important factor in building support for your program is the school board. Although the board members may seem far removed, they're the ones who ultimately determine whether a school district will employ physical education specialists for their elementary schools. The time to gain the board's support is not when it's considering eliminating the physical education program at the elementary schools—that's often too late. Get to know the members, and let them get to know you and your program long before then.

- Attend one or two school board meetings each year. They won't be your most entertaining evenings, but you'll learn much about how decisions are made in school districts. If there's an opportunity, try to speak to one or more of the board members so you get to know them. Don't ask for anything; just introduce yourself and talk about the current business before the board. If you ever have an occasion to speak to the board, the fact that you understand how the meetings are conducted and know a few members of the board will make things substantially easier for you.
- Whenever you're offering a special program at your school, send the board a written invitation. Be sure you've attended enough board meetings so you can recognize the members and call them by name if they come to your program. If you know in advance that the members will attend, try to have someone, such as the principal or another teacher, available to serve as a host.
- If you come across an article you think the school board members should read, send them a copy with a brief note. The article should be short, well written, and important to the board members.
- NASPE's Web site (www.naspeinfo.org) contains "advocacy resources" if you need up-to-date facts and figures for a presentation to the school board or a legislative group.

Your relationship with the school board will be somewhat distant. It's important, however, to cultivate a relationship if your program of physical education is going to thrive within a school district.

The Community at Large

Realistically, the community at large is less important than the populations discussed so far. You can potentially enhance your program, however, by conducting a program with community appeal. Typically, these are major undertakings that require substantial time and effort. The workload can be lightened by conducting programs with other schools in your district.

- If your community has a shopping mall, check with the managers; the managers of malls are often looking for demonstrations. Such a presentation will give your program a great deal of public visibility. It's a good idea to have handouts available so that people who stop by for a few minutes to watch the program know exactly what they're watching. The children who aren't currently in action can distribute these leaflets.
- The halftime of basketball games is a good opportunity for displaying some of the highlights of your program. For the program to be effective, the announcer's script needs to be well done and rehearsed. Many children from different grades will make the program more appealing for the spectators. Contemporary loud music is also stimulating. Be sure to include the younger children because they have enormous crowd appeal to help get your message across. Also, the children really enjoy performing, and their parents, grandparents, friends, and neighbors enjoy watching them.

Legislators

One of the eternal truths about teaching physical education is the seemingly endless need to convince others that physical education is important in the lives of children. There are times when, in addition to parents, administrators, and school boards, it is important to contact a legislator about an impending bill that will have an impact on physical education programming. In recent years, for example, some states have considered legislation to substitute activities such as marching band, athletics, and/or Reserve Officers' Training Corps (ROTC) for secondary physical education. If this happens in your state, contact your legislator(s) to explain why you do not support a particular piece of legislation. There are a number of Web sites that list the contact information for both state and national legislators. When you do, there are several guidelines to follow.

- Mention the legislation specifically by its title—for example, House Bill 402.

- Be certain the letter or e-mail is well written. Be especially careful that all words are correctly spelled and that the grammar and format follow recommended guidelines.
- Be concise and straightforward. Legislators may receive hundreds of letters about a piece of legislation, and long rambling letters are not as effective as ones that stick to the facts.
- Often a form letter is circulated by a professional association to be sent to legislators. Although it is acceptable to use the form letter, it is probably less effective than modifying the letter to make it more personal and unique.
- A handwritten letter may attract more attention than a typed letter. It will stand out from computer-generated letters.
- Finally, if it can be arranged, a personal visit is also an effective way to advocate for legislation. Again, it is best to be concise and straightforward as the visit will be limited in length and you will need to know your facts.

Children as Advocates

We've saved the most important component until the end: the children. Obviously, if you hope to build support from the six populations just described, the children will have to benefit from and enjoy the program. If the children aren't avid supporters of your program, you'll have difficulty gaining support from others in the immediate community.

Children become advocates and talk positively about teachers who help them learn and improve in any subject, not only physical education. In any school, the best teachers are both known and respected by the children, other teachers, and the principal. The word gets out when a teacher and a program are good.

Unfortunately, building a quality program of physical education requires more than being a successful teacher. To cultivate all the other populations that contribute to the success of a program, a teacher also needs to be part politician, part public relations director, and part fund-raiser. Some teachers find that part of the job distasteful, but it is necessary, especially when one is beginning a program of physical education.

Summary

One role teachers of successful physical education programs play is that of generating support. Seven different populations need to be aware and supportive of physical education if the programs are to be successful: school administration, other teachers in the school, parents, the school board, the community at large, legislators, and the children. Children are the most important advocates of a program, so a program must be of high quality if support from the other six groups is to be developed.

Reading Comprehension Questions

1. Why are seven different populations identified for building support for a program? Which of the seven do you think is least important? Why?
2. What's the first step a teacher must take to develop a program with widespread support?
3. What does the phrase *principal education* mean? Why do you think many principals are not well informed about quality physical education programs?
4. Locate two elementary school Web sites from your state that have a physical education section. Write a brief review of the physical education section. Was it helpful? Comprehensive? Did it answer questions parents might ask?
5. Why is the school board so important to the success of a physical education program?
6. Why are the children the most important factor in developing support for a program?

References/Suggested Readings

[CDC] Centers for Disease Control and Prevention. 2011. *Physical activity and health: The benefits of physical activity.* **http://www.cdc.gov/physicalactivity/everyone/health/**

[CDE] California Department of Education. 2002. The relationship of reading, math and physical fitness scores in 5th, 7th, and 9th grade children. Available at **http://www.cahperd.org.**

Cone, T. P., P. Werner, S. L. Cone, and A. M. Woods. 1998. *Interdisciplinary teaching through physical education.* Champaign, IL: Human Kinetics.

Diller, S. 1994. Newsletters make parents and professionals take note. *Strategies* 8(1): 18–20.

Giles-Brown, E. 1993. Teach administrators why physical education is important. *Strategies* 6(8): 23–25.

Graham, G., J. M. Wilkins, S. Westfall, S. Parker, R. Fraser, and M. Tembo. 2002. The effects of high-stakes testing on elementary school art, music and physical education. *Journal of Physical Education, Recreation and Dance* 73(8): 51–54.

Grissom, J. B. Physical fitness and academic achievement. 2005. *Journal of Exercise Physiology-online* 8(1): 11–25. **http://www.asep.org/files/Grissom.pdf.**

Holt/Hale, S. 2010. *On the move: Lesson plans to accompany Children Moving.* 8th ed. New York: McGraw-Hill.

McFarland, A. 2001, December. Developing a marketing plan for physical education. *The Physical Educator.*

[NASPE] National Association for Sport and Physical Education. 2004. *Moving into the future: National standards for physical education.* 2nd ed. Reston, VA: National Association for Sport and Physical Education.

[NASPE] National Association for Sport and Physical Education. 2009. *Appropriate practices for elementary school physical education.* 3rd ed. Reston, VA: National Association for Sport and Physical Education.

[NASPE] National Association for Sport and Physical Education. 2011. *Key points of quality physical education.* **http://www.aahperd.org/naspe/publications/teachingTools/key-points-of-QPE.cfm.**

Ratey, J., with E. Hagerman. 2008. *Spark: The revolutionary new science of exercise and the brain.* New York: Little, Brown.

Schneider, R. E. 1992. Don't just promote your profession—market it. *Journal of Physical Education, Recreation and Dance* 63(5): 70–71.

Sims, S., and K. Dowd. 2010, July/August. Using a report card as an advocacy tool. *Strategies* 36–37.

Stevens, D. 1994. Movement concepts: Stimulating cognitive development in elementary students. *Journal of Physical Education, Recreation and Dance* 65(8): 16–23.

Stodden, D. F., J. D. Goodway, S .J. Langendorfer, M. Roberton, M. E. Rudisill, C. Garcia, and L.G. Garcia. 2008. A developmental perspective on the role of motor skill competence in physical activity. *Quest* 60(2): 290–306.

Tamm, P. 1993. Dear physical educator: Writing letters makes a difference. *Strategies* 6(8): 13–15.

Tenoschok, M., and S. Sanders. 1984. Planning an effective public relations program. *Journal of Physical Education, Recreation and Dance* 55: 48–49.

[USDHHS] U.S. Department of Health and Human Services. 1996. *Physical activity and health: A report of the Surgeon General.* Atlanta: Centers for Disease Control and Prevention, National Center for Chronic Disease Prevention and Health Promotion.

Ward, P. 1999. The saber-tooth project [monograph]. *Journal of Teaching Physical Education* 18(4).

Physical Education for Tomorrow's Children

Some see things as they are and say why. I dream things that never were and say why not.

—Robert F. Kennedy

Key Concepts

- Successful children's teachers are by nature optimists and innovative thinkers who dream about the future.

- This chapter provides a series of dreams with the hope that it will stimulate readers to develop their own dreams about the future of physical education for children.

- Since the first edition of *Children Moving* was published in 1980, some of these dreams have become realities for some teachers and children.

This final chapter in *Children Moving* is different from what you will find in most books. We are dreamers. We want the best for children and their teachers, so we continue to dream about how things might be. Since 1980, when the first edition of *Children Moving* was published, the profession of physical education has made great progress. Today, as never before, the important benefits of becoming and remaining physically active for a lifetime are widely understood. There is also an increasing recognition that the skill theme approach, as described in *Children Moving*, has the potential to provide the movement foundation critical for enjoyable and ongoing participation in sports and physical activity as adolescents and adults. We are delighted with the progress that has been made. We are not satisfied, however. We will continue to dream about ideal physical education programs and want to share those dreams with you as the last chapter in the book. Some will call our dreams unrealistic, perhaps even unnecessary. We hope you will understand, however, the feeling that exists so strongly in us to never be satisfied with anything but the best.

We believe it is as important to continue to dream as it is to see our dreams realized. Perhaps our hopes for the future will stimulate you to think and dream about the way things could be. The following dreams describe the world of children's physical education as we would like it to be—for every child and every teacher.

- Every physical education program would be designed to lead children to develop the knowledge, skills, and attitudes that provide the foundation for a lifetime of enjoyable physical activity.
- Stakeholders, parents, and administrators would understand that quality programs of physical education consist of far more than physical activity and require credentialed teachers to implement these programs.

- Every physical education program would be designed for all children, not only the athletes and physically fit youngsters.
- The public would continue to understand and value the important role regular physical activity can play in the prevention of cardiovascular disease, diabetes, certain types of cancer, alcohol and drug addiction, and obesity. For these reasons they would demand quality daily physical education for their children
- K–12 physical education would be designed to assist children to discover their personal tendencies, interests, and joys related to physical activity and then guide them to develop the competence that leads to confidence and regular participation in a sport or physical activity.
- Parents would limit "screen time" (television viewing and computer usage) to a maximum of two hours a day, thereby encouraging youngsters to increase their physical activity at home.
- Negative physical education programs that discourage and humiliate youngsters would be banned from schools, along with their teachers.
- Every child would have positive instruction in physical education every day.
- All physical education programs, recreation programs, and youth-serving agencies would collaborate to provide interesting, enjoyable, and easily accessible opportunities for children to be physically active outside of the school day.
- All parents would become involved in their children's physical education. The concepts and skills introduced at school would be valued, enhanced, and embellished at home, through parent–child activity nights, after-school programs for parents, and parent volunteer programs.
- Children would be grouped—by interest in a specific activity, by ability, by experience—to accomplish the specific goals of a series of lessons, then regrouped when the teacher decides to move to a new skill theme. For example, some upper-grade children might be interested in putting on a dance performance for lower-grade children. Those upper-grade children could be grouped to meet together for two weeks to prepare their dance and perform it. When they accomplish that goal, they could be regrouped as appropriate for another activity.
- There would be time during the day for teachers to cooperatively plan a personalized curriculum with each child. This would help children learn to make significant decisions about what they want to learn and how they want to learn it.
- Physically challenged children would benefit from programs and activities designed specifically for

them to help them lead fuller lives. These activities may, or may not be, traditional sports.

- Assistance would be readily available for those children who require special remedial attention. This program would include instruction for parents so they could help their children at home.
- Discrimination of any type would no longer exist in physical education.
- There would be times during each school day, beyond scheduled physical education classes, when children could choose to come to the gymnasium to practice skills or activities in which they were interested.
- Classes would be scheduled to facilitate cross-age teaching—fifth graders working with first graders, or children at the proficiency level working with those at the precontrol level, for example.
- Classes would be scheduled so that beginnings and endings were determined by the children's interest and involvement in a lesson rather than by an impersonal and insensitive time schedule.
- Teachers would have adequate time between lessons to jot down a few notes about the progress the last class made, rearrange equipment, review lesson plans, and shift their thoughts to the next class.
- Administrators and others who schedule classes would understand that physical education is intended to be an instructional experience, not a loosely organized recess. This understanding would be reflected by scheduling only one class rather than two or three classes with 60 or even 90 children at a time.
- Teachers would be able to arrange frequent visits to other schools and teachers to gain new ideas for their programs.
- Teachers would be able to make arrangements to switch teaching assignments with other teachers for a day or a week. This would provide more experiences working in different environments and with children from various ethnic and socioeconomic backgrounds.
- Teachers would collaborate and organize their curriculum into organic, natural contexts (consistent with the way children view the world), rather than artificially separating learning into compartmentalized subjects like reading, mathematics, art, and physical education. For example, building a house involves reading, mathematics, climbing, balancing, and cooperating with others.
- All classroom teachers would understand that a quality program of physical education can significantly contribute to children's total development, especially cognitive functioning. They wouldn't prevent children from going to physical education

class because they hadn't finished their work or because they misbehaved.

- All colleagues, parents, and administrators would be vitally interested in our teaching and physical education programs. They would demonstrate this interest by visiting our classes regularly, not only at the first PTA meeting of the year or during school lunch week.
- It would be common practice for individuals from the community to share their expertise and experiences with children. Children might learn about mountain climbing, hang gliding, Wii Fit, Dance Dance Revolution (DDR), hiking, human spatial ecology, and weightless gymnastics, for example.
- Schools would become community centers that involve parents and children in educational projects of mutual interest and benefit. These would include child/parent-designed and -constructed playscapes, child/parent-designed and -implemented field days for preschool children or underserved children, and child–parent programs designed for senior citizens.
- There would be no more grades in physical education. Children's progress would be reported to parents communicating what was to be learned and what children had learned.
- Physical education, in both elementary and secondary schools, would receive as much emphasis as high school athletics. Communities would understand that an appropriate program of physical education for every child is at least as important as athletic programs for the gifted. And so all schools would have appropriate equipment, facilities, and budgets for physical education programs.
- All school districts would understand the differences between teaching children and teaching adolescents and would refuse to hire individuals whose primary interest and expertise is in coaching or teaching at a high school. Instead, school districts would hire, as elementary instructors, only reflective teachers who are professionally qualified and dedicated to a career of teaching physical education to children.
- Preservice teachers would work in elementary schools for several years before going to college so they learn the right questions to ask about children and teaching when they enter college.
- Teacher-education institutions would offer professional preparation programs for elementary school physical education specialists; these programs would be different from those for secondary school physical education teachers.
- College teachers would regularly trade teaching assignments with elementary school teachers, allowing the teachers to study current theories and practices at

a college and share their wisdom with preservice teachers while giving the professors realistic opportunities to translate their theories into practice and gain experience about teaching today's children.

- Teachers and professors would collaborate and be supported to collaborate in the development of professional learning groups aimed at discovering better ways to enhance the learning experiences of children, preservice teachers, and in-service teachers.
- Teachers would be involved in conceptualizing and conducting action research. The resulting studies would have the potential for finding answers to the questions that teachers want answered.
- Research results would be disseminated in forms that teachers of children would find useful, practical, and interesting, for example, in weekly pamphlets, newsletters, or podcasts that would use layperson's language, not professional jargon or advanced concepts related to experimental design or statistics.
- Every school would have a gymnasium designed specifically for children's physical education that would not have to be vacated for lunch, school assemblies, or plays.
- Every school would have the quantity and variety of equipment that would allow every child maximum practice at his or her level of physical development.
- Schools will continue to use laptop computers and tablets with the children, and physical educators will continue to discover ways to use these devices to motivate and encourage children to become and remain physically active.
- Portable environments would be made available to schools throughout the year. Children would have opportunities to use portable swimming pools for swimming lessons, portable ski slopes for skiing lessons, and portable antigravity chambers to experience moving in a weightless atmosphere.
- A national association designed specifically for teachers of children's physical education would be started. The conferences, newsletter, research, and other functions would be designed to specifically address and answer the questions teachers in the schools are asking.
- Mentors would be available to teachers who want to improve their teaching effectiveness and be supported in their early years of teaching.
- Adequate funds would be made available for resource centers operated by teachers for teachers. Such centers would offer assistance in making materials or equipment, opportunities to hear visiting lecturers, professional development courses, discussion and sharing sessions, and up-to-date professional libraries.
- Computers would be readily available in gyms for children to keep track of their own progress and for teachers to design better programs and report the children's progress to the parents.
- All gyms would be equipped with the latest technology, such as digital video and still cameras, permanently mounted television monitors, pedometers, heart rate monitors, and wireless handheld and laptop computers linked to the Internet.
- Cell phone technology will continue to develop to make it easier for teachers to use their cell phones to record the children's progress, share ideas with others, and feel less isolated.
- Physical educators will continue to find ways to use social media like Facebook and Twitter to enhance their programs and meet and keep in touch with other educators.

We continue to dream about and search for better ways of teaching children. And we would like to hear your dreams and ideas about children, teaching, and physical education. If you would like to communicate with us, please e-mail us at george.graham.2010@gmail.com.

One other dream emerged as we were writing this book. Wouldn't it be great if the ideas from our book help you become a more effective teacher of children? We've done our part—now it's up to you. Make a positive difference in the lives of the children you teach! We wish you all the best!

Sample School-Year Content Overviews (Scope and Sequence)

This Appendix contains two sample yearly overviews (scopes and sequences). The process of developing these overviews is described in detail in Chapter 6. The sample overviews are for a two-day-a-week program (72 lessons a year) for primary grade classes (inexperienced) and a five-day-a-week (180 lessons a year) overview for intermediate grades (experienced) classes. Obviously you will need to adapt these overviews. If, for example, your classes meet once a week you will need to adapt the two-day-a-week outline to 36 lessons a year. That is why we provide percentages in the overviews to aid with the adaptations that will need to be made. We think you will find these overviews to be a useful place to start outlining the content you will be teaching in a school year. As you study these overviews, keep these important points in mind:

1. The content overviews show how to organize your school year using skill themes, movement, and fitness concepts. We suggest they be used as starting points for developing your own yearly scopes and sequences.
2. In these examples, primary (inexperienced) generally refers to K–2 classes, and experienced to grades 3–5.
3. The day–to-day content is intended to be the major focus of that day's lesson, but in many instances other content will be taught during a lesson as well—for example, a review of a skill theme or concept from the previous day or a skill that needs to be worked on frequently but for short periods of time, such as jumping rope and transferring weight from feet to hands.
4. In both overviews, the first few lessons are devoted to establishing a learning environment as outlined in Chapter 8. Several other lessons throughout the year are devoted to "reviewing" the learning environment. The period after winter or spring break, for instance, is often a good time to review the learning environment. Review days give you a chance to check the environment to determine if some areas,

such as immediately stopping at the stop signal and paying careful attention when you are talking, need additional practice.
5. The sequencing of the skill themes and movement concepts takes typical weather patterns into account. Outdoor activities are grouped at the beginning and end of the school year, indoor activities toward the middle of the year. For the most part, the movement concepts are introduced early in the year and are revisited throughout the year when time permits.
6. Fitness concepts (Chapter 27) are taught throughout the year on Wednesdays in the five-day-a-week example and every other week in the two-day-a-week scope. Obviously they could be grouped differently, but this placement allows you to teach a concept or two and set aside time for the children to incorporate the concept into their lifestyle before you introduce another fitness concept. It also allows you to review and reinforce concepts throughout the year instead of lumping them into a block of lessons.
7. In our program, time is allowed throughout the year for special events that take time away from teaching. (In most of the elementary schools in which we have taught, there are days when physical education must be missed because of field trips, holiday shows or assemblies, voting, or picture days.)
8. Notice that skill themes tend to be massed at the beginning (several days combined) and then distributed throughout the remainder of the year. Notice too that in the programs for the experienced classes, several days in a row are sometimes spent on a single skill theme. As children improve in skill proficiency, they tend to want to spend more days on the same skill because their success rate is much higher. When success rates are low, children seem to concentrate better when the skill themes are changed frequently and reviewed regularly.

Sample Two-Day-a-Week Scope (72 Lessons) for Primary Grade Classes

Topic of Lesson/Activity	Percentage of School Year[a]	Number of Days
Establishing a Learning Environment	4	3
Space Awareness	9	6
Effort	5	4
Relationships	5	4
Traveling	7	5
Chasing/Fleeing/Dodging		
Bending, Stretching, Twisting, Curling	4	3
Jumping and Landing	5	4
Rolling	7	5
Balancing	5	4
Transferring Weight	5	4
Kicking and Punting	7	5
Throwing and Catching	7	5
Volleying	3	2
Dribbling	3	2
Striking with Rackets	4	3
Striking with Hockey Sticks	2	1
Striking with Golf Clubs	2	1
Striking with Bats	3	2
Fitness and Wellness	8	6
Field Day and Other Events	5	3
	100	72

[a]Percentages are approximate.

Sample Two-Day-a-Week Lesson Topics for Primary Grade Classes (72 Days a Year)

Week	Chapter	Day	
1	8	1	Establishing an Environment for Learning (pgs. 99–125)
	8	2	Establishing an Environment for Learning (cont.) (pgs. 99–125)
2	13	1	Exploring Self-Space (p. 212)
	13	2	Exploring General Space (p. 214)
3	13	1	Traveling in Different Directions (p. 217)
	13	2	Traveling and Freezing at Different Levels (p. 218)
4	27	1	Teaching Physical Fitness, Physical Activity, and Wellness (p. 561)
	23	2	Throwing at a Large Target (p. 439)
5	23	1	Catching a Rolling Ball (p. 440); Catching from a Skilled Thrower (p. 440)
	16	2	Traveling with Different Locomotor Patterns (p. 271): Sliding; Galloping; Hopping; Skipping (p. 274)
6	16	1	Performing Locomotor Sequences (p. 276)
	17	2	Traveling to Flee (p. 295); Fleeing from a Partner (p. 296)
7	17	1	Traveling to Dodge (p. 295); Dodging the Obstacles (p. 296)
	22	2	Kicking a Stationary Ball from a Stationary Position (p. 408)
8	22	1	Approaching a Stationary Ball and Kicking (p. 409); Kicking in the Air (p. 410)
	22	2	Dropping, Bouncing, and Kicking Lightweight Balls (p. 425); Dropping and Punting (p. 425)
9	19	1	Jumping and Landing: Basic Patterns (p. 326)
	27	2	Teaching Physical Fitness, Physical Activity, and Wellness (p. 561)
10	24	1	Volleying Balloons in the Air (p. 466)
	24	2	Volleying a Ball Upward (Underhand Pattern) (p. 468)
11	24	1	Bouncing a Ball Down (Dribbling) Continuously (p. 483)
	24	2	Dribbling and Walking (p. 483)
12	14	1	Exploring Time (p. 229)
	14	2	Exploring Force (p. 234)
13	14	1	Traveling and Changing Force Qualities (p. 234)
	8	2	Establishing an Environment for Learning (p. 101)
14	13	1	Exploring Pathways (p. 219)
	13	2	Exploring Extensions (p. 223)
15	16	1	Moving to Rhythms (p. 276)
	27	2	Teaching Physical Fitness, Physical Activity, and Wellness (p. 561)
16	25	1	Striking Down; Striking Up (pp. 504, 505)
	25	2	Striking Up and Down (p. 505)
17	19	1	Jumping over Low Obstacles: Hoops (p. 329); Jumping over Low Obstacles: Hurdles (p. 329)
	19	2	Jumping a Turned Rope (p. 330); Jumping a Self-Turned Rope (p. 331)
18	15	1	Identifying Body Parts (p. 244); Balancing on Matching and Nonmatching Parts (p. 245)
	15	2	Traveling and Freezing in Different Body Shapes (p. 247)
19	27	1	Teaching Physical Fitness, Physical Activity, and Wellness (p. 561)
	16	2	Leaping (p. 268)
20	15	1	Over, Under, Around, In Front Of, and Behind Concepts (p. 252)
	16	2	Locomotors and Rhythm: The Follow-Me Dance (p. 280)
21	21	1	Rocking on Different Body Parts (p. 388); Rocking to Match a Partner (p. 387)
	21	2	Rolling Sideways (p. 387); Rolling Forward (p. 389)
22		1	Special Event
	15	2	Matching (p. 256); Mirroring (p. 257); Matching and Mirroring (p. 257)
23	20	1	Balancing on Different Bases of Support (pp. 345, 348)
	20	2	Balancing in Different Body Shapes (pp. 346, 349)
24	21	1	Rolling in a Long, Narrow Position (Log Roll) (p. 387)
	21	2	Rocking Backward (p. 389); Rocking Backward over the Shoulders (p. 391)
25	21	1	Transferring Weight to Hands Momentarily (p. 370)
	21	2	Transferring Weight to Hands Across Mats (p. 371)
26	23	1	Throwing Overhand (p. 441); Throwing Underhand (p. 441); Throwing Sidearm (p. 442)
	23	2	Throwing a Ball Against a Wall and Catching the Rebound (p. 448)

(continued)

Sample Two-Day-a-Week Lesson Topics for Primary Grade Classes (72 Days a Year) (continued)

Week	Chapter	Day	
27	20	1	Traveling on Low Gymnastics Equipment (p. 346)
	20	2	Balancing Sequence (p. 357)
28	14	1	Traveling and Flow (p. 236)
	21	2	Rolling After Jumping Off Equipment and Landing (p. 396)
29	21	1	Transferring Weight from Feet to Combinations of Body Parts (p. 372)
	21	2	Transferring off Low Apparatus (Bench, Crate, or Low Table) (p. 374)
30	22	1	Kicking a Rolling Ball from a Stationary Position (p. 414); Kicking to a Partner (p. 414)
	22	2	Punting Different Types of Balls (p. 426)
31	27	1	Teaching Physical Fitness, Physical Activity, and Wellness (p. 561)
	17	2	Dodging the Obstacles (p. 296)
32	23	1	Throwing and Catching with a Partner (p. 449)
	25	2	Striking a Ball Rebounding from a Wall (p. 513)
33	19	1	Jumping for Distance (p. 326); Jumping for Height (p. 326)
	26	2	Striking a Stationary Ball (p. 525); First Swings Golf (p. 553)
34	26	1	Striking for Distance—Hockey (p. 528)
	26	2	Striking a Stationary Ball—Bats (p. 542)
35	27	1	Teaching Physical Fitness, Physical Activity, and Wellness (p. 561)
	26	2	Striking a Pitched Ball—Bats (p. 547)
36		1	Field Day
		2	Field Day

**Sample Five-Day-a-Week Scope (180 Lessons)
for Intermediate Grade Classes**

Topic of Lesson/Activity	Percentage of School Year[a]	Number of Days
Establishing a Learning Environment	3	6
Space Awareness	3	6
Effort	5	9
Relationships	4	7
Traveling	4	7
Chasing/Fleeing/Dodging		
Bending, Stretching, Twisting, Curling	4	7
Jumping and Landing	5	9
Rolling	7	12
Balancing	5	9
Transferring Weight	7	12
Kicking and Punting	7	12
Throwing and Catching	8	15
Volleying	5	9
Dribbling	4	7
Striking with Rackets	7	12
Striking with Hockey Sticks	3	6
Striking with Golf Clubs	3	6
Striking with Bats	4	7
Fitness and Wellness	9	16
Field Day and Other Events	3	6
	100	180

[a]Percentages are approximate.

Five-Day-a-Week Program for an Experienced Class (180 Days a Year)

Week	Chapter	Day	
1	8	8	Establishing an Environment for Learning (pgs. 99–125)
	8	2	Establishing an Environment for Learning (pgs. 99–125)
	8	3	Establishing an Environment for Learning (pgs. 99–125)
	13	4	Traveling Over, Under, and Around Obstacles in General Space (p. 215)
	13	5	Turning While Moving in Different Directions (p. 218)
2	13	1	Traveling While Rising and Sinking (p. 219)
	13	2	Traveling Pathways and Obstacles (p. 221)
	14	3	Combining Imagery and Time (p. 231)
	14	4	Differentiating Among Time Words (p. 232)
	14	5	Combining Sport Skills and Time (p. 232)
3	17	1	Dodging Stationary Obstacles (p. 298)
	17	2	Dodging and Faking Moves to Avoid a Chaser (p. 299)
	20	3	Performing Inverted Balances (p. 352)
	20	4	Performing Inverted Balances (cont.) (p. 352)
	19	5	Jumping a Self-Turned Rope (p. 331)
4	22	1	Kicking to a Partner (p. 414)
	22	2	Tap/Dribble: Traveling in Pathways (p. 415)
	24	3	Dribbling and Traveling (p. 487)
	21	4	Transferring Weight to Hands Across Mats (p. 371)
	21	5	Transferring Weight to Hands: Walking (p. 378)
5	23	1	Throwing Overhand (p. 441); Throwing Underhand (p. 441); Throwing Sidearm (p. 442)
	23	2	Throwing a Ball against a Wall and Catching the Rebound (p. 448)
	27	3	Teaching Physical Fitness, Physical Activity, and Wellness (p. 561)
	23	4	Throwing for Distance (p. 448)
	22	5	Punting with an Approach (p. 426); Punting for Distance (p. 427)
6	22	1	Punting for Accuracy (p. 427); Punting for Height (p. 428)
	17	2	Dodging While Manipulating an Object (p. 301)
	17	3	Dodging While Manipulating an Object (cont.) (p. 301)
	23	4	Throwing and Catching over a Net with a Partner (p. 449)
	23	5	Throwing and Catching While Traveling (p. 452)
7	23	1	Throwing to Make a Partner Move to Catch (p. 453)
	13	2	Combining Pathways, Levels, and Directions (p. 222)
	27	3	Teaching Physical Fitness, Physical Activity, and Wellness (p. 561)
	13	4	Traveling and Extensions (p. 223)
	22	5	Tap/dribble: Control of Ball and Body (p. 416)
8	22	1	Traveling and Kicking for a Goal (p. 417)
	25	2	Striking Up, Down, and Forward (p. 506)
	25	3	Striking to Different Places (p. 512)
	25	4	Striking an Object to Send It over a Net (p. 512)
	25	5	Striking a Ball Rebounding from a Wall (p. 513)
9	25	1	Hitting Cooperatively and Continuously with a Partner (p. 514)
	26	2	Striking a Pitched Ball—Bats (p. 547)
	27	3	Teaching Physical Fitness, Physical Activity and Wellness (p. 561)
	26	4	Striking a Pitched Ball—Bats (cont.) (p. 547)
	24	5	Dribbling, traveling, and switching hands (p. 487)
10	24	1	Dribbling Around Stationary Obstacles in General Space; Dribbling Around Stationary Obstacles in Limited Space (p. 491)
	24	2	Volleying to a Partner (Overhead Pattern) (p. 472); Cooperative Volleys (Overhead Pattern) (p. 473)
	24	3	Obstacle-Course Volley (p. 473)
	24	4	Volleying for Direction and Accuracy: Four Square, Two Square (p. 470)
	24	5	Volleying with a Bounce (p. 473)

Five-Day-a-Week Program for an Experienced Class (180 Days a Year)

Week	Chapter	Day	
11	24	1	Striking a Ball Continuously with Different Body Parts (p. 475)
	20	2	Balancing Symmetrically and Nonsymmetrically (p. 349)
	27	3	Teaching Physical Fitness, Physical Activity and Wellness (p. 561)
	20	4	Balancing on Crates (p. 360)
	20	5	Traveling into and out of Balances by Rolling (p. 362)
12	19	1	Jumping a Self-Turned Rope (p. 331)
	8	2	Establishing an Environment for Learning (p. 101)
	26	3	Striking for Distance—Hockey (p. 528)
	26	4	Striking for Distance—Hockey (cont.) (p. 528)
	14	5	Showing Contrasts of Force (p. 235); Using Imagery and Force (p. 235)
13	16	1	Changing Speeds to Music (p. 281)
	16	2	Traveling with Changes in Speed: A Dance of Water, Steam, and Ice (p. 281)
	27	3	Teaching Physical Fitness, Physical Activity and Wellness (p. 561)
	16	4	Traveling in Slow Motion: The Sports Dance (p. 281)
	19	5	Jumping Using Buoyant and Yielding Landings (p. 331); Jumping on and off Equipment Using Buoyant and Yielding Landings (p. 334)
14	19	1	Jumping and Landing Task Sheet (p. 335)
	19	2	Jumping and Landing Task Sheet (cont.) (p. 335)
	20	3	Performing Inverted Balances on Equipment (p. 362)
	20	4	Performing Sequences That Combine Stationary Balances and Traveling on Mats (p. 362)
	20	5	Balancing While Supporting the Weight of a Partner (p. 363)
15	20	1	Balancing on Hanging Ropes (p. 364)
	21	2	Transferring Weight to Hands and Forming a Bridge (p. 378)
	27	3	Teaching Physical Fitness, Physical Activity and Wellness (p. 561)
	21	4	Transferring Weight onto Large Apparatus (p. 378)
	26	5	Pathways, Speeds, and Directions—Hockey (p. 535)
16		1	Special Event
	21	2	Rolling After Jumping over Equipment and Landing (p. 396)
	21	3	Rolling, Levels, Directions, and Jumping (p. 398)
	21	4	Rolling While Traveling, Jumping, and Landing (p. 398)
	21	5	Rolling After Jumping from Different Heights (p. 397)
17	21	1	Rolling and Traveling Quickly (p. 400)
	8	2	Establishing an Environment for Learning (p. 101)
	27	3	Teaching Physical Fitness, Physical Activity and Wellness (p. 561)
	16	4	Traveling with a Partner: Matching Pathways (p. 282)
	21	5	Transferring Weight to Head and Hands on Apparatus (Box, Beam, Table) (p. 379)
18	26	1	Striking While Dodging Stationary Obstacles—Hockey (p. 533)
	14	2	Following Flow Sentences (p. 237); Practicing Flow Sequences (p. 237)
	14	3	Using Flow for Movement Conversations (p. 238)
	14	4	Combining Time, Force, and Flow (p. 238)
	24	5	Dribbling in General Space While Changing Directions (p. 488)
19	24	1	Dribbling While Stopping, Starting, and Turning (Pivots and Fakes) (p. 490)
	21	2	Rolling, Jumping, and Traveling in Relationship to Others (p. 400)
	27	3	Teaching Physical Fitness, Physical Activity and Wellness (p. 561)
	21	4	Rolling on Low Equipment; Rolling over Low Hurdles (p. 401)
	16	5	Shadowing a Partner's Travel (p. 285)
20	16	1	Performing Rhythmical Patterns (p. 285)
	15	2	Creating Postcard Sculptures (p. 248)
	15	3	Creating Body Shapes in the Air (p. 249)
	21	4	Traveling and Rolling Between Pieces of Equipment (p. 402)
	21	5	Rolling, Balancing, and Rolling (p. 402)

(continued)

Five-Day-a-Week Program for an Experienced Class (180 Days a Year) (continued)

Week	Chapter	Day	
21	15	1	Creating Postcard Sculptures (cont.) (p. 248)
	21	2	Rolling to Express an Idea (p. 403)
	27	3	Teaching Physical Fitness, Physical Activity and Wellness (p. 561)
	21	4	Rolling to Express an Idea (cont.) (p. 403)
	24	5	Dribbling Against an Opponent: One on One (p. 493)
22	24	1	Dribbling Against Opponents: Moving Defenders (p. 494)
	16	2	Traveling to Tell a Story: The Fountain of Youth Dance (p. 286)
	21	3	Transferring Weight on Bars (p. 382)
	21	4	Transferring Weight over Apparatus (Vaulting Box) (p. 380)
	21	5	Transferring Weight along Apparatus (p. 381)
23		1	Special Event
	24	2	Dribble Tag (p. 494)
	27	3	Teaching Physical Fitness, Physical Activity and Wellness (p. 561)
	26	4	Striking to a Stationary Partner—Hockey (p. 530)
	19	5	Jumping to an Accented Beat (p. 339)
24	19	1	Jumping with a Partner to Mirror Actions (p. 339); Jumping with a Partner to Match Actions (p. 340)
	26	2	Traveling and Striking While Changing Pathways—Hockey (p. 532)
	15	3	Traveling Along Equipment (p. 252)
	15	4	Forming Cooperative and Collaborative Relationships (p. 259)
	15	5	Forming Cooperative and Collaborative Relationships (cont.) (p. 259)
25	15	1	Meeting and Parting in a Cooperative Group (p. 259)
	8	2	Establishing an Environment for Learning (p. 101)
	27	3	Teaching Physical Fitness, Physical Activity and Wellness (p. 561)
	21	4	Rolling onto Low Equipment (p. 404)
	23	5	Throwing to a Moving Target (p. 453)
26	23	1	Throwing for Distance and Accuracy (p. 454)
		2	Special Event
	21	3	Transferring Weight on Bars (p. 382)
	21	4	Combining Skills on Mats (p. 382)
	21	5	Combining Weight Transfer and Balances into Sequences on Mats and Apparatus (p. 383)
27	21	1	Combining Weight Transfer and Balances into Sequences on Mats and Apparatus (cont.) (p. 383)
	19	2	Jumping to Catch (p. 366); Jumping to Throw (p. 337)
	27	3	Teaching Physical Fitness, Physical Activity and Wellness (p. 561)
	19	4	Throwing and Catching While Jumping (p. 338)
	22	5	Tap/Dribble and Kick: Playing Soccer Golf (p. 419)
28	17	1	Dodging Semistationary Obstacles (p. 299)
	24	2	Volleying with a Volleybird (p. 477)
	24	3	Striking to the Wall—Varying Levels, Force, and Body Position (p. 477)
	24	4	Volleying Continuously to a Partner (p. 478)
	24	5	Volleying Three-on-Three (p. 479)
29	22	1	Playing One-on-One Soccer (p. 418)
	26	2	Striking from a Stationary Position to a Moving Target—Hockey (p. 537)
	27	3	Teaching Physical Fitness, Physical Activity and Wellness (p. 561)
	26	4	Striking to Small Targets—Hockey (p. 534)
	26	5	Striking to varying distances—Golf (p. 554)
30	17	1	Dodging and Chasing One Person in a Mass (p. 300)
	23	2	Catching to Throw Quickly to a Partner (p. 456)
	23	3	Throwing and Catching in a Field, Run, and Score Gamelike Situation (p. 457)
	23	4	Throwing to Avoid a Defender (p. 458)
	23	5	Throwing and Catching in a Small-Sided Invasion Game (p. 459)

Five-Day-a-Week Program for an Experienced Class (180 Days a Year) (continued)

Week	Chapter	Day	
31	23	1	Throwing at a Stationary Object While Being Defended (p. 459)
	25	2	Striking to Different Places Around a Partner (p. 515)
	27	3	Teaching Physical Fitness, Physical Activity and Wellness (p. 561)
	25	4	Striking Upward in a Dynamic Situation (p. 517)
	25	5	Striking to One Wall with a Partner (p. 518)
32	17	1	Dodging in a Dynamic Situation (p. 301)
	25	2	Striking at Angles to Two Walls with a Partner (p. 519)
	25	3	Partner Striking Across a Net (p. 520)
	25	4	Partner Striking Across a Net (cont.) (p. 520)
	25	5	Self-Designed Racket Games (p. 522)
33	25	1	Self-Designed Racket Games (cont.) (p. 522)
	22	2	Punting Within a Limited Time (p. 430)
	27	3	Teaching Physical Fitness, Physical Activity and Wellness (p. 561)
	22	4	Punting Quickly: Rush the Circle (p. 431)
	22	5	Playing Two-on-One Soccer (p. 420)
34	26	1	Striking so the Ball Travels in the Air: Air Ball—Golf (p. 553)
	26	2	Striking so the Ball Travels in the Air: Air Ball—Golf (cont.) (p. 553)
	26	3	Playing Hoop Golf (p. 555)
	26	4	Hitting to Open Spaces—Bats (p. 549)
	26	5	Striking a Pitched Object Varying the Distance—Bats (p. 550)
35	26	1	Directing the Pathway, Distance, and Speed of an Object—Bats (p. 551)
	23	2	Throwing and Catching with a Flying Disc in a Small-Sided Invasion Game (p. 460)
	23	3	Throwing and Catching a Flying Disc in Different Places Around the Body with a Partner (p. 457)
	27	4	Teaching Physical Fitness, Physical Activity and Wellness (p. 561)
	26	5	Six-Player Striking and Fielding in a Gamelike Situation (p. 551)
36	26	1	One-Base Baseball (p. 552)
		2	Special Event
		3	Special Event
		4	Special Event
		5	Field Day

Note: Page numbers followed by italicized letters refer to boxes (*b*), figures (*f*), footnotes (*n*), or tables (*t*).